T0393624

HOW THE SECULARIZATION OF RELIGIOUS HOUSES TRANSFORMED
THE LIBRARIES OF EUROPE, 16th–19th CENTURIES

BIBLIOLOGIA

ELEMENTA AD LIBRORUM STUDIA PERTINENTIA

Collection publiée sous les auspices de
l'Institut de recherche et d'histoire des textes, Paris.

VOLUME 63

Comité de rédaction
André Binggeli, CNRS, Institut de recherche et d'histoire des textes, Paris
Paola Degni, Alma Mater Università di Bologna
Michele C. Ferrari, Friedrich-Alexander-Universität Erlangen
Françoise Fery-Hue, CNRS, Institut de recherche et d'histoire des textes, Paris
Xavier Hermand, Université de Namur
Marilena Maniaci, Università degli studi di Cassino e del Lazio meridionale
Donatella Nebbiai, CNRS, Institut de recherche et d'histoire des textes, Paris
Judith Olszowy-Schlanger, École Pratique des Hautes Études, Paris
Teresa Webber, Trinity College, Cambridge

How the Secularization of Religious Houses Transformed the Libraries of Europe, 16th–19th Centuries

Edited by

CRISTINA DONDI, DORIT RAINES, AND † RICHARD SHARPE

BREPOLS

© 2022, Brepols Publishers n. v., Turnhout, Belgium.

All rights reserved. No part of this publication may be reproduced, stored in a retrieval system, or transmitted, in any form or by any means, electronic, mechanical, photocopying, recording, or otherwise without the prior permission of the publisher.

D/2022/0095/30
ISBN 978-2-503-59392-0
e-ISBN 978-2-503-59560-3
DOI 10.1484/M.BIB-EB.5.124554
ISSN 1375-9566
e-ISSN 2565-9286

Printed in the EU on acid-free paper

In memoriam

Richard Sharpe (1954–2020)
Presenting in Convocation House, the Bodleian Library, Oxford,
during the 2012 conference (Credit: D. Raines)

Table of Contents

Part 7
Tools for Research

Introduction

Throughout the medieval and early-modern periods monasteries were often active cultural workshops, centres of fundamental importance for reading and writing. At different periods they built up and maintained collections of books, sometimes large libraries. Their scribes and scriptoria multiplied copies of texts, ensuring their circulation and in many cases their survival. Monks and canons wrote countless new works. The longevity and security of monastic libraries ensured the preservation of texts that had become rare, and some of these libraries became resources to scholars beyond their own communities. While the management and development of such libraries was not constant over the centuries, and some religious communities often alienated books no longer of use to them, across Europe as a whole the libraries of religious institutions proved themselves vital to the survival of written learning. Even if humanist scholars sometimes berated monks for their negligence, benign neglect enabled ancient texts to survive until they were rediscovered. The Henrician Reformation in England and Wales was the first break in this tradition, but in Catholic Europe the religious orders continued to provide a home for scholars and to cultivate up-to-date libraries. Large numbers of printed books were acquired, in some cases added to historic collections of manuscript books, in others replacing them. Some houses of different orders and disciplines, Benedictine, Cistercian, Dominican, Jesuit, retained living libraries in which a vast learning,

ancient, medieval, and modern was preserved. Some libraries became famous in the seventeenth and eighteenth centuries and attracted the interest of scholars from far and wide.

The deliberate closure of religious houses, in varying circumstances, affected all of Europe at some point between the sixteenth and nineteenth centuries (indeed, secularizations continued into the twentieth century). At different times and in different countries the state actively intervened to bring monastic life to an end, thereby creating a sudden and traumatic fracture in the cultural fabric of each country where this happened. The consequences for the libraries of the suppressed institutions varied widely: in some cases, medieval and early-modern collections were preserved intact; in others, books were abandoned to their fate, or transferred piecemeal into new ownership to serve different cultural purposes, creating new opportunities for enhanced circulation and the formation of civic or national collections. Integral preservation or dispersal may each be viewed in positive or negative terms. For religious, political, and economic history there are many large-scale factors involved in secularization, and its effects worked on many aspects of life beside libraries and books. None the less, by focusing on the fate of books and libraries through these changes a particular narrative emerges of great cultural importance. It is the most important book-historical story for the survival and accessibility of Europe's heritage of the written word, one that interacts with major historical shifts and still connects with future issues for the continuing role of books and libraries in the European heritage.

The conference held at the University of Oxford in 2012 brought together more than thirty speakers with expertise in various aspects of this process or with knowledge of its impact in different countries and at different periods. The result was to assemble and share for the first time the similar and different experiences of European countries, from Portugal and Spain in the west to Poland and Ukraine in the east, from Finland and Sweden in the north to Rome and Naples in the south. The untested expectation was that the differences between secularization events at different dates would be greater than between events occurring contemporaneously in different countries; but this was not how matters turned out. Dissolution under the impact of the protestant Reformation in the sixteenth century produced very dissimilar results in England, Germany, Switzerland, the Netherlands, and Scandinavia; dissolution happening in Catholic countries in the eighteenth and nineteenth centuries produced further contrasting results. The comparisons are instructive. In the early period some countries made no state-sanctioned attempt to preserve the libraries of dissolved institutions (England, the Netherlands, Zurich); in others, the aim was to secularize the books in public libraries without any deaccessions. At a later date and with much higher volumes to deal with, there was a tendency to segregate manuscripts and incunabula, as heritage resources, from the mass of more modern printed books: the former were more regularly preserved, the latter might be preserved or disposed of, and disposals took various forms. The European process was replicated in Latin America in the nineteenth century, and from the middle of the century some American, as well as European, buyers began to take advantage of European disposals. In some countries national libraries were created to absorb the dissolved books, in others a network of local libraries became repositories for

the heritage books and a range of different trade developments dealt with disposals. Our capacity to trace the history of books from medieval and early-modern institutions to current libraries is variable once again. Libraries broken up at a later date are more likely to have recognizable bookplates and their books stand a better chance of appearing in surviving inventories (Venice, Munich); but even so, in the context of wide dispersal the tracing of provenances for high volumes of printed books is not viable. Where libraries were entirely subsumed into public libraries, however, even such later imprints will often remain identifiable, and a sequence of book-plates, stamps, and sometimes pre-dissolution catalogues or accession lists may be assembled to allow strays to be located and even the history of the former library to be understood.

This variety of circumstance was represented in the conference programme, and is reflected in the papers in this volume. Part 1 begins with the territorial and temporal map of the dissolved collections, seen across a wide perspective that includes both the political and economic contexts that led to the phenomenon of monastic dissolution, and also the mapping of different territorial processes over the *longue durée*. Part 2 examines state policy towards book collections, that is the different formation of official approaches to the dissolution of monasteries. Were governments aware of library treasures and of their patrimonial or cultural value? Did they plan beforehand on how to deal with them? Part 3 focuses on sequestration, redistribution, or contribution to the foundation of public libraries. Here we look at the dissolution from the perspective of libraries. What material was reused and in what ways? How did the dissolution contribute to the opening of new public libraries or influence the contents of those already established? Part 4 shifts the attention to changes occurring in the book trade due to the massive flow of books and manuscripts on to the market. It also looks at changes in collecting habits and the emergence of a new type of collector. In part 5 the focus is on the migration of books, the monastic practice of "rejuvenating" the collections, the change in reading habits, and the new publics gaining access to the books. Part 6 investigates the different outcomes when the state was indifferent to the fate of libraries from dissolved institutions and saw collections broken up: clandestine removal of books from the monastic library, confiscation of the library for private uses, or destruction. Finally, part 7 presents some of the tools and methodologies that exist for furthering research into the dispersal and virtual reconstruction of lost libraries.

Much of the relevant information has been known, case by case, to curators in the institutions that received high-volume transfers of former monastic books, and the conference made a point of inviting participation from curators as well as researchers. Significant value arose in the sharing of knowledge across this permeable boundary, and still more in the sharing of national experiences. The subject had not previously been approached from a comparative international angle. Bringing together experts from countries where secularization took place at different periods reinforced in all our minds the degree to which this slow historical process changed over time in varying circumstances, when different factors led to an outcome that was similar in the sense that religious houses had their endowments sequestered, different in the sense that their intellectual patrimony was subject to very different levels of control. Market forces in the ultimate phases of secularization had a further impact. Another common feature lay in the challenges that scholars and librarians experience today in tracing back the collections from their identified books, virtually of course, in writing and in collective digital resources that can overcome geographical barriers.

The reader may notice a disparity in the evidence that each author has been able to bring to bear upon their subject. Provenance research is well advanced in some territories, less so in others. In the decade since the conference and this publication, we have attempted to bridge some of the gaps in the evidence by means of newly created digital resources (detailed in Part 7 of this volume). But in the end, these differences have to be accepted. They are an indication of where more research is needed. There has in general been little new work in the years since the conference took place. We anticipate that the publication of this volume will stimulate further research, such that, eventually, some of the gaps visible in the evidence presented here will be able to be bridged.

The overall intention of the conference's convenors was to understand the mechanisms of dissolution, and beyond that, to investigate how the variegated reality of the dissolutions had changed the role of libraries as centres for education and the circulation and preservation of knowledge. Multiple avenues for further investigation open up in historical and cultural studies, such as the impact of the secularization on non-religious libraries, private and court libraries, and the change in attitude with respect to certain disciplines and even to erudition itself.

Looking at the secularization phenomenon from an historical perspective, two processes highlighted by the conference emerge as principal areas for further investigation. First, there is the role assumed by books and libraries in the overall pattern of dissolution of religious houses. Since books represent collateral damage, not having been the principal target of the authorities, it is worthwhile to examine the dynamics of their treatment in the complex dismantling of often venerable institutions. The second lies in the differences between the secularizations that resulted from religious conflicts in the sixteenth century and those that happened under Napoleonic and national governments from the eighteenth century onwards. Rather than being primarily religious in motivation, the latter clearly had to do first and foremost with economic considerations related to the property of religious houses. The need to deal with formerly monastic book collections was only a side effect of a much larger phenomenon, both political and economic, and an awareness of libraries' existence (and the need to deal with them by either redistribution or sale) occurred in some cases only after the act of secularization itself, as in the case of the 1768 secularizations in Venice.

A richly detailed picture emerges from the secularization phenomenon using cultural and book-historical approaches. Confronting the sixteenth-century monastic suppressions with those imposed by Napoleon and the national governments, four elements emerge strongly: the logistics of dissolution; the criteria applied during the selection and inventorying of the books; the decision on acquisition or sale; and the role of those involved in the process of the dissolution. For the Reformation and its impact, the departure point was the question of whether it should be considered a destructive or innovative force for change in libraries and book production (or both at the same time). Points of interest for further research which arise from these papers include: the different treatment reserved to libraries of male or female religious institutions; the role played by language (Latin versus vernacular) in the process of retention or disposal of books in libraries, and whether it varied according to different countries and communities (e.g. scholars versus parish commoners); the role played by the date of the works (classical, patristic, medieval, modern) and the date of the manuscripts or editions (medieval and modern manuscripts, incunabula, sixteenth-century editions, later editions); the role played by subject-class (history and classics versus theology, liturgy, devotional literature), as well as the nature of the texts themselves (academic versus popular); and finally the format of the books, larger versus smaller formats, single works versus miscellanies.

Observable emphases may also clarify the changing perceptions of manuscript and print. For example, when books were selected for preservation was any preference given to manuscripts over printed books, or vice versa? Did new material relocated to existing libraries affect the balance between these two typologies? Where a manuscript was discarded, what kind of reuse were its leaves destined for? Did the destruction of Catholic or Protestant liturgical books lead to a new wave in the production of printed editions to replace the loss? And more specifically: did these changes affect the rise in production in the printing industry? Was the increased income used to invest in improving the technology or in expanding or diversifying the types of books printed? How did the practice of librarianship adapt to the quantity of books librarians had to deal with? Finally, new flows of books may be examined in light of their contribution to the rise of city or university libraries. Criteria of rarity and utility were both dependent on the times and the individuals involved in the selection. For example, literary works tended to be favoured over the theological, liturgical, and legal, considered less relevant or outdated. It explains why today texts of the classics are well represented on the shelves of our special collections while legal and liturgical texts survive more often as fragments in bindings.

While the dissolutions of the Reformation period were principally the result of the clash between two rival Christian churches, and consequently the redistribution or destruction of books and manuscripts followed the violence of that seizure, the Napoleonic and national dissolutions beginning in the eighteenth century were different in their primary motivation, essentially economic in character (excepting the case of the suppression of the Jesuits as occurred in Belgium and Catalonia), although Enlightenment ideas also played a part and influenced deaccessioning policies and the provision of books for a modernized and rationalized educational system.

With the secularizations carried out by liberal governments, books considered to be important, useful or valuable were destined for the main public libraries, less valuable material, or duplicates, were directed to schools, seminaries and the like, while books considered as useless (cheap printing, liturgy, the contents of most libraries of female religious) were sold or destroyed. It is interesting how retention criteria in the early-modern and the modern period matched. Beyond this general trend, if conquered countries were involved, as, for example, Italy under Napoleon, very rare specimens were sequestered and taken away to Paris. Moreover, at every step of the process outlined above, books could be abstracted by various means and in different circumstances, to find themselves on the developing local, national or international antiquarian market.

Assessing the dissolutions from the point of view of their management, it is possible to detect different local stories: for example, distribution of books to local libraries in Rome as against being sent to Paris from Venice, or the picture of complete disorder in Catalonia against the well managed process in Venice. What also emerges are the different treatments of religious libraries: the way that personal interest could enhance elements of dissolution, as in the Swedish and Spanish cases, or else a preference exists for large or valuable libraries over small ones, as in the Venetian case. Moreover, the differing personal approaches of those in charge (Gerard in Belgium, Morelli in Venice, von Aretin in Bavaria) and the role they played in the process should be considered and examined: were they mere executors of the authorities' policies and directives or did they express personal opinions and prejudices, revolutionary or reformist? Were they in a position to influence the process in which they were involved?

The later period of European secularizations, covering a span of some 150 years from the 1759 expulsion of the Jesuits in Portugal to the Spanish *Desamortización* of the 1920s, presents certain similarities to the preceding age of Reformation as regards the criteria for the selection of books for new homes. In much the same way, it asks to be considered as a destructive or innovative force for change in the life of libraries. It seems that the overwhelming quantity of books involved, coupled with state handling that could be organized but was mostly too hasty, brought about a more rapid release of books that in turn produced a decisive cultural change. New public and national libraries arose, as in Italy, France, and Poland, with a change in reading habits and the enhancement of public education due to the creation of new school and academic libraries. The book market substantially increased too. Sometimes the disposals took place in an orderly fashion, by public auctions either with printed catalogues (as in Bavaria, Belgium, France, Switzerland, Portugal), or without (Venice); however the sheer quantity of rare books available for sale changed the nature of the book market: the period witnesses new buyers, prices and the rise of the figure of the collector as known today. The modern shape and composition of European public libraries (and American special collections departments) is a reflection of these major events and the choices that operated chiefly in the period from the sixteenth to the nineteenth centuries.

Monastic libraries grew almost organically, evolving over time and under the influence of cultural, political, economic, and technological shifts. Already before the Reformation the shift from manuscript to print caused what Gerhardt Powitz has called the "book extinction" of the period around 1500, in which great numbers of manuscript books, especially liturgical ones, were discarded in favour of printed editions. However, the secularizations accelerated this evolutionary potential to extreme realities.

It is clear that at least three different contrary modes were dominant at all times: dissolution and regeneration, sequestration and repurposing; relocation and patrimonialization. Whereas these processes are mostly documented and can be analysed sometimes in great detail, evidence for one further treatment of the books, i.e. destruction, is rather lacking, unless we confront, on a European level, old library inventories that will report books since lost.

Significant progress has instead taken place, so far as methodology and digital resources are concerned, to trace the many books that once formed part of a monastic library, those which still survive today and those which we have now lost. Databases such as MLGB3, MEI, and RICI are reconstructing that dispersal through the assessment of a successful combination of primary sources: documentary, bibliographical, and pertaining to the material evidence of the books themselves. With the scholarship and digital resources now available to us, it is our duty properly to trace and identify the many hundreds of thousands of volumes which were affected by the secularizations – and which probably survived to later centuries because of them. The work of identification and systematization will enable us to trace the impact on our culture of the circulation of these books.

* * *

The results of this research are timely, as we perceive the impact of technological change on our own evolving society, in a highly volatile political landscape and impending economic retrenchment, accelerated by the Covid-19 pandemic. The initial findings in this volume spell out the devastating effects of the policies of the past, as well as the extensive, expensive, and time-consuming efforts which are demanded today to piece collections back together, a work of research that can now be advanced with the support of digital resources. This is not merely an exercise in bibliography, it is the necessary reconstruction of the cultural and intellectual heritage of institutions and nations. This picture, and these data, are indispensable for libraries and governments grappling today with the ongoing process of preservation and disposal of knowledge and books wrought by the digital

shift. But also, by the reappearance and application of the old concept of "useful knowledge" and its counterpart, "useless knowledge".

Books are mobile objects, and their potential for movement over time and space is part of their very nature. The libraries into which they move are like living organisms, reflecting the changing intellectual achievements and needs of communities and societies over time, intensely susceptible to external factors, political and economic as well as cultural. As is abundantly clear from the papers gathered in this volume, politics had tremendous effects on the dispersal of the cultural and intellectual heritage in the past. And it continues to do so today. If the effects of technological change combined with political and economic upheavals will again disperse vast quantities of our heritage – something many would argue is part of the life-cycle of books, even beneficial in the formation of new libraries – let us at least be prepared. Let us use the experience we have acquired in the understanding of the preservation and disposal of knowledge and the digital resources of today at least to track the dispersals, and prevent the unnecessary destruction and loss of collective memory (and evidence).

* * *

We are extremely grateful to have had our authors' patience and the patience of our publisher. It has taken far too long to bring this volume to publication. Gaps in the literature are entirely the editors' fault. In particular, we are aware that the phenomenon of the impact of the Reformation on the formation of public city libraries in northern and southern Germany should have required a dedicated space which we were not able to provide. We thank most warmly our colleagues Martin Davies, Stephen Parkin, and James Willoughby for reading through a number of the papers. Finally, we gratefully acknowledge the financial support towards the organization of the original conference received from the British

Academy, the Gladys Krieble Delmas Foundation, the John Fell Fund of the University of Oxford, and the Fritz Thyssen Stiftung received via the Bodleian Library.

As we bring this volume to a close at last, though sadly too late to benefit from Richard Sharpe's incisive and profound understanding of historical libraries, established collections are still being dispersed on the market. The catastrophe of pandemics is something we did not discuss in the book, but we are aware it may lead to a new chapter in the preservation, dispersal, and destruction of knowledge.

"The preservation of knowledge is ultimately … about having faith in the future"

(Richard Ovenden, *Burning the Books. A History of Knowledge Under Attack* [London, 2020], 151).

Cristina Dondi, Dorit Raines, † Richard Sharpe

Chronology

Date	Country	Authority	Libraries
1516	France	Francis I	Concordat of Bologna allowed Francis I to appoint abbots *in commendam*, effectively secularizing much of the endowment of French religious houses
1521	Germany		Luther's *De votis monasticis* published
Early 1524	Germany		Luther's pamphlet, *An die Ratsherren aller Städte Deutschlands, dass sie christliche Schulen aufrichten und halten sollen* (Wittenberg, 1524), denounced monastic learning but advocated "gutte librareyen odder bücher heuser"
1524–25; 1527–28	England	Papacy	Cardinal Wolsey obtained papal consent to dissolve thirty small religious houses to support his school and college
1524	Zurich	Protestant city council	The abolition of the various monasteries was a gradual development that lasted from February to December 1524
1525	Germany/Switzerland		Peasants' War, destruction of libraries. While dozens of monasteries were devastated in Germany, only two small monastic libraries were affected in Switzerland
1525–30	German-speaking Switzerland	Protestant city councils	Closure of monasteries in Zurich, Bern, Basel, and Schaffhausen
1527–37	Sweden	Gustav I Vasa	Diet of Västerås adopted protestant position and allowed the crown to take over the property of the church. Gråmunkeholmen OFM dissolved in 1527, Stockholm OP in 1528, and others between then and 1537, leaving only the nuns of Vadstena and of Nådendal
1527–38	Denmark	Frederik I and his son Christian III	Dissolution of religious houses began in 1527, as protestant towns petitioned the king to dissolve Franciscan houses, and by 1538 all religious houses had closed
1528	Basel, Bern	Protestant city council	Abolition of monasteries
1529	Schaffhausen	Protestant city council	Abolition of monasteries
1530	Switzerland		An attempt to dissolve the Abbey of St Gallen failed

Date	Country	Authority	Libraries
1532	Zurich	Reform of the chapter library of the Grossmünster	Conrad Pellikan reorganised the chapter library. By 1551 he had catalogued 771 volumes with 66 manuscripts and 854 printed works, most of them from the dissolved monasteries of the city and canton of Zurich
1532	England	voluntary	Holy Trinity Aldgate surrendered its endowments and is dissolved. Library disappeared.
1532	Scotland	Pope Clement VII	Papacy allowed abbacies *in commendam*
1534–35	England	Henry VIII	"Valor Ecclesiasticus" documented the value of ecclesiastic revenues
1535	England	Henry VIII	Visitation of monasteries
1536	England	parliament	Act for the suppression of smaller monasteries, February 1535/36
1537	Ireland	Irish Parliament	First suppression of a few monasteries
1537	Scotland	James V	James V refused the English envoys' encouragement to dissolve monasteries
1539	England	Parliament	Act for the suppression of the greater monasteries, April 1539
1541	Ireland	Irish Parliament	Suppression of further monasteries
1553	England	Mary I	Temporary restoration of religious life at Westminster OSB, Syon OSS, and Greenwich OFM Obs
1572–78	Netherlands	Protestant city councils	Alteration Act(i.e. change from Roman Catholicism to Protestantism) from 1572 onwards in most Dutch cities, finally in Amsterdam (1578)
1618–48	German territories		Thirty Years War
1652	Italy	Pope Innocent X	Following the bull *Instaurandae regularis disciplinae*, suppression of some regular congregations and other small convents
1712	Zurich and Bern	City councils	Toggenburg War: The army of the Protestant cantons of Zurich and Bern took books of St Gallen Abbey as part of their spoils
26 Dec 1754	Tuscany	Francis I, Holy Roman Emperor	Law to ban the export of books and works of art
June 1758	Portugal	Marquis of Pombal, Secretary of State for Internal Affairs	Jesuits deprived of all possession in Portuguese territories
6 Aug 1762 / 1 Apr 1763	France	Parliament	French Parliament ruled against the Jesuits in France. Jesuit colleges were closed on 1 Apr 1763
Nov 1764	France	Louis XV	Jesuit order extinguished in France by royal decree
27 Feb 1767	Spain	Carlos III	Jesuits expelled from Spain and the Two Sicilies. Libraries inventoried and confiscated
1767–68	Austria	Maria Theresa	Jesuit drama schools suppressed in Austria and territories
1768	Parma, Piacenza and Guastalla (Duchy)	Ferdinand	Jesuits expelled from Parma and their book collections confiscated
7 Sept 1768	Republic of Venice	Senate	Suppression of monasteries with fewer than twelve religious or lacking sufficient income: mostly from the Capuchins, Reformed Friars Minor, Friars Minor of the Observance, Franciscan Tertiaries and Carthusians

Date	Country	Authority	Libraries
23 Aug 1770	Republic of Venice	Senate	Closure of the houses of the Carmelites of the Mantuan Congregation
5 Dec 1770	Republic of Venice	Senate	Closure of the houses of the Cassinese Congregation (Benedictines)
5 Sept 1772	Republic of Venice	Senate	Closure of the houses of the Augustinians, Girolamini, Minims, and the Servites
21 July 1773	Europe	Pope Clement XIV	Clement XIV's bull *Dominus ac redemptor* led to the confiscation of Jesuit possessions in the rest of Catholic Europe, i.e. Italy, Austrian territories including Belgium, and further east the Polish–Lithuanian commonwealth
29 Sep 1773	Republic of Venice	Senate	Following the Pope's bull, suppression of the Jesuits in the Venetian territories
1780	Prussia	Frederick II the Great	Suppression of the Jesuits extended to the Prussian territories
1781–85	Austria	Joseph II	Closure of the contemplative orders and a number of prelate orders, reducing the number of religious houses by one third. Various instructions concerning books and archives followed
1781	Grand Duchy of Tuscany	Peter Leopold	Closure of the orders of Celestines (1781), Augustinian hermits (1782), Cistercians (1783), and Theatines (1785)
1782	Republic of Venice	Senate	Closure of the houses of the Canons Regular (Augustinians)
2 Nov 1789	France	Assemblée constituante	Nationalization of the property of the clergy
13 Feb 1790	France	Assemblée constituante	Suppression of religious houses
15 Oct 1794	France / Belgium		During the War of the First Coalition French authorities authorized officials to seize the cultural goods of defeated enemies, starting in Brussels, then also in the Netherlands and Rhineland
7 May 1796	France / Italy	Directorate	Similar seizures authorized in Italy
1795–96	Ruthenia	Catherine II the Great	Basilian Order forced to convert to Russian Orthodox observance
16 May 1797	France/Republic of Venice	Napoleon/Venetian envoys	Peace Treaty forcing the Republic to hand over 20 paintings and 500 manuscripts to the French commissaries
2 Aug 1797	France/Republic of Venice	French army	Some monastic libraries plundered by the French and their followers
11 Feb 1798	Roman Republic	French army	Military expropriation of a number of Roman religious institutions
10 May 1798	Roman Republic	Direttorio	French occupiers decree the confiscation of monastic goods in Rome during the period of the First Roman Republic
1802	Papal state – Rome	Pope Pius VII	10–12,000 printed duplicates are returned to the Franciscans of the Aracoeli
1802–03	Bavaria	Prince Elector Maximilian IV Joseph	Closure of mendicant houses in Bavaria by Count Joseph von Montgelas. In Feb. 1803 the government decides to secularize the prelate orders too. Between 1802 and 1810 over 200 monasteries in Bavaria were suppressed

Date	Country	Authority	Libraries
8 June 1805	Napoleonic Kingdom of Italy	Napoleon	Reorganization of the secular and regular clergy
10 June 1806	Napoleonic Kingdom of Italy (Territories of the former Republic of Venice)	Eugène de Beauharnais, Viceroy of Italy	Sealing off all libraries and archives and preparation of inventories
July 1806	France/Venice	Napoleon	Thirty monasteries in Venice suppressed
24 Mar 1808	Napoleonic Grand Duchy of Tuscany	Napoleon	Suppression of some religious orders in Tuscany, with further orders concerning the seizure of cultural goods – by 1810 it is extended to all orders
4 Dec 1808	Spain	Napoleon	Order to reduce the number of monasteries in Spain by one third
18 Aug 1809	Spain	Joseph Bonaparte	Order of suppression of all monasteries in the Spanish lands
1810	France/Venice	Napoleon	All remaining monasteries in Venice suppressed
7 May 1810	French empire – Department of Rome	Napoleon	Suppression of religious orders
15 Oct 1810	French empire – Department of Rome	Consulta Straordinaria per gli Stati romani	French authorities opened to the public the religious libraries at Santa Maria sopra Minerva OP, Angelica OSA, and Aracoeli OFM
30 Oct 1810	Silesia	Frederick William III, King of Prussia	Prussian authorities seized church property in Silesia in order to pay war-damages to Napoleon. A royal commission appointed to collect monastic books from Silesia at Breslau in 1811
1811–1814	French Empire – Department of Rome	Consulta Straordinaria per gli Stati romani, then Intendenza per i beni della Corona	Requisition of libraries belonging to religious orders
17 June 1812	Spain	Consejo de Regencia	Liberals ordered the confiscation of monastic property
1814	Papal state – Rome	Pope Pius VII	Restitution of the books to the religious orders
7 Aug 1814	Europe	Pope Pius VII	Jesuit society restored by bull of Pius VII, *Solicitudo omnium ecclesiarum*
4 Dec. 1815	Grand Duchy of Tuscany	Ferdinand III	Convention with the Papacy to re-open 77 convents in Tuscany and return the books
17 Apr 1819	Kingdom of Poland (under Russia)	Primate Franciszek Skarbek-Malczewski	Following pope Pius VII's bull *Ex imposita Nobis*, count Stanisław Kostka Potocki ordered the dissolution of selected monasteries, including many ancient foundations
13 Mar 1820	Russia	Tsar Alexander I	Jesuits suppressed in the Russian territories
6 Sept 1820	Spain	Liberal government	Recently restored Jesuits are suppressed by the Liberal Triennium (*Trienio liberal*)
1 Oct 1820	Spain	Liberal government	All monastic orders suppressed (again)
19 July 1832	Russia	Tsar Nicholas I	Tsar Nicholas I ordered the suppression of Roman Catholic monasteries in Russian lands, slowly implemented in 1830s and 1840s
1833	Oporto	Dom Pedro IV	Preparation for a public library to receive the books from the religious orders

Date	Country	Authority	Libraries
1834	Portugal	Liberal government	Under Joaquim António de Aguiar the government nationalized lands and possessions of religious orders
4 July 1835	Spain	Liberal government	Under Juan Álvarez Mendizábal the Jesuits were suppressed in Spain (again)
25 July 1835	Spain	Liberal government	Under Juan Álvarez Mendizábal the government issued the *Desamortización eclesiástica*. All small monasteries were suppressed
8 Mar 1836	Spain	Liberal government	Under Juan Álvarez Mendizábal Piarists, hospital orders, and small nunneries were suppressed with effect from 29 July 1837
1840–50	Switzerland	Liberal governments	Abolition of monasteries in the cantons of Aargau, Thurgau, Lucerne, Freiburg, and Ticino
1848	Sardinia		Jesuits suppressed
1849	Second Roman Republic	Triumvirate	Intended confiscations, especially due to Giuseppe Mazzini who called for the confiscation of the landholdings of the Church, not yet carried out but some inventories made
29 May 1855 (-1866)	Kingdom of Sardinia (then Kingdom of Italy)	King Vittorio Emanuele II	Law of suppression of religious institutions which were not dedicated to the activities of preaching, education, and assisting the sick, progressively extended to the whole Italian territory
1862	Zurich	Government	Dissolution of Rheinau Abbey
8 Nov 1864	Kingdom of Poland (under Russia)	Tsar Alexander II	A decree ordered the dissolution of a large number of remaining monasteries
7 July 1866	Italy	King Vittorio Emanuele II	Royal Decree valid throughout the national territory – with the exception of Rome which had not yet been annexed – for the suppression of religious houses and the transfer of their assets to state property
1872	Germany	Prussian Parliament (Reichstag)	Start of the Kulturkampf between Prussia led by chancellor Otto von Bismarck and the Roman Catholic Church led by pope Pius IX, which lasted until 1879 and during which the Jesuits were expelled (4 July 1872) and the dissolution of religious orders took place (31 May 1875). On 26 April 1887 all orders were readmitted except for the Jesuits
19 June 1873	Italy	King Vittorio Emanuele II	After the annexation of Rome to the Kingdom of Italy (20 Sept. 1870), a new Decree applied to the province of Rome promulgated the suppression of religious houses, but preparations to confiscate libraries had been already in train since 1871

PART 1

The Territorial and Temporal Map of the Dissolved Collections

▾ INTRODUCTION OF THE ARGUMENT IN A LARGE
PERSPECTIVE THAT INCLUDES BOTH THE POLITICAL AND
ECONOMIC CONTEXT THAT LED TO THE PHENOMENON
OF MONASTIC DISSOLUTION, AND ALSO THE MAPPING
OF THE DIFFERENT TERRITORIAL PROCESSES IN A *LONGUE
DURÉE* PERSPECTIVE.

FIORENZO LANDI

The Dissolution of Monasteries and Convents in Europe. An Overview of the Economic Implications

The structural presence of ecclesiastical property in the economy of the Catholic countries of *ancien régime* Europe has frequently raised the question of the exact composition of the regular clergy's patrimony. In the sixteenth to the eighteenth centuries, when church property in general was expanding, as well as during the Napoleonic era and the subsequent course of the nineteenth century, when liberal governments embarked on wholesale seizures, the statistical survey was a tool widely employed by both secular and religious authorities. From the English prototype, the *valor ecclesiasticus* used by Henry VIII for the seizure of monastic property, the large number of sixteenth and eighteenth-century Spanish surveys, the eighteenth-century French surveys, and the statistics compiled by Austro-Hungarian rulers, the property of the regular clergy was closely monitored in light of the important role that it played in the economy of the *ancien régime*.

Although a vast bibliography dealing with the economic history of the regular clergy exists[1],

it mainly deals with individual convents and monasteries or with orders and congregations in their local or national contexts. What has hitherto been completely missing is an international perspective on the phenomenon, which presents some common traits: in the first place the manner in which assets and income were acquired is similar throughout Europe and in colonial territories; second, the management and accounting systems applied are very much the same everywhere; and third, the fate of such patrimony and revenues is always the same: confiscation.

The regular clergy represented a kind of globalization *ante litteram*: they had a centralized administration based in Rome, Latin as common language, and common economic interests and cultural objectives. This means that we can choose between two different strategies of inquiry: a local and a general or global one. By using two different perspectives, we can obtain two similar but opposite results. For example, if we examine a large city such as Seville at the beginning of sixteenth century with a population of about 50,000 inhabitants and some seventy monasteries and convents, we can easily find out that each of

[1] For a large European bibliography divided by countries in Fiorenzo Landi, *Storia economica del clero in Europa. Secoli XV–XIX* (Roma, 2005).

Fiorenzo Landi • Professor of Economic History at the University of Bologna. fiorenzo.landi@unibo.it

How the Secularization of Religious Houses Transformed the Libraries of Europe, 16th–19th Centuries, ed. by Cristina Dondi, Dorit Raines, and † Richard Sharpe, BIB, 63 (Turnhout, 2022), pp. 27–38.

BREPOLS ✠ PUBLISHERS   DOI 10.1484/M.BIB-EB.5.128476

them had divergent economic interests, social ties and goals. Even two monasteries located near one another in the same street could operate and manage their resources in a very different way. But if we compare a Benedictine monastery in Seville with a Benedictine monastery in Krakow, or an observant Franciscan monastery in Seville with a convent of the same order in Sweden, they appear to be quite similar.

For many years I have studied regular clergy from an economic perspective with a team of historians from several European countries and from Latin America. We have tried to find an international perspective and to discover the common economic, social, and cultural aspects of the regular clergy. All orders and congregations have been analysed[2]. In my judgement there are four main questions, which I will discuss below. First I shall examine the socio-cultural function of religious orders; second, the forms of wealth and income accumulation, and third the timing of the processes that led to eventual confiscation. Finally, I shall look at the relationship between official acts concerning confiscations, the property actually owned, and the confiscated property – all this with a focus on books and their trade.

1. The Socio-cultural Function of Religious Orders

In the modern age, from the beginning of the sixteenth century to the end of the eighteenth century, the Catholic Church carried out its proselytizing and social control through a network of institutions of both regular and secular clergy, which covered the territory of Europe in an extensive and widespread form. At the beginning

of the sixteenth century, before the Protestant Reformation, forty to fifty thousand monasteries and friaries, nunneries, many parishes, and a whole variety of other institutions, such as brotherhoods, oratories and so on, constituted an established infrastructure to which the secular state also delegated important functions such as educational programs, schools and a wide range of support for the poor, the sick, outcasts, orphans and widows. This sort of *ancien régime* welfare was not based on the principle of equality and solidarity, but on the concepts of privilege, protection, and access to charity. In particular, for those receiving alms and aids, receipt of charity involved an attitude of gratitude which in turn manifested itself in social relationships. Helping and assisting people in need consequently became a way to control minds and behaviour, a process called by historians of the Church "disciplining" ("disciplinamento")[3], and translated into precise behavioral rules by the Council of Trent. The historical category of "disciplining" is closely linked with the confessionalisation model and the instruments used to achieve it: the Inquisition tribunals and the Index of Forbidden Books[4].

2. Forms of Wealth and Income Accumulation of the Religious Institutions

The economic basis that enabled the huge institutional apparatus of the Catholic Church to function consisted for the most part in existing inherited property and income. They were used to

---

2   *Accumulation and Dissolution of Large Estates of the Regular Clergy in Early Modern Europe*, ed. Fiorenzo Landi (Rimini, 1999); Idem, *Confische e sviluppo capitalistico. I grandi patrimoni del clero regolare in età moderna in Europa e nel continente americano* (Milano, 2004).

3   *Disciplina dell'anima, disciplina del corpo e disciplina della società tra medioevo ed età moderna*, ed. Paolo Prodi (Bologna, 1994).

4   Jörg Deventer, '"Confessionalisation" – a useful theoretical concept for the study of religion, politics, and society in early modern East-Central Europe?', *European Review of History: Revue Européenne d'Histoire*, 11, no. 3 (2004), 403–25.

pay the costs of over 100,000 religious institutions, which supported not only religious personnel but a wide range of staff and property as well. "Just as the body does not live without the soul, so too neither do the corporeal goods of the Church exist long without spiritual goods", wrote the canon lawyer William of Saint-Amour at the beginning of the thirteenth century in his treatise *Tractatus brevis de periculis novissimorum temporum ex scripturis sumptus* against the mendicant order (referring to Saint Paul in 1 Corinthians 9:13: "Do you not know that those who perform sacred services eat the food of the temple, and those who attend regularly at the altar have their share from the altar?")[5]. In fact, throughout the modern age the endowment of these religious houses continued to come from institutions of the secular state. Original patrimonies were generally the result of generous donations by sovereign rulers, kings and emperors, to Benedictine abbeys, priories, and nunneries. From the thirteenth century, the emergence and expansion of the mendicant orders, Franciscans, Dominicans, Augustinians, Carmelites, spread a new way of regular life, characterized by the abandonment of collective property just as much as of individual property. This was very soon reconsidered. On the one hand the Catholic Church distrusted choices of pauperism which often degenerated into uncontrollable forms of heretical resistance (from Cathars to Waldensians to Patarines), and so it encouraged the mendicant orders to relax

their elective poverty; on the other hand, the strict rule was closely associated with the heroic phase of the initial mendicant profession, a phase which was gradually fading away.

Consequently, with a few exceptions such as the Minorites or Capuchins, the accumulation of property by mendicant orders went hand in hand with the accumulation of property by traditional orders. After the Counter-Reformation regular priests contributed to a wave of new foundations. Religious followers of a *formula vitae* akin to the traditional rules, they did not however wear habits and did not live in convents. They accomplished their mission in nursing the sick, like the Camillians, and in teaching in Catholic schools, like the Jesuits and Piarists. As had already happened with Mendicants and Benedictines, the new orders did not replace their predecessors but joined them.

3. The Timing of the Procedures Leading to the Eventual Confiscation

The genesis of the rich endowment of religious orders as well as their dissolution are trends common to all European countries and, in this case, to the American colonies too. Forms, times, and reasons are different, but the destiny of large ecclesiastical estates is usually the same, namely confiscation or forced alienation. Bearing in mind that the processes attendant on both the growth and the dissolution of the religious patrimony have many points in common, we can identify at least four waves of confiscation: from 1530 to 1550, from 1770 to 1789, from 1790 to 1820 and from 1820 to 1870. But in fact, as one may see from Tables 1.1 and 1.2[6], both secular governments and the Church itself resorted very frequently to

5   Michel-Marie Dufeil, 'Guglielmo di Sant'Amore', in *Dizionario degli Istituti di perfezione* (= DIP), ed. Guerrino Pelliccia and Giancarlo Rocca, 10 vols (Roma, 1974–2003), IV 1484–1489. Cf. Jonathan Robinson, '*Qui praedicat periculum in illo peribit*: William of St-Amour's Anti-Mendicant Sermons', in *Weapons of Mass Instruction: Secular and Religious Institutions Teaching the World*, Proceedings of a St Michael's College Symposium (25–26 November 2005), ed. Joseph Goering, Francesco Guardiani, and Giulio Silano (Ottawa, 2008), 51–63; Virpi Mäkinen, *Property Rights in the Late Medieval Discussion on Franciscan Poverty* (Leuven, 2001), 19–53.

6   Domingo Javier Andrés, 'Soppressioni e diritto canonico', in *Dizionario degli Istituti di perfezione*, as note 5, VIII 1801–07.

confiscation. Finally, beginning in the second half of the twentieth century, the Catholic Church changed its economic strategy, transferring its interest to financial investments and ending the systematic confiscation of real estates. Naturally from this time onward, the evaluation of the economic activity of the Catholic Church becomes much more difficult because its main objective is the diversification of wealth internationally using non-traceable forms to prevent further seizures[7].

When, in different stages, from about 1530 to the middle of the nineteenth century, the inherited real estate and revenues of the regular clergy were confiscated, the legal justifications adopted focused mainly on two arguments. First, there was a need to eliminate contemplative institutions that were a burden on society; and, secondly, it became essential to restore to secular control the functions that had been delegated to the regular clergy, especially in the fields of charity and social assistance. In both cases the legal arguments were pretexts used to prevent the seizures from appearing as a denial of property rights[8]. The real common objective, however,

of all confiscations was the raising of funds for various purposes: Henry VIII used them to tie the gentry to the Crown, Napoleon to finance military campaigns, nineteenth-century liberal governments to avoid financial default.

The seizures carried out by the secular state followed the same methods from the sixteenth century to the middle of the nineteenth century. They began by considering a list of patrimonies and revenues of individual institutions, generally obtained by the imposition of an affidavit to the parties concerned; then, officials in charge of the seizure proceeded to divide property into lots and sell each portion separately; finally they made a list of what remained unsold and decided how it was to be used.

The first act of this confiscation procedure was established under oath by the prior or abbot of a convent or a monastery on the basis of the administrative records contained in ledgers, inventories, or catalogues of the friary or monastery. The purpose of the procedure was obvious, and the religious could defend themselves by failing to report anything that could be omitted. The kind of property to be confiscated made a real difference: it was obviously very difficult to hide the ownership of land or buildings, whether urban or rural, but it was relatively easy to get rid of documents relating to loans of money or to hide artefacts made of gold and silver[9]. In

---

7   Giancarlo Rocca, 'Le strategie anticonfisca degli istituti religiosi in Italia dall'Unità al Concordato del 1929: appunti per una storia', in *Clero, economia e contabilità in Europa tra Medio Evo ed età contemporanea*, ed. Roberto Di Pietra and Fiorenzo Landi (Roma, 2007), 226–47; Benny Lai, *Finanze e finanzieri vaticani tra l'Ottocento e il Novecento da Pio IX a Benedetto XV* (Milano, 1979); John Francis Pollard, *Money and the Rise of the modern Papacy: Financing the Vatican, 1850–1950* (Cambridge, 2005).

8   The debate on the possibility of abolishing the right of ownership of ecclesiastical persons or entities without questioning the right of ownership in general was particularly intense and important in France during the Revolution. These arguments were also used during the Napoleonic confiscation and those of the liberal governments in the course of the nineteenth century. This apparent contradiction was resolved according to the principle expressed by Charles-Maurice de Talleyrand-Périgord (1754–1838) by which the clergy is not an owner in the same way as other owners, since the goods they enjoy, which they cannot dispose of, are given to them not as personal possessions but only in

order to fulfil their functions. See Louis Bergeron, 'Beni nazionali', in *Dizionario critico della rivoluzione francese*, ed. François Furet and Mona Ozouf (Milano, 1994), 525–33. On the Catholic Church's position: Andrés, 'Soppressioni e diritto canonico', as note 6 and relating bibliography.

9   For example, it was widely known in Ravenna that when General Augereau, Napoleon's army commander, ordered the preparation of the inventory of all property owned by the rich Benedictine monastery of San Vitale, the abbot's relatives, members of the local noble family Guiccioli, shut themselves in the archives for some days in order to falsify documents regarding property ownership, inventories of valuables and loan-at-interest

any case, the most important confiscations took place in a climate of widespread lawlessness and violence under the pressing need for money. The Catholic Church threatened excommunication for buyers of confiscated properties. The most massive confiscations, those of the Napoleonic period and those by liberal governments, took place in a time of change when the political leadership gave no security to the buyers. The result was that often, if not every time, the most important financial transactions were handled by speculators and profiteers, sometimes using accounting tricks and forged records. The Italian historian Pasquale Villani, who conducted some of the most relevant research on the subject of confiscation, considered that only 10% of the wealth taken from the regular clergy was sold in a transparent manner to the actual buyers at auction[10]. Then there were goods that could not find buyers and became property of the state, such as most of the buildings used for urban schools, high schools, courthouses, jails, but also goods of small commercial value, such as a large part of the libraries.

Of course, from the point of view of our historical investigation, the context of widespread lawlessness associated with the dismantling of confiscated church property makes it very difficult to reconstruct the precise facts. The difficulty of finding reliable sources causes a mismatch between the economic reality, documented, for example, through internal accounts of monasteries and convents, statements of abbots and priors under oath, and what we find reported in the lists of seized goods. In other words, almost all sources relating to property confiscated from monasteries and convents are insufficient and incomplete. If we follow the official sources, the image we obtain is distorted because most of the sources are false and unreliable. On the other hand, if we try to understand the hidden mechanisms, there is lack of evidence to demonstrate alternative truths. Historians seem to have solved the problem by not investigating the deep reasons: out of the numerous studies devoted to the regular clergy in general, those focusing on the dynamics and effects of the crisis represent not more than 5–10 per cent[11]. And practically none of these few studies are devoted to libraries and book confiscation in their economic context.

4. Relationship between Official Acts concerning Confiscations and the Confiscated Books

Before we see what kind of evidence of the library holdings of religious institutions can be found in the extant confiscation records, it is worthwhile considering beforehand the kind of religious institutions that may have owned large book collections. In this context the relationship between regular clergy and the development of library collections depended on two aspects: resources and specific mission. The availability of resources had to do with the economic strength of the religious institutions. Many of them in fact had very limited economic resources, especially money, and could not afford to own an expensive asset such as a collection of books. As for the religious institution's mission, if the responsibility assigned to them required engagement in a particular social function rather than in education or some other intellectual duty, the time and effort dedicated to poor

contracts before submitting the list to the French. Fiorenzo Landi, *Un'accumulazione senza sviluppo* (Lugo, 1979), 180.

10   Pasquale Villani, *Italia napoleonica. Guida* (Napoli, 1978), 73.

11   On the confiscation mode, destination and dispersion of confiscated property: Bernard Bodinier and Éric Teyssier, *L'événement le plus important de la Révolution. La vente des biens nationaux* (Paris, 2000); Germán Rueda Hernanz, *La Desamortización en Espana: un balance (1766–1924)* (Madrid, 1997).

relief or helping economically disadvantaged, marginalized, or disabled people would generally have prevented them from acquiring libraries beyond a strictly personal religious one. Studying library holdings of these religious institutions is in consequence quite a hazardous task. Conversely, those institutions that had educational duties or a role in defending theological orthodoxy, and those that more generally represented different social models of religious aspiration, had a need for large library collections. The creation and preservation of large libraries depended to a large extent on institutional stability and continuity of management: a monastery, a friary, or a nunnery could easily maintain important libraries down the centuries with little annual outlay.

We should not, however, expect surviving records to tell us the full story of library collections. Books are one of those categories of property for which there was neither a steady preservation policy nor systematic registration in inventories. The book, as an economic good, had a value for unlawful predators as well as for lawful confiscators. As happened with stolen paintings and other works of art, the most ancient books were rare, attractive and sometimes considered of value to collectors. If such an interest was shown toward library items no longer of direct use for the religious community, its members were not necessarily keen on keeping them in the collection. Illicit transactions were sometimes encouraged by the fact that though the cataloguing of library material was systematically practised in most major monastic libraries, that took place much less frequently in smaller libraries. In fact, the most frequently read books were often borrowed from the library and kept in individual cells; when a member of one community moved to another, he sometimes took the borrowed books with him. The administrative provisions regarding the purchase of books, as well as guidelines for the safekeeping of library material, were rare and sporadic. In the accounts, which always tend to be precise and careful particularly when they concern purchases paid for in cash, references to the purchase of books are almost always absent, even when significant investments were being made to acquire them[12]. We should not forget that monastic accounts were public. This does not mean that they were published, but rather that they were subject to checks carried out by the auditors of congregations and orders, in order to guarantee their correctness. A certain proportion of various items was accordingly frequently modified and made to disappear using simple accounting tricks. These aimed at improving the image of each monastery or abbey by avoiding the disclosure of the real number of merchandise items and artefacts that had disappeared.

The careers of abbots and priors who were entrusted with the direction of convents and monasteries also depended on how well they managed the institutions they administered. Presenting a positive economic balance was therefore of clear interest for them. Evidence of such an attitude, whether direct or indirect, is frequent and convincing: the accounting manuals illustrated budget tricks, even as they deprecated them; auditors and comptrollers of orders and congregations were often on the payroll of the same institutions they were auditing and were rewarded with cash and gifts for favorable assessments; we find reports against abbots or priors responsible for the use of accounting tricks in order to falsify

---

12   The accounting system of double registration should not be confused with the double entry one. Double entry requires that all items are reported under debits and credits. In other words, each item must show a debit or a credit. On the contrary, in case of double registrations, debits and credits are grouped considering costs or revenue centres and only the most important items are autonomous. For example, if the itemizing of expenses for books in a convent included completely alien and heterogeneous subjects, such as the hire of horses for threshing wheat, the expenses of libraries were largely undervalued and the running costs given as much lower than the actual ones. Fiorenzo Landi, *Il Tesoro dei regolari. L'inchiesta sui conventi d'Italia del 1650* (Bologna, 2013).

their accounts; and finally, when the Roman Curia investigated the economic condition of monasteries and convents, they bypassed the ordinary accounting processes, which was always on a cash basis, and instead requested direct economic data, not filtered by the accounting system, which they obviously found untrustworthy.

The above consideration leads us to the conclusion that the affidavits issued by monasteries and convents in relation to confiscation of books are usually very general and in part faulty. If we want to have a more reliable representation of the library collections actually held, it would therefore be better to start from the internal documents of the individual religious houses, in order to get to know at least the general accounting tools and the recording techniques used.

I have already stressed how singular it is not to have records of expenditure related to the purchase of books in the accounting records of religious orders, even where we are certain that books were bought. The absence of records should not surprise us though. Let us consider, for example, the Jesuits. Their objectives were proselytizing missions and education. To manage colleges and apply the *ratio studiorum* they had to buy books in large quantities. And yet the costs for books are not reported in their accounting. In the accounts of Jesuit colleges it is common to find legacies, bequests, which are sums of money intended for predefined purposes. If someone left a legacy of 500 *scudi* per year for buying books, we should need to go back to the original notarial deed unless we happen to be lucky enough to find a random record of the fact[13]. The only reference otherwise is to the *Legatum* item, not the purchase of books. Another example is the number of books that were kept not in libraries but in the individual cells of

monks, nuns, or friars. Some of these had been borrowed, but some had been purchased by the monk or friar, others and others were inherited or obtained in some other way. In these cases there are no traces of such acts until the death of the particular friar or monk. On death, the convent or monastery took possession of the personal property of the deceased. And even in such circumstances libraries were not very often the final destination, since books could simply be transferred to other monks or friars to keep as their own. These are the reasons why the acquisition of hundreds of books was not reported directly but only as *spolium mortuorum*.

Furthermore, there was a problem of *peculium*. The monks and the friars, depending on the order or congregation, were allowed by the internal management to have a *peculium* or a "wage", which is a sum of money for their personal needs: in this way books could be purchased without leaving traces in the record[14]. In other cases the use of ambiguous words helped to obscure such indications: while we are looking for entries such as "library", "buying books", and similar keywords, the books bought may have been recorded under the item *studium*. In other cases the purchase of books is simply to be found under "extraordinary expenses" alongside candle-wax or fees for illegal grazing[15]. At the same time there is a lack of economic interest in purchased books, which

---

13 The *scudo* was the currency of the Papal States until 1866; it was subdivided into 100 *baiocchi*, each subdivided into 5 *quattrini*.

14 Michele Miele, 'Il costo della vita consacrata: la polemica sul peculio nel Settecento', in *Chiesa e denaro tra Cinquecento e Settecento: possesso, uso, immagine*: atti del 13. Convegno di studio dell'Associazione italiana dei professori di storia della Chiesa, Aosta 9–13 settembre 2003 (Milano, 2004), 281–304.

15 In the 6200 investigation reports on the regular clergy's property in Italy in 1650, which lists in detail the income and expenses for each monastery and convent, a specific item indicated the purchase of books, but similar terms may often appear, the most common of which is the study or "stadium". Vatican City, Archivio segreto vaticano, Sacra Congregazione sopra lo stato dei Regolari, *Relationes*, I-48, 1650.

is evident, for example, in the rules regarding the investigation of the economic condition of the regular clergy by Pope Innocent X[16]. The inquest attached economic importance to almost everything – with the exception of books. In the section referring to income and expenditure are also recorded smaller costs: the costs of riding a donkey, amounting to ten *scudi* per annum, the purchase of ten brooms, the cost of some notebooks and ink to write, but there are no recordings of hundreds of *scudi* used to buy books.

It seems that books were considered as personal goods, also when they were placed in a library. All these elements serve to highlight, in my opinion, the difficulties and limitations attached to research on confiscations and, in particular, the difficulty of reconstructing specific movements of library collections from monasteries and convents into public libraries and the losses attendant on such movements. Nevertheless, I should like to conclude with at least one positive note: the similarity of proceedings in this business of confiscation, which affected all European countries and even America, enables us to use case studies in a such a way that we may generalize from them. In other words, individual cases can represent what normally happened in this case much more than in many other contexts.

---

16 Landi, *Il tesoro dei regolari*, as note 12; Emanuele Boaga, *La soppressione innocenziana dei piccoli conventi in Italia* (Roma, 1971).

Table 1.1. Dissolutions ordered by the State[17]

Years	State	Orders
1305–12	France	Templar
1414	England	foreign priories
1522–23	Germany	all orders
1527	Sweden-Finland	all orders
1527–90	Prussia	all orders
1527–90	Norway	all orders
1527–90	Switzerland	all orders
1527–90	Ireland	all orders
1527–90	Scotland	all orders
1527–90	Netherlands	all orders
1527–90	Hungary	all orders
1536	England	all orders
1536	Denmark-Iceland	all orders
1593	France	Jesuits
1606	Venice	Jesuits
1759	Portugal	Jesuits
1761	Kingdom of Naples	
1764	France	Jesuits
1766–80	France	small convents
1767	Spain	Jesuits
1767	Kingdom of Naples	Jesuits
1768	France	various orders
1768	Malta	Jesuits
1768	Duchy of Parma	Jesuits
1768–74	Kingdom of Naples	various convents
1769	Portugal	Oratorians
1769–70	Venice	small convents
1770	Venice	various orders
1770–85	Grand Duchy of Tuscany	Cassinesi
1772	Venice	all orders
1773	Venice	various orders
1773–89	Poland	all orders
1784	Kingdom of Naples	Calabria
1787	Spain	
1789	France	all orders
1798	Ligurian Republic	all orders
1799	Kingdom of Naples	various orders
1803	Germany	all orders
1805	Kingdom of Italy	various orders

---

17   The lists were compiled on the basis of data reported in *Dizionario degli Istituti di perfezione*, as note 5, 'Soppressioni', VIII 1782–1891.

YEARS	STATE	ORDERS
1806	Duchy of Lucca	various orders
1806	Duchy of Parma	Jesuits
1806–15	Kingdom of Naples	all orders
1808–09	Spain	
1820	Russia	Jesuits
1820–23	Spain	various orders
1833–34	Greece	Orthodox
1833–37	Spain	all orders
1834	Portugal	all orders
1841	Switzerland	Canton of Aargau
1848	Kingdom of Sardinia	Jesuits
1848	Switzerland	all orders
1848	Sicily	Jesuits and Redemptorists
1855	Kingdom of Sardinia	all orders
1860–87	Germany	Prussia
1866	Kingdom of Italy	all orders
1868	Spain	all orders

Table 1.2. Dissolutions ordered by the Holy See

YEARS	ORDERS	GEOGRAPHICAL AREA	COUNCIL OR POPE
1274	Mendicants	Catholic Europe	Second Council of Lyons
1312	Beguines and Beghards	Catholic Europe	Council of Vienna
1489	Order of the Holy Sepulchre	Catholic Europe	Innocent VIII
1525	small convents	England	Cardinal Wolsey
1566	Minor Conventual priests	Spain	Pius V
1566	Religious houses without vows and cloistered	Catholic Europe	Pius V
1568	Third Order Regular	Catholic Europe	Pius V
1569	Camaldolese Congregation of Fonte Avellana		Pius V
1570	Florensians	Catholic Europe	Pius V
1571	Humiliati	Catholic Europe	Pius V
1572	Order of Saint Lazarus	Northern Italy	Gregory XIII
1579	Some Camaldolese convents	Italy	Gregory XIII
1626	Reformed Conventual	Catholic Europe	Adrian VIII
1631	"Jesuitesses"	England	Adrian VIII
1645	Order of St Ambrose and St Barnabas	Italy	Innocent X
1650	Basilian Armenians	Catholic Europe	Innocent X
1651	Clerks Regular of the good Jesus	Ravenna	Innocent X
1652	small convents	Italy	Innocent X
1656	Crociferi Canons Regular of the Holy Cross		Alexander VI
1668	Reformed Conventual	Catholic Europe	Clement IX
1668	Jesuati and other	Venice	Clement IX
1751	Coloritani Hermits	Kingdom of Naples	Benedict XIV
1773	Jesuits	Catholic Europe	Clement XIV

Selective Bibliography

Archival sources

Vatican City, Archivio segreto vaticano, Sacra Congregazione sopra lo stato dei Regolari, *Relationes*, I-48, 1650.

Secondary Works

Accumulation and Dissolution of Large Estates of the Regular Clergy in Early Modern Europe, ed. Fiorenzo Landi (Rimini, 1999).

Domingo Javier Andrés, 'Soppressioni e diritto canonico', in *Dizionario degli Istituti di perfezione*, (DIP), ed. Guerrino Pelliccia and Giancarlo Rocca, 10 vols (Roma, 1974–2003), VIII 1801–07.

Louis Bergeron, 'Beni nazionali', in *Dizionario critico della rivoluzione francese*, ed. François Furet and Mona Ozouf (Milano, 1994), 525–33.

Emanuele Boaga, *La soppressione innocenziana dei piccoli conventi in Italia* (Roma, 1971).

Bernard Bodinier and Éric Teyssier, *L'événement le plus important de la Révolution. La vente des biens nationaux* (Paris, 2000).

Jörg Deventer, '"Confessionalisation" – a useful theoretical concept for the study of religion, politics, and society in early modern East-Central Europe?', *European Review of History: Revue Européenne d'Histoire*, 11, no. 3 (2004), 403–25.

Disciplina dell'anima, disciplina del corpo e disciplina della società tra medioevo ed età moderna, ed. Paolo Prodi (Bologna, 1994).

Dizionario degli Istituti di perfezione (= DIP), ed. Guerrino Pelliccia and Giancarlo Rocca, 10 vols (Roma, 1974–2003).

Michel-Marie Dufeil, 'Guglielmo di Sant'Amore', in *Dizionario degli Istituti di perfezione*, (DIP), ed. Guerrino Pelliccia and Giancarlo Rocca, 10 vols (Roma, 1974–2003), IV 1484–89.

Benny Lai, *Finanze e finanzieri vaticani tra l'Ottocento e il Novecento da Pio IX a Benedetto XV* (Milano, 1979).

Fiorenzo Landi, *Un'accumulazione senza sviluppo* (Lugo, 1979).

Fiorenzo Landi, *Confische e sviluppo capitalistico. I grandi patrimoni del clero regolare in età moderna in Europa e nel continente americano* (Milano, 2004).

Fiorenzo Landi, *Storia economica del clero in Europa. Secoli XV–XIX* (Roma, 2005).

Fiorenzo Landi, *Il Tesoro dei regolari. L'inchiesta sui conventi d'Italia del 1650* (Bologna, 2013).

Virpi Mäkinen, *Property Rights in the Late Medieval Discussion on Franciscan Poverty* (Leuven, 2001).

Michele Miele, 'Il costo della vita consacrata: la polemica sul peculio nel Settecento', in *Chiesa e denaro tra Cinquecento e Settecento: possesso, uso, immagine*: atti del 13. Convegno di studio dell'Associazione italiana dei professori di storia della Chiesa, Aosta 9–13 settembre 2003 (Milano, 2004), 281–304.

John Francis Pollard, *Money and the Rise of the modern Papacy: Financing the Vatican, 1850–1950* (Cambridge, 2005).

Germán Rueda Hernanz, *La Desamortización en Espana: un balance (1766–1924)* (Madrid, 1997).

Jonathan Robinson, '*Qui praedicat periculum in illo peribit*: William of St-Amour's Anti-Mendicant Sermons', in *Weapons of Mass Instruction: Secular and Religious Institutions Teaching the World*, Proceedings of a St Michael's College Symposium (25–26 November 2005), ed. Joseph Goering, Francesco Guardiani, and Giulio Silano (Ottawa, 2008), 51–63.

Giancarlo Rocca, 'Le strategie anticonfisca degli istituti religiosi in Italia dall'Unità al Concordato del 1929: appunti per una storia', in *Clero, economia e contabilità in Europa tra Medio Evo ed età contemporanea*, ed. Roberto Di Pietra and Fiorenzo Landi (Roma, 2007), 226–47.

Pasquale Villani, *Italia napoleonica. Guida* (Napoli, 1978).

RICHARD SHARPE († 2020)

Dissolution and Dispersion in Sixteenth-Century England: Understanding the Remains

The words monastic and medieval tend to go together in English history. Between 1535 and 1540 nine centuries of medieval monasticism were brought to an end by act of parliament, and title to all monastic property was vested in the Crown. It is usually seen as a side-effect of the Reformation and in particular of those acts whereby King Henry VIII was declared to be "the only supreme head in earth of the Church of England" (1534) just as he was "only the supreme head of this his realm of England immediately under God" (1536)[1]. The king was to have authority to reform the church within his kingdom. The stimulus is linked to the king's wish to divorce his Spanish queen, Katharine of Aragon, a great matter that had been in train since 1527 – failure to secure annulment from the pope led the king to break with the Church of Rome in 1533 – but, as in other countries, the negative perception of monasteries combined a wide range of different views, economic and social as much as religious, and their dissolution was an act of tactical opportunism as well as part of the long-term historical process that would drastically reduce the role of Catholic monasteries all over Europe and beyond.

Early in 1535, visitors, most of them lawyers, men close to the king's minister Thomas Cromwell, visited the monasteries in England, Wales, and parts of Ireland to report on their revenues and on other matters that caught their attention[2]. Libraries

---

[1] Quotations from An Act concerning the King's Highness to be Supreme Head of the Church of England, 26 Henry VIII, c. 1 (1534), An Act extinguishing the authority of the bishop of Rome, 28 Henry VIII, c. 10 (1536), printed in *Statutes of the Realm*, 12 vols, Record Commission (London, 1810–28), iii. 492, 663–66; abridged in Geoffrey R. Elton, *The Tudor Constitution. Documents and Commentary*, 2nd edn (Cambridge, 1982), 364–65, 365–67.

[2] M. David Knowles, *The Religious Orders in England*, 3 vols (Cambridge, 1948–59), iii. 268–90. This resulted in the *Valor Ecclesiasticus*. Knowles's third volume provides a convenient, footnoted narrative of the whole dissolution process, but, despite its broad scope as monastic history, there is no discussion of monastic libraries in the sixteenth century (though Prior More's book-buying for Worcester is mentioned, p. 122). What happened to libraries at the dissolution gets one footnote (p. 383).

Richard Sharpe († 2020) • Formerly Professor of Diplomatic, University of Oxford

How the Secularization of Religious Houses Transformed the Libraries of Europe, 16th–19th Centuries, ed. by Cristina Dondi, Dorit Raines, and † Richard Sharpe, BIB, 63 (Turnhout, 2022), pp. 39–66.

BREPOLS ❦ PUBLISHERS   DOI 10.1484/M.BIB-EB.5.128477

were of no interest, but letters occasionally provide mention of a book or two, apparently sought out[3]. It is likely that monks realized already that the continuity of monastic life was coming to an end. The act, passed in 1536, that dissolved and secularized all religious houses with an income of less than £200 per year allowed that the king, as well as taking possession of all their landed endowments, "shall have and enjoy to his own proper use all the ornaments, jewels, goods, chattels, and debts", pertaining to the dissolved monasteries[4]. Commissioners were appointed in each county to survey these smaller monasteries, and instructions were issued to them, "to make a just inventory betwixt them and the governor or other head officer [of each religious house], by indenture, of the ornaments, plate, jewels, chattels, ready money, stuff of household, corn as well severed as not severed, stock and store in the farmers' hands and the value thereof"; the instructions further mention lead (from the roofs) and bells, all of which was to be sold, "plate and jewels only excepted"[5]. Many returns survive, some have been published. Furniture was sold on the spot, and from some places there are detailed inventories, including

items that fetched no more than a few pence[6]. Books very rarely feature at all, and even library furniture is scarcely mentioned[7]. One frustratingly brief entry differentiates fifty-two books in the library, valued at a mere 5 shillings, and fifty-four parchment books in the choir, valued at 66s 8d[8]. Gold, silver, and precious stones went to the king's jeweller, Sir John Williams (d. 1559), to be put to secular use[9]. It may be noted that

---

3 William Holleway, prior of Bath, to Thomas Cromwell, dated 24 Sept 1535, below, note 79.

4 An Act whereby all religious houses of monks, canons, and nuns which may not dispend above the clear yearly value of £200 are given to the King's Highness, 27 Henry VIII, c. 28 (1536), sect. 4; *Statutes of the Realm*, iii. 575–78; Elton, *Tudor Constitution*, as note 1, 383–87; Joyce A. Youings, *The Dissolution of the Monasteries* (London, 1971), 155–59. The commissioners from sample counties are listed by Knowles, *Religious Orders*, as note 2, iii. 478–79.

5 An example of such instructions from 1536 is printed by Youings, *Dissolution*, as note 4, 160–63; others, including a draft by Thomas Wriothesley (1505–1550), are noted in *Letters and Papers, Foreign and Domestic. Henry VIII* [hereafter *LP*], 21 vols in 28 (London, 1863–1910), x, no. 721.

6 Samples have appeared in print, for example: Mackenzie E. C. Walcott, 'Inventories and valuations of religious houses at the time of the dissolution', *Archaeologia* 43 (1871), 201–49; Francis A. Hibbert, *The Dissolution of the Monasteries as illustrated by the suppression of the religious houses of Staffordshire* (London, 1910), 224–57, where, apart from the occasional mass-book, one finds only this, at Grey Friars, Stafford, "old books and a coffer in the library, 2s. […] old books in the vestry 8d" (pp. 246–47).

7 Nigel L. Ramsay, '"The manuscripts flew about like butterflies": the break-up of English libraries in the sixteenth century', in *Lost Libraries: The Destruction of Great Book Collections since Antiquity*, ed. James E. Raven (Basingstoke, 2004), 127, 141, cites an example from the inventory of goods at the Grey Friars at Chichester, dissolved on 8 October 1538, which mentions old books in connection with new furniture: "Item in the library four stalls and a half substantially new made with divers old books. Item a goodly new press with almers [*cupboards*] for books" (*Victoria County History* [= VCH] *of Sussex*, ii (London, 1907), 95; *LP*, as note 5, xiii, pt 2, no. 562).

8 Dissolution inventory (1536) from the Premonstratensian abbey of Cockersand, cited by William Farrer, *The Chartulary of Cockersand Abbey*, 7 parts, Chetham Society (1898–1909), iii, pt 3, 1171–72. Since choir-books were now useless, their value can only have been for the parchment; the implication, therefore, is that the library books were "in papiro", that is, most likely printed books.

9 Much appears in the accounts returned by commissioners from individual houses, and the plate and jewels were too much for the Jewel House, so they were stored in the former Hospital of St Mary in Cripplegate, London, dissolved in 1536. The memoir of Williams (Sybil M. Jack, 'Williams, John, Baron Williams (c 1500–1559)', *Oxford Dictionary of National Biography* [=ODNB], https://doi.org/10.1093/ref:odnb/29514) shows him to have been unable to provide cumulative accounts to King Henry. A belated account was presented in 5 Edward VI (1552), 'The declaracion off thaccompt off

vestments and works of art surviving from the monasteries are rare indeed. The stripping of lead from the roofs often yielded a considerable sum of money as well as rendering the buildings of no immediate use except, in many cases, as a source of building stone. This act dissolved the majority of monastic houses, including almost all nunneries, though some bought respite. Late in 1537 a new three-pronged campaign began. This involved the pillage of shrines and relics, even in churches that were not suppressed, seizing a very large sum in gold and silver. It dealt with the mendicant orders, already depleted by emigration: on 6 February 1537/1538 Richard Ingworth OP (d. 1545), was commissioned as visitor of the four mendicant orders, and over the next twelve months the friars were pushed into surrendering their houses[10]. And from the beginning of 1538 the heads of greater monastic houses were subject to pressure by Cromwell's visitors to surrender themselves into the king's hands. New commissions were issued, in this case to experienced visitors and to officials of the court of augmentations, to take possession of the monasteries[11]. The second act of dissolution, which was passed in May 1539, vested in the Crown all monastic possessions surrendered or still to be surrendered[12]. Almost all the greater abbeys had surrendered by January 1539/1540. The process was not without martyrs: the Carthusians resisted even the oath of supremacy in 1535 and perished

for it, the Cistercian abbot of Woburn died in the same cause despite the surrender of his abbey in 1538, the Cluniac prior of Lenton was hanged, and three Benedictine abbots resisted surrender; they were hanged as traitors and their abbeys of Colchester, Glastonbury, and Reading seized in November and December 1539. The last abbey to surrender was Waltham on 23 March 1539/1540. The speed and efficiency with which religious houses, monastic or mendicant, were destroyed represented one of the largest transfers of resources ever seen in the country. Through the court of augmentations, established in 1536, the Crown sold much of the land so acquired into the hands of a newly empowered gentry, changing the social history of England. Monastic ruins remained a symbol of an old monkish era left behind, but the protestant reformation had changed attitudes, and there was only limited regret.

Synopsis of Discussion

Books are not mentioned in any of the statutes or in the instruments for their implementation, though they would have fallen within the category of goods, broadly defined, and might have found buyers as readily as did household furniture. Monastic reading was not well regarded by reformers, and the only books in which the commissioners took a regulated interest were cartularies and registers that preserved evidence of title to lands. Liturgical books of monastic use would serve no purpose. And library books were left to their fates. I have seen no English evidence to show whether anyone knew what had been done in Germany or Switzerland, Denmark or Sweden, to transfer books into other libraries or into the hands of the state[13]. The

Syr John Williams', [ed. William Barclay D. D. Turnbull], *Account of the Monastic Treasures, confiscated at the Dissolution of the various houses in England, by Sir John Williams*, Abbotsford Club (Edinburgh, 1836), which records many thousand ounces of gold and silver.

10 Knowles, *Religious Orders*, as note 2, iii. 360–66.

11 An example concerning specified houses in Lincolnshire, dated 21 February 1539, is printed by Youings, *Dissolution of the Monasteries*, as note 4, 176–77.

12 An Act for dissolution of abbeys, 31 Henry VIII, c. 13 (1539); *Statutes of the Realm*, iii. 733–39; abridged in Elton, *Tudor Constitution*, as note 1, 388–91, and Youings, *Dissolution of the Monasteries*, as note 4, 191–94.

13 Events in Germany, Denmark, Sweden, and Switzerland are discussed by Knowles, *Religious Orders*, as note 2, iii. 165–71, as necessary historical context but without claiming that news from abroad had any impact in

immediate past experience in England, when a major London priory, crippled by insurmountable debt, surrendered to the Crown in 1532, was no different: its books disappeared[14]. Other houses, all small, that were dissolved in the 1520s so that their endowments could be used to support other institutions, probably had little in the way of book-collections. The only house where one might have expected much of a library was St Frideswide's priory in Oxford, which was taken over by Cardinal Wolsey for his Cardinal College, refounded after his fall as Christ Church[15]. It is not known what happened to any library books from the priory[16].

Knowing that King Henry VIII, like his father King Henry VII, had a taste for books, modern books for the most part, one may be surprised that the royal officials took so very little interest in monastic libraries. We shall consider below the evidence for the transfer of some books from dissolved monasteries into the royal library, which happened on a small scale, apparently unsystematically, and in any case in a manner unconnected with the actual dissolution. The evidence available to understand English libraries more broadly in this period tells a story of neglect, decay, closure. All of this makes sense in the light of changes in the use of books and in books themselves, so that, once it is understood that the books in monastic libraries were seen by most people as useless and therefore valueless, it is not surprising that the Crown's agents did not concern themselves.

Antiquarian interest in the medieval past or in well-made medieval manuscripts existed here and there, and it is now realized that individuals in some places were motivated to rescue some books, but it was haphazard. In the very hour of dissolution, one commissioner, the Welsh lawyer John Prise, had sufficient interest to keep for himself manuscripts from the libraries of houses he dismantled[17]. Men of such antiquarian tastes were not usually commissioned by the king's minister Thomas Cromwell for this task, and Prise's interest is known to us only from

England and without mention of books.

14   This was Holy Trinity, Aldgate, whose prior surrendered in February 1532 (Eliza Jeffries Davis, 'The beginning of the dissolution: Christchurch, Aldgate, 1532', *Transactions of the Royal Historical Society* 4th ser. 8 (1925), 127–50). Its buildings were swiftly sold for development, its revenues went to the Crown, and the last canons received pensions. The one book now known from its library has a shelfmark, "de vj ordine xlij"; by 1610 it was in the hands of Archbishop Bancroft, now Lambeth Palace, MS 51, but it seems to have escaped the notice of Leland in London in the 1530s and '40s. One might have expected the London book-trade to have taken more interest. Another London house, the collegiate church of St Martin-le-Grand, had been appropriated by Henry VII in 1503 to support the running of his chapel attached to Westminster abbey, and it was suppressed in 1542 (VCH, as note 7, *London*, 1909, i. 555–66). An inventory shows its richness in plate and vestments, but the only books were service books and a grammar-book chained in the choir (James M. W. Willoughby, *The Libraries of Collegiate Churches*, Corpus of British Medieval Library Catalogues 15 [London, 2013], 292–99, [SC262]).

15   See James M. W. Willoughby, 'Thomas Wolsey and the books of Cardinal College', *Bodleian Library Record* 28 (2015), 114–34.

16   This was one of thirty houses suppressed by Wolsey with papal consent in 1524–1525 and 1527–1528 to fund his colleges at Oxford and Ipswich; with the exception of the Cluniac priory at Daventry, the rest were small (Knowles, *Religious Orders*, as note 2, iii. 470). In most cases evidence of libraries does not exist. Lessness in Kent is the only one of these houses from which library

books have survived. It is interesting to note, however, that four old liturgical books from Bromehill priory were transferred into Wolsey's new college in Ipswich (Willoughby, *Collegiate Churches*, as note 14, 261, 266). In 1531 it was parliament – papal consent would no longer be sought – that allowed Henry VIII to suppress several small houses to support Henry VI's foundation at Eton College. None of this was secularization but conversion of use, a long-established tradition.

17   Neil R. Ker, 'Sir John Prise', *The Library* 5th ser. 10 (1955), 1–24, repr. in his *Books, Collectors, and Libraries* (London, 1985), 471–95, with addenda, 496.

the modern recognition of surviving monastic books that passed through his hands.

The evidence available to us dictates what can be learnt. Historical records from the sixteenth century for the most part show libraries coming to an end, even in institutions not affected by the dissolution of the religious houses. This evidence has been brought together by Nigel Ramsay, and it leaves no doubt that the dissolution could hardly have happened at a worse time for the conservation, even the selective conservation, of monastic libraries[18]. The one context that could provide continuity did little to save libraries from before the dissolution: just two Benedictine houses that became secular cathedrals have retained to this day a significant proportion of their medieval books, namely Durham and Worcester. Twelve other religious houses that became secular cathedrals kept little or nothing[19]. Occasionally one can find evidence to show that former religious kept books for themselves, in some cases hoping that monastic life would be restored, but in only one case, Lanthony priory, is there reason to think that this preserved a significant cluster of books, and the route to preservation cannot be reconstructed. The major part of the evidence for what happened to monastic libraries is not the historical record but actual books, still in existence, that contain evidence to associate them with a religious house. Since the libraries were broken up, there is no predictable line of transmission for such books and no general reason why they should survive in large groups.

It was not until the last years of the nineteenth century that scholarship in England began to recognize and record such information with any view to framing lists of what has survived from this or that library and comparing such lists of surviving books with monastic library catalogues drawn up in the middle ages. Montague Rhodes James (1862–1936) was the pioneer, who began the recording of such evidence in his descriptive catalogues of manuscripts and who made an effort to print the major extant medieval catalogues annotated with references to those books that have survived and could be cross-matched. His list of books from the abbey of Bury St Edmunds published in 1895 was the first of its kind, but his work proved influential over the next forty years. On the eve of the Second World War an effort was made to inspect all medieval manuscripts in English collections, or in displaced collections, so that such evidence could be systematically gathered. The result was brought together by Neil R. Ker (1908–1982) as *Medieval Libraries of Great Britain. A List of Surviving Books*, first published in 1941, revised in 1964, supplemented in 1987, and now with a digital third edition available online[20]. This work has borne fruit in several ways. The identification of former monastic books in the old royal collection, which includes what has survived from the libraries of King Henry VIII, has made possible a study of the rescue of medieval books for the king on the eve of the dissolution. The identification of such books more broadly and their listing according to their medieval provenances shows what libraries are represented by substantial numbers of books and invites one to ask the question why they are so represented. Where books survive, even in small numbers, it is important to ask by what route they survived. What Ker himself calls the *descent* of the books, and especially of batches of books, is usually the key to understanding their fate around the time of the dissolution and after[21]. Without this synthesis of physical

---

18 Ramsay, "The manuscripts flew about like butterflies", as note 7, 125–44.

19 Bristol, Canterbury, Carlisle, Chester, Ely, Gloucester, Oxford, Norwich, Peterborough, Rochester, Westminster, and Winchester.

20 James M. W. Willoughby, in this volume.

21 Neil R. Ker, *Medieval Libraries of Great Britain. A List of Surviving Books* (London, 1941), x–xv, and with revisions on the same pages in the second edition. This preface

evidence, what happened to the books could not have been told. Just as the king's agents were not concerned with books, so students of the dissolution have not been concerned with libraries[22]. A lecture delivered to the London Bibliographical Society by Ker in 1942 began the process of reconstructing the story of what had happened to monastic books and how some thousands of them could be found and identified in institutional collections[23]. To read his listings with a knowledge of what religious houses once existed, of their wealth, the number of their monks, perhaps even the number of their books recorded in medieval catalogues, reveals how much has been lost.

Book and Library Environment

This brief sketch outlines the difficulty of the subject and explains the structure of this paper. Contemporary historical evidence for what happened to monastic books, as we have seen, is very scarce. There was simply no official interest, and we can consider the reasons for that. Unofficial interest is very rarely documented, but it existed here and there, as we infer from the fact that some thousands of former monastic books have survived. We have had to learn to interpret this material evidence and to make of it what sense we can in relation to the perceived historical background.

Circumstances were extraordinarily unfavourable. Most old learning was out of fashion, commentaries on the Sentences of Peter Lombard and the works of Duns Scotus were scorned by the king's visitors at Oxford in 1535, and the whole field of canon law had become obsolete[24]. Even where works of learning were not out of date, most sixteenth-century readers saw little reason to use old handwritten copies, which became vulnerable to disposal, even before the dissolution. The early sixteenth-century catalogue of the library of the brethren of Syon abbey provides a conspicuous demonstration: founded in 1417, the abbey had acquired manuscripts for sixty years, but from as early as 1468 the brethren started to acquire printed books[25]. After 1516 more than two hundred entries in the catalogue were erased and rewritten as new books took the place of old[26]. Where books were chained to lectern desks, the space was probably fully utilized by this period, and to bring in any new book meant the removal of an old one[27]. The Syon catalogue was not maintained after 1524, so that any subsequent accessions were unrecorded in the extant evidence[28]. This catalogue depicts

---

sets out the method very clearly.

22   Even in the work of a medievalist such as Dom David Knowles (see n. 2 above).

23   Neil R. Ker, 'The migration of manuscripts from the English medieval libraries', *The Library* 4th ser. 23 (1942), 1–11, repr. in his *Books, Collectors, and Libraries* (London, 1985), 459–69, with addenda, 470.

24   The visitation of Oxford in September 1535 by Dr Richard Layton and Dr John Tregonwell (*LP*, as note 5, ix, nos 350, 351; M. Claire Cross, 'Oxford and the Tudor state', in *History of the University of Oxford*, ed. Trevor Henry Aston, 8 vols [Oxford, 1984–2000], iii. 117–49, at 128–29).

25   The catalogue was first edited by Mary Bateson, *Catalogue of the Library of Syon Abbey, Isleworth* (Cambridge, 1898). Her preface says that she began the work with no sense of the bibliographical challenge it presented; it is fortuitous that she was able to draw on advice from both Montague Rhodes James and George F. Warner, who were just beginning to shape the new study of monastic bibliography in England. The edition was superseded by Vincent A. Gillespie, *Syon Abbey*, Corpus of British Medieval Library Catalogues 9 (London, 2001). The date when printed books begin to be acquired is inferred from the index of imprints (pp. 679–95) in conjunction with the list of donors (pp. 567–94). Of course, donors who brought books acquired before profession complicate the picture.

26   Gillespie, *Syon Abbey*, as note 25, 439–502, recovers the content of 262 erased entries from the unamended index to the primary catalogue.

27   As observed by Ramsay, "The manuscripts flew about like butterflies", as note 7, 132.

28   Gillespie, *Syon Abbey*, as note 25, xlix–l.

an unusually modern library. In many monastic libraries manuscripts continued in use for decades after they had been outmoded. For example at Canterbury cathedral in 1508 money was invested in repairs and chaining of a collection of nearly three hundred books, for the most part manuscripts dating from the twelfth and thirteenth centuries[29].

Books of newer learning were not necessarily to be found in religious houses, but even where they were, printed books were not seen as valuable. By the 1520s and '30s readers could very often afford to own the books they needed to an extent that cannot be observed a generation earlier, perhaps not even a decade earlier[30]. More than two hundred volumes gifted to Corpus Christi College, Cambridge, "ad usum magistri et sociorum", by its former master Peter Nobys, after 1525 and perhaps as late as 1542, illustrate the point; this represents far more books than appear in the college inventory[31]. By the 1560s and '70s students were owning even more books

and doing so earlier in their careers[32]. If we look at evidence from the university colleges of Oxford and Cambridge, where for two centuries – roughly 1320 to 1520 – small institutions had used communal resources to provide students and scholars with sufficient books for their studies, investment in libraries more or less ceased[33]. Books chained to desks languished or worse, and lending stocks were depleted and not replenished. Readers who needed current texts had no use for books inherited from the previous generation, let alone from forebears four centuries before. While college libraries languished, university libraries closed. In Cambridge no money was spent on books for the university library between 1530 and 1573; it was in effect abandoned in 1546–1547[34]. The older university library in Oxford faded away in the same period, almost unvisited after the 1530s, though the antiquary and bibliographer John Bale (1495–1563) was there at some time between 1548 and 1553, hunting for little-known medieval works among the neglected books[35].

29 The list, arranged by desk, was drawn up by William Ingram in 1508. Printed by Montague Rhodes James, *Ancient Libraries of Canterbury and Dover* (Cambridge, 1903); discussion by Ker, 'The migration of manuscripts', as note 23, 10–11, and by Christopher F. R. de Hamel, 'The dispersal of the library of Christ Church, Canterbury, from the fourteenth to the sixteenth century', in *Books and Collectors, 1200–1700. Essays Presented to Andrew Watson*, ed. James P. Carley and Colin G. C. Tite (London, 1997), 263–79, at 269–70.

30 David J. McKitterick, 'Two sixteenth-century catalogues of St John's College library', *Transactions of the Cambridge Bibliographical Society* 7 (1978), 135–55, at 138, 140–41; Kristian Jensen, 'Universities and colleges', in *The Cambridge History of Libraries in Britain and Ireland*, ed. Elisabeth Leedham-Green and Teresa Webber, 3 vols (Cambridge, 2006), i. 345–62, at 351.

31 The record of Nobys's books is printed by Peter D. Clarke, *The University and College Libraries of Cambridge*, Corpus of British Medieval Library Catalogues 10 (London, 2002), 211–39 (UC22); this may be compared with the list of just over one hundred books on the six stalls of the college library refitted in the 1560s, ibid. 241–54 (UC25).

32 Neil R. Ker, 'The provision of Books', in *History of the University of Oxford*, ed. Trevor Henry Aston, 8 vols (Oxford, 1984–2000), iii. 441–519, at 477. An earlier example of expanding private libraries is provided by the case of John Bateman (d. 1559), who left nearly 500 books (Elisabeth S. Leedham-Green, *Books in Cambridge Inventories: Book Lists from Vice-Chancellor's Court Probate Inventories in the Tudor and Stuart Periods*, 2 vols (Cambridge, 1986), i. 234–44 (no. 105).

33 Neil R. Ker, 'Oxford college libraries in the sixteenth century', *Bodleian Library Record* 6 (1957–61), 459–515; id., 'Provision of books', as note 32.

34 John Claude T. Oates, *Cambridge University Library. A History. From the beginnings to the Copyright Act of Queen Anne* (Cambridge, 1986), 73, 81; Jensen, 'Universities and colleges', as note 30, 347.

35 The notebook in which John Bale recorded titles is now Bodl. MS Selden Supra 64; rearranged into alphabetic order, this was printed by Reginald Lane Poole and Mary Bateson, *John Bale's Index of British and Other Writers* (Oxford, 1902), repr. with introduction by James P. Carley and Caroline Brett (1989). Titles noted "Ex bibliotheca Academie Oxon." appear at pp. 14, 38, 82, 178, 242, 247, 299, 309, 321, 400; "Ex bibliotheca gymnasii

Soon afterwards, protestant reformers cleared the desks of books, and in January 1556 even the furniture was sold off; it was bought to equip a new college library for the recent foundation of Christ Church, though this was perhaps a rearguard action more than an early sign of recovery[36]. The famous collection of books given by Duke Humfrey had simply melted away[37]. For fifty years and more institutional libraries were neglected, in many cases to the point of extinction.

This academic context sheds light on what happened in the monasteries of the university towns, where one might have thought that monastic books could have found new secular use. The religious houses of Oxford had once had important libraries. Black Friars and Grey Friars had been major repositories of texts in the middle ages. In the latter case, John Leland visited in 1535 to see the famous library and found only filth and neglect, saying that the important books had been alienated long since by the friars themselves[38]. Little survives now,

and how even that survived is not deducible[39]. From Osney abbey, near Oxford castle, a dozen books survive at Magdalen College. Canterbury College books, sent to Oxford from Canterbury cathedral priory for the use of monks at the university, were inventoried at intervals; the inventories made in 1501 show the library at its largest, with some 340 volumes, and the books were listed for the last time in 1534, when there were still some 260 manuscripts and a dozen printed books[40]. The college was surrendered along with its parent, the cathedral priory at Canterbury, in 1540, and the books were at once disposed of. They are now best represented as parchment leaves used by local book-binders, an ironic testimony to the thriving market for sixteenth-century books in Oxford[41].

The learned clerks of the university were still major buyers and users of books, modern books, but libraries as such had become largely irrelevant. When whole libraries of old books became ownerless, no one picked up what could be had for little or nothing[42]. Neither the colleges

---

Oxon.", p. 39; "Ex collegio Academie Oxon.", p. 65; "Ex bibliotheca Oxoniensi", pp. 69–70. Poole and Bateson sought each title in the lists of Duke Humfrey's books; they found two still present from 1439 (pp. 242, 299, and 321), one from 1444 (p. 309); given the slightness of Bale's record, this does not mean that there were not more of the duke's books still at their desks.

36 Ker, 'Provision of books', as note 32, 465–66; Jensen, 'Universities and colleges', as note 30, 347. The library furniture was bought by Richard Marshall, dean of Christ Church, in order to set up a college library in the former monastic refectory of St Frideswide's. Marshall was dean only under Queen Mary, his catholic views were often to the fore, and he may have wished to create an old-fashioned home for books displaced by more forward-looking heads. See further, Ralph Hanna and David G. Rundle, *A Descriptive Catalogue of the Western Manuscripts, to c. 1600, in Christ Church, Oxford* (Oxford, 2017), 38–39.

37 David G. Rundle, 'Habits of manuscript-collecting: the dispersals of the library of Humfrey, duke of Gloucester', in *Lost Libraries*, as note 7, 106–24.

38 John Leland, *De uiris illustribus*, ed. James P. Carley (Toronto, 2010), 480–83; Carley, lxii, for date of his visit.

39 Eight books survive, all in different places, with an *ex libris* from the Oxford Grey Friars; see Neil R. Ker, *Medieval Libraries of Great Britain: A List of Surviving Books* (London, 1941) [= *MLGB*], 142, none from the Black Friars. The small library at the end of the dormitory in the Austin Friars' house is represented by three books with donor inscriptions.

40 William Abel Pantin, *Canterbury College, Oxford*, 4 vols, Oxford Bibliographical Society new ser. 6–8, 30 (Oxford, 1947–85). 1. 39–44, 75–76.

41 Neil R. Ker, *Fragments of Medieval Manuscripts used as Pastedowns in Oxford Bindings*, 2nd edn, Oxford Bibliographical Society 3rd ser. 5 (Oxford, 2004 for 2000), passim; de Hamel, 'The Dispersal of the library of Christ Church', as note 29, 264–69. The buildings of Canterbury College were acquired for Christ Church – Canterbury Quad occupies the site – but the new college inherited none of its books; Hanna and Rundle, *Catalogue of Christ Church*, as note 36, 35.

42 For the example of a learned foreign buyer, Marcello Cervini, acquiring English manuscripts in bulk probably in the Low Countries, see James M. W. Willoughby, 'Cardinal Marcello Cervini (1501–1555) and English

nor their individual fellows were interested in such books around 1540.

It is clear that the dissolution of the monasteries occurred at what was, in England, the worst possible time for their books. The modern medium of print, new learning, and new protestant attitudes were three reasons why most older books and all older libraries were outmoded. The new affordability of printed books meant that old books were unwanted. Even in a case such as Syon, where the brethren had many modern books, there is no evidence of selective survival, even when located so close to the London book-trade. Between 1536 and 1540 the dissolution might have brought tens of thousands of books into the market if there had been buyers, but it has become a commonplace to say that the buyers were mostly the book-binders, the glovers, the chandlers, anyone who could use cheaply-available scrap parchment.

Survival

Only two circumstances favoured the preservation of monastic library collections. One of these was where the institution itself continued with a new secular community, which could keep the library, or some of it, if it chose to, for as long as there was space available. The other was where individual religious retained substantial numbers of books, but as individuals they could not provide continuity. These two factors have shaped the best preserved collections of monastic books, but the survivors are few, little more than a thousand books in total.

First, then, some religious houses enjoyed a degree of institutional continuity. In medieval England seven cathedrals had, instead of a chapter

of secular canons, a Benedictine cathedral priory, headed by a prior who was in effect dean of the cathedral. One cathedral, Carlisle, was a priory of Austin canons. In all these cases the monastic house surrendered to the king, but the cathedral remained, and in most cases the conventual buildings remained, while a secular chapter of dean and canons replaced the monastic chapter[43]. There was even some continuity of personnel as former monks accepted prebends and became secular canons. In addition, six former abbeys survived under new constitutions: four Benedictine abbeys and two Augustinian abbeys became new cathedrals, though the see of Westminster did not endure[44]. Out of these fourteen houses, with annual incomes ranging from £418 at Carlisle to £2,349 at Canterbury and £3,470 at Westminster, just two have retained a substantial number of books, Durham and Worcester. Durham has what is probably the highest survival ratio of any monastic collection, with more than six hundred manuscript books still in existence, two thirds of them still in Durham[45]. Perhaps as many as one hundred printed books survive with evidence of having belonged to monks of Durham; Ushaw College, a Catholic seminary founded four miles from Durham in 1804, now has most of these, but how and when they reached the college is unknown[46]. In the

---

libraries', in *Books and Bookmen in Early Modern Britain. Essays Presented to James P. Carley*, ed. James M. W. Willoughby and Jeremy Catto (Toronto, 2018), 119–49.

43   The former Benedictine cathedral priories are Canterbury, Durham, Ely, Norwich, Rochester, Winchester, and Worcester.

44   Chester, Gloucester, and Peterborough, all Benedictine, and Bristol and Oxford, both Austin canons, became the sees of new dioceses in 1542. The royal abbey at Westminster, which became a cathedral late in 1540, lost its bishop but retained its canons in 1550; the Benedictine rule was restored here by Queen Mary in 1556, but in 1559 it became again a college of secular canons and has remained since 1579 a royal peculiar.

45   Figures from *MLGB3*; for which see James M. W. Willoughby in this volume.

46   Alan J. Piper, 'Dr Thomas Swalwell, monk of Durham, archivist and bibliophile (d. 1539)', in *Books and Collectors, 1200–1700*, as note 29, 71–100. The late Ian Doyle had

case of Worcester, the inconvenient location of the medieval library, high in the south transept, allowed benign neglect to preserve books that no one in the sixteenth century is likely to have wanted, making it an unusual cache of more than one hundred volumes that survived precisely because they were unwanted, and now bearing a precious witness to the late medieval connexions between the cathedral priory and Oxford university[47]. On the whole, however, the senior men appointed to canonries in the cathedrals in the sixteenth century had no more interest in keeping up old libraries than their younger counterparts in the universities. They had the money to own the books they wanted.

Individual religious who kept communal books are not so easy to observe. At the London Charterhouse in November 1538 surviving brethren "were licensed by the visitors to take such things as were meet for them"; beds and books are mentioned[48]. In Yorkshire, a few former monks from the Cluniac priory of Monk Bretton maintained communal life in private in a house at Worsbrough, and in July 1558 one of them drew up a list of books in their house, bought ("empti") by the former prior, subprior, and two surviving former monks. There are nearly one hundred and fifty items on the list, a mixture of medieval and modern reading, but almost all of them printed books[49]. Where particular

editions can be identified, they date from before the priory surrendered in 1538, so that it may be supposed, but cannot be proven, that the books were monastic books, perhaps bought from the commissioners at the time of the surrender. If so, these monks had modernized their library. Four Yorkshire monks may have hoped that the brief catholic restoration under Queen Mary (1553–1558) would lead to a resumption of monastic life, but it did not. They had no successors, and none of their books can now be traced. Such former monks in Yorkshire have been the subject of study, and several mentioned monastic books in their testaments[50]. At the time of his death in 1544 William Vavasour, last warden of the Grey Friars in York, had a library (as a probate inventory shows): "Item eight score (160) printed books in the study, £8; item other bookes in parchment and paper written, 8s; item desks in the study, 2s". He left twenty books to one priest in the city, six to another, and the remainder, together with the desks and "all things thereunto belonging", he bequeathed to another former friar, Ralph Clayton[51]. The valuation of the printed books at 1s each is low, and one can only wonder how many manuscripts added up to 8s. Edward Heptonstall, sometime Cistercian of Kirkstall abbey, making his will in August 1558, wanted "all the books in a chest at the foot of his bed and all the other books then

been working on the printed books of Ushaw College and had found many more with Swalwell's annotations. The College closed as a seminary in 2011 but the library remains *in situ* and is now overseen by the University of Durham Library, the books newly catalogued.

47 The manuscripts were catalogued by Rodney M. Thomson, *A Descriptive Catalogue of the Medieval Manuscripts in Worcester Cathedral Library* (Cambridge, 2001). See further Joan Greatrex, *Everyday Sermons from Worcester Cathedral Priory. An Early Fourteenth-Century Collection in Latin* (Amsterdam, 2019).

48 *LP*, as note 5, xiii, pt 2, no. 903.

49 Printed with notes by Richard Sharpe in *English Benedictine Libraries. The Shorter Catalogues*, Corpus of British Medieval Library Catalogues 4 (London, 1996), 266–87.

50 Discussion by M. Claire Cross, 'Community solidarity among Yorkshire religious after the Dissolution', in *Monastic Studies. The Continuity of Tradition*, ed. Judith Loades (Bangor, 1990), 245–54; details of the individuals in M. Claire Cross and Noreen Vickers, *Monks, Friars, and Nuns in Sixteenth-Century Yorkshire*, Yorkshire Archaeological Society Record Series 150 (Leeds, 1995), 455 (Vavasour), 456–57 (Clayton), 146 (Heptonstall), 101 (Barker). The manuscripts that survive from Greyfriars York, Kirkstall abbey, and Byland abbey cannot be directly associated with any former religious.

51 M. Claire Cross, *York Clergy Wills 1520–1600* (York, 1984–1989), ii. 33–35 (will, dated 13 Nov. 1544, proved 16 Jan 1544/1545), 35–36 (inventory).

in his custody, which had once belonged to the abbey", to be looked after in case the abbey should be restored. And Robert Barker, last prior of Byland abbey, is inferred to have kept monastic books from the fact that a namesake, vicar of Driffield from 1558, making his will in 1581, listed nearly ninety titles and "fortye other olde written bookes which ar of small valewe"; he left them to trustees until some member of his family might "be able to understand them"; it is inferred from his otherwise modest inventory that these had come down to him from the Cistercian abbey, whose restoration was now beyond hope[52]. To judge from the titles, some items were undoubtedly manuscripts, probably dating from the early thirteenth century, and one perhaps earlier[53]. One of his trustees, John Nettleton (d. 1597), was also a man who owned former monastic books, which came into the hands of Henry Savile (1568–1617), of Banke, Yorkshire, whose own family had also been able to keep monastic books[54]. Research into

clerical wills from other counties would no doubt reveal similar examples of former religious who retained what were or at least may have been monastic books.

From the Austin canons of Lanthony priory in the suburbs of Gloucester we have books but must guess at their descent. More than one hundred books from the priory were acquired by Archbishop Richard Bancroft at the beginning of the seventeenth century, but one can only speculate how so many were kept together for sixty years after the priory surrendered to the king's agent in 1539. This large group was one of the first of its kind to be recognized, and M. R. James looked for an explanation. The seventeenth-century memoirist Anthony Wood had long since suggested that the last prior of Lanthony had a collection of manuscripts, which passed to his nephew and so descended to John Theyer (1597–1673), the subject of Wood's memoir. Testing this, James confirmed that the last pensioned prior Richard Hart *alias* Hempsted, in his will dated 1545, bequeathed "all his bookes of latyn" to one Thomas Morgan, which could mean that he had retained monastic books; Hart also names as one of his executors his sister's husband, Thomas Theyer, whose grandson, the aforementioned John Theyer, had a considerable library of manuscripts, sold by his grandson Charles in 1678 and acquired for the

---

52 M. Claire Cross, 'A medieval Yorkshire library', *Northern History* 25 (1989), 281–90.

53 "Explanatio magistri Stephani Cantuariensis in Isaia propheta" (p. 287) is a work of Stephen Langton never printed; "Alexander super Ecclesiasten" (p. 287) is probably Alexander Nequam's work in five books, part of which was printed for the first time in 1863, the rest is still unprinted. Both are likely to be manuscripts from the thirteenth century. Behind another item, "Epistola de postulanda expositione in Lucam" (p. 290), one may recognize Bede's commentary on Luke, and it may be noted that a high-quality Cistercian copy, s. xii[3/4], of his commentaries on Acts and the Catholic Epistles survives from Byland abbey, now in the library at Wormsley Park (*The Wormsley Library. Catalogue of an Exhibition held at the Pierpont Morgan Library, New York, 27 January–2 May 1999* (New York, NY, 1999), 8–11). This Byland Bede is first visible in the hands of one Thomas Bateman (1821–1861), of Bakewell; its whereabouts for the previous three centuries are unknown.

54 The executor, John Nettleton, of Hutton Cranswick, and his family were recusants; Hugh Aveling, *Post Reformation Catholicism in East Yorkshire 1558–1790*, East Yorkshire Local History Series xi (1960), 60.

Andrew G. Watson, *The Manuscripts of Henry Savile of Banke* (London, 1969), 56: BL MS Harley 524, a thirteenth-century volume of sermons and theological texts without evidence of medieval provenance, has Nettleton's name (fol. 4r) in the hand of the next owner, Henry Savile of Banke. Cyril E. Wright, 'The dispersal of the libraries in the sixteenth century', in *The English Library before 1700*, ed. Francis Wormald and Cyril E. Wright (London, 1958), 157–58 and n. 25, mentions that he owned a late-fifteenth-century book of hours, citing a sale catalogue from 1949 (and since resold, Sotheby's, 1 Dec. 1970, lot 2871, where the Nettleton inscription is reproduced, and Sotheby's, 8 Dec. 1975, lot 96, "England, perhaps London, after 1457").

royal library by Charles II. Yet among the Theyer manuscripts in the royal library James found "not more than two or three that are Lanthony books"[55]. Small groups of Lanthony manuscripts passed through the hands of men connected with Gloucester cathedral in the late sixteenth and early seventeenth centuries. Of these the most substantial is a clutch of more than twenty manuscripts given to Corpus Christi College, Oxford, in the early seventeenth century by Henry Parry, whose father, of the same name, a protégé of Bancroft, had been bishop of Gloucester from 1607 to 1610[56]. The Porter family, who obtained the site of the priory and lived there, does not feature, so the books had surely not remained *in situ*[57]. Yet someone must have kept this large group of books together, which probably passed through more than one owner before reaching Bancroft. The fact that books from Gloucester abbey did not do so well, let alone books from the friaries in the city, may be a pointer that it was a member of the monastic community rather than just someone in the neighbourhood who was collecting monastic books. A local bibliophile of

antiquarian tastes might have formed a collection of more diverse provenance.

Most monastic collections were simply abandoned to their fates. There was no conversion to secular use such as happened in Zurich, no policy of sequestration such as happened in Sweden, but nor was there any policy of sale or destruction. If former monks or incoming owners of monastic buildings did not want the books, anyone could have them, and in some places we can infer that there were men of antiquarian taste who kept books. The colossal dispersion was not always immediate: it has been shown at Canterbury cathedral, which continued as a secular foundation, that books were being removed from the claustral buildings over three generations. It is known that nearly five thousand books survive that bear evidence of medieval monastic ownership, of which four fifths survived without any perceptible institutional connexion[58]. From a very few abbeys, hundreds of books survive, from some, dozens, from many, one, two, a few books. The scale of survival is not always related to the size and wealth of institutions, but the great majority of religious houses were small and their libraries perhaps proportionately insignificant. From most houses nothing can now be recognized, but there are recognizable books from over four hundred abbeys, priories, and friaries. Even where large numbers of books have survived, it is evident that they were being dispersed among different takers and keepers, so that no one line of descent explains survival. Their preservation over the centuries is not necessarily distinct from that of other medieval books, held by secular institutions or by successive

---

55   Montague Rhodes James, *The Manuscripts in the Library at Lambeth Palace* (Cambridge, 1900), 1–6. In fact, one certain and two probable books from Lanthony had reached the Royal Library before 1542 (James P. Carley, *The Libraries of King Henry VIII*, Corpus of British Medieval Library Catalogues 7 (London, 1999), H2. 651, 686, 1422), only one came through the Theyer collection (BL MS Royal 8 D. VIII). R. Ian Jack, 'An archival case history: the cartularies and registers of Llanthony priory in Gloucestershire', *Journal of the Society of Archivists* 4 (1972), No. 5, 370–83, at 371, makes the supposition that Bancroft acquired the books now at Lambeth "from the Theyers", but this is not very probable: it is scarcely credible that Bancroft persuaded Thomas Theyer's father or grandfather to relinquish books selected for their shared provenance.

56   Rodney M. Thomson, *A Descriptive Catalogue of the Medieval Manuscripts of Corpus Christi College, Oxford* (Cambridge, 2011), xxiv.

57   Andrew G. Watson, *The Libraries of the Augustinian Canons*, Corpus of British Medieval Library Catalogues 6 (London, 1998), 35.

58   A figure of 4,900 is given by David N. Bell, 'Monastic libraries 1400–1557', in *Cambridge History of the Book in Britain*, 6 vols (Cambridge, 1999–2011), iii. 229–54, at 243, counting from *Medieval Libraries of Great Britain* and excluding secular institutions. He adds that about 320 of these known monastic books are printed (pp. 245, 249–50).

private owners. Nearly five centuries since the dissolution, we now seek to recover the complex stories of how monastic books have survived[59].

Reconstructing Lost Libraries

What happened to monastic books became a story worth telling only when scholars began to take a systematic interest in the marks of ownership in medieval manuscripts. The key date in England was 1895, when Montague Rhodes James, a fellow of King's College, Cambridge, published a list of manuscripts that had belonged to the great Suffolk abbey of Bury St Edmunds[60]. James had grown up six miles away at Great Livermere, but his work was not merely sentimental. In his day King's College, MS 7, was a mid-twelfth-century copy of Bede on Revelation with the *ex libris* of Bury and a class-mark B. 292; from this James learnt to recognize books from Bury and set out to look for them. He found a hundred at Pembroke College, given in 1599 by an Ipswich merchant named William Smart, and in one of these, MS 47, there was a list of books written in the second half of the twelfth century and continued by later hands. James was well on the way to reconstructing a lost library. Moreover, Boston of Bury, someone who was supposed to have lived in the early fifteenth century, was a

name known to medieval bibliography since the sixteenth century, when John Bale had cited his work[61]. His catalogue of authors aroused much interest among scholars in the seventeenth century, though very few saw it. James identified Boston as the author of bibliographical notes at the front of many Bury books. In 1898 he discovered a transcript of Boston's work made in 1694 by Thomas Tanner (1674–1735), from which excerpts had been published[62].

Much more recently "Boston" has been shown to be a ghost, created by Bale, who had obtained an anonymous copy of his catalogue from a pensioned former monk of Bury, Ailot Holt; the writer is now recognized as Henry de Kirkestede, mid-fourteenth-century librarian of the abbey, whose name or initials are included in some of his notes[63]. Henry used author and subject class-marks in these notes, and he wrote his class-marks in the books, of which he also compiled a (now lost) register[64]. The numbers further allow us to estimate the size of the library in his day at some 2,100 volumes[65]. His work in

---

59 Wright, 'Dispersal', as note 54, 148–75. There are valuable recent discussions by James P. Carley, 'Monastic collections and their dispersal', in *Cambridge History of the Book in Britain*, as note 58, iv. 339–47; id. 'The dispersal of the monastic libraries and the salvaging of the spoils', in *Cambridge History of Libraries*, as note 30, i. 265–91; Richard Sharpe, *Libraries and Books in Medieval England: The Role of Libraries in a Changing Book Economy* (Oxford, 2023), from his Lyell Lectures 2019.

60 Montague Rhodes James, *On the Abbey of Bury St Edmunds* (Cambridge, 1895), 42–99. Thirty years on he produced a longer list of manuscripts bearing marks that identified them with Bury St Edmunds, 'Bury St Edmunds manuscripts', *English Historical Review* 41 (1926), 251–60.

61 Bale's notebook has an entry for Boston of Bury, *John Bale's Index of British and Other Writers*, ed. Poole and Bateson, as note 35, 49, and cites "Ex Bostoni Buriensis catalogo", "Ex catalogo Buriensi", &c., very frequently.

62 Thomas Tanner, *Bibliotheca Britannico-Hibernica*, ed. David Wilkins (London, 1748), xvii–xliii.

63 Richard H. Rouse, 'Bostonus Buriensis and the author of the *Catalogus scriptorum ecclesiae*', *Speculum* 41 (1966), 471–99. The catalogue of authors was edited by Richard H. Rouse and Mary A. Rouse, *Henry of Kirkestede. Catalogus de libris autenticis et apocrifis*, Corpus of British Medieval Library Catalogues 11 (London, 2004), with an important introduction.

64 Richard Sharpe, 'Reconstructing the medieval library of Bury St Edmunds: the lost catalogue of Henry of Kirkstead', in *Bury St Edmunds: Medieval Art, Architecture, Archaeology, and Economy*, ed. Antonia Gransden, British Archaeological Association Transactions ([Leeds], 1998), 204–18.

65 Sharpe in *English Benedictine Libraries*, as note 49, 44; id., 'Accession, classification, location: press-marks in medieval libraries', *Scriptorium* 50 (1996), 279–87, at 285–86.

various ways has left us able to know a great deal about the library especially in the 1350s. An active librarian is crucial to the creation of evidence, whether by marking the books themselves or by compiling catalogues, without which we should be hard pressed to know anything at all about medieval libraries.

What led James to do the work he did is not spelt out, but he was a considerable traveller. It is likely that he was on the one hand inspired by his travels on the Continent, where he could see great abbeys both ruined and living, and on the other hand informed by studying the recent catalogues of some French libraries into which huge numbers of monastic books had been transferred after the Revolution. The books from the abbey of Jumièges, for example, were described in great numbers in the Rouen catalogue by Henri Omont (1857–1940), which appeared in 1886[66]. James was aware of the scholarship of such men as Léopold Delisle (1826–1910), Omont's superior in Paris, but his attention was particularly caught by Omont's paper, "Anciens catalogues de bibliothèques anglaises", which printed a late-fourteenth-century catalogue of more than four hundred books in the library of the Austin canons at Lanthony[67]. There is no sign that Omont knew that many books from Lanthony were in Lambeth Palace library, a collection formed by successive archbishops of Canterbury in the early seventeenth century, but James knew that. In 1900 he produced what

amounts to a provenance list for the medieval manuscripts at Lambeth Palace, including a hundred or so from Lanthony, whose descent is still unexplained. James had made two very important discoveries, first that by recognizing marks of provenance it was possible to draw up a list of books identifiable as surviving from a dispersed library, and second, that comparison with a medieval catalogue allowed one to judge what proportion of a library's holdings could still be identified. Medieval books and medieval catalogues complement one another and allow one to form a complex picture of the diversity of monastic libraries. James went on to print the largest medieval library catalogues, including several catalogues from Canterbury cathedral priory, made at different dates; the very large catalogue of the library of St Augustine's abbey outside the walls of Canterbury, now dated to the 1370s with later additions; the tripartite catalogue of Dover priory drawn up in 1389; the rich catalogue of the books held by the Austin friars in York in 1372, including the largest and most eclectic private library known from medieval England, that of John Argam; the curious but detailed fourteenth-century catalogue from Peterborough abbey; and finally William Charite's catalogue from Leicester abbey datable to 1477 × 1494[68]. Four of these were from Benedictine houses, one a house of canons regular, and one of friars.

---

66 *Catalogue général des manuscrits des Bibliothèques Publiques de France. Départements.* Tome 1, *Rouen,* compiled by Henri Omont (Paris, 1886).

67 Henri Omont, 'Anciens catalogues de bibliothèques anglaises', *Centralblatt für Bibliothekswesen* 9 (1892), 201–22, printed four lists, from the Benedictine abbey of Burton (*c.* 1175), an unidentified house, now recognized as the Augustinian priory of Bridlington, the Cistercian abbey of Flaxley (early 13th cent.), and (pp. 207–22) the Augustinian priory of Lanthony; these are all re-edited in respective volumes of the Corpus of British Medieval Library Catalogues.

68 Montague Rhodes James, *The Ancient Libraries of Canterbury and Dover* (Cambridge, 1903); id., 'The catalogue of the library of the Augustinian friars of York', in *Fasciculus Joanni Willis Clark dicatus* (Cambridge, 1909), 2–96; id., *Lists of manuscripts formerly in Peterborough abbey library,* Transactions of the Bibliographical Society, Supplement 5 (1926); Montague Rhodes James and Alexander Hamilton Thompson, 'Catalogue of the library of Leicester abbey', *Transactions of the Leicestershire Archaeological Society* 19 (1936–1937), 111–61, 378–440; 21 (1940–1941), 1–88. All except the catalogues of Christ Church cathedral priory at Canterbury have now been superseded by volumes in the Corpus of British Medieval Library Catalogues.

And it was with guidance from James that Mary Bateson in 1898 prepared an edition of the very extensive early sixteenth-century catalogue of the brothers' library from the Brigittine abbey of Syon[69]. In all of these editions notes were added where there was knowledge to cross-match entries in the medieval catalogues with surviving books, building a concise sense of what could still be examined, but rarely seeking to exploit the comparison between a book itself and its medieval description. James focused on the larger medieval catalogues, and he searched far and wide for books that had survived from libraries broken up at the dissolution. Great monastic libraries appealed to his antiquarian sensibilities, but he had little interest in categorization of libraries by type or in finding and understanding the evidence that would shed light on the typology of medieval libraries or their evolution over time.

Meanwhile, building on discoveries made by James, two scholars trained in his benign shadow developed a far more systematic approach to medieval bibliography. With Roger Aubrey Baskerville Mynors (1903–1989) and Neil R. Ker (1908–1982), it may be said that the science of manuscript provenance had reached England. The story has been well told by Mary and Richard Rouse[70]. James had prepared many catalogues of the western manuscripts in Cambridge libraries and elsewhere, including Lambeth Palace, in which he made a point of recording evidence of provenance. During the same period, George F. Warner (1845–1936), and his able assistant Julius P. Gilson (1868–1929), began a catalogue of the manuscripts in the old royal collection in 1894, finally published in 1921. This was particularly thorough in recording and indexing evidence of provenance[71]. It is difficult to know whether James's work was a necessary influence here or whether they had simultaneously begun to gather such evidence. Warner and Gilson, however, did little to synthesize. The discovery of a late-thirteenth-century union catalogue that had been available to Br Henry de Kirkestede prompted R. A. B. Mynors to want systematic evidence of what books could be shown to have survived from what medieval libraries. He prepared an edition of the union catalogue, *Registrum Anglie*, subsequently annotated by Mary and Richard Rouse, who showed that it was the work of Oxford Franciscans, who visited scores of monastic libraries. And it was Mynors who recruited a small team and began to collect provenance data on record-cards, which soon became *Medieval Libraries of Great Britain*, arranged as a book by one of the compilers, Neil Ker, and printed in 1941. With this as a tool much more could be learnt.

First to benefit from the new tool was the old royal collection, one of the foundation collections of the British Museum. While the collection of data was under way, J. R. Liddell printed a short report, preserved among the royal manuscripts, which lists religious houses in Lincolnshire and records titles seen there and required for the king. With the help of Warner and Gilson's catalogue and of the record-cards to which Liddell himself had contributed, he was able to show that books marked for confiscation could often be found in the old royal collection, so demonstrating for the first time an apparent effort on the king's behalf to take selected books from monastic libraries. He associated the list with the work of John Leland,

---

69 Mary Bateson, *Catalogue of the Library of Syon Monastery, Isleworth*, as note 25.

70 *Registrum Anglie*, ed. Roger A. B. Mynors, Richard H. Rouse, and Mary A. Rouse, Corpus of British Medieval Library Catalogues 2 (London, 1991). The introduction to this book gives a rich survey of the work stimulated by Mynors's discovery of *Registrum Anglie*.

71 George F. Warner and Julius P. Gilson, *British Museum, Catalogue of Western Manuscripts in the Old Royal and King's Collections*, 4 vols (London 1921). The index even includes the press-marks of unidentified monastic houses.

the king's antiquary, in and after 1533; the houses visited were in some cases dissolved in 1536, which provided him with a *terminus ad quem*. This realization put an end to any assumption that the sequestration of manuscripts for the royal library was contingent on the dissolution. A campaign of visiting libraries appears to have been envisaged, of which this return is the only documentary evidence. It is headed, "Tabula librorum de historiis antiquitatum ac diuinitate tractantium in librariis et domibus religiosis subscriptis reportorum"[72]. There are thirty-six headings in this record, representing no more than half the religious houses within Lincolnshire. The occasion of this search has recently been redated by James Carley to 1528 on the grounds that the *pestis* which kept the visitor out of some houses was rife in that year[73]. This is important. Not only does it mean that this search took place too early to have any connexion with the dissolution of the monasteries, it takes it back to a time when Cardinal Wolsey was still chancellor. The brevity of the returns indicates that the search focused on relatively scarce works. Historical works might point to the king as much as to Leland, and in particular some books may have been selected for their relevance to the annulment of the king's

marriage, Wolsey's most pressing concern in 1528[74]. The report was not to include anything "de libris communiter impressis seu de materiis predictis minime tractantibus". In nine houses the agent reported finding only books not relevant to his purpose or common printed books, and in five houses he reported only common printed books; in just one he said there were manuscript books, though nothing to his purpose. It is an accidental revelation, therefore, that this record characterizes so many small houses as having printed books, a rare witness to the fact of modernization in smaller monastic libraries[75]. The search was not concerned with recent books but with old texts unavailable in print. Titles that attracted the attention of the

---

72 J. R. Liddell, "'Leland''s lists of manuscripts in Lincolnshire monasteries', *English Historical Review* 55 (1939), 88–95 (quotations from the heading, p. 89).

73 Mention of *pestis*, which kept the agent away from two infected houses, points specifically to 1528 (John Leland, *De uiris illustribus*, ed. Carley, as note 38, lxii n. 198, following John A. H. Wylie and Leslie H. Collier, 'The English sweating sickness (Sudor Anglicus): a reappraisal', *Journal of the History of Medicine and Allied Sciences* 36 (1981), 425–45, at 431). His earlier judgement, "end of 1530 or slightly later", depends on associating particular titles with the king's concerns in "the second part of Henry's campaign" (Carley, *The Libraries of King Henry VIII*, as note 55, xxxiv–xxxv). The latter date ties in closely with payments for the fetching of books from specific religious houses in different parts of the country, but there are no payments from 1528.

74 Two such items are remarked on by Carley, *The Libraries of King Henry VIII*, as note 55, xxxiv. First, the commentary on Leviticus by Ralph of Flaix taken from Kirkstead (Lincs), now BL MS Royal 3 D. ix (s. xii) [reported Z11. 6 = H2. 844], has an obvious connexion to marrying one's brother's wife. Ker, 'The Migration of manuscripts', as note 23, 9, "wondered what the king, or whoever was responsible for his library, wanted with four copies" of this work, noting this and three others: Bodl. MS Bodley 245 (*SC* 2127) did belong to Henry VIII, Cambridge, Corpus Christi College, MS 87, and Cambridge, Trinity College, MS B. 4. 24 are both in the same "Old Royal" binding. The obvious deduction is that different agents gathered these copies, and that selection from reports was not necessarily in the hands of one person. Second, Carley remarks on the notes, some apparently by Henry VIII, in a copy of William of Malmesbury's *Gesta pontificum Anglorum*, from Thornton (Lincs), now BL MS Harley 2 (s. xiii¹) [reported A34. 4], as touching on the king's concerns.

75 The five where he mentions only printed books are the Premonstratensian abbey of Newsham (with an income of £99 p.a.), the Austin canons of Thornholme (£105), the Grey Friars of Grimsby, the Carmelites of Boston, and the Gilbertines of Haverholme (£70). The eight cases where he mentions irrelevant books or printed books are the Austin friars of Lincoln, the Benedictines of Humberston (£32), the Austin canons of Newstead by Stamford (£38), Elsham (£70), Wellow (£95), and Kyme (£101), the Gilbertines of Ormsby (£80), the Austin Friars of Grimsby (where he found "codices uetustissimi tamen uel impressi seu ad rem non pertinentes", the very old books evidently not desirable), the Cistercians of Louth Park (£147) ("complures libri neque ad materias

king's agents were reported, and someone – perhaps the king himself – chose which ones were to be taken; ninety-five titles were noted in eighteen religious houses, and forty-four of them were marked, representing thirty-six books, which were required to be handed over and were added to one of the royal libraries. Ker made the point that no monastery north of Lincolnshire was represented among the provenanced books surviving in the old royal collection; this is not strictly correct, but books reached the royal library at different times and in different ways[76]. Among those not on the visitor's route are the Benedictines of Spalding priory and the Gilbertines of Sempringham priory, yet books from these two south Lincolnshire houses still survive in the old royal collection. They do not come from a second visitor's touring the rest of the country at the same time. Payments were made for bringing books from Sempringham on 12 February 1530/1531, those from Spalding on 4 June 1531[77]. No payments were made in respect of the houses visited in 1528, but these are not the only ones from 1530 and 1531. A list of titles was sent to the king from Reading abbey in 1530, and a payment was made to a servant of the abbey on 29 November for delivering books to Hampton Court palace – the procedure is different from the earlier tour in Lincolnshire – and this may be linked to at least five books from Reading in the royal library at Westminster palace in 1542[78]. Others relate

to books from Ramsey abbey, 27 January 1530/1531; Gloucester abbey, 17 February 1530/1531; Evesham abbey, 18 March 1530/1531, and all these houses are represented in the 1542 inventory of the king's books at Westminster. This appears to represent a second trawl of monastic libraries, in different circumstances, more than a year after Wolsey's dismissal.

It is impossible to know how many such reports and deliveries there may have been, but we may not extrapolate from this limited evidence to a well-organized but entirely undocumented national visitation. As late as September 1535 we hear that William Tyldesley, who among other duties kept the king's books at Richmond palace, had found a book in the priory at Bath, which the king commanded[79]. And a week later the prior of Christchurch was still looking for copies of William of Malmesbury to add to a copy of Bede's *Historia ecclesiastica* already sent to Thomas Cromwell[80].

There are nearly four hundred books still in the royal library and bearing evidence of a monastic provenance that were already at Westminster in 1542[81]. The inventory does not invite one

---

pertinentes nisi sint litteris impressi"). Only at Nocton priory does he mention that the canons had irrelevant books, "saltem non impressi".

76 Ker, 'Revised Preface' to *Medieval Libraries of Great Britain 2* [*MLGB2*] (London, 1964), xi–xii; Carley, *Libraries of King Henry VIII*, as note 55, xxxiii–xxxix.

77 Carley, *The Libraries of King Henry VIII*, as note 55, xxxvii. Four manuscripts from Sempringham and four from Spalding passed into the old royal collection at this time (ibid. 321); a further book from Spalding, now BL MS Royal 8 E. vi, arrived later through Thomas Cranmer and John Lumley.

78 Carley, *The Libraries of King Henry VIII*, as note 55, xxxvi– xxxvii. Of seventeen identified books from Reading now in the Royal Library, five were certainly there in 1542;

---

ten more may have arrived as part of this delivery, and two arrived only with the Theyer manuscripts in 1678.

79 William Holleway, prior of Bath, to Thomas Cromwell, dated 24 Sept 1535: "I have send your Mastership herein an old book *Opera Anselmi* which one William Tildysleye after scutiny made here in my library willed me to send unto you by the King's grace and commandment" (*LP*, as note 5, ix, no. 426; Warner and Gilson, *British Museum*, as note 71, vol. i, xiv; Carley, *The Libraries of King Henry VIII*, as note 55, xli–xlii). All books from Bath now in the royal library arrived only with John Lumley's books in 1609.

80 John Draper, prior of Christchurch, to Cromwell, 3 October 1535 (*LP*, as note 5, ix. 529; Carley, *The Libraries of King Henry VIII*, as note 55, xlii).

81 The index to *Medieval Libraries of Great Britain* records nearly five hundred manuscripts in the royal collection that still bear evidence of their medieval provenance. From this number must be subtracted those that only arrived in the royal library as part of two large acquisitions in the seventeenth century, the libraries of

to conjecture a large number of others, now lost or lacking evidence of provenance. Some forty-seven houses are represented, of which thirteen are accounted for by the one visitation of Lincolnshire in 1528. Six more are explained by the payments made in 1530–1531. Of the other twenty-eight houses, only four provided books in some numbers, Worcester cathedral priory (eight in the 1542 inventory), St Augustine's abbey in Canterbury (fifteen), St Albans abbey (twenty-five), but the most striking group came from the library of the Benedictine cathedral priory at Rochester: a hundred books from here can be recognized in the royal library[82]. Two theories have been advanced to explain their removal, either in connexion with the arrest of John Fisher, bishop of Rochester, in 1534 or/ and with the king's plan to convert the monastic buildings into a royal residence in 1540: if either is correct, their sequestration was not related to the dissolution of the priory[83].

A synopsis of the provenances of monastic books in the library at Westminster, shows that among small houses those of the Lincolnshire list form a large proportion. From this it appears that the list is not a lone survivor from many such returns: the haul of books from that county stands out in comparison with the scarcity of books from minor houses elsewhere in England. It would be mistaken to imagine that there was a nationwide harvest, carried out with the same acquisitive efficiency as the dissolution itself in the 1530s. In 1533 John Leland, the king's antiquary, began his searches in monastic libraries, looking for books that told the story of learning and literature in England[84]. Monastic libraries were the oldest and most conservative in the country and offered the best prospect of his finding such books. Over a period of four years, during which he toured England and Wales, he was able to take for himself books that caught his eye, some of which have survived, but he was not collecting books for the king's library[85]. There may be little doubt that Henry VIII knew that his French contemporary François I was building a royal library at Fontainebleau, while Leland was surely aware of the activity of François's agent Jean de Gagny in collecting books for the royal library[86]. If there was emulation, however, it was on a small scale. Neither king contemplated the nationalization of the manuscript patrimony. Indeed, it must be as good as certain that in 1536 Henry VIII had little interest in adding more monastic books to his library and Thomas

---

John Lumley (1533–1609), whose books were purchased by King James in 1609, and John Theyer (1597–1673), acquired by King Charles II in 1678. More than sixty of these monastic books came through John Lumley (Sears Jayne and Francis R. Johnson, *The Lumley Library. The Catalogue of 1609* (London, 1956)), more than fifty through the Theyer family (Warner and Gilson, *British Museum*, as note 71, vol. i, xxxviii–xxxix). These books account for more than forty monastic houses, which can be discounted as the source of Royal Library manuscripts in Henry VIII's time.

82   Carley quoted the *ex libris* of Rochester from Royal 1 B. IV, adding "Et hujusmodi Anathemata in plurimis reperiuntur Codicibus"; many others were quoted, but former monastic owners were not indexed nor commented on in the preface.

83   *The History of the King's Works*, ed. Howard M. Colvin, 6 vols (London, 1963–82), iv, pt 2: 1485–1660, 237, suggests that the books were sent to Westminster because, after the surrender of the priory on 31 March 1540, the king intended to convert the cloister into a royal palace. James P. Carley proposed instead that they were taken selectively, as books had been taken in and after 1528, perhaps in the specific circumstances of the arrest of Bishop John Fisher in April 1534 (*The Libraries of King Henry VIII*, as note 55, xl–xli).

84   John Leland, *De uiris illustribus*, ed. Carley, as note 38, li–c.

85   Manuscripts described by John Bale in his *Index* (as n. 34) as being "ex bibliotheca" or "ex museo Jo. Lelandi" are conveniently listed by Alfred B. Emden, *A Biographical Register of the University of Oxford A.D. 1501 to 1540* (Oxford, 1974), 723–25.

86   André Jammes, 'Un bibliophile à découvrir, Jean de Gagny', *Bulletin du bibliophile* (1996), 35–81; André Jammes and Nicolas Barker, 'Jean de Gagny: a bibliophile re-discovered', *The Library* 7th ser. 11 (2010), 405–46.

Cromwell had none. An old and easy assumption that the dissolution of the monasteries brought books into the king's hands rests on no evidence at all[87]. All the evidence for the king's acquiring monastic books relates to the years before the dissolution.

If the king had simply wanted to build a library for show, he could have easily taken possession of the books in abbeys close to his palaces. Besides thirteen religious houses in London itself, there were important houses nearby, especially Westminster abbey itself but also Bermondsey, Chertsey, and Syon. No London house is represented by a single known book in the royal library, and only Syon has any significant number of surviving books.

Only a part of Henry VIII's libraries has survived[88]. His heirs took no interest in such books, and in Edward VI's time even the royal collection was purged of some conspicuously Roman Catholic books.

One of the earliest individuals known to us as having acquired manuscripts from a number of monastic libraries is Thomas Cranmer, the reforming archbishop of Canterbury appointed to succeed the conservative William Warham, who died in 1532. His manuscripts in one sense form a footnote to the royal library, because his library passed into the hands of John Lumley and so came into the royal collection in 1609. But might there be an older connexion? Cranmer owned manuscripts from two clusters of religious houses. One is easily explained. He had eight or

nine from Canterbury cathedral priory, which, as archbishop, he could have taken for himself; one from All Saints' College in nearby Maidstone and printed books from Canterbury houses may be explained in the same way. He also had eight or nine manuscripts from Bath cathedral priory, three from Bristol abbey, and one each from Gloucester abbey, Athelney abbey, and Hinton charterhouse – five religious houses in Somerset or Gloucestershire, which may add up to a visitation, though the king had books only from Gloucester, and those were delivered by a servant of the abbey in 1531. Given that most of Cranmer's library was a working library, not an antiquarian collection, one can only wonder how he came to have these manuscripts. It would not be inconceivable that some had been brought to Westminster for the king but were allowed to fall into the archbishop's hands instead.

Ker was the first to be fully alert to the profile of monastic books surviving from different religious houses. He sought to explain some of the distortions in what has survived as a reflection of the interests of sixteenth-century readers. The condition of monastic libraries at the time of the dissolution varied, as it had always varied. There were still some libraries filled with well-made and useful books: those most likely to appeal to collectors in sixteenth-century England were copies of the Latin Fathers made in the twelfth century, books whose large format and stately script made them still attractive and whose biblical or patristic contents were old enough to be accepted as part of the common heritage of the church rather than catholic books filled with doctrine unacceptable to protestant readers. Some houses had never had good libraries, some that may have had in the past had neglected them, others had updated them with printed books less likely to appeal to the taste of the new collectors. Some collectors were lucky enough to find whole groups of manuscripts still together decades after the dissolution. In some

---

87 Warner and Gilson, *British Museum,* as note 71, i. 14, describing BL MS Royal 1 C. III, a large fourteenth-century bible in French, records the *ex libris* of Reading abbey and adds, "The MS. was presumably written in Reading Abbey, and passed (like other MSS now in the Royal Library) to Henry VIII at the Dissolution". No one would now assume that such a book was written in the abbey, and all the evidence goes against supposing any large-scale "passing" of manuscripts to the king during or after 1536–1540.

88 Jayne and Johnson, *The Lumley Library,* as note 81.

cases such books may even have been sheltered by the continued existence of unused monastic buildings, which appears to have been the case at Christ Church, Canterbury[89]. Chester abbey books are represented by two clutches attested in the early seventeenth century, traced back to the Bostock family[90]. These circumstances were surely exceptional. Batches of more than a dozen or so books from a single source are rare, and for the most part collectors were gathering up manuscripts that had been dispersed among many hands. Ker was also aware very early that such collections had for the most part stabilized in institutional libraries during the seventeenth and early eighteenth centuries.

Only in the closing years of the sixteenth century do we begin to see conditions become more favourable to conservation. There was a revival in libraries. New learning was accumulating, and by the later sixteenth century scholars began to want to read in depth in their subject, not simply in the latest editions. What had been written fifty years before, even a hundred years before, might again command attention. Even in the interpretation of ancient texts, understanding was advancing, and a scholar might want to compare the work of different editors and commentators. More than a century's accumulation of printed books could not be bought to meet the needs of an individual. Libraries were needed again, and they began to appear in the universities, where colleges invested once more in books. The revival of libraries provided a setting for the conservation of books even when their historic owners were no longer interested. Two examples are secular rather than monastic, the canons of Exeter cathedral and of St George's

Chapel, Windsor, who gave their older books to the Bodleian in 1605 and 1612[91].

Also, from about the 1580s in England, general interest in the past increased, and study of the past became better informed. The first circle of men who called themselves antiquaries appeared. Books could begin to be valued because they were old or because they carried works that no one had read for generations, and the university colleges are the first institutions to be seen as repositories for literary antiquities. This trend spread to some of the cathedrals, where individual canons begin to foster corporate libraries. Where Matthew Parker and John Whitgift, successive archbishops of Canterbury, and Thomas Nevile, dean of Canterbury cathedral, had given manuscripts to Cambridge colleges, Archbishop Richard Bancroft aimed to build a new library for himself and his archiepiscopal successors at Lambeth Palace. The largest and most durable campaign was that of Sir Thomas Bodley, whose eponymous library for the University of Oxford opened in 1602 and quickly became the favoured beneficiary for those with manuscripts to donate.

By the early seventeenth century collectors of medieval manuscripts were active whose names still resonate, chief among them Sir Robert Cotton (1571–1631). While the new antiquarian interest fostered the discovery and conservation of older books, manuscripts, even monastic manuscripts, the new need for libraries to maintain the depth of human learning created a setting to house old books whose interest may not have lain in their contents so much as in their physical antiquity. During roughly one hundred and fifty years, between the 1570s and the 1720s, there was a persistent current that brought old books, particularly medieval manuscripts, towards

---

89 De Hamel, 'The Dispersal of the library of Christ Church', as note 29, 263–79.

90 See Ralph Hanna, 'The descent of some Chester libraries', *The Library*, 7th ser. 22 (2021), 57–68.

91 On this gift of books by the canons of St George's, see Willoughby, *The Libraries of Collegiate Churches*, as note 14, 878–80; on the gift from Exeter, see id. *The Libraries of the Secular Cathedrals*, Corpus of British Medieval Library Catalogues 17, forthcoming.

collectors and through them into institutions. In a lecture to the Bibliographical Society on 23 March 1942, Neil Ker argued that by *c.* 1720 a large part of what had escaped destruction around the time of the dissolution was once again, as he put it, "immobilized"[92]. The seventeenth century was a great period for libraries and for scholarship in England, with new and lasting libraries created in the universities and cathedrals, as well as in particular contexts such as the creation of the libraries at Lambeth Palace and at Sion College in London, and not excluding the more esoteric opening of the Cotton Library at Westminster. Besides Cotton one should name Sir Kenelm Digby, Sir Simonds D'Ewes, John Selden, Bishop Thomas Barlow, and in the early eighteenth century Dr Hans Sloane and Robert and Edward Harley, earls of Oxford. The collections of Digby and Selden and Barlow became part of the Bodleian Library, those of D'Ewes and others were absorbed by Harley, and his library in turn was merged with the small but choice antiquarian library of Sir Robert Cotton, the Royal Library at St James's that housed what had survived from Henry VIII's collections, and the vast library of manuscripts and printed books formed by Sir Hans Sloane to create a national library in the newly founded British Museum in 1753.

Interest in monastic books as such, however, was haphazard and sentimental. Where a collector was aware of the monastic *ex libris*, the association with an old abbey was attractive but in isolation it was hardly meaningful.

In the eighteenth century disdain for monkish learning reached its peak. If one were to identify a low point in interest in monastic libraries, one could hardly do better than refer to the comments of John Nichols (1745–1826), printer, publisher, and fosterer of antiquarian studies, who handled transcripts made from William Charite's late-fifteenth-century library catalogue of Leicester abbey. The catalogue itself, now in the Bodleian Library, MS Laud Misc. 623, describes some nine hundred volumes, all (so far as we can tell) manuscripts. It may in fact represent the library as it stood around 1463[93]. Nichols thought the loss of the library insignificant; even the books themselves were insignificant, "many have only two folia. The first words of some are given; and, after all our enquiries, many of the writers here enumerated must remain as unknown as they are uninteresting; and perhaps posterity has very little reason to regret the loss of the Library of Leicester Abbey"[94]. This antiquary had no idea what "2° fo." entered against each book signified, and his guess was completely absurd[95]. Half a century later, a monastic provenance had become a selling-point for manuscripts at auction, but there was still no sign that understanding monastic libraries was on the historian's agenda.

It was not until a century after Nichols's remark that Montague Rhodes James began the process of scholarly recovery.

The printed books from British monastic libraries remained a nearly invisible category despite the late-eighteenth-century craving for incunabula[96].

92 Ker, 'The Migration of manuscripts', as note 23, 2. It is coincidental that the seventieth anniversary of this lecture occurred during the 2012 conference from which the present volume resulted.

93 It was edited by Teresa Webber and Andrew G. Watson, *Libraries of Augustinian Canons*, Corpus of British Medieval Library Catalogues 6 (London, 1998), 109–399 (A20).

94 John Nichols, *The History and Antiquities of the County of Leicester*, 4 volumes in 8 (London, 1795–1815), i, pt 2, app. xvii, 101 (quoted by Montague Rhodes James, 'Catalogue of the library of Leicester abbey', as note 68, 118); Richard Sharpe, 'Henry Ellis, Richard Gough's protégé', *Bodleian Library Record* 22 (2009), 191–211, at 197–98.

95 James M. W. Willoughby, 'The *secundo folio* and its uses, medieval and modern', *The Library*, 7th ser. 12 (2011), 237–58.

96 Kristian Jensen, *Revolution and the Antiquarian Book: Reshaping the past, 1780–1815* (Cambridge, 2011), from his Lyell Lectures 2008, 'Collecting Incunabula: Enlightenment, Revolution, and the Market'.

There was no interest in framing a picture of what a monastic library might have held. Indeed, so completely were printed books ignored that even today the perception in England is that monastic books were manuscript books from the middle ages[97]. Printed books from the monasteries were rarely retained in 1540, and if they were – for example by monks displaced to live as secular clergy – their long-term preservation was unlikely[98]. The copy of Jean de Gagny's Primasius, printed in 1537, and owned by William Buckland, monk of Abingdon, is an interesting case, because he

obviously kept the book after the dissolution[99]. It has only his inscriptions, not the *ex libris* of the abbey. Such books were simply second-hand books with no institutional protection. And even if they have survived, evidence of their monastic provenance has attracted less attention than the equivalent evidence in manuscripts; indeed, sixteenth-century monastic books may be less likely to have institutional ownership-marks and more likely to bear only the names of individual monks[100]. We may add manuscript, therefore, to the alliterative association of monastic and medieval.

---

97 Ker, 'Revised Preface' to *MLGB2*, as note 76, xi, made the point that *MLGB* included ninety-two manuscripts from Scottish libraries, while John Durkan and Anthony Ross, *Early Scottish Libraries* (Glasgow, 1961), recorded several hundred printed books from Scottish libraries before 1560. Comparison with the impression given by *MLGB* for books from English libraries will mean nothing unless an equivalent effort of recording printed books is made. For our purposes figures from both countries should be limited to books from religious houses, and the difference between the dates of dissolution in England and Scotland must be taken into account.

98 Ker, 'The migration of manuscripts', as note 23, 11, mentions three or four printed books from Merton priory given by a former canon, Thomas Paynell, to St John's College, Oxford. Another example is a group of four manuscripts from the Bonshommes at Ashridge, Bucks, in the Huntington Library, discussed by Herbert C. Schulz, 'The monastic library and scriptorium at Ashridge', *Huntington Library Quarterly* 1 (1937–1938), 305–11, which appear to have been kept by the pensioned rector, Thomas Waterhouse, after he surrendered the house on 6 November 1539, and bequeathed in the first instance to his nephew's family. In one of them, Huntington Library, MS EL 9 H. 15, a custumal, Waterhouse wrote after 28 July 1540, "Hoc anno nobilis domus de Asscherugge destructa fuit et fratres expulsi sunt in die S. Leonardi. Hoc anno decapitatus fuit ille eximius haereticus et proditor Thomas Cromwell, qui causa fuit destruccionis omnium domorum religiosorum in Anglia" (Henry John Todd, *The History of the College of Bonhommes at Ashridge* (London, 1823), 25). Ker cautioned: "This sort of evidence needs collecting and weighing. I do not feel justified in drawing conclusions from it at present" ('The migration of manuscripts', as note 23, 11).

99 A dozen books printed between 1532 and 1537 with monastic provenances are noted by Bell, 'Monastic libraries, 1400–1557', as note 58, 250, including two from as late as 1537. The evidence, however, is inscriptions that name individual monks, so these were not part of any monastic library. This copy of Primasius on the Pauline epistles, edited by Jean de Gagny, Lyon: S. Gryphius, 1537, now in Pembroke College, Cambridge (Herbert M. Adams, *Catalogue of books printed on the continent of Europe, 1501–1600, in Cambridge libraries*, 2 vols (London, 1967), P2094), is inscribed as the property of William Buckland, monk of Abingdon, who retained the book after the abbey surrendered in 1539, describing himself in a second inscription as servant of Henry, Lord Stafford (*MLGB2*, as note 76, 226). In 1556 Lord Stafford, a catholic, listed some three hundred Latin books in his own possession (Andrew H. Anderson, 'The books and interests of Henry, Lord Stafford (1501–63)', *The Library* 5th ser. 21 (1966), 87–114, at 97–114); some of these are old enough to have come from monastic libraries, but I am not aware that any have been identified.

100 The monastic house that can boast the largest number of surviving printed books is Durham cathedral priory, where a dean and secular chapter replaced the prior and monks. More than six hundred manuscripts survive, most of them still in the cathedral library. The recognition of printed books from the conventual library is less secure, but some still there were marked with an *ex libris* in the 1520s (e.g. B. V. 58, Cologne 1524; D. VII. 23–24, Basel 1527). By this date, however, printed books without *ex libris* are often recognized by the annotating hand of Br Thomas Swallwell, who enters inscriptions in Durham books between 1510 and 1538 (Neil R. Ker, *Medieval Libraries of Great Britain 2 [MLGB2]. Supplement to the second edition*, ed. Andrew G. Watson (London, 1987), 97); see further above, note 46.

Conclusion

A second wave of dissolutions followed ten years later. Where a few moribund collegiate churches had been dissolved in the early 1540s, Henry VIII's Chantries Act of 1545 sought to organize by statute what had hitherto been a piecemeal process. The act lapsed with his death in 1546, but in the reign of his young son, King Edward VI, the Second Chantries Act (1547) made formally forfeit every institution – whether collegiate church, chantry, guild, or fraternity – whose central intercessory function belonged to a purgatorial doctrine that no longer had any validity in protestant theory[101].

Another possible route to survival for old catholic books from England has never been investigated. It is perhaps unlikely to prove an abundant channel of preservation, but there is limited evidence that books may have been taken abroad by catholic exiles. A late-twelfth-century volume of Augustine and Anselm, written in England, survives now in Brussels, but in the sixteenth century it had belonged to the Flemish cartographer Abraham Ortelius (1527–1598); when his books were auctioned, it was bought by a Jesuit, whose note at the front refers to its being saved "ex Angliae calamitate uastatis ab iconoclastis ecclesiis sub Henrico VIII rege"[102]. It contains no evidence of its earlier provenance, but it is interesting as an observation on what had happened to English religious houses and their books.

---

101   King Edward VI would legislate to dissolve "all manner of colleges, free chapels, and chantries" (1 Edward VI, c. 14, 1547; *Statutes of the Realm*, iv. 24–33; abridged in Elton, *Tudor Constitution*, as note 1, 391–94).

102   Now Brussels, Bibliothèque Royal, MS 8386–96 (cat. 1111). In 1598 it was bought by Andreas Schott, SJ, Antwerp; a generation later the Jesuit house in Antwerp was the base for the work of Rosweyde and Bolland, and the manuscript has survived as part of the seventeenth-century working library of the Bollandists (Bart Op de Beeck, in this volume).

Bibliography

Manuscripts and Archival Sources

Brussels, Bibliothèque Royal, MS 8386–96 (cat. 1111).

Cambridge, Corpus Christi College, MS 87.

Cambridge, Trinity College, MS B. 4. 24.

London, BL MS Harley 2.

London, BL MS Harley 524.

London, BL MS Royal 1 C. III.

London, BL MS Royal 3 D. IX.

London, BL MS Royal 8 D. VIII.

London, BL MS Royal 8 E. VI.

Oxford, Bodl. MS Bodley 245.

Oxford, Bodl. MS Selden Supra 64.

San Marino, California, Huntington Library, MS EL 9 H. 15.

Secondary Works

Account of the Monastic Treasures, confiscated at the Dissolution of the various houses in England, by Sir John Williams, ed. William Barclay D. D. Turnbull, Abbotsford Club (Edinburgh, 1836).

Herbert M. Adams, *Catalogue of books printed on the continent of Europe, 1501–1600, in Cambridge libraries*, 2 vols (London, 1967).

Andrew H. Anderson, 'The books and interests of Henry, Lord Stafford (1501–63)', *The Library* 5th ser. 21 (1966), 87–114.

Hugh Aveling, *Post Reformation Catholicism in East Yorkshire 1558–1790*, East Yorkshire Local History Series xi (1960).

Mary Bateson, *Catalogue of the Library of Syon Monastery, Isleworth* (Cambridge, 1898).

David N. Bell, 'Monastic libraries 1400–1557', in *Cambridge History of the Book in Britain*, 6 vols (Cambridge, 1999–2011), iii. 229–54.

James P. Carley, *The Libraries of King Henry VIII*, Corpus of British Medieval Library Catalogues 7 (London, 1999).

James P. Carley, 'Monastic collections and their dispersal', in *Cambridge History of the Book in Britain*, 6 vols (Cambridge, 1999–2011), iv. 339–47.

James P. Carley, 'The dispersal of the monastic libraries and the salvaging of the spoils', in *Cambridge History of Libraries in Britain and Ireland*, ed. Elisabeth Leedham-Green and Teresa Webber, 3 vols (Cambridge, 2006), i. 265–91.

Catalogue général des manuscrits des Bibliothèques Publiques de France. Départements, ed. Henri Omont, Tome 1, *Rouen* (Paris, 1886).

Peter D. Clarke, *The University and College Libraries of Cambridge*, Corpus of British Medieval Library Catalogues 10 (London, 2002).

M. Claire Cross, *York Clergy Wills 1520–1600* (York, 1984–1989).

M. Claire Cross, 'Oxford and the Tudor state', in *History of the University of Oxford*, ed. Trevor Henry Aston, 8 vols (Oxford, 1984–2000), iii. 117–49.

M. Claire Cross, 'A medieval Yorkshire library', *Northern History* 25 (1989), 281–90.

M. Claire Cross, 'Community solidarity among Yorkshire religious after the Dissolution', in *Monastic Studies. The Continuity of Tradition*, ed. Judith Loades (Bangor, 1990), 245–54.

M. Claire Cross and Noreen Vickers, *Monks, Friars, and Nuns in Sixteenth-Century Yorkshire*, Yorkshire Archaeological Society Record Series 150 (Leeds, 1995).

Christopher F. R. de Hamel, 'The dispersal of the library of Christ Church, Canterbury, from the fourteenth to the sixteenth century', in *Books and Collectors, 1200–1700. Essays Presented to Andrew Watson*, ed. James P. Carley and Colin G. C. Tite (London, 1997), 263–79.

John Durkan and Anthony Ross, *Early Scottish Libraries* (Glasgow, 1961).

Geoffrey R. Elton, *The Tudor Constitution. Documents and Commentary*, 2nd edn (Cambridge, 1982).

Alfred B. Emden, *A Biographical Register of the University of Oxford A.D. 1501 to 1540* (Oxford, 1974).

William Farrer, *The Chartulary of Cockersand Abbey*, 7 parts, Chetham Society (1898–1909).

Vincent A. Gillespie, *Syon Abbey*, Corpus of British Medieval Library Catalogues 9 (London, 2001).

Joan Greatrex, *Everyday Sermons from Worcester Cathedral Priory. An Early Fourteenth-Century Collection in Latin* (Amsterdam, 2019).

Ralph Hanna, 'The descent of some Chester libraries', *The Library* 7th ser. 22 (2021), 57–68.

Ralph Hanna and David G. Rundle, *A Descriptive Catalogue of the Western Manuscripts, to c. 1600, in Christ Church, Oxford* (Oxford, 2017).

Francis A. Hibbert, *The Dissolution of the Monasteries as illustrated by the suppression of the religious houses of Staffordshire* (London, 1910).

The History of the King's Works, ed. Howard M. Colvin, 6 vols (London, 1963–82).

R. Ian Jack, 'An archival case history: the cartularies and registers of Llanthony priory in Gloucestershire', *Journal of the Society of Archivists* 4 (1972), No. 5, 370–83.

Sybil M. Jack, 'Williams, John, Baron Williams (c 1500–1559)', *Oxford Dictionary of National Biography*, https://doi.org/10.1093/ref:odnb/29514

Montague R. James, *On the Abbey of Bury St Edmunds* (Cambridge, 1895).

Montague R. James, *The Manuscripts in the Library at Lambeth Palace* (Cambridge, 1900).

Montague R. James, *Ancient Libraries of Canterbury and Dover* (Cambridge, 1903).

Montague R. James, *The Ancient Libraries of Canterbury and Dover* (Cambridge, 1903).

Montague R. James, 'The catalogue of the library of the Augustinian friars of York', in *Fasciculus Joanni Willis Clark dicatus* (Cambridge, 1909), 2–96.

Montague R. James, 'Bury St Edmunds manuscripts', *English Historical Review* 41 (1926), 251–60.

Montague R. James, *Lists of manuscripts formerly in Peterborough abbey library*, Transactions of the Bibliographical Society, Supplement 5 (1926).

Montague R. James and Alexander Hamilton Thompson, 'Catalogue of the library of Leicester abbey', *Transactions of the Leicestershire Archaeological Society* 19 (1936–7), 111–61, 378–440; 21 (1940–1), 1–88.

André Jammes, 'Un bibliophile à découvrir, Jean de Gagny', *Bulletin du bibliophile* (1996), 35–81.

André Jammes and Nicolas Barker, 'Jean de Gagny: a bibliophile re-discovered', *The Library* 7th ser. 11 (2010), 405–46.

Sears Jayne and Francis R. Johnson, *The Lumley Library. The Catalogue of 1609* (London, 1956).

Eliza Jeffries Davis, 'The beginning of the dissolution: Christchurch, Aldgate, 1532', *Transactions of the Royal Historical Society* 4th ser. 8 (1925), 127–50.

Kristian Jensen, 'Universities and colleges', in *The Cambridge History of Libraries in Britain and Ireland*, ed. Elisabeth Leedham-Green and Teresa Webber, 3 vols (Cambridge, 2006), i. 345–62.

Kristian Jensen, *Revolution and the Antiquarian Book: Reshaping the past, 1780–1815* (Cambridge, 2011).

John Bale's Index of British and Other Writers, ed. Reginald Lane Poole and Mary Bateson, (Oxford, 1902), repr. with introduction by James P. Carley and Caroline Brett (1989).

Neil R. Ker, *Medieval Libraries of Great Britain. A List of Surviving Books* (London, 1941).

Neil R. Ker, 'The migration of manuscripts from the English medieval libraries', *The Library* 4th ser. 23 (1942), 1–11.

Neil R. Ker, 'Sir John Prise', *The Library* 5th ser. 10 (1955), 1–24.

Neil R. Ker, 'Oxford college libraries in the sixteenth century', *Bodleian Library Record* 6 (1957–61), 459–515.

Neil R. Ker, 'Revised Preface' to *Medieval Libraries of Great Britain 2 [MLGB2]* (London, 1964).

Neil R. Ker, 'The provision of Books', in *History of the University of Oxford*, ed. Trevor Henry Aston, 8 vols (Oxford, 1984–2000), iii. 441–519.

Neil R. Ker, *Books, Collectors, and Libraries* (London, 1985).

Neil R. Ker, *Medieval Libraries of Great Britain 2 [MLGB2]. Supplement to the second edition*, ed. Andrew G. Watson (London, 1987).

Neil R. Ker, *Fragments of Medieval Manuscripts used as Pastedowns in Oxford Bindings*, 2nd edn, Oxford Bibliographical Society 3rd ser. 5 (Oxford, 2004 for 2000).

M. David Knowles, *The Religious Orders in England*, 3 vols (Cambridge, 1948–59).

Elisabeth S. Leedham-Green, *Books in Cambridge Inventories: Book Lists from Vice-Chancellor's Court Probate Inventories in the Tudor and Stuart Periods*, 2 vols (Cambridge, 1986).

John Leland, *De uiris illustribus*, ed. James P. Carley (Toronto, 2010).

Letters and Papers, Foreign and Domestic. Henry VIII, 21 vols (London, 1863–1910)

J. R. Liddell, '"Leland"'s lists of manuscripts in Lincolnshire monasteries', *English Historical Review* 55 (1939), 88–95.

David J. McKitterick, 'Two sixteenth-century catalogues of St John's College library', *Transactions of the Cambridge Bibliographical Society* 7 (1978), 135–55.

John Nichols, *The History and Antiquities of the County of Leicester*, 4 vols (London, 1795–1815).

John Claude T. Oates, *Cambridge University Library. A History. From the beginnings to the Copyright Act of Queen Anne* (Cambridge, 1986).

Henri Omont, 'Anciens catalogues de bibliothèques anglaises', *Centralblatt für Bibliothekswesen* 9 (1892), 201–22.

William Abel Pantin, *Canterbury College, Oxford*, 4 vols, Oxford Bibliographical Society new ser. 6–8, 30 (Oxford, 1947–85).

Alan J. Piper, 'Dr Thomas Swalwell, monk of Durham, archivist and bibliophile (d. 1539)', in *Books and Collectors, 1200–1700. Essays Presented to Andrew Watson*, ed. James P. Carley and Colin G. C. Tite (London, 1997), 71–100.

Nigel L. Ramsay, '"The manuscripts flew about like butterflies": the break-up of English libraries in the sixteenth century', in *Lost Libraries: The Destruction of Great Book Collections since Antiquity*, ed. James E. Raven (Basingstoke, 2004), 125–44.

Registrum Anglie, ed. Roger A. B. Mynors, Richard H. Rouse, and Mary A. Rouse, Corpus of British Medieval Library Catalogues 2 (London, 1991).

Richard H. Rouse, 'Bostonus Buriensis and the author of the *Catalogus scriptorum ecclesiae*', *Speculum* 41 (1966), 471–99.

Richard H. Rouse and Mary A. Rouse, *Henry of Kirkestede. Catalogus de libris autenticis et apocrifis*, Corpus of British Medieval Library Catalogues 11 (London, 2004).

David G. Rundle, 'Habits of manuscript-collecting: the dispersals of the library of Humfrey, duke of Gloucester', in *Lost Libraries: The Destruction of Great Book Collections since Antiquity*, ed. James E. Raven (Basingstoke, 2004), 106–24.

Herbert C. Schulz, 'The monastic library and scriptorium at Ashridge', *Huntington Library Quarterly* 1 (1937–1938), 305–11.

Richard Sharpe, *English Benedictine Libraries. The Shorter Catalogues*, Corpus of British Medieval Library Catalogues 4 (London, 1996).

Richard Sharpe, 'Accession, classification, location: press-marks in medieval libraries', *Scriptorium* 50 (1996), 279–87.

Richard Sharpe, 'Reconstructing the medieval library of Bury St Edmunds: the lost catalogue of Henry of Kirkstead', in *Bury St Edmunds: Medieval Art, Architecture, Archaeology, and Economy*, ed. Antonia Gransden, British Archaeological Association Transactions ([Leeds], 1998), 204–18.

Richard Sharpe, 'Henry Ellis, Richard Gough's protégé', *Bodleian Library Record* 22 (2009), 191–211.

Richard Sharpe, *Libraries and Books in Medieval England: The Role of Libraries in a Changing Book Economy* (Oxford, 2023).

Statutes of the Realm, 12 vols, Record Commission (London, 1810–28).

Thomas Tanner, *Bibliotheca Britannico-Hibernica*, ed. David Wilkins (London, 1748).

Rodney M. Thomson, *A Descriptive Catalogue of the Medieval Manuscripts in Worcester Cathedral Library* (Cambridge, 2001).

Rodney M. Thomson, *A Descriptive Catalogue of the Medieval Manuscripts of Corpus Christi College, Oxford* (Cambridge, 2011).

Henry John Todd, *The History of the College of Bonhommes at Ashridge* (London, 1823).

Victoria County History of Sussex, i (London, 1909); *London*, ii (London, 1907).

Letters and Papers, Foreign and Domestic. Henry VIII, 21 vols in 28 (London, 1863–1910).

Mackenzie E. C. Walcott, 'Inventories and valuations of religious houses at the time of the dissolution', *Archaeologia* 43 (1871), 201–49.

George F. Warner and Julius P. Gilson, *British Museum, Catalogue of Western Manuscripts in the Old Royal and King's Collections*, 4 vols (London 1921).

Andrew G. Watson, *The Manuscripts of Henry Savile of Banke* (London, 1969).

Andrew G. Watson *The Libraries of the Augustinian Canons*, Corpus of British Medieval Library Catalogues 6 (London, 1998), 35.

Teresa Webber and Andrew G. Watson, *Libraries of Augustinian Canons*, Corpus of British Medieval Library Catalogues 6 (London, 1998).

James M. W. Willoughby, 'The *secundo folio* and its uses, medieval and modern', *The Library*, 7th ser. 12 (2011), 237–58.

James M. W. Willoughby, *The Libraries of Collegiate Churches*, Corpus of British Medieval Library Catalogues 15 (London, 2013).

James M. W. Willoughby, 'Thomas Wolsey and the books of Cardinal College', *Bodleian Library Record* 28 (2015), 114–34.

James M. W. Willoughby, 'Cardinal Marcello Cervini (1501–1555) and English libraries', in *Books and Bookmen in Early Modern Britain. Essays Presented to James P. Carley*, ed. James M. W. Willoughby and Jeremy Catto (Toronto, 2018), 119–49.

James M. W. Willoughby, *The Libraries of the Secular Cathedrals*, Corpus of British Medieval Library Catalogues 17, forthcoming.

The Wormsley Library. Catalogue of an Exhibition held at the Pierpont Morgan Library, New York, 27 January–2 May 1999 (New York, NY, 1999).

Cyril E. Wright, 'The dispersal of the libraries in the sixteenth century', in *The English Library before 1700*, ed. Francis Wormald and Cyril E. Wright (London, 1958), 157–58.

John A. H. Wylie and Leslie H. Collier, 'The English sweating sickness (Sudor Anglicus): a reappraisal', *Journal of the History of Medicine and Allied Sciences* 36 (1981), 425–45.

Joyce A. Youings, *The Dissolution of the Monasteries* (London, 1971).

RUDOLF GAMPER

Klosteraufhebungen und das Schicksal ihrer Bibliotheken in der Deutschschweiz*

Klöster wurden bei ihrer Gründung auf unbeschränkte Dauer angelegt, dennoch kam es aus verschiedenen Gründen bereits vor der Reformation zur Aufhebung von Klöstern. In der Deutschschweiz löste die Reformation in den Jahren 1525 bis 1530 eine erste Welle von Klosteraufhebungen aus, eine zweite Welle stand im Zusammenhang mit der Gründung der modernen Schweiz im Jahrzehnt von 1840 bis 1850. Die Entscheidung zur Aufhebung und Säkularisierung der Klöster fällten in beiden Zeitabschnitten die Regierungen der einzelnen eidgenössischen Orte[1] bzw. Kantone, denn die Schweiz war bis 1848 (mit Ausnahme der Jahre 1798 bis 1803) eine Konföderation von weitgehend unabhängigen, republikanisch organisierten Orten

bzw. Kantonen ohne zentrale Regierungsgewalt[2]. Die einzelörtischen bzw. kantonalen Regierungen konfiszierten die Vermögen der Klöster und damit auch die Bibliotheken. Die folgende Übersicht konzentriert sich auf diese beiden Zeiten, weitere Klosteraufhebungen im 18. und 19. Jahrhundert werden nur beiläufig erwähnt.

1. Die Klosteraufhebungen in der Reformationszeit

Bereits vor der Reformation griffen die Regierungen der eidgenössischen Orte häufig in Entscheidungen der Kirche ein und hoben Klöster auf[3]. In der Reformationszeit bestimmten sie allein über die Einführung der kirchlichen

---

* Für zahlreiche Hinweise und wertvolle Diskussionen danke ich Gertraud Gamper, Winterthur, Martin Germann, Zürich, Verena Müller, Zürich, Ian Holt, Solothurn, Martin Steinmann, Basel, und Katrin Wenig, Würzburg.

1 Zum Begriff Orte für die Bündnispartner der frühen Eidgenossenschaft siehe Andreas Kley, Artikel 'Kantone', in *Historisches Lexikon der Schweiz*, Bd. 7 (Basel, 2008), 66–67.

2 Zur politischen Struktur der Schweiz: Thomas Maissen, *Geschichte der Schweiz* (Baden, 2010); Volker Reinhardt, *Kleine Geschichte der Schweiz* (München, 2010).

3 Jürg Leuzinger, 'Berns Griff nach den Klöstern', in *Berns grosse Zeit. Das 15. Jahrhundert neu entdeckt*, hrsg. v. Ellen J. Beer u. a. (Bern, 1999), 360–65; Heinzpeter Stucki, 'Die vorreformatorische Kirche', in *Geschichte*

Rudolf Gamper • Ehemals Bibliothekar der Vadianischen Sammlung St. Gallen. Rudolf.Gamper@gmail.com

How the Secularization of Religious Houses Transformed the Libraries of Europe, 16th–19th Centuries, ed. by Cristina Dondi, Dorit Raines, and †Richard Sharpe, BIB, 63 (Turnhout, 2022), pp. 67–81.

BREPOLS ꬓ PUBLISHERS   DOI 10.1484/M.BIB-EB.5.128478

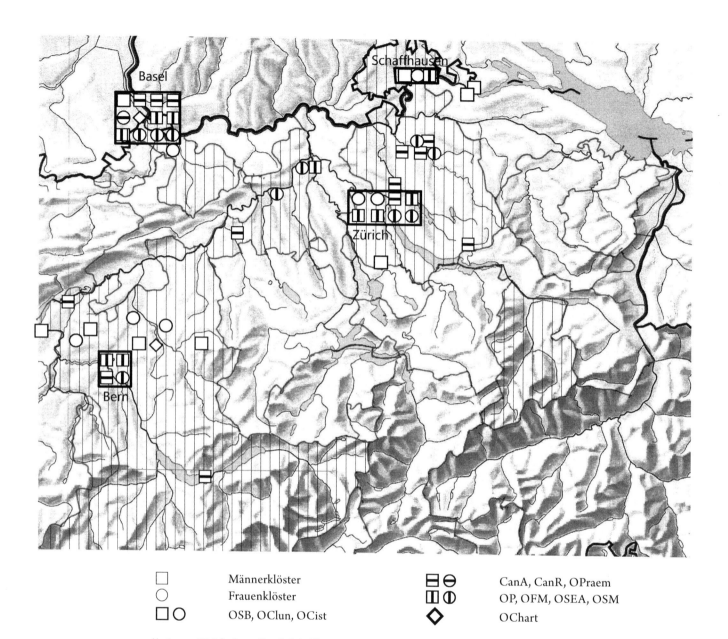

Männerklöster
Frauenklöster
OSB, OClun, OCist

CanA, CanR, OPraem
OP, OFM, OSEA, OSM
OChart

Karte 3.1. Zürich, Bern, Basel, Schaffhausen: aufgehobene Klöster (1525–1530)

Neuerungen. Die im schweizerischen Mittelland und am Oberrhein gelegenen grossen und reichen Städtekantone entschieden sich in den 1520er

Jahren für die Einführung der Reformation und hoben die Klöster in ihrem Gebiet auf[4]; die kleinen und stärker ländlich geprägten Kantone lehnten

des Kantons Zürich, Bd. 2: Frühe Neuzeit – 16. bis 18. Jahrhundert, hrsg. v. Nikolaus Flüeler und Marianne Flüeler-Grauwiler (Zürich, 1996), 186–88.

4   Zur Reformation: Caroline Schnyder, Artikel 'Reformation', in Historisches Lexikon der Schweiz, Bd. 10 (Basel, 2011), 168–70.

die Neuerungen ab und bewahrten die Klöster in ihrem Gebiet[5]. 1532 ging die Ausbreitung der Reformation in der Deutschschweiz wegen einer militärischen Niederlage der Reformierten zu Ende[6]; von 1530 bis ins 19. Jahrhundert wurden nur noch wenige Klöster aufgehoben. In den Untertanengebieten, den so genannten Gemeinen Herrschaften, blieben die Klöster ebenfalls erhalten[7].

Die Karte 3.1 zeigt die 1525 bis 1530 aufgehobenen Klöster in den drei Städteorten Zürich, Bern, Basel sowie dem kleineren Ort Schaffhausen[8]. In den Gebieten dieser Orte lagen mehr als 60 Prozent aller Klöster der Deutschschweiz.

Die meist kleinen Niederlassungen der Ritterorden und die "Sammlungen" (Beginen und vergleichbare Gruppen) sind nicht berücksichtigt; Prädikatur- und andere Kirchenbibliotheken sind ebenfalls ausgeschlossen.

2. Klosterbibliotheken und Liturgica vor der Reformation

Über die Grösse und Zusammensetzung der vorreformatorischen Stifts- und Klosterbibliotheken in der Deutschschweiz ist wenig bekannt. Nur wenige Bibliotheken in Basel, St. Gallen und vielleicht

in Bern[9] besassen neue, aktuelle Bücherkataloge. Vollständig erhalten sind die Kataloge der Basler Kartäuser und der St. Galler Dominikanerinnen. Demnach besassen die Basler Kartause rund 2100 Bände und die St. Galler Dominikanerinnen 323 Bände[10]. Ein älterer, nicht vollständig erhaltener Katalog der St. Galler Benediktiner von 1461 verzeichnet rund 500 Handschriften[11]. Dies sind stattliche Bibliotheken. Von den übrigen Stiften und Klöstern sind keine Kataloge überliefert und man darf annehmen, dass die meisten keine hatten. Neuere Untersuchungen lassen vermuten, dass zu Beginn des 16. Jahrhunderts die Bibliotheken der meisten übrigen Klöster klein waren, einige waren auch arg vernachlässigt[12].

---

5 Die beiden konfessionell gemischten Orte Appenzell und Glarus hatten keine Klöster in ihren Herrschaftsgebieten.

6 Helmut Meyer, *Der Zweite Kappeler Krieg. Die Krise der Schweizerischen Reformation* (Zürich, 1976).

7 André Holenstein, Artikel 'Gemeinde Herrschaften', in *Historisches Lexikon der Schweiz*, Bd. 5 (Basel, 2006), 200–01. Vorübergehende Klosteraufhebungen werden hier nicht berücksichtigt.

8 Eine differenzierte kartografische Aufnahme findet sich in *Helvetia Sacra*, Abt. 2, Teil 2: *Die weltlichen Kollegiatstifte der deutsch- und französischsprachigen Schweiz*, redigiert v. Guy P. Marchal (Bern, 1977), Kartenbeilage, sowie in *Helvetia Sacra*, Abt. 10: Register, hrsg. v. Arthur Bissegger u. a. (Basel, 2007), Carte 4, nach 696.

9 In Bern ist der Auftrag zur Erstellung eines Verzeichnisses erhalten, nicht aber das Verzeichnis. Albert Bruckner, *Scriptoria medii aevi Helvetica*, Bd. 11: *Schreibschulen der Diözese Lausanne* (Genf, 1967), 75. Von den Liturgica ist ein Verzeichnis erhalten. Martin Germann, 'Zwischen Konfiskation, Zerstreuung und Zerstörung. Schicksale der Bücher und Bibliotheken in der Reformationszeit in Basel, Bern und Zürich', *Zwingliana*, 27 (2000), 63–77, hier 77.

10 Zum Aufbau der Kartäuserbibliothek Basel: Max Burckhardt, 'Bibliotheksaufbau, Bücherbesitz und Leserschaft im spätmittelalterlichen Basel', in *Studien zum städtischen Bildungswesen des späten Mittelalters und der frühen Neuzeit*, hrsg. v. Bernd Moeller u. a. (Göttingen, 1983), 33–52; Schätzungen für weitere Bibliotheken: St. Leonhard in Basel: 1000 (Beat von Scarpatetti, 'Ex Bibliotheca Leonardina', *Basler Zeitschrift für Geschichte und Altertumskunde* 74 (1974), 271–310, hier 281), Dominikaner Basel, über 600: Bernhard Neidiger, in *Die Dominikaner und Dominikanerinnen in der Schweiz*, redigiert v. Petra Zimmer unter Mitarb. von Brigitte Degler-Spengler, Helvetia Sacra, Abt. 4, Bd. 5 (Basel, 1999), Bd. 1, 225–27; zu den Dominikanerinnen in St. Gallen: Magdalen Bless-Grabher, in *Dominikaner und Dominikanerinnen*, Bd. 2, 732–34 und 768–71.

11 *Mittelalterliche Bibliothekskataloge Deutschlands und der Schweiz*, Bd. 1: *Die Bistümer Konstanz und Chur*, bearb. v. Paul Lehmann (München, 1918), 101–18.

12 Im Doppelband der Helvetia Sacra über *Die Dominikaner und Dominikanerinnen*, wie Anm. 10, wird jeder Klosterbibliothek ein eigenes Kapitel gewidmet. Zum Niedergang der Bibliotheken in nicht observanten dominikanischen Frauenklöstern im 15. Jahrhundert

Neben den Stifts- und Konventsbibliotheken gewannen die privaten Bibliotheken an Bedeutung. Bei den Kanonikern und bei den Benediktinern, z. T. auch bei den Dominikanern, wurden Bücher als Privatbesitz behandelt und als Privatbesitz verschenkt oder vererbt[13]. Einige Kanoniker oder Konventualen bzw. deren Erben schenkten oder verkauften die Bücher dem Konvent. Seit die gedruckten Bücher die handschriftlichen ab ca. 1480 mehr und mehr verdrängten, nahm die Bedeutung der privaten Bibliotheken in Stiften und Klöstern zu.

Die liturgischen Bücher standen (oder lagen) in der Regel nicht in der Bibliothek, sondern in der Kirche bzw. in der Sakristei. Auch hier brachte der Buchdruck eine einschneidende Veränderung. Er ermöglichte die Produktion einheitlicher liturgischer Bücher. Die Bischöfe gaben seit den 1480er-Jahren neue Missale und Breviere heraus, schrieben die Benutzung der neuen liturgischen Bücher vor und verboten die Verwendung der alten. Auch für die Ordensliturgien wurden neue Breviere gedruckt und verbindlich erklärt. Alte liturgische Handschriften wurden in grosser Zahl ausgeschieden und als Buchbindermakulatur verwendet, und zwar bereits vor der Reformation[14].

Die rasche Ablösung der handschriftlichen Textüberlieferung durch Drucke veränderte auch die Klosterbibliotheken. Gerhardt Powitz nennt den Wandel "das 'Büchersterben' der Zeit um 1500": ein beträchtlicher Teil der bis dahin tradierten mittelalterlichen Handschriften wurde um 1500 innert weniger Jahrzehnte vernichtet[15]. Die Makulierung der Handschriften und die Privatisierung des Buchbesitzes setzten sich in der Reformationszeit fort.

3. Die Liturgica in der Reformation

Die Reformation manifestierte sich für die Bevölkerung zuerst in der Abschaffung des Messgottesdienstes und des Stundengebets. Altäre, Bilder und Statuen wurden aus den Kirchen entfernt, der Kirchenschatz (Kelche, Patenen, Monstranzen, etc.) konfisziert. Dies geschah fast überall in geregelter, von der Regierung und den tonangebenden Pfarrern überwachter Form. Die Stifter konnten an vielen Orten die der

---

allgemein: Wolfram Schneider-Lastin, a.a.O., Bd. 2, 1032–35; weitere Angaben enthalten die Artikel über das Basler Frauenkloster Klingental OP (*Bücher im Privatbesitz der Nonnen*, Bd. 2, 571) und über das Basler Frauenkloster St. Maria Magdalena OP (*Klosterbibliothek von mindestens 52 Bänden*, Bd. 2, 599), vgl. auch: Claudia Engler, 'Die Stadtklöster – Tradition und Erneuerung. "Ein news puch." Die "Bibliothek" des Dominkanerinnenklosters St. Michael in der Insel', in *Berns grosse Zeit*, wie Anm. 3, 482–89, hier 484.

13 Albert Bruckner, 'Zur Geschichte der Stiftsbibliothek von St. Peter zu Basel', in *Classical and Medieval Studies in Honor of Edward Kennard Rand*, hrsg. v. Leslie Webber Jones (New York, 1938), 33–40, hier 33–37; Hans von Greyerz, 'Studien zur Kulturgeschichte der Stadt Bern am Ende des Mittelalters', *Archiv des historischen Vereins des Kantons Bern*, 35 (1940), 177–491, 355.

14 Nach den Beobachtungen von Gerhardt Powitz können liturgische Fragmente mehr als die Hälfte der Makulaturmasse ausmachen. Gerhardt Powitz, 'Libri

inutiles in mittelalterlichen Bibliotheken. Bemerkungen über Alienatio, Palimpsestierung und Makulierung', *Scriptorium*, 50 (1996), 288–304, hier 303.

15 Powitz, 'Libri inutiles', wie Anm. 14, 299. Die Einbandfragmente der Bestände der Zentralbibliothek Zürich wurden in den 1940er-Jahren von Rudolf Steiger fotografisch erfasst (vgl. *Katalog der Handschriften der Zentralbibliothek Zürich*, Bd. 1: Leo Cunibert Mohlberg, *Mittelalterliche Handschriften* (Zürich, 1952), VIII). Eine Durchsicht der Sammlung im Jahr 2003 hat ergeben, dass ein beträchtlicher Teil der Fragmente für Einbände des späten 15. und des frühen 16. Jahrhunderts verwendet wurde, z. B. für die Bibliotheken von Peter Numagen und Gerold Edlibach. Interessant ist, dass Edlibach vor der Reformation keinen Anstoss an der Makulierung von Pergamenthandschriften nahm, die Zerstörung der Liturgica in der Reformation aber stark beklagte. Dazu: "Da beschachend vil grosser endrungen". Gerold Edlibachs Aufzeichnungen über die Zürcher Reformation 1520–1526, hrsg. v. Peter Jezler, in *Bilderstreit. Kulturwandel in Zwinglis Reformation*, hrsg. v. Hans-Dietrich Altendorf und Peter Jezler (Zürich, 1984), 41–74, hier 65.

Kirche übergebenen Bilder zurücknehmen. Die verbliebenen Bilder wurden in oft tumultartigen Aktionen verbrannt, die Statuen zerstört, die Wandgemälde übermalt, der Kirchenschatz eingeschmolzen. Die Zerstörungsrituale befestigten den Bruch mit der spätmittelalterlichen visuellen Frömmigkeit[16].

In Zürich – und nur in Zürich – wurden unter der Aufsicht der Pfarrer die liturgischen Bücher, Drucke und Handschriften, demonstrativ zerschnitten und die Blätter verkauft, z. B. als Verpackungsmaterial oder als Einbandmaterial an die Buchbinder, nicht aber verbrannt. Damit war sichergestellt, dass man Messe und Stundengebet endgültig überwunden hatte[17]. Es wurden aber bei weitem nicht alle liturgischen Bücher vernichtet. Selbst im Zürcher Grossmünster, dem Zentrum der Reformation, in dem Huldrych Zwingli predigte und lehrte, blieb der Leitfaden der vorreformatorischen Liturgie, der Liber ordinarius, vollständig erhalten[18]; auch einige Breviere sind noch intakt[19]. In Bern und Schaffhausen wurden wertvolle liturgische Handschriften absichtlich verschont und in katholisch gebliebene Gebiete verkauft.

Eine Quantifizierung der Zerstörung von liturgischen Büchern in der Reformationszeit ist nur in wenigen Fällen möglich[20]. Es ist zu vermuten, dass die Verluste in der älteren Literatur stark überzeichnet wurden. Sowohl die katholische wie die reformierte Geschichtsschreibung hatte ein Interesse daran, die Vernichtung der liturgischen Bücher möglichst drastisch zu schildern. Die katholische Geschichtstradition beklagte das erlittene Unrecht durch das Zerstörungswerk der Reformation, die reformierte Geschichtstradition unterstrich den Erfolg der Abschaffung der Messe und des Stundengebets, wozu auch die Beseitigung der dazu notwendigen Bücher gehörte. Aus quellenkritischer Sicht ist Vorsicht geboten; es wäre falsch, die Makulierung liturgischer Handschriften unbesehen den Umwälzungen der frühen Reformationszeit zuzuschreiben[21].

---

16 Sergiusz Michalski, 'Die Ausbreitung des reformatorischen Bildersturms 1521–1537', in *Bildersturm. Wahnsinn oder Gottes Wille?*, hrsg. v. Cécile Dupeux, Peter Jezler und Jean Wirth, Ausstellungskatalog (Zürich, 2000), 46–51; Peter Jezler, *Der Bildersturm in Zürich 1523–1530*, ebd. 75–83.

17 Martin Germann, 'Bibliotheken im reformierten Zürich. Vom Büchersturm (1525) zur Gründung der Stadtbibliothek (1629)', in *Beiträge zur Geschichte des Buchwesens im konfessionellen Zeitalter*, hrsg. v. Herbert G. Göpfert u. a. (Wiesbaden, 1985), 189–212, hier 190.

18 *Der Liber Ordinarius des Konrad von Mure. Die Gottesdienstordnung am Grossmünster in Zürich*, hrsg. v. Heidi Leuppi (Freiburg / Schweiz, 1995).

19 St. Gallen, Stiftsbibliothek, Cod. 526–29; Beat Matthias von Scarpatetti, *Die Handschriften der Stiftsbibliothek St. Gallen. Beschreibendes Verzeichnis*, Bd. 2 (Wiesbaden, 2008), 350–63.

20 Heinrich Bullinger überliefert, gestützt auf Felix Frey, den damaligen Propst des Zürcher Grossmünsters, in der 50 Jahre nach den Ereignissen entstandenen Tiguriner-Chronik die Zahl von 50 weggenommenen liturgischen Pergamenthandschriften. Martin Germann, *Zwischen Konfiskation*, wie Anm. 9, 65; vgl. Germann, *Bibliotheken*, wie Anm. 17, 190.

21 Es ist auffällig, dass seit den 1520er-Jahren bis ins 17. Jahrhundert zahlreiche Bucheinbände mit Pergamentfragmenten bezogen und Koperteinbände mit Pergamentfragmenten hergestellt wurden, besonders für Archivmaterial. Die Pergamente stammen oft aus liturgischen Handschriften, aus Brevieren, Missalen, Gradualen und Antiphonaren, bei weitem nicht alle aus der ersten Säuberungswelle der 1520er-Jahre, wie früher gelegentlich vermutet wurde. Die Wiederverwendung des Pergaments von nicht mehr gebrauchten liturgischen Handschriften setzte – wie oben gesagt – bereits im späten 15. Jahrhundert ein, dort vor allem als Spiegelblätter in Einbänden von Inkunabeln und Frühdrucken. Nach der Reformation ging die Makulierung von liturgischen Handschriften bis ins 17. Jahrhundert weiter, denn nach der Liturgiereform des Konzils von Trient waren viele liturgische Handschriften auch im katholischen Gottesdienst nicht mehr brauchbar.

4. Die Klosterbibliotheken in der Reformation

Die Reformatoren waren in der Regel Bücher-liebhaber und förderten die Errichtung von neuen Studienbibliotheken. Martin Luther forderte Anfang 1524 in einer Broschüre die städtischen Regierungen ausdrücklich auf, "gutte libra-reyen odder bücher heuser" einzurichten[22]. Die Broschüre wurde in der Deutschschweiz gelesen und beachtet. In allen reformierten Hauptstädten wurden Studienbibliotheken auf- oder ausgebaut. Darin blieben Teile der Klosterbibliotheken erhalten, allerdings in ganz unterschiedlichem Ausmass. Die Reformatoren der Deutschschweiz hatten für Handschriften in der Regel kein Interesse; in ihren privaten Bibliotheken standen nur wenige Handschriften, z. B. Chroniken, deren Texte nicht gedruckt waren. Dies gilt auch für die neuen Studienbibliotheken. Sie nahmen zwar auch Texte der gelehrten theologischen Scholastik, der Jurisprudenz und der volkstüm-lichen vorreformatorischen Heiligenverehrung in die neuen Studienbibliotheken auf, aber nur selektiv. In den Bibliotheken der aufge-hobenen Klöster standen zu einem guten Teil Handschriften mit genau diesen Texten. Es bestand nur ein geringes Interesse an ihrer Erhaltung[23].

Die Zürcher Regierung überliess denn auch bei der Aufhebung der Klöster die Bücher grund-sätzlich den Chorherren und Chorfrauen, den Mönchen und Nonnen. Als Beispiel sei ein Besitzeintrag im ersten Band der "Postilla super totam Bibliam" des Nicolaus de Lyra von 1481 genannt.

Ille liber est ecclesie S. Jacobi in Monte Sancto [Heiligenberg / Winterthur]. Et pervenit ad eam a domino Heinrico Haggenberg, eiusdem ecclesie quondam canonico. [Andere Hand:] Atque dum per verbum dei cultus iste templumque destruerantur, domini mei Thuricenses etiam libros illos nobis donaverunt. Plebanus igitur et nos omnes prebendarii Montis Sancti divisimus inter nos singula patronorum nostrorum dona, et bona pace liber iste mihi Laurencio Boßhart novissimo prebendario senioris s. Martini assignatus est anno domini 1525[24].

Der erste Besitzer des Buches war demnach der Chorherr Heinrich Haggenberg, der das Buch dem Chorherrenstift schenkte. 1525 verfügte die Regierung die Aufteilung der Bibliothek[25]. Dabei ging das Buch an Laurenz Bosshard, der aber nur den ersten Band des zweibändigen Werkes erhielt. Das Kolophon steht am Ende des zweiten Bandes. Deshalb kopierte Bosshard am Schluss des ersten Bandes den Druckort und das Druckdatum aus dem Kolophon. Das zweibändige Werk gehörte also zuerst zur Privatbibliothek von Heinrich Haggenberg und ging in die gemein-same Bibliothek des Chorherrenstifts ein. Der erste Band gelangte bei deren Auflösung in die Privatbibliothek von Laurenz Bosshard; das Werk, das auch nach der Reformation seinen Wert behielt, gelangte nicht als Ganzes, sondern bandweise zur Verteilung.

Die Privatisierung der Klosterbibliotheken durch die Aufteilung unter die Chorherren und Chorfrauen, Mönche und Nonnen, ver-kleinerte die Chancen, dass die Bücher erhal-ten blieben, ganz wesentlich. Im Gegensatz zu Lyras Postilla wurden die meisten nicht mehr verwendet; sie blieben in der Regel nur dann

---

22 Martin Luther, 'An die Ratherren aller Städte deutsches Lands, daß sie christliche Schulen aufrichten und halten sollen, 1524', in Martin Luther, *Weimarer Ausgabe*, Bd. 15 (Weimar, 1899), 9–53, hier 49.

23 Martin Germann, *Die reformierte Stiftsbibliothek am Grossmünster Zürich im 16. Jahrhundert und die Anfänge der neuzeitlichen Bibliographie* (Wiesbaden, 1994), 106.

24 Inge Dahm, *Aargauer Inkunabelkatalog* (Aarau, 1985), Nr. 661, korrigiert nach dem Original.

25 *Die Chronik des Laurencius Bosshart von Winterthur 1185–1532*, hrsg. v. Kaspar Hauser (Basel, 1905), 316.

erhalten, wenn sie als Geschenke in eine kirchliche oder staatliche Institution kamen, die sie aufbewahrte, auch wenn sie keinen aktuellen Gebrauchswert hatten. Für vorsätzliche und systematische Bücherzerstörungen in klösterlichen Bibliotheksbeständen, wie sie in der älteren Literatur häufig angenommen wurden, fehlen nach neuen Untersuchungen hinreichende Indizien[26].

Bedeutend besser als die Bibliotheksbestände sind die Archive mit den Urkunden und Büchern der Verwaltung erhalten. Sie erlitten in der Reformation praktisch keine Verluste. Nur in den zwei oder drei Klöstern, die zu Beginn der Reformation überfallen und angezündet wurden und fast völlig ausbrannten, wurden auch die meisten Archivalien zerstört; in einigen weiteren Klöstern nahmen vertriebene Konventualen die Archivalien mit sich ins Exil[27]. Von den Klosterbibliotheken dagegen sind nur wenige erhalten. Der Unterschied ist leicht zu erklären: Die Regierungen der Kantone sicherten die Dokumente, die für die Verwaltung und für die Erhebung der Abgaben wichtig waren; mit diesen Ressourcen konnte die Regierung die

staatliche Ordnung neu gestalten. Die Bücher für den Gottesdienst dagegen hatten keinen Wert mehr und die Bücher für die Erbauung und das Studium waren für die Regierungen ohne Interesse.

5. Die Klosterbibliotheken in den reformierten eidgenössischen Orten

Die Regierungen der reformierten Orte der Eidgenossenschaft behandelten die Klosterbibliotheken unterschiedlich.

Im ganzen Herrschaftsgebiet der Stadt Zürich wurden die Bücher der Stifts- und Klosterbibliotheken aufgeteilt. Die Bibliotheken wurden dadurch zerstreut. Die aus den Stiften und Klöstern austretenden Geistlichen erhielten das Gut zurück, das sie beim Eintritt ins Klostervermögen eingebracht hatten; Bücher dienten ausserdem als Teil der Abfindung beim Austritt aus dem Stift oder Kloster. In der Stadt Zürich besass Huldrych Zwingli, die unbestrittene Führungsgestalt der Zürcher Reformation, eine Privatbibliothek von über 150 Bänden. Nach seinem Tod 1531 wurde sie zum Kern der Studienbibliothek des Grossmünsters, der Stiftsbibliothek[28]. Diese Bibliothek bildete in den folgenden Jahren eine Art Sammelbecken für die zerstreuten Handschriften und Drucke aus den Zürcher Klöstern (vgl. den Beitrag von Martin Germann in diesem Band).

Bern, der wichtigste und mächtigste Kanton der Eidgenossenschaft, hob die Klöster 1528 auf. Der Bildersturm in der Hauptkirche, im Münster, entglitt zeitweise der Kontrolle der Regierung, sonst sorgte der Rat für einen geordneten

26 Schneider-Lastin, *Dominikanerinnen*, wie Anm. 10, 1033 zum Kloster Ötenbach; seine Forschungsergebnisse dürften auch auf andere, nicht observante Klöster übertragbar sein. Einzig bei den Büchern für den Gottesdienst sind gezielte Zerstörungen gut belegt.

27 Die Überlieferung der Klosterarchive ist in den Artikeln der Helvetia Sacra beschrieben, während zu den Bibliotheken, die dominikanischen ausgenommen, meistens nur dürftige Angaben zu finden sind. Für Basel: Heiligensetzer, Nicht ein blettlin, wie Anm. 35, 141, Anm. 11. Anzumerken bleibt, dass zerstreute Bestände aus Klosterbibliotheken erst teilweise durch die Provenienzforschung identifiziert wurden. So wurden beträchtliche Teile der Franziskanerbibliotheken von Zürich und Schaffhausen erst in den 1990er-Jahren entdeckt. Germann, Stiftsbibliothek, wie Anm. 23, 153–55; Rudolf Gamper, Gaby Knoch-Mund, Marlis Stähli, *Katalog der mittelalterlichen Handschriften der Ministerialbibliothek Schaffhausen* (Dietikon / Zürich, 1994), 45–47.

28 Germann, *Stiftsbibliothek*, wie Anm. 23, 166–68; *Handbuch der historischen Buchbestände in der Schweiz*, hrsg. v. der Zentralbibliothek Zürich, bearb. v. Urs B. Leu u. a., 3 Bde (Hildesheim, 2011), hier Bd. 3, 365–66.

Ablauf[29]. Die Bibliotheken wurden aufgelöst wie in Zürich und die Bücher durch die Abgabe an die Kanoniker, Mönche und Nonnen zerstreut. Die neue Studienbibliothek[30] erlangte nicht die Bedeutung der Zürcher Stiftsbibliothek, die Handschriften und Frühdrucke wurden häufiger als in Zürich in die umliegenden katholischen Gebiete verbracht. Ein Kartäusermönch aus Thorberg nahm nicht weniger als 33 Werke in sein neues Kloster Ittingen mit[31]. Viele blieben so erhalten. Der einzige geschlossene Bestand aus einem Kloster in der Berner Studienbibliothek sind rund 40 Bände mit 64 Drucken und Handschriften aus der Kartause Thorberg[32]. Bemerkenswert – und gut dokumentiert – ist der Verkauf der sechs prächtigen Antiphonare der Berner Hauptkirche, des Münsters, nach Estavayer und an eine weitere Kirche. So blieb ein wichtiges Werk der Berner Buchproduktion um 1490 erhalten[33].

In Schaffhausen wurden die Klöster 1529 geschlossen. Die liturgischen Bücher wurden rasch zum Handelsgut. Die Regierung verbot den Handel innerhalb des Kantons, in fremde Gebiete durften die Liturgica verkauft werden. Die Bibliotheken der Männerklöster wurden – anders als in Zürich und Bern – nicht aufgelöst, sondern blieben offenbar mehr oder weniger unbeachtet liegen, die Bücher des einzigen städtischen Frauenklosters sind weitgehend verschwunden. Nach rund zehn Jahren, um 1540, wurde eine Studienbibliothek gegründet. Man sammelte die noch vorhandenen Bücher der Klöster ein. Die neue Bibliothek enthielt anfänglich mehrheitlich Handschriften. Diese wurden von reformierten Pfarrern für das Studium gebraucht, bis die Studienbibliothek die Texte in neuen Druckausgaben erworben hatte[34].

Basel war zu Beginn des 16. Jahrhunderts eine Stadt der Bücher mit leistungsfähigen Druckereien und grossen Klosterbibliotheken. Hier zog sich die Auflösung der zahlreichen Klöster nach der Reformation 1529 über längere Zeit hin. Die grossen Bibliotheken blieben während Jahrzehnten ohne Betreuung in den Klostergebäuden liegen, die liturgischen Handschriften wurden nach und nach ausgesondert[35]. In der Domstiftbibliothek sind studentische Bücherdiebstähle gut dokumentiert[36]. Die Basler Büchersammlungen sind dennoch bedeutend besser erhalten als jene in den anderen reformierten Kantonen. Eine grosse Ablieferung aus der Bibliothek der Dominikaner an die Universitätsbibliothek ist für 1559 bezeugt, weitere, umfangreichere Ablieferungen aus den Bibliotheken der Kartäuser, der Chorherren von St. Leonhard und aus dem Domstift wurden 1590 durchgeführt[37]. Die Universitätsbibliothek Basel hat seitdem den weitaus grössten Bestand an

---

29   Franz-Josef Sladeczek, 'Bern 1528. Zwischen Zerstörung und Erhaltung', in *Bildersturm*, wie Anm. 16, 97–103.

30   *Handbuch der historischen Buchbestände*, wie Anm. 28, Bd. 1, 240–41.

31   Urs B. Leu, 'Europäischer Inkunabeldruck und Thurgauer Lesekultur', in Marianne Luginbühl und Heinz Bothien, *Meisterwerke des frühen Buchdrucks. Die Inkunabel-Schätze der Kantonsbibliothek Thurgau aus den Klöstern von Ittingen, Fischingen und Kreuzlingen* (Frauenfeld, 2011), XII–XLI, hier XXXVI–XL.

32   von Greyerz, *Studien*, wie Anm. 13, 334–40; Germann, *Zwischen Konfiskation*, wie Anm. 9, 75 (mit korrigierten Bestandeszahlen).

33   Joseph Leisibach, 'Die Antiphonare des Berner Münsters St. Vinzenz. Eine nicht erhoffte Neuentdeckung', *Zeitschrift für Schweizerische Kirchengeschichte*, 83 (1989), 177–204.

34   Rudolf Gamper, 'Die Schaffhauser "Liberey" im 16. Jahrhundert', *Schaffhauser Beiträge zur Geschichte*, 67 (1990), 241–54; Gamper, Knoch-Mund, Stähli, *Katalog Ministerialbibliothek Schaffhausen*, wie Anm. 27, 50–52; *Handbuch der historischen Buchbestände*, wie Anm. 28, Bd. 2, 260–61.

35   Lorenz Heiligensetzer, '"Nicht ein blettlin Bergaments mehr". Der Einbruch in die verwaiste Domstiftbibliothek 1581', *Basler Zeitschrift für Geschichte und Altertumskunde*, 109 (2009), 139–50, hier 141; Germann, *Zwischen Konfiskation*, wie Anm. 9, 70.

36   Heiligensetzer, 'Nicht ein blettlin', wie Anm. 35, 145–50.

37   Germann, *Zwischen Konfiskation*, wie Anm. 9, 70–72; Heiligensetzer, 'Nicht ein blettlin', wie Anm. 35, 140–44; *Handbuch der historischen Buchbestände*, wie Anm. 28, Bd. 1, 121–23.

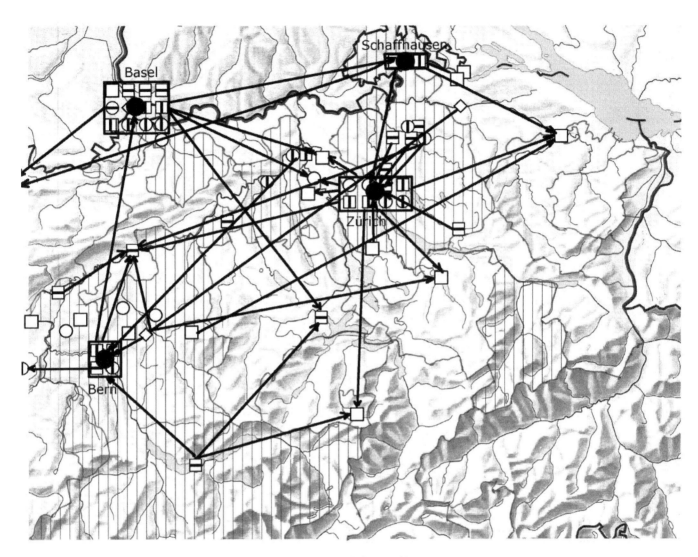

Karte 3.2. Deutschschweiz: Verschiebung von Buchbeständen aus aufgehobenen Klöstern

mittelalterlichen Handschriften und Inkunabeln aller Schweizer Bibliotheken. – Von den Beständen der übrigen Klöster, vor allem der Frauenklöster, sind nur wenige Handschriften bekannt, die zum Teil in die Universitätsbibliothek, zum Teil in verschiedene Klöster ausserhalb von Basel gelangten.

Ergebnisse

In der Reformationszeit wurden rund 60 Prozent der Klöster in der Deutschschweiz aufgehoben, darunter viele in den reichen Städten, deren Klöster grössere Bibliotheken besassen als jene auf dem Lande. Die Klosteraufhebungen bewirkten die grösste Umschichtung des Buchbesitzes in der gesamten Geschichte der Schweiz. Es ist zu vermuten, dass in den Jahren 1525 bis 1530 zwischen einem Drittel und zwei Dritteln des gesamten Buchbestandes in der Deutschschweiz den Besitzer wechselte.

Die Karte 3.2 zeigt die bisher bekannten Verschiebungen innerhalb der Deutschschweiz an. Über 90 Prozent der Bücher stammen aus Männerklöstern, die Bücher aus Frauenklöstern galten in der Reformationszeit offensichtlich nicht viel. Solothurn erweist sich als wichtigste Sammelstätte für versprengte Bücher aus Klosterbibliotheken[38].

Von den Büchern, die den austretenden Chorherren und Chorfrauen, Mönchen und Nonnen mitgegeben wurden, sind Einzelstücke im Laufe der Zeit in andere Klosterbibliotheken und in staatliche Bibliotheken gelangt. Die Karte zeigt die bisher bekannten Verschiebungen innerhalb der Deutschschweiz an. Die Erforschung der Besitzgeschichte ist bei weitem nicht abgeschlossen; jeder Handschriften- und Inkunabelkatalog, jede Neukatalogisierung alter Bestände bringt neue Identifikationen von Vorbesitzern. Sicher ist aber, dass die meisten Bibliotheksbestände der aufgehobenen Klöster nicht in der Reformation zerstört, sondern durch die Zerstreuung und mangelndes Interesse nach und nach zugrunde gingen.

6. Die Klosteraufhebungen 1840–1850

Vom 1530 bis 1840 wurden nur wenige Klöster aufgehoben. Den grössten Einschnitt bildete die Aufhebung des Jesuitenordens 1773; die Jesuiten führten aber ihre Tätigkeit vorerst als Weltpriester und Lehrer weiter und die Bibliotheken verblieben in den Lehranstalten[39]. Die Französische Revolution

bereitete der 13-örtigen Eidgenossenschaft 1798 ein Ende und legte mit der Helvetik (1798 bis 1803) die Grundlage für die Entwicklung der modernen Schweiz. Die meisten Klöster überstanden die Revolutionszeit und ihre Bibliotheken erlitten keine Verluste, einzig die Benediktinerabtei St. Gallen 1805 wurde durch einen Parlamentsbeschluss säkularisiert, wobei die Stiftsbibliothek als eigenständige Institution weitergeführt wurde[40].

Die Bibliotheken der grossen Männerklöster in der Deutschschweiz waren zu Beginn des 19. Jahrhunderts gut organisiert. Im 18. und frühen 19. Jahrhundert hatten sie neue, repräsentative Bibliothekssäle erhalten, die Bestände waren nach Fachgebieten aufgestellt und in Katalogen von unterschiedlicher Qualität erfasst. Grosse Klöster wie Muri und St. Urban besassen ca. 15'000 Bände, kleine wie Wettingen ca. 2700 Bände[41]. In den katholischen Gebieten und den ehemaligen Untertanenländern gab es – anders als in den reformierten Gebieten – keine staatlichen Bibliotheken von Bedeutung; die Bibliotheken der grossen Männerklöster und die Lehranstalten, die die Jesuitenbibliotheken weiterführten, waren, zusammen mit einigen Privatbibliotheken, die einzigen

---

38   Die wichtigsten Provenienzen sind: Bern, Dominikaner und Dominikanerinnen; Gottstatt, Prämonstratenser; Thorberg, Kartause; Basel, Augustinerchorherren von St. Leonhard, Kartause und Franziskaner; Zürich, Dominikanerinnen; Zürichberg, Augustinerchorherren; Wädenswil, Johanniterkommende, evtl. auch Töss, Dominikanerinnen. Freundliche Mitteilung von Ian Holt, Zentralbibliothek Solothurn.

39   *Helvetia Sacra*, Abt. 7: *Der Regularklerus. Die Gesellschaft Jesu in der Schweiz*, bearb. v. Ferdinand Strobel (Bern, 1976), 127–28. (Luzern), 169 (Fribourg), 212–13. (Porrentruy) und 314–15. (Solothurn); *Handbuch der historischen Buchbestände*, wie Anm. 28, Bd. 1,

476–77. (Porrentruy), Bd. 2, 49 (Luzern), Bd. 2, 352–53. (Solothurn), dazu auch: Ian Holt, 'Die Solothurner Jesuitenbibliothek (1646–1773) und ihre Gönner. Die Bibliothek Franz Haffners und weitere Schenkungen und Vermächtnisse', *Jahrbuch für Solothurnische Geschichte*, 80 (2007), 247–77.

40   *Fürstabtei St.Gallen. Untergang und Erbe 1805/2005* (St. Gallen, 2005); zur Bibliothek: Karl Schmuki, *Die Schicksale der Klosterbibliothek St.Gallen zwischen 1797 und 1811*, ebd. 107–20.

41   Muri: ca. 15,000 Bände (Charlotte Bretscher-Gisiger und Rudolf Gamper, *Katalog der mittelalterlichen Handschriften der Klöster Muri und Hermetschwil* (Dietikon-Zürich, 2005), 51–52. und 70, Anm. 244); Sankt Urban: 15,000–18,000 Titel, (siehe unten, Anm. 48); Wettingen: 2,700 Bände nach dem Verkauf der Dubletten (Charlotte Bretscher-Gisiger und Rudolf Gamper, *Katalog der mittelalterlichen Handschriften des Klosters Wettingen. Katalog der mittelalterlichen Handschriften in Aarau, Laufenburg, Lenzburg, Rheinfelden und Zofingen* (Dietikon-Zürich, 2009), 67–68, Anm. 286).

Grundlagen für wissenschaftliche Studien[42]. Deshalb bestand aus der Sicht der Regierungen grundsätzlich ein Interesse, diese Buchbestände zu erhalten und sie – wenn Klöster aufgehoben wurden – in die neu gegründeten Kantonsbibliotheken zu integrieren. An den Beständen der Frauenklöster dagegen hatten die Regierungen wenig oder kein Interesse. Die Nonnen besassen nur wenige wissenschaftliche Werke – und für die fromme Erbauungsliteratur hatte man in den neuen kantonalen Bibliotheken keine Verwendung.

Der Druck auf die Klöster nahm in den 1830er-Jahren stark zu. Die liberalen Kräfte erstarkten mit der beginnenden Industrialisierung. Die politische Organisation der Schweiz beruhte seit 1803 wieder auf den weitgehend unabhängigen Kantonen. Die Kleinräumigkeit behinderte die wirtschaftliche Entwicklung; ein wichtiges Ziel der liberalen Bewegung bestand darin, eine neue, zeitgemässe politische Organisation des Landes zu erreichen. Sie hatte ihre Hochburgen in den reformierten Kantonen. Gegen diese Erneuerung der Schweiz wehrten sich die katholisch-konservativen Kräfte. Sie lehnten die Stärkung der Zentralgewalt strikte ab und bekämpften den zunehmenden staatlichen Einfluss auf die Kirche, besonders auch auf die Klöster. Diese galten – nicht zu Unrecht – als Zentren des Widerstands gegen die Modernisierung der staatlichen Ordnung. Der Kampf um die Erneuerung der staatlichen Ordnung spitzte sich in den 1840er-Jahren zu[43].

In diesem Zusammenhang kam es zu Klosteraufhebungen, zuerst im Kanton Aargau. Nach einem Aufstand im Freiamt hob das kantonale Parlament Anfang 1841 alle Klöster im Kanton auf, musste aber unter äusserem Druck den Nonnen 1843 die Rückkehr gestatten. Die Männerklöster blieben aufgehoben. Deren Bibliotheken wurden 1845/1846 in die Kantonsbibliothek verbracht. Sie wurden dort neu katalogisiert; die Dubletten sonderte man aus und verkaufte sie[44].

Nach dem kurzen Bürgerkrieg 1847, dem so genannten Sonderbundskrieg, hoben die mehrheitlich liberalen Parlamente in den Kantonen 1848 Thurgau, Luzern, Freiburg und – unter etwas anderen Vorzeichen – im Kanton Tessin[45] zahlreiche Klöster auf. In allen Kantonen waren finanzielle Gründe ausschlaggebend. Im konfessionell gemischten Thurgau war das Interesse an den Bibliotheken anfänglich gering; bedeutende Handschriften aus dem Dominikanerinnenkloster St. Katharinental kamen 1850/1851 auf den Antiquariatsmarkt[46]. Die Regierung wollte anfänglich auch die grossen Bibliotheken der Männerklöster Fischingen, Ittingen und Kreuzlingen verkaufen, was einige im Bildungswesen engagierte Theologen und Historiker verhindern konnten. Die Bücher wurden erst 1852/1862 in den Kantonshauptort Frauenfeld transportiert, als man die Klostergebäude veräusserte und

---

42 In der Schweiz existiert kein Werk, das einen zusammenfassenden Überblick über die Entwicklung der Bibliotheken gibt. Deshalb sei auf die Artikel über die Stadt- und Kantonsbibliotheken im Handbuch der historischen Buchbestände (wie Anm. 28) verwiesen.

43 Maissen, Geschichte, wie Anm. 2, 186–204; Reinhardt, Kleine Geschichte, wie Anm. 2, 127–33.

44 Bretscher-Gisiger und Gamper, Katalog Muri, wie Anm. 41, 52–56; *Handbuch der historischen Buchbestände*, wie Anm. 28, Bd. 1, 16.

45 Der Kanton Tessin war mehrheitlich liberal und katholisch. Angesichts der Krise der Staatsfinanzen wurden die religiösen Körperschaften schrittweise enteignet. Einige Konventsbibliotheken gelangten in die Biblioteca cantonale in Lugano. Adriana Ramelli, *Catalogo degli incunaboli della Biblioteca Cantonale di Lugano* (Firenze, 1981), 11f; Raffaello Ceschi, *Geschichte des Kantons Tessin* (Frauenfeld, 2003), 65–66; *Handbuch der historischen Buchbestände*, wie Anm. 28, Bd. 2, 426–27.

46 Das Dominikanerinnerkloster St. Katharinental blieb 1848 erhalten dank seinem Grundbesitz, der zum Teil in Deutschland lag und bei der Auflösung verloren gegangen wäre. Es wurde erst 1869 aufgehoben; die Vermögensverwaltung unterstand aber bereits früher dem Kanton Thurgau. Erich Trösch, Artikel 'Sankt Katharinental', in *Historisches Lexikon der Schweiz*, Bd. 10 (Basel, 2011), 755–56; Cordula M. Kessler, *Gotische Buchkultur. Dominikanische Handschriften aus dem Bistum Konstanz* (Berlin, 2010), 10–28.

neuen Nutzungen zuführte. 1862 bis 1865 wurden der gesamte Bestand katalogisiert; rund 12'000 Titel wurden in die Kantonsbibliothek integriert, darunter rund 360 Inkunabeln. Nach der Aussonderung der Dubletten verkaufte man rund 2400 Bände; zusätzlich wurden die zwei kantonalen Schulen mit Büchern ausgestattet[47]. Die Klöster der Zisterzienserinnen in Feldbach, Kalchrain und Tänikon sowie die Benediktinerinnen in Münsterlingen wurden ebenfalls säkularisiert; aus ihren Bibliotheken sind nur vereinzelte Bände bekannt.

In den katholischen Kantonen Luzern und Freiburg wurden die Klöster aufgehoben, um finanzielle Mittel zur Deckung der Kriegsschuld des Sonderbundskriegs zu erhalten. Die Luzerner Regierung säkularisierte 1848 die Zisterzienserabtei St. Urban und das Frauenkloster Rathausen. Die Bibliothek von St. Urban mit über 15'000 Titeln, darunter 63 Handschriften, blieb erhalten; sie gelangte zusammen mit der grossen Kupferstich- und der ansehnlichen Münzsammlung integral in die Kantonsbibliothek Luzern[48]. Im Kanton Freiburg wurden bereits Ende 1847 die Jesuiten vertrieben, 1848 folgte die Aufhebung des Zisterzienserklosters Hauterive, der Kartause Part-Dieu sowie des Augustinerklosters in Freiburg. Die Bibliotheken dieser Klöster bildeten den Grundstock der neuen, 1848 gegründeten Kantonsbibliothek von rund 40'000 Titeln, darunter rund 100 Handschriften[49]. – Bei den Klosteraufhebungen von 1840 bis 1850 sind die Vorgänge für die grossen Männerklöster, deren Bibliotheken von den Kantonen übernommen wurden, gut dokumentiert. Was mit den Büchern in den kleinen Männerklöstern und den Frauenklöstern geschah, deren Bibliotheken nicht mehr vorhanden sind, ist noch weitgehend unerforscht.

Im 19. Jahrhundert sind einige weitere Klosteraufhebungen vor 1840 und nach 1850 anzufügen, vor allem die Benediktinerabtei Pfäfers (1838), das Luzerner Franziskanerkloster In der Au (1838), sowie die Benediktinerabtei Rheinau (1862). Aus der Pfäferser Bibliothek blieb der Handschriftenbestand und ein kleiner Teil der Drucke erhalten, die beiden anderen Bibliotheken gingen zum grössten Teil den Kantonsbibliotheken auf[50].

Der Überblick zeigt, dass in beiden Wellen der Klosteraufhebungen die Bibliotheken mit einem hohen Anteil von wissenschaftlichen Werken die beste Erhaltungschance hatten, das sie für die Reformatoren des 16. Jahrhunderts mit ihrem humanistischen Hintergrund wie für die Liberalen des 19. Jahrhunderts für die Studien- und Kantonsbibliotheken einen Gebrauchswert darstellten, während die Bestände der Frauenklöster mit Geringschätzung behandelt wurden.

---

47 Alois Schwager, 'Die Klosterpolitik des Kantons Thurgau 1798–1848', 2. Teil, *Thurgauische Beiträge zur vaterländischen Geschichte*, 119 (1982), 65–248, hier 191–95; Marianne Luginbühl und Heinz Bothien: *'Auch Bücher haben ihr Schicksal'. Die Geschichte der thurgauischen Klosterbibliotheken seit dem 19. Jahrhundert* (Frauenfeld, 1999); *Handbuch der historischen Buchbestände*, wie Anm. 28, Bd. 2, 489–90.

48 *Sankt Urban, 1194–1994. Ein ehemaliges Zisterzienserkloster*, hrsg. im Auftr. des Regierungsrates des Kantons Luzern (Bern, 1994), 91 und 170; Charlotte Bretscher-Gisiger, Peter Kamber, und Mikkel Mangolt, *Katalog der mittelalterlichen Handschriften des Klosters St. Urban*, in *Vorbereitung*.

49 Romain Jurot, *Catalogue des manuscrits médiévaux de la Bibliothèque cantonale et universitaire de Fribourg* (Dietikon-Zürich, 2006), 13–14.

50 Pfäfers: Romain Jurot, *Katalog der Handschriften der Abtei Pfäfers im Stiftsarchiv St. Gallen* (Dietikon-Zürich, 2002), 28–29; Luzern: *Kloster und Pfarrei zu Franziskanern in Luzern*, hrsg. v. Clemens Hegglin und Fritz Glauser (Luzern, 1989), Bd. 1, 132–33; Rheinau: 'Gelehrte Mönche im Kloster Rheinau. Inkunabeln, Drucke und Handschriften', mit Beiträgen von Marlies Stähli, Urs Leu u. a., *Librarium*, 52 (2009), 67–133; zum Rheinauer Bestand, der 1863 nach Einsiedeln kam: Odo Lang, *Katalog der Handschriften in der Stiftsbibliothek Einsiedeln*, 2. Teil, Codices 501–1318 (Basel, 2009), XIII.

Bibliography

Manuscripts and Archival Sources

St. Gallen, Stiftsbibliothek, Cod. 526–29.

Secondary Works

Magdalen Bless-Grabher, in *Dominikaner und Dominikanerinnen in der Schweiz*, redigiert v. Petra Zimmer unter Mitarb. von Brigitte Degler-Spengler, Helvetia Sacra, Abt. 4, Bd. 2 (Basel, 1999), 732–34 und 768–71.

Charlotte Bretscher-Gisiger und Rudolf Gamper, *Katalog der mittelalterlichen Handschriften der Klöster Muri und Hermetschwil* (Dietikon-Zürich, 2005).

Charlotte Bretscher-Gisiger und Rudolf Gamper, *Katalog der mittelalterlichen Handschriften des Klosters Wettingen. Katalog der mittelalterlichen Handschriften in Aarau, Laufenburg, Lenzburg, Rheinfelden und Zofingen* (Dietikon-Zürich, 2009).

Charlotte Bretscher-Gisiger, Peter Kamber, und Mikkel Mangolt, *Katalog der mittelalterlichen Handschriften des Klosters St. Urban* (Zürich, 2013).

Albert Bruckner, 'Zur Geschichte der Stiftsbibliothek von St. Peter zu Basel', in *Classical and Medieval Studies in Honor of Edward Kennard Rand*, hrsg. v. Leslie Webber Jones (New York, 1938), 33–40.

Albert Bruckner, *Scriptoria medii aevi Helvetica*, Bd. 11: *Schreibschulen der Diözese Lausanne* (Genf, 1967).

Max Burckhardt, 'Bibliotheksaufbau, Bücherbesitz und Leserschaft im spätmittelalterlichen Basel', in *Studien zum städtischen Bildungswesen des späten Mittelalters und der frühen Neuzeit*, hrsg. v. Bernd Moeller u. a. (Göttingen, 1983), 33–52.

Raffaello Ceschi, *Geschichte des Kantons Tessin* (Frauenfeld, 2003).

Inge Dahm, *Aargauer Inkunabelkatalog* (Aarau, 1985).

Claudia Engler, 'Die Stadtklöster – Tradition und Erneuerung. "Ein news puch." Die "Bibliothek" des Dominikanerinnenklosters St. Michael in der Insel', in *Berns grosse Zeit. Das 15. Jahrhundert neu entdeckt*, hrsg. v. Ellen J. Beer u. a. (Bern, 1999), 482–89.

Fürstabtei St.Gallen. Untergang und Erbe 1805/2005 (St. Gallen, 2005).

Rudolf Gamper, 'Die Schaffhauser "Liberey" im 16. Jahrhundert', *Schaffhauser Beiträge zur Geschichte*, 67 (1990), 241–54.

Rudolf Gamper, Gaby Knoch-Mund, und Marlis Stähli, *Katalog der mittelalterlichen Handschriften der Ministerialbibliothek Schaffhausen* (Dietikon / Zürich, 1994).

'Gelehrte Mönche im Kloster Rheinau. Inkunabeln, Drucke und Handschriften', mit Beiträgen von Marlies Stähli, Urs Leu u. a., *Librarium*, 52 (2009), 67–133.

Martin Germann, 'Bibliotheken im reformierten Zürich. Vom Büchersturm (1525) zur Gründung der Stadtbibliothek (1629)', in *Beiträge zur Geschichte des Buchwesens im konfessionellen Zeitalter*, hrsg v. Herbert G. Göpfert u. a. (Wiesbaden, 1985), 189–212.

Martin Germann, *Die reformierte Stiftsbibliothek am Grossmünster Zürich im 16. Jahrhundert und die Anfänge der neuzeitlichen Bibliographie* (Wiesbaden, 1994).

Martin Germann, 'Zwischen Konfiskation, Zerstreuung und Zerstörung. Schicksale der Bücher und Bibliotheken in der Reformationszeit in Basel, Bern und Zürich', *Zwingliana*, 27 (2000), 63–77.

Hans von Greyerz, 'Studien zur Kulturgeschichte der Stadt Bern am Ende des Mittelalters', *Archiv des historischen Vereins des Kantons Bern*, 35 (1940), 177–491.

Handbuch der historischen Buchbestände in der Schweiz, hrsg. v. der Zentralbibliothek Zürich, bearb. v. Urs B. Leu u. a., 3 Bde (Hildesheim, 2011).

Kaspar Hauser, hrsg. v., *Die Chronik des Laurencius Bosshart von Winterthur 1185–1532* (Basel, 1905).

Lorenz Heiligensetzer, '"Nicht ein blettlin Bergaments mehr". Der Einbruch in die verwaiste Domstiftbibliothek 1581', *Basler Zeitschrift für Geschichte und Altertumskunde*, 109 (2009), 139–50.

Helvetia Sacra, Abt. 2, Teil 2: *Die weltlichen Kollegiatstifte der deutsch- und französischsprachigen Schweiz*, redigiert v. Guy P. Marchal (Bern, 1977).

Helvetia Sacra, Abt. 7: *Der Regularklerus. Die Gesellschaft Jesu in der Schweiz*, bearb. v. Ferdinand Strobel (Bern, 1976).

Helvetia Sacra, Abt. 10: Register, hrsg. v. Arthur Bissegger u. a. (Basel, 2007).

André Holenstein, 'Gemeinde Herrschaften', in *Historisches Lexikon der Schweiz*, Bd. 5 (Basel, 2006), 200–01.

Ian Holt, 'Die Solothurner Jesuitenbibliothek (1646–1773) und ihre Gönner. Die Bibliothek Franz Haffners und weitere Schenkungen und Vermächtnisse', *Jahrbuch für Solothurnische Geschichte*, 80 (2007), 247–77.

Peter Jezler, hrsg. v., '"Da beschachend vil grosser endrungen". Gerold Edlibachs Aufzeichnungen über die Zürcher Reformation 1520–1526', in *Bilderstreit. Kulturwandel in Zwinglis Reformation*, hrsg. v. Hans-Dietrich Altendorf und Peter Jezler (Zürich, 1984), 41–74.

Peter Jezler, *Der Bildersturm in Zürich 1523–1530*, in *Bildersturm. Wahnsinn oder Gottes Wille?*, hrsg. v. Cécile Dupeux, Peter Jezler und Jean Wirth, Ausstellungskatalog (Zürich, 2000), 75–83.

Romain Jurot, *Katalog der Handschriften der Abtei Pfäfers im Stiftsarchiv St. Gallen* (Dietikon-Zürich, 2002).

Romain Jurot, *Catalogue des manuscrits médiévaux de la Bibliothèque cantonale et universitaire de Fribourg* (Dietikon-Zürich, 2006).

Katalog der Handschriften der Zentralbibliothek Zürich, Bd. 1: Leo Cunibert Mohlberg, *Mittelalterliche Handschriften* (Zürich, 1952), VIII.

Cordula M. Kessler, *Gotische Buchkultur. Dominikanische Handschriften aus dem Bistum Konstanz* (Berlin, 2010).

Andreas Kley, 'Kantone', in *Historisches Lexikon der Schweiz*, Bd. 7 (Basel, 2008), 66–67.

Kloster und Pfarrei zu Franziskanern in Luzern, hrsg. v. Clemens Hegglin und Fritz Glauser (Luzern, 1989).

Odo Lang, *Katalog der Handschriften in der Stiftsbibliothek Einsiedeln*, 2. Teil, Codices 501–1318 (Basel, 2009).

Joseph Leisibach, 'Die Antiphonare des Berner Münsters St. Vinzenz. Eine nicht erhoffte Neuentdeckung', *Zeitschrift für Schweizerische Kirchengeschichte*, 83 (1989), 177–204.

Urs B. Leu, 'Europäischer Inkunabeldruck und Thurgauer Lesekultur', in Marianne Luginbühl und Heinz Bothien, *Meisterwerke des frühen Buchdrucks. Die Inkunabel-Schätze der Kantonsbibliothek Thurgau aus den Klöstern von Ittingen, Fischingen und Kreuzlingen* (Frauenfeld, 2011), XII–XLI.

Heidi Leuppi, hrsg. v., *Der Liber Ordinarius des Konrad von Mure. Die Gottesdienstordnung am Grossmünster in Zürich* (Freiburg / Schweiz, 1995).

Jürg Leuzinger, 'Berns Griff nach den Klöstern', in *Berns grosse Zeit. Das 15. Jahrhundert neu entdeckt*, hrsg. v. Ellen J. Beer u. a. (Bern, 1999), 360–65.

Marianne Luginbühl und Heinz Bothien, '*Auch Bücher haben ihr Schicksal*'. *Die Geschichte der thurgauischen Klosterbibliotheken seit dem 19. Jahrhundert* (Frauenfeld, 1999).

Martin Luther, 'An die Ratherren aller Städte deutsches Lands, daß sie christliche Schulen aufrichten und halten sollen, 1524', in Martin Luther, *Weimarer Ausgabe*, Bd. 15 (Weimar, 1899), 9–53.

Thomas Maissen, *Geschichte der Schweiz* (Baden, 2010).

Helmut Meyer, *Der Zweite Kappeler Krieg. Die Krise der Schweizerischen Reformation* (Zürich, 1976).

Sergiusz Michalski, 'Die Ausbreitung des reformatorischen Bildersturms 1521–1537', in *Bildersturm. Wahnsinn oder Gottes Wille?*, hrsg. v. Cécile Dupeux, Peter Jezler und Jean Wirth, Ausstellungskatalog (Zürich, 2000), 46–51.

Mittelalterliche Bibliothekskataloge Deutschlands und der Schweiz, Bd. 1: *Die Bistümer Konstanz und Chur*, bearb. v. Paul Lehmann (München, 1918).

Bernhard Neidiger, '*Basel BS, Dominikaner*', in *Die Dominikaner und Dominikanerinnen in der Schweiz*, redigiert v. Petra Zimmer unter Mitarb. von Brigitte Degler-Spengler, Helvetia Sacra, Abt. 4, Bd. 5 (Basel, 1999), Bd. 1, 188–284.

Gerhardt Powitz, 'Libri inutiles in mittelalterlichen Bibliotheken. Bemerkungen über Alienatio, Palimpsestierung und Makulierung', *Scriptorium*, 50 (1996), 288–304.

Adriana Ramelli, *Catalogo degli incunaboli della Biblioteca Cantonale di Lugano* (Firenze, 1981).

Volker Reinhardt, *Kleine Geschichte der Schweiz* (München, 2010).

Sankt Urban, 1194–1994. Ein ehemaliges Zisterzienserkloster, hrsg. im Auftr. des Regierungsrates des Kantons Luzern (Bern, 1994).

Beat Matthias von Scarpatetti, 'Ex Bibliotheca Leonardina', *Basler Zeitschrift für Geschichte und Altertumskunde* 74 (1974), 271–310.

Beat Matthias von Scarpatetti, *Die Handschriften der Stiftsbibliothek St. Gallen. Beschreibendes Verzeichnis*, Bd. 2 (Wiesbaden, 2008).

Karl Schmuki, 'Die Schicksale der Klosterbibliothek St.Gallen zwischen 1797 und 1811', in *Fürstabtei St.Gallen. Untergang und Erbe 1805/2005* (St. Gallen, 2005), 107–20.

Caroline Schnyder, 'Reformation', in *Historisches Lexikon der Schweiz*, Bd. 10 (Basel, 2011), 168–70.

Alois Schwager, 'Die Klosterpolitik des Kantons Thurgau 1798–1848', 2. Teil, *Thurgauische Beiträge zur vaterländischen Geschichte*, 119 (1982), 65–248.

Franz-Josef Sladeczek, 'Bern 1528. Zwischen Zerstörung und Erhaltung', in *Bildersturm. Wahnsinn oder Gottes Wille?*, hrsg. v. Cécile Dupeux, Peter Jezler, und Jean Wirth, Ausstellungskatalog (Zürich, 2000), 97–103.

Heinzpeter Stucki, 'Die vorreformatorische Kirche', in *Geschichte des Kantons Zürich*, Bd. 2: Frühe Neuzeit – 16. bis 18. Jahrhundert, hrsg. v. Nikolaus Flüeler und Marianne Flüeler-Grauwiler (Zürich, 1996), 186–88.

Erich Trösch, 'Sankt Katharinental', in *Historisches Lexikon der Schweiz*, Bd. 10 (Basel, 2011), 755–56.

JEFFREY GARRETT

The Expropriation of Monastic Libraries in German-Speaking Europe, 1773–1817*

The princes of the Lutheran north and east of Germany had already suppressed their monasteries – and appropriated their libraries – during the Reformation. By the eighteenth century, the court libraries of northern and eastern Germany, the libraries of the ancient cities of the north, such as Hamburg and Magdeburg, and even – one might say especially – the university libraries (with rare exceptions such as Göttingen) were in no way comparable to the great ecclesiastical collections of the Catholic South[1].

Before the successive waves of dissolutions which I will be considering in this paper, monasteries and their libraries were flourishing across a wide belt of Central Europe as seldom before in their history: from the smattering of Habsburg enclaves, including Freiburg, in what was called Further Austria (*Vorderösterreich*); eastward and northward across Baden, the Duchy of Württemberg, and along the upper and central Rhine Valley (Cologne, Mainz, Trier); in the Catholic regions of Westphalia; across all of Bavaria; and then throughout the vast Austrian Empire, including not only the German-speaking hereditary lands (*Erblande*) in the centre, but also the predominantly Catholic areas of the Slavic east, including Galicia (now in modern-day Poland and Ukraine)[2], and in the southeast Slovenia and Croatia. In the imperial

---

* This paper brings together findings published in earlier articles by the author, among them: 'Bibliophiles with an Attitude: French Influences on Bavarian Library Secularization Policy, 1800–1810', *RLA Romance Languages Annual*, 4 (1994), 33–39; 'Aufhebung im doppelten Wortsinn: The Fate of Monastic Libraries in Central Europe, 1780–1810', *Verbum Analecta Neolatina*, 2 (1999), 15–27; 'Bavarian State Library', *International Dictionary of Library Histories*, ed. David H. Stam, vol. 1 (Chicago, London, 2001), 202–07. This paper also reflects the enormous body of research published to commemorate the 200th anniversary of the *Säkularisation* in Bavaria, Württemberg, Baden, Westphalia et al., between 2002 and 2005. See esp. the literature survey in Engelbert Plassmann,

Büchervernichtung – Bücherverschiebung – neuer Aufbruch: eine Nachlese zum Säkularisationsjubiläum 2003, Berliner Arbeiten zur Bibliothekswissenschaft (Berlin, 2005). German-speaking Switzerland is covered by Gamper, in this volume.

1 *Büchervernichtung*, as note above, 12, 15.

2 See Derwich and Dukh in this volume.

Jeffrey Garrett • Formerly Associate University Librarian for Special Libraries at Northwestern in Chicago and director of Northwestern's Department of Special Collections and Archives. jgarrett@northwestern.edu

How the Secularization of Religious Houses Transformed the Libraries of Europe, 16th–19th Centuries, ed. by Cristina Dondi, Dorit Raines, and † Richard Sharpe, BIB, 63 (Turnhout, 2022), pp. 83–97.

BREPOLS ❧ PUBLISHERS   DOI 10.1484/M.BIB-EB.5.128479

capital of Vienna, the number of monasteries had soared from 25 in 1660 to no fewer than 125 forty years later[3]. All told, 2,163 abbeys, monasteries, hermitages, and other houses of monastic orders were counted in the Habsburg Empire around 1770. In neighbouring Bavaria, a much smaller European power, there were 382 monasteries in 235 locations around the year 1800 within Bavaria's modern borders[4], including the imperial abbeys, wealthy and *reichsunmittelbar*, answerable only to the emperor, among them Sankt Emmeram in Regensburg, founded in 739. Between Austria and Bavaria – and of enormous relevance for the progress of the Enlightenment in the Bavarian-Austrian border region and indeed throughout Central Europe – were the ancient and powerful ecclesiastical states of Passau and Salzburg and the universities they maintained.

One monastery with a trajectory typical for the entire region was the Benedictine abbey of Altenburg, founded in the twelfth century in the hill country of northern Austria near Horn[5]. Altenburg had rebounded from the ferment and decline of the Reformation era and the depredations of the Thirty Years War to expand greatly in the late seventeenth and early to mid-eighteenth centuries. In the early 1730s, Altenburg's abbot Placidus Much commissioned an extraordinary new library to be built in the Baroque style to accompany an imposing new east-facing facade.

Altenburg can stand for hundreds of other religious foundations of the region. Leaving the Jesuits aside for the moment, the central European monasteries of the prelate orders – Benedictines, Cistercians, Augustinian Canons,

and Premonstratensians – almost all had libraries of note, with holdings often numbering in the tens of thousands of volumes[6]. Perhaps the most prominent of these was Polling, an Augustinian abbey in Upper Bavaria between Munich and the Alps, with a library of close to 80,000 volumes[7], not far from the Benedictine abbeys of Tegernsee and Benediktbeuern with between 25,000 and 40,000 volumes. The abbeys of Württemberg also had fabulous libraries, perhaps most importantly the Cistercian abbey of Salem, with 40,000 to 60,000 volumes. In Westphalia, monastic collections were also notable, such as those of Corvey and Klarholz[8]. But these were just the most salient collections. To focus just on Bavaria for a moment, probably the most heavily researched Central European region, modern estimates have placed the total number of books in the libraries of the prelate orders alone at 1.2 million. Even the property-shunning mendicant orders – again just considering Bavaria – had an estimated 342,000 volumes by 1800[9].

---

3   *Die Habsburger: eine europäische Familiengeschichte*, ed. Brigitte Vacha (Graz, Vienna, Cologne, 1992), 333.

4   Rainer Braun, *Klöster in Bayern um 1800: eine Bestandsaufnahme*, Forum Heimatforschung: Ziele, Wege, Ergebnisse (Munich, 2005), 11.

5   Gerhard Stenzel, *Von Stift zu Stift in Österreich* (Vienna, 1977), 47–51.

6   On the "foundational role" (*tragende Rolle*) of the monasteries, their monks, and their libraries for the scholarly life of Bavaria by 1800, see Dieter Kudorfer, 'Die Säkularisation und das Bibliothekswesen. Traditionsbruch und Neuanfang für die Wissenschaft', in *Lebendiges BücherErbe: Säkularisation, Mediatisierung und die Bayerische Staatsbibliothek. Ausstellungskataloge*, ed. Dieter Kudorfer (Munich, 2003), 9–20 at 13. For Württemberg, see Gerhard Römer, *Bücher, Stifter, Bibliotheken: Buchkultur zwischen Neckar und Bodensee* (Stuttgart, 1997).

7   Cf. Kudorfer, 'Die Säkularisation und das Bibliothekswesen', as note 6, 10–11.

8   *Die Bibliothek des Praemonstratenserklosters Clarholz*, ed. Reinhard Feldmann (Münster, 1996); Johannes Meier, '… wie die geistlichen Herren in den meisten Zweigen der Wissenschaft und der Literatur wohl bewandert und mit ihrer Zeit fortgeschritten waren: zum geistigen und religiösen Standort des adligen Clarholzer Prämonstratenserkonventes in den letzten Jahrzehnten vor der Säkularisation der alten Reichskirche', *Analecta Praemonstratensia*, 73 (1997), 201–31.

9   Ladislaus Buzás, *German Library History, 800–1945*, trans. William D. Boyd (Jefferson NC, 1986), 159–60.

In little more than forty years, that is between the papal suppression of the Jesuits in 1773 and the last monastic secularization mandated by the Principal Decree of the Imperial Deputation (the *Reichsdeputationshauptschluss*) of 1803, namely the dissolution of Höglwörth near Salzburg in 1817[10], this entire culture would almost disappear from the map. It was replaced by a totally new "order of books," as Roger Chartier might have called it[11], one characterized by huge state-owned collections and smaller regional and university libraries with increasing relevance for science and teaching, a knowledge infrastructure that remained in place for the following 200 years.

On 21 July 1773, Pope Clement XIV, with his brief *Dominus ac Redemptor*, formally abolished the Society of Jesus. Already in the 1760s the Bourbon kings of Portugal, France, and Spain had moved against the powerful order in much of Europe and especially in their domains in Asia and the New World, but in Central Europe, the major Catholic powers of Austria and Bavaria had been waiting for this final step before seizing and disposing of Jesuit properties. In the Habsburg lands, the government of Maria Theresa had already been thinking of libraries and archives when suppression was known to be imminent, but when the day came, different imperial offices reacted differently and even inconsistently[12]. An imperial patent of 9 September 1773, just two months after the Pope's suppression order,

specifically mentions books and archives as part of the wealth of the order (*Ordensvermögen*) and threatens "the most severe pecuniary and corporal punishment" upon those who would steal or destroy them. Yet just ten days later, in a decree dated 19 September 1773, the Imperial Court mandated that all manuscripts and other materials which solely treated *de moribus, disciplina et correctione* of Jesuits should be destroyed. On 4 December, however, yet another court office, the Chancellery, reversed this order, though by then in numerous Austrian cities, among them Graz and Klagenfurt, everything which qualified as useless and harmful had already been burned[13]. Still, overall, the suppression of the Jesuits meant mainly a change of legal title to the books and libraries which for the most part stayed in their existing locations, namely at the secondary schools (*Gymnasien*) and universities that had been maintained by the Jesuits – this was the case in Munich, for example – or they were simply transferred *en bloc* to the possession of states or cities where they resided, as in Fulda, Trier, Mainz, Cologne, and Bamberg[14]. Benedictines and other learned orders stepped into the roles of Jesuits, replacing them in schools and elsewhere. In the Habsburg-controlled southwest of Germany, books from confiscated Jesuit libraries in Freiburg, Rottenburg, Feldkirch, and Konstanz became additions to the library of the University of Freiburg[15].

---

10 Cornelia Jahn, 'Mühsam erworbene Schätze. Der Ablauf der Büchersäkularisation', in *Lebendiges BücherErbe*, as note 6, 21–46 at 27.

11 Roger Chartier, *The Order of Books: Readers, Authors, and Libraries in Europe between the Fourteenth and Eighteenth Centuries*, trans. Lydia G. Cochrane (Stanford, 1994).

12 For a summary of the actions against the Jesuits in the Habsburg hereditary lands, see the still authoritative account by Simon Laschitzer, 'Die Verordnungen über die Bibliotheken und Archive der aufgehobenen Klöster in Österreich', *Mittheilungen des Instituts für Österreichische Geschichte*, 2 (1881), 403–40. The present account largely follows Laschitzer.

13 Laschitzer, 'Die Verordnungen über die Bibliotheken', as note 12, 404–06.

14 Klemens Löffler, *Deutsche Klosterbibliotheken*, Bücherei der Kultur und Geschichte, 2nd, greatly expanded and improved ed. (Bonn, Leipzig, 1922), 74.

15 Elmar Mittler, *Die Universitätsbibliothek Freiburg i. Br., 1795–1823: Personal, Verwaltung, Übernahme der säkularisierten Bibliotheken* (Freiburg, 1971); Albert Raffelt, 'University Library of Freiburg in Breisgau', trans. James H. Stam, *International Dictionary of Library Histories*, ed. David H. Stam, vol. 2 (Chicago, London, 2001), 762–64.

If the suppression of the Jesuits was the result of traditional European court intrigue and *Machtpolitik* with a little bit of *Zeitgeist* mixed in – one commentator speaks of the "inner secularization" of the earlier eighteenth century, which preceded the secularization of state and society later on[16] – the waves of suppressions that followed upon the dissolution of the Jesuit order were decidedly not. They were in large measure ideologically motivated. The Enlightenment was becoming increasingly unfriendly to monkery as a decadent holdover of the Dark Ages. In an age when reason and utility were held high, Voltaire commented scathingly on the monks' contribution to society with the following words: "They sing, they eat, they digest"[17]. In Austria, the views of Maria Theresa and especially those of her son Joseph towards monks were only slightly less caustic than Voltaire's, especially with regard to the contemplative and mendicant orders. In a 1765 *Denkschrift* to Maria Theresa on the condition of the monarchy – Joseph was at the time an impressionable young man in his early 20s – the future emperor shows how well he had absorbed the anti-monastic teachings of his tutor Johann Christoph Bartenstein[18]:

> Je ferais examiner par une commission impartiale toutes les fondations qui existent. Dans les endroits où on agirait contre les intentions du fondateur, je les réformerais

et les employerais pour des pieuses causes, qui fussent en même temps utiles à l'État, nommément l'éducation des enfants, qui, en faisant des chrétiens, les feraient en même temps des bons sujets.

By then, however, Maria Theresa's ministers were already preparing a "great remediation" (*eine große Remedur*) of Austria's monastic landscape[19], for, as Imperial Chancellor Wenzel Anton von Kaunitz put it, "the population and the production of goods is suffering due to the great number of these celibates …"[20]. Apart from the confiscation of the Jesuit properties, however, there was no action taken during the Empress's lifetime.

Soon after her death in 1780, however, Joseph II issued a decree dissolving the monasteries of the contemplative orders. Joseph also dissolved a number of monasteries of the prelate orders, such as St Paul in Carinthia, whose finances had fallen into disarray[21]. In the following years, a total of 738 monasteries were dissolved across the monarchy, with much of the proceeds from the sale of their possessions given over to a new state foundation called the "Fund for Religion" (*Religionsfonds*), established in 1782, which continued to pay for much of the expenses of the Church in Austria until well into the twentieth century. This reallocation strategy shows clearly that Joseph, though anti-monastic, was not fundamentally

---

16   Kudorfer, 'Die Säkularisation und das Bibliothekswesen', as note 6, 14.

17   Voltaire's original comment on the social utility of monks reads in context "… mais ce sont de trop grands saints pour travailler. Que font-ils donc? … Ils chantent, ils boivent, ils digèrent … Que cela est utile à un État!" *Des embellissements de la ville de Cachemire*, Œuvres complètes de Voltaire / Complete works of Voltaire, ed. Ulla Kölving et al. (Geneva, Banbury, Oxford, 1968–), vol. 31B, 261.

18   *Maria Theresia und Joseph II. Ihre Correspondenz sammt Briefen Joseph's an seinen Bruder Leopold*, ed. Alfred Ritter von Arneth, 3 vols (Vienna, 1867–1868), III 350–51.

19   Gerhard Winner, *Die Klosteraufhebungen in Niederösterreich und Wien*, Forschungen zur Kirchengeschichte Österreichs, 3 (Wien, 1967), 17.

20   *Denkschriften des Fürsten Wenzel Kaunitz-Rittberg*, ed. Adolf Beer (Vienna, 1872), 107; see also Josef Hrazky, 'Johann Christoph Bartenstein, der Staatsmann und Erzieher', *Mitteilungen des österreichischen Staatsarchivs*, 11 (1958), 221–51.

21   Waltraud Krassnig, 'Die Aufhebung des Stiftes 1782–1787', in *Schatzhaus Kärntens: Landesausstellung St Paul 1991: 900 Jahre Benediktinerstift*, ed. Günther Hödl and Johannes Grabmayer, vol. 2: Beiträge (Klagenfurt, 1991), 207–16; Adam Wolf, *Die Aufhebung der Klöster in Innerösterreich 1782–1790: ein Beitrag zur Geschichte Kaiser Joseph's II* (Vienna, 1871).

anti-clerical. As his biographer Derek Beales has pointed out, "one of the principles of [Joseph's] legislation was that much of the proceeds from his suppressions of contemplative monasteries should go to funding more parish clergy. He was not atheist, deist, or Protestant, but a Catholic reformer"[22]. Joseph's fundamental attitude was not to destroy or eradicate, but to reapportion resources within the Church, away from the unproductive monks of the contemplative orders and into the hands of parish priests and the more productive monastic orders. This was therefore not a "secularization", but a reform – in the medieval sense, a *renovation* – or, in Maria Theresa's words, a *Remedur*.

This Josephine attitude is manifested in the statements of Habsburg officials sent across the land to close monastic libraries and sell or repurpose their collections. One of the most prominent of these officials was Joseph Valentin von Eybel (1741–1805), who wrote in one of his many anti-monastic pamphlets in 1782, *Was ist ein Pfarrer?* ("What Is a Pastor?"), the following[23]:

Especially in every parish house one should find a library of good books permanently maintained for the necessary use of the priest for pastoral care and in which parish priests and chaplains may find the appropriate means to fortify the genuine principles they have learned and for their further education. The libraries in the abbeys, used by only very few, could become more socially useful as parish libraries.

How did these policies look in actual practice, and what happened to the books? This is at times difficult to trace, for, as Simon Laschitzer observed in his still-useful 1881 study of the confiscations in the Austrian province of Carinthia, research on the paths of monastic books in Austria is made difficult because lists of confiscated books, which would have been so important, were not archived and are rarely available[24].

But some records do exist, and research based on these records is available. Let us consider just one well-documented example, the small collegiate foundation of Ardagger, founded by Emperor Heinrich III near Amstetten in Lower Austria in 1059[25]. Once a thriving religious centre, a slow decline set in during the Reformation period, and the canons increasingly neglected their pastoral duties, preferring to pay vicars to perform them. Its reputation as a sinecure no doubt played a role in the decision of the Austrian government to dissolve Ardagger in October of 1784.

Upon the closing of Ardagger, its library of 500 volumes was packed into five wooden bookcases and soon forgotten[26]. Two years later, however, the local magistrate, Franz Moritz

---

22 Derek Beales, 'Christians and "philosophes": The Case of the Austrian Enlightenment', in *History, Society and the Churches: Essays in Honour of Owen Chadwick*, ed. Derek Beales and Geoffrey Best (Cambridge, 1985), 169–94 at 189. Beales's superb two-volume biography of Joseph II also provides key insights for understanding the Josephine *Klostersturm* of the 1780s: Derek Beales, *Joseph II* (Cambridge, New York, 1987, 2009).

23 The original reads: "Insonderheit soll in jedem Pfarrhofe eine alldort beständig zu verbleibende Bibliothek von guten Büchern angetroffen werden, die den Seelsorgern nothwendig sind, und in welcher Pfarrer, und Kapläne zur Befestigung der erlernten ächten Grundsätze und zu ihrer weiteren Ausbildung die gehörigen Mittel finden können. Die in den Klöstern vielleicht nur von ein und anderem benützten Bibliotheken könnten gemein-nützlichere Pfarrbibliotheken werden." Joseph Valentin von Eybel, *Was ist ein Pfarrer?* (Wien, 1782), 41–42.

24 Laschitzer, 'Die Verordnungen über die Bibliotheken', as note 12, 404.

25 Johannes Landlinger, *Stift Ardagger*, 2nd ed. (St Pölten, 1966); Stenzel, *Von Stift zu Stift in Österreich*, as note 5, 61–63, 170–72.

26 The following account is based on Benedikt Wagner, O.S.B., 'Der Religionsfonds versteigert eine alte Stiftsbibliothek', in *Translatio studii. Manuscript and Library Studies Honoring Oliver L. Kapsner, O.S.B.*, ed. Julian G. Plante (Collegeville MN, 1973), 235–43.

Danzer, requested permission from the prefecture for Lower Austria to dispose of the "useless" books in order to make room in the bookcases for his own files. After much bureaucratic to and fro, which eventually involved the Imperial Court Chancellery and a detailed, item-by-item, woefully inaccurate appraisal, the Court in Vienna agreed to an auction of the better pieces and the sale of the rest as waste paper. The public auction took place at Ardagger on 20 August 1787. Only two bidding parties were present, two *patres* representing the nearby Benedictine monastery of Seitenstetten and the parish priest of the neighbouring market community of Amstetten. Seitenstetten acquired the entire library for 27 fl., a sum roughly equivalent to the market price for three pigs. Among the books auctioned off to Seitenstetten were 42 medieval manuscripts (including illuminated works from Ardagger's own scriptorium), 94 incunabula, and about 50 printed works from the sixteenth century, some of which are now the most interesting pieces in Seitenstetten's library of 50,000 volumes; others of the books from Ardagger remained at Seitenstetten until they were sold during the great inflation of the 1920s and wandered off, many into American libraries or into private collections[27]. The meagre proceeds from the auction in 1787 were transferred to the *Religionsfonds*, used at the time to finance new rural parishes as well as to endow the new bishoprics of Linz and St Pölten.

The fate of the Ardagger library was not unusual in Austria, and surviving monasteries were often the heirs of their less fortunate neighbours. For example, the libraries of the dissolved Upper Austrian monasteries Garsten and Gleink became the possession of the Diocesan Library in Linz, though some of the most valuable pieces were acquired by the libraries of the monasteries St Florian, Göttweig, Heiligenkreuz, and (again) Seitenstetten[28]. This explains the glories of libraries such as Melk today, the fact that many manuscripts and old printed books reside even today in Austrian parish-house libraries, and finally why the Austrian court library, the *Hofbibliothek*, largely overlooked in the reallocation of library resources other than for the most beautiful *cimelia* – a very conservative and aristocratic approach to library collection development – never attained the research significance of its peers in Munich, Paris, or London[29].

Two years after the Ardagger auction, all hell broke loose in France. Even before the Revolution, 400 monasteries had been dissolved there. In 1790, all the rest were liquidated, in part with great brutality, loss of life, and the often chaotic displacement and frequent destruction of libraries and other cultural assets. With regard to books, a pronounced radicalization of attitudes took place. The revolutionaries' hatred for the order of the *ancien regime* informed their disposition towards the books housed in the libraries of the old order. Typical of this inflamed attitude was that of Urbain Domergue (1745–1810), a commissioner of the *Bureau de bibliographie*, the agency charged with channelling the enormous flow of books from ecclesiastical and aristocratic libraries to Paris and administering the so-called "dépôts littéraires". Domergue spoke of "counter-revolutionaries" hiding in the libraries of France, by which, however, he did not mean monarchist librarians but rather many of the books that had been in their care. A simple and time-honored solution

27 Franz Unterkircher, 'Die älteren Bibliotheken Österreichs', in *Die Bibliotheken Österreichs in Vergangenheit und Gegenwart*, ed. Franz Unterkircher et al., Elemente des Buch- und Bibliothekswesens, 7 (Wiesbaden, 1980), 1–83 at 23.

28 Eduard Straßmayr, 'Schicksale oberösterreichischer Klosterbibliotheken', *Oberösterreichische Heimat-blätter*, 1 (1947), 119–30.

29 Cf. Christiane Tropper, 'Schicksale der Büchersammlungen niederösterreichischer Klöster nach der Aufhebung durch Joseph II. und Franz (II.) I.', *Mitteilungen des Instituts für österreichischen Geschichts-forschung*, 91 (1983), 95–150.

to the problem could have been, of course, to destroy them. But instead Domergue advocated something far more devious, namely that the evil contained in them be sent to France's enemies abroad[30]:

> Rejetons au sein de nos ennemis le poison de nos livres de théologie, de mysticité, de royalisme, de féodalité, de législation oppressive; et tandis que nos phalanges républicaines portent la destruction parmi leurs satellites, achevons de porter dans leurs esprits, par le moyen de nos livres, le vertige et le délire.

Directing the poison of these books into the enemies' camp would at once purge France of error and drive counterrevolutionary Europe into fevered insanity[31].

Domergue's opposite number in Bavaria ten years later was Court Librarian Baron Johann Christoph von Aretin (1772–1824), one of the most fascinating and controversial figures of nineteenth-century Bavarian intellectual history[32]. Historian, member of the academies in both Munich and Göttingen, an aggressive anti-Austrian and anti-Prussian pamphleteer, and a notorious womanizer, Aretin had already made a name for himself as a firebrand and sympathizer both of the French Revolution and the radical *Illuminati*. His biographer (and

great-grandnephew) Erwein von Aretin described him as "one of the best-hated men of intellectual Munich"[33]. His life abounded with intrigue and scandal. Even his transfer from Munich to a judgeship in provincial Neuburg in later life was shrouded in allegations concerning a stabbing incident in which one of his many northern German enemies, the pedagogue Friedrich Tiersch, was the victim[34]. An interesting twist in Aretin's character and the cornerstone of the career we will be examining now more closely was that Aretin was a fanatical lover of books, or in the parlance of the day: a *bibliomane*[35]. Hot tempers and affection for books are a pairing of personal qualities that may have gone out of style today, but they were documentably rampant in France and elsewhere in Europe during the eighteenth and early nineteenth centuries[36].

Following the defeat of Bavarian armies at Hohenlinden in December of 1800 and the occupation of the country by the French, Aretin was appointed liaison officer to (the later) Marshal Ney in Mühldorf, 50 miles east of Munich. As revealed by their correspondence, a "calm, even friendly" relationship developed between them[37]. Ney, too, was a notorious book-lover, like other Napoleonic generals including Neveu, Delmas, Joba, Lecourbe, Thomas, and Villatte, whose visits were feared by librarians all across occupied Europe from Madrid to Vienna[38]. It was probably with Ney's encouragement and patronage that Aretin travelled to Paris for three months in 1801

30   *Procès-verbaux du Comité de l'Instruction publique de la Convention nationale*, ed. James Guillaume, 7 vols (Paris, 1891–1907), II 799.

31   Cf. Emmet Kennedy, *A Cultural History of the French Revolution* (New Haven, 1989), 214.

32   Erwein von Aretin, 'Christoph Freiherr von Aretin. Ein Lebensbild aus der Zeit des Ministers Montgelas', *Gelbe Hefte*, 3.1 (1926), 15–34, 100–33, 317–29; E[dwin] Heyse Dummer, 'Johann Christoph von Aretin: A Re-evaluation', *Library Quarterly*, 16.2 (1946), 108–21; Paul Ruf, *Säkularisation und Bayerische Staatsbibliothek*, vol. I: *Die Bibliotheken der Mendikanten und Theatiner (1799–1802)* (Wiesbaden, 1962), 5–48.

33   Aretin, 'Christoph Freiherr von Aretin', as note 32, 21.

34   Aretin, 'Christoph Freiherr von Aretin', as note 32, 129–31.

35   Ruf, *Säkularisation und Bayerische Staatsbibliothek*, as note 32, 7. On bibliomania and bibliomaniacs, see also Daniel Desormeaux, *La Figure du bibliomane: histoire du livre et stratégie littéraire au XIXᵉ siècle*. St.-Genouph, 2001.

36   Jean Viardot, 'Naissance de la bibliophilie: les cabinets de livres rares', in *Histoire des bibliothèques françaises. Les bibliothèques sous l'Ancien Régime 1530–1790*, ed. Claude Jolly ([Paris], 1988), 269–89.

37   Aretin, 'Christoph Freiherr von Aretin', as note 32, 26.

38   Buzás, *German Library History, 800–1945*, as note 9, 155.

for a visit to the Bibliothèque Nationale to study the organization and structure of this suddenly hypertrophic library, at the time the largest aggregation of books in human history. Just as surely as he was struck by the sheer magnitude of bibliographic resources that had flowed to Paris from ecclesiastical and aristocratic libraries throughout France – estimates range as high as eight million volumes – Aretin was to become a disciple of the French revolutionary ideal for libraries, namely "la mise à la disposition de la nation" of all collections of the land[39]. His exposure to the French model would find almost immediate application back home. Even before the very first wave of monastic secularizations was officially announced in Bavaria, Aretin drew the attention of his sovereign to the need for special and immediate attention to be given to the books in monastic libraries. In a petition dated 6 February 1802, drafted by Aretin (though signed by his superior at the library, Kasimir von Haeffelin), we find the following argumentation which clearly reflects Aretin's apprenticeship in Paris[40]:

> it would be extremely important to have experts inspect these libraries and to have lists prepared of the most notable books so that the literary treasures often to be found

there do not fall into the hands of the outside speculators who are already lying greedily in wait for them and which in this unworthy manner would be lost, both to the detriment and to the disgrace of the fatherland.

Aretin's request was fulfilled beyond his dreams. Within weeks of his petition, he was entrusted with the confiscation of valuable books for the *Hofbibliothek* in Munich from the hundreds of monasteries in Bavaria, additionally with the coordination of confiscations for the university library in Landshut as well as for school and other public libraries across Bavaria, and with the disposal of the rest. His goal as representative of the state's bibliographical interests, analogous to that of other Francophile Bavarian leaders, was to emulate the achievements of the Revolution in destroying the monopoly of monasteries over the library resources of the land – without, however, the blood, which in France had also become that of the Revolution's creators. Not that this student of France's library policies was averse to using force. Indeed, in Aretin, we find the same haughty, rigorous, leathery, tradition-breaking spirit as in France. He was to become, in the words of his contemporary Friedrich Jacobs, "a hard-hearted persecutor of the monks"[41].

Aretin, of course, saw this quite differently. He described his expeditions to the monastic libraries of Bavaria as nothing other than a "literarische Geschäftsreise", a literary business trip, with the goal of freeing up the library resources of the land from the deadly grip of the mortmain – in German "die tote Hand" – of monasterial possession[42]. Delighted upon learning of the government's

---

39 Viardot, 'Naissance de la bibliophilie', as note 36, 26.
40 The original reads: "... so wäre es doch höchst nöthig, diese Bibliotheken durch Sachverständige besichtigen und die merkwürdigsten Bücher aufzeichnen zu lassen, damit nicht die Schätze der Literatur, die sich haüfig daselbst vorfinden werden, auswärtigen Spekulanten, die schon begierig darauf lauern, in die Hände fallen, und zum Schaden ebenso wohl als zur Schande des Vaterlandes auf unwürdige Art distrahirt werden können." Quoted in Ruf, *Säkularisation und Bayerische Staatsbibliothek*, as note 32, 58–59. For more on the influences of the French Revolution on the *Säkularisation* of monastic libraries in Bavaria, see Jeffrey Garrett, 'Bibliophiles with an Attitude: French Influences on Bavarian Library Secularization Policy, 1800–1810', *RLA Romance Language Annual*, 4 (1994), 33–39.

41 Quoted in Aretin, 'Christoph Freiherr von Aretin', as note 32, 132. In German: "ein hartherziger Verfolger der Mönche."
42 Johann Christoph Freiherr von Aretin, *Briefe über meine literarische Geschäftsreise in die baierischen Abteyen. Mit einer Einführung herausgegeben von Wolf Bachmann*, Bibliotheca Bavarica (Munich, 1971); John A. S. Phillips,

decision (in February 1803) to secularize not only the monasteries of the mendicant orders but also those belonging to the prelate orders, until then privileged and protected Bavarian Estates, or *Landstände*, Aretin wrote the following from the Premonstratensian abbey of Schäftlarn, where he was busily, even joyously, engaged in plundering the library[43]:

> Yesterday and today were separated by a chasm of a thousand years. Today the gigantic step over this chasm has been ventured. Today begins a new era of Bavarian history, important like none other that can be found. From now on, the moral, intellectual, and physical culture of this land will be entirely transformed. In a thousand years, the consequences of this step will still be felt. Historians of philosophy will speak of the dissolution of the monasteries just as we now look upon the lifting of the right to private warfare [300 years before, by the *Ewiger Landfriede* of 1495]. They will mark the beginning of a new age and will approach the ruins of the abbeys with the same mixed feelings with which we now contemplate the ruins of the castles of the old robber barons.

On a very fundamental level, this is the statement of a revolutionary, not a *reformator*. In the years between 1802 and 1810, over 200 monasteries in Bavaria were suppressed, including several that even then dated back a thousand years: Tegernsee, Benediktbeuern, Polling, Weltenburg, and St Emmeram, to name but a few. Some of these, like St Emmeram in Regensburg, should have enjoyed protection of the highest order, since they were *Reichsabteien*, "imperial abbeys". But the Holy Roman Empire had ceased to exist in 1806, and the imperial abbeys vanished within the next few years. The quantity of books that flooded out of these institutions is staggering even by today's standards, as suggested by the numbers I mentioned at the beginning of this article. Aretin selected about 200,000 volumes for the *Hofbibliothek*, making it within a few years, in the estimation of many contemporaries such as the British Museum's Antonio Panizzi, second only to the Bibliothèque Nationale in Paris as the foremost library of Europe[44]. This deliberate, planned appropriation was only thinkable against the background of the revolutionary developments in France ten years before[45].

'Die literarische Geschäftsreise des Barons von Aretin. Auf den Spuren der bayerischen Säkularisation', *Bayerland*, 73.2 (1971), 1–4.

43 "Zwischen gestern und heute stand eine Kluft von tausend Iahren: Heute ist der Riesenschritt über diese unermessliche Kluft gewagt. Von heute an datirt sich eine Epoche der baierischen Geschichte, so wichtig, als in derselben bisher noch keine zu finden war. Von heute an wird die sittliche, geistige und physische Kultur des Landes eine ganz veränderte Gestalt gewinnen. Die philosophischen Geschichtschreiber werden von Auflösung der Klöster, wie sie es von der Aufhebung des Faustrechts thaten, eine neue Zeitrechnung anfangen, und man wird sich dann den Ruinen der Abteyen ungefähr mit eben dem gemischten Gefühle nähern, mit welchem wir jezt die Trümmer der alten Raubschlösser betrachten". Johann Christoph Freiherr von Aretin, *Beyträge zur Geschichte und Literatur vorzüglich aus den Schätzen der pfalzbaierischen Centralbibliothek zu München*, 9 vols (Munich, 1803–1807), I 98–99.

44 Hermann Hauke, 'Die Bedeutung der Säkularisation für die bayerischen Bibliotheken', in *Glanz und Ende der alten Klöster: Säkularisation im bayerischen Oberland 1803*, ed. Josef Kirmeier and Manfred Treml, Veröffentlichungen zur Bayerischen Geschichte und Kultur, 21 (Munich, 1991), 87–97 at 94.

45 The deliberate nature of the Bavarian library confiscations and their etatist motivation have been carefully examined in recent research, cf. Hauke, 'Die Bedeutung der Säkularisation', as note 44, 87: "The liquidation of Bavaria's monastic and corporative libraries at the beginning of the 19th century was not just a side effect of closing the monasteries. The change was intentional... The purpose was to gain control of the intellectual potential which the monastic libraries represented and to harness it for the purposes of the state." ["Die Auflösung der Kloster- und Korporationsbibliotheken Bayerns zu Beginn des 19. Jahrhunderts ist nicht bloß ein Nebeneffekt der Klosteraufhebung gewesen. Die Veränderung war beabsichtigt... Es ging also darum,

As we did for Austria during the 1780s, let us take the case of a single, relatively minor monastery in Bavaria and trace the fate of its books. One hundred and fifty miles upstream along the Danube from Ardagger, the monastery of the mendicant Capuchins in Straubing, Lower Bavaria, was dissolved just eighteen years later, in February 1802[46]. On June 2, 1802, four months after the decree of dissolution, the conventuals were removed to a transitional "central monastery", which the Bavarian government had established for their order in Altötting, about 50 miles to the south[47]. As at Ardagger, the books were sold off, but only after an incunabula specialist, dispatched from Munich by Aretin, Johann Baptist Bernhart (1759–1821), had visited the library, pronounced it "very significant", and selected 407 volumes for the court library. The total receipts from the sale of the remaining 6,000 books amounted to 72 fl., 38 xr. – a little more than 2 Kreuzer per volume[48].

If the French model was as significant for Bavaria as I have contended, it could be argued at this point, how was it possible for all of this theological "poison" to be so simply distributed to the highest bidders at an auction? Ultimately, it was not. Within months of the auction in Straubing, such sales were halted by the Bavarian General Directorate for Schools and Studies, following reports that peddlers, fitted out with licenses issued by the Bavarian government, were going door to door hawking books and

calendars filled "with the most nonsensical monks' notions"[49]. The result of the intercession by the school ministry can be seen in reports filed by government agents from then on, like those submitted on 3 July and 4 September 1803 by a school inspector named Bruninger, responsible for disposing of the books of the Franciscan convent at Zeilhofen, Lower Bavaria. Before being sold, we read here, the cover, title page, and index of each book were carefully detached. The books were then torn into 20 to 30 pieces which were thrown individually into different piles scattered across the room[50]. In this way, so Bruninger continues, about two hundredweight of waste paper were produced, which could then be sold without subversive side-effects[51]. One might say, in keeping with what was clearly the dominant imagery of this operation, that the library had to be detoxified before it could be sold. Bruninger concluded his report with the remark that he had kept some of the most remarkable "outgrowths" (Auswüchse) of the library "for future historical research as a vivid document ... of the past monks' age"[52]. Again, the use of the term "outgrowth" in relation to books is taken from the vocabularies of gardening and of

---

das geistige Potential, das die Klosterbibliotheken darstellten, unter Kontrolle zu bringen und für die Ziele des Staates einzusetzen".]

46   Ruf, *Säkularisation und Bayerische Staatsbibliothek*, as note 32, 517–20.

47   These were also known as "Aussterbeklöster" – literally "monasteries to die out in" – among contemporaries.

48   By comparison, horses belonging to monasteries went for around 35 fl. each, which made one horse the market equivalent of over 4,000 pounds of monastery books. Maria Bernarda Wagner, 'Die Säkularisation der Klöster im Gebiet der heutigen Stadt Passau 1802–1836', Diss., Universität München, 1935, 49.

---

49   "... mit den widersinnigsten Mönchsbegriffen angefüllt ..." Quoted in Ruf, *Säkularisation und Bayerische Staatsbibliothek*, as note 32, 87.

50   Ruf, *Säkularisation und Bayerische Staatsbibliothek*, as note 32, 610.

51   For "subversive," Bruninger uses here "volksschädlich," a word with a long and inglorious history ahead of it.

52   "Aus der Absicht, daß es für die zukünftige Geschichtsforschung zu weiterer Beurtheilung der Vergangenen Mönchsalter ein anschauliches Document sein werde, habe ich die Vorzüglichen Auswüchse gesammelt ..." Ruf, *Säkularisation und Bayerische Staatsbibliothek*, as note 32, 611. Compare Bruninger's report to the comments of French "bibliographer" Urbain Domergue, who explicitly compared his library work to that of a botanist: "nous croyons qu'il faut conserver un ou deux exemplaires de toutes les productions de la sottise humaine, soit comme monuments historiques, soit comme objet de curiosité. C'est ainsi que le botaniste place dans son herbier,

medicine, suggesting cancers and cysts in need of excision to prevent their spread[53].

More explicit use of horticultural and pharmacological vocabulary occurs in a letter to the Bavarian government written by Maximilian von Ockel, a judge (*Landrichter*) from Rauhenlechsberg and the *Kommissar* appointed to oversee the dismantling of one of the truly great monasteries of Bavaria, Benediktbeuern, situated in the Isar Valley at the foot of the Alps. In good revolutionary manner, Ockel makes explicit negative reference to the pre-revolutionary Habsburg ruler Joseph II and the failure of his policies as a warning against the dangers of moderation, and then writes: "If this weed is not entirely eradicated, then sooner or later it will take root again, grow, and, with redoubled energy, bring back the age of darkness and all the horrors thereof"[54]. An aside to the secularization of Benediktbeuern and the destruction of its library is that one of the manuscripts Aretin rescued – virtually from the teeth of the paper-mill – was a collection of over 300 medieval Latin songs, which many years later was given the name *Carmina burana*, made world-famous in the choral work of Carl Orff which premiered in 1937[55].

It may not have escaped the reader's attention that there is a schizophrenic aspect to the treatment of monastic books in the French and Bavarian library secularizations under examination here, which is to say France in the 1790s and then France's eager student and *adlatus* – Bavaria – in the first decade of the 1800s. It is found in the extremes of contempt for the monkish libraries on the one hand, which often led to the massive sale or destruction of these libraries, and, on the other, the awe and delight felt by the bibliophiles and scholars under the secularizers at the riches that they were able to take into the state's possession, a wealth which was to form the core of state libraries in Munich, Stuttgart, as well as several great provincial and university libraries.

In conclusion, the consequences of library secularizations for the history of librarianship in Germany and indeed for the world were also epochal. This is because the sheer mass of books to be organized and managed brought an end to the model of the librarian as "le vivant catalogue", a sobriquet once applied to the Paris librarian Joseph Van Praet (1754–1837), as well as to the notion that the order of libraries could be visually represented, as it was in the great hall libraries of the Baroque. This in turn heralded the end of librarianship as a primarily mnemonic art or craft, and its rebirth as a science based on Kantian philosophy, a development pioneered by Martin Schrettinger (1772–1851) – himself, ironically, a former Benedictine monk and librarian of the abbey of Weißenohe, who had gone into the Bavarian state service under Aretin after the secularization of his monastery. As his diaries reveal, Schrettinger watched, both bemused and horrified, as the successive efforts of his superiors in Munich – Aretin, Hamberger, and Scherer – failed disastrously to create order out of bibliographic chaos, until he himself was put in charge during the 1820s. Schrettinger relied on heavily cross-referenced catalogues as opposed to shelf order to ensure multi-dimensional access to scholarly literature.

parmi une foule de plantes, l'acouit qui donne la mort". *Procès-verbaux du Comité de l'Instruction publique de la Convention nationale*, as note 30, 799.

53 Compare Domergue's medical imagery in France eleven years before: "Portons le scalpel révolutionnaire dans nos vastes dépôts de livres et coupons tous les membres gangrénés du corps bibliographique". *Procès-verbaux du Comité de l'Instruction publique de la Convention nationale*, as note 30, 798.

54 "… daß dieses Unkraut, wenn es nicht gänzlich ausgerottet wird, früher oder später wieder Wurzeln schlägt, aufkeimt und mit vermehrten Kräften die Zeiten der Finsternis und alle Schrecknisse derselben herbeiführt". Quoted in Wolfgang Jahn, 'Die Aufhebung des Klosters Benediktbeuern', in *Glanz und Ende der alten Klöster*, as note 44, 70–77 at 77.

55 *Thesaurus librorum: 425 Jahre Bayerische Staatsbibliothek. Ausstellung München 18. August – 1. Oktober 1983*, ed. Karl Dachs and Elisabeth Klemm (Wiesbaden, 1983), 106.

To consider this bibliographic revolution now, other than to observe the causal connexion linking it back to the secularization of monastic libraries, would go beyond the parameters of this overview, but it is a lasting legacy of this era no less significant than the distribution of European monastic library resources across the globe[56].

---

56 Schrettinger's diaries (*Tagebuch*) from 1792 on as well as his various unpublished histories of the court (and later: state) library in Munich all reside in the *Handschriftenabteilung* of the Bavarian State Library in Munich. They constitute a central resource for the study of his thought. Especially interesting are the earliest diary entries documenting his reception of Immanuel Kant's philosophical works while still a monk in Weißenohe, a Benedictine monastery near Regensburg. They provide numerous examples of the resistance of Schrettinger's superiors to the young monk's interest in Kant's philosophy – as well as Schrettinger's growing cynicism toward the clerical assertion of primacy for the *sapientia divina* over secular knowledge. On Schrettinger and his contributions, see Michael K. Buckland, 'Information Schools: A Monk, Library Science, and the Information Age', in Bibliothekswissenschaft – Quo Vadis?/Library Science – Quo Vadis?, ed. Petra Hauke (Berlin, 2010), 19–32; Jeffrey Garrett, 'Redefining Order in the German Library, 1775–1825', *Eighteenth-Century Studies*, 33.1 (1999), 103–23; Uwe Jochum, *Bibliotheken und Bibliothekare 1800–1900* (Würzburg, 1991); Stephan Kellner, 'Vom "künstlichen Chaos" zur Ordnung "in Reih und Glied". Der schwierige Weg zur Katalogiserung der Druckschriften', in *Lebendiges BücherErbe*, as note 6; Sandro Uhlmann, 'Martin Schrettinger: Wegbereiter der modernen Bibliothekswissenschaft', in *Handbuch der Bibliothek-Wissenschaft. Neudruck der Ausgabe Wien 1834 mit einem Nachwort und einer Bibliographie*, ed. Holger Nitzscher, Stefan Seeger, and Sandro Uhlmann (Hildesheim, 2003).

Bibliography

Erwein von Aretin, 'Christoph Freiherr von Aretin. Ein Lebensbild aus der Zeit des Ministers Montgelas', *Gelbe Hefte*, 3.1 (1926), 15–34, 100–33, 317–29.

Johann Christoph Freiherr von Aretin, *Beyträge zur Geschichte und Literatur vorzüglich aus den Schätzen der pfalzbaierischen Centralbibliothek zu München*, 9 vols (Munich, 1803–1807).

Johann Christoph Freiherr von Aretin, *Briefe über meine literarische Geschäftsreise in die baierischen Abteyen. Mit einer Einführung herausgegeben von Wolf Bachmann*, Bibliotheca Bavarica (Munich, 1971).

Derek Beales, 'Christians and "philosophes": The Case of the Austrian Enlightenment', in *History, Society and the Churches: Essays in Honour of Owen Chadwick*, ed. Derek Beales and Geoffrey Best (Cambridge, 1985), 169–94.

Derek Beales, *Joseph II*, 2 vols (Cambridge, New York, 1987, 2009).

Rainer Braun, *Klöster in Bayern um 1800: eine Bestandsaufnahme*, Forum Heimatforschung: Ziele, Wege, Ergebnisse (Munich, 2005).

Michael K. Buckland, 'Information Schools: A Monk, Library Science, and the Information Age' in Bibliothekswissenschaft – Quo Vadis?/Library Science – Quo Vadis?, ed. Petra Hauke (Berlin, 2010), 19–32.

Ladislaus Buzás, *German Library History, 800–1945*, trans. William D. Boyd (Jefferson NC, 1986).

Roger Chartier, *The Order of Books: Readers, Authors, and Libraries in Europe between the Fourteenth and Eighteenth Centuries*, trans. Lydia G. Cochrane (Stanford, 1994).

Denkschriften des Fürsten Wenzel Kaunitz-Rittberg, ed. Adolf Beer (Vienna, 1872).

Des embellissements de la ville de Cachemire, Œuvres complètes de Voltaire / Complete works of Voltaire, ed. Ulla Kölving et al. (Geneva, Banbury, Oxford, 1968–).

Daniel Desormeaux, *La Figure du bibliomane: histoire du livre et stratégie littéraire au XIXe siècle*. St.-Genouph, 2001.

E[dwin] Heyse Dummer, 'Johann Christoph von Aretin: A Re-evaluation', *Library Quarterly*, 16.2 (1946), 108–121.

Joseph Valentin von Eybel, *Was ist ein Pfarrer?* (Vienna, 1782).

Reinhard Feldmann, ed., *Die Bibliothek des Praemonstratenserklosters Clarholz* (Münster, 1996).

Jeffrey Garrett, 'Bibliophiles with an Attitude: French Influences on Bavarian Library Secularization Policy, 1800–1810', *RLA Romance Languages Annual*, 4 (1994), 33–39.

Jeffrey Garrett, 'Aufhebung im doppelten Wortsinn: The Fate of Monastic Libraries in Central Europe, 1780–1810', *Verbum Analecta Neolatina*, 2 (1999), 15–27.

Jeffrey Garrett, 'Redefining Order in the German Library, 1775–1825', *Eighteenth-Century Studies*, 33.1 (1999), 103–23.

Jeffrey Garrett, 'Bavarian State Library', *International Dictionary of Library Histories*, ed. David H. Stam, vol. 1 (Chicago, London, 2001), 202–07.

Hermann Hauke, 'Die Bedeutung der Säkularisation für die bayerischen Bibliotheken', in *Glanz und Ende der alten Klöster: Säkularisation im bayerischen Oberland 1803*, ed. Josef Kirmeier and Manfred Treml, Veröffentlichungen zur Bayerischen Geschichte und Kultur, 21 (Munich, 1991), 87–97.

Josef Hrazky, 'Johann Christoph Bartenstein, der Staatsmann und Erzieher', *Mitteilungen des österreichischen Staatsarchivs*, 11 (1958), 221–51.

Cornelia Jahn, 'Mühsam erworbene Schätze. Der Ablauf der Büchersäkularisation', in *Lebendiges BücherErbe: Säkularisation, Mediatisierung und die Bayerische Staatsbibliothek. Ausstellungskataloge*, ed. Dieter Kudorfer (Munich, 2003), 21–46.

Wolfgang Jahn, 'Die Aufhebung des Klosters Benediktbeuern', in *Glanz und Ende der alten Klöster: Säkularisation im bayerischen Oberland 1803*, ed. Josef Kirmeier and Manfred Treml, Veröffentlichungen zur Bayerischen Geschichte und Kultur, 21 (Munich, 1991), 70–77.

Uwe Jochum, *Bibliotheken und Bibliothekare 1800–1900* (Würzburg, 1991).

Stephan Kellner, 'Vom "künstlichen Chaos" zur Ordnung "in Reih und Glied". Der schwierige Weg zur Katalogiserung der Druckschriften', in *Lebendiges BücherErbe: Säkularisation, Mediatisierung und die Bayerische Staatsbibliothek. Ausstellungskataloge*, ed. Dieter Kudorfer (Munich, 2003), 72–79.

Emmet Kennedy, *A Cultural History of the French Revolution* (New Haven, 1989).

Waltraud Krassnig, 'Die Aufhebung des Stiftes 1782–1787', in *Schatzhaus Kärntens: Landesausstellung St Paul 1991: 900 Jahre Benediktinerstift*, ed. Günther Hödl and Johannes Grabmayer, vol. 2: Beiträge (Klagenfurt, 1991), 207–16.

Dieter Kudorfer, 'Die Säkularisation und das Bibliothekswesen. Traditionsbruch und Neuanfang für die Wissenschaft', in *Lebendiges BücherErbe: Säkularisation, Mediatisierung und die Bayerische Staatsbibliothek. Ausstellungskataloge*, ed. Dieter Kudorfer (Munich, 2003), 9–20.

Johannes Landlinger, *Stift Ardagger*, 2nd ed. (St Pölten, 1966).

Simon Laschitzer, 'Die Verordnungen über die Bibliotheken und Archive der aufgehobenen Klöster in Österreich', *Mittheilungen des Instituts für Österreichische Geschichte*, 2 (1881), 403–40.

Klemens Löffler, *Deutsche Klosterbibliotheken*, Bücherei der Kultur und Geschichte, 2nd, greatly expanded and improved ed. (Bonn, Leipzig, 1922).

Maria Theresia und Joseph II. Ihre Correspondenz sammt Briefen Joseph's an seinen Bruder Leopold, ed. Alfred Ritter von Arneth, 3 vols (Vienna, 1867–1868).

Johannes Meier, '… wie die geistlichen Herren in den meisten Zweigen der Wissenschaft und der Literatur wohl bewandert und mit ihrer Zeit fortgeschritten waren: zum geistigen und religiösen Standort des adligen Clarholzer Prämonstratenserkonventes in den letzten Jahrzehnten vor der Säkularisation der alten Reichskirche', *Analecta Praemonstratensia*, 73 (1997), 201–31.

Elmar Mittler, *Die Universitätsbibliothek Freiburg i. Br., 1795–1823: Personal, Verwaltung, Übernahme der säkularisierten Bibliotheken* (Freiburg, 1971).

Holger Nitzscher, Stefan Seeger, and Sandro Uhlmann, ed., *Handbuch der Bibliothek-Wissenschaft. Neudruck der Ausgabe Wien 1834 mit einem Nachwort und einer Bibliographie* (Hildesheim, 2003).

John A. S. Phillips, 'Die literarische Geschäftsreise des Barons von Aretin. Auf den Spuren der bayerischen Säkularisation', *Bayerland*, 73.2 (1971), 1–4.

Engelbert Plassmann, *Büchervernichtung – Bücherverschiebung – neuer Aufbruch: eine Nachlese zum Säkularisationsjubiläum 2003*, Berliner Arbeiten zur Bibliothekswissenschaft (Berlin, 2005).

Procès-verbaux du Comité de l'Instruction publique de la Convention nationale, ed. James Guillaume, 7 vols (Paris, 1891–1907).

Albert Raffelt, 'University Library of Freiburg in Breisgau', trans. James H. Stam, *International Dictionary of Library Histories*, ed. David H. Stam, vol. 2 (Chicago, London, 2001), 762–64.

Gerhard Römer, *Bücher, Stifter, Bibliotheken: Buchkultur zwischen Neckar und Bodensee* (Stuttgart, 1997).

Paul Ruf, *Säkularisation und Bayerische Staatsbibliothek*, vol. I: *Die Bibliotheken der Mendikanten und Theatiner (1799–1802)* (Wiesbaden, 1962).

Gerhard Stenzel, *Von Stift zu Stift in Österreich* (Vienna, 1977).

Eduard Straßmayr, 'Schicksale oberösterreichischer Klosterbibliotheken', *Oberösterreichische Heimatblätter*, 1 (1947), 119–30.

Thesaurus librorum: 425 Jahre Bayerische Staatsbibliothek. Ausstellung München 18. August – 1. Oktober 1983, ed. Karl Dachs and Elisabeth Klemm (Wiesbaden, 1983).

Christiane Tropper, 'Schicksale der Büchersammlungen niederösterreichischer Klöster nach der Aufhebung durch Joseph II. und Franz (II.) I.', *Mitteilungen des Instituts für österreichischen Geschichtsforschung*, 91 (1983), 95–150.

Sandro Uhlmann, 'Martin Schrettinger: Wegbereiter der modernen Bibliothekswissenschaft', in *Handbuch der Bibliothek-Wissenschaft. Neudruck der Ausgabe Wien 1834 mit einem Nachwort und einer Bibliographie*, ed. Holger Nitzscher, Stefan Seeger, and Sandro Uhlmann (Hildesheim, 2003), 1–48.

Franz Unterkircher, 'Die älteren Bibliotheken Österreichs', in *Die Bibliotheken Österreichs in Vergangenheit und Gegenwart*, ed. Franz Unterkircher et al., Elemente des Buch- und Bibliothekswesens, 7 (Wiesbaden, 1980), 1–83.

Brigitte Vacha, ed., *Die Habsburger: eine europäische Familiengeschichte* (Graz, Vienna, Cologne, 1992).

Jean Viardot, 'Naissance de la bibliophilie: les cabinets de livres rares', in *Histoire des bibliothèques françaises. Les bibliothèques sous l'Ancien Régime 1530–1790*, ed. Claude Jolly ([Paris], 1988), 269–89.

Benedikt Wagner, O.S.B., 'Der Religionsfonds versteigert eine alte Stiftsbibliothek', in *Translatio studii. Manuscript and Library Studies Honoring Oliver L. Kapsner, O.S.B.*, ed. Julian G. Plante (Collegeville MN, 1973), 235–43.

Maria Bernarda Wagner, 'Die Säkularisation der Klöster im Gebiet der heutigen Stadt Passau 1802–1836', Diss., Universität München, 1935.

Gerhard Winner, *Die Klosteraufhebungen in Niederösterreich und Wien*, Forschungen zur Kirchengeschichte Österreichs, 3 (Vienna, 1967).

Adam Wolf, *Die Aufhebung der Klöster in Innerösterreich 1782–1790: ein Beitrag zur Geschichte Kaiser Joseph's II* (Vienna, 1871).

JAVIER ANTÓN PELAYO

The Secularization of Spanish Religious Libraries (1767–1836): The Catalan Case[*]

1. Introduction

The secularization of church properties in Spain from the end of the eighteenth century to the mid-nineteenth century has usually been studied in economic, juridical, political, and ideological perspectives. Historians have focused their studies on the large legislation arising from the process; the sale of properties, buildings, and possessions; the Church's participation in party politics during the first Liberal era; and the growth of the secular movement and anti-clericalism[1]. Very few studies, and all of them recent, have analysed the consequences of confiscation for the cultural property of the Church: monuments, works of art, books, and archives. Although there have been a few excellent studies concerning the impact on paintings and architecture, few have looked at what happened to the enormous book holdings of the dissolved monasteries[2].

All religious establishments owned libraries, many of them in existence since the middle ages, with large and rare collections. According to the 1797 census, by which time the Jesuits already had been suppressed, Spain had 2,051 convents and monasteries; there were 238 in Catalonia,

---

[*] Text translated by Ruth Mackay. A close version of this article was published, in Spanish, with the title 'La desamortización de las bibliotecas conventuales en Cataluña durante la crisis del Antiguo Régimen', *Memoria y Civilización. Revista de Historia*, 21 (2018), 611–51.

[1] Germán Rueda Hernanz, *La desamortización en España: un balance (1766–1924)* (Madrid, 1997); Francisco Martí Gilabert, *La desamortización española* (Madrid, 2003).

[2] Genaro Luis García López, 'La administración territorial ante la política cultural y la recogida de los bienes nacionales durante la revolución liberal: análisis especial de su actuación en materia bibliotecaria', in *El municipio constitucional* (Madrid, 2003), 349–60; Agustín Hevía Ballina and Ramón Rodríguez Álvarez, 'Desamortización y bibliotecas eclesiásticas', *Memoria Ecclesiae*, 22 (2003), 225–42; Miguel C. Muñoz Feliu, 'Liberalismo, desamortización y política bibliotecaria. El caso valenciano', *Anales de documentación*, 9 (2006), 133–41.

Javier Antón Pelayo • Profesor titular de Historia Moderna en la Universidad Autónoma de Barcelona. Javier.Anton@uab.cat

How the Secularization of Religious Houses Transformed the Libraries of Europe, 16th–19th Centuries, ed. by Cristina Dondi, Dorit Raines, and † Richard Sharpe, BIB, 63 (Turnhout, 2022), pp. 99–124.

BREPOLS ✥ PUBLISHERS   DOI 10.1484/M.BIB-EB.5.128480

and many of these were famous for their libraries, including Montserrat, Poblet, Santes Creus, Ripoll, Bellpuig de les Avellanes, Sant Cugat, and the Barcelona monasteries of Santa Catalina, San Agustín, San Francisco, and San José.

The confiscation campaign by civil authorities had financial objectives, principally to pay off the government's debts and pay for the wars, but the legislation did not make provision for auctions of artistic or intellectual heritage; rather, the state was to take possession of these and make them part of Spain's national patrimony. This noble gesture, however, ran up against the unpleasant fact that, with the exception of Jesuit properties after the 1767 expulsion, which was handled quite efficiently, confiscation in the first half of the nineteenth century was hindered by various wars, economic difficulties, and the bureaucratic inability of successive governments to handle and take charge of objects whose profits were not to be realised in financial terms.

This article analyses the impact that four campaigns of confiscation had on libraries in Catalan religious establishments during the transition from the old regime to liberalism. The first of the campaigns, the seizure of Jesuit properties after the expulsion of the order in 1767, can be judged a success, for it was limited in scope and it took place during a period of political stability. The second campaign took place during resistance to the Napoleonic invasion of 1808–1814, referred to in Spanish as *la Guerra de la Independencia* and in English as the Peninsula War; it comprised two initiatives with common objectives but which ended up opposing one another because of political and military circumstances, the legislation enacted by Joseph Bonaparte in 1809 and by the Cortes of Cádiz in 1812. The third campaign came during the Liberal Triennium (1820–1823), an attempt to revisit the Cádiz proposal that was cut short by various European countries, whose governments supported Ferdinand VII's absolutist rule. And, in 1835, the fourth campaign initiated by the Conde

de Toreno and prime minister Juan Álvarez Mendizábal was curtailed by the Carlist War (1833–1840) and by popular revolts, especially in Catalonia during the summer of 1835.

The secularization of conventual and monastic libraries led to an unprecedented loss and destruction of Spain's patrimony, both manuscript and printed, but the books that were saved went on to form part of university and church libraries. The inherited books, however, were of little interest at first to common readers, and during the early decades of the nineteenth century they were essentially held in storage, at most used by a few scholars who did little to educate society about liberal cultural values.

2. The Expulsion of the Jesuits in 1767

In the wake of similar royal initiatives in Portugal in 1759 and in France in 1762, the Society of Jesus was expelled from His Catholic Majesty's dominions in 1767. In a royal decree dated 27 February, Charles III ordered that the Jesuits leave Spain and that their properties be seized. The order was kept secret until 2 April, however, when provincial governors (*corregidores*) and mayors (*alcaldes mayores*) were ordered to open a sealed document that had been sent to them and to execute it that very night. The document contained precise instructions on how to take possession of the Jesuits' belongings. In general, the operation was a success, and the members of the Society were quickly taken to ports and sent into exile.

Once the Jesuits had vacated their buildings and schools (*colegios*), local authorities, following the government's detailed directions, moved in to dispose of their movable goods. The authorities proceeded diligently to obtain maximum benefit from this property while pointing to the exceptional nature of the measures, but at the same time orders were issued to respect the libraries and works of art. In most *colegios* there were libraries with good, well-organized collections of printed books, if we may judge from evidence earlier than the confiscation and from the inventories drawn afterwards[3].

2.1. Legal edicts regarding the Jesuit libraries

A royal writ (*real provisión*) dated 7 April 1767 provided for a general inventory of all property belonging to each Jesuit establishment; regarding books and papers, article 7 called for a specific inventory of each establishment including a list of the communal library holdings. Specifying further, a writ on 23 April provided detailed instructions on how to inventory the books and papers. The instructions consisted of twenty-four points outlining how to draw up one index of printed books and another of manuscripts. Both indexes had to be in alphabetical order by author's surname, which was to be followed by the author's first name (in parenthesis), and words describing the format of each volume. The list of printed works had to contain the complete title with the place and year of publication. The list of manuscripts was to include the first two and last two lines of each work and an indication of

how many folios it contained. Manuscripts were to be examined carefully to see whether several works were bound together in one volume, in which case the start and finish of each work was to be transcribed. Smaller works such as sermons, prayers, and current affairs were to be indexed individually; books printed in black letter (i.e. incunabula) should be included in the list of manuscripts.

These inventories were to be carried out in the libraries and archives of the *colegios* and in any dwelling attached to them. In every establishment authorities were to collect both books and any private papers (such as account books, invoices, correspondence, poetry, satirical writings, etc.), which would be inventoried and then transferred to a public library. It was recommended that the index of printed books and their valuation be undertaken by a skilled archivist and that an impartial man of letters carefully review the work carried out. Finally, the printing presses and bookshops in some of the schools were dealt with, and it was suggested that universities take charge of Jesuit libraries if in the same city. Already during summer 1767, some inventories of manuscripts were sent to the Archivo de San Isidro in Madrid, in accordance with government instructions (*carta circular*) dated 20 April, though the bundles of documents themselves and the rest of the inventories were not sent until after issuance of a later *carta circular* on 2 May 1769[4]. The custody of such documents clearly had an investigative purpose; by examining them the authorities hoped to find proof of actions to justify retroactively the exceptional measures taken against the Jesuits.

---

3   Margarita Becedas González and Óscar Lilao Franca, 'Noticias sobre la biblioteca del Colegio Real de la Compañía de Jesús de Salamanca', in *Homenaje al padre Benigno Hernández Montes* (Salamanca, 1999), 511–38; María Dolores García Gómez, 'La biblioteca del colegio de jesuitas de Albacete en el trance de la expulsión (1767)', *Hispania Sacra*, LII/105 (2000), 229–58; María Victoria Játiva Miralles, *La biblioteca de los jesuitas del colegio de San Esteban de Murcia* (Murcia, 2008); Gerardo Luzuriaga Sánchez, 'Inventario de la biblioteca del Colegio de los jesuitas de Oñati', *Boletín de la Real Sociedad Bascongada de Amigos del País*, 51.2 (2005), 435–57; Ramón Sánchez González, 'La biblioteca del colegio San Bernardo de la Compañía de Jesús en Oropesa (Toledo)', *Hispania Sacra*, LXIII, 127 (2011), 41–74; Javier Vergara, 'El proceso de expropiación de la biblioteca de los jesuitas en Pamplona (1767–1774)', *Revista de Historia Moderna. Anales de la Universidad de Alicante*, 26 (2008), 325–42.

4   The inventories of books and manuscripts in the Jesuit *colegio* of Adoración de los Reyes, in Tarragona, were completed on 16 December 1770. The indexes were very detailed, taking up five large volumes, which can be seen in the Archivo Histórico Nacional [Madrid], Códices y Cartularios, books 540–44 [available for consultation online].

Orders regarding libraries were more careful and deliberate, so much so that the same *carta circular* of 2 May 1769 asked that municipal governments take exceptional care in storing the books, making sure they were not damaged or lost during a period of waiting before they could be transferred to their final destination. The *real provisión* of 1 August 1771 insisted that "until the final destination of the collections is decided upon, they should be carefully cleaned and preserved".

Plans for the Jesuit libraries grew more concrete with a royal decree (*real cédula*) issued 17 February 1771, drafted by Manuel Ventura Figueroa (1708-1783), a priest whom the king trusted, and who was in charge of seizing any unclaimed properties. This decree, aside from reducing the cost of papal bulls on the occasion of the appointment of bishops and archbishops, expropriated prelates' personal libraries upon their death and directed the income to diocesan revenues (*la mitra*) for the benefit of successors, relatives, and parishioners. In this way new public libraries would be created, which were to receive those Jesuit books not assigned to other institutions.

The government debated this measure, however, deciding to add some exceptions and alterations regarding those Jesuit libraries still awaiting assignment. As a result, a *real provisión* issued 2 May 1772 laid out the destination of the remaining Jesuit libraries still unassigned. The regulation confirmed that the books of the expelled order should go into public libraries under the jurisdiction of bishops, with the following exceptions: first, the *colegios* of Loyola and Villagarcía would become seminaries for missionaries to the Indies and would keep books from Jesuit libraries, especially from those in the provinces of Valladolid and Guipuzcoa; second, approved universities could inherit libraries from *colegios* in their city, with the exception of the two *colegios* in Palma de Mallorca, whose holdings would go to that city's university even if it was

not yet approved; and third, the library in the *colegio* in Toledo would go to a seminary planned for that city. The government also decided that manuscripts were to go to the Archivo de San Isidro el Real in Madrid, and that before handing over the libraries to the *mitras* (i.e. dioceses), universities, and seminaries, the book collections should be reviewed, setting aside those containing "maxims and doctrines prejudicial to the dogma, religion, good customs, and privileges of His Majesty" as well as textbooks of the "so-called Jesuit school".

2.2 Jesuit libraries in Catalonia

The royal decrees were implemented fairly uniformly throughout the 147 establishments and schools run by the Jesuits in Spain in 1767. Twelve of these were in Catalonia[5]. Though there were some exceptions and unexpected developments, for the most part the measures were put into practice efficiently and strictly. The Catalan libraries were disposed of in exact accordance with the decree.

We know very little about some of these *colegio* libraries or what happened to them after 1767. María Dolores García Gómez has written about the difficulty of locating Jesuit library inventories in the archives where, in theory, they were kept. She was also frequently disappointed at not finding documents mentioned in older studies and catalogues[6]. For this reason we

---

5 Enrique Giménez López and Francisco Javier Martínez Naranjo, 'La expulsión de los jesuitas de Cataluña', *Butlletí de la Societat Catalana d'Estudis Històrics*, 20 (2009), 115–36.

6 María Dolores García Gómez, 'Un acopio documental: los inventarios de temporalidades de las bibliotecas de la Compañía de Jesús en la provincia de Aragón', in *Aspectos de la política religiosa en el siglo XVIII. Estudios en Homenaje a Isidoro Pinedo Iparraguirre, S.J.*, Enrique Giménez López, ed. (Alicante, 2010), 151–84 and *Testigos de la memoria. Los inventarios de las bibliotecas de la Compañía de Jesús en la expulsión de 1767* (Alicante, 2011).

Table 5.1. Transfer sites of Catalan Jesuit libraries after the 1767 expulsion

JESUIT ESTABLISHMENT	LIBRARY TRANSFER SITE
1. Colegio de Belén (Barcelona)	Barcelona episcopal seminary library
2. Colegio de Cordellas (Barcelona)	[unknown or lost]
3. Colegio de los Santos Reyes (Tarragona)	Tarragona seminary library
4. Colegio de San Ignacio (Lérida)	Lérida seminary library
5. Colegio de San Martín (Gerona)	Gerona seminary library
6. Colegio de San Ignacio (Manresa)	Vic episcopal library
7. Residencia de la Cueva (Manresa)	
8. Colegio de San Andrés (Vic)	
9. Residencia de San Guim (near Cervera)	
10. Colegio de San Bernardo (Cervera)	University of Cervera
11. Colegio de la Concepción (Tortosa)	[unknown]
12. Colegio de San Andrés (Seo de Urgell)	Seo de Urgell episcopal library

shall concentrate here on libraries in Barcelona, Gerona, Cervera, and on the several that ended up in the episcopal library of Vic.

In 1772, the enormous library of the Colegio de Belén in Barcelona was merged into the city's episcopal seminary library. In 1775 it became public, and in January 1776, under the direction of Féliz Amat, it opened its doors. Although revolutionary events in the nineteenth and twentieth centuries led to the loss or dispersal of many of its holdings, to this day it retains most of the original collection. In contrast, the library of the Colegio de Cordellas in the same city has left no trace[7].

In the library at the Colegio de San Martín, in Gerona, the librarian Anton Oliva and the public receiver or delegate (*síndico personero*) Josep de la Valette in April 1773 examined and listed all the books, separating those written by Jesuits and their followers from the rest. Their labours were officially supervised by Bishop Manuel Antonio Palmero; the bishop was ill, however, and he delegated this responsibility to La Valette, recommending that he should not be

too detailed or spend too much time deciding what to do with the Jesuit books on this or that topic. The prelate's particular aversion to the Jesuits meant that two thirds of the books were blacklisted. He also tried to convince the two men of the great honour implicit in working for the king, even without payment. A commissioner (*comisionado*) had to intervene, ordering the bishop to pay the two men with one third of the books, which would be given to their seminary. The other two thirds were locked up in the archive of the *colegio*[8]. The bishop took charge of the books on 9 November 1777, and six months later the city council asked the bishop to make the library public, though it appears this request was not acted upon[9]. Although the Gerona diocesan archive catalogue states that a bundle of documents (no. 516, section S) contains the inventory of the books from San Martín, the document is not there now, and its location is unknown.

The scope and contents of the libraries at Vic are better known, thanks to the work of Antoni

---

7 Antoni Borràs i Feliu, 'L'expulsió dels jesuïtes de la ciutat de Barcelona en el marc general del seu desterrament d'Espanya per Carles III', *Pedralbes. Revista d'Història Moderna*, 8.2 (1988), 403–30 at 422.

8 Javier Antón Pelayo, *La herencia cultural. Alfabetización y lectura en la ciudad de Girona (1747–1807)* (Bellaterra, 1998), 71–72.

9 Lluís Batlle i Prats, 'Notícia de la biblioteca dels jesuïtes a Girona l'any 1779', *Revista de Girona*, 103 (1983), 81–83.

Pladevall[10]. After the *real provisión* of 2 May 1772 was issued, Bishop Bartolomé de Sarmentero asked three individuals to catalogue the holdings of the Jesuit libraries in Vic, Manresa, and San Guim. They gave him their inventories in the autumn of 1774, but the only ones to survive in the Vic episcopal archive are those from Vic and San Guim; documents regarding the Colegio de San Ignacio and the Cueva de Manresa residency have been lost. The indexes for the *colegio* at San Andrés show that 899 books were found in the Jesuits' rooms, along with 966 in the general library, for a total of 1,865. The inventory from San Guim lists 578 titles. As for Manresa, Pladevall studied the *ex libris* of books now in the Vic episcopal library and concluded that the numbers coming from the Jesuit house would be similar to those from San Andrés. All in all, the confiscation of Jesuit properties meant that some 4,500 volumes entered the Vic episcopal library.

The library of the Colegio de San Bernardo in Cervera was transferred to that university in the city, which had been created by Philip V in 1717, when upon his orders the six older universities in Catalonia were merged into one. The Jesuit collection transferred to the university in 1772 comprised 1,054 works in 1,884 volumes[11].

3. Confiscation Policies of Spanish Governments 1808–1814

The entry of the French army into Spain on its way to conquer Portugal, England's ally, and the abdications of Spain's King Charles IV in March 1808 and of his son, King Ferdinand VII, in May 1808 allowed Napoleon to hand the Spanish crown to his brother Joseph Bonaparte. These circumstances, along with deep economic and fiscal difficulties, led to a popular uprising against the invaders in May 1808.

Although the French suffered some defeats that summer, Napoleon's entry into Spain with an army of 300,000 men served to curb the insurrection, restore his brother to the throne, and undertake governmental action. French troops occupied nearly the entire country, but they exercised control only in the cities and on the main roads. Rural Spain remained in the hands of guerrillas, who tirelessly harried the French army.

From late 1808 to early 1814, Spain was ruled by two governments: that of Joseph I in Madrid and that of the Junta Suprema Central in Cádiz, in the name of Ferdinand VII, who was a prisoner in France. Measures taken by both governments were severely limited by the war; death, violence, and pillaging were accompanied by terrible losses to the country's cultural patrimony.

Along with works of art, very many libraries were destroyed or damaged during the *Guerra de la Independencia*[12]. Many books were burned; the most valuable ones were stolen or sold, and some ended up being used for bullet cartridges, wrapping food, mattresses, and other practical uses.

The historical record regarding the destruction of religious libraries is full of examples, and as a result it is very difficult to draw up an exhaustive list of the books that were lost. In Catalonia, we know of the near or total destruction of libraries in the monasteries of San Martí de Riudeperes, Santo Domingo (Lérida), San Agustín (Gerona), San Francisco de Asís (Tarragona and Lérida) and Santa María de Jesús (Reus), as well as the monastery of the Anunciación (Gerona), the Hieronymite monasteries of Vall d'Hebron and Murtra, and the great Benedictine abbey of Montserrat.

---

10 Antoni Pladevall i Arumí, *La il·lustració a Vic. Les aportacions de Francesc Veyan i Mola i Llucià Gallissà i Costa* (Cabrera de Mar, 2000), 94–99.

11 José María Benítez i Riera, *Jesuïtes i Catalunya: fets i figures* (Barcelona, 1996), 91.

12 Hipólito Escolar Sobrino, *Historia de las bibliotecas* (Madrid, 1990), 432; Ana Jesús Mateos Gil, 'Expolios y saqueos. Consecuencias de la Guerra de la Independencia en el patrimonio artístico calagurritano', *Kalakorikos*, 13 (2008), 71–106.

Though the efforts of both governments regarding seized books were limited and short-lived, they would end up being a reference point in the future.

3.1 Napoleonic confiscation

The basis of Joseph I's religious policy was Napoleon's plan to reform the Spanish church. One of his priorities, inspired by the recent French example, was to reduce the number of the regular clergy. Arguing that "too many [clergy] is harmful to the State's prosperity", on 4 December 1808 Napoleon himself signed a decree reducing the number of monasteries in Spain by one third. The properties of the suppressed houses were to be used to offset royal debts, maintain the French army, and compensate cities for losses suffered during the war[13].

A few months later, however, Joseph I attempted to implement far more drastic measures. With a decree on 18 August 1809, he ordered that all religious, monastic, mendicant, and clerical orders in all of Spain's dominions were to be suppressed in the space of two weeks. He also ordered that their properties should be handed over to the state, though their cultural patrimony would, at least at first, be put at the disposal of the public.

Although there was no general, uniform legislation regarding what to do with the confiscated libraries, in 1811 there was a plan to create public libraries based on the holdings of the monasteries. The plan was part of a draft decree, though it was never approved, which proposed that public libraries should be established in large cities and in those where "more than four religious communities have been suppressed, with their libraries going to this purpose"[14].

The probable objective was to bring into line the various initiatives that local authorities in 1810 and 1811 had attempted to put into effect. We know there were efforts to establish public libraries in Madrid[15], Vizcaya[16], Pamplona[17], Burgos[18], Valencia[19], Seville, Ávila, Córdoba, Palencia, Sanlúcar de Barrameda, and Tarancón[20]. In nearly all these cases, the books from the suppressed monasteries, gathered together apparently to inspire the public to read, were returned to their legitimate owners after 1814.

In Catalonia, the French prefect of Gerona tried to establish a public library in 1812 with books from the city's monasteries[21]. The initiative in Barcelona, however, was even more ambitious.

3.2 The libraries of Barcelona's religious establishments under the Napoleonic government, and plans to create a public library

The suffering of the city of Barcelona under Bonaparte was described by Raimon Ferrer, a friar at San Felipe Neri, who wrote a long diary, *Barcelona cautiva*, "Captive Barcelona", describing the difficult circumstances undergone

13 Luis Barbastro Gil, 'Plan de reforma de la iglesia española impulsado por Napoleón Bonaparte', *Hispania Sacra*, LX-121 (2008), 267–95.

14 Luis García Ejarque, *Historia de la lectura pública en España* (Gijón, 2000), 42.

15 Manuel Carrión Gutiez, *La Biblioteca Nacional* (Madrid, 1996), 41–42.

16 Lartaun Eguibar Urrutia, 'El sistema napoleónico en el espacio vasco: del ordenamiento foral a un nuevo régimen. Implantación y alcance', *Historia constitucional. Revista electrónica de historia constitucional*, 9 (2008), 25–59 at 55.

17 Antonio Pérez Goyena, 'La primera biblioteca pública de Pamplona', *Príncipe de Viana*, II/3 (1941), 33–37; Roberto San Martín Casi, 'Inicios de la lectura pública en Navarra: la primera biblioteca (1810–1813) y fray Pedro María Navarro', *TK*, 6 (1998), 9–28.

18 Cristina Borreguero Beltrán, *Burgos en la Guerra de la Independencia: enclave estratégico y ciudad expoliada* (Burgos, 2007), 137–38.

19 María Pilar Hernando Serra, *El ayuntamiento de Valencia y la invasión napoleónica* (Valencia, 2004), 179.

20 García Ejarque, *Historia de la lectura*, as note 14, 43–46.

21 Carles Rahola, *La ciutat de Girona* (Barcelona, 1929), vol. 2, 12.

by monasteries in the city and their libraries[22]. After the king's decree of 18 August 1809, which extinguished religious communities, General Duhesme in October ordered that an inventory of their properties should be drawn up. First the libraries were closed and locked, and then, after November, detailed inventories began to be drawn up. With the common good in mind, on 8 May 1810 the new governor of Barcelona, Jean-Pierre Lacombe, issued a decree, published two days later in the official Catalan government record, ordering that books from suppressed monasteries should be used to form a public library and that duplicate copies should be sold. The law also established an Arts and Sciences Commission comprising ten members: Colonel Fabre (who chaired the commission), the Augustinian Father Malcobal, the Dominican Father Sopena, a canon of the cathedral named Comas, a priest named Godayol, a medical doctor named Ignasi Ametller, criminal court judges Antón Camps and Mariano Ubach, an army inspector named Durand (the commission's archivist and secretary), and Josep Tastu, a bookseller and printer (and vice-secretary of the commission). Their service, honorary and non-remunerated, consisted of gathering and classifying books from religious establishments and from emigrants abroad, with powers to investigate missing works and those stolen during the turmoil. Because of the war, the tasks moved ahead slowly, and by November 1812 they had gathered only the collections of San Angelo (Calced Carmelites), San Pablo (Benedictines), Santa Catalina (Dominicans), and San Francisco de Asís. In all, these libraries numbered between 18,000 and 20,000 volumes[23]. The carelessness with which the books were shipped meant the libraries were out of order and many volumes had parts missing ("truncados").

3.3 The confiscation policy of the Cortes of Cádiz

The Consejo de Regencia de España e Indias, the government body that succeeded the Junta Suprema Central in 1810, summoned a meeting of the Extraordinary and Constitutive Cortes, which opened in September 1810 on the island of León (present-day San Fernando) but had then to move to Cádiz in February 1811 on account of the war. Its principal task was to draw up a constitution, which was approved in March 1812. It also established an organization for the government based on liberal principles.

One of its reforms was ecclesiastical confiscation, which commenced with a decree dated 17 June 1812 ordering that all properties belonging to religious houses that had been dissolved, suppressed, or reformed "as a result of the enemy invasion or of rulings by the invading government" should be seized by the state. There was an attempt to apply the policy in Andalusia and in territories not controlled by the French, but many monasteries had been reoccupied by regular clergy, despite the fact that their buildings were sometimes in ruins[24].

The libraries of the suppressed religious establishments were to form part of a new network of provincial public libraries, a plan devised by

22 Raimon Ferrer, *Barcelona cautiva, o sea, diario exacto de lo ocurrido en la misma ciudad mientras la oprimieron los franceses, esto es, desde el 13 de febrero de 1808 hasta el 28 de mayo de 1814*, 7 vols (Barcelona, 1815–1821) and Antoni Moliner Prada, *La Guerra del Francès a Catalunya segons el diari de Raimon Ferrer* (Bellaterra, 2010).

23 Cayetano Barraquer y Roviralta, *Los religiosos en Cataluña durante la primera mitad del siglo XIX*, 4 vols (Barcelona, 1915–1917), vol. 1.

24 Juan Manuel Barrios Rozúa, 'Los conventos andaluces frente a la desamortización de las Cortes de Cádiz y el anticlericalismo', in *La desamortización: el expolio del patrimonio artístico y cultural de la Iglesia en España*: Francisco Javier Campos y Fernández de Sevilla, coord. (San Lorenzo del Escorial, 2007), 119–38.

Bartolomé José Gallardo y Blanco and approved in November 1813. But efforts were directed mainly at gathering, preserving, and protecting displaced books and therefore were aimed more at the interests of scholars than at a public readership[25]. In any case, the measures were not implemented because on 4 May 1814 Ferdinand VII struck down all the legislation passed by the Cortes of Cádiz and restored the absolutist regime. Most of the suppressed monasteries were reopened, and in 1815 the Society of Jesus was re-established in accordance with the bull of Pope Pius VII.

4. Disentailment During the Liberal Triennium 1820–1823

After various conspiracies and military *pronunciamientos* against Ferdinand VII, there was a liberal revolt in January 1820 at Las Cabezas de San Juan (Seville), led by Lt Colonel Rafael del Riego (1784–1823), after which the king was forced to accept the 1812 Constitution in March 1820. Liberal-minded ministers were appointed and so began the period referred to as the *Trienio liberal*. During its brief existence, the liberal government tried to further the legislative work of the first constitutional era. Ecclesiastical reform, especially of the regular clergy, was a priority, and those first affected were the Jesuits, who had been reinstated in 1815 by the king. Just five years later, the Jesuit order had seventeen open establishments in Spain, two of them in Catalonia: the novitiate at Manresa and the *colegio* in Tortosa. The Jesuits' relative success was not well received by the liberals, who responded with a suppression decree, which the king was forced to accept on 6 September 1820.

The regular clergy were alarmed at all this and, fearing their imminent suppression, secretly sold whatever properties they could, even if the decree of 7 May 1820 had prohibited them from selling their property. Local authorities sent numerous complaints to the Cortes about illegal sales, particularly in September, October, and November. Provincial and municipal leaders sent reports about monks who were sneaking away with provisions, livestock, jewels, valuable books, and, in general, anything they could carry[26]. The clergy's fears materialised on 1 October 1820 with a decree suppressing all monastic orders, the regular clergy of San Benito, the cloistered communities of Tarragona and Zaragoza, those of San Agustín, and the Premonstratensians; and establishments pertaining to the four military orders, St John of Jerusalem, San Juan de Dios, and the other hospital orders. Houses not affected by the suppression order had to have at least twenty-four religious in priests' orders; if they had fewer, the monks were to be transferred to the nearest continuing monastery of their order. In Spain as a whole, 324 houses were closed down; and from the orders that were not suppressed the inhabitants of 801 abandoned monasteries moved to the 860 which, for the time being, were allowed to continue.

Meanwhile, the houses' landed estates and other possessions were confiscated. A royal order on 29 October 1820, followed by a provisional instruction on 4 November, specified the procedure for drawing up inventories. Property was to be treated in five categories: 1) buildings and dwellings; 2) deeds, mortgages, tithes, and similar documents; 3) personal property; 4) archives, libraries, paintings, statues, etc.; and 5) liturgical furnishings and other objects for religious services.

Once the archives, libraries, and paintings had been properly inventoried and put at the disposal of the Cortes library, they were to be transferred

---

25 García Ejarque, *Historia de la lectura*, as note 14, 32–39.

26 Manuel Revuelta González, *Política religiosa de los liberales en el siglo XIX. Trienio Constitucional* (Madrid, 1973), 223–27; Gaspar Feliu i Montfort, *La clerecia catalana durant el Trienni Liberal* (Barcelona, 1972), 93.

to provincial libraries, museums, academies, and other public institutions of learning. The intention was reiterated in a royal order on 9 December 1820, which instructed provincial authorities to give intelligent and trustworthy individuals responsibility for the inventories of the libraries, archives, and works of art belonging to the suppressed religious communities and to guard the items when necessary. But the authorities pointed to difficulties in complying with these orders, for example that many of the suppressed monasteries were located in small and isolated towns where there was no one to whom they could assign these tasks. Therefore, they requested funds to pay for staff from elsewhere and to cover the costs of transporting seized goods. A royal order of 10 January 1821 provided that these such things could be paid for, when absolutely necessary, with public funds.

4.1 Implementation of the legislation in Catalonia

The decree of 1 October 1820 in Catalonia led to the elimination of twenty-four monasteries belonging to the entirely suppressed orders, of which sixteen were Benedictine, three were Cistercian, two were Hieronymite, two were Carthusian, and one was Premonstratensian. The Benedictine abbey of Montserrat and the Cistercian abbey in Poblet were allowed to remain open, because they were considered hospice monasteries, so designated by the government, for aged and sick religious[27].

A few months later, an order on 17 May 1821 identified further religious houses in Catalonia that also had to be eliminated; eighty-six more were shut down, among them thirteen Dominican, eleven Calced Augustinian, ten Calced Mercedarian, nine Lesser Observant

Franciscan, and eight Capuchin. Ninety religious houses remained open[28].

By mid-1821, around one hundred monasteries in Catalonia had been dissolved. Government financial authorities took charge of the religious houses, their estates and revenues, and their belongings, but as they were mostly interested in selling goods and had little margin of time or money, the inventories marked with the number 4, signifying libraries, archives, and paintings, were undertaken hastily. Nor were the collection and custody of these items carried out with the necessary care.

For most of the church, this confiscation by a liberal government amounted to pillage and the church reform laws to radical anticlericalism. If the liberals aired anticlerical satires in the press, the church responded with erudite treatises and, especially, with fervent sermons that had a profound impact among the mostly pious population. The war of words escalated. Some members of the church actively collaborated with armed units in Catalonia fighting against the constitutional regime. In response, starting in early 1822, the liberals authorized a series of violent acts against the clergy: attacks on monasteries, harassment, arrests, deportations, and even murder. In this situation, many monks abandoned their houses, either to seek protection elsewhere or to join royalist insurrectionists, which meant their communities fell below the minimum number required in the royal decree of 1 October 1820 to escape closure. By early 1823, there were almost no religious houses still functioning in Catalonia; some, such as Poblet, were actually sacked by the local residents.

With civil war raging, on 2 November 1822 Bishop Félix Torres Amat sent a report to the Real Academia de la Historia in Madrid about the state of the archives and libraries from suppressed houses in Catalonia. The bishop, who wished to

---

27 Revuelta, *Política religiosa*, as note 26, 406–07.

28 Revuelta, *Política religiosa*, as note 26, 446–51.

preserve Catalonia's patrimony, proposed to the Real Academia de la Historia that it ask Próspero de Bofarull, who was in charge of the historic Archivo General de la Corona de Aragón, in Barcelona, to undertake an inspection and move the most valuable books and papers into his own archive. As a result, the government instructed Bofarull, by royal order dated 22 November, to do just that: he was to move "all the documents and books, both printed and manuscript, from the archives and libraries of the monasteries and convents suppressed in Catalonia's four provinces", in order to ensure their protection. The order also authorized 6,000 *reales* to pay for this task.

In mid-December 1822, Bofarull contacted the leading Catalonian local authorities (Jefes Superiores Políticos de Cataluña) to tell them about his new task and to introduce them to those who would be acting in his name in each province. He asked that authorities collaborate with his delegates and give them access to the archives and libraries, so that they could inspect and classify their holdings and then send the books and documents to the Archive of the Crown of Aragon.

In order to achieve some degree of uniformity in the selection of books and documents in the four provinces, the delegates were given the following orders:

1) They were to begin their inspection in the archives and libraries of the four provincial capitals (Barcelona, Tarragona, Lérida, and Gerona) and then, so far as was possible, to extend their efforts throughout the province, although it was further recommended that people be appointed in the smaller towns where libraries and archives were located.

2) They were to separate manuscripts, early printed books, documents, historical dictionaries (a very popular type of work among the educated classes of the eighteenth and nineteenth centuries), and books written in Arabic, Greek, and Hebrew.

3) Given the difficulty of a close examination *in situ* of all these works, generally speaking all the bulls, donations, and other documents granted by popes and kings, unusual lawsuits, and other particularly interesting muniments should be grouped together.

4) Delegates were to be extremely careful not to disturb the arrangement of libraries and archives, and their inventory was to reflect the original order. This inventory was to be sent to the Archive of the Crown of Aragon, clearly identifying which book came from which library or archive. The selected items were to be stored in a safe place until they could be safely sent to Barcelona.

With the exception of the delegate in Gerona, who will be discussed below, we know nothing about the activities of Bofarull's representatives, who were supposed to save the most valuable holdings of the Catalan libraries. We do know that their mission was generally successful; many early manuscripts and documents from Santa María de Ripoll and San Cugat del Vallés entered the Archive of the Crown of Aragon. After Ferdinand VII restored his absolutist rule, however, they were returned to their former owners.

4.2 The Marquis of Capmany's mission in Gerona[29]

In late December 1822, Mariano Sabater y de Vilanova, marquis of Capmany and the delegate for the Archive of the Crown of Aragon in the province of Gerona, contacted Francisco Ignacio Feliu, lieutenant commissioner for public credit

---

29 The following section is based on Archivo Histórico de Gerona, Gobierno Civil de Gerona, D 4468/6 and 7; Diputación Provincial de Gerona, Libro de Actas, 17 April 1823, fol. 58; and Enric Mirambell i Belloch, 'Projecte de biblioteca provincial (1820–1823)', *Revista de Girona*, 136 (1989), 75–82.

Table 5.2. Libraries of suppressed convents and monasteries in the province of Gerona, January 1823 (excluding the three convents in Puigcerdà)

	MONASTERIES/CONVENTS	VOLUMES	STORAGE SITE	PERSON IN CHARGE
1	Calced Augustinians of Gerona	150		
2	Mínims of Gerona	196		
3	Mercedarians of Gerona	211		
4	Discalced Carmelites of Gerona	400		
5	Capuchins of Gerona	335	Gerona	Francisco Ignacio Feliu
6	Franciscans of Gerona	400		
7	Dominicans of Gerona	825		
8	Carmelites of Gerona	391		
9	Monastery of San Pedro de Galligans of Gerona	224		
10	Franciscans of San Salvio	200	San Salvio en San Miguel de Cladells	Antonio de Borés y Bages
11	Calced Augustinians of Palamós	100	Palamós	Salvador Prats
12	Minims of Bagur	95	Bagur	Pedro Puig y Mundo
13	Minims of Hostalric	6	Gerona	Francisco Ignacio Feliu
14	Franciscans of Figueras	–	Figueras	
15	Capuchins of Figueras	–		
16	Benedictines of San Pedro de Rodas	–		
17	Calced Carmelites of Perelada	–	Perelada	
18	Dominicans of Perelada	–		Antonio Delaygua
19	Dominicans of Castellón de Ampúrias	–	Castellón de Ampurias	
20	Agustinians of Castellón de Ampúrias	–		
21	Franciscans of Castellón de Ampúrias	100		
22	Servites of Ampurias	–	Ampurias	
23	Servites of Bañolas	[384]	Bañolas	Miguel Frigola y Mirambell
24	Benedictines of Bañolas	[197]	Bañolas	
25	Augustinians of Torroella de Montgrí	–	Torroella de Montgrí	Salvio Palau
26	Franciscans of Santa Coloma de Farners	–	Santa Coloma de Farners	Local judiciary
27	Benedictines of Sant Feliu de Guixols	–	Sant Feliu de Guixols	?
28	Benedictines of Amer	–	Amer	?
29	Benedictines of Besalú	–	Besalú	[Antonio Gafas]
30	Calced Carmelites of Olot	–	?	[Attached to the
31	Capuchins of Olot	–	?	subsidiary commission
32	Benedictines of Camprodón	–	?	of the Vic regional Public Credit Junta]

in Gerona and Figueras. The marquis asked him for a precise report regarding the suppressed monasteries in the area and the names of those responsible for the sites where their libraries and archives were now stored. Feliu stalled, saying he needed to get the authorization of the commis-

sioner, so Capmany was compelled to call upon the services of José Perol, the highest political authority (Jefe Político) in the province. As a result of pressure by the latter, on 7 January 1823 Feliu gave him a list of the holdings of all the suppressed religious houses, the books and manuscripts in each, where they were stored, and who was in charge of them.

In drawing up this catalogue, Feliu used the No. 4 inventories, which the government finance office had drawn up when they took over the religious houses. The list specified that the works often had parts missing as a result of looting during the War of Independence, but there also were deficiencies and irregularities in the creation of the inventories for monasteries outside the capital city. Some did not give the total number of books, others had not been delivered to the government authority, while still others had not even been started.

The marquis of Capmany thought the list sent by Francisco Ignacio Feliu was insufficient, because it contained nothing about archives. He requested the keys to the buildings where the books and documents were stored, and at the same time he asked the mayors of the provincial towns where religious houses had been suppressed to undertake another inventory and to transfer books and documents to Gerona, requisitioning horses and carriages if necessary. The local mayors objected to this order, partly because they did not want to pay for the transfer and also because they did not want to give up objects they thought belonged to their communities and that might be useful for educational purposes among their own people.

By early March 1823 the marquis of Capmany had finished examining all the libraries in the city of Gerona. After setting aside a few volumes for the Archive of the Crown of Aragon, he said he believed the remaining "five to six thousand volumes" were liable to be lost because they were incorrectly located or to be stolen due to inadequate security in the Capuchin church where they were stored. He ordered them therefore to be moved to San Francisco de Asís to form the nucleus of a new public library. Capmany enthusiastically volunteered to further this plan, and the leading provincial political authority ("Jefe Político de la Provincia") accepted. The

provincial government (*la Diputación*), despite ongoing economic difficulties, agreed to finance some of the expenses.

The room in San Francisco de Asís chosen to store the library was leased to Capmany by government financial authorities. Fitting out the space and transporting the books cost 1,304 *reales de vellón* (a copper and silver alloy.

By early April Capmany had all the books from all the monasteries in the city, totaling 4,051 volumes, but he insisted that all books from all libraries in the province should also be transferred, and he lamented the inadequate authority demonstrated by politicians ("Jefes Políticos de la Provincia") over their staff, who were not properly obeying orders. By the middle of April the only books to have arrived in the city of Gerona were from poor libraries in Bañolas: 197 volumes from the Benedictines "were in such bad shape that they were useless", and 384 from the Servites, in a similarly lamentable state, were described as "very used … some torn, all of them damaged".

In the end, counting the books that arrived from Bañolas, 4,636 books were gathered in San Francisco de Asís. A printer, Agustín Figueró, delivered 6,000 labels for the books, though they probably were never used. On 14 April 1823, the army of the Holy Alliance – Austria, Prussia, Russia, and France – crossed the border between France and Catalonia to restore King Ferdinand VII and topple the liberal government. A royal order on 11 June 1823 re-established the religious orders and returned to them all the properties seized during the Liberal Triennium.

5. The Desamortización under the Count of Toreno and Juan Álvarez Mendizábal (1835–1838)

After Ferdinand VII died in 1833, his daughter Isabella II took the throne, but until she came of age in 1843, at first her mother, María Cristina de Borbón, acted as regent, followed from 1840 by General Espartero. During that decade, legislative efforts by the moderate liberals and the progressive liberals were limited by a coup attempt by absolutists, who proclaimed Ferdinand's brother, Charles, as the rightful king Charles V. This Carlist uprising spread through much of the Basque Country and Navarre, as well as through parts of Catalonia, Aragón, and Valencia.

The Carlist movement's fierce defense of Catholicism drew the sympathies of much of the church, and particularly of the regular clergy. This attitude, by the friars in particular, made the liberals even more anticlerical, thinking that the church's properties should help the country get through difficult financial times and pay for the war effort. It became one of the liberal governments' priorities to nationalize the monasteries, while popular pressure further radicalized the measures as they were initially conceived.

The men responsible for the secularization were José María Queipo de Llano y Ruiz de Sarabia (1786–1843), 7th Conde de Toreno, and Juan Álvarez Mendizábal (1790–1853). Toreno was a moderate liberal who served as prime minister for barely three months, from 7 June to 13 September 1835. In that brief period he carried out two crucial measures regarding the religious orders, which, though they originally had been proposed a year earlier by the government of the moderate Francisco Martínez de la Rosa, were aimed at calming the waters of both the progressives and the far right: on 4 July he suppressed the Company of Jesus, and on 25 July he suppressed all monasteries with fewer than a dozen vowed religious.

In July and August of that year, the more radical liberals, disappointed with the government's timid stance vis-à-vis the friars, stirred up trouble in Catalonia and other parts of Spain. Many disturbances ended with attacks, often arson, against convents and monasteries and the murder of the religious inhabitants. In such a revolutionary context, many regular clergy abandoned their

establishments to save their own lives, and local authorities urged them to do so. On 10 August in Barcelona an "Auxiliary Consultative Junta" comprising civilians and military personnel was created to govern the capital city and Catalonia, independent of the central government, until 22 October. During that period, the Junta ordered that all monasteries and convents should be closed down and their properties seized, which Toreno's government reinforced by issuing a royal decree on 11 August 1835. Besides those affected by the royal decree of 25 July, now the measure would include "those which, due to current circumstances, are closed or abandoned"[30].

By the time Mendizábal, a liberal of fame, took charge of the government in September, nearly all religious houses had been suppressed, either by the juntas or through implementation of the 11 August royal decree. Nevertheless, Mendizábal wished to show his support for the revolutionary suppression of the monastic orders, regardless of how many members they had, by issuing a royal decree on 11 October according to which monastic properties (except for cultural objects and those used during religious services) would become state property, to be used to pay off the public debt.

By late 1835 there were very few monasteries still open in Spain, and in Catalonia they were all closed. Most of their patrimony was in state hands. On 8 March 1836 yet another decree was issued, this one ordering the "suppression of all monasteries, convents, *colegios*, congregations, and other religious institutions and communities for men, including the regular clergy and the four military orders and the Order of St John of Jerusalem, throughout the peninsula, adjacent islands, and Spanish possessions in Africa".

---

30 Josefina Bello, *Frailes, intendentes y políticos. Los bienes nacionales, 1835–1850* (Madrid, 1997), 70; Manuel Revuelta González, *La exclaustración (1833–1840)* (Madrid, 1976); Joan Portet i Pujol, 'L'exclaustració de religiosos de l'any 1835', *Ausa*, 151 (2003), 29–49.

The only exceptions were to be the Piarists and hospital orders that remained open, houses in the Holy Land, and missionaries working in Asia. In Catalonia, the order affected 207 religious houses: twenty-seven monasteries, one collegiate church, 163 mendicant houses, and sixteen houses for regular clergy[31]. The measure also affected female orders, though with so many exceptions that it amounted to a reduction in numbers rather than a suppression.

The decree of 8 March 1836 became law on 29 July 1837, when it included confiscation of the secular clergy as well, along with the elimination of the Piarists, the hospital orders, and convents of nuns with fewer than twelve vowed religious.

As for the libraries and cultural and artistic objects, between 1835 and 1840 several provisions were issued to save and protect these objects and make them available to the public. Nevertheless, a large number disappeared in the chaos, devastation, and pillage[32].

5.1 Legal provisions and instructions regarding cultural objects and specifically libraries

As with previous confiscation orders, the royal decrees of 4 July and 25 July 1835 earmarked the properties and rents of the suppressed monasteries to pay off the public debt and repay loans. An exception was made for libraries, archives, paintings, and other objects of use to institutions of arts and sciences. With the aim of occupying the religious houses, an order (*carta circular*) on 12 August instructed *intendentes provinciales*, along with their financial aides, to draw up inventories of goods and rights for each house according to the same five categories as in 1820. They were told to review with care documents affecting public credit (deeds, account books, rents and mortgages, etc.). Anything relating to category no. 4, in which cultural items were listed, was the responsibility of civil governors, according to a royal order of 29 July, which prescribed commissions of three to five members (ideally educated men) who would identify, inventory, and gather libraries, archives, and artistic objects they deemed worthy of preservation. One of the commissions' priorities was to amass all inventoried items in a safe place in the provincial capitals.

But the execution of these orders was hampered by various circumstances. First, the time elapsed between the writing of the orders and their arrival in the provinces allowed the religious to hide much of their personal property, including books. Also, the lack of specialized administrative staff, who could properly assess the value of the objects of art, meant inventories were done hastily and carelessly. Third, there was little co-ordination between the relevant ministries (Finance and Public Administration), and fourth, the expelled religious did little or nothing to co-operate with the commissioners. All this meant that many cultural goods had not been inventoried and were vulnerable to theft and deterioration. Taking advantage of this disorder, foreign collectors tried to acquire objects, books, and medieval manuscripts. Several orders were issued to stop the plundering (2 and 4 September 1836, 28 April 1837, and 20 August 1838), but it is difficult to say whether they had any effect.

We have little exact information about how these commissions worked in Catalonia. The most active was in Barcelona; the members

---

31 Joan Bada and Genís Samper, *Catalònia Religiosa. Atles històric: dels orígens als postres diez* (Barcelona, 1991), 24.

32 Vicente Bécares Botas, *Las bibliotecas monásticas y la desamortización en la provincia de Zamora* (Zamora, 1999); J. D. Buján Núñez, 'Desamortización y bibliotecas en la provincia de Pontevedra', *Pontevedra. Revista de Estudios Provinciais*, 8–9 (1992), 264–74; Carmen Rodrigo Zarzosa, Carmen, 'Desamortización de pinturas, libros y "alajas" en los conventos suprimidos en Valencia (1835–1837)', in *La desamortización: el expolio del patrimonio artístico y cultural de la iglesia en España*: Francisco Javier Campos y Fernández de Sevilla, coord. (San Lorenzo del Escorial, 2007), 699–722.

of the group (established on 28 August 1835) were Joan Agell, Josep Arrau, Josep Antoni Llobet, Antoni Montmany, and Andreu Avel·lí Pi. Between 29 August and 13 September they took charge of the books, documents, and works of art from eighteen convents and one monastery in the city, along with several religious houses in nearby towns[33]. Despite the commission's zeal, one month had already passed since the houses were emptied, and though the city council had tried to protect them, in the confusion there were thefts and vandalism. Andreu Avel·lí Pi years later remembered the wealth and beauty of the library in the Dominican house of Santa Catalina, in Barcelona, and the painful work of the commission among its ruins: "What did we have before our eyes? Oh! Empty bookshelves, valuable books piled up everywhere, their covers damaged, their illustrations ripped out, their pages shredded ..."[34]. But despite the difficulties, the authorities managed to bring nearly 134,000 volumes to St John of Jerusalem in Barcelona, though many were damaged by moths and worms after having been dealt with improperly[35]. The commission's draft inventory of books today sits in the University of Barcelona library (MS 1522). It details the volumes collected from each establishment, and though the numbers do

not always add up[36], the total appears correct. Table 5.3 contains the numbers from Rodríguez Parada's doctoral thesis, based on the inventory:

The Gerona commission was appointed on 1 September 1835; its members were Benito Calero, Segimon Amich, Salvi Cabruja, Lluís Barnoya, and Antoni Bertrán. Its labours were brief, since the monasteries they inspected were practically empty. Almost nothing is known about the commissions in Tarragona and Lérida[37]. We do know, however, that in Tarragona there was a "central commission of archives, libraries, and works of art of the expelled regular clergy of this province" and that in May 1836 it asked the *Diputación* for a room from the Convent of San Francisco with which to establish a public library and museum[38].

The royal order of 19 July 1835 was implemented unevenly, which prompted local authorities to send multiple memoranda to the central government. For that reason, and to ensure the safety of the artistic and literary patrimony, as well as to further the construction of libraries and museums in the provincial capitals, the royal order of 27 May 1837 was issued, by which local authorities were to establish commissions in each town where there was a suppressed monastery. These commissions were to draw up inventories of their cultural properties which they would then send to the provincial capital. There, pro-

33 Josefina Bello, *Frailes, intendentes y político*, as note 30, 114 and Pilar Vélez, *El desvetllament de la conciència de patrimonio històric a Catalunya. Lliçó inaugural del curs 2003–2004* (Barcelona, 2003), 24.

34 Andrés Avelino Pi y Arimon, *Barcelona antigua y moderna. Descripción e historia de esta ciudad desde su fundación hasta nuestros días*, 2 vols (Barcelona, 1854), vol. 1, 566.

35 Agustí Duran i Sampere, 'La primera Biblioteca Pública Municipal de Barcelona', in *Barcelona i la seva historia*, 3 vols (Barcelona, 1973–1975), vol. 3, 559–62 at 562. A note from Richard Sharpe: One surely does not acquire such infestation in a few weeks; we may wonder whether this was long-tern neglect by the religious, or was it the same old rhetoric that we had from Poggio Bracciolini about monks' leaving their old manuscripts to the grubs and beetles?

36 Jordi Torra i Miró, 'La biblioteca de la Universitat de Barcelona i el breviari benedictí (Montserrat: Rosenbach, 1519) Norton 418', *Miscellània Litúrgica Catalana*, 5 (1994), 43–48 at 45; Valentí Serra de Manresa, 'Aproximació a les biblioteques dels caputxins setcentistes del Principat: clàssics, escolàstics i novatores', *Pedralbes. Revista d'Història Moderna*, 15 (1995), 265–77 at 267; Concepción Rodríguez Parada, *La biblioteca del convento de Barcelona de la orden de la Merced: una herramienta para la formación de los frailes* (Barcelona, 2009), 307.

37 Antoni Jordà Fernández, *Las diputaciones provinciales en sus inicios. Tarragona, 1836–1840* (Madrid, 2002), 262–63.

38 Jordà, *Las diputaciones provinciales*, as note 37, 261–63.

Table 5.3. Inventory of books from convents in the city and province of Barcelona (1835)

	MONASTERIES/CONVENTS	NO. OF VOLUMES
1	Convent of San Agustín (Austin friars)	15.971
2	Convent of San José (Austin friars)	2.898
3	Convent of San Pablo del Campo (Benedictines)	1.399
4	Monastery of Sant Benet, Bages (Benedictines)	945
5	Convent of Santa Madrona (Capuchins)	5.395
6	Convent of Santa Eulalia, Sarria (Capuchins)	3.302
7	Convent of San Francisco (Franciscans)	15.565
8	Jesuits, Manresa	4.694
9	Convent of La Merced (Mercedarians)	5.736
10	Convent of San Francisco de Paula (Minims)	4.905
11	House of San Severo o Paules (mission congregation)	928
12	Monastery of San Carlos Borromeo, Manresa (Capuchins)	351
13	Convent of La Madre de Dios del Carmen (Calced Carmelites)	9.539
14	Convent of San José (Discalced Carmelites)	10.624
15	Convent of Grace (Discalced Carmelites)	2.452
16	Cartuja de Montalegre, Tiana (Carthusians)	3.565
17	Convent of Santa Catalina (Dominicans)	20.130
18	Convent of Sant Felipe Neri (Oratorians)	6.452
19	Convent of La Madre de Dios del Buen Suceso (Servites)	4.102
20	Clerics	1.914
21	Convent of the Trinity (Calced Trinitarians)	5.700
22	Convent of La Madre de Dios de la Bona Nova (Discalced Trinitarians)	1.332
	TOTAL	133.854

vincial authorities would appoint a five-member scientific and artistic commission to replace the commissions appointed in 1835, and would comprise members who were "knowledgeable in literature, sciences, and arts." The chairman would be from either the provincial *Diputación* or the city council. The new commission was to gather all the inventories and compile them into one, and from that they would decide which works should be transferred to the capital to be preserved in the new library and museum. The cost of drawing up these inventories, transferring the works, and constructing the new buildings would come from the proceeds of auctions of works rejected by the scientific and artistic commission. Since the finance would depend on rejected works – of which there were few, and they were worth very little – the latest royal order was scarcely implemented. Yet another royal

order, therefore, on 8 March 1838, insisted that the 27 May order be respected and extended to include Choir books, most of which had been seriously damaged out of ignorance.

In Barcelona, however, there was no need to set up a new commission, because the royal order of 22 September 1838 stated that the books should be handed over to the universities. The previous year, the government had approved the provisional transfer of the university of Cervera to Barcelona, which became permanent in 1842. The 22 September order provided that the university professors would replace the scientific and artistic commissions which otherwise continued in provinces without universities. At the same time, it stated that the seized books should form part of a public library. The Public and Provincial Library, which opened in 1837 in St John of Jerusalem, was under the jurisdiction of the

Diputación and the Barcelona city council until 1847, when it became subject to the university.

In Tarragona, the royal order of 27 May 1837 spurred the local political chief into action. In July the *Diputación* nominated as deputy Rafael de Magriñá, though it ended up appointing Antoni Batlle Puiggener as commission chairman at the end of the year. The commission did very little, however, given the enormous destruction already suffered by convents and monasteries in Tarragona[39].

In Lérida, meanwhile, the provincial commission was established on 8 June 1837; its members were Francisco Jover (chair), José Castel, Jaime Nadal, Joaquín de Gomar, José Ymbert de Maniarés, and Pedro Casals. Their first task was to write an inventory of the episcopal library; Bishop Julián Alonso was gone, having been accused of supporting the Carlists. The group then took over the libraries in the monasteries of Tárrega, Cervera, Balaguer, and Bellpuig de les Avellanes. By May 1839 it had managed to bring together 6,000 volumes and various paintings then stored in the old Discalced Carmelite convent in Lérida, today Lérida's diocesan museum[40].

The *Jefe Político* in Gerona strictly complied after the issuance of the March 1838 royal order. In late April, together with a representative of the "Junta in charge of buildings and properties from suppressed monasteries in the Province of Gerona", he sent orders to town mayors that they and their local priests and other authorities (such as "un representante del comisionado subalterno de amortización del Partido") should undertake inventories of archives, libraries, Choir books, statues, paintings, and other objects previously owned by religious establishments. The list of books should include title, author, translator (where relevant), the number of volumes, place and year of publication, the type of binding, the size, and the condition of the book. Though these specifications were almost entirely ignored, the inventories arrived in Gerona over the following months. There they were examined by the scientific and artistic commission in charge of deciding which objects should go to the library and museum in Gerona. The commission, established on 4 May, had the following members: Josep Antoni Barraquer (chairman), Francesc Escarrá, Francesc Battle, and three men who had been members of the commission in 1835: Antoni Bertrán, Lluis Barnoya, and Salvi Cabruja.

Of the nineteen towns with suppressed monasteries in the province, the commission requested that only Figueras, Olot, San Feliu de Guizols, Amer, Blanes, and Besalú transfer their books to the capital. In all, 4,249 volumes went to Gerona; the establishments that yielded the most were the Benedictine monasteries of San Feliu de Guizols (2,636 volumes) and Amer (1,009). Blanes had 401, Olot 100, Besalú 88, and Figueras just fifteen. Some mayors, such as in Bañolas, Palamós, Hostalric, Santa Coloma de Farners, Comprodón, and Puigcerdà, were relieved of the task once they declared that the suppressed houses in their jurisdiction had neither books nor works of art. Books from the Benedictine and Servite monasteries in Bañolas had already been sent to Gerona in 1823 on the orders of the marquis of Capmany. Other mayors said the books they had inventoried were useless. The mayor of Torroella de Montgrí said the fifty-five volumes in the Canon regulars of St Augustine had no bindings and were missing pages; the mayor of Begur said the small number of books in the Minim establishment had parts missing and were "in very bad condition"; the mayor of Ripoll said that part of the archive and

39 Jordà, *Las diputaciones provinciales*, as note 38, 264 and Salvador-J. Rovira i Gómez, *La desamortització dels béns de l'església a la província de Tarragona (1835–1845)* (Tarragona, 1979), 293–304.

40 Carmen Berlabé Jové, *El Museu Diocesà de Lleida. La seva formació i la legitimitat del seu patrimonio artístic* (Barcelona, 2009), 37–38 and Genaro Luis García López, *Libros para no leer: el nacimiento de la política documental en España* (Gijón, 2004), 103.

some library books had been saved from a fire in 1835, at a time when they were stored in private dwellings in town, but they were burned a second time, on this occasion by the Carlists, leaving that monastery's documentary patrimony reduced to "a few useless papers and volumes with missing parts from the Theology Faculty"; and the mayor of Breda said that when the national militia took over his town's monastery, they burned the books along with the altars and the images. In these cases, the commission decided to store what little had survived in the local finance offices.

Nothing is known of the fate of the libraries in Castellón de Ampurias or La Escala. Books from the Franciscan monastery in La Bisbal, amounting to 1,071 volumes, were deposited in the home of the town's parish priest (*capellán mayor*) until 1857, when they were transferred to the public library.

5.2 The fate and resting place of libraries from Catalan religious houses: public libraries

Some of the books from suppressed religious houses were transferred, not without mishaps, to the shelves of public libraries; others disappeared as a result of fires, pillaging, or decay caused by ignorance and indolence on the part of the authorities; still others ended up in private libraries, having been bought, stolen, or donated.

Anticlerical assaults during the summer of 1835 placed religious libraries in danger. In Catalonia, the attacks began in the town of Reus, in the province of Tarragona. On 22 July around one hundred rioters attacked and burned the Franciscan and Discalced Carmelite establishments there. That day, twenty-two religious were murdered, and the libraries of both houses were seriously damaged by flames and later by pillaging[41]. The disturbances, instigated by the

so-called "Cristinos", the anti-Carlist forces allied with the queen regent, María Cristina de Borbón, continued for many days in convents and monasteries near Reus, in Alcover, Selva del Camp, Valls, Riudoms, Escornalbou, Santes Creus, and Scala Dei.

On 25 July, the feast day of St James of Compostela, it was Barcelona's turn. The convents of the Discalced Carmelites, Calced Carmelites, Dominicans, Calced Trinitarians, Calced Augustinians, and Minims were all burnt, though in this case their books did not serve as kindling. The authorities attempted to halt the attacks, but sixteen religious were killed. On 26 July the violence spread to several towns near Barcelona – Sarrià, Vall d'Hebron, Gràcia, Martorell, and Montalegre – as well as to the Benedictine monasteries of Sant Cugat del Vallès and Sant Jeroni de Murtra, in Badalona, both of which were burnt[42]. In the following weeks, given the dangerous turn of events, religious men and women began to leave their establishments. Cayetano Barraquer's masterpiece describes their travails in detail, as well as what happened to many of their books[43].

Many convents and monasteries had sufficient time to attend to their movable goods, because the displaced religious carried them away with them, managed to hide them, or left them with trustworthy people. Among the houses that succeeded in hiding their books or leaving them in other friendly religious establishments were the Calced Trinitarians of Avinganya, the Calced Carmelites of Manresa, the Franciscans of Riudeperes, the Dominicans of Cervera, the Hieronymites of Hostalric, and the Capuchins of Vilanova and Calella-Pineda. Barraquer writes that the religious of Calella-Pineda "took away their considerable library, which filled many carts". They left it in the

---

41   Eduard Toda i Güell, *Los convents de Reus y sa destrucción en 1835* (Reus, 1930).

42   Manuel Santirso, *Revolució liberal i guerra civil a Catalunya (1833–1840)* (Lérida, 1999), 150–59.

43   Barraquer, *Los religiosos en Cataluña*, as note 23, vol. 4, 211.

grand hall of a large private house in Teixidor[44]. Barraquer did not know what happened to the library from Vilanova but, he said, "according to a choir member, Guiu, before receiving the mayor's last warning, the friars hid some books in the church vault. As for the other things, when the religious fled, some people took them"[45].

The irrational devastation by the mob or by mindless youths destroyed books in many monasteries, all painfully chronicled in Barraquer's work. According to a witness, in the monastery of San Salvador de Breda, the crowd "threw the books out the windows, forming mountains of books in the courtyards of the monastery, and this lasted for many days"[46]. In Santes Creus, once the monastery was abandoned, "children cut the beautiful illuminations from parchments and played with them as if they were *aleluyas*" (religious picture cards) tossed in the air[47]. There also were lootings in Tárrega, Poblet, Sant Hilari de Cardó, and many more.

The widespread pillage meant that a large part of the libraries ended up in private hands. Some of the rioters ruined their spoils or used them to wrap food. After the sack of the Charterhouse at Montalegre, for example, "in many houses in Tiana one could see pages of books being used as kindling or to wrap lard and similar things"[48]. Others took books and other objects and hid them in their homes, as at Santa Coloma de Farners, where even today inhabitants own books that probably came from the looting of the Franciscan monastery of Nuestra Señora de Bellver. The town's historical archive has books and Choir books from there, donated by individuals who had come into their possession[49].

Many books from the suppressed convents and monasteries never ended up where the government's plans intended them to go. But others did, going to centralized storage areas that later became public libraries, or to other authorized libraries. In Catalonia, seven libraries became responsible for most of the nationalized book collections.

5.2.1 The Provincial Library, University of Barcelona

In 1836, books from the suppressed monasteries of the city of Barcelona, along with books from other religious houses in the province (see Table 5.3) were transferred to St John of Jerusalem. In all, as we have seen, there were nearly 134,000 volumes, though the number decreased after the sale of duplicates and owing to the bad condition of many of the books. The Public Library of Barcelona opened on 2 April 1840 with 34,000 books in place, and in 1847 the library passed to the jurisdiction of the University of Barcelona.

Books from suppressed monasteries and convents throughout the province were sent there, along with a portion of those from the now-abolished University of Cervera. In the latter case, books deemed appropriate for university education were shipped to Barcelona, and the rest were sent to the University of Lérida, which was established in 1840 but would not last long. In 1843, some 1,600 books from there were sent to the University of Barcelona, and 2,000 were sent to the Lérida provincial library. That same year, books from monasteries in the Penedés region, except duplicates, especially from the Franciscan monastery of Vilafranca and the Dominican monastery of Sant Ramon de Penyafort, also were transferred. Soon after, they were joined by books from San Cugat del Vallés that had been saved from the sack. Many contained ex libris,

44   Barraquer, *Los religiosos en Cataluña*, as note 23, vol. 4, 211.
45   Barraquer, *Los religiosos en Cataluña*, as note 23, vol. 4, 239.
46   Barraquer, *Los religiosos en Cataluña*, as note 23, vol. 3, 134.
47   Barraquer, *Los religiosos en Cataluña*, as note 23, vol. 3, 383.
48   Barraquer, *Los religiosos en Cataluña*, as note 23, vol. 3, 329.
49   Xavier Pérez Gómez, 'La desamortització eclesiàstica', in *Història de la Selva*: Narcís Figueras y Capdevila and Joan Llinàs y Pol, coords. (Girona, 2011), 499–502 at 500.

generally handwritten, though provenance can also be determined from the bindings[50].

5.2.2 The Gerona Provincial Library

In 1823, the marquis of Capmany gathered 4,636 volumes in San Francisco de Asís from the nine monasteries in the city of Gerona and two in Bañolas. It is not known whether the books were returned after the restoration of the absolutist regime or remained together. Fifteen years later, they were transferred, and by the end of 1839, a further 4,249 volumes had arrived in the capital.

The whereabouts of these 8,885 volumes, the sum of both joint libraries, between 1840 and 1848 is unknown. Aside from possible thefts, many were in very bad state, nearly useless, and others were duplicates. Nevertheless it is known that between 5,000 and 6,000 volumes were temporarily held in the diocesan seminary, while the rest, the smaller part, may have been in the Civil Governor's offices[51].

The Provincial Library was finally established in 1848 in the former Capuchin convent, which had also housed the secondary school for the past three years. The initial collection was 1,300 volumes, though in early 1848 they were joined by 4,541 volumes from the diocesan seminary[52]. In all, there were 5,841 volumes, to which we must add the 1,071 volumes from La Bisbal,

which arrived in 1856. Theoretically, by then the library had 6,912 volumes. The figures basically coincide with an inventory taken in 1859, which stated that there were 7,579 books, and one in 1865, by which time there were 8,800 books[53].

Altogether, the suppressed monasteries provided around 7,000 volumes to the Gerona Public Library, a small fraction of all the books owned by religious houses at the end of the eighteenth century.

5.2.3 The Tarragona Provincial Library

Salvador J. Rovira has written that the suppression was "a true calamity" for convent and monastery libraries in Tarragona[54]. A large part of the surviving bibliographic patrimony went to the Tarragona Provincial Library, founded in 1846 by Father Joaquín Caballero for the purpose of gathering all the holdings of the suppressed religious houses. The collection included books from the monasteries of Santes Creus (2,000 volumes), Poblet[55], and Scala Dei; the Carmelites and San Francisco de Paula de Valls; the Franciscan monasteries of Escornalbou and Tarragona; and the Mercedarian monastery of Tortosa. The Provincial Library was housed in the former San Francisco, and by 1857 it had 6,000 volumes[56]. According to Barraquer, in

50 Neus Verger Arce, 'La Biblioteca de reserva de la Universitat de Barcelona', *Bid: Textos Universitaris de Biblioteconomia i Documentació*, 21 (2008), <http://www.ub.edu/bid/21/verger.htm> [Consulted: 31-01-2012]. See also now the database of former owners: https://crai.ub.edu/sites/default/files/posseidors/home_eng.htm and the records created in MEI.

51 Enric Mirambell i Belloc, 'La biblioteca pública de Girona, fruit de la desamortització', *Revista de Girona*, 113 (1985), 36–39 and Lluís Buscató i Somoza, *De l'antiquarisme a l'arqueologia. La protecció del patrimonio històric i arqueològic a la província de Girona (1835–1876)* (Girona, 2011), 257–62.

52 García Ejarque, *Historia de la lectura*, as note 14, 80.

53 Pedro Martínez Quintanilla, *La provincia de Gerona. Datos estadísticos* (Gerona, 1865), 160.

54 Rovira, *La desamortització dels béns de l'església*, as note 40, 302.

55 In 1835 the monastery library in Poblet contained 8,002 volumes, of which 4,322 were part of the legacy of Father Antoni de Aragón. Part of these holdings passed into the hands of Jacint Pla, nicknamed *xafa-rucs* (someone who overloads burros), who took them to his warehouse in Reus, where they were damaged, Rovira, *La desamortització dels béns de l'església*, as note 40, 303.

56 Bernabé Bartolomé Martínez, 'Las bibliotecas públicas provinciales (1835–1885). Un intento de promoción de la lectura en España', *Revista de Educación*, 288 (1989), 271–304, at 299.

the Tarragona seminary library there were also books from the suppressed houses[57].

5.2.4 The Lérida Provincial Library

This library was founded in 1842 in the former Dominican monastery of Roser, a building that also served as a secondary school. Though it had space to hold 15,000 volumes, in 1844 it had only 2,500, despite the fact that the previous year part of the University of Cervera holdings (2,000 volumes) were supposed to be transferred there and that some 6,000 volumes were still being held in the former Discalced Carmelite convent[58]. In 1857 its holdings had risen to 5,608 volumes[59].

5.2.5 The Vic Episcopal Library

When Francesc de Veyan y Mola, bishop of Vic, founded the library in 1806, its holdings were around 7,000 volumes, of which 4,500 came from the Jesuit houses in Manresa, Vic, and San Guim de Cervera. Barraquer believed that after the desamortización in 1835, the books from Vic's monasteries were transferred to the Episcopal Library[60].

5.2.6 The library of the Tortosa seminary

The Santiago and San Matías college became a seminary in 1824, the same year that Víctor Damián Sáez became bishop of Tortosa. He established what Barraquer called a "grand library" there, in whose collection there were books from the city's suppressed convents and monasteries[61].

5.2.7 The Seo de Urgell Episcopal Library

According to Barraquer, books from some establishments in the diocese of Urgell ended up in the episcopal library thanks to the efforts of Bishop Simón de Guardiola[62]. In 1849 it had some 7,000 volumes[63].

6. Conclusion

During the first half of the nineteenth century, cultural properties held by Spanish religious houses were swept up in expropriation and confiscation campaigns led by a series of governments, all of which, despite their ideological differences, wished to resolve the profound financial problems of the state. In order to pay off their public debts and pay for the wars, governments seized the properties of the regular clergy and auctioned off their landed estates.

But the artistic, bibliographic, and archival holdings of the monasteries, now part of the national patrimony, quickly became burdensome for the administration. Although legislation was issued regarding the protection and custody of the books, similar to measures taken in other European countries, the state's financial and bureaucratic inability to take proper charge of treasures from religious establishments led to irreparable losses. Thousands of books were pillaged, damaged, or destroyed, and those that were saved owed their survival to the altruism of a small group of intellectuals.

The provincial libraries where the seized books were eventually sent became warehouses of old books on theological, juridical, and spiritual matters of little interest to a new generation of readers, who preferred novels, the daily press, and

57 Barraquer, *Los religiosos en Cataluña*, as note 23, vol. 4, 106.
58 Carmen Berlabé Jové, as note 41, 39.
59 Bartolomé, 'Las bibliotecas públicas', as note 57, 298.
60 Barraquer, *Los religiosos en Cataluña*, as note 23, vol. 3, 482 and 522.
61 Barraquer, *Los religiosos en Cataluña*, as note 23, vol. 3, 449, 560 and 661.

62 Barraquer, *Los religiosos en Cataluña*, as note 23, vol. 3, 677.
63 Pascual Madoz, *Diccionario geográfico-estadístico-histórico de España y sus provincias de Ultramar* (Madrid, 1849), vol. 14, 433.

modern textbooks. As a result, "popular libraries" during the nineteenth century attempted to make up for the deficiencies of these public libraries and better meet readers' demands[64].

Though Catalonia tried to apply the measures dictated by the national governments, its particular social, political, and military circumstances during the first half of the nineteenth century led to a radicalization and to an even greater loss of books than that suffered by the rest of Spain.

---

64 J. A. Martínez Martín, J. A, 'La lectura en la España contemporánea: lectores, discursos y prácticas de lectura', *Ayer*, 58 (2005), 15–34.

Bibliography

Manuscripts and Archival sources

Archivo Histórico de Gerona, Gobierno Civil de Gerona, D 4468/6 and 7.
Diputación Provincial de Gerona, Libro de Actas, 17 April 1823, fol. 58.
Madrid, Archivo Histórico Nacional [AHN], Códices y Cartularios, books 540–44 [available for consultation online].

Secondary Works

Javier Antón Pelayo, *La herencia cultural. Alfabetización y lectura en la ciudad de Girona (1747–1807)* (Bellaterra, 1998).
Javier Antón Pelayo, 'La desamortización de las bibliotecas conventuales en Cataluña durante la crisis del Antiguo Régimen', *Memoria y Civilización. Revista de Historia*, 21 (2018), 611–51.
Andrés Avelino Pi y Arimon, *Barcelona antigua y moderna. Descripción e historia de esta ciudad desde su fundación hasta nuestros días*, 2 vols (Barcelona, 1854).
Joan Bada and Genís Samper, *Catalònia Religiosa. Atles històric: dels orígens als postres diez* (Barcelona, 1991).
Luis Barbastro Gil, 'Plan de reforma de la iglesia española impulsado por Napoleón Bonaparte', *Hispania Sacra*, LX-121 (2008), 267–95.
Cayetano Barraquer y Roviralta, *Los religiosos en Cataluña durante la primera mitad del siglo XIX*, 4 vols (Barcelona, 1915–1917).
Juan Manuel Barrios Rozúa, 'Los conventos andaluces frente a la desamortización de las Cortes de Cádiz y el anticlericalismo', in *La desamortización: el expolio del patrimonio artístico y cultural de la Iglesia en España*: Francisco Javier Campos y Fernández de Sevilla, coord. (San Lorenzo del Escorial, 2007), 119–38.
Bernabé Bartolomé Martínez, 'Las bibliotecas públicas provinciales (1835–1885). Un intento de promoción de la lectura en España', *Revista de Educación*, 288 (1989), 271–304.
Lluís Batlle i Prats, 'Notícia de la biblioteca dels jesuïtes a Girona l'any 1779', *Revista de Girona*, 103 (1983), 81–83.
Vicente Bécares Botas, *Las bibliotecas monásticas y la desamortización en la provincia de Zamora* (Zamora, 1999).
Margarita Becedas González and Óscar Lilao Franca, 'Noticias sobre la biblioteca del Colegio Real de la Compañía de Jesús de Salamanca', in *Homenaje al padre Benigno Hernández Montes* (Salamanca, 1999), 511–38.
Josefina Bello, *Frailes, intendentes y políticos. Los bienes nacionales, 1835–1850* (Madrid, 1997).
José María Benítez i Riera, *Jesuïtes i Catalunya: fets i figures* (Barcelona, 1996).
Carmen Berlabé Jové, *El Museu Diocesà de Lleida. La seva formació i la legitimitat del seu patrimonio artístic* (Barcelona, 2009).

Antoni Borràs i Feliu, 'L'expulsió dels jesuïtes de la ciutat de Barcelona en el marc general del seu desterrament d'Espanya per Carles III', *Pedralbes. Revista d'Història Moderna*, 8.2 (1988), 403–30.

Cristina Borreguero Beltrán, *Burgos en la Guerra de la Independencia: enclave estratégico y ciudad expoliada* (Burgos, 2007).

J. D. Buján Núñez, 'Desamortización y bibliotecas en la provincia de Pontevedra', *Pontevedra. Revista de Estudios Provinciais*, 8–9 (1992), 264–74.

Lluís Buscató i Somoza, *De l'antiquarisme a l'arqueologia. La protecció del patrimonio històric i arqueològic a la provincia de Girona (1835–1876)* (Girona, 2011).

Manuel Carrión Gutiez, *La Biblioteca Nacional* (Madrid, 1996).

Agustí Duran i Sampere, 'La primera Biblioteca Pública Municipal de Barcelona', in *Barcelona i la seva historia*, 3 vols (Barcelona, 1973–1975), vol. 3, 559–62.

Lartaun Eguibar Urrutia, 'El sistema napoleónico en el espacio vasco: del ordenamiento foral a un nuevo régimen. Implantación y alcance', *Historia constitucional. Revista electrónica de historia constitucional*, 9 (2008), 25–59.

Hipólito Escolar Sobrino, *Historia de las bibliotecas* (Madrid, 1990).

Gaspar Feliu i Montfort, *La clerecia catalana durant el Trienni Liberal* (Barcelona, 1972).

Raimon Ferrer, *Barcelona cautiva, o sea, diario exacto de lo ocurrido en la misma ciudad mientras la oprimieron los franceses, esto es, desde el 13 de febrero de 1808 hasta el 28 de mayo de 1814*, 7 vols (Barcelona, 1815–1821).

Luis García Ejarque, *Historia de la lectura pública en España* (Gijón, 2000).

María Dolores García Gómez, 'La biblioteca del colegio de jesuitas de Albacete en el trance de la expulsión (1767)', *Hispania Sacra*, LII/105 (2000), 229–58.

María Dolores García Gómez, 'Un acopio documental: los inventarios de temporalidades de las bibliotecas de la Compañía de Jesús en la provincia de Aragón', in *Aspectos de la política religiosa en el siglo XVIII. Estudios en Homenaje a Isidoro Pinedo Iparraguirre, S.J.*: Enrique Giménez López, ed. (Alicante, 2010), 151–84.

María Dolores García Gómez, *Testigos de la memoria. Los inventarios de las bibliotecas de la Compañía de Jesús en la expulsión de 1767* (Alicante, 2011).

Genaro Luis García López, 'La administración territorial ante la política cultural y la recogida de los bienes nacionales durante la revolución liberal: análisis especial de su actuación en materia bibliotecaria', in *El municipio constitucional* (Madrid, 2003), 349–60.

Genaro Luis García López, *Libros para no leer: el nacimiento de la política documental en España* (Gijón, 2004).

Enrique Giménez López and Francisco Javier Martínez Naranjo, 'La expulsión de los jesuitas de Cataluña', *Butlletí de la Societat Catalana d'Estudis Històrics*, 20 (2009), 115–36.

María Pilar Hernando Serra, *El ayuntamiento de Valencia y la invasión napoleónica* (Valencia, 2004).

Agustín Hevía Ballina and Ramón Rodríguez Álvarez, 'Desamortización y bibliotecas eclesiásticas', *Memoria Ecclesiae*, 22 (2003), 225–42.

María Victoria Játiva Miralles, *La biblioteca de los jesuitas del colegio de San Esteban de Murcia* (Murcia, 2008).

Antoni Jordà Fernández, *Las diputaciones provinciales en sus inicios. Tarragona, 1836–1840* (Madrid, 2002).

Gerardo Luzuriaga Sánchez, 'Inventario de la biblioteca del Colegio de los jesuitas de Oñati', *Boletín de la Real Sociedad Bascongada de Amigos del País*, 51.2 (2005), 435–57.

Pascual Madoz, *Diccionario geográfico-estadístico-histórico de España y sus provincias de Ultramar* (Madrid, 1849).

Francisco Martí Gilabert, *La desamortización española* (Madrid, 2003).

J. A. Martínez Martín, J. A, 'La lectura en la España contemporánea: lectores, discursos y prácticas de lectura', *Ayer*, 58 (2005), 15–34.

Pedro Martínez Quintanilla, *La provincia de Gerona. Datos estadísticos* (Gerona, 1865).

Ana Jesús Mateos Gil, 'Expolios y saqueos. Consecuencias de la Guerra de la Independencia en el patrimonio artístico calagurritano', *Kalakorikos*, 13 (2008), 71–106.

Enric Mirambell i Belloc, 'La biblioteca pública de Girona, fruit de la desamortització', *Revista de Girona*, 113 (1985), 36–39.

Enric Mirambell i Belloch, 'Projecte de biblioteca provincial (1820–1823)', *Revista de Girona*, 136 (1989), 75–82.

Antoni Moliner Prada, *La Guerra del Francès a Catalunya segons el diari de Raimon Ferrer* (Bellaterra, 2010).

Miguel C. Muñoz Feliu, 'Liberalismo, desamortización y política bibliotecaria. El caso valenciano', *Anales de documentación*, 9 (2006), 133–41.

Xavier Pérez Gómez, 'La desamortització eclesiàstica', in *Història de la Selva*: Narcís Figueras y Capdevila and Joan Llinàs y Pol, coords. (Girona, 2011), 499–502.

Antonio Pérez Goyena, 'La primera biblioteca pública de Pamplona', *Príncipe de Viana*, II/3 (1941), 33–37.

Antoni Pladevall i Arumí, *La il·lustració a Vic. Les aportacions de Francesc Veyan i Mola i Llucià Gallissà i Costa* (Cabrera de Mar, 2000).

Joan Portet i Pujol, 'L'exclaustració de religiosos de l'any 1835', *Ausa*, 151 (2003), 29–49.

Carles Rahola, *La ciutat de Girona* (Barcelona, 1929).

Manuel Revuelta González, *Política religiosa de los liberales en el siglo XIX. Trienio Constitucional* (Madrid, 1973).

Manuel Revuelta González, *La exclaustración (1833–1840)* (Madrid, 1976).

Concepción Rodríguez Parada, *La biblioteca del convento de Barcelona de la orden de la Merced: una herramienta para la formación de los frailes* (Barcelona, 2009).

Carmen Rodrigo Zarzosa, 'Desamortización de pinturas, libros y "alajas" en los conventos suprimidos en Valencia (1835–1837)', in *La desamortización: el expolio del patrimonio artístico y cultural de la iglesia en España*: Francisco Javier Campos y Fernández de Sevilla, coord. (San Lorenzo del Escorial, 2007), 699–722.

Salvador-J. Rovira i Gómez, *La desamortització dels béns de l'església a la província de Tarragona (1835–1845)* (Tarragona, 1979).

Germán Rueda Hernanz, *La desamortización en España: un balance (1766–1924)* (Madrid, 1997).

Ramón Sánchez González, 'La biblioteca del colegio San Bernardo de la Compañía de Jesús en Oropesa (Toledo)', *Hispania Sacra*, LXIII, 127 (2011), 41–74.

Roberto San Martín Casi, 'Inicios de la lectura pública en Navarra: la primera biblioteca (1810–1813) y fray Pedro María Navarro', *TK (Asociación Navarra de Bibliotecarios)*, 6 (1998), 9–28.

Manuel Santirso, *Revolució liberal i guerra civil a Catalunya (1833–1840)* (Lérida, 1999).

Valentí Serra de Manresa, 'Aproximació a les biblioteques dels caputxins setcentistes del Principat: clàssics, escolàstics i novatores', *Pedralbes. Revista d'Història Moderna*, 15 (1995), 265–277.

Eduard Toda i Güell, *Los convents de Reus y sa destrucción en 1835* (Reus, 1930).

Jordi Torra i Miró, 'La biblioteca de la Universitat de Barcelona i el breviari benedictí (Montserrat: Rosenbach, 1519) Norton 418', *Miscellània Litúrgica Catalana*, 5 (1994), 43–48.

Pilar Vélez, *El desvetllament de la conciència de patrimonio històric a Catalunya. Lliçó inaugural del curs 2003–2004* (Barcelona, 2003).

Javier Vergara, 'El proceso de expropiación de la biblioteca de los jesuitas en Pamplona (1767–1774)', *Revista de Historia Moderna. Anales de la Universidad de Alicante*, 26 (2008), 325–42.

Neus Verger Arce, 'La Biblioteca de reserva de la Universitat de Barcelona', *Bid: Textos Universitaris de Biblioteconomia i Documentació*, 21 (2008), <http://www.ub.edu/bid/21/verger.htm>

Digital Sources

Barcelona, CRAI, Former Owners, https://crai.ub.edu/sites/default/files/posseidors/home_eng.htm.

Material Evidence in Incunabula (MEI), https://data.cerl.org/mei/_search.

LUÍS CABRAL

Case study 1: Portugal, Porto – State Policy Concerning the Dissolution of Monastic Book Collections in Portugal, Especially during the Nineteenth Century

Partiti sunt vestimenta mea sibi

Ps. 22 (21), 19

1. Introduction

Portugal as an independent country is a successful example of a balanced long-term partnership between the kingdom and the Catholic Church, not only pope and bishops but also military and non-military religious orders. As a matter of fact, the unity of the state relied upon the unity of territory, religion, language, and culture. Yet there were several periods of conflict and crisis instead of partnership.

There were valuable repositories of books in the Middle Ages apart from the royal archives and library. The monastery of Santa Cruz de Coimbra, founded in 1131 as a house of Canons Regular of Saint Augustine, had a manuscript library which since 1834 has been part of the Biblioteca Pública Municipal de Porto in the city of Porto[1]. The Cistercian monastery of Alcobaça, founded by royal charter in 1153, had a library which is now in the Biblioteca Nacional de Portugal[2]. There were also the archives of the archbishop and chapter of Braga, which are still kept in Braga[3].

---

1 Aires Augusto do Nascimento and José Francisco Meirinhos, *Catálogo dos Códices da Livraria de Mão do Mosteiro de Santa Cruz de Coimbra na Biblioteca Pública Municipal do Porto* (Porto, 1997).
2 *Tesouros da Biblioteca Nacional* (Lisboa, 1992).
3 António de Sousa Araújo and Armando B. Malheiro da Silva, *Inventário do Fundo Monástico-Conventual* (Braga, 1985). Bernardo Vasconcelos e Sousa ed., *Ordens Religiosas em Portugal: das origens a Trento: guia histórico* (Lisboa, 2005).

Luís Cabral • Formerly Director of Biblioteca Pública Municipal do Porto. luisborgescabral@gmail.com

How the Secularization of Religious Houses Transformed the Libraries of Europe, 16th–19th Centuries, ed. by Cristina Dondi, Dorit Raines, and † Richard Sharpe, BIB, 63 (Turnhout, 2022), pp. 125–133.

BREPOLS ❦ PUBLISHERS

DOI 10.1484/M.BIB-EB.5.128481

During the sixteenth century, and specifically during the reign of Manuel I (1495–1521) and João III (1521–1557) and therefore twenty years before the union with Spain (1580), a large State and Church reorganization occurred as part of a more general policy of centralization. This event had a substantial impact on the written heritage of archives and libraries. A detailed revision of the national legislative corpus ("ordenações") was followed by a general restructuring of the charters from the municipalities ("forais"). Also the Church produced a relatively large number of normative texts ("constituições sinodais"). At Church level, a general reformation and often a regrouping of monasteries and convents took place, not only in male but also in female religious houses. Among the latter we should mention, in 1536, the case of the monastery of São Bento de Avé-Maria in Porto, as an example of the merging of four rural medieval monasteries into a single and much larger house, placed within the confines of the country's second city.

2. The Time of the Jesuits: The Marquis of Pombal's Reforms, Eighteenth century

It is precisely during the eighteenth century that we can find to a large extent the first signs of the well-planned suppression of religious orders which would take place mostly from 1832 onwards.

Several events and other circumstances influenced the country during the Age of Enlightenment:

a) Freemasonry appeared in Portugal in 1735. A century later it would have among its members a relatively large number of people from the government, from the new liberal administration and even some leading figures from the Church.

b) The Lisbon earthquake in 1755, obviously a natural phenomenon, was however an opportunity for the government to implement quite significant political reforms. The consequences of the earthquake were very serious in terms of the damage caused to people and to public and private properties, archives, libraries and many other cultural assets. The real dimension of this disaster for the capital city and for a meaningful part of the country consisted in the rebuilding of most of the town and the need was felt to replace the former Royal Library with a new national library.

c) As early as 1756, the suppression of some of the financially less secure religious houses was the first act of what became a never-ending drama. Through Pombal's regalist policy the State adopted a more direct intervention in Church affairs. The Crown's right to appoint bishops, among many other issues, caused frequent problems and threatened to provoke schism with Rome, a situation which persisted over the two following centuries.

d) The French Revolution (1789) had a large impact all over Europe and also in America. The Portuguese Royal Court moved to Brazil (1807–1821), during the so-called Peninsular War (1807–1813), taking with it a large number of manuscripts and printed books which belonged mainly to the Royal Library of Ajuda in Lisbon. A few private libraries and some archives were also transferred to Brazil.

e) The suppression of the Jesuits (1759).

The most important part of the Jesuits' wealth was without a doubt their estates and revenues. They owned and directed several colleges, each one with its own library and other educational equipment. In these famous colleges the young elites were formed. The influence of Jesuits in society was also seen in different religious activities and practices such as confession and spiritual direction.

The Marquis of Pombal, Prime Minister between 1750 and 1777, persecuted not only the Society of Jesus, a persecution which had wide repercussions all over Europe, but also some of the most important Portuguese noble families, such as the Távora, Aveiro, and Alorna. Their involvement in the plot against King José I (1714–1777) was the official reason for this persecution. There were several arrests and executions which greatly affected the public, bringing as a result the enhancement of the royal power.

As a "side effect" of the expulsion of the Jesuits, the State took possession of their property, libraries included, which passed to the University of Coimbra. The University of Évora (1559–1759), Portugal's second university, owned by the Jesuits themselves, was also suppressed.

3. The Liberal Regime: Nineteenth century

As early as 1814, a "Project of a plan for the suppression of the Religious Orders in Portugal" was published in London, in the *O Investigador Portuguez em Inglaterra*, a journal produced by a liberal emigrant group, which was also, it is interesting to note, supported by the Portuguese court, then in Rio de Janeiro[4].

After the Liberal Revolution (Porto, 1820) general elections were held and the first Parliament in 1821 stopped admissions for novices. The Inquisition was dismantled in the same year. In 1822, when Brazil became independent, the first laws concerning the suppression of religious orders were issued in Portugal. At that time there were 401 male religious houses with 5,621 friars and monks, while the female ones were 132 and included 2,980 nuns.

Once installed, the Liberal Government (1829–1834) produced a detailed legislative package in order to dismantle some of the main structures of the Catholic Church such as real

estate and moveable assets, in other words libraries, archives and other cultural artefacts.

First, it is important to point out that the legislation abolishing religious orders was addressed more immediately to male houses and it took longer to affect women's convents.

Second, the State also interfered with many other important ecclesiastical matters, such as the appointment of bishops and church officials, the different organizational aspects of religious institutions, from dioceses to parishes and even in the aspect of inheritance law.

In this period not only ecclesiastical libraries but also a number of private libraries were sequestered from individuals of high social standing and cultural prominence. There is somehow a tendency to emphasize the value of the libraries of the religious orders over the latter. But, as a matter of fact, some of these libraries were of paramount importance. If we consider the situation in the south of Portugal, mainly in Lisbon, we can find a relatively large number of libraries of this type. In the north, especially in Porto, there were a lower number of private libraries. However, two of them were very large and valuable as far as Portugal is concerned: the libraries of Bishop Avelar and Viscount Balsemão which, until the mid 1830s and together with some other libraries belonging to religious orders, constituted a kind of single library resource in itself for the city of Porto.

The decree dated 5 December 1832 issued in Porto, ordering the sequestration of the properties belonging to people accused of high treason, was applied with immediate effect to Bishop Avelar's library. Its safety was a real concern for the Municipality since religious houses were prey to thefts. D. João de Magalhães e Avelar (1754–1833) was a professor of Law at the University of Coimbra as well as a famous historian. He was Bishop of Porto between 1816 and 1833. His library had more than 36,000 volumes and was considered the most important private book collection in Portugal. Luís Pinto

---

4 *O Investigador Portuguez em Inglaterra*, 10 (July 1814).

de Sousa Coutinho (1774–1833), 2nd Viscount Balsemão, was a military man[5]; his library comprised some 12,000 volumes, before the second French invasion. Both men used to import books especially from France. These two libraries were among the founding collections of Porto Public Library.

The decree that ordered the suppression of religious orders was published in Lisbon on 30 May 1834. It seems to have had the strong personal support of D. Pedro IV (1798–1834). It was preceded by various acts of legislation, not only under the Angra government, the Liberal Government which first took power in the Azores, but also in Porto, the government's headquarters during the period 1832–1833.

The Azores Decree of 17 May 1832 declared the suppression of religious orders in the Azores. It stated that "All properties belonging to the suppressed convents and monasteries in the Islands of the Azores are now considered national property". This document supplied a very detailed list of the suppressed houses and those contents which were to be preserved. Sacred vessels and vestments were to be donated to poorer parishes.

This legislative text already included various decisions relating to women's religious houses. New admissions to religious orders were generally forbidden and the text also stressed the role of the State in managing the financial aspects of the Church.

In Porto the decree dated 15 May 1833 was issued when the Liberal Government was installed in the city. This decree stipulated that monasteries, convents, and hospices, both male and female, which had been abandoned were to be suppressed in the Porto area.

After setting up an initial commission, the Government created a new one on 12 December 1832, under the chairmanship of Father Marcos Pinto Soares Vaz Preto (1782–1851)[6], with the responsibility of ensuring "good care for libraries, sacred vessels, and other property belonging to the convents and monasteries of this city as well as for the conservation of the buildings".

This new commission exercised an important role in the administration of the moveable and immoveable properties of religious orders. Its members were politically and socially important and represented the liberal spirit of the time. The commission was particularly involved in the management of the book collections which from then on were the property of the State, as the examination of one of its records will show, a 1833 register or *Copiador*[7].

During the siege of Porto, the situation appeared to be under control but was in fact very confused. From the records in this register we have selected two examples of the work of this commission.

The first example is a short description of the excesses caused by the English troops billeted in the convent of Santo António da Cidade, that would become the new public library:

"that it appears that there is no religious sacrilege too shocking for these people [i.e. the

---

5 He was born in Falmouth, England, where his father was Portuguese Ambassador in London. His mother, D. Catarina de Lencastre, was a well-known poetess. He had a degree in Philosophy and was Captain General in Brazil and Secretary of State.

6 Father Marcos was a very influential person. Exiled in London, he was appointed as Archbishop of Lacedemónia in 1835 and was also a royal confessor. Charged with high treason in 1836, he was elected as deputy in 1834–1835, 1842–1846 and 1848–1851. As early as 1831, he had collected statistics about religious members (men and women), and about the income of each religious house.

7 The 1833 *Copiador* was acquired by the District Archive of Porto in 2013; Luís Cabral, 'O Porto do Cerco (1832–1833): um livro da Comissão Administrativa dos Conventos Extintos ou Abandonados', *Boletim Cultural Amigos do Porto*, 31 (2013).

English] unrestrained by religious sentiment, to carry out. We are not used to seeing people breaking altars, smashing images, forcing doors and selling objects of worship in public taverns."

The second example deals with the shortage of paper. The Commission suggested to the King that books such as Mercator´s *Decretales* could be used for cartridges.

Books whose titles contained the word "moral" were considered by them as "immoral and against the Catholic faith". The same Commission should also expurgate from "the libraries titles against social mores and the government." Here we find censorship alongside the immediate satisfaction of urgent military requirements.

4. The Porto Royal Public Library

On 9 July 1833 a decree was issued concerning the foundation of the *Real Biblioteca Pública do Porto* (Porto Royal Public Library)[8].

The idea of a public library was quite new in the country's history. Despite its being new, it seems not to have had any major supporters. The plan was to establish a public library and at the same time a second Portuguese national library. To some extent the library was also the aspiration of the King, D. Pedro, who was personally involved

in the foundation of an extensive library as a sign of his royal authority and prestige.

The *memorandum* introducing this decree contains various proposals and values which are typical of a liberal programme:

a) It starts with a proclamation: "Ignorance is the worst enemy of freedom".
b) The government's mission is to educate people (with a reference to the former Azores laws: intellectual freedom of public teaching, freely available to everyone).
c) Libraries are seen as one of the most effective means of educating the members of society (that is to say its elites): "The creation of public libraries must be the accompaniment of every educational system. There is no doubt that an accurate assessment of the relative level of instruction of a country's inhabitants can be made by reference to the existing number of this kind of facility".

This decree dated 9 July states clearly the mission of the Porto Library:

a) Its purpose is public education.
b) Its foundation collections are not only those from the suppressed religious orders but also the sequestered private libraries of individuals who have been subject to judgement for high treason.
c) The library is established both under the responsibility of the State and the Porto City Council 9 the Library became fully municipal only in 1876).
d) The collections, apart from the libraries of the religious orders and some libraries which had been sequestered, include acquisitions, gifts and also legal deposit.
e) There is a special concern about the question of what to do with duplicate books. The decree encourages the redistribution of such items to the two main higher education schools in Porto – the Royal Naval and Commercial Academy and the School of Medicine and

---

8 *Memoria ácerca da livraria dos herdeiros do Bispo do Porto, D. João de Magalhães e Avelar* … (Lisboa: Typ. de Antonio José da Rocha, 1846); Sampaio Bruno, 'A Bibliotheca Publica do Porto', *Serões*, 16 (Oct. 1906) – 20 (Fev. 1907); Biblioteca Pública Municipal do Porto, *Documentos para a sua História* (Porto, 1933); Biblioteca Pública Municipal do Porto, *Exposição no 150º aniversário da sua fundação, 1833–1983* (Porto, 1984); Luís Cabral and Maria Adelaide Meireles, *Tesouros da Biblioteca Pública Municipal do Porto* (Lisboa, 1998); Luís Cabral, 'A Real Biblioteca Pública do Porto: um projecto liberal', *Páginas a & b*, 3 (2009), 29–38.

Surgery (from 1911 a part of the University of Porto).

As a consequence, a tradition of gifts to other libraries was theoretically inaugurated with this decree but was not actually put into effect until the beginning of the twentieth century. Other duplicate books were collected in a store, in order to be delivered elsewhere. Between 1866 and 1869 Porto Library organized six auctions (with catalogues), something which had already taken place in Lisbon. We know that several items were not real duplicates (even if we accept that such a bibliographical concept indeed exists). The income resulting from the auctions was used to buy "new and useful" books and periodicals.

From a quantitative point of view, the bibliographical heritage collected by the State as far as the Porto area is concerned has been estimated at 100,000 volumes, relating roughly to twenty convents and monasteries, a figure that may not be too far from reality, when we compare the distribution of religious houses across the country. The figures from the subsequent general Depósito das Livrarias ("Deposit of Libraries") in Lisbon, organized as the liberal revolution spread from north to south, were of 180,000 volumes at the time.

We would like to refer, albeit briefly, to a group of decrees issued in Lisbon on 5 August 1833:

a) All clergy, secular or regular, who abandoned their parishes, chapels, convents, monasteries and hospices on the occasion of the installation of the liberal government were to be treated as rebels and traitors.

b) All posts for archbishops and bishops which had been confirmed by Rome during the absolutist period were declared vacant, creating a schism with the Church. The decision also included all other church posts down to the parish level.

c) All admissions to sacred orders and the novitiate were banned.

d) The power to appoint archbishops, bishops and church officials was henceforth an exclusive prerogative of the government.

The "Junta do Exame do Estado Actual e Melhoramento Temporal das Ordens Religiosas" had existed since the end of the eighteenth century to advise the Government, but had been suppressed by the absolutist government. It was restored on 23 August 1833, with Father Marcos as the chairman. By the end of the year (28 December 1833), the government was attempting to solve the difficult problem of the lack of clergymen in the provinces of Africa and Asia. There was a need for parish work, catechesis and for Portuguese language teaching. Moreover it was also the Junta's wish to give to the overseas churches the sacred vessels, vestments and utensils of worship coming from the suppressed convents and monasteries.

The Decree of 30 May 1834 came out immediately after the end of the Civil War (1828–1834) and the fall of the absolutist government.

Its highly political text reflects the personal will of the monarch. It is worth stressing that this law was received with a unanimous negative judgment from the advising *Junta*.

Based on the values of "civilization" and supported by "the lights of the century" it tried to balance population, church and property. The report on the decree is a relatively long one, presenting strong arguments for the suppression. The decree itself is brief in its statements but was far-reaching in its consequences:

a) The suppression of religious orders in Portugal, the Atlantic Islands and overseas dominions.

b) It covered all convents, monasteries, colleges, hospices and other houses belonging to the regular orders.

c) Their properties were generally incorporated by the State.

d) The sacred utensils were reserved for the poorer churches, as was the case in the earlier legislation.

e) It provided a pension for religious members except for those who had collaborated with the absolutist government.

A few days later (4 July 1834) an ordinance containing more detailed instructions on the way the 30 May decree should be applied was published. It said that specific inventories of book and manuscript collections must be drawn up and that libraries were excluded from being sold together with other goods at public auction.

It is interesting to note that this ordinance was addressed in the first place to the Governor of the Province of Douro who had a prominent role in the selection of the best place to house the Porto Library. His role expanded beyond the boundaries of his province, since he became responsible for coordinating several libraries and archives across the country from north to south[9].

The establishment of the Library in the ancient monastery of Santo António da Cidade, where it is still located, was something new for the time. In the same building were installed not only the Royal Library, but also a Museum with collections of objects which had belonged to religious orders.

5. Republican Legislation: Twentieth century

During the last years of the monarchy several anti-clerical measures were promulgated, among which there was the decree issued on 10 March 1901, which:
a) ordered the civil governors in the kingdom to enquire into the existence of religious

institutions dedicated to the monastic life, according to the May 1834 decree;
b) established a similar enquiry regarding educational and charitable institutions owned by religious communities;
c) ordered an investigation into the admissions into religious orders and monastic novitiates.

The new Republican regime in 1910 brought what we can call the *grand finale* for the long process of dismantling an important part of the structure of the Roman Catholic Church. To a large extent, the new regime preserved the anti-clerical approach pursued over the two previous centuries.

The decree issued on 8 October 1910, just a few days after the Republican revolution, echoed the eighteenth-century laws and the 1834 liberal legislation, in making particular reference to the Jesuits.

The State interfered strongly from the highest level of diocesan administration to the daily business of parish life. Some bishops were even forced into exile, a move which caused conflict with the Vatican.

The most important law from this period is the Law of Separation of Church and State, dated 20 April 1911, underwritten by all the members of the provisional Republican government.

It includes almost two hundred articles from which we will mention a few which are relevant to our topic:
a) All religious buildings, namely cathedrals, churches and chapels, were declared public property;
b) Commissions to deal with questions of worship in churches were set up. They were also intended to control the financial income of the Church;
c) Matters such as funerals and cemeteries were also regulated;
d) The Jesuits are specifically mentioned in the decree.

9 Luís Cabral, 'Alexandre Herculano e o Património Cultural: reflexões "entre Douro e Minho"', *Forum*, 46 (2011), 37–59. On the most important librarian of Porto Library in this period see also Luís Cabral, *Alexandre Herculano e a Biblioteca do Porto: um caso exemplar* (Porto, 2013).

One of the consequences of this radical legislation was the acquisition by the Government of some very important archives previously owned by the bishops and chapters of some dioceses. Their acquisition lies at the origin of the present-day regional archives[10].

The Government attained a much more direct control over the internal and organizational aspects of the Catholic Church in Portugal with a special emphasis being laid on patrimonial matters. The secular clergy now suffered the largest blow.

6. Conclusions

New information continues to become available and makes drawing any definitive conclusions difficult and premature[11]. However, some indicative suggestions can be put forward. We have considered the suppression of religious orders in Portugal as a three-step process:

a) eighteenth century – The expulsion of the Jesuits from Portugal and its Empire.

b) nineteenth century – The Liberals' policy towards the suppression of religious orders.

c) twentieth century – The Republican laws impacting mainly on the secular clergy.

    1. Libraries provoked considerable interest, even if as moveable property they were regarded as secondary. Two examples of this interest: the attention paid to Bishop Avelar's library and the fact that the direct sale or auction of the contents of the libraries of religious orders was prohibited.

2. The history of several of Portugal's libraries and archives is closely linked to the suppression of religious orders.

3. War had an important impact on the security and conservation of the collections.

4. The lack of control over book collections on the part of the government and of the administrative authorities can be considered as destructive as the more common risks of theft, fire, bombardmens, water damage and negligence.

5. Censorship recurs sporadically in various degrees.

6. The main libraries were seen as libraries which generated other libraries since their collections were often redistributed to other libraries.

7. Political and social changes caused internal problems as well as with the country's foreign relations (for example with the Vatican).

8. The empire of Brazil and the Portuguese-speaking countries in Africa deserve further investigation.

---

10 Fernanda Ribeiro, *O acesso à informação nos arquivos* (Lisboa, 2003).

11 Luís A. Oliveira Ramos, 'A extinção das ordens religiosas: consequências culturais', *Bibliotheca Portucalensis*, 7 (1992) 7–25; Paulo J. S. Barata, *Os livros e o Liberalismo: da biblioteca conventual à biblioteca pública: uma alteração de paradigma* (Lisboa, 2003); Paulo J. S. Barata, 'As bibliotecas no liberalismo: definição de uma política cultural de regime', *Análise Social*, 174 (2005), 37–63.

Bibliography

Paulo J. S. Barata, *Os livros e o Liberalismo: da biblioteca conventual à biblioteca pública: uma alteração de paradigma* (Lisboa, 2003).

Paulo J. S. Barata, 'As bibliotecas no liberalismo: definição de uma política cultural de regime', *Análise Social*, 174 (2005), 37–63.

Biblioteca Pública Municipal do Porto, *Documentos para a sua História* (Porto, 1933). Biblioteca Pública Municipal do Porto, *Exposição no 150º aniversário da sua fundação, 1833–1983* (Porto, 1984).

Luís Cabral and Maria Adelaide Meireles, *Tesouros da Biblioteca Pública Municipal do Porto* (Lisboa, 1998).

Luís Cabral, 'A Real Biblioteca Pública do Porto: um projecto liberal', *Páginas a & b*, 3 (2009), 29–38.

Luís Cabral, 'Alexandre Herculano e o Património Cultural: reflexões "entre Douro e Minho"', *Forum*, 46 (2011), 37–59.

Luís Cabral, 'O Porto do Cerco (1832–1833): um livro da Comissão Administrativa dos Conventos Extintos ou Abandonados', *Boletim Cultural Amigos do Porto*, 31 (2013).

Luís Cabral, *Alexandre Herculano e a Biblioteca do Porto: um caso exemplar* (Porto, 2013).

Memoria ácerca da livraria dos herdeiros do Bispo do Porto, D. João de Magalhães e Avelar ... (Lisboa: Typ. de Antonio José da Rocha, 1846).

Aires Augusto do Nascimento and José Francisco Meirinhos, *Catálogo dos Códices da Livraria de Mão do Mosteiro de Santa Cruz de Coimbra na Biblioteca Pública Municipal do Porto* (Porto, 1997).

O Investigador Portuguez em Inglaterra, 10 (July 1814).

Luís A. Oliveira Ramos, 'A extinção das ordens religiosas: consequências culturais', *Bibliotheca Portucalensis*, 7 (1992) 7–25.

Fernanda Ribeiro, *O acesso à informação nos arquivos* (Lisboa, 2003).

Sampaio Bruno, 'A Bibliotheca Publica do Porto', *Serões*, 16 (Oct. 1906) – 20 (Fev. 1907).

António de Sousa Araújo and Armando B. Malheiro da Silva, *Inventário do Fundo Monástico-Conventual* (Braga, 1985).

Tesouros da Biblioteca Nacional (Lisboa, 1992).

Bernardo Vasconcelos e Sousa ed., *Ordens Religiosas em Portugal: das origens a Trento: guia histórico* (Lisboa, 2005).

MARIA LUISA LOPEZ VIDRIERO

Case study 2: Spain, Seville and Madrid – The Formation of New Libraries

Chronology

Strictly speaking, it was over the last four decades of the eighteenth century that the abolition of religious orders and the suppression of their houses impacted on Spanish libraries. Subsequently, the great political upheavals of the nineteenth century, caused in particular by the confrontation between constitutional liberalism and absolutist conservatism, as well as by the Carlist Wars[1], had a direct effect on the religious orders in Spain, which experienced both suppression and restoration. In 1835 and 1836, the *Desamortización Eclesiástica*, or Nationalization of Church Property under the prime ministership of Juan Álvarez Mendizábal (1790–1853), a progressive who briefly held office during the three-year liberal interlude of Ferdinand VII's reign was, in fact, only the best-known of a long series of expropriations of ecclesiastical land and property that had begun in the eighteenth century and would continue throughout the nineteenth and into the twentieth

century. It was, for instance, followed by further confiscations under other progressive ministers Joaquín Fernández-Espartero (1793–1879) in 1841, and then under Pascual Madoz (1806–1870) in 1855. This was a gradual process which can be divided into three stages differentiated by the sort of property that was seized and put up for sale: 1767–1836, from Charles III (1716–1788) to Mendizábal, confiscation of estates associated with the Church and of the property of ecclesiastical institutions that had been suppressed; 1836–1841, from Mendizábal to Espartero, confiscation of property of the regular and secular clergy; 1855–1924, from Madoz to Primo de Rivera (1870–1930), confiscation of any remaining ecclesiastical, and also the sale of State-owned, property.

These expropriations formed part of a policy of transferring property ownership with a view to increasing the nation's wealth and, in the short and medium terms, to securing a windfall that would reduce public debt. The seizure and auctioning of property said in Spanish to be "en manos muertas", that is, until then, legally inalienable possessions of the Church and the religious orders which held it in perpetuity, was officially decreed to be

---

[1] A series of civil wars that took place in Spain during the period 1833–1876.

Maria Luisa Lopez Vidriero • Formerly Directora de la Real Biblioteca of Madrid. marialuisavidriero@gmail.com

How the Secularization of Religious Houses Transformed the Libraries of Europe, 16th–19th Centuries, ed. by Cristina Dondi, Dorit Raines, and †Richard Sharpe, BIB, 63 (Turnhout, 2022), pp. 135–143.

BREPOLS ❧ PUBLISHERS   DOI 10.1484/M.BIB-EB.5.128482

permissible by law. These decrees had the purpose of financing the liberal government.

The Expropriation of Jesuit Libraries

In 1767, under King Charles III, the Jesuits were expelled[2]. Voltaire would celebrate this in a letter of the time exclaiming, "On a coupé les griffes au monstre!" For him, a world without Jesuits or Jansenists was a spring which had sprung back as the terrible weight of superstition was lifted from it[3]. The importance of the expulsion for the history of the book in Spain is almost incalculable; it affected everything to do with books, both the ideas they conveyed and their material form.

The closure of the large number of Jesuit houses in the territories of the Spanish Crown – that is to say Spain itself, its colonies in the Americas, and the Philippines – resulted, on the one hand, in the disposal by sale of the order's extraordinarily rich collections and, on the other, in educational reform and the urgent need to produce new works for new *mentalités*. In 1773, Pope Clement XIV declared the abolition of the Jesuit order wherever papal authority prevailed. The order was restored in all Catholic countries by order of Pope Pius VII in 1814, and the Jesuits returned to Spain in 1815, during the reign of Ferdinand VII[4].

From 1767, the expropriation of Jesuit collections meant that a veritable flood of books was released, and the government, and society in general, had to deal with them. A large number of library-inventories, together with papers and documents from Jesuit houses that were suppressed at this time, are preserved in the Jesuit Sections of the Real Academia de la Historia and of the Archivo Histórico Nacional, both in Madrid. In April of that same year of 1767, the reformist finance minister Pedro Rodríguez de Campomanes (1723–1802) had drawn up detailed instructions, which had the force of law behind them, to ensure that the inventories of books and documents sequestered from Jesuit houses conformed to strict and uniform bibliographical guidelines[5].

After the expulsion of the Society of Jesus in Spain, the administrative elite took charge of Jesuit property and drew up plans for its disposal. With the exception of those of the Society's buildings that had been earmarked for official use, the remainder of its property that didn't go to other institutions was auctioned off, the resulting income being used, in part, to maintain the former members of the order[6].

The Jesuits' Imperial College in Madrid enjoyed enormous prestige and played a unique role in education in the capital. The fate of its library therefore provides a model of how the State sought to deal with an educational library

2 España. Rey. Carlos III. Pragmática Sanción. El Pardo, 2 abril 1767. *Pragmática sanción de su Magestad en fuerza de ley para el estrañamiento de estos Reynos a los Regulares de la Compañía, ocupación de sus Temporalidades, y prohibición de su restablecimiento en tiempo alguno, con las demás prevenciones que expresa.* En Madrid: en la Imprenta Real de la Gazeta, 1767.

3 Voltaire [François-Marie Arouet], *Lettre CLXVII a M. le Marquis de Villevieille* (1775), in *Œuvres complètes: Recueil des lettres de M. de Voltaire*, 13: 1775–78, v. 68, A Gotha, Chez Charles-Guillaume Ettinger, Libraire, 1789, 295–96.

4 Iglesia Católica. Papa, Clemente XIV. Breve. 1773. *Dominus ac Redemptor.* Iglesia Católica. Papa, Pio VII. Bula. 1814. *Solicitudo omnium ecclesiarum.*

5 Short inventory in: Antonio Rodríguez Villa, *Catálogo general de manuscritos de la Real Academia de la Historia.* There is also an extensive catalogue: Real Cédula, 23 de abril 1767. "Instrucciones de lo que se deberá observar para inventariar libros y papeles que han sido de los regulares de la Compañía de Jesús en todos los dominios de S.M.". Published in: *Colección general de las providencias tomadas por el gobierno sobre extrañamiento y ocupación de los regulares de la Compañía que existían en los dominios de S.M. de España, Indias y Filipinas* (Madrid, 1967).

6 Francisco Aguilar Piñal, *La Universidad de Sevilla en el s. xviii. Estudio sobre la primera reforma universitaria moderna* (Sevilla, 1969), 313; Francisco Aguilar Piñal, *La Sevilla de Olavide* (Sevilla, 1966).

of such great standing. In 1770 this famous Jesuit school was converted into the Royal College of San Isidro with the remit to educate the capital's elite. It subsequently became the library of the Complutensian University (formerly known as the Universidad Central), and nowadays it forms the core of the holdings of rare books owned by the Complutense and is called the Biblioteca Histórica "Marqués de Valdecilla"[7].

We have to remember that the sudden availability of such an extraordinary number of manuscripts and printed books coincided with the Enlightenment, when being a learned collector was considered a mark of distinction, and when the Spanish State was encouraging the cultivation of knowledge about national culture and also striving to dignify that culture. The unique opportunity to acquire works of art and substantial amounts of books attracted both individuals and the nation's great store-house of books, the Biblioteca Pública del Rey, which the Crown conceived of as a repository of national memory accessible to its citizens. Confiscation in France in 1764, three years before the sequestrations took place in Spain, had provided Spanish booksellers – and especially the librarians of the Biblioteca Pública del Rey and those in charge of the King's private library – with the opportunity to acquire large numbers of books. The Italian bookseller Angelo Corradi, acting on behalf of Juan de Santander (1712–1783), librarian of the Royal Public Library, acquired a substantial part of the collection of the Collège de Clermont in Paris[8]. As booksellers and travellers frequently reported, old books such as the ones coming

from Jesuit libraries were eagerly snapped up by individuals and institutions in Spain.

If we now focus on Seville and treat it as a case study, we can gauge the impact of the suppression of the Jesuits and the sale of their books on the two public libraries in that city, the university and the episcopal one, and also on individual collections which were later to find their way into the private library of Charles IV, king from 1788 to 1808, who was a great bibliophile and also a keen expropriator.

Seville

The Jesuits had owned many houses in Seville: the convent of Santa María Anunciata, the College of San Hermenegildo, the College and Novitiate of San Luis, the Redcoat College for lay students – Santa María de la Concepción –, and two Colleges for foreign lay students: Santa María de la Concepción para los irlandeses (or the Irish College) and San Gregorio el Magno (for the English)[9].

Three officials in the city of Seville, Pablo Olavide (1725–1803), Francisco de Bruna (1719–1807), and Melchor Gaspar de Jovellanos (1744–1811), respectively Intendente, Alcaide (governor), and Fiscal Mayor (principal judge) of the city, were directly involved in carrying out government's orders to confiscate paintings, other works of art, and books belonging to the Jesuits in the city, as well as disposing of their buildings, rents, and other property. Jovellanos had just been posted to Seville, and had been charged with the task of disposing of the assets of the Colegio de las Becas, which was the Jesuits' seminary for the diocese of Seville[10]. It fell to

7   José Simón Díaz, *Historia del Colegio Imperial de Madrid*. 2 vols (Madrid, 1952–1959); Aurora Alonso de Miguel, *La Biblioteca de los Reales Estudios de San Isidro. Su historia hasta la integración en la Universidad Central* (Madrid, 1996).

8   Gabriel Sánchez Espinosa, 'Los libreros Ángel Corradi y Antoine Boudet y la importanción de libros franceses para la academia de San Fernando', *Bulletin Hispanique*, 114–1 (2012), 195–216.

9   Francisco Aguilar Piñal, *La Sevilla*, as note 6, 74–77.

10   Jovellanos arrived in Seville in 1768, as 'Alcalde del Crimen de la Audiencia' and remained there until 1778, when he moved to Madrid as 'Alcalde de Casa y Corte'; see Javier Varela, *Jovellanos* (Madrid, 1988).

him to organize the public sale of the College's library. Thanks to Rodríguez de Campomanes, the finance minister who had passed the decree ordering the expulsion of the Jesuits, and on the recommendation of the royal painter Rafael Mengs (1728–1779), Antonio Ponz (1725–1792) was ordered to draw up an inventory of the Jesuits' possessions in Andalusia. Only a few years later, in 1771, Jovellanos undertook his literary travels throughout Spain, when he was warm in his praise of Francisco de Bruna's marvellously rich collection of books and paintings, many of which had come from Jesuit Colleges[11].

The expulsion of the Jesuits, the disposal of their property, and the sale of some of their books at bargain prices, had a profound impact on the sort of collecting that ensued. It was associated with the Bourbon reforms and was characterized by courtly antiquarianism. Melchor Gaspar Jovellanos, who started his collection at just this time, bought former Jesuit books just as eagerly as did Bruna. The library of the College of San Hermenegildo passed in large part to Jovellanos's collection in which his classical and scholarly tastes, shared with Bruna, went hand in hand with the intellectual interests of somebody who was absolutely up-to-date with the latest ideas, something he shared with Pablo Olavide[12]. Jovellanos's collection, built up over the ten years when he lived in Seville, therefore shared some aspects of those of his two friends, Bruna and Olavide.

However, the sale of the Jesuits' books did not attract Pablo Olavide as a private collector because, as both bibliophile and reader, he identified himself with the French elite who were close to the *philosophes*, and so he was much more cosmopolitan in his taste. Although he felt no particular enthusiasm for the Seville Jesuits' books (and they were of no interest to him personally as a collector), as the official responsible for confiscating those books Olavide was conscious of their importance and decided that they should be made widely available. He was aware that Seville society as a whole would benefit greatly if they were made accessible in a public library. So, while Bruna was interested in them for his private collection, Olavide stated that if his own library, which contained the best up-to-date publications, were combined with the old books sequestered from Jesuit houses, Seville would have the finest book collection in Spain[13].

Along with the sale of Jesuit books to individuals, the government envisaged that confiscated books should be made accessible to the public. In 1769 the inventory of sequestered books had still not been completed, and two years later Bruna asked the University to request the Provincial Committee to hand over the list of books from the Convent of Santa María Anunciata and from the College of San Hermenegildo so he could select the ones he wanted[14]. A royal decree of 1772 ordered Jesuit collections from all the Society's houses within the kingdom of Seville to be transferred to the Librería Episcopal, while those from Jesuit houses in the city itself were to go to the University[15]. However, by the

---

11   Antonio Ponz, *Viaje por España*, ed. Casto Maria del Rivero (Madrid, 1947), t. ix carta ix, and t. xvii carta v.

12   When José Cevallos had addressed this request to him in February 1769, the Regent replied that José de Aroca, in charge of drawing up the index, had not yet completed it; see Bonifacio Chamorro, 'Breve historia de la biblioteca de Jovellanos', *Bibliografía Hispánica*, 11 (1944), 755.

13   AHN, Inquisición de Corte leg 4210. Marcelin Defourneaux, *Inquisición y censura de libros en la España del siglo XVIII* (Madrid, 1973), 63.

14   AMS, Papeles importantes del s. xviii, t. 17. Cf. Aguilar Piñal, *Historia de la Universidad* de Sevilla (Sevilla, 1991), 269.

15   The "kingdom" ("reino") of Seville was a territorial jurisdiction of the Crown of Castile from the time it was won from Muslim rule in 1248 during the *Reconquista* until Javier de Burgos (1778–1848)' provincial division of Spain in 1833. The Crown of Castile consisted of several such kingdoms. Seville was one of the Four Kingdoms

time this measure was implemented most of the books had already been auctioned off to individual collectors. In 1781, Bruna complained that neither the Cardinal Archbishop Francisco de Solís y Folch de Cardona (1713–1775) nor the Cardinal Patriarch of the West Indies Francisco Javier Delgado Venegas (1714–1781), successive archbishops of Seville, had ordered the books to be brought to the city or had created space in the Archbishop's Palace for them, despite the instructions sent to them by the Regente and the Presidente de la Junta Provincial for confiscated property[16].

The final piece of the jigsaw we should take into account when studying the impact of the confiscation of Jesuit libraries on a single city – in our case Seville – is the fate of the libraries of the nobility or of leading members of the Administration: they were absorbed by the royal collections. For instance, the majority of Francisco de Bruna's books selected by librarians in 1807 for the King's Private and Public Libraries originally came from Jesuit houses in Seville.

To sum up, then, those who eventually benefited from the confiscation of the Jesuits' books were, in this order: first, private collectors interested in the regeneration of Spain, in scholarship and with an antiquarian disposition; second, the royal collections; and third, public education.

All three groups acquired material from Jesuit libraries that contained choice manuscript and printed books that were international in character and often had interesting bindings.

The sales of ecclesiastical property decreed in 1798 by Charles IV went on right up to 1808 and was the first full-blown confiscation of its kind in Spain. During those years no less than a sixth of the ecclesiastical buildings and lands were publicly auctioned. This process was made possible because the Pope had granted the King permission to expropriate a wide range of property: hospitals, hospices, poor houses, and university colleges. The aim of the expropriation was to improve public finances, and it went much further than the earlier confiscations carried out under liberal reformist governments during the reign of Charles III. All this has been thoroughly studied by Richard Herr and I refer you to his publications[17].

As an example let us look at the fate of the fine collections of books from university College libraries. In 1798, a royal decree by Charles IV ordered the dissolution of the Colleges that Charles III had previously reorganised. There were six such university Colleges in Spain, four of them were in Salamanca, the other two in Valladolid and Alcalá[18]. The library of the College of Santa Cruz in Valladolid, into which books from Jesuit houses throughout that province had been incorporated, and which now came under the jurisdiction of the Chancellery, passed in 1807 to the University of Valladolid. An inventory of this library was drawn up, and the 13,000 printed books and 336 manuscripts listed in it give some idea of the College's holdings. The books from the College of San Ildefonso in Alcalá de Henares were similarly incorporated into the library of the University of Alcalá. The "Inventory of books in the University Library to which have been added those from the College of San Ildefonso", made at that time, is another source allowing

---

of Andalusia. Falling largely within the present day autonomous region of Andalucia, it included roughly the territory of the present-day provinces of Huelva, Seville, and Cádiz, the Antequera Depression in the present-day province of Málaga, and also some municipalities in the present-day autonomous region of Extremadura in the province of Badajoz (source: Wikipedia [accessed Aug. 2021]).

16 RAH, col. Vargas Ponce, t. xiv. Cf. Aguilar Piñal, *La Universidad*, as note 6, 492.

17 Richard Herr, 'Hacia el derrumbe del Antiguo Régimen: crisis fiscal y desamortización bajo Carlos IV', *Moneda y crédito*, 118 (1971), 37–100.

18 *Novísima Recopilación*, Leyes 6ª, 7ª y 8ª, tit. 3º, lib. 8.- Real Cédula de 25 de septiembre de 1798.

us to appreciate the cultural importance of the libraries built up by those elite institutions that were the Colleges[19]. But what gives the clearest idea of the impact of Charles IV's expropriations is the history of the manuscripts once owned by the four university Colleges at Salamanca – San Bartolomé, Fonseca, Cuenca, and Oviedo. These important manuscripts were so valuable that, after they had been inventoried between 1799 and 1802, they were transferred to the King's private library. Loewe-Hartel's and Kristeller's catalogues show the enormous significance of this collection[20].

Expropriation was also carried out under Napoleon's brother, who sat on the Spanish throne as Joseph I during the French occupation between 1808 and 1813, and it continued under the nationalist Spanish Parliament. This paved the way for the two great nineteenth-century expropriations, which were the ones that had the greatest consequences for books and libraries in Spain. Mendizábal's, in 1835 to 1836, during the reign of Ferdinand VII (1784–1833), and Madoz's under Queen Isabel II (1830–1904), changed the face of the nation's book collections, and it is this new face that we still recognise in Spanish libraries today.

The Nineteenth-Century Confiscations: Madrid

These confiscations gave rise to a new urban and industrial society in Spain, and they changed the character of the country's institutions. By the middle of the nineteenth century, a conservative bourgeoisie, which had become a property-owning class thanks to the expropriations, was making its presence felt in the country. Among those who were buyers at the auctions of sequestered property the most notable were, on the one hand, the middle classes (merchants, lawyers, civil servants, industrialists and politicians), and on the other the aristocracy, especially those members of it who had been newly ennobled by Queen Isabel II, who succeeded Ferdinand VII in 1833. During her reign ancient titles, such as that of grandee of Spain, were reinstated and it became possible to enjoy such distinctions without possessing the landed estates that once went with them[21]. The grandees created by Isabel II speak for themselves: out of fifty such titles conferred during her reign, twenty went to generals and the remainder to courtiers whose names we immediately associate with book collecting and the ownership of magnificent private libraries. For instance we may name the financier José María de Salamanca (1811–1883), Count of Llanos and Marquis of Salamanca, who built the luxury quarter of Madrid that bears his name, and José María Pérez de Guzmán y Liaño (c. 1798–1876), Duke of T'Serclaes. The latter's sons – the second Duke and the Marquis of Jerez de los Caballeros – built up two of the best private libraries in Spain. The second Duke's collection is now one of the most important in the Hispanic Society of America. The library created by his twin brother was dispersed among various heirs; until recently books from it could still be bought at auction[22].

19 By royal decree of 20 February 1798, the duplicates resulting from this merger were put on sale. The measure had a dubious application. AHN, Universidades, Libro 1094.

20 Margarita Becedas, *El VII Centenario de la Universidad de Salamanca en la Biblioteca Universitaria* (Salamanca, 2011), 107–22. Gustav Loewe, *Bibliotheca Patrum Latinorum Hispaniensis*. Herausgegeben und bearbeitet von Wilhelm von Hartel (Vienna, 1887); Paul Oskar Kristeller, *Iter Italicum* (London, 1963).

21 Real Orden 4 diciembre 1864.

22 Palafox, duque de Zaragoza; Espartero, duque de la Victoria; Narváez, duque de Valencia; Prim, marqués de los Castillejos; Pezuela, conde de Cheste; Goyeneche, conde de Guaquil; Tacón, duque de la Unión de Cuba; Esteva, marqués de Esteva de las Delicias; Serrano, duque de la Torre; Gutiérrez de la Concha, marqués de la Habana. The other group consists of titles derived from marriage with the royal family: general Muñoz, second husband of Queen María Cristina, duque de

Madoz's expropriation coincided with economic disaster in Spain and the loss of its last colonies. Confiscated ecclesiastical and monastic libraries, as well as those of the ruined nobility, supplied a lucrative market dominated by traffickers in books rather than by scrupulous booksellers. Many items were sold in Paris, London and the US, feeding a collecting frenzy among foreign Hispanists[23].

But many confiscated collections were transferred to public and university libraries. The Biblioteca Nacional in Madrid holds not only many of the books themselves but also a large number of inventories of expropriated collections that came to it. At the same time books were bought, or simply "arrived" in the private libraries of a bourgeoisie with aristocratic aspirations, for whom a book-lined room was a status symbol. Or they were incorporated into the libraries of a new nobility that wished to identify itself with a practice of their longer-established peers, the building of a fine collection.

The history of old library collections mirrors the profound changes in Spanish society that took place during the nineteenth century and, with it, the consolidation of a system of public libraries in which the Biblioteca Nacional became the key player.

Riansares y de Tarancón and his sons, and the marqueses de Bondad Real (Gurowski y Borbón), and de Valcarlos (Güell y Borbón).

23 María Luisa López-Vidriero Abelló, 'Naturalismo bibliófilo: el portentoso hurto de la Real Biblioteca particular de Su Majestad'; John O'Neill, 'Archer M. Huntington y las primeras publicaciones de la HSA', in *Bibliofilia y nacionalismo: nueve ensayos sobre las artes contemporáneas del libro*, ed. Maria Luisa López-Vidriero Abelló, coord. Pablo Andrés Escapa (Salamanca, 2011), 85–146 and 244–71.

Bibliography

Manuscripts and Archival Sources

Madrid, Archivo Histórico Nacional [AHN], Inquisición de Corte leg 4210.
Madrid, Archivo Histórico Nacional [AHN], Universidades, Libro 1094.
Madrid, Real Academia de la Historia [RAH], col. Vargas Ponce, t. xiv.
Sevilla, Archivo Municipal de Sevilla [AMS], Papeles importantes del s. xviii, t. 17.

Secondary Works

Francisco Aguilar Piñal, *La Sevilla de Olavide* (Sevilla, 1966).
Francisco Aguilar Piñal, *La Universidad de Sevilla en el s. xviii. Estudio sobre la primera reforma universitaria moderna* (Sevilla, 1969).
Francisco Aguilar Piñal, *Historia de la Universidad* de Sevilla (Sevilla, 1991).
Aurora Alonso de Miguel, *La Biblioteca de los Reales Estudios de San Isidro. Su historia hasta la integración en la Universidad Central* (Madrid, 1996).
Margarita Becedas, *El VII Centenario de la Universidad de Salamanca en la Biblioteca Universitaria* (Salamanca, 2011).
Bonifacio Chamorro, 'Breve historia de la biblioteca de Jovellanos', *Bibliografía Hispánica*, 11 (1944), 17–36.
Colección general de las providencias tomadas por el gobierno sobre extrañamiento y ocupación de los regulares de la Compañía que existían en los dominios de S.M. de España, Indias y Filipinas (Madrid, 1967).
Marcelin Defourneaux, *Inquisición y censura de libros en la España del siglo XVIII* (Madrid, 1973).
España. Rey. Carlos III. Pragmática Sanción. El Pardo, 2 abril 1767.
Richard Herr, 'Hacia el derrumbe del Antiguo Régimen: crisis fiscal y desamortización bajo Carlos IV', *Moneda y crédito*, 118 (1971), 37–100.
Iglesia Católica. Papa, Clemente XIV. Breve. 1773. *Dominus ac Redemptor.*
Iglesia Católica. Papa, Pio VII. Bula. 1814. *Solicitudo omnium ecclesiarum.*
Paul Oskar Kristeller, *Iter Italicum* (London, 1963).
Maria Luisa López-Vidriero Abelló, 'Naturalismo bibliófilo: el portentoso hurto de la Real Biblioteca particular de Su Majestad', in *Bibliofilia y nacionalismo: nueve ensayos sobre coleccionismo y artes contemporáneas del libro*, ed. Maria Luisa López-Vidriero Abelló, coord. Pablo Andrés Escapa (Salamanca, 2011), 86–146.
Gustav Loewe, *Bibliotheca Patrum Latinorum Hispaniensis*. Herausgegeben und bearbeitet von Wilhelm von Hartel (Vienna, 1887).

Novísima recopilacion de las leyes de España: dividida en XII. libros, en que se reforma la Recopilacion publicada por el Señor Don Felipe II. en el año de 1567, reimpresa últimamente en el de 1775, 6 vols (Madrid, 1805–1807).

John O'Neill, 'Archer M. Huntington y las primeras publicaciones de la HSA', in *Bibliofilia y nacionalismo: nueve ensayos sobre las artes contemporáneas del libro*, ed. Maria Luisa López-Vidriero Abelló, coord. Pablo Andrés Escapa (Salamanca, 2011), 244–71.

Antonio Ponz, *Viaje por España*, ed. Casto Maria del Rivero (Madrid, 1947).

Antonio Rodríguez Villa, *Catálogo general de manuscritos de la Real Academia de la Historia* [online publication: https://www.rah.es/wp-content/uploads/2016/09/Cat_gen_manuscritos1.pdf].

Gabriel Sánchez Espinosa, 'Los libreros Ángel Corradi y Antoine Boudet y la importancistón de libros franceses para la academia de San Fernando', *Bulletin Hispanique*, 114–1 (2012), 195–216.

Jose Simón Díaz, *Historia del Colegio Imperial de Madrid*, 2 vols (Madrid, 1952–1959).

Javier Varela, *Jovellanos* (Madrid, 1988).

Voltaire [François-Marie Arouet], *Lettre CLXVII a M. le Marquis de Villevieille* (1775), in *Œuvres complètes: Recueil des lettres de M. de Voltaire*, 13: 1775–1778, v. 68, A. Gotha, Chez Charles-Guillaume Ettinger, Libraire, 1789, 295–96.

PEDRO RUEDA RAMÍREZ

The Secularization of Religious Houses in Latin America from Independence to the New Republics: Continuity and Fragmentation of Library Collections

During the process of secularization or confiscation of religious property, part of Latin American monastic and religious school libraries were turned over to the state. In this paper, we address three key periods: first, the expulsion of the Jesuits in 1767; second, independence from the Spanish Crown, which promoted the first secularization movement in Bolivia and Peru; and third, the secularization laws of the second half of the nineteenth century, which had a major impact on monastic collections in Mexico. In addition, we look at how the confiscated books became part of libraries and private collections, with a particular focus on some establishments that hold considerable numbers of books from the monasteries. Finally, we analyse some catalogues and some research on the provenance of books that can help us to reconstruct the former monastic collections. In particular, studies on ownership marks enable us to identify copies that are now preserved in South American public, university and national libraries and trace their monastic origins.

The process of nationalizing religious property was extremely complicated and unfolded in very different ways in different countries[1]. Here we provide a general overview that focuses on the main characteristics of the change that these books underwent when they left the Church and were transferred to a new owner. In these changes, the books' original use and target readership altered dramatically. The monastic libraries were used to teach doctrine to regular clergy, and they also provided education for students in religious school and support for the arguments with which to win over unbelievers and enemies; when the collections changed hands, they were removed from the context that

---

[1] Miranda Lida, 'La Iglesia católica en las más recientes historiografías de México y Argentina. Religión, modernidad y secularización', *Historia Mexicana*, 56, 4 (2007), 1393–1426.

Pedro Rueda Ramírez • Professor. University of Barcelona. pedrorueda@ub.edu

How the Secularization of Religious Houses Transformed the Libraries of Europe, 16th–19th Centuries, ed. by Cristina Dondi, Dorit Raines, and † Richard Sharpe, BIB, 63 (Turnhout, 2022), pp. 145–159.

BREPOLS ❧ PUBLISHERS   DOI 10.1484/M.BIB-EB.5.128483

had given them value and meaning for centuries. It would be a long time before these volumes were recognized as cultural heritage. In fact, they were frequently consigned to storerooms, and many books were lost or sold illegally. There are considerable gaps in knowledge about this rich bibliographical heritage, but researchers are increasingly interested in its study[2].

Jesuit Libraries after the Expulsion: the First Attempt at Secularization

A total of 2,606 Jesuits, scattered over a large area, were expelled from the territories of the Americas and the Philippines following an edict from the Spanish Crown in 1767[3]. Forty Jesuit schools and houses, as well as one hundred and fourteen missions, were closed in Mexico, Cuba and Guatemala alone[4]. The instructions sent by Charles III of Spain to the viceroys were passed on immediately to those responsible for confiscating the buildings. The orders stated that all assets had to be inventoried, including the books in the libraries and chambers. In Puebla de los Ángeles (Mexico), an inventory was drawn up of the Colegio del Espíritu Santo library (which is now preserved in the Biblioteca Lafragua at the Universidad Autónoma de Puebla). The inventory contained detailed information on 2,546 titles in the library. These books were transferred to other religious schools in the city and continued

to be used to train clergy and students[5]. The Spanish Crown took over the management of Jesuit properties. In many cases, it sold the goods and assets, but on occasions it distributed the churches and teaching establishments to other religious orders, which maintained the original activity[6].

The libraries of the Jesuit schools were given to other institutions belonging to the Crown or the Church. In Chile and Peru, Jesuit books were handed over to the universities that existed at that time[7]. This was the case of the books in the library of the Jesuit school the Colegio Máximo de San Pablo, which went to the Universidad de San Marcos de Lima. Indeed, a number of Latin American universities continue to have large collections that originally came from Jesuit schools (and other centres), such as the collection of the Biblioteca Central of the Universidad Nacional de San Antonio Abad del Cuzco[8]. In these cases, the confiscation radically altered the books' functional value, as they no longer fulfilled their original purpose of educating in the disciplines of the *Ratio Studiorum* (the Jesuit plan of studies). The expelled Jesuits had no option but to return to Europe, without their books or possessions. They left behind all their

---

2 Idalia García Aguilar, 'Imprenta y librerías jesuitas en la Nueva España', in *El libro en circulación en la América colonial: producción, circuitos de distribución y conformación de bibliotecas en los siglos XVI al XVIII* (México, 2014), 205–37.

3 Teófanes Egido, *Las causas "gravísimas" y secretas de la expulsión de los jesuitas por Carlos III* (Madrid, 1994).

4 Javier Burrieza Sánchez, *Jesuitas en Indias: entre la utopía y el conflicto: trabajos y misiones de la Compañía de Jesús en la América moderna* (Valladolid, 2007), 511.

5 Manuel E. Santiago Hernández, 'Biblioteca Histórica "José María Lafragua" de la Benemérita Universidad Autónoma de Puebla', *Pecia Complutense*, 7, 12 (2010), 38–53 (here 43): https://eprints.ucm.es/10036/1/pecia2.pdf, accessed 28 Nov. 2021.

6 Ignacio Osorio Romero, *Historia de las bibliotecas novohispanas* (México, 1986), 65–99. Carmen Castañeda, 'Libros: modernidad e Independencia', in Gladys Lizama Silva ed., *Modernidad y modernización en América Latina: México y Chile, siglos XVIII al XX* (Guadalajara, 2001), 249–75.

7 Luis Enrique Rodríguez San Pedro Bezares, 'Las Universidades Hispánicas: líneas de investigación e historiografía: siglos XV-XVIII', in *Historiografía y líneas de investigación en historia de las universidades: Europa mediterránea e Iberoamérica* (Salamanca, 2012), 17–78.

8 Pedro M. Guibovich Pérez, *Censura, libros e inquisición en el Perú colonial, 1570–1754* (Sevilla, 2003), 244.

papers, books, educational establishments and university chairs. This left a gap that was rapidly filled by other religious people, many of whom were secular clergy under the vigilant supervision of the Crown[9]. This process of secularization directly affected dozens of libraries throughout Latin America and the Philippines, which, in a matter of days, lost all their users.

At the beginning of the nineteenth century, some of the governments of the new republics, such as the Argentine government, promoted the recovery from educational establishments of books that had belonged to the Jesuits and their subsequent inclusion in national libraries. The main idea behind the opening of national libraries was to create places "for the use of inhabitants"[10]. The revolutionary committees of the first independent governments copied the models of European public libraries[11], and included a political component that clearly reflected the constitutional concepts. The opening of national libraries went hand in hand with the transformation of the people from subjects of the Spanish Crown to citizens of new nations. A spirit of freedom meant that books were considered objects that should be available to all citizens interested in culture or knowledge. In this new political climate, the libraries were regarded as bastions of knowledge to be entrusted with safeguarding national culture. This is reflected in the news articles and institutional speeches

related to the foundation and inauguration of the national libraries of Argentina and Mexico[12]. Yet the libraries did not always have sufficient material resources or librarians to meet these objectives. In many cases, the Jesuit books were included as a rich, varied resource used to form a solid base for the collections. For example, after the expulsion, Jesuit books in Chile were handed over to the Universidad de San Felipe. However, in 1818, Bernardo O'Higgins (1778–1842), the director of the Biblioteca Nacional de Chile, managed to get the books transferred to this library[13]. In Peru, the Colegio de San Pablo that had belonged to the Jesuits became the home of the National Library in 1821. The general and politician José de San Martín (1778–1850) wanted to open a public centre "for all people to use", in order to foster the "prosperity of the State"[14]. Consequently, after various vicissitudes, Jesuit books in Peru were transferred to this National Library.

Problems with these secularized assets would recur in different places and at different times. After independence, the Jesuits had very different relationships with the government in each country. In some cases, there were major confrontations. In Uruguay, for instance, in 1858, the president Gabriel Antonio Pereira (1794–1861) authorized the opening of Jesuit schools, but in the following year, a decree forced Jesuits to leave the Republic immediately[15]. Each time this cycle started again, the Jesuits formed new collections of books. Some of these have survived

9   Lucrecia Raquel Enríquez, 'El clero y la Independencia de Chile', in Josep-Ignasi Saranyana and Juan Bosco Amores Carredano eds, *Política y religión en la Independencia de la América hispana* (Madrid, 2011), 187–218; Enrique Villalba Pérez, *Consecuencias educativas de la expulsión de los jesuitas en América* (Madrid, 2003).

10 Gonzalo B. Catalán and Bernardo Jorquera, 'Biblioteca Nacional de Chile', in *Historia de las bibliotecas nacionales de Iberoamérica* (México, 1995), 133–92 (here 162).

11 Alejandro E. Parada, *De la biblioteca particular a la biblioteca pública: libros, lectores y pensamiento bibliotecario en los orígenes de la Biblioteca Pública de Buenos Aires, 1779–1812* (Buenos Aires, 2002).

12 J.-F. Finó and Luis A. Hourcade, *Evolución de la bibliotecología en la Argentina: 1757–1952* (Santa Fe, 1952).

13 Catalán and Jorquera, 'Biblioteca Nacional de Chile', as note 10, 133–92.

14 Gladys Padró Montezuma and José Tamayo Herrera, 'Biblioteca Nacional del Perú', in *Historia de las bibliotecas nacionales de Iberoamérica* (México, 1995), 419–39 (here 420).

15 Tomás Sansón Corbo, 'La Iglesia y el proceso de secularización en el Uruguay moderno (1859–1919)', *Hispania Sacra*, 63, 127 (2011), 283–303 (here 292).

until present times, such as the Eusebio F. Kino library of the Mexican Province of the Society of Jesus, whose particularly diverse and valuable collection comes from donations, acquisitions on the second-hand book market, and other such sources[16].

Fragmentation: the New Republics

During the years 1804–1809, measures ordered by King Charles IV of Spain led to the confiscation in the Americas of the properties and ground rents of charitable institutions, including hospitals, hospices, and houses of mercy for the relief of the poor. The aim of this reform was to obtain money for the Crown[17]. Then the period of war against Napoleon (1808–1814) completely changed the political map. At this time, measures were implemented such as the abolition of the Inquisition and the transfer of its assets to the State. After the war, King Ferdinand VII (1784–1833) returned to power and immediately reinstated the Inquisition[18]. Pope Pius VII rescinded the suppression of the Society of Jesus, and the Jesuits returned to the Americas, and some of their assets, particularly churches and schools, were given back to them. Thus, the absolute monarchy overruled many of the liberal proposals[19]. However, on their return in 1816, they found many of their buildings in ruins[20]. Subsequently, political changes happened

very rapidly and the independence of the new American republics opened new perspectives in the relationships between the Church and the state[21]. For example, although the new states needed to rebuild diplomatic relations with Rome, in many cases this process became a source of tension and conflict when the liberal factions argued for various changes, including the separation between the Church and the state and the renegotiation of the clergy's privileges.

Political debates on the relationships between the Church and the new states involved both liberals and conservatives. The proposals, which were gathered in constitutional texts, focused on the role that the new leaders should play in their relationship with the churches in each national territory and on the contribution of clergy to the patriotic construction of the republics. Another priority was to rebuild relationships with Rome and, consequently, for the pope to recognize the new nations. In the case of Mexico, Rosas Salas proposes that this happened in two stages: first, in the period between the end of the War of Independence and 1855, which was characterized by the religious agreements between ecclesiastical leaders and republican governments and by the close ties that existed between the interests of the religious elite and leading political groups; and second, in the period that began in 1859 with the promulgation of the *Leyes de Reforma* (Reform Laws), which favoured the legal separation of the Church and the state. In Mexico, as we will see, this was accompanied by a far-reaching process of secularization, which affected the religious libraries[22].

In addition, there was intense debate on the reform and state control of secular and regular clergy. The question of state control was

16 Leticia Ruiz Rivera, *Catálogo de sermones mexicanos de la Biblioteca Eusebio F. Kino de la provincia mexicana de la Compañía de Jesús* (Madrid, 2006).

17 Juvenal Jaramillo Magaña, 'Fiscalidad en Nueva España. El obispo y el Cabildo Catedral de Michoacán ante la crisis fiscal borbónica', *América Latina en la Historia Económica*, 20, 3 (2013), 56–89; Germán Rueda, *La desamortización en España: un balance: 1766-1924* (Madrid, 1997).

18 Ibid.

19 Ibid.

20 Burrieza Sánchez, *Jesuitas en Indias*, as note 4, 540.

21 Manuel Revuelta González, *La exclaustración, 1833–1840* (Madrid, 1976).

22 Sergio Francisco Rosas Salas, 'De la República católica al Estado laico: Iglesia, Estado y secularización en México, 1824–1914', *Lusitania Sacra*, 25 (2012), 227–44. http://hdl.handle.net/10400.14/9838, accessed 21 Jan. 2022.

particularly controversial. In Chile, there was an attempt in 1818 to bring regular clergy under the authority of the diocesan, rather than the orders' generals[23]. In Argentina, the religious reform of 1822 aimed to constitute a "republican church" that would make clergy government employees[24]. This created constant conflicts with the orders and with Rome. The solutions were different in each of the new republics.

In some cases, these relationships deteriorated, and the monasteries and libraries were abolished. Antonio José de Sucre (1795–1830) proclaimed the Republic of Bolivia in the area of Upper Peru (Charcas) including an area that occupied much of what is modern day Bolivia and southern Peru. On 29 March 1826, he ordered the abolition of monasteries of regular clergy, stating that "the district governors will preserve all the archives, paintings, books and other possessions of the abolished monasteries and will send inventories to the government"[25]. The idea was that the new Bolivian state would find new uses for these possessions. In these early times, the secularization process was linked to the work of a committee on the Church, which was republican in this case. These first measures were extended to all Peruvian territories in the first period of the country's independence. In a decree published on 28 September 1826, the new republican state ordered the closure of all the monasteries which

had fewer than eight resident clerics and declared that no town or village could have more than one convent of any religious order[26]. Between 1826 and 1840, 61 monasteries were closed down (28 in the diocese of Lima, 14 in Trujillo, seven in Huamanga, five in Cuzco, four in Arequipa and one in Chachapoyas). The process affected the orders that had the most establishments, Dominicans, Fransciscans and Mercedarians. In 1775, the Mercedarians had 15 monasteries. In the secularization process, they lost ten establishments as well as several schools[27]. The buildings were taken over by national schools and state offices, and their income was used for seminaries, parish churches, or charitable institutions.

In the rest of Latin American territories, the leaders tried to get the Church to support the recently established constitutional policies[28]. In this case, the safeguarding of religious property by the states was essential to the Church. In territories in which there was successful collaboration between bishops and politicians, the Church managed to keep many of its properties intact. In Peru, liberal sectors began a reform in 1848, but its scope was limited and its nature pragmatic. In this new phase, the Peruvian leaders, many of whom were traders, landowners or professionals,

23 Enríquez, 'El clero y la Independencia de Chile', as note 9, 209.

24 Francisco Di Stefano, 'El clero de Buenos Aires en la primera mitad del siglo XIX', in Valentina Ayrolo ed., *Estudios sobre el clero iberoamericano, entre la Independencia y el Estado-Nación* (Salta, 2006), 203–26 (here 213).

25 *Colección oficial de leyes, decretos, órdenes, & de la República Boliviana: años 1825 y 1826* (La Paz, [c. 1827]), 145: https://scholarship.rice.edu/jsp/xml/1911/27090/1/aa00380.tei.html, accessed 17 Apr. 2020. Alicia Fraschina, 'Reformas en los conventos de monjas de Hispanoamérica: 1750–1865. Cambios y continuidades', *Hispania Sacra*, 60, 122 (2008), 445–66.

26 Fernando Armas Asín, 'Iglesia, Estado y economía en la coyuntura independentista en el Perú', *Anuario de Historia de la Iglesia*, 17 (2008), 163–78 (here 168). Pilar García Jordán, '¿Poder eclesiástico frente a poder civil? Algunas reflexiones sobre la Iglesia peruana ante la formación del estado moderno (1808–1860)', *Boletín Americanista*, 26, 34 (1984), 45–74.

27 Ibid., 169–70.

28 Agustín Sánchez Andrés, 'El marco constitucional de las relaciones entre Iglesia y Estado en América del Sur (1811–1900)', *Hispania Sacra*, 50, 102 (1998), 589–610 (here 590). Francisco Di Stefano, 'Disidencia religiosa y secularización en el siglo XIX Iberoamericano: cuestiones conceptuales y metodológicas', *Projeto História. Revista do Programa de Estudos de Pós-Graduação em História*, 37 (2008). https://revistas.pucsp.br/index.php/revph/article/view/3050 accessed 28 Nov. 2021.

were not interested in creating conflicts with the Church[29]. The Peruvian Constitution of 1860 introduced measures such as secular schools and the abolition of ecclesiastical courts, but the Church kept its assets and some degree of autonomy. In other states, such as Mexico, this situation did not arise, and the negotiations intensified. A number of cases are analyzed below.

Political Disputes: Religious Identity and Secularization

Cooperation with the Church deteriorated as positions became more radical. Liberal newspapers began very critical campaigns against the clergy's wealth and the payments that the faithful had to make (payment of church fees and tithes, among others), on freedom of religion, and on the role of the Church in education. In this debate, bills began to be drawn up that declared all assets held in mortmain to belong to the nation. This included all assets, and land in particular, that were not on the market as they were tied up as Church properties. This idea fuelled the practice of confiscation, in which the aim was to free up assets so that they could be auctioned. Hence, such assets would be put on the market for the bourgeois to acquire, which would free up land and boost the economy. These liberal principles were rejected by the Church. Upon setting out for Mexico during the reign of Emperor Maximilian I, the apostolic nuncio Pier Francesco Meglia was advised by the secretary of state to Pius IX, Cardinal Giacomo Antonelli, that Mexico's liberal and conservative factions wanted the same reforms and differed only in their opinion of how quickly their government should change its

relations with the Holy See[30]. Bishop José María de Jesús Belaunzarán (1772–1857) considered that church property was outside of civil authority and inalienable by nature[31]. These arguments were refuted. The Mexican Finance Minister Guillermo Prieto (1818–1897) stated that the clergy's assets had not become national property on a specific date but had always belonged to the nation[32]. In Latin American countries, arguments that were pro-secularization and pro-nationalization of church property were to gain strength, particularly after the victory of liberal governments in the latter part of the nineteenth century.

The timing of this process varied from country to country. The extent of the changes and reforms depended on the balance of power between conservatives and liberals, and on the power of the Church itself. In 1871, Joaquín Blengio (1834–1901), who was rector of the Campechano Institute (Campeche, Mexico), stated in a very rhetorical speech on libraries that "electricity is now made everywhere. Today, everyone reads, everyone broadens their mind. Knowledge is no longer the exclusive privilege of a small circle … science is no longer the property of a priestly caste". With these arguments, Professor Blengio considered that books were overcoming "absolutism and tyranny and achieving democracy and freedom of thought"[33]. This speech illustrates Blengio's liberal ideology, which was similar to that of many other supporters of secularization. His rather utopian idea was to diminish the role of the clergy and the role of the military as he wanted "armouries to become libraries, and barracks, universities"[34].

---

29 Jeffrey Klaiber, 'La reorganización de la Iglesia ante el estado liberal en el Perú (1860–1930)', in *Historia general de la Iglesia en América Latina* (Salamanca, 1987), vol. 8, 277–307 (here 282).

30 Marta Eugenia García Ugarte, *Poder político y religioso: México, siglo XIX* (México, 2010), 12.

31 Moisés González Navarro, *Anatomía del poder en México, 1848–1853* (México, 1977), 106–15 (here 106).

32 Robert J. Knowlton, *Los bienes del clero y la reforma mexicana: 1856–1910* (México, 1985), 127.

33 *Inauguracion de la Biblioteca Nacional de México: abril 2 de 1884* (México, 1884), 72.

34 Ibid., 75.

In any case, weapons also played a role in some countries. In Guatemala, the president and dictator Justo Rufino Barrios (1835–1885) had gained power by military means. In 1872, he expelled the religious orders and seized the Church's property[35].

Secularization and the Expropriation of Church Property

As in Catholic Europe, the clergy in the new Latin American republics were divided into secular and regular clergy. In Mexico, in 1852, secular clergy predominated and were strongly established in the country. In total, there was one archbishopric and ten bishoprics, the collegiate church of Guadalupe, 1,229 parish churches and 3,223 ecclesiastics. The regular clergy from different orders also had a long tradition in the country, but less overall influence. There were 146 monasteries (with 1,139 individuals), 59 nunneries (with 1,541 nuns, 879 female servants, etc.) and eight *Colegios de Propaganda Fide* (schools for the propagation of the faith) for preparing missions[36]. The data are approximate and changed over time.

These two hundred and more Mexican monasteries were the target of the *Leyes de Reforma* (Reform Laws) approved between 1855 and 1874, which began the process of secularization of church property. The act of 12 July 1859 dealt with the expropriation of church property and the abolition of religious corporations, such as orders, institutes, brotherhoods and other entities[37]. Among the expropriated or "nationalized" possessions were "the books and documents kept

in the many colonial monasteries, which had to be transferred to public institutions such as existing museums, secondary schools, and libraries"[38].

Scattered Heritage: the Breaking up of Collections

In Mexico, the Reform Laws marked the end of the monastic use of churches and chapels, the closure of schools run by clergy, and the loss of all their property – including the libraries. Secularization had already taken place in Spain as a result of the confiscation laws there[39]. However, it occurred later in Mexican territories, in the context of patriotic politics that sought to "nationalize" church property and reduce the clergy's influence on educational institutions, charities, etc. From then on, these tasks would be carried out by the federal states of the Mexican Republic[40].

The federal structure of Mexico is one reason why the nationalization and sale of property developed in different ways depending on the state. In some cases, church buildings were boarded up and fell into disrepair. The disappearance of paintings, sculptures, and altarpieces began to be noted[41]. In other cases, monastic books were transferred to other institutions, such as public libraries, university libraries, or other teaching and research centres. This process affected many collections

35   Jean Meyer, 'La Iglesia', in *Historia general de América Latina* (Madrid, 1999–2008), vol. 6 (2003), 227–50 (here 241).

36   González Navarro, *Anatomía del poder en México*, as note 31, 114–15.

37   Julio César Olivé Negrete and Bolfy Cottom, *INAH, una historia* (México, 2003), vol. 3: *Leyes, reglamentos, circulares y acuerdos*, 219–27 (Ley de nacionalización de bienes eclesiásticos).

38   Idalia García Aguilar, 'Llover sobre mojado: la Librería del Colegio Apostólico de Nuestro Padre San Francisco de Pachuca', in Jaime Ríos Ortega ed., *7º Seminario Hispano Mexicano de Investigación en Bibliotecología y Documentación* (México, 2011), 101–33 (here 102).

39   Ramiro Lafuente López, *Un mundo pocos visible: imprenta y bibliotecas en México durante el siglo XIX* (México, 1992).

40   Carmen Vázquez Mantecón, Alfonso Flamenco Ramírez and Carlos Herrero Bervera, *Las bibliotecas mexicanas en el siglo XIX* (México, 1987).

41   Jan Bažant, *Alienation of church wealth in Mexico: social and economic aspects of the liberal revolution, 1856–1875* (Cambridge, 1971), 217.

from monasteries and nunneries and occurred in stages. The eight most important monasteries in the city of Mexico were seized by government administrators in just a few hours, following orders given on 5 February 1861. On 26 February 1863, President Benito Juárez (1806–1872) declared that "all communities of nuns" were abolished. Nuns from the convent of San José de Gracia de México had eight days to hand over the place and leave. Their convent library was secularized, although we do not know what happened to the books, but, like many other monastic libraries, traces of the collection were lost over the years. However, in the twentieth century, a lot of 145 titles from this library were purchased to be incorporated into the "José María Basagoiti" Historical Archive[42].

In terms of the treatment of books, the Reform Laws were not implemented in a careful, controlled way, and much of the monastic heritage was lost. Books were taken to various storerooms and libraries with no control or supervision. This disorganized transfer led to many books being stolen, lost or damaged. In Zacatecas (Mexico) the monastic books were given to the public library to create a special collection. This is now called the Biblioteca de Colecciones Especiales "Elías Amador" (The Elías Amador Library of Special Collections). The transfer of these books to the State Public Library was described by the historian Cuauhtémoc Esparza Sánchez in the *Compendio histórico del Colegio Apostólico de Propaganda Fide, de Nuestra Señora de Guadalupe de Zacatecas*. His statement indicates that the books were transported in carts, and that no care was taken to protect them:

The pillage reached its peak in the library. To improve the State Public Library, all the books were removed and taken to the city of Zacatecas in open carts. Many books were lost, as with every jolt of the vehicles, volumes fell to the ground and were picked up by passers-by, with the knowledge and consent of the driver, who sometimes acted with even greater generosity, as he lavishly handed out piles of books to those who requested them. Another sizeable part [of the collection] was taken in the same way to Tlaltenango, for the parish priest Rafael Herrera, who obtained them as a result of his friendship with General González Ortega[43].

According to the editor and bibliographer Felipe Teixidor (1895–1980), the beginning of secularization in 1861 was "the year of abundance for Mexican bibliophiles", as some of the books fell into private hands, particularly those of booksellers and collectors[44]. These individuals took advantage of the circumstances to appropriate many books, both when the Reform Laws were implemented and at a later date. In addition, books were taken out of Mexico and sold in auctions in London, Paris, and the United States. In 1868, a sales catalogue was published (*Bibliotheca Mejicana. Catalogue d'une riche collection… réunie au Mexique*, Paris, 1868) that listed the books of an anonymous "attaché à la Cour de Maximilien". Auctions of Mexican books were held in Leipzig and London in 1869 (*Bibliotheca Mejicana; a catalogue of an extraordinary collection of books and manuscripts … particularly Mexico*, London, 1869; *Catalogue de la riche bibliothèque de D. José María Andrade*, Leipzig, 1869)[45]. The books on offer included many copies of works that had been published in Mexico, which were rare in the European book market. This was the case with books in indigenous languages. These books

42   Ana Rita Valero de García Lascuráin and Nora Deveaux Cabrera, 'Vizcaínas: un proyecto de conservación, desarrollo social y cultural mexicano con 280 años de historia', *Corpus*, 3, 2 (2013): http://corpusarchivos.revues.org/589, accessed 17 Apr. 2020.

43   García Aguilar, 'Llover sobre mojado', as note 38, 102.
44   Felipe Teixidor, *Ex libris y bibliotecas de México* (México, 1931).
45   Ibid., xxii.

became part of the collections of the Bibliothèque Nationale de France, the Hof-Bibliothek in Vienna, and the Bancroft Collection at Berkeley in California[46]. The high numbers of monastic volumes in the book market were observed by Adolph Sutro (1830–1898), a US millionaire, on a visit to Mexico in 1889. Sutro bought the entire stock of the bookseller Eufemio Abadiano and transported it to California[47]. The books he purchased included volumes from the Colegio Imperial de Santa Cruz de Tlatelolco library, an educational establishment founded in 1536. After the destruction of a large part of the collection in the 1906 earthquake, Sutro's heirs donated the Mexican books which remained intact to the California State Library. Other monastic books, with the ownership "fire marks" (*marcas de fuego*) of each school, house or monastery, were scattered in collections worldwide[48].

National Libraries and Secularized Collections

The media and political parties played a key role in all the ideological conflicts on secularization. On 2 January 1861, the newspaper *El Monitor Republicano* suggested that it was necessary "to draw up and implement plans for a National Library that is worthy of Mexico, in which

are used the wealth of documents that must now be gathered"[49]. This statement reveals the expectations of the press, which proposed that the National Library would be an ideal place for the monastic collections. However, things were not so easy for the people responsible for managing these collections. The Mexican National Library was to suffer enormously from political upheavals in the nineteenth century. Like a tapestry, it was formed and then frequently dismantled. In 1833, its creation was ordered and it was established that it should include the books from the Colegio Mayor de Santa María de Todos los Santos, which had been closed in 1829, and collections from the Real y Pontificia Universidad de México. However, the complex political circumstances in Mexico meant that plans for the new library could not be consolidated. The foundation of a National Library was ordered again in a decree on 30 November 1867. This was to be established in different premises, a former monastery building. Nevertheless, the building was not opened as the National Library until 1884, seventeen years after its foundation had been decreed. This new building should, as its director indicated, have received the books "from the former monasteries and from the library that had belonged to the Cathedral"[50]. The opening event was a celebration with laudatory poems and symphonic music, but there were numerous problems with the new library building, whose design was inadequate for its purpose and lacked the resources required to fully implement the library archiving policies of the day. For this reason, although the volumes were stored there they were not actually ordered or catalogued for a considerable period of time. Without going into further detail, however, it

46 Ignacio Osorio Romero and Boris Berenzon Gorn, 'Biblioteca Nacional de México', in *Historia de las bibliotecas nacionales de Iberoamérica* (México, 1995), 325–63 (here 333).

47 W. Michael Mathes, 'La colección mexicana de la biblioteca Sutro de San Francisco, California', *Quinto centenario*, 2 (1981), 213–18: https://dialnet.unirioja.es/ejemplar/137786, accessed 17 Apr. 2020.

48 The practice of burning marks into the fore edge of books with a hot metal stamp was in use in Mexican religious libraries from the late sixteenth until the early nineteenth century. See *Catálogo colectivo de marcas de fuego*: www.marcasdefuego.buap.mx/, accessed 17 Apr. 2020.

49 Teixidor, *Ex libris y bibliotecas de México*, as note 44, 393. Idalia García Aguilar, *Miradas aisladas, visiones conjuntas: defensa del patrimonio documental mexicano* (México, 2001).

50 *Inauguracion de la Biblioteca Nacional de México*, as note 33, 10.

is enough to say that this library now has an extraordinary collection from the monasteries. The library itself calculates that there are 90,000 volumes, which form part of a collection called *Fondo de Origen* (the Original Collection)[51]. This name is due to the 1867 decree to establish that the monastic collections should be moved into the new library.

The Recovery of Lost Heritage from the Monasteries

One of the first studies on the provenance of monastic books was that of Rafael Sala, who published *Marcas de fuego de las antiguas bibliotecas mexicanas* (The fire marks of Mexican monastic libraries, 1925). This essay described the ownership marks of the monasteries that had been closed down. The author, however, was not concerned to link these "fire marks" with the books that he had examined or to provide information on the libraries and collections in which he had seen them. Felipe Teixidor researched in greater depth the fire marks and *ex libris* in books from the former monasteries that were owned by booksellers and bibliophiles. Teixidor's book, published in 1931, was one of the first studies of the origin of monastic collections. These marks were of more interest to bibliophiles than to librarians, as they could be used to find out about (and value) the books that could be purchased on the antique market and in the Mexican bookshops of the time. However, some librarians did realize the enormous value of these marks for reconstructing collections[52]. In general, very little

has been published on this topic at local level in Mexico, and the scattered collections have not been connected or reconstructed[53]. As a result, researchers and librarians have collaborated to create the *Catálogo Colectivo de Marcas de Fuego* (Joint Catalogue of Fire Marks)[54]. This project will lead to considerable advances in the reconstruction of the collections and in the preservation of heritage assets.

There are other challenges for bibliographic heritage from the former monasteries. In some cases, the measures needed to safeguard and monitor the books have not been implemented. In other cases, the books have been treated as museum pieces that can be visited as part of a tourist route. This can be seen in the Palafoxiana Library in Puebla[55] or the Elías Amador Library in Zacatecas (both in Mexico)[56]. It has not always been easy for researchers to consult the material. These difficulties have delayed access to the collections and dissemination of knowledge about them. In Latin America, there are many descriptive publications (printed book catalogues and institutional studies on some libraries, among others), but there is no comprehensive analysis of the heritage problems resulting from secularization. One important

---

51   Biblioteca Nacional de México, *La Biblioteca Nacional de México: testimonios y documentos para su historia*, ed. María del Carmen Ruiz Castañeda, Luis Mario Schneider and Miguel Ángel Castro (México, 2004).

52   Rafael Sala, *Marcas de fuego de las antiguas bibliotecas mexicanas* (México, 1925). Manuel Villagrán Reyes, *Marcas de fuego de las librerías conventuales en la*

Biblioteca 'Elías Amador' de Zacatecas (Zacatecas, 1992).

53   Idalia García Aguilar, 'El fuego y la tinta, testimonios de bibliotecas conventuales novohispanas', *Inventio, la génesis de la cultura universitaria en Morelos*, 11 (2010), 101–09: https://dialnet.unirioja.es/descarga/articulo/3235828.pdf, accessed 17 Apr. 2020.

54   Which can be consulted at: http://www.marcasdefuego. buap.mx:8180/xmLibris/projects/firebrand/, accessed 17 Apr. 2020. Mercedes Isabel Salomón Salazar, and Andrew Green, 'Las marcas de fuego: propuesta de una metodología para su identificación', in Idalia García and Pedro Rueda eds, *Leer en tiempos de la Colonia: imprenta, bibliotecas y lectores en Nueva España* (México, 2010), 341–67.

55   http://web.archive.org/web/20071011201620/http://www.bpm.gob.mx/inicio.asp, accessed 17 Apr. 2020.

56   https://www.zacatecas.gob.mx/biblioteca-elias-amador-tesoro-invaluable-de-america/, accessed 29 Nov. 2021.

centre for monastic collections is the Mexican Instituto Nacional de Antropología e Historia (INAH), which has a very large collection of manuscripts and printed works. The Biblioteca Nacional de Antropología e Historia "Dr Eusebio Dávalos Hurtado"[57] (Dr Eusebio Dávalos Hurtado National Library of Anthropology and History), a part of the INAH, received collections from former monasteries that were brought together in the *Fondo Conventual* (Monastic Collection). This collection includes books from at least 77 monasteries belonging to ten religious orders and contains a total of 28,966 volumes.

Some private institutions have played an important role in drawing up catalogues of monastic heritage collections. The Spanish Fundación Histórica Tavera[58] funded the cataloguing of the old collections of several Peruvian or Bolivian libraries[59]. In Mexico, Apoyo al Desarrollo de Archivos y Bibliotecas de México (Support for the Development of Mexican Archives and Libraries) has published numerous catalogues for each one of the institutions that it has been involved with in Mexico[60]. In some cases, the religious orders themselves set up projects to recover their heritage. One of these is the Biblioteca Franciscana (Franciscan Library), which is housed in the *Portal de Peregrinos* building of the San Gabriel Cholula monastery in Puebla (Mexico). The aim of the Franciscan Library is to "preserve, research, and disseminate the bibliographic heritage of the Order"[61]. This is an interesting model that has brought together the books that make up the heritage of the order, after signing an agreement with the Universidad de Las Américas. Thus, private initiatives and the desire to disseminate knowledge about bibliographic heritage are contributing to increasing knowledge about the collections.

Nevertheless, most of the catalogues are local, and union catalogue projects do not have a wide scope. The *Catálogo Colectivo de Fondos Antiguos de las Bibliotecas Nacionales de Iberoamérica* (Union Catalogue of Old Collections in Latin American National Libraries), which is promoted by the *Asociación de Bibliotecas Nacionales de Iberoamérica* (ABINIA), has only limited results[62]. In 2012 this organization inaugurated the portal *Biblioteca Digital del Patrimonio Iberoamericano*, which provides access to digital collections of the bibliographic and documental heritage of eight different national libraries in Ibero-America[63]. Another interesting project that is in its early stages is the *Catálogo Colectivo de Fondos Antiguos* (Union Catalogue of Old Collections, Mexican bibliographic heritage). Since 2001, this catalogue has brought together the collections of several institutions[64]. It can be used to locate editions, but the local catalogues still need to be searched to find

---

57   https://www.bnah.inah.gob.mx/index.php?id=19, accessed 17 Apr. 2020.

58   http://www.larramendi.es/cms/elemento.cmd?id=ms/menendezpelayo/paginas/m_pelayo_fund_tavera.html, accessed 11 May 2017.

59   *Catálogos bibliográficos: fondo antiguo del Archivo y Biblioteca Nacionales de Bolivia, fondo antiguo del Archivo-Biblioteca Arquidiocesanos Monseñor Taborga de Sucre* (*Bolivia*) ([Madrid], 2003); *Catálogos: fondo antiguo de la Biblioteca de la Universidad Nacional de San Antonio Abad del Cuzco* (*Perú*). *Fondo antiguo de la Biblioteca del Convento Franciscano de Tarata* (*Bolivia*) ([Madrid], 1998).

60   The inventories and catalogues are online at https://www.adabi.org.mx/index.php/publicaciones-menu.html, accessed 17 Apr. 2020.

61   https://biblio.udlap.mx/franciscana/, accessed 17 Apr. 2020.

62   Luisa Orera Orera, 'El control y acceso al patrimonio bibliográfico a través de los catálogos disponibles en Internet', *Documentación de las ciencias de la información*, 30 (2007), 9–23 (here 19).

63   http://www.iberoamericadigital.net/BDPI/, accessed 29 Nov. 2021.

64   Rosa María Fernández de Zamora, 'Hacia el catálogo colectivo nacional de fondos antiguos: patrimonio bibliográfico mexicano', in *XXXIV Jornadas Mexicanas de Biblioteconomía, Puerto Vallarta, Jalisco* (*México*) (México, 2003), 151–56. http://eprints.rclis.org/6105/, accessed 17 Apr. 2020.

information about specific copies (including their ownership marks). This is the case with monastic books in the Original Collection of the National Library of Mexico (which has been associated with the Universidad Nacional Autónoma de México since 1914)[65]. Information about these books can be found in the Nautilo catalogue[66].

There are insufficient studies on the provenance of the preserved collections. The lack of planning at national level, the legal ambiguity in heritage assets, and the libraries' lack of resources have hindered the consolidation of projects. However, some important initiatives have been set up, which indicate that the trend is positive.

---

65 http://bnm.unam.mx/, accessed 17 Apr. 2020.
66 https://catalogo.iib.unam.mx/F/-/?func=find-b-0&local_base=BNM, accessed 17 Apr. 2020.

Bibliography

Andrés Agustín Sánchez, 'El marco constitucional de las relaciones entre Iglesia y Estado en América del Sur (1811–1900)', *Hispania Sacra*, 50, 102 (1998), 589–610.

Fernando Armas Asín, 'Iglesia, Estado y economía en la coyuntura independentista en el Perú', *Anuario de Historia de la Iglesia*, 17 (2008), 163–78.

Jan Bažant S., *Alienation of church wealth in Mexico: social and economic aspects of the liberal revolution, 1856–1875* (Cambridge: Cambridge University Press, 1971).

Biblioteca Nacional de México, *La Biblioteca Nacional de México: testimonios y documentos para su historia*. Compilación y edición, María del Carmen Ruiz Castañeda, Luis Mario Schneider, Miguel Ángel Castro (México, D.F.: UNAM, Biblioteca Nacional, 2004).

Javier Burrieza Sánchez, *Jesuitas en Indias: entre la utopía y el conflicto: trabajos y misiones de la Compañía de Jesús en la América moderna* (Valladolid: Universidad de Valladolid. Secretariado de Publicaciones e Intercambio Editorial, 2007).

Carmen Castañeda, 'Libros: modernidad e Independencia', in Gladys Lizama Silva (ed.), *Modernidad y modernización en América Latina: México y Chile, siglos XVIII al XX* (Guadalajara, Jalisco: Universidad de Guadalajara: Centro de Investigaciones Diego Barros Arana, 2001), 249–75.

Gonzalo Catalán B., and Bernardo Jorquera, 'Biblioteca Nacional de Chile', in *Historia de las bibliotecas nacionales de Iberoamérica* (México, D.F.: Universidad Nacional Autónoma de México, 1995), 133–92.

Colección oficial de leyes, decretos, órdenes, & de la República Boliviana: años 1825 y 1826 (La Paz: Imprenta artística, [c. 1827]). http://books.google.es/ accessed 27 January 2012.

Francisco Di Stefano, 'Disidencia religiosa y secularización en el siglo XIX Iberoamericano: cuestiones conceptuales y metodológicas', *Projeto História. Revista do Programa de Estudos de Pós-Graduação em História*, 37 (2008) https://revistas.pucsp.br/index.php/revph/article/view/3050 Accessed 29 Nov. 2021.

Francisco Di Stefano, 'El clero de Buenos Aires en la primera mitad del siglo XIX', in Valentina Ayrolo (ed.), *Estudios sobre el clero iberoamericano, entre la Independencia y el Estado-Nación* (Salta: Universidad Nacional de Salta. Centro Promocional de Investigaciones en Historia y Antropología, 2006), 203–26.

Teófanes Egido, *Las causas "gravísimas" y secretas de la expulsión de los jesuitas por Carlos III* (Madrid: Fundación Universitaria Española, 1994).

Lucrecia Raquel Enríquez, 'El clero y la Independencia de Chile', in Josep-Ignasi Saranyana, and Juan Bosco Amores Carredano (eds), *Política y religión en la Independencia de la América hispana* (Madrid: Biblioteca de Autores Cristianos: Universidad de Navarra, 2011), 187–218.

Rosa María Fernández de Zamora, 'Hacia el catálogo colectivo nacional de fondos antiguos: patrimonio bibliográfico mexicano', in *XXXIV Jornadas Mexicanas de Biblioteconomía, Puerto Vallarta, Jalisco*

(*México*) (México, D.F.: Asociación Mexicana de Bibliotecarios, A.C., 2003), 151–56 http://eprints.rclis. org/7562/1/34jornadas.pdf accessed 29 Nov. 2021.

J.-F. Finó, and Luis A. Hourcade, *Evolución de la bibliotecología en la Argentina: 1757–1952* (Santa Fe: Imprenta de la Universidad, 1952).

Alicia Fraschina, 'Reformas en los conventos de monjas de Hispanoamérica: 1750–1865. Cambios y continuidades', *Hispania Sacra*, 60, 122 (2008), 445–66.

Idalia García Aguilar, 'El fuego y la tinta, testimonios de bibliotecas conventuales novohispanas', *Inventio, la génesis de la cultura universitaria en Morelos*, 11 (2010), 101–09 https://dialnet.unirioja.es/servlet/fichero_ articulo?codigo=3235828&orden=0 accessed 21 Feb. 2012.

Idalia García Aguilar, 'Imprenta y librerías jesuitas en la Nueva España', in *El libro en circulación en la América colonial: producción, circuitos de distribución y conformación de bibliotecas en los siglos XVI al XVIII* (México, 2014), 205–37.

Idalia García Aguilar, 'Llover sobre mojado: la Librería del Colegio Apostólico de Nuestro Padre San Francisco de Pachuca', in Jaime Ríos Ortega (ed.), *7º Seminario Hispano Mexicano de Investigación en Bibliotecología y Documentación* (México, 2011), 101–33.

Idalia García Aguilar, *Miradas aisladas, visiones conjuntas: defensa del patrimonio documental mexicano* (México, 2001).

Pilar García Jordán, '¿Poder eclesiástico frente a poder civil? Algunas reflexiones sobre la Iglesia peruana ante la formación del estado moderno (1808–1860)', *Boletín Americanista*, 26, 34 (1984), 45–74.

Marta Eugenio García Ugarte, *Poder político y religioso: México, siglo XIX* (México, 2010).

Moisés González Navarro, *Anatomía del poder en México, 1848–1853* (México, 1977), 106–15.

Pedro M. Guibovich Pérez, *Censura, libros e inquisición en el Perú colonial, 1570–1754* (Sevilla, 2003).

Inauguracion de la Biblioteca Nacional de México: abril 2 de 1884 (México, 1884).

Juvenal Jaramillo M., 'Fiscalidad en Nueva España. El obispo y el Cabildo Catedral de Michoacán ante la crisis fiscal borbónica', *América Latina en la Historia Económica*, 20, 3 (2013), 56–89.

Jeffrey Klaiber, 'La reorganización de la Iglesia ante el estado liberal en el Perú (1860–1930)', *Historia general de la Iglesia en América Latina* (Salamanca, 1987), VIII, 277–307.

Robert J. Knowlton, *Los bienes del clero y la reforma mexicana: 1856–1910* (México, 1985).

Ramiro Lafuente López, *Un mundo pocos visible: imprenta y bibliotecas en México durante el siglo XIX* (México, 1992).

Miranda Lida, 'La Iglesia católica en las más recientes historiografías de México y Argentina. Religión, modernidad y secularización', *Historia Mexicana*, 56, 4 (2007), 1393–1426.

W. M. Mathes, 'La colección mexicana de la biblioteca Sutro de San Francisco, California', *Quinto centenario*, 2 (1981), 213–18 https://dialnet.unirioja.es/servlet/articulo?codigo=2038078&orden=1&info=link accessed 29 Nov. 2021.

Jean Meyer, 'La Iglesia', in *Historia general de América Latina* (Madrid, 1999–2008), VI, 227–50.

Julio César Olivé Negrete and Bolfy Cottom, *INAH, una historia* (México, 2003), III: leyes, reglamentos, circulares y acuerdos, 219–27 (Ley de nacionalización de bienes eclesiásticos).

Luisa Orera Orera, 'El control y acceso al patrimonio bibliográfico a través de los catálogos disponibles en Internet', *Documentación de las ciencias de la información*, 30 (2007), 9–23.

Ignacio Osorio Romero and Boris Berenzon Gorn, 'Biblioteca Nacional de México', in *Historia de las bibliotecas nacionales de Iberoamérica* (México, 1995), 325–63.

Ignacio Osorio Romero, *Historia de las bibliotecas novohispanas* (México, 1986).

Gladys Padró Montezuma and José Tamayo Herrera, 'Biblioteca Nacional del Perú', in *Historia de las bibliotecas nacionales de Iberoamérica* (México, 1995), 419–39.

Alejandro E. Parada, *De la biblioteca particular a la biblioteca pública: libros, lectores y pensamiento bibliotecario en los orígenes de la Biblioteca Pública de Buenos Aires, 1779–1812* (Buenos Aires, 2002).

Manuel Revuelta González, *La exclaustración, 1833–1840* (Madrid, 1976).

Luis Enrique Rodríguez San Pedro Bezares, 'Las Universidades Hispánicas: líneas de investigación e historiografía: siglos XV-XVIII', in *Historiografía y líneas de investigación en historia de las universidades: Europa mediterránea e Iberoamérica* (Salamanca, 2012), 17–78.

Sergio Francisco Rosas Salas, 'De la República católica al Estado laico: Iglesia, Estado y secularización en México, 1824–1914'. *Lusitania Sacra*, 25 (2012), 227–44. http://hdl.handle.net/10400.14/9838

Germán Rueda, *La desamortización en España: un balance: 1766–1924* (Madrid, 1997).

Leticia Ruiz Rivera, *Catálogo de sermones mexicanos de la Biblioteca Eusebio F. Kino de la provincia mexicana de la Compañía de Jesús* (Madrid, 2006).

Rafael Sala, *Marcas de fuego de las antiguas bibliotecas mexicanas* (México, 1925).

Mercedes I. Salomón Salazar and Andrew Green, 'Las marcas de fuego: propuesta de una metodología para su identificación', in Idalia García and Pedro Rueda (eds), *Leer en tiempos de la Colonia: imprenta, bibliotecas y lectores en Nueva España* (México, 2010), 341–67.

Tomás Sansón Corbo, 'La Iglesia y el proceso de secularización en el Uruguay moderno (1859–1919)', *Hispania Sacra*, 63, 127 (2011), 283–303.

Manuel E. Santiago Hernández, 'Biblioteca Histórica "José María Lafragua" de la Benemérita Universidad Autónoma de Puebla', *Pecia Complutense*, 7, 12 (2010), 38–53. https://eprints.ucm.es/10036/ accessed 22 Jan. 2012.

Felipe Teixidor, *Ex libris y bibliotecas de México* (México, 1931).

Ana Rira Valero de García Lascuráin and Nora Deveaux Cabrera, 'Vizcaínas: un proyecto de conservación, desarrollo social y cultural mexicano con 280 años de historia', *Corpus*, 3, 2 (2013). http://corpusarchivos.revues.org/589

Carmen Vázquez Mantecón, Alfonso Flamenco Ramírez, and Carlos Herrero Bervera, *Las bibliotecas mexicanas en el siglo XIX* (México, 1987).

Manuel Villagrán Reyes, *Marcas de fuego de las librerías conventuales en la Biblioteca 'Elías Amador' de Zacatecas* (Zacatecas, 1992).

Enrique Villalba Pérez, *Consecuencias educativas de la expulsión de los jesuitas en América* (Madrid, 2003).

PART 2

State Policy toward Book Collections

▼ THE DIFFERENT APPROACHES OF GOVERNMENT POLICY
TOWARDS THE DISSOLUTION OF MONASTERIES. WERE
GOVERNMENTS AWARE OF THE LIBRARY TREASURES AND
OF THEIR PATRIMONIAL OR CULTURAL VALUE? DID THEY
PLAN BEFOREHAND HOW TO DEAL WITH THEM?

The Dissolution of the Libraries of Venetian Religious Houses and the Keeper of the Library of St Mark, Jacopo Morelli, under Venetian, French, and Austrian Governments (1768–1819)

The dissolution of the religious houses' libraries in Venice started in 1768 and went on until the beginning of the second period of Austrian rule in 1814. Under the Venetian government some 320 manuscripts and 80 incunabula had been removed from those libraries and made their way to the Library of St Mark (Libreria di San Marco). During the French rule, an estimated number of 173,000 manuscripts, incunabula and printed books had been confiscated, out of which 63.5% (around 110,000) had been put on sale[1].

An entire book collection culture disappeared but due to the exceptional foresight of one man, the remaining 36.5% of the confiscated material was either deposited in the Library of St Mark or helped to found a number of still existing libraries in Venetian schools, cultural institutes and academies.

The mastermind behind the re-destination of an incredible quantity of books from religious libraries in the period from 1782 to 1819 was the Keeper of the Library of St Mark in Venice, the renowned scholar Jacopo Morelli (1745–1819), who played a key role in this affair under three governments: Venetian (until May 12, 1797),

---

[1] The data are based on the calculation made by Pietro La Cute, 'Le vicende delle biblioteche monastiche veneziane dopo la soppressione napoleonica', *Rivista di Venezia*, A. VIII, no. 10 (October 1929), 645–46, the tables "Tavola dimostrativa delle distribuzioni di libri fatte negli anni 1806-7-8" (which covers a total of 44,706 books) and "Tavola dimostrativa dei libri distribuiti o venduti dopo la soppressione del 1810"

(with a total of 113,075 books). I have added to these data the number of books taken away by the French in 1797 and not included in La Cute's tables. See Tables 9.1–9.2 in the Annex.

Dorit Raines • Associate Professor of History of Libraries and Documentation, Dipartimento di Studi Umanistici, Università Ca' Foscari, Venezia. raines@unive.it

How the Secularization of Religious Houses Transformed the Libraries of Europe, 16th–19th Centuries, ed. by Cristina Dondi, Dorit Raines, and †Richard Sharpe, BIB, 63 (Turnhout, 2022), pp. 163–194.
BREPOLS ❧ PUBLISHERS
DOI 10.1484/M.BIB-EB.5.128484

French (from May to December 1797 and from 1806 to 1814) and Austrian (from December 1797 to 1805 and from 1814 until his death in 1819). Morelli, operating in a constantly changing political context, used his scholarly prestige to impose his ideas and convictions on the Venetian (and the Veneto) book and library landscape. His critical attitude toward the obsolescence of numerous religious houses' libraries and his strong belief in a rational book redistribution made him a perfect ally of the governments under which he continued to serve until his death.

Morelli as a Scholar

Morelli began his education with a Jesuit priest, Federigo Testa, yet his real mentor was the illustrious scholar and librarian, the friar Bernardo Maria De Rubeis (1687–1775) from the order of the Observant Dominicans on the Zattere in Venice[2]. The circumstances of their acquaintance were strongly related to Morelli's growing passion for the book world. According to his biographer, the abbot Giannantonio Moschini (1773–1840)[3], after he had frequented lessons held in the Dominican monastery by well-known scholars, Morelli bought for next to nothing two manuscripts through the mediation of one of them. He then discovered the manuscripts were a copy of the Latin correspondence of the Venetian humanist and diplomat Francesco Barbaro

(1390–1454)[4]. The young Morelli, inspired by genuine passion and curiosity, collated them with the edition of the Barbaro correspondence which had been published two decades earlier by the influential Venetian cardinal Angelo Maria Querini (1680–1755), and discovered imperfections and omissions in it[5]. Embarrassed, he sought the advice of De Rubeis who, appreciative of the young scholar, introduced him to the Dominican monastic library and the collection of Apostolo Zeno which many considered to be already obsolete[6].

Morelli's encounter with the Zeno library, whose owner (1668–1750) was a well-known "letterato" and imperial poet, as well as one of the founders in 1710 of the "Giornale de' letterati d'Italia", was a turning point in the

---

2   On De Rubeis, Paolo Preto, 'De Rubeis, Bernardo Maria', in *Dizionario biografico degli Italiani*, 39 (1991), 238–40; more up-to-date information, especially on his role and importance within the order, in Antonella Barzazi, *Gli affanni dell'erudizione. Studi e organizzazione culturale degli ordini religiosi a Venezia tra Sei e Settecento* (Venezia, 2004), 197–214.

3   Giannantonio Moschini, 'Narrazione intorno alla vita e alle opere di D. Iacopo Morelli', in *Operette di Iacopo Morelli, bibliotecario di S. Marco, ora insieme raccolte con opuscoli di antichi scrittori* (Venezia, 1820), I, IV–V.

4   On the acquisition by Morelli and in general on the fate of the Barbaro family's manuscripts: Dorit Raines, 'La biblioteca manoscritta di Daniele Barbaro: raccolta, uso e dispersione di una collezione veneziana', in *Daniele Barbaro 1514–1570: letteratura, scienza e arti nella Venezia del Rinascimento*, Susy Marcon and Laura Moretti eds (Crocetta del Montello (TV), 2015), 101–13 (especially 104–05).

5   *Epistolae: Diatriba Praeliminaris in duas partes divisa ad Francisci Barbari et aliorum ad ipsum Epistolas: Ab Anno Chr. MCCCCXXV. ad An. MCCCCLIII, nunc primum editas ex duplici Ms. cod. Brixiani, &.Vaticano uno*, Brixiae: Excudebat Joannes-Maria Rizzardi, 1741. The volume does not mention Querini, although the fact that he was cardinal of Brescia and his book collection was located in the same city suggest he may have been behind the publication. The second volume appeared two years later: *Francisci Barbari et aliorum ad ipsum Epistolae*, Brixiae: Exc. Joan. Maria Rizzardi, 1743. See Margaret L. King, *Umanesimo e patriziato a Venezia nel Quattrocento, vol. II: circolo umanistico veneziano. Profili* (Roma, 1989), 462–66.

6   Moschini, 'Narrazione', as note 3, V. On Apostolo Zeno and his library, Marino Zorzi, *La Libreria di San Marco. Libri, lettori, società nella Venezia dei Dogi* (Milano, 1987), 324, 367–68, 373–74; Antonella Barzazi, 'Libertino o devoto? Apostolo Zeno nello specchio della sua biblioteca', in *Il «Giornale de' Letterati d'Italia» trecento anni dopo. Scienza, storia, arte, identità (1710–2010)*, Atti del convegno, Padova, Venezia, Verona, 17–19 novembre 2010, Enza del Tedesco ed. (Pisa-Roma, 2012), 133–44.

young man's cultural development, to the extent that subsequently it was the only collection from the suppressed religious houses which he insisted had to be transferred in its entirety to the Library of St Mark. With Zeno's rare books and manuscripts, library catalogues and bibliographies of all kinds, historical works, the transactions of academies, as well as periodicals and dictionaries[7] – Morelli felt fortunate in having had access to that rich and stimulating collection[8]. His frequentations though were not limited only to books he found there but also to the circle of scholars who were constantly present in the monastery and its library. He furthermore used to visit the libraries of other religious houses: the Somaschan library which was part of S. Maria della Salute, as well as those of S. Francesco della Vigna and S. Michele in Murano, where he saw how rich those collections were for scholars[9]. Using the same technique of commentary and collation which he had employed in working on the Barbaro correspondence and presenting his work to the circle of Venetian "letterati", he quickly distinguished himself for his extensive knowledge of ancient Latin and Greek writings. His scholarship convinced other colleagues to entrust him with other editorial projects. The Latinist Natale Dalle Laste (1707–1792) solicited

Morelli in 1774 to celebrate the memory of the humanist scholar Vittorino da Feltre (1373–1446), one of the teachers at the University of Padua, by editing and publishing the manuscript biography of him by the Mantuan Francesco Prendilacqua. Dalle Laste asked a contact to make a copy of the manuscript in the Vatican Library and Morelli briefly annotated it[10].

In the same years, Morelli managed to have the support of a rich Venetian patrician: Tommaso Giuseppe Farsetti (1710–1792), a bibliophile and the owner of an important manuscript collection, whose circle of friends included the French philosophers Voltaire, Montesquieu and Jean-Jacques Rousseau, the Italian "letterati" Giovanni Maria Mazzuchelli, Francesco Algarotti, Marco Forcellini, and Girolamo Tartarotti as well as the Venetians Carlo Goldoni and the Gozzi brothers[11]. Reluctant to leave Venice, Morelli nevertheless travelled with Farsetti visiting Padua, Milan, Bologna, Vicenza and Verona where he was introduced to Farsetti's important friends. Already in 1771, they published together the catalogue of Farsetti's manuscript library where in the preface authored by Morelli[12], he

---

7   The library catalogue can be found in: Biblioteca Nazionale Marciana, Venezia (BNM), Cod. Marc. It. XI, 288–93 (= 7273–7278) [già Riservati 31–36].

8   Moschini, 'Narrazione', as note 3, VIII.

9   Ibid., VIII–XI. On the Somaschan congregation: Barzazi, *Gli affanni dell'erudizione*, as note 2, 73–196; on the Camaldolese congregation, ibid., 255–332 and the article in the present book; on the Somaschan library: Rudj Gorian, *Nascosti tra i libri: I periodici antichi della Biblioteca del Seminario patriarcale di Venezia (1607–1800)* (Venezia, 2017); on the S. Francesco della Vigna library: Costanzo Albasini, 'La biblioteca di san Francesco della Vigna in Venezia', in *Le Venezie francescane*, 19 (1952), 4, 177–81; on the S. Michele in Murano library: Lucia Merolla, *La Biblioteca di san Michele di Murano all'epoca dell'abate Giovanni Benedetto Mittarelli. I codici ritrovati* (Manziana, 2012).

10   Jacopo Morelli, 'Narrazione intorno all'abate Natale Lastesio', in *Operette di Iacopo Morelli, bibliotecario di S. Marco, ora insieme raccolte con opuscoli di antichi scrittori* (Venezia, 1820), III, 78–79. The publication referred to is: *De Vita Victorini Feltrensis dialogus Francisci Prendilaquae Mantuani ex codice Vaticano. Annotationes adjecit Jacobus Morellius*, Patavii: Typis Seminarii, apud Joannem Manfre, 1774. Dalle Laste wrote the dedication letter.

11   Paolo Preto, 'Farsetti, Tommaso Giuseppe', in *Dizionario biografico degli Italiani*, 45 (1995), 184–86. On the circumstances of Morelli's acquaintance with Farsetti, Moschini, 'Narrazione', as note 3, XII.

12   *Biblioteca manoscritta di Tommaso Giuseppe Farsetti patrizio Veneto e Balì del Sacr' Ordine Gerosolimitano*, in Venezia: Nella Stamperia Fenzo, 1771, V–XXII. The second volume appeared some years later: *Della biblioteca manoscritta di Tommaso Giuseppe Farsetti patrizio veneto, e balì del sagr'ordine Gerosolimitano. Parte seconda*, in Venezia: presso Pietro Savioni, 1780. Morelli and Farsetti collaborated again and published: *Catalogo*

attacked those who considered manuscripts to be outdated and obsolete and who shamelessly left them to gather dust and be eaten by mice. He furthermore pointed an accusing finger against some of the private owners of libraries for selling Venetian literary treasures to foreigners. The example he gave concerned the manuscript "De praestantia venetae politiae" by Giovanni Caldiera (or Calderia) acquired by Archbishop William Laud and later donated to the Bodleian Library[13], adding the scandalized comment that "we are forced to see such a useful work which honours our homeland ending up in foreign hands"[14]. This comment which shows the young Morelli's passion for Venetian bibliographical treasures and echoes the contemporary and prevalent alarm at the continuous acquisition of Venetian collections by foreigners[15], seems

somewhat sinister to judge from the post-1797 events.

Urged by Farsetti, Morelli cultivated the ambition to become the Keeper of the Library of St Mark and for that reason hurriedly worked on a history of the library for publication, although he knew that the current Keeper, the old and infirm Anton Maria Zanetti (1706–1778), intended to publish his own version[16]. The latter in fact was already suspicious of the young man's intentions and became hostile. Yet Morelli, of strong character and convictions, pursued his intellectual career. Rigorous and hard-working, he went on to author (sometimes in collaboration with

dei libri italiani, in Venezia: appresso Modesto Fenzo, 1785 and *Catalogo di libri latini*, in Venezia: appresso Antonio Graziosi, 1788, which included a list of printed books as well as the collection's remaining Latin and Italian manuscripts.

13   Today Oxford, Bodleian Library, MS Laud. Misc. 717, fols 101r–150v. On Caldiera, Juliana Hill Cotton, 'Caldiera (Calderia), Giovanni', in *Dizionario biografico degli Italiani*, 16 (1973), 626–28. Laud purchased in 1635, probably through the English bookseller John Fetherstone, a group of Venetian manuscripts. On the provenance, H. O. Coxe, *Bodleian Library. Quarto catalogues*, II. *Laudian Manuscripts, reprinted from the edition of 1858–1885, with corrections and additions, and an historical introduction by R. W. Hunt* (Oxford, 1973), XX–XXI.

14   "Nientedimeno opera sì utile, ed alla patria nostra onorevole in altrui mano siamo costretti a vedere". Introduction by Morelli to *Biblioteca manoscritta di Tommaso Giuseppe Farsetti*, XII (the Caldiera manuscript affair is at VIII–XII).

15   Morelli probably alludes to the sale in 1762 of the collection owned by the British consul in Venice, Joseph Smith (1674?-1770), to King George III (See Federico Montecuccoli degli Erri, 'Il console Smith. Notizie e documenti', *Ateneo Veneto*, ns., 33 (1995), 111–81). Two other important sales occured in the 1780s: first the library of the Venetian Giacomo Soranzo (4,000 manuscripts and 20,000 rare printed books), part of

which entered the English book market through the Canonici collection (Vittorio Rossi, 'La biblioteca manoscritta del senatore veneziano Jacopo Soranzo', *Il libro e la stampa*, I (1907), 1, 3–8; 5, 122–33; Irma Merolle, *L'Abate Matteo Luigi Canonici e La Sua Biblioteca. I Manoscritti Canonici e Canonici-Soranzo delle biblioteche fiorentine* (Roma-Firenze, 1958). Then in 1788, the entire collection of the Venetian bibliophile Maffio Pinelli (12,000 printed and rare books), was purchased by the London bookseller James Edwards and sold at auction (*Bibliotheca Pinelliana. A catalogue of the magnificent and celebrated library of Maffei Pinelli, late of Venice: comprehending an unparalleled collection of the Greek, Roman, and Italian authors, from the origin of printing … a considerable number of curious Greek and Latin manuscripts, of the 11. 12. 13. 14. 15. and 16. centuries; … on Monday March 2, 1789, and the twenty-two following days, (Sunday excepted); … at the great room, opposite the chapel, in Conduit Street, Hanover square, London … catalogues to be had of mess. Robson and Clarke, booksellers New Bond Street; Mr Edwards, booksellers, Pall Mall; and of the principal booksellers throughout Europe*, [London], [1789]).

16   *Della pubblica libreria di San Marco in Venezia dissertazione storica di D. Jacopo Morelli …*, In Venezia: presso Antonio Zatta, 1774. On this episode, Zorzi, *La Libreria*, as note 6, 288. The Library of St Mark had usually during the eighteenth century two distinct figures: the Keeper ("custode"), who was a professional librarian and who was responsible for the daily management, and the Librarian ("Bibliotecario"), a patrician, usually Procurator of St Mark, nominated by the Senate to forsee to the budget and the development of the collections.

others) prestigious publications. In 1776 he published with Farsetti a catalogue of Italian comedies[17], and then in the same year, this time as sole author, the two volumes dedicated to the description of the Nani di San Trovaso manuscript collection[18], one of the most prestigious family collections in Venice, part of which arrived in the Library of St Mark in 1800[19], while the archival part ended up in the hands of Lord Guilford and was destined for Corfù[20]. The remainder went

to various owners, including the abbot Daniele Francesconi, librarian of the University of Padua[21].

Morelli as a Library Keeper under the Venetian Government (1778–1797)

When the Keeper of the Library of St Mark, the old Zanetti, died in 1778, Morelli was clearly a strong candidate to succeed him. Already known as the "Magliabecchi of the eighteenth century"[22] he was strongly backed by his patron Farsetti as well as by the *Riformatore dello studio di Padova*[23], Pietro Barbarigo, against the candidacy of Zanetti's brother, Girolamo, whose promotion was solicited by the Procurator of St Mark Alvise II Piero Contarini, future Librarian of the Library of St Mark. The Senate eventually decided to nominate Morelli as Keeper of the Library on 30 November 1778[24].

Morelli quickly realized that the library's reputation had diminished somewhat over the previous years on account of its continuing closures; as the authors of the *Encyclopédie* put it in 1781: "La Bibliothéque de S. Marc est impenetrable"[25]. It also lacked important books and manuscripts as well as updated catalogues, while other private libraries such as the Pisani di San Vidal, which opened to the public three

17 *Catalogo di commedie italiane*, Venezia: nella stamperia di Modesto Fenzo, 1776. Gaetano Melzi, *Dizionario di opere anonime e pseudonime di scrittori italiani o come che sia aventi relazione all'Italia*, In Milano: Coi torchi di Luigi di Giacomo Pirola, 1848, v. 1 (A-G), 185, credits Farsetti and Morelli with the authorship of the compilation. In fact, the preface first uses the singular pronoun (p. III) and then moves to "us" (from p. IV onwards).

18 *Codices manuscripti latini bibliothecae Nanianae a Iacobo Morellio relati. Opuscula inedita accedunt ex iisdem deprompta*, Venetiis: typis Antonii Zattae, 1776; *I codici manoscritti volgari della libreria Naniana riferiti da don Iacopo Morelli. S'aggiungono alcune operette inedite da essi tratte*, In Venezia: nella stamperia d'Antonio Zatta, 1776. On the collection and a profile of the owners: the brothers Bernardo and Giacomo Nani, see Giannantonio Moschini, *Della letteratura veneziana del secolo 18. fino a' nostri giorni opera di Giannantonio Moschini*, In Venezia: dalla stamperia Palese, 1806, II, 49–51; Filippo Nani-Mocenigo, 'Giacomo Nani. Memorie e documenti', in *Agostino, Battista e Giacomo Nani (Ricordi storici)*, (Venezia, 1917²), 387–597; Piero Del Negro, 'Giacomo Nani. Appunti biografici', *Bollettino del Museo Civico di Padova*, 60 (1971), 2, 115–47, Zorzi, *La Libreria*, as note 6, 342. The Greek collection was first described by Luigi Mingarelli, *Graeci Codices Manu Scripti Apud Nanios Patricios Venetos Asservati*, Bononiae: Typis Laelii a Vulpe, 1784, while the description in two volumes of the Oriental manuscripts was carried out by the Orientalist and professor at Padua University Simone Assemani: *Museo cufico Naniano illustrato dall'abate Simone Assemani professore di lingue orientali...*, In Padova: nella stamperia del Seminario, 1787–1788.

19 Zorzi, *La Libreria*, as note 6, 309–15.

20 Today in the National Library of Greece. On this complicated story see Andrea Nanetti, *Il fondo archivistico Nani nella Biblioteca Nazionale di Grecia ad Atene: euristica documentaria sulla Morea veneta* (Venezia, 1996).

21 Emmanuele Antonio Cicogna, *Delle iscrizioni veneziana raccolta ed illustrate*, VI, pt. I, Venezia: Presso la Tipografia Andreola, 1853, 115.

22 Moschini, *Della letteratura*, as note 3, II, 50.

23 Magistracy established in 1528 to supervise the University of Padua. Over the course of the years it assumed other responsibilities such as the control over printing and censorship, supervision of the Public Library and of public historiography.

24 Zorzi, *La Libreria*, as note 6, 288.

25 *Encyclopédie, ou Dictionnaire raisonné des sciences, des arts et des métiers, par une Société des gens de lettres. Mis en ordre & publié par M. Diderot; & quant à la partie mathematique, par M. D'Alembert*, A Lausanne et à Berne: chez les Sociétés typographiques, vol. 36, 1781, 754.

times a week, were able to satisfy the curiosity of scholars[26]. He immediately initiated an acquisition policy: six months after his arrival he could proudly announce that he had bought eleven precious manuscripts from the abbot Matteo Luigi Canonici[27]. Morelli though needed to do much more in order to make the Library of St Mark central to the scholarly community. Help came unexpectedly.

On 20 September 1767 the Venetian Senate, desperately looking for ways to replenish the disastrous state of its public debt, adopted the report of the newly created *Deputazione ad pias causas*, established in 1766 in order to reform the entire patrimony of religious houses in the Venetian State. The magistrates counted 441 religious houses in Venice and its mainland belonging to 35 different orders made up of 7,733[28] monks, and 45,773 between seculars and regulars (2% of the whole population) and specified their sources of revenue and their estates[29]. Subsequently, on

7 September 1768 the Senate decreed the criteria to be applied for the suppression of religious houses, targeting those with fewer than twelve religious or lacking sufficient income. They were to be enacted across the whole territory of the Veneto[30]. Between June and July 1769, the initial suppressions comprised 21 out of 41 religious houses belonging to the Capuchin order; four out of 28 belonging to the Reformed Friars Minor; and 22 out of 31 to the Friars Minor of the Observance. Measures were also taken to suppress the Franciscan Tertiaries (seven houses) and the Carthusians (two houses)[31]. In 1770, the Senate ordered the closure of religious houses belonging to the Carmelites of the Mantuan Congregation[32] and four houses of the Cassinese Congregation (Benedictines)[33]. In 1772 the gradual suppression took place of houses belonging to the orders of the Augustinians (only four houses were allowed to continue their activities in the Province of Venice and accommodate the remaining 157 regulars), the Girolamini (five houses out of nine were suppressed, but the remaining four were meant to be closed down too), the Minims (the friars of St Francis of Paola were allowed to keep five out of seven houses) and the Servites (the

---

26   Dorit Raines, 'Book Museum or Scholarly Library? The "Libreria di San Marco" in a Republican Context', in *Ateneo Veneto*, 3 ser, 197, (2010), 9/II, 31–50.

27   On the Canonici collection, see note 15. On the purchase see Zorzi, *La Libreria*, as note 6, 290 and Biblioteca Nazionale Marciana, Cod. Marc. Lat. XIV, 110 (= 4533), nos LV–LXV; Ibid., Cod. Riservato 190.

28   Cecchetti provides two different numbers: Bartolomeo Cecchetti, *La Republica di Venezia e la corte di Roma nei rapporti della religione*, vol. II: *Documenti*, Venezia: Prem. stabilim. tipogr. di P. Naratovich, 1874, 114: 7,703 religious cited in the 29 December 1766 report of the *Magistrato Sopra Monasteri* and Ibid., vol. I, 215: 7,733 religious – a number taken from the 12 June 1767 report of the *Deputazione ad pias causas*.

29   Calculation in the report of the *Deputazione ad pias causas* dated 12 June 1767 (Cecchetti, *La Republica di Venezia e la corte di Roma*, as note 28, vol. II, 138; vol. I, 214–17). The June 1767 report pointed out the fact that another survey, carried out in 1764 by the Venetian patrician Zuan Antonio da Riva from the *Magistrato Sopra Monasteri*, had furnished slightly different figures (7,638 monks) and explained the discrepancy by asserting that religious houses wished to exaggerate their numbers for fear of closure. The difference between 7,733 monks and 20,871 regulars (part of the 45,773 ecclesiastics who

were either regulars or seculars) is explained by the fact that the Venetians calculated only those who wore the monastic habit and lived in monasteries while other regulars lived in communities or had the title of abbot without practising the role.

30   Cecchetti, *La Republica di Venezia e la corte di Roma*, as note 28, vol. I, 218–39.

31   Ibid., vol. I, 223; II, 152: decrees of 1 June 1769 and 20 July 1769. In 1772 the *Deputazione ad pias causas* requested the immediate suppression of the houses of Verona and Noventa Padovana. Cecchetti, *La Republica di Venezia e la corte di Roma*, vol. II, 157: "Scrittura" dated 12 June 1772.

32   The decree is dated 23 August 1770. Cecchetti, *La Republica di Venezia e la corte di Roma*, as note 28, vol. II, 152.

33   The decree is dated 5 December 1770. Cecchetti, *La Republica di Venezia e la corte di Roma*, as note 28, vol. I, 224.

Friar Servants of Mary were allowed to keep six out of 13 houses in the province of Venice for 154 regulars)[34]. On 21 July 1773 Clement XIV's suppression of the Jesuit order was promulgated and the Senate enacted it on 29 September of the same year[35].

The outcome was the closure between 1770 and 1793 of 127 religious houses across the whole Venetian territory and the reduction of about 2,000 seculars (9% – from 22,307 in 1766 to 20,274 in 1790) and of 3,468 regulars (44,8% – from 7,733 to 4,265 in the same period)[36].

In all the decrees or regulations concerning the closure of religious houses in the Veneto only brief references were made to the fate of the books which belonged to the suppressed religious houses, or rather specifically those which belonged to deceased friars. When on 1 June 1769, the Venetian Senate ordered the institution of a fund for religious works (*Cassa Civanzi*) that would collect the surplus revenue coming from the suppressed houses, it specifically addressed the question of deceased religious and their property (i.e. investments held in their name or in the name of the religious house, as well as silverware and other valuable property belonging to them), emphasizing that "books and other articles of common use belonging to the deceased will be kept for the benefit of the whole community"[37]. It may be presumed that the merger of small religious houses, each one of which probably owned a minimal book collection or was accustomed to let each friar possess a small number of volumes, resulted in a sort of common book repository in the order's remaining houses, as testified by the ownership inscriptions on the books[38]. The books themselves, however, were not considered worthy of inventory by the Venetian government (although in the case of

34 The decree is dated 5 September 1772. Cecchetti, *La Republica di Venezia e la corte di Roma*, as note 28, vol. II, 160–62. Cf. ibid., 151–60: "Scrittura" of the *Deputazione ad pias causas* dated 12 June 1772.

35 Cecchetti, *La Republica di Venezia e la corte di Roma*, as note 28, vol. I, 229, 239; Giuseppe Cappelletti, *I Gesuiti e la Republica di Venezia. Documenti diplomatici relativi alla Società gesuitica raccolti per decreto del Senato 14 giugno 1606 e pubblicati per la prima volta dal cav. pr. Giuseppe Cappelletti*, Venezia: Tipografia Grimaldo, 1873, 399–403.

36 Samuele Romanin, *Storia documentata di Venezia*, Venezia: Dalla Tipografia di Pietro Naratovich, 1859, vol. VIII, 177–80; Giuseppe Gullino, 'Il giurisdizionalismo dello Stato veneziano: gli antichi problemi e la nuova cultura', in *La Chiesa di Venezia nel Settecento*, Bruno Bertoli ed., Contributi alla storia della Chiesa di Venezia, 6 (Venezia, 1993), 30–33; Renata Targhetta, 'Secolari e regolari nel Veneto prima e dopo la legislazione antiecclesiastica (1765–84)', *Studi Veneziani*, 19 (1991), 171–84. On the reform and the legal debate regarding ecclesiastical property: Giovanni Zalin, 'Ricerche sulla privatizzazione della proprietà ecclesiastica nel Veneto. Dai provvedimenti Tron alle vendite laiche', in AA.VV., *Studi in memoria di Luigi Dal Pane* (Bologna, 1982), 538 (537–55); Giovanni Tabacco, *Andrea Tron e la crisi dell'aristocrazia senatoria a Venezia* (Udine, 1980), 130–55.

37 Cecchetti, *La Republica di Venezia e la corte di Roma*, as note 28, vol. I, 223.

38 The presence of different eighteenth-century monastic "ad usum" inscriptions on the books' title pages, especially in the case of Franciscan houses, which were previously hostile to any form of ownership, is a valuable testimony to the migration of books following the voluntary or obligatory change of the religious' place of residence. This is found, for example, in a number of volumes, today in the collection of the Municipal Library of Monselice near Padua, with provenances from the house of the Reformed Friars Minor of S. Maria delle Grazie in Conegliano (550 volumes deposited after its suppression in 1769 in the monastery of St Bernardino di Collalto) and the Friars Minor (Franciscans) of S. Maria delle Grazie in Piove di Sacco (suppressed in 1769). Elisa Veronese, *Storia del Gabinetto di Lettura di Monselice 1857–1939*, Laurea thesis under the supervision of Prof. Dorit Raines, Venezia, Università Ca' Foscari, a.a. 2012–2013, 32, 70, 73, 76–77; Federica Benedetti, *La biblioteca francescana di San Michele in Isola e le "sue biblioteche" (1829–2008). Il modello delle biblioteche di Santa Maria delle Grazie di Conegliano, San Bernardino di Collalto, San Francesco di Ceneda*, Biblioteca S. Francesco della Vigna, 1 (Milano, 2013), 206. Cf. Pietro M. Candeo, *I Santuari Mariani della Diocesi di Padova* (Villa del Conte (PD), 1986).

large libraries, the authorities did ask for one)[39], as was the case with other assets or valuables, because of the modest profits expected at their sale and due to the legal distinction, in cases of property transmission, between a library collection and a quantity of books[40].

According to the Justinian *Digest* a library was part of a building and therefore considered to be a whole[41]. This view was revived by the eminent seventeenth-century jurist Giovanni Battista De Luca (1614–1683) who placed libraries in the category of "solid movable objects", such as statues or paintings, and therefore considered them as integral collections[42]. Books or volumes which did not belong to a library were then tacitly considered, either by the *Digest* or by De Luca, of being of common use[43]. This legal distinction between a library collection and a quantity of books is probably the reason for the lack of documentation and the chaotic dispersion of the collections of books which belonged to the religious houses suppressed between the 1760s and the 1770s.

As already mentioned, Jacopo Morelli became Keeper of the Library of St Mark in 1778, some years after the process of closing religious houses was moving towards conclusion. He could not have interfered with the closure before his nomination, but he was determined to at least make the Library of St Mark the repository of the valuable books and manuscripts from the collections belonging to the Canons Regular (Augustinians) when in 1782 the Venetian government decided to suppress the order. In 1783 Morelli, by order of the *Magistrato Sopra Monasteri*, chose for the Library of St Mark 587 manuscripts and 40 incunabula from S. Giovanni di Verdara in Padua, arguing that the Library of St Mark was "well-known for its prerogative in receiving manuscripts into its collections" and that moreover, "manuscripts, which very often contain unpublished texts, are considered a rarity and an ornament to cities and also attract foreigners who wish to study them"[44].

39   See for example the decree issued on 29 September 1773 regarding the Jesuit expulsion, which assigned to the *Deputazione ad pias causas* the duty to "carry out the inventory and the assemblage of all the assets belonging to these orders, such as ornaments, silver, all sort of furnishings, and more, eventually selling them in order to compensate the Fund *ad pias causas* for the aforementioned valuables". Cecchetti, *La Republica di Venezia e la corte di Roma*, as note 28, vol. II, 239. The three magistrates *ad pias causas*, however, in the document submitted to the Senate on 25 September 1773 specifying in detail how the secularization of the Jesuit company was to take place, referred to the need to make an inventory of all "immovable as well as movable property, gold, silver, ornaments, [and] libraries [...] of the said company". Cappelletti, *I Gesuiti e la Republica di Venezia*, as note 35, 416.

40   On the question see Dorit Raines, 'Sotto tutela. Biblioteche vincolate o oggetto di fedecommesso a Venezia, XV–XVIII secoli', *Mélanges de l'École française de Rome. Italie et Méditerranée*, 124 (2013), no. 2, 536–37.

41   According to the Justinian *Digest* a bookcase attached to the wall is part of the building: "It is also forbidden by this decree to bequeath property which the legatee cannot deliver without detaching it from a building; that is to say, blocks of marble, or columns. The Senate decided that this also applied to tiles, to beams, and to doors, as well as to libraries attached to walls". *The Digest or Pandects*, Book XXX, Title I: "Concerning legacies and trusts", 41 (9).

42   Giovanni Battista De Luca, *Il dottor volgare ovvero il compendio di tutta la legge civile, canonica, feudale e municipale nelle cose più ricevute in pratica del cardinale*

Giambatista De Luca e dal medesimo moralizzato in lingua italiana, Firenze: coi tipi di V. Batelli e compagni, 1839, vol. 3, 105.

43   *The Digest or Pandects*, Book XXXIII, Title X. Concerning bequests of household goods: "7. *Celsus, Digest, Book XIX*: Labeo says that the term 'supellex' is derived from the custom of persons who, when about to start on a journey, were accustomed to place in skins such articles as would be of use to them. Tubero attempts to explain the term 'household goods' as utensils destined for the daily use of the head of the family, which do not come under some other designation, as, for example, provisions, silver plate, clothing, ornaments, implements intended for farming or for a house".

44   "Questi manoscritti convengono affatto alla Libreria di S. Marco, perché questa sola è famosa per la prerogativa di contenere codici manoscritti, e per questi si è resa

In 1784 twenty-two manuscripts and 200 printed books (out of which 42 incunabula) arrived after a careful selection from the Canons Regular of the Congregation of the Most Holy Savior in S. Michele di Candiana near Padua and the Canons Regular of the Lateran of S. Leonardo in Monte Donico[45]. By this point the Venetian State regarded Morelli – also because of his network of correspondents – as the only competent person to administer the vast book collections which were present on its territory and make an appropriate selection[46]: in 1786 he coordinated the transfer of material considered to be of a literary and historical nature and "not pertinent for the purposes of the Prince [i.e., Doge]" from the

archives of the Council of Ten and the *Cancelleria Inferiore* to the Library of St Mark[47].

Morelli's key idea of the library as a place of study that would attract scholars and honour the Venetian State led him to implement at times an aggressive acquisition policy. One such incident occurred in 1789 when the Council of Ten received a denunciation made by the Prior of the SS. Giovanni e Paolo Dominican monastery that precious manuscripts, incunabula and other books had disappeared from the library. The *Inquisitori di Stato* were soon instructed to investigate the matter. The evidence they gathered revealed a long-term state of negligence in the way the library had been run[48]. The 80-year old librarian, Domenico Maria Berardelli, who was not always present due to infirmity, had entrusted a fellow friar with the keys to the library with the consequence that unscrupulous friars had sold precious manuscripts and incunabula to distinguished collectors such as the cardinal Loménie de Brienne, Matteo Luigi Canonici, Maffeo Pinelli and an unidentified Russian government minister[49]. Morelli was asked by the Council of Ten on 25 September 1789 to report

celebre […] Inoltre li manoscritti, contenendo spesso opere inedite, si riguardano come rarità ed ornamenti delle città ed attraggono lo studio anche de' forestieri". BNM, Archivio della biblioteca, busta anno 1783, fasc. 66. Cf. La Cute, 'Le vicende delle biblioteche monastiche', as note 1, 600; Zorzi, *La Libreria*, as note 6, 294–95. Morelli suggested moreover that the nearly 6,000 books should be given to the Library of the University of Padua "which must be supplied with books relating to all branches of knowledge".

45 Zorzi, *La Libreria*, as note 6, 294–95. The rest of the books were given to various educational institutions.

46 Morelli had an intense correspondence with German Bible scholars and theologians like Adler, Beck, Böckh and Creuzer; French scholars and historians like Boissonade; the Spanish scholar Juan Andrés; English philologists such as Blomfield and Burgess, and the bibliographer and bookseller Edwards; Italian scholars such as Bettinelli, Silvestri, the Tuscan poet D'Elci, the Cardinal Garampi, and also scholars such as Tomitano and Valsecchi, the printer Bodoni and the sculptor Antonio Canova; booksellers such as Pietro Brandolese, the French Antoine Augustin Renouard and Carlo Scapin from Padua, or the book collectors Antonio Marsand and Gaetano Melzi, as well as directors of the major European libraries. All in all, over 50 years of activity Morelli had 216 correspondents. On the esteem his fellow scholars had for him, as expressed by Andrés: "but where can one find another ocean of erudition like yours?", Alessia Giachery, *Jacopo Morelli e la repubblica delle lettere attraverso la sua corrispondenza (1768–1819)* (Venezia, 2012), 30–36.

47 BNM, Archivio della Biblioteca, busta "Governo Veneto", fasc. 101, report of the Librarian Francesco Pesaro to the Senate, 16 June 1789.

48 The Librarian, Domenico Maria Berardelli had already denounced the absence of some valuable materials (he called it "sacrilego furto") in his 1779 catalogue of manuscripts: *Codicum omnium latinorum et italicorum qui manuscripti in bibliotheca SS. Joannis et Pauli Venetiarum apud PP. Praedicatores asservantur catalogus, sectio secunda*, in *Nuova raccolta di opuscoli scientifici e filologici*, 33, 1779, pt. III, 4. See Antonella Barzazi, 'Berardelli, Domenico Maria', in Enzo Bottasso, *Dizionario dei bibliotecari e bibliografi italiani dal XVI al XX secolo*, Roberto Alciati ed. (Montevarchi, 2009), 56–57.

49 Rinaldo Fulin, 'Vicende della libreria in SS. Gio. e Paolo', *Atti dell'Ateneo Veneto*, ser. II, 5 (1868), 273–94; Graziano Ruffini, *La chasse aux livres: Bibliografia e collezionismo nel viaggio in Italia di Étienne-Charles de Loménie de Brienne e François-Xavier Laire (1789–1790)* (Firenze, 2012), 75–90.

on what steps needed to be taken to avoid further thefts or improper alienations and to transfer to the Library of St Mark those manuscripts and books that "are of no use at all for the friars' studies, or incomprehensible to them"[50].

Morelli, in compliance with this specific order from the Council of Ten, carried it out firmly and promptly. He visited fifteen libraries which he thought would have valuable material[51]. A brief quantitative survey of the libraries' holdings, based on scattered and sometimes rather partial information, may help to shed light on Morelli's administrative and intellectual capacities in dealing with a massive number of books: he was able to review and select valuable material out of a total of approximately 144,000 manuscripts and printed books. The libraries visited were: S. Giorgio Maggiore (Benedictines), S. Michele (Camaldolese), S. Mattia (Camaldolese) and S. Pietro Martire (Dominicans) – all three on the island of Murano –, Sant'Andrea della Certosa (Carthusians), the Somaschan Library of the Salute, the Gesuati (Observant Dominicans on the Zattere), S. Francesco della Vigna (Friars Minor of the Observance), S. Maria Gloriosa dei Frari (Franciscans), Santo Stefano (Augustinian Hermits), S. Maria dei Carmini (Carmelites), S. Nicola da Tolentino (Theatines), S. Maria di Nazareth (Discalced Carmelites), S. Bonaventura (Friars Minor), and SS. Giovani e Paolo (Dominicans)[52]. Another seventeen libraries which he did not manage to visit belonged to convents that had minor collections: S. Giobbe (Friars Minor of the Observance), S. Giorgio in Alga (Discalced Carmelites), S. Domenico di Castello (Dominicans), S. Nicoletto dei Frari (Friars Minor Conventual), S. Francesco di Paola (Minims), Sant'Elena (Olivetans), S. Secondo in Isola (Dominicans), S. Giacomo della Giudecca (Servants of Mary – Servites), S. Cristoforo in Isola (Augustinian Hermits), Santo Spirito in Laguna (Friars Minor of the Observance), S. Francesco del Deserto (Reformed Friars Minor), S. Salvador (Canons Regular), S. Maria dei Servi (Servites), Redentore in the Giudecca (Friars Minor Capuchins), Fava (Oratorian Fathers of S. Philip Neri), S. Clemente in Isola (Camaldolese), and S. Sebastiano (Girolamini). In total there were approximately 32,000 books in all of the minor libraries[53].

Morelli's approach was quite intrusive: he not only made a survey of all the Venetian religious libraries which had been selected (pinpointing missing books and manuscripts), but also drew up lists of rare items which were *desiderata* for the Library of St Mark in the event of their closure. He showed himself to be extremely well-organized in his survey, creating for each library a "note of the best manuscripts and the rarest printed books in the library" and then making the Prior sign the list alongside his own signature. A marginal note contained the Prior's written commitment to see that the books were "to be always thoroughly taken care of and conserved in the library of the convent"[54]. He also stamped those he wished to have with the

50 BNM, Archivio della Biblioteca, busta "Governo Veneto", fasc. 105a.

51 ASV, Consiglio dei Dieci, b. 195, report of Morelli to the Council of Ten: Carlo Castellani, *Parole dette dal Prefetto della Biblioteca Nazionale di S. Marco quando il R. Istituto di Scienze, Lettere ed Arti inaugurava nel Pantheon Veneto il busto dell'Ab. Jacopo Morelli* (Venezia, 1893), 8–11; Fulin, 'Vicende', as note 49, the report is on 289–94 (here 289–90). Cf. Zorzi, *La Libreria*, as note 6, 302.

52 See Tables 9.1–9.2 in the Annex.

53 See Tables 9.1–9.2 in the Annex.

54 BNM, Archivio della Biblioteca, folder "Biblioteche delle corporazioni religiose soppresse 1789–1812", fasc. 1: "Nota Libri frati 25 settembre 1789". Cf. Zorzi, *La Libreria*, as note 6, 557; Carlo Campana, 'Manoscritti e incunaboli delle biblioteche camaldolesi verso la Marciana', in *San Michele in Isola – Isola della conoscenza: ottocento anni di storia e cultura camaldolesi nella laguna di Venezia: Mostra organizzata in occasione del millenario della fondazione della congregazione camaldolese*, Marcello Brusegan, Paolo Eleuteri, and Gianfranco Fiaccadori eds (Torino, 2012), 222–27.

Venetian lion of St Mark[55]: 232 manuscripts and 641 printed books in total[56]. He was moreover able to put pressure on the Council of Ten to allow him to take under his care carefully selected manuscripts and books – judged to be extremely valuable – from libraries such as SS. Giovanni and Paolo (303 manuscripts and 78 rare books), S. Pietro Martire in Murano (2 valuable incunabula[57]), and Sant'Andrea della Certosa (12 rare books, mostly incunabula). The rest of the surveyed libraries would then – according to the report – be subject to a careful periodical control by Morelli.

As for the other Regulars book collections, no other information emerges from the official documentation preserved in the Library of

St Mark's archive nor in the State archives in relation to any survey made after 1789 by Morelli or by the Venetian authorities regarding their library holdings. However, as emerges from owner signatures on the Canonici manuscript collection in the Bodleian library in Oxford, Bernardo Trevisan, Giacomo Soranzo at the beginning of the eighteenth century and especially Matteo Luigi Canonici in the period from 1773–1789 managed to acquire manuscripts from these smaller collections, some of which we know nothing about: S. Salvador[58], Sant'Andrea del Lido or La Certosa[59], Sant'Alvise[60], S. Daniele[61], S. Maria Maggiore[62], S. Bartolomeo[63], Santo Spirito[64], S. Chiara in Murano[65], and S. Sebastiano[66] – all rather small religious houses, some of which however had precious collections (like La Certosa)[67] that had served their predecessors but were no longer

---

55 See an example placed on a number of incunables from S. Giorgio Maggiore in the article by Dondi-Prosdocimi-Raines in this volume, nos 15, 62, 72, 81, 138 and 145 in the catalogue.

56 Fulin, 'Vicende', as note 49, 290, with the number of manuscripts taken from S. Mattia corrected by Zorzi: Zorzi, *La Libreria*, as note 6, 507, note 140. Cf. Edoardo Barbieri, 'Produrre, conservare, distruggere: per una storia dei libri e della biblioteca di S. Mattia di Murano', in *L'Ateneo Veneto*, n.s. 184 (1997), 35, 13–55 (here 42, note 125).

57 Morelli refers to Homer's *Batrachomyomachia*, printed in Venice by Laonicus and Alexander in 1486 (GW 12901; ISTC ih00301000), saying it was the first Greek book to be printed in Venice and that the copy in Sant'Andrea della Certosa was the only one in the city. He added that another "very rare" book was bound with it without specifying which one, but he may have meant the verses by Michele Apostolis inserted at the end of the volume. Fulin, 'Vicende', as note 49, 293; Caterina Carpinato, *Varia posthomerica neograeca. Materiali per il corso di lingua e letteratura neogreca* (Milano, 2006), 40. The volume is today in the Marciana Library in Venice with shelfmark Inc. V. 685 (*Homerou Batrachomyomachia en de tisi Tigretos tou Karos*, (Eis Benetian: Laonicou Kretos kai protothytou Chanion, 1486. Meni aprillio eicoste deutera). On the recto of the front blank leaf a note in Morelli's hand: "Venetiis, apud Laonicum Cretensem, 1486" (MEI 02121831). The digital edition is online: http://www.internetculturale.it/jmms/iccuviewer/iccu.jsp?id=oai%3A193.206.197.21%3A18%3AVE0049%3AVEAE127312&mode=all&teca=marciana.

58 Bodleian Library, Oxford, MS Canon. Ital. 51, from the Soranzo collection, no. 285 in 4° and MS Canon. Ital. 247, bought by Canonici himself. The identification of Canonici's manuscripts from the Soranzo and Trevisan collections is based on J. B. Mitchell, 'Trevisan and Soranzo: some Canonici manuscripts from two Eighteenth-Century Venetian collections', in *The Bodleian Library Record*, VIII (1969), 3, 125–35 and the card catalogue prepared by him at the Bodleian Library.

59 Ibid., MS Canon. Class. Lat. 152.

60 Ibid., MS Canon. Ital. 172, from the Soranzo collection, no. 400 in 4°.

61 Ibid., MS Canon. Ital. 192 and 246, from the Soranzo collection, no. 529 in 4°.

62 Ibid., MS Canon. Ital. 203, from the Soranzo collection, no. 418 in 4°.

63 Ibid., MS Canon. Pat. Lat 58.

64 Ibid., MS Canon. Pat. Lat 12, from the Trevisan collection no. 114, probably sold to Soranzo.

65 Ibid., MS Canon. Ital. 164.

66 Ibid., MS Canon. Pat. Lat 42, from the Soranzo collection, no. 459.1 in 4°.

67 See Morelli's remark in 1789 regarding La Certosa in his report after his survey of the religious houses' library collections, asking to transfer to the Library of St Mark what remained from this collection (12 books) "from which in the past these Regulars had sold the best volumes". Morelli's report in Fulin, 'Vicende', as note 49, 293.

useful for late eighteenth-century monks. The shift in role which was taking place between the book collections in religious houses to public libraries as the centre of knowledge transmission was already well established in the second half of the eighteenth century[68].

Morelli was far from regarding the libraries of religious houses as monuments to Venetian culture or identity, and therefore as integral and homogeneous collections. His criterion of judgement was more based on public interest and on the evaluation of the utilitarian aspect of each book or manuscript: those judged to be valuable and rare were, in his view, best made part of the State library (under whatever government, as we shall see), while others could be reused by cultural institutions, schools or academies and the rest sold off at the best price. I would like to underline the words: "public" and "utility", since these terms may help to understand not only the government's (or governments') approach but also Morelli's towards the dissolution of religious houses and their libraries. The idea of "public" dimension was very much present already in the eighteenth century through people's growing awareness of the power of information, news and therefore, of public opinion, but it was also slowly reaching the realm of learning with the founding of new public libraries that were intended to serve not only the narrow circle of scholars who were part of the Republic of Letters but a wider cultivated public of readers[69]. The monastic libraries were now a distant memory; as one of the delegates to the suppressed libraries put it: "the financial setbacks of the regular orders caused their inability to buy books that are being published

every day. It is not strange therefore if one finds their libraries lacking in modern publications"[70]. Morelli was also well aware of this factor but equally he argued for the dissolution of religious libraries also on the grounds that most of the friars "through ignorance or unwillingness were not fit to preserve with proper care the treasures they had in their possession and make the best out of them"[71]. Yet there was the other side of the coin: the public libraries, in Morelli's view, needed excellent books in order to stimulate Italian cultural production, which he judged to be "decadent", a subject to which he had paid particular attention in his correspondence, especially with the German historian and philologist Barthold Georg Niebuhr[72].

Morelli under the Provisional Municipal Government (1797) and the First Period of Austrian Rule (1798–1805)

Morelli, who had the complete trust of the Venetian government, had become both in the political arena and in the intellectual sphere, an (if not "the") authority on libraries and books. Everything changed after the abdication of the Venetian Great Council on 12 May 1797 and with the entrance of French troops into the

---

68 See Antonella Barzazi's article in the present volume.

69 Dorit Raines, 'La cultura libraria della Repubblica di Venezia nel Settecento', in *Un'istituzione dei Lumi: la biblioteca. Teoria, gestione e pratiche biblioteconomiche nell'Europa dei Lumi*, Frédéric Barbier and Andrea De Pasquale eds (Parma, 2013), 85–104 (here 88–89, 98–104).

70 Letter of Sebastiano Ongin to the *Dipartimento di Finanza* after a visit to the monastic libraries, 17 September 1808. ASV, Demanio, 1806–1813, b. 328, fasc. "Biblioteche e Belle Arti [1808–11]".

71 Report of Morelli to the Council of Ten, in Fulin, 'Vicende', as note 49, 292: Morelli refers to the friars of SS. Giovanni and Paolo.

72 Stefano Trovato, 'Una lettera a Barthold Georg Niebuhr di Jacopo Morelli: la decadenza culturale dell'Italia all'inizio della Restaurazione', *Ateneo Veneto*, 3 ser., 193 (2006), 5/II, 204: "maxime de ingeniis Italorum dolendum est, studium Philologiae et Criticae in Scriptoribus antiquis Graecis et Latinis emendandis et illustrandis iamdiu neglectum apud nostrates fuisse".

city. Morelli's power was considerably curtailed and "his" library – once the predator of the libraries belonging to religious houses – itself became prey to the French commissaries who were disposed to execute to the letter the peace treaty signed on 16 May 1797 between general Bonaparte and the Republic of Venice. Article V of the Treaty specified that "la république de Venise remettra enfin aux commissaires à ce destinés vingt tableaux et cinqcent manuscrits au choix du général en chef"[73]. Morelli received the visit of the secretary of the French delegation Alexandre Villetard on 17 June. The latter told him that in a few days he would receive the list of the desired manuscripts. Morelli then hurried to suggest to the Committee of Public Instruction that at least part of the material to be handed over to the French should come from the religious houses' collections[74]. On 21 June, he was then invited to assist the French representative, the chemist Claude-Louis Berthollet, to select the required material from fifteen Venetian religious houses' collections: SS. Giovanni e Paolo (Dominicans), Gesuati (Observant Dominicans on the Zattere), S. Domenico di Castello (Dominicans), S. Giorgio Maggiore (Benedictines), Santo Stefano (Augustinian Hermits), S. Salvador (Canons Regular), S. Maria dei Carmini (Carmelites), S. Maria di Nazareth (Discalced Carmelites), S. Maria Gloriosa dei Frari (Franciscans), S. Francesco della Vigna (Friars Minor of the Observance), S. Michele in Murano (Camaldolese), S. Bonaventura (Reformed Friars Minor), S. Nicola da Tolentino (Theatines), the Somaschan Library of the Salute, Fava (Oratorian Fathers of S. Philip Neri), as well as from the S. Giustina di Padua Library, and the Treviso

and Padua chapter cathedral libraries[75]. A total of 289 rare books, 50 musical books and 54 manuscripts made their way to the Library of St Mark to await the selection.

After the arrival of these confiscated manuscripts and books in the Library of St Mark, Berthollet and the mathematician Gaspard Monge made their selection in September: Morelli carefully noted on the 1789 selection list made by him all the titles handed over to the French commissaries[76]. He managed to persuade the French to include 268 titles[77] from the religious houses' libraries: 22 manuscripts came mostly from S. Giorgio Maggiore, S. Michele in Murano, the Somaschan Salute and the cathedral library of the Chapter of Padua, and another 17 from the convent of S. Giustina in Padua[78], while 50 musical volumes originated from the Salute library[79] and 120 incunabula were also handed over out of which ten were printed on vellum and 53 were first editions[80]; in addition there were 59 Aldine editions – one of which printed

73   M. de Clercq, *Recueil des traités de la France, tome 1: 1713–1802*, Paris: A. Durand et Pedone-Lauriel, 1880, 326.

74   BNM, Archivio della Biblioteca, busta "Governo Democratico", doc. 7; Zorzi, *La Libreria*, as note 6, 352.

75   Giuseppe Valentinelli, *Bibliotheca manuscripta ad S. Marci Venetiarum. Codices MSS Latini*, Venetiis: ex typographia commercii, 1868, I, 107.

76   An examination of the titles crossed out by Morelli on his 1789 list for S. Giorgio Maggiore clearly indicates that the 1789 selection list served as the basis for the 1797 French selection and that the signs of cancellation or the + signs in the margins refer to the 1797 selection. See in the present volume the article by Dondi-Prosdocimi-Raines.

77   In the end only 258 went to the French as ten Aldine editions from S. Giustina in Padua were left behind.

78   Valentinelli, *Bibliotheca manuscripta*, as note 75, I, 110, note 3.

79   The "Liste des ouvrages de musique imprimés, divisée par la Commission des sciences et arts pour faire partie des 500 volumes dus par Venise à la République française. Ex Bibliotheca Monasterii dicti della Salute" is in the Archive of the Bibliothèque Nationale de France, AM 269.

80   Ibid., Valentinelli, *Bibliotheca manuscripta*, as note 75, I, 109, note 7 for the vellum copies and note 8 for the first editions, where he enumerates 47 copies.

on vellum[81] – of which 32 came from S. Giustina in Padua (ten of these, however, remained in Venice for obscure reasons), eight were from the cathedral library of the Chapter of Padua and the same number from that of Treviso, and the remaining eleven came from libraries of different Venetian religious houses[82]. The remaining 202 volumes came from the collection of the Library of St Mark (171 Greek manuscripts, 23 in Latin, two in Italian, two in French, two in Arabic and two printed musical books)[83]. Morelli who had

already tried to get hold of the treasures from monastic libraries in 1789 understood that these collections were no longer safe. He did not lose any time: first, he kept all the remaining material in the Library of St Mark which had been sent from the religious houses and not handed over to the French (consisting of 15 manuscripts and 110 printed books) and then he was successful in demanding in September 1797 that the Committee of Public Instruction issue a decree stating that in the event of a dissolution of the regular orders he would have first choice from their collections for the "National Library" (as it was now renamed)[84].

Other material was confiscated by the "citoyen Brunet" who was at the time "agent des contributions et finances" of the French revolutionary army under Napoleon[85]. Morelli was ordered on 21 December 1797 (on the eve of the French troops' departure and the arrival of the Austrians) by the "Commissione dei V cogli Aggiunti" in charge of

81 Archive of the Bibliothèque Nationale de France, AM 269: "Liste des éditions Aldines que la Commission des sciences et arts a choisies dans les Bibliothèques de Venise, de Padoue et de Trévise pour faire partie des 500 volumes dus à la République Française".

82 BNM, Archivio della Biblioteca, busta "Biblioteche delle Corporazioni Religiose Soppresse", fasc. 1; Zorzi, *La Libreria*, as note 6, 352 and 528, note 38. In note 36 the same author suggests that the French took away all the documentation relating to the 1797 confiscation. In fact, in the Archives of the Bibliothèque Nationale de France, AM 269, Fasc. "envoi d'Italie", we find the "Liste des éditions du xve siècle que la Commission des sciences et arts a choisies dans les Bibliothèques de Venise, de Padoue et de Trévise pour faire partie des 500 volumes dus à la République Française": 117 titles are annotated although at the bottom of the list it is stated that the total number amounts to 120 (perhaps some titles were in more than one volume). There follow other pages with lists of titles arriving from each religious house. These probably refer to the first selection of titles made by the French, which arrived in the Library of St Mark and on the basis of which the final selection of 268 titles was made. In ASV, Demanio 1806–1813, b. 328, fasc. "Biblioteche. Libri cessi a biblioteche, licei etc. anno 1811 n. 219", in a document called "Biblioteche. Libri trasportati in Francia l'anno 1797", (extracted from Morelli's report dated 30 August 1806 no. 2822, fol. 49), a reference is made to 1,357 books: "S. Maria del Carmine 11; Domenicani alle Zattere 15; Sta Maria dei Frari 17; S. Francesco della Vigna 615; S. Giorgio Maggiore 24; S. Michele di Murano 26; Somaschi alla Salute 618; S. Stefano 9; S. Nicola ai Tolentini 22".

83 Archive of the Bibliothèque Nationale de France, AM 269: pages probably written by the librarian Joseph Van Praet: "Note de quelques livres rares qui manquent à la Bibliothèque Nationale [25 Therm. An 5] – Extrait du Catalogue des Mss. Grecs et Latins de la Bibliothèque de

S. Marc à Venise"; Valentinelli, *Bibliotheca manuscripta*, as note 75, I, 109–10, for the complete list of manuscripts and books' shelfmarks from the Library of St Mark handed over to the French. Valentinelli counts 203 pieces in all; Zorzi, *La Libreria*, as note 6, 352 counts 203 manuscripts and two printed books. As for the other 30 pieces due to be handed to the French following the peace treaty, Berthollet and Monge agreed to confiscate instead the famous gem with the head of Zeus and the aegis (*Giove egioco*).

84 See Valentinelli, *Bibliotheca manuscripta*, as note 75, I, 112, decree issued on 20 September 1797, article 2; Zorzi, *La Libreria*, as note 6, 528, note 39, citing from BNM, Archivio della Biblioteca, busta "Governo Democratico", doc. 53.

85 Michel Bruguière and Pierre-François Pinaud, *Guide du chercheur pour la période 1789–1815: les sources de l'histoire financière et économique* (Genève, 1992), 121; Archives Nationales, France, *Pièces isolées, collections et papiers d'érudits*, tome 5: sous-série AB, XIX3371, Dossier 3: *Padoue (gouvernement central et municipalité)*: "Lettres adressées au gouvernement central du Padouan, de la Polésine, de Rovigo et d'Adria: Brunet, agent des contributions et finances en Italie (8 juillet 1797)".

fairly imposing the tax burden on the citizens, to hand over to Brunet five rare editions[86] and two

manuscripts[87], part of the material originating from the libraries of the religious houses, as well as a famous manuscript by Niccolò Manuzzi, from the Library of St Mark collection. These volumes were never returned by the French, as they had not been part of the signed treaty between the Venetian Republic and Napoleon[88].

During the first period of Austrian rule (1798–1805), Morelli was obliged already in June 1798 to hand back all the "treasures" he had obtained from the religious libraries due to the abolition of the French decree[89]. The list preserved in the Marciana Library's archives enumerates the volumes as follows: Gesuati (Observant Dominicans on the Zattere) – 15;

---

86 Three incunabula: Marcus Fabius Quintilianus, *Institutiones oratoriae*, [Venice], Nicolaus Jenson, 21 May 1471 (GW M36818; ISTC iq00026000); Aulus Gellius, *Noctes Atticae*, Venice, Nicolaus Jenson, 1472 (GW 10594; ISTC ig00120000) bound with Priscianus, *Opera*, [Venice, Vindelinus de Spira], 1472 (GW M35406; ISTC ip00961000); *Breviarium Romanum*, Venice, Nicolaus Jenson, [before 6 May] 1478 (GW 5101; ISTC ib01112000) and two rare editions: Francesco Marchi, *Della architettura militare… libri tre. Nelli quali si descrivono li veri modi, del fortificare, che si usa a' tempi moderni. Con un breve, et utile trattato, nel quale si dimostrano li modi del fabricar l'artigliaria, et la prattica di adoperarla, da quelli che hanno carico di essa*, Brescia, Comino Presegni per Gaspare dall'Oglio, 1599; *Geographiae veteris Scriptores græci minores*, Oxonii, E theatro Sheldoniano, 1698–1712, 4 vols. Valentinelli, *Bibliotheca manuscripta*, as note 75, I, 112, notes 1–2. The case of the Quintilian volume printed by Jenson in 1471 is quite indicative of the confusion in 1797. It is certain that two copies arrived in the Library of St Mark in 1797: one from the library of S. Giorgio Maggiore (as in BNM, Archivio della Biblioteca, busta "Biblioteche delle Corporazioni Religiose Soppresse", fasc. 1: Morelli's 1789 selection list, p. 6) and another from S. Michele di Murano (Bibliothèque Nationale de France, AM 269, "Note de plusieurs livres rares qui se trouvent dans quelques bibliothèque de Venise et que la Bibliothèque Nationale se commande aux soins des citoyens commissaires du Gouvernement pour la recherche des Mouvemens des arts en Italie, le 25 thermidor an 5"; BNM, Archivio della Biblioteca, busta "Biblioteche delle Corporazioni Religiose Soppresse", Morelli's note: "Nota di libri a stampa e Manoscritti estratti dalla Libreria di San Michele di Murano, a richiesta delli Cittadini Berthollet e Monge, Commissarii della Rep. Francese, poi da essi lasciati in dietro" – yet both Quintilian and Aulus Gellius are crossed out). One copy, printed on vellum, is reported to have been handed over to the French in 1797 as part of the 500 confiscated volumes (Bibliothèque Nationale de France, AM 269, "Liste des éditions du xvᵉ siècle que la Commission des sciences et arts a choisies dans les Bibliothèques de Venise, de Padoue et de Trévise pour faire partie des 500 volumes dus à la République Française"). As the copy from S. Giorgio Maggiore was not printed on vellum (according to Morelli's 1789 selection list), it is possible that the removed copy was the one belonging to S. Michele di Murano. Yet, if the "citoyen Brunet" took away the S. Giorgio Maggiore copy

(left behind, as the S. Michele di Murano copy had been chosen), it is strange that a Quintilian copy belonging to the same monastic library was handed over on 4 September 1806 by Morelli to Giovanni Rossi, in charge of the warehouse located in S. Maria dell'Umiltà. Morelli stated that "the following eight books once belonging to the library of S. Giorgio Maggiore, have been handed over to him [i.e. Morelli] on July 20 of the current year" ("li seguenti otto libri già appartenenti alla Biblioteca di S. Giorgio Maggiore, a lui stati provisoriamente consegnati addì 20 luglio prossimo passato"). (BNM, Archivio della Biblioteca, busta "Governo Italico" among documents listing books sent to Milan, Ministry of Public Education: "No. 27"). See also note 90. Moreover, in the list of books which returned to Venice in 1815, we find at no. 334 an Aldine edition of Quintilian (1514) but not the 1471 Jenson edition (Bibliothèque Nationale de France, AM 272: "Fascicule Etat des livres imprimés tirés des Bibliothèques de Venise pour la Bibliothèque du Roi, et restitués le 5 octobre 1815" signed "Baron d'Ottenfels, Commissaire de S.M.I et R. Observatoire"). The Bibliothèque Nationale de France has today three copies: Res. X. 598 (no indication of provenance); Res. Vel. 534 (provenance: Lazzaro Bonamico, 1 May 1535; Pierre et Jacques Du Puy; Bibliothèque Royale; with illumination); Res. Vel. 535 (provenance: Zen family (Venice?); with illumination). I am grateful to Cristina Dondi and Sabrina Minuzzi for their help and observations.

87 "*Biblia sacra* et *Evangeliae quatuor*". Valentinelli, *Bibliotheca manuscripta*, as note 75, I, 111, note 2.

88 See Giovanni Rossi's testimony in Cicogna, *Delle iscrizioni*, as note 21, IV (1834), 601–02.

89 See note 84.

S. Michele in Murano (Camaldolese) – 14; S. Giorgio Maggiore (Benedictines) – 13; the Somaschan Library of the Salute – 12; S. Francesco della Vigna (Friars Minor of the Observance) – 9; S. Maria Gloriosa dei Frari (Franciscans) – 4; S. Nicola da Tolentino (Theatines) – 3; Santo Stefano (Augustinian Hermits) – 2; S. Maria dei Carmini (Carmelites) – 1: all in all 73 volumes (manuscripts and printed books) out of the 110 printed books and 15 manuscripts that remained in the "Public Library" (as it was now called) after the 1797 selection by the French commissaries[90].

By the time the French returned in 1806, now under Napoleon Bonaparte, things had radically changed. As we shall see, contrary to Pietro La Cute's descriptions of the complete chaos regarding the dissolution of the monastic libraries under Napoleonic rule, the documents tell a completely different story[91]. From the outset, the French had clear cultural and educational objectives in mind and pursued them with an astonishing organizational capability. Morelli, too, followed his own cultural plan, trying to fit into the larger French one.

Morelli under the Napoleonic Kingdom of Italy (1806–1814)

On 1 May 1806 Venice and the mainland were annexed to the Napoleonic Kingdom of Italy. The 8 June 1805 decree of the new French ruler regarding the reorganization of the secular and regular clergy, including nuns, was extended on 23 March 1806 to all the territories of the ex-Republic of Venice[92]. And already on 10 June the Viceroy of Italy, Eugène de Beauharnais, promulgated a decree ordering all libraries and archives to be sealed off (article III) as well as inventories of their possessions to be prepared by the governmental department which managed state-owned land and property (*Demanio*) (article II). Moreover, the decree invited the Head of the *Dipartimento della Pubblica Istruzione* (Education department) to communicate to the *Demanio* the choice of manuscripts that should be sent to Milan (article IV), and the books needed for school libraries (article V). All other books were destined to be sold in public auctions (article VI)[93]. When on 19 June 1806 the Director General of the *Demanio* in Milan asked the Venetian local office to send him all the catalogues and inventories of the libraries belonging to religious[94], Morelli acted immediately: on 21 June he sent a letter to the authorities asking for the books not to be sent to Milan but to the "library which has the sovereign right", i.e., the Library of St Mark[95]. The Venetian librarian also informed the governor General Sextius Alexandre François de Miollis of his request and the latter, finally convinced, wrote on 8 July 1806 a letter to the Viceroy Beauharnais in which he asked that the books remain "sur le sol qu'ils ont embelli des fruits eclatans de leur travaux"[96]. The

---

90　BNM, Archivio della Biblioteca, busta "Biblioteche delle Corporazioni Religiose Soppresse", fasc. 2. Cf. Zorzi, *La Libreria*, as note 6, 529, note 53.

91　La Cute, 'Le vicende delle biblioteche monastiche', as note 1, 598.

92　*Bollettino delle leggi del Regno d'Italia*, Milano: Regis stamperia Veladini, 1805, I, no. 45, 123–40; 1806, II, no. 56, 393; on 28 July 1806 more specific orders were

---

issued regarding the monasteries to be suppressed (ibid., 1806, II, no. 160, 809–20); finally on 25 April 1810, a decree was issued which extended the suppressions to the whole territory of the Kingdom of Italy (ibid., 1810, I, no. 77, 264–67).

93　*Bollettino delle leggi del Regno d'Italia*, Milano: Dalla Reale Stamperia, 1806, pt. II, no. 100, 609–11.

94　ASV, Demanio 1806–1813, b. 328, fasc. "Biblioteche. Libri cessi a biblioteche, licei etc. anno 1811 n. 219", letter dated 19 June 1806.

95　BNM, Archivio della Biblioteca, busta "Governo Italico", doc. 13; published by La Cute, 'Le vicende delle biblioteche monastiche', as note 1, 7–10; cf. Zorzi, *La Libreria*, as note 6, 530, note 91.

96　BNM, Archivio della Biblioteca, busta "Governo Italico", fasc. 16, published by La Cute, 'Le vicende delle biblioteche monastiche', as note 1, 10; cf. Zorzi, *La Libreria*, as note 6, 530, note 93.

request was denied[97]. Morelli was forced to hand over in September the rare volumes already in his possession to be sent later on to a book warehouse in S. Maria dell'Umiltà[98]. Perhaps at this point he realized that he should review his priorities and try to secure the most he could in the circumstances.

A few days after Morelli's request, the *Demanio* in Milan was already alarmed – a well-known bookseller named Salvi was headed to Venice to buy an entire monastic collection: the library of the Camaldolese order of S. Michele in Murano, which had been offered to him for a thousand *zecchini*. The police followed the bookseller, who in fact got to Murano only to discover that unfortunately for his business the library had already been sealed off[99]. This episode convinced the head of the *Demanio* of the need to act quickly and he asked the local Venetian head of the department to take proper measures. The only person the latter could turn to was Jacopo Morelli who was politely requested to indicate the names of various individuals who could diligently record the books and carry out an intelligent selection. Morelli was by no means seen as officially heading this operation at this point of time; he was merely considered to be the best-informed person on the subject[100].

Morelli proposed three names: Giovanni Rossi, the abbot Sebastiano Ongin Polacco and Paolo Giaxich[101]. Giovanni Rossi (1776–1852), Venetian by birth, had trained as a lawyer but never practised the profession; he was a founder of the Accademia Letteraria and a collector of books and manuscripts and had had past experience in rearranging the archives of the Procurators of St Mark. Together with the appointment to manage the religious libraries, he was also called by the head of the State Archives, Carlo Antonio Marin, to assist him and the archivist Jacopo Chiodo in rearranging the Venetian Republic archives moved by the French from the Doge's Palace to the Scuola Grande (or Confraternity) of S. Teodoro in 1807[102]. As for Ongin Polacco, not much is known about him, except for his extensive learning, judged by the criteria he applied in selecting books and registering them in the destination catalogues he prepared according to standards which are still used today. Later he left Venice to become a *Censore* in a boarding school which used to be the College of the Nobility – renamed the Regio Liceo Convitto Metaurense in Urbino in 1811[103]. The third name is that of Paolo Giaxich, nephew of the *Delegato*

97   Alvise Zorzi, *Venezia scomparsa* ([Vicenza] and Milano, 1972), 84.

98   See also note 89 for the June 1798 request made by the Austrians.

99   ASV, Demanio 1806–1813, b. 328, fasc. without title, letters exchanged between Milan, Treviso and Venice dated 14 June (no. 178); 5 July (nos 10–11); 9 July (no. 246); 13 July (no. 374); 15 July (no. 12); 17 July (no. 7); 17 July (no. 15); 20 July 1806 (n.n.).

100 Perosa, head of the *Demanio* wrote to Morelli: "non so a chi meglio dirigermi che a Lei, S.r Abb. Preg.mo, affinché voglia sollecitamente indicarmi le persone ch'ha il fondamento delle sue distinte analoghe conoscenze credesse le più opportune". ASV, Demanio 1806–1813, b. 328, fasc. marked "Monumenti, Belle Arti, Biblioteche e stampe", letter dated 25 June 1806 (no. 563).

101 Cicogna, *Delle iscrizioni*, as note 21, IV (1834), 601.

102 Dorit Raines, 'La bibliothèque manuscrite de Giovanni Rossi. Un gardien du passé vénitien et sa collection', *Miscellanea Marciana*, 5 (1990), 77–205; Francesca Cavazzana Romanelli, 'Topografia del potere, topografia della memoria. I luoghi della politica e dell'amministrazione della Serenissima nella rievocazione ottocentesca di Giovanni Rossi', in *Tempi uomini ed eventi di storia veneta. Studi in onore di Federico Seneca*, Sergio Perini et al. eds (Rovigo, 2003), 457–76; Luigi Ferro, 'Jacopo Chiodo, fondatore dell'archivio di stato di Venezia', in *Ad Alessandro Luzio gli archivi di stato italiani: miscellanea di studi storici* (Firenze, 1933), 364–69.

103 ASV, Demanio 1806–1813, b. 328, fasc. marked "Biblioteche e Belle Arti [1808–11]", Ongin's letter dated 7 July 1810 to Francesco Vendramin, *Intendente di Finanza del Dipartimento dell'Adriatico*; Letter of the *Dipartimento di Finanza* dated 7 October 1810 to the *Direttore generale del Demanio, Boschi e Diritti Uniti*, no. 23542/7202.

per Culto, Dipartimento dell'Adriatico, a scholar and Rossi's friend[104].

The task of all three (each always signed his reports as "Delegate of the suppressed religious houses' libraries"), was to be divided into three stages: 1. Select the material according to the specifications supplied by the authorities (but in fact, as we shall see, by Morelli) and prepare the destination catalogues; 2. Prepare the material to be sent to the chosen warehouse: the monastery of St Anna in Padua (where the libraries of forty different monasteries would be accumulated during the Napoleonic period) and the provenance catalogues; 3. Prepare the remaining material for public sale[105]. It seems that the work was divided up between the three so that they could finish more quickly: Rossi and Giaxich (who suffered from frail health) were to deal with: S. Giacomo della Giudecca (the Servite friars), S. Maria dei Carmini (the Carmelites), S. Secondo and S. Pietro in Murano (Dominicans), S. Giorgio Maggiore (Benedictines), Sant'Elena (the Olivetan Congregation), while Ongin was responsible for S. Giobbe (Friars Minor of the Observance), S. Giorgio in Alga and S. Maria di Nazareth (both of these institutions belonged to the mendicant Discalced Carmelites). The outcome after four months of work by Ongin was a total of twelve bookcases sent in November 1806 to Padua (3,675 books from S. Giobbe including eleven manuscripts and twenty-six incunabula) and 1,093 from S. Giorgio in Alga[106], while Rossi (helped by Giaxich who was at times ill) continued until March 1807 and sent fifty-seven bookcases[107].

At this point, an enormous quantity of material had accumulated in the warehouse of St Anna and the *Demanio*'s strategy changed: it was decided to move the volumes from the other Venetian religious houses to a warehouse situated in Venice: S. Maria dell'Umiltà, from which the Benedictine sisters had been removed in June 1806. This time the religious libraries in question were those of S. Domenico in Castello, S. Francesco di Paola, S. Nicoletto dei Frari, S. Francesco del Deserto, la Certosa, SS. Giovanni e Paolo (book collection sent back and deposited in the S. Maria della Fava oratory, a part of which is still there), S. Salvador, Santo Stefano and S. Francesco della Vigna. The volumes were transported to the Venetian warehouse where the *Dipartimento di Finanza* had set a guard. Giovanni Rossi was assigned to the task of selection, working from October 1807 to June 1808. From his report we can deduce that inside the warehouse each suppressed library was allocated its own space and that the selection was made after a provenance catalogue had been carefully prepared, dividing the material into "good", "mediocre" and "discarded" volumes. The idea was to store the books according to the institution of provenance and select the material according to the following procedure: first, manuscripts, incunabula and other printed books were separated, with the first two categories regarded as material to be sent to the Paduan warehouse. As for the other printed books: Rossi chose from each library those which he regarded as "good" (*buoni*) either because of their edition or for the quality of their contents. The material chosen was carefully listed in a destination catalogue and put into cases to be sent to Padua. As for "the mediocre" volumes (*mediocri*), which could be given to schools and other cultural institutions, Rossi did not think it worthwhile to compile a catalogue but only noted how many there were according to format. Finally, the items designated as "discarded" (*scarti*) went immediately for sale. One cannot avoid observing a similarity between this *modus*

---

104   Girolamo Dandolo, *La Caduta della Repubblica di Venezia ed i suoi ultimi cinquant'anni: studii storici* (Venezia, 1855), 252.

105   BNM, Archivio della Biblioteca, busta "Governo Italico", doc. 13; see note 93.

106   ASV, Demanio 1806–1813, b. 328, fasc. marked "Anno 1807 Biblioteche. Spedizioni Libri Padova n. 220", 1st fasc., dated 26 November 1806 and signed Ongin Polacco.

107   Ibid., 2nd fac., dated 7 March 1807 and signed Giovanni Rossi.

operandi and Morelli's selection methods in the 1780s[108].

The books selected to be sent to Padua were placed in cases (2,194 from S. Domenico in Castello, 1,060 from S. Nicoletto dei Frari, 559 from S. Francesco di Paola, and 8,782 from the remaining religious libraries). Rossi reported that he was still unable to make a selection from the libraries of SS. Giovanni e Paolo, S. Salvador, Santo Stefano and S. Francesco della Vigna, because of the amount of work they demanded. He noted that almost all the libraries had been subject to previous spoliations of rare and valuable material, especially manuscripts and incunabula, so that he regarded what he had examined as the "leftovers" from those libraries. He observed, however, that the library of S. Giorgio Maggiore was the most valuable. Rossi placed 1,800 books from this library into seventeen cases to be sent to Padua, among which he mentioned 85 incunabula (some in a deteriorated condition) and 180 manuscripts (mostly "cartacei", "on paper", from the sixteenth century onwards). The other library he mentioned in detail was that of S. Nicoletto dei Frari which had four incunabula and one parchment manuscript. Rossi then tried to sum up everything that had been sent to Padua by himself and Ongin in three lots dated November 1806, March 1807 and June 1808. All together, 17,918 books were sent to Padua[109]. The rest was destined either for cultural institutions or for sale.

After sending the material to Padua Giovanni Rossi was no longer involved in the selection of books. In September 1808 Sebastiano Ongin reappeared and sent his own report in which he bitterly criticized Rossi for his disorderly work and equally pointed out the precarious state of the warehouse in Venice and the potential damage the ambience could cause to the delicate materials[110]. The *Direttore generale del Demanio* in Milan asked Ongin to send him books on specific topics; Ongin then moved on to deal with the books intended for public auction[111]. Later on he was assigned a new task: to select books for various schools and academies from the "mediocre" category created by Rossi from the remaining libraries that the latter had not had time to go over: S. Salvador, Santo Stefano and S. Francesco della Vigna. He compiled a destination catalogue for the Società di Medicina (that in 1812 would become the Ateneo Veneto) comprising 2,095 volumes: 955 from S. Francesco della Vigna, 600 from S. Salvador and 540 from Santo Stefano[112]. And it is at this point that Morelli comes back to centre stage.

Morelli, who had been practically forced to participate in the systematic closure of religious houses, had to make a choice: whether to sacrifice most of the material in order to obtain what he really thought worthwhile: the libraries of S. Michele in Murano (one of the richest in precious manuscripts), the Capuchins in the Giudecca (containing Tommaso Rangone's collection or what remained of it) and above all, Apostolo Zeno's library in the Gesuati (Observant Dominicans on the Zattere). As soon as the authorities took the decision to distribute the books to different cultural academies, they

---

108 ASV, Demanio 1806–1813, b. 328, fasc. marked "Biblioteche. An. 1808, Elenco di Padova 1819 n. 218", Rossi's report dated 5 June 1808; ibid., fasc. marked "Biblioteche e Belle Arti [1808–11]", letter dated 26 June 1810 no. 17417 of the *Direttore generale del Dipartimento di Finanza*.

109 Ibid., fasc. marked "Biblioteche. An. 1808, Elenco di Padova 1819 n. 218", Rossi's report dated 5 June 1808.

110 ASV, Demanio 1806–1813, b. 328, fasc. marked "Biblioteche e Belle Arti [1808–11]", Ongin's report dated 27 October 1808.

111 ASV, Demanio 1806–1813, b. 328, fasc. marked "Biblioteche e Belle Arti [1808–11]", letter dated 21 September 1808, signed by Ongin; letter of the Director General of the *Demanio* dated 26 September 1808.

112 ASV, Demanio 1806–1813, b. 326, fasc. I, 1/5; b. 328, fasc. marked "An. 1809. Biblioteche Scarti n. 223".

announced to Morelli in January 1809 that the Accademia di Belle Arti would have the first choice of the books from the Gesuati library. Morelli though had already made his choice of the books he wanted from there and was waiting for the authorization to move them to the Library of St Mark. He became furious and practically threatened to denounce the *Demanio* in Venice for not having the necessary authorization to intervene. He also asked them to refrain from any action until the *Dipartimento della Pubblica Istruzione* had been informed. His letter was so vehement in its tone that Morelli won the first round[113]. The Gesuati library was for the time secure.

By that time Ongin Polacco had finished compiling the catalogues and asked for a period of leave and proper remuneration which was refused by Milan on the grounds that he had never been appointed as the Delegate of the suppressed libraries, a title which was reserved only for Giovanni Rossi[114]. After Ongin's departure Morelli now found himself directly in charge of the situation, signing off documents as the Delegate himself. He received all the provenance catalogues from the remaining libraries, but his attention was now concentrated mainly on the Gesuati, S. Michele in Murano and the Capuchin libraries to which he paid visits and selected books. The tenor of the official correspondence changed drastically in the years 1810–1811: the administration seemed to have accepted Morelli's opinion that the best haven for the valuable items

was the Library of St Mark and not Milan and the authorities patiently waited until Morelli had finished selecting the books he thought fit. At the same time other matters got neglected: although the books for the Società di medicina had already been selected in April 1809, the handover letter was signed in March 1811 and the items left for their new location only in December of that year after recurrent requests to move the material which was already in a deteriorating state[115]. Likewise, Morelli visited all the remaining libraries, made selections and handed over to the other institutions designated to receive them the books they had requested: the Seminario patriarcale, Collegio navale and Convitto S. Caterina[116].

All in all, apart from the books and manuscripts sold by the friars before the juggernaut of dissolution intervened in the libraries of the religious houses, the final figures were: 1,319 manuscripts and rare editions which left the city in 1797 and were subsequently partially restituted by the French; 17,918 volumes sent in 1806 and 1808 to the warehouse of St Anna in Padua and a further 1,949 sent in 1811 to Milan; 31,581 volumes given to cultural institutions in the city in 1806 and 1811; 179 handed back to friars in 1806 and the remaining put up for sale: in 1806 (28,832 volumes) and from 1811 to 1814 (81,150 volumes)[117].

* * *

If we now return to our initial question about how the cultural impact of the dissolution of

113 ASV, Demanio 1806–1813, b. 328, fasc. marked "Biblioteche e Belle Arti [1808–11]", letter dated 31 January 1809, no. 372 of the Director General of the *Dipartimento della Pubblica Istruzione* to Morelli and a letter dated 9 February 1809, no. 3896 of the Director General of the *Demanio* to the *Dipartimento di Finanza*; Morelli's answer to the *Dipartimento di Finanza* is dated 16 February 1809.

114 ASV, Demanio 1806–1813, b. 328, fasc. marked "Biblioteche e Belle Arti [1808–11]", letter dated 26 June 1810, no. 17417 of the Director General of the *Dipartimento di Finanza*.

115 ASV, Demanio 1806–1813, b. 328, fasc. marked "Biblioteche. Libri cessi a biblioteche, licei etc. anno 1811, no. 219", no. F.

116 ASV, Demanio 1806–1813, b. 328, fasc. marked "Biblioteche. Libri cessi a biblioteche, licei etc. anno 1811, no. 219". This explains how these and other similar institutions preserve special collections material still today.

117 See Tables 9.1–9.2 in the Annex.

the religious libraries in Venice can be assessed, the least we can say is that out of this massive confiscation, Morelli succeeded in obtaining for "his" library up until 1812 3,462 printed books and 631 manuscripts. While most of his claims were satisfied, he did not succeed in preventing the transfer of the Library of St Mark to the Doge's palace[118] nor in obtaining what he cherished most: Apostolo Zeno's collection in its entirety. The return of the Austrians in 1814 partially reinstated the situation: the spoils of war taken by the French were partially returned in 1815; the library obtained further space in its new home (but did not regain its original building), and Morelli secured the Emperor's promise that Apostolo Zeno's collection would be entrusted to him. The promise was partially fulfilled only after his death: in 1820 the Library of St Mark received 315 books from the Somaschan library of the Salute, and in 1823 and then again in 1832 a further 196 manuscripts and 20,759 volumes from the Zeno collection. The total number of volumes from the suppressed religious houses which came into the Library of St Mark from 1797 to 1832 is 24,536 books and 827 manuscripts[119]. The books deposited in Padua during the period of French rule were initially neglected, then slowly put up for sale or transferred at the request of religious seminaries in the Veneto until 1862 when the warehouse of St Anna in Padua was finally closed[120]. The remaining books were dispersed among municipal and school libraries all over the Veneto region. The remaining catalogues prepared under the period of French rule can be of great help in tracing the whereabouts of these entirely dispersed collections.

118 See Zorzi, *La Libreria*, as note 6, 363–64.

119 Zorzi, *La Libreria*, as note 6, 365–68; BNM, Archivio della Biblioteca, busta 1815, fasc. 109, report dated 13 December 1815.

120 Lavinia Prosdocimi, 'Sulle tracce di antichi inventari e note manoscritte. Codici da librerie claustrali nella Biblioteca Universitaria di Padova', in *Splendore nella regola: codici miniati da monasteri e conventi nella Biblioteca Universitaria di Padova*, Federica Toniolo and Pietro Gnan eds (Padova, 2011), 55.

Table 9.1. Holdings, confiscation and book sales of the Venetian Religious orders' libraries – the 1797–1808 dissolutions

LEGEND

vols – printed books
ms. – manuscripts
inc. – incunabula
rare – rare books (mostly inc.)
Given back – to friars.
ACC – Accademia di Belle Arti, Venezia
ASV – Archivio di Stato, Venezia
AV – Ateneo Veneto (Scuola Medica), Venezia
BCMC – Biblioteca Civica Museo Correr, Venezia
BNM – Biblioteca Marciana, Venezia (1811, 1823, 1832)
LIC – Liceo Convitto di Venezia
MAR – Collegio di Marina, Venezia
SEM – various religious seminaries (Venice, Concordia, Chioggia, Comacchio, Rovigo, Ceneda).

NAME OF LIBRARY AND ORDER	BEFORE 1789 – N. OF BOOKS IN CATALOGUES	1789 – NUMBER OF BOOKS IN LIBRARY	1789 – MORELLI'S SELECTION[121]	1797 – TAKEN AWAY BY THE FRENCH[122]	1806–08 – SENT TO PADUA[123]	1806–08 – GIVEN TO INSTITUTIONS	1806–08 – SOLD IN AUCTIONS
S. Giorgio Maggiore (Benedictines) 1806			19 ms.; 62 rare	ASV: 24 titles	5,448 vols (213 ms.; 78 inc.)		10,088 vols
S. Pietro Martire – Murano (Dominicans) 1806			2 inc. – moved to BM		305 vols		1,168 vols
S. Maria dei Carmini (Carmelites) 1806			11 rare	1 ms, 3 inc., 9 rare (ASV: 11 titles)	954 vols (29 ms.; 47 inc.)		1809 – 4,510 vols
S. Giobbe (Friars Minor of the Observance) 1806					3,675 vols (11 ms.; 26 inc.)		
S. Giorgio in Alga (Discalced Carmelites) 1806					1,093 vols		

121   In this column the "rare" category includes incunabula.

122   Sources: Romanin, *Storia documentata*, vol. X, 396–446. Transcribed from BCMC, Ms. Correr, no. 1167/1937 (Miscellanea, n. XXXVIII); ASV, Direzione del Demanio, 1806–13, b. 328, fasc. 2: "Biblioteche. Libri cessi a biblioteche, licei etc. anno 1811 n. 219: "Biblioteche. Libri trasportati in Francia l'anno 1797". [Note in margin by unidentified person that these books were transported to Paris in 1797 along with 50 manuscripts as in Morelli's report dated 30 August 1806, no. 2822, fol. 49 (2B)].

123   The number of manuscripts and incunabula in brackets are included in the overall number of volumes.

NAME OF LIBRARY AND ORDER	BEFORE 1789 – N. OF BOOKS IN CATALOGUES	1789 – NUMBER OF BOOKS IN LIBRARY	1789 – MORELLI'S SELECTION[121]	1797 – TAKEN AWAY BY THE FRENCH[122]	1806–08 – SENT TO PADUA[123]	1806–08 – GIVEN TO INSTITUTIONS	1806–08 – SOLD IN AUCTIONS
S. Domenico di Castello (Dominicans) 1806					2,194 vols		2,916 vols
S. Nicoletto dei Frari (Friars Minor Conventual) 1806					1,060 vols		886 vols
S. Francesco di Paola (Minims) 1806					559 vols (13 inc.)		1,167 vols
Sant'Elena (Olivetans) 1806	734 vols; 10 ms.[124]				1,069 vols (13 ms.)		947 vols
S. Secondo in Isola (Dominicans) 1806		1798–1611 vols; 2 ms.[125]			559 vols		2,088 vols
S. Giacomo della Giudecca (Servants of Mary – Servites) 1806					447 vols		744 vols
Sant'Andrea della Certosa (Carthusians) 1806	1600–100 ms, 1,300 vols[126] the rare vols sold before 1789[127]		12 rare – moved to BM		—	—	—
S. Cristoforo in Isola (Augustinian Hermits) 1806					—	—	—
S. Spirito in Laguna (Friars Minor of the Observance) 1806					—	—	—

124 The catalogue is in Cod. Marc. It. VII, 1562 (=7843).
125 The Catalogue is in Cod. Marc. Lat. X, 333 (=3757).
126 Biblioteca Apostolica Vaticana, Vat. Lat.11276, cc. 502r–515v.
127 Zorzi, *La Libreria*, as note 6, 517, note 79.

NAME OF LIBRARY AND ORDER	BEFORE 1789 – N. OF BOOKS IN CATALOGUES	1789 – NUMBER OF BOOKS IN LIBRARY	1789 – MORELLI'S SELECTION[121]	1797 – TAKEN AWAY BY THE FRENCH[122]	1806–08 – SENT TO PADUA[123]	1806–08 – GIVEN TO INSTITUTIONS	1806–08 – SOLD IN AUCTIONS
S. Francesco del Deserto (Reformed Friars Minor)					—	—	—
S. Salvador (Canons Regular) 1808					118 vols	AV – 600 vols	
S. Francesco della Vigna (Friars Minor of the Observance) 1808			18 ms.; 60 rare	1 ms.; 20 inc.; 21 rare (ASV: 615 titles)	226 vols	AV – 955 vols Given back to friars – 179 vols	
Santo Stefano (Augustinian Hermits) 1808			2 ms.; 21 rare	1 ms., 1 inc.; 14 rare (ASV: 9 titles)	211 vols	AV – 540 vols	
Deposit at Convent dell'Umiltà							1809–4,318 vols

Table 9.2. Holdings, confiscation and book sales of the Venetian Religious orders' libraries – the 1810 dissolution

NAME OF LIBRARY AND ORDER	BEFORE 1789 – N. OF BOOKS IN CATALOGUES	1789 – NUMBER OF BOOKS IN LIBRARY	1789 – MORELLI'S SELECTION	1797 – TAKEN AWAY BY THE FRENCH[128]	1811 – SENT TO MILAN[128]	1811–32 – GIVEN TO INSTITUTIONS[129]	1811–14 – SOLD IN AUCTIONS
S. Mattia – Murano (Camaldolese)	12,000 volumi catalogo 1777 Francesco Rogantini, see Barbieri – Zorzi, 327, 40,000 vols (out of which 2,352 ms. and 1,203 inc.)		15 ms.; 20 rare	3 ms.; 3 inc., 11 rare		BNM – 6 vols; 3 ms. SEM – 25 vols	3,089 vols (792 in f°, 864 in 4°, 1,433 in 12°) + 31 vols to G.B. Ferro = 3,120 vols
the Somaschan Library of the Salute	30,000 vols[130]		41 ms.; 116 rare	2 ms.; 81 doges' illuminations; 25 inc.; 97 rare; 268 musical editions; 6,883 engravings (Romanin, X, 437 counts 6,175 engravings); app. 3,000 drawings (ASV: 618 titles)	795 vols (not mentioned by La Cute, 48)	BNM – 448 vols; 135 ms. BNM (1820) – 315 vols AV – 62 vols MAR – 381 vols SEM – 193 vols; (1820) – 1,198 vols	1813–14,106 vols + 618 vols to Ant. Vianello (1814) + 236 vols in 1820 = 14,960 vols
Gesuati (Observant Dominicans on the Zattere) 1811, 1823, 1832	30,000 vols[131]		63 ms.; 217 rare	67 ms.; 217 inc.; 37 rare (ASV: 15 titles)	810 vols (not mentioned in ASV, Direzione..., doc. 2C)	ACC – 208 vols BNM – 1,859 vols; 477 ms BNM (1823) – 13,479 vols; 196 ms BNM (1832) – 7,280 vols	1832–9,701 vols

128 Source: ASV, Direzione del Demanio, 1806–13, b. 328, fasc. 2: "Biblioteche. Libri cessi a biblioteche, licei etc. anno 1811 n. 219", doc. dated 10 February 1812: "Elenco dei libri da spedire a Milano, Direzione Generale della Pubblica Istruzione, consegnati al sig. r Fuchz da Bettio". Numbers slightly different from those published by La Cute, 'Le vicende delle biblioteche monastiche', as note 1, 48. Riccardo Quinto, *Manoscritti medievali nella Biblioteca dei Redentoristi di Venezia (S. Maria della consolazione, detta della 'Fava')* (Padova, 2006).

129 Unless otherwise specified in this column and the following one – the number of books refers to 1811.

130 Zorzi, *La Libreria*, as note 6, 334.

131 Ibid., 334.

NAME OF LIBRARY AND ORDER	BEFORE 1789 – N. OF BOOKS IN CATALOGUES	1789 – NUMBER OF BOOKS IN LIBRARY	1789 – MORELLI'S SELECTION	1797 – TAKEN AWAY BY THE FRENCH	1811 – SENT TO MILAN[128]	1811–32 – GIVEN TO INSTITUTIONS[129]	1811–14 – SOLD IN AUCTIONS
S. Maria Gloriosa dei Frari (Franciscans)	6,000 vols in fol. all with Dutch binding[132]		3 ms.; 23 rare	2 ms.; 3 inc.; 104 rare (ASV: 17 titles)	122 vols (also La Cute, 48)	BNM – 151 vols, 1 ms. MAR – 85 vols AV – 24 vols SEM – 248 vols	1811, 1814 – 3,522 vols + aprx. 20 vols to G. B. Cavallini + 17 vols to Ant. Vianello = 3,559 vols
S. Nicola da Tolentino (Theatines)			28 ms.; 29 rare	ASV: 22 titles	42 vols (La Cute, 48: 40 vols)	BNM – 63 vols MAR – 15 vols SEM – 88 vols	5,224 vols
S. Maria di Nazareth (Discalced Carmelites)			1 ms.; 16 rare		103 vols (La Cute, 48: 102 vols)	BNM – 277 vols; 2 ms. MAR – 20 vols AV – 10 vols SEM – 124 vols	1811–13 – 6,376 vols (2,100 in f°, 1,750 in 4°, 2,300 in 12°, 236 – unknown format) +12 vols to G.B. Ferro = 6,388 vols
S. Michele – Murano (Camaldolese)			37 ms.; 55 rare	82 ms.; 54 inc. (ASV: 26 titles)		BNM – 264 vols; 12 ms ACC – 250 vols LIC – 957 vols SEM – 41 vols	16,000 vols
S. Maria dei Servi (Servites)						BNM – 27 vols	1813 – 3,428 vols (633 in f°, 874 in 4°, 1,921 in 12°) +20 vols to G.B. Ferro = 3,448 vols

132 La Cute, 'Le vicende delle biblioteche monastiche', as note 1, 598.

NAME OF LIBRARY AND ORDER	BEFORE 1789 – N. OF BOOKS IN CATALOGUES	1789 – NUMBER OF BOOKS IN LIBRARY	1789 – MORELLI'S SELECTION	1797 – TAKEN AWAY BY THE FRENCH	1811 – SENT TO MILAN[128]	1811–32 – GIVEN TO INSTITUTIONS[129]	1811–14 – SOLD IN AUCTIONS
Redentore in the Giudecca (Friars Minor Capuchins)					38 vols (La Cute, 48: 37 vols)	BNM – 54 vols MAR – 11 vols AV – 22 vols SEM – 32 vols	1813–3,681 vols (1,462 in f°, 1,219 in 4°, 1,000 in 12°) + 613 vols to G.B. Ferro = 4,294 vols
Fava (Oratorian Fathers of S. Philip Neri)					39 vols (La Cute, 48: 49 vols)	BNM – 210 vols MAR – 23 vols AV – 5 vols SEM – 102 vols	1812–5,295 vols
S. Bonaventura (Reformed Friars Minor)			5 ms.; 11 rare	3 rare		BNM – 37 vols	1813–4,152 vols (1,216 in f°, 1,406 in 4°, 1,530 in 12°) +617 vols to G.B. Ferro = 4,769 vols
S. Clemente in Isola (Camaldolese)						BNM – 4 vols	3,111 vols + 27 vols to Ant. Vianello in 1814 = 3,138 vols
SS. Giovanni e Paolo (Dominicans)	1777–84 Beradelli Gk – 155 ms.; Lat and It – 643 ms. (Morelli – 716) plus other 5 identified by provenance note by Quinto, 351–72)		303 ms.: 78 inc. – moved to BM			BNM (1810) – 25 vols BNM (1812) – 37 vols	1812–3,138 vols (deposited in Fava convent)
S. Sebastiano (Girolamini)							1813–1,238 vols (362 in f°, 396 in 4°, 480 in 12°) +16 vols to G.B. Ferro = 1,254 vols

Bibliography

Manuscripts and Archival Sources

Oxford, Bodleian Library, MS Canon. Class. Lat. 152.
Oxford, Bodleian Library, MS Canon. Ital. 51.
Oxford, Bodleian Library, MS Canon. Ital. 164.
Oxford, Bodleian Library, MS Canon. Ital. 172.
Oxford, Bodleian Library, MS Canon. Ital. 192.
Oxford, Bodleian Library, MS Canon. Ital. 203.
Oxford, Bodleian Library, MS Canon. Ital. 246.
Oxford, Bodleian Library, MS Canon. Ital. 247.
Oxford, Bodleian Library, MS Canon. Pat. Lat 12.
Oxford, Bodleian Library, MS Canon. Pat. Lat 42.
Oxford, Bodleian Library, MS Canon. Pat. Lat 58.
Oxford, Bodleian Library, MS Laud. Misc. 717.

Paris, Archive of the Bibliothèque Nationale de France, AM 269.
Paris, Archive of the Bibliothèque Nationale de France, AM 272.
Paris, Archives Nationales, *Pièces isolées, collections et papiers d'érudits*, tome 5: sous-série AB, XIX3371, Dossier 3: *Padoue (gouvernement central et municipalité)*.

Roma, Biblioteca Apostolica Vaticana, Vat. Lat. 11276

Venezia, Archivio di Stato, Consiglio dei Dieci, b. 195.
Venezia, Archivio di Stato, Demanio 1806–1813, b. 326.
Venezia, Archivio di Stato, Demanio 1806–1813, b. 328.
Venezia, Biblioteca Nazionale Marciana, Archivio della biblioteca, busta anno 1783.
Venezia, Biblioteca Nazionale Marciana, Archivio della Biblioteca, busta anno 1815.
Venezia, Biblioteca Nazionale Marciana, Archivio della Biblioteca, busta "Biblioteche delle Corporazioni Religiose Soppresse 1789–1812".
Venezia, Biblioteca Nazionale Marciana, Archivio della Biblioteca, busta "Governo Veneto".
Venezia, Biblioteca Nazionale Marciana, Archivio della Biblioteca, busta "Governo Democratico".
Venezia, Biblioteca Nazionale Marciana, Archivio della Biblioteca, busta "Governo Italico". '
Venezia, Biblioteca Nazionale Marciana, Cod. Marc. It. VII, 1562 (=7843).

Venezia, Biblioteca Nazionale Marciana, Cod. Marc. It. XI, 288–93 (= 7273–7278).

Venezia, Biblioteca Nazionale Marciana, Cod. Marc. Lat. X, 333 (=3757).

Venezia, Biblioteca Nazionale Marciana, Cod. Marc. Lat. XIV, 110 (= 4533).

Venezia, Biblioteca Nazionale Marciana, Cod. Riservato 190.

Primary Sources

Breviarium Romanum, Venice: Nicolaus Jenson, [before 6 May], 1478. GW 5101; ISTC ib01112000.

Aulus Gellius, *Noctes Atticae*, Venice: Nicolaus Jenson, 1472. GW 10594; ISTC ig00120000.

Homerus, *Batrachomyomachia*, Venice: Laonicus [and Alexander], 1486. GW 12901; ISTC ih00301000; MEI 02121831; Venice, Biblioteca Nazionale Marciana, INC. V. 685.

Priscianus, *Opera*, [Venice: Vindelinus de Spira], 1472. GW M35406; ISTC ip00961000.

Marcus Fabius Quintilianus, *Institutiones oratoriae*, [Venice]: Nicolaus Jenson, 21 May 1471. GW M36818; ISTC iq00026000.

Secondary Works

Costanzo Albasini, 'La biblioteca di san Francesco della Vigna in Venezia', in *Le Venezie francescane*, 19 (1952), 4, 177–81.

Simone Assemani, *Museo cufico Naniano illustrato dall'abate Simone Assemani professore di lingue orientali…*, In Padova: nella stamperia del Seminario, 1787–88.

Edoardo Barbieri, 'Produrre, conservare, distruggere: per una storia dei libri e della biblioteca di S. Mattia di Murano', in *L'Ateneo Veneto*, n.s. 184 (1997), 13–55.

Antonella Barzazi, *Gli affanni dell'erudizione. Studi e organizzazione culturale degli ordini religiosi a Venezia tra Sei e Settecento* (Venezia, 2004).

Antonella Barzazi, 'Berardelli, Domenico Maria', in Enzo Bottasso, *Dizionario dei bibliotecari e bibliografi italiani dal XVI al XX secolo*, Roberto Alciati ed. (Montevarchi, 2009), 56–57.

Antonella Barzazi, 'Libertino o devoto? Apostolo Zeno nello specchio della sua biblioteca', in *Il «Giornale de' Letterati d'Italia» trecento anni dopo. Scienza, storia, arte, identità (1710–2010)*, Atti del convegno, Padova, Venezia, Verona, 17–19 novembre 2010, Enza del Tedesco ed. (Pisa-Roma, 2012), 133–44.

Federica Benedetti, *La biblioteca francescana di San Michele in Isola e le "sue biblioteche" (1829–2008). Il modello delle biblioteche di Santa Maria delle Grazie di Conegliano, San Bernardino di Collalto, San Francesco di Ceneda, Biblioteca S. Francesco della Vigna*, 1 (Milano, 2013).

[Domenico Maria Berardelli], *Codicum omnium latinorum et italicorum qui manuscripti in bibliotheca SS. Joannis et Pauli Venetiarum apud PP. Praedicatores asservantur catalogus, sectio secunda*, in *Nuova raccolta di opuscoli scientifici e filologici*, 33, 1779, pt. III.

Bibliotheca Pinelliana. A catalogue of the magnificent and celebrated library of Maffei Pinelli, late of Venice: comprehending an unparalleled collection of the Greek, Roman, and Italian authors, from the origin of printing … a considerable number of curious Greek and Latin manuscripts, of the 11. 12. 13. 14. 15. and 16. centuries; … on Monday March 2, 1789, and the twenty-two following days, (Sunday excepted); … at the great room, opposite the chapel, in Conduit Street, Hanover square, London … catalogues to be had of mess. Robson and Clarke, booksellers New Bond Street; Mr Edwards, booksellers, Pall Mall; and of the principal booksellers throughout Europe, [London, 1789].

Bollettino delle leggi del Regno d'Italia, Milano: Regis stamperia Veladini, 1805–1806.

Michel Bruguière and Pierre-François Pinaud, *Guide du chercheur pour la période 1789–1815: les sources de l'histoire financière et économique* (Genève, 1992).

Carlo Campana, 'Manoscritti e incunaboli delle biblioteche camaldolesi verso la Marciana', in *San Michele in Isola – Isola della conoscenza: ottocento anni di storia e cultura camaldolesi nella laguna di Venezia: Mostra organizzata in occasione del millenario della fondazione della congregazione camaldolese*, Marcello Brusegan, Paolo Eleuteri, and Gianfranco Fiaccadori eds (Torino, 2012), 222–27.

Pietro M. Candeo, *I Santuari Mariani della Diocesi di Padova* (Villa del Conte (PD), 1986).

Giuseppe Cappelletti, *I Gesuiti e la Republica di Venezia. Documenti diplomatici relativi alla Società gesuitica raccolti per decreto del Senato 14 giugno 1606 e pubblicati per la prima volta dal cav. pr. Giuseppe Cappelletti*, Venezia: Tipografia Grimaldo, 1873.

Caterina Carpinato, *Varia posthomerica neograeca. Materiali per il corso di lingua e letteratura neogreca* (Milano, 2006).

Carlo Castellani, *Parole dette dal Prefetto della Biblioteca Nazionale di S. Marco quando il R. Istituto di Scienze, Lettere ed Arti inaugurava nel Pantheon Veneto il busto dell'Ab. Jacopo Morelli* (Venezia, 1893).

Francesca Cavazzana Romanelli, 'Topografia del potere, topografia della memoria. I luoghi della politica e dell'amministrazione della Serenissima nella rievocazione ottocentesca di Giovanni Rossi', in *Tempi uomini ed eventi di storia veneta. Studi in onore di Federico Seneca*, Sergio Perini et al. eds (Rovigo, 2003), 457–76.

Bartolomeo Cecchetti, *La Republica di Venezia e la corte di Roma nei rapporti della religione*, Venezia: Prem. stabilim. tipogr. di P. Naratovich, 1874.

Emmanuele Antonio Cicogna, *Delle iscrizioni veneziana raccolta ed illustrate*, VI, pt. I, Venezia: Presso la Tipografia Andreola, 1853.

H. O. Coxe, *Bodleian Library. Quarto catalogues, II. Laudian Manuscripts, reprinted from the edition of 1858–1885, with corrections and additions, and an historical introduction by R. W. Hunt* (Oxford, 1973).

Girolamo Dandolo, *La Caduta della Repubblica di Venezia ed i suoi ultimi cinquant'anni: studii storici* (Venezia, 1855).

M. de Clercq, *Recueil des traités de la France, tome 1: 1713–1802*, Paris: A. Durand et Pedone-Lauriel, 1880.

Piero Del Negro, 'Giacomo Nani. Appunti biografici', *Bollettino del Museo Civico di Padova*, 60 (1971), 2, 115–47.

Giovanni Battista De Luca, *Il dottor volgare ovvero il compendio di tutta la legge civile, canonica, feudale e municipale nelle cose più ricevute in pratica del cardinale Giambatista De Luca e dal medesimo moralizzato in lingua italiana*, Firenze: coi tipi di V. Batelli e compagni, 1839.

De Vita Victorini Feltrensis dialogus Francisci Prendilaquae Mantuani ex codice Vaticano. Annotationes adjecit Jacobus Morellius, Patavii: Typis Seminarii, apud Joannem Manfre, 1774.

Encyclopédie, ou Dictionnaire raisonné des sciences, des arts et des métiers, par une Société des gens de lettres. Mis en ordre & publié par M. Diderot; & quant à la partie mathematique, par M. D'Alembert, A Lausanne et à Berne: chez les Sociétés typographiques, vol. 36, 1781.

Epistolae: Diatriba Praeliminaris in duas partes divisa ad Francisci Barbari et aliorum ad ipsum Epistolas: Ab Anno Chr. MCCCCXXV. ad An. MCCCCLIII, nunc primum editas ex duplici Ms. cod. Brixiani, &. Vaticano uno, Brixiae: Excudebat Joannes-Maria Rizzardi, 1741.

Giuseppe Tommaso Farsetti, *Biblioteca manoscritta di Tommaso Giuseppe Farsetti patrizio Veneto e Balì del Sacr' Ordine Gerosolimitano*, in Venezia: Nella Stamperia Fenzo, 1771.

Giuseppe Tommaso Farsetti, *Della biblioteca manoscritta di Tommaso Giuseppe Farsetti patrizio veneto, e balì del sagr'ordine Gerosolimitano. Parte seconda*, In Venezia: presso Pietro Savioni, 1780.

[Giuseppe Tommaso Farsetti], *Catalogo dei libri italiani*, in Venezia: appresso Modesto Fenzo 1785.

[Giuseppe Tommaso Farsetti], *Catalogo di libri latini*, In Venezia: appresso Antonio Graziosi, 1788.

[Giuseppe Tommaso Farsetti, Jacopo Morelli], *Catalogo di commedie italiane*, Venezia: nella stamperia di Modesto Fenzo, 1776.

Luigi Ferro, 'Jacopo Chiodo, fondatore dell'archivio di stato di Venezia', in *Ad Alessandro Luzio gli archivi di stato italiani: miscellanea di studi storici* (Firenze, 1933), 364–69.

Francisci Barbari et aliorum ad ipsum Epistolae, Brixiae: Exc. Joan. Maria Rizzardi, 1743.

Rinaldo Fulin, 'Vicende della libreria in SS. Gio. e Paolo', *Atti dell'Ateneo Veneto*, ser. II, 5 (*1868*), 273–94.

Geographiae veteris Scriptores græci minores, 4 vols, Oxonii, E theatro Sheldoniano, 1698–1712.

Alessia Giachery, *Jacopo Morelli e la repubblica delle lettere attraverso la sua corrispondenza (1768–1819)* (Venezia, 2012).

Rudj Gorian, *Nascosti tra i libri: I periodici antichi della Biblioteca del Seminario patriarcale di Venezia (1607–1800)* (Venezia, 2017).

Giuseppe Gullino, 'Il giurisdizionalismo dello Stato veneziano: gli antichi problemi e la nuova cultura', in *La Chiesa di Venezia nel Settecento*, Bruno Bertoli ed., Contributi alla storia della Chiesa di Venezia, 6 (Venezia, 1993), 23–38.

Juliana Hill Cotton, 'Caldiera (Calderia), Giovanni', in *Dizionario biografico degli Italiani*, 16 (1973), 626–28.

Margaret L. King, *Umanesimo e patriziato a Venezia nel Quattrocento*, vol. II: *circolo umanistico veneziano. Profili* (Roma, 1989).

Pietro La Cute, 'Le vicende delle biblioteche monastiche veneziane dopo la soppressione napoleonica', *Rivista di Venezia*, A. VIII, no. 10 (October 1929), 645–46

Francesco Marchi, *Della architettura militare… libri tre. Nelli quali si descrivono li veri modi, del fortificare, che si usa a' tempi moderni. Con un breve, et utile trattato, nel quale si dimostrano li modi del fabricar l'artigliaria, et la prattica di adoperarla, da quelli che hanno carico di essa*, Brescia, Comino Presegni per Gaspare dall'Oglio, 1599.

Gaetano Melzi, *Dizionario di opere anonime e pseudonime di scrittori italiani o come che sia aventi relazione all'Italia*, In Milano: Coi torchi di Luigi di Giacomo Pirola, 1848, vol. I (A-G).

Lucia Merolla, *La Biblioteca di san Michele di Murano all'epoca dell'abate Giovanni Benedetto Mittarelli. I codici ritrovati* (Manziana, 2012).

Irma Merolle, *L'Abate Matteo Luigi Canonici e La Sua Biblioteca. I Manoscritti Canonici e Canonici-Soranzo delle biblioteche fiorentine* (Roma-Firenze, 1958).

Luigi Mingarelli, *Graeci Codices Manu Scripti Apud Nanios Patricios Venetos Asservati*, Bononiae: Typis Laelii a Vulpe, 1784.

J. B. Mitchell, 'Trevisan and Soranzo: some Canonici manuscripts from two Eighteenth-Century Venetian collections', in *The Bodleian Library Record*, VIII (1969), 3, 125–35.

Federico Montecuccoli degli Erri, 'Il console Smith. Notizie e documenti', *Ateneo Veneto*, ns., 33 (1995), 111–81.

Jacopo Morelli, *Della pubblica libreria di San Marco in Venezia dissertazione storica di D. Jacopo Morelli …*, In Venezia: presso Antonio Zatta, 1774.

Jacopo Morelli, *Codices manuscripti latini bibliothecae Nanianae a Iacobo Morellio relati. Opuscula inedita accedunt ex iisdem deprompta*, Venetiis: typis Antonii Zattae, 1776.

Jacopo Morelli, *I codici manoscritti volgari della libreria Naniana riferiti da don Iacopo Morelli. S'aggiungono alcune operette inedite da essi tratte*, In Venezia: nella stamperia d'Antonio Zatta, 1776.

Jacopo Morelli, 'Narrazione intorno all'abate Natale Lastesio', in *Operette di Iacopo Morelli, bibliotecario di S. Marco, ora insieme raccolte con opuscoli di antichi scrittori* (Venezia, 1820), III, 3–92.

Giannantonio Moschini, *Della letteratura veneziana del secolo 18. fino a' nostri giorni opera di Giannantonio Moschini*, In Venezia: dalla stamperia Palese, 1806, vol. II.

Giannantonio Moschini, 'Narrazione intorno alla vita e alle opere di D. Iacopo Morelli', in *Operette di Iacopo Morelli, bibliotecario di S. Marco, ora insieme raccolte con opuscoli di antichi scrittori* (Venezia, 1820).

Andrea Nanetti, *Il fondo archivistico Nani nella Biblioteca Nazionale di Grecia ad Atene: euristica documentaria sulla Morea veneta* (Venezia, 1996).

Filippo Nani-Mocenigo, '*Giacomo Nani. Memorie e documenti*', in *Agostino, Battista e Giacomo Nani* (*Ricordi storici*), (Venezia, 1917²), 387–597.

Paolo Preto, 'De Rubeis, Bernardo Maria', in *Dizionario biografico degli Italiani*, 39 (1991), 238–40.

Paolo Preto, 'Farsetti, Tommaso Giuseppe', in *Dizionario biografico degli Italiani*, 45 (1995), 184–86.

Lavinia Prosdocimi, 'Sulle tracce di antichi inventari e note manoscritte. Codici da librerie claustrali nella Biblioteca Universitaria di Padova', in *Splendore nella regola: codici miniati da monasteri e conventi nella Biblioteca Universitaria di Padova*, Federica Toniolo and Pietro Gnan eds (Padova, 2011), 53–70.

Riccardo Quinto, *Manoscritti medievali nella Biblioteca dei Redentoristi di Venezia (S. Maria della consolazione, detta della 'Fava')* (Padova, 2006).

Dorit Raines, 'La bibliothèque manuscrite de Giovanni Rossi. Un gardien du passé vénitien et sa collection', *Miscellanea Marciana*, 5 (1990), 77–205.

Dorit Raines, 'Book Museum or Scholarly Library? The "Libreria di San Marco" in a Republican Context', in *Ateneo Veneto*, 3 ser, 197, (2010), 9/II, 31–50.

Dorit Raines, 'Sotto tutela. Biblioteche vincolate o oggetto di fedecommesso a Venezia, XV–XVIII secoli', *Mélanges de l'École française de Rome. Italie et Méditerranée*, 124 (2013), no. 2, 533–50.

Dorit Raines, 'La cultura libraria della Repubblica di Venezia nel Settecento', in *Un'istituzione dei Lumi: la biblioteca. Teoria, gestione e pratiche biblioteconomiche nell'Europa dei Lumi*, Frédéric Barbier and Andrea De Pasquale eds (Parma, 2013), 85–104.

Dorit Raines, 'La biblioteca manoscritta di Daniele Barbaro: raccolta, uso e dispersione di una collezione veneziana', in *Daniele Barbaro 1514–1570: letteratura, scienza e arti nella Venezia del Rinascimento*, Susy Marcon and Laura Moretti eds (Crocetta del Montello (TV), 2015), 101–13.

Samuele Romanin, *Storia documentata di Venezia*, Venezia: Dalla Tipografia di Pietro Naratovich, 1859.

Vittorio Rossi, 'La biblioteca manoscritta del senatore veneziano Jacopo Soranzo', *Il libro e la stampa*, I (1907), 1, 3–8; 5, 122–33.

Graziano Ruffini, *La chasse aux livres: Bibliografia e collezionismo nel viaggio in Italia di Étienne-Charles de Loménie de Brienne e François-Xavier Laire (1789–1790)* (Firenze, 2012).

Giovanni Tabacco, *Andrea Tron e la crisi dell'aristocrazia senatoria a Venezia* (Udine, 1980).

Renata Targhetta, 'Secolari e regolari nel Veneto prima e dopo la legislazione antiecclesiastica (1765–84)', *Studi Veneziani*, 19 (1991), 171–84.

Stefano Trovato, 'Una lettera a Barthold Georg Niebuhr di Jacopo Morelli: la decadenza culturale dell'Italia all'inizio della Restaurazione', *Ateneo Veneto*, 3 ser., 193 (2006), 5/II, 193–210.

Elisa Veronese, *Storia del Gabinetto di Lettura di Monselice 1857–1939*, Laurea thesis under the supervision of Prof. Dorit Raines, Venezia, Università Ca' Foscari, a.a. 2012–2013.

Giuseppe Valentinelli, *Bibliotheca manuscripta ad S. Marci Venetiarum. Codices MSS Latini*, Venetiis: ex typographia commercii, 1868, vol. I.

Giovanni Zalin, 'Ricerche sulla privatizzazione della proprietà ecclesiastica nel Veneto. Dai provvedimenti Tron alle vendite laiche', in AA.VV., *Studi in memoria di Luigi Dal Pane* (Bologna, 1982), 537–55.

Alvise Zorzi, *Venezia scomparsa* ([Vicenza] and Milano, 1972).

Marino Zorzi, *La Libreria di San Marco. Libri, lettori, società nella Venezia dei Dogi* (Milano, 1987)

VINCENZO TROMBETTA

La politica delle soppressioni e le nuove biblioteche a Napoli tra illuminismo regalista e restaurazione (1767–1815)

L'abate cistercense Placido Troyli (1688–1757) consegna alle pagine della sua monumentale *Istoria Generale del Reame di Napoli* – undici tomi in quarto tirati, senza sottoscrizione tipografica, tra il 1747 e il 1754 – una puntuale ricognizione delle biblioteche di Napoli, vasta e popolosa capitale del regno borbonico delle Due Sicilie. Centro di antica tradizione culturale e fulcro della produzione editoriale dell'intero Mezzogiorno d'Italia, la città partenopea vanta una fitta trama di librerie dislocate nei suoi diversi quartieri. Oltre alla Biblioteca Reale – ragguardevole "per la rarità de' Libri, e per la quantità de' medesimi" trasferiti dal ducato di Parma da Carlo di Borbone (1716–1788) assieme al "dovizioso Museo di Medaglie e di Antichità, e a una Galleria rinomatissima di eccellenti Pitture" di Casa Farnese – l'autore descrive: la pubblica biblioteca dei Regi Studi, destinata ai docenti e agli studenti dell'Ateneo, ma all'epoca ancora in via di costituzione; la Libreria di S. Angelo a Nilo istituita sul finire del Seicento per volontà testamentaria del cardinale Francesco Maria Brancaccio vescovo di Viterbo, autorevole membro

della Congregazione dell'Indice dei Libri proibiti e "amantissimo di buoni libri"; e la biblioteca di Ferdinando Vincenzo Spinelli principe di Tarsia, aperta nel 1747 a selezionati studiosi tre giorni alla settimana nel suo sontuoso palazzo a Salita Pontecorvo, edificato dall'architetto Domenico Antonio Vaccaro. Numerose, poi, le domestiche librerie di aristocratici, eruditi e professionisti capaci di accumulare cospicue raccolte: nella categoria dei "Secolari", Troyli menziona, tra le altre, quelle di Matteo Egizio, Giambattista Vico, Francesco Vargas Macciucca, Costantino Grimaldi, Niccolò Capasso, Niccolò Fraggiani, Lorenzo Brunasso.

Ma la quota più ingente del patrimonio librario – per valore storico e pregio bibliografico – viene custodita nei numerosi complessi monastici e conventuali. La rassegna comprende: la biblioteca di S. Giovanni a Carbonara degli Agostiniani, che merita il "primo luogo tra le librerie celebri per li tanti Manoscritti, e Libri d'ogni sorta"; dei SS. Apostoli dei padri Teatini con "volumi di Autori molto rari e di tutte le Scienze"; di S. Efrem Nuovo dei Cappuccini provvista di scelte opere acquisite

Vincenzo Trombetta • Ha insegnato Storia del Libro e dell'Editoria all'Università degli Studi di Salerno. trolen@alice.it

How the Secularization of Religious Houses Transformed the Libraries of Europe, 16th–19th Centuries, ed. by Cristina Dondi, Dorit Raines, and † Richard Sharpe, BIB, 63 (Turnhout, 2022), pp. 195–221.

BREPOLS ❧ PUBLISHERS   DOI 10.1484/M.BIB-EB.5.128485

per sapiente cura di Giambattista Centurioni; di S. Domenico Maggiore, "la più grande, e la più ricca di libri di quante ne sono oggidì in Napoli"; dei padri Zoccolanti dell'Ospedaletto, che dispongono di una "libreria considerevole"; di Monte Oliveto dove era confluita la "considerabile libreria" dei sovrani aragonesi con codici "degni di essere veduti da ogni amante di belle lettere tutti scritti a Penna in Pergamena, di ottimi Caratteri"; di S.a Teresa degli Scalzi con "Libri per ogni Scienza"; di S.a Caterina a Formello per le "tante rare edizioni"; di S. Severino dei Benedettini fornita di "Manoscritti antichi, che altrove avere non si possono"; di S. Lorenzo dei Minori Conventuali, che raccoglie "Libri d'ogni sorta, e in abbondanza e molti Manoscritti"; dei padri di S. Filippo Neri della Congregazione dell'Oratorio, che "si ammira numerosissima in un Vaso ben disposto" avendo incorporato, grazie all'intermediazione di Vico, la ricca libreria dell'avvocato Giuseppe Valletta, punto d'incontro e di studio dei *novatores* napoletani tra fine Seicento e inizi del Settecento. Degne di attenzione pure le biblioteche dei Gesuiti, come "la grandissima libreria" del Collegio Massimo al Gesù Vecchio che conserva, in riservate scansie, "solamente i libri composti da' Padri della Compagnia, tutti coverti ad una maniera di color rosso", e quella della Casa Professa considerata, non a torto, "di somma considerazione"[1].

In meno di mezzo secolo, però, l'articolata struttura bibliotecaria di proprietà ecclesiastica subisce una radicale trasformazione indotta dalle più generali vicende che investono le comunità religiose, come l'espulsione dei Gesuiti nella seconda metà del Settecento; le requisizioni effettuate in taluni conventi e monasteri all'in-

domani della Repubblica del 1799; e l'abolizione degli ordini religiosi nel Decennio francese. Tre fasi, connotate da differenti istanze politiche e da peculiari finalità sociali e culturali, ma tuttavia riconducibili a eventi di portata europea, come la secolarizzazione dell'istruzione da sottrarre ai tradizionali modelli scolastici e pedagogici della *Ratio Studiorum*[2], l'ondata giacobina che travolge gli assetti politici di antico regime e l'insediamento di nuove monarchie nella temperie napoleonica.

1. Le biblioteche gesuitiche e la loro dispersione

L'espulsione dell'Ordine di Sant'Ignazio – sull'esempio del Portogallo, esteso alla Francia e fino alla "cattolicissima" Spagna – rappresenta, nella realtà meridionale, l'esito della politica anticurialista intrapresa dal governo borbonico e, con solerte determinazione, perseguita dal marchese Bernardo Tanucci ministro di Casa Reale che, con il consenso dei gruppi intellettuali e del potente ceto forense, avversa i privilegi della nobiltà e contrasta l'ingerenza della Roma papale. All'interno del fronte cattolico, attraversato da innovative correnti filosofiche e teologiche, la Compagnia di Gesù si era arroccata nell'intransigente difesa dei propri privilegi esercitando, con l'egemonia dell'educazione, un ruolo morale e culturale ritenuto di ostacolo a quel riformismo regalista, che incoraggiava lo sviluppo delle condizioni economiche e sociali del paese e l'ammodernamento del suo apparato scolastico. A opinione dei suoi tanti detrattori, il gesuitismo era contrario al riconoscimento dei diritti della sovranità e, forte di "immense ricchezze" e di una "smisurata potenza", aveva

---

1 Placido Troyli, *Delle varie biblioteche del Reame di Napoli*, in., Id., *Istoria Generale del Reame di Napoli. Ovvero Stato antico, e moderno delle Regioni, e Luoghi, che 'l Reame di Napoli compongono, una colle loro prime Popolazioni, Costumi, Leggi, Polizia, Uomini Illustri, e Monarchi* (Napoli, 1752), IV/4, 229–47.

2 Cf. *Gesuiti e Università in Europa (secoli XVI–XVIII)*, atti del Convegno di studi, Parma, 13–15 dicembre 2001, a cura di Gian Paolo Brizzi e Roberto Greci (Bologna, 2002).

creato un autonomo Stato svincolato da ogni forma di controllo politico[3].

In particolare l'abolizione – il cui piano operativo scatta nella notte tra il 20 e il 21 novembre del 1767 – sradica un'articolata struttura nella quale capaci precettori e insegnanti, con il supporto di cospicue biblioteche, avevano plasmato, per circa due secoli, la vita intellettuale con indiscusso prestigio e autorevolezza: nelle scuole gesuitiche, infatti, si era educata la gioventù d'estrazione tanto popolare quanto aristocratica e proprio a quest'ultima veniva affidato il compito di occupare, con fedeltà e competenza, i ranghi elevati di una gerarchia al servizio della corte e dell'amministrazione dello stato. La Giunta degli Abusi, organo dipendente dalla prima Segreteria di Stato e costituito da altissime personalità[4], riceve mandato di definire le questioni inerenti allo scioglimento della Compagnia e di provvedere alla gestione delle sue immense proprietà, non solo librarie, custodite nel Collegio Massimo al Salvatore[5], nella

Casa Professa[6], nella Casa di Probazione della

3 Vedi Michelangelo Schipa, *Il Regno di Napoli al tempo di Carlo di Borbone* (Napoli, 1904), 114–15. Sul tema dell'abolizione rimandiamo a: Michele Volpe, *I Gesuiti nel Napoletano* (Napoli, 1914), I, 15–33; Umberto Antonio Padovani, *La soppressione della Compagnia di Gesù* (Napoli, 1962); Enrica Robertazzi Delle Donne, *L'espulsione dei Gesuiti dal Regno di Napoli* (Napoli, 1970); Domenico Ambrasi, 'L'espulsione dei Gesuiti dal Regno di Napoli nelle lettere di Bernardo Tanucci a re Carlo III', *Campania Sacra. Studi e Documenti*, 2 (1971), 211–50; Michele Miele, 'Ricerche sulla soppressione dei religiosi nel Regno di Napoli nel 1767', *Campania Sacra. Studi e Documenti*, 4 (1973) 1–144; Egidio Papa, 'I beni dei Gesuiti e i preliminari della loro espulsione dal Regno di Napoli nel 1767', *Rivista di Storia della Chiesa*, 30 (1976), 81–113.

4 Cf. Francesco Trinchera, *Degli archivi napoletani. Relazione a S.E. il Ministro della Pubblica Istruzione* (Napoli, 1872), 375; *Stato delle rendite e pesi degli aboliti collegi della Capitale e Regno dell'espulsa Compagnia detta di Gesù*, a cura di Carolina Belli (Napoli, 1981), 3, nota 9.

5 La biblioteca del Collegio Massimo, dotata di un regolamento per le mansioni del personale e per la consultazione, era dislocata in un grande vaso su due livelli – lungo 146 palmi e largo 43 – iniziato nel 1688 e terminato nel corso del 1700. Il piano inferiore, con una sequenza continua di vetrine e colonne doriche a

parete e scansie, realizzate in legno di noce e di olivo da Corrado Guden "insignis faber lignarius", contenevano due distinti nuclei librari: uno di autori vari e l'altro di scrittori dell'Ordine, notevole per le preziose legature in pelle cremisi e oro. La Sezione Manoscritti e Rari della Biblioteca Nazionale "Vittorio Emanuele III" di Napoli conserva i tomi in folio dei suoi cataloghi settecenteschi *Libraria del SS. Salvatore* (Ms. III. A. 33, cc. 226), con l'*Inventario di una Scanzia straordinaria in mezzo alla Libraria* (cc. 227–29): registro topografico (con aggiunte, inserzioni, correzioni, lacune, spostamenti, duplicati) che riporta un ordinamento in diciotto classi disposte in ventotto scansie, segnalate con cifre romane su cartellini sporgenti dal margine destro, con la sequenza alfabetica, all'interno di ogni singola classe, per nome di battesimo degli autori: I. Biblia Sacra; II. Concilia, et Canones; III. Sancti Patres; IV. Interpretes Sacrae Scripturae; V. Concionatores; VI. Ascetici; VII. VIII. IX. X. XI. Historici; XII. XIII. Polyhistores; XIV. XV. Miscellanei; XVI. XVII. XVIII. Philologi; XIX. Mathematici; XX. Medici, et Philosophi; XXI. Philosophi; XXII. XXIII. Jurisperiti; XXIV. Canonistae; XXV. Morales; XXVI. Polemici; XXVII. XXVIII. Teologi. Utili notizie in Guerriera Guerrieri, *La Biblioteca Nazionale Vittorio Emanuele III* (Milano-Napoli, 1974), 151–52. Vedi anche: Mario Rotili, *Il cortile del Salvatore* (Roma, 1955); Maria Giuseppina Castellano Lanzara, 'La casa del Salvatore in Napoli', in *Miscellanea di scritti vari in memoria di Alfonso Gallo* (Firenze, 1956), 239–47; Michele Errichetti, 'L'architetto Giuseppe Valeriano (1542–1596) progettista del Collegio Napoletano del Gesù Vecchio', *Archivio Storico per le Province Napoletane*, 34 (1959), 325–52; Giancarlo Alisio, 'Il Gesù Vecchio a Napoli', *Napoli Nobilissima*, 5 (1966), V–VI, 211–19; Michele Errichetti, 'L'antico Collegio Massimo dei Gesuiti a Napoli (1552–1806)', *Campania Sacra. Studi e Ricerche*, 7 (1976), 170–264; Aldo Pinto, 'Il Museo di Mineralogia e l'antica biblioteca gesuitica del Collegio Massimo', *Rendiconto della Accademia delle Scienze Fisiche e Matematiche*, 132, ser. IV, vol. LX (1993), 121–46.

6 La libreria della Casa Professa al Gesù Nuovo – collocata nel settecentesco vaso realizzato da Cristoforo Schor collaboratore dell'architetto Arcangelo Guglielmelli – conteneva soprattutto opere in lingue orientali per le cui notizie rinviamo a: Carlo D'Engenio, *Napoli Sacra* (Napoli, 1624), 228; Francesco Schinosi, 'Fondazione in Napoli della Casa de' Professi', in Id., *Istoria della Compagnia di Giesù. Appartenente al Regno di Napoli*, Parte Prima (Napoli, 1706), 371–81; Filippo Iappelli, 'Gesuiti e Seicento Napoletano. II. Congregazioni del

Nunziatella a Pizzofalcone[7] e nei diversi collegi della capitale. Le prime direttive riguardano la vendita di tutti i mobili non preziosi, che escludono espressamente i libri, gli argenti, i quadri e altri oggetti di valore per garantire la loro tutela. L'accorpamento della dote libraria, da convogliare nell'istituendo Collegio Reale al Salvatore, viene disposto il 22 aprile 1768 prevedendo, a trasferimento ultimato, la redazione di più indici:

> i libri de' Collegi del Carminiello, di S. Giuseppe a Chiaja e di S. Francesco Saverio, oggi detto S. Ferdinando, si uniscano co' libri del Collegio Massimo, o sia Casa del Salvatore di questa Capitale, e se ne facciano tre indici, uno de' duplicati, l'altro de' libri degli Autori Gesuiti, e il terzo di tutti gli altri libri[8].

Lo *Stato in ristretto dell'Azienda Gesuitica dal giorno dell'espulsione, col Piano di tutte le Opere disposte da Sua Maestà*, impresso nel 1774, rimarca la finalità dei beni requisiti, ora dispensati "a beneficio del Pubblico": i quadri per la formazione di una pinacoteca, gli strumenti scientifici per attrezzare un moderno osservatorio astronomico e i libri da destinare al "servizio della gioventù studiosa":

> Altresì sono tutti esistenti i quadri, le librerie, e gli strumenti matematici, destinati da Sua Maestà a beneficio del Pubblico: cioè i quadri per formarsene una speciosa galleria nell'abolita casa del Noviziato di Pizzofalcone, ove sta destinato un Convitto per la gioventù di ragguardevole distinzione; le Librerie, e gli strumenti matematici, radunati tutti nella Casa del Salvatore per servizio della gioventù studiosa, e per l'osservatorio astronomico, che sta ordinato di costruirsi.

Le difficoltà di riscontrare volumi pervenuti in duplice o anche in triplice copia, di catalogare la rilevante quantità di opere antiche e di ripartire gli autori in base all'appartenenza all'Ordine rallentano le procedure d'inventariazione, peraltro, già avviate in ritardo. La *Dimostrazione in ristretto dello Stato attuale dell'Azienda di Educazione*, stampata il 30 aprile 1774 senza indicazioni tipografiche, conferma il prosieguo dei lavori di registrazione, ma inserisce pure un riferimento alle librerie degli aboliti collegi nelle altre province del Regno che, contrariamente a quelle napoletane, devono conservarsi nelle rispettive sedi di origine:

> Le librerie rinvenute negli aboliti Collegj del Regno nell'istessi Collegj si conservano a comodo della Gioventù studiosa; e le librerie degli Aboliti Collegj della Capitale, radunate tutte nella Casa di S. Salvatore, dove al presente se ne formano i Registri, serviranno al maggior comodo del Pubblico.

Gli anni seguenti rappresentano un periodo denso di significativi avvenimenti per le istituzioni culturali napoletane, come la riforma dell'Ateneo che, incrementato il numero delle cattedre,

---

Gesù Nuovo e Oratorio dei Nobili', *Societas. Rivista bimestrale dei Gesuiti dell'Italia Meridionale*, 34.3 (1985), 90.

7   Nel 1711 era stata inaugurata la "nuova" Libreria con un lascito annuale di trenta ducati che il padre Isidoro Cicala aveva devoluto per l'acquisto di opere moderne. Alla data del 30 settembre 1762 – si legge nel *Libro delle Consulte* – uno dei padri "pregò che si mettessero in buon'ordine e registro li Libri nella Libreria Comune, e che si formasse catalogo più esatto de' libri di detta Libreria per maggior facilità di trovarli, e poi riporli nelle proprie scanzie. Lo che si sta eseguendo". NAPOLI, *Archivio Napoletano Societatis Jesu. Libro / Delle Consulte / della / Casa di Probazione / della Compagnia di Giesv / di Napoli / Principiato a Gennaro / MDCCXI*, c. 123r. Cf. pure Filippo Iappelli, 'La Nunziatella. Da Noviziato dei Gesuiti a Scuola Militare (1587–1787). II', *Societas. Rivista bimestrale dei Gesuiti dell'Italia Meridionale*, 36. 1–2 (1987), 72–73.

8   NAPOLI, *Archivio di Stato*, Casa Reale Antica, Giunta degli Abusi, fascio 1298, ora in Filippo Iappelli, 'Il Palazzo delle Congregazioni e l'"insula" del Gesù Nuovo. I', *Societas. Rivista bimestrale dei Gesuiti dell'Italia Meridionale*, 35.3 (1986), 68.

viene traslocato nel Collegio Reale al Salvatore sorto sulle ceneri di quello gesuitico; il trasferimento della Biblioteca Reale da Capodimonte al Palazzo degli Studi fuori la porta di S. Maria di Costantinopoli; la fondazione dell'Accademia delle Scienze inaugurata, con fastosa cerimonia, alla presenza dei sovrani. L'accavallarsi e il sovrapporsi di tanti progetti, però, stravolge il primitivo piano di salvaguardia delle librerie ignaziane per le quali s'introduce un criterio che ne determina l'inevitabile dispersione: i materiali correnti e privi di valore bibliografico vengono assegnati alla libreria del Collegio Reale – affidata al bibliotecario Michele Torcia (1736–1808) – per "uso scolastico", o redistribuiti ad altre comunità ecclesiastiche; gli altri, rari e pregevoli, o ben legati, o solo di buona edizione, invece, sono riservati alla Reale Biblioteca, allora ancora alloggiata nella residenza di Capodimonte, diretta dal padre somasco Giovanni Maria della Torre (1712–1782). Disponendo di un solo addetto, "che attualmente fatica a poner l'indice per ordine alfabetico", il della Torre chiede, con la lettera del 12 aprile 1780, l'ausilio di idoneo personale per "scrivere l'indice grande degli espulsi": prova evidente, a questa data, dell'avvenuta consegna dei materiali librari dei Gesuiti, trasportati da carri trainati da buoi lungo un tragitto che, oltrepassate le mura della città, scendeva al vallone della Sanità per risalire sulla verdeggiante collina di Capodimonte. Immediato l'accoglimento dell'istanza se già il 18 aprile 1780 può chiedere la retribuzione degli addetti che "travagliano agli Indici e Inventari delle Librerie Gesuitiche". Alla successiva richiesta di un "piano ragionato", il della Torre replica il 25 aprile 1780, fornendo il quadro degli impiegati con la specifica delle mansioni e del soldo corrispondente: nell'elenco di "quelli che faticano all'Indice per scegliere i libri e farne notare i frontespizi" figurano Alessio Pelliccia, Pasquale Baffi e Giuseppe Cestari senza "soldo, ma a' quali è stato promesso, che nelle vacanze saranno collocati a tenore delle fatiche fatte". Alla catalogazione dei volumi – ai quali intere

generazioni di studenti erano ricorse per la loro formazione culturale – attendono, quindi, alcuni tra i più noti esponenti di quella intellighenzia che, senza riserve, aderirà alle insorgenze giacobine, in molti casi, versando il proprio contributo di sangue alla causa della Repubblica Napoletana nel 1799. Nella lista di coloro "che sono applicati a fare l'Indice de' libri degli espulsi", rimesso con la lettera del 2 maggio 1780, viene incluso pure Donato Campo, valente tipografo, e persona di fiducia del regio bibliotecario.

Con la lettera del 14 settembre 1780 – nella quale si attesta la revoca dell'iniziale proposito di preservare tutti i depositi librari nei relativi complessi soppressi nelle altre province – il ministro Giuseppe Beccadelli Bologna (1726–1813) riceve notizia del sopralluogo di Emanuele Terres e Vincenzo Altobelli, commercianti di libri di comprovata esperienza, effettuato nei locali superiori del Collegio Massimo al Salvatore dove erano stati confusamente ammassati i materiali sequestrati in altre diciotto case gesuitiche, tra cui quelli della ricca libreria del collegio di Capua[9],

---

9 La biblioteca del collegio capuano – riferisce Carlo Paletti funzionario governativo incaricato delle operazioni di esproprio – manca ancora dell'inventario perché la sua compilazione "richiede più tempo" del previsto, come precisa nella lettera a Tanucci dell'8 febbraio 1768. Il protrarsi delle registrazioni inventariali conferma, indirettamente, la ricchezza della libreria che Francesco Granata aveva già descritto nella *Storia sacra della Chiesa Metropolitana di Capua* tirata, nel 1766, dalla Stamperia Simoniana: "Nello stesso Collegio vi è un'ottima Libreria, arricchita di molti, rari ed utilissimi libri; anzi a nostro giudizio può paragonarsi alle migliori che sono in Napoli, non solo per la rarità de' libri, ma ancora per la ricca dote [tramite la quale] si comprano di giorno in giorno nuove opere di valore e di buon gusto". Si conserva un frammento dell'*Inventario de' libri ritrovati / nella Libraria del Collegio degli / espulsi Gesuiti di Capua*: i tre fascicoli sciolti, compilati da mani diverse e privi di paginazione, registrano a partire "dalla Scansia 1 a destra nell'/entrare nella Libraria" alcune centinaia di volumi con descrizioni molto sommarie. Cf. CAPUA, *Biblioteca del Museo Campano*, Ms. busta 292. Per una sua ipotesi ricostruttiva vedi Annamaria Robotti, 'La

"acciocché – scrive il della Torre – sulla faccia del luogo facessero uno scandaglio ragionato di ciò, che potrebbe importare in fare un confronto tra l'Indice già quasi compito di tutti i libri, co' libri stessi esistenti; per vedere in un'occhiata quanti libri potessero mancare". Per eseguire la gravosa verifica bibliografica l'Altobelli preventiva una spesa di ottanta ducati, poi ridotta a sessanta per le insistenze del prefetto, ma il riscontro subisce imprevisti ritardi. Raccogliendo l'invito a non trascurare altri librai, in grado di eseguire il medesimo lavoro in minor tempo e a costi più contenuti, il padre della Torre, dopo aver interpellato persone esperte "di queste materie", propone, per maggior "cautela legale", l'"accenzione della candela" – una pubblica licitazione – vinta, il 30 settembre 1780, dal libraio Carlo Mormile con l'offerta ribassata a 29 ducati e altri 20 per pagare i facchini a fronte di un lavoro da concludere in due mesi[10].

Le indagini archivistiche rivolte all'individuazione degli elenchi di esproprio restituisce – purtroppo incompleto perché ritrovato, ad oggi, solo il manoscritto del secondo volume – quello del Collegio dei Nobili, istituito nel 1679 da Giovan Battista Manso marchese di Villa (1569–1645), "uomo di gran sapere e letteratura", e affidato ai padri della Compagnia. Infatti, dopo

aver sostenuto la creazione del Pio Monte della Misericordia nel 1608, il Manso, sensibile alla diffusione del sapere, fonda per i giovani dell'aristocrazia napoletana il *Seminarium Nobilium*, dove alunni e convittori apprendono "non solamente le buone lettere, e religiosi costumi", ma possono praticare "ancora molti esercizi cavallereschi, come del ballo, della scherma, e del torneo" sul modello del Collegio dei Nobili di Parma.

Intorno alla metà del Settecento il Collegio napoletano, provveduto della biblioteca appartenuta allo stesso marchese di Villa e da lui donata per volontà testamentaria[11], viene completamente ristrutturato, ma non si tralascia l'aspetto della didattica approntando nuovi programmi per le classi di grammatica, umanità, retorica e filosofia. Sorge, tra i convittori, pure un'Accademia di Scienze e Belle Lettere nella quale – pubblicamente – si gareggia nelle dissertazioni di fisica, di matematica, di legge, o con componimenti poetici spesso in greco e in latino, o con rappresentazioni teatrali.

Il secondo volume dell'inventario redatto nel corso delle procedure di requisizione consente una più appropriata analisi della ricchezza bibliografica donata, e poi incrementata dalla Compagnia di Sant'Ignazio, senza però riflettere l'interna arti-

---

biblioteca settecentesca del Collegio dei Gesuiti in Capua', *Societas. Rivista bimestrale dei Gesuiti dell'Italia Meridionale*, 51.5–6 (2003), 237–40.

10 "Colla presente mia dichiaro di contentarmi di rivedere stanze dicisette di libri esistenti nel SS. Salvatore coll'inventario, e riscontrarli col medesimo tra lo spazio di mesi due, cioè dalli 2 ottobre 1780 fino alli 2 di dicembre di d:o anno, poco più, o poco meno. E mi contento per ducati ventinove da pagarsi dopo fatto il lavoro, ben inteso, che d.o confronto lo debba fare di due altre stanze unite alla diciesette sud.e, perchè nulla manchi allo esatto generale riscontro. Napoli li 30 settembre 1780. Carlo Mormile". NAPOLI, *Archivio di Stato*, Badia di Mileto, fascio 283, fac.lo 3, ora in Vincenzo Trombetta, 'Lettere di Giovanni Maria della Torre "custode" della Real Biblioteca di Napoli (1777–178)', *Rendiconti della Accademia di Archeologia Lettere e Belle Arti di Napoli*, 67 (1997–1998), 341–67.

11 Così la sua disposizione testamentaria: "Lascio al detto Monte mio erede tutta la mia libreria, così dei libri stampati come dei mss … e voglio che i libri si debbano conservare nel palagio da me donato … e non si possano estraere né per vendita né per prestanza, ma debbano sempre ivi conservarsi per uso … così dei signori Accademici oziosi, come degli alunni del mio Seminario". Michele Manfredi, *Gio. Batista Manso nella vita e nelle opere* (Napoli, 1919), 254. Sull'influente mecenate e sodale di maghi, astronomi e alchimisti, tra i fondatori dell'Accademia degli Oziosi, vedi pure: Angelo Borzelli, *Giovan Battista Manso Marchese di Villa* (Napoli, 1916); Carolina Belli, 'La Fondazione del Collegio dei Nobili di Napoli', in *Chiesa, Assistenza e Società nel Mezzogiorno moderno*, a cura di Carla Russo, prefazione e introduzione di Giuseppe Galasso (Galatina, 1994), 183–280; Carlo Lanza, 'Il Collegio dei Nobili e l'espulsione dei Gesuiti nella Napoli del 1767', *Capys. Bollettino interno degli "Amici di Capua"*, 33 (2000), 79–88.

colazione della biblioteca che, senz'altro, differiva dalla struttura di quella del Collegio Massimo (libreria "secreta", libreria riservata ai padri, e ai novizi). Datato 28 novembre 1767 e sottoscritto dall'attuario Giosuè Salvati, il manoscritto espone la titolazione: *Napoli / 1768 / Inventario della Libraria del Collegio / Seminario dei Nobili / Vol: Secondo / Giosue Salvati / Att.rio*[12]. Alle cc. 1–71 sono ordinate, per formato, circa mille e duecento opere, di prevalente edizione cinque e seicentesca. Nella prima carta, sul margine superiore sinistro, si legge: *Inventario de Libri / ritrovati nella Libra/ria di q.to Semina/rio e Collegio de No/bili*. Questa la suddivisione tematica delle quattordici scansie:

I. De Libri Poetici. II. [mancante]. III–IV. Miscellanea Selecta. V. Rhetores. VI. Historici. VII. Concilia, et Patres. VIII–IX. Philosophi. X. Ascetici. XI. Rhetores. XII. [mancante]. XIII. Juristae. XIV. Casuistae.

Le indicizzazioni, complete di data di stampa, ammontano a 1.129 così ripartite: 7 incunaboli, 676 cinquecentine, 412 secentine, 34 settecentine. Le quote maggiori si concentrano nelle classi dei Rethores (284 pari al 25%), Poetici (270 pari al 24%), Philosophi (136 pari al 12%), Historici (131 pari all'12%), Casuistae (124 pari al 11%); poco affollate, al contrario, quelle dei Juristae (34 pari al 3%), Concilia, et Patres (37 pari al 3%), Ascetici (54, pari al 4%), oltre alla Miscellanea Selecta (59, pari a 6%). Una biblioteca capace di compensare la sua palese "inattualità" con il pregio delle edizioni: il notamento, infatti, elenca un nutrito numero di volumi usciti dai torchi delle più famose officine tipografiche italiane tra Cinque e Seicento[13],

oltre alle tirature di famosi stampatori europei: Christophe Plantin ad Anversa, Sebastian Gryphius a Lione, Robert Estienne a Parigi.

Cospicua la quantità, nelle scansie della libreria, dei classici del mondo greco e latino: Omero, i tragici greci Eschilo, Sofocle, Euripide; i commediografi Plauto e Terenzio; i lirici Catullo, Virgilio, Properzio, Ovidio; gli storici Senofonte, Tucidide, Tito Livio, Plutarco, Appiano Alessandrino; i filosofi da Aristotele a Boezio. Le opere letterarie partono dalle istituzioni di lingua greca ed ebraica ai lexicon greco-latini oltre a rimari, grammatiche, tesauri, e dizionari. Ricchissimo il settore con manuali sull'arte del versificare, sulla retorica, e sulla poesia e, ancora, elogi, sonetti, madrigali, panegirici, novelle, poemi eroici, tragedie, commedie amorose e burlesche. Modesta, invece, l'entità di annali ecclesiastici, di commentari biblici, di scritti dei Padri e Dottori della Chiesa, di testi teologici, agiografici e devozionali – forse più significativamente contenuti nella prima parte del catalogo non ancora emersa dello scavo d'archivio – che risalta al diretto confronto con l'insieme delle opere di giurisprudenza, di filosofia (etica, morale, metafisica, logica), di belle arti (pittura e architettura, antiquaria e musica), di scienze (geografia, medicina, fisica, matematica, geometria, astronomia, nautica, agricoltura, zoologia). Largo spazio è accordato alla storia napoletana declinata in genealogie, biografie di uomini illustri, vicende belliche e cronache del regno, e altrettanto numerosi i libri d'apparato: descrizioni di tornei cavallereschi, feste, matrimoni e teatri di nobiltà[14].

---

12 NAPOLI, *Archivio di Stato*, Azienda Gesuitica. Collegio dei Nobili, in via di ordinamento.

13 Basti citare quelle di Aldo Manuzio, Gabriele Giolito de' Ferrari, Francesco Marcolini, Michele Tramezzino, Vincenzo Valgrisi, Giovan Battista Ciotti (Venezia); Comin da Trino (Monferrato); Filippo Giunti, Lorenzo Torrentino, Bartolomeo Sermatelli (Firenze); Vincenzo

Colombara (Perugia); Paolo Manuzio e Antonio Blado (Roma); Ottavio Beltrani, Giuseppe Cacchi, Giacomo Carlino, Costantino Vitale, Antonio Pace, Nicola Stigliola, Lazzaro Scoriggio, Orazio Salviani, Domenico Roncagliolo (Napoli).

14 Cf. Vincenzo Trombetta, 'La libreria del Collegio dei Nobili e le biblioteche dei Gesuiti, a Napoli, tra Sette e Ottocento', in *Educare la nobiltà*, atti del Convegno

Il documento, alle cc. 72–78, presenta un ulteriore *Inventario de' libri particolari, ritrovati nelle Camere dei / PP. Gesuiti, che stanziavano in questo Collegio, e Sem- / minario de Nobili*, che enumera altri settantaquattro titoli, così ripartiti: 13 cinquecentine, 36 secentine e 25 settecentine. La libreria, anche in questo secondo segmento, conserva un carattere "antico" – a testimonianza di un'educazione fondata sullo studio di opere di lunga e consolidata tradizione – con una irrisoria percentuale di tirature settecentesche, non a caso presenti proprio nelle singole celle dei padri, lettori di testi indispensabili al loro continuo aggiornamento.

Analogo a Palermo, nella capitale dei domini al di là del faro, il problema della riconversione delle librerie gesuitiche. Per evitare che i materiali librari degli espulsi "si perdano, rosi dalla polvere, e da' tarli", la Giunta delle Scuole di Palermo, il 13 giugno 1771, propone al viceré di formare "una Biblioteca pubblica a comodo di que' Letterati, poiché vendendosi i sud.ti libri, poco se ne ritrarrebbe, e sfiorato il meglio, il rimanente sarebbe inutile, ed invendibile"[15]. Con reale dispaccio del 31 agosto 1778 viene ordinata a Gabriele Lancellotto Castelli principe di Torremuzza, la figura più rappresentativa della Deputazione degli Studi, la costituzione, nello stesso abolito Collegio Gesuitico, di una biblioteca "in ampie proporzioni, ben provveduta, per farla servire ad utile del pubblico, della cultura, delle scienze e dei discenti che in gran numero accorrevano dalla vicina Regia Accademia"[16], accorpandovi

anche i volumi requisiti nei collegi della Val di Mazara incamerati fin dal 1769. Pure la Pubblica Libreria del Senato – istituita da Alessandro Vanni principe di San Vincenzo nel 1760 "a esclusivo uso pubblico […] dove senz'alcun privilegio né vincolo tutti egualmente potessero attingere alle infinite sorgenti della sapienza" – beneficia della soppressione, incamerando i duplicati "che non fossero necessarj a quella della Accademia dei Regj Studj"[17] e ottenendo due ampi locali della Casa Professa, per collocarvi l'intero fondo librario, concessi fin dal 1774 dallo stesso ministro Tanucci. La biblioteca viene aperta alla pubblica consultazione grazie all'infaticabile attività del suo prefetto Tommaso Maria Angelici, che per l'occasione recita l'*Orazione pel riaprimento della Pubblica Libreria di Palermo*, poi stampata, in quarto, nel 1780.

Anche nel dipartimento di Bari, in adempimento alle disposizioni della Prima Segreteria di Stato emanate il 15 settembre 1788, Emanuele Zeuli, in qualità di amministratore dell'Azienda di Educazione, ordina "colla possibile sollecitudine" l'indice delle librerie gesuitiche requisite nel capoluogo barese. Il manoscritto in folio di cc. 76 e intitolato *Bari / Real Azienda di Educazione / Libreria / Tavola de' Libri* elenca oltre duemila e trecento opere – in gran parte di edizione seicentesca e di argomento religioso – di cui,

---

Nazionale di studi, Perugia, Palazzo Sorbello, 18–19 giugno 2004, a cura di Gianfranco Tortorelli (Bologna, 2005), 123–63; Id., 'Libri e biblioteche della Compagnia di Gesù a Napoli dalle origini all'Unità d'Italia', *Hereditas Monasteriorum Journal*, 4 (2014), 127–59.

15 NAPOLI, *Archivio di Stato*, Casa Reale Antica, fascio 1330.

16 "Come luogo più acconcio per la pubblica Biblioteca scelse il Torremuzza la grande sala al primo piano ove quei padri tenevano le ricreazioni, le premiazioni, i letterarii e scientifici convegni. L'architetto G. V. Marvuglia l'ampliò e decorò. La Biblioteca per le

---

proporzioni dell'ampia sua sala, pel numero delle spaziose finestre, per la elegante doratura della soffitta, per lo scaffale di noce ben scompartito e meglio intagliato, riuscì veramente bella, e di lunga mano superiore alle sale della Comunale e fra le migliori che allora esistessero in Italia". Luigi Sampolo, *La R. Accademia degli Studi di Palermo. Narrazione Storica* (Palermo, 1888), 108–09. Vedi pure: Niccolò Domenico Evola, *Sulla Biblioteca Nazionale di Palermo* (Palermo, 1872); Id., 'Cenni storici della Biblioteca Nazionale di Palermo', in *Ricordo del primo centenario della Biblioteca Nazionale di Palermo* (Palermo, 1882).

17 Cf. Gioacchino Di Marzo, *Primo centenario della Biblioteca comunale di Palermo addì XXV Aprile MDCCCXXV. Relazioni, Poesie, Iscrizioni* (Palermo, 1875).

sommariamente, si segnalano pure le condizioni di conservazione (*tarlato, molto tarlato*)[18].

Sul destino delle librerie ignaziane a Napoli grava una fragile e indecisa politica di tutela incapace di opporsi a un orientamento che, sebbene mai esplicitato, intende cancellare la memoria storica del sistema d'istruzione gesuitico e i suoi pertinenti strumenti culturali: l'affermazione dei gretti interessi di Casa Reale, la penuria di validi bibliotecari e le ruberie degli stessi addetti, poi, concorrono all'irrimediabile perdita di un inestimabile tesoro bibliografico sedimentato e custodito da secoli, ma disperso in pochi anni. Accorate le pagine del Giustiniani che, nelle sue *Memorie storico-critiche della Real Biblioteca Borbonica* edite nel 1818, denuncia le impunite ruberie in molti casi indotte da danarosi bibliofili; l'inutile stampa di cataloghi di vendita, mal compilati e con titoli di ben poco richiamo per collezionisti e librai, con ricavi economici di assai modesta entità; infine, la definitiva eliminazione, per mezzo di aste pubbliche, di quintali di libri, ormai inservibili, a peso di carta straccia:

I libri de' *Gesuiti* erano in gran numero, e per la massima parte ancor di pregio. Gl'incumbenzati alla scelta, e quelli di maggior conoscenza mostrarono meno interesse per la gloria del Re e della Nazione. La medesima dovea riuscire ricchissima, ed ottima; ma (salvi alcuni biblici, SS. Padri, e classici pochissimi) consistette in teologi, canonisti, ascetici, predicabili, legali, non tutti ancora delle migliori stampe. Chi può dubitare, che gl'Ignaziani non avessero avute nelle loro raccolte taluni libri benanche rarissimi? Tra i libri gesuitici si rinvenne una copia di *Girolamo Morlino*, che comprò poi il Duca di *Cassano Serra* per ducati 120 da mano di uno di questi destinati a fare il detto

assortimento. Di tutti quei libri, che i *Gesuiti* appellavano *Rubri* per ragione delle loro legature, e che erano i più scelti ed interessanti, ne furono assai pochi incorporati a quelli della Farnesiana, che in oggi a colpo d'occhio si possono osservare nella nostra R. Biblioteca. Non furono venduti i libri identici, ed ottimi, ma francamente involati: val quanto dire, che le librerie de' *Gesuiti* si posero piuttosto a saccheggio da tutti quegl'impiegati, i quali eransi destinati a fare la dovuta scelta, e vendere poi i duplicati, per acquistare altri libri da rendere sempreppiù ricca e di utilità al pubblico la novella R. Biblioteca. De' mediocri rimasti non se ne fece benanche buon uso; perché dall'infinito lor numero poteasene pure ricavare qualche profitto, onde impiegarne il denaro a compra di altri corpi utili a completare le classi in essa nostra Real Biblioteca; ma si venderono con poco giudizio ed intelligenza bibliografica, e con pochissimo profitto del Fisco. Finalmente della rimasta putredine ne formarono tanti cataloghetti, usciti però da mano imperitissima, che posero a stampa; e non so, se dalla vendita fatta di pochi di essi libri se ne fosse ricuperata la spesa della stampa. Nel pian terreno della Real Biblioteca ne rimasero, come roba anche inservibile, da circa 300 cantara; e, dopo di essere stati così ammonticchiati per lungo tempo, si trasportarono nel braccio nuovo della medesima, dove rimasero pure senza mai più essere osservati, e furono alla fine consegnati alla bilancia[19].

18 NAPOLI, Biblioteca Nazionale "Vittorio Emanuele III", Sezione Manoscritti e Rari, Ms. III. A.45; alle carte 59–67 segue *Altro Indice di / Libri*.

19 Lorenzo Giustiniani, *Memorie storico-critiche della Real Biblioteca Borbonica di Napoli* (Napoli, 1818), 84–85, ristampa anastatica a cura di Vincenzo Trombetta (Sala Bolognese, 2008). Nel ricostruire le vicende della Biblioteca Reale, in occasione dell'Esposizione Universale di Vienna, Vito Fornari scriverà: "Peggior sorte toccò alla libreria de' gesuiti, la quale dopo la loro cacciata dal regno era stata eziandio destinata in dote alla nuova biblioteca. La più parte di que' volumi fu sottratta e venduta. Ma ne furono salvati alquanti, manoscritti

Eppure, nell'Europa colta di quegli anni, non mancano esempi di segno contrario: a Vienna, la ricca biblioteca del Collegio Teresiano – severa fucina dell'educazione aristocratica austriaca – viene preservata dagli effetti della soppressione (anche se chiusa tra il 1773 e il 1797), l'unica a non essere incamerata nell'università o venduta alle pubbliche aste[20].

2. Le requisizioni dopo la caduta della Repubblica nel 1799

Diversi gli obiettivi delle requisizioni di talune biblioteche religiose all'indomani della sanguinosa repressione della Repubblica Napoletana del 1799: una breve stagione politica e ideale, dolorosamente costellata da episodi di violenza e saccheggio. I lazzari inferociti, già all'avvicinarsi delle truppe francesi, assaltano il palazzo della famiglia della Torre, a largo S. Giovanni Maggiore, accusata di voler consegnare la città al generale Jean-Etienne Championnet senza opporre resistenza. Assieme alla pinacoteca e al gabinetto vesuviano – rarissima e preziosa raccolta di reperti vulcanici, materiali lavici, stampe e *guaches* del Vesuvio – viene devastata la libreria di Ascanio Filomarino duca della Torre, gentiluomo di camera di Ferdinando IV di Borbone e illustre geologo, che aveva ereditato i codici e i manoscritti del cardinale Ascanio, suo illustre avo, asceso al soglio cardinalizio alla metà del Seicento[21]. Il 19 gennaio 1799, dopo aver

assistito impotente allo scempio delle sue amate collezioni, Ascanio, assieme al fratello Clemente, viene condotto al Porto Salvo per essere fucilato; ai loro cadaveri, viene barbaramente appiccato il fuoco con la pece.

La caduta della Repubblica segna il naufragio degli ideali illuministi e la sconfitta del suo più generale progetto politico e culturale, ma anche la fine violenta di alcune di quelle domestiche librerie, che avevano costituito i centri di formazione e di aggregazione degli intellettuali giacobini. Nelle turbolente giornate del '99 vengono devastate le biblioteche di Domenico Potenza, luogotenente della Regia Camera; di Gaetano Manso con "le più belle edizioni dei classici, e di altre ottime opere, e delle stampe migliori"; di Marcantonio Carafa principe di Stigliano nelle cui scaffalature – secondo il Giustiniani – oltre a "una ottima raccolta di libri scelti, e di rarità" era custodita "la bella e rarissima edizione della *biblia* fatta in *Napoli* nel 1470 [ma 1476] da Mattia di Olmoutz". Saccheggiate e depredate pure le biblioteche di Giuseppe Zurlo, direttore delle Finanze e di quelle appartenute a Gaetano Filangieri, rinomato estensore della *Scienza delle Legislazione*[22]; e a Domenico Cirillo,

e stampati, e tra gli altri alcuni di non piccolo pregio". Vito Fornari, *Notizia della Biblioteca Nazionale di Napoli* (Napoli, 1874), 66–67.

20 Cf. Antonio Trampus, *I Gesuiti e l'Illuminismo. Politica e religione in Austria e nell'Europa Centrale (1773-1798)* (Firenze, 2000), 75.

21 Nella romanzata ricostruzione del Dumas, la libreria filomariniana avrebbe custodito, oltre a una nutrita raccolta di autografi, la più completa collezione italiana di edizioni elzeviriane: "Accanito bibliomane, collezionava libri rari e manoscritti preziosi. La stessa biblioteca reale – quella di Napoli, ovviamente – non

aveva nulla di paragonabile alla sua collezione di Elzevir, o per parlare più correttamente, di Elzevier. Aveva infatti una raccolta quasi completa, di tutte le edizioni pubblicate da Luigi, Isacco e Daniele, ossia da padre, figlio e nipote. [...] mostrava agli intenditori con orgoglio quella collezione quasi unica in cui si susseguivano nel frontespizio l'angelo che tiene in una mano un libro e nell'altra una falce, il ceppo di vite che avvolgeva un olmo col motto *Non solus*, la Minerva e l'olivo con l'esergo *Ne extra oleas*, il fiorone con la maschera di bufalo che gli Elzevier adottarono nel 1629, la sirena che gli successe nel 1634, il finalino raffigurante la testa di Medusa, la ghirlanda di malvarose, e per finire, i due scettri incrociati su uno scudo, il loro ultimo contrassegno. Le sue edizioni, inoltre, tutte scelte, erano notevoli per la grandezza e la larghezza dei margini, alcuni dei quali raggiungevano quindici o diciotto righe". Alexandre Dumas, *La Sanfelice* (Napoli, 1998), 239–40.

22 Cf. 'Il Catalogo della biblioteca di Gaetano Filangieri', a cura di Renato Bruschi, in Istituto Italiano per gli Studi Filosofici, *Gaetano Filangieri. Lo Stato secondo*

illustre botanico che, gelosamente, conservava i cinquecenteschi erbari di Ferrante Imparato.

Appena debellato il pericolo giacobino, l'amministrazione borbonica, con il decreto del 20 luglio 1799, stabilisce la soppressione di alcune case religiose perchè "ridotte per le passate infelicissime circostanze nel più alto grado di confusione"[23]. Non si sottovaluta la questione libraria: da Palermo – dove si era rifugiato il sovrano e tutta la corte borbonica – si ordina, nel gennaio del 1800, la requisizione dei "manoscritti, libri antichi, quelli di rara edizione [...] e specialmente quelli di S. Martino, di S. Giovanni a Carbonara e que' libri e Manoscritti degli Espulsi [immessi] nel Monistero dei SS. Sossio e Severino" per destinarli alla Biblioteca Reale

che ne incamera pure i doppi, giacché "con dei baratti possono farci degli altri acquisti", così come i capienti "Armarj di S. Pietro a Majella" per collocare gli esuberi e i futuri incrementi. I regi bibliotecari, pertanto, sono tenuti a redigere un esatto "supplemento al catalogo de' Libri, che si incorporano" e a provvedere al loro ordinamento. Si vara, dunque, un insieme di misure, di cui non sfugge la portata politica, per potenziare la prima biblioteca del regno, affinché "riluca la protezione della M.S. accordata alle Arti, ed alle Scienze, e possa la med.a contribuire a formare sudditi illuminati ne' loro doveri, e fedeli al Re, che nulla tralascia per renderli tali"[24].

In particolare, il monastero dei Ss. Severino e Sossio, "sotto il pretesto del *giacobinismo* dei monaci", era stato saccheggiato, divenendo, in seguito, provvisorio alloggio dell'esercito della Santa Fede radunato nelle province calabresi dal cardinale Fabrizio Ruffo per abbattere il governo repubblicano[25]. L'acquartieramento dei sanfedisti nel complesso benedettino, però, aveva causato ingenti danni: pergamene, incunaboli e antiche opere a stampa, assieme a varia suppellettile, erano state date alle fiamme per cucinare zuppe e riscaldare i vasti ambienti. Punitivo, invece, il sequestro della biblioteca dei Certosini a S. Martino – dotata di un catalogo a stampa fin dal 1764[26] – colpevoli di aver ospitato, in una

ragione. Catalogo della Mostra, a cura di Renato Bruschi e Saverio Ricci (Napoli, 1992), 153–84; Eugenio Lo Sardo, 'La Biblioteca Filangieri', in Id., *Il mondo nuovo e le virtù civili. L'epistolario di Gaetano Filangieri* (Napoli, 1999), 299–324. L'Archivio del Museo Civico "Principe Filangieri" conserva il *Catalogo della Libreria del fu Cav. re D. Gaetano Filangieri. 29 settembre 1788*: il manoscritto in ottavo, di sole carte 8 numerate con una rilegatura di epoca posteriore, presenta un ordinamento per formato con la sola citazione del nome dell'autore o del titolo, mentre raramente figurano la città e la data di edizione. A parte i classici della letteratura greca e latina, gli strumenti di consultazione, i manuali e le grammatiche, i testi della biblioteca del Filangieri ripercorrono l'intera vicenda del pensiero settecentesco: da Vico a Giannone, da Verri a Beccaria fino a Galanti e Pagano. Fitta la presenza di autori francesi: spiccano le opere di Rousseau, Mably, Helvétius, Diderot, d'Alambert e Voltaire; ma anche quelle della *côterie* di d'Holbac, Condillac, Marat, Brissot e Linguet, più volte citato nella sua *Scienza della Legislazione* pubblicata nel 1780.

23 Le case religiose soppresse dal provvedimento risultano: S. Martino, Monteoliveto degli Olivetani, S. Severino e Sossio (ristabilita nel 1804), S. Pietro Martire dei Domenicani, S. Pietro a Majella, S. Pietro ad Aram dei Canonici Lateranensi, S. Gaudioso delle Benedettine, S. Giovanni a Carbonara "per sequestrarne le rendite, onde invertirle a sollevare i popoli dai danni sofferti". Cf. Elisa Novi Chiavarria, 'I religiosi napoletani tra repubblica e prima restaurazione', in *Il Cittadino Ecclesiastico. Il clero nella repubblica napoletana del 1799*, a cura di Pierroberto Scaramella (Napoli, 2000), 155–78.

24 NAPOLI, *Archivio di Stato*, Casa Reale Antica, fascio 1515.

25 Già nelle prime congiure giacobine del 1794 il monastero di S Severino e Sossio, assieme a quello di S.a Maria delle Grazie a Caponapoli, era stato motivatamente sospettato di aver ospitato affollate riunioni clandestine per leggere "libri proibiti", accreditando la tesi della partecipazione di non pochi ecclesiastici ai clubs giacobini. Vedi Maria Aurora Tallarico, 'Una "Memoria sullo stato delle Chiese di Napoli" del vescovo E. C. Minutolo all'indomani della Repubblica Partenopea del '99', *Rivista di Storia della Chiesa in Italia*, 31.1 (1977), 101–27.

26 Vedi il *Bibliothecae Regalis Carthusiae S. Martini Catalogus in quo singuli singularum artium et scientiarum libri qui in quavis fere lingua exstant autorumque cognomina ordine alphabetico recensentur*, stampato dalla Tipografia Simoniana.

delle gallerie del Quarto del Priore, un ballo di patrioti per festeggiare la nascita della Repubblica e di aver apertamente parteggiato per gl'insorti giacobini.

Rientra, nell'ordinanza, anche l'antica libreria agostiniana costituita con i fondi dell'umanista Aulo Giano Parrasio e del cardinale Girolamo Seripando. Famosa per i suoi tesori bibliografici, la biblioteca, durante gli anni del viceregno austriaco (1707–1734), aveva dovuto alienare, a favore della Palatina di Vienna, i suoi codici più pregevoli per "cesareo compiacimento". Proprio al fine di salvaguardare l'inestimabile patrimonio, con il dispaccio del 29 agosto 1792 – emanato per il partecipe interessamento di Francesco Daniele, regio istoriografo – era stata dichiarata "reale". Il convento, il 13 giugno 1799, veniva depredato da una folla esagitata che, per puro caso, aveva risparmiato la libreria[27]; e già il 28 luglio dello stesso anno, l'incaricato Goffredo de Bellis comunica di aver completato l'inventario dei codici: "Ritrovai che i codici Latini sono 367, e i Greci 66; ed oltre ad essi vi è un'altra singolare raccolta di manoscritti, altri opera del celebre Cardinal Seripando, altri di sua mano scritti e altri da lui raccolti ascendenti in tutto al numero di 59". Secondo il resoconto del *Giornale* di Diomede Marinelli, nei primi giorni d'agosto del 1800, "si sono principiati a trasportare i celebri manoscritti della libreria di s. Giovanni a Carbonara ne' regi studi, osia nella Libreria reale. Essi sono sopra i 500 manoscritti"[28]. Quasi un anno dopo, Giuseppe Vespoli marchese di Montagano, in qualità di soprintendente ai monasteri soppressi, riferisce:

In seguito di quanto ha disposto Vs. Ill.ma relativamente al passaggio de' MSS. sistenti nella Libreria dell'abolito Monastero di G. Giovanni a Carbonara, nel nuovo Real Museo, mi do il piacere di parteciparle, che sabato 2 corrente furono trasportati nella Real Biblioteca gli anzidetti MSS. al numero di 590 fra Latini, Greci, e Arabi, quelli soprattutto del Cardinal Seripando Caracciolo, de' quali ne fu fatta la dovuta consegna a' Regi Bibliotecari D. Andrea Belli, e D. Antonio Perrotti, li quali diedero il corrispondente ricivo[29].

I provvedimenti del governo, imposti dalla situazione di grave pericolosità, si configurano come un primo intervento di tutela e salvaguardia, sebbene isolato e sporadico, atto a preservare da ogni forma di vandalismo e d'indebita appropriazione l'integrità fisica di famose raccolte librarie, che avevano richiamato l'attenzione di eruditi viaggiatori e di celebri bibliografi, come gli abati maurini Jean Mabillon, in visita alla città e alle sue ricche biblioteche nell'ottobre del 1685, e Bernard de Montfaucon, a Napoli nell'ottobre del 1698.

---

27 Così riferisce una cronaca ottocentesca: "Riguardo poi agli Agostiniani di S. Gio: a Carbonara, Ella si ricorderà benissimo che quel Monistero fu saccheggiato dalla plebe nel giorno preciso de' 13 Giugno 1799, ma siccome l'ingresso alla Biblioteca era occupato da un pedale del Coro, il popolo ignorandolo non lo forzò, e la Biblioteca restò salva. Questa però scampata dal furore distruttore di gente volgare, ebbe la disgrazia di essere sfiorata da mani più accorte, che l'ebbero dopo que' giorni in potere, finché avvertitone il Nostro Sovrano, fu disposto che fosse tosto trasferita nella Reg.a Biblioteca Borbonica, ma già depredata, come si può raccogliere dal confronto, e di ciò che ne dice il P. Montfaucon quando la visitò, e di quell'Inventario che se ne fece poi". NAPOLI, *Archivio di Stato*, Ministero degli Interni, I Inventario, fascio 941.

28 Cf. Diomede Marinelli, *I giornali di Diomede Marinelli. Due codici della Biblioteca Nazionale di Napoli (XV.D. 43–44), pubblicati per cura di A. Fiordalisi (1794–1800)* (Napoli, 1901), 333.

29 NAPOLI, *Archivio di Stato*, Rei di Stato, fascio 42. Sul tema rinviamo a Vincenzo Trombetta, 'Le biblioteche e il 1799', in Soprintendenza Archivistica per la Campania – Regione Campania, *Omaggio alla Repubblica Napoletana del 1799. Fonti e Ricerche* (Napoli, 2000), 49–60.

3. La requisizione delle biblioteche ecclesiastiche nel Decennio francese

Le procedure di esproprio degli ordini religiosi sistematicamente attuate dai governi dei Napoleonidi – il cui carattere ideologico e politico rinvia al processo di secolarizzazione avviato nella Francia rivoluzionaria – rendono disponibile ai bisogni del paese l'enorme patrimonio ecclesiastico, sia pure a costo di inevitabili dispersioni[30]. Lo smantellamento degli insediamenti religiosi che, supplendo alle carenze dello stato, aveva comunque permesso l'accesso alla pubblica lettura e al lavoro intellettuale – "Or tali biblioteche essendo collocate in siti diversissimi della nostra capitale, offrivano agli studiosi non piccola comodità per leggere e riscontrare, trovando sempre ciascuno una biblioteca prossima alla sua abitazione" scriverà un zelante funzionario borbonico dopo la Restaurazione del 1815[31] – con l'attivazione di un nuovo e più avanzato sistema bibliotecario senza nulla concedere alla rapace politica imperiale francese: la pianificata requisizione di codici, manoscritti e libri rari condotta, nel 1796–1798, da Gaspard Monge, commissario francese per le Scienze e le Arti nei dipartimenti italici, non sarà mai consentita nel regno di Napoli.

Per evitare dolose sottrazioni, Giuseppe Napoleone promulga il decreto del 26 agosto 1806 che prevede, in tutte le province, la redazione di "esatti" inventari delle biblioteche col divieto di asportare libri senza autorizzazione per desti-narli alle case di educazione e agli stabilimenti scientifici[32]; ma il decreto del 13 febbraio 1807 ammette l'eccezione per le badie di Montevergine, Montecassino e Cava, delegando la salvaguardia dei loro archivi e biblioteche agli stessi monaci con il compito di "classificare e porre in ordine libri e manoscritti"[33]. Sull'approssimazione e le insufficienze dei dati bibliografici, però, deve intervenire lo stesso ministro degli Interni dopo aver verificato, negli inventari consegnati, che "manca assolutamente il luogo e l'anno delle edizioni e molti titoli sono guasti e mal espressi": deve quindi raccomandare agli intendenti di avvalersi "di persona istruita in materia bibliografica"[34].

I notamenti redatti nelle operazioni di sequestro, tra il 1807 e il 1809, forniscono una panoramica quanto mai eterogenea della dotazione monastica, dalle più modeste librerie di provincia alle biblioteche di grande tradizione, come quelle di S. Maria La Nova, di S. Efremo vecchio, di S. Agostino alla Zecca, del Carmine Maggiore, di S. Caterina a Formello, di S. Pietro Martire, di S. Lorenzo, di S. Agostino Maggiore, di S. Domenico. Gli espropri ricevono una prima sistemazione nella sconsacrata chiesa di Croce di Palazzo, a Monteoliveto e al Gesù Vecchio ove si organizza la distribuzione tra le varie biblioteche, secondo una prestabilita gerarchia, e la vendita a peso di tutti quei "libri stimati inutili". Questa massa di volumi, benché frazionata, costituisce il presupposto per potenziare le biblioteche pubbliche (Biblioteca Reale, Biblioteca di S. Angelo a Nilo) e quelle a carattere speciale (Collegio di Musica di S. Pietro a Majella, Scuola

30 Maria Aurora Tallarico, 'La tutela del patrimonio artistico e librario delle Congregazioni soppresse a Napoli durante il decennio francese (1806–1815)', *Atti della Accademia di Scienze Morali e Politiche di Napoli*, 89 (1978), 237–50.

31 Vincenzo Flauti, 'Memorie critiche su la istruzione pubblica del Regno di Napoli dal principio del secolo corrente fino a' nostri giorni per servire di norma ad una riforma necessaria di essa', in Id., *Anecdota ad publicam eruditionem spectantia post auctoris fata inter amicos evulganda* (Neapoli, 1837), 20–21.

32 *Collezione degli editti, determinazioni, decreti e leggi di S.M. Dà 15 febbraio a' 31 dicembre*, seconda edizione (Napoli, 1813), 303.

33 *Bullettino delle Leggi del Regno di Napoli. Anno 1807*, Tomo I, *Dal mese di gennaio a tutto il mese di giugno* (Napoli, 1807), 25.

34 Lettera del ministro Miot all'Intendente della Provincia di Principato Citeriore del 6 aprile 1808. SALERNO, *Archivio di Stato*, Intendenza, busta 2465, fasc.lo 9.

Militare Politecnica, Accademia di Marina); per riqualificare biblioteche storiche pure a gestione ecclesiastica (Oratoriana dei padri Filippini – Congregazione esclusa dalla soppressione perché senza voti solenni, al pari dei Dottrinari e dei Pii Operai), e per impiantare la nuova Biblioteca della Croce e quella del Collegio Reale da aprire agli studenti universitari.

Il convinto sostegno governativo alle istituzioni bibliotecarie – in termini di mezzi economici, competenze professionali e assegnazione di materiali – incentiva la domanda di lettura, la cui sensibile crescita viene opportunamente registrata dal "Monitore delle Due Sicilie" che, il 4 novembre 1808, riporta in prima pagina:

> Un concorso straordinario si osserva da qualche tempo a questa parte di giovani studiosi nelle pubbliche biblioteche di questa capitale, e particolarmente nella Reale, sita nell'edifizio detto degli Studj, e nella Brancacciana di S. Angelo a Nilo: argomento sicuro dell'impegno, che desta nei giovani l'alta protezione, che dà alle lettere, ed a' letterati, il Governo.

La Biblioteca Reale diretta dall'abate gesuita Juan Andrés – in carica dal 24 aprile del 1806 per volere di Giuseppe Bonaparte favorevolmente impressionato dalla profondità del suo sapere enciclopedico – si arricchisce, in particolare, di codici, incunaboli e cinquecentine provenienti anche da lontane province, come dall'antica Certosa di S. Lorenzo a Padula[35].

D'indubbio rilievo la formazione della biblioteca del Collegio Reale e degli Studi che, pur avendo già incamerato una esigua porzione dei libri gesuitici dopo l'espulsione della Compagnia in epoca borbonica, non disponeva ancora di una struttura organizzata e una dotazione adeguata a svolgere un servizio pubblico a vantaggio della "gioventù studiosa". Il progetto di una biblioteca istituzionalmente deputata all'istruzione accademica viene rilanciato dal governo francese che nomina un nuovo responsabile – il naturalista Giuseppe Antonio Ruffa originario di Tropea – e provvede a incrementarne il patrimonio grazie appunto alle risorse rese utilizzabili dalle soppressioni. Tra il novembre e il dicembre del 1808 il prefetto sottoscrive la ricevuta della consegna di un migliaio di volumi: 163 titoli da S. Lorenzo (20 novembre); 188 da S.a Maria degli Angeli (23 novembre); 191 da S. Teresa (24 novembre); 175 da S. Pietro Martire (27 novembre); 250 da S. Domenico alla Sanità (3 dicembre); 36 da Sant'Agostino Maggiore (12 dicembre)[36]. I relativi inventari solo parzialmente restituiscono la fisionomia delle biblioteche d'origine dal momento che presuppongono la precedente cernita effettuata dall'abate Andrès per la Biblioteca Reale in base alla valutazione del pregio bibliografico dei singoli volumi e alla necessità di completare edizioni scomplete e lacunose collezioni. Ciò nonostante, l'analisi della seconda scelta operata dagli addetti dell'Intendenza consente di confermare le diversità tematiche presenti nelle librerie monastiche e d'identificare le opere più idonee ad essere impiegate a sostegno dei corsi universitari.

Da S. Lorenzo[37] giunge alla Biblioteca del Collegio e dei Regi Studi una discreta quantità di

---

35 Per una più ampia disamina cf. Guerriera Guerrieri, *Per il recupero del patrimonio bibliografico, archivistico, artistico e sacro della Certosa di Padula disperso nell'Ottocento*, Quaderni del centro di studi salernitani "Raffaele Guariglia" (Salerno, 1974).

36 Vedi le *Carte attinenti al travaglio eseguito dal Sig.r Gaetano Gagliardi nelle cennate Biblioteche per ripartire i libri delle medes.me in quelle della Croce; Reale; e Gesù Vecchio. Del peso de' libri di scarto, e da conto finalmente dello stato de' stigli ove riposti eran i libri di ciascun Monistero*, NAPOLI, Archivio di Stato, Ministero degli Interni, II Inventario, fascio 5064, ora in Vincenzo Trombetta, *Storia della Biblioteca Universitaria di Napoli. Dal viceregno spagnolo all'Unità d'Italia* (Napoli, 1995), 65 e passim.

37 Il monastero di S. Lorenzo, alla metà del Seicento, disponeva di una Libraria tra "le più famose di Napoli, per l'ampiezza, e capacità della stanza, e per la numerosità, e sceltezza de' libri che vi sono". Carlo De

classici greci e latini in edizioni cinque e secentesche, come: le *Opere* di Cicerone (Basilea, 1553, Napoli, 1777), le *Commedie* di Terenzio (Venezia, 1573) e di Aristofane (Ginevra, 1607), le *Opere* di Virgilio (Venezia, 1578) e di Orazio (Basilea, 1595), gli *Epigrammi* di Marziale (Parigi, 1617), le *Metamorfosi* di Ovidio (Anversa, 1618) con l'*Istoria dei Poeti Greci* di Lorenzo Crasso stampata a Napoli, da Antonio Bulifon, nel 1678. Non mancano i testi dei Padri della Chiesa e volumi di area religiosa[38]. Un accentuato orientamento letterario è ricavabile dalla lista dei libri ricevuti da S.a Maria degli Angeli dei Chierici Regolari, a Pizzofalcone[39]; mentre sicuramente differente

si rivela l'orientamento culturale della raccolta libraria di S. Teresa degli Scalzi, fuori la porta di S.a Maria di Costantinopoli[40]: accanto alle opere dei Padri della Chiesa e ai testi del mondo classico con diverse edizioni del sedicesimo secolo – (Tito Livio 1539; Cicerone 1540; Senofonte 1555; Omero 1561; Strabone 1571, tutti pubblicati a Basilea; Plauto, Parigi, 1576; Seneca, Parigi, 1599; Virgilio, Augusta, 1599) – figurano numerose opere di storia, tra cui: il *Corpus Historiae Byzantinae*, Francoforte, 1568; Giulio Cesare Capaccio, *Neapolitanae Historiae*, Napoli, 1607; Gregorio Rosso, *Istoria delle cose di Napoli sotto l'imperio di Carlo V*, Napoli, 1635; *Storia Universale de' Concili*, Venezia, 1696; *Memorie istoriche de' Monarchi ottomani*, Venezia, 1697. Ma grande spazio viene riservato alla cultura scientifica, nella sua più ampia accezione.

In base alla documentazione inventariale, la libreria di S. Pietro Martire fornisce opere classiche e, in particolare, una selezionata raccolta di testi medici[41],

---

Lellis, *Parte seconda O' vero Supplemento a Napoli sacra di d. Cesare D'Engenio Caracciolo* (Napoli, 1654), 69. Anche il canonico Carlo Celano, nelle sue *Notizie del Bello, dell'Antico, e del Curioso della Città di Napoli per gli signori forestieri* (Napoli, 1692) la ricorda per i "vari libri antichi di sommo pregio".

38 Per i primi si elencano: le opere di S. Cirillo Alessandrino (Basilea, 1566 e Parigi, 1638), Tertulliano (Parigi, 1608), Origene (Parigi, 1619), S. Gregorio Magno (Parigi, 1705), Ireneo (Venezia, 1734), S. Girolamo (Venezia, 1772), e ancora: la *Bibliothèque des auteurs ecclésiastiques* di Louis Ellies Dupin in cinquantasei tomi (Parigi, 1707), gli *Annales Ordinis S. Benedicti* di Jean Mabillion in cinque libri in-folio (Lucca, 1739–1740), una *Biblia sacra* in ventidue volumi (Venezia, 1755), la *Storia Ecclesiastica* di Claude Fleury (prima edizione napoletana tirata a partire dal 1767) e le *Opere tradotte in italiano* di Jacques-Bénigne Bossuet (Napoli, 1778).

39 La biblioteca, ricordiamo, era stata frequentata da Niccolò Toppi alla ricerca di materiali utili per la compilazione della sua *Biblioteca Napoletana* tirata dal Bulifon nel 1678. Questi i titoli più significativi pervenuti ai Regj Studi: *Grammatica greca* (Lione, 1605 e Padova, 1765); *Vocabolario italiano e spagnuolo* (Roma, 1620) e *Grammatica spagnuola e italiana* di Lorenzo Franciosini (Roma, 1638); *Vocabolario della Crusca*, (nella terza impressione della Stamperia dell'Accademia, Firenze, 1691); *Dittionario italiano-francese e francese-italiano* di Antoin Oudin e Lorenzo Ferretti (Venezia, 1693); *Dictionarum septem linguarum* di Ambrogio Calepino (Padova, 1718). Ma anche i *Principi della lingua latina* (Venezia, 1550); *L'Arte Poetica* [...] *con la dottrina de' Sonetti, e postille del Valvassori* di Antonio Minturno (Venezia, 1563); il *Tesoro della lingua toscana* (Venezia,

1594); il *Parnasus Poeticus* (Roma, 1595); *Del modo di comporre in versi nella lingua toscana* di Girolamo Ruscelli (Venezia, 1612); il *Trattato della lingua* di Giacomo Pergamini (Venezia, 1641); *Della lingua toscana* di Benedetto Buonmattei (Napoli, 1723).

40 Così nelle *Aggiunzione* al Celano: "Un tempo la libreria che questi religiosi avevano, era ricca assai e di gran pregio [...] i quali libri poscia nella soppressione dell'Ordine per grandissima parte furon riposti nella grande biblioteca denominata Borbonica, e gli altri venduti".

41 Sul finire del diciottesimo secolo, la biblioteca aveva ricevuto un "dono che molto soddisfece i monaci per la qualità del donatore, che fu re Ferdinando IV. Il dono consistette in 10 volumi *in folio* del museo Farnesiano, insieme ad altri dello stesso genere, che il priore ordinò fossero accuratamente rilegati e messi in un posto d'onore". Giuseppe Cosenza, 'La Chiesa e il Convento di S. Pietro Martire. III. Epoca Moderna', *Napoli Nobilissima*, 9.1 (1900), 27. Dalle sue scansie pervengono: Galeno, *Ars medica* (Venezia, 1549) e *Chirurgica* (Valencia, 1624); Giovanni Battista Da Monte, *Consultationes medicinales* (Venezia, 1559); Gabriele Falloppio, *De morbo gallico* (Venezia, 1574); Sebastiano Ajello, *Breve discorso sopra l'imminente peste nel Regno di Napoli* (Napoli, 1577); Diomede Amico, *Opera medica*

come anche di carattere scientifico le rimesse librarie pervenute dalla Sanità dei Domenicani[42]. Assai modesta, invece, la quantità dei volumi proveniente da S. Agostino Maggiore alla Zecca[43].

Un'altra ondata di soppressioni viene disposta da Gioacchino Murat: la legge del 7 agosto 1809 prescrive a tutti i religiosi l'obbligo di deporre l'abito e di lasciare il proprio convento, consentendo di portar via solo gli effetti personali e qualche suppellettile, ma non "i metalli, le cose preziose, i quadri, le biblioteche, gli archivi e simili oggetti di arte o di museo, gli arredi sacri, le macchine, i vasi ed altri utensili esistenti nelle spezierie", che dovranno essere inventariati con un'approssimativa stima economica[44]. Il decreto interessa vari complessi, tra cui: S. Domenico Maggiore, Madonna dei Sette Dolori, S. Nicola Tolentino, Crociferi ai Mannesi, S. Maria in Portico, S. Orsola a Chiaia, S. Brigida, Rosariello, Speranzella, Montesanto, Gesù e Maria. Anche stavolta le librerie vengono incamerate, secondo una preordinata ripartizione, tra la Biblioteca Reale, la Biblioteca dei Regi Sudi, quella di S. Angelo a Nido (Brancacciana) e dei Girolamini. Ruffa registra queste assegnazioni, con le rispettive date di consegna:

> Montesanto, Rosariello e Speranzella, Monastero della Concordia (5 novembre 1810), Gesù e Maria (12 novembre), Monastero di S. Maria in Portico (13 novembre), Monastero dei SS. Apostoli e di S. Anna a Capuana (19 novembre), Madonna de' Sette Dolori, S. Nicola Tolentino, Monastero di S. Orsola (21 novembre), Crociferi ai Mannesi (22 novembre), S. Brigida, Monastero de' Barnabiti, S. Domenico Maggiore (senza data)[45].

Le accessioni, sul piano quantitativo, oscillano dai 6 titoli del Monastero dei Barnabiti ai 14 di

---

(Venezia, 1599); *De morbis veneficius* (Milano, 1618); *De febribus* (Napoli, 1627); Giulio Cesare Claudini, *Opera medica* (Venezia, 1628); Maxentius Piccinus, *De usu medicamenti expurgantis in febris* (Napoli, 1628); Joseph Du Chesne, *Pharmacopea* (Venezia, 1638); *Historia anatomica* (Lione, 1650); Lazare Riviere, *Praxis medica* (Leida, 1660); Paolo Zacchia, *De mali ipochondriaci* (Roma, 1664); Teofrasto Paracelso, *Opera medica* (Genova, 1668).

42 La "famosa libreria in ogni sorta di scienze" custodisce "due globi celesti e terrestri che simili in grandezza non abbiamo a Napoli". Nel novero delle opere scientifiche vedi: la *Breve e universale risoluzione d'aritmetica per ritrovare ogni sorta di misura di terra* di Lorenzo Bonocchio (Brescia, 1597); la *Trigonometria* di Bartolomeo Pitisco (Francoforte, 1612); *Corso matematico* (Palermo, 1661); la *Pratica di aritmetica e geometria* di Lorenzo Forestani (Siena, 1682); le *Operazioni del Compasso* di Galileo Galilei (Padova, 1694); le *Esercitazioni geometriche* di Paolo Mattia Doria (Parigi, 1719). Nutrito il settore astronomico: Girolamo Balduini, *Quaesitum de forma caeli* (Venezia, 1522); *Ephemerides caelestium motum* (Venezia, 1582); Giovanni Paolo Gallucci, *Caelestium corporum* (Venezia, 1603); Tolomeo, *De praedicationibus astronomicis* (Francoforte, 1622); *Astrologia naturalis* (Marsiglia, 1645); Francesco Levera, *Prodromus universae astronomiae* (Roma, 1663); Giuseppe Rosaccio, *Teatro del cielo e della terra* (Trevi, 1686). Ed inoltre: Giovanni Battista Vimercati, *Dialogo degli orologi solari* (Venezia, 1567); *Ragionamenti de' flussi e riflussi del mare oceano* (Venezia, 1574); Petrus Apianus, *Cosmographia* (Anversa, 1584); Leonardo Fioravanti, *Capricci medicinali* (Venezia, 1595); Daniello Bartoli, *Del suono de' tremori armonici e dell'udito* (Roma, 1679); Antonio Bulifon, *Lettera sull'eruzione del Vesuvio del 1692* (Napoli, 1694); Pietro Antonio de Martino, *De omnibus morbis humani corporis tractatus* (Napoli, 1699).

43 All'ingresso, una lapide – oggi al Museo di San Martino – ammoniva: "Urbano P.P. VIII / Scomunica papale con la pri / vatione di voce attiva e passiva / a chi si sia di qualsivoglia grado / dignità e condizione ch'ardirà / di cacciare fuora dalla libreria / di S. Agostino Maggiore di Napoli / libri o vero quinterni tanto scritti / a mano quanto stampati di qual / si voglia materia si siano / Spedita il dì XI aprile 1644 / nell' XXI anno del suo /

pontificato". Giuseppe Consoli Fiego, *Itinera Literaria, Ricerche sulle biblioteche napoletane del XVII Secolo* (Napoli, 1934), 162.

44 *Bullettino delle Leggi del Regno di Napoli, Anno 1809*, Tomo II, *Da luglio a tutto dicembre* (Napoli, 1809), 805–11.

45 NAPOLI, *Archivio di Stato*, Ministero degli Interni, Appendice II, fascio 1915.

S. Nicola Tolentino, dai 15 di S. Orsola ai 49 dei Crociferi, dai 236 dei SS. Apostoli fino ai 642 di S. Maria in Portico. La quota sicuramente più rilevante e bibliograficamente più pregiata, però, giunge da S. Domenico Maggiore[46]: oltre duecento le edizioni del sedicesimo secolo, identificate dall'inconfondibile bollatura oblunga con la scritta "Biblioteca S. Dominici Majoris"[47].

Nel gennaio del 1810, inoltre, il Ruffa redige l'*Inventario de' libri scelti in Monteoliveto per uso della Biblioteca Universitaria* che, senza riportare le originarie provenienze, enumera 1767 titoli, corredati dal nome dell'autore, titolazione quasi sempre abbreviata, luogo e data di edizione, suddivisi per formato: n. 912 in folio, n. 522 in quarto, n. 255 in ottavo, n, 90 in sedicesimo. Un'altissima quota è assorbita da annali ecclesiatici, bollari, catechismi, breviari, omelie, sinodi diocesani, volumi di apologetica, diritto canonico, storia delle congregazioni, di vite di santi, oltre a opere predicabili, panegirici, esercizi spirituali e sermoni. Pochi i testi non riconducili all'area religiosa, e tra questi: l'*Opera Omnia* di Marsilio Ficino (Basilea, 1561), le *Opere* di Svetonio (Parigi, 1616), *Le isole più*

---

46   Nella biblioteca – che conservava i codici di Gioviano Pontano fecondissimo scrittore umanista – avevano studiato, alla fine del Cinquecento, Tommaso Campanella e Giordano Bruno che vi "rinvenne non poco di ciò che gli potesse occorrere" tra le "pregevolissime opere, di cui parecchie mancavano nelle altre biblioteche della città". Vincenzo Spampanato, *Vita di Giordano Bruno. Con documenti editi e inediti* (Messina, 1921), I, 227–28. La "famosa, e ricca libraria di diverse scienze" si accrebbe con i lasciti di Deodato Marone, teologo di corte, revisore dei libri esteri, ed esaminatore delle R. Scuole del Regno, e di Eustachio D'Afflitto, "destinato per la scelta de' libri de' Gesuiti, e per formar la Real Biblioteca". Giustiniani, *Memorie storico-critiche*, come alla nota 19, 59–60. Nel 1718 soffre la perdita di rari codici a favore della Palatina di Vienna, che Carlo VI progetta di trasformare in una delle più ricche d'Europa. Nel 1807, afferma il Giustiniani, la biblioteca, consultabile solo in alcuni giorni della settimana, "fu tolta al pubblico, e quei PP. giudiziosamente la spogliarono innanzi tempo del miglior, che vi era". Dopo la soppressione del 1809 si apprende che "molti libri e manoscritti erano stati involati", e tra questi anche il manoscritto autografo di S. Tommaso d'Aquino, in seguito ritrovato grazie "alla somma vigilanza della Polizia, cui riuscì di scovrire un deposito di moltissimi volumi furtivamente involati". Cf. Michele Miele, 'Un intervento della polizia murattiana per arrestare la dispersione del patrimonio librario dei conventi soppressi', *Campania Sacra*, 2 (1971), 251–69, poi in Id., *La Chiesa del Mezzogiorno nel decennio francese. Ricerche* (Napoli, 2007), 317–26. E Agostino Gervasio, antiquario e bibliofilo, nel suo *Saggio di una storia napoletana* aggiunge: "i libri con gli altri sono andati a male e venduti a picciole partite. Io ne ho acquistati non pochi che formano il miglior ornamento della mia collezione di libri di storia letteraria". Il passo in Consoli Fiego, *Itinera Literaria*, come alla nota 43, 137.

47   Da citare almeno: Aristotile, *Libri Physicorum* (Lugduni, apud Jacobum Giuntam, 1542); Erasmo da Rotterdam, *De duplici copia verborum ac rerum commentarii duo* (Venetiis, in aedibus Francisci Bindanei et Maphei

Pasinei, 1542); Albertus Pighius, *Hierarchiae Ecclesiasticae assertio* (Coloniae, excudebat Melchior Nouesianus, 1544); Sallustio, *De Catilinae coniuratione ac Bello Jugurthino* (Lugduni, apud Seb. Gryphium, 1551); Giuseppe Flavio, *De Bello judaico* (Anvers, en casa de Martin Nucio, 1551); Polibio, *Historiarum* (Lugduni, Seb. Gryphium, 1554); Appiano, *Delle guerre civili et esterne de' Romani* (In Vinegia, appresso Domenico de' Farri, 1555); Girolamo Cardano, *Liber de libris propriis* (Lugduni, apud Guglielmum Rouillium, sub scuto Veneto, 1557); Diodoro Siculo, *Bibliotheca Historicae* (Basileae, per Henricum Petri, 1559); Pietro Galatino, *Opus de Arcanis Catholicae Veritatis* (Basilea, per Joannem Hernagium, 1561); Antoine Du Pinet, *Historiae plantarum* (Lugduni, apud Gabrielem Coterium, 1561); Giovanni Della Casa, *Rime et prose* (In Venetia, appresso Domenico Farri, 1563); Virgilio, *Universum poema* (Venetiis, apud Joannem Mariam Bonellum, 1566); S. Tommaso d'Aquino, *Opera* (Romae, apud Julium Accoltum, 1570); Pietro Bembo, *Gli Asolani* (Venezia, appresso Gabriele Giolito, 1575); Ovidio, *Metarmophoseon* (Venetiis, apud Jo. Cryphium, 1580); Serafino Razzi, *Istoria de gli huomini illustri, così nelle prelature come nelle dottrine del Sacro Ordine de gli Predicatori* (Lucca, per il Busdrago, 1596). Sulla più complessiva ricognizione bibliografica rinviamo a Eugenio Canone, 'Contributo per una ricostruzione dell'antica 'Libraria' di S. Domenico Maggiore. Manoscritti, incunaboli, cinquecentine conservati nelle biblioteche napoletane', in *Giordano Bruno. Gli anni napoletani e la 'peregrinatio' europea. Immagini, Testi, Documenti*, a cura di Eugenio Canone (Cassino, 1992), 190–247.

famose del mondo di Fortunato Porcacchi (Padova, 1620), la *Storia di Luigi IX Re di Francia* di Pietro Mattei (Venezia, 1688), i *Frammenti storiali del Tribunale della Real Camera di Napoli* di Nicolò Doti (Napoli, 1693), l'*Historia della Repubblica di Venezia* di Michele Foscarini (Venezia, 1696), *Intorno alla geometria di Cartesio* del Doria (Venezia, 1721), il *Kalendarium* del Mazzocchi (Napoli, 1743), la *Raccolta delle vite e famiglie degli uomini illustri del Regno di Napoli* del Muratori (Milano, 1755), *Del dialetto napoletano* di Ferdinando Galiani (Napoli, 1779), il *Trattato dell'eloquenza* di Giuseppe Maria Platina (Bologna, 1791)[48].

Caposaldo del sistema bibliotecario cittadino e cardine della pubblica istruzione, la Gioacchina – la Biblioteca della Nazione Napoletana istituita con il decreto del 26 febbraio 1812 nell'abolito monastero di Monteoliveto e destinata a raccogliere l'organica raccolta di libri, manoscritti, carteggi, stampe, busti e ritratti degli uomini illustri del Regno di Napoli, al fine di documentare la storia e la letteratura delle regioni meridionali[49] – incamera una quota dei

fondi monastici. In particolare, il prefetto Luigi Carlo Federici, responsabile pure della Libraria di S. Angelo a Nido, accertando il progressivo esaurirsi delle fonti di approvvigionamento nella capitale, valuta, con la dovuta attenzione, un "notamento delle librerie de' Monasteri soppressi della Provincia di Terra di Lavoro", nel quale, comunque, "de' molti e ricchi monasteri che esistevano in Aversa non si fa alcuna menzione, ad eccezione de' soli Cappuccini". Quindi, con la missiva datata 26 aprile, informa il ministro degli Interni Giuseppe Zurlo del proposito di recarsi a Aversa per recuperare i libri ivi

---

48 Cf. Vincenzo Trombetta, 'I fondi monastici nella formazione della Biblioteca Universitaria di Napoli (1806–1810)', *Fridericiana*, 3 (1991–1992), 75–90.

49 L'ordinanza reale delinea gli orientamenti e le prospettive della prima biblioteca napoletana a carattere "nazionale". Per la sua realizzazione sono stanziati adeguati finanziamenti e previsti gli strumenti per favorirne lo sviluppo: la nuova biblioteca pubblica, infatti, gode dell'assegnazione di ottomila lire annue – mentre la Municipalità è tenuta alle ordinarie spese di gestione – e del diritto di stampa e può aggiungere, a libri e manoscritti, altre varie testimonianze delle vicende patrie attraverso il reperimento di monete battute a partire dalla decadenza dell'impero romano, di medaglie celebrative e di ritratti, oltre a stampe e busti degli uomini illustri del regno. La biblioteca, secondo il programma, avrebbe ospitato anche la sede della cattedra di Biografia letteraria e bibliografia, prima e unica in tutt'Italia, per la formazione professionale dei futuri bibliotecari. *Bollettino delle Leggi del Regno di Napoli. Anno 1812*, Semestre I. *Da gennaio fino a tutto giugno* (Napoli, 1812), 227–30. Così il passo che il ministro Zurlo inserisce nel suo *Rapporto sullo stato del*

Regno di Napoli per gli anni 1810, e 1811 presentato al Re nel suo Consiglio di Stato del Ministro dell'Interno, pubblicato dalla tipografia del Trani nel 1812: "Finalmente Vostra Maestà ha voluto coronare gli stabilimenti fatti per l'istruzione pubblica con tutti quei mezzi d'insegnamento che convengono ad una gran capitale, ed alla numerosa gioventù che v'è raccolta. Dopo d'aver riordinate, accresciute ed aperte all'uso pubblico tutte le antiche biblioteche della capitale, V.M. trovandole poco proporzionate al bisogno del gran numero di studiosi che vi concorrono, e poco ben distribuite pel sito, volendo dare alla sua amata città di Napoli una testimonianza perenne della cura che ha presa per l'istruzione generale, e specialmente per la cultura e pel lustro di lei, ha concepito l'idea di formare colla sua particolare borsa sotto il nome di *Biblioteca Gioacchina* una grandiosa biblioteca municipale nella sala dell'antica biblioteca di Monteoliveto e nelle altre sale a questa adiacenti. V.M. vuole che essa contenga non solo una collezione generale di libri d'ogni genere, ma anche la collezione particolare di tutti gli scrittori patrj, dei manoscritti i più pregevoli che si trovano tuttavia nelle mani de' particolari, delle monete battute dai Principi e Monarchi delle Sicilie dalla caduta dell'impero romano sin oggi, di tutte le medaglie coniate in onore de' grandi uomini della nazione, o per l'occasione de' pubblici avvenimenti, de' ritratti, busti e stampe degli uomini illustri di Napoli che possano rinvenirsi. Il dono che con questo nuovo stabilimento farà alla città di Napoli come per monumento della cultura nazionale, e di ciò che V.M. ha fatto per promuoverla, dee contenere, ha detto V.M., la storia delle sue lettere e delle vicende che queste hanno sofferto. Ella si occupa in questo momento di mandare ad effetto una così belle e generosa idea" (48–49).

depositati. Al suo rientro, rimette una dettagliata relazione indicando, sulla scorta "de' sommari ed infelici notamenti che se ne son fatti", quelle biblioteche monastiche che ancora "promettono contenere delle opere d'importanza", come dei Cappuccini e degli Alcantarini di Venafro, dei Francescani di Piedimonte, e dei Riformati di Centurano[50]. Previo avviso delle autorità locali, quindi, propone d'inviare "una persona capace addetta al servizio di questa Biblioteca, insieme con le ceste per caricarveli", disponendo pure la vendita di tutti gli altri volumi per non lasciarli "più perire nei luoghi ove sono ormai da più anni rinchiusi". Filippo Federici, fratello del prefetto e anch'egli in servizio a S. Angelo a Nido in qualità di sottobibliotecario, provvede al trasporto dei libri da Casamarciano e da Centurano. Munito, poi, di un dispaccio dell'intendente di Terra di Lavoro, nella prima settimana di ottobre raggiunge, "dopo un dispendioso ed infelice viaggio", il Collegio di Maddaloni dove già era stata selezionata quella parte "dei corpi più insigni per le Reali Biblioteche di Napoli": ma il rettore dell'Istituto, riconoscendo valida la sola autorizzazione della Pubblica Istruzione, si rifiuta di consegnare i volumi colà accatastati e, all'inviato, ne concede soltanto una frettolosa ispezione. Il 13 ottobre Filippo Federici redige un puntuale rapporto sull'accaduto ed esprime il vivo rincrescimento per le "circa 40 cantaia di libri la maggior parte di opere pregevolissime di Scrittori Sacri e Profani [...] ammonticchiati in due stanze sotterranee dove cominciavano di già a marcire, oltre al maltrattamento ricevuto dai topi"[51]. L'intoppo burocratico, comunque, si risolve in pochi mesi e l'8 gennaio 1814 l'abate Federici può dichiarare concluso sia l'accorpamento di tutti i libri provenienti dalla Terra di Lavoro, che "la scelta di tutti quegli articoli che ho giudicato

poter convenire alle Reali Biblioteche di questa Capitale, e uniti insieme gli ho riserbati per distribuirli secondo il bisogno di ciascheduna". Allega agli atti il *Notamento di libri scelti dal Deposito del R.l Collegio di Maddaloni per uso delle Reali Biblioteche Giovacchina e Brancacciana* comprendente circa centocinquanta titoli[52].

"Nella speranza di rinvenire que' volumi mancanti alle opere pervenutemi", lo stesso Federici, il 15 febbraio, giunge a Maddaloni. Recupera ben pochi libri per la Gioacchina, ma collabora fattivamente per aprire la biblioteca del Collegio: opera uno scarto del materiale da vendersi nella "migliore maniera" e organizza il trasporto di dodici armadi dal vicino convento di S.a Lucia per sistemarvi "una collezione di libri bellissimi in ogni materia sacra e profana".

***

Gli studi sulle requisizioni librarie, nel decennio napoleonico, sono state concentrate – con poche e meritevoli eccezioni[53] – nella capitale del Regno e solo di recente si sono programmate ricognizioni a più vasto raggio, tuttora in corso, per un'analisi quantitativa e una valutazione bibliografica dei materiali librari provenienti da monasteri e conventi delle altre regioni meridionali. In questa sede possiamo anticipare alcuni dati raccolti che, sebbene d'indubbio interesse, meritano ancora indispensabili approfondimenti.

50 Lettera del 7 agosto 1813. NAPOLI, *Archivio di Stato*, Ministero degli Interni, II Inventario, fascio 5065.

51 *Ivi.*

52 Nella lista si distinguono: le *Opere* di Sant'Anselmo, nell'edizione parigina del 1675 e quelle di San Bonaventura in dodici tomi stampati a Venezia; le *Lettere senesi sulle Belle arti* di Andrea da Valle; *Della forza della immaginazione nelle donne gravide* di Blondel; la *Sylloge epistolarum Sanctorum Patrum*; le *Vite de' Santi dell'Antico Testamento*; le *Riflessioni sul diluvio universale* di Costantini; il *Giornale ecclesiastico* di Roma, in sette tomi.

53 Cf. Candido Cuomo, *Le leggi eversive del secolo XIX e le vicende degli Ordini Religiosi della Provincia di Principato Citeriore (Ricerche Storiche)*, Tomo IX, *Le Biblioteche degli Ordini Religiosi soppressi* (Mercato S. Severino, 1973).

Il fondo Intendenza dell'Archivio di Stato di Salerno conserva alcuni degli elenchi relativi ai sequestri effettuati nella Provincia di Principato Citeriore. Questa una prima tabella riepilogativa che indica località, anno della compilazione degli inventari (laddove annotato), comunità religiosa, quantità dei volumi, note e commenti dei compilatori:

Balvano (1812), Osservanti, 227 opere enumerate secondo la progressione topografica;

Bracigliano (1815), Riformati di S. Francesco, 80 opere "più varj libercoli di diversa grandezza e di varj argomenti, in numero 250";

Campagna (1807), Domenicani di S. Bartolomeo, circa 60 opere;

Campagna (1807), Agostiniani della Ss. Annunziata, 200 opere, tra cui numerose miscellanee;

Campagna (1811), Osservanti della Ss. Concezione, circa 480 opere enumerate secondo la progressione topografica, ma indicate, spesso, solo con nome dell'autore;

Castelluccio (1811), Cappuccini e Riformati. Cappuccini circa 160 opere. Riformati 30 titoli mentre "diversi altri i quali perché laceri, e trattano quasi tutti di materie inette, non si sono creduti necessari a scriversi, per non obbligare il Comune alla spese del trasporto, ed il Collegio a fare acquisto di Libri di nessunissima considerazione";

Eboli (1812), Cappuccini, circa 40 opere "oltre li suddetti Libri, ve ne sono altri antichi, e logori in ottavo, de' quali, o non se conosce l'Autore o sono di nessuna valuta";

Laurino (1815), Minori Osservanti di S. Antonio, 160 opere;

Marsiconuovo (1808), Conventuali, 200 opere;

Mercato S. Severino (1809), Conventuali di S. Francesco "esistono nella Biblioteca di detto Monistero libri numero 150 riguardanti Materie di Teologia, Filosofia, e Prediche per lo più dispari, di cattivissime edizioni, e piene di rancidezze, vantando la più famosa vetustà, che non presentano niun valore, menocchè quello di carta vecchia";

Montecorvino Rovella (1809), Riformati di S. Maria della Pace, "Opere numero Seicento, i quali essendosi ritrovati scritti la maggior parte in lingua Gotica e Spagnola, e niuno Autore Classico, non si è stimato espediente di farne la descrizione";

Montecorvino Rovella (1809), Basiliani di Materdomini, circa 600 opere comprese molte "dimezzate, ed altri Libri Ecclesiastici, o divoti, anche maltrattati nelle coverte";

Oliveto, Riformati 60 opere riposte in "sette scansie di noce, cinque grandi, e due piccole";

Pagani (1809), Carmelitani Scalzi di S. Maria del Carmine, "nella libreria si son trovati esistenti libri n. 454, maltenuti, di cattiva ligatura, riguardantino materie Ecclesiastiche, e vite de' SS. Padri, e di pochissimo valore";

Palomonte, Minori Osservanti, circa 60 opere e "vari altri volumi tutti dimezzati che né si conoscono gli Autori";

Policastro (1812), Minori Osservanti, "pochi ed inutili libri esistenti nel soppresso Convento de' Minori Osservanti di Battipaglia. Libri vecchi e laceri, numero trentatré, tra quali vi sono tre Breviarj";

Polla, Cappuccini, circa 100 opere, enumerate secondo la progressione topografica;

S. Nicola la Palma (1811), Osservanti, circa 430 opere;

S. Angelo Fasanella (1813), Osservanti, circa 130 opere suddivise in "Libri legali", "Istoria dell'Ordine", "Predicatori", "S.S. Padri" e "Filosofia";

Salerno (1808), Teresiani, 155 opere e "scaffali pieni di libri "di pochissimo conto, vecchi e rosi dal tempo";

Salerno (1809), convento di S. Antonio, circa 60 opere;

San Severino (1808), conservatorio delle Donne Monache del villaggio Penta, circa 80 opere;

Santomenna (1808), Cappuccini, circa 110, opere enumerate secondo la progressione topografica;

Sicignano (1815) Cappuccini, circa 100 opere;
Teggiano (1811), Minori Osservanti della SS. Pietà, circa 30 opere e "altri libri morali antichi logori e consunti";
Vallo (1811), Cappuccini, circa 180 opere;
Vallo, Domenicani di S. Maria delle Grazie, la "Libreria sita nella Camera Priorale" contiene circa 100 opere enumerate secondo la progressione topografica[54].
Vibonati (1810), monastero di S. Francesco di Paola, circa 200 opere con l'indicazione del prezzo approssimativo;
Vietri sul Mare (1809), Conventuali di S. Antonio, 85 opere.

L'Archivio di Stato di Potenza, per la Basilicata, conserva l'inedito notamento della biblioteca del Convento di S. Sofia dei Francescani a Noja redatto il 10 ottobre del 1809 dall'ex guardiano Antonio Salerno. Il documento – aperto dalla specifica "Nel detto suppresso monistero non vi sono trovati quadri, o altri oggetti di scienze o art[icoli] all'infuori de' soli quadri appartenenti al culto rapportati nel rispettivo inventario, ma solamente i seguenti libri, esistenti nella camera detta della Libreria" – elenca circa 80 titoli. Ai padri Minori Conventuali di S. Antonio di Pescopagano, secondo l'inventario del 23 settembre 1809, viene requisita una libreria comprendente un centinaio di opere per un valore stimato in 58 ducati e 75 grana[55].

Di ben più cospicua entità i sequestri nella provincia dell'Aquila come si ricava dagli inediti *Notamenti de' libri esistenti ne' / monisteri degli ordini possidenti / soppressi col Real decreto de' 7 agosto / dell'anno 1809, in quelli soppressi degli ordini mendicanti, ed in quelli / non soppressi /*

della Provincia di Aquila / Anno 1811 preceduti dall'*Indice degli inventari compresi / nel presente Volume / de' Monisteri soppressi col decreto de' 7 agosto 1809*[56] di cc. 426. Dalle oltre cinquanta comunità religiose, sparse in tutta la provincia, emerge un rimarchevole dato quantitativo: circa mille e cinquecento le opere sottratte ai Riformati di Sulmona; oltre mille e seicento le opere requisite nel convento degli Agostiniani dell'Aquila, elencate quasi sempre senza data e luogo di stampa; e poco meno di tremila quelle confiscate ai Domenicani (cc. 47–101). Significativo il settore, forte di circa centoventi titoli, delle materie mediche possedute dagli Agostiniani: cura delle febbri e delle afflizioni muliebri, trattati di anatomia, aforismi, dispute, responsi, consigli, osservazioni e trattamenti sui mali ipocondriaci, sul morbo gallico, sulla pestilenza, sulla podagra, sulla farmacopea, sulla medicina pratica, sugli effetti curativi dei bagni. Di grande qualità e vastità di argomenti la biblioteca domenicana forse frequentata anche da un pubblico di studenti: grammatiche greche, latine, ebraiche e francesi fino a un vocabolario turco, istituzioni grammaticali e oratorie, trattati sulla lingua italiana e sull'ortografia, dizionario dei sinonimi, poetica e retorica, filosofia, elementi di storia, geografia, matematica, astronomia, scienze fisiche e naturali, diritto civile, iconologia, economia, biografia.

4. La Restaurazione

La Restaurazione borbonica del 1815 eredita il sistema bibliotecario creato nel Decennio francese, limitandosi a riconvertire la Biblioteca della Croce – destinata all'istruzione dei principi reali dove il prefetto Domenico Romanelli aveva sperimentato nuove procedure di classificazione bibliografica[57] – e a sopprimere la Gioacchina

---

54   SALERNO, *Archivio di Stato*, Intendenza, busta 2467 (fascc. 1, 3); 2468 (fascc. 1, 2, 4, 6); 2469 (fascc. 2, 9, 14); 2470 (fascc. 1, 8, 11); 2471 (2, 7, 9, 10, 13); 2472 (fascc. 6, 7, 11, 13); 2473 (1, 4, 7, 8, 10); 2474 (fascc. 53, 55, 64).

55   POTENZA, *Archivio di Stato*, Intendenza, Intendenza, busta 1286.

56   NAPOLI, *Archivio di Stato*, Monasteri soppressi, vol. 5671.

57   Vedi Vincenzo Trombetta, 'La figura del bibliotecario tra mestiere e professione', in *Cultura e lavoro intellettuale: istituzioni, saperi e professioni nel Decennio Francese*, a

troppo compromessa ideologicamente con la monarchia napoleonide. E, negli anni successivi, non sarà neppure dato seguito alle richieste di restituzione pervenute da numerosi centri religiosi, riaperti in tutto il Mezzogiorno, per la pratica impossibilità di risalire alle originarie provenienze dei libri, ormai disordinatamente distribuiti tra le varie biblioteche cittadine.

Nel primi mesi del 1828, trovandosi "nella necessità di formare una mediocre libreria, necessaria ai Religiosi per attendere allo studio, e senza mezzi a poterla formare", il padre Fedele del Gelso, provinciale dei Cappuccini di Chieti, e il padre Giovan Michele Quaranta superiore degli Agostiniani di S. Giovanni a Carbonara, "ripristinati in S. Carlo e nella Maddalena dei Spagnoli", chiedono la riconsegna dei libri requisiti negli anni francesi, o, altrimenti, di ottenere un adeguato compenso[58]. Nell'inedita missiva del 14 giugno 1828 diretta al Ministero degli Interni e firmata dall'abate Federici rientrato nella direzione della Biblioteca di S. Angelo a Nilo – al quale era stata indirizzata la nota dei libri abruzzesi per l'eventuale riscontro – si accenna ad un ulteriore smistamento dei duplicati rimessi ad alcune comunità religiose, e in particolare ai Gesuiti, per consentire l'impianto di nuove librerie:

L'esposto del Padre Provinciale de' Cappuccini di Abruzzo è vero, sebbene il notamento de' libri da lui descritti non sia esattamente, poiché ve ne sono diversi che non furono presi per servizio della Biblioteca di questa capitale [...] mentre non solamente qui esistevano ma ve ne erano tanti, che furono venduti a' bottegai. Il sig. D. Mario Giardini impiegato allora, cioè nel 1813, nella Biblioteca di Monteoliveto oggi di codesta Università fu incaricato di portarsi negli Apruzzi a scegliere nelle Biblioteche de' Monisteri soppressi quelle opere che potevano interessare le Biblioteche pubbliche di Napoli, ed egli di fatto eseguì il suo incarico con saviezza e discrezione avendo recato in Napoli preziosi manoscritti, e quattrocentisti, ed altre opere d'importanza, la maggior parte delle quali furono consegnate alla Biblioteca Borbonica, ed alcune di minore conto furono aggiunte a cotesta Biblioteca della Regia Università, ed a quella di S. Angelo a Nilo di mio carico. Ma Ella da ciò che dico vede bene che poco o nulla vi è di que' segnati da' PP. cappuccini, essendo tutti articoli di pochissimo conto. In conseguenza quante volte si avesse per Sovrana clemenza a conceder loro un compenso di que' librj che furon da essi tolti, e qui trasportati / avendo presente il med.o lor notamento / il di lor valore ascenderebbe non più che ad una cinquantina di ducati. Intanto i PP. Agostiniani si sono avvisati troppo tardi a ridomandare de' libri della Biblioteca poiché anche dopo la incorporazione fattavi in quella della Croce, detta poi de' Ministeri, tutte quelle opere che vi si trovavano duplicate, sono state già per Sovrana determina.e accordate e consegnate a diversi altri stabilimenti religiosi e precisamente a PP. Gesuiti[59].

Più stringata e burocratica la risposta di Vincenzo Flauti – responsabile della Biblioteca della Regia Università alla quale l'amministrazione borbonica aveva assegnato i doppi e le opere di minor pregio bibliografico della Gioacchina e aperta alla cittadinanza il 2 gennaio 1827[60] – che, il 27 giugno, scrive:

Con due suoi pregiatissimi uffizi degli 11 corrente mi ha Ella inviate le dimande del

cura di Anna Maria Rao, atti del primo Seminario di Studi "Decennio Francese (1806–1815)", Napoli, 26–27 gennaio 2007 (Napoli, 2009), 149–82.

58 NAPOLI, *Archivio di Stato*, Ministero degli Interni, I Inventario, fascio 941.

59 *Ivi.*

60 Vedi l'Avviso al pubblico per l'apertura della Biblioteca della Regia Università degli Studi', comparso nel *Giornale del Regno delle Due Sicilie* del 7 febbraio 1827.

Padre Giovanni Quaranta Superiore attuale de' PP. Agostiniani a S. Giovanni a Carbonara, e del Padre Fedele del Gelso attuale Provinciale de' Cappuccini d'Apruzzo i quali sono ricorsi a Sua Maestà per aver restituiti taluni libri appartenenti un tempo ai loro rispettivi Conventi, e che credevano ritrovarsi al presente nella nostra biblioteca. In vista di ciò ho l'onore di risponderle, che io nulla so della provenienza de' libri della Biblioteca dell'Università compresi nell'inventario che si ha di essa. Posso però assicurarla, che avendo fatto riscontrare nel catalogo la nota de' libri che richiede il Provinciale de' Cappuccini, né men vestigio della maggior parte di essi ho potuto ritrovare[61].

***

La ramificata trama delle biblioteche monastiche e conventuali, creata a Napoli tra Cinque e Settecento, viene alterata da una serie di espropri che, in un breve arco cronologico, ridisegnano l'assetto degli istituti bibliotecari. Sebbene di differente segno politico e ideologico e al di là degli intendimenti, le stesse modalità organizzative delle requisizioni da una parte provocano significativi danneggiamenti del patrimonio librario – la cui entità non sappiamo ancora valutare – ma, dall'altra, creano le oggettive premesse per la creazione di un moderno sistema di centri di studio fruibile da un più ampio pubblico di lettori.

61 NAPOLI, *Archivio di Stato*, Ministero degli Interni, I Inventario, fascio 941.

Bibliography

Manuscripts and Archival Sources

Capua, *Biblioteca del Museo Campano*, Ms. busta 292: *Inventario de' libri ritrovati / nella Libraria del Colleggio degli / espulsi Gesuiti di Capua.*

Napoli, Archivio del Museo Civico "Principe Filangieri", *Catalogo della Libreria del fu Cav.re D. Gaetano Filangieri. 29 settembre 1788.*

Napoli, *Archivio di Stato*, Badia di Mileto, fascio 283.

Napoli, *Archivio di Stato*, Azienda Gesuitica. Collegio dei Nobili, in via di ordinamento.

Napoli, *Archivio di Stato*, Casa Reale Antica, fascio 1330.

Napoli, *Archivio di Stato*, Casa Reale Antica, fascio 1515.

Napoli, *Archivio di Stato*, Casa Reale Antica, Giunta degli Abusi, fascio 1298.

Napoli, *Archivio di Stato*, Ministero degli Interni, I Inventario, fascio 941.

Napoli, *Archivio di Stato*, Ministero degli Interni, II Inventario, fascio 5064: *Carte attinenti al travaglio eseguito dal Sig.r Gaetano Gagliardi nelle cennate Biblioteche per ripartire i libri delle medes.me in quelle della Croce; Reale; e Gesù Vecchio. Del peso de' libri di scarto, e da conto finalmente dello stato de' stigli ove riposti eran i libri di ciascun Monistero.*

Napoli, *Archivio di Stato*, Ministero degli Interni, II Inventario, fascio 5065.

Napoli, *Archivio di Stato*, Ministero degli Interni, Appendice II, fascio 1915.

Napoli, *Archivio di Stato*, Monasteri soppressi, vol. 5671.

Napoli, *Archivio di Stato*, Rei di Stato, fascio 42.

Napoli, *Archivio Napoletano Societatis Jesu.*: *Libro / Delle Consulte / della / Casa di Probazione / della Compagnia di Giesv / di Napoli / Principiato a Gennaro / MDCCXI.*

Napoli, Biblioteca Nazionale "Vittorio Emanuele III", Sezione Manoscritti e Rari, Ms. III. A. 33, *Libraria del SS. Salvatore; Inventario di una Scanzia straordinaria in mezzo alla Libraria.*

Napoli, Biblioteca Nazionale "Vittorio Emanuele III", Sezione Manoscritti e Rari, Ms. III. A.45.

Potenza, *Archivio di Stato*, Intendenza, busta 1286.

Salerno, *Archivio di Stato*, Intendenza, busta 2465, fasc.lo 9: Lettera del ministro Miot all'Intendente della Provincia di Principato Citeriore del 6 aprile 1808.

Salerno, *Archivio di Stato*, Intendenza, busta 2467 (fascc. 1, 3); 2468 (fascc. 1, 2, 4, 6); 2469 (fascc. 2, 9, 14); 2470 (fascc. 1, 8, 11); 2471 (2, 7, 9, 10, 13); 2472 (fascc. 6, 7, 11, 13); 2473 (1, 4, 7, 8, 10); 2474 (fascc. 53, 55, 64).

Secondary Works

Giancarlo Alisio, 'Il Gesù Vecchio a Napoli', *Napoli Nobilissima*, 5 (1966), V–VI, 211–19.

Domenico Ambrasi, 'L'espulsione dei Gesuiti dal Regno di Napoli nelle lettere di Bernardo Tanucci a re Carlo III', *Campania Sacra. Studi e Documenti*, 2 (1971), 211–50.

Tommaso Maria Angelici, *Orazione pel riaprimento della Pubblica Libreria di Palermo* (Palermo, 1780).

'Avviso al pubblico per l'apertura della Biblioteca della Regia Università degli Studi', *Giornale del Regno delle Due Sicilie* del 7 febbraio 1827.

Carolina Belli, 'La Fondazione del Collegio dei Nobili di Napoli', in *Chiesa, Assistenza e Società nel Mezzogiorno moderno*, a cura di Carla Russo, prefazione e introduzione di Giuseppe Galasso (Galatina, 1994), 183–280.

Bibliothecae Regalis Carthusiae S. Martini Catalogus in quo singuli singularum artium et scientiarum libri qui in quavis fere lingua exstant autorumque cognomina ordine alphabetico recensentur (Napoli, 1764).

Angelo Borzelli, *Giovan Battista Manso Marchese di Villa* (Napoli, 1916).

Bullettino delle Leggi del Regno di Napoli. Anno 1807, Tomo I, *Dal mese di gennaio a tutto il mese di giugno* (Napoli, 1807).

Bullettino delle Leggi del Regno di Napoli, Anno 1809, Tomo II, *Da luglio a tutto dicembre* (Napoli, 1809).

Bollettino delle Leggi del Regno di Napoli. Anno 1812, Semestre I. *Da gennaio fino a tutto giugno* (Napoli, 1812).

Eugenio Canone, 'Contributo per una ricostruzione dell'antica "Libraria" di S. Domenico Maggiore. Manoscritti, incunaboli, cinquecentine conservati nelle biblioteche napoletane', in *Giordano Bruno. Gli anni napoletani e la 'peregrinatio' europea. Immagini, Testi, Documenti*, a cura di Eugenio Canone (Cassino, 1992), 190–247.

Maria Giuseppina Castellano Lanzara, 'La casa del Salvatore in Napoli', in *Miscellanea di scritti vari in memoria di Alfonso Gallo* (Firenze, 1956), 239–47.

'Il Catalogo della biblioteca di Gaetano Filangieri', a cura di Renato Bruschi, in Istituto Italiano per gli Studi Filosofici, *Gaetano Filangieri. Lo Stato secondo ragione. Catalogo della Mostra*, a cura di Renato Bruschi e Saverio Ricci (Napoli, 1992), 153–84.

Carlo Celano, *Notizie del Bello, dell'Antico, e del Curioso della Città di Napoli per gli signori forestieri* (Napoli, 1692).

Collezione degli editti, determinazioni, decreti e leggi di S.M. Dà 15 febbraio a' 31 dicembre, seconda edizione (Napoli, 1813).

Giuseppe Consoli Fiego, *Itinera Literaria, Ricerche sulle biblioteche napoletane del XVII Secolo* (Napoli, 1934).

Giuseppe Cosenza, 'La Chiesa e il Convento di S. Pietro Martire. III. Epoca Moderna', *Napoli Nobilissima*, 9.1 (1900).

Candido Cuomo, *Le leggi eversive del secolo XIX e le vicende degli Ordini Religiosi della Provincia di Principato Citeriore (Ricerche Storiche)*, Tomo IX, *Le Biblioteche degli Ordini Religiosi soppressi* (Mercato S. Severino, 1973).

Camillo De Lellis, *Parte seconda O' vero Supplemento a Napoli sacra di d. Cesare D'Engenio Caracciolo* (Napoli, 1654).

Carlo D'Engenio, *Napoli Sacra* (Napoli, 1624).

Gioacchino Di Marzo, *Primo centenario della Biblioteca comunale di Palermo addì XXV Aprile MDCCCXXV. Relazioni, Poesie, Iscrizioni* (Palermo, 1875).

Alexandre Dumas, *La Sanfelice* (Napoli, 1998).

Michele Errichetti, 'L'architetto Giuseppe Valeriano (1542–1596) progettista del Collegio Napoletano del Gesù Vecchio', *Archivio Storico per le Province Napoletane*, 34 (1959), 325–52.

Michele Errichetti, 'L'antico Collegio Massimo dei Gesuiti a Napoli (1552–1806)', *Campania Sacra. Studi e Ricerche*, 7 (1976), 170–264.

Niccolò Domenico Evola, *Sulla Biblioteca Nazionale di Palermo* (Palermo, 1872).

Niccolò Domenico Evola, 'Cenni storici della Biblioteca Nazionale di Palermo', in *Ricordo del primo centenario della Biblioteca Nazionale di Palermo* (Palermo, 1882).

Vincenzo Flauti, 'Memorie critiche su la istruzione pubblica del Regno di Napoli dal principio del secolo corrente fino a' nostri giorni per servire di norma ad una riforma necessaria di essa', in Id., *Anecdota ad publicam eruditionem spectantia post auctoris fata inter amicos evulganda* (Neapoli, 1837), 20–21.

Vito Fornari, *Notizia della Biblioteca Nazionale di Napoli* (Napoli, 1874).

Gesuiti e Università in Europa (secoli XVI–XVIII), atti del Convegno di studi, Parma, 13–15 dicembre 2001, a cura di Gian Paolo Brizzi e Roberto Greci (Bologna, 2002).

Lorenzo Giustiniani, *Memorie storico-critiche della Real Biblioteca Borbonica di Napoli* (Napoli, 1818), ristampa anastatica a cura di Vincenzo Trombetta (Sala Bolognese, 2008).

Francesco Granata, *Storia sacra della Chiesa Metropolitana di Capua* (Napoli, 1766).

Guerriera Guerrieri, *La Biblioteca Nazionale "Vittorio Emanuele III"* (Milano-Napoli, 1974).

Guerriera Guerrieri, *Per il recupero del patrimonio bibliografico, archivistico, artistico e sacro della Certosa di Padula disperso nell'Ottocento*, Quaderni del centro di studi salernitani "Raffaele Guariglia" (Salerno, 1974).

Filippo Iappelli, 'Gesuiti e Seicento Napoletano. II. Congregazioni del Gesù Nuovo e Oratorio dei Nobili', *Societas. Rivista bimestrale dei Gesuiti dell'Italia Meridionale*, 34.3 (1985).

Filippo Iappelli, 'Il Palazzo delle Congregazioni e l'"insula" del Gesù Nuovo. I', *Societas. Rivista bimestrale dei Gesuiti dell'Italia Meridionale*, 35.3 (1986).

Filippo Iappelli, 'La Nunziatella. Da Noviziato dei Gesuiti a Scuola Militare (1587–1787). II', *Societas. Rivista bimestrale dei Gesuiti dell'Italia Meridionale*, 36, 1–2 (1987), 72–73.

Carlo Lanza, 'Il Collegio dei Nobili e l'espulsione dei Gesuiti nella Napoli del 1767', *Capys. Bollettino interno degli "Amici di Capua"*, 33 (2000), 79–88.

Eugenio Lo Sardo, 'La Biblioteca Filangieri', in Id., *Il mondo nuovo e le virtù civili. L'epistolario di Gaetano Filangieri* (Napoli, 1999), 299–324.

Michele Manfredi, *Gio. Batista Manso nella vita e nelle opere* (Napoli, 1919).

Diomede Marinelli, *I giornali di Diomede Marinelli. Due codici della Biblioteca Nazionale di Napoli (XV.D. 43–44), pubblicati per cura di A. Fiordalisi (1794–1800)* (Napoli, 1901).

Michele Miele, 'Un intervento della polizia murattiana per arrestare la dispersione del patrimonio librario dei conventi soppressi', *Campania Sacra*, 2 (1971), 251–69, poi in Id., *La Chiesa del Mezzogiorno nel decennio francese. Ricerche* (Napoli, 2007), 317–26.

Michele Miele, 'Ricerche sulla soppressione dei religiosi nel Regno di Napoli nel 1767', *Campania Sacra. Studi e Documenti*, 4 (1973), 1–144.

Elisa Novi Chiavarria, 'I religiosi napoletani tra repubblica e prima restaurazione', in *Il Cittadino Ecclesiastico. Il clero nella repubblica napoletana del 1799*, a cura di Pierroberto Scaramella (Napoli, 2000), 155–78.

Umberto Antonio Padovani, *La soppressione della Compagnia di Gesù* (Napoli, 1962).

Egidio Papa, 'I beni dei Gesuiti e i preliminari della loro espulsione dal Regno di Napoli nel 1767', *Rivista di Storia della Chiesa*, 30 (1976), 81–113.

Aldo Pinto, 'Il Museo di Mineralogia e l'antica biblioteca gesuitica del Collegio Massimo', *Rendiconto della Accademia delle Scienze Fisiche e Matematiche*, 132, ser. IV, vol. LX (1993), 121–46.

Enrica Robertazzi Delle Donne, *L'espulsione dei Gesuiti dal Regno di Napoli* (Napoli, 1970).

Annamaria Robotti, 'La biblioteca settecentesca del Collegio dei Gesuiti in Capua', *Societas. Rivista bimestrale dei Gesuiti dell'Italia Meridionale*, 51.5–6 (2003), 237–40.

Mario Rotili, *Il cortile del Salvatore* (Roma, 1955).

Luigi Sampolo, *La R. Accademia degli Studi di Palermo. Narrazione Storica* (Palermo, 1888).

Francesco Schinosi, 'Fondazione in Napoli della Casa de' Professi', in Id., *Istoria della Compagnia di Giesù. Appartenente al Regno di Napoli*, Parte Prima (Napoli, 1706), 371–81.

Michelangelo Schipa, *Il Regno di Napoli al tempo di Carlo di Borbone* (Napoli, 1904).

Vincenzo Spampanato, *Vita di Giordano Bruno. Con documenti editi e inediti* (Messina, 1921).

Stato delle rendite e pesi degli aboliti collegi della Capitale e Regno dell'espulsa Compagnia detta di Gesù, a cura di Carolina Belli (Napoli, 1981).

Maria Aurora Tallarico, 'Una "Memoria sullo stato delle Chiese di Napoli" del vescovo E. C. Minutolo all'indomani della Repubblica Partenopea del '99', *Rivista di Storia della Chiesa in Italia*, 31.1 (1977), 101–27.

Maria Aurora Tallarico, 'La tutela del patrimonio artistico e librario delle Congregazioni soppresse a Napoli durante il decennio francese (1806–1815)', *Atti della Accademia di Scienze Morali e Politiche di Napoli*, 89 (1978), 237–50.

Antonio Trampus, *I Gesuiti e l'Illuminismo. Politica e religione in Austria e nell'Europa Centrale (1773–1798)* (Firenze, 2000).

Francesco Trinchera, *Degli archivi napoletani. Relazione a S.E. il Ministro della Pubblica Istruzione* (Napoli, 1872).

Vincenzo Trombetta, 'I fondi monastici nella formazione della Biblioteca Universitaria di Napoli (1806–1810)', *Fridericiana*, 3 (1991–1992), 75–90.

Vincenzo Trombetta, *Storia della Biblioteca Universitaria di Napoli. Dal viceregno spagnolo all'Unità d'Italia* (Napoli, 1995).

Vincenzo Trombetta, 'Lettere di Giovanni Maria della Torre "custode" della Real Biblioteca di Napoli (1777–178)', *Rendiconti della Accademia di Archeologia Lettere e Belle Arti di Napoli*, 67 (1997–1998), 341–67.

Vincenzo Trombetta, 'Le biblioteche e il 1799', in Soprintendenza Archivistica per la Campania – Regione Campania, *Omaggio alla Repubblica Napoletana del 1799. Fonti e Ricerche* (Napoli, 2000), 49–60.

Vincenzo Trombetta, 'La libreria del Collegio dei Nobili e le biblioteche dei Gesuiti, a Napoli, tra Sette e Ottocento', in *Educare la nobiltà*, atti del Convegno Nazionale di studi, Perugia, Palazzo Sorbello, 18–19 giugno 2004, a cura di Gianfranco Tortorelli (Bologna, 2005), 123–63.

Vincenzo Trombetta, 'La figura del bibliotecario tra mestiere e professione', in *Cultura e lavoro intellettuale: istituzioni, saperi e professioni nel Decennio Francese*, a cura di Anna Maria Rao, atti del primo Seminario di Studi "Decennio Francese (1806–1815)", Napoli, 26–27 gennaio 2007 (Napoli, 2009), 149–82.

Vincenzo Trombetta, 'Libri e biblioteche della Compagnia di Gesù a Napoli dalle origini all'Unità d'Italia', *Hereditas Monasteriorum Journal*, 4 (2014), 127–59.

Placido Troyli, 'Delle varie biblioteche del Reame di Napoli', in Id.,, *Istoria Generale del Reame di Napoli. Ovvero Stato antico, e moderno delle Regioni, e Luoghi, che 'l Reame di Napoli compongono, una colle loro prime Popolazioni, Costumi, Leggi, Polizia, Uomini Illustri, e Monarchi* (Napoli, 1752).

Michele Volpe, *I Gesuiti nel Napoletano* (Napoli, 1914).

Giuseppe Zurlo, *Rapporto sullo stato del Regno di Napoli per gli anni 1810, e 1811 presentato al Re nel suo Consiglio di Stato del Ministro dell'Interno* (Napoli, 1812).

MARIE-PIERRE LAFFITTE

Napoléon et les confiscations de livres dans les monastères italiens

J'ai étudié la question des confiscations à l'étranger en 1989, pour une exposition que la Bibliothèque nationale a consacrée à ses acquisitions révolutionnaires. J'ai aussi publié à cette occasion un bilan des manuscrits originaires d'Italie qui sont restés à Paris en 1815[1]. Je vais essayer de présenter ici cette question de façon un peu différente, en soulignant le rôle qu'a pu jouer Bonaparte, d'abord comme général en chef des armées d'Italie en 1796–1797 et en 1799–1800, puis comme consul et comme empereur à partir de 1800 et en évoquant rapidement les conséquences des décisions prises entre 1796 et 1814 sur l'histoire des bibliothèques italiennes[2].

L'intérêt pour les collections de manuscrits et d'imprimés anciens conservées depuis le Moyen Âge dans des institutions religieuses et leur spoliation ne sont pas une nouveauté pendant la période révolutionnaire puis sous le Consulat et le Ier Empire, même si l'importance numérique et la signification symbolique en sont bien différentes selon les années. Avant de parler de l'Italie, je voudrais donner quelques exemples antérieurs à la Révolution et un aperçu des premières confiscations révolutionnaires, qui éclairent ce qui s'est passé dans la péninsule.

Du Moyen Âge à 1794

Dès le Moyen Âge, les savants s'intéressent au contenu des collections ecclésiastiques et surtout à celles des monastères, qui possèdent souvent les copies les plus anciennes des auteurs de l'Antiquité ou des débuts de l'ère chrétienne, qu'ils veulent copier et étudier[3]. Cet intérêt s'amplifie à l'époque

---

1   1789. Le Patrimoine libéré. 200 trésors entrés à la Bibliothèque Nationale de 1789 à 1799 (Paris, 1989); Marie-Pierre Laffitte, 'La Bibliothèque nationale et les conquêtes artistiques de la Révolution et de l'Empire: les manuscrits d'Italie', Bulletin du Bibliophile, 2 (1989), 272–323.

2   Voir en particulier les contributions sur ce sujet dans ces actes.

3   Marie-Pierre Laffitte, 'La redécouverte des manuscrits carolingiens par les érudits et les collectionneurs français (xvie-xviiie siècles)', Actes de la journée d'études carolingiennes, Paris, 4 mai 2007, réd. en collab. avec Jean-Pierre Caillet (Turnhout, 2009), 141–58.

Marie-Pierre Laffitte • Formerly Chef du service médiéval du département des Manuscrits de la BnF. marie-pierre.laffitte@orange.fr

How the Secularization of Religious Houses Transformed the Libraries of Europe, 16th–19th Centuries, ed. by Cristina Dondi, Dorit Raines, and †Richard Sharpe, BIB, 63 (Turnhout, 2022), pp. 223–244.
BREPOLS ❧ PUBLISHERS   DOI 10.1484/M.BIB-EB.5.128486

humanistique: Le Pogge (Giovanni Francesco Poggio Bracciolini, 1380–1459) cherche des textes à travers l'Europe, à Cluny en 1415, à Saint-Gall à l'été 1416, où il copie un exemplaire du IXe siècle aujourd'hui perdu des *Commentaires* d'Asconius sur les discours de Cicéron[4]. En juillet 1417, il trouve un Ammien Marcellin du IXe siècle provenant de l'abbaye de Fulda qu'il emporte en Italie pour le copier; le manuscrit ne retournera pas à Fulda[5].

Par ailleurs, ces bibliothèques monastiques aux fonds précieux n'ont pas toujours bonne réputation, comme en témoigne quelques années auparavant le chagrin de Boccace devant l'état pitoyable de la bibliothèque du Mont-Cassin. Son élève Benvenuto d'Imola (1320?-1388) le rapporte vers 1375 dans son commentaire sur le *Paradis* de Dante[6]:

> Avidus videndi librariam quam audiverat ibi esse nobilissimam, petivit ab uno monacho humiliter, velut ille, qui suavissimus erat, quod deberet ex gratia sibi aperire bibliothecam. At ille rigide respondit, ostendens sibi altam scalam: "Ascende quia aperta est". Ille laetus

ascendens, invenit locum tanti thesauri sine ostio vel clavi; ingressusque vidit herbam natam per fenestras, et libros omnes cum bancis coopertos pulvere alto. Et mirabundus coepit aperire et volvere nunc istum librum, nunc illum, invenit que ibi multa et varia volumina antiquorum et peregrinorum librorum. Ex quorum aliquibus erant detracti aliqui quinterni, ex aliis recisi margines chartarum, et sic multipliciter deformati. Tandem miseratus, labores et studia tot inclytorum ingeniorum devenisse ad manus perditissimorum hominum, dolens et illacrymans recessit...

Il semble que Boccace se soit consolé en mettant la main sur quelques manuscrits qui se trouvaient alors au Mont-Cassin, si l'on en croit la présence aujourd'hui à Florence de plusieurs manuscrits en écriture bénéventine, dont un Tacite du XIe siècle qui se trouvait encore dans l'abbaye au XIVe siècle[7].

Au XVIe siècle, en France, l'aumônier du roi de France François Ier Jean de Gagny accuse quant à lui les moines de cacher leurs trésors. Ce théologien et philologue averti spécialiste des *Épîtres* de saint Paul tient des propos sévères dans la préface de sa traduction en français d'un commentaire de ce livre de la Bible, dédicacée au souverain:

> les moines claustriers qui leurs librairies jadis par leurs anciens doctes plantées de beaux et singuliers livres obstinement gardent et ferment [...]. Commencay à fouiller et fueilleter toutes les libraries des monasteres et chapitres[8]....

---

4   Madrid, Bibliothèque Nationale, ms. 8514 (la copie de Poggio); Berthold Louis Ullman, *The Origin and development of humanistic script* (Rome, 1960), 21–57; *Inventario general de manuscritos de la Biblioteca nacional* (Madrid, 1995), XIII 10; *Texts and transmission. A Survey of the Latin Classics*, éd. Leighton D. Reynolds (Oxford, 1983), 24–25; Albinia C. de la Mare, *The Handwriting of Italian humanists*, 1/1, *Francesco Petrarca, Giovanni Boccacio, Coluccio Salutati, Niccolo Niccoli...* (Paris, 1973), 78; Jacques Stiennon, *Paléographie du Moyen Âge* (Paris, 1973), 122–24.

5   Rome, Bibliothèque Vaticane, ms. Vat. Lat. 1873; Leighton D. Reynolds et Nigel G. Wilson, *D'Homère à Erasme, la transmission des classiques grecs et latins* (Paris, 1986), 92–94; la copie du XVe siècle se trouve à la Bibliothèque Nationale de Florence, conv. soppr. I.V.43.

6   Paris, BnF, ms. italien 77, *La Divina Comedia con un raffazzonamento delle note di Benvenuto Rambaldi* (ms. daté de 1393 provenant du pape Pie VI), fol. 175; Lodovico Antonio Muratori, *Antiquitates italicae medii aevi, sive Dissertationes de moribus, ritibus, religione, regimine...* (Milan, 1738–1742), I, col. 1292.

7   Florence, Bibliothèque Laurentienne, ms. Plut. 68.2; cf. Cornelia C. Coulter, 'Boccaccio and the Cassinese manuscripts of the Laurentian Library', *Classical Philology*, XLIII,4 (1948), 217–30; Francis Newton, *The Scriptorium and library at Monte Cassino, 1058–1105* (Cambridge, 1999), 96–107 et *passim*.

8   Paris, BnF, ms. français 935, fol. 2–2v: 'Briefve et fructueuse exposition sur les epistres de sainct Paul par Primasius, evesque de Uticque en Affrique, disciple de saint Augustin'; Jean de Gagny dit avoir travaillé

Ces propos sans aucun doute très exagérés marqueront les esprits et un officier français de l'armée d'Italie, l'écrivain helléniste Paul-Louis Courier, dira la même chose de la bibliothèque de la Badia Fiorentina, où il avait vu un manuscrit du *Daphnis et Chloé* de Longus peu avant la suppression de l'abbaye en 1808: dans une lettre célèbre adressée au libraire parisien Antoine-Augustin Renouard (1765–1853), il raconte

> L'abbaye de Florence, d'où vient dans l'origine de texte de Longus, était connue dans toute l'Europe comme contenant les manuscrits les plus précieux qui existassent. Peu de gens les avaient vus; car, pendant plusieurs siècles cette bibliothèque resta inaccessible: il n'y pouvait entrer que des moines, c'est à dire qu'il n'y entrait personne. La collection qu'elle renfermait, d'autant plus intéressante qu'on la connaissait moins, était une mine toute neuve à exploiter pour les savans[9]. . . .

Jean de Gagny rapporte aussi dans sa préface que François Ier l'a chargé de visiter les abbayes royales et d'y repérer des textes latins rares afin de les apporter à la Bibliothèque du roi qui se trouve alors à Fontainebleau, comme d'autres représentants du roi de France achetaient en Italie et envoyaient en France des manuscrits grecs destinés aux études hellénistiques. Sa récolte entrera dans la Bibliothèque du roi peu après sa mort en 1549; les volumes, pour la plupart

des textes théologiques datables du IXe au XIIIe siècle provenant de diverses abbayes françaises, seront immédiatement reliés aux armes du roi Henri II[10].

Les Guerres de Religion fournissent un terrain propice aux écumeurs de bibliothèques: à partir des années 1560, des manuscrits commencent à sortir de sanctuaires détruits. Au moment du saccage de l'abbaye de Fleury-sur-Loire par les années huguenotes en 1562 certains volumes sont mis à l'abri; ils ne retourneront jamais dans l'abbaye. Les reîtres du prince de Condé occupent et dévastent Saint-Denis à l'automne 1567, et des manuscrits de Saint-Denis sont vendus à Paris dès la fin de la même année. Savants et collectionneurs profitent de cette aubaine. Des exemplaires très anciens, qui témoignent du rôle primordial de Saint-Denis et de Fleury dans la connaissance et la transmission des auteurs antiques, entrent alors dans des collections privées. Un Lactance du IXe siècle portant l'ex-libris de Fleury et un Justinien datable vers 800 qui contient des lettres d'Abbon de Fleury figurent dans celle de l'humaniste Aymar de Ranconnet[11], et à la fin du XVIe siècle, le plus ancien témoin conservé du traité *De Officiis* de saint Ambroise de Milan, daté du VIIe siècle, passe avec une soixantaine d'autres manuscrits de Saint-Denis dans les mains du parlementaire Jacques-Auguste de Thou[12]. A la fin du XVIIe siècle, Etienne Baluze

---

d'après un manuscrit en latin aujourd'hui perdu, qu'il a trouvé dans l'abbaye de Saint-Chef-en-Dauphiné; André Jammes, 'Un bibliophile à découvrir, Jean de Gagny', *Bulletin du bibliophile*, 1 (1996), 35–80; Laffitte, 'La redécouverte des manuscrits carolingiens', voir note nr. 3, 143–44.

9   Florence, Bibliothèque Laurentienne, ms. conv. soppr. 627; Paul-Louis Courier, *Collection complète des pamphlets politiques et opuscules littéraires...* (Bruxelles, 1827), 48; cf. Rudolf Blum, *La Biblioteca della Badia Fiorentina e i codici di Antonio Corbinelli*, Studi e Testi 155 (Rome, 1951), 9.

10   Marie-Pierre Laffitte et Fabienne Le Bars, *Reliures royales de la Renaissance. La Librairie de Fontainebleau 1544–1570* (Paris, 1999), 22–23 et n° 53.

11   Paris, BnF, mss latins 1663 et 4568; cf. Marco Mostert, *The Library of Fleury, a provisional list of manuscripts* (Hilversum, 1989), 200, 206 et *passim*; les manuscrits de Ranconnet seront saisis par le roi François II après la mort de leur propriétaire à la Bastille en 1559 et reliés aux armes de François II ou de Charles IX pour la Bibliothèque du roi; cf. Laffitte et Le Bars, *Reliures royales de la Renaissance*, voir note nr. 10, 24 et n° 114, 116b, 119, 122a, 124a et b.

12   Paris, BnF, ms. latin 1732; cf. Elias Avery Lowe, *Codices latini antiquiores, a palaeographical guide to latin manuscripts prior to the ninth century: France*

dépouille aussi les bibliothèques bénédictines ou cisterciennes normandes étranglées par les embarras financiers, pour Jean-Baptiste Colbert, ministre de Louis XIV[13]. Les Mauristes eux-mêmes se serviront ici ou là pour leurs travaux d'érudits.

La politique révolutionnaire jusqu'en 1796

Il s'agissait là d'initiatives personnelles, ponctuelles et conjoncturelles. Cependant, ces prélèvements dans les bibliothèques de monastères présentent des points communs avec la vision des bibliothèques qu'ont les révolutionnaires français, qui comptent dans leurs rangs des savants reconnus. Ils sont aussi influencés par la nationalisation qui commence en Europe avec l'empereur d'Autriche Joseph II, et donc dans l'Italie sous domination autrichienne, où les biens des Jésuites et des congrégations religieuses sont confisqués au bénéfice de l'église séculière à partir de 1768[14].

Dès le début de la Révolution en France, l'Assemblée constituante vote le 2 novembre 1789 la nationalisation des biens du clergé:

Tous les biens ecclésiastiques sont à la disposition de la Nation, à la charge de pourvoir d'une manière convenable aux frais du culte, à l'entretien de ses ministres et au soulagement des pauvres, sous la surveillance et d'après les instructions des provinces[15].

Cette décision inspirée par l'ancien évêque d'Autun Charles-Maurice de Talleyrand-Périgord (qui négociera et signera en 1814 le traité de Paris!) met à la disposition de la Nation l'ensemble des biens ecclésiastiques. Ces nationalisations ont un aspect économique, mais pour ce qui est des bibliothèques, elles sont menées dans un souci d'ouverture et de mise à disposition d'un large public de toutes les richesses cachées dans leurs murs, comme le suggéraient les propos des savants depuis le XIVe siècle. Elles sont complétées par la suppression des ordres monastiques le 13 février 1790:

L'Assemblée décrète, comme article constitutionnel, que la loi ne reconnaîtra plus de vœux monastiques solennels de personnes de l'un ni de l'autre sexe; déclare en conséquence que les ordres et congrégations réguliers, dans lesquels on fait de pareil vœux, sont et demeureront supprimés en France, sans qu'il puisse en être établi de semblables à l'avenir[16].

Bien qu'elles soient décidées pour des raisons différentes, les décisions prises à l'encontre des collections d'émigrés et de condamnés vont amplifier ce processus de nationalisation de toutes sortes de collections.

En 1794, au début des conquêtes territoriales dans le Nord de l'Europe, les pratiques sont différentes à l'étranger de celles qui sont appliquées en France, et en Belgique les saisies commencent

---

(Paris-Oxford, 1950), V, n° 534; Donatella Nebbiai-Della Guarda, *La Bibliothèque de l'abbaye de Saint-Denis* (Paris, 1985), 126–28, 130–36, 145, 300, 312; Marie-Pierre Laffitte, 'Les manuscrits de la collection de Thou', *Histoire des bibliothèque françaises. II, Les bibliothèques sous l'Ancien Régime 1530–1789*, 2e éd. (Paris, 2008), 155–57; Veronika Von Büren, 'Ambroise de Milan dans la bibliothèque de Cluny', *Scriptorium*, 47 (1993), 141–60 *passim*.

13 Marie-Pierre Laffitte, 'Les manuscrits normands de Colbert. Reliures cisterciennes', *Actes du colloque Manuscrits et enluminures dans le monde normand*, octobre 1995 (Caen, 1999), 197–205.

14 À Milan, l'installation en 1778 de l'actuelle Bibliothèque Brera dans le collège Jésuite, occupant jusqu'en 1773 du palais Brera, illustre bien cette situation; cf. Maria Luisa Grossi Turchetti, *I Manoscritti datati della Biblioteca nazionale Braidense di Milano* (Florence, 2004), 4; une partie des fonds *Conventi Suppressi* des bibliothèques de Florence provient de ces premières suppressions.

15 *Archives parlementaires de 1787 à 1860. Assemblée nationale constituante*, IX, *16 septembre 1789–11 novembre 1789* (Paris, 1877), 649.

16 *Ibid.*, X, *24 décembre 1789–1er mars 1790* (Paris, 1880), 591.

dans les collections princières ennemies, comme cela s'est déjà passé sous Charles VIII en 1495 à Naples chez les rois aragonais[17] et sous Louis XII en 1498 à Pavie chez les ducs de Milan pendant les premières guerres d'Italie[18]. Des raisons dynastiques étaient alors invoquées pour justifier les saisies.

Après la victoire de Fleurus le 8 messidor an II (26 juin 1794), des commissaires choisis parmi les savants et les artistes dévoués à la Révolution doivent aller chercher "les chefs d'œuvre créés par l'homme" dans les pays vaincus[19]. Ils reçoivent des instructions très générales, parfaitement résumées dans une lettre circulaire du Comité d'Instruction publique du 15 vendémiaire an III (5 octobre 1794): les disciplines mises en valeur sont "… Bibliographie, Histoire naturelle, Peinture…". Des livres et des tableaux seront envoyés en France, mais aussi des objets de toutes sortes, plantes, outils, animaux empaillés, etc. Le bibliothécaire de la Bibliothèque Mazarine, l'abbé Michel Leblond, fait partie de ces érudits séduits par les idées révolutionnaires[20]; il s'occupe des livres, manuscrits, incunables et autres imprimés précieux.

Le Comité d'instruction publique avait chargé Michel Leblond de reprendre à Bruxelles les manuscrits à peintures de la bibliothèque des ducs de Bourgogne, qui avaient déjà été saisis en 1748 puis rendus en 1770[21]. Les premières caisses reçues à Paris contiennent près de mille ouvrages de la bibliothèque ducale. Puis Leblond élargit rapidement sa mission de façon empirique et il continue son périple près de Bruxelles, dans les abbayes de Dieleghem et Affligem, où il s'empare d'un évangéliaire couvert d'une reliure précieuse[22]. Quelques mois plus tard, il expliquera sa technique dans une lettre envoyée de Coblence le 12 nivôse an III (7 janvier 1795) à un correspondant inconnu:

mais il me suffit d'abord d'apercevoir des clochers: ils me servent de guide. J'ai donc pris le parti de visiter les maisons de moines et j'ai trouvé environ trois cents volumes assez précieux chez les Carmes, les Récollets et surtout chez les Dominicains… Je suis passionné pour les bibliothèques de jésuites[23].

Les saisies sont entreposées dans les dépôts littéraires parisiens[24] où les bibliothécaires peuvent choisir des documents. Le même processus a lieu ensuite aux Pays-Bas et en Rhénanie.

17 Tammaro De Marinis, *La biblioteca napoletana dei Re d'Aragona…*, 4 vols (Milan, 1947–1952); *Idem, Supplemento*, avec la participation de Denise Bloch, Charles Astruc, Jacques Monfrin et José Ruysschaert, 2 vols (Vérone, 1969).

18 Elisabeth Pellegrin, *La Bibliothèque des Visconti et des Sforza, ducs de Milan, au XVᵉ siècle* (Paris, 1955); *Eadem, Supplément* (Florence-Paris, 1969).

19 Ferdinand Boyer, 'L'organisation des conquêtes artistiques de la Convention en Belgique', *Revue belge de philologie et d'histoire*, 49 (1971), 490–500; *Idem*, 'Les conquêtes scientifiques de la Convention en Belgique et dans les pays rhénans (1794–1795)', *Revue d'histoire moderne et contemporaine*, 18 (1971), 354–74.

20 Ségolène Chambon, 'Le rôle de l'abbé Leblond dans les commissions de savants', catalogue de l'exposition *Antiquités, Lumières et Révolution. L'abbé Leblond (1738–1809) "second fondateur de la Bibliothèque Mazarine"* (Paris, 2009), 65–72.

21 Anne-Marie Legaré, 'Les cent quatorze manuscrits de Bourgogne choisis par le comte d'Argenson pour le roi Louis XV. Édition de la liste de 1748', *Bulletin du Bibliophile* (1998), 241–329; Marie-Pierre Laffitte, 'Cadeaux, spoliations, achats, un aperçu des manuscrits "parisiens" provenant des ducs de Bourgogne et de leur entourage', in *Miniatures flamandes 1404–1482*, éd. Bernard Bousmanne et Thierry Delcourt (Paris, 2011), 55–65.

22 Paris, Bibliothèque de l'Arsenal, ms. 1184 rés; cf. 1789, *Le Patrimoine libéré*, voir note nr. 1, n° 238.

23 Boyer, 'Les conquêtes scientifiques', voir note nr. 19, 370.

24 Jean-Baptiste Labiche, *Notice sur les dépôts littéraires et la révolution bibliographique de la fin du dernier siècle* (Paris, 1880); Dominique Varry, 'Les confiscations révolutionnaires', *Histoire des bibliothèques françaises. III, Les Bibliothèques de la Révolution et du XIXᵉ siècle 1789–1914* (Paris, 1991), 9–27.

L'Italie

Les choses se passent différemment en Italie, en deux étapes totalement indépendantes. Pendant la première campagne d'Italie menée par Bonaparte, on imite ce qui s'est passé en Belgique, en plus organisé, et pendant la deuxième campagne d'Italie et les années d'occupation de la péninsule par l'administration napoléonienne, on reprend ce qui s'est passé en France au tout début de la Révolution.

La première campagne d'Italie (1796–1797) est à l'origine une diversion contre l'Autriche qui menace la nouvelle République, mais elle marque surtout le début de la carrière de Napoléon Bonaparte. Âgé seulement de 27 ans, il est nommé général en chef de l'armée d'Italie le 12 ventôse an IV (2 mars 1796) et prend son commandement à Nice le 1er germinal (21 mars). Son armée est mal en point, les officiers supérieurs l'acceptent difficilement, mais il montre ses capacités et la campagne se termine dix-huit mois plus tard avec le traité de Campo Formio, signé le 18 octobre 1797 par l'Autriche et la France. Stendhal salue son succès dans le premier paragraphe de la *Chartreuse de Parme*:

> le 15 mai 1796 le général Bonaparte fit son entrée dans Milan à la tête de cette jeune armée qui venait de passer le pont de Lodi et d'apprendre au monde qu'après tant de siècles César et Alexandre avaient un successeur[25].

En novembre 1797, Bonaparte quitte l'Italie pour l'Égypte. La résistance des Italiens et les succès des armées autrichiennes font refluer les Français mais une seconde campagne commence en 1799; Bonaparte reprend la tête de l'armée d'Italie au printemps 1800 et la péninsule reste sous domination française jusqu'en 1814.

---

25 1ère édition (Paris, 1839) I, 7.

Première époque: les saisies destinées à la France

Pendant la première campagne, et comme en Europe du Nord, les victoires militaires françaises sont accompagnées d'une politique de saisies d'œuvres d'art. Qu'en est-il exactement du rôle de Bonaparte dans cette affaire?

Le 18 floréal an IV (7 mai 1796), le Directoire exécutif (la plus haute instance politique française composée de 5 membres élus depuis octobre 1795), envoie à Bonaparte des instructions générales, assez semblables à celles données en 1794. On n'y parle pour le moment que de ce qui deviendra plus tard le Musée du Louvre, et les confiscations de livres ne sont pas évoquées clairement:

> Le directoire exécutif est persuadé, citoyen général, que vous regardez la gloire des beaux-arts comme attachée à celle de l'armée que vous commandez. L'Italie leur doit en grande partie ses richesses et son illustration; mais le temps est arrivé où leur règne doit passer en France pour affermir et embellir celui de la liberté. Le Museum national doit renfermer les monuments les plus célèbres de tous les arts et vous ne négligerez pas de l'enrichir de ceux qu'il attend des conquêtes actuelles de l'armée d'Italie, et de celles qui lui sont encore réservées. Cette glorieuse campagne, en mettant la République en mesure de donner la paix à ses ennemis, doit encore réparer les ravages du vandalisme en son sein et joindre à l'éclat des trophées militaires le charme des arts bienfaisants et consolateurs.
> Le Directoire exécutif vous invite donc, citoyen général, à choisir un ou plusieurs artistes, destinés à rechercher, à recueillir et à faire transporter à Paris les objets de ce genre les plus précieux et à donner des ordres précis pour l'exécution éclairée de ces dispositions, dont il désire que vous lui rendiez compte Le Tourneur, Carnot, L.-M. Revellière-Lépeaux.

Le troisième signataire, Louis-Marie de la Revellière-Lépeaux, est un anticlérical notoire, spécialiste des affaires culturelles et religieuses. Dans une autre lettre datée du même jour, les trois mêmes directeurs soulignent "la direction savante et glorieuse… que le génie seul de la Liberté a pu inspirer" qu'ils souhaitent voir appliquée au cours de la campagne d'Italie confiée à Bonaparte[26].

Ce n'est donc pas le général qui décide des saisies en Italie en 1796; c'est d'ailleurs le Directoire qui se charge de trouver les six commissaires qui doivent être envoyés en Italie le 22 floréal an IV (11 mai 1796)[27]. Cependant, Bonaparte sait certainement ce qui s'est passé en Belgique puis dans le nord de l'Europe. Si d'un côté, il est intraitable pour les soldats pris à voler, de l'autre, par conviction peut-être, par calcul sûrement, il anticipe la décision du Directoire Exécutif et s'intéresse beaucoup, du moins au début, à cet aspect de sa mission: dès le 9 floréal (28 avril 1796), avant même d'avoir reçu des instructions écrites de Paris, il envisage d'intégrer la remise d'un tableau dans les clauses de l'armistice de Cherasco conclu avec le roi de Sardaigne, et le 12 floréal (1er mai 1796) il évoque cette question dans une lettre envoyée d'Acqui à Guillaume-Charles Faipoult, ambassadeur de France à Gênes depuis 1795, qui connaît mieux que lui les richesses artistiques de l'Italie:

> Envoyez-moi une note sur les ducs de Parme, de Plaisance et de Modène; les forces qu'ils ont sur pied… Surtout envoyez-moi une note des tableaux, statues, cabinets et curiosités qui se trouvent à Milan, Parme, Plaisance et Bologne[28]….

Bonaparte introduit ensuite systématiquement, comme un barème préétabli, une demande de vingt tableaux, dans les armistices avec le duc de Parme le 9 mai 1796, puis avec le duc de Modène le 11 mai. Dans plusieurs lettres envoyées de Plaisance puis de Milan au Directoire exécutif, il rend compte des différentes phases de ces opérations. Ainsi, le 20 et le 29 floréal (9 et 18 mai), il écrit

> Je vous enverrai le plus tôt possible les plus beaux tableaux du Corrège, entre autres un saint Jérôme que l'on dit être son chef d'œuvre. J'avoue que ce saint prend un mauvais temps pour arriver à Paris

et encore,

> Il part pour demain, citoyens directeurs, vingt superbes tableaux à la tête desquels se trouve le célèbre Saint Jérôme du Corrège, qui a été vendu, à ce qu'on m'assure, 200.000 livres. J'en ferai partir à peu près autant de Milan, entre autres les tableaux de Michel-Ange[29].

Il n'est pas encore question de livres à ce moment-là. Le ton et les termes employés sont révélateurs de la nature de l'intérêt du général pour les œuvres d'art. Bonaparte évoque pour la première fois des manuscrits dans une lettre au Directoire exécutif expédiée de Milan le 19 plairial (7 juin 1796):

> Je serai bientôt à Bologne. Voulez-vous que j'accepte alors, pour accorder l'armistice au Pape, 25 millions de contributions en argent, 5 millions en denrées, trois cents cadres, des statues et des manuscrits en proportion[30]….

---

26 *Recueil des actes du Directoire exécutif*, publiés et commentés par Antonin Debidour (Paris, 1910–1917), I, 333 et 333–34; Marie-Louise Blumer, 'La commission pour la recherche des objets de sciences et arts en Italie (1796–1797)', *La Révolution française*, 87 (1934), 62–88, 124–50, 222–59.

27 Blumer, 'La commission', voir note nr. 26, 70–76.

28 Napoléon Bonaparte, *Correspondance générale*. I, *Les apprentissages 1784–1797*, sous la direction de Thierry Lentz (Paris, 2004), 377, n° 557.

29 *Ibid.*, 391, n° 584 et 406–07, n° 609.

30 *Ibid.*, 431–32, n° 656.

C'est un avant-goût des clauses de l'armistice de Bologne du 23 juin,

> Art. VIII. Le Pape livrera à la République française cent tableaux, bustes, vases ou statues, au choix des commissaires qui seront envoyés à Rome, parmi lesquels objets seront notamment compris le buste en bronze de Junius Brutus et celui en marbre de Marcus Brutus, tous les deux placés au Capitole, et cinq cents manuscrits au choix desdits commissaires[31],

entériné par le traité de Tolentino signé avec le pape le 19 février 1797 :

> Art. XIII. L'article VIII du traité d'armistice signé à Bologne, concernant les manuscrits et objets d'art, aura son exécution entière et la plus prompte possible[32].

La cohérence de ces trois textes est évidente. Mais dans les lettres qui suivent, Bonaparte s'intéresse plus à d'autres collections, et en particulier à des serpents qui se trouvent à Bologne. La seule autre mention de sa part à des manuscrits se lit dans une lettre adressée de Castiglione le 3 thermidor (21 juillet 1796) au diplomate François Cacault, qui a signé avec lui le traité de Tolentino. Il cite les "… savants et artistes qui doivent faire le choix des tableaux, manuscrits et statues…" que Cacault doit prendre en charge pour leur transport et leur subsistance[33].

On constate donc que comme dans le nord de l'Europe, les premières confiscations concernent surtout des tableaux et des objets d'art provenant des collections des vaincus. Les choses ne changent que quand les commissaires nommés par le Directoire exécutif arrivent à Milan le 7 juin et se mettent au travail, même si le peintre Jacques-Pierre Tinet qui a été choisi par Bonaparte le 30 floréal an VI (19 mai 1796) a déjà visité la Bibliothèque Ambrosienne à Milan[34]. Mais, contrairement à ce qui s'est passé dans le nord de l'Europe, l'organisation des saisies est clairement prévue dans les traités signés par la République et les puissances italiennes. Elle doit peu au hasard et a comme arrière-fond un projet d'enrichissement des collections françaises existantes, qui explique sans doute la part des biens du clergé dans les confiscations qui commencent à l'été 1796. Et ce phénomène nouveau a pour point central les livres. On y reconnaît le même zèle érudit que dans les spoliations faites en France dans des collections monastiques très anciennes à partir du XVIe siècle. Dans son rapport sur la bibliographie prononcé en mars 1794, l'abbé Grégoire soulignait déjà l'intérêt à la fois intellectuel et financier de ces saisies:

> Les faits suivans donneront une idée de la rareté et de la cherté de certains ouvrages que l'ignôrance voudroit renvoyer au rebut sous prétexte qu'ils sont mal reliés, vieux, gothiques etc.
> Un exemplaire de la première édition de Pline le naturaliste, Venise, 1469 fut acheté en 1769 par Lavalière au prix de 750 livres. En 1784 le même exemplaire a été vendu 1700 livres et en 1786 un autre exemplaire moins beau a été vendu à un Anglais pour 3000 livres.
> En 1791 on a vendu
> Marci Tullii Ciceronis Epistolae familiares, Venise, 1469, en parchemin, 2000 livres.
> Grammaticae methodus, Mayence, 1468, in-folio, 1121 livres.

31 Christophe-Guillaume de Koch, *Histoire abrégée des traités de paix entre les puissances de l'Europe* (Bruxelles, 1837), I, 576.

32 https://napoleon-empire.net/texte-officiel/traite-tolentino.php ; Marie-Louise Blumer, 'Le transport en France des objets d'art cédés par le traité de Tolentino', *Revue des études italiennes*, 1 (janvier-mars 1936), 11–23.

33 Bonaparte, *Correspondance*, voir note nr. 28, 516–17, n° 802.

34 Blumer, 'La commission', voir note nr. 26, 76–78.

Sancti Hieronimi Epistolae in-folio, 1199 livres 19 sous etc.

Nota. Cette note et les deux précédentes m'ont été fournies par le citoyen Van Praët, sous garde des imprimés à la Bibliothèque nationale[35]!

Les archives de la Bibliothèque nationale gardent la trace de la préparation des prélèvements de livres qui lui sont destinés. L'Italie offre un large choix de collections et les professionnels s'attachent moins à leur statut qu'à l'importance et à la rareté des ouvrages qu'elles contiennent.

Les échanges sont fréquents entre les bibliothécaires qui réfléchissent à Paris et les commissaires qui font le travail sur le terrain. Les conservateurs de la Bibliothèque Nationale utilisent des travaux publiés depuis la fin du XVIIe siècle dont ils connaissent bien l'intérêt. Ils se font attribuer des exemplaires de catalogues trouvés dans les dépôts littéraires: dans une demande un peu postérieure aux confiscations en Italie, figure l'ouvrage de Thomas Hyde sur les éditions imprimées de la Bibliothèque Bodléienne, publié à Oxford en 1674[36] et dont l'examen est peut-être destiné à préparer les suites de l'invasion de la Grande-Bretagne, l'un des rêves napoléoniens inassouvis.

Pour les manuscrits, l'*Iter italicum*, récit du voyage de Jean Mabillon (1632–1707) en Italie au cours des années 1685 et 1686[37], est complété par le *Diarium italicum* de Bernard de Montfaucon (1698–1701), beaucoup plus détaillé que celui de Mabillon et surtout par les deux tomes de la *Bibliotheca bibliothecarum*, où Montfaucon publie de nombreux inventaires de manuscrits conservés dans toute l'Europe, réalisant ainsi une

source de première importance pour l'Italie[38]. Pour Venise, les catalogues de Zanetti, publiés en 1740 pour les manuscrits grecs et en 1741 pour les latins, italiens et français, sont aussi certainement utilisés[39].

Les incunables sont repérés dans des ouvrages spécialisés récents, comme ceux de Giovanni Battista Audiffredi[40] et de François-Xavier Laire[41], bibliothécaire du cardinal Loménie de Brienne, sur les incunables imprimés en Italie et sur les éditions aldines. Pour Bologne, on utilise le catalogue des imprimés publié en 1695.

Le conservateur Joseph Van Praet (1754–1837), qui rédigera en 1805 le catalogue des vélins de la Bibliothèque impériale et en 1831 celui des manuscrits de Louis de Bruges[42], joue un rôle important dans cette affaire. Avant d'entrer à

---

35 Henri Grégoire, *Rapport sur la bibliographie*. Séance du 22 germinal l'an II... (Paris, [avril 1794]), 9.

36 Thomas Hyde, *Impressorum librorum bibliothecae Bodleianae in Academia Oxoniensi* (Oxford, 1674).

37 Dom Jean Mabillon et Dom Michel Germain, *Iter Italicum litterarium... annis 1685 et 1686* (Paris, 1687).

38 Dom Bernard de Montfaucon, *Diarium italicum, sive Monumentorum veterum, bibliothecarum, musaeorum, &c.* (Paris, 1702); *Bibliotheca bibliothecarum manuscriptorum nova, ubi quae innumeris pene manuscriptorum bibliothecis continentur*, 2 vols (Paris, 1739).

39 Antonio Maria Zanetti, *Graeca D. Marci Bibliotheca codicum manuscriptorum* (Venise, 1740) et *Latina et italica D. Marci bibliotheca codicum manu scriptorum...* (Venise, 1741); Marino Zorzi, *Venetiae quasi alterum Byzantium: Collezioni veneziane di codici greci* (Venezia, 1993), 30.

40 *Catalogus historico-criticus romanarum editionum saeculi XV...* (Rome, 1783); *Specimen historico-criticum editionum italicarum saeculi XV...* (Rome, 1794).

41 *Specimen historicum typographiae romanae XV. saeculi* (Rome, 1778); *Serie dell' edizioni aldine per ordine cronologico ed alfabetico* (Pisa, 1790); *Index librorum ab inventa typographia ad annum 1500, chronologice dispositis cum notis historiam typographico-litterariam illustrantibus. Catalogue des livres de la bibliothèque de M*** [le cardinal Loménie de Brienne]* (Paris, 1791–1792); cf. François Dupuigrenet-Desroussilles, 'Les trésors d'Italie, (1796–1798)', in *1789. Le patrimoine libéré*, voir note nr. 1, 264–65 et *passim*.

42 *Catalogue des livres imprimés sur vélin de la Bibliothèque impériale* (Paris, 1805); *Recherches sur Louis de Bruges, seigneur de la Gruthuyse..., suivies de la notice des manuscrits qui lui ont appartenu et dont la plus grande partie se conserve à la Bibliothèque du roi* (Paris, 1831); Dominique Varry, 'Joseph Van Praet', *Histoire des*

la Bibliothèque du roi en 1784, Van Praet, dont le père était libraire-imprimeur à Bruges, avait travaillé pendant plusieurs années pour Guillaume de Bure, un célèbre libraire parisien fournisseur habituel de la Bibliothèque du roi, et rédigé pour lui, entre autres catalogues de vente, celui de la bibliothèque du duc de La Vallière[43]. Il décide donc des critères à appliquer pour le choix des documents dans une note qui reflète bien les intérêts des savants depuis le XVIᵉ siècle, les textes de l'Antiquité et les manuscrits de haute époque, la paléographie et les exemplaires illustrés, les incunables, les éditions sur vélin, mais aussi son expérience personnelle de bibliographe et de bibliophile averti:

> prendre généralement tous les manuscrits d'histoire, d'auteurs classiques grecs et latins, de poësies en quelque langue qu'ils soient; négliger les manuscrits des pères de l'église et des théologiens, à moins qu'ils ne soient assez anciens pour servir à l'histoire de la diplomatique; tout manuscrit de ce genre qui est postérieur au 10ᵉ siècle ne peut avoir aucune valeur, et ne mérite pas qu'on s'en occupe; on en excepte ceux qui sont parfaitement exécutés, enrichis de miniatures ou qui ont quelque mérite particulier; [...] peu de manuscrits sur papier du 13ᵉ, un manuscrit sur papier ne peut être beaucoup plus ancien que du 14ᵉ siècle; il en existe peu du 13ᵉ; les miniatures [...] datent de la fin du 14ᵉ siècle. [...] s'attacher de préférence aux éditions du 15ᵉ siècle; les plus précieuses sont celles qui datent depuis

1457 jusqu'à 1473; les éditions grecques sont moins anciennes elles ne remontent qu'à l'année 1476 et jusqu'en 1500, elles sont toutes recherchées; les livres imprimés sur velin ou parchemin doivent être mis au nombre des livres rares ainsi que ceux tirés en grand papier surtout les auteurs classiques grecs et latins; on ne doit pas négliger un livre bien relié en maroquin et les collections de pièces fugitives concernant l'histoire des Pays-Bas[44].

Une note plus tardive de Van Praet sur les choix à accomplir à Turin et les établissements "intéressants", envoyée à Aubin-Louis Millin, employé comme lui de la Bibliothèque nationale, le 3 floréal an VII (22 avril 1799), montre que les bibliothèques religieuses et en particulier monastiques sont en première ligne, car c'est là qu'on peut trouver les exemplaires recherchés:

> remis au c. Millin le 3 floréal an 7. La Bibliothèque nationale désireroit en outre qu'on fit choix parmi les éditions du 15ᵉ siècle que possèdent les différentes bibliothèques de Turin, savoir celles de l'Université, des Pères de la Mission de S. Vincent de Paul, des Augustins, des Dominicains, des Recolets de S. Thomas, des Carmes à la Porte Jovine, de la Congrégation de S. Bernard à la Consolata, des clercs réguliers de S. Paul dits de S. Dalmas, des Carmes déchaussés de Ste Thérèse, des Augustins déchaussés de S. Charles, des Réformés de S. François dits de la Madonne des Anges, des Religieux de la rédemption de S. Michel, des Capucins hors les murs:
> 1/ tous les livres latins datés depuis 1457 jusqu'en 1480.
> 2/ les grecs depuis 1476 jusqu'en 1512, y compris ceux sortis des presses d'Alde et des Juntes.

bibliothèques françaises. III, *Les Bibliothèques de la Révolution et du XIXᵉ siècle, 1789–1914*, 1ᵉʳᵉ éd. (Paris, 1991), 302–03.

43 *Catalogue des livres de la bibliothèque de feu monsieur le duc de La Vallière*, 3 vols (Paris, 1783); Dominique Coq, 'Le parangon du bibliophile français: le duc de La Vallière et sa collection', *Histoire des bibliothèques françaises. II, Les bibliothèques sous l'Ancien Régime 1530–1789*, 2ᵉ éd. (Paris, 2008), 409–25.

44 Paris, BnF, Archives modernes 269, acquisitions d'imprimés, livres acquis ou saisis à l'étranger. Révolution et Premier Empire: imprimés saisis dans les bibliothèques étrangères (Italie, Espagne).

3/ tous les livres imprimés sur velin ou parchemin de quelque date qu'ils puissent être et de quelque matière qu'ils traitent; on assure qu'il se trouve dans la Bibliothèque ci-devant royale deux articles de ce genre savoir
1/ la bible polyglotte de Philippe II imprimée à Anvers en 15(..) par Plantin en plusieurs volumes in folio[45],
2/ Rabbi Jacob Ben Ascerarbakkurim (hebraice) (1478) in fol.[46].

Pour les imprimés, la recherche menée par le spécialiste qu'est Van Praet est axée sur les éditions anciennes manquantes ou mal représentées à la Bibliothèque nationale. Les documents en langues orientales ne sont pas signalés expressément dans ses notes, mais il est manifeste qu'ils font l'objet de l'attention de tous. Les manuscrits grecs sont nombreux dans les saisies, surtout à Venise et à Rome et en 1811 à Gênes; de même, les textes en hébreu et en arabe sont recherchés et il s'en trouve dans les saisies de Bologne, Mantoue, Padoue[47].

La visite des bibliothèques se fait dans la foulée de l'armée occupante, en Haute-Italie et en Lombardie. Pour Venise, un article resté secret du traité signé par les représentants de la Sérénissime et les autorités françaises à Milan le 16 mai 1797 stipule que les Français recevront 20 tableaux (toujours 20 tableaux!) et 500 manuscrits[48],

que le mathématicien Gaspard Monge, qui fait partie des commissaires en Italie, choisit pour la Bibliothèque nationale au cours de l'été et de l'automne 1797 dans les bibliothèques vénitiennes, à Padoue et à San Daniele del Friuli. Pour les États Pontificaux, outre Bologne, les apports sont romains: Bibliothèque Vaticane, Cabinet du pape Pie VI, collection Albani… Des saisies ponctuelles à Turin et Florence mettent un point final à cette première époque en 1799 (voir la chronologie des saisies italiennes à la fin de cet article).

J'ai publié il y a vingt ans les listes des manuscrits restés à la Bibliothèque nationale de Paris après 1815, mais je voudrais citer ici des exemples d'ouvrages restés ou non à Paris, qui permettent de comprendre comment les commissaires en Italie appliquent les consignes et les demandes précises de leurs informateurs parisiens.

À Bologne, Mabillon avait vu les bibliothèques des chanoines réguliers de Saint-Sauveur et des Dominicains. Montfaucon en avait fait de même quelques années plus tard et c'est grâce à ses descriptions plus précises que les commissaires prennent un Pentateuque en rouleau de plus de 12 m de long sur 55 cm de large puis réclament la note en latin et en hébreu que le Bénédictin avait vue et que les Bolonais avaient gardée. On suit les péripéties de cette réclamation dans la correspondance entre les bibliothécaires parisiens, les commissaires en Italie et leur intermédiaire Charles Delacroix, ministre des relations extérieures:

> Parmi les objets tirés de chez les Dominicains de Florence [sic], Citoyen [Millin], il se trouve une Bible hebraïque expédiée avec une caisse numérotée 20 par les commissaires pour les sciences et arts et qui ne m'est point encore parvenue.
> A cette Bible devrait être jointe une note dont parle Montfaucon, note partie en latin et partie en hébreu, que les Dominicains avaient enlevée pour la conserver comme un témoignage de l'existence de cette Bible.

45 *Biblia Sacra hebraice, chaldaice, graece & latine…*: tomus primus-[octvavus] / [cura et studio Benedicti Ariae Montani], Antuerpiae: Christophorus Plantinus excudebat, 1568–1572.

46 *Ibid.* Apparemment il s'agit d'une erreur de la part de Van Praet et l'édition recherchée est: Jacob ben Asher, *Arba'ah Turim*, Piove di Sacco: Meshullam Cuzi, 3 July 1475. Folio (GW M10386; ISTC ij00000200). La BnF ne possède pas une copie de l'édition.

47 Laffitte, 'La Bibliothèque nationale et les conquêtes artistiques de la Révolution et de l'Empire: les manuscrits d'Italie', voir note nr. 1.

48 *Correspondance inédite, officielle et confidentielle de Napoléon Bonaparte avec les cours étrangères, les princes, les ministres et les généraux français et étrangers en Italie, en Allemagne et en Égypte*, [V]: *Venise* (Paris, 1819), 179.

Le Citoyen Monge se plaignit de cette sous-traction et la note fut envoyée c'est la même que celle que je vous adresse et dont je vous prie de bien vouloir m'accuser la réception … Charles Delacroix[49].

Le Grand Duc de Toscane essaiera sans succès de racheter un magnifique exemplaire peint d'Avicenne, confisqué lui aussi chez les Dominicains. Ces documents exceptionnels repartiront à Bologne en 1815[50].

Les éditions les plus anciennes du traité sur l'orthographe de Jean Tortellius et de la *Cosmographie* de Ptolémée figurent pratiquement dans toutes les listes établies à Paris. Plusieurs exemplaires de Tortellius sont toujours à la Bibliothèque nationale, dont trois de l'édition vénitienne de 1471. Imprimée sur vélin, la première est un bon exemple d'une collection aristocratique; provenant de la Bibliothèque Malatesta de Césène, elle avait été signalée par Van Praet dans les saisies possibles: "A Cesene dans la bibliothèque des Cordeliers. 1. Tortellii Aretini de orthographia … Venetiis Nicolaus

Jeanson 1471 grand in fol. superbe exemplaire imprimé sur velin tablette 21 n.º 4". Deux autres non illustrées et tirées sur papier illustrent bien ce qu'étaient les collections monastiques plus austères de Sainte-Justine de Padoue et de San Giorgio Maggiore de Venise; d'autres éditions plus récentes proviennent des Ognissanti à Florence, de Saint-Sauveur de Bologne et de San Benedetto Po[51].

Sitôt arrivés à la Bibliothèque nationale, les manuscrits d'Italie sont rangés par provenance dans une pièce réservée, catalogués, estampillés de l'estampille aux lettres "RF" utilisée de 1792 à 1802[52]. Cette marque reste encore aujourd'hui imprimée en rouge dans de nombreux volumes repartis par la suite dans leur bibliothèque d'origine. Ils sont aussi communiqués aux lecteurs: l'archéologue Quatremère de Quincy, dont on connaît les prises de position courageuses contre les saisies en Italie, y consulte des manuscrits orientaux du Vatican en l'an XIII[53]. L'opération sera plus longue et compliquée pour les imprimés. Certains volumes sont intégrés à des trains

---

49 BnF, Archives modernes 269.

50 Biblioteca Universitaria di Bologna, Pentateuque, hébreu 1 (Ms. 3569) et Avicenne, hébreu 18 (Ms. 2197); cf. Leonello Modona, *Catalogo dei codici ebraici della Biblioteca della R. Università di Bologna* (Florence, 1889); *Catalogo de' capi d'opera di pittura, sculptura, antichità, libri etc. trasportati dall'Italia in Francia* … (Venise, 1799), Libri, xxv; Giovanna Murano, 'I libri di uno Studium generale: l'antica libraria del convento di San Domenico di Bologna', *Annali di Storia delle Università italiane*, 13 (2009) http://www.cisui.unibo.it/frame_annali.htm; *Nuovo catalogo dei manoscritti ebraici della Biblioteca Universitaria di Bologna*, éd. Mauro Perani et Giacomo Corazzol (Argelato, Bologna, 2013), 74–76 (Ms. 17 [B]) et 35–38 (Ms. 3 [M]). Voir aussi Maria Cristina Bacchi and Laura Miani, *Vicende del patrimonio librario bolognese: manoscritti e incunaboli della biblioteca universitaria di Bologna*, in *Pio VI Braschi e Pio VII Chiaramonti. Due Pontefici cesenati nel bicentenario della Campagna d'Italia. Atti del Convegno internazionale* (maggio 1997), éd. Andrea Emiliani, Luigi Pepe, et Biagio Dradi Maraldi (Bologna, 1998), 369–475.

51 BnF, Archives modernes 269; édition de Venise 1471 (CIBN T-290; GW M47219; ISTC it00395000) sur vélin, Réserve des Livres Rares, Vélins 526; édition de Venise 1471 sur papier, Réserve des Livres Rares, X. 630 (bénédictins de Sainte-Justine de Padoue) et X. 629 (bénédictins de S. Giorgio Maggiore à Venise); édition de Rome, 1471 (CIBN T-291; GW M47210; ISTC it00394000), Réserve des Livres Rares, X. 631 (Ognissanti de Florence); édition de Trévise 1477 (CIBN T-292; GW M47213; ISTC it00396000), Réserve des Livres Rares, X. 632 (Saint-Sauveur de Bologne); édition de Vicence 1479 (CIBN T-293; GW M47233; ISTC it00397000), Réserve des Livres Rares, X. 633 (San Benedetto Po).

52 Pierre Josserand et Jean Bruno, 'Les Estampilles du département des imprimés de la Bibliothèque nationale', *Mélanges d'histoire du livre et des bibliothèques offerts à Monsieur Franz Calot* (Paris, 1960), n° 17.

53 BnF, Archives modernes 560. Département des Manuscrits. Enregistrement chronologique des prêts. 1785–180; Antoine Quatremère de Quincy, *Lettres à Miranda sur le déplacement des monuments de l'art de l'Italie*, introd. et notes par Edouard Pommier, 2ᵉ éd. (Paris, 1996).

de reliures, les plus importants faisant l'objet de reliures luxueuses. Ainsi, en août 1809, le relieur parisien Lefebvre relie en "maroquin bleu doubler" [*sic*] de moire deux exemplaires de Virgile, l'un annoté par Pétrarque et illustré par Simone Martini et l'autre dit Virgile des Médicis, qui seront rendus respectivement à Milan et à Florence en 1815[54]. Un tirage sur vélin du traité *De proprietate latini sermonis* de Marcellus Nonius, imprimé par Jenson à Venise en 1476 et provenant de San Giorgio Maggiore rentrera lui aussi à Venise, mais à la Biblioteca Marciana; il est toujours couvert d'une reliure et de tranches dorées caractéristiques de l'Empire, sans doute semblable à celles des Tortellius restés à Paris[55].

Même si Bonaparte fait preuve de volontarisme dans cette phase des confiscations, il n'en est pas vraiment le commanditaire, en particulier pour les livres qui ne l'intéressent pas beaucoup. Ses intérêts sont avant tout politiques et financiers.

La seconde période: la politique impériale

Les envois en France s'arrêtent après l'application des traités de paix avec le roi de Sardaigne, l'empereur d'Autriche et le Pape: il n'y a plus de transfert de livres en France, à l'exception d'un petit lot de manuscrits surtout en grec, qui sont prélevés en 1811 chez les Missionnaires urbains de Gênes, à l'intention de la Bibliothèque impériale[56].

Mais les saisies ne s'arrêtent pas là. Le projet centralisateur mais aussi les soucis financiers des nouvelles institutions consulaire puis impériale s'exercent d'une autre manière: elles reprennent à leur compte la politique de nationalisation des biens du clergé et de suppression des ordres monastiques appliquée en France qu'elles confient aux gouvernements des républiques créées peu à peu en Italie à la suite de la conquête des territoires, et les bibliothèques supprimées sont regroupées dans celles qui servent en quelque sorte de dépôts littéraires et deviendront par la suite des bibliothèques communale, universitaire ou nationale, comme cela s'est passé en France. Il est difficile de faire un tableau précis de ces opérations car cela dépend et de l'avancée de l'occupation et du statut des états italiens concernés. J'évoquerai cependant deux exemples pour souligner la variété des situations, l'un précoce, l'autre tardif.

Le cas de Bologne, qui faisait partie des États pontificaux, est réglé très rapidement. Dès fin 1796 Bonaparte demande la réduction des couvents, montrant bien où est pour lui l'intérêt financier de l'opération:

> Ordonnez qu'il n'y ait dans l'Etat de Bologne qu'un seul couvent de meme ordre, supprimez toux ceux, qui auraient moint de 15 religieux; resserez les couvents des religieuses et servez vous des ressources considerables que cela vous donnera pour remplacer dans votre trésor le defficit[57].

54   Milan, Bibliothèque Ambrosienne, ms. A 79 inf.; Florence, Bibliothèque Laurentienne, ms. Plut. 39.1; BnF, Archives modernes 624. Département des Manuscrits. Listes de trains de reliure, factures, lettres et notes diverses concernant les volumes reliés à l'extérieur. 1806–1835; pour le Virgile dit des Médicis, voir Henry Rushton Fairclough, 'Some notes on "The value of the medicean Codex of Vergil"', *Classical Philology*, 27.4 (1932), 399–401; Max Hoffmann, *Der Codex Mediceus Pl. XXXIX n. 1 des Vergilius. I* (Leipzig, 1889).

55   Venise, Biblioteca Nazionale Marciana, Membr. 21; cf. MEI 02008357: n. 262 de la liste de restitution, Biblioteca Nazionale Marciana, Archivio, b. 1816. Voir Dondi-Prosdocimi-Raines dans ces actes.

56   Annaclara Cataldi Palau, *Catalogo dei manoscritti greci della Biblioteca Franzoniana (Genova)*, 2 vols, Bollettino dei Classici, Accademia nazionale dei Lincei, suppl. n° 8 e 17 (Rome, 1990, 1996), II, *Aggiunte e correzioni*, 185–96.

57   *Œuvres de Napoléon Bonaparte, texte intégral, Lettre du 11 décembre 1796 au quartier-général à Milan et au Sénat de Bologne*, 22. http://www.gutenberg.org/files/12230/12230-h/12230-h.htm

Les congrégations religieuses sont donc rapidement supprimées dans la foulée et un décret du sénat de Bologne du 6 juin 1798 confirme l'ordre du gouvernement de la République cisalpine pour la suppression des Olivétains de S. Michele in Bosco, des chanoines de S. Sauveur, et des Dominicains. Le 16 juin 1798 ces derniers doivent quitter les bâtiments transformés en caserne et en bibliothèque municipale. Une nouvelle vague de décisions a lieu après la paix de Lunéville le 9 février 1801 et l'organisation définitive de la République cisalpine. Le 30 avril 1801 une bibliothèque publique départementale est créée dans le couvent des Dominicains. Comme en France, des inventaires de tous les fonds conservés doivent être rédigés. En décembre 1801, on adopte des règles de tri des documents copiées sur celles qui ont été fixées en France à partir de 1790 dans plusieurs publications (dont le rapport sur la bibliographie de l'abbé Grégoire, prononcé en mars 1794 déjà cité): conservation systématique des manuscrits anciens et des éditions en langues étrangères et pour les autres imprimés, de tous les ouvrages antérieurs à 1550 et des tirages sur vélin

2. Essi sceglieranno ad uso pubblico

1. Tutti i manoscritti quando non siano scolastici moderni val a dire di due secoli in quà

2. Tutti i libri stampati avanti il 1500…

3. Tutti gli autori classici Greci, Latini ed Italiani…

4. Tutti i libri di scienze…

4. Delle infinite opere teologiche e riguardanti le materie Ecclesiastiche, non conserveranno che

1. Tutte le Bibbie…

2. I Santi Padri quando siano di prima Edizione e d'Edizione Maurina…

5. Preserveranno su questo principio generale tutte le edizioni di Aldo, di Stefano, di Wechelio… et d'altri stampatori famosi del secolo XVI

6. … tutti i libri relativi alle lingue orientali[58] …

En Toscane, l'application des lois françaises commence dix ans après avec l'annexion à l'Empire en décembre 1807. La suppression des ordres religieux par décret impérial du 24 mars 1808 puis la nationalisation de tous les biens par les ordonnances de l'administrateur général de Toscane Edouard Dauchy des 16 et 29 avril 1808 sont confirmés par le décret impérial signé à Saint-Cloud le 13 septembre 1810

Il consiglier di Stato…, Amministratore della Toscana…
- titolo primo: Soppressione dei conventi
art. I. Sono soppressi i conventi di religiosi e religiose di Toscana
- titolo quarto: stipendio dei religiosi e religiose
art. XXI. I Signori Prefetti nomineranno dei commisari, che saranno caricati di trasportarsi nelle biblioteche dei conventi per farvi…, la scelta dei libri e manoscritti che meritano d'essere per la pubblica istruzione conservati…
Firenze, li 29 aprile 1808 Dauchy[59]
Napoleone imperatore dei Francesi etc.
Art. I. Tutti gli ordini monastici e congregazioni d'uomini e di donne sono definitivamente ed interamente soppresse nei dipartimenti dell'Arno, del Mediterraneo e dell'Ombrone…
Saint-Cloud, li 13 settembre 1810 Napoleone…

Pour les livres et les manuscrits l'ordonnance du 29 avril indique que les commissaires doivent aller chercher les documents des couvents supprimés. A Florence, les manuscrits sont réunis dans plusieurs dépôts; ils sont ensuite distribués dans les fonds dits *conventi soppressi* des Bibliothèques Laurenziana, Marucelliana et Nazionale. A la

---

58 Albano Sorbelli, dans *Inventari dei manoscritti delle biblioteche d'Italia* 30 (Florence, 1924), 4.
59 Antonio Zobi, *Storia civile della Toscana dal MDCCXXXVII al MDCCCXLVIII* (Florence, 1851), III, Appendice di documenti, 323–27.

Bibliothèque nationale de Florence, les manuscrits portent la grosse estampille noire ornée de l'aigle impériale de la *Commissione degli oggetti d'arti e scienze* (Commission des objets d'arts et de science), bien différente de celles qui sont imprimées en rouge à la même époque sur les collections de la Bibliothèque impériale de Paris[60].

Les États italiens partagent cette histoire avec les autres territoires annexés en Europe du Nord, comme le Luxembourg actuel, devenu département français. Les principes sont ceux de la Révolution, le Directoire, le Consulat puis l'Empire les conservent. L'empereur signe les décrets mais délègue leur application aux administrations locales, et son but principal est l'homogénéisation de l'Empire. Cet aspect de la politique napoléonienne survivra à sa chute, ce qui n'est pas le cas pour les envois en France.

Les restitutions

En effet, dès le printemps 1814, avant même la signature le 31 mai du traité de Paris qui entérine la restitution des confiscations envoyées en France,

> Art. 31. Les archives, cartes, plans et documens quelconques appartenans aux pays cédés, ou concernant leur administration, seront fidèlement rendus en même temps que le pays, ou, si cela était impossible, dans un délai qui ne pourra être de plus de six mois après la remise des pays mêmes[61],

le roi de Prusse puis les autres souverains vainqueurs envoient leurs représentants à Paris pour récupérer ce dont ils avaient été spoliés. Pour la Bibliothèque nationale, les restitutions ont lieu en octobre 1815. L'"État des manuscrits rendus par MM. les Conservateurs administrateurs de la Bibliothèque du roi de France, à Mrs les Commissaires de LL. MM. les Souverains alliés"[62], dont voici l'extrait concernant les retours en Italie

S. M. l'Empereur d'Autriche

– Florence (au grand duc de Toscane)
  le fameux manuscrit de Virgile connu sous le nom de Virgile de Florence [déposé 20 fructidor an VII/ rendu 5 octobre 1815]
– Mantoue, les manuscrits de Mantoue sont au nombre de sept [déposés an V et an VII/ rendus 5 octobre 1815]
  grec: 1 / latins: 5 / italien: 1 = 7
– Milan, Bibliothèque Ambrosienne… [déposés frimaire an VII/ 8 mss rendus 5 octobre 1815]
  latins: 3 / italiens: 7 = 10
– Modène (au grand duc de Modène) [déposés thermidor an V/ rendus 21 octobre 1815]
  orientaux: 2 / grecs: 32 / latins: 30 / italiens: 3 / allemand: 1 = 68
– Monza [déposés fructidor an V/ rendus 5 octobre 1815]
  latins: 114 / français: 1 = 115
– Venise [déposés 11 octobre 1797/ rendus 5 octobre 1815]
  les manuscrits provenant de la Bibliothèque de Saint Marc de Venise…
  orientaux: 3 / grecs: 167+ 4 / latins: 23 / françois: 2 / italiens: 2 = 201
  les manuscrits provenant des monastères à Venise…
  grecs: 12 / latins: 7 / italiens: 3 = 22
– Vérone, les manuscrits provenant de la bibliothèque du chapitre de Vérone… [déposés fructidor an V/ rendus 5 octobre 1815]
  latins: 24 / italiens: 5 = 29

S. M. le Roi de Sardaigne

---

60 *I Manoscritti datati del fondo conventi soppressi della Biblioteca nazionale centrale di Firenze* (Florence, 2002), 8–11, 47, 49, 52 et *passim*, pl. LXV, LXVI, CIII, CXVII, CLXII, CLXXXVIII.

61 de Koch, *Histoire abrégée des traités de paix entre les puissances de l'Europe depuis la paix de Westphalie*, voir note nr. 31, III (1838), 364: section IV: Traité de Paris, 1814.

62 BnF, Archives modernes 495.

– les manuscrits venant de Turin [déposés 13 germinal an VII et 16 floréal an X/ rendus 18 octobre 1815]

latins: 18 / italiens: 30 = 48

Le pape

– Rome, les manuscrits provenant de la Bibliothèque du Vatican... [déposés 1797/ rendus 2 septembre 1815]

orientaux: 191 / grecs: 133 / latins: 154 / italiens: 15 / français: 8 = 501

– Bologne, les manuscrits provenant de Bologne (abbaye de Saint-Sauveur) [déposés 1797/ rendus 23 octobre 1815]

hébreux: 9 / latins: 421 / italiens: 76 = 506

donne pour les manuscrits une idée de l'ampleur des saisies et des restitutions. À part quelques erreurs de destination pour les retours, des oublis et les manuscrits de la Bibliothèque Vaticane offerts à Louis XVIII par le pape Pie VII[63], tous les manuscrits sont rendus. En Italie, ils sont confiés aux bibliothèques désignées avant 1814 pour conserver les fonds anciens confisqués et centralisés par l'administration impériale. Pour les livres imprimés et en particulier les incunables, il n'existe pas de listes comme pour les manuscrits et il est plus difficile de préciser ce que Van Praet a rendu ou non.

C'est la politique de suppressions appliquée entre 1797 et 1810 qui explique que certains lots, et pas uniquement des manuscrits ou des imprimés d'origine monastique, soient restés à Paris après la chute de l'Empire: en 1814, les institutions religieuses et les collections privées auxquelles ils appartenaient n'existent plus depuis plusieurs années et ils n'apparaissent pas dans les exigences de l'Empereur d'Autriche, du roi de Sardaigne, du pape et du duc de Modène.

Les manuscrits restés à la Bibliothèque nationale sont faciles à repérer. Ils correspondent aux critères donnés par Van Praet et proviennent de collections particulières romaines, le cabinet personnel du pape Pie VI (à la Bibliothèque nationale et à Sainte-Geneviève)[64] et la collection Albani[65], de San Daniele del Friuli et pour les couvents, des bibliothèques de Sainte-Justine de Padoue et de Polirone (San Benedetto Po), visitées par les Français en 1796–1797, puis transférées pour la première en 1807 à la Bibliothèque Brera, et pour la seconde dès 1797 à la Biblioteca Teresiana de Mantoue[66].

Pour ce qui concerne les livres imprimés, le catalogue des incunables de la Bibliothèque nationale de France donne de nombreuses informations sur ce sujet, mais l'identification systématique des exemplaires reste encore un chantier à mener.

Chronologie des saisies en Italie, 1796–1799

15 mai 1796 entrée des troupes à Milan

26 mai 1796 Biblioteca Ambrosiana

14 juin 1796 Biblioteca Nazionale Braidense fondée par les Jésuites (1571), donnée au gouvernement en 1773

5 juin 1796 occupation de Bologne

23 juin 1796 armistice avec Pie VI

14 juillet 1796 Bibliothèque des chanoines réguliers de Saint-Sauveur, Dominicains de Bologne, Institut des Sciences

63 Léopold Delisle, 'Les archives du Vatican', *Journal des Savants* (août 1892), 498; Jeanne Bignami-Odier, *La Bibliothèque Vaticane de Sixte IV à Pie XI...*, Studi e Testi 272 (Vatican, 1973), 162–63, 174 et 303.

64 Laffitte, 'La Bibliothèque nationale et les conquêtes artistiques de la Révolution et de l'Empire: les manuscrits d'Italie', voir note nr. 1, 309–13; Françoise Zehnacker, dans *Trésors du Vatican. La papauté à Paris* (Paris, 1990), 187–89.

65 Marie-Pierre Laffitte, 'Quelques manuscrits de la bibliothèque Albani', *Bulletin du Bibliophile*, 1 (1985), 35–40.

66 Laffitte, 'La Bibliothèque nationale et les conquêtes artistiques de la Révolution et de l'Empire: les manuscrits d'Italie', voir note nr. 1, 300–02 et 314–15; Charles Astruc, 'Benedetto Bacchini et les manuscrits de Sainte-Justine de Padoue', *Italia medioevale e umanistica*, 3 (1960), 345–46; 1789. *Le patrimoine libéré*, voir note nr. 1, n° 109.

29 juillet 1796 arrivée des commissaires français à Rome

4 octobre 1796 rupture de l'armistice avec Modène et occupation de la ville

1er novembre 1796 Biblioteca Estense

16 janvier 1797 Abbaye de St Benedetto de Polirone

3 février 1797 capitulation de Mantoue

19 février 1797 traité de Tolentino avec le pape

5–6 mars 1797 saisie du trésor de la cathédrale de Monza fondée à la fin du VIᵉ siècle par la reine lombarde Théodelinde de Bavière

31 mars 1797 saisies à Massa e Carrara (propriété de la duchesse Marie-Béatrice d'Este, duchesse de Massa, qui avait épousé un archiduc d'Autriche)

17 avril 1797 Pâques véronaises et occupation de Vérone

mai 1797 saisies à Vérone

printemps 1797 reprise de la saisie au Vatican

15 mai 1797 entrée des Français à Venise

16 août 1797 saisies à Mantoue

11 septembre 1797 saisie à San Daniele del Friuli

11 octobre 1797 saisies à Venise, Padoue, Trévise

novembre 1797 départ de Bonaparte

10 février 1798 entrée des Français à Rome

été 1798 saisies dans les collections romaines autres que celles du Vatican

décembre 1798 abdication de Charles-Emmanuel roi de Piémont

hiver 1798–1799 saisies de livres à Turin

26 mars 1799 entrée dans Florence

6 septembre 1799 saisie du Virgile de Florence

Bibliography

Manuscripts and Archival Sources

Bologna, Biblioteca Universitaria, Ms. 3.

Bologna, Biblioteca Universitaria, Ms. 17.

Bologna, Biblioteca Universitaria, Ms. 2197.

Bologna, Biblioteca Universitaria, Ms. 3569.

Florence, Bibliothèque Laurentienne, ms. conv. soppr. 627.

Florence, Bibliothèque Laurentienne, ms. Plut. 39.1.

Florence, Bibliothèque Laurentienne, ms. Plut. 68.2.

Florence, Bibliothèque Nationale, conv. soppr. I.V.43.

Madrid, Bibliothèque Nationale, ms. 8514.

Milan, Bibliothèque Ambrosienne, ms. A 79 inf.

Paris, Bibliothèque de l'Arsenal, ms. 1184 rés.

Paris, BnF, Archives modernes 269, acquisitions d'imprimés, livres acquis ou saisis à l'étranger. Révolution et Premier Empire: imprimés saisis dans les bibliothèques étrangères (Italie, Espagne).

Paris, BnF, Archives modernes 495.

Paris, BnF, Archives modernes 560. Département des Manuscrits. Enregistrement chronologique des prêts. 1785–180.

Paris, BnF, Archives modernes 624. Département des Manuscrits. Listes de trains de reliure, factures, lettres et notes diverses concernant les volumes reliés à l'extérieur. 1806–1835.

Paris, BnF, ms. français 935.

Paris, BnF, ms. italien 77.

Paris, BnF, ms. latin 1663.

Paris, BnF, ms. latin 1732.

Paris, BnF, ms. latin 4568.

Rome, Bibliothèque Vaticane, ms. Vat. Lat. 1873.

Primary Sources

Jacob ben Asher, *Arba'ah Turim*, Piove di Sacco: Meshullam Cuzi, 3 July 1475. Folio. ISTC ij00000200.

Nonius Marcellus, *De proprietate latini sermonis*, Venice: Nicolaus Jenson, 1476. Folio. ISTC in00265000; MEI 02008357. Venise, Biblioteca Nazionale Marciana, Membr. 21.

Tortellius, Johannes, *Orthographia*, Venice: Nicolaus Jenson, 1471. Folio. CIBN T-290; ISTC it00395000.

Tortellius, Johannes, *Orthographia*, Rome: Ulrich Han (Udalricus Gallus) and Simon Nicolai Chardella, [after 10 Aug.] 1471. Folio. CIBN T-291; ISTC it00394000.

Tortellius, Johannes, *Orthographia*. (Ed: Hieronymus Bononius), Treviso: Hermannus Liechtenstein, for Michael Manzolus, 2 Apr. 1477. Folio and 4°. CIBN T-292; ISTC it00396000.

Tortellius, Johannes, *Orthographia*. (Ed: Hieronymus Bononius), Vicenza: Stephan Koblinger, 13 Jan. 1479. Folio. CIBN T-293; ISTC it00397000.

Secondary Works

1789. Le Patrimoine libéré. 200 trésors entrés à la Bibliothèque Nationale de 1789 à 1799 (Paris, 1989).

Archives parlementaires de 1787 à 1860. Assemblée nationale constituante, IX, *16 septembre 1789–11 novembre 1789* (Paris, 1877).

Archives parlementaires de 1787 à 1860. Assemblée nationale constituante, X, *24 décembre 1789–1er mars 1790* (Paris, 1880).

Charles Astruc, 'Benedetto Bacchini et les manuscrits de Sainte-Justine de Padoue', *Italia medioevale e umanistica*, 3 (1960), 341–51.

Maria Cristina Bacchi et Laura Miani, 'Vicende del patrimonio librario bolognese: manoscritti e incunaboli della biblioteca universitaria di Bologna', in *Pio VI Braschi e Pio VII Chiaramonti. Due Pontefici cesenati nel bicentenario della Campagna d'Italia. Atti del Convegno internazionale* (maggio 1997), éd. Andrea Emiliani, Luigi Pepe, Biagio Dradi Maraldi (Bologna, 1998), 369–475.

Biblia Sacra hebraice, chaldaice, graece & latine…: tomus primus-[octvavus] / [cura et studio Benedicti Ariae Montani], Antuerpiae: Christophorus Plantinus excudebat, 1568–1572.

Bibliotheca bibliothecarum manuscriptorum nova, ubi quae innumeris pene manuscriptorum bibliothecis continentur, 2 vols (Paris, 1739).

Jeanne Bignami-Odier, *La Bibliothèque Vaticane de Sixte IV à Pie XI…*, Studi e Testi 272 (Vatican, 1973).

Rudolf Blum, *La Biblioteca della Badia Fiorentina e i codici di Antonio Corbinelli*, Studi e Testi 155 (Rome, 1951).

Marie-Louise Blumer, 'La commission pour le recherche des objets de sciences et arts en Italie (1796–1797)', *La Révolution française*, 87 (1934), 62–88, 124–50, 222–59.

Marie-Louise Blumer, 'Le transport en France des objets d'art cédés par le traité de Tolentino', *Revue des études italiennes*, 1 (janvier-mars 1936), 11–23.

Napoléon Bonaparte, *Correspondance générale*. I, *Les apprentissages 1784–1797*, sous la direction de Thierry Lentz (Paris, 2004).

Ferdinand Boyer, 'L'organisation des conquêtes artistiques de la Convention en Belgique', *Revue belge de philologie et d'histoire*, 49 (1971), 490–500.

Ferdinand Boyer, 'Les conquêtes scientifiques de la Convention en Belgique et dans les pays rhénans (1794–1795)', *Revue d'histoire moderne et contemporaine*, 18 (1971), 354–74.

Annaclara Cataldi Palau, *Catalogo dei manoscritti greci della Biblioteca Franzoniana (Genova)*, 2 vols, Bollettino dei Classici, Accademia nazionale dei Lincei, suppl. n° 8 e 17 (Rome, 1990, 1996).

Catalogo de' capi d'opera di pittura, sculptura, antichità, libri etc. trasportati dall'Italia in Francia… (Venise, 1799), Libri, xxv.

Catalogue des livres de la bibliothèque de feu monsieur le duc de La Vallière, 3 vols (Paris, 1783).

Catalogue des livres imprimés sur vélin de la Bibliothèque impériale (Paris, 1805).

Catalogus historico-criticus romanarum editionum saeculi XV… (Rome, 1783).

Ségolène Chambon, 'Le rôle de l'abbé Leblond dans les commissions de savants', catalogue de l'exposition *Antiquités, Lumières et Révolution. L'abbé Leblond (1738–1809) "second fondateur de la Bibliothèque Mazarine"* (Paris, 2009), 65–72.

Dominique Coq, 'Le parangon du bibliophile français: le duc de La Vallière et sa collection', *Histoire des bibliothèques françaises. II, Les bibliothèques sous l'Ancien Régime 1530–1789*, 2ᵉ éd. (Paris, 2008), 409–25.

Correspondance inédite, officielle et confidentielle de Napoléon Bonaparte avec les cours étrangères, les princes, les ministres et les généraux français et étrangers en Italie, en Allemagne et en Égypte, [V]: *Venise* (Paris, 1819).

Cornelia C. Coulter, 'Boccaccio and the Cassinese manuscripts of the Laurentian Library', *Classical Philology*, XLIII, 4 (1948), 217–30.

Paul-Louis Courier, *Collection complète des pamphlets politiques et opuscules littéraires…* (Bruxelles, 1827).

Christophe-Guillaume de Koch, *Histoire abrégée des traités de paix entre les puissances de l'Europe* (Bruxelles, 1837).

Albinia de la Mare, *The Handwriting of Italian humanists*, 1/1, *Francesco Petrarca, Giovanni Boccacio, Coluccio Salutati, Niccolò Niccoli…* (Paris, 1973).

Léopold Delisle, 'Les archives du Vatican', *Journal des Savants* (août 1892).

Tammaro De Marinis, *La biblioteca napoletana dei Re d'Aragona…*, 4 vols (Milan, 1947–1952). *Supplemento*, avec la participation de Denise Bloch, Charles Astruc, Jacques Monfrin et José Ruysschaert, 2 vols (Vérone, 1969).

François Dupuigrenet-Desroussilles, 'Les trésors d'Italie, (1796–1798)', in *1789. Le Patrimoine libéré. 200 trésors entrés à la Bibliothèque Nationale de 1789 à 1799* (Paris, 1989), 264–65.

Henri Grégoire, *Rapport sur la bibliographie. Séance du 22 germinal l'an II…* (Paris, [avril 1794]).

Maria Luisa Grossi Turchetti, *I Manoscritti datati della Biblioteca nazionale Braidense di Milano* (Florence, 2004).

Max Hoffmann, *Der Codex Mediceus Pl. XXXIX n. 1 des Vergilius. I* (Leipzig, 1889).

Thomas Hyde, *Impressorum librorum bibliothecae Bodleianae in Academia Oxoniensi* (Oxford, 1674).

Index librorum ab inventa typographia ad annum 1500, chronologice dispositis cum notis historiam typographico-litterariam illustrantibus. Catalogue des livres de la bibliothèque de M*** [le cardinal Loménie de Brienne] (Paris, 1791–1792).

Inventari dei manoscritti delle biblioteche d'Italia 30 (Florence, 1924).

Inventario general de manuscritos de la Biblioteca nacional (Madrid, 1995).

André Jammes, 'Un bibliophile à découvrir, Jean de Gagny', *Bulletin du bibliophile*, 1 (1996), 35–80.

Pierre Josserand et Jean Bruno, 'Les Estampilles du département des imprimés de la Bibliothèque nationale', *Mélanges d'histoire du livre et des bibliothèques offerts à Monsieur Franz Calot* (Paris, 1960), 261–98.

Jean-Baptiste Labiche, *Notice sur les dépôts littéraires et la révolution bibliographique de la fin du dernier siècle* (Paris, 1880).

Marie-Pierre Laffitte, 'Quelques manuscrits de la bibliothèque Albani', *Bulletin du Bibliophile*, 1 (1985), 35–40.

Marie-Pierre Laffitte, 'La Bibliothèque nationale et les conquêtes artistiques de la Révolution et de l'Empire: les manuscrits d'Italie', *Bulletin du Bibliophile*, 2 (1989), 272–323.

M.-P. Laffitte et Fabienne Le Bars, *Reliures royales de la Renaissance. La Librairie de Fontainebleau 1544–1570* (Paris, 1999).

Marie-Pierre Laffitte, 'Les manuscrits normands de Colbert. Reliures cisterciennes', *Actes du colloque Manuscrits et enluminures dans le monde normand*, octobre 1995 (Caen, 1999), 197–205.

Marie-Pierre Laffitte, 'Les manuscrits de la collection de Thou', *Histoire des bibliothèque françaises. II, Les bibliothèques sous l'Ancien Régime 1530–1789*, 2ᵉ éd. (Paris, 2008), 155–57.

Marie-Pierre Laffitte, 'La redécouverte des manuscrits carolingiens par les érudits et les collectionneurs français (XVIᵉ-XVIIIᵉ siècles)', *Actes de la journée d'études carolingiennes*, Paris, 4 mai 2007, réd. en collab. avec Jean-Pierre Caillet (Turnhout, 2009), 141–58.

Marie-Pierre Laffitte, 'Cadeaux, spoliations, achats, un aperçu des manuscrits "parisiens" provenant des ducs de Bourgogne et de leur entourage', in *Miniatures flamandes 1404–1482*, éd. Bernard Bousmanne et Thierry Delcourt (Paris, 2011), 55–65.

Anne-Marie Legaré, 'Les cent quatorze manuscrits de Bourgogne choisis par le comte d'Argenson pour le roi Louis XV. Édition de la liste de 1748', *Bulletin du Bibliophile* (1998), 241–329.

Elias Avery Lowe, *Codices latini antiquiores, a palaeographical guide to latin manuscripts prior to the ninth century: France* (Paris-Oxford, 1950).

Dom Jean Mabillon et Dom Michel Germain, *Iter Italicum litterarium… annis 1685 et 1686* (Paris, 1687).

I Manoscritti datati del fondo conventi soppressi della Biblioteca nazionale centrale di Firenze (Florence, 2002).

Leonello Modona, *Catalogo dei codici ebraici della Biblioteca della R. Università di Bologna* (Florence, 1889).

Dom Bernard de Montfaucon, *Diarium italicum, sive Monumentorum veterum, bibliothecarum, musaeorum, &c.* (Paris, 1702).

Marco Mostert, *The Library of Fleury, a provisional list of manuscripts* (Hilversum, 1989).

Giovanna Murano, 'I libri di uno Studium generale: l'antica libraria del convento di San Domenico di Bologna', *Annali di Storia delle Università italiane*, 13 (2009) http://www.cisui.unibo.it/frame_annali.htm

Lodovico Antonio Muratori, *Antiquitates italicae medii aevi, sive Dissertationes de moribus, ritibus, religione, regimine…* (Milan, 1738–1742).

Donatella Nebbiai-Della Guarda, *La Bibliothèque de l'abbaye de Saint-Denis* (Paris, 1985).

Francis Newton, *The Scriptorium and library at Monte Cassino, 1058–1105* (Cambridge, 1999).

Nuovo catalogo dei manoscritti ebraici della Biblioteca Universitaria di Bologna, éd. Mauro Perani et Giacomo Corazzol (Argelato, Bologna, 2013).

Oeuvres de Napoléon Bonaparte, texte intégral, Lettre du 11 décembre 1796 au quartier-général à Milan et au Sénat de Bologne, 22. https://www.gutenberg.org/files/12230/12230-h/12230-h.htm

Elisabeth Pellegrin, *La Bibliothèque des Visconti et des Sforza, ducs de Milan, au xve siècle* (Paris, 1955); Eadem, *Supplément* (Florence-Paris, 1969).

Antoine Quatremère de Quincy, *Lettres à Miranda sur le déplacement des monuments de l'art de l'Italie*, introd. et notes par Edouard Pommier, 2e éd. (Paris, 1996).

Recherches sur Louis de Bruges, seigneur de la Gruthuyse…, suivies de la notice des manuscrits qui lui ont appartenu et dont la plus grande partie se conserve à la Bibliothèque du roi (Paris, 1831).

Recueil des actes du Directoire exécutif, publiés et commentés par Antonin Debidour (Paris, 1910–1917).

Leighton D. Reynolds et Nigel G. Wilson, *D'Homère à Erasme, la transmission des classiques grecs et latins* (Paris, 1986).

Henry Rushton Fairclough, 'Some notes on "The value of the medicean Codex of Vergil"', *Classical Philology*, 27.4 (1932), 399–401.

Serie dell' edizioni aldine per ordine cronologico ed alfabetico (Pisa, 1790).

Specimen historico-criticum editionum italicarum saeculi XV… (Rome, 1794).

Specimen historicum typographiae romanae XV. Saeculi, éd. François-Xavier Laire (Rome, 1778).

J. Stiennon, *Paléographie du Moyen Âge* (Paris, 1973).

Texts and transmission. A Survey of the Latin Classics, éd. Leighton D. Reynolds (Oxford, 1983).

Trésors du Vatican. La papauté à Paris (Paris, 1990).

Berthold Louis Ullman, *The Origin and development of humanistic script* (Rome, 1960).

Dominique Varry, 'Les confiscations révolutionnaires', *Histoire des bibliothèques françaises*. III, *Les Bibliothèques de la Révolution et du xixe siècle 1789–1914* (Paris, 1991), 9–27.

Dominique Varry, 'Joseph Van Praet', *Histoire des bibliothèques françaises*. III, *Les Bibliothèques de la Révolution et du xixe siècle, 1789–1914*, 1ère éd. (Paris, 1991), 302–03.

Veronika Von Büren, 'Ambroise de Milan dans la bibliothèque de Cluny', *Scriptorium*, 47 (1993), 141–60.

Antonio Maria Zanetti, *Graeca D. Marci Bibliotheca codicum manuscriptorum* (Venise, 1740).

Antonio Maria Zanetti, *Latina et italica D. Marci bibliotheca codicum manu scriptorum …* (Venise, 1741).

Antonio Zobi, *Storia civile della Toscana dal MDCCXXXVII al MDCCCXLVIII* (Florence, 1851).

Marino Zorzi, *Venetiae quasi alterum Byzantium: Collezioni veneziane di codici greci* (Venezia, 1993).

Digital Sources

Napoléon & Empire, https:// napoleon-empire.net/texte-officiel/traite-tolentino.php.

PART 3

Sequestration, Redistribution, or Contribution to the Foundation of Public Libraries

▼ THE DISSOLUTION FROM THE PERSPECTIVE OF
LIBRARIES. WHAT MATERIAL WAS REUSED AND IN WHAT
WAYS? HOW DID THE DISSOLUTION CONTRIBUTE TO THE
OPENING OF NEW PUBLIC LIBRARIES OR INFLUENCE THE
CONTENTS OF THOSE ALREADY ESTABLISHED?

JOS A. A. M. BIEMANS

The Foundation of the City Library of Amsterdam (1578) and the Confiscation of Manuscripts and Printed Books from Ecclesiastical and Monastic Libraries. Fact or Fiction?

The University of Amsterdam was founded in 1877. Nevertheless the *library* of the University of Amsterdam carries its history back to at least the last quarter of the sixteenth century. The traditional explanation for this remarkable fact is as follows. After the Alteration (Dutch: *Alteratie*) of the city, i.e., its change in 1578 from Roman Catholicism to Protestantism, a city library was established for the educated and learned people in town. Some decades later, in 1632, Amsterdam was allowed to establish an institution for higher education. Unfortunately, the city and University of Leiden effectively blocked the foundation of a second university in the Northern Netherlands, so Amsterdam had to be satisfied with starting an Illustrious High School (*Athenaeum Illustre*) and the city library was put at the disposal of this school. In 1877, almost 250 years later, the Athenaeum was raised to the status of a university. Consequently the library of the city and of the Athenaeum of Amsterdam became a University Library. And indeed, a small number of manuscripts and hundreds of early printed books that were in the city library from its very beginnings, still form part of the University Library's department of Special Collections. In this retrospect the line from present times to medieval times is uninterrupted. And the University Library functions for both the academic community and the well-educated citizens, in other words, it is still the city library of Amsterdam[1].

The literature on the subject, traditionally and almost without exception, tells us that this city library

---

[1] Besides the library of the University of Amsterdam there is also the great public library of the city, serving everyone in town and region: the Openbare Bibliotheek Amsterdam (OBA).

Jos A. A. M. Biemans • Professor emeritus of Manuscript Studies and formerly curator of manuscripts at the Library of the University of Amsterdam. j.a.a.m.biemans@uva.nl

How the Secularization of Religious Houses Transformed the Libraries of Europe, 16th–19th Centuries, ed. by Cristina Dondi, Dorit Raines, and † Richard Sharpe, BIB, 63 (Turnhout, 2022), pp. 247–271.

BREPOLS ❧ PUBLISHERS   DOI 10.1484/M.BIB-EB.5.128487

Figure 12.1. Amsterdam, New Church *c.* 1500, with at the right an adjacent new building with three latticed windows: the second location of the sacristy and library; engraving in: M. Fockens, *Beschryvinge der wijdt-vermaarde Koop-stad Amstelredam* (Amsterdam 1664, between pp. 550–51).

was founded by the new burgomasters immediately or at least shortly after the Alteration in 1578. We also learn that its first collection of books consisted of the greater part of books confiscated from the previous Roman Catholic monasteries and churches and that these books were brought together in the city's New Church (Fig. 12.1)[2]. Yet, official documents which may serve as a "birth certificate" for the city library, are lacking. The municipal archives are silent

regarding *who* decided to start a library, or *when* such a decision was made, not to mention the question *why* a library was considered necessary for the city. The archives and financial administration of the New Church were lost during a tremendous fire in 1645. Shortly after, in 1652, the old Town Hall entirely burned down. Happily the oldest archives with the medieval charters and other records were safely kept in a highly secure room at the Old Church: they

2   Hendrik Cornelis Rogge, *Geschiedenis der Stedelijke Boekerij van Amsterdam* (Amsterdam, 1882); [Combertus Pieter Burger Jr.], 'Geschiedenis der Bibliotheek', in *Gids voor de Bibliotheek der Universiteit van Amsterdam*

(Amsterdam, 1919), V–XVI; Herman de la Fontaine Verwey, 'The City Library of Amsterdam in the Nieuwe Kerk 1578–1632', *Quærendo* 14 (1984), 163–206.

survived the fire and are still available for research. Unfortunately these precious documents provide nothing relevant to the present research.

Since January 2011 I have been engaged in writing a new history of Amsterdam University Library, from its earliest times[3]. Of course I do not want to reproduce the stories of my predecessors, but the question is whether I will be able to find something new. The main questions are: can we be sure about a foundation of the City Library in 1578? Did the new burgomasters really take the initiative to start such a municipal institution? Is it possible to confirm the notion that its initial collection consisted mainly of confiscated books? In fact, the lack of records makes it impossible to verify previous reconstructions of what may have happened in the world of the book in Amsterdam around 1578. The only way to reach my goal is raising new questions and following new avenues of inquiry. For instance, by scrutinizing the reports of several architectural restorations of the New Church I hope to be a little bit more precise about the original location and housing of the library. Visual representations can be valuable but they may also mislead. Also, I will compare the available information about what happened elsewhere in the Northern Netherlands, particularly in the County of Holland, with the few things we know about the situation in Amsterdam, hoping to see the thick fog lifting. And of course, another important source of information will be the actual books that originally belonged to the city library and have survived to the present time.

Historical Background

Before approaching the history of the Amsterdam library, it seems necessary to sketch the historical background and to pay some attention to the political and religious developments that form the backdrop. For a century the Netherlands or Low Countries were ruled by the rich and powerful dukes of Burgundy, vassals of the kings of France. In 1477, when Duke Charles the Bold had died and was succeeded by his daughter Duchess Mary of Burgundy, the king of France seized the opportunity and without any hesitation took possession of the French parts of the vastly extended territories of the Burgundian dukes. Mary kept the other parts of the duchy and had meanwhile married Maximilian I of Habsburg, by which the Low Countries came under the rule of the house of Habsburg. To cut a long story short, in the first half of the sixteenth century the Netherlands formed part of the vast European empire of Charles V who was born in 1500, son of Philip the Handsome and Joanna of Castile and Aragon. In 1506 – at the age of six – he inherited the Low Countries as part of the Habsburg dominions, including the Austrian lands. Already in 1515 – at the age of 14 – he received his legal adulthood and took up government by himself. One year later he inherited from his maternal grandfather Aragon and Castile, by which he actually was forced to accept the Spanish crown. In addition, in 1519 his paternal grandfather Maximilian had passed away and in 1521 Charles also became emperor of the Holy Roman or German empire.

Charles was born in Gent, in the Southern Netherlands, and he took a great interest in these regions. In those days Flanders and Brabant were tremendously prosperous and, between the many travels he had to make into many regions and corners of his empire, Charles felt at home in Brussels. Being an orthodox member of the Church of Rome he saw it as his task to protect the church from all sorts of heresy, for instance the – in his view – highly objectionable thoughts and deeds of the former monk in Germany, Martin Luther. In Spain he carried out a thorough religious purge, thus creating a solid foundation for a rather totalitarian kind of Catholicism. In the Netherlands the emperor did not succeed in repelling Luther's

---

3 My study on the Amsterdam municipal library until 1632 and books for learned citizens was recently published: Jos A. A. M. Biemans, *Boeken voor de geleerde burgerij. De stadsbibliotheek van Amsterdam tot 1632.* [Nijmegen, 2019].

influences, which caused him great disappointment. In 1555, at the age of 55, exhausted, he abdicated as emperor during an impressive ceremony in Brussels, leaning – as history tells – on the arm or shoulder of his pupil and friend, William of Orange. Charles was succeeded by his son Philip II, who was born and raised in Spain and who in 1556 also succeeded his father as king of Spain. Unlike his father he had no personal connexion to the Low Countries; he spoke only Spanish and Portuguese, no Dutch or German, and he did not understand at all the mentality of his Northern European subjects. And in his turn he too undertook the arduous task of protecting the Roman Catholic Church against both the expansive activities of the Islamic Ottoman empire and the growing influence of northern Protestantism.

As far as affects the Netherlands Philip's answers to the Protestant movements were merely military ones. Shortly after the iconoclastic fury that occurred in 1566, a war began, which would last for eighty years and would strongly influence the long-term future of the Low Countries. Ironically, the Prince of Orange just mentioned as a close friend of Charles V would become one of the most prominent leaders of the insurrection and the opponent to Charles's son and successor Philip II of Spain[4].

The Data

Let us return to Holland and examine the table in the Appendix. A detailed explanation of this table will be useful. The first column from the left contains the names of *cities*, first the cities in the County of Holland, then a few cities in other regions. The second and the third columns

---

4 *De Tachtigjarige Oorlog. Opstand en consolidatie in de Nederlanden (ca. 1560–1650)*, ed. Simon Groenveld, Huib L. Ph. Leeuwenberg, M. E. H. Nicolette Mout and Wilhelmus M. Zappey (Zutphen, 2008); Jan Juliaan Woltjer, *Tussen vrijheidsstrijd en burgeroorlog. Over de Nederlandse Opstand 1555–1580* ([n. p.], 1994).

inform us about the numbers of *monasteries* in these cities, first the "male" monasteries, then the "female" ones. Included are the houses of the brethren and the sisters of the so-called movement of the Modern Devotion. The next three columns give information about the *parish library* and any possible *chapter library* in these cities, preceded by an indication of the time of their foundation. A parish library primarily served the needs of the priests, the staff of the parish school, and the magistracy. A chapter library most of all was at the disposal of the canons, who both had to advise the bishop in theological, legal, political, and financial affairs, and who usually took care of the education of prospective priests and of talented sons from usually upper class families.

Then we arrive at the column with the most important information in this table: it shows the dates when the cities in the revolt against Spain officially took the side of the Prince of Orange, making the change from Roman Catholicism to Protestantism. Usually this *change*, reform, or Alteration also meant that church property was confiscated by the new municipal magistracy, both movable and immovable, or real estate, property. It is assumed that this reformation proved to be an excellent opportunity in many cities to start or re-start a public library. The last but one column of the table tells us the year in which a *city library* was more or less officially founded or made a restart under the new regime. The explanation for the number of question marks will be addressed later on. In the last column, the *location* of these city libraries has been indicated.

Gathering all the data for this scheme proves to be very helpful in order to make understandable what happened to the libraries of the former parishes and monasteries in many Dutch cities during the sixteenth century. If we observe the last column on the right, we can see that most of the "new" city libraries were housed in a confiscated church, in most cases the main church of the town. The two exceptions are Haarlem and Deventer (Latin *Daventria*), cases to be discussed later on.

Let us first examine the data in the "change" column, which underpins the chronological order of the whole table. This column does not list all the cities that took the side of the Prince of Orange. I have only incorporated cities that are relevant for the purpose of my research, which is to reconstruct what might have happened in Amsterdam with respect to the foundation of the city library after the Alteration. For in doing so we have to answer the question whether books from the monasteries of Amsterdam did or did not enter the new, that is "reformed", municipal library, and how. In this "change" column the chronological arrangement of the cities is based on the moment a particular city officially changed political and religious colours. The sequence reflects the footsteps or the sails of Protestant soldiers and seamen, marching or sailing on the Dutch cities to persuade their city governments to join the cause for freedom of power and belief.

Regarding the cities in the County of Holland we may take note that all but one of these towns took the side of the Prince in 1572. The only exception was Amsterdam. This city, or more precisely its government, chose still to remain Roman Catholic. It was not until 1578 that the *people* dismissed the catholic burgomasters and expelled the monks from their monasteries[5]. The emphasis on the word people needs some explanation. We have to realise that in fact only a minority of the citizens in Amsterdam and elsewhere longed for such a profound political and religious change. The majority of the population had remained Roman Catholic, which meant also staying loyal to the Spanish government. Militant Protestant minorities in the Dutch towns did their utmost to bring the insurrection inside the city walls. Their purpose was not only political freedom and the expulsion of Roman Catholicism with its many abuses, but – as we shall see – their striving was also caused by some social-economic motives.

Every fact and figure in this table represents a story. Let us go to Alkmaar. First of all we may notice that the number of "male" monasteries is just one, whereas there are five "female" institutions[6]. We may observe more or less the same with respect to the other cities in the survey. We could speak of a general feature of the institutional religious life in Dutch cities during the transition from late medieval to early modern times. Now one might ask, why incorporate into the table this information about the number of medieval monasteries existing in this era? The reason is that in studying the rise of city libraries we need at least to have some idea about the size or extent of the total quantity of institutional library-books in a particular city. (Private book collections must be left aside.) It goes without saying that libraries of male monasteries in general were larger than those in female houses. And we all know the many differences between the books in these two categories of monastic libraries: their size, the nature and the language of their texts, the purpose for which the collection was established, and hence the various ways in which the books were used. But in my judgement these figures give us an overall impression (out of focus and unclear of course) of the small or large quantities of books that – once a city had made the decision to change political and religious colours – so to speak became available for confiscation. Later on I will discuss whether or not monastic books really entered the city libraries.

Let us now examine the column concerning parish libraries. As is well known, the Fourth Lateran Council in 1215 had not only renewed the ordinance of the Council of 1179 on free schools for clerics in connexion with every cathedral but

5 Hendrik van Nierop, 'Van wonderjaar tot Alteratie 1566–1578', in *Geschiedenis van Amsterdam tot 1578. Een stad uit het niets*, ed. Marijke Carasso-Kok (Amsterdam, 2004), 479–81; Joke Spaans, 'Stad van vele geloven 1578–1795', in *Geschiedenis van Amsterdam 1578–1650. Centrum van de wereld*, ed. Willem Frijhoff and Maarten Prak (Amsterdam, 2004), 385–88.

6 *Geschiedenis van Alkmaar*, ed. Diederik Aten, Jan Drewes, Joop Kila and Harry de Raad (Zwolle, 2007).

had further determined that in other churches too, with sufficient resources, a suitable master should be appointed to teach grammar and other branches of study to the clerics of those and other churches. This concerned the schools of cathedral and collegiate chapters as well as schools of the official parishes. In general, every city formed one parish, with only one parish church, supporting only one school. This was a Latin school, or – using the appropriate term still common in England – a grammar school. Only boys could go to this kind of school, where teaching was done in Latin. Of course some cities had more than one church, that is apart from the churches and chapels of monasteries, but these other churches were subordinate to the main church; they were usually of minor importance and did not support a school or keep a book collection of any importance. Nevertheless there were more schools than the official parish school. In Amsterdam, for example, several teachers had their private French or Dutch schools, in which the children, besides reading, writing, and arithmetic, were also taught French and book-keeping for boys or sewing for girls[7].

In the larger cities, such as Utrecht, Leiden, and Amsterdam, special permission had been received from the secular and ecclesiastical authorities to divide their devout inhabitants between two or more parishes. In those cases there could – or even should – have been established two or more Latin parish schools and parish libraries. That is why we have an Old Church and a New Church in Amsterdam. The centre of ecclesiastical life in the Northern Netherlands was the large and important city of Utrecht. From way back in time here stood the seat of the archbishop, and in the fifteenth and sixteenth centuries this city counted

four parishes and no less than five chapters. Presumably there were four parish schools and four parish libraries, though only one of these libraries truly deserved the name – the library of the Buurkerk. On the other hand the chapter libraries in Utrecht must each have had quite an extensive collection of good books[8].

City, church, and school represented the corners of a triangle, not to say they formed a trinity, of course a profane one. At the Latin school the boys also received a thorough training in performing Gregorian chant, which accompanied the celebration of Mass and other ritual services in church. They sometimes also added musical lustre to festivities and parties organized by the city government. Having an excellent choir therefore contributed strongly to the fame of the city and its main church. The parish library was meant for study, first of all by the priests and those studying to become priests. Then there was the rector of the Latin school and possibly other school teachers. Thirdly, the collection of books could be consulted by the city magistrates, by well-educated citizens, by theologians (for instance those of the monasteries in or outside the town), by medical doctors, lawyers, and so on. In this respect the parish library of the main city church also served as a city library *avant la lettre*, just as the Latin parish school at the same time was the official school of the city.

Regarding the management of the library, we might say that the churchwardens together with the rector of the Latin school were in charge of it, whereas the sacristan or sacrist served as the day-to-day custodian; this also explains why in many churches sacristy and library were located close to one another. Both the city church council and the city government were supervising procedures

---

7 Annemarieke Willemsen, *Back to the schoolyard. The daily practice of medieval and renaissance education* (Turnhout, 2008); Erika Kuijpers, 'Lezen en schrijven. Onderzoek naar het alfabetiseringsniveau in zeventiende-eeuws Amsterdam', *Tijdschrift voor sociale geschiedenis* 23 (1997), 490–522.

8 Llewellyn C. J. J. Bogaers, *Aards, betrokken en zelfbewust. De verwevenheid van cultuur en religie in katholiek Utrecht, 1300–1600*, 2 vols (Utrecht, 2008); Ada van Deijk, Flip Delemarre and Pieter van Traa, *Middeleeuwse kerken in Utrecht* (Zutphen, 1988).

Figure 12.2. Interior of the library in the Great Church of St Nicholas in Edam.

from a distance. The same more or less applies to the chapter libraries, where the canons served in the choir of their church, participated in teaching at the Latin school, and from the very nature of their position were the most important users of the chapter library. Sometimes a chapter was connected to a parish church and then parish, chapter, and city library could be one and the same.

Many churches kept two collections of books: the necessary liturgical books on the one hand and the books for study and learning on the other. The first, rather small, collection was available in the choir of the church or in the sacristy nearby. The other collection of books was often much larger. It had to be kept in a separate room in the church or in an extension made to the building. In both situations a parish library was usually only accessible from within the church. For storage and at the same time for consulting the books, there existed a number of possibilities. Books could be put on *plutei*, as in the parish library of Edam (Fig. 12.2). This city, like Amsterdam and Hoorn, was one of the ports to what used to be called the

South Sea (*Zuider Zee*), now the IJsselmeer[9]. The other possibility was to store them in book cases, on open shelves above a lectern, as at Enkhuizen (Fig. 12.3)[10]. In both situations, the books could be chained. The same applies to chapter libraries, but – returning to our first table in the Appendix – we can see that apart from Leiden none of the cities in the County of Holland had a chapter with canons within its walls.

Turning again to the city of Alkmaar, the year shown for the foundation of its parish library is not a secure fact. We lack any information about this library; all we know is that there actually *was* a library. The date 1518–1520 is based on the fact that the building was completed in those years. The same goes for Edam, where the Church of

9 Ben Speet, *Edam, duizend jaar geschiedenis van een stad* (Zwolle, 2007).

10 Elly Faber, Alice de Vries, Jan Doedes and Adrie Brinkkemper, *De St Gommarus- of Westerkerk te Enkhuizen* (Enkhuizen, 2003); Robert P. Zijp, *De Librije van Enkhuizen* (Enkhuizen, 1991).

Figure 12.3. Interior of the library in the Western Church (of St Gomarus) in Enkhuizen.

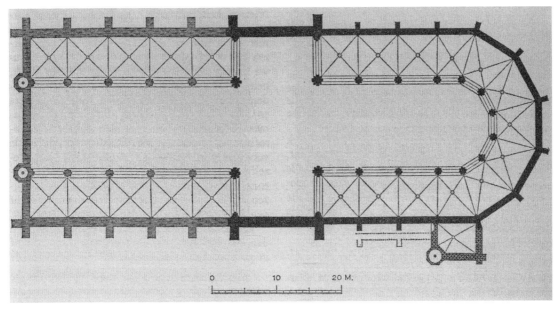

Figure 12.4. Reconstruction of the original ground plan for the New Church of Amsterdam c. 1418, showing the protrusion for the sacristy and the winding stairs to the library above it (from: R. Meischke, 'De Nieuwe Kerk te Amsterdam', in *Bulletin van de Koninklijke Nederlandsche Oudheidkundige Bond* 15 (1962), 319).

St Nicholas was (mostly?) completed in the year shown, around 1518. The indication "<1495 or 1496" with respect to the foundation of a library in the Old Church at Amsterdam refers to an archival document dating from that particular year (or new style 1496) which for the first time mentions that there existed a "liberaria antique ecclesie parochialis sancti Nicolay"[11]. This concerns the old library, possibly dating from the first quarter of the fifteenth century, for in the years 1512–1516 the Old Church received a new library whose construction provided also for a new south porch.

Regarding the library location inside the church, we must observe that the libraries at Alkmaar, Enkhuizen, Edam, and, as we have seen, in the Old Church at Amsterdam are all situated at the southern side of the choir of these churches. In Alkmaar we still find the space that originally served as the library in a specific room, created on the floor above the south entrance. In Haarlem, Edam as well as in Enkhuizen it is in a room above the sacristy, in both cases in an extension built next to the south porch. Ever since the Reformation the former Roman Catholic church of St Nicholas in Edam has not been referred to by its Protestant users by the name of its catholic patron but simply as the Great Church, a pattern seen in many Dutch cities. It is remarkable that the Latin school of Edam was on the same floor as the library inside the same extension to the church rather than in a separate building elsewhere in town[12].

Locating libraries at the south side of churches, above the southern entrance or on a floor above the sacristy, proves to be a traditional place for a parish library, that is to say at least in the

11 Herman Janse, *De Oude Kerk te Amsterdam.*
Bouwgeschiedenis en restauratie (Zeist, Zwolle [2004]),
46.

12 A comparable situation can be found in Amersfoort.

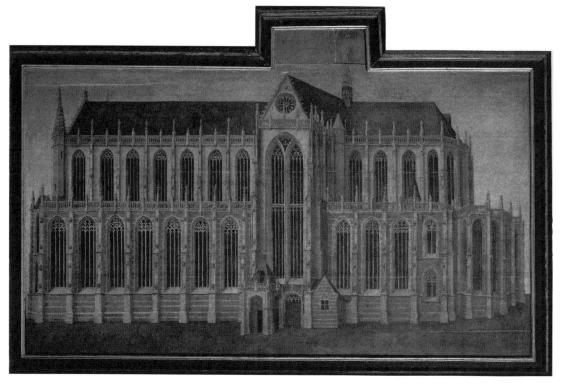

Figure 12.5. Painted design for the New Church of Amsterdam, *c.* 1480–1490 (Amsterdam, Nieuwe Kerk).

Netherlands[13]. Another example of this situation we find in Amsterdam. A reconstruction of the original ground plan for the New Church of Amsterdam, of which the first parts were built before 1418, shows only one extending part, with at its left corner a small tower with a spiral staircase made of stone (Fig. 12.4). This square protrusion was designed and meant to house the sacristy on the ground floor and the library above. That is exactly what we see on a painted architectural model for this church (Fig. 12.5)[14]. Starting from the right side of the south transept

we have the high windows of three added chapels and then we have the original extension, divided into two levels.

As always there are exceptions. The chapter library at Zutphen was originally housed on the floor above the chapter house, but in 1560–1564 a new building was added with a library at ground level (Fig. 12.6). The church council in Zutphen did their best to create a Roman Catholic book collection in order to help their citizens stay on the right, orthodox, path. But it did not work. In 1591 even Zutphen became Protestant[15].

13 I know of some Italian church libraries that are also at this side of the building, without doubt because it is the warmer side with the best light till sunset; but I have not made a study of this phenomenon.

14 Gérard Roosegaarde Bisschop, 'De geschilderde maquette in Nederland', *Nederlands kunsthistorisch jaarboek* (1956), 167–217, ill. 2.

15 Jos A. A. M. Biemans, 'Zutphen: de librije van de Walburgiskerk. Kennis en wetenschap in een middeleeuwse stad', in *Plaatsen van herinnering. Nederland van prehistorie tot Beeldenstorm*, ed. Wim Blockmans and Herman Pleij (Amsterdam, 2007), 362–73; *De Sint-Walburgiskerk in Zutphen. Momenten uit de geschiedenis van een middeleeuwse kerk*, ed. Michel Groothedde [et al.] (Zutphen, 1999).

Figure 12.6. Interior of the library in the Church of St Walburga in Zutphen.

Back to Alkmaar. In the "change" column we find *two* dates with respect to this town. The explanation is that Alkmaar had joined the revolt on 21 June 1572, but in 1573 the town was besieged and captured by Spanish troops. Shortly after June 1576 the town and its inhabitants were liberated by the Protestants. The same happened to the cities of Leiden[16], Haarlem[17], and above all

to Deventer[18]. Two examples. During the siege of Leiden people were suffering severely and by the end were starving to death, but they did not open the gates and did not let the Spanish come in. After being freed by Protestant troops in 1574, the city was gratefully honoured by the Prince of Orange for its outstanding perseverance when he gave his permission for the foundation of a Protestant university, the first one in the Low Countries. As already mentioned, the confiscation of ecclesiastical property usually took place shortly after the Alteration, but in some places there was a certain delay. In Haarlem some ecclesiastical property had been confiscated straight after its Alteration, but in 1573 the city was captured by Spanish troops and then of course

16 *Leiden. De geschiedenis van een Hollandse stad: Leiden tot 1574*, ed. Jan W. Marsilje (Leiden, 2002). *Leiden. De geschiedenis van een Hollandse stad*, ed. Rudi C. J. van Maanen, vol. 1; *Leiden. De geschiedenis van een Hollandse stad: 1574–1795*, ed. Simon Groenveld (Leiden, 2003). *Leiden. De geschiedenis van een Hollandse stad*, ed. Rudi C. J. van Maanen, vol. 2.

17 *Deugd boven geweld. Een geschiedenis van Haarlem, 1245–1995*, ed. Gineke F. van der Ree-Scholtens (Hilversum, 1995); Gerard Jaspers, *De zestiende eeuw in de Stadsbibliotheek Haarlem* (Amsterdam, Haarlem 1997).

18 Henk Slechte, *Geschiedenis van Deventer*, 2 vols (Zutphen, 2010).

any further confiscation was stopped. Happily liberated in 1577, William of Orange proclaimed that Haarlem's ecclesiastical property should not be taken. However, this decision was overruled by the general council of the States of Holland. Another round of confiscation then took place between 1578 and 1581 (in the Appendix table dates concerning a confiscation at a later time are placed between round brackets).

Apart from the few cities that had been under fire or were besieged, in most places the Alteration took place without bloodshed. In Amsterdam the Roman Catholic burgomasters and some prominent catholic members of the city council were assembled at the central place at the Dam, together with the Franciscan friars and some priests who would remain faithful to their catholic belief. They were forced to leave the city and were deported in small boats. Though many of these deportees feared for their lives, they were released on a dyke outside the city's territory, finding only their pride wounded, for not a hair on anyone's head was touched.

Finally, examining the data in the column "city library", the reader must have noticed that with respect to some cities a date is given from *before* the Alteration: Hoorn (1535), Zutphen (1564), and Deventer (1560). In these towns parish or chapter libraries functioned more or less as a city library already in those days. After the Alteration of the cities, their books changed ownership but remained on their lecterns or on their shelves; for the time being nothing really changed except control, though in the course of time some catholic books had to make room for Protestant ones.

Another thing one may have already noticed is that in only a few cases did the foundation of a new city library take place shortly after the Alteration or the confiscation of church property (books included). This is the case, for instance, in the city of Utrecht[19] or the city of Groningen[20]. In most cities however, it took a few years, sometimes one or two decades, before a city library was officially founded as distinct from a parish library that had also served as library for the city. In Leiden the foundation of a city library never happened because of the initiative to establish a university library. Something comparable happened in Franeker. The parish library in the Church of St Martin was transported in 1586 to the former monastery of the canons regular of the Holy Cross, which had been confiscated to house the Franeker university[21].

So far I have used the words confiscation of religious or ecclesiastical goods as a self-evident phrase. Of course, we understand that Roman Catholic churches were occupied and given to Protestants. And yes, we can imagine that the Protestants wanted to take formal leave of the priests, the monks, and the sisters or nuns, as well as of their saints and so on. And whereas Protestant books had been treated as heretical literature that had to be exterminated, now of course it was the turn of papist and monkish books to be put away.

But there is more to that. I have already mentioned that only a minority of the population in Dutch cities showed any eagerness for change. Apart from the militant Protestants, there were other people who worked hard for a revolution or at least for radical changes. Some of

---

19 'Een paradijs vol weelde'. Geschiedenis van de stad Utrecht, ed. Renger Evert de Bruin [et al.] (Utrecht, 2000).

20 Alex C. Klugkist and Sybren Sybrandy, *Van knekelhuis tot kloppend hart. Geschiedenis van de Bibliotheek van de Rijksuniversiteit Groningen – 1615 tot heden* (Groningen, 2012), 7–8; *Aan de ketting. Boek en bibliotheek in Groningen voor 1669*, ed. Jos M. M. Hermans and Gerda C. Huisman (Groningen, 1996), 10, 26–33; Jos M. M. Hermans, *Boeken in Groningen voor 1600. Studies rond de librije van de Sint-Maarten*. [PhD-Thesis Groningen 1987], 183–85.

21 Jacob van Sluis, *The Library of Franeker University in context, 1585–1843* (Leiden, 2020).

them – sometimes even forming part of the city governments – did have specific economic and social motives. In many old cities, for example, there was a need for more space to build houses, hospitals, and the like. Enlarging the city and making new fortifications would have cost a fortune, urban renewal seemed a better solution.

Some people, therefore, were looking enviously at the many premises and plots of land that were in the possession of different monasteries. In Utrecht for instance there were as many as eight male and thirteen female monasteries. The confiscation of their houses, chapels, and other buildings, together with the sometimes large grounds in which they stood, in this case meant that approximately one third of the city's surface area now became public property[22]. Some monastic buildings and chapels were reused for new functions, others were razed to the ground to make space for new houses. In Amsterdam, with a comparable number of religious institutions within its walls, we find the same phenomenon: complete neighbourhoods were changed, the infrastructure was renewed, and there was a new social and economic flowering. The confiscation of the Roman Catholic premises is still considered the biggest handover of real estate property in the history of the Northern Netherlands[23]. Destroying the images of saints, selling or melting down the precious gold and silver religious or liturgical objects, as well as confiscating the monastic and ecclesiastical libraries, helped to get rid of these things and to empty the confiscated buildings to refit them for new functions or simply to demolish them.

Confiscated Books

The next obvious question that comes to mind is what was actually done with the confiscated books, whether older manuscripts or newer printed books? Returning to the data in the table we may notice that apparently the books were collected and stored in places where there were people acquainted with books, in other words in the existing parish or city libraries. It seems that the official founding of a new, that is protestant, library was not immediately considered necessary. For – as I have already touched on – it is striking that the majority of the dates given in the column "city library" fall at the end of the century, in other words not shortly after the Alteration of the cities but quite some time later: at Edam in or before 1585, at Enkhuizen in or before 1588, at Alkmaar and Gouda in 1594, at Haarlem in 1596 and at Deventer in 1597; Rotterdam only followed in 1604. So far I do not have a single general explanation for this. For instance, I do not know whether there was a specific event or reason that stimulated the official foundation of city libraries just at that period, particularly in the final decade of the century. I am presenting the provisional results of a work in progress. The date "in or before 1588" for Enkhuizen is based on the earliest mention of a reformed city library in an archival document[24]. In all other cities the local magistrates decided to start or to renew a – naturally protestant – city

22 Antonius Hendricus Maria van Schaik, 'Een nieuwe heer en een andere leer', in *'Een paradijs vol weelde'. Geschiedenis van de stad Utrecht*, ed. Renger Evert de Bruin [et al.], (Utrecht, 2000), 225–28.

23 Boudewijn Bakker, 'De zichtbare stad 1578–1813', in *Geschiedenis van Amsterdam 1578–1650. Centrum van de wereld*, ed. Willem Frijhoff and Maarten Prak (Amsterdam, 2004), 17–31.

24 Jaap Keppel, 'Enkhuizen. De Enkhuizer stadsbibliotheek', in *Historische stadsbibliotheken in Nederland. Studies over openbare stadsbibliotheken in de Noordelijke Nederlanden vanaf circa 1560 tot 1800*, ed. Ad Leerintveld and Jan Bedaux (Zutphen, 2016), 37–44. Concerning the bookcases in this library, i.e the absence of influence from the English Stall-system, see now: Jos A. A. M. Biemans, 'De lectrijnkasten in de librije van Enkhuizen: een Enkhuizer type?', in Jan Bos, Marieke van Delft (et al., eds), *Een oud Boeck is oud Goud. Studies over bijzondere werken bij het afscheid van Ad Leerintveld als conservator moderne Handschriften van de Koninklijke Bibliotheek* (Den Haag, Amsterdam) 2017, 26–36.

library around the same time. In Gouda after the Alteration many difficulties had to be solved before a city library could be opened in the Great Church of St John. Gouda appears twice in the table, because the city library in the Great Church ought not to be considered just as a continuation of the former parish library in the same church[25]. In Alkmaar the previous library had deteriorated and a new start was necessary[26]. In Deventer things went slowly until the city magistracy and church council eventually took the initiative to solve the problems[27]. In Rotterdam the construction of a new space for the manuscripts and printed books caused the start of a new library[28]. An interesting case is presented by the city of Edam. The year 1585 marks an initiative by the new city council to relocate the municipal library next to the Latin school[29]. Without any doubt the situation regarding the former parish library had not changed much since 1572. The parish priest, Fr Meinert Jansz, had to leave most of his flock, with only a small number of his sheep following him. He was immediately succeeded by Pauwel Pietersz, his former colleague in the same parish, who from a Roman Catholic priest became the first clergyman in his now reformed church at Edam[30].

In conclusion, in those cities where we do not know whether or when a new city library was founded, we may safely assume that the confiscated books were also kept in the existing parish libraries. This is the reason why in the Appendix I indicated such cases, including Amsterdam, with a question mark.

Storing books in an existing library environment, however, is not the same as incorporating books into a library collection. In what way and to what extent did confiscated books enter the new, maybe even modern, city libraries? That question is rather difficult to answer. Let us examine first what happened in Utrecht: they confiscated the whole lot of book collections immediately after the Alteration in 1580. That does not imply that all of those libraries were handed in straightaway, but in 1584 the Utrecht City Library was officially founded. As we know, Utrecht before the Reformation counted eight male and thirteen female monasteries, and besides there were five chapters. In 1580 the chapter of St John had been stormed; part of its library was destroyed and the books that remained were sold. The other chapters successfully resisted confiscation. With respect to the eight male institutions unfortunately the monasteries of the Franciscans and the Dominicans had already been demolished in 1566 and their books burned. The brothers of the House of St Jerome succeeded in keeping back part of their library, and even out of the books that they had been forced to hand over, in no time at all some were simply taken back by brothers visiting the city library.

The history of the book collections from two much smaller male monasteries lies outside our range of vision. With respect to the four other male monasteries in Utrecht we luckily have a lot of information[31].

25 Jan Willem Klein, 'De oudste boeken van de Goudse stadslibrije', *De schatkamer*, 16 (2002), 1–17.

26 G. Ineke Plenckers-Keyser and C. Streefkerk, 'De librije van Alkmaar', in *Glans en glorie van de Grote Kerk. Het interieur van de Alkmaarse Sint Laurens*, ed. Leo Noordegraaf, Alkmaarse Historische Reeks 10 (Hilversum, 1996), 263–74.

27 Hans Peeters, *Romantiek en mythevorming rond een bibliotheek. 450 jaar Stads- en Athenaeumbibliotheek 1560–2010* (Deventer, 2010), 155–60.

28 Jacob Willem Charles Besemer, 'De bouwgeschiedenis van de Sint-Laurenskerk (1449 – tot 1940)', in *De Laurens in het midden. Uit de geschiedenis van de Grote Kerk van Rotterdam*, ed. Frederik Angenientus van Lieburg, Johan Cornelis Okkema and Heinrich Schmitz (Rotterdam, 1996), 67 and Johanna J. M. Meyers, 'Erasmiana in de Laurenslibrije van Rotterdam', in Ibidem, 346–47.

29 Speet, *Edam*, as note 9, 141.

30 Speet, *Edam*, as note 9, 110–13.

31 Daniël Grosheide, Adriaan D. A. Monna and Pierre N. G. Pesch, *Vier eeuwen Universiteitsbibliotheek Utrecht*. Vol. 1: *De eerste drie eeuwen* (Utrecht, 1986); *Handschriften en oude drukken van de Utrechtse Universiteitsbibliotheek. Catalogus bij de tentoonstelling in het Centraal Museum*

Table 12.1. Books from Utrecht monasteries in the City Library of 1584, now in the University Library of Utrecht

LIBRARIES	MANUSCRIPTS	PRINTED BOOKS
Carthusians	145	68
Regular Canons	144	70
House of St Jerome	3	27
Abbey of St Paul	37	66
Total	**329**	**231**

Table 12.2. Manuscripts and printed books from Amsterdam monasteries, still extant*

MONASTERIES	MANUSCRIPTS (volumes)	PRINTED BOOKS (volumes)	TOTAL
female monasteries: 17	MD: 74, of which 0 in Cat.-1612	MD: 10, of which 0 in Cat.-1612	84
	L: 15, of which 2 in Cat.-1612	L: 0	15
male monasteries: 5	MD: 6, of which 0 in Cat.-1612	MD: 0	6
	L: 3, of which 1 in Cat.-1612	L: 24, of which 12 in Cat.-1612	27
total	**98, of which 3 in Cat.-1612**	**34, of which 12 in Cat.-1612**	**132**

* included are two manuscripts with texts in both Middle Dutch and Latin, as well as one manuscript in medieval Low German.

What may we conclude from the figures in this table with respect to the confiscated books in Utrecht? First of all, in 1584 apparently only books from male monasteries entered the city library, in other words only Latin books were chosen. Any clue or trace regarding the vernacular books or any possible Latin books from female monasteries is lacking. In addition we may conclude that the collections of the house of St Jerome (founded in 1475) and the venerable abbey of St Paul (founded in 1050) were probably a bit more up to date than the other two monastic libraries, judging from the confiscated books and looking at the numbers of printed books compared to the collection of manuscripts. The books from the library of St Paul's abbey were the most modern one, handing over almost the same number of printed books as the libraries of the Carthusians (founded in 1392) and Regular canons (founded 1292) but with far fewer manuscripts.

Turning back to Amsterdam we may bring together the relevant information about books in Middle Dutch (MD) and Latin (L) from Amsterdam monasteries in the table above[32]. In addition, one finds the number of books that can be identified in the first printed catalogue of the Amsterdam City Library, published in 1612[33].

First of all, the table shows that the information about books in the vernacular quantitatively exceeds the data concerning the Latin books. Secondly and with respect to this corpus of Amsterdam books, the provenance of manuscripts is better known than that of the printed books. Thirdly, and just like we saw in Utrecht, none of the handwritten and printed books with texts in Middle Dutch entered the collection of the city library. Only three manuscripts and twelve volumes with printed books, all with texts in Latin, can be identified in the catalogue of 1612. The question here is at what precise date these books were incorporated into the city library?

te Utrecht ter gelegenheid van het 400-jarig bestaan van de bibliotheek der Rijksuniversiteit, 1584–1984, ed. Koert van der Horst, Loes C. Kuiper-Brussen en Pierre N. G. Pesch (Utrecht, 1984).

32 I used Karl Stooker and Theo Verbeij, *Collecties op orde. Middelnederlandse handschriften uit kloosters en semi-religieuze gemeenschappen in de Nederlanden*. Vol. I: *Studie*, vol. II: *Repertorium*, Miscellanea Neerlandica XV–XVI (Leuven, 1997) and – after having corrected and augmented the data – *Amsterdamse kloosters in de Middeleeuwen*, ed. Marian Schilder (Amsterdam, 1997), 183–89.

33 *Catalogus Bibliothecæ Amstelredamensis* (Lugduni Batavorum [Leiden], 1612).

Figure 12.7. The seven volumes of the Amsterdam Choir bible, each measuring approximately 505 × 345–55 mm (Allard Pierson, University of Amsterdam, Special Collections, MS I A 1–7).

Immediately or shortly after the Alteration of 1578 or later on, but before 1612?

The three manuscripts are a large and beautifully decorated Latin Bible in seven volumes (Fig. 12.7), undoubtedly from the monastery of the Carthusians, and two much smaller volumes each containing some books of the Bible, both of them with marks to show that they had belonged to the monastery of St Cecile, inhabited by sisters of the Third Order of St Francis. Of the twelve volumes, each comprising several printed books in Latin, one had belonged to the library of the Franciscan friars, four had been the property – or at least in the possession or use – of an individual Franciscan, named Petrus Wantenus. The seven

remaining volumes came from the library of the monastery of St Paul, inhabited by brothers of the Third Order of St Francis.

I am inclined to say that the books from the seventeen female monasteries in Amsterdam proved to be irrelevant or at least may be considered irrelevant for a new city library. Although buildings and land were confiscated after the Alteration and although a number of monasteries received new functions, now serving as a hospital, an orphanage, a new Latin School, a storehouse, a guesthouse for official visitors of the city and so on, the sisters were usually allowed to stay in – a part of – their buildings. Only in cases where their monastery had to make space, for instance, in order to build many family houses, they had to find new premises. So, most likely the nuns had kept their personal prayer books, their books containing devotional tracts as well as texts for meditation. Besides, for the greater part the texts in these books were in Middle Dutch, forming a category without any value for a city library. It is almost certain that in Amsterdam – just as in Utrecht – books from female monasteries were not confiscated at all. The two Latin Bible manuscripts from the monastery of St Cecile may have been donated or sold to the city library later on as antiquities rather than as books for use.

With respect to the five male monasteries in Amsterdam four of them had already been plundered: their books were simply not there to be confiscated … The library of the Carthusians was demolished already in 1566. The monastery of the Franciscan friars was looted twice. And so on. Most of their books – and those from the other male monasteries – left behind when the monks or friars were expelled, had been stolen by 1578, had been sold, and were never to be seen again. Why, when, or how the four volumes bearing the name or device of Br Petrus Wantenus became part of the city library we do not know. The property of the monastery of St Paul, including their books, was all sold to the new trustees of one of the poorhouses. Later on the board of this poorhouse had disposed of the books. Obviously a few printed books from it were bought for the city library.

But, despite of the demolition in 1566, how did the seven volume Bible from the Carthusians, originally each measuring *c.* 500 × 370 mm, come – undamaged – into the possession of the city library? In 1566, before the iconoclastic furies broke out, the city government had instructed the monasteries to transport their precious religious objects such as silver or golden statues, chalices, and monstrances to safer places elsewhere. The Carthusians must have listened to this advice: their splendid altarpiece, a painted panel by the

famous Amsterdam painter Jacob van Oostsanen, can still be admired in the Museo di Capodimonte at Naples. Presumably this set of large and richly decorated books had also been safeguarded in time, and one way or another it was acquired later on by the city library. In short, the widespread story that tells how the city library of Amsterdam started with the confiscated books from its monasteries turns out to be a myth.

What remains are the books of the two parish libraries. The books of the Old Church must have been transferred to the New Church, but we do not know their number, for we cannot identify these copies. One thing is certain: within a few days following the Alteration, the Old Church was given to the Protestants, and reformed services began to take place immediately[34]. The books of the parish library at the New Church were allowed to stay on their shelves, waiting for inspection, deselection, and the consequences of further decisions. My conclusion is that the initial collection of the city library of Amsterdam consisted of the books from the two previous parish libraries, which before the Alteration had already functioned more or less as a library respectively for the old and the new parts of town.

The Foundation of the City Library

Again I return to the remarkable phenomenon that for many of the libraries mentioned in the Appendix table we have no information at all about what happened between the moment of confiscation and the foundation of a new city library. In most cities, I think, for a while *nothing* happened. Only in Utrecht and Groningen was a new city library founded immediately or shortly after the Alteration, at Utrecht in 1584 and at Groningen in 1594. In other cities, including Amsterdam, books were confiscated or brought

---

34 Spaans, as note 5, 385–414.

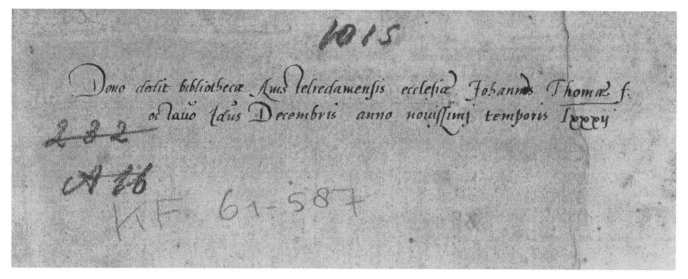

Figure 12.8. Note of donation made in 1582 to the library of Amsterdam of the *Novum Testamentum* in Greek, edited and annotated by Theodorus Beza, Genève, Henry Estienne, 1582 (Allard Pierson, University of Amsterdam, Special Collections, KF 61–587).

together, but any further steps apparently did not have a high priority. A new era had begun, new municipal and national infrastructures – such as protestant organizations and institutions – were necessary. But the confiscated or otherwise collected books, despite their being no longer chained to the furniture, did not run away. Actually, we may observe a similar attitude at the University of Leiden during its earliest period. After the foundation Prince William of Orange in 1575 presented the first books to start the university library, namely the precious *Biblia Regia* or *Polyglot Bible* in eight volumes, printed and published between 1569 and 1572 by the famous house of Plantin at Antwerp. But we have to wait until 1587 before an appropriate space was found to set up a physical setting for the library and start collecting more books[35].

I presume that in Amsterdam, just as in some other cities in the Northern Netherlands, only after a while – may be after a couple of years? and

in several steps? – a start was made with sorting out the confiscated or collected books. Books considered useful in the new circumstances were selected for the library, whereas others were deselected and sold. This assumption has implications for the question when precisely the city library was founded. The former catholic library in the New Church may have been enriched with many books or just a few from the parish library in the Old Church, it may have changed gradually into a protestant book collection. Apparently, however, these changes did not constitute sufficient reason for an official inauguration of the renewed city library, not even for a certificate of its rebirth. This may seem plausible, but more important is the question whether we have any evidence or at least some reasonable arguments for these assumptions? Asking the question requires an answer.

In May 1580 the Revd Martin Lydius, a protestant clergyman, and Laurens Jacobsz Reael, corn merchant and churchwarden, were charged by the protestant church council of Amsterdam with the task of visiting the well-known bookshop of Cornelis Claesz. Obviously he had bought several books from the book collection in the

35 Christiane Berkvens-Stevelinck, *Magna Commoditas. Leiden University's Great Asset. 425 Years Library Collections and Services* (Leiden, 2012), 13–17.

New Church. It turned out however, that some of these had been sold by mistake (or had wrongfully been deselected by Cornelis Claesz?). Lydius and Reael had to negotiate about exchanging these books for other ones that surely could be spared from the library. We do not know what resulted from their efforts, but we may suppose that in 1580 the new church council was in charge of the library in the New Church[36].

In 1582 a new edition of the *New Testament* in Greek with the annotations by Theodore de Bèze or Beza was published. Before the year was over one copy of this bulky edition was donated to the Amsterdam Library in the New Church. It contains the following note of donation: "Dono dedit bibliothecae Amstelredamensis ecclesiae Johannes Thomae filius octavo Idus Decembris anno novissimi temporis lxxxij" (Fig. 12.8)[37]. The most remarkable word of this note is *ecclesiae* and not *oppidi* or *civitatis*. In other words the book was presented to what apparently was still called the library of the church, not that of the city.

In addition, some fourteen years later, there was another remarkable acquisition. In 1596 an important source for the study and practice of the law was purchased from an Amsterdam bookseller, the famous *Oceanus Juris*, printed and published in Venice in 1584–1586[38]. This ocean of legal knowledge, consisting of numerous studies by a great number of authors, collected in twenty-eight volumes, supplied the Amsterdam magistracy, its clergy, lawyers, merchants, and many other learned men, with the most recent and complete information about international matters of both civil and canon law. The Amsterdam copy requires a space of about three metres on the shelves. The cost of this invaluable reference work was met by the two Protestant communities together, that is by the Old Church and the New Church. Happily or wisely, the city church council agreed to place the twenty-eight volumes in the library room of the New Church[39]. On the front cover we may read in gold, "Ex dono Templi Veteris et Novi", a gift by the Old and the New Church (Fig. 12.9). A gift to their own library, that is the library of the Protestant community in Amsterdam? Or the library of the city? Just as before the Alteration, there was no difference between the two.

It goes without saying that the Amsterdam library was also visited by scholars from elsewhere. One of them was a Leiden professor of history, Paulus Merula (1558–1607). In 1598 he brought out the *editio princeps* of the paraphrase of *Cantica Canticorum* or the Song of Songs by Willeram (d. 1085), abbot of Ebersberg[40]. The edition has a Latin dedication to the Senate and the people of Amsterdam, in which Merula praises both because of their love for scholarship, which becomes visible, among other things, in the "Public Library" of the city. He was impressed by the presence of the *Oceanus Juris* and by the availability of excellent books in all fields of learning. These laudatory words came from an unimpeachable authority, for Merula was himself librarian of Leiden University Library[41]. It is

36 Combertus Pieter Burger, 'Een oud bericht over de "Liberie" in de Nieuwe Kerk te Amsterdam', *Het Boek*, 15 (1926), 148.

37 UBA, Bijzondere Collecties, KF 61–587; see Kees Gnirrep and Garrelt Verhoeven, 'Hier spreken de doden. De Oudheid in de Stedelijke Bibliotheek', in *Boek en Oudheid*, ed. René van Beek, Geralda Jurriaans-Helle and Frits van der Meij (Amsterdam, 2008), 106; de la Fontaine Verwey, as note 2, 202.

38 UBA, Bijzondere Collecties, KF 61–1653 to 1669, KF 61–5233 to 5243.

39 Ernest Wilhelm Moes and Combertus Pieter Burger, *De Amsterdamsche boekdrukkers en uitgevers in de zestiende eeuw*, 4 vols (Amsterdam, 1900–1915), vol. 4, 246; Rogge, as note 2, 4, note 3.

40 Willerami Abbatis in Canticum Canticorum Paraphrasis gemina: Prior rhythmis Latinis, altera veteri lingua Francica [...] Edente Paullo G. F. P. N. Merula. Lugduni Batavorum, 1598.

41 "Amorem autem, qui Vobis in Studia singularis, testatur etiam, inter alia, publica illa, quam ante annos aliquot instituistis, Bibliotheca: eam optimis

Figure 12.9. Note of donation on the front cover of the *Oceanus Juris*, volume 1 (Allard Pierson, University of Amsterdam, Special Collections, KF 61–1653).

striking that Merula addressed himself to the city council and the people of Amsterdam even as he refers to the Public Library. Again, the civic library and the church library were one and the same, a scholarly instrument in the hands of city and church[42].

Conclusion

My conclusion is that, shortly after the Alteration, the two Roman Catholic parish libraries of Amsterdam were transformed gradually into one Protestant church library – housed in the New Church – and that this library still served as the library for the well-educated citizens. In this view, at Amsterdam, just as elsewhere in the Northern Netherlands, a new city library was founded, tacitly, without any formal decree by the new magistracy. Most likely the only decision that was made concerned the transfer of books from the Old Church to the New Church in anticipation of things to come in the fullness of time. In this case and mostly in the other ones, at the very most we may consider the Alteration in 1578 as a new starting point of the already existing church library that in due course would become a more or less "protestant" library that continued to serve the citizens as their city library of Amsterdam.

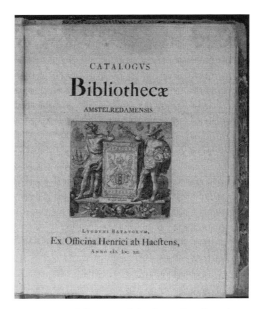

Figure 12.10. Title page of the first printed catalogue of the Amsterdam City Library in the New Church, made in Leiden anno 1612 (Allard Pierson, University of Amsterdam, Special Collections, O 06–1773).

---

et selectissimis Scriptoribus nuper ita stipatam vidi, ut cum instructissimis jure committi possit."; see – more extensively – Combertus Pieter Burger in Maurits Benjamin Mendes da Costa, *De handschriften der Stedelijke Bibliotheek met de latere aanwinsten. Vooraf enige mededeelingen over de geschiedenis van de bibliotheek en hare handschriftenverzameling, door den Bibliothecaris Dr C. P. Burger Jr.* (Amsterdam, 1902). Bibliotheek der Universiteit van Amsterdam, Catalogus der Handschriften II (1902), VII.

42 Recently, a number of studies on several city libraries in the Low Countries such as Amsterdam, Haarlem, Alkmaar, Enkhuizen, Edam, Gouda, Rotterdam, Utrecht, Deventer, Zutphen, etc. was published: *Historische stadsbibliotheken in Nederland*, as note 24.

Appendix: Parish Libraries and City Libraries before and after the Political and Religious Changes in the Netherlands during the Sixteenth century

(the order of appearance is chronological, according to column 7 which starts with the word "change")

city	monas-teries male	monas-teries female	foundation first parish or chapter library	parish library	chapter library	change (usually with confiscation of catholic property)	city library	location (actual name, "Great Church" = "Reformed" name)
County of Holland								
Hoorn	1	8	< 1482	+	-	20–5–1572	1535	Great Church, Ch. of St Cyriacus
Enkhuizen	1	3	?	+	-	21–5–1572	< 1588	Western Church, Ch. of St Gomarus
Alkmaar	1	5	1518–20	+	-	21–6–1572; 8–10–1573	1594	Great Church of St Lawrence
Gouda	4	7	< 1487	+	-	21–6–1572; (1572–73)	-	Great Church of St John the Baptist
Gouda							1594	Great Church of St John the Baptist
Leiden	1	c. 10	< 1462	+	+	23–6–1572; 3–10–1574	[1587	University Library]
Haarlem	2	8	< 1428	+	-	24–6–1572; 24–3–1577	?	Great Church of St Bavo
Haarlem						(1573–81)	1596	previous Dominican monastery
Edam	-	1	c. 1518	+	-	26–6–1572	< 1585	Great Church of St Nicholas
Rotterdam	2	4	?	+	-	25–7–1572	1604	Great Church of St Lawrence
Delft	2	9	< 1434	+	-	26–7–1572	?	Old Church
Amsterdam	5	17	< 1495/96	+	-	26–5–1578	-	Old Church
Amsterdam			c. 1418	+	-		1578?	New Church
Other regions								
Utrecht	8	13	< 1415	2 or >	5	18–6–1580 (1581–84)	1584	Church of St John the Baptist
Franeker	1	-	< 1512	+	-	31–3–1580	[1585	University Library]
Zutphen	5	6	< 1492	+	+	30–5–1591	1564	Church of St Walburga
Deventer	-	-	> 1334	-	+		1375?	Great Church, Ch. of St Lebuinus
Deventer				private collection bought by the city			1560	presbytery of † Phoconius
Deventer	1	5	c. 1380	in Houses of the Modern Devotion			1569	Master Florens' House
Deventer	1	1	-	-	-	1566–91 (1591–97)	1597	Master Florens' House
Groningen	4	5	< 1470	+	+	22–7–1594	1594	Great Church of St Martin

Bibliography

Archival Sources

Amsterdam, University Library (UBA), Bijzondere Collecties, KF 61–587; 61–1653 to 1669, 61–5233 to 5243.

Secondary Works

Aan de ketting. Boek en bibliotheek in Groningen voor 1669, ed. Jos M. M. Hermans and Gerda C. Huisman (Groningen, 1996).

Amsterdamse kloosters in de Middeleeuwen, ed. Marian Schilder (Amsterdam, 1997).

Boudewijn Bakker, 'De zichtbare stad 1578–1813', in *Geschiedenis van Amsterdam 1578–1650. Centrum van de wereld*, ed. Willem Frijhoff and Maarten Prak (Amsterdam, 2004), 17–31.

Christiane Berkvens-Stevelinck, *Magna Commoditas. Leiden University's Great Asset. 425 Years Library Collections and Services* (Leiden, 2012).

Jacob Willem Charles Besemer, 'De bouwgeschiedenis van de Sint-Laurenskerk (1449 – tot 1940)', in *De Laurens in het midden. Uit de geschiedenis van de Grote Kerk van Rotterdam*, ed. Frederik Angenientus van Lieburg, Johan Cornelis Okkema and Heinrich Schmitz (Rotterdam, 1996), 11–103.

Jos A. A. M. Biemans, 'Zutphen: de librije van de Walburgiskerk. Kennis en wetenschap in een middeleeuwse stad', in *Plaatsen van herinnering. Nederland van prehistorie tot Beeldenstorm*, ed. Wim Blockmans and Herman Pleij (Amsterdam, 2007), 362–73.

Jos A. A. M. Biemans, De lectrijnkasten in de librije van Enkhuizen: een Enkhuizer type?, in Jan Bos, Marieke van Delft (et al., eds), *Een oud Boeck is oud Goud. Studies over bijzondere werken bij het afscheid van Ad Leerintveld als conservator moderne Handschriften van de Koninklijke Bibliotheek* (Den Haag, Amsterdam, 2017), 26–36.

Jos A. A. M. Biemans, *Boeken voor de geleerde burgerij. De stadsbibliotheek van Amsterdam tot 1632* [Nijmegen, 2019].

Llewellyn C. J. J. Bogaers, *Aards, betrokken en zelfbewust. De verwevenheid van cultuur en religie in katholiek Utrecht, 1300–1600*, 2 vols (Utrecht, 2008).

[Combertus Pieter Burger Jr.], 'Geschiedenis der Bibliotheek', in *Gids voor de Bibliotheek der Universiteit van Amsterdam* (Amsterdam, 1919), V–XVI.

Combertus Pieter Burger, 'Een oud bericht over de "Liberie" in de Nieuwe Kerk te Amsterdam', *Het Boek*, 15 (1926), 148–149.

Catalogus Bibliothecæ Amstelredamensis (Lugduni Batavorum [Leiden], 1612).

Herman de la Fontaine Verwey, 'The City Library of Amsterdam in the Nieuwe Kerk 1578–1632', *Quærendo* 14 (1984), 163–206.

De Sint-Walburgiskerk in Zutphen. Momenten uit de geschiedenis van een middeleeuwse kerk, ed. Michel Groothedde [et al.] (Zutphen, 1999).

De Tachtigjarige Oorlog. Opstand en consolidatie in de Nederlanden (ca. 1560–1650), ed. Simon Groenveld, Huib L. Ph. Leeuwenberg, M. E. H. Nicoletta Mout and Wilhelmus M. Zappey (Zutphen, 2008).

Deugd boven geweld. Een geschiedenis van Haarlem, 1245–1995, ed. Gineke F. van der Ree-Scholtens (Hilversum, 1995).

'*Een paradijs vol weelde'. Geschiedenis van de stad Utrecht*, ed. Renger Evert de Bruin [et al.] (Utrecht, 2000).

Elly Faber, Alice de Vries, Jan Doedes and Adrie Brinkkemper, *De St Gommarus- of Westerkerk te Enkhuizen* (Enkhuizen, 2003).

Geschiedenis van Alkmaar, ed. Diederik Aten, Jan Drewes, Joop Kila and Harry de Raad (Zwolle, 2007).

Kees Gnirrep and Garrelt Verhoeven, 'Hier spreken de doden. De Oudheid in de Stedelijke Bibliotheek', in *Boek en Oudheid*, ed. René van Beek, Geralda Jurriaans-Helle and Frits van der Meij (Amsterdam, 2008), 98–119.

Daniël Grosheide, Adriaan D. A. Monna and Pierre N. G. Pesch, *Vier eeuwen Universiteitsbibliotheek Utrecht*. Vol. 1: *De eerste drie eeuwen* (Utrecht, 1986).

Handschriften en oude drukken van de Utrechtse Universiteitsbibliotheek. Catalogus bij de tentoonstelling in het Centraal Museum te Utrecht ter gelegenheid van het 400-jarig bestaan van de bibliotheek der Rijksuniversiteit, 1584–1984, ed. Koert van der Horst, Loes C. Kuiper-Brussen and Pierre N. G. Pesch (Utrecht, 1984).

Jos M. M. Hermans, *Boeken in Groningen voor 1600. Studies rond de librije van de Sint-Maarten* [PhD-Thesis Groningen 1987].

Jaap Keppel, 'Enkhuizen. De Enkhuizer stadsbibliotheek', in *Historische stadsbibliotheken in Nederland. Studies over openbare stadsbibliotheken in de Noordelijke Nederlanden vanaf circa 1560 tot 1800*, ed. Ad Leerintveld and Jan Bedaux (Zutphen, 2016), 37–44.

Jan Willem Klein, 'De oudste boeken van de Goudse stadslibrije', *De schatkamer*, 16 (2002), 1–17.

Alex C. Klugkist and Sybren Sybrandy, *Van knekelhuis tot kloppend hart. Geschiedenis van de Bibliotheek van de Rijksuniversiteit Groningen – 1615 tot heden* (Groningen, 2012).

Erika Kuijpers, 'Lezen en schrijven. Onderzoek naar het alfabetiseringsniveau in zeventiende-eeuws Amsterdam', *Tijdschrift voor sociale geschiedenis* 23 (1997), 490–522.

Herman Janse, *De Oude Kerk te Amsterdam. Bouwgeschiedenis en restauratie* (Zeist, Zwolle [2004]).

Gerard Jaspers, *De zestiende eeuw in de Stadsbibliotheek Haarlem* (Amsterdam, Haarlem 1997).

Leiden. De geschiedenis van een Hollandse stad, ed. Rudi C. J. van Maanen et al., 4 vols (Leiden 2002–2004).

Maurits Benjamin Mendes da Costa, *De handschriften der Stedelijke Bibliotheek met de latere aanwinsten. Vooraf enige mededeelingen over de geschiedenis van de bibliotheek en hare handschriftenverzameling, door den Bibliothecaris Dr C. P. Burger Jr.* (Amsterdam, 1902). Bibliotheek der Universiteit van Amsterdam, Catalogus der Handschriften II.

Johanna J. M. Meyers, 'Erasmiana in de Laurenslibrije van Rotterdam', in *De Laurens in het midden. Uit de geschiedenis van de Grote Kerk van Rotterdam*, ed. Frederik Angenientus van Lieburg, Johan Cornelis Okkema and Heinrich Schmitz (Rotterdam, 1996), 345–352.

Ernest Wilhelm Moes and Combertus Pieter Burger, *De Amsterdamsche boekdrukkers en uitgevers in de zestiende eeuw*, 4 vols (Amsterdam, 1900–1915).

Hans Peeters, *Romantiek en mythevorming rond een bibliotheek. 450 jaar Stads- en Athenaeumbibliotheek 1560–2010* (Deventer, 2010).

G. Ineke Plenckers-Keyser and C. Streefkerk, 'De librije van Alkmaar', in *Glans en glorie van de Grote Kerk. Het interieur van de Alkmaarse Sint Laurens*, ed. Leo Noordegraaf, Alkmaarse Historische Reeks 10 (Hilversum, 1996), 263–74.

Hendrik Cornelis Rogge, *Geschiedenis der Stedelijke Boekerij van Amsterdam* (Amsterdam, 1882).

Gérard Roosegaarde Bisschop, 'De geschilderde maquette Nederland', *Nederlands kunsthistorisch jaarboek* (1956), 167–217.

Henk Slechte, *Geschiedenis van Deventer*, 2 vols (Zutphen, 2010).

Jacob van Sluis, *The Library of Franeker University in context, 1585–1843* (Leiden, 2020).

Joke Spaans, 'Stad van vele geloven 1578–1795', in *Geschiedenis van Amsterdam 1578–1650. Centrum van de wereld*, ed. Willem Frijhoff and Maarten Prak (Amsterdam, 2004), 385–414.

Ben Speet, *Edam, duizend jaar geschiedenis van een stad* (Zwolle, 2007).

Karl Stooker and Theo Verbeij, *Collecties op orde. Middelnederlandse handschriften uit kloosters en semi-religieuze gemeenschappen in de Nederlanden*. Vol. I: *Studie*, vol. II: *Repertorium*, Miscellanea Neerlandica XV–XVI (Leuven, 1997).

Ada van Deijk, Flip Delemarre and Pieter van Traa, *Middeleeuwse kerken in Utrecht* (Zutphen, 1988).

Hendrik van Nierop, 'Van wonderjaar tot Alteratie 1566–1578', in *Geschiedenis van Amsterdam tot 1578. Een stad uit het niets*, ed. Marijke Carasso-Kok (Amsterdam, 2004), 479–81.

Antonius Hendricus Maria van Schaik, 'Een nieuwe heer en een andere leer', in *'Een paradijs vol weelde'. Geschiedenis van de stad Utrecht*, ed. Renger Evert de Bruin [et al.], (Utrecht, 2000), 225–28.

Annemarieke Willemsen, *Back to the schoolyard. The daily practice of medieval and renaissance education* (Turnhout, 2008).

Willerami Abbatis in Canticum Canticorum Paraphrasis gemina: Prior rhythmis Latinis, altera veteri lingua Francica [...] Edente Paullo G.F.P.N. Merula. Lugduni Batavorum, 1598.

Jan Juliaan Woltjer, *Tussen vrijheidsstrijd en burgeroorlog. Over de Nederlandse Opstand 1555–1580* Amsterdam, 1994).

Robert P. Zijp, *De Librije van Enkhuizen* (Enkhuizen, 1991).

EMMANUELLE CHAPRON

Bibliothèques et suppressions ecclésiastiques en Toscane de Pierre-Léopold à Napoléon

Le grand-duché de Toscane est un observatoire doublement intéressant de ce qui se joue, en matière de bibliothèques, dans les suppressions ecclésiastiques. Comme d'autres États italiens, il connaît une succession de trois vagues de suppressions en moins d'un demi-siècle, ce qui permet d'aborder de manière comparée les modalités de leur mise en œuvre et l'évolution des réflexions sur le sort à donner aux livres. Après l'expulsion des jésuites, qui vide en 1773 les neuf couvents toscans, les suppressions ordonnées par le grand-duc Pierre-Léopold (1765–1790) touchent dans les années 1780 près de la moitié des établissements. Vingt ans plus tard, les deux phases des suppressions napoléoniennes, en 1808 puis en 1810, aboutissent à la fermeture des 460 couvents et monastères de Toscane. Bien avant les suppressions du Royaume d'Italie, dans les années 1860, ce demi-siècle constitue donc un laboratoire de la sécularisation des bibliothèques et des œuvres d'art[1].

En second lieu, le grand-duché est, avec les États pontificaux, le seul État de la péninsule où

---

[1] La bibliographie concerne surtout le sort des bâtiments et des œuvres d'art: Roberta Lapucci, 'Fonti d'archivio per la storia delle arti durante la soppressione napoleonica a Firenze', *Rivista d'arte*, série 4, 39 (1987), 475–93. Osanna Fantozzi Micali et Piero Roselli, *Le soppressioni dei conventi a Firenze. Riuso e trasformazioni dal sec. XVIII in poi* (Florence, 2000). Fabio Bisogni, 'Da Pietro Leopoldo a Napoleone: tutela e dispersione di beni culturali a Siena e in Toscana', in *Ideologie e patrimonio storico-culturale nell'età rivoluzionaria e napoleonica: a proposito del trattato di Tolentino* (Rome, 2000), 563–605. Sur les bibliothèques, Marielisa Rossi, 'Sulle tracce delle biblioteche: i cataloghi e gli inventari (1808–1819) della soppressione e del ripristino dei conventi in Toscana. Parte prima[-seconda]', *Culture del testo*, IV, 12 (1998), 85–123 et *Culture del testo e del documento*, I, 2 (2000), 109–45. Je me permets de renvoyer aussi à Emmanuelle Chapron, 'Il patrimonio ricomposto. Biblioteche e soppressioni ecclesiastiche in Toscana da Pietro Leopoldo a Napoleone', *Archivio storico italiano*, 2 (2009), 299–345.

Emmanuelle Chapron • Professeur d'histoire moderne à Aix-Marseille Université, AMU, CNRS, UMR 7303 Telemme et directrice d'études cumulante à l'École pratique des hautes études (chaire d'Histoire et civilisation du livre). emmanuelle.chapron@univ-amu.fr

How the Secularization of Religious Houses Transformed the Libraries of Europe, 16th–19th Centuries, ed. by Cristina Dondi, Dorit Raines, and † Richard Sharpe, BIB, 63 (Turnhout, 2022), pp. 273–286.
BREPOLS ❧ PUBLISHERS   DOI 10.1484/M.BIB-EB.5.128488

se trouve mise en place dès le XVIIIe siècle une législation destinée à protéger, non seulement les œuvres d'art et les antiquités, mais également les manuscrits et les ouvrages rares, voire des bibliothèques entières en tant qu'elles participent au "decoro pubblico". Le pivot de cette législation est l'édit du 26 décembre 1754, qui interdit de faire sortir de l'État les manuscrits, antiquités, œuvres d'art "et autres œuvres et choses rares" sans la permission du Conseil de Régence. L'édit est utilisé pour empêcher l'exportation de la bibliothèque de la famille Gaddi (1755), la dispersion des raretés de la bibliothèque de l'érudit Anton Maria Biscioni (1756) et l'expatriation des manuscrits de la bibliothèque des franciscains de Montepulciano (1757)[2]. Le pouvoir fait alors appel à l'expertise d'érudits ou à celle des bibliothécaires des deux grandes bibliothèques publiques de Florence, la Laurentienne et la Magliabechiana, qui sont également les grandes bénéficiaires de ces sauvetages[3].

La représentation collective et politique qui identifie l'histoire de Florence à son rôle dans les progrès de l'art du dessin est centrale dans la genèse de cette législation. Elle est à l'origine des premiers édits médicéens en matière de patrimoine artistique, comme celui du 24 octobre 1602 qui interdit l'exportation des tableaux de maîtres. Dans la première moitié du XVIIIe siècle, le développement des fouilles et l'intérêt pour

les incunables et imprimés rares conduisent à faire évoluer la représentation de ce qui fait la "civilisation toscane" et à élargir le périmètre des biens protégés[4]. La législation romaine en matière de manuscrits a pu également constituer un modèle opératoire, à une époque où les circulations érudites sont denses entre les deux capitales[5]. En 1737, le traité sanctionnant la transmission du grand-duché des Médicis aux Habsbourg-Lorraine interdit l'exportation de ce qui, dans l'héritage du défunt grand-duc Jean-Gaston, s'y trouve "pour l'ornement de l'Etat, pour l'utilité du public, et pour attirer la curiosité des étrangers". En 1747, la loi sur les fidéicommis aménage des dispositifs particuliers pour la transmission, à l'intérieur des familles, des "collections de choses rares et précieuses, qu'il importe de conserver avec soin dans nos États". L'édit de 1754 place finalement l'ensemble de ces biens sous le contrôle direct du pouvoir politique, qui peut interdire la vente à l'étranger des collections les plus précieuses. Dans le sillage du patrimoine artistique et antiquaire, un "patrimoine écrit" se trouve défini, au sens que lui donne Dominique Poulot d'un ensemble d'œuvres et de monuments jugés dignes d'être transmis à la postérité, dont les contours relèvent de la réflexion savante mais aussi d'une volonté politique, sanctionnées toutes deux par l'opinion[6]. Au nom de ce même principe supérieur, le pouvoir politique intervient pour protéger des collections en péril, comme celle des franciscains de Santa

---

2 Sur la genèse et l'application de cette politique aux bibliothèques dans la seconde moitié du XVIIIe siècle, Emmanuelle Chapron, *Ad utilità pubblica. Politique des bibliothèques et pratiques du livre à Florence au XVIIIe siècle* (Genève, 2009), chap. 5.

3 La Laurentienne (Biblioteca Medicea Laurenziana), installée dans un bâtiment construit par Michel-Ange au flanc de la basilique San Lorenzo, est ouverte au public en 1571. Elle conserve les manuscrits rassemblés par Côme l'Ancien et Laurent le Magnifique. La bibliothèque publique Magliabechiana, fondée par le testament du bibliothécaire grand-ducal Antonio Magliabechi (1633–1714), est inaugurée en 1747. En 1861, elle est unie à la bibliothèque Palatine pour former la Biblioteca Nazionale Centrale de Florence.

4 Marcello Verga, 'La cultura del Settecento. Dai Medici ai Lorena', in Furio Diaz (dir.), *Storia della civiltà toscana*, V, *I Lumi del Settecento* (Florence, 1999), 125–52.

5 L'édit du cardinal Spinola du 30 septembre 1704 impose un contrôle préalable sur toute vente de papiers ou de volumes. Andrea Emiliani, *Leggi, bandi e provvedimenti per la tutela dei beni artistici e culturali negli antichi stati italiani, 1571–1860* (Bologne, 1978), 83–86.

6 Dominique Poulot, 'La représentation du patrimoine des bibliothèques', in Jean-Paul Oddos (dir.), *Le Patrimoine. Histoire, pratiques et perspectives* (Paris, 1997), 17–42: 20.

Croce, dont les érudits florentins constatent l'incurie[7].

Les suppressions ecclésiastiques viennent mettre à l'épreuve les principes et les modalités d'application de cette politique patrimoniale. En s'inscrivant dans une politique ecclésiastique aux enjeux plus larges, elles impliquent des acteurs plus nombreux et plus divers. En libérant des collections parfois anciennes et précieuses, mais souvent de qualité médiocre, elles confrontent les autorités à la nécessité du tri. Élaborées en l'espace d'un demi-siècle, elles permettent enfin d'appréhender les relations complexes entre l'irruption de nouvelles pratiques politiques (celles des Habsbourg-Lorraine puis de l'époque napoléonienne), l'infléchissement des contours de ce patrimoine écrit et ce que ces choix disent de la représentation collective de la civilisation toscane.

L'épisode jésuite: un laboratoire?

Dans la péninsule italienne, la dissolution des bibliothèques jésuites s'est principalement faite en 1773 au profit de trois instances: les institutions scolaires et universitaires, les bibliothèques publiques locales et les bibliothèques centrales des États[8]. Celles des jésuites toscans ne connaissent

pas un sort différent. Le grand-duché compte alors neuf collèges, dont deux sont situés à Sienne, les autres à Florence, Livourne, Prato, Borgo San Sepolcro, Pistoia, Arezzo et Montepulciano. L'administration du patrimoine jésuite est confiée en septembre 1773 au comte Federico Barbolani da Montauto (1742–1788). Les mesures qu'il propose de prendre au sujet des bibliothèques varient en fonction de leur qualité intellectuelle, de l'existence de structures locales susceptibles de racheter les livres et des dispositions testamentaires qui pèsent sur certains fonds[9]. Le plus souvent, Montauto souligne l'issue incertaine qu'aurait la mise en vente de ces collections d'une valeur et d'un intérêt assez minces. Il suggère que la bibliothèque publique de la ville rachète le fonds ou, lorsqu'il n'y en a pas, que les livres soient revendus à la nouvelle communauté enseignante. Ainsi à Arezzo, la bibliothèque publique pourrait acheter les ouvrages dont elle a besoin, le reste serait proposé aux frères de Vallombreuse qui ont repris le collège. De fait, en septembre 1774, un ensemble d'ouvrages est vendu pour 800 l. aux nouveaux occupants du bâtiment[10]. À Pistoia, la majeure partie des livres du collège est achetée par la Pia Casa di Sapienza (aujourd'hui Biblioteca Comunale Forteguerriana), et le reste revendu aux libraires et aux particuliers[11]. À Borgo San Sepolcro, où la bibliothèque des jésuites est inaliénable (comme l'a stipulé le testament du

7 Chapron, *Ad utilità pubblica*, voir note nr. 1, 62–63. Les manuscrits sont transférés à la Laurentienne en 1766 (le bibliothécaire Angelo Maria Bandini en publie l'inventaire dans le t. V de son catalogue, qui paraît en 1778), la partie la moins précieuse en est restituée aux religieux en 1772. La bibliothèque reconstituée à Santa Croce conflue à nouveau dans les bibliothèques publiques Magliabechiana et Laurentienne lors des suppressions de 1808–1810.

8 Outre la bibliographie citée plus bas, voir par exemple Luigi Marchini, 'Biblioteche pubbliche a Genova nel Settecento', *Atti della società ligure di storia patria*, n.s., 20, 2 (1980), 40–67, Giuseppe Biadego, *Storia della biblioteca comunale di Verona* (Vérone, 1892), Emilio Nasalli Rocca, 'I più antichi regolamenti della biblioteca di Piacenza', *Accademie e biblioteche d'Italia*, 39, 1 (1971), 5–21, Valentino Romani, 'Tra Giansenisti ed ex-Gesuiti:

Note sulle origini della Biblioteca Pubblica di Macerata', *Nuovi Annali della Scuola speciale per archivisti e bibliotecari*, 13 (1999), 91–101, Simonetta Riccio, 'L'istituzione della biblioteca comunale a Tivoli nel 1773', *Atti e memorie della Società Tiburtina di Storia e d'Arte*, 71 (1998), 87–126.

9 Archivio di Stato di Firenze [désormais ASF], Reggenza, 371, ins. 15.

10 Il s'agit de "vari corpi di libri alcuni completi, ed altri mancanti, per la maggior parte ascetici, e molti duplicati" (ASF, Compagnie religiose soppresse da Pietro Leopoldo [désormais Comp. rel.], 1142, ins. 644, fasc. A, ins. 10, n° 459).

11 Mario Bencivenni, *L'architettura della Compagnia di Gesù in Toscana* (Florence, 1996), 121–23.

donateur Giovan Battista Monfalconi, en 1636), les livres sont confiés à la commune, qui manque justement d'un fonds public[12]. À Livourne, dont la bibliothèque publique manque de fonds pour acheter les livres, ils sont mis à l'encan. La piètre réputation de la collection jésuite livournaise ne facilite pas les choses: estimée à 3700 l., proposée aux enchères à 2900 l. en septembre 1774, elle ne trouve aucun acheteur malgré trois rabais successifs de 5%, 8% et 15% et n'est vendue qu'en avril 1775 à un libraire de Florence, Casimiro Tarpi, recommandé par Montauto[13]. La solution mise en œuvre dans la capitale suit les mêmes lignes. Les pères des Écoles Pies apportant avec eux leur propre bibliothèque, celle du collège San Giovannino est mise en vente, après que la Magliabechiana a exercé son droit de préemption. La bonne tenue intellectuelle du fonds des jésuites florentins est attestée par le déroulement de la vente: estimée entre 850 et 1000 écus, mise à prix à 700 écus, la bibliothèque est achetée 1000 écus par le libraire Bastiano Volpini qui en commence dès le lendemain la vente au détail[14].

Deux éléments doivent être finalement soulignés. Tandis que la réforme scolaire tend à mettre sur pied un système éducatif relativement homogène, le sort des anciennes bibliothèques jésuites s'adapte plus étroitement aux réalités du tissu culturel local, sans tentative d'unification institutionnelle ou de mise en réseau. La voie toscane diffère là sensiblement de la politique lombarde, dont les nouvelles bibliothèques doivent former les maillons d'un réseau fortement coordonné et hiérarchisé[15]. Par ailleurs, alors que la Magliabechiana s'impose progressivement comme la "bibliothèque centrale" du grand-duché de Toscane, elle n'occupe pas dans cette politique une place différente de celle des autres bibliothèques publiques du territoire[16]. Ses prérogatives sont en tout cas très inférieures à celles dont jouissent la bibliothèque impériale de Vienne et les bibliothèques princières des autres États italiens, à Modène, Naples ou Parme, qui obtiennent un droit de préemption sur tous les fonds jésuites de leur État[17]. Dans le grand-duché même, ce privilège n'est octroyé qu'à la Galerie des Offices, dont le directeur reçoit la mission de visiter toutes les maisons jésuites et d'en prélever les œuvres d'art intéressantes. Il récupère à cette occasion des livres d'antiquités et de beaux-arts, ce qui représente un discret élargissement de sa mission originelle. Ces quelque cent quarante ouvrages, qui constituent le premier noyau de la bibliothèque de la Galerie des Offices, sont le seul fruit centralisé de cette première vague de suppressions.

Les suppressions léopoldiennes: entre politique ecclésiastique et administration du patrimoine

Les modalités des suppressions des années 1780 marquent une certaine continuité avec l'épisode

---

12 ASF, Comp. rel., 1156, ins. 697.
13 ASF, Comp. rel., 1150, ins. 671, fasc. B.
14 ASF, Comp. rel., 966, n° 30, ins. B.
15 Silvia Furlani, 'Maria Teresa fondatrice di biblioteche', *Accademie e biblioteche d'Italia*, 50, 6 (1982), 459–74.

16 Cette centralité croissante se manifeste par exemple dans les modalités du dépôt légal. En 1743, la loi sur la censure impose aux imprimeurs toscans de remettre un exemplaire de chaque ouvrage à la bibliothèque du palais Pitti (la Palatine) et un autre à la bibliothèque publique de leur ville "s'il y en a une, et s'il n'y en a pas, à celle de Florence, dite la Magliabechiana". En 1771, le grand-duc Pierre-Léopold réunit la Palatine à la Magliabechiana, qui reçoit désormais tous les exemplaires de ce dépôt légal.
17 Vincenzo Trombetta, *Storia e cultura delle biblioteche napoletane. Librerie private, istituzioni francesi e borboniche, strutture postunitarie* (Naples, 2002), 144–51. *Notizie e documenti per una storia della Biblioteca palatina di Parma* (Parme, 1962), 63. Paola Di Pietro Lombardi, *Girolamo Tiraboschi* (Rimini, 1996), 71. Gerhard Winner, *Die Klosteraufhebungen in Niederösterreich und Wien* (Vienne, 1967). Walter Pongratz, 'Die Mariatheresianische Bibliotheksreform und ihre Folgen', in Paul Haegbein et Peter Vodosek (dir.), *Staatliche Initiative und Bibliotheksentwicklung* (Wolfenbüttel, 1985), 129–54.

jésuite de 1773. Exactes contemporaines de celles qui sont mises en œuvre en Autriche après la mort de Marie-Thérèse, ces suppressions s'inscrivent dans une nouvelle phase de la politique ecclésiastique léopoldienne. Appliquée par étapes à partir de 1781, la suppression de près de la moitié des monastères du grand-duché participe du projet de rationaliser la trame monastique, de discipliner les religieux, de réorienter leurs activités vers des tâches socialement utiles. Certains ordres sont complètement supprimés, les autres sont rassemblés dans un nombre restreint de maisons. Une administration du Patrimoine ecclésiastique est instituée dans chaque diocèse en octobre 1784 pour gérer les patrimoines des établissements supprimés: la moitié des biens est affectée à l'entretien du clergé, un quart sont rendus à la congrégation d'origine, le reste est consacré au fonctionnement des séminaires, des écoles publiques et des hôpitaux[18].

Que deviennent les bibliothèques des couvents? Il faut relativiser l'ampleur de la redistribution livresque: si un certain nombre de collections sont anciennes et importantes, la plupart sont en réalité très minces. L'inventaire du monastère olivétain de San Bernardo d'Arezzo, dressé en 1767, ne signale ainsi dans la bibliothèque qu'une mauvaise table, un tabouret et trois étagères de vieux livres[19]. Comme lors de l'épisode jésuite, aucune directive générale n'est prise en Toscane pour organiser la collecte et la redistribution de ces fonds de livres, alors que d'autres États (et notamment les domaines héréditaires des Habsbourg) font au même moment le choix d'une gestion centralisée[20]. La différence entre les politiques toscane et autrichienne peut s'expliquer en partie par le caractère très progressif des suppressions léopoldiennes. *A contrario*, lorsque Pierre-Léopold ordonne en 1785 la suppression de toutes les compagnies de piété laïques, une disposition générale concerne les œuvres d'art et les livres[21].

Pour les établissements religieux, l'absence d'un schéma organisateur laisse libre cours aux revendications des institutions, qui font jouer leurs appuis dans les milieux ecclésiastiques et administratifs. Les livres des dominicains de Montepulciano sont ainsi disputés en 1785 entre la bibliothèque publique d'Arezzo et les écoles publiques de Montepulciano, qui obtiennent finalement les livres, avec le soutien du vicaire et de l'administrateur du Patrimoine ecclésiastique[22]. De manière générale pourtant, plus qu'aux établissements scolaires et aux bibliothèques publiques, privilégiés en 1773, c'est aux séminaires et aux nouvelles académies ecclésiastiques que semblent aller en priorité les livres, lorsqu'ils ne sont pas vendus. Cette solution témoigne de l'importance accordée dans les années 1780 à la formation du clergé séculier, appelé à devenir un auxiliaire du pouvoir pour le maintien de l'ordre social et le bon déroulement des réformes[23]. La bibliothèque des dominicains d'Arezzo est ainsi répartie en 1785 entre l'académie ecclésiastique et le séminaire archiépiscopal[24]. La bibliothèque des augustins de Cortone revient en 1787 au

18 Diana Toccafondi, 'La soppressione leopoldina delle confraternite tra riformismo ecclesiastico e politica sociale', *Archivio storico pratese*, 61 (1985), 143–72. Carlo Fantappié, *Il monachesimo moderno tra ragion di Chiesa e ragion di Stato. Il caso toscano (XVI–XIX sec.)* (Florence, 1993).

19 ASF, Comp. rel., 2329, fol. 182–97, 187v°.

20 Winner, *Die Klosteraufhebungen*, voir note nr. 17, 91–95.

21 *Bandi e Ordini da osservarsi nel granducato di Toscana, stampati in Firenze e pubblicati dal di 12 luglio 1737 [al di otto febbraio 1790]* (Florence, 1747–1790), n° CL, 30 juillet 1785, art. XXVI.

22 ASF, Segreteria di Stato, 429, protocole 45 n° 37 et 455, protocole 8 n° 5.

23 Carlo Fantappié, 'Promozione e controllo del clero nell'età leopoldina', in Zeffiro Ciuffoletti, Leonardo Rombai (dir.), *La Toscana dei Lorena. Riforme, territorio, società* (Florence, 1989), 233–50.

24 ASF, Regio Diritto, 5373: V. Martini à Pierre-Léopold, 3 décembre 1784.

séminaire de la ville, et non à sa bibliothèque publique[25].

Les suppressions des années 1780 diffèrent également de l'épisode jésuite par le rôle qu'y jouent à nouveau les deux principales bibliothèques florentines, la Magliabechiana et la Laurentienne. À l'instar d'autres bibliothèques centrales de la péninsule, elles reçoivent alors de nombreux ouvrages des couvents supprimés. Leur intervention est pourtant loin d'être systématique, car elles ne prélèvent de livres que dans une douzaine de maisons. Aucun texte général ne régit en effet ces acquisitions: elles se font toujours à la suite d'une requête particulière des bibliothécaires, qui agissent en fonction des informations dont ils disposent. Ainsi, ce n'est qu'après avoir appris certaines suppressions par le biais de la *Gazzetta toscana* que le bibliothécaire de la Magliabechiana, Ferdinando Fossi (1720–1800), adresse sa requête à l'administration grand-ducale[26].

Quoique peu nombreux, ces prélèvements sont intéressants car ils illustrent l'évolution de l'administration des fonds patrimoniaux sous le règne de Pierre-Léopold. Ils s'inscrivent d'abord dans la tendance à la spécialisation des fonds précieux qui se dessine depuis les années 1770: à la Laurentienne sont réservés les manuscrits antérieurs à l'invention de l'imprimerie, à la Magliabechiana revenant les incunables et les manuscrits plus récents[27]. En juillet 1783, après la disparition des deux dernières abbayes cisterciennes de Toscane, San Salvatore a Settimo et San Frediano in Cestello, ordre est donné de transférer les imprimés au séminaire archiépiscopal de Florence, les parchemins à l'Archivio diplomatico, les incunables à la Magliabechiana, et de répartir les manuscrits, selon leur mérite, entre la Magliabechiana et la Laurentienne[28]. Mais ces prélèvements sont également l'occasion pour la Magliabechiana d'affirmer son rôle de "bibliothèque centrale" du grand-duché. Alors qu'Angelo Maria Bandini (1726–1803) fait de la bibliothèque Laurentienne une référence universelle pour la "République des philologues", la Magliabechiana se conçoit de plus en plus comme le conservatoire de la culture toscane, habilitée à exercer un droit de préemption sur les collections emblématiques de sa civilisation, dans son acception politique et savante. En mai 1778, ayant eu vent de la suppression de la Badia de Fiesole, Ferdinando Fossi signale au gouvernement l'existence d'une bibliothèque qui pourrait être placée dans la Magliabechiana, dans la mesure où elle a été réunie pour les chanoines par Côme l'Ancien. Au printemps 1789, il réclame de pouvoir choisir des livres dans la bibliothèque des alcantarins de l'Ambrogiana, "parce qu'elle fut acquise grâce à la munificence du grand-duc Côme III et que le savant Magliabechi prêta son aide au choix des livres"[29]. Les 116 ouvrages qu'il en reçoit (dont un seul incunable) constituent les témoins d'une entreprise bibliographique singulière, au croisement des attachements

---

25 ASF, Segreteria di Stato, 487, protocolo 4 n° 11, 29 novembre 1787.

26 Biblioteca nazionale centrale di Firenze [désormais BNCF], Archivio Magliabechiano XII, fol. 521: F. Fossi à V. Martini (secrétaire du Regio Diritto), [sans date mais 1785] annoté: "non mi ricordo del giorno della data di questo biglietto ma fu appena che dalla Gazzetta [seppi] essere stati soppressi i due qui enunciati conventi" (il s'agit du couvent dominicain de Sant'Agnese de Montepulciano et du couvent des servites de Scrofiano, près de Chiusi). Sur Fossi, Carlo Fantappiè, 'Fossi, Ferdinando', in *Dizionario biografico degli Italiani*, 49 (1997), 505–07.

27 Sur cette politique patrimoniale, Chapron, *Ad utilità pubblica*, voir note nr. 1, chapitre 6.

28 ASF, Segreteria di Stato, 362, ins. 82 et 377 bis, protocolo 49 n° 60.

29 ASF, Segreteria di Stato, 529, protocolo 4 n° 40: supplique de F. Fossi, 14 février 1789 ("perché fu acquistata dalla munificenza del granduca Cosimo III, come anco perché nella scelta v'intervenne, come mi viene asserito, l'assistenza dell'intendente Magliabechi").

religieux du grand-duc Côme III (1670–1723), qui installa les franciscains de la réforme de saint Pierre d'Alcantara près de sa résidence favorite, et de l'expertise intellectuelle de son bibliothécaire Antonio Magliabechi (1633–1714), que toute l'Europe reconnaissait comme une "bibliothèque vivante"[30].

Les suppressions napoléoniennes

Les suppressions napoléoniennes, deux décennies plus tard, marquent à bien des égards une franche rupture par rapport aux pratiques politiques et savantes précédentes. Avec la centralisation, la constitution de commissions *ad hoc* et l'institution de grands dépôts, ce sont les procédures de la France révolutionnaire et des autres États italiens sous domination napoléonienne qui font désormais autorité.

Cette politique se déroule dans un cadre recomposé. Le grand-duché organisé autour de sa capitale est devenu en mars 1808 un ensemble de trois départements, l'Arno (Florence), l'Ombrone (Sienne) et la Méditerranée (Livourne)[31]. Alors que les bibliothèques des couvents supprimés étaient restées à la marge des préoccupations du gouvernement léopoldien, la question est abordée très rapidement par les autorités napoléoniennes. Un mois seulement après le décret impérial de suppression du 24 mars 1808, une ordonnance de l'Administrateur général Luc Jacques Édouard Dauchy (1757–1817) fixe la marche à suivre pour les bibliothèques. Les livres les plus intéressants seront mis de côté pour former une bibliothèque

"per la pubblica istruzione" dans chaque chef-lieu de préfecture. Le reste sera remis à la disposition des couvents maintenus, ou vendu avec les meubles des établissements supprimés[32]. Les choix mis en œuvre dans la sélection des livres s'avèrent en fait très restrictifs, bien plus proches de la pratique patrimoniale des Habsbourg-Lorraine que des bibliothèques d'instruction publique sur le modèle français. Dans le Val di Chiana, le commissaire choisit les seuls livres "d'une édition rare", tandis que le comte bibliophile Fabrizio Orsini de' Rilli (1742–1826) ne retient que vingt-et-un manuscrits et un incunable de la bibliothèque des mineurs de San Lorenzo de Bibbiena[33].

L'étape suivante marque une rupture plus franche avec la période léopoldienne. Le 6 octobre 1808, la Junte impériale (organe de gouvernement mis en place par Napoléon) ordonne la suspension de toute vente de livres et d'objets d'art et institue une "Commission pour la conservation des objets d'art et de sciences". Le nom du nouvel organe rappelle celui du conseil actif en France sous le Directoire, ainsi que celui d'autres structures du même genre actives ailleurs en Italie, notamment à Rome[34]. Pour la première fois en Toscane, le choix des livres à préserver est confié à un groupe

---

30 Carlo Fantappié, *Il monachesimo moderno*, voir note nr. 18. Sur Magliabechi, Caroline Callard, 'Diogène au service des princes: Antonio Magliabechi à la cour de Toscane (1633–1714)', *Histoire, Économie, Société*, 19, 1 (2000), 85–103.

31 De manière générale sur la période: Ivan Tognarini (dir.), *La Toscana nell'età rivoluzionaria e napoleonica* (Naples, 1985).

32 Ordonnance du 29 avril 1808, article XXI (I Signori Prefetti nomineranno dei commissari, che saranno incaricati di trasportarsi nelle biblioteche dei Conventi per farvi, prima che sia scomposta la mobilia, la scelta dei libri e manoscritti che meriteranno d'essere per la pubblica istruzione conservati, onde formarne una biblioteca in ogni capo-luogo di Prefettura, ove questi saranno trasportati; l'avanzo di questi libri resterà a disposizione dei Conventi che restano, o destinati sono a ricevere i religiosi riuniti; quelli dei Conventi soppressi saranno venduti come mobilia), publiée dans Antonio Zobi, *Storia civile della Toscana dal 1737 al 1848* (Florence, 1850–1852), t. III, Appendice di documenti, 323–27.

33 ASF, Prefettura dell'Arno, 213.

34 Monica Calzolari, 'Le commissioni preposte alla conservazione del patrimonio artistico e archeologico di Roma durante il periodo napoleonico (1809–1814).

d'experts, et la procédure est alignée sur celle des collections artistiques[35]. Constituée des directeurs des institutions culturelles florentines (bibliothèques Riccardiana, Laurentienne et Marucelliana, Académie des beaux-arts, Galerie des Offices), la commission est chargée de se rendre dans les couvents des trois départements et de choisir les objets dignes d'être conservés. Ils les marquent de leur sceau (un aigle impérial blanc sur fond noir, entouré de la légende "Conservazione degli oggetti di arti e scienze") et ceux des couvents supprimés sont transférés dans un local fourni par le préfet[36].

En cinq mois (octobre 1808-février 1809), les commissaires visitent trente-trois maisons dans la sous-préfecture de Florence. Pour accélérer les démarches dans le reste du territoire, la Commission est suppléée, à partir de mars 1809, par des délégués choisis parmi les notabilités sociales et intellectuelles locales et munis d'instructions précises. Ces derniers sont chargés d'extraire des bibliothèques "tous les

manuscrits et tous les parchemins, les livres rares et particulièrement ceux imprimés au XVe siècle, les textes de langue, les éditions des plus célèbres imprimeurs, les corpus les plus respectables d'art et de science"[37]. Il faut donc sauver ce qui est rare, mais également ce qui est utile: deux critères dont les délégués provinciaux sentent bien le caractère arbitraire, lié tant à la valeur très variable des collections ecclésiastiques qu'au jugement personnel du délégué. Le compte-rendu dressé par deux délégués d'Arezzo éclaire la manière dont ceux-ci ont procédé. Ils ont délimité quelques certitudes (tous les incunables et les "textes de langue toscane" cités dans le dictionnaire de la Crusca) et assumé des choix (parmi les classiques latins et les *Cinquecentine*). Pour le reste, ils ont construit une définition personnelle de ce qui fait le patrimoine écrit, à partir des critères de l'utilité publique, mais aussi de l'histoire des mondes savants et de la bibliographie matérielle, en choisissant par exemple des volumes qui "attestent des infatigables souffrances et des vastes connaissances de leurs auteurs", ainsi que "des dépenses non ordinaires de l'édition"[38]. Les termes du choix reflètent plus largement la manière dont les élites cultivées se représentent la civilisation toscane. La sélection intégrale des "textes de langue", c'est-à-dire des auteurs qui font référence pour le bon usage et la pureté de la langue toscane, témoigne de la primauté de la dimension linguistique dans cette définition. Elle fait écho au récent rétablissement de l'académie de la Crusca (supprimée en 1783

Nuove ricerche sui fondi documentari dell'Archivio di Stato di Roma', in *Ideologie e patrimonio storico-culturale*, voir note nr. 1, 515–59.

35 Il n'a jamais été question, en Toscane, de reconnaître à une institution ou à un individu une fonction publique en matière de patrimoine livresque, alors que le dispositif existe pour les œuvres d'art (par l'édit du 24 octobre 1602, Ferdinand Ier confie à l'Académie de dessin le soin de délivrer les autorisations de sortie du territoire pour les tableaux) ou les antiquités (par la loi du 5 août 1780, le grand-duc Pierre-Léopold charge le directeur de la Galerie des Offices d'examiner et d'acheter tout vestige antique trouvé sur le territoire et intéressant le musée). Pierre-Léopold refuse à l'été 1783 une suggestion faite en ce sens par l'érudit Lorenzo Mehus (1716–1802), qui proposait d'instituer une surintendance aux bibliothèques publiques, et de conférer à son titulaire le droit de préempter tous les manuscrits et éditions anciennes qu'il jugerait dignes d'intérêt, afin d'endiguer les exportations (ASF, Reggenza, 1051, ins. 13: Regolamento per le librerie pubbliche di Firenze).

36 ASF, Prefettura dell'Arno, 214, non num.: Extrait des registres des délibérations de la Junte extraordinaire de Toscane, séance du 6 octobre 1808.

37 Biblioteca comunale di Cortona, ms. 552, fol. 256, cité par Trombetta, *Storia e cultura delle biblioteche napoletane*, voir note nr. 17, 212 (si toglieranno tutti i codici e tutte le pergamene, i libri rari, e specialmente quelli stampati nel sec. XV, i testi di lingua, l'edizioni de' più celebri stampatori, i corpi più rispettabili di arti e scienze [...]).

38 Archivio dell'Accademia delle Belle Arti di Firenze [désormais AABA], 23, ins. "Arezzo": Processo verbale, 30 mai 1809 (l'instancabile sofferenza, e il vaste cognizioni dei loro autori, e spesse volte le spese non ordinarie dell'edizione).

par Pierre-Léopold et ressuscitée en 1808 par Napoléon), ainsi qu'à une question politique brûlante, celle de la langue officielle pratiquée en Toscane, réglée à peu près au même moment par un décret impérial qui autorise conjointement le français et le toscan.

Alors que la première suppression avait encore un caractère partiel, l'ordre général de fermeture de tous les couvents d'hommes et de femmes des trois départements toscans est donné par le décret de Saint-Cloud du 13 septembre 1810, qui révoque les dernières exceptions[39]. Comme lors de la première vague de suppressions, mais cette fois sans délai, une "Commissione dei monumenti delle Arti della città di Firenze" est chargée des bibliothèques, manuscrits, antiquités et objets d'art du département de l'Arno. L'expérience de la première suppression a porté ses fruits et les commissaires procèdent beaucoup plus rapidement. En deux mois, la commission visite 95 couvents dans vingt communes différentes, dont 43 dans la seule ville de Florence[40]. Une telle rapidité ne se comprend que si l'on considère que dans les deux tiers des cas (pour l'essentiel des monastères de femmes), les commissaires ne retiennent aucun livre et seulement quelques tableaux. Lors de cette seconde phase, plus de 16 000 ouvrages imprimés et manuscrits, provenant de 32 établissements, sont prélevés, puis redistribués un an plus tard entre les différentes institutions culturelles de Florence[41]:

les bibliothèques publiques Magliabechiana et Marucelliana, la Laurentienne, les académies de la Crusca, du Cimento et des Georgofili, les bibliothèques de l'hôpital Santa Maria Nuova, de la Galerie des offices, de la Cour impériale et de la Préfecture de l'Arno, l'archevêché et le collège Eugeniano. Cette répartition, qui élargit ce qui avait déjà été pratiqué en 1808[42], apparaît bien éloignée dans ses principes du projet initial de bibliothèque départementale. Plus proche de ce qui s'est pratiqué à Paris, elle prend acte du suréquipement culturel de la ville de Florence. Mais elle entérine également une évolution longue du paysage bibliothécaire européen, contemporaine des processus de professionnalisation des activités intellectuelles, qui aboutit à la constitution de fonds spécialisés dans les établissements de formation ou d'exercice professionnel. Sous le règne de Pierre-Léopold, le Musée de physique et d'histoire naturelle, l'hôpital Santa Maria Nuova et la Galerie des offices avaient mis en place des fonds de travail propres, qui sont considérablement enrichis par les suppressions[43].

Dès la première suppression napoléonienne, les délégués de la Commission avaient dégagé, entre les livres rares et les livres de rebut, une troisième catégorie: celle des ouvrages inutiles pour les institutions de la capitale, mais susceptibles d'être conservés à l'usage de la population locale. C'est autour de ces livres que se joue la dernière évolution, capitale, de la période. En novembre 1810, la Commission demande au préfet de l'Arno Jean Antoine Joseph Fauchet que les ouvrages et tableaux choisis par les délégués de la commission puissent être conservés dans les "cités subalternes" du département[44]. En reconnaissant l'existence

---

39   Le décret, propre aux départements toscans, exclut tout de même les congrégations sans vœux perpétuels dont les membres se consacrent au soin des malades et à l'éducation. Décret publié dans Fantozzi Micali, Roselli, *Le soppressioni dei conventi*, voir note nr. 1, 297.

40   Les comptes-rendus figurent dans AABA, 25.

41   Les chiffres viennent du 'Catalogo dei libri e manoscritti scelti dalla commissione degli Oggetti d'Arti e Scienze nelle Librerie Monastiche del Dipartimento dell'Arno disposto da Francesco Tassi Parte prima A-K Firenze 1811', puis 'parte seconda L-Z Firenze 1811', 2 vol., qui inclut 14311 notices d'imprimés et 1912 de manuscrits (décrit dans Rossi, 'Sulle tracce delle biblioteche… Parte prima', voir note nr. 1, notice [13]).

42   Au bénéfice du Musée impérial de physique et d'histoire naturelle, de la Cour d'appel et du lycée de Florence.

43   Chapron, *Ad utilità pubblica*, voir note nr. 1, chapitre 4.

44   AABA, 27, fol. 120: G. degli Alessandri à J. Fauchet, 20 novembre 1810. Fauchet (1763–1834) est préfet de l'Arno du 15 mars 1809 à l'évacuation de l'Italie par les

d'un patrimoine municipal qu'il est légitime de laisser sur place, la Commission pose les bases d'un véritable maillage bibliothécaire et muséal du territoire, instrument d'une nouvelle culture civique et de ce que le gardien des mineurs observants de Radicondoli appelle "l'âme du citoyen tranquille"[45]. L'accord du préfet, obtenu dès le 30 novembre, semble modifier la stratégie des délégués de la Commission. Dès lors qu'il ne s'agit plus de prélever les seuls morceaux de choix pour les institutions florentines, mais de constituer le fonds d'une bibliothèque indigène, un certain nombre de collections ecclésiastiques sont prélevées "dans leur totalité" par les délégués[46]. À Arezzo, l'ancien couvent Saint-Ignace des bénédictins devient au printemps 1811 le siège du collège, de l'école de dessin, de la bibliothèque municipale et du dépôt des objets d'art et de sciences[47]. Le sort de la célèbre bibliothèque de l'ermitage de Camaldoli est réglé suivant les mêmes logiques administratives. La bibliothèque, dont les origines remontent au XIe siècle, est alors riche de quelque 7000 ouvrages imprimés, 400 manuscrits et plus de 700 incunables[48]. En juin puis en septembre 1808, elle est visitée à la demande du préfet par Orsini de' Rilli, qui dresse une longue liste de livres à prélever[49]. Deux ans plus tard, la Commission met à son tour de côté les ouvrages les plus précieux. Les commissaires renferment le reste des livres "en attendant que se présente l'occasion de disposer de cette bibliothèque à l'usage et à l'avantage d'une respectable population voisine, selon les principes déjà exprimés par [le préfet]", tout en soulignant la nécessité d'intervenir rapidement

pour éviter que les livres ne se dégradent sous les rigueurs de l'hiver apennin[50]. Orsini de' Rilli propose alors de les conserver dans sa propre bibliothèque, qu'il a l'intention de léguer à la commune de Poppi, mais il suffit au maire et au conseil municipal de Bibbiena de manifester leur intention de constituer une bibliothèque publique, et de faire valoir que l'ermitage relève administrativement de leur ressort, pour que le reliquat du fonds leur soit attribué[51].

Comme précédemment, les livres que les membres de la Commission ou leurs délégués considèrent comme sans valeur pour la capitale et inutiles pour les populations locales, sont destinés à être vendus. Les maires qui souhaitent retenir ces reliquats pour leur commune se trouvent le plus souvent déboutés par l'administration préfectorale. Le problème récurrent posé par ces collections conduit finalement les autorités à mettre en place une solution plus générale. L'arrêté pris le 15 janvier 1812 par le préfet de l'Arno autorise les maires à conserver les bibliothèques supprimées, après prélèvement et sous l'autorité de la Commission des arts et des sciences. Les fonds n'en appartiennent pas pour autant à la commune et pourront être réaffectés à tout moment par le gouvernement, mais ils sont laissés à la disposition et à la charge financière de l'administration municipale, pour servir à l'instruction des habitants[52]. Cette décision rappelle tout à fait la situation qui prévaut en France depuis le décret de 1803. En réalité, la faible valeur marchande et intellectuel des fonds de livres n'incite guère les maires à constituer des dépôts, d'autant que l'arrêté ne les y oblige pas.

---

armées françaises.

45 Archivio di Stato di Siena, Prefettura, 36, n° 233 (l'animo del tranquillo cittadino).

46 AABA, 25, fasc. 17, 19, 81, dans les dépôts de Castiglion Fiorentino, de Cortone et de Fojano.

47 AABA, 27, fol. 293: décret du 21 mars 1811.

48 Sur les origines de la bibliothèque, Maria Elena Magheri Cataluccio et Antonio Ugo Fossa, *Biblioteca e cultura a Camaldoli: dal Medioevo all'umanesimo* (Rome, 1979).

49 ASF, Prefettura, 519, avec liste.

50 AABA, 27, fol. 115 (fintantoché non si presentasse l'occasione di assicurare in qualche modo questa Libreria, coerentemente ai principi già esternati all'E.V., ad uso, e vantaggio di qualche rispettabile vicina Popolazione).

51 AABA, 27, fol. 314: arrêté du 26 mars 1811.

52 ASF, Demanio francese, misc. B, 19, ins. 2563.

Par ajustements progressifs entre le monde savant et le personnel politique d'une part, entre les autorités centrales et municipales d'autre part, les pratiques connaissent en trois décennies une triple évolution. La première est celle des objets à sauver, qui passe des seuls manuscrits et éditions rares, sous le règne de Pierre-Léopold, à la conservation locale de la quasi-totalité des fonds, dans la dernière phase des suppressions napoléoniennes. La seconde concerne ses bénéficiaires – d'une affectation ciblée aux établissements scolaires ou ecclésiastiques, congruente aux objectifs de la politique léopoldienne, à l'institution de bibliothèques de proximité. La troisième regarde le rôle des bibliothèques centrales, Magliabechiana et Laurentienne au premier chef, qui s'affirment comme les conservatoires d'un patrimoine écrit dont leurs bibliothécaires contribuent à définir le sens et le périmètre. Les pratiques bibliothéconomiques s'adaptent à l'évolution des prélèvements: tandis que Ferdinando Fossi fait imprimer et apposer des étiquettes rappelant l'origine des ouvrages collectés dans les années 1780 (*Ex Bibliotheca Augustinianorum Cortenensiis, Ex Bibliotheca Augustiniana Montisilicini anno 1787*, etc.), les manuscrits provenant des suppressions de 1808 constituent, au sein de la Biblioteca Nazionale Centrale de Florence héritière de la Magliabechiana, un fonds particulier, celui des "Conventi soppressi". Cette évolution n'aboutit pourtant pas à enraciner localement un réseau de bibliothèques publiques. En 1814, lorsque Ferdinand III reprend le trône de Toscane qu'il avait dû céder en 1801 à Louis Ier de Bourbon-Parme, une partie des opérations est remise en cause. La convention signée le 4 décembre 1815 avec la papauté prévoit la réouverture de 77 couvents et la restitution des ouvrages nécessaires aux études des religieux, à retirer des bibliothèques où ils avaient été déposés après les suppressions[53].

---

53   Sur cette phase, Rossi, 'Sulle tracce delle biblioteche… parte seconda', voir note nr. 1. Le texte de la convention est publié dans Fantozzi Micali et Roselli, *Le soppressioni dei conventi*, voir note nr. 1, 299–301.

Bibliography

Manuscripts and Archival Sources

Firenze, Archivio dell'Accademia delle Belle Arti, 23.

Firenze, Archivio dell'Accademia delle Belle Arti, 25.

Firenze, Archivio dell'Accademia delle Belle Arti, 27.

Firenze, Archivio dell'Accademia delle Belle Arti, non coté. 'Catalogo dei libri e manoscritti scelti dalla commissione degli Oggetti d'Arti e Scienze nelle Librerie Monastiche del Dipartimento dell'Arno disposto da Francesco Tassi Parte prima A-K Firenze 1811', puis 'parte seconda L-Z Firenze 1811', 2 vol.

Firenze, Archivio di Stato, Reggenza, 371, ins. 15.

Firenze, Archivio di Stato, Compagnie religiose soppresse da Pietro Leopoldo, 1142, ins. 644, fasc. A, ins. 10, n° 459.

Firenze, Archivio di Stato, Comp. rel., 1156, ins. 697.

Firenze, Archivio di Stato, Comp. rel., 1150, ins. 671, fasc. B.

Firenze, Archivio di Stato, Comp. rel., 966, n° 30, ins. B.

Firenze, Archivio di Stato, Comp. rel., 2329, fol. 182–97, 187v°.

Firenze, Archivio di Stato, Demanio francese, misc. B, 19, ins. 2563.

Firenze, Archivio di Stato, Prefettura, 519.

Firenze, Archivio di Stato, Prefettura dell'Arno, 213.

Firenze, Archivio di Stato, Prefettura dell'Arno, 214.

Firenze, Archivio di Stato, Reggenza, 1051, ins. 13: Regolamento per le librerie pubbliche di Firenze.

Firenze, Archivio di Stato, Regio Diritto, 5373: V. Martini à Pierre-Léopold, 3 décembre 1784.

Firenze, Archivio di Stato, Segreteria di Stato, 362, ins. 82 et 377 bis, protocole 49 n° 60.

Firenze, Archivio di Stato, Segreteria di Stato, 429, protocole 45 n° 37 et 455, protocole 8 n° 5.

Firenze, Archivio di Stato, Segreteria di Stato, 487, protocole 4 n° 11, 29 novembre 1787.

Firenze, Archivio di Stato, Segreteria di Stato, 529, protocole 4 n° 40: supplique de F. Fossi, 14 février 1789.

Firenze, Biblioteca nazionale centrale, Archivio Magliabechiano XII, fol. 521: F. Fossi à V. Martini (secrétaire du Regio Diritto), [sans date mais 1785].

Cortona, Biblioteca comunale, ms. 552, fol. 256.

Siena, Archivio di Stato, Prefettura, 36, n° 233.

Secondary Works

Bandi e Ordini da osservarsi nel granducato di Toscana, stampati in Firenze e pubblicati dal di 12 luglio 1737 [*al di otto febbraio 1790*] (Florence, 1747–1790).

Mario Bencivenni, *L'architettura della Compagnia di Gesù in Toscana* (Florence, 1996).

Giuseppe Biadego, *Storia della biblioteca comunale di Verona* (Vérone, 1892).

Fabio Bisogni, 'Da Pietro Leopoldo a Napoleone: tutela e dispersione di beni culturali a Siena e in Toscana', in *Ideologie e patrimonio storico-culturale nell'età rivoluzionaria e napoleonica: a proposito del trattato di Tolentino* (Rome, 2000), 563–605.

Caroline Callard, 'Diogène au service des princes: Antonio Magliabechi à la cour de Toscane (1633–1714)', *Histoire, Économie, Société*, 19, 1 (2000), 85–103.

Monica Calzolari, 'Le commissioni preposte alla conservazione del patrimonio artistico e archeologico di Roma durante il periodo napoleonico (1809–1814). Nuove ricerche sui fondi documentari dell'Archivio di Stato di Roma', in *Ideologie e patrimonio storico-culturale nell'età rivoluzionaria e napoleonica: a proposito del trattato di Tolentino* (Rome, 2000), 515–59.

Emmanuelle Chapron, 'Il patrimonio ricomposto. Biblioteche e soppressioni ecclesiastiche in Toscana da Pietro Leopoldo a Napoleone', *Archivio storico italiano*, 2 (2009), 299–345.

Emmanuelle Chapron, *Ad utilità pubblica. Politique des bibliothèques et pratiques du livre à Florence au XVIIIe siècle* (Genève, 2009).

Paola Di Pietro Lombardi, *Girolamo Tiraboschi* (Rimini, 1996).

Andrea Emiliani, *Leggi, bandi e provvedimenti per la tutela dei beni artistici e culturali negli antichi stati italiani, 1571–1860* (Bologne, 1978).

Carlo Fantappié, 'Promozione e controllo del clero nell'età leopoldina', in Zeffiro Ciuffoletti et Leonardo Rombai (dir.), *La Toscana dei Lorena. Riforme, territorio, società* (Florence, 1989), 233–50.

Carlo Fantappié, *Il monachesimo moderno tra ragion di Chiesa e ragion di Stato. Il caso toscano (XVI–XIX sec.)* (Florence, 1993).

Carlo Fantappiè, 'Fossi, Ferdinando', in *Dizionario biografico degli Italiani*, 49 (1997), 505–07.

Osanna Fantozzi Micali et Piero Roselli, *Le soppressioni dei conventi a Firenze. Riuso e trasformazioni dal sec. XVIII in poi* (Florence, 2000).

Silvia Furlani, 'Maria Teresa fondatrice di biblioteche', *Accademie e biblioteche d'Italia*, 50, 6 (1982), 459–74.

Roberta Lapucci, 'Fonti d'archivio per la storia delle arti durante la soppressione napoleonica a Firenze', *Rivista d'arte*, série 4, 39 (1987), 475–93.

Maria Elena Magheri Cataluccio et Antonio Ugo Fossa, *Biblioteca e cultura a Camaldoli: dal Medioevo all'umanesimo* (Rome, 1979).

Luigi Marchini, 'Biblioteche pubbliche a Genova nel Settecento', *Atti della società ligure di storia patria*, n.s., 20, 2 (1980), 40–67.

Emilio Nasalli Rocca, 'I più antichi regolamenti della biblioteca di Piacenza', *Accademie e biblioteche d'Italia*, 39, 1 (1971), 5–21.

Notizie e documenti per una storia della Biblioteca palatina di Parma (Parme, 1962).

Walter Pongratz, 'Die Mariatheresianische Bibliotheksreform und ihre Folgen', in Paul Haegbein et Peter Vodosek (dir.), *Staatliche Initiative und Bibliotheksentwicklung* (Wolfenbüttel, 1985), 129–54.

Dominique Poulot, 'La représentation du patrimoine des bibliothèques', in Jean-Paul Oddos (dir.), *Le Patrimoine. Histoire, pratiques et perspectives* (Paris, 1997), 17–42.

Simonetta Riccio, 'L'istituzione della biblioteca comunale a Tivoli nel 1773', *Atti e memorie della Società Tiburtina di Storia e d'Arte*, 71 (1998), 87–126.

Valentino Romani, 'Tra Giansenisti ed ex-Gesuiti: Note sulle origini della Biblioteca Pubblica di Macerata', *Nuovi Annali della Scuola speciale per archivisti e bibliotecari*, 13 (1999), 91–101.

Marielisa Rossi, 'Sulle tracce delle biblioteche: i cataloghi e gli inventari (1808–1819) della soppressione e del ripristino dei conventi in Toscana. Parte prima[-seconda]', *Culture del testo*, IV, 12 (1998), 85–123 et *Culture del testo e del documento*, I, 2 (2000), 109–45.

Diana Toccafondi, 'La soppressione leopoldina delle confraternite tra riformismo ecclesiastico e politica sociale', *Archivio storico pratese*, 61 (1985), 143–72.

Ivan Tognarini (dir.), *La Toscana nell'età rivoluzionaria e napoleonica* (Naples, 1985).

Vincenzo Trombetta, *Storia e cultura delle biblioteche napoletane. Librerie private, istituzioni francesi e borboniche, strutture postunitarie* (Naples, 2002).

Marcello Verga, 'La cultura del Settecento. Dai Medici ai Lorena', in Furio Diaz (dir.), *Storia della civiltà toscana*, V, *I Lumi del Settecento* (Florence, 1999), 125–52.

Gerhard Winner, *Die Klosteraufhebungen in Niederösterreich und Wien* (Vienne, 1967).

Antonio Zobi, *Storia civile della Toscana dal 1737 al 1848* (Florence, 1850–1852).

ANDREINA RITA

La Biblioteca Vaticana e la dispersione delle biblioteche dei religiosi romani nella prima Repubblica Romana e nell'età napoleonica

La soppressione degli ordini religiosi, imposta dai francesi durante la prima Repubblica Romana e nuovamente in età napoleonica, seppure formalmente motivata da ragioni ideologiche volte alla secolarizzazione del contesto sociale, venne di fatto realizzata principalmente per interessi economici. Decretata per ben due volte, a distanza di poco più di un decennio, comportò in pratica la confisca dei beni mobili e immobili dei religiosi, incamerati dal Governo con l'espropriazione, talvolta immediata, dei loro edifici, che vennero adibiti ad altro uso. Furono requisiti anche quelli che oggi chiameremo beni culturali e tra essi le biblioteche. Si mise in atto così la prima grande dispersione moderna del patrimonio librario degli ordini religiosi. Dispersione che a Roma riguardò specificamente gli ordini maschili. Solo una piccola parte dei libri smembrati venne trasferita a Parigi. Il resto si disperse all'interno della città: alcuni volumi furono portati nella Biblioteca Vaticana, altri in Casanatense, altri ancora, forse la maggior parte, finirono sul mercato librario; molti andarono dispersi e perduti. Talvolta furono

gli stessi religiosi a smembrare furtivamente le loro biblioteche, nella speranza di salvare dalla requisizione almeno i libri più preziosi e quelli ritenuti testimoni fondamentali della loro storia.

Si assistette dunque a un imponente movimento librario di cui beneficiarono principalmente librai e bibliofili. Tra i tanti, Monaldo Leopardi (1776–1847), padre del ben più noto Giacomo, testimone diretto di quegli eventi:

> Nel 1798 gli eserciti francesi invasero lo Stato pontificio, e costituirono il fantoccio politico chiamato Repubblica romana. Questo fu tempo felicissimo per l'acquisto di libri, perché se ne mise in commercio una massa immensa, spettante non solo ai conventi soppressi, ma ai cardinali, prelati, avvocati e gente di ogni classe, che sloggiò in folla da Roma[1].

---

[1] Alessandro Avòli, 'Monaldo e la sua biblioteca', in Monaldo Leopardi, *Autobiografia*, introduzione di Giulio Cattaneo ([Roma], 1997), 227–53, a 233–34.

Andreina Rita • Direttore del Dipartimento degli Stampati, Biblioteca Apostolica Vaticana. rita@vatlib.it

How the Secularization of Religious Houses Transformed the Libraries of Europe, 16th–19th Centuries, ed. by Cristina Dondi, Dorit Raines, and †Richard Sharpe, BIB, 63 (Turnhout, 2022), pp. 287–312.

BREPOLS ❧ PUBLISHERS   DOI 10.1484/M.BIB-EB.5.128489

Ma non fu un tempo altrettanto felice per chi, come i religiosi, assistette impotente alla dispersione delle proprie biblioteche, ricevute in eredità, curate e nel tempo accresciute, e in quel contesto espropriate e svendute "per un prezzo inferiore al valore intrinseco della carta"[2].

La prima Repubblica Romana (1798–1799)

La prima confisca libraria delle case religiose romane fu formalmente avviata il 10 maggio 1798, con decreto del Direttorio[3]. La disposizione, nota anche come legge sul noviziato – per il fatto di prescrivere ai novizi di entrambi i sessi l'uscita dai chiostri entro il termine di dieci giorni – decretava "l'accentramento" dei religiosi di ciascun Ordine in un istituto specificamente deputato[4] e contestualmente sanciva con l'articolo VII la soppressione diretta e definitiva di

33 case romane[5]. Riguardo a queste veniva tra l'altro disposto che le statue e i quadri che vi si trovavano fossero raccolti nel museo pubblico, i manoscritti nella Biblioteca Vaticana e i libri a stampa nella cosidetta Libraria della Minerva, ossia la Casanatense. Ma specificamente per quest'ultimo aspetto, gli eventi si svolsero in modo diverso da quanto prescritto dalla legge.

A Roma l'espropriazione di conventi e monasteri avvenne infatti in più fasi e in alcuni casi addirittura prima dell'emanazione della legge sul noviziato. L'11 febbraio 1798, all'indomani dell'occupazione, quando papa Pio VI non aveva ancora lasciato Roma, i Francesi invasero in modo estremamente violento "l'Ospizio" dell'Aracoeli sul Campidoglio, dove insediarono il quartier generale dell'*Armée*. Fu poi la volta del convento di San Pietro in Montorio, occupato alla fine dello stesso mese, e di San Francesco a Ripa, per restare in ambito francescano[6]. Seguì la presa della

---

2 Ivi.

3 Venne pubblicato il giorno successivo (22 fiorile, anno VI); una copia in *Collezione di carte pubbliche, proclami, editti, ragionamenti ed altre produzioni tendenti a consolidare la rigenerata Repubblica romana* (Roma, 1798–99), I, 456–59; sulla recezione del decreto anche 'Annali di Roma 1798–1799', in *Due diari della Repubblica Romana del 1798–1799*, a c. di Carlo Gasbarri e Vittorio Emanuele Giuntella, Collectanea urbana, 4 (Roma, 1958), 22.

4 Vennero conservate le case di Gesù e Maria al Corso, degli Agostiniani scalzi; Santa Maria in Traspontina e San Martino ai Monti, dei Carmelitani; Santa Maria della Scala dei Carmelitani scalzi; Santa Croce in Gerusalemme dei Cistercensi; Santa Maria sopra Minerva, dei Domenicani; Santa Maria in Vallicella degli Oratoriani; Sant'Andrea delle Fratte e San Francesco di Paola, dei Minimi; Santi XII Apostoli, dei Minori Conventuali; San Francesco a Ripa, dei Minori Osservanti Riformati; Missione a Monte Citorio, dei Vincenziani; Santa Maria a' Monti, dei Pii Operai; Santi Cosma e Damiano, del Terz'Ordine regolare di San Francesco; Trinità a Strada Condotta, dei Trinitari spagnoli; San Carlo alle Quattro Fontane dei Trinitari scalzi spagnoli.

5 Santa Prisca, San Giorgio al Velabro, San Nicola da Tolentino, San Idelfonso, Santa Maria in Montesanto, San Crisogono in Trastevere, Santa Maria della Vittoria, San Pancrazio, Sant'Anna alle Quattro Fontane, Ospizio a' Carbognani, Santa Maria in Carinis, Ospizio ad Ara Coeli, San Bernardo alle Terme, Santa Sabina all'Aventino, San Clemente, San Sisto, Santa Maria in Monte Mario, San Girolamo della Carità, Trinità dei Monti, Santa Maria della Luce, San Giovanni a Porta Latina, Santa Dorotea, Sant'Ephrem Siro, San Bartolomeo all'Isola, San Pietro in Montorio, Sant'Andrea a Monte Cavallo, San Giuseppe alla Lungara, Santa Balbina, San Silvestro, San Paolo alla Regola, San Dionigio, Santa Francesca Romana, Santa Maria delle Fornaci. Per queste e per le altre soppressioni ecclesiastiche avvenute a Roma nel 1798–1799, con specifica attenzione alla confisca dei beni artistici, cf. Pier Paolo Racioppi, *Arte e Roma. Città e patrimonio artistico nella Repubblica Romana (1798–99)* (Roma, 2018), 85–120.

6 Per la storia dei conventi francescani romani durante la Repubblica Romana, cf. Luigi Sergio Mecocci, 'La *Repubblica Romana* del 1798–1799 ed i frati minori della Provincia Romana', *Archivum Franciscanum Historicum*, 91 (1998), 169–227 (specificamente per l'Aracoeli: 178–84; per San Pietro in Montorio: 207–09; per San Francesco a Ripa: 184–96; per San Bartolomeo all'Isola:

casa dei Carmeliatani scalzi di San Pancrazio, dei Cistercensi Foglianti di San Bernardo alle Terme, dei Teatini di San Silvestro al Quirinale, degli Agostiniani scalzi di San Nicola da Tolentino e ancora di numerosi altri ordini. Spesso i conventi e i monasteri occupati risultavano essere sede di case generalizie e provinciali degli ordini, e in qualche caso ospitavano anche collegi, noviziati e *studia* teologici, filosofici e di preparazione missionaria. Erano dunque case di "residenza" e di "formazione" in cui si custodivano ricche collezioni librarie, che in quegli "anni funesti" subirono pesantissime dispersioni.

Stando a quanto attestato dalle fonti, molte di queste biblioteche avevano ancora un impianto generale rispondente in parte ai dettami del Concilio di Trento. Talvolta avevano un nucleo storico che nel tempo era stato accresciuto per acquisto e/o dono, in base a disposizioni specifiche dettate da ciascun Ordine. Spesso erano a uso interno del convento o del monastero ma, su richiesta, disponibili anche per studiosi esterni. Per lo più e da tempo, erano costituite quasi prevalentemente da stampati, in genere organizzati in classi. Conservavano anche libri proibiti, quasi sempre collocati in una specifica sezione. Talvolta la loro gestione era affidata a un religioso, incaricato anche della stesura e dell'aggiornamento dell'inventario, spesso redatto in duplice copia (una era conservata in archivio e aveva forse una valenza patrimoniale). In qualche caso il bibliotecario svolgeva anche la funzione di archivista: poteva succedere infatti che non esistesse una separazione netta tra archivio e biblioteca e che carte e materiali archivistici fossero collocati negli stessi ambienti dei libri a stampa e dei manoscritti.

Il decreto del 10 maggio 1798 stabiliva che dopo l'allontanamento dei religiosi e la confisca formale delle loro case e di tutto ciò che in esse era conservato, una commissione di cinque membri, nominata dall'Istituto Nazionale[7] che soprintendeva alla pubblica istruzione, dovesse scegliere da ciascuna raccolta gli eventuali libri da conservare. La destinazione dei materiali selezionati variava in rapporto alla tipologia di libro requisito: i manoscritti venivano destinati alla Biblioteca Vaticana, mentre gli stampati alla Casanatense; i volumi restanti sarebbero stati venduti. Infatti, già nell'estate 1798 furono organizzate e pubblicate almeno cinque aste librarie: a luglio fu la volta delle biblioteche di San Paolino alla Regola, poi di San Pancrazio e di San Pietro in Montorio, messe in vendita insieme al mobilio e assegnate "all'ultimo e migliore oblatore"[8]. Entrambe queste ultime raccolte furono anche pesantemente disperse per vie non ufficiali[9]. Toccò poi ai libri di San

---

7 Sulla nascita e sulle competenze dell'Istituto: Luigi Pepe, 'L'Istituto nazionale della Repubblica Romana', *Mélanges de l'École française de Rome. Italie et Méditerranée*, 108 (1996), 703–30.

8 *Collezione di carte pubbliche, proclami*, come alla nota 3, II, 283.

9 Molti libri della biblioteca di San Pietro in Montorio – almeno 700 volumi – così come alcuni di quelli di San Paolino alla Regola, di Santa Dorotea, di Santa Maria delle Fornaci, di San Silvestro al Quirinale, di Santa Sabina e di Trinità dei Monti, finirono nelle mani del poco onesto libraio Giuseppe Nave, che se ne impossessò in parte furtivamente, in parte acquistandoli 'ad un prezzo vilissimo' e li raccolse e nascose presso il convento femminile delle *Convertite al Corso*, utilizzato come suo magazzino: cf. Fabio Tarzia, *Libri e rivoluzioni: figure e mentalità nella Roma di fine ancien régime (1770–1800)*, Studi e ricerche di storia dell'editoria, 7 (Milano, 2000), *ad indicem* a 102–05; a 104 nt 130 e Rita, *Biblioteche e requisizioni librarie a Roma*, come alla nota 6, 329–30; a 330 nt. 1252 indicazioni bibliografiche sul Nave. Sui materiali d'archivio e sui manoscritti di San Pancrazio finiti ai 'salumieri di Campo Marzio e di Campo dei Fiori' e poi recuperati grazie all'interesse e all'operato dei carmelitani: *ibid.*, 338 nt. 1283.

209–11). Cf. anche *Due diari della Repubblica Romana del 1789–1799*, come alla nota 3, con due sommarie cronache degli avvenimenti accaduti nel periodo in cui Roma era 'in mano dei Francesi', redatte direttamente dai religiosi. Altre indicazioni bibliografiche in Andreina Rita, *Biblioteche e requisizioni librarie a Roma in età napoleonica. Cronologia e fonti romane*, Studi e testi, 470 (Città del Vaticano, 2012), 20 nt. 7.

Giuseppe alla Lungara, di San Crisogono e di Santa Dorotea[10]. Altre quattro collezioni andarono vendute a settembre; tra esse la ricca biblioteca dei Minimi del convento della Trinità dei Monti, che fu messa all'asta insieme ai "legni della Sagrestia"[11].

La confisca delle biblioteche dei religiosi romani nella fase iniziale fu dunque attuata così come prevedeva la legge; lo documenta anche il racconto di un uomo interno all'ambiente papale, Giuseppe Antonio Sala (1762–1839)[12], che solo molti anni dopo riceverà la porpora cardinalizia:

L'Istituto Nazionale sceglie i manoscritti nelle biblioteche soppresse per trasportarli al Vaticano, dove vengono ora collocati anco i libri in stampa, non essendovi luogo di riporli nella Casanatense, né danaro per aumentarne a tale oggetto la fabrica. Tutti i libri poi, che rimangono dopo una tal scelta, si vendono d'ordinario a un prezzo anco più vile di quello che vendevasi in addietro la cartaccia, e di fatto per la maggior parte finiscono in mano de' pizzicaroli, o di altri bottegari[13].

Secondo la cronaca del Sala si derogò dunque alla legge in un solo aspetto e, sembrerebbe, per necessità: a causa della mancanza di spazi in cui collocare i volumi, almeno una parte degli stampati che la commissione ritenne utile conservare fu raccolta in Vaticana e non in Casanatense, come inizialmente prescritto.

La variazione nel *modus operandi* è confermata anche da un resoconto di Gaetano Marini (1742–1815), prefetto degli Archivi Vaticani, e in seguito anche primo custode della Biblioteca, che nel 1810 si trasferì a Parigi per l'allestimento degli Archivi Imperiali[14]. Il documento, finora inedito e privo di data, ma probabilmente successivo alla caduta della prima Repubblica Romana, fu stilato dallo stesso Marini per attestare e giustificare il suo operato "in servigio della S. Sede e della causa pubblica [...] nell'assenza di Nostra Santità da Roma"[15]. Riguardo alle dispersioni librarie, il Marini si attribuisce, in particolare, il merito di

---

10   *Collezione di carte pubbliche, proclami*, come alla nota 3, II, 514.

11   *Ibid.*, 546.

12   Per un primo approccio biografico, cf. Philippe Boutry, *Souverain et Pontife. Recherches prosopographiques sur la Curie Romaine à l'âge de la Restauration (1814–1816)*, Collection de l'École française de Rome, 300 (Rome, 2002), 461–63.

13   Giuseppe Antonio Sala, *Diario romano degli anni 1798–1799*, ristampa con premessa di Vittorio Emanuele Giuntella e indice analitico di Renata Tacus Lancia, Miscellanea della Società romana di storia patria, 1–3. Scritti di Giuseppe Antonio Sala pubblicati sugli autografi da Giuseppe Cugnoni, 1–3 (Roma, 1980), III, 25.

14   Per un profilo biografico: Domenico Rocciolo, *Marini, Gaetano*, in *Dizionario biografico degli italiani*, 70 (Roma, 2008), 451–54; anche Boutry, *Souverain et Pontife*, come alla nota 12, 583–85 e Marco Buonocore, *Tra i codici epigrafici della Biblioteca Apostolica Vaticana*, Epigrafia e antichità, 22 (Faenza, 2004), *ad indicem*; per la bibliografia 86 nt. 117. Sul Marini e sulla sua attività in Vaticana cf. Andreina Rita 'Tra Rivoluzione e Restaurazione. La Vaticana di Marini, Battaglini e Baldi', in *Storia della Biblioteca Apostolica Vaticana, V: La Biblioteca Vaticana dall'occupazione francese all'ultimo papa re (1797–1878)*, a c. di Andreina Rita (Città del Vaticano, 2020), 55–103, che in particolare per il § 2.4 prende avvio da questo lavoro; specificamente per il periodo della prima occupazione francese, anche: Marco Maiorino, 'L'unione dei due Archivi segreti. Gaetano Marini e il trasferimento dell'Archivio di Castel Sant'Angelo nel Vaticano', in *Gaetano Marini (1742–1815), protagonista della cultura europea. Scritti per il bicentenario della morte*, a c. di Marco Buonocore, I, Studi e testi, 492 (Città del Vaticano, 2015), 327–55; per la Biblioteca Vaticana vista dal primo custode nel periodo in cui si trovava a Parigi: Antonio Manfredi e Andreina Rita, 'Notizie sulla Vaticana in età napoleonica da dieci lettere inedite di Gaetano Marini ad Angelo Battaglini (Parigi 1810–1815)', *ibid.*, 515–85.

15   Il documento, in copia di mano di Angelo Battaglini, secondo custode della Biblioteca Vaticana ai tempi di Marini, si conserva sciolto, tra altri materiali legati al Marini, all'interno del codice Città del Vaticano, *Biblioteca Apostolica Vaticana*, Arch. Bibl. 52, pt. A, ed è segnato fol. Ir-v; è qui edito in *Appendice documentaria*, I. Una stesura più breve, con alcune varianti, fu data alle

avere "messo in sicuro" nella Biblioteca Vaticana numerosi codici greci dell'abbazia di Grottaferrata, alcuni "rinomatissimi" di quelli di Farfa, "14 gran tomi di antiche pergamene dell'Archivio di S. Francesca Romana", tutti i manoscritti e gli incunaboli del Collegio Capranica[16]. E ancora, grazie al suo interessamento e al suo operato – sostiene infatti di essere intervenuto con "iterate istanze e memorie" – furono trasferiti in Vaticana "circa 26 mila libri stampati, scelti da alcuni membri dell'Istituto dalle soppresse librerie, i quali, stati da prima deposti in alcune stanze della Minerva, vi soffrivano continue e pubbliche ruberie"[17].

Molti dei libri requisiti agli ordini religiosi romani furono quindi raccolti in Vaticana: i manoscritti, secondo quanto prescritto dalla legge, ma anche una gran quantità di stampati, che invece sarebbe dovuta giungere in Casanatense. Nella biblioteca pontificia i libri a stampa furono suddivisi in classi e collocati[18].

Di questo ingente spostamento librario e del conseguente accrescimento della Vaticana avvenuto tra il 1798 e il 1799, non sono tuttavia note finora fonti dirette: in particolare, tranne piccole e sporadiche menzioni, non se ne trova

traccia nell'Archivio della Biblioteca. Eppure il passaggio dei libri degli ordini religiosi avvenne; lo attestano le cronache coeve, alcune redatte dai testimoni diretti di quegli eventi, e soprattutto lo documentano i moltissimi volumi provenienti dalle biblioteche religiose romane che si conservano ancora in Vaticana.

La mancanza di fonti non permette al momento di delineare analiticamente l'intera vicenda. Non sono note con certezza neppure tutte le case religiose da cui, durante l'occupazione giacobina, furono confiscati libri. Non è chiaro se il trasferimento fu diretto o se, come riferito dal Marini, i libri a stampa furono dapprima portati e accatastati in Casanatense e solo in un secondo momento trasferiti in Vaticana, per garantirne la conservazione e preservarli da ulteriori smembramenti. Non si conoscono i nomi di coloro che operarono per individuare i volumi da trasferire e di quelli che organizzarono lo spostamento e non è certo se il provvedimento di confisca abbia riguardato intere raccolte o una scelta di volumi, come prescritto dal decreto del Direttorio e, in questo caso, con quali criteri ne sia stata effettuata la selezione. Probabilmente si procedette secondo poche regole generali e ciascuna raccolta libraria ebbe una sorte propria.

Ad esempio, la biblioteca dei Francescani dell'Aracoeli[19] subì una pesantissima dispersione.

---

stampe nel 1822 dal nipote del Marini: Marino Marini, *Degli aneddoti di Gaetano Marini. Commentario di suo nipote Marino* (Roma, 1822), 188–93.

16 I libri del Collegio Capranica e le pergamene degli Olivetani di Santa Francesca Romana furono richiesti 'alle Municipalità e ai commissari classificatori', cf. la lettera a Gaetano Marini, 28 settembre 1798, in Città del Vaticano, *Biblioteca Apostolica Vaticana*, Arch. Bibl. 101, fols 22r–23v. I materiali 'messi al sicuro' dal Marini in Vaticana vennero restituiti ai precedenti proprietari tra il dicembre 1799 e l'agosto 1800, cf. Rita, *Biblioteche e requisizioni librarie a Roma*, come alla nota 6, 287 nt. 1005, con indicazione delle fonti; anche Antonio Manfredi, 'I Vaticani latini nel secolo XIX. Dispersioni, acquisizioni e inventari. Una prima ricognizione', in *Storia della Biblioteca Apostolica Vaticana, V*, come alla nota 14, 455–58.

17 Città del Vaticano, *Biblioteca Apostolica Vaticana*, Arch. Bibl. 52, pt. A, fol. 1r.

18 Ivi.

19 Sulla storia della biblioteca francescana durante le due occupazioni francesi e sulle confische librarie: cf. Rita, *Biblioteche e requisizioni librarie a Roma*, come alla nota 6, 51–57; sui libri passati in Vaticana anche Manfredi, 'I Vaticani latini nel secolo XIX', come alla nota 16, 457–58; sulla storia della biblioteca, in generale: Marina Venier, 'The monastic libraries in Rome, from the Lists of the Religious Orders for the Sacred Congregation of the Index to the Confiscation in 1873: the reconstruction of the Eborense Library in the Monastery of Santa Maria in Aracoeli belonging to the Friars Minor Observant', in *Virtual visits to lost libraries: reconstruction of and access to dispersed collections. Papers presented on 5 November 2010 at the CERL Seminar hosted by the Royal Library of Denmark, Copenhagen*, ed. Ivan Boserup e David J. Shaw, Cerl Papers, 11 (London, 2011), 95–112; per il periodo

Come già accennato, la casa fu occupata prima della soppressione formale, e molti frati vennero allontanati; il convento, e la sua "libraria" furono saccheggiati: "si rubò a piene mani" e la biblioteca fu anche depredata dal "popolaccio [...] che tutto ne asportò, non rimanendovi che i muri e la porta"[20].

Parte dei libri dell'Aracoeli venne salvata in Vaticana[21]. I frati sperarono che questo trasferimento garantisse la conservazione di ciò che restava della loro ricca collezione libraria. Non furono trasferiti solo i manoscritti[22], come comunemente si credeva, ma anche una consistente quantità di stampati di cui per molto tempo si è ignorato il passaggio. Analogamente vennero portati in Vaticana molti dei libri a stampa della biblioteca di San Bartolomeo all'Isola, di San Bernardo alle Terme, di San Pietro in Montorio, di San Nicola da Tolentino, di San Silvestro al Quirinale, della Trinità dei Monti al Pincio. Dalle stesse raccolte furono contestualmente trasferiti anche libri manoscritti. Questo elenco di biblioteche monastiche e conventuali, allestito sulla base delle note di possesso tracciate sui volumi conservati nelle varie sezioni del fondo

Raccolta Generale[23] della Biblioteca, potrebbe essere ulteriormente accresciuto. Non si sa quando i libri vennero effettivamente trasferiti e neppure quanti furono complessivamente quelli acquisiti dalla Vaticana. L'unica cifra finora nota è trasmessa dal Marini che, come è stato già detto, riferisce di aver fatto portare nella biblioteca del papa, oltre ad altri gruppi di volumi estrapolati da specifiche collezioni, 26.000 "libri stampati"[24]. Certo è che parte di quei libri, proprio grazie al Marini, nel frattempo nominato primo custode, in seguito non rimase in Vaticana.

Infatti nel 1800, all'indomani della parentesi rivoluzionaria, ripristinato il governo pontificio, il Marini sottopose a Pio VII la proposta di conservare in Biblioteca i manoscritti e i libri trasferiti dalle collezioni degli ordini religiosi durante la prima Repubblica Romana. Contestualmente chiese l'autorizzazione per "distribuire a' conventi, che più degli altri ne abbisognano" i moltissimi stampati posseduti dalla Vaticana in duplice o triplice copia che erano stati accumulati in seguito al trasferimento delle varie biblioteche dei religiosi, spesso sovrapponibili per tipologia e posseduto. In particolare propose di beneficiare di quei volumi – che si ritenevano essere tra i 10 e i 12 mila[25] – i conventi francescani dell'Aracoeli e di San Bartolomeo all'Isola, tanto "più che dalle loro librerie si è avuta la miglior parte di tali libri".

qui considerato, 102–03, 110–11 nt. 40, con diversa lettura delle fonti. Sul convento dell'Aracoeli anche: Marianna Brancia di Apricena, *Il complesso dell'Aracoeli sul colle Capitolino (IX–XIX secolo)* (Roma, 2000); in particolare sulla biblioteca, 243–65.

20   Ottorino Montenovesi, 'La biblioteca del convento dell'Aracoeli e le sue vicende. Ricordi storici', in *La madonna d'Aracoeli negli eventi storici celebrati solennemente il 30 maggio 1948 sul colle Capitolino* (Roma, 1949), 51–53, a 52.

21   "I libri, tranne una piccola parte che alla fine riuscì a varcare le soglie del Vaticano e vi rimase, furono venduti a peso di carta, o, per pochi baiocchi, ad ebrei ed amatori di codici": ivi.

22   Il passaggio dei manoscritti alla Vaticana è stato ricostruito anche da Paolo Vian, 'Altri codici Aracoelitani nella Biblioteca Vaticana', in *Miscellanea Bibliothecae Apostolicae Vaticanae*, 2, Studi e testi, 331 (Città del Vaticano, 1988), 287–311, con identificazione e descrizione dei codici.

23   Per la struttura del fondo, articolato in molteplici sezioni, con alcune note storiche, cf. Massimo Ceresa, 'Raccolta Generale', in *Guida ai fondi manoscritti, numismatici a stampa della Biblioteca Vaticana*, a c. di Francesco D'Aiuto e Paolo Vian, Studi e testi, 466–67 (Città del Vaticano, 2010) II, 840–58. *Specimina* di queste note in Rita, 'Tra Rivoluzione e Restaurazione', come alla nota 14, 88–94.

24   Città del Vaticano, *Biblioteca Apostolica Vaticana*, Arch. Bibl. 52, pt. A, fol. 1r; lo stesso Marini in un'altra *Memoria per la Biblioteca Vaticana*, parla di '25 mila volumi, scielti dalle molte librerie de' conventi soppressi [...], e salvati per tal modo dal comun naufragio': Città del Vaticano, *Biblioteca Apostolica Vaticana*, Arch. Bibl. 37, fol. 285r.

25   Ivi.

La richiesta presentata al papa fu accolta il 12 agosto 1800 e rimessa al cardinale bibliotecario Francesco Saverio de Zelada (1717–1801), che ne autorizzò l'esecuzione[26]. Nel 1802[27], la Vaticana consegnò i volumi al superiore dell'Ordine francescano, destinandoli al convento dell'Aracoeli al Campidoglio e a quello di San Bartolomeo all'Isola Tiberina. Tuttavia, è probabile che tutti i libri siano rimasti nel convento al Campidoglio, perché la casa francescana sull'Isola Tiberina in quegli anni era in ristrutturazione[28].

Il passaggio dei libri a stampa dalla Vaticana all'Aracoeli non fu una restituzione, ma una sorta di risarcimento simbolico. I Francescani infatti non riebbero i propri libri, ma i libri trasferiti dalle altre biblioteche religiose romane. Per questo, in seguito i frati dell'Aracoeli tentarono di riavere i loro volumi, "con tutti gli attrezzi annessi", rivolgendosi direttamente a Pio VII[29]. La dispersione avvenuta durante la prima Repubblica Romana segnò dunque uno strappo nella storia della biblioteca francescana: venne meno infatti

la continuità tra la raccolta antica – fondata a metà Quattrocento e poi accresciuta fino alle magnificenze del vescovo portoghese José Maria Ribeiro da Fonseca de Évora (1690–1752) – e quella ottocentesca, costituita da ciò che restava della collezione precedente, dai numerosi duplicati ricevuti dalla Vaticana e da successive acquisizioni, databili dall'inizio del secolo XIX[30].

Ma non tutti i volumi entrati in Vaticana durante l'occupazione giacobina vi rimasero. Per esempio, vennero restituiti ai precedenti proprietari i volumi e le carte dei cosiddetti *Musici di Palazzo*[31] – in seguito riacquisiti dalla Vaticana, costituiscono ora il fondo *Cappella Sistina* –, i 242 tra libri e codici avuti dal Collegio Capranica[32] e i vari manoscritti dei Basiliani di Grottaferrata[33] e dell'Abazia di Farfa[34]. I libri trasferiti dalle biblioteche degli ordini religiosi che rimasero in Vaticana furono inseriti nei fondi aperti e ordinati prescindendo dalla loro provenienza. I manoscritti vennero collocati nei fondi *Vaticano arabo*[35], *latino*[36], *greco*, *ebraico* e *indiano*. Gli stampati inizialmente furono sistemati

---

26   Il documento è trasmesso in Città del Vaticano, *Biblioteca Apostolica Vaticana*, Arch. Bibl. 37, fol. 185r-v. In calce alla *Memoria*, il rescritto del cardinale Aurelio Roverella; segue (fol. 186r) l'ordine di esecuzione a firma del cardinal bibliotecario de Zelada, indirizzato a Gaetano Marini. La documentazione è edita in Leonhard Lemmens, 'De sorte Archivi generalis Ordinis Fratrum Minorum et Bibliothecae Aracoelitanae tempore Reipublicae Tiberinae (an. 1798–1799)', *Archivum Franciscanum historicum*, 17 (1924), 30–54, a 51–52.

27   La data è indicata in una inedita minuta di mano del secondo custode della Biblioteca Vaticana Giuseppe Baldi († 1831). Il documento non datato, si colloca probabilmente alla fine del secondo decennio dell'Ottocento: Città del Vaticano, *Biblioteca Apostolica Vaticana*, Arch. Bibl. 38, fol. 137r.

28   Ivi.

29   L'istanza che rivolsero al Santo Padre si conserva in Città del Vaticano, *Biblioteca Apostolica Vaticana*, Arch. Bibl. 37, fols 170–71. Il documento, sia pure privo di data, sembrerebbe riferibile, anche per motivi storici, alla confisca libraria avvenuta durante la prima Repubblica Romana (1798–1799). L'istanza non sembrerebbe però aver avuto seguito.

30   All'indomani della prima Repubblica Romana, l'anziano frate bibliotecario Giovanni Battista Dassori si adoperò con grande caparbietà per il ripristino della raccolta, impegnando anche "500 scudi di propria borsa", cf. Montenovesi, *La biblioteca del convento dell'Aracoeli e le sue vicende*, come alla nota 20, 52. Sulla storia della biblioteca, *supra* nt. 19.

31   Città del Vaticano, *Biblioteca Apostolica Vaticana*, Arch. Bibl. 37, fol. 181v.

32   Città del Vaticano, *Biblioteca Apostolica Vaticana*, Arch. Bibl. 37, fols 176r–77v.

33   Città del Vaticano, *Biblioteca Apostolica Vaticana*, Arch. Bibl. 37, fols 32r–33v.

34   Città del Vaticano, *Biblioteca Apostolica Vaticana*, Arch. Bibl. 37, fol. 174r.

35   Per l'elenco dei codici vaticani arabi provenienti dalla biblioteca di San Pietro in Montorio, cf. Delio Vania Proverbio e Andreina Rita, 'Vaticani arabi', in *Guida ai fondi manoscritti, numismatici, a stampa della Biblioteca Vaticana*, come alla nota 23, I, 553–64.

36   Per i manoscritti dell'Aracoeli ora nel fondo *Vaticano latino*: cf. Vian, 'Altri codici Aracoelitani', come alla nota 22.

nella cosiddetta *Seconda Raccolta*, che durante la prefettura (1895–1914) del gesuita Franz Ehrle, venne riorganizzata e suddivisa nelle varie sezioni dell'attuale *Raccolta Generale*[37].

I libri a stampa provenienti dall'Aracoeli ebbero nella fase iniziale una sorte un po' diversa: furono conservati fino alla fine dell'Ottocento in un fondo unitario col titolo di *Collezione Aracoeli*[38]; in seguito anche questo fu suddiviso nella *Raccolta Generale*.

Dunque i manoscritti e gli stampati, trasferiti in Vaticana dalle biblioteche degli ordini religiosi durante la prima Repubblica Romana, non hanno oggi una collocazione sequenziale. Inoltre, non essendo finora noti eventuali elenchi di versamento che permettano almeno l'identificazione delle opere e delle edizioni, i libri provenienti dagli ordini religiosi possono essere individuati soltanto attraverso l'analisi diretta degli esemplari. Gli eventuali elementi riconducibili alla storia dell'esemplare – note di possesso, *ex libris*, antiche segnature, annotazioni presenti sull'unità fisica – costituiscono la prova o almeno l'indizio per suggerire la provenienza del volume. Segni, spesso tracciati nelle periferie del libro, attraverso cui ricostruire la storia dell'esemplare; segni che mettono in relazione il singolo volume con l'intera

raccolta di cui era parte, definendone nel caso specifico la provenienza fisica e culturale.

L'occupazione napoleonica (1808–1814): la Biblioteca imperiale e la Biblioteca municipale[39]

Le premesse alla successiva confisca libraria furono gettate nel febbraio 1808, quando, dopo un breve e apparente ritorno alla "normalità", Roma fu di nuovo occupata dalle truppe francesi; annessa poi all'Impero, fu proclamata "ville imperiale et libre" (17 maggio 1809). Il conflitto tra il papa e Napoleone, esploso già dal 1805, sia sul piano politico che su quello religioso, culminò nell'assalto *manu militari* del Palazzo del Quirinale e nella deportazione di Pio VII avvenuta nella notte tra il 5 e il 6 luglio 1809. Poi, a distanza di circa un anno, gli ordini religiosi romani furono di nuovo soppressi, per legge imperiale (7 maggio 1810). Di nuovo, la soppressione significò la confisca del patrimonio immobiliare e dei beni mobili, libri compresi. Tutto venne censito e valutato. Anche la questione delle biblioteche dei frati e dei monaci venne disciplinata dalla Consulta Straordinaria – l'organo temporaneamente incaricato dell'amministrazione e del governo del Dipartimento[40].

---

37 Per la descrizione del fondo nelle sue articolazioni, con introduzione storica, cf. Ceresa, 'Raccolta Generale', come alla nota 23.

38 L'esistenza di tale fondo è attestata da una rara pianta topografica delle due sale della Biblioteca Vaticana allestite durante il pontificato di Leone XIII, edita in Mariano Ugolini, 'La nuova biblioteca Leonina in Vaticana Memoria', in *Nel giubileo episcopale di Leone XIII. Omaggio della Biblioteca Vaticana* (Roma, 1893); ripubblicata più recentemente in Raffaele Farina, '"Splendore veritatis gaudet ecclesia". Leone XIII e la Biblioteca Vaticana', *Miscellanea Bibliothecae Apostolicae Vaticanae*, 11, Studi e testi, 423 (Città del Vaticano, 2004), 285–370, a 313, e in Andreina Rita, 'La Biblioteca Vaticana nelle sue architetture', in *Biblioteca Apostolica Vaticana: libri e luoghi all'inizio del terzo millennio* (Città del Vaticano, 2011), 70–123, a 100, è in entrambi riferita per errore ad altra opera.

39 Per la ricostruzione analitica delle requisizioni librarie avvenute in questo periodo mi permetto di rimandare a Rita, *Biblioteche e requisizioni librarie a Roma*, come alla nota 6, con bibliografia e fonti dettagliate, qui omesse per brevità; un cenno generale anche in Eadem, 'Tra Rivoluzione e Restaurazione', come alla nota 14, 74–76, in cui si sintetizza parte di questo lavoro.

40 Sull'attività della Consulta Straordinaria cf. Carla Nardi, *Napoleone e Roma. La politica della Consulta Romana*, Collection de l'École française de Rome, 115 (Roma, 1989); ora, in particolare per gli interventi relativi alle arti, anche Ilaria Sgarbozza, *Le spalle al Settecento. Forma, modelli e organizzazione dei musei nella Roma napoleonica (1809–1814)* (Città del Vaticano, 2013), 23–49.

Il 15 ottobre 1810, fu stabilita con decreto[41] l'apertura alla pubblica consultazione di tre biblioteche romane appartenute a congregazioni religiose ormai soppresse: la Casanatense o Minerva dei Domenicani, l'Angelica degli Agostiniani e l'Aracoeli al Campidoglio dei Francescani. Le tre raccolte librarie confiscate ai religiosi e gli edifici che le ospitavano passarono dunque nelle competenze della Municipalità, su cui ricadde, oltre all'onere di garantirne la "publicità" anche quello di mantenerle, gestirle e accrescerle, fornendole anche "de' libri moderni, di cui mancano assolutamente". Ma, delle tre, la Casanatense fu di fatto considerata l'unica Biblioteca Municipale, forse anche per motivazioni pratiche quali lo stato di conservazione degli ambienti e dei libri posseduti, la notorietà e la prassi (aveva avuto un ruolo preminente anche durante la prima Repubblica Romana). La sua gestione fu affidata al consigliere di Prefettura Luigi Marini (1778–1838)[42] che la diresse avvalendosi, anche se in forma non ufficiale, dei due precedenti bibliotecari domenicani. La Consulta e gli organi di governo che si succedettero nell'amministrazione di Roma durante l'occupazione napoleonica, dibatterono a lungo sulle sorti della Biblioteca Angelica e dell'Aracoeli, ma sembrerebbe senza alcuna ripercussione pratica[43].

Nel frattempo, il 19 novembre 1810, il prefetto degli Stati Romani, Camille de Tournon (1778–1833), in applicazione del precedente decreto della Consulta, aveva stabilito di raccogliere presso la Casanatense i "manuscritti e i libri preziosi" conservati nelle case religiose soppresse, non solo di Roma ma di tutto il Dipartimento del Tevere[44]. Si decise di non trasferire integralmente nella Biblioteca Municipale le collezioni librarie di ciascun istituto religioso, come forse era stato fatto nella precedente occupazione francese, ma di scegliere alcuni volumi – per lo più i codici e gli stampati preziosi ed eventualmente quelli mancanti – selezionati secondo precisi criteri da una commissione specificamente nominata. Per legge, ogni requisizione era documentata in un processo verbale, allestito in duplice copia, nel quale si elencavano "sommariamente il numero e la specie delle opere rimesse". Per evitare l'accumulo di duplicati, si vietava addirittura la confisca di due esemplari della stessa opera. Il catalogo generale dei volumi trasportati in Casanatense sarebbe stato redatto, successivamente al versamento, dal bibliotecario responsabile dell'istituzione.

Così, per meglio rispondere ai "bisogni dell'istruzione", si allestiva a Roma, come nelle altre maggiori città dell'Impero, una "libraria municipale" nella quale raccogliere, per "pubblica utilità" e dunque a disposizione di tutti i lettori, i libri che prima erano disponibili soltanto per pochi, smembrati in più conventi e monasteri "chiusi e inaccessibili" – ma quest'ultima affermazione si dimostrò in realtà un pregiudizio[45].

---

41 *Bollettino delle leggi e decreti imperiali pubblicati dalla Consulta Straordinaria negli Stati Romani*, 12 (1810), 124, 223–25. Il decreto fu pubblicato anche nel *Giornale del Campidoglio*, 20 ottobre 1810, 509.

42 Cavaliere della Corona di Ferro, fu nominato direttore della Biblioteca Municipale il 12 novembre 1810: Roma, *Archivio di Stato*, Archivio Marini-Clarelli, b. 75, 1. Su di lui: Camillo Ravioli, *Della vita e delle opere di Luigi Marini* (Roma, 1858); ora anche Fausta Dommarco, 'Profilo di un burocrate: Luigi Marini direttore generale dei Catasti', in *Roma fra la Restaurazione e l'elezione di Pio IX. Amministrazione, economia, società e cultura*, a c. di Anna Lia Bonella, Augusto Pompeo e Manola Ida Venzo (Roma, 1997), 119–33, interessato soprattutto alle vicende post napoleoniche, ma con ampi riferimenti agli anni precedenti; data la nomina a direttore della Casanatense al 1811 (p. 123).

43 Rita, *Biblioteche e requisizioni librarie a Roma*, come alla nota 6, 52–53.

44 *Bollettino delle leggi*, 13.1 (1810), 128, 99–101.

45 Sull'organizzazione delle maggiori biblioteche romane e sulla loro apertura al pubblico, si veda la *Memoria sopra le Biblioteche* redatta il 7 agosto 1809 dal conservatore della Vaticana Filippo Aurelio Visconti (1754–1831) su richiesta dell'erudito Joseph Marie de Gérando

In questa prospettiva, a partire dal novembre 1811 furono avviate le requisizioni delle biblioteche degli ordini religiosi soppressi. Diversamente da quanto avvenne per le carte requisite dagli archivi, trasferite e accentrate a Parigi[46], i libri furono dunque raccolti in Casanatense. Si iniziò dalla collezione libraria dei Domenicani di Santa Sabina da cui furono presi circa 100 titoli. Si passò poi a scegliere da quella degli Agostiniani lombardi di Santa Maria del Popolo e da quella degli Agostiniani scalzi del convento di Gesù e Maria al Corso. Fu poi la volta delle biblioteche dei Passionisti dei Santi Giovanni e Paolo al Celio e dei Gerolamini dei Santi Bonifacio e Alessio all'Aventino. In quello stesso periodo furono confiscati e trasferiti in Casanatense circa 5.000 titoli scelti dalle diverse raccolte librarie custodite nel convento francescano dei Santi XII Apostoli. Ci si apprestava poi a scegliere dalla nota e preziosa biblioteca dei Cistercensi di Santa Croce in Gerusalemme, famosa per la quantità e il pregio dei manoscritti greci conservati, quando le confische librarie furono bruscamente interrotte a causa di un contenzioso giuridico insorto tra la Corona e la Municipalità.

Nella primavera 1811 era giunto a Roma il barone Martial Daru (1774–1827)[47], con nomina imperiale di intendente dei beni della Corona nei Dipartimenti del Tevere e del Trasimeno.

In aperto contrasto con il Governo Municipale, l'alto funzionario rivendicava alla Corona il possesso di gran parte del patrimonio mobile e immobile confiscato dall'Impero al papato, tra cui addirittura la basilica di San Pietro[48]. La *querelle* tra le due autorità governative si risolse con l'assegnazione alla Corona di alcuni palazzi pontifici – tra cui il Quirinale e le sue pertinenze, i Musei, la Biblioteca, l'Archivio, la Calcografia – e di tutti gli oggetti d'arte e di antichità conservati negli edifici pubblici di Roma e del Vaticano. Per questi ultimi, il Daru chiese un dettagliato censimento che, in funzione della presa di possesso, ne determinasse l'esatta e reale consistenza e lo stato di conservazione. Fu eseguita anche la ricognizione del posseduto della Biblioteca Vaticana. Venne affidata a due verificatori esterni[49] – Michelangelo Lanci (1779–1867)[50] e Raffaele Scaramucci (1786–1863)[51] – entrambi professori alla Sapienza, ma l'Intendente, e non solo lui, non fu soddisfatto del loro operato[52].

Il Daru aveva progetti ambiziosi per quella importante biblioteca dalla storia secolare, che era stata dei pontefici e che ora era dell'Imperatore, e di cui lui stesso era stato nominato amministratore. Voleva farne una grandiosa e

(1772–1842), membro della Consulta Straordinaria: Città del Vaticano, *Biblioteca Apostolica Vaticana*, Arch. Bibl. 56, fols 3r–8v (copia calligrafica autografa); il testo è edito in Rita, *Biblioteche e requisizioni librarie a Roma*, come alla nota 6, 435–37.

46 Sull'ambizioso progetto di raccogliere a Parigi tutti gli archivi dell'Impero, cf. Maria Pia Donato, *L'archivio del mondo. Quando Napoleone confiscò la storia* (Bari, 2019); per la documentazione relativa alle case religiose romane, offre ancora valide indicazioni Odoric-Marie Jouve, 'Odyssée des archives monastiques de Rome, 1810–1814', *La France Franciscaine*, 6 (1923), 1–46.

47 Su di lui da ultimi: Henri Daru, *Martial Daru baron d'Empire, 1774–1827: maître et bienfaiteur de Stendhal* (Paris, 2009) e Sgarbozza, *Le spalle al Settecento*, come alla nota 40, 121–26.

48 Sulla questione anche Carla Nardi, *Napoleone e Roma. Dalla Consulta Romana al ritorno di Pio VII (1811–1814)* (Roma, 2005), 67–76.

49 Cf. la disposizione del barone Laurent-Marie Janet (1768–1841) del 28 aprile 1811 conservata in Paris, *Arch. Nat.*, Maison de l'Empereur. Domaine étranger, Italie, Belgique, Hollande, O², 1072, fol. 112r ora edita in Sgarbozza, *Le spalle al Settecento*, come alla nota 40, 260–61: *Appendice documentaria XI*.

50 Riferimenti biografici corredati da bibliografia in Rita, *Biblioteche e requisizioni librarie a Roma*, come alla nota 6, 94 nt. 3; ora anche in *Storia della Biblioteca Apostolica Vaticana*, V, come alla nota 14, *ad indicem*.

51 Riferimenti biografici corredati da bibliografia in Rita, *Biblioteche e requisizioni librarie a Roma*, come alla nota 6, 58–59 nt. 34.

52 Daru, *Martial Daru*, come alla nota 47, 271; Rita, *Biblioteche e requisizioni librarie a Roma*, come alla nota 6, 70–71.

scelta collezione libraria, fornita dei libri più preziosi e delle rarità bibliologiche, degna della seconda città dell'Impero. Un simbolo della magnificenza artistica e culturale della Roma napoleonica. Per questo intendeva trasferirvi i volumi delle biblioteche degli ordini religiosi romani, notoriamente ricche di libri rari e pregevoli. Ma il desiderio dell'Intendente si scontrava con quanto progettato e parzialmente realizzato dalla Municipalità. Così le biblioteche degli ordini religiosi soppressi divennero un ulteriore oggetto del contendere. Il contenzioso tra Corona e Municipalità fu risolto nel giugno 1812 anche grazie all'intervento dell'intendente generale *de la Maison de l'empereur*, Jean-Baptiste Nompère de Champagny[53], duca di Cadore (1756–1834), al quale il Daru si rivolse per appoggiare la sua causa, e che ottenne dal ministro dell'interno, Jean-Pierre Bachasson conte di Montalivet (1766–1823), l'agognata decisione[54].

La priorità nella confisca libraria fu concessa alla Biblioteca Imperiale e dunque alla Vaticana, che per prima effettuò il sopralluogo delle raccolte e la selezione dei libri da requisire. Dopo questa prima scelta, le biblioteche dei religiosi romani vennero sottoposte a un'ulteriore valutazione da parte dei funzionari della Casanatense. I libri restanti, ossia quelli non scelti per la confisca, – spesso la gran parte della collezione – furono lasciati nelle case religiose; inizialmente affidati alla custodia del Demanio, passarono poi nelle competenze del Commissario per le requisizioni librarie. In seguito molti di quei volumi, considerati di scarto, vennero trasportati e "accatastati" nel Collegio Urbano di Propaganda Fide, nel frattempo trasformato in una sorta di grande

deposito librario. Si pensava di venderli, ma di fatto solo una piccola parte venne effettivamente messa all'asta[55].

Dall'inverno 1812, la requisizione dei libri dei religiosi romani fu eseguita da una specifica commissione coordinata da un funzionario nominato *ad hoc*. L'incarico fu assegnato al dotto marchese Agricol-Joseph Fortia d'Urban (1756–1843)[56], alla cui presenza prima i conservatori della Vaticana e poi il direttore della Casanatense scelsero i libri da trasferire. Era nella commissione anche il rappresentante del Demanio Luigi Montanari. La confisca a favore della Vaticana fu materialmente eseguita dagli stessi funzionari che operarono nella Biblioteca papale anche in età pontificia, prima e dopo Napoleone. Si trattava dei conservatori Angelo Battaglini (1759–1842)[57], Angelo Uggeri (1754–1837)[58] e Filippo Aurelio Visconti[59]. I volumi destinati alla Casanatense furono invece

---

53 Su di lui, cf. la voce nel *Dictionnaire Napoléon*, sous la direction de Jean Toulard (Paris, 1987), 398–99.

54 Daru, *Martial Daru*, come alla nota 47, 272. Sul conte di Montalivet, cf. il sito della Fondation Napoléon, all'indirizzo online: https://www.napoleon.org/FR/salle_lecture/biographies/files/Montalivet_allegret_RSN46061.asp (ultima consultazione luglio 2020).

55 Certamente fu venduta al pubblico incanto l'intera biblioteca dei Serviti di San Marcello al Corso: lo dimostra *l'avviso di vendita* stampato da Luigi Perego Salvioni, conservato in Città del Vaticano, *Archivio storico della Congregazione "De Propaganda Fide"*, Acta 175, fol. 497v.

56 Per le indicazioni bio-bibliografiche cf. Rita, *Biblioteche e requisizioni librarie a Roma*, come alla nota 6, 33–34 nt. 48. In una lettera del luglio 1813 al Conte di Cadore il Daru lamenterà la negligenza del Fortia e proporrà di sopprimerne il ruolo: cf. Daru, *Martial Daru*, come alla nota 47, 272.

57 Soprannumerario dal 1791, fu tra i protagonisti della storia della Biblioteca Vaticana nell'età napoleonica: cf. Rita, *Biblioteche e requisizioni librarie a Roma*, come alla nota 6, *ad indicem* e in particolare, 72–73 e anche *Storia della Biblioteca Apostolica Vaticana, V*, come alla nota 14, *ad indicem*.

58 Sull'attività in Biblioteca: Rita, *Biblioteche e requisizioni librarie a Roma*, come alla nota 6, 74 nt. 19; anche Manfredi e Rita, 'Notizie sulla Vaticana', come alla nota 14, 534 nt. 111 e *Storia della Biblioteca Apostolica Vaticana, V*, come alla nota 14, *ad indicem*.

59 Per le indicazioni bio-bibliografiche: Rita, *Biblioteche e requisizioni librarie a Roma*, come alla nota 6, 74 nt. 20 e *Storia della Biblioteca Apostolica Vaticana, V*, come alla nota 14, *ad indicem*.

scelti da Francesco Saverio Magno (1728–1841)[60] e Pietro Paolo Buttaoni (1775–1859)[61], i due Domenicani responsabili della biblioteca prima dell'occupazione napoleonica. Tuttavia i nomi dei due frati compaiono nei verbali di confisca solo prima della nomina del Fortia; in seguito la documentazione relativa alle confische destinate alla Casanatense sarà sempre sottoscritta dal direttore Luigi Marini.

Per evitare l'accumulo di duplicati – avvenuto nel 1798–1799 – e secondo quanto aveva già fatto applicare il de Tournon, le raccolte non vennero requisite integralmente, ma furono scelti i volumi da trasferire. La selezione fu eseguita dapprima sugli inventari, se esistenti, e poi con il sopralluogo alla raccolta. Furono presi i libri di maggior pregio bibliologico, bibliografico e storico e quelli mancanti alla biblioteca di destinazione. Per ogni confisca fu redatto un verbale[62] con allegata la lista delle opere requisite. Un primo elenco di biblioteche da cui prendere libri fu stilato dai conservatori della Vaticana nell'aprile 1811 su richiesta del Daru[63]. Essi indicarono come particolarmente interessanti solo poche raccolte librarie: quella di Santa Croce in Gerusalemme, segnalata per la notevole quantità di manoscritti greci posseduti; la Vallicelliana alla Chiesa Nuova e la collezione dei Benedettini di San Callisto, in cui si custodivano "tanto manoscritti, quanto buone,

e rare edizioni"; la collezione del monastero di Sant'Alessio sull'Aventino e quella del Collegio di San Bonaventura in Ss. Apostoli, ricordate per la presenza di stampati rari. Precisarono inoltre che in quasi tutte le biblioteche dei religiosi romani, "anche le meno scelte, può rinvenirsi qualche cosa di pregievole" e per questo sostennero l'opportunità di "confrontare di ciascuna i cataloghi". Il suggerimento fu accolto: la lista definitiva delle raccolte da requisire, allestita poi dal commissario Fortia, era infatti molto più nutrita di quella stilata dai conservatori. Vi erano elencate le biblioteche di tutti gli ordini religiosi che avevano una casa romana: Passionisti, Domenicani, Gesuiti, Francescani – Alcantarini, Conventuali, Osservanti, Osservanti riformati, Terziari – Agostiniani e Carmelitani scalzi e calzati, Cistercensi, Benedettini di tutte le numerose congregazioni, Canonici regolari, Scolopi, Teatini, Camilliani, Caracciolini, Somaschi, Barnabiti, Oratoriani, Chierici regolari della Madre di Dio, Girolamini, Pii operai, Trinitari, Mercedari e Scalzetti. Talvolta furono confiscate più biblioteche dello stesso Ordine.

Tra il 1811 e il 1814, i funzionari di Vaticana e Casanatense valutarono per la requisizione complessivamente 67 biblioteche romane di ordini religiosi maschili. In qualche caso, le raccolte, sebbene segnalate come potenzialmente "interessanti", non furono trovate perché già in precedenza smembrate, per lo più durante l'occupazione giacobina. In altri casi, le biblioteche vennero lasciate intatte perché i libri che le costituivano furono considerati privi di qualsiasi valore e quindi non confiscati.

I conservatori della Vaticana scelsero da 54 biblioteche religiose romane. Da esse trasferirono oltre 6.100 opere a stampa e 817 codici per un totale di circa 20.000 volumi[64]. Il computo

---

60 Per un inquadramento bibliografico: Rita, *Biblioteche e requisizioni librarie a Roma*, come alla nota 6, 63–64 nt. 53.

61 Al secolo Domenico, alcuni anni dopo fu nominato Maestro del Sacro Palazzo: *ibid.*, 64 nt. 54.

62 Il formulario utilizzato variava in funzione della natura istituzionale della biblioteca di destinazione: imperiale la Vaticana, municipale la Casanatense. Per qualche esempio, cf. Rita, *Biblioteche e requisizioni librarie a Roma*, come alla nota 6, 447–52.

63 La richiesta del Daru e la risposta dei conservatori vaticani è trasmessa in copia di mano del Battaglini in Città del Vaticano, *Biblioteca Apostolica Vaticana*, Arch. Bibl. 52, pt. A, 75–76; entrambi i testi sono editi in Rita, *Biblioteche e requisizioni librarie a Roma*, come alla nota 6, 453–54.

64 Il totale delle opere a stampa e dei manoscritti scelti è calcolato sui verbali di confisca; il numero dei volumi è tratto dalle stime dei conservatori vaticani.

non includeva i 1.330 manoscritti trasferiti dalla Vallicelliana, la biblioteca romana degli Oratoriani di San Filippo Neri, e i materiali provenienti dall'Archivio dei cantori della Cappella Sistina. In Vaticana i volumi di queste due istituzioni vennero infatti sempre conservati separatamente e in un unico blocco e per questo, dopo la caduta di Napoleone, la restituzione ai precedenti possessori fu estremamente lineare, non essendo necessaria l'individuazione dei singoli esemplari.

Durante il triennio 1811–1814, furono formalmente trasferite in Casanatense circa 16.000 opere, ma la cifra, calcolata sui verbali di confisca finora noti, potrebbe essere molto maggiore. Provenivano da 41 biblioteche romane.

Moltissimi altri volumi furono raccolti nei locali del Collegio Urbano di Propaganda Fide per essere venduti all'asta. Negli stessi luoghi vennero accatastati anche i mobili e le scansie di alcune delle biblioteche soppresse.

Altri libri rimasero nelle case religiose, ridotte ormai a crisalidi vuote, in balia dei "tarli" e dei "ladri".

Nella primavera 1814, Napoleone abdicò, e dopo la breve e poco significativa parentesi del Governo Napoletano, il 24 maggio Pio VII rientrò trionfalmente a Roma. Papa e curia cercarono di ristabilire per quanto possibile una sorta di *status quo ante* nel tentativo di incoraggiare la ripresa degli ordini religiosi disgregati e profondamente provati dalle due devastanti occupazioni francesi che si erano succedute nel giro di poco più di un decennio. Le Congregazioni furono ripristinate e papa Pio VII volle che il patrimonio librario requisito durante il periodo napoleonico fosse restituito ai precedenti proprietari, quasi a sottolineare, nonostante la frattura subita, la continuità nell'identità culturale e nella storia degli ordini. Ma i bibliotecari della Vaticana – in pratica le stesse persone che avevano praticamente operato la confisca libraria delle biblioteche degli ordini soppressi sotto l'egida napoleonica – tentarono di cambiare la decisione papale, che annullava

completamente il loro lavoro e rendeva più povera la Biblioteca. Così, come era riuscito ad ottenere al termine della prima Repubblica Romana Gaetano Marini, avrebbero desiderato lasciare in Vaticana tutti i volumi che vi erano stati trasferiti tra il 1811 e il 1814. Tuttavia, nonostante le obiezioni e le molte difficoltà che avanzarono, alcune reali e altre addotte, il papa fu irremovibile e ordinò che i libri dei religiosi ritornassero nelle biblioteche da cui erano stati confiscati. Le restituzioni furono avviate già a partire dal 1814, almeno da parte della Casanatense. Poi anche i libri trasferiti in Vaticana furono resi ai precedenti possessori. Lo attestano le brevi note stilate per ricevuta dai religiosi al momento della consegna dei volumi. La ricevuta fu infatti posta come condizione alla restituzione. Tuttavia alcuni ordini religiosi non furono soddisfatti: sentendosi defraudati di parte dei loro volumi, lamentarono restituzioni fortemente lacunose, e talvolta indicarono precise mancanze. In qualche caso la mancata consegna fu rivendicata più volte, con caparbietà e per lungo tempo. È il caso del codice quattrocentesco latore del *Teseida* di Boccaccio confiscato dai conservatori della Vaticana agli Scolopi di San Pantaleo, che continuarono a richiederne la restituzione fino all'inizio del 1822, quando finalmente riuscirono a riaverlo[65]. Gli stessi religiosi non ricevettero invece altri volumi, manoscritti e a stampa, di cui non rivendicarono la restituzione, probabilmente perché non ebbero tempestiva consapevolezza della loro mancanza[66].

65 Città del Vaticano, *Biblioteca Apostolica Vaticana*, Arch. Bibl. 38, fols 198r–99r. Il manoscritto oggi è custodito presso la Biblioteca Nazionale Centrale di Roma (Roma, *Biblioteca Nazionale Centrale*, S. Pantaleo 11), dove è finito in seguito a una successiva confisca, quella del 1873, effettuata dallo Stato italiano.

66 Per i volumi di San Pantaleo rimasti in Vaticana, cf. Rita, *Biblioteche e requisizioni librarie a Roma*, come alla nota 6, 372–73. In particolare per il *Filocolo* del Boccaccio: eadem, 'Il Filocolo di Celso Cittadini (Vat. lat. 8506)

Non tutti gli ordini si dimostrarono interessati a riavere i propri volumi, forse perché nel frattempo alcune case "erano passate in altra religione" o forse per ignoranza dei nuovi superiori, che talvolta non sapevano neppure "d'aver avuto libri"[67]. L'autorità pontificia impose alla Vaticana comunque la restituzione.

Tuttavia, nonostante l'esplicito volere del papa e le ricevute attestanti la restituzione ai religiosi precedenti possessori, alcuni libri confiscati in età napoleonica rimasero in Vaticana, dove ancora oggi si trovano. Secondo una stima dell'allora secondo custode Giuseppe Baldi[68] si tratterebbe di circa 1.300 volumi su un totale di 20.000 confiscati. Probabilmente rimasero nella Biblioteca pontificia non solo per l'oggettiva difficoltà di individuarne la provenienza – difficoltà più volte lamentata dai conservatori – ma anche per l'arbitrio di chi effettuò le restituzioni che ritenne di trattenere alcuni manoscritti – comprese carte d'archivio – e numerosi stampati di pregio, soprattutto incunaboli, pensando che così si potesse garantire nel tempo una migliore conservazione e una maggiore fruibilità di quei materiali.

Un esempio: San Carlino alle Quattro Fontane

Il 22 ottobre 1813 i conservatori della Vaticana si recarono nel convento dei Trinitari scalzi spagnoli di San Carlino alle Quattro Fontane. La biblioteca era sita nell'ambiente progettato e realizzato alla metà del Seicento da Francesco Borromini (1599–1667), uno dei più originali e importanti architetti del barocco italiano, che

ne disegnò anche la scaffalatura lignea disposta in origine in una metà della sala[69]. Nello spazio, non particolarmente ampio – era "longo palmi 58, largo 21, e alto seconda la sua simmetria" – era collocata la raccolta libraria che nel 1726 constava di circa 4.500 volumi, suddivisi e collocati in 12 classi[70]. Quei libri erano stati già in precedenza descritti in un catalogo alfabetico per autore, privo di data, ma redatto probabilmente nella seconda metà del Seicento[71]. Da quella collezione, nell'autunno 1813, i conservatori scelsero oltre 60 opere, sommariamente descritte nella lista allegata al processo verbale della confisca. Questo elenco[72], finora noto in un unico testimone stilato dal Battaglini, che lo allestì per copia conforme, consta in realtà di 58 voci numerate. Ma le opere requisite furono di più perché talvolta – forse

---

67 Città del Vaticano, *Biblioteca Apostolica Vaticana*, Arch. Bibl. 105, fol. 42r. Sulle restituzioni: cf. Rita, *Biblioteche e requisizioni librarie a Roma*, come alla nota 6, 355–78.

68 Su di lui *ibid.*, 76–77 e nt. 33.

e l'identità dell'abate de Rossi', in *Studi in onore del cardinale Raffaele Farina*, a c. di Ambrogio M. Piazzoni, Studi e testi, 478 (Città del Vaticano, 2013), 1043–65.

69 La struttura architettonica della biblioteca così come disegnata dal Borromini è descritta nel *Libro de las fabricas del Convento de S. Carlos a las 4 Fontanas* redatto da Juan de s. Buenaventura (Roma, *Archivio di S. Carlino alle Quattro Fontane*, ms. 77); per una descrizione del vaso librario, cf. Fiammetta Sabba, 'I saloni librari Borrominiani fra architettura e decoro', in *Bibliothèques, décors, XVIIᵉ–XIXᵉ siècle*, ed. Frédéric Barbier, István Monok e Andrea De Pasquale (Paris 2016), 225–47 a 227–28; in generale, sulla biblioteca dei Trinitari cf. Rita, *Biblioteche e requisizioni librarie a Roma*, come alla nota 6, 297–99.

70 Città del Vaticano, *Archivio Apostolico Vaticano*, Congr. Visita Ap. 108, 7.

71 Roma, *Archivio di Stato*, Biblioteca, Manoscritti, 150: *Index librorum omnium cum annotatione auctorum qui in hac sancti Caroli ad quatuor Fontes de Urbe ordinis Discalceatorum Sanctissime Trinitatis Redemptionis Captivorum Bibliotheca sunt*. Il codice trasmette due diverse stesure dell'*Index*. La più antica fu in seguito copiata e integrata nell'altra che sembrerebbe databile alla prima metà del Settecento. Alla stesura originaria è premessa un'istruzione metodologica: *Annotationes ad huius libri intelligentiam, ad que facilitatem reperiendi libros*. Nella parte centrale del codice sono aggiunte alcune liste redatte probabilmente all'inizio del Settecento.

72 Città del Vaticano, *Biblioteca Apostolica Vaticana*, Arch. Bibl. 36, fols 18r–19v. Il testo è edito in *Appendice documentaria*, II.

nei casi in cui l'unità fisica era miscellanea – in un'unica voce vennero descritte più edizioni. Tra l'altro furono requisiti sei codici cartacei[73] e sette incunaboli[74]. Due sole opere vennero scelte per la Casanatense nel dicembre 1813[75].

Dopo la caduta di Napoleone e la restaurazione dello Stato pontificio, i Trinitari spagnoli, attraverso il superiore del convento, Antonio del beato Simone de Rojas, introdussero al papa la richiesta formale per avere "il benigno permesso di poter quelli [libri] riprendere a beneficio de [...] religiosi"[76]. L'istanza, accolta il 12 marzo 1816 con rescritto *ex audientia Sanctissimi*[77], avviò la procedura per la restituzione. Il successivo 23 aprile, il delegato dell'Ordine, Marco De Cupis, riceveva dai funzionari della Vaticana "78 pezzi

di libri appartenuti a detti padri e convento" e ne stilava la relativa ricevuta[78].

Eppure, nonostante la suddetta attestazione, alcuni dei volumi requisiti dai conservatori vaticani alla biblioteca conventuale di San Carlino sono ancora conservati nella collezione pontificia. È il caso per esempio del codice cartaceo settecentesco *Vat. lat.* 8616, latore della *Relazione de tumulti accaduti in Roma l'anno 1736. Loro origine e sequela*[79], corrispondente alla descrizione numero 53 dell'elenco di requisizione[80]. Rimasero in Vaticana anche alcuni stampati della raccolta trinitaria, come dimostra la traduzione italiana dell'*Opera Medicinalia* di Johannes Mesue (Yuhanna ibn Māsawayh), uscita a Venezia il 12 dicembre 1493 dai torchi di Pietro Quarenghi[81], descritta al numero 5 dell'elenco di confisca napoleonico[82] e ora *Inc.* III.44. Analogamente, anche l'esemplare *Inc.* III.45, latore delle *Vitae et sententiae philosophorum* di Diogene Laerzio nell'edizione bresciana di Jacopo de' Britannici del 1485[83], proviene dalla biblioteca di San Carlino ed entrò in Vaticana in seguito alla requisizione del 1813. A differenza del manoscritto individuato,

73   Descritti ai numeri 6, 8, 17, 18, 22 e 53 dell'elenco di confisca.

74   Corrispondenti ai numeri 2, 4, 5 e 12. Due edizioni descritte al numero 2: 'Diogenes Laertius latine, Brixiae 1485' (ISTC id00221000; BAVI D-94) e 'Persius Satyrae cum notis Fontii, Venetiis 1485' (ISTC: ip00347000); tre al numero 4, di cui soltanto una inequivocabilmente identificabile: 'Theophili Brixii Carmen, Brixiae 1496' (ISTC: it00154000; BAVI T-54); la mancanza di elementi non permette l'identificazione certa di 'Pomponius Mela Cosmographia, sine loco, et anno'; nella citazione 'Macer Philosophus, De virtutibus herbarum, Brixiae 1496' alcuni elementi descrittivi non risultano corretti; il riferimento potrebbe anche rinviare a un'edizione del primo Cinquecento e le note tipografiche essere state copiate erroneamente dalla citazione precedente. Per l'*Opera medicinalia* descritta al numero 5, cf. *infra*. Rimanda presumibilmente ai *Sermones de tempore et de sanctis* del santo domenicano Vincent Ferrer (ISTC: if00132000; BAVI F-19), la citazione trasmessa dalla voce 12: 'S. Vincentius Ordinis Praed. Sermones, Argentinae 1489'.

75   Verbale ed elenco della confisca sono trasmessi da *Roma, Archivio di Stato*, Archivio Marini-Clarelli, b. 75, 4, [non foliato]; solo l'elenco anche in *Roma, Biblioteca Casanatense*, Ms. Cas. 489, fols 249r–250v.

76   Città del Vaticano, *Biblioteca Apostolica Vaticana*, Arch. Bibl. 37, fol. 62r.

77   Città del Vaticano, *Biblioteca Apostolica Vaticana*, Arch. Bibl. 37, fol. 63v.

78   Città del Vaticano, *Biblioteca Apostolica Vaticana*, Arch. Bibl. 37, fol. 64r. Il numero 78 indicato nella ricevuta, presumibilmente si riferisce al numero dei volumi e non a quello delle opere consegnate.

79   Una descrizione manoscritta del codice, estremamente sommaria, è disponibile nell'*Inventarium codicum Latinorum Bibliothecae Vaticanae, tomus XI a n. 8472 ad 9019*, opera et studio Giovanni Battista De Rossi – Francesco Massi, Paolo Scapaticci e Luigi Vincenzi, 91; riproduzione fotografica: Città del Vaticano, *Biblioteca Apostolica Vaticana*, Sala Cons. Mss. rosso 312; originale: Città del Vaticano, *Biblioteca Apostolica Vaticana*, Vat. lat. 15349 (11); anche Rita, *Biblioteche e requisizioni librarie a Roma*, come alla nota 6, 300 nt. 1071.

80   Città del Vaticano, *Biblioteca Apostolica Vaticana*, Arch. Bibl. 36, fol. 19r: 'Codice cartaceo in 4. Tumulti accaduti in Roma nel 1736'.

81   ISTC: im00521000; BAVI M-239.

82   Città del Vaticano, *Biblioteca Apostolica Vaticana*, Arch. Bibl. 36, fol. 18v: 'Mesue Io., Della consolazione delle medicine semplici, Venezia 1493'.

83   Cf. *supra* nt. 74.

che non presenta note di possesso o segni che ne attestino la precedente appartenenza, in calce al foglio IIr di entrambi gli incunaboli è tracciato a penna un *ex libris* che conferma in modo inequivocabile la provenienza dei due volumi: *Conventus S. Caroli ad 4 Fontes de Urbe.*

Trascorsero alcuni anni dal termine dell'occupazione napoleonica e molti dei libri requisiti alle biblioteche religiose romane ritornarono presso gli ordini. Una piccola parte rimase in Vaticana, forse "occultata"[84] dai conservatori. Altri volumi, la gran parte, furono venduti e comunque andarono dispersi. Si consumò così la seconda significativa dispersione ottocentesca delle biblioteche degli ordini religiosi romani.

Anche i libri restituiti ai religiosi rimasero per poco tempo presso le loro case: a distanza di poco più di mezzo secolo gli ordini furono di nuovo soppressi e le loro raccolte librarie definitivamente smembrate dal nascente Stato italiano che le destinò alla costituenda Biblioteca Nazionale di Roma. Di alcune di esse oggi si è persa totalmente traccia, e nei migliori dei casi, ne resta il nome legato a un fondo librario della Biblioteca Nazionale. Ma prima di questo smembramento definitivo, nel 1849, durante la seconda Repubblica Romana sorta nei territori dello Stato Pontificio, si tentò un'ulteriore confisca libraria, oggetto di uno dei saggi presentati in questo volume[85].

---

84 È questo il termine utilizzato da Giuseppe Baldi in una sua nota priva di data, ma databile anteriormente all'agosto 1829: Città del Vaticano, *Biblioteca Apostolica Vaticana*, Arch. Bibl. 38, fol. 70r.

85 Marina Venier, *The dispersal of monastic libraries in Rome. The laws of suppression during the Roman Republic of 1849 and after the annexation of the city as the capital of the Kingdom of Italy in 1873*, in the present volume.

Appendice documentaria

Nella trascrizione sono state normalizzate secondo criteri moderni soltanto le maiuscole.

I[86]

Breve e sincera indicazione dell'operato dall'ab. Marini nell'assenza di N. S. da Roma in servigio della S. Sede, e della causa pubblica, e di quanto esiste affidato alla di lui custodia, diligenza, e onoratezza.

L'ab. Marini, stato prefetto degli archivi secreti pontifici per 26 anni, all'entrar de' Francesi in Roma seguitò a ritenerne la custodia, ne questi furono giammai biffati dal nuovo governo, che pur aveva biffato la Biblioteca, ed il Museo Vaticano, ne esso chiamato a darne conto. Però si stava molto incerto della sua sorte, e sarebbe volentieri partito per ritornarsene alla patria se non l'avesse trattenuto l'attaccamento a detti archivi, e il desiderio di vedere in sicuro luoghi, ne' quali sono i più antichi, ed i più preziosi ed originali monumenti della Religione, e della Sede Apostolica. E questi abbandonati, Dio sa a quali mani sarebbero capitati, ed a quali rovine esposti.

Nel tempo dunque, che viveva nelle maggiori angustie di spirito, ed in un totale ritiro, videsi improvvisamente eletto dal general S. Cyr con una pubblica stampa de' 19 marzo 1798, membro dell'Istituto Nazionale per la storia ed antichità, senza essere prima stato richiesto intorno a ciò, e senza neppur sapere a chi dovesse una tal distinzione. Non ringraziò ne il General ne altri, ma col fatto accettò la carica, ed intervenne alle adunanze, che l'Istituto faceva nel Palazzo Vaticano. Pochi giorni dopo allo stesso modo, e con altra stampa fu confermato nella prefettura degli Archivi, che prima aveva, con di più la sopraintendenza alla Biblioteca, e Museo Vaticano, ne per tal cosa pure si presentò, ne rendè grazie ad alcuno, lietissimo per altro della oppinione, in cui si avvide di essere presso la Rep. Romana, di persona dotta ed onesta, ne ciò senza un'aperta disposizione della Provvidenza, che voleva salvi gli Archivi segreti, i quali altrimente perivano senza meno. E veramente potè con suo credito conseguire per mezzo del commissario Monge, che il comandante di Castello non avesse le chiavi dell'Archivio di quel Forte, che gli mandò a chiedere imperiosamente lo stesso giorno in cui fu nominato prefetto di esso. E fu allora che, conoscendo il pericolo grandissimo, al qual era questo soggetto, si maneggiò per riportare dal generale il permesso di trasferirlo tutto nell'Archivio Vaticano, siccome egli eseguì sollecitamente ed in un sol giorno. E fu cosa prossima al prodigio che questi si fosse mantenuto chiuso ed intatto per tre e più mesi che era stato in poter de' Francesi.

---

86 Il documento, in copia di mano di Angelo Battaglini, custode della Biblioteca Vaticana, si conserva sciolto, all'interno del codice Città del Vaticano, *Biblioteca Apostolica Vaticana*, Arch. Bibl. 52, pt. A, provvisoriamente segnato fol. Ir-v; corrisponde parzialmente al testo edito in Marino Marini, *Degli aneddoti di Gaetano Marini. Commentario di suo nipote Marino* (Roma, 1822), 188–93.

La Prefettura accordatagli di tali archivi lo mise in istato di aver modo, onde serbare illesi anche gli altri archivi ecclesiastici, avendo destramente mostrato l'interesse, che vi era di ritenerli quali monumenti di storia, della quale egli era professore nell'Istituto. Fece quindi intendere ad un certo Capponi, dichiarato archivista generale della Nazione, che di questi avea esso presa la custodia, ed ai rispettivi archivisti, che gli mandassero le chiavi, e fossero tranquilli. Per tal guisa andò al possesso di cinque archivi della Dataria, e di quelli della Penitenzieria, de' Vescovi e Regolari, del Concilio, della Immunità, de' Riti, della Sacra Visita, che dalle camere di monsig. Tria all'Orso fece venire a S. Pietro, e trasportò nell'Archivio Vaticano quello del Concistoro, che cominciava a dissiparsi, redento con poche libre d'argento dai commissari francesi, che abitavano il Palazzo, e in detto archivio fece medesimamente entrar quello de' Musici della Cappella, unico nel genere suo. Da' pizzicagnoli, e da altri rivenditori di commestibili ricuperò moltissime ed importantissime carte della Secretaria di Stato, e da (!) 150 grossi volumi di lettere scritte dalla Consulta. Molto operò eziandio per divenir padrone degli archivi di Propaganda e del S. Offizio occupati dai Francesi, e gli (!) avea già ottenuti, ma a principio gli mancaro i mezzi per le spese de' trasporti, ed in appresso, la Commission Francese, non essendo più la medesima, la nuova oppose varie difficoltà. Dopo iterate istanze e memorie ebbe ordine di far passare alla Vaticana da (!) circa 26 mila libri stampati, scelti da alcuni membri dell'Istituto dalle soppresse librerie, i quali, stati da prima deposti in alcune stanze della Minerva, vi soffrivano continue e pubbliche ruberie, e con questi senza danari, solo ed in poco tempo, ma con lavoro assiduo di più ore in ciascun giorno, ha formato un'assai pregevole biblioteca, distinta nelle sue classi, ed insigne massimamente per la copia e varietà delle cose ecclesiastiche. Ha meso in sicuro tutti i manoscritti e libri stampati del sec. XV del Collegio Capranica, più codici

greci del Monastero di Grotta Ferrata, ed alcuni rinomatissimi di quello di Farfa e 14 gran tomi di antiche pergamene dell'Archivio di S. Francesca Romana, che sono un vero e raro tesoro diplomatico. Tutti i bei quadri delle chiese o distrutte o chiuse ha pur ritirati nel Vaticano, facendoli per maggior sicurezza porre nell'appartamento del Card. Bibliotecario, assegnatogli per sua abitazione, ma dove non andò mai, contento delle camere che abitava in tempo de' Papi. Ottenne ancora di poter custodire uno stupendo e sommamente venerato Cristo di avorio di S. Paolino alla Regola, le stampe della Galleria della Certosa, le madri de' caratteri esotici, ed alcuni ponzoni de' latini della insigne Stamperia di Propaganda, e i marmi preziosi, ch'erano in alcune delle chiese abolite. E quanto ebbe poc'anzi a fare perché non fossero venduti i bei porfidi di S. Pancrazio e strappati barbaramente dalle lor pergamene e libri i sigilli d'oro e d'argento, che si stanno nell'archivio già di Castello. Gli si presentò nella scorsa mattina di s. Michele Arcangelo, mandato dal Comitato, un giudice criminale, un perito argentiere, uno scrivano ed un giovine che portava le bilancie, coll'ordine in iscritto di recarsi tosto nell'archivio e portar via, dopo averli pesati, i detti sigilli, stati allora allora, non si sà come, denunciati al Governo del valore di sopra mille scudi. O quale e quanta amarezza non provò egli per tal cosa! Seppe però, coll'aiuto di Dio specialissimo, sì ben fare e dire, e furono coloro sì discreti, che non fu preso nulla in quel giorno, e nel seguente non vi fu più Repubblica. Assistito poi sempre dalle efficaci premure e dal buon volere di chi presedeva alla Fabbrica di S. Pietro, alla quale era stata data la cura del Palazzo Vaticano, ha riparato in conveniente maniera agl'immensi danni recati dal tempo, dalla negligenza de' custodi e delle truppe napoletane all'Archivio, Biblioteca e Museo, e alle occasioni che i Ministri dell'Interno gli hanno commesso d'installare in detta Biblioteca tre novelli scrittori, si è loro opposto sempre vigorosamente con dire (il che era verissimo) che non avevano quelli i necessari requisiti per tale impiego, e che ogni ragione voleva si pensasse agli antichi. E così niuna novità si è fatta in essa sotto di lui, e vi si è anche ritenuto sempre alla vista di tutti il ritratto di Pio VI. Ond'è che ha egli la dolce compiacenza di poter affermare con verità, che malgrado le perdite fatte, l'Archivio, la Libraria, ed il Museo Vaticano sono ora sicuramente i soli luoghi pubblici in tutta Roma, che si siano conservati, e facciano tuttavia mostra a forestieri del loro antico splendore e magnificenza.

La maggior parte delle cose sin qui narrate le ha il Papa sapute per mezzo di mons. Spina, e ne ha goduto. E perché a questo scrisse un giorno l'ab. Marini che pensava sicuramente di ripatriare, non sapendo più come vivere, avendo perduto tutto, ne potendo per alcuna via riscuotere l'annuo assegnamento fattogli di 500 piastre, il prelato, alli 5 di marzo 1799, gli rispose che per carità non avesse abbandonato il suo posto. Ubbidì[87], ed avutasi allora dal Papa la condanna del noto giuramento e l'obbligo di ritrattarlo pubblicamente, ed avendo già Marini con sicura coscienza e sull'esempio di probi e dotti ecclesiastici prestato in voce tal giuramento con tutto l'Istituto nel maggio 1798, replicò a monsignor Spina, che voleva in ogni maniera sottomettersi alle decisioni e agli ordini del capo della Chiesa, ma che facendolo sarebbe stato immediatamente deposto dall'impiego in cui era, e conseguentemente in pericolo gli Archivi e tante altre cose con tanta sollicitudine ed industria conservate. Chiedea pertanto da Sua Santità medesima una secreta assoluzione. Ma il Papa dovette allora abbandonare Firenze e però ebbe Marini ricorso al di lui delegato, monsig. Di Pietro, il quale, informato di tutto ciò, con un singolarissimo rescritto de' 7 aprile 1799 *proprio oratoris confessario commisit, ut extra Poenitentiariae tribunal, et coram duobus testibus*

ab oratore scripto recipiat retractationem iuramenti ab ipso praestiti firma obbligatione retractationem praefatam manifestandi publice ac palam ubi primum licebit, e tal ritrattazione privata fece egli alli 10 dello stesso mese nella Cappella della casa de' Penitenzieri di S. Pietro, e la pubblica alli 3 di ottobre nella Secreteria del Vicariato.

II

Per il verbale e l'annesso elenco di requisizione è stata adottata una trascrizione conservativa (senza scioglimento delle abbreviazioni e senza normalizzazioni). Per le opere descritte nell'elenco non è stato ritenuto necessario indicare citazioni o riferimenti bibliografici perché la descrizione datane è sembrata sufficientemente identificativa. Fanno eccezione gli incunaboli, per i quali ci si è riferiti all'*Incunabula Short Title Catalogue* (ISTC). Sono state segnalate in nota soltanto le eventuali inesattezze e gli elementi mancanti. Solo nei casi certi, in nota è stata indicata anche l'eventuale identificazione dell'esemplare vaticano.

Verbale della requisizione della biblioteca del convento
di San Carlino alle Quattro Fontane
eseguita a favore della Biblioteca Vaticana il 22 ottobre 1813[88]

In nome di Sua Maestà l'Imperatore de' Francesi, Re d'Italia e protettore della Confederazione del Reno.

L'anno mille ottocentotredici, il giorno 22 ottobre all'una ora pomeridiana. Noi cavaliere Fortia, commissario nominato a consegnare alla Biblioteca Imperiale del Vaticano i manoscritti e libri stampati delle Corporazioni soppresse reputati degni dai sigg. conservatori della mede-

---

87 Da questo punto il testo manoscritto non corrisponde a quello edito, per il quale cf. *supra* nt. 1.

88 Il documento in *copia conforme* di mano di Angelo Battaglini, custode della Biblioteca Vaticana, si conserva in Città del Vaticano, *Biblioteca Apostolica Vaticana*, Arch. Bibl. 36, fols 18r–19v.

sima di aver luogo in detta Biblioteca, come da lettera de' 27 ottobre 1812, ci siamo portati unitamente co' sig.[ri] Angelo Battaglini, Filippo Aurelio Visconti, conservatori dell'Imperiale Biblioteca del Vaticano, e col sig.[r] Luigi Montanari, ricevitore del Demanio, alla Libreria del soppresso Convento di <u>S. Carlino alle quattro Fontane</u>, ed avendo il sig.[r] Montanari tolta la biffa della porta della detta libreria, ci siamo introdotti co' nominati soggetti, ed i sig.[ri] conservatori dell'Imperiale Biblioteca Vaticana hanno scelto le opere segnate nella qui annessa nota in numero di cinquantotto articoli, quali abbiamo loro dati e consegnati, ed hanno trasportati al Vaticano, di che abbiamo formato il presente processo verbale in triplice copia da ritenersi da noi, dalli sig.[ri] conservatori sudetti e dal sig.[r] Montanari.

L'anno, mese, giorno ed ora sudetta.

Fortia d'Urban
Angelo Battaglini
Filippo Aurelio Visconti
Montanari

Nota de' libri scelti dalli sig.[ri] conservatori dell'Imperiale Biblioteca Vaticana provenienti dalla Libreria del soppresso Convento di S. Carlino alle Quattro Fontane e consegnati alli medesimi sig.[ri] conservatori per la detta Imperiale Biblioteca del Vaticano.

1. Aldovrandus Ulysse, Historia animalium, Bononiae 1646, t. 13, ch. max, fig.
2. Diogenes Laertius latine, Brixiae 1485, fol.[89]; Persius, Satyrae cum notis Fontii, Venetiis 1485, fol.[90]
3. Ant. Musa, De Herba vetonica et L. Apuleius, De Medicaminibus herbarum, sine loco et anno, in 4.[91].
4. Macer Philosophus, De virtutibus herbarum, Brixiae 1496, 4.[92]; Theophili Brixi Carmen, Brixiae 1496, in 4.[93]; Pomponius Mela, Cosmographi,a sine loco et anno, in 4.[94].
5. Mesue Io., Della Consolazione delle medicine semplici, Venezia 1493, fol.[95]
6. Codice cartaceo manoscritto miscellaneo, in 4.
7. La difesa de' libri santi contro Voltaire, Venezia 1750[96], in 4.
8. Volateranus, Opera, cod. chart. mss., t. 2, fol.
9. Bartolomei, L'America. Poema eroico, Roma 1650, fol.
10. Innocentius III, Decretales, tom. I, Romae Priscian. Florent. 1543, fol. max.
11. S. Iustinus, Opera, Basileae Froben 1555, fol.
12. S. Vincentius Ordinis Praed., Sermones, Argentinae 1489, fol.[97].
13. Daniel latinae et Syro-Estranghelio idiomate a Bugato, Mediolani 1788, in 4.
14. Rycuius Iustus, De anno saeculari iubileo, Antuerpiae 1625, 8.
15. Buccius Ant., De instituenda regendaque mente, Romae 1772, in 8.

89 Diogenes Laertius, *Vitae et sententiae philosophorum*. Tr: Ambrosius Traversarius. Brescia: Jacobus Britannicus, 23 Nov. 1485. Folio. BAVI D-94; GW 8380; ISTC id00221000; corrisponde all'esemplare: Città del Vaticano, *Biblioteca Apostolica Vaticana*, Inc. III.45.

90 Persius Flaccus, Aulus, *Satyrae* (Comm: Bartholomaeus Fontius). Venice: Antonius Battibovis, 17 Sept. 1485. Folio. GW M31371; ISTC ip00347000.

91 Potrebbe riferirsi all'edizione curata da Gabriel Humelberg, stampata a Zurigo da Christoph Froschauer nel 1537.

92 Cf. *supra* nt. 74.

93 Theophilus Brixianus, *Carmina de vita solitaria et civili*. Brescia: Bernardinus de Misintis, [not before Oct.] 1496. 4°. BAVI T-54; GW M45901; ISTC it00154000.

94 Cf. *supra* nt. 74.

95 Mesue, Johannes, *Opera medicinalia* [Italian] *Il libro della consolatione delle medicine semplici solutive*. Venice: Petrus de Quarengiis, Bergomensis, 12 Dec. 1493. Folio. GW M23025; ISTC im00521000; corrisponde all'esemplare: Città del Vaticano, *Biblioteca Apostolica Vaticana*, Inc. III.44.

96 Errore per 1770, data corretta dell'edizione.

97 Ferrerius, Vincentius, S, *Sermones de tempore et de sanctis*. Strasbourg: [Printer of the 1483 Jordanus de Quedlinburg (Georg Husner)], 1488–89. Folio. BAVI F-19; GW 9837; ISTC if00132000.

16. Cancalloni[98] Gio. Battista, Vita di s. Severini, senza luogo ed anno.

17. Codice cartaceo in 4, miscellaneo.

18. Codice cartaceo in 4. Cose riguardanti il card. Mazzarini.

19. De Tamayo Salazar Juan, Vida de s. Epifacio[99], Madrid 1646, in 4.

20. Salvianus, Opera cum Baluzio, Pedeponti 1743, in 4.

21. Ganganelli et Braschi, Dialogo, Tibet antica 1784, 4.

22. Codice cartaceo Critica sui cinque volumi del Diritto libero della Chiesa, in 8.

23. Raccolta di diverse materie per la vita del card. Mazzarini, Lione, in 4.

24. Sergardus Ludovicus, Sectani Satyrae, Lucae 1783, t. 4, in 8 max.

25. Arteaga Stefano, Rivoluzioni del teatro musicale italiano, Venezia 1785, t. 3, in 8.

26. Borsa Matteo, Il gusto presente in letteratura italiana con osservazioni dell'Arteaga, in 8.

27. Mancinus Io. Alois[100]., De vita Michaelis Guthieri, Bononiae 1795, in 8.

28. Giovenale e Persio volgarizzati dal Silvestri, Padova 1711, in 8.

29. Denina Carlo, Bibliopea, Turino 1776, in 8.

30. Diario de los literator de España, en Madrid 1736, t. 7, in 8.

31. Barbeyrac Jean, Traité de la morale des Pères de l'Eglise, Amsterdam 1728, in 4.

32. Ughus Petrus Alex. M.ª, De Honorio I pontifice, Bononiae 1784, in 8.

33. Piazza Carlo Bart., Necrologia, Roma 1711, in 4.

34. Fabiano Alessandro[101], Interpretazione del libro di Giobbe, Roma 1774, in 8.

35. De Pineda fray Juan[102], Chronologia hospitalaria de la religion de s. Juan de Dios, a Madrid 1715, t. 2, fol.

36. Statuti della religione Gerosolimitana, Borgo Novo 1676, fol.

37. Chronologia Romanor. Pontificum in pariete S. Pauli[103], Romae 1751, fol. fig.

38. Fiestas de la Iglesia de Seivilla, en Seivilla 1671, fol. fig.

39. Notitia dignitatum utriusque Imperii cum Pancirolo, excudebat Steph. Gamonetus 1623, fol. fig.

40. Seifridus Io., Arbor Aniciana, Viennae 1613, fol.

41. De Solis d. Ant., Historia de la nueva España, 1684, fol.

42. Paleotto Alfonso, Espicazione[104] del lenzuolo del Signore, Bologna 1598, in 4.

43. Istorici delle cose veneziane, da Sabellico, Bembo, Paruta e Morosini, Venezia 1718–1719, t. 5, in 4.

44. Verus Io. Baptista, Rerum Venetarum, Venet. 1678, in 4.

45. Real Accademia de Buenas Lettras de Barcellona, Barcellona senz'anno, t. 2, in 4.

46. Tumultus illustratus Fl. Clementis, Urbini 1727, in 4.

47. Risposta alle memorie di Cesi del Contelorio, Napoli 1676, in 4.

48. Commentarius de Francorum regis dominiis, Lugd. Batav. Elzev. 1629, in 24.

49. Res Publica Hungariae, Lugd. Elzev. 1634, in 24.

50. M. Aurelio imperatore, I dodici libri, Roma 1675, in 12.

51. Livius, Historiarum pars nuper inventa, Romae Mazochius 1519, in 8.

52. Bracci Ignazio, Etimologia de' nomi Papa e Pontefice, Roma 1630, in 12.

---

98 *Cancalloni*: errore per Cancellotti.
99 *Epifacio*: errore per Epitacio.
100 *Mancinus*: errore per Maneiro (Juan Luis).
101 Il nome completo dell'autore è Alessandro Fabiano De Sanctis.

102 L'autore dell'opera è Juan Santos; Juan de Pineda è l'autore del prologo.
103 L'autore dell'opera è Giovanni Marangoni.
104 *Espicazione*: errore per Esplicazione.

53. Codice cartaceo in 4. Tumulti accaduti in Roma nel 1736[105].

54. Historia del card. Albornoz escritta en lengua latina da Juan Ghines[106], en Bolonia 1612, in 4.

55. Fontana Aldighiero, L'origine della religione gerosolimitana.

56. Alidosi Pasquali Gio. Niccolò, Instruzione delle cose notabili di Bologna, ivi 1621, in 4.

57. Raccolta di tutti i bandi di Bologna, ivi 1631, in 4.

58. Istoria del cielo tradotta dal francese, Venezia 1747, in 8.

Noi sottoscritti abbiamo ricevuto i suddetti libri.
Angelo Battaglini
Filippo Aurelio Visconti
Conservatori della Biblioteca Vaticana
Per copia conforme
Angelo Battaglini Primo conservatore
dell'Imperiale Biblioteca del Vaticano

---

105 Città del Vaticano, *Biblioteca Apostolica Vaticana*, Vat. lat. 8616.

106 L'autore dell'opera è Juan Ginés de Sepúlveda.

Bibliography

Manuscripts and Archival Sources

Città del Vaticano, *Archivio Apostolico Vaticano*, Congr. Visita Ap. 108, 7.

Città del Vaticano, *Archivio storico della Congregazione "De Propaganda Fide"*, Acta 175.

Città del Vaticano, *Biblioteca Apostolica Vaticana*, Arch. Bibl. 36.

Città del Vaticano, *Biblioteca Apostolica Vaticana*, Arch. Bibl. 37.

Città del Vaticano, *Biblioteca Apostolica Vaticana*, Arch. Bibl. 38.

Città del Vaticano, *Biblioteca Apostolica Vaticana*, Arch. Bibl. 52, pt. A.

Città del Vaticano, *Biblioteca Apostolica Vaticana*, Arch. Bibl. 56.

Città del Vaticano, *Biblioteca Apostolica Vaticana*, Arch. Bibl. 101.

Città del Vaticano, *Biblioteca Apostolica Vaticana*, Arch. Bibl. 105.

Città del Vaticano, *Biblioteca Apostolica Vaticana*, Vat. lat. 8616.

Città del Vaticano, *Biblioteca Apostolica Vaticana*, Vat. lat. 15349 (11): *Inventarium codicum Latinorum Bibliothecae Vaticanae, tomus XI a n. 8472 ad 9019,* opera et studio Giovanni Battista De Rossi, Francesco Massi, Paolo Scapaticci e Luigi Vincenzi, 1852–1855.

Paris, *Arch. Nat.*, Maison de l'Empereur. Domaine étranger, Italie, Belgique, Hollande, O², 1072.

Roma, *Archivio di S. Carlino alle Quattro Fontane*, ms. 77: *Libro de las fabricas del Convento de S. Carlos a las 4 Fontanas* redatto da Juan de s. Bonaventura.

Roma, *Archivio di Stato*, Archivio Marini-Clarelli, b. 75.

Roma, *Archivio di Stato*, Biblioteca, Manoscritti, 150: *Index librorum omnium cum annotatione auctorum qui in hac sancti Caroli ad quatuor Fontes de Urbe ordinis Discalceatorum Sanctissime Trinitatis Redemptionis Captivorum Bibliotheca sunt.*

Roma, *Biblioteca Casanatense*, Ms. Cas. 489.

Roma, *Biblioteca Nazionale Centrale*, S. Pantaleo 11.

Primary Sources

Diogenes Laertius, *Vitae et sententiae philosophorum*. Tr: Ambrosius Traversarius. Brescia: Jacobus Britannicus, 23 Nov. 1485. Folio. BAVI D-94; GW 8380; ISTC id00221000.

Ferrerius, Vincentius, S, *Sermones de tempore et de sanctis*. Strasbourg: [Printer of the 1483 Jordanus de Quedlinburg (Georg Husner)], 1488–89. Folio. BAVI F-19; GW 9837; ISTC if00132000.

Mesue, Johannes, *Opera medicinalia* [Italian] *Il libro della consolatione delle medicine semplici solutive.* Venice: Petrus de Quarengiis, Bergomensis, 12 Dec. 1493. Folio. BAVI M-239; GW M23025; ISTC im00521000.

Persius Flaccus, Aulus, *Satyrae* (Comm: Bartholomaeus Fontius). Venice: Antonius Battibovis, 17 Sept. 1485. Folio. GW M31371; ISTC ip00347000.

Theophilus Brixianus, *Carmina de vita solitaria et civili.* Brescia: Bernardinus de Misintis, [not before Oct.] 1496. 4°. BAVI T-54; GW M45901; ISTC it00154000.

Secondary Works

Alessandro Avòli, 'Monaldo e la sua biblioteca', in Monaldo Leopardi, *Autobiografia*, introduzione di Giulio Cattaneo ([Roma], 1997), 227–53.

Bollettino delle leggi e decreti imperiali pubblicati dalla Consulta Straordinaria negli Stati Romani, 12 (1810).

Marianna Brancia di Apricena, *Il complesso dell'Aracoeli sul colle Capitolino (IX–XIX secolo)* (Roma, 2000).

Marco Buonocore, *Tra i codici epigrafici della Biblioteca Apostolica Vaticana*, Epigrafia e antichità, 22 (Faenza, 2004).

Philippe Boutry, *Souverain et Pontife. Recherches prosopographiques sur la Curie Romaine à l'âge de la Restauration (1814–1816)*, Collection de l'École française de Rome, 300 (Rome, 2002).

Massimo Ceresa, 'Raccolta Generale', in *Guida ai fondi manoscritti, numismatici a stampa della Biblioteca Vaticana*, a. c. di Francesco D'Aiuto e Paolo Vian, Studi e testi, 466–67 (Città del Vaticano, 2010) II, 840–58.

Collezione di carte pubbliche, proclami, editti, ragionamenti ed altre produzioni tendenti a consolidare la rigenerata Repubblica romana (Roma, 1798–99).

Henri Daru, *Martial Daru baron d'Empire, 1774–1827: maître et bienfaiteur de Stendhal* (Paris, 2009).

Dictionnaire Napoléon, sous la direction de Jean Toulard (Paris, 1987).

Fausta Dommarco, 'Profilo di un burocrate: Luigi Marini direttore generale dei Catasti', in *Roma fra la Restaurazione e l'elezione di Pio IX. Amministrazione, economia, società e cultura*, a. c. di Anna Lia Bonella, Augusto Pompeo e Manola Ida Venzo (Roma, 1997), 119–33.

Maria Pia Donato, *L'archivio del mondo. Quando Napoleone confiscò la storia* (Bari, 2019).

Due diari della Repubblica Romana del 1798–1799, a. c. di Carlo Gasbarri – Vittorio Emanuele Giuntella, Collectanea urbana, 4 (Roma, 1958).

Raffaele Farina, '"Splendore veritatis gaudet ecclesia". Leone XIII e la Biblioteca Vaticana', *Miscellanea Bibliothecae Apostolicae Vaticanae*, 11, Studi e testi, 423 (Città del Vaticano, 2004), 285–370.

Odoric-Marie Jouve, 'Odyssée des archives monastiques de Rome, 1810–1814', *La France Franciscaine*, 6 (1923), 1–46.

Leonhard Lemmens, 'De sorte Archivi generalis Ordinis Fratrum Minorum et Bibliothecae Aracoelitanae tempore Reipublicae Tiberinae (an. 1798–1799)', *Archivum Franciscanum historicum*, 17 (1924), 30–54.

Marco Maiorino, 'L'unione dei due Archivi segreti. Gaetano Marini e il trasferimento dell'Archivio di Castel Sant'Angelo nel Vaticano', in *Gaetano Marini (1742–1815), protagonista della cultura europea. Scritti per il bicentenario della morte*, a. c. di Marco Buonocore, I, Studi e testi, 492 (Città del Vaticano, 2015), 327–55.

Antonio Manfredi, 'I Vaticani latini nel secolo XIX. Dispersioni, acquisizioni e inventari. Una prima ricognizione', in *Storia della Biblioteca Apostolica Vaticana, V: La Biblioteca Vaticana dall'occupazione francese all'ultimo papa re (1797–1878)*, a. c. di Andreina Rita (Città del Vaticano, 2020), 445–76.

Antonio Manfredi – Andreina Rita, 'Notizie sulla Vaticana in età napoleonica da dieci lettere inedite di Gaetano Marini ad Angelo Battaglini (Parigi 1810–1815)', in *Gaetano Marini (1742–1815), protagonista della cultura europea. Scritti per il bicentenario della morte*, a c. di Marco Buonocore, I, Studi e testi, 492 (Città del Vaticano, 2015), 515–85.

Marino Marini, *Degli aneddoti di Gaetano Marini. Commentario di suo nipote Marino* (Roma, 1822).

Luigi Sergio Mecocci, 'La Repubblica Romana del 1798–1799 ed i frati minori della Provincia Romana', *Archivum Franciscanum Historicum*, 91 (1998), 169–227.

Ottorino Montenovesi, 'La biblioteca del convento dell'Aracoeli e le sue vicende. Ricordi storici', in *La madonna d'Aracoeli negli eventi storici celebrati solennemente il 30 maggio 1948 sul colle Capitolino* (Roma, 1949), 51–53.

Carla Nardi, *Napoleone e Roma. La politica della Consulta Romana*, Collection de l'École française de Rome, 115 (Roma, 1989).

Carla Nardi, *Napoleone e Roma. Dalla Consulta Romana al ritorno di Pio VII (1811–1814)* (Roma, 2005).

Luigi Pepe, 'L'Istituto nazionale della Repubblica Romana', *Mélanges de l'École française de Rome. Italie et Méditerranée*, 108 (1996), 703–30.

Delio Vania Proverbio e Andreina Rita, 'Vaticani arabi', in *Guida ai fondi manoscritti, numismatici a stampa della Biblioteca Vaticana*, a c. di Francesco D'Aiuto e Paolo Vian, Studi e testi, 466–67 (Città del Vaticano, 2010), I, 553–64.

Pier Paolo Racioppi, *Arte e Roma. Città e patrimonio artistico nella Repubblica Romana (1798–99)* (Roma, 2018).

Camillo Ravioli, *Della vita e delle opere di Luigi Marini* (Roma, 1858).

Andreina Rita, 'La Biblioteca Vaticana nelle sue architetture', in *Biblioteca Apostolica Vaticana: libri e luoghi all'inizio del terzo millennio* (Città del Vaticano, 2011), 70–123.

Andreina Rita, *Biblioteche e requisizioni librarie a Roma in età napoleonica. Cronologia e fonti romane*, Studi e testi, 470 (Città del Vaticano, 2012).

Andreina Rita, 'Il Filocolo di Celso Cittadini (Vat. lat. 8506) e l'identità dell'abate de Rossi', in *Studi in onore del cardinale Raffaele Farina*, a c. di Ambrogio M. Piazzoni, Studi e testi, 478 (Città del Vaticano, 2013), 1043–65.

Andreina Rita, 'Tra Rivoluzione e Restaurazione. La Vaticana di Marini, Battaglini e Baldi', in *Storia della Biblioteca Apostolica Vaticana, V: La Biblioteca Vaticana dall'occupazione francese all'ultimo papa re (1797–1878)*, a c. di Andreina Rita (Città del Vaticano, 2020), 55–103.

Domenico Rocciolo, *Marini, Gaetano*, in *Dizionario biografico degli italiani*, 70 (Roma, 2008), 451–54.

Giuseppe Antonio Sala, *Diario romano degli anni 1798–1799*, ristampa con premessa di Vittorio Emanuele Giuntella e indice analitico di Renata Tacus Lancia, Miscellanea della Società romana di storia patria, 1–3. *Scritti di Giuseppe Antonio Sala pubblicati sugli autografi da Giuseppe Cugnoni*, 1–3 (Roma, 1980).

Fiammetta Sabba, 'I saloni librari Borrominiani fra architettura e decoro', in *Bibliothèques, décors, XVIIe–XIXe siècle*, éd. Frédéric Barbier, István Monok e Andrea De Pasquale (Paris 2016), 225–47.

Ilaria Sgarbozza, *Le spalle al Settecento. Forma, modelli e organizzazione dei musei nella Roma napoleonica (1809–1814)* (Città del Vaticano, 2013).

Fabio Tarzia, *Libri e rivoluzioni: figure e mentalità nella Roma di fine ancien régime (1770–1800)*, Studi e ricerche di storia dell'editoria, 7 (Milano, 2000).

Mariano Ugolini, 'La nuova biblioteca Leonina in Vaticana Memoria', in *Nel giubileo episcopale di Leone XIII. Omaggio della Biblioteca Vaticana* (Roma, 1893).

Marina Venier, 'The monastic libraries in Rome, from the Lists of the Religious Orders for the Sacred Congregation of the Index to the Confiscation in 1873: the reconstruction of the Eborense Library in the

Monastery of Santa Maria in Aracoeli belonging to the Friars Minor Observant', in *Virtual visits to lost libraries: reconstruction of and access to dispersed collections. Papers presented on 5 November 2010 at the CERL Seminar hosted by the Royal Library of Denmark, Copenhagen*, ed. Ivan Boserup e David J. Shaw, Cerl Papers, 11 (London, 2011), 95–112.

Paolo Vian, 'Altri codici Aracoelitani nella Biblioteca Vaticana', in *Miscellanea Bibliothecae Apostolicae Vaticanae*, 2, Studi e testi, 331 (Città del Vaticano, 1988), 287–311.

Digital Sources

Fondation Napoléon, https://www.napoleon.org/FR/salle_lecture/biographies/files/Montalivet_allegret_RSN46061.asp.

MARINA VENIER

The Dispersal of Monastic Libraries in Rome. The Laws of Suppression during the Roman Republic of 1849 and after the Annexation of the City as the Capital of the Kingdom of Italy in 1873

In the course of the nineteenth century Rome was the theatre of two major historical events, which overwhelmed the city: in 1849 the proclamation of the second Roman Republic in the wake of the revolutions that had swept across Europe in the previous year, and in 1870 the conquest and annexation of the city as the new capital of the unified Kingdom of Italy. These events led to the suppression of the religious houses and the subsequent confiscation of their possessions, but the effects on their libraries varied widely.

The first, in fact, unlike the second, can have had no impact on their library collections, since the Republic lasted only five months, from 9 February to 4 July. Its legislation concerning religious houses none the less generated records that provide a valuable witness to their book collections in 1849. After the upheavals at the end of the eighteenth and beginning of the nineteenth centuries the libraries had begun to be painfully and gradually reconstructed, but the second suppression had a devastating effect on them and led to the complete and definitive dispersal of huge numbers of the books which they housed.

After the Executive Committee Decree, dated 13 February 1849, forbidding the alienation of church property, on the following day the Interior Ministry issued an Implementing Regulation to order all convents and affiliated institutions to compile an accurate and detailed inventory of their ordinary and valuable possessions including all the sacred objects used for liturgical purposes and other furnishings[1]. The inventories had to be drawn up

---

1 Seconda Repubblica Romana, Ministro dell'Interno, Circolare del 14 febbraio 1849. See: Daniele Arru, *La legislazione della Repubblica romana del 1849 in materia ecclesiastica* (Milano, 2012), 63–73; Biblioteca di Storia moderna e contemporanea di Roma [website], http://www. repubblicaromana-1849.it/index.php?1/home/ accessed

Marina Venier • Formerly Head of the Cataloguing Department of Rare Books at the National Central Library of Rome (BNC Roma). m.venier55@gmail.com

How the Secularization of Religious Houses Transformed the Libraries of Europe, 16th–19th Centuries, ed. by Cristina Dondi, Dorit Raines, and † Richard Sharpe, BIB, 63 (Turnhout, 2022), pp. 313–324.

BREPOLS ❦ PUBLISHERS   DOI 10.1484/M.BIB-EB.5.128490

quickly and in cases where they were not provided, the government itself would compile an inventory with the costs defrayed by the institution. The full and swift inventory of the church properties was a prerequisite both to any decision that the Republic needed to take on what to do with them and also to their preservation and protection[2]. During March and April 1849 inspections of churches, monasteries, convents, religious institutions, and confraternities were carried out, and inventories of the contents duly drawn up. The initiative met with resistance from the clergy, who tried to hide their possessions or refused to give access to certain rooms[3]. The inventories compiled in this way are kept today in the city's State Archives[4]. The descriptions of the rooms and of the objects they contain are more or less detailed; among the rooms described are the libraries of the institutions where these existed. These lists rarely give an estimate of the size of these *librerie*, but the description together with the list of furnishings helps to give us an approximate sense of how large they were. The existence of library catalogues is often mentioned but, as we shall see in the context of the 1873 suppressions these frequently disappeared.

The inventory of the library of the monastery of the Discalced Augustinians in Gesù e Maria al Corso, compiled between 15 and 20 March 1849, gives us the number of the books in the library (924), which was calculated by counting the volumes on the shelves and in the existing catalogue. This catalogue disappeared in 1873[5]. On 15 March 1849 the inventory of the library of the Cistercian monastery in Santa Croce in Gerusalemme was compiled. In this list two distinct *librerie* are mentioned, one small, the other large, as well as the existence of two catalogues, one for printed books and a second, more descriptive catalogue, in two volumes, of the monastery's "old manuscripts"[6]. The library of the Observant Franciscans in the monastery of San Bonaventura on the Palatine hill also had a catalogue, bound in vellum, in which the books were listed in alphabetical order of author headings, of which there were approximately 1,800. There were also two globes, one terrestrial and one celestial[7]. The library of the Barnabites (Clerics Regular of St Paul) in the monastery of Santi Biagio e Carlo ai Catinari is recorded as being in two rooms; for this collection too, the inventory indicates that a catalogue existed, compiled from 1829 onwards by Fr Prospero Duelli, in two volumes, A to K in 617 pages and L to Z in 653 pages[8]. In the inventory for the monastery of the Reformed Observant Franciscans of San Francesco a Ripa drawn up on 27 March 1849, two closed bookcases are recorded as containing "many books on different subjects", and there was also a "bookseller's" wooden press for binding[9].

6 December 2021); the documents in Archivio di stato di Roma (ASR), Camerale III, Chiese e conventi, Busta 1882 and *Miscellanea della Repubblica romana. 1848–1849*.

2 *Almanacco della Repubblica: storia d'Italia attraverso le tradizioni, le istituzioni e le simbologie repubblicane*, a cura di Maurizio Ridolfi (Milano, 2003), 84–96; Giuseppe Leti, *La Rivoluzione e la Repubblica romana (1848–1849)* (Milano, 1913), 496; Giuseppe Monsagrati, 'L'arte in guerra. Monumenti e politica a Roma al tempo dell'assedio del 1849', in *Roma repubblicana 1798–99, 1849*, a cura di Marina Caffiero, *Roma moderna e contemporanea*, 9 (2001), 1–3, 217–62. Daniele Arru, as note 1, 64–65, 328–30.

3 ASR, Repubblica Romana (1848–1849), Miscellanea, Busta 8: Lettera n. 2369, 13 marzo 1849.

4 ASR, Camerale III, Roma – Chiese e monasteri, under the name of the church or the monastery.

5 ASR, Camerale III, Roma – Chiese e monasteri, Busta 1874: Gesù e Maria al Corso, 15 marzo 1849.

6 ASR, Camerale III, Roma – Chiese e monasteri, Busta 1877: S. Croce in Gerusalemme, 6 aprile 1849.

7 ASR, Camerale III, Roma – Chiese e monasteri, Busta 1899: S. Bonaventura al Palatino (o alla polveriera), 26 marzo 1849. The books are listed in the following way: "A n. 125 volumi autori, B n. 203, C n. 228, D n. 83, E n. 39, F n. 82, G n. 149, H n. 33, I n. 57, K n. 8, L n. 101, M n. 166, N n. 41, O n. 32, P n. 164, Q n. 4, R n. 122, S n. 153, T rinvenuta senza numerare gli autori, U, V, X e Y come T, Z n. 6 autori". At the end, there was the list of banned books.

8 ASR, Camerale III, Roma – Chiese e monasteri, Busta 1899: S. Carlo ai Catinari, 24 marzo 1849.

9 ASR, Camerale III, Roma – Chiese e Conventi. Busta 1900: S. Francesco a Ripa, 27 marzo 1849. "Passati nella Libreria. Un giro di scanzie di albuccio tinto

The Republican government was responsible for the sequestration of palaces and monasteries in order to use them as barracks but it showed no tolerance towards or complicity with criminal acts that might be perpetrated by private individuals or public officials. It took great pains to protect the artistic and historical heritage of the city. Pietro Sterbini, minister for public works, did all he could to ensure that nothing was taken from libraries and archives and that the contents of museums and galleries remained intact. But contemporary sources reveal that many dealers, especially English ones, flocked to the city ready to pick up art objects at bargain prices.

There were serious threats, and there was real destruction as a result of the siege and eventual surrender of the city as well as being caused by the gangs of mercenaries which the government, especially towards the end, found it impossible to restrain. The French had launched 3500 missiles – bombs and grenades – against the city. Reports of the works of art and monuments that were hit, particularly around the Janiculum, can be found in the pages of the *Monitore romano*, especially after 19 June 1849. Once the French had entered Rome, a "Commission spéciale" was established to draw up a report on the damage that the city had suffered. The report was published in Paris in 1850. Its main purpose was to contradict the information on damage to the city that had been published in the *Monitore romano*. Indeed, from archival sources it emerges that many churches and monasteries later asked the restored papal government for funds to repair war damages[10].

The results of law No. 1402, passed on 19 June 1873, to suppress the religious foundations in the city were far more effective. This law decreed the suppression of all the religious houses in Rome and the confiscation of their properties, libraries, archives, buildings, and art collections[11].

The negative consequences of this law in Rome can be ascribed in part to the fact that similar laws were already in effect in the other parts of the Kingdom of Italy, with the result that the Roman clergy were forewarned and had time to shelter the most precious items in their collections from the threatened sequestration. The effects of legislation regarding the Church passed under the Kingdom of Italy were first applied in the Kingdom of Sardinia[12]. In 1848 the Society of Jesus was suppressed (L. n. 777/25

---

noce con sportelli con 'sue' ramate. Entro le medesime una quantità di libri di materie diverse. Un torchio di legno da libraro con viti simili e cavicchie di ferro. Una tavola grande di noce, un castelletto con suoi ferri, un telaro di legno, diciotto sedie di noce imbottite e fodere di corame in pessimo stato. Una scala a pioli, altra a gradini, una credenza chiusa con entro libri proibiti. Alle quattro finestre quattro tele di mussola. Alle pareti sei quadri dipinti in olio rappresentanti santi e ritratti." See also: Rosa Maria Servello, 'Habent sua fata libelli. Testimonianze di provenienza e possessori nei fondi librari', in *Dalla notitia librorum degli inventari agli esemplari. Saggi di indagine su libri e biblioteche dai codici Vaticani latini 11266–11326*, a cura di Rosa Marisa Borraccini (Macerata, 2009), 72–122.

10 ASR, Computisteria generale della Reverenda Camera Apostolica, Personale Affari generali, *Atti distribuiti per luoghi* (1835–1870), Pratiche avviate da alcune chiese romane per ottenere fondi per restauri.

11 Italo Mario Laracca, *Il patrimonio degli ordini religiosi in Italia. Soppressione e incameramento dei loro beni (1848–1873)* (Roma, 1936), 139–62; Carlo Maria Fiorentino, *Chiesa e Stato a Roma negli anni della destra storica 1870–1876. Il trasferimento della capitale e la soppressione delle Corporazioni religiose* (Roma, 1996), 393–94. Antonella Gioli, *Monumenti e oggetti d'arte nel regno d'Italia. Il patrimonio artistico degli enti religiosi soppressi tra riuso, tutela e dispersione. Inventario dei Beni delle corporazioni religiose 1860–1890*, Quaderni della rassegna degli archivi di Stato, 80 (Roma, 1997), 254–55. Archivi di Stato, DGA - Direzione Generale Archivi [website], http://www.archivi.beniculturali.it/dga/uploads/documents/Quaderni/Quaderno_80.pdf (accessed 6 December 2021).

12 Cosimo Semeraro, 'Il contesto politico culturale dei rapporti Chiesa-Sato nell'Ottocento', in *La memoria silenziosa. Formazione, tutela e status giuridico degli archivi monastici nei monumenti nazionali. Atti del Convegno. Veroli, Abbazia di Casamari 6–7 novembre 1998. Ferentino, Palazzo comunale 8 novembre 1998*, Saggi 62 (Roma, 2000), 29. Archivi di Stato, DGA

August 1848), while in 1855 a law was passed whereby "the houses of religious orders", listed here, lost their status as legally recognised entities, while "religious institutions which were not dedicated to the activities of preaching, education, and assisting the sick" were suppressed and the administration of their assets handed over to the "Cassa Ecclesiastica" (L. n. 878 29 May 1855). Over time, as further Italian regions were annexed, the law was extended to Umbria (December 1860), to the Marche (January 1861), to Naples and its surrounding territory (February 1861), and, after the constitution of the new Kingdom of Italy, to the Veneto region in 1866. Finally, the Royal decree of 7 July 1866, n. 3036, promulgated over the whole of the national territory – apart from Rome which had not yet been annexed – the suppression of religious institutions and the transfer of their assets to State property[13].

The bibliographical patrimony received by the State as a consequence was of considerable size. An enquiry carried out at the end of 1865 – excluding the city of Rome therefore – calculated that it consisted of more than 4 million volumes, 4,149,281 to be exact, which, after the Veneto region was annexed to the national territory in 1870, was the largest in Europe. And with the annexation of Rome, where most religious orders had their general houses, this patrimony grew even further[14].

In the immediate aftermath of the city's capture in 1870, the Italian government appointed Enrico Narducci (1832–1893) to study the situation of the city's libraries[15]. Narducci was the librarian of Prince Baldassarre Boncompagni, he wrote about bibliography and catalogues, and he proposed a universal catalogue of Italian libraries. He was appointed "Delegato governativo per le biblioteche di Roma" (22 March 1871). From 5 September 1872 he was a member of the "Commissione Governativa per le biblioteche" and one year later, 2 October 1873, he was made the representative of the Ministry of Education on the "Commissione speciale per le biblioteche monastiche di Roma". He was also director of the Biblioteca Alessandrina (1872). Therefore he played an important role in the events that preceded and followed the law of confiscation. As government delegate on behalf of the Public Education Ministry, he wrote three reports: "Rapporto sulle biblioteche romane" (Report on the libraries in Rome), dated 6 October 1870; "Piano per la fondazione in Roma di una Biblioteca Nazionale" (Plan for the foundation of a National Library in Rome), dated 16 March 1871; and "Informazione sommaria" (Summary information), dated 12 July 1871. The second of these reports describes the circumstances he found in some Roman libraries, the number of books and, where available, the existence of catalogues as the main tool to check the completeness of the holdings. He was also aware of the importance of preserving the historical memory of particular collections. One of Narducci's suggestions was

- Direzione Generale Archivi [website], http://www.archivi.beniculturali.it/dga/uploads/documents/Saggi/Saggi_62.pdf (accessed 6 December 2021), 29–41.

13 Legge n. 878 del 29 maggio 1855. See the extensive bibliography, discussion and their texts in Gianpaolo Romanato, 'Le leggi antiecclesiastiche negli anni dell'unificazione italiana', in *Ordini religiosi tra soppressioni e ripresa (1848–1950) I servi di Maria*, Atti del Convegno – Roma, 3–6 ottobre 2006, *Studi storici dell'ordine dei Servi di Maria*, 56–57 (2006–2007), 1–120.

14 *Le biblioteche governative italiane nel MDCCCXCVIII. Notizie storiche, bibliografiche e statistiche pubblicate a cura del Ministero della Pubblica Istruzione* (Roma, 1900), 41–43. Mauro Tosti Croce, 'Lo Stato e le biblioteche: un percorso istituzionale dall'Unità al 1975', in *Tra*

passato e futuro. Le biblioteche pubbliche statali dall'Unità d'Italia al 2000, a cura di Francesco Sicilia (Roma, 2004), 17–72. The first lists 210 libraries, of which most are in central/northern Italy. The Braidense of Milano, the Universitaria of Torino and the Magliabechiana of Firenze had each more than 200,000 volumes.

15 Giovanni Solimine, 'Enrico Narducci e le biblioteche nei primi decenni dell'Italia unita', in *Nuovi annali della Scuola speciale per archivisti e bibliotecari*, 8 (1994), 195–218.

that the provenance of each copy should be recorded on the catalogue cards and in the inventory of the nascent National Library, but his sound advice went unheeded[16].

Three years elapsed between the capture of Rome in 1870 and the law to suppress the religious houses, passed on 19 June 1873. During this period, the clergy tried to hide as many volumes as possible, especially the most valuable ones, while destroying others or transferring them to other locations. Official inspections of the libraries had already started in September 1872 and the process of actually taking possession of them began in September, 1873. Between July 1874 and May 1875 about fifty-two libraries were transferred from the places where they had been housed hitherto, in part to the Dominican convent of Santa Maria sopra Minerva then, when the space available there was full, to the nearby Collegio Romano[17]. At the same time, the clergy had also initiated protracted legal disputes, which continually delayed the delivery of other collections to the National Library, even after its formal opening, which took place on 14 March 1876. This episode was named at the time "the war of the codices"[18]. The library of the

Camaldolesi in the monastery of San Gregorio al Celio had an early-nineteenth-century catalogue, probably compiled by Fr Mauro Cappellari, who became Pope Gregory XVI in 1831. The monks declared that it had gone missing, but it is more likely that, on the contrary, they kept it and concealed it: of the 12,000 volumes reported in the 1871 inspection, just 4,500 were delivered to the National Library[19]. The library of the Franciscan friars of the Collegio di San Bonaventura, located in the convent of the Santi dodici Apostoli, was concealed in the Antoniana vineyard outside the Porta San Sebastiano; out of 16,000 volumes reported in the 1871 inspection, a mere 4,435 were delivered to the National Library[20]. The legal dispute which started in 1874 between Italy and Portugal over the Eborense library of the Franciscans in Santa Maria in Ara Coeli, named after its founder Bishop Josè Maria Fonseca da Evora, ended only nine years later, in 1883, when the collection of 19,906 volumes was finally delivered to the National Library. Thanks to this, it was the only monastic library which was both transported and stored as a whole, being given its own section as part of the National Library's collections[21].

16 Enzo Esposito, *Biblioteca Nazionale Centrale Vittorio Emanuele II* (Roma, 1974), 22: "Peraltro come ricordo storico stimerei utilissimo che in apposita finca del catalogo alfabetico e dell'inventario fosse indicata la provenienza di ciascuna delle opere provenute dalla detta soppressione, come a cagion d'esempio: Arac. Biblioteca già Aracoelitana, Coll. Rom. Biblioteca già del Collegio Romano, SS.Apost. Biblioteca già di S. Bonaventura nel Convento de' SS.Apostoli e così per le altre biblioteche".

17 The library of the Collegio Romano was transferred to the Giunta liquidatrice dell'asse ecclesiastico on 20 October 1873, and was sealed off. A year later, 1874, it was opened and transferred to the Director of the Casanatense library, Gilberto Govi.

18 See Virginia Carini Dainotti, *La Biblioteca Nazionale Vittorio Emanuele al Collegio Romano* (Firenze, 1956), 16. Margherita Breccia Fratadocchi, 'Antichi cataloghi, libri e biblioteche nei fondi manoscritti della Nazionale

di Roma', in *Dalla notitia librorum degli inventari agli esemplari. Saggi di indagine su libri e biblioteche dai codici Vaticani latini 11266–11326*, a cura di Rosa Marisa Borraccini (Macerata, 2009), 27–59.

19 Carini Dainotti, as note 18, 25 nota 9, 50–52.

20 Carini Dainotti, as note 18, 24 nota 4, 43.

21 Marina Venier, 'The monastic libraries in Rome, from the lists of the religious orders for the Sacred Congregation of the Index to the confiscation in 1873: the reconstruction of the Eborense Library in the monastery of Santa Maria in Aracoeli belonging to the Friars Minor Observant', in *Virtual visits to lost libraries: reconstruction of and access to dispersed collections*, Papers presented on 5 November 2010 at the CERL Seminar hosted by the Royal Library of Denmark, Copenhagen, edited by Ivan Boserup and David J. Shaw (London, 2011), 95–112. Carini Dainotti, as note 18, 24, 58–61. Breccia Fratadocchi, as note 18, 42–47. BNCRoma – Archive – Posizione 7/C n. 3 1883 - Lettere di Domenico

In 1883, Domenico Gnoli (1838–1915), who had been appointed Prefect of the Biblioteca Nazionale Vittorio Emanuele in the previous year, explained, in several letters to the Ministry of Public Education, that some 18,000 volumes of the Eborense library had been delivered to the National Library and that some books, duplicates among the Eborense collection or the works of Franciscan authors, were requested by the Franciscan mother-house of the Aracoeli. It is interesting that the Prefect informs the Ministry that the Eborense library had been kept in its entirety (in accordance with the resolutions taken by the Italian and Portuguese governments) and that the National Library was using the older monastic catalogue, changing only the shelf marks of the volumes.

These deliberate reductions in the monastic collections, which took place between 1871 and 1873, affected even the main historical nucleus of the National Library, the Jesuit library in the Collegio Romano. Out of approximately 110,000 volumes only 50,000 were transferred to the National Library, despite the existence of earlier catalogues and the fact that the library did not have to be moved[22].

By 1874 the books from the libraries of the suppressed religious houses had been gathered to form the first nucleus of the newly established National Library. The libraries of sixty-nine religious houses, situated in Rome and in its province, amounting to some 650,000 books, were moved first to the Dominican convent of Santa Maria sopra Minerva, then to the nearby Jesuit Collegio Romano, and stored in makeshift spaces, such as the cells vacated by the members of the order. About 380,000 books were reallocated to the libraries from which they had come (200,000 volumes to the Casanatense library, 150,000 to the Angelica, and 30,000 to the Vallicelliana), while 277,674 books remained in the Collegio Romano, which was the first seat of the new National Library[23].

Through all these upheavals, manuscripts for the most part retained a connexion with their

---

Gnoli al Ministro della Pubblica Istruzione, n. 2 del 24 marzo, n. 3 del 18 giugno, n. 4 del. 21 giugno 1883. The catalogue in *Antichi cataloghi* 1/ 1–3 ('Catalogo della biblioteca Aracoeliana Eborense' A-M, L-Z, Appendice), from the first half of the nineteenth century, shows on the right side, next to each title, as Gnoli wrote, the current shelf mark. The sections are: 31, 32, 37 (the 6,285 volumes have the stamp of Bishop Fonseca), 42 (from 42.1 to 42.7.G.2), 43. In the National library, the volumes from these sections (about 17,000 volumes) contain the labels of the "Eborense" [and Aracoelitana] library. There are other older catalogues: *Antichi cataloghi* 2/ 1–3 (1844, 1845), "Indice alfabetico dei libri della Biblioteca Araceliana", a catalogue with the stamp of Bishop Fonseca; *Antichi cataloghi* 45–48 (in arabic numbers) they consist of lists of books, bibliographies, bibliographical cuttings (sec. XIX). The cataloguing in the SBN catalogue of the books and the digitization of some volumes and of the historical catalogues are now in progress.

22 *Le biblioteche governative italiane nel MDCCCXCVIII*, 47 nota 1. BNC-Roma, *Antichi cataloghi* 21 (subject catalogue in 27 volumes), 23 (author catalogue in 12 volumes), 57 (topographic catalogue in 2 volumes). See also: *Antichi cataloghi* 25, 36, 50, 51 and MS Gesuitico 882. Jacob Diamond, S. I., 'A catalogue of the old Roman college library and a reference to another', in *Gregorianum*, 32 (1951), 109–14. Alda Spotti, 'Guida storica ai fondi manoscritti della Biblioteca Nazionale Centrale Vittorio Emanuele II di Roma', in *Pluteus* 4–5 (1986–1987) [1990], 359–86 and in *I fondi, le procedure, le storie. Raccolta di studi della Biblioteca* (Roma, 1993), 4–31. Breccia Fratadocchi, as note 18, 29–38.

23 A complete bibliography (to 1992) of the history of the National Library can be found in 'La Biblioteca Nazionale Centrale Vittorio Emanuele II di Roma: una bibliografia, 1870–1992', a cura di Sergio Masti, Ludovica Mazzola, Marcella Pisano, in *I fondi, le procedure, le storie. Raccolta di studi della Biblioteca* (Roma, 1993), 293–317. See also: Paolo Veneziani, 'La Biblioteca Nazionale Centrale Vittorio Emanuele II', in *Il Collegio Romano dalle origini al Ministero per i Beni e le Attività culturali* (Roma, 2003), 397–425. Breccia Fratadocchi, as note 18, 29–59.

provenance[24]. The original order of the collections of the printed books, however, underwent much disruption, and the obliteration of the books' former identities was most intense at the point when they were incorporated unsystematically into the new National Library and placed in large sections arranged first by subject and, within each subject, by format. The way this occurred is well described in a letter written in 1929 by Giuliano Bonazzi (1863–1956), prefect of the Biblioteca Nazionale Vittorio Emanuele during the years 1909 to 1933, to the Minister for Education on the subject of returning volumes that had been requested by the Carmelites of Santa Maria della Scala[25]. Immediately after the law suppressing the monasteries in the city was passed, Bonazzi wrote that the libraries:

> were incorporated unsystematically into the Vittorio Emanuele collections; the former ownership of the volumes can only be recovered from the former library's stamps on the title-pages. In ordering the National Library's collections, the best volumes were selected from among the books coming from the various monastic libraries and placed in large sections arranged by subject such as literature, history, jurisprudence, etc. For this reason it is impossible to establish which volumes – and how many – come from former monastic libraries. Moreover, a large number of duplicates have been sold at various times at auction – sales for which there was a special

law which allowed the proceeds to be used for further acquisitions for the National Library's collections.

So there was another factor which affected the dispersal of the monastic collections. Already in 1874 Ruggero Bonghi, when he was the Minister for Education, said in his budget report on 26 May 1874: "Out of those 400,000 volumes […] I can assure you that at least 200,000 are not worth the cost of moving them […] since the friars read only books which are 200 years old!"[26]. Thus the way was opened for the sale of duplicates. Some 19,000 volumes were sold at four auctions held between 1879 and 1914[27] and another 100,000 were weeded out and left in storage in the National Library, where they can still be found uncatalogued. In this way the monastic libraries of Rome underwent a double dispersal, first, when the clergy tried to hide and subtract the volumes to avoid handing them over to the Italian State, and again once they had arrived in the National Library. In the light of this double loss, both external and internal, how might we begin today to reconstruct these collections? As we have said, manuscripts were kept separately as collections from the various

24 Livia Martinoli, 'Per la storia e la catalogazione dei fondi manoscritti della Biblioteca Nazionale Centrale di Roma', in *Manoscritti antichi e moderni*, Quaderni della Biblioteca nazionale centrale di Roma 11 (Roma, 2005), 117–48.

25 Archivio BVE, Posizione 7 D, 17 agosto 1900. About Giuliano Bonazzi, see: Armando Petrucci, 'Bonazzi, Giuliano', in *Dizionario biografico degli italiani* [website], https://www.treccani.it/enciclopedia/giuliano-bonazzi_(Dizionario-Biografico) (accessed 6 December 2021).

26 Atti Parlamentari, Sessione 1873–1874, IV, 4000, in Paolo Veneziani, as note 23, 402, nota 13.

27 *Catalogo delle opere duplicate di teologia appartenenti alla Biblioteca Nazionale V.E. di Roma che si offrono in vendita al pubblico incanto. Vol. I* (Roma, 1879). Only the first volume was published, containing 5.497 titles on theology and ecclesiastical history and 3,095 on lives of the saints (BNCRoma 200.H.64); *Catalogo di opere duplicate della Biblioteca Vittorio Emanuele di Roma*, lotto primo (Roma, 1895); lotto secondo (Roma 1897) about 3,200 books were sold (BNCRoma 200.K.231); *Catalogo dei duplicati della Biblioteca Nazion. Vittorio Emanuele di Roma da vendersi alla pubblica auzione* (Roma, 1913–1914), it lists 5,150 titles (BNCRoma 200.F.5). Attilio Nardecchia, 'Il commercio antiquario specie dei libri ecclesiastici', in *Il libro e le biblioteche. Atti del primo congresso bibliologico francescano internazionale 20–27 febbraio 1949* (Romae, 1950), 387.

monastic libraries. In searching, one can use the inventories of manuscripts drawn up for each monastery and the related hand-written indexes that were created when the volumes were rearranged in the National Library. These manuscripts are now being catalogued online in MANUS[28], in which the records include a field for provenance notes. Several collections have already been included; in two years' time about 3000 manuscripts will have been catalogued from a total of 8,000 now held by the National Library. The situation with the printed books is different, but many books from the suppressed religious orders now in the National Library still show evidence of their former ownership. Due mainly to subsequent rebinding – especially during the 1970s, when a devastating conservation programme was undertaken in the National Library – provenance evidence has been lost from a great many books, especially incunabula, when older bindings were removed. The kinds of evidence we find in these volumes comprise printed book labels, ink stamps made with metal, wooden, or rubber tools, inscriptions in ink along the bottom edge, old shelf marks, and distinctive bindings[29].

All the books from the Jesuit library of the Collegio Romano carry a printed book label, centrally positioned inside the front cover, with the inscription *Ex biblioteca Majori Coll. Rom. Societ. Jesu*, sometimes combined with the ex libris inscription and with different kinds of stamps on the title page. During the seventeenth century, the normative use of *ex libris* was already prescribed by the Collegio Romano.

The Jesuits' books still show many of their old shelf marks. On some volumes the shelf mark is traced with a brush on the spine, within a blue band divided by two red stripes, and comprises a capital letter and Arabic numerals. This is the shelfmark relating to the first Subject Catalogue made in the eighteenth century.

On other volumes, inside the front cover, at the lower left, we can find two different stages of shelfmarks. The older is formed by three pen-written Arabic numerals, the first followed by an apostrophe, all positioned on the same line. This has then been superseded by a new line comprising an Arabic numeral, a lower-case letter, and another Arabic numeral. This is the shelfmark that we find in the eighteenth-century printed books catalogue of the Collegio Romano. Both catalogues are now in the National Library.

The books coming from the library of the Collegio di San Pantaleo (Order of Poor Clerics Regular of the Mother of God of the Pious Schools) have two kinds of stamps and the *ex libris* inscription on the title page. We know that manuscripts from this collection had a green vellum binding and a shelf mark consisting simply of a number in Arabic figures. On the printed books, on the other hand, we have a shelf mark comprising a capital letter, a Roman numeral, and an Arabic numeral, written one above the other.

As far as the books in the library of the Collegio di San Bonaventura in the monastery of the Santi dodici Apostoli are concerned, we find in them the stamp and/or the characteristic vertical shelf mark comprising the letters C. (Camera), S. (Scrinium), followed by the capital letter, O. (Ordo) and N. (Numerus), followed by Arabic numerals. Felice Peretti, elected pope in 1585 as Pope Sixtus V, donated to the Collegio a new library, the so called Feliciana, amounting to 16,000 volumes. Only 4,000 books reached the National Library, together with the old catalogue, which gives us evidence of the previous shelf mark.

---

28 ICCU [website], http://manus.iccu.sbn.it/, accessed 6 December 2021). See: Martinoli, as note 24, 117–48.

29 Marina Venier, *Librerie dei conventi riunite nella Vittorio Emanuele*, in Biblioteca Nazionale Centrale di Roma [website], http://www.bncrm.beniculturali.it/getFile.php?id=795 (accessed 6 December 2021). See also: CERL, Online Provenance resources, Geographical areas, Italy, Rome, Biblioteca Nazionale Centrale [website], https://www.cerl.org/web/en/resources/provenance/geographical (accessed 6 December 2021).

In 1994 the National Library started to catalogue its historical printed collections book in hand, for inclusion in the union catalogue of the Servizio bibliotecario nazionale (SBN), the network of Italian libraries[30]. The database for early printed material, containing records of editions from the early days of printing up to 1830, records the names of former owners and the most recent owners or provenances, linked to one or more inventory numbers identifying each copy[31].

At present the database of owners includes some 1,300 headings, the result of cataloguing almost all the copies of sixteenth- and seventeenth-century editions in the National Library. The entire collection of incunabula, 1683 editions in 2153 copies, has been described in the *Material Evidence in Incunabula* (MEI) database; owners and provenances are now also available in the CERL Thesaurus.

30 ICCU [website], https://www.iccu.sbn.it/opencms/opencms/it/main/sbn/ (accessed 6 December 2021).
31 ICCU [website], https://www.sbn.it/ (accessed 6 December 2021). Servello, as note 9, 61–72.

Bibliography

Manuscripts and Archival Sources

Roma, Biblioteca Nazionale Centrale – Archive – Posizione 7C/ 1883 n. 3, 3 bis, 4 – Lettere di Domenico Gnoli al Ministro della Pubblica Istruzione.

Roma, Biblioteca Nazionale Centrale – Archive – Posizione 7 D, 17 agosto 1900.

Atti Parlamentari, Sessione 1873–1874, IV.

Archivi di Stato, DGA- Direzione Generale Archivi [website], http://www.archivi.beniculturali.it/index.php/cosa-facciamo/pubblicazioni/cerca-nelle-pubblicazioni (accessed 6 December 2021).

Biblioteca di Storia moderna e contemporanea di Roma [website], http://www.repubblicaromana-1849.it/index.php?1/home (accessed 6 December 2021).

Roma, Archivio di stato (ASR), Camerale III, Roma – Chiese e conventi.

Roma, Archivio di stato (ASR), Camerale III, Roma – Chiese e monasteri.

Roma, Archivio di stato (ASR), Computisteria generale della Reverenda Camera Apostolica, Personale Affari generali, *Atti distribuiti per luoghi* (1835–1870), Pratiche avviate da alcune chiese romane per ottenere fondi per restauri.

Roma, Archivio di stato (ASR), Repubblica Romana (1848–1849), Miscellanea, Busta 8: Lettera n. 2369, 13 marzo 1849.

Secondary Works

Almanacco della Repubblica: storia d'Italia attraverso le tradizioni, le istituzioni e le simbologie repubblicane, a cura di Maurizio Ridolfi (Milano, 2003).

Daniele Arru, *La legislazione della Repubblica romana del 1849 in materia ecclesiastica* (Milano, 2012).

'La Biblioteca Nazionale Centrale Vittorio Emanuele II di Roma: una bibliografia, 1870–1992', a cura di Sergio Masti, Ludovica Mazzola, Marcella Pisano, in *I fondi, le procedure, le storie. Raccolta di studi della Biblioteca* (Roma, 1993), 293–317.

Le biblioteche governative italiane nel MDCCCXCVIII. Notizie storiche, bibliografiche e statistiche pubblicate a cura del Ministero della Pubblica Istruzione (Roma, 1900).

Margherita Breccia Fratadocchi, 'Antichi cataloghi, libri e biblioteche nei fondi manoscritti della Nazionale di Roma', in *Dalla notitia librorum degli inventari agli esemplari. Saggi di indagine su libri e biblioteche dai codici Vaticani latini 11266–11326*, a cura di Rosa Marisa Borraccini (Macerata, 2009), 27–59.

Virginia Carini Dainotti, *La Biblioteca Nazionale Vittorio Emanuele al Collegio Romano* (Firenze, 1956).

Catalogo delle opere duplicate di teologia appartenenti alla Biblioteca Nazionale V.E. di Roma che si offrono in vendita al pubblico incanto. Vol. I (Roma, 1879).

Catalogo dei duplicati della Biblioteca Nazion. Vittorio Emanuele di Roma da vendersi alla pubblica auzione (Roma, 1913–1914).

Catalogo di opere duplicate della Biblioteca Vittorio Emanuele di Roma, lotto primo (Roma, 1895); lotto secondo (Roma, 1897).

Jacob Diamond, S. I., 'A catalogue of the old Roman college library and a reference to another', *Gregorianum*, 22 (1951), 103–14.

Enzo Esposito, *Biblioteca Nazionale Centrale Vittorio Emanuele II* (Roma, 1974).

Carlo Maria Fiorentino, *Chiesa e Stato a Roma negli anni della destra storica 1870–1876. Il trasferimento della capitale e la soppressione delle Corporazioni religiose* (Roma, 1996).

Antonella Gioli, *Monumenti e oggetti d'arte nel regno d'Italia. Il patrimonio artistico degli enti religiosi soppressi tra riuso, tutela e dispersione. Inventario dei "Beni delle corporazioni religiose 1860–1890*, Quaderni della rassegna degli archivi di Stato, 80 (Roma, 1997). Archivi di Stato, DGA- Direzione Generale Archivi [web site], http://www.archivi.beniculturali.it/dga/uploads/documents/Quaderni/Quaderno_80.pdf (accessed 6 December 2021).

Italo Mario Laracca, *Il patrimonio degli ordini religiosi in Italia. Soppressione e incameramento dei loro beni (1848–1873)* (Roma, 1936).

Giuseppe Leti, *La Rivoluzione e la Repubblica romana (1848–1849)* (Milano, 1913).

Livia Martinoli, 'Per la storia e la catalogazione dei fondi manoscritti della Biblioteca Nazionale Centrale di Roma', in *Manoscritti antichi e moderni*, Quaderni della Biblioteca nazionale centrale di Roma, 11 (Roma, 2005), 117–48.

Giuseppe Monsagrati, 'L'arte in guerra. Monumenti e politica a Roma al tempo dell'assedio del 1849', in *Roma repubblicana 1798–99, 1849*, a cura di Marina Caffiero, *Roma moderna e contemporanea*, 9 (2001), 1–3, 217–62.

Attilio Nardecchia, 'Il commercio antiquario specie dei libri ecclesiastici', in *Il libro e le biblioteche*. Atti del primo congresso bibliologico francescano internazionale 20–27 febbraio 1949 (Roma, 1950).

Armando Petrucci, 'Bonazzi, Giuliano', in Dizionario biografico degli italiani [website], https://www.treccani.it/enciclopedia/giuliano-bonazzi_(Dizionario-Biografico) (accessed 22 July 2013).

Gianpaolo Romanato, 'Le leggi antiecclesiastiche negli anni dell'unificazione italiana', in *Ordini religiosi tra soppressioni e ripresa (1848–1950) I servi di Maria*. Atti del Convegno – Roma, 3–6 ottobre 2006, *Studi storici dell'ordine dei Servi di Maria*, 56–57 (2006–2007), 1–120.

Cosimo Semeraro, 'Il contesto politico culturale dei rapporti Chiesa-Sato nell'Ottocento', in *La memoria silenziosa. Formazione, tutela e status giuridico degli archivi monastici nei monumenti nazionali*. Atti del Convegno. Veroli, Abbazia di Casamari 6–7 novembre 1998, Saggi 62 (Roma, 2000), 29–42. Archivi di Stato, DGA - Direzione Generale Archivi [website], http://www.archivi.beniculturali.it/dga/uploads/documents/Saggi/Saggi_62.pdf (accessed 6 December 2021).

Rosa Maria Servello, 'Habent sua fata libelli. Testimonianze di provenienza e possessori nei fondi librari', in *Dalla notitia librorum degli inventari agli esemplari. Saggi di indagine su libri e biblioteche dai codici Vaticani latini 11266–11326*, a cura di Rosa Marisa Borraccini (Macerata, 2009), 72–122.

Giovanni Solimine, 'Enrico Narducci e le biblioteche nei primi decenni dell'Italia unita', in *Nuovi annali della Scuola speciale per archivisti e bibliotecari*, 8 (1994), 195–218.

Alda Spotti, 'Guida storica ai fondi manoscritti della Biblioteca Nazionale Centrale Vittorio Emanuele II di Roma', *Pluteus* 4–5 (1986–1987) [1990], 359–86.

Mauro Tosti Croce, 'Lo Stato e le biblioteche: un percorso istituzionale dall'Unità al 1975', in *Tra passato e futuro. Le biblioteche pubbliche statali dall'Unità d'Italia al 2000*, a cura di Francesco Sicilia (Roma, 2004), 17–72.

Paolo Veneziani, 'La Biblioteca Nazionale Centrale Vittorio Emanuele II', in *Il Collegio Romano dalle origini al Ministero per i Beni e le Attività culturali* (Roma, 2003), 397–425.

Marina Venier, 'The monastic libraries in Rome, from the lists of the religious orders for the Sacred Congregation of the Index to the confiscation in 1873: the reconstruction of the Eborense Library in the monastery of Santa Maria in Aracoeli belonging to the Friars Minor Observant', in *Virtual visits to lost libraries: reconstruction of and access to dispersed collections*, Papers presented on 5 November 2010 at the CERL Seminar hosted by the Royal Library of Denmark, Copenhagen, edited by Ivan Boserup and David J. Shaw (London, 2011), 95–112.

Digital Sources

CERL, Online Provenance resources, Geographical areas, Italy, Rome, Biblioteca Nazionale Centrale, https://www.cerl.org/web/en/resources/provenance/geographical.

CERL Thesaurus, https://data.cerl.org/thesaurus/_search.

ICCU, https://www.iccu.sbn.it/opencms/opencms/it/main/sbn.

Manus Online, http://manus.iccu.sbn.it.

SBN, https://opac.sbn.it/opacsbn/opac/iccu/free.jsp.

Material Evidence in Incunabula (MEI), https://data.cerl.org/mei/_search.

Marina Venier, *Librerie dei conventi riunite nella Vittorio Emanuele*, in Biblioteca Nazionale Centrale di Roma, http://www.bncrm.beniculturali.it/getFile.php?id=795.

MAREK DERWICH

The Dissolution of Monasteries in Silesia and Poland

Range of Dissolution

In 1772, the lands of the Polish–Lithuanian Commonwealth were partitioned with territory being taken by three states, Prussia, the Austrian empire, and the Russian empire, leaving a much reduced territory still under the rule of King Stanisław II August. A second partition in 1793 further reduced the territory under the king's rule, and a third partition in 1795 divided the remainder of the territory between the three partitioning powers. The dissolution of religious houses was first imposed in the Polish lands during exactly this period; it is therefore the case that the dates, occasions, and policies driving the dissolution varied according to the jurisdiction under which particular houses came after the partition. Yet to take a long-term view one cannot consider the fate of Polish and Lithuanian monasteries and their libraries only as part of the dissolution processes in Prussia, Austria, and Russia. After the Napoleonic wars a new Kingdom of Poland was created on newly defined borders, and the dissolution of religious houses continued under successive Polish governments. These

circumstances make for a very complicated picture. This paper is concerned with what happened in the lands that form the country now called Poland including the area whose territorial name is Silesia[1]. In terms of different jurisdictions, therefore, we shall have to deal first with the dissolution of religious houses by a Catholic government within the remaining Polish–Lithuanian Commonwealth between 1772 and 1795, secondly with what happened in Polish lands under the rule of Catholic Austria, particularly under Emperor Joseph II, and thirdly with the effects of Protestant Prussian government.

Catholic religious in the lands of the Polish–Lithuanian commonwealth that came under Russian rule, lands that belonged historically to the Grand Duchy of Lithuania, had a very different experience, under a nationalist Russian government closely linked to the Orthodox Church. This territory is treated in a separate paper by Oleh Dukh.

---

[1] A region of Central Europe located mostly in Poland, with small parts in the Czech Republic and Germany.

Marek Derwich • Formerly professor in the History Department of the University of Wrocław (Poland).
marek.derwich@uwr.edu.com

How the Secularization of Religious Houses Transformed the Libraries of Europe, 16th–19th Centuries, ed. by Cristina Dondi, Dorit Raines, and † Richard Sharpe, BIB, 63 (Turnhout, 2022), pp. 325–335.
BREPOLS ❧ PUBLISHERS   DOI 10.1484/M.BIB-EB.5.128491

In 1772, just before the first partition of the lands of the Polish-Lithuanian Commonwealth, the number of religious in the territory of the Polish-Lithuanian Commonwealth (the Poles, Lithuanians and, in fact, also part of the Ruthenians[2]), was about 14,540; they lived in some 990 monasteries that belonged to twenty-nine different male religious orders. At the same time in the area of Silesia there were 1,334 religious in seventy-three monasteries belonging to seventeen male religious orders. In total, the Polish-Lithuanian Commonwealth and Silesia had at that moment thirty male religious orders of 1,063 monasteries of various sizes and 15,874 religious, most of whom were mendicants.

In 1914, at the dawn of Polish independence, several phases of dissolution had reduced the numbers in the same territory to 188 monasteries (19% of the 1772 figure) with 2,252 religious (only 14% of the number in 1772). These figures disguise the real scale of the dissolution, however, because 133 of the remaining religious houses (126 friars convents), with 1,830 religious, were situated in Galicia, the land between Cracow and Lviv, which had been under the jurisdiction of the Catholic Austro-Hungarian Empire[3]. These figures have been calculated for men's houses; unfortunately, in the case of female religious life we do not have such detailed data.

The Dissolution in the Polish-Lithuanian Commonwealth, 1772–1795

The belief that there were too many monasteries and religious, and the need to strengthen diocesan structures, very apparent in the reforms of emperor Joseph II and presented in the case of the dissolution of other monasteries, was not alien to the Polish episcopate. In July 1773 there were no reservations in accepting the papal bull suppressing the Jesuits. Their suppression produced funds and buildings for the creation of the Commission of National Education[4]. The collections of Jesuit books were divided. Some of them, deemed necessary for the schools, were taken over by the Commission of National Education. Other books landed in gradually emerging local public libraries (mostly provincial). The significant part of the collections, recognised as valuable and useful, was taken over by the newly established seminary libraries. The rest was dispersed[5].

---

2   An area bordering the south of Poland, Ukraine, Romania, Hungary and Slovakia.

3   Piotr Paweł Gach, 'Soppressioni 1773–1879, Polonia', in *Dizionario degli istituti di perfezione*, ed. Guerrino Pelliccia and Giancarlo Rocca, 10 vols (Roma, 1974–2003), VIII 1830–34; idem, 'Le réseau des monastères de moines et chanoines réguliers en Pologne et en Silésie (1700–1914)', in *Naissance et fonctionnement des réseaux monastiques et canoniaux. Actes du Premier Colloque international du CERCOM, Saint-Étienne, 16–18 septembre 1985. CERCOR, Travaux et recherches, 1 (Saint-Étienne, 1991), 271–98 Marek Derwich, *Klasztory i mnisi* [Monasteries and monks], A to Polska właśnie (Wrocław, 2004), 101, 192.

4   Agata Demkowicz, 'Stan badań nad kasatą jezuitów w Polsce' [State of research on the suppression of the Jesuits in Poland], in *Prace Humanistyczne* [Towarzystwa Naukowego w Rzeszowie], S. 1, fol. 31, ed. Piotr Żbikowski (Rzeszów, 2004), 155–74.

5   Radosław Lolo, 'Kasata kolegium jezuitów w Pułtusku a losy tutejszej szkoły (1772–1781)' [Dissolution of the Jesuit monastery in Pułtusk and fate of its school], in *Kasaty klasztorne na obszarze dawnej Rzeczypospolitej Obojga Narodów i na Śląsku na tle procesów sekularyzacyjnych w Europie (XVIII–XX wiek)* [Dissolution of monasteries in the territory of the old Polish and Lithuanian Commonwealth and of Silesia against the background of secularization processes in Europe (XVIII–XX centuries)], ed. Marek Derwich, 4 vols (Wrocław, 2014), I 99–104, and summary in *Pruskie kasaty klasztorne na Śląsku na tle procesów sekularyzacyjnych w Polsce i Europie. Międzynarodowa konferencja naukowa, Wrocław, 18–21 listopada 2010. Księga streszczeń = The Prussian dissolution of monasteries in Silesia against a background of secularization processes in Poland and Europe. International conference, Wrocław, 18–21 November 2010. Abstracts*, ed. Marek Derwich and Marek L. Wójcik (Wrocław, 2010), 98–99.

The first dissolution of monasteries in the lands of the Polish-Lithuanian Commonwealth was conducted in the 1780s by primate Michał Jerzy Poniatowski – the brother of the last king of pre-partition Poland. During the years 1781–1788 he dissolved seven monasteries, including five in Cracow, and in four other female convents he shut down novitiates[6]. The book collections from these institutions became the property of other monasteries of the same order in Cracow[7].

The Dissolution of Monasteries in Galicia under the Emperor Joseph II

Enlightened monarchies ruling Protestant Prussia and Catholic Austria from the mid-eighteenth century began to exert a sometimes far-reaching intervention into religious life, especially in the economy. This policy of subjugation of the Church to the State, institutionalised by Emperor Joseph II, is called Josephinism after him[8]. As a result of the partitions in 1772 and 1795 and the provisions of the Congress of Vienna in 1815 the territory of Galicia, extending from Cracow to Lviv, also saw the implementation of that policy. Joseph's suppression led to the liquidation of

over half of the male and two thirds of the female monasteries respectively, which after the first partition had come under Austrian rule. After the death of Joseph II in 1790, the rate of dissolution decreased; however, until the repeal of his law in 1852, several dozen more monasteries were dissolved[9].

It took almost ten years before the Austrian Imperial administration turned to deal with monastic libraries, with the decree dated 12 January 1782, and the "Klostersturm", the second phase of the dissolution, which lasted until 1787. Joseph II appointed commissioners to draw up catalogues of early printed books, manuscripts, and archives, and to take possession of existing catalogues and inventories. The commissioners also drew up summary lists for easier access to information required for allocating confiscated collections to new homes. On the basis of the summary lists the most valuable books and manuscripts were selected for the Hofbibliothek in Vienna. Other collections of printed books were to be transferred to the nearest high school or university library. These book collections helped to establish new libraries, such as the University library of Lviv, capital of Galicia, established in 1785. Books which were neither sent to Vienna nor to other libraries were put on sale and ended up in private hands.

From the beginning of the nineteenth century, when the relaxation of Joseph's policy allowed, the books confiscated from dissolved monasteries were transferred to the libraries of monasteries of the same order that continued to function, or, if none existed to receive them, to the libraries of seminaries under the direction of diocesan bishops[10].

---

6 Piotr Paweł Gach, *Kasaty klasztorne na ziemiach dawnej Rzeczypospolitej i Śląska 1773–1914* [Dissolution of monasteries in the territory of the old Polish and Lithuanian Commonwealth and of Silesia 1773–1914] (Lublin, 1984), 17–21.

7 Hermina Święch, 'Przyczyny i przebieg kasat żeńskich klasztorów w Krakowie w drugiej połowie XVIII i na początku XIX w.' [The causes and the development of the dissolutions of the female monasteries in Cracow in the second half of the 18th and the beginning of 19th century], in *Kasaty klasztorne*, as note 5, I 159–78, and summary in *Pruskie kasaty klasztorne*, as note 5, 162–63.

8 Stanisław Jujeczka, 'Kasaty dóbr kościelnych w nowożytnej Europie (połowa XVII – początek XIX wieku)' [Secularisation of the ecclesiastical estate in modern Europe (mid 17th – early 19th century)], in *Kasaty klasztorne*, as note 5, I 61–78, and summary in *Pruskie kasaty klasztorne*, as note 5, 66–67.

9 Derwich, *Klasztory i mnisi*, as note 3, 184. See Gach, *Kasaty klasztorne*, as note 6, 22–35, 120–24, 145–50.

10 Jolanta Gwioździk, 'Pokasacyjne losy księgozbiorów klasztornych na obszarze Rzeczypospolitej Obojga Narodów' [The fate of the monastic libraries in the territory of the old Polish and Lithuanian

The Dissolution in the Prussian Partition

Initially, the policy of Prussia towards the religious orders, as outlined by Frederick II (1712–1786; king from 1740), was characterized by cold pragmatism. Monasteries were generally allowed to function, but their endowments were taken away by the state, which in return provided an allowance fixed at about half the level of their income at this date. In the territories newly acquired as a result of the partition of Poland, the Prussian authorities were looking for buildings to house various state institutions, and with this in view they closed down twenty-nine monasteries (only two of them for women) and moved the religious and sisters to other houses of their orders[11].

The libraries of dissolved monasteries, after their inventories were completed, were left in place for the time being. Small parts of the collections, mostly books of theology, philosophy, liturgy, usually under the control of the church authorities were allocated to the emerging needs of the libraries of diocesan seminaries. Those that remained in place, were dispersed, either by purchase, theft, or donation, or – especially in the case of the less valuable – destroyed when the buildings were allocated for different state purposes, such as military barracks, warehouses, and administrative offices[12].

After 1815 the Prussian dissolution was limited only to the Polish lands taken during the annexations of the years 1773–1795, namely the Grand Duchy of Poznań, and Western and Eastern Prussia.

Again after 1815, the Prussian authorities increasingly began to believe that the Catholic Church, including the monasteries, was a major obstacle to the implementation of a policy to integrate the Polish lands into Prussia. First the novitiates were closed down, then the state proceeded to the liquidation of the monasteries. By 1830, twenty-six of them, including two female, were closed. During the years 1833–1841 sixty-one monasteries were closed: forty-six male and fifteen female, including all the old medieval monasteries which still had large and valuable collections of books[13].

Secularisation Committees prepared detailed inventories of the libraries, which were given to the administrative authorities after which books were sent by them to certain institutions to complement their collections – first of all to the Royal Library in Berlin, followed to the University Libraries in Breslau (Wrocław), capital of Silesia and Königsberg (Kaliningrad), capital of Eastern Prussia, finally to the libraries of local secondary schools. The rest was transferred to diocesan bishops who mostly issued instructions to include them in seminary libraries. Books which served no purpose, books in bad condition and duplicates were left in place. Their subsequent fate was, in general, one of dispersal.

At the same time, the race to gain valuable manuscripts, incunabula and early printed books, by the above-mentioned central libraries, was joined by local antique dealers, librarians and book collectors, often with success. By this means, Titus Działyński and Edward Raczyński, aristocrats, politicians and protectors of arts,

---

Commonwealth after the dissolutions], in *Kasaty klasztorne*, as note 5, III 137–50, and summary in *Pruskie kasaty klasztorne*, as note 5, 56–57.

11   See Jürgen Peter Ravens, *Staat und katholische Kirche in Preussens polnischen Teilungsgebieten (1772–1807)*, Veröffentlichungen des Osteuropa Institutes München, 21 (Wiesbaden, 1963); Gach, *Kasaty klasztorne*, as note 6, 36–42; Derwich, *Klasztory i mnisi*, as note 3, 185.

12   Krzysztof Walczak, 'Wpływ kasat klasztorów na losy bibliotek dziewiętnastowiecznego Kalisza' [Influence of the secularization on the fate of the libraries in Kalisz in nineteenth century], in *Kasaty klasztorne*, as note 5, III 221–227, and summary in *Pruskie kasaty klasztorne*, as note 5, 164–65; Gwioździk, 'Pokasacyjne losy', as note 10.

13   Derwich, *Klasztory i mnisi*, as note 3, 185. Gach, *Kasaty klasztorne*, as note 6, 137–44.

gained a portion of the book collections for their large emerging libraries: the Działyński Library in Kórnik and the Raczyński Library in Poznań[14].

The dissolution policy, intensified by the aspirations towards Germanisation of the Polish lands, was revived during the Kulturkampf (The Battle of Cultures 1872–1879)[15]. It eliminated the remaining fifty-six monasteries, nine male and forty-seven female. Their collections of books, mostly from the nineteenth century, were dispersed[16].

The Dissolution in Silesia under the Rule of Prussia

The immediate cause of the dissolution of Silesian monasteries was the need to pay war contributions by Prussia after their defeat in the war with Napoleon in the years 1806–1807. An edict of the Prussian King Frederick William III (1770–1840; king from 1797), of 30 October 1810, dissolved sixty-nine monasteries – fifty-six male (96%) and thirteen female (76%)[17].

On 8 November, 1811, Johann Gustav Gottlieb Büsching[18] was designated as the "Königlicher Comissarius" for the acquisition of all Silesian book collections kept in monasteries. He was to make an inspection of the collections, organise and catalogue them all and to ensure their proper storage. Büsching's appointment was not accidental – even before the secularisation edict was issued, he had developed a project to create a Silesian Central Library, which was to include collections from all the libraries in Breslau (Wrocław) and other principal libraries in Silesia.

Initially all catalogued book collections, bearing the provenance labels, were packed into crates with marked sections and transported to Breslau. The incoming books were compared with the catalogues of the well structured library of St Vincent monastery in Breslau. The duplicates were immediately directed to a separate department. However, this *modus operandi* was later changed: books were to be catalogued immediately, on the spot, and only the catalogues were to be sent to Breslau. Based on the catalogues, the books needed in the Central Library were chosen. On 20 April 1812 Büsching was dismissed and transferred to the archive in Breslau, where he successfully sorted out the archive materials left from the dissolved monasteries. His removal from the organisation of book collections had a

---

14   Piotr Paweł Gach, *Mienie polskich zakonów i jego losy w XIX wieku* [The property of the Polish monastic orders and its vicissitudes in the 19th Century], Mozaika. Seria Monografii, 1 (Rzym, 1979), 73–74.

15   Georg Franz, *Kulturkampf. Staat und katholische Kirche in Mitteleuropa von der Säkularisation bis zum Abschluss preusischen Kultrkampfes* (München, 1954).

16   Lech Trzeciakowski, 'The Prussian State and the Catholic Church in Prussian Poland 1871–1914', *Slavic Revue*, 26 (1967), 4, 618–37; Zygmunt Zieliński, 'Ustawy antyzakonne kulturkampfu i ich wykonanie na terenie Wielkopolski' [The law against religious orders during the Kulturkampf and its implementation in Greater Poland], *Roczniki Teologiczno-Kanoniczne*, 16 (1969), 4, 75–91; Derwich, *Klasztory i mnisi*, as note 3, 185, 188; Zygmunt Zieliński, *Kulturkampf w archidiecezji gnieźnieńskiej i poznańskiej w latach 1873–1887* [Kulturkampf in the Archdiocese of Gniezno and Poznań in 1873–1887] (Poznań, 2012).

17   Josef Joachim Menzel, 'Die Säkularisation in Schlesien 1810', in *Säkularisationen in Ostmitteleuropa. Zur Klärung des Verhältnisses von geistlicher und weltlicher Macht*

im Mittelalter, von Kirche und Staat in der Neuzeit, ed. Joachim Köhler, Forschungen und Quellen zur Kirchen- und Kulturgeschichte Ostdeutschlands, 19 (Köln-Weimar, 1984), 85–102; Gach, *Kasaty klasztorne*, as note 6, 69–78; idem, 'Kasata zakonów na Śląsku Pruskim w latach 1810–1811' [Dissolution of religious orders in Prussian Silesia in 1810–1811], *Roczniki Humanistyczne*, 26 (1978), 2, 233–48.

18   Marek Hałub, *Johann Gustav Gottlieb Büsching 1783–1829. Ein Beitrag zur Begründung der schlesischen Kulturgeschichte*, Acta Universitatis Wratislaviensis, 1978 (Wrocław, 1997); Brigitte Bönisch-Brednich, *Büschings Volkskundliche Forschungen in Schlesien. Eine Wissenschaftsgeschichte* (Marburg, 1994).

negative effect on their fate. Progress faltered and a significant part of the collections was stolen and dispersed. Fortunately most of the collections of major monasteries had been already sent to Breslau by Büsching.

On 14 September 1815 the process of confiscating the book collections left from the dissolved monasteries was considered finished. A total of 150,000 to 200,000 volumes had been inventoried, out of which approximately 70,000 found their place in the Königliche und Universitäts-Bibliothek in Breslau. The others ended up in the Stadtbibliothek in Breslau, the most valuable ones, in provincial libraries and, finally, in school libraries or gymnasia.

Many of the duplicates owned by the Königliche and Universitäts-Bibliothek, which were not essential to the library, were transferred to the Royal Library in Berlin and Königsberg, and later to the libraries of the newly established universities in Bonn and Greifswald. They were also included in the libraries of secondary schools in Silesia, mainly in Neisse, Glatz and Leobschütz. Duplicates also became an important source for raising funds to purchase new books. On 10 May 1945 two thirds of the collection of the Königliche and Universitäts-Bibliothek was destroyed by fire. Only about 45,000 volumes were saved, which were then integrated to the 150,000 volumes of the Stadtbibliothek in Breslau and collections kept in other Silesian libraries, creating in this way the Library of Wrocław University, which now has 230,000 volumes, including 12,500 early printed books from the monasteries dissolved in 1810[19].

Secularisation in the Kingdom of Poland

In the Kingdom of Poland (known as Congress Poland or the Russian Poland), unified with Russia by personal union (i.e. a combination of two or more states that have the same monarch while their boundaries, laws, and interests remain distinct), the dissolution of monasteries was announced by the decree of 17 April 1819. Thirty-five monasteries were liquidated: twenty-nine male (of the 180 existing in the Kingdom) and six female (of the thirty-three existing). Quantitatively, the dissolution was relatively small, but it covered most of the old, rich, twelfth-and thirteenth-century monastic and canonical foundations, such as the Benedictines from Łysa Góra and Siechiechów, the Cistercians from Jędrzejów, Koprzywnica, Ląd, Sulejów and Wąchock, the Canons Regular from Czerwińsk,

---

19   Mieczysław Walter, 'Pruska sekularyzacja klasztorów w dziejach Biblioteki Uniwersyteckiej we Wrocławiu' [Die preussische Säkularisation der Klöster in der Gechichte der Universitätsbibliothek zu Wrocław = The prussian secularization of monasteries in the history of Wrocław University Library], in *Druga Konferencja Naukowa Komisji Bibliografii i Bibliotekoznawstwa Wrocławskiego Towarzystwa Naukowego. Wrocław*

3–5 listopada 1954. Referaty i dyskusja, Śląskie Prace Bibliograficzne i Bibliotekoznawcze, 4 (Wrocław, 1957), 179–94; Weronika Karlak, 'Pokasacyjne zasoby starych druków w Bibliotece Uniwersyteckiej we Wrocławiu – działalność J. G. Büschinga a stan obecny' [Old prints from the suppressed monasteries in the Wrocław University Library. J. G. Büsching's activities and the current situation], in *Kasaty klasztorne*, as note 5, III 245–262, and summary in *Pruskie kasaty klasztorne*, as note 5, 72–73; Bożena Kumor-Gomułka, 'Wrocławskie księgozbiory kościelne w projekcie Śląskiej Biblioteki Centralnej – dlaczego tak, dlaczego nie? Kształtowanie idei zorganizowania zjednoczonej Biblioteki Miejskiej we Wrocławiu w okresie przed – i posekularyzacyjnym' [Church libraries from Wrocław and the project of Silesian Central Library – The Idea of the Municipal Library in Wrocław before and immediately following the dissolution], in *Kasaty klasztorne*, as note 5, III 229–243, and summary in *Pruskie kasaty klasztorne*, as note 5, 96–97; Grzegorz Pisarski, 'Druki z dawnej biblioteki opactwa cystersów w Krzeszowie w zbiorach biblioteki Zakładu Narodowego im. Ossolińskich we Wrocławiu' [Prints from the old library of the Cistercian abbey in Krzeszów in the collection of National Ossoliński Institute library in Wrocław], paper delivered, but not published in *Kasaty klasztorne*, as note 5, and summary in *Pruskie kasaty klasztorne*, as note 5, 128–29.

Miechów, Hebdów, and Witów[20]. These large, old religious houses had not only very significant estates and extensive complexes of monastic buildings, but also great Polish book and archival collections, numbering several thousand rare books and hundreds of medieval manuscripts, as well as a few thousand documents in parchment and paper in each abbey[21].

As early as 4 May 1819 the provincial committees for Religion and Public Education were obliged to seal immediately the libraries of the monasteries and to draw up within 20 days the catalogues of their books. Afterwards Samuel Bogumił Linde, the principal director of the Public Library at the University of Warsaw, was sent to look through these monastic libraries and to select from them the manuscripts and books needed for the library he managed, which it was planned would be transformed into the National Library. Selected books were loaded into crates and barrels and sent to larger stores, from where they were transported to Warsaw. Linde wrote in his report that during 114 days he travelled 274 miles and processed about 80,000 volumes of books. The Public Library in Warsaw received in total 46,134 books and significant quantities of incunabula (about 6,000) and manuscripts (about 1,500) from forty-eight monastic libraries, 3,659 books from fifteen libraries of collegiate churches, as well as 260 books from two parish libraries.

Following the collapse of the November Uprising in 1831, during the years 1832–1834 most of the book collections of the libraries in Warsaw,

including the Public Library, were transported to the Imperial Public Library in St Petersburg[22].

More books followed, from monasteries dissolved in 1864 after the fall of the January Uprising. A decree of 8 November 1864, and especially the related regulations for its implementation, led to the liquidation of 129 monasteries (125 male and four female) in the Kingdom of Poland[23]. By then the abolished monasteries did not have rich and valuable book collections such as those dissolved by the decree in 1819, so most of the books remained in the country. They went to various ecclesiastical institutions[24].

Under the peace treaty between Poland and the Soviet Union signed in 1921 in Riga, most of these collections returned to Poland and entered the nascent National Library in Warsaw. During the Second World War the German occupiers separated the manuscripts, incunabula and early printed books, which were placed in the basement of the building of the former Krasinski Library. They were burned in the first half of October 1944 by German special forces as a reprisal for the Warsaw Uprising. Hundreds of thousands of early printed books and about 15,000 manuscripts were destroyed[25].

---

20 Gach, *Kasaty klasztorne*, as note 6, 87–114.

21 Franciszek Tadeusz Borowski, 'Dekret kasacyjny z z roku 1819 i jego wykonanie w stosunku do zakonów diecezji sandomierskiej' [Decree of Cassation of the year 1819 and its implementation in relation to the orders of the Diocese of Sandomierz], *Studia Sandomierskie*, 18 (2011), 1, 7–162.

22 Bożena Koredczuk, 'Spory wokół losów bibliotek po kasacie klasztorów w Królestwie Polskim w latach 1815–1830' [Controversies around the fates of the libraries after the dissolution of monasteries in the Kingdom of Poland from 1815 to 1830], in *Kasaty klasztorne*, as note 5, III 151–160, and summary in *Pruskie kasaty klasztorne*, as note 5, 80–81; Małgorzata Kośka, 'Losy księgozbiorów klasztornych po kasacie 1819 r. Misja Samuela Bogumiła Lindego' [The fate of monastic libraries after their dissolution in 1819. Mission of S. B. Linde], in *Kasaty klasztorne*, as note 5, III 73–78, and summary in *Pruskie kasaty klasztorne*, as note 5, 86–87.

23 Gach, *Kasaty klasztorne*, as note 6, 175–204.

24 Gach, *Mienie polskich zakonów*, as note 14, 36–37.

25 *Straty bibliotek i archiwów warszawskich w zakresie rękopiśmiennych źródeł historycznych* [Loss of libraries and archives in Warsaw in the manuscript register of historical sources], ed. Piotr Bańkowski, vol. 3: Biblioteki [Libraires] (Warszawa, 1955); Barbara

From the books chosen by Linde there remained about 4,000 duplicates, which in time were transferred to the new University Library in Warsaw. The remaining part of the book collections, from the monasteries abolished by the decrees in 1819 and 1864, were given to seminary libraries. However, the libraries of diocesan seminaries received only parts of the collection – the rest was dispersed or destroyed[26].

Bieńkowska, *Losses of Polish libraries during WorldWar II*, transl. Krystyna Cękalska, Polish Cultural Heritage. Series A, Losses of Polish Culture (Warsaw, 1994).

26 Marek Derwich, *Benedyktyński klasztor św. Krzyża na Łysej Górze w średniowieczu* [Benedictine Monastery of St Cross on Bald Mountain in the Middle Ages] (Warszawa-Wrocław, 1992), 92–105; Maria Cubrzyńska-Leonarczyk, 'Kolekcje klasztorne w zbiorze starych druków Biblioteki Uniwersyteckiej w Warszawie – historia i współczesność' [Monastic collections in the early imprints department of Warsaw University Library: the historical and the current situation], in *Kasaty klasztorne*, as note 5, III 173–183, and summary in *Pruskie kasaty klasztorne*, as note 5, 30–31; Elżbieta Bylinowa, 'Pocysterskie księgozbiory z Koprzywnicy, Sulejowa i Wąchocka w zbiorach Biblioteki Uniwersyteckiej w Warszawie' [Post-Cistercian libraries from Koprzywnica, Sulejów and Wąchock in the collection of Warsaw University Library], in *Kasaty klasztorne*, as note 5, III 185–203, and summary in *Pruskie kasaty klasztorne*, as note 5, 28–29; Marianna Czapnik, 'Losy księgozbiorów klasztornych Łowicza' [The fate of the monastic libraries from Łowicz], in *Kasaty klasztorne*, as note 5, III 205–220, and summary in *Pruskie kasaty klasztorne*, as note 5, 32–33. On the history of the collections forming at different stages the National Library of Poland see now also Michał Spandowski, *Catalogue of Incunabula in the National Library of Poland*, 2 vols (Warsaw, 2020), I 7-21.

Bibliography

Barbara Bieńkowska, *Losses of Polish libraries during WorldWar II*, transl. Krystyna Cękalska, Polish Cultural
  Heritage. Series A, Losses of Polish Culture (Warsaw, 1994).

Brigitte Bönisch-Brednich, *Büschings Volkskundliche Forschungen in Schlesien. Eine Wissenschaftsgeschichte*
  (Marburg, 1994).

Franciszek Tadeusz Borowski, 'Dekret kasacyjny z z roku 1819 i jego wykonanie w stosunku do zakonów diecezji
  sandomierskiej' [Decree of Cassation of the year 1819 and its implementation in relation to the orders of the
  Diocese of Sandomierz], *Studia Sandomierskie*, 18 (2011), 1, 7–162.

Elżbieta Bylinowa, 'Pocysterskie księgozbiory z Koprzywnicy, Sulejowa i Wąchocka w zbiorach Biblioteki
  Uniwersyteckiej w Warszawie' [Post-Cistercian libraries from Koprzywnica, Sulejów and Wąchock in the
  collection of Warsaw University Library], in *Kasaty klasztorne*, III 185–203, and summary in *Pruskie kasaty
  klasztorne*, 28–29.

Maria Cubrzyńska-Leonarczyk, 'Kolekcje klasztorne w zbiorze starych druków Biblioteki Uniwersyteckiej w
  Warszawie – historia i współczesność' [Monastic collections in the early imprints department of Warsaw
  University Library: the historical and the current situation], in *Kasaty klasztorne*, III 173–83, and summary in
  Pruskie kasaty klasztorne, 30–31.

Marianna Czapnik, 'Losy księgozbiorów klasztornych Łowicza' [The fate of the monastic libraries from Łowicz],
  in *Kasaty klasztorne*, III 205–20, and summary in *Pruskie kasaty klasztorne*, 32–33.

Agata Demkowicz, 'Stan badań nad kasatą jezuitów w Polsce' [State of research on the suppression of the Jesuits
  in Poland], in *Prace Humanistyczne* [Towarzystwa Naukowego w Rzeszowie], S. 1, f. 31, ed. Piotr Żbikowski
  (Rzeszów, 2004), 155–74.

Marek Derwich, *Benedyktyński klasztor św. Krzyża na Łysej Górze w średniowieczu* [Benedictine Monastery of St
  Cross on Bald Mountain in the Middle Ages] (Warszawa-Wrocław, 1992).

Marek Derwich, *Klasztory i mnisi* [Monasteries and monks], A to Polska właśnie (Wrocław, 2004).

Georg Franz, *Kulturkampf. Staat und katholische Kirche in Mitteleuropa von der Säkularisation bis zum Abschluss
  preusischen Kultrkampfes* (München, 1954).

Piotr Paweł Gach, 'Kasata zakonów na Śląsku Pruskim w latach 1810–1811' [Dissolution of religious orders in
  Prussian Silesia in 1810–1811], *Roczniki Humanistyczne*, 26 (1978), 2, 233–48.

Piotr Paweł Gach, *Mienie polskich zakonów i jego losy w XIX wieku* [The property of the Polish monastic orders and
  its vicissitudes in the 19th Century], Mozaika. Seria Monografii, 1 (Rzym, 1979).

Piotr Paweł Gach, *Kasaty klasztorne na ziemiach dawnej Rzeczypospolitej i Śląska 1773–1914* [Dissolution of
  monasteries in the territory of the old Polish and Lithuanian Commonwealth and of Silesia 1773–1914]
  (Lublin, 1984).

Piotr Paweł Gach, 'Soppressioni 1773–1879, Polonia', in *Dizionario degli istituti di perfezione*, ed. Guerrino Pelliccia and Giancarlo Rocca, 10 vols (Roma, 1974–2003), VIII 1830–34.

Piotr Paweł Gach, 'Le réseau des monastères de moines et chanoines réguliers en Pologne et en Silésie (1700–1914)', in *Naissance et fonctionnement des réseaux monastiques et canoniaux*. Actes du Premier Colloque international du CERCOM, Saint-Étienne, 16–18 septembre 1985. CERCOR, Travaux et recherches, 1 (Saint-Étienne, 1991), 271–98.

Jolanta Gwioździk, 'Pokasacyjne losy księgozbiorów klasztornych na obszarze Rzeczypospolitej Obojga Narodów' [The fate of the monastic libraries in the territory of the old Polish and Lithuanian Commonwealth after the dissolutions], in *Kasaty klasztorne*, III 137–50, and summary in *Pruskie kasaty klasztorne*, 56–57.

Marek Hałub, *Johann Gustav Gottlieb Büsching 1783–1829. Ein Beitrag zur Begründung der schlesischen Kulturgeschichte*, Acta Universitatis Wratislaviensis, 1978 (Wrocław, 1997).

Stanisław Jujeczka, 'Kasaty dóbr kościelnych w nowożytnej Europie (połowa XVII – początek XIX wieku)' [Secularisation of the ecclesiastical estate in modern Europe (mid 17th – early 19th century)], in *Kasaty klasztorne*, I 61–78, and summary in *Pruskie kasaty klasztorne*, 66–67.

Weronika Karlak, 'Pokasacyjne zasoby starych druków w Bibliotece Uniwersyteckiej we Wrocławiu – działalność J.G. Büschinga a stan obecny' [Old prints from the suppressed monasteries in the Wrocław University Library. J.G. Büsching's activities and the current situation], in *Kasaty klasztorne*, III 245–262, and summary in *Pruskie kasaty klasztorne*, 72–73.

Kasaty klasztorne na obszarze dawnej Rzeczypospolitej Obojga Narodów i na Śląsku na tle procesów sekularyzacyjnych w Europie (XVIII–XX wiek) [Dissolution of monasteries in the territory of the old Polish and Lithuanian Commonwealth and of Silesia against the background of secularization processes in Europe (XVIII–XX centuries)], ed. Marek Derwich, 4 vols (Wrocław, 2014).

Bożena Koredczuk, 'Spory wokół losów bibliotek po kasacie klasztorów w Królestwie Polskim w latach 1815–1830' [Controversies around the fates of the libraries after the dissolution of monasteries in the Kingdom of Poland from 1815 to 1830], in *Kasaty klasztorne*, III 151–160, and summary in *Pruskie kasaty klasztorne*, 80–81.

Małgorzata Kośka, 'Losy księgozbiorów klasztornych po kasacie 1819 r. Misja Samuela Bogumiła Lindego' [The fate of monastic libraries after their dissolution in 1819. Mission of S.B. Linde], in *Kasaty klasztorne*, III 73–88, and summary in *Pruskie kasaty klasztorne*, 86–87.

Bożena Kumor-Gomułka, 'Wrocławskie księgozbiory kościelne w projekcie Śląskiej Biblioteki Centralnej – dlaczego tak, dlaczego nie? Kształtowanie idei zorganizowania zjednoczonej Biblioteki Miejskiej we Wrocławiu w okresie przed- i posekularyzacyjnym' [Church libraries from Wrocław and the project of Silesian Central Library – The Idea of the Municipal Library in Wrocław before and immediately following the dissolution], in *Kasaty klasztorne*, III 229–43, and summary in *Pruskie kasaty klasztorne*, 96–97.

Radosław Lolo, 'Kasata kolegium jezuitów w Pułtusku a losy tutejszej szkoły (1772–1781)' [Dissolution of the Jesuit monastery in Pułtusk and fate of its school], in *Kasaty klasztorne*, I 99–104, and summary in *Pruskie kasaty klasztorne*, 98–99.

Josef Joachim Menzel, 'Die Säkularisation in Schlesien 1810', in *Säkularisationen in Ostmitteleuropa. Zur Klärung des Verhältnisses von geistlicher und weltlicher Macht im Mittelalter, von Kirche und Staat in der Neuzeit*, ed. Joachim Köhler, Forschungen und Quellen zur Kirchen- und Kulturgeschichte Ostdeutschlands, 19 (Köln-Weimar, 1984), 85–102.

Grzegorz Pisarski, 'Druki z dawnej biblioteki opactwa cystersów w Krzeszowie w zbiorach biblioteki Zakładu Narodowego im. Ossolińskich we Wrocławiu' [Prints from the old library of the Cistercian abbey in Krzeszów in the collection of National Ossoliński Institute library in Wrocław], paper delivered, but not published in *Kasaty klasztorne*, summary in *Pruskie kasaty klasztorne*, 128–29.

Pruskie kasaty klasztorne na Śląsku na tle procesów sekularyzacyjnych w Polsce i Europie. Międzynarodowa konferencja naukowa, Wrocław, 18–21 listopada 2010. Księga streszczeń = *The Prussian dissolution of monasteries in Silesia against a background of secularization processes in Poland and Europe.* International conference, Wrocław, 18–21 November 2010. Abstracts, ed. Marek Derwich and Marek L. Wójcik (Wrocław, 2010).

Jürgen Peter Ravens, *Staat und katholische Kirche in Preussens polnischen Teilungsgebieten (1772–1807),* Veröffentlichungen des Osteuropa Institutes München, 21 (Wiesbaden, 1963).

Michał Spandowski, *Catalogue of Incunabula in the National Library of Poland,* 2 vols (Warsaw, 2020).

Straty bibliotek i archiwów warszawskich w zakresie rękopiśmiennych źródeł historycznych [Loss of libraries and archives in Warsaw in the manuscript register of historical sources], ed. Piotr Bańkowski, vol. 3: Biblioteki [Libraires] (Warszawa, 1955).

Hermina Święch, 'Przyczyny i przebieg kasat żeńskich klasztorów w Krakowie w drugiej połowie XVIII i na początku XIX w.' [The causes and the development of the dissolutions of the female monasteries in Cracow in the second half of 18th and the beginning of 19th century], in *Kasaty klasztorne,* I 159–178, and summary in *Pruskie kasaty klasztorne,* 162–63.

Lech Trzeciakowski, 'The Prussian State and the Catholic Church in Prussian Poland 1871–1914', *Slavic Revue,* 26 (1967), 4, 618–37.

Krzysztof Walczak, 'Wpływ kasat klasztorów na losy bibliotek dziewiętnastowiecznego Kalisza' [Influence of the secularization on the fate of the libraries in Kalisz in nineteenth century], in *Kasaty klasztorne,* III 221–27, and summary in *Pruskie kasaty klasztorne,* 164–65.

Mieczysław Walter, 'Pruska sekularyzacja klasztorów w dziejach Biblioteki Uniwersyteckiej we Wrocławiu' [Die preussische Säkularisation der Klöster in der Gechichte der Universitätsbibliothek zu Wrocław = The prussian secularization of monasteries in the history of Wrocław University Library], in *Druga Konferencja Naukowa Komisji Bibliografii i Bibliotekoznawstwa Wrocławskiego Towarzystwa Naukowego. Wrocław 3–5 listopada 1954.* Referaty i dyskusja, Śląskie Prace Bibliograficzne i Bibliotekoznawcze, 4 (Wrocław, 1957), 179–94.

Zygmunt Zieliński, 'Ustawy antyzakonne kulturkampfu i ich wykonanie na terenie Wielkopolski' [The law against religious orders during the Kulturkampf and its implementation in Greater Poland], *Roczniki Teologiczno-Kanoniczne,* 16 (1969), 4, 75–91.

Zygmunt Zieliński, *Kulturkampf w archidiecezji gnieźnieńskiej i poznańskiej w latach 1873–1887* [Kulturkampf in the Archdiocese of Gniezno and Poznań in 1873–1887] (Poznań, 2012).

OLEH DUKH

The dissolution of Roman-Catholic and Uniate Monasteries in the Western guberniyas of the Russian Empire and the fate of their libraries*

The partitions of Poland of 1772, 1793, and 1795 not only changed the configuration of political power in East-Central Europe, but also reshaped the religious and ethnic structure of the partitioners: Austria, Prussia and Russia. The major part of the territory of the Polish-Lithuanian Commonwealth, inhabited chiefly by followers of the Uniate Church and the Roman Catholic Church, fell within the boundaries of the Russian Empire. As a result of the First Partition, in Russia there were 37 Roman Catholic monasteries and 20 Uniate ones[1]. The non-Orthodox population continued to increase after the Second and Third Partitions. At the beginning of the nineteenth century the western guberniyas (governorates)[2] of the Russian Empire had a population of about 1.5 million followers of the Uniate Church[3] and the Roman Catholic Church[4] each. According

---

* Scientific work financed by the Ministry of Science and Higher Education (Republic of Poland) under the name "National Programme of Development in the Humanities" in the years 2012–2016.

1 Piotr Paweł Gach, *Kasaty zakonów na ziemiach Rzeczypospolitej i Śląska 1773–1914* [Dissolution of religious orders in the territories of the Polish-Lithuanian Commonwealth and Silesia in 1773–1914] (Lublin, 1984), 52. It is worth mentioning that until the beginnings of

the 20th century the Uniate Church had only one order, of the Basilians, founded in 1617 thanks to the activity of Josyf Veliamyn Rutsky, Metropolitan of Kyiv (1613–1637).

2 The western guberniyas or the Western Krai are understood here as the territories that became part of the Russian Empire as a result of three partitions of the Polish-Lithuanian Commonwealth (excluding Kingdom of Poland, or Congress Poland); *Западные окраины Российской империи* [Western territories of the Russian Empire] (Москва [Moscow], 2006), 103–04. In the Polish historiography those lands are referred to as Ziemie Zabrane [Stolen Lands].

3 After a forced conversion to the Orthodox faith of a considerable number of Uniates in the years 1794–1796.

4 Marian Radwan, *Carat wobec Kościoła greckokatolickiego w zaborze rosyjskim 1796–1839* [Russian Empire and the Uniate Church within the former territories of Poland,

---

Oleh Dukh • Lecturer at the Faculty of History at the Ivan Franko National University of Lviv (Ukraine).
o_duch@yahoo.com

How the Secularization of Religious Houses Transformed the Libraries of Europe, 16th–19th Centuries, ed. by Cristina Dondi, Dorit Raines, and †Richard Sharpe, BIB, 63 (Turnhout, 2022), pp. 337–355

DOI 10.1484/M.BIB-EB.5.128492

to the research conducted by Piotr Paweł Gach, in 1803 within the former territories of Poland, incorporated into the Russian state, there were 323 Roman Catholic monasteries and 40 Roman Catholic convents[5]. In total, there were 22 active orders for men and 10 for women in that area. The Basilians, who formed part of the Uniate Church, had 85 monasteries[6].

Until the 1830s, Roman Catholic monasteries enjoyed relative tolerance in the Russian Empire. The same cannot be said, though, of the Basilians, who suffered repressions as the first one among the orders of the Catholic Church. In 1795–1796 ten monasteries from the Ruthenian Province of the Order of Saint Basil the Great were forced to convert to the Orthodox faith[7]. It came as a part of the first wave of persecutions of the Uniates in the Russian Empire. In 1794–1796 more than 1.3 million Uniate Church believers were converted, often forcibly, to Orthodoxy, mainly in Podolia and Volyn[8]. At the current state of research, little is known about the fate of the Basilian libraries. Bearing in mind that the monasteries were not dissolved, but only changed their religious affiliation, their book collections did not disperse; they simply became the property of the Orthodox community. In a document dated 4 July 1799 the superior of the Holovchyntsi monastery, Fr. Damaskin, wrote

that he had received books from the Basilians[9]. The traces of the first attempts of transferring the collections to religious institutions date back to the end of the eighteenth century. It was to become a relatively common practice in the following century. The collection of the Ostroh Basilian monastery became the property of the Orthodox seminary founded there in 1796[10]. Probably a similar situation took place in Sharhorod, where next to an Orthodox, previously Uniate monastery, an Orthodox seminary was founded in 1797 for the eparchy of Bratslav and Podolia[11].

It was the Society of Jesus that benefited the most from the favourable attitude of the Russian authorities towards the Roman Catholic orders. In 1773 Empress Catherine II (1764–1796) did not allow the proclamation of Clement XIV's papal brief *Dominus ac Redemptor* (aimed at the dissolution of the Jesuits) to be enacted within the territory of the Russian Empire[12]. Thus, Orthodox Russia, after the suppression of the Jesuits in Protestant Prussia in 1780, became the only country in which the Society of Jesus could operate legally. In 1775 there were 13 Jesuit

---

incorporated into the Russian state in 1796–1839] (Lublin, 2004), 69; Сергій Іванович Жилюк, *Російська православна церква на Волині (1793–1917)* [Serhiy Ivanovych Zhylyuk, Russian Orthodox Church in Volyn (1793–1996)] (Житомир [Zhytomyr], 1996), 80.

5 Gach, *Kasaty zakonów*, as note 1, 60.

6 *Нарис історії Василіянського Чину Святого Йосафата* [History outline of the Basilian Order of St Josaphat] (Рим [Rome], 1992), 258.

7 The ten monasteries were located in Ostroh, Zahaitsi, Chetvertivka, Sharhorod, Korzhivtsi, Holovchyntsi, Sataniv, Kamianets-Podilsky, Bilylivka, Hraniv; see Radwan, *Carat wobec Kościoła greckokatolickiego*, as note 4, 78.

8 Ibid., 29.

9 Евфимий Иосифович Сецинскій, *Матеріалы для исторіи монастырей Подольской епархіи* [Evfimiy Iosifovich Syetsinskiy, Materials for the history of the monasteries in the Eparchy of Podolia] (Каменецъ-Подольскъ [Kamyanets-Podilskyy], 1891), 78.

10 Тетяна Євгеніївна Мяскова, 'Бібліотека Острозького єзуїтського колегіуму: історія виникнення, функціонування та сучасний стан' [Tetiana Yevheniyivna Myaskova, Jesuit College Library in Ostroh: origins, activity and current state], *Рукописна та книжкова спадщина України* [Manuscript and book heritage of Ukraine], 11 (2007), 127.

11 Сецинскій, *Матеріалы для исторіи*, as note 9, 207.

12 Михаил Яковлевич Морошкинъ, *Іезуиты въ Россіи съ царствованія Екатерины II-й и до нашего времени* [Mikhail Yakovlevich Moroshkin, The Jesuits in Russia since the Rule of Catherine II to the present day] (Санкт-Петербургъ [Saint Petersburg], 1867), vol. 1, 85–86.

institutions in the Russian Empire[13], including 6 colleges: Dinaburg[14], Mahilyow, Mstislavl, Orsha, Vitsyebsk and Polatsk[15]. During the following 40 years the order had the opportunity to freely expand under the reign of the Romanovs. In 1820 there were already 20 Jesuit institutions in Russia[16]. Also, the number of Jesuit fathers was increasing considerably. In 1775 there were 148 of them, whereas in 1820 there were 358[17]. One of the reasons of this increase was the influx of Jesuits from Europe, America and Asia, which followed the suppression of the order. As they were coming to Russia, they were bringing along their own book collections, contributing to the growth of the Jesuit libraries. It must be noted, though, that the process was favoured by the policy of both the college rectors and the state authorities, interested in buying books, which was necessary for their educational activity. It explains the expansion of the Jesuit college libraries in the Belorussian[18] Province. Polatsk can serve as a good example: despite the 1750 fire at the college, which destroyed almost the entire collection, in 1787 it already had 5576 volumes[19]. Moreover, various benefactors made donations to the colleges. The archbishop of Gniezno Ignacy Raczyński (1806–1818), a former Jesuit, purchased around eight thousand books from

the libraries of the monasteries dissolved by the Prussian authorities. Later on he donated the books to the Russian Jesuits[20].

Under the rule of the Romanovs the Society of Jesus, like other Roman Catholic orders, had favourable conditions for expanding their educational activity, which, in turn, contributed to the acquisition of new volumes, necessary for teaching. The main educational institution of the Russian Jesuits was the Polatsk Academy, founded in 1812 after the reorganization of a local college[21]. According to an ex-Piarist Antoni Moszyński, the libraries of the Academy had a total of forty thousand volumes at that time[22]. The remaining Jesuit educational institutions had a much smaller number of books. The library in Vitsyebsk had three and a half thousand volumes in 1820. Even smaller was the library of the Mahilyow college, which had one thousand and seven hundred volumes around 1818[23]. Nevertheless, these were among the largest monastic library collections

13 In 1772, after the First Partition of the Polish-Lithuanian Commonwealth, Livonia, the entire Vitsyebsk and Mahilyow voivodeships, as well as parts of Polatsk and Minsk voivodeships were incorporated into the Russian Empire.

14 Today: Daugavpils (Latvia).

15 Gach, *Kasaty zakonów*, as note 1, 44–45.

16 Ibid., 45.

17 Ibid., 47.

18 A historical name of Belarus (together with its adjectival form) will be used in contexts referring to the period before the year 1991 (translator's note).

19 Franciszek Radziszewski, *Wiadomość historyczno-statystyczna o znakomitych bibliotekach i archiwach publicznych i prywatnych* [Historical and statistical information on great libraries and archives, both public and private] (Kraków, 1875), 62.

20 Bolesław Breżgo, 'Losy bibliotek jezuickich w Połocku i Witebsku' [The fate of the Jesuit Libraries in Polatsk and Vitsyebsk], *Przegląd Powszechny*, 43 (1926), 89.

21 *Materyały do dziejów Akademii Połockiej i szkół od niej zależnych* [Materials for the history of the Academy of Polatsk and schools that depended on] (Kraków, 1905), 57.

22 Breżgo, *Losy bibliotek*, as note 20, 88; Татьяна Владимировна Говорова, *Библиотека Полоцких иезуитов: факты, сведения, документы* [Tatyana Vladimirovna Govorova, Jesuit Library in Polatsk: facts, information, documents], in *Материалы 14-й Международной Конференции "Крым 2007"* [Materials from the 14th International Conference "Crimea 2007"] (Москва [Moscow], 2007); http://www.gpntb.ru/win/inter-events/crimea2007/cd/131.pdf.

23 Тамара Борисовна Блинова, *Иезуиты в России (Их роль в организации образования и просвещения)* [Tamara Borisovna Blinova, Jesuits in Russia (their role in the organization of education and enlightenment)] (Гродно [Hrodna], 2002), 229; Urszula Paszkiewicz, *Inwentarze i katalogi bibliotek z ziem wschodnich Rzeczypospolitej do 1939 roku. Suplement 2* [Inventory and catalogues of libraries in the eastern territories of Poland until 1939. Supplement 2] (Poznań 2006), 523.

in the territories of the western guberniyas of the Russian Empire.

Alexander I's (1801–1825) ukase (a tsarist edict) from 13 March 1820 put an end to the Jesuit schooling in Russia. It made the Society of Jesus illegal in the Russian Empire, and the Jesuits were expelled from the country[24]. This decision had a negative impact on the fate of their libraries. The examples of the Polatsk Academy and the Vitsyebsk college offer an insight into their history. The Polatsk Academy had the largest library among Roman Catholic monasteries in Russia. According to Antoni Moszyński, after the closing of the Academy "a real plunder began. […] Within a couple of days the library was remorselessly pillaged. […] Rare and precious volumes were sold for nothing. Even the police helped in that ransacking." It was only a commission which was set up in order to inventory and take over the Jesuit property that put an end to the plunder. The commission was headed by the headmaster of the Vitsyebsk gymnasium, Kirill Kanarovsky-Sohovich[25]. After the Polatsk Academy closed, its library was managed for some time by the Vitsyebsk Treasury Office. In 1822 it was handed down to the Piarists, who had taken over a former Jesuit school[26]. However, in 1830 the Piarist school ceased to exist, and in 1835 it was replaced by a Cadet Corps[27]. The closedown of the Piarist school created conditions which

inevitably meant that the vast Jesuit collection would be dispersed. It aroused the interest of the most important persons in the state, including Emperor Nicholas I (1825–1855), as well as the head of the Department for Religious Affairs of Foreign Faiths count Dmitry Bludov (1826–1832) and the Minister of Public Enlightenment Prince Karl Lieven (1828–1833). On 17 February 1830 the Emperor ordered Dmitry Bludov to collect detailed data about the ex-Jesuit library in Polatsk and to examine the possibilities of handing over its collection to the main libraries of the Empire, except for those books which were supposed to stay in Polatsk for the use of the Cadet Corps[28]. Two months later, on 26 April 1830, Dmitry Bludov informed Karl Lieven that he had looked into the matter thoroughly. According to Bludov, most of the books, namely dictionaries of ancient and modern languages, as well as works on canon law, should be transferred to the Department for Religious Affairs of Foreign Faiths at the Ministry of Public Enlightenment. His plans also included the university libraries of Saint Petersburg and Moscow. The former was to obtain mainly volumes on Oriental studies, the latter – medical books for the Faculty of Medicine. Part of the collection was intended for the Imperial Public Library in Saint Petersburg, which was supposed to "receive books by ancient and modern authors which it does not have, particularly the best and valuable volumes, or rare books, that may embellish and enrich the library."[29] The rest of the books were to be distributed among the Polatsk Cadet Corps (writings on chemistry, physics, mathematics, as well as dictionaries and grammars of European languages), the Roman Catholic Ecclesiastical College (volumes on theology) and local gymnasia (Polish-language literary and

---

24 *Полное Собраніе Законовъ Россійской имперіи, съ 1649 года* [A complete collection of laws of the Russian Empire until 1649] (Санкт-Петербургъ [Saint Petersburg], 1830), vol. 37, 113–19, no. 28198.

25 Блинова, *Иезуиты в России*, as note 23, 227–28. He was also the head of a commission which was supposed to take over the library of the Vitsyebsk Jesuit college (Ibid. 229).

26 Breżgo, *Losy bibliotek*, as note 20, 89.

27 Сергей Поляков, *Полоцкий кадетский корпус. История в лицах* [Sergey Polyakov, Polatsk Cadet Corps. The history of the people] (Полоцк [Polatsk], 2010), 14; Алексей Парфёнович Сапунов, 'Заметка о коллегии и Академии иезуитов в Полоцке' [Alexei Parfyonovich Sapunov, Notes on the Jesuit College and Academy in

Polatsk], in *Иезуиты в Полоцке. 1580–1820* [Jesuit in Polatsk. 1580–1820] (Полоцк [Polatsk], 2005), vol. 2, 29–30.

28 Блинова, *Иезуиты в России*, as note 23, 240.

29 Ibid., 240–41.

historical works)[30]. In 1830 a committee was set up to divide the collection. It consisted of the professor of the University of Saint Petersburg Dmitry Popov (representative of the Ministry of Public Enlightenment), collegial secretary Shepelevich (member of the Department for Religious Affairs of Foreign Faiths) and captain Talyzin (delegate from the General Staff). Dmitry Popov's report from 29 June 1830 presents the following data regarding the number of books which passed from the former Jesuit library in Polatsk to other library collections (excluding the libraries of the gymnasia)[31].

According to research by Bolesław Breżgo, the first volumes to be selected were the ones for the Polatsk Cadet Corps. In 1831, the books intended for the universities, the Imperial Public Library and the Department for Religious Affairs of Foreign Faiths were dispatched to Saint Petersburg and Moscow. Afterwards, a division was made of the books for the Vitsyebsk gymnasium and the Roman Catholic Ecclesiastical College. The set intended for the Ecclesiastical College was stored in the buildings of a dissolved Dominican monastery in Polatsk until 1833, after which they were shipped to Saint Petersburg and distributed among the Roman Catholic seminaries in Mahilyow, Minsk and Samogitia[32].

The Jesuit college library in Vitsyebsk met a similar fate. After its closedown in 1820

No.	Institution	Complete volumes	Incomplete volumes
1	Imperial Public Library in Saint Petersburg	266	-
2	University of Saint Petersburg	3878	576
3	University of Moscow	343	22
4	Polatsk Cadet Corps	1149	328
5	Department for Religious Affairs of Foreign Faiths at the Ministry of Public Enlightenment	1396	240
6	Roman Catholic Ecclesiastical College	3219	345

the headmaster of the Vitsyebsk gymnasium Kirill Kanarovsky-Sohovich made a request to the Ministry of Religious Affairs and Public Enlightenment for the Jesuit collection to be given to the institution of which he was the head[33]. Contrary to what he wanted, in 1822 the collection was taken over by the Basilians, who were running a district school in town. It was only in 1832, after the closing of the Basilian monastery, that the collection became the property of the Vitsyebsk gymnasium[34]. Its later fortunes turned out to be complicated. Following the directive of Nikolai Sergievsky, curator (chief education officer) of the Vilnius Educational District (1869–1899), the Vilnius Public Library received around 800 books from the former Jesuit collection of the Vitsyebsk gymnasium. After the October Revolution (1917), the gymnasium was converted into a military hospital. The books, early printed books in particular, started to be plundered and then sold. Only thanks to the vigorous activities of the Vitsyebsk Department of the

---

30 Breżgo, *Losy bibliotek*, as note 20, 90. Cf. *Путеводитель по Императорской Публичной Библиотеке* [Guide to the Imperial Public Library] (Санкт-Петербургъ [Saint Petersburg], 1860), 6.

31 Блинова, *Иезуиты в России*, as note 23, 241–42. Bolesław Breżgo offers different data. According to him, Polatsk Cadet Corps obtained 2080 volumes, the Imperial Public Library 389, the University of Saint Petersburg 6260, the University of Moscow 454, the Department for Religious Affairs of Foreign Faiths 3056. The remaining books were transferred to the Vitsyebsk gymnasium and the Roman Catholic Ecclesiastical College (Breżgo, *Losy bibliotek*, as note 20, 90–91).

32 Ibid., 92.

33 Блинова, *Иезуиты в России*, as note 23, 229; Radziszewski, *Wiadomość historyczno-statystyczna*, as note 19, 118.

34 Breżgo, *Losy bibliotek*, as note 20, 92–93. Cf. Urszula Paszkiewicz, *Inwentarze i katalogi bibliotek z ziem wschodnich Rzeczypospolitej: spis za lata 1510–1939* [Inventories and catalogues of libraries in the eastern territories of Poland: registers from 1510–1939] (Warszawa, 1998), 189.

Moscow Archeological Institute did around two thousand volumes survive. In 1924 they became part of the collection of the Vitsyebsk branch of the Belorussian State Museum, the present-day Vitsyebsk Heritage Museum[35].

In connection with the fate of the former Jesuit library collections in the Russian Empire, one must not neglect to mention the collections of the Society of Jesus colleges closed down in 1773 in the eastern territories of the Polish-Lithuanian Commonwealth. After the dissolution of the order, the Commission of National Education, established in 1774, took charge of the former Jesuit educational institutions, including their libraries. It was thanks to the Commission's endeavours that the Vilnius Academy of the Society of Jesus was converted into the Principal School of the Grand Duchy of Lithuania, and its collection was taken over by the new institution[36]. The library kept growing as it incorporated collections from other dissolved Jesuit monasteries in Lithuania and Belorussia: Kražiai, Kaunas and Hrodna[37]. The Ukrainian colleges in Bar, Ostroh, and Ovruch passed on to the Basilians, who continued the educational activity of the Jesuits[38], but also became owners of their collections[39]. In the nineteenth century the books collected by the Jesuits often circulated among various ecclesiastical and secular libraries. For instance, the former Jesuit

collection of the college in Ostroh was taken over by the Basilians in 1773, and in 1796, in turn, by the Volyn Orthodox Seminary, set up that year. The seminary, together with its library, changed its location several times. In 1825 it moved to Annopol, in 1836 – to Kremenets, and finally in 1902 – to Zhytomyr[40]. During Napoleon's invasion of Russia in 1812 the library was taken away to the Poltava Governorate, but part of the collection, including the former Jesuit volumes, was lost. In the nineteenth century the seminary suffered several fires (the largest one in 1821), which impeded the expansion of the library[41]. After the Soviets came to power, the seminary was closed down in 1919. Its library became the property of the Zhytomyr Institute of Public Enlightenment, and in 1925 the Volyn Heritage Museum. Eventually, at the beginning of the 1930s, the most valuable parts of the museum's collection, including the ones inherited from the seminary, moved to the All-National Library of Ukraine (today the Vernadsky National Library of Ukraine), where they remain to the present day[42]. 110 books are currently attested as coming from the Ostroh Jesuit collection, although in 1889 the library of the Volyn Seminary owned 214 such volumes[43].

The Russian authorities, for various reasons, supported educational activities in the territories annexed as a result of the partitions. At

35 Breżgo, *Losy bibliotek*, as note 20, 93.
36 Michał Eustachy Brensztejn, *Bibljoteka uniwersytecka w Wilnie do roku 1832-go* [Vilnus University Library until 1832] (Wilno, 1922), 15.
37 Józef Łukaszewicz, *Historya szkół w Koronie i w Wielkiem księstwie Litewskiem aż do roku 1794* [The history of schools in the Polish-Lithuanian Commonwealth until 1794] (Poznań, 1851), vol. 4, 42.
38 Maria Pidłypczak-Majerowicz, *Bazylianie w Koronie i na Litwie. Szkoły i książki w działalności zakonu* [The Basilian order in the Polish-Lithuanian Commonwealth. Schools and books in the activities of the Order] (Warszawa-Wrocław, 1986), 40.
39 Мяскова, *Бібліотека Острозького єзуїтського колегіуму*, as note 10, 127; Łukaszewicz, *Historya szkół*, as note 37, vol. 4, 48, 125, 263, 266.
40 Ірина Володимирівна Мілясевич, 'Бібліотека Волинської духовної семінарії. Острозький період (1796–1836 pp.)' [Iryna Volodymyrivna Milyasevych, Volyn Theological Seminary Library. Period called 'Ostrogsky' (1796–1836)], *Вісник Книжкової палати* [Chamber of Books Information], 3 (2002), 28–30; ead., 'Бібліотека Волинської духовної семінарії. Кременецький період (1836–1901 pp.)' [Volyn Theological Seminary Library. Period called 'Kremenetsky' (1836–1901)], *ibidem*, 11 (2001), 37–39.
41 Ead., *Бібліотека Волинської духовної семінарії. Острозький період (1796–1836)*, as note 40, 29–30.
42 Мяскова, *Бібліотека Острозького єзуїтського колегіуму*, as note 10, 130–31.
43 Ibid., 129, 132.

the beginning of the nineteenth century two higher education institutions were set up in the western guberniyas of the Russian Empire: the University of Vilnius and the Volyn Higher Gymnasium (which later became the Volyn Lyceum). The libraries at these schools also owned former Jesuit collections. In accordance with the Emperor Alexander I's decree, in 1803 the University of Vilnius was founded, following a reorganisation of the Vilnius Principal School (formerly the Principal School of the Grand Duchy of Lithuania). The aforementioned collection of the Vilnius Academy of the Society of Jesus and of other Jesuit colleges constituted a considerable part of the university's library collection[44]. Two years later in Kremenets, thanks to the efforts of Tadeusz Czacki, the Volyn Higher Gymnasium was founded, and in 1819 turned into the Volyn Lyceum. From the very beginning it had a library, whose collection was composed mainly of the books of the last King of Poland Stanisław August Poniatowski[45]. The gymnasium library also obtained the Kremenets Jesuit collection. After the dissolution of the Society of Jesus, for a period of time it was owned by the Basilians, who were running a district school in town. After the establishment of the gymnasium, the collection, amounting to 694 volumes at the time, was incorporated into its library[46]. It is worth mentioning that after 1827 75 books from the Kremenets Jesuit collection were transferred from the library of the Volyn Lyceum to the

library of the University of Helsinki, founded by the Emperor Alexander I[47].

Before moving on to the discussion of other libraries of Roman Catholic monasteries it must be observed that in the first quarter of the nineteenth century, in the western guberniyas of the Russian Empire, the fewest number of Roman Catholic monasteries were dissolved in comparison with the remaining regions of contemporary Poland. Arvydas Pacevičius claims that their situation under the rule of the Romanovs did not change significantly as compared to the Polish-Lithuanian era. They only had to put more emphasis on educational activity[48]. As has been already remarked, it was the Jesuits that suffered the greatest losses over that period. According to Piotr Paweł Gach, in 1825 in the western guberniyas of the Russian Empire there were 329 Roman Catholic monasteries, which constituted 50 per cent of all the existing monasteries in Poland and Silesia at the time[49].

44 Adam Łysakowski, 'Uniwersytecka bibljoteka publiczna w Wilnie (Zarys ogólny)' [Public University Library in Vilnus. (General outline)], *Ateneum Wileńskie*, 8 (1931–1932), 233.

45 Евгения Алексеевна Колесник, *Книжные коллекции Центральной научной библиотеки Академии Наук УССР* [Evgeniya Alekseevna Kolyesnik, Book collections of the Central Scientific Library of the USSR Academy of Sciences] (Киев [Kyiv], 1998), 18.

46 Ibid., 31.

47 Ірина Олегівна Ціборовська-Римарович, 'Книги из библиотек иезуитских коллегий в фондах Национальной библиотеки имени В.И. Вернадского: происхождение, исторические судьбы пути поступления' [Iryna Olehivna Ciborovska-Rymarovych, Books from the libraries of Jesuit colleges in the collections of the Vernadsky National Library of Ukraine: origin, historical fate, directions of leaving], in *Библиотеки национальных академий наук: проблемы функционирования, тенденции развития: Научно-практический и теоретический сборник* [Libraries of National Academies of Sciences: problems of functioning, tendencies of development. Collection of academic, theoretical and practical works] (Киев [Kyiv], 2008), vol. 6, 424.

48 Arvydas Pacevičius, 'Zaginiony świat książki: biblioteki klasztorne na Litwie pod władzą carów' [Lost world of the Book: monastic libraries in Lithuania under the rule of the Tsars], in *Wspólnota pamięci. Studia z dziejów kultury ziem wschodnich dawnej Rzeczypospolitej* [Community of the memory. Studies in the history of culture of the eastern regions of the former Polish-Lithuanian Commonwealth], ed. Jolanta Sylwia Gwioździk, Jan Malicki (Katowice, 2006), 246.

49 Gach, *Kasaty zakonów*, as note 1, 132.

Only after Nicholas I's succession to the throne did the situation in Russia begin to deteriorate. At the beginning of the 1830s on, the doctrine of "the official nationality", invented by the then Deputy Minister (and later Minister) of Public Enlightenment Sergey Uvarov, becomes the official state ideology[50]. It can be summarised as follows: "Orthodoxy – Autocracy – Nationality". It was supposed to embody the idea of the harmony of the imperial power, the Orthodox Church, and the Russian people. The imposition of the ideology had a devastating impact on both the Roman Catholic and Uniate Churches. They were seen as undermining the principle of the threefold unity: religious, political, and national. The most important factor, however, in the changing policy of the Russian authorities towards the Roman Catholics, was the November Uprising (1830–1831). The basis for the mass suppression of Roman Catholic monasteries in the western guberniyas of the Russian Empire was Nicholas I's ukase from 19 July 1832 entitled *On dissolving some*

of the Roman Catholic monasteries. The formal reasons for their dissolution were certain affairs inside the monasteries that allegedly needed resolving. The ukase mentions, among other things, an insufficient number of monks in some monasteries, or lack of discipline, but it does not make any references to the Uprising[51].

In the first half of the 1830s 60 per cent of the Roman Catholic monasteries in the western guberniyas of the Russian Empire suffered dissolution. The heaviest losses were incurred by the Canons Regular of Penance (the so-called white Augustinians), the Dominicans, the Franciscans, the Calced Carmelites and the Friars Minor of the Observance (Observants). The dissolutions continued in later years. In 1836–1863 the lands in question saw the closure of another 66 per cent of the Roman Catholic monasteries and 30 per cent of the Roman Catholic convents. This time those who were affected most adversely were the Piarists, the Brothers Hospitallers of St John of God, the Dominicans and the Observants, and as far as the convents are concerned – the Mariae Vitae Congregation, nuns who had the largest number of convents. In 1863 there were only 46 Roman Catholic monasteries and 39 Roman Catholic convents in the western guberniyas of the Russian Empire[52].

The suppression affected the Order of Saint Basil the Great too. At the end of the 1820s it still had 83 monasteries. Josyf Semashko's plan from 22 December 1827 was for 60 Basilian monasteries to be closed down in the territories of the western guberniyas of the Russian Empire[53]. The plan, though, was never carried out. As had been the case with the Roman Catholic orders, the

---

50 Cf. Максим Михайлович Шевченко, 'Понятие "теория официальной народности" и изучение внутренней политики императора Николая I' [Maxim Mikhailovich Shevchenko, The term 'theory official nationality' and the study of the internal policy of the Emperor Nicolas I], *Вестник Московского университета. Серия 8: История* [Bulletin of Moscow University. Series 8th. History], 4 (2002), 89–104; Сергей Валерьевич Удалов, 'Теория официальной народности: механизмы внедрения' [Sergei Valerievich Udalov, 'Theory official nationality: mechanisms of introduction], in *Освободительное движение в России. Межвузовский сборник научных трудов* [Liberation Movement in Russia: intercollegiate collection of papers], ed. Н. Троицкий (Саратов [Saratov], 2006), vol. 21, 73–81; Ричард Вортман, '"Официальная народность" и национальный миф российской монархии XIX века' [Richard Wortman, 'Official nationality' and the national myth of the Russian monarchy in 19th century], in *Россия / Russia* (Москва [Moscow], 1999), vol. 3 (11): *Культурные практики в идеологической перспективе. Россия, XVIII – начало XX века* [Cultural practices in ideological perspective. Russia, 18th-the beginning of 19th century], 233–44.

51 *Полное Собраніе Законовъ Россійской имперіи. Собраніе второе* [A complete collection of laws of the Russian Empire. The second collection] (Санкт-Петербургъ [Saint Petersburg], 1833), vol. 7: *1832*, 507–10, no. 5506.

52 Gach, *Kasaty zakonów*, as note 1, 158, 169.

53 Radwan, *Carat wobec Kościoła greckokatolickiego*, as note 4, 116.

decision of the authorities was influenced by the Basilians' participation in the November Uprising. In 1830–1834 44 Basilian monasteries were dissolved[54]. Finally, the Order of Saint Basil the Great ceased to exist in the western guberniyas along with the eradication of the Uniate Church in Russia, which took place in 1839.

The mass dissolution of the Roman Catholic and Uniate monasteries in the 1830s and the 1840s undoubtedly had an adverse effect on the subsequent fates of monastic book collections. After the proclamation of the 1832 imperial ukase, the governors were ordered to inventory in detail all the movables and immovables of the dissolved monasteries, including their libraries. They were obliged to send the inventories to the Ministry of State Domains and the Department for Religious Affairs of Foreign Faiths, which at that time was already subordinate to the Ministry of the Interior[55]. In 1834 Pyotr Medeksha, a teacher of Russian in the gymnasium in Hrodna, enacting the order of the Hrodna governor, made an inventory of the library at the Dominican monastery in Dziarechyn, which consisted of around 300 books[56]. The inventories provided the state administration with the knowledge of the size of the monastic property, including the library collections. The Minister of the Interior count Alexander Stroganov (1838–1841) wrote that in the period 1832–1839 reports on the property of 191 Roman Catholic monasteries were sent to Saint Petersburg[57]. However, until the end of

the 1830s the state authorities, in fact, did not engage in the affairs of the monastic libraries; they were only interested in the property the monasteries had been deprived of as such. The collections were stored mainly in the spaces of the monasteries under the supervision of the governorate Treasury or the local police[58]. This was the period in which the first mass dispersal of the library collections took place. The books were often taken along by the monks leaving the monastery, or they ended up in private collections. The last prior of the Carthusian monastery in Biaroza, Paweł Geniusz, took with him to Lunin a considerable part of the monastery collection, and after his death the books were sold off[59]. The collection of the aforesaid ex-Piarist Antoni Moszyński consisted, to a large extent, of books from closed-down monastic libraries, chiefly from Lyubeshiv[60]. The library of Ivan Yastriebtsov, headmaster of the Hrodna gymnasium, and later the Dinaburg gymnasium, amounting to around five thousand volumes, was composed to a high degree of books from the Piarist monastery in Shchuchyn[61]. Those books that were handed over to the still functioning centres of a given order fared better. The collection of the Calced Carmelites in Vyshnivets was transferred to Berdychiv. Part of the books (283 volumes, 195 titles) went to private collections. They were taken over by the Mniszech family, who had a mansion in Vyshnivets[62]. The 1838 inspection of

54 Ibid., 132, 138–40.

55 Piotr Paweł Gach, *Mienie polskich zakonów i jego losy w XIX wieku* [Property of polish religious orders and its fate in the 19th century] (Rzym, 1979), 40.

56 Urszula Paszkiewicz, *Inwentarze i katalogi bibliotek z ziem wschodnich Rzeczypospolitej do 1939 roku. Suplement 1* [Inventory and catalogues of Libraries in the eastern territories of Poland until 1939. Supplement 1] (Warszawa, 2000), 40.

57 Bronisław Ussas, 'Z dziejów grabieży i niszczenia polskiego mienia kościelnego przez Rosjan w świetle świadectw rosyjskich (1655–1925)' [From the History of

plunder and destruction of Polish ecclesiastical property by the Russians in the light of Russian testimonies (1655–1925)], *Przegląd Powszechny*, 53 (1936), 63.

58 Ussas, *Z dziejów grabieży*, as note 57, 63.

59 Radziszewski, *Wiadomość historyczno-statystyczna*, as note 19, 2.

60 Ibid., 58–59.

61 Ibid., 12, 82.

62 Ірина Олегівна Ціборовська-Римарович, 'Книгозбірня монастиря Ордену босих кармелітів у Вишнівці: історія та книгознавча характеристика фонду' [Iryna Olehivna Ciborovska-Rymarovych, Collection of books from the Discalced Carmelite monastery in Wiśniowiec:

the Observant monastery in Dubno discovered that aside from the monastic library (in a rather run-down condition), volumes from the dissolved monastery in Varkovychi were found in the wardrobes[63]. These are only several examples of a very common phenomenon. The monastery of the Order of Reformed Friars Minor in Dederkaly, closed down only at the end of the nineteenth century, accommodated the books from the dissolved monasteries in Boćki and Kremenets[64]. The closed-down Observant monastery in Telšiai handed its volumes to Kretinga[65].

In the 1830s ex-monastic collections started to enlarge seminary libraries, both Orthodox and Roman Catholic. After the dissolution of the monasteries in Mezhyrichi (the Piarists), Lutsk (the Trinitarians), and Horodyshche (the Discalced Carmelites), part of their collections was accommodated by the Volyn Roman Catholic Seminary in Zhytomyr[66]. A large portion of the collections from dissolved Basilian monasteries

became the property of Orthodox seminary libraries. The books from the closed-down monasteries in Hoshcha, Lutsk, Horodyshche, and Bilostok, in compliance with a decree of the ecclesiastical authorities, in 1834 were transferred to the Volyn Orthodox Seminary[67]. After the Lithuanian Orthodox Seminary moved in 1845 from Zhyrovychy to Vilnius to the buildings of a former Basilian (and then Orthodox) monastery dedicated to the Holy Trinity, five thousand books that used to belong to the Basilians were taken over by the seminary[68]. Soon the library expanded with a subsequent 225 volumes coming from the dissolved Basilian convent in Vilnius[69].

Not until 1839 did the state authorities exhibit increased interest in the monastic collections. The Ministries of the Interior, Public Enlightenment, and State Domains agreed that part of the books would be transferred to the Roman Catholic clergy, another part to gymnasium libraries, and the rest would become the property of governorate public libraries[70]. It must be remarked that in the 1830s public libraries in Russia were only beginning to be established and to function as a network. One of the initiators of that process was Nikolai Mordvinov (1754–1845), chairman of the Free Economic Society. On 23 April 1830, he suggested to the Minister of the Interior count Arseny Zakrevsky (1828–1832) that governorate libraries be established. They were intended to be created on the basis of existing local centres, without financial support from the state Treasury. The minister readily accepted the proposal and as early as 5 July of the same year he sent to all the governors a circular *On the foundation of public libraries for reading in the guberniyas*, in which he gave orders that the matter be investigated in

history and characteristics], *Рукописна та книжкова спадщина України* [Manuscript and book heritage of Ukraine], 13 (2009), 145–46.

63 Paszkiewicz, *Inwentarze i katalogi… Suplement 1*, as note 56, 51.

64 Radziszewski, *Wiadomość historyczno-statystyczna*, as note 19, 4, 36–37.

65 Ibid., 34.

66 Ірина Олегівна Ціборовська-Римарович, 'Бібліотеки римо-католицьких монастирів Волині XVI–XVIII ст.: історична доля, роль у монастирській діяльності, сучасний стан фондів (за фондами Національної бібліотеки України ім. В. І. Вернадського)' [Iryna Olehivna Ciborovska-Rymarovych, Libraries of the Roman Catholic monasteries of Volyn from 16th to 18th century: historical fates, role in the activities of the monastery, the current state of the collections (by the collections of Vernadsky National Library of Ukraine)], in *Актуальні питання культурології. Альманах наукового товариства "Афіна" кафедри культурології Рівненського державного гуманітарного університету* [Current questions of culture studies. Almanac of the Scientific Society 'Athena', in the Cultural Departement of the State Humanistic University. in Rivne] (Рівне [Rivne], 2010), vol. 9, 9–14; Radziszewski, *Wiadomość historyczno-statystyczna*, as note 19, 46, 48, 123.

67 Мілясевич, *Бібліотека Волинської духовної семінарії. Острозький період (1796–1836 рр.)*, as note 40, 38.

68 Radziszewski, *Wiadomość historyczno-statystyczna*, as note 19, 101.

69 Ibid.

70 Ussas, *Z dziejów grabieży*, as note 57, 64.

detail in each locality[71]. As a result, in the 1830s, about 40 libraries were set up in the governorate capitals. In the Belarusian territories, the first public library was established as early as 1833 in Mahilyow. In 1837, the library in Hrodna opened its doors to the public. In the mid 1830s the process of setting up the Governorate Public Library in Minsk began, even though it was not until 1845 that it made its collection available to readers[72]. Unlike the dissolution of the monasteries carried out in the 1860s, when a substantial portion of the books were transferred to the Vilnius Public Library, in the 1830s only a small number of volumes ended up in public libraries in Russia.

Special governorate commissions were set up in order to allocate the collections left by the closed-down monasteries[73]. The governorate committee in Hrodna turned out to operate most efficiently, as it completed its work by the end of 1840. The committee transferred most of the volumes (3618) from the fourteen monastic libraries[74] it was in charge of to the Vilnius Roman Catholic Seminary. A much smaller number

of books became the property of governorate public libraries, which obtained 696 volumes. The fewest books (only 431) were allocated to school libraries[75]. The governorate committee in Minsk completed its proceedings in 1841. The collections of 23 monastic libraries, according to their proposal, were to be distributed among the Minsk Roman Catholic Seminary, the Minsk gymnasium, and the local governorate public library[76]. Unfortunately, all the books stored in Minsk were irretrievably lost in a fire in 1842[77]. The governorate committee in Vilnius was established as late as 1843[78], and ceased to operate in 1849. In the span of five years it decided the fate of fourteen monastic collections[79]. Most books, namely 2892 volumes were transferred, as had been the case with the Hrodna committee, to the Vilnius Roman Catholic Seminary. The remaining ones were shared out among governorate public libraries and school libraries[80]. According to the statement of the Minister of the Interior Pyotr Valuyev (1861–1868), in 1853 the Department for Religious Affairs of Foreign Faiths had still not received a report on the state of the monastic libraries from three governorate committees from the territory of the Vitsyebsk Governorate

71 Иван Сергеевич Коннов, 'Публичные библиотеки в культурной среде российской провинции во второй половине XIX – начале XX века (на примере Пензенской, Самарской и Симбирской губерний)' [Ivan Sergeevich Konnov, Public libraries in the cultural environment of the Russian province in the second half of the 19th and early 20th centuries (on the examples of the Penza, Samara and Simbirsk Governorate)], Известия Российского государственного педагогического университета им. А. Н. Герцена [News of the Herzen State Pedagogical University of Russia], 119 (2009), 56.

72 Наталья Березкина, 'Из истории библиотечного дела Беларуси' [Natalia Beryezkina, Extracts from the history of librarianship in Belarus], Вестник ББА [Herald of BLA], 1 (1996), http://www.bla.by/herald_bla.

73 Gach, Mienie polskich zakonów, as note 55, 50.

74 Located in: Bukhavichy, Kanyukhi, Valeuka, Vasilishki, Ziembin (the Dominicans), Drohiczyn, Lapenitsa, Sheybakpol, Svislach (the Franciscans), Kalesniki, Lida, Zhaludok (the Calced Carmelites), Shchuchyn (the Piarists), Kremyanitsa (the Canons Regular of the Lateran).

75 Gach, Mienie polskich zakonów, as note 55, 50–51.

76 Ussas, Z dziejów grabieży, as note 57, 65.

77 Ibid., 186.

78 Arvydas Pacevičius, 'Biblioteki klasztorne na Litwie w końcu XVIII i pierwszej połowie XIX wieku: stan – rozwój – losy' [Monastic Libraries in Lithuania in the late 18th and first half of the 19th century: the state – developement – the fates], in Zakony i klasztory w Europie Środkowo-Wschodniej. X–XX wiek [Religiuos Orders and Monasteries in Central and Eastern Europe. 10th-20th century], ed. Henryk Gapski, Jerzy Kłoczowski (Lublin, 1999), 372.

79 In the following localities: Palevene (the Dominicans), Gelvonai, Halshany, Kaltanėnai, Valkininkai, Žaiginys (the Franciscans), Jūžintai, Papilys, Salakas, Tverečius (the Canons of Penance), Antalieptė (the Discalced Carmelites), Pumpėnai (the Calced Carmelites), Panevėžys (the Piarists).

80 Gach, Mienie polskich zakonów, as note 55, 50.

General: the ones in Vitsyebsk, Mahilyow and Smolensk[81].

After the November Uprising (1830–1831), apart from numerous monasteries being dissolved, two main higher schools in the western guberniyas, the University of Vilnius and the Volyn Lyceum, were closed down. In 1834, however, the Russian-language University of Saint Vladimir in Kyiv was founded. It was endowed with the thirty-five thousand-volume collection of the Volyn Lyceum, closed down two years earlier. In 1834–1840 the Kyiv University library was enlarged by the collections from the University of Vilnius, as well as from the Vilnius Roman Catholic Seminary. Between 1842 and 1843, after the closure of the Vilnius Medical-Surgical Academy, its entire library, amounting to 17556 books, was transferred to Kyiv[82]. All the collections passed on to Kyiv included books from monastic libraries. As has already been said, the library of the University of Vilnius was based on the collection of the Vilnius Academy of the Society of Jesus and of other colleges, whereas the library of the Volyn Lyceum had a substantial collection of Jesuit books from Kremenets. Among the books belonging to the Vilnius Medical-Surgical Academy there were early printed books on medical subjects, which came from some of the dissolved monasteries, including the Carthusian monastery in Biaroza[83]. Hence, we can conclude that the dispersal of monastic collections was accompanied by a reverse process: their accumulation in the country's main libraries.

After the suppression of the January Uprising (1863–1864), the second wave of dissolutions of Roman Catholic monasteries began in the Russian Empire. In June 1864 Mikhail Muravyov, governor-general of the Northwestern Krai, obtained a permission to dissolve all those monasteries whose monks had been involved in the Uprising[84]. In the western guberniyas of the Russian Empire 24 monasteries and 23 convents were closed at the time[85]. Not long afterwards a considerable number of the monastic libraries came under the management of the curator of the Vilnius Educational District (1864–1868) Ivan Kornilov. Being in charge of such an enormous collection, in 1864 he requested from Muravyov permission to open a public library in Vilnius. He claimed that the library, apart from having educational functions, could also serve ideological purposes. Kornilov assumed that as Vilnius did not have a university, the library would become the centre of the country's intellectual activity, in such a way that "pure Russian science [would be able to] contend with Polish science."[86] In January 1865 Pyotr Bezsonov (1828–1898) was appointed the first director of the library, and was soon replaced by Alexander Vladimirov[87]. In compliance with Mikhail Muravyov's decision, the library obtained several rooms in the

81 Ussas, *Z dziejów grabieży*, as note 57, 185.
82 Тетяна Євгеніївна Мяскова, 'Заснування та комплектування бібліотеки Університету св. Володимира (1834–1841)' [Tetiana Yevheniyivna Myaskova, Foundation and equipment of the St Vladimir Univeristy Library (1834–1841)], *Рукописна і книжкова спадщина України* [Manuscript and book heritage of Ukraine], 4 (1998), 296–97; Колесник, *Книжные коллекции*, as note 45, 5, 38.
83 Колесник, *Книжные коллекции*, as note 45, 38.
84 Андрей Иванович Ганчар, *Римско-католический костел в Беларуси (1864–1905)* [Andrey Ivanovich Ganchar, The Roman Catholic Church in Belarus (1864–1905)] (Гродно [Hrodna], 2008), 51.
85 Gach, *Kasaty zakonów*, as note 1, 193.
86 *Краткій отчетъ о Виленской Публичной Библиотеке* [A brief report on the Vilnus Public Library] (Вильна [Vilnius], 1867), 1; Александр Иванович Миловидовъ, *Рукописное отделеніе Виленской Публичной Библиотеки. Его исторія и составъ* [Alexander Ivanovich Milovidov, Manuscripts Department of the Vilnus Public Library. Its history and contents] (Вильна [Vilnius], 1910), 16.
87 Stanisław Lisowski, 'Uniwersytecka Bibljoteka Publiczna w Wilnie za czasów rosyjskich' [Public University Library in Vilnus in Russian times], *Ateneum Wileńskie*, 8 (1931–1932), 245.

building of the former "Institute for Nobles". The report on the library's activity for the year 1867 reveals that around 150 thousand books had been brought to Vilnius, chiefly from dissolved Roman Catholic monasteries, as well as from closed-down district schools and gymnasia, and from confiscated private collections. In a short period of time the Vilnius collection amounted to two hundred thousand volumes. The books were brought in cases and sacks, frequently in a poor state and without adequate preparation and documentation[88]. Paweł Kubicki describes the ways in which Vilnius Public Library expanded with the accession of early printed books and manuscripts brought from dissolved Roman Catholic monasteries. According to the report of the head of the Trakai uyezd (district), after the dissolution of the Paparćiai Dominican monastery, 58 chests on carts were sent to the education office of the Vilnius Educational District[89]. In the following year an official notified the head of the Brest uyezd that following the directive of the the Hrodna uyezd he had donated to the Vilnius Committee of Censorship 20 *poods* (over 320 kilograms) of books from the dissolved Marian monastery in Rasna[90]. In 1866, the headmaster of a district school in Slonim announced that after the closedown of the local Observant monastery, the archive and the books were handed over to the Vilnius Public Library[91]. Such was the case with the volumes from the Vilnius Museum of Antiquities (closed down a year earlier) too. The collection of the Museum had about twenty thousand books, including twelve thousand titles

in Latin, mainly theological works. A substantial part of those had been inherited from dissolved Roman Catholic monasteries[92].

The Vilnius Public Library was officially opened on 24 May 1867, an event which was linked to Emperor Alexander II's (1855–1881) planned visit to Vilnius[93]. The preparation and description of the collection was going to take much longer. The curator of the Vilnius Educational District (1869–1899) Nikolai Sergievsky reported that as late as in 1872 "piles of books were stacked in the storage areas, and there was not enough space to organise them."[94] By 1874 only 14640 early printed books and 1525 manuscripts had been catalogued[95]. The cataloguers' attention was focused on manuscripts and early printed books written in Old Slavonic. An anonymous author observed in 1905 in the newspaper *Kurjer Litewski* that the readership of the Vilnius Public Library were virtually unable to use Polish texts. No printed catalogue had been made either, and the manuscript one was incomplete and inaccurate[96].

In the second half of the nineteenth century the ex-monastic collections enriched other libraries of the western guberniyas of the Russian Empire as well. One of the largest ones in the Southwestern Krai (Kyiv Governorate General) was the library of the University of Saint Vladimir in Kyiv. In the 1870s it obtained an immense collection from the Discalced Carmelite monastery in Berdychiv. After its dissolution in 1866, its library was

88 *Краткій отчетъ о Виленской Публичной Библіотеке*, as note 86, 5; Lisowski, *Uniwersytecka Bibljoteka Publiczna*, as note 87, 244–45, 261.

89 Paweł Franciszek Kubicki, *Bojownicy kapłani za sprawę Kościoła i Ojczyzny w latach 1861–1915* [Priests fighting for Church and Homeland in 1861–1915] (Sandomierz, 1938), part 2: *Dawna Litwa i Białoruś* [Former Lithuania and Belarus], vol. 4, 327.

90 Ibid., 251.

91 Ibid., 238.

92 *Краткій отчетъ о Виленской Публичной Библіотеке*, as note 86, 2–3; *Отчетъ о Виленской Публичной Библіотеке и Музее за 1867 годъ* [A report on the Vilnius Public Library and Museum for the year 1867] (Вильна [Vilnius], 1868), 4.

93 *Краткій отчетъ о Виленской Публичной Библіотеке*, as note 86, 13; Lisowski, *Uniwersytecka Bibljoteka Publiczna*, as note 87, 248.

94 Lisowski, *Uniwersytecka Bibljoteka Publiczna*, as note 87, 248.

95 Ibid., 250.

96 Ibid., 257.

entrusted to the secular clergy, which had taken over the ex-Carmelite church of the Immaculate Conception of the Blessed Virgin Mary. In 1877, the curator of the Kyiv Educational District requested the Kyiv governor-general Alexander Dondukov-Korsakov (1869–1878) for the collection to be donated to the University of Saint Vladimir. After the consent was given, a special commission, headed by Professor Alexander Kotlarevsky, director of the Historical Society of Nestor the Chronicler, came to Berdychiv[97]. The following year the collection of the Berdychiv monastery, composed of 6502 volumes, was transferred to Kyiv[98].

The policy of the Soviet authorities towards religious institutions in the following century was a dire conclusion of the processes initiated in the nineteenth-century Russian Empire. Mass dissolutions of monasteries by the Bolsheviks caused many of the monastic libraries either to fall into decay or become dispersed. At best, their collections were acquired by academic and public libraries. After 1919, the collections from the dissolved ecclesiastical institutions from the territories of the former Volyn Governorate begin to find their way to the Volyn Heritage Museum in Zhytomyr. As has already been mentioned, its library incorporated the collection of the Volyn Orthodox Seminary. Furthermore, the museum library accommodated the collection of the Volyn Roman Catholic Chapter and the Volyn Roman Catholic Seminary. In this way the museum acquired extremely valuable volumes from the former Roman Catholic monasteries dissolved in

the nineteenth century from the regions of Volyn and Podolia, including the centres of the following orders: the Trinitarians (Lutsk, Berestechko, Teofipol, Brahin, Kamianets-Podilsky), the Jesuits (Ostroh), the Capuchins (Brusyliv, Vinnytsia), the Order of Reformed Friars Minor (Dederkaly, Kremenets), the Observants (Janów)[99]. By order of the People's Commissariat for Education of the Ukrainian SSR, in 1931–1932, all the manuscripts and early printed books of Volyn Heritage Museum moved to the All-National Library of Ukraine[100]. As a result, the library in Kyiv was increased by ninety thousand titles, including 32320 books from the libraries of dissolved Roman Catholic institutions and 9176 books from the old Orthodox seminary[101]. Thus the main research library in Ukraine acquired a large number of volumes left by the Roman Catholic and Uniate monasteries dissolved in the nineteenth century. Another channel through which the monastic libraries became part of the All-National Library of Ukraine after 1917 was the acquisition of the collection of the University of Saint Vladimir, which had obtained the Jesuit collections from Kremenets and Vilnius. After World War I, the Kyiv library came into the possession of the collection from the Vyshnivets castle, which

---

97 More about him in Надія Любовець, 'Олександр Олександрович Котляревський: матеріали до бібліографії' [Nadiya Lyubovets, Ołeksandr Ołeksandrowycz Kotlarevsky: materials for a bibliography], in Українська біографістика: збірник наукових праць інституту біографічних досліджень [Biography in Ukraine: a collection of scientific papers from the Institute for Biografical Research] (Київ [Kyiv], 2010), vol. 6, 55–80.

98 Колесник, *Книжные коллекции*, as note 45, 41.

99 Cf. Сергій Миколайович Міщук, *Бібліотека Волинського краєзнавчого музею у Житомирі (1900–1932): походження, склад, доля. Автореф. дисертації на здобуття наукового ступеня кандидата історичних наук* [Serhiy Mykolayovych Mishchuk, Library of Volyn Heritage Museum in Zhytomyr (1900–1932): origins, content, fates. Paper into dissertation to obtain the academic degree of PhD (candidate of historical sciences)] (Київ [Kyiv], 2003); Ціборовська-Римарович, *Бібліотеки римо-католицьких монастирів Волині*, as note 66, 9–14.

100 Любов Андріївна Дубровіна, *Історія Національної Бібліотеки України ім. В.І. Вернадського. 1918–1941* [Lyubov Andriyivna Dubrovina, History of the Vernadsky National Library of Ukraine. 1918–1941] (Київ [Kyiv], 1998), 160–61.

101 Мяскова, *Бібліотека Острозького єзуїтського колегіуму*, as note 10, 132.

partly consisted of the books from the local Discalced Carmelite monastery[102].

In the 1920s and the 1930s, a similar process of aggregation of ex-monastic collections was taking place in Belarus. In 1921 in Minsk the library of the Belarusian State University was founded, and in the following year became the Belarusian State and University Library (later on, in 1926, the Belarusian State Library, and in 1932 the Lenin State Library of the Belarusian SSR. It is today the National Library of Belarus). The collections of the religious and ecclesiastical institutions (including monasteries and seminaries) dissolved after the establishment of Soviet rule constituted the basis for the department of manuscripts and early printed books of the State library. Additionally, the library came into the possession of the books from the former Jesuit college in Polatsk and the libraries of the Minsk and Vitsyebsk seminars, which themselves consisted of ex-monastic collections[103]. After World War I, the collection of the Vilnius Public Library was transferred to the Stefan Batory University Library, founded in Vilnius in 1919[104].

As the USSR annexed Lithuania in 1940, the library was turned into the Academic Library of the Vincas Kapsukas State University.

In the twentieth century, a substantial part of the collections that had come from the libraries of Roman Catholic and Uniate monasteries dissolved in the previous century were eventually incorporated into the research libraries of the USSR. They, in turn, after the declaration of independence of the Soviet republics, became the most important scholarly libraries in the newly emerged independent states of Eastern Europe. At present, most of the ex-monastic collections can be found in the Vernadsky National Library of Ukraine in Kyiv (Ukraine), the National Library of Belarus in Minsk (Belarus), the Vilnius University Library (Lithuania) and the National Library of Russia in Saint Petersburg (the Russian Federation). The concentration of these collections in a small number of locations undoubtedly favours a more detailed study and documentation. Yet a substantial portion of the monastic collections are still in smaller regional libraries and require further research.

102   Ірина Олегівна Ціборовська-Римарович, *Родові бібліотеки Правобережної України XVIII ст. (Вишневецьких–Мнішків, Потоцьких, Мікошевських): історична доля та сучасний стан* [Iryna Olehivna Ciborovska-Rymarovych, Libraries belonging to the families from the Right-bank Ukraine (Wiśniowieckich-Mniszchów, Potockich, Mikoszewskich): historical fates and current status)] (Київ [Kyiv], 2006), 46–47.

103   Татьяна Ивановна Рощина, 'Белорусские исторические книжные коллекции в фондах Национальной библиотеки Белоруссии (проблемы изучения)' [Tatyana Ivanovna Roshchina, Belarusian historical collections of books in the collections of the National Library of Belarus (research problems)], in *Белорусский сборник: статьи и материалы по истории и культуре Белоруссии* [Belarusian Collection: articles and materials on the history and culture of Belarus] (Санкт-Петербург [Saint Petersburg], 2002), vol. 2, 199–202.

104   Łysakowski, *Uniwersytecka bibljoteka publiczna*, as note 44, 236.

Bibliography

Michał Eustachy Brensztejn, *Bibljoteka uniwersytecka w Wilnie do roku 1832-go* [Vilnus University Library until 1832] (Wilno, 1922).

Bolesław Breżgo, 'Losy bibliotek jezuickich w Połocku i Witebsku' [Fate of the Jesuit Libraries in Polatsk and Vitsyebsk], *Przegląd Powszechny*, 43 (1926), 88–94.

Piotr Paweł Gach, *Kasaty zakonów na ziemiach Rzeczypospolitej i Śląska 1773–1914* [Dissolution of religious orders in the territories of the Polish-Lithuanian Commonwealth and Silesia in 1773–1914] (Lublin, 1984).

Piotr Paweł Gach, *Mienie polskich zakonów i jego losy w XIX wieku* [Property of polish religious orders and its fate in the 19th century] (Rzym, 1979).

Paweł Franciszek Kubicki, *Bojownicy kapłani za sprawę Kościoła i Ojczyzny w latach 1861–1915* [Priests fighting for Church and Homeland in 1861–1915] (Sandomierz, 1938), part 2: *Dawna Litwa i Białoruś* [Former Lithuania and Belarus], vol. 4.

Stanisław Lisowski, 'Uniwersytecka Bibljoteka Publiczna w Wilnie za czasów rosyjskich' [Public University Library in Vilnus in russian times], *Ateneum Wileńskie*, 8 (1931–1932), 241–46.

Józef Łukaszewicz, *Historya szkół w Koronie i w Wielkiem księstwie Litewskiem aż do roku 1794* [The history of schools in the Polish-Lithuanian Commonwealth until 1794] (Poznań, 1851).

Adam Łysakowski, 'Uniwersytecka bibljoteka publiczna w Wilnie (Zarys ogólny)' [Public University Library in Vilnus. (General outline)], *Ateneum Wileńskie*, 8 (1931–1932), 231–40.

Materyały do dziejów Akademii Połockiej i szkół od niej zależnych [Materials for the history of the Academy of Polatsk and schools that depended on] (Kraków, 1905).

Arvydas Pacevičius, 'Biblioteki klasztorne na Litwie w końcu XVIII i pierwszej połowie XIX wieku: stan – rozwój – losy' [Monastic Libraries in Lithuania in the late 18th and first half of the 19th century: the state – developement – the fates], in *Zakony i klasztory w Europie Środkowo-Wschodniej. X–XX wiek* [Religiuos Orders and Monasteries in Central and Eastern Europe. 10th-20th century], ed. Henryk Gapski, Jerzy Kłoczowski (Lublin, 1999), 370–72.

Arvydas Pacevičius, 'Zaginiony świat książki: biblioteki klasztorne na Litwie pod władzą carów' [Lost world of the Book: monastic libraries in Lithuania under the rule of the Tsars], in *Wspólnota pamięci. Studia z dziejów kultury ziem wschodnich dawnej Rzeczypospolitej* [Community of the memory. Studies in the history of culture of the eastern regions of the former Polish-Lithuanian Commonwealth], ed. Jolanta Sylwia Gwioździk, Jan Malicki (Katowice, 2006), 243–54.

Urszula Paszkiewicz, *Inwentarze i katalogi bibliotek z ziem wschodnich Rzeczypospolitej do 1939 roku. Suplement 1* [Inventory and catalogues of Libraries in the eastern territories of Poland until 1939. Supplement 1] (Warszawa, 2000).

Urszula Paszkiewicz, *Inwentarze i katalogi bibliotek z ziem wschodnich Rzeczypospolitej do 1939 roku. Suplement 2* [Inventory and catalogues of libraries in the eastern territories of Poland until 1939. Supplement 2] (Poznań 2006).

Urszula Paszkiewicz, *Inwentarze i katalogi bibliotek z ziem wschodnich Rzeczypospolitej: spis za lata 1510–1939* [Inventory and catalogues of libraries in the eastern territories of Poland: registers from 1510–1939] (Warszawa, 1998).

Maria Pidłypczak-Majerowicz, *Bazylianie w Koronie i na Litwie. Szkoły i książki w działalności zakonu* [The Basilian order in the Polish-Lithuanian Commonwealth. Schools and books in the activities of the Order] (Warszawa-Wrocław, 1986).

Marian Radwan, *Carat wobec Kościoła greckokatolickiego w zaborze rosyjskim 1796–1839* [Russian Empire and the Uniate Church within the former territories of Poland, incorporated into the Russian state in 1796–1839] (Lublin, 2004).

Franciszek Radziszewski, *Wiadomość historyczno-statystyczna o znakomitych bibliotekach i archiwach publicznych i prywatnych* [Historical and statistical information about great libraries and archives, both public and private] (Kraków, 1875).

Bronisław Ussas, 'Z dziejów grabieży i niszczenia polskiego mienia kościelnego przez Rosjan w świetle świadectw rosyjskich (1655–1925)' [From the History of plunder and destruction of Polish ecclesiastical property by the Russians in the light of Russian testimonies (1655–1925)], *Przegląd Powszechny*, 53 (1936), 44–56, 185–203.

Наталья Березкина, 'Из истории библиотечного дела Беларуси' [Natalia Beryezkina, Extracts from the history of librarianship in Belarus], *Вестник ББА* [Herald of BLA], 1 (1996), http://www.bla.by/herald_bla.

Тамара Борисовна Блинова, *Иезуиты в России (Их роль в организации образования и просвещения)* [Tamara Borisovna Blinova, Jesuits in Russia (their role in the organization of education and enlightenment)] (Гродно [Hrodna], 2002).

Ричард Вортман, '"Официальная народность" и национальный миф российской монархии XIX века' [Richard Wortman, 'Official nationality' and the national myth of the Russian monarchy in 19th century], in *Россия / Russia* (Москва [Moscow], 1999), vol. 3 (11): *Культурные практики в идеологической перспективе. Россия, XVIII – начало XX века* [Cultural practices in ideological perspective. Russia, 18th-the beginning of 19th century], 233–44.

Андрей Иванович Ганчар, *Римско-католический костел в Беларуси (1864–1905)* [Andrey Ivanovich Ganchar, The Roman Catholic Church in Belarus (1864–1905)] (Гродно [Hrodna], 2008).

Татьяна Владимировна Говорова, *Библиотека Полоцких иезуитов: факты, сведения, документы* [Tatyana Vladimirovna Govorova, Jesuit Library in Polatsk: facts, information, documents], in *Материалы 14-й Международной Конференции "Крым 2007"* [Materials from the 14th International Conference "Crimea 2007"] (Москва [Moscow], 2007); http://www.gpntb.ru/win/inter-events/crimea2007/cd/131.pdf.

Любов Андріївна Дубровіна, *Історія Національної Бібліотеки України ім. В.І. Вернадського. 1918–1941* [Lyubov Andriyivna Dubrovina, History of the Vernadsky National Library of Ukraine. 1918–1941] (Київ [Kyiv], 1998).

Сергій Іванович Жилюк, *Російська православна церква на Волині (1793–1917)* [Serhiy Ivanovych. Zhylyuk, Russian Orthodox Church in Volyn (1793–1917)] (Житомир [Zhytomyr], 1996).

Западные окраины Российской империи [Western territories of the Russian Empire] (Москва [Moscow], 2006).

Евгения Алексеевна Колесник, *Книжные коллекции Центральной научной библиотеки Академии Наук УССР* [Evgeniya Alekseevna Kolyesnik, Book collections of the Central Scientific Library of the USSR Academy of Sciences] (Киев [Kyiv], 1998).

Иван Сергеевич Коннов, 'Публичные библиотеки в культурной среде российской провинции во второй половине XIX – начале XX века (на примере Пензенской, Самарской и Симбирской губерний)' [Ivan Sergeeevich Konnov, Public libraries in the cultural environment of the Russian province in the second half of the 19th and early 20th centuries (on the examples of Penza, Samara and Simbirsk Governorate)], *Известия Российского государственного педагогического университета им. А. Н. Герцена* [News of the Herzen State Pedagogical University of Russia], 119 (2009), 55–60.

Краткій отчетъ о Виленской Публичной Библіотеке [A brief report on the Vilnus Public Library] (Вильна [Vilnius], 1867).

Надія Любовець, 'Олександр Олександрович Котляревський: матеріали до бібліографії' [Nadiya Lyubovets, Ołeksandr Ołeksandrowycz Kotlarevsky: materials for a bibliography], in *Українська біографістика: збірник наукових праць інституту біографічних досліджень* [Biography in Ukraine: a collection of scientific papers from the Institute for Biografical Research] (Київ [Kyiv], 2010), vol. 6, 55–80.

Александр Иванович Миловидовъ, *Рукописное отделеніе Виленской Публичной Библиотеки. Его исторія и составъ* [Alexander Ivanovich Milovidov, Manuscripts Department of the Vilnus Public Library. Its history and contents] (Вильна [Vilnius], 1910).

Ірина Володимирівна Мілясевич, 'Бібліотека Волинської духовної семінарії. Кременецький період (1836–1901 рр.)' [Iryna Volodymyrivna Milyasevych, Volyn Theological Seminary Library. Period called 'Kremenetsky' (1836–1901)], *ibidem*, 11 (2001), 37–39.

Ірина Володимирівна Мілясевич, 'Бібліотека Волинської духовної семінарії. Острозький період (1796–1836 рр.)' [Iryna Volodymyrivna Milyasevych, Volyn Theological Seminary Library. Period called 'Ostrogsky' (1796–1836)], *Вісник Книжкової палати* [Chamber of Books Information], 3 (2002), 28–30.

Сергій Миколайович Міщук, *Бібліотека Волинського краєзнавчого музею у Житомирі (1900–1932): походження, склад, доля. Автореф. дисертації на здобуття наукового ступеня кандидата історичних наук* [Serhiy Mykolayovych Mishchuk, Library of Volyn Heritage Museum in Zhytomyr (1900–1932): origins, content, fates. Paper into dissertation to obtain the academic degree of PhD (candidate of historical sciences)] (Київ [Kyiv], 2003).

Михаил Яковлевич Морошкинъ, *Іезуиты въ Россіи съ царствованія Екатерины II-й и до нашего времени* [Mikhail Yakovlevich Moroshkin, The Jesuits in Russia since the Rule of Catherine II to the present day] (Санкт-Петербургъ [Saint Petersburg], 1867).

Тетяна Євгеніївна Мяскова, 'Бібліотека Острозького єзуїтського колегіуму: історія виникнення, функціонування та сучасний стан' [Tetiana Yevheniyivna Myaskova, Jesuit College Library in Ostroh: origins, activity and current state], *Рукописна та книжкова спадщина України* [Manuscript and book heritage of Ukraine], 11 (2007), 122–135.

Тетяна Євгеніївна Мяскова, 'Заснування та комплектування бібліотеки Університету св. Володимира (1834–1841)' [Tetiana Yevheniyivna Myaskova, Foundation and equipment of the St Vladimir Univeristy Library (1834–1841)], *Рукописна і книжкова спадщина України* [Manuscript and book heritage of Ukraine], 4 (1998), 292–302.

Нарис історії Василіянського Чину Святого Йосафата [History outline of the Basilian Order of St Josaphat] (Рим [Rome], 1992).

Отчетъ о Виленской Публичной Библіотеке и Музее за 1867 годъ [A report on the Vilnius Public Library and Museum for the year 1867] (Вильна [Vilnius], 1868).

Полное Собраніе Законовъ Россійской имперіи, съ 1649 года [A complete collection of laws of the Russian Empire until 1649] (Санкт-Петербургъ [Saint Petersburg], 1830).

Полное Собраніе Законовъ Россійской имперіи. Собраніе второе [A complete collection of laws of the Russian Empire. The second collection] (Санкт-Петербургъ [Saint Petersburg], 1833).

Сергей Поляков, *Полоцкий кадетский корпус. История в лицах* [Sergey Polyakov, Polatsk Cadet Corps. The history of the people] (Полоцк [Polatsk], 2010).

Путеводитель по Императорской Публичной Библиотеке [Guide to the Imperial Public Library] (Санкт-Петербургъ [Saint Petersburg], 1860).

Татьяна Ивановна Рощина, 'Белорусские исторические книжные коллекции в фондах Национальной библиотеки Белоруссии (проблемы изучения)' [Tatyana Ivanovna Roshchina, Belarusian historical collections of books in the collections of the National Library of Belarus (research problems)], in *Белорусский сборник: статьи и материалы по истории и культуре Белоруссии* [Belarusian Collection: articles and materials on the history and culture of Belarus] (Санкт-Петербург [Saint Petersburg], 2002), vol. 2, 199–202.

Алексей Парфёнович Сапунов, 'Заметка о коллегии и Академии иезуитов в Полоцке' [Alexei Parfyonovich Sapunov, Notes on the Jesuit College and Academy in Polotsk], in *Иезуиты в Полоцке. 1580–1820* [Jesuit in Polatsk. 1580–1820] (Полоцк [Polatsk], 2005), vol. 2, 7–40.

Евфимий Иосифович Сецинскій, *Матеріалы для исторіи монастырей Подольской епархіи* [Evfimiy Iosifovich Syetsinskiy, Materials for the history of the monasteries in the Eparchy of Podolia] (Каменецъ-Подольскъ [Kamyanets-Podilskyy], 1891).

Ірина Олегівна Ціборовська-Римарович, 'Бібліотеки римо-католицьких монастирів Волині XVI–XVIII ст.: історична доля, роль у монастирській діяльності, сучасний стан фондів (за фондами Національної бібліотеки України ім. В. І. Вернадського)' [Iryna Olehivna Ciborovska-Rymarovych, Libraries of the Roman Catholic monasteries of Volyn from 16th to 18th century: historical fates, role in the activities of the monastery, the current state of the collections (by the collections of the Vernadsky National Library of Ukraine)], in *Актуальні питання культурології. Альманах наукового товариства "Афіна" кафедри культурології Рівненського державного гуманітарного університету* [Current questions of culture studies. Almanac of the Scientific Society 'Athena' in the Cultural Department of the State Humanistic University. in Rivne] (Рівне [Rivne], 2010), vol. 9, 9–14.

Ірина Олегівна Ціборовська-Римарович, 'Книги из библиотек иезуитских коллегий в фондах Национальной библиотеки имени В.И. Вернадского: происхождение, исторические судьбы пути поступления' [Iryna Olehivna Ciborovska-Rymarovych, Books from the libraries of Jesuit colleges in the collections of the Vernadsky National Library of Ukraine: origin, historical fate, directions of leaving], in *Библиотеки национальных академий наук: проблемы функционирования, тенденции развития: Научно-практический и теоретический сборник* [Libraries of National Academies of Sciences: problems of functioning, tendencies of development. Collection of academic, theoretical and practical works] (Киев [Kyiv], 2008), vol. 6, 411–430.

Ірина Олегівна Ціборовська-Римарович, 'Книгозбірня монастиря Ордену босих кармелітів у Вишнівці: історія та книгознавча характеристика фонду' [Iryna Olehivna Ciborovska-Rymarovych, Collection of books from the Discalced Carmelite monastery in Wiśniowiec: history and characteristics], *Рукописна та книжкова спадщина України* [Manuscript and book heritage of Ukraine], 13 (2009), 139–55.

Ірина Олегівна Ціборовська-Римарович, *Родові бібліотеки Правобережної України XVIII ст. (Вишневецьких–Мнішків, Потоцьких, Мікошевських): історична доля та сучасний стан* [Iryna Olehivna Ciborovska-Rymarovych, Libraries belonging to the families from the Right-bank Ukraine (Wiśniowieckich-Mniszchów, Potockich, Mikoszewskich): historical fates and current status)] (Київ [Kyiv], 2006).

Максим Михайлович Шевченко, 'Понятие "теория официальной народности" и изучение внутренней политики императора Николая I' [Maxim Mikhailovich Shevchenko, The term 'theory official nationality' and the study of the internal policy of the Emperor Nicolas I], *Вестник Московского университета. Серия 8: История* [Bulletin of Moscow University. Series 8th. History], 4 (2002), 89–104.

Сергей Валерьевич Удалов, 'Теория официальной народности: механизмы внедрения' [Sergei Valerievich Udalov, 'Theory official nationality: mechanisms of introduction], in *Освободительное движение в России. Межвузовский сборник научных трудов* [Liberation Movement in Russia: intercollegiate collection of papers], ed. Н. Троицкий (Саратов [Saratov], 2006), vol. 21, 73–81.

PART 4

Impact on Book Trade and the Emergence of Private Collections

▾ CHANGES OCCURRING IN THE BOOK TRADE DUE TO
THE MASSIVE FLOW OF BOOKS AND MANUSCRIPTS INTO
THE MARKET. CHANGE IN COLLECTING HABITS AND THE
EMERGENCE OF A NEW TYPE OF COLLECTOR

DOMINIQUE VARRY

Le commerce du livre d'antiquariat en France après la Révolution

Á la mémoire de Giles Gaudard Barber

Le commerce du livre d'antiquariat dans la France du XIXe siècle est encore très mal connu, et a été peu étudié. Il n'a guère été évoqué que par de rares textes et mémoires émanant de collectionneurs. Nous devons l'avouer d'entrée de jeu, les pages qui suivent sont exploratoires, et ne prétendent pas donner une vision synthétique et définitive de la question. Il est en tout cas avéré que ce commerce du livre ancien au XIXe siècle a pour l'essentiel été alimenté par des livres confisqués, au moins théoriquement, sous la Révolution, et ayant subi depuis de multiples péripéties. Cette masse de livres provenait à la fois de biens nationaux de première origine, c'est-à-dire confisqués au clergé par le décret des 2–4 novembre 1789, et de biens nationaux de seconde origine, confisqués ultérieurement aux émigrés, déportés, condamnés… Mélangés dans les dépôts littéraires de la Révolution, ils l'ont également été par la suite dans les boutiques des libraires de seconde main et sur les étals des bouquinistes. Comment ces livres ont-ils été distraits des collections publiques pour échouer chez les revendeurs? Telle sera notre première interrogation. Nous essaierons ensuite de dresser une typologie de ces derniers.

Avant d'évoquer les confiscations révolutionnaires et leurs conséquences, il nous faut rappeler une pratique assez générale au XVIIIe siècle, et dans les années qui précédèrent la Révolution: celle, pour les bibliophiles de haut parage, de faire écumer monastères et maisons religieuses par leurs bibliothécaires ou des mercenaires, pour proposer l'échange d'ouvrages récents contre des éditions anciennes, et tout spécialement incunables. Ce faisant, ils marchaient sur les pas d'illustres prédécesseurs, tels l'archevêque de Rouen Jacques-Nicolas Colbert (1655–1707), qui avait agi de même au XVIIe siècle.

On peut ainsi citer le cas du Père François-Xavier Laire, bibliothécaire du cardinal Loménie de Brienne depuis 1786, qui sévit dans un certain

Dominique Varry • Formerly agrégé d'histoire and professeur des Universités, Enssib (Lyon). dominique.varry@enssib.fr

How the Secularization of Religious Houses Transformed the Libraries of Europe, 16th–19th Centuries, ed. by Cristina Dondi, Dorit Raines, and † Richard Sharpe, BIB, 63 (Turnhout, 2022), pp. 359–370.

BREPOLS ⚜ PUBLISHERS   DOI 10.1484/M.BIB-EB.5.128493

nombre de maisons religieuses françaises[1], et qui assista son cardinal de patron dans une expédition italienne qui, en 1789 et 1790, permit une abondante moisson dans les bibliothèques religieuses de la péninsule, dont environ quatre cents incunables[2]. Un des intermédiaires de Loménie de Brienne et de Laire était dom Maugérard, un bénédictin qui trafiqua dès 1765 en Allemagne, et poursuivit cette activité sous la Révolution et l'Empire. Né à Auzéville, dans la Meuse, le 29 avril 1735, Jean-Baptiste Maugérard avait pris l'habit bénédictin à Mouzon en 1751. Il fut ordonné prêtre en 1759, et devint bibliothécaire de l'abbaye Saint Arnould de Metz. Il fut aussi le précepteur des fils du duc de Montmorency, qui étaient neveux du cardinal de Montmorency-Laval évêque de Metz. Il commença à jouer les intermédiaires en livres anciens, en particulier en Allemagne, à partir de 1765. Prêtre réfractaire sous la Révolution, il suivit son évêque en Allemagne, et se fit libraire d'ancien et particulièrement d'incunables. De 1802 à 1806, sur nomination du ministre Chaptal, il fut commissaire du gouvernement pour les œuvres d'art et les objets scientifiques dans les quatre départements du Rhin. Il demeura ensuite trafiquant et marchand de manuscrits et d'incunables jusqu'à son décès survenu à Metz le 15 juillet 1815. Un de ses arrières petits neveux a publié sa biographie à la fin du XIXe siècle[3].

Avant d'émigrer à la suite de son évêque, dom Maugérard avait dû vendre sa bibliothèque personnelle un peu précipitamment. Le catalogue anonyme de cette vente a été dévoilé par Van-Praët sur l'exemplaire de la Bibliothèque nationale[4], pour laquelle il acheta un certain nombre de lots.

Nombreux furent les candidats à l'émigration qui, comme dom Maugérard, livrèrent leurs bibliothèques au feu des enchères avant leur départ. Mais cela fut aussi le cas de hauts personnages demeurés en France, mais dont la situation financière avait eu à pâtir des événements. Tel fut, par exemple, le cas du cardinal Loménie de Brienne soudainement privé d'appréciables revenus de ses abbayes par la nationalisation des biens du clergé. A peine rentré de sa campagne de chasse bibliographique italienne, au printemps 1790, il dut se résoudre à se dépouiller… y compris de ses acquisitions les plus récentes. Une première vente, dont le Père Laire rédigea le catalogue en deux volumes, intervint en 1791[5]. Une seconde, dont le catalogue rédigé par Guillaume de Bure l'aîné, se présente comme le troisième tome des précédents, se tint en mars 1792[6]. Cinq autres ventes intervinrent dans les années suivantes, jusqu'en 1797[7].

Ces ventes furent l'occasion d'acquisitions par la Bibliothèque nationale, mais également par des étrangers: Lord Spencer, le libraire londonien Edwards, le trafiquant russe Petr Dubrowski[8]… Dans une correspondance du 26 juin 1795 au bibliophile franc-comtois Vernier, le Père Laire

1 Michel Vernus, *Une vie dans l'univers du livre. François-Xavier Laire (1738–1801)* (Lons le Saunier, 2001), 72–84.

2 Graziano Ruffini, *La chasse aux livres. Bibliografia e collezionismo nel viaggio di Étienne-Charles de Loménie de Brienne e François-Xavier Laire (1789–1790)* (Florence, 2012).

3 Jean-Baptiste Buzy, *Dom Maugérard, Histoire d'un bibliographe lorrain* (Châlons-sur-Marne, 1882); Kristian Jensen, *Revolution and the Antiquarian Book: Reshaping the Past, 1780–1815* (Cambridge, 2011), ad indicem.

4 *Notice de livres rares, la plupart imprimés dans le quinzième siècle, dont la vente se fera rue des deux écus, à l'hôtel saint-Antoine, le 16 janvier 1792, et jours suivans après midi* (Paris, [1792]).

5 François-Xavier Laire, *Index librorum ab inventa typographia ad annum 1500… Prima [Secunda] pars*, 2 vols (Sens, 1791).

6 Guillaume de Bure l'aîné, *Catalogue des livres de la bibliothèque de M***. Faisant suite à l'Index librorum ab inventa typographia… dont la vente se fera le lundi 12 mars 1792… Tome III* (Paris, 1792).

7 *Catalogue d'une partie des livres de la bibliothèque du cardinal de Loménie de Brienne…* (Paris, an V [1797]), BnF Q8206.

8 Annie Charon, 'Un amateur russe, Doubrovski à la vente Loménie de Brienne', in *Le Siècle des Lumières. I. Espace culturel de l'Europe à l'époque de Catherine II*, éd. Sergueï Karp (Moscou, 2006), 213–30.

évoquant le catalogue en deux volumes de 1791 écrivait[9]: "[...] Quant aux monumens qui y étaient rapportés, ils ont été vendus à Paris en 1791 et on a vendu en détail la plus belle collection de livres du XVe siècle qu'on eut fait jusqu'à présent et la plupart a été transporté [sic] en Angleterre [...]". Une tradition non vérifiée rapporte d'ailleurs que nombre de ces ventes des débuts de la Révolution ont profité aux acheteurs anglais.

Avant même les confiscations révolutionnaires, les bibliothèques de certaines communautés religieuses avaient donc déjà fait l'objet de soustractions, et ces volumes se retrouvèrent très vite sur le marché. Dès la confiscation de 1789, les autorités révolutionnaires successives ont pris des mesures destinées à exclure livres, œuvres d'art et objets scientifiques des ventes, et à les protéger contre les altérations ou la destruction. Tel fut le cas pour les biens du clergé par le décret des 23–28 octobre 1790. Deux ans plus tard, le 10 octobre 1792, un nouveau décret étendait cette interdiction aux biens des émigrés. A l'initiative du conventionnel Gilbert Romme, un décret du 24 octobre 1793 proscrivait les mutilations des reliures pour en enlever les symboles monarchiques et féodaux. Cette décision faisait suite à l'initiative de certains relieurs de remplacer les armes de France par des symboles révolutionnaires sur les ouvrages de la ci-devant Bibliothèque du roi devenue Bibliothèque nationale. Les trois rapports de l'abbé Grégoire, à l'été et à l'automne 1794, sur le vandalisme ont cependant relevé un certain nombre d'exemples où ces décrets protecteurs n'avaient empêché ni destructions ni détournements. Ainsi, par exemple, de cette vente illégale des 1684 volumes et des meubles de la bibliothèque des récollets de Gisors, survenue le 7 mars 1791[10]. Dans ce cas précis, nous

avons pu identifier 17 des 23 acheteurs des volumes qui, pour une part ont été remis sur le marché, et pour l'autre ont servi de papier d'emballage. Deux libraires, l'un de Gisors l'autre de Beauvais, acquirent 481 volumes. Une demi-douzaine de fripiers et d'épiciers emportèrent 525 volumes. Trois hommes de loi, le sacristain, un apothicaire et sept inconnus se partagèrent les 678 volumes restants.

Les dépôts littéraires eux-mêmes, dans lesquels étaient regroupés les ouvrages confisqués ont parfois été mis au pillage par ceux qui en avaient la garde. Parmi bien d'autres cas, nous avons étudié celui du citoyen Dambreville[11], directeur du dépôt parisien des Cordeliers, qui à la suite d'une dénonciation, de surveillances et de filatures en cabriolets à travers Paris, fut arrêté le 4 juin 1801 pour avoir soustrait un nombre important mais inconnu d'ouvrages du dépôt dont il avait la charge, et être en relation avec un huissier priseur. L'enquête s'arrêta subitement lorsqu'on constata que le suspect avait rendu plusieurs visites, des livres sous le bras, à Lucien Bonaparte!

Certains de ces dépôts littéraires ont d'ailleurs vu, dans les premières années du XIXe siècle, leurs collections vendues pour aider à payer des retards de salaire de leurs bibliothécaires. Tel fut, par exemple, le cas aux Andelys (Eure) où, le 14 mars 1805, un ordre du sous-préfet, approuvé deux jours plus tard par le préfet du département, ordonna la vente des livres pour cette raison. Un courrier de 1817 du préfet au ministère de l'Intérieur nous informe de ce que cette vente avait rapporté 2 620 francs[12]. Ce cas ne fut sans doute pas unique.

Les années du Consulat et de l'Empire ont, par ailleurs, été caractérisées par la vente d'un nombre important, mais impossible à évaluer, tant à Paris qu'en province, de volumes essentiellement religieux

---

9   Michel Vernus, *Une vie dans l'univers du livre*, voir note nr. 1, 126.

10 Dominique Varry, *"Sous la main de la Nation". Les bibliothèques de l'Eure confisquées sous la Révolution française* (Ferney-Voltaire, 2005), 222–23.

11 Dominique Varry, 'Une ténébreuse affaire: les curieux agissements du citoyen Dambreville', *Bulletin du bibliophile* 1 (1994), 82–102.

12 Dominique Varry, *"Sous la main de la Nation"*, voir note nr. 10, 225.

et juridiques qui ont été cédés au prix du papier. C'est ainsi que le 5 mai 1807, le préfet de la Meuse annonçait la vente, le 21 mai suivant à la mairie de Bar-sur-Onain de 4 000 kg de vieux livres dont le papier pouvait être utilisé à emballer des marchandises. Des dossiers des Archives nationales conservent des propositions d'achat de livres au poids: 20 francs le quintal d'*in-folios* ou d'*in-quarto*, 8 francs le quintal de petits formats à partir de l'*in-octavo*[13].

Une nouvelle période de ventes importantes de livres, elles aussi impossibles à quantifier, s'est ouverte dans les années de la Restauration puis de la Monarchie de Juillet, tout spécialement à partir de 1832, quand le gouvernement a conditionné son aide aux bibliothèques municipales à la publication des catalogues de leurs collections. Nombreux furent alors les catalogues dont les préfaces firent état de ventes de prétendus "doubles" bien entendu non vérifiés. Celui de Louviers (Eure) rappelle que par délibération du 21 novembre 1832, le conseil municipal avait décidé la vente des doubles. Celle-ci est intervenue au début de l'année 1833. Dix ans plus tard, lorsque le catalogue de la bibliothèque de Louviers fut publié, la collection ne comportait plus que 5 000 volumes, un nombre équivalent d'ouvrages avait été vendu. Le même texte évaluait à environ 14 000 le nombre des volumes confisqués aux maisons religieuses du district de Louviers par le décret de novembre 1789[14]. Les 9 000 volumes manquants en 1843, par rapport à ce chiffre initial, dont les 5 000 vendus en 1833, ont vraisemblablement été remis dans le circuit du livre d'antiquariat.

Ces ventes sauvages furent théoriquement interdites par les autorités dans une ordonnance royale de 1839. Les instructions données le 20 avril 1840 par le ministre Victor Cousin à l'inspecteur des bibliothèques Félix Ravaisson à l'occasion de sa tournée dans l'Ouest de la France entre mai et juillet 1840, et reproduites par ce dernier dans son rapport, étaient on ne peut plus claires[15]:

"[…] Vous aurez encore à vous assurer, Monsieur, s'il ne se fait pas, contrairement aux dispositions de l'article 40 de l'ordonnance royale du 22 février 1839, des ventes de livres doubles ou autres, et, s'il s'en fait, vous vous y opposerez, au nom du ministre. Vous inviterez l'administration locale à mettre les doubles à la disposition du ministère, en échange des livres provenant des souscriptions et du dépôt légal, conformément à l'arrêté ministériel du 23 juillet 1838. La bibliothèque de Nantes, entre autres, possède un grand nombre de doubles pour l'échange desquels une correspondance s'est établie entre l'administration centrale et le conseil municipal; il y aurait lieu d'intervenir pour déterminer ce conseil à faire l'abandon de ses doubles, et, surtout, pour rappeler la défense qui a été faite au préfet d'en autoriser la vente. […]"

De fait, ces mesures venaient trop tard, et un nombre très important de volumes, qu'on ne pourra jamais évaluer, avaient été mis durant un demi-siècle, soit entre les années 1790 et 1840, sur le marché. Signe de la vitalité de ce dernier, les premières années du XIXᵉ siècle virent paraître plusieurs manuels et instruments de travail importants, et destinés à un long usage.

Alors que la *Bibliographie instructive ou Traité de la connaissance des livres rares et singuliers* de Guillaume-François Debure, publiée en sept volumes *in-octavo* entre 1763 et 1768 s'adressait en priorité aux collectionneurs dont elle cherchait, d'une certaine

---

13   Dominique Varry, 'Vicissitudes et aléas des livres placés sous la main de la Nation', in *Révolution française et "vandalisme révolutionnaire". Actes du colloque international de Clermont-Ferrand (15–17 décembre 1988)*, Simone Bernard-Griffiths, Marie-Claude Chemin et Jean Ehrard éd. (Paris, 1992), 277–84.

14   Louis Bréauté, *Catalogue de la bibliothèque de la ville de Louviers…* (Rouen, 1843), 3–5.

15   Félix Ravaisson, *Rapports au ministre de l'Instruction publique sur les bibliothèques des départements de l'Ouest, suivis de pièces inédites* (1841), 6.

manière, à façonner le goût, il est significatif que les premières années du XIXᵉ siècle aient vu la publication des premiers manuels expressément destinés aux libraires, même s'ils ont également pu être utilisés par les bibliophiles. Leurs titres sont en tout cas éloquents quant au lectorat visé en priorité. C'est en 1804 et 1805 que l'imprimeur-libraire parisien Martin Silvestre Boulard[16], né en 1748 et décédé en 1809, publia sur ses presses les deux volumes *in-octavo* de son *Traité élémentaire de bibliographie…* Le titre long de l'ouvrage en résume le propos: *Traité élémentaire de bibliographie, contenant la manière de faire les inventaires, les prisées, les ventes publiques et de classer les catalogues. Les bâses [sic] d'une bonne bibliothèque, et la manière d'apprécier les livres rares et précieux. Ouvrage utile à tous les bibliographes, et particulièrement aux bibliothécaires et aux libraires qui commencent. Pouvant servir d'introduction à toutes les bibliographies qui ont paru jusqu'à ce jour*. On signalera, en particulier, dans la première partie des chapitres sur la rareté des livres (chapitre 5), la dépréciation des livres (chapitre 6), le choix des éditions et des exemplaires (chapitre 7), la reliure (chapitre 8).

Le second ouvrage important à paraître, en 1809 en trois volumes, fut le *Manuel du libraire et de l'amateur de livres* de Jacques Charles Brunet (1780–1867). En plus de descriptions bibliographiques des ouvrages recensés, il donnait des indications sur leur rareté et sur leur valeur pécuniaire. Destiné prioritairement, comme son titre l'indique aux libraires, il est rapidement devenu l'ouvrage de référence indispensable du bibliophile, et a conservé ce rôle jusqu'à nos jours. Il a fait l'objet de quatre rééditions jusqu'à celle de 1860 en six volumes. Il est aujourd'hui proposé par la maison "Classiques Garnier" sous forme de CD-Rom.

Ultérieurement sont apparus les périodiques spécialisés. Le premier fut, en 1834, le *Bulletin du*

bibliophile. A l'origine, il s'agissait d'une simple feuille publicitaire du libraire Techener, que nous évoquerons ultérieurement, agrémentée d'un article d'érudition de Charles Nodier. Son abonnement annuel élevé, douze francs, en faisait une publication relativement confidentielle réservée à de riches collectionneurs. Parmi ses premiers collaborateurs, on relève les noms de Charles Nodier, Gabriel Peignot, Jacques Charles Brunet… Il est très vite devenu une vraie revue, et parait encore aujourd'hui, deux fois l'an. La librairie parisienne Giraud-Badin, héritière de la librairie Techener, est toujours propriétaire du titre.

Le second fut lancé en 1857 à l'initiative du libraire Auguste Aubry, sous le titre de *Bulletin du bouquiniste*. Il publiait deux fois par mois des listes de livres mis en vente, et disparut en 1896. Son abonnement annuel plus modique, trois francs, lui donnait un lectorat plus large que le précédent. Pour leur part, les frères Charavay lancèrent en 1862 *L'Amateur d'autographes*. Il connut une interruption de publication entre 1893 et 1897, et disparut en 1914.

Le commerce de la librairie française d'antiquariat au XIXᵉ siècle est encore très mal connu, faute d'études sérieuses. Une des premières à s'être penchée sur cette question, rencontrée lors de la préparation de sa thèse consacrée au bibliophile Charles de Spoelberch de Lovenjoul (1836–1907), est Catherine Gaviglio-Faivre d'Arcier, auteur d'un article[17] publié dans la récente *Histoire de la librairie française*.

Une première réalité à ne pas oublier est le fait que nombre de libraires traditionnels, tant dans la capitale qu'en province, adjoignaient un rayon de livres d'occasion à ceux des nouveautés. Tel était par exemple le cas dans la célèbre librairie parisienne Bossange dans les années 1830. Tel

---

16 Frédéric Barbier, Sabine Juratic et Annick Mellerio, *Dictionnaire des imprimeurs, libraires et gens du livre à Paris 1701–1789: A-C* (Genève, 2007), 294–95. Le patronyme est parfois orthographié Boullard.

17 Catherine Gaviglio-Faivre d'Arcier, 'Les libraires d'ancien et d'occasion', in *Histoire de la librairie française*, éd. Patricia Sorel et Frédérique Leblanc (Paris, 2008), 128–39.

fut aussi le cas de Paul Klincksieck qui, en 1888, adjoignit le livre d'antiquariat à sa double activité de libraire et d'éditeur d'ouvrages scientifiques.

Les vendeurs qui se limitaient au commerce de livres anciens peuvent être répartis en trois catégories. La plus éminente était celle des libraires d'antiquariat. Ils diffusaient des catalogues à prix marqués, et organisaient des ventes publiques. Venaient ensuite les libraires d'occasion, également appelés bouquinistes au XIXe siècle. La plupart de ceux qui exercèrent dans la capitale étaient d'origine provinciale. Honoré Champion, parisien de naissance, fait exception dans ce groupe. Anatole Claudin (1833–1906) était natif d'Orléans, les frères Charavay étaient lyonnais… Ces deux catégories de libraires tenaient boutique, sur les quais de la Seine à Paris, aux environs de l'Hôtel-Dieu et quai de l'Hôpital à Lyon. Elles furent toutes deux soumises à l'obtention d'un brevet de librairie entre 1810 et 1870.

Les vendeurs de la catégorie la plus humble étaient de simples étalagistes qui conservaient et exposaient leur marchandise dans des "boîtes", coffres de bois accrochés au parapet des quais de la Seine. C'est à eux que s'applique aujourd'hui l'appellation de "bouquinistes".

Parmi les libraires d'antiquariat émerge la figure de Jacques Joseph Techener[18]. Il était né à Orges (Haute-Marne) en mars 1802 d'un père autrichien. Il mourut à Paris en juin 1873. Après avoir servi comme commis chez Jean-François Royez, il ouvrit sa propre librairie en 1827. Ami de Charles Nodier, nous avons déjà évoqué son rôle dans la création du *Bulletin du bibliophile*. Il publia aussi, avec son fils et successeur Léon Techener, une *Histoire de la bibliophilie* en 1861–1863[19]. Il avait

acheté de très nombreux livres confisqués sous la Révolution et vendus, comme nous l'avons évoqué, au poids du papier. Dans les années 1830, il acquit de nombreux "doubles" dont les bibliothèques se débarrassaient. Avec ce double apport, il donna une nouvelle impulsion au commerce d'antiquariat, et publia plus de quatre cents catalogues. Il était lui-même collectionneur et essaya de vendre sa bibliothèque par l'intermédiaire de Sotheby's. Malheureusement, une partie des ouvrages destinés à cette vente disparut dans un incendie survenu à Londres le 29 juin 1865. Sa collection fut finalement dispersée à Paris, la même année, en quatre ventes successives. Il s'était retiré en 1863, et son fils Léon (1832–1888) lui succéda.

Le XIXe siècle fut aussi celui du développement des grandes salles des ventes parisiennes. L'une des plus célèbres en matière de livres fut la Salle Silvestre située au 28 de la rue des Bons Enfants, dans l'ancien hôtel de La Guillonière. Elle avait été créée vers 1796–1798 par le libraire L. Silvestre qui organisait des ventes aux enchères à son domicile. Elle fut, jusqu'en 1815 à peu près le seul lieu de ventes publiques de livres à Paris. Cette année là, le libraire Debure, qui utilisait la salle Silvestre mais la trouvait trop exiguë, transféra ses ventes à l'hôtel de Bullion, 3 rue Jean-Jacques Rousseau. Bâti dans le premier tiers du XVIIe siècle pour le surintendant des finances Claude de Bullion, cet hôtel abritait des ventes publiques depuis les années 1780. Il fut en grande partie détruit en 1880, à l'occasion du percement de la rue du Louvre. Pour sa part, la salle Silvestre continua néanmoins de fonctionner, en soirée (19–20 heures), jusqu'en 1935. On y vendait trois types de marchandises: des livres, des estampes, et des autographes. Au milieu du siècle apparut un nouveau lieu de ventes publiques: l'hôtel Drouot, construit entre 1850 et 1852, qui offrit d'abord quatorze, puis dix-huit salles d'enchères éclairées au gaz et chauffées au charbon.

Les libraires de seconde main constituaient une autre catégorie de pourvoyeurs de livres anciens. Le Père Lécureux, surnommé "la modeste

---

18 Catherine Gaviglio-Faivre d'Arcier, 'Portrait d'un libraire d'ancien: Techener', in *Histoire de la librairie française*, voir note nr. 17, 130.

19 Jacques Joseph Techener et Léon Techener, *Histoire de la bibliophilie. Reliures. Recherches sur les bibliothèques des plus célèbres amateurs. Armorial des bibliophiles* (Paris, 1861–1864), 10 livraisons.

providence des bibliophiles", en représente sans doute l'archétype. Il était né à Paris en 1795, et y mourut en novembre 1875. Il s'était fait une spécialité des exemplaires dépareillés qu'il achetait dans les ventes et chaque fois que l'occasion se présentait. Les libraires tant parisiens que provinciaux recouraient souvent à ses services pour se procurer un tome manquant et compléter une suite. Son biographe, Alexandre Piedagnel[20], a ainsi dépeint sa boutique:

"Au n° 20 de la rue des Grands-Augustins, tout au fond d'une cour silencieuse, se trouvait le vaste et poudreux magasin du digne bouquiniste. Sans cérémonie et à toute heure du jour, on pouvait pénétrer dans le temple, situé au rez-de-chaussée, en tournant le bouton d'une porte vitrée dont les carreaux étaient constamment couverts d'une vénérable poussière. Une marche à descendre, cinq ou six pas à faire dans une demi-obscurité, et le visiteur apercevait ou plutôt devinait soudain le père Lécureux, assis gravement devant un petit bureau de sapin noirci, placé près d'une fenêtre ayant vue sur une seconde cour, où s'étiolaient de compagnie quelques lilas et un platane, au centre d'une maigre pelouse. Le bureau vermoulu était surchargé de registres écornés et de liasses de papiers jaunis, du milieu desquels émergeait la tête chenue du bonhomme. Dans deux grandes pièces contiguës et peu élevées, l'œil rencontrait partout de nombreux rayons pliant sous le poids de volumes brochés ou reliés, et ficelés soigneusement par séries, avec de larges étiquettes sur chaque paquet. A terre, près du seuil, des pyramides de bouquins; sous les tables boiteuses, sur les chaises branlantes, encore des livres empilés; dans les encoignures, tapissées de toiles d'araignées, devant les fenêtres aux vitre verdâtres, tout le long des salles lézardées, toujours des livres et des brochures! […] On trouvait tout (ou du moins des échantillons de tout) dans ce capharnaüm, où il semblait, par exemple, terriblement difficile de circuler. De petits sentiers sinueux y étaient ménagés cependant, mais il fallait, pour s'y reconnaître, avoir une certaine habitude du logis."

Après avoir présenté les lieux, Piedagnel[21] campait le personnage, tout aussi haut en couleurs:

"Nous avons donné une idée du sanctuaire; voici maintenant le profil du grand-prêtre. Sec, courbé, de moyenne taille, la figure parcheminée et sillonnée de rides profondes, les pommettes saillantes, les cheveux blancs, et assez rares, les yeux vifs derrière ses lunettes rondes, le nez long et légèrement busqué, barbouillé de tabac; la bouche fine et souvent souriante d'un bon sourire bien franc, tel était le père Lécureux, vêtu dès l'aube, l'hiver aussi bien que l'été, d'une redingote noire lustrée par l'usage, et dont les manches étroites étaient protégées par des fourreaux en percaline, tachés d'encre et passablement fatigués. D'une poche de cette redingote, d'une coupe démodée depuis longtemps, s'échappait à demi un ample mouchoir à carreaux; un gilet noir étriqué, un vieux pantalon de même couleur, une cravate en soie très-mûre, entourant un col de chemise en toile rousse, et des pantoufles de lisière fanées complétaient ce costume sans prétention, on le voit du reste! Le père Lécureux, en effet, ne songeait point du tout à s'habiller; absorbé par ses recherches et ses classements incessants, il voulait simplement se couvrir à la hâte et tant bien que mal, pour se mettre en règle vis-à-vis de la société."

---

20 Alexandre Piedagnel, *Un bouquiniste parisien le Père Lécureux* (Paris, 1878), 18–20.

21 *Idem*, 22–23.

Le père Lécureux estimait son fonds à plus de 30 000 francs, mais ne trouva personne pour lui succéder lorsqu'il voulut se retirer. Après sa mort, les livres furent vendus en bloc, au poids, à un marchand de papier, pour dix centimes le kilo!

Á un niveau encore inférieur, on trouvait les étaleurs ou étalagistes, que nous appelons aujourd'hui "bouquinistes". Là encore, la tradition a retenu, pour le début du siècle, la figure de Nicolas Louis Achaintre. Né en 1771, mort en 1836, il avait été un des meilleurs latinistes de son temps, traducteur et annotateur de Juvénal et d'Horace. Il avait été professeur de latin, et correcteur d'imprimerie chez Didot. La rumeur attribuait sa déchéance qui l'avait conduit sur les quais à son goût pour la boisson. Dans les années 1810–1811, il tenait des boîtes de livres sur le quai Malaquais:

"[…] Tout en face du palais de l'Institut, à côté de la guérite de péage et sur le parapet même du quai, s'étalaient sans crainte du froid, bien qu'ils fussent pour la plupart dépouillés de leurs couvertures, d'innombrables volumes, ouverts au hasard et maintenus contre les lutineries du vent par une ficelle protectrice. Devant cette friperie littéraire, allait et venait, comme un soldat en faction, un vieillard long et maigre dont le costume s'harmonisait admirablement avec le déplorable accoutrement de ses livres. Le pauvre homme n'avait pour toute égide contre les rafales du nord qu'un mince carrick d'une nuance sans nom; et dont le frottement des années avait tellement dénudé le tissu qu'il en était devenu diaphane. Cette étroite enveloppe collait de toutes parts sur ses membres grêles et anguleux comme les draperies mouillées de l'école de David, alors à l'apogée de sa vogue. Du reste le propriétaire du triste vêtement en tirait tout le parti possible: il était parvenu à s'y cacher tout entier, de telle sorte que le collet, dressé par-dessus les oreilles, adhérait immédiatement à une casquette affaissée dans sa forme, avec une visière en abat-jour; et

ce qui laissait voir dans l'interstice de cette visière et des parois du collet ressemblait moins à une figure humaine qu'à la tranche quinticolore d'un code Napoléon, tant le froid avait bizarrement crispé et nuancé le visage du pauvre hère. […]"[22]

Comme le soulignait le bibliophile Jacob[23], l'étalagiste pouvait être aussi bien un jeune homme destiné à un avenir plus brillant dans la librairie, qu'un ancien libraire déchu:

"[…] Là enfin c'est un ancien libraire, un ancien homme de lettres, qui se consolent de leur décadence en vivant encore avec des livres, malgré le tort que les livres leur ont fait […] Pour les uns, l'étalage est le piédestal de la librairie; pour les autres, c'en est le dernier échelon. Beaucoup de libraires sont partis de là, beaucoup sont arrivés là."

Pour certains bibliophiles, ces bouquinistes des quais offraient davantage d'heureuses surprises que les libraires en boutiques plus traditionnels. Charles Asselineau dans *L'Enfer du bibliophile*, sous la rubrique "la damnation" donnait des exemples des pépites qu'on pouvait parfois trouver chez ces étaleurs:

"[…] Enfin voyez-le sur les quais, notre amateur. – Il sait et répète avec tout le monde depuis vingt ans qu'on ne trouve rien sur les quais. Mais il peut se faire qu'en dix ans une seule occasion se présente. Et cette occasion-là, il ne veut pas que d'autres que lui en profitent. Il a pour lui les autorités: Nodier et Parison, par exemple, qui trouvèrent sur les quais l'un

22 Henri Bruneel, 'Le bouquiniste. Anecdote bibliographique', *Le Bibliologue de la Belgique et du Nord de la France*, 3 (novembre–décembre 1839), 33–39, voir 35.

23 Paul Lacroix dit le Bibliophile Jacob, *Les amateurs de vieux livres* (Paris, 1994), 30–31. Texte publié pour la première fois en 1840 et 1841 dans le *Bulletin du bibliophile*.

le *Marot* d'Étienne Dolet, l'autre le *César* de Montaigne, payé à sa vente *quinze cent cinquante francs*, et qui lui avait coûté dix-huit sous!"[24]

Et il ajoutait en note:

"Nous aurions pu citer des témoins plus récents, par exemple M. de Fontaine de Resbecq, qui trouva, il y a quatre ou cinq ans, sur les quais, et paya *six sous*, un charmant exemplaire du *Pastissier françois*, Elzevir 1655, qui atteint quelquefois jusqu'à cinq cents francs dans les ventes. (Voy. l'intéressant petit ouvrage intitulé *Voyages littéraires sur les quais de Paris*, Durand 1857, in-18)."[25]

Le témoignage du comte Adolphe Charles Théodore de Fontaine de Resbecq (1813–1865), évoqué par Asselineau, est en effet précieux sur ce commerce des quais. Dans ses *Voyages littéraires sur les quais de la Seine*, il racontait à travers vingt-sept lettres adressées à un ami bibliophile de province ses visites quotidiennes aux bouquinistes des quais de la Seine, ses rencontres, ses découvertes, ses coups de cœur et ses achats. Pour lui, l'un des premiers mérites de ces bouquinistes était les heureuses surprises que pouvait recéler leurs boîtes, dont des raretés inattendues et insoupçonnées:

"[...] J'avouerai cependant que mon cœur bat plus fort devant les boîtes que dans une bibliothèque riche et bien distribuée, parce qu'en parcourant les unes j'ai la pensée, l'espérance de découvrir une rareté, tandis que dans les autres, si cette rareté s'y trouve, on la connaît, on en sait le prix [...]"[26]

Il s'extasiait ensuite sur la masse de volumes que ces soixante-huit bouquinistes parisiens alors répertoriés pouvaient proposer au chaland, soit, selon ses dires, autant qu'une grande bibliothèque publique du temps:

"[...] Terme moyen, les bouquinistes occupent quinze mètres avec douze à quinze boîtes; il y en a qui en ont plus. 68 fois 15 font 1020. Ces 1020 boîtes (d'un mètre chacune) étant rapprochées les unes des autres, donneraient donc une étendue de plus d'un kilomètre. D'après des renseignements que j'ai pris, une boîte peut contenir de 75 à 80 volumes. Ainsi, terme moyen, un bouquiniste expose de 1000 à 1200 volumes, ce qui fait pour les soixante-huit environ 70 000 volumes [...]"[27]

Il insistait enfin sur leur plus grande disponibilité envers les éventuels vendeurs, alors que les libraires patentés refusaient souvent de se déplacer s'ils jugeaient que les livres qu'on leur offrait n'avaient pas un intérêt de premier ordre:

"[...] Souvent le libraire auquel on vient offrir des livres ne se soucie pas de se déranger s'il n'y en a qu'un petit nombre. Il demande les titres; s'ils ne lui conviennent pas il ne veut même pas qu'on les lui porte. Le bouquiniste, au contraire, viendra volontiers chez vous; il achètera même cinq ou six volumes seulement, parce que, pour lui, tout est de vente; c'est ainsi que l'un d'eux a acheté d'une femme de ménage à laquelle un pauvre moribond l'avait donné avec d'autres livres, le Rommant de la Rose (sans lieu ni date), in-folio goth., fig. sur bois. [...]"[28]

L'ouvrage du comte de Resbecq constitue sans doute un des plus beaux hommages alors rendus à ces humbles étaleurs. Il témoigne également de

24 Charles Asselineau, *L'enfer du bibliophile* (Paris, 1860), 15–16.
25 *Idem.*
26 Adolphe de Fontaine de Resbecq, *Voyages littéraires sur les quais de Paris. Lettres à un bibliophile de province* (Paris, 1857), 20.
27 *Idem*, 36–37.
28 *Ibidem*, 112.

la passion de ces collectionneurs du temps, qui demeurent aujourd'hui bien méconnus. Seules des personnalités de l'importance de Lovenjoul[29] ou du duc d'Aumale[30], ou le cercle provincial des bibliophiles lyonnais[31] ont été véritablement étudiées. De la foule des amateurs plus anonymes, qui attendent toujours leur historien, on a cependant conservé le souvenir de quelques personnalités sortant de l'ordinaire, telle celle du bibliomane Antoine-Marie-Henry Boulard. Il était né le 5 septembre 1754 et décéda le 6 mai 1825 à Paris[32]. Noble, il exerça la profession de notaire, et fut maire du 11ème arrondissement de Paris en 1800. Il avait entrepris d'"opérer le sauvetage des vieux livres", en achetant 500 à 600 000 volumes qu'il entreposait dans six maisons différentes. A sa mort, il fallut trois ans de travail pour établir le catalogue de sa bibliothèque, en cinq volumes *in-octavo*. Les ventes de ses livres s'étalèrent de 1829 à 1833. La section des livres d'histoire et des voyages, qui constitue le tome 5 du catalogue, fut achetée en bloc par un autre bibliomane, l'anglais Sir Richard Heber. Comme le souligne son biographe Descuret:

"Après la vente de M. Boulard, les étalagistes de Paris furent tellement encombrés, que pendant plusieurs années les livres d'occasion ne se vendaient plus que la moitié de leur valeur habituelle."

Cet exemple nous amène à souligner un phénomène que nous avons déjà rencontré avec Lord Spencer et le libraire Edwards et qui attend encore d'être étudié et élucidé: celui de l'intervention de nombreux bibliophiles anglais sur le marché français, et de la vente en Angleterre de collections françaises, ceci dès les premiers temps de la Révolution. On pourrait ainsi, parmi d'autres, rappeler le cas de William Beckford (1760–1844) qui séjourna à Paris à partir de 1788, et bénéficia pour ses acquisitions bibliophiliques du concours du libraire Charles Chardin (1742–1826) lui-même collectionneur.

À ces diverses considérations, on ajoutera que le nombre de libraires de toutes catégories spécialisés dans l'antiquariat ne cessa d'augmenter, surtout après 1850, de même que celui des bibliophiles, ce qui entraina une raréfaction progressive des ouvrages mis sur le marché, et une augmentation des prix. Une des innovations qui a alors participé à cet accroissement des amateurs est l'introduction vers le milieu du siècle, par le libraire Pierre Janet, des catalogues à prix marqués.

Au terme de ces quelques lignes, force nous est de constater que le commerce du livre ancien dans la France du XIXe siècle est encore bien mal connu. Mis à part quelques grandes figures, les marchands demeurent des anonymes. On pourrait en dire à peu près autant des collectionneurs. Il a en tout cas été prospère fort longtemps, même s'il s'est quelque peu tassé après 1850. Il s'est surtout alimenté, tout au long du siècle des livres que la Révolution avait confisqués tant dans les maisons religieuses que chez les particuliers, et qui au hasard de multiples aléas ont échappé aux collections publiques. Ce marché français n'est pas demeuré qu'hexagonal, mais a eu des liens encore mystérieux, avec le marché anglais. Il y a là, parmi d'autres, et pour peu que la documentation s'y prête, des pistes à explorer.

29 Catherine Gaviglio-Faivre d'Arcier, *Charles de Spoelberch de Lovenjoul (1836–1907): biographie*, thèse de doctorat de l'université Paris IV, 2002. Publiée sous le titre le titre *Lovenjoul (1836–1907). Une vie, une collection* (Paris, 2007).

30 Denis Galindo, 'Le duc d'Aumale et la Société des bibliophiles lyonnais: érudition et mondanité au royaume des amis des livres', *Bulletin de la Société historique, archéologique et littéraire de Lyon*, 33 (2003), 173–98.

31 Denis Galindo, *Érudition et bibliophilie en France au XIXe siècle: la société des Bibliophiles lyonnais (1885–1914), cénacle d'amis des livres, société savante et association d'éditeurs amateurs en province sous la Troisième République*, thèse de doctorat sous la direction de Dominique Varry, université Lyon 2, 2008.

32 J.-B. F. Descuret, *Boulard bibliomane ou La médecine des passions* (Paris, 1991).

Bibliography

Charles Asselineau, *L'enfer du bibliophile* (Paris, 1860).

Frédéric Barbier, Sabine Juratic et Annick Mellerio, *Dictionnaire des imprimeurs, libraires et gens du livre à Paris 1701–1789: A-C* (Genève, 2007).

Louis Bréauté, *Catalogue de la bibliothèque de la ville de Louviers…* (Rouen, 1843).

Henri Bruneel, 'Le bouquiniste. Anecdote bibliographique', *Le Bibliologue de la Belgique et du Nord de la France*, 3 (novembre-décembre 1839), 33–39.

Jean-Baptiste Buzy, *Dom Maugérard, Histoire d'un bibliographe lorrain* (Châlons-sur-Marne, 1882).

Catalogue d'une partie des livres de la bibliothèque du cardinal de Loménie de Brienne… (Paris, an V [1797]).

Annie Charon, 'Un amateur russe, Doubrovski à la vente Loménie de Brienne', in *Le Siècle des Lumières. I. Espace culturel de l'Europe à l'époque de Catherine II*, éd. Serguëi Karp (Moscou, 2006), 213–30.

Guillaume de Bure l'aîné, *Catalogue des livres de la bibliothèque de M***. Faisant suite à l'Index librorum ab inventa typographia… dont la vente se fera le lundi 12 mars 1792… Tome III* (Paris, 1792).

Adolphe de Fontaine de Resbecq, *Voyages littéraires sur les quais de Paris. Lettres à un bibliophile de province* (Paris, 1857).

J.-B. F. Descuret, *Boulard bibliomane ou La médecine des passions* (Paris, 1991).

Denis Galindo, 'Le duc d'Aumale et la Société des bibliophiles lyonnais: érudition et mondanité au royaume des amis des livres', *Bulletin de la Société historique, archéologique et littéraire de Lyon*, 33 (2003), 173–98.

Denis Galindo, *Érudition et bibliophilie en France au XIXᵉ siècle: la société des Bibliophiles lyonnais (1885–1914), cénacle d'amis des livres, société savante et association d'éditeurs amateurs en province sous la Troisième République*, thèse de doctorat sous la direction de Dominique Varry, université Lyon 2, 2008.

Catherine Gaviglio-Faivre d'Arcier, *Charles de Spoelberch de Lovenjoul (1836–1907): biographie*, thèse de doctorat de l'université Paris IV, 2002. Publiée sous le titre le titre *Lovenjoul (1836–1907). Une vie, une collection* (Paris, 2007).

Catherine Gaviglio-Faivre d'Arcier, 'Les libraires d'ancien et d'occasion', in *Histoire de la librairie française*, éd. Patricia Sorel et Frédérique Leblanc (Paris, 2008), 128–39.

Catherine Gaviglio-Faivre d'Arcier, 'Portrait d'un libraire d'ancien: Techener', in *Histoire de la librairie française*, éd. Patricia Sorel et Frédérique Leblanc (Paris, 2008), 130.

Kristian Jensen, *Revolution and the Antiquarian Book: Reshaping the Past, 1780–1815* (Cambridge, 2011).

Paul Lacroix dit le Bibliophile Jacob, *Les amateurs de vieux livres* (Paris, 1994).

François-Xavier Laire, *Index librorum ab inventa typographia ad annum 1500… Prima [Secunda] pars*, 2 vols (Sens, 1791).

Notice de livres rares, la plupart imprimés dans le quinzième siècle, dont la vente se fera rue des deux écus, à l'hôtel saint-Antoine, le 16 janvier 1792, et jours suivans après midi (Paris, [1792]).

Alexandre Piedagnel, *Un bouquiniste parisien le Père Lécureux* (Paris, 1878).

Félix Ravaisson, *Rapports au ministre de l'Instruction publique sur les bibliothèques des départements de l'Ouest, suivis de pièces inédites* (1841).

Graziano Ruffini, *La chasse aux livres. Bibliografia e collezionismo nel viaggio di Étienne-Charles de Loménie de Brienne e François-Xavier Laire (1789–1790)* (Florence, 2012).

Jacques Joseph Techener et Léon Techener, *Histoire de la bibliophilie. Reliures. Recherches sur les bibliothèques des plus célèbres amateurs. Armorial des bibliophiles* (Paris, 1861–1864).

Dominique Varry, 'Vicissitudes et aléas des livres placés sous la main de la Nation', in *Révolution française et "vandalisme révolutionnaire". Actes du colloque international de Clermont-Ferrand (15–17 décembre 1988)*, Simone Bernard-Griffiths, Marie-Claude Chemin et Jean Ehrard éd. (Paris, 1992), 277–84.

Dominique Varry, 'Une ténébreuse affaire: les curieux agissements du citoyen Dambreville', *Bulletin du bibliophile*, 1 (1994), 82–102.

Dominique Varry, *"Sous la main de la Nation". Les bibliothèques de l'Eure confisquées sous la Révolution française* (Ferney-Voltaire, 2005).

Michel Vernus, *Une vie dans l'univers du livre. François-Xavier Laire (1738–1801)* (Lons le Saunier, 2001), 72–84.

The Book Market in Nineteenth-century Venice

The fall of the Venetian Republic in May 1797 had almost immediate consequences for the monastic libraries of the city. On 6 July, the new Municipality (called *Municipalità Provvisoria*, dependent on the French), to which the government of the Republic had transferred its power, promulgated a decree directed to the superiors and librarians of the fourteen monasteries that were considered to possess the best collections, prohibiting them from selling or exchanging their books, medals, globes, scientific instruments, and any other objects of value in their possession. Their patrimony was to remain intact, at the disposal of the revolutionary forces that had subdued Venice. Subsequently, many precious books were taken away from these libraries, by order of the Municipality, to be given to the French[1].

With the arrival of the Austrians, to whom Napoleon had ceded Venice in January 1798,

religious institutions (churches, convents, and confraternities known as *scuole*) and private property were respected. Yet, the economic situation of the patrician families continuously deteriorated with the diminishing of their revenues. The new political occupiers spared private libraries; yet the owners were constrained to sell for financial reasons. A bad omen for the world of books was the loss of the best part of the family library of the Foscarini of Carmini, which had belonged to the erudite doge Marco Foscarini (1696–1763): the manuscripts were sent to Vienna in 1800 to reduce the large debt that the Foscarini had accumulated towards the imperial government for unpaid taxes; the printed books were sold[2]. There followed next the dispersal of the valuable library of Francesco Pesaro (1739–1799), a prominent political figure, which was sold in England after his death by

---

1 At the end of the Venetian Republic, in Venice there were 41 monasteries. Al least seven monastic libraries were very important: see in this volume the essay by Dorit Raines, whom I would like to thank for her generous and friendly help in identifying the archival material mentioned in notes 20 and 52.

2 Tommaso Gar, 'I codici storici della collezione Foscarini conservata nella imperiale biblioteca di Vienna', *Archivio storico italiano*, 5 (1843), 281–476. The printed books catalogue bears the title: *Catalogo della biblioteca Foscarini ai Carmini vendibile a Venezia nell'anno 1800* [Venezia, 28 novembre 1799?].

Marino Zorzi • Formerly Director of the Biblioteca Nazionale Marciana of Venice. marinozorzi@gmail.com

How the Secularization of Religious Houses Transformed the Libraries of Europe, 16th–19th Centuries, ed. by Cristina Dondi, Dorit Raines, and † Richard Sharpe, BIB, 63 (Turnhout, 2022), pp. 371–388.
BREPOLS ☙ PUBLISHERS   DOI 10.1484/M.BIB-EB.5.128494

his brother Piero, who had moved to London, brokenhearted, after the fall of the Republic[3].

The booksellers continued their activity: already before the fall of the Venetian Republic there were hundreds of them in the city, according to the Spanish scholar Juan Andrés (1740–1817), who spoke enthusiastically of the Venetian book market in his *Cartas familiares*, published in 1790[4]. He had made excellent acquisitions, just as the British Consul, Joseph Smith (1682–1770), and Amadeus Schweyer (1727–1791), a merchant and Consul of Augsburg, had done some years before[5]. Now, under Austrian rule, the book market continued to prosper, as documented by the catalogues printed by booksellers, which describe both old and recent books. Following the decline of the printing industry, year by year many printers either left the city or continued to trade only as booksellers[6].

Some optimism about the future was still shared by a few: the priest and scholar Giannantonio Moschini (1773–1840), in the second volume of his work on Venetian literature, published in 1806, registered with satisfaction that some noblemen and citizens were still increasing their collections, moved by their love for knowledge; he named Antonio Correr and

3 On Pesaro and his library: Lorenza Perini, 'Per la biografia di Francesco Pesaro (1740–1799)', *Archivio Veneto*, 145 (1995), 65–98; Dorit Raines, 'Prodromi neo-classici. Anticomania, natura e l'idea del progresso nella cultura libraria settecentesca del patriziato veneziano', in *Committenti, mecenati e collezionisti di Canova*, I, eds Giuliana Ericani and Fernando Mazzocca, Studi, Istituto di Ricerca per gli studi su Canova e il Neoclassicismo, vol. 6 (Bassano del Grappa, 2008), 47–68. The catalogue bears the title: *Catalogo di una Libreria che si trova vendibile in Venezia nell'anno MDCCXCIX*, s.n.t.

4 *Cartas familiares del abate D. Juan Andrés a su hermano D. Carlos Andrés dándole noticia del viage que hizo a Venecia y otras ciudades de aquella republica en el año 1788, publicadas por el mismo Don Carlos*, vol. 3, In Madrid: por Don Antonio de Sancha, 1790, 200–14.

5 On the Smith collection in Venice: *Catalogo di libri raccolti dal fu Signor Giuseppe Smith e pulitamente legati*, Venezia: MDCCLXXI; Federico Montecuccoli degli Erri, 'Il console Smith. Notizie e documenti', *Ateneo Veneto*, 33 (1995), 111–81; Lotte Hellinga, 'The Bibliotheca Smithiana', in *Libraries within the Library. The Origins of the British Library's Printed Collections*, eds. Giles Mandelbrote and Barry Taylor (London, 2009), 261–79; on the Schweyer or Svajer collection: *Catalogo di Libreria posta in vendita in Venezia nell'anno MDCCXCIV*, [S.l., ma Venezia]: [s.n.], [1794]; Stefano Ferrari, 'Libri, storia e Altertumswissenschaft. Amadeo Svaier e gli eruditi danesi a Venezia sul finire del Settecento', *Analecta romana instituti danici*, 28 (2001), 135–52; idem, 'L'Accademia Roveretana degli Agiati e la cultura di lingua tedesca (1750–1795)', in *La cultura tedesca in Italia, 1750–1850*, edited by Alberto Destro e Paola Maria Filippi (Bologna, 1995), 217–76.

6 Some of the established printers became booksellers. See the catalogues of Antonio Zatta (1798): *Catalogo di libri latini, e italiani, che trovansi vendibili nel negozio di Antonio Zatta e figli libraj e stampatori di Venezia. Contenente tanto quelli di propria che di altre venete edizioni de' quali è fornito in maggior numero, ed inoltre i libri di forestiera antica e moderna impressione. Si aggiunge nel fine un elenco dei libri francesi, ed un altro copioso delle immagini e stampe in rame a bulino, carte geografiche, e musica vocale e strumentale fin'ora pubblicata, e il tutto a moneta veneta*, Stampato a Venezia da Antonio Zatta e figli, 1791; *Catalogo de' libri latini italiani e francesi che si trovano vendibili presso la ditta Antonio Zatta qu. Giacomo di Venezia, da esso stampati...*, Venezia, [tip. Zatta], 1806; of Pietro Zerletti (1798): *Catalogo di libri con prezzi, mancante di frontespizio, interfoliato, con annotazioni autografe di Francesco Milli; ad uso di Zerletti Pietro*, Venezia, [s.n.], 1798; of Giovanni Antonio Curti (1804): *Catalogo dei libri latini, italiani, francesi e di altre lingue straniere che trovansi vendibili da Gio. Antonio Curti q. Vito libraio in Merceria di S. Giuliano*, Venezia, [s.n.], 1804; of Simone Occhi (1806): *Catalogo di libri latini, ed italiani, che si trovano in maggior numero nel negozio di Simon Occhi*, Venezia, 1806; and of Francesco Andreola (1807): *Catalogo dei libri latini, italiani e francesi che si trovano vendibili da Francesco Andreola libraio e stampatore veneto in campo S. Angelo*, Venezia, [s.n.], 1807. Among the books sold by Curti, for instance, one notes the works of Carlo Gozzi in 12 volumes (48 *lire venete*, equivalent to about 24 *lire italiane*), the *Narrazione apologetica* by Pier Antonio Gratarol, a self-declared victim of the *Ancien Régime* (16 *lire venete*). A demand for such titles apparently existed. On the printing industry and its decline see Michele Gottardi, *L'Austria a Venezia* (Milano, 1993), 249–61 (for the booksellers, 255).

Lorenzo Antonio da Ponte (1758–1821). Moreover, according to him, a group of young patricians, among them Barbon Morosini, Girolamo Silvio Martinengo (1753–1834), Giannantonio Gambara, the Manins, were starting to collect new libraries for their own use. He also mentioned some scholarly booksellers, such as Giandomenico Coleti (1727–1798), Girolamo Mantovani, Leonardo Bassaglia, who helped these lovers of culture[7].

Two years later, in the fourth volume of his work, published in 1808, Moschini presented a desolate picture: "if libraries were a happy topic when I discussed them before, they now fill me with bitterness, as most of them have been dispersed"[8]. And in reality a cataclysm had struck the city: Napoleon, triumphant at Austerlitz, had annexed the Venetian region to his empire in December 1805. Venice and its territory had become a province of the Kingdom of Italy. The consequences were disastrous for the city. Immediately, in the spring of 1806, the devotional *scuole* (lay confraternities of a charitable and cultural character) were all suppressed and their properties passed to the *Demanio*, the State property office[9]. A little later the *scuole di mestiere*, trade guilds in which artisans and workers found mutual protection, were suppressed too: this meant unemployment and poverty for thousands[10]. Enormous sums were exacted from the city and its population[11].

The Church was also struck heavily. The parish churches were reduced in number from seventy to forty, then to thirty; the suppressed churches passed into the hands of the *Demanio*. On 28 July, 1806 thirty religious houses were suppressed, and their buildings, including their churches, and all their properties passed to the *Demanio*. In 1810 all monasteries and convents were suppressed in the entire Napoleonic empire, including the Kingdom of Italy and Venice[12]. The consequence was the use of the buildings for military or administrative purposes, which brought about major transformation, or even demolition, carried out in order to sell the building materials.

The Venetian churches and *scuole* were richly decorated with works of art. These were removed and distributed in accordance with French policy. The paintings considered not worthy of being exhibited in Brera (the national museum of the new Kingdom, created in Milan, on the model of the Louvre in Paris), were given to the Gallery of the Accademia, established in Venice in 1807, to which some works considered good but of secondary importance were reserved. The enormous quantity of other paintings was sold for derisory sums. Sculptures, altars, choirs, furniture were assigned to churches on the mainland or simply destroyed; reliquiaries were sold for their metal[13].

The books received, at least in theory, somewhat better treatment. A decree of the Kingdom of Italy, dated 10 June 1806, ordered the most careful preservation of the manuscripts and rare

7 Giannantonio Moschini, *Della letteratura veneziana nel secolo XVIII*, vol. II (Venezia, 1806), 69–74.

8 *Ibidem*, vol. IV (Venezia, 1808), 116–17.

9 Gastone Vio, *Le Scuole Piccole nella Venezia dei Dogi* (Costabissara/Vicenza, 2001); *1806. La Scuola Grande salvata*, ed. Maria Agnese Chiari Moretto Wiel (Venezia, 2006). Alvise Zorzi, in his *Venezia scomparsa* (Milano, 1972), 544–93, still essential for the history of the destructions in Venice after 1797, describes 51 buildings – altered or destroyed – which used to be the seats of *Scuole*.

10 Massimo Costantini, *L'albero della libertà economica. Il processo di scioglimento delle corporazioni veneziane* (Venezia, 1987).

11 In March 1806, the French government exacted immediately 1.500.000 *lire* from the new province, a little later five million, soon raised to seven: Evgenij Tarle, *Le*

Blocus continentale et le Royaume d'Italie (Paris, 1928), 191. Eleven "ducati gran feudi" were created in the former Venetian State, for the benefit of marshals and great officials of the Empire: the rent foreseen for the dukes was 60.000 or 100.000 *franchi*, equivalent to about the same sum in *lire*, at the expense of the population.

12 Bruno Bertoli, *La soppressione di monasteri e conventi a Venezia dal 1797 al 1810* (Venezia, 2002).

13 Alvise Zorzi, *Venezia scomparsa*, as note 9, 70–137.

books contained in the libraries of the suppressed convents in the Venetian provinces recently annexed. The powerful minister of finance, Giuseppe Prina, recommended in particular the preservation of books and ancient manuscripts in a letter to the director of the *Demanio* of Venice, dated 24 June 1806; the minister also ordered the director to take care of "pictures and sculptures of distinguished authors"[14], but this order was interpreted in a different way. The scholar Giovanni Rossi was appointed as commissary to choose the appropriate books from the suppressed monastic libraries, to be distributed among public libraries, academies, or schools. He worked diligently, visiting ten monasteries, where he selected a great number of books, 17,363 in all. Nor did he spare the National Library, as the Library of St Mark's was now called: the decree applied to its treasures too, some of which were to be handed over to the French. All the selected books were sent to Padua, deposited in the suppressed church of S. Anna, to be assigned to various institutions of the region. The distribution proved to make only slow progress: there were still books in S. Anna, unused but often damaged, almost half a century later, in 1862[15].

One can only imagine the fate of the 24,514 books considered "di scarto" (second rate). Some were gathered in the suppressed convent of Umiltà, where they were found in 1808, soaked by the rain, which was coming through an open window and the roof; a part of this collection was sold at auctions (for example a group of books of the monastery of S. Giorgio Maggiore were bought by two second-hand dealers), but many of the books were stolen. Venice became a paradise for profiteers of any kind, as Giovanni Rossi testifies. He bemoaned in particular the destruction of objects, pieces of furniture, relics, books, all hoarded together in suppressed churches and convents with no respect. But what could one expect, he writes, from people greedy for loot and lacking any principle of honesty?[16]

A second suppression occurred in 1810. A new Napoleonic decree issued in Compiègne on 25 April ordered the suppression of all remaining religious houses except for seminaries, cathedral and collegiate chapters, sisters of charity, and other female education institutions[17]. This turned out to be profitable for the Library of St Mark's, where the librarian Jacopo Morelli (1745–1819), a scholar highly esteemed even by the new government, was able to secure many precious books for the library. Others were distributed to various cultural institutions and schools[18]. The great library of the Dominicans on the Zattere, which contained the precious collection of the scholar and poet Apostolo Zeno (1668–1750), was left intact for the moment[19]. The remaining books were auctioned off. In January 1813 there took place no fewer than six auction sales for the books of the monasteries of S. Mattia in Murano, S. Bonaventura, the Discalced Carmelites, the Servite Friars, the Capuchins at the Redentore, and S. Sebastiano: the number of volumes to be

14 "... pitture e sculture di insigni autori". Vincenzo Trombetta, *L'editoria a Napoli nel decennio francese* (Milano, 2011), 20, gives the text of the decree. For the difference between theory and practice see A. Zorzi, *Venezia scomparsa*, as note 9, 106.

15 See the essays by Dorit Raines and by Dondi-Prosdocimi-Raines in this book.

16 Venezia, Biblioteca Nazionale Marciana, Cod. It. VII, 614 (= 9220), Giovanni Rossi, *Leggi e costumi dei Veneziani*, vol. XIV, cc. 161–62; cf. Marino Zorzi, *La Libreria di San Marco. Libri, lettori, società nella Venezia dei Dogi* (Milano, 1987), 332. Rossi also names some of the worst profiteers, such as the former canon Luigi Bossi, who made a great career under the Kingdom of Italy.

17 Pietro La Cute, 'Le vicende delle biblioteche monastiche veneziane dopo la soppressione napoleonica', *Rivista di Venezia*, A. VIII, no. 10 (October 1929), 617.

18 See the essay by Dorit Raines in this volume.

19 Francesca Cavazzana Romanelli – Stefania Rossi Minutelli, 'Archivi e biblioteche', in *Storia di Venezia*, vol. VIII, *L'Ottocento*, eds Mario Isnenghi and Stuart Woolf (Roma, 2002), II, 1081–1122 (see 1097–1101).

sold daily varied between three and six thousand: a total of 21,738 volumes were to be sold with an accumulated valuation of 7,471 lire. The auctions were to take place in the convents themselves, but these were probably already deserted; so instead of being auctioned the whole mass of books was sold to G. B. Ferro, for 6,900 lire[20].

In the autumn it was the turn of the Franciscans of S. Maria Gloriosa (known simply as the Frari) (3,500 volumes, auctioned on 27 October 1810), the Somaschi of S. Maria della Salute (14,000 volumes, on 28 October), the Camaldolese of S. Clemente (3,200 volumes, on 29 October). The total valuation had been 12,178 lire, but the auction was deserted. Then followed an offer by Pietro Marini of 4,580 lire for the whole lot, then a second offer of 4,809 lire. The director of the *Demanio* wrote to the Prefect of Monte Napoleone in Milan (responsible for the administration of the public debt of the Kingdom of Italy), proposing to refuse the offer, judging it too low. Eventually two merchants made more substantial offers, G. B. Toscan and Antonio Vianello; the last eventually concluded the purchase for 13,000 lire[21].

To gain an idea of the nature of these sales let us look at the catalogue of an earlier auction, held on 15 November 1809. It probably involved books coming from private libraries, for it lacked any indication of their provenance: the catalogue has 268 pages, 3,820 items; it includes 719 books in Latin, 543 in Italian, 2,558 in various other languages, French, English, German, even Dutch. The auction was to be held from twelve o'clock to three p.m.: three hours for the whole mass of books. Apparently only substantial bidders could take part, invited to bid for big lots or for

the whole, which inevitably led to a reduction in price[22].

In order to understand the meaning of the sums offered and paid for the books at auction, a useful instrument of comparison is provided by the salaries of civil servants. Clerks in charge of records and similar minor officers were paid 2,000 lire a year; in the higher positions salaries ranged from 2,700 to 4,500 lire; university professors could earn 6,000 lire; while a director general might receive 9,000 lire. In 1810 one pound of flour cost 25 cents, of beef 50, of oil 96, of wine 80[23]. Even if we consider that the lots included books of all kinds, old and modern, rare and common, the prices obtained seem very low: on average less than half a lira per book. But even so low, they were much higher than those of works of art. The fate of these was worse by comparison with that of books: paintings and sculptures were destroyed in great number, and a painting would often fetch only the price of a printed book or less: in July 1811, 1,305 paintings were sold for 791 lire; in September others were given up in a single lot; and on 18 March 1814 a group of works by Paris Bordon, Jacopo Bassano, Palma il Giovane, and others, was sold for 43 lire. These are only a few examples out of many that are documented[24]. We can suppose that the fashion of the times influenced the prices: works of art from the Middle Ages, the baroque, the eighteenth

20 Venezia, Archivio di Stato, *Direzione del Demanio*, 1806–1813, b. 328, fasc.I. 1/9. See also A. Zorzi, *Venezia scomparsa*, as note 9, 122.

21 Venezia, Archivio di Stato, *Direzione del Demanio*, 1806–1813, b. 328, fasc.I. 1/9.

22 The catalogue is today in Biblioteca Nazionale Marciana in Venice with shelfmark 220 D 200: *Catalogo di libri latini, italiani e francesi che si vendono al pubblico incanto in Venezia… il giorno 15 novembre 1809*, [S.n.t.].

23 On salaries, Ugo Tucci, 'Stipendi e pensioni dei pubblici impiegati nel Regno lombardo-veneto dal 1824 al 1866', *Archivio economico dell'unificazione italiana*, 10 (1960), fasc. 4; Marino Berengo, *Intellettuali e librai nella Milano della Restaurazione* (Torino, 1980), 375–76. For the prices of goods, Bartolomeo Cecchetti, 'Saggio sui prezzi delle vettovaglie e altre merci a Venezia', *Atti dell'Istituto Veneto di Scienze, Lettere ed Arti*, ser. IV, vol. 3 (1874), 1465–1492.

24 A. Zorzi, *Venezia scomparsa*, as note 9, 119–24.

century were disregarded or utterly despised, because they did not meet the modern taste for neoclassicism. The same criteria were applied in architecture: even the great sixteenth-century architect Jacopo Sansovino (1486–1570) was now considered to be "incorretto". The church of S. Geminiano, built by him at the opposite end of the Piazza from the church of St Mark, was demolished along with dozens of other medieval, Renaissance, and baroque buildings, while sculptures and monuments were also destroyed, leaving intellectuals of the time utterly indifferent. For the same reasons, nobody was interested in buying furniture or works of art: neither collectors nor dealers were to be found, either in Milan or abroad. The government's haste to have the buildings emptied further contributed to the destruction: all the magnificent furniture of the monastic libraries was broken up and sold as wood[25]. One exception was the Benedictine library of S. Giorgio Maggiore, given to be used by the Liceo of S. Caterina, now Liceo Foscarini, and restored in its original place by Count Vittorio Cini in 1950 (although some statues are missing).

The book market was over-populated with sellers of every kind. The monasteries could not sell, but single monks sometimes tried to do so, when they realised the destiny that awaited them and their brethren: to be sent to their former family homes, poor and humiliated. When Giovanni Rossi made his visits to the convents after the first suppression, he found many books missing,

either taken by the French, stolen, or sold. The Somaschi order, already experiencing a first alienation of books from the library in 1797, and foreseeing the worst – their convent would actually be suppressed in 1810 – sold some of their books to the bookseller Adolfo Cesare. The agreement was that the bookseller could take 3,000 books of his own choosing, paying them a ducat per book, about six Italian lire. Many of the remaining books were sold by the government after the suppression: as we have seen, 14,000 volumes were auctioned in 1813; others ended up in the hands of fishmongers and sellers of pepper, to be used as wrapping paper, according to the diaries of the great scholar Emmanuele Antonio Cicogna (1789–1868)[26]. Another order which obtained the permission of their superiors to sell some books and prints, in order to survive, having been deprived of all their properties, were the Camaldolese of S. Michele in Murano, whose library was particularly rich in medieval manuscripts[27].

A great part of the patricians and of the *cittadini originari*, the former ruling class of the Republic, sold everything: paintings, sculptures, books, and subsequently their houses and landed property. The patricians in possession of a modest fortune were the worst affected, having also lost their employment. Those who still had some fortune left were obliged to abandon the city and to live in their estates in the countryside in order to survive. Their Venetian homes, including the art and book collections, were then left abandoned, because they were not able to pay

---

25 A moving description of the demolition of the mediaeval furniture of the library of S. Giobbe is given by Giovanni Rossi, *Leggi e costumi*, as note 16, 152–53. The magnificent furniture of the library of SS. Giovanni e Paolo, adorned with wooden statues of the XVII century, was destroyed and sold as "ammasso di legname", a heap of wood, in 1807, when the Director of the *Demanio* ordered the room to be cleared "sul momento", immediately. E. A. Cicogna, in his *Saggio di bibliografia veneziana* (Venezia, 1847), 693, writes that an Englishman, "signor Brown", bought some of the ornaments. Their present whereabouts are unknown.

26 The *Diario* of Emmanuele Antonio Cicogna is today in Venezia, Biblioteca del Civico Museo Correr, in four volumes. It is the main source for the history of books in the first half of the nineteenth century; for our research particularly relevant are the first volume: MCC, Cod. Cicogna 2844 (from 1 January 1810 to 4 March 1816), and the second one: MCC, Cod. Cicogna 2845 (from 5 March 1816 to 5 October 1835).

27 Lucia Merolla, *La biblioteca di San Michele di Murano all'epoca dell'abate G. B. Mittarelli. I codici ritrovati* (Manziana / Roma, 2010), 129.

the high taxes imposed on them. Many sold even their mainland estates, bought in general by the local bourgeoisie or by the managers of the farms. In Venice at least eighty *palazzi* were sold by their old owners and demolished by the buyers, usually speculators or building contractors, in order to obtain bricks, stones, and other building materials[28].

A similar fate lay ahead for private family archives: every patrician family had one, to be used in the course of their political or administrative activity; their old purpose being no longer relevant, these papers became obsolete and they were often sold simply as paper, paid for by weight. Cicogna recorded seeing a valuable manuscript from the Da Ponte archive in the hands of a seller of cheese and butter, and documents concerning the Arsenal in a grocer shop[29]. The same happened, much later, in 1865, with the archive of the family Duodo of S. Maria Zobenigo[30]. All in all, in 1847 the number of patrician archives still surviving was only nineteen[31]: a paltry few

when compared with the number of 173 noble families existing in 1797.

When the Austrians returned in 1814, they found the city in a very poor state, after a siege of six months, a situation that lasted at least until 1830[32]. Private libraries continued to disappear. The library of the Venier family at the Gesuiti was sold to a Paduan bookseller in 1817. The young Paduan student Antonio Rosmini, who would make his name as a Catholic philosopher, obtained from his parents in Rovereto the money to rescue the library from the bookseller who was totally indifferent to the extraordinary historical interest of the collection. The rather high sum paid by Rosmini was 800 fiorini, equivalent to 2,400 lire, but he was convinced, and rightly so, that he had made a magnificent acquisition[33]. The Nani family library was sold in the years 1820–1821, and the same happened to the famous museum of antiquities collected by the family. The Tiepolo family, heirs of the Nani, did the same with its library. The Persico collection of coins and medals was sold to a merchant from Trieste in 1820[34].

The market was thus continually provided with more and more collections put up for sale. The Austrian empire was poor and had no money to devote to culture: libraries and collections of art offered for sale to the government were regularly refused, sometimes after long and diligent proceedings. Some acquisitions were made by the Library of St Mark's at modest prices using its endowment for buying modern

28 Giuseppe Gullino, 'Economia e finanza dallo scorcio della Repubblica all'età napoleonica', in *Le metamorfosi di Venezia. Da capitale di Stato a città del mondo* (Firenze, 2001), 113–27; Renzo Derosas, 'Aspetti economici della crisi del patriziato veneziano tra fine Settecento e primo Ottocento', in *Venezia nell' Ottocento*, ed. Massimo Costantini (Mantova, 1991), 11–61. 80 palaces were destroyed in Venice, according to Antonio Lamberti, *Memorie degli ultimi cinquant'anni della Repubblica di Venezia*, a manuscript in Biblioteca Nazionale Marciana, Cod. marc. It. VII, 1454 (= 9345), c. 7r (now edited: *Memorie degli ultimi cinquant'anni della Repubblica di Venezia*, eds Manlio Pastore Stocchi and Marino Zorzi (Venezia 2019), note 5). A. Zorzi, *Venezia scomparsa*, as note 9, 440–75, enumerates 59 of them. The destructions extended beyond Venice to the whole Venetian State.

29 Marino Zorzi, 'Le biblioteche a Venezia nel secondo Settecento', *Miscellanea Marciana*, 1 (1986), 253–324, at 275.

30 Rinaldo Fulin, *E. A. Cicogna: festa letteraria nel R. Liceo Marco Polo* (Venezia, 1873), 17–18.

31 Giuseppe Cadorin, 'Archivi pubblici e privati', in *Venezia e le sue lagune*, vol. II, parte II (Venezia, 1847), 3–75, at 39–52.

32 The Austrians found a skinned carcass, "uno spolpato carcame", as A. Lamberti, as note 28, writes, 4 (same page of the printed edition). The situation improved when Venice became a free port. Adolfo Bernardello, *Venezia nel Regno Lombardo-Veneto. Un caso atipico (1815–1866)* (Milano 2015), 223–80.

33 Antonio Rosmini, *Epistolario* (Casale, 1887), vol. I, 270–76; Berengo, *Intellettuali e librai*, as note 23, 119.

34 Marino Zorzi, 'La gestione del patrimonio librario', in *Venezia e l'Austria*, eds Gino Benzoni and Gaetano Cozzi (Venezia, 1999), 265–90.

books as requested by scholars: for example, in 1821 a print of the magnificent bird's eye view of Venice, a woodcut made in 1500 by Jacopo de' Barbari, was bought for 15 lire[35].

The book market was also choked with contemporary publications from what was left of the Venetian printing industry, yet the prices of these books were high in comparison with those of old books: modern books usually cost two or three *lire*[36]. The most expensive item in the catalogue of one of the biggest Venetian booksellers, Adolfo Cesare, issued in 1812, was the *Encylopédie méthodique*, printed in 154 volumes in Padua: 616 lire. With such a sum one could buy hundreds of old paintings or entire collections of old books. Printers then tried to accommodate the problem by offering new books for sale in parts. The *Inscrizioni Veneziane* by Emmanuele Antonio Cicogna came out in *fascicoli*, at a price of 20 cents for one *foglio* of eight pages[37]. Not much, but more than the cost of old books sold in auctions. For recent books there was apparently still demand from scholars such as schoolteachers and university professors. Naturally the magnificent illustrated editions issued in the course of the eighteenth century, frequently financed by patrician capitalists, did not appear any longer.

A question which deserves an answer is the identity of the buyers of old books, leaving out shopkeepers who bought entire archives in order to use documents as wrapping material. One can identify two distinct groups. The first is a group of professional dealers based in Venice, who had

available resources. They acted as first buyers, aiming to sell on to collectors[38]. The second group includes dealers based in other cities. Let us try to see who these dealers were and also to form a profile of who the final buyers were.

During the Napoleonic period, the "prince" of Venetian book-dealers was clearly Adolfo Cesare, already mentioned. He could afford to buy the best libraries. In 1810 he bought from two Jewish dealers the large library that Giacomo Collalto had collected in his palazzo at S. Stin. The number of books, mainly bound in vellum, amounted to 80,000, perhaps even to 150,000, "mole immensa di libri" ("enormous number of books"), commented Cicogna[39]. The first dealers had paid for the whole lot, in August 1810, 8,000 ducats (about 25,000 lire); Cesare paid 52,000 lire, which means 50 or 60 cents per book, or even less. Cicogna reports that Cesare kept the best for himself. He divided the remaining books into three groups and sold them to other booksellers: for the books in 12° and in 8° he asked one *lira veneta*, for those in 4° two *lire*, and for the *books in folio*, four *lire*.

In the same year 1810 Cesare made another important acquisition, the Pisani library at S. Vidal, one of the largest private libraries, which had been open to scholars three days a week and run by expert librarians such as the priest Antonio Bonicelli[40]. Cesare paid 22,000 lire for the five thousand choice books and the

---

35 Archivio della Biblioteca Marciana, year 1821.

36 Berengo, *Intellettuali e librai*, as note 23, 142, for similar prices in Milan.

37 Subscribers were vital to the economic continuity and survival of renowned works of erudition. For the *Inscrizioni* by Cicogna the "associati" were initially 271 in 1822, but in 1842 their number dwindled to 120: Stefania Rossi Minutelli, 'Emmanuele Antonio Cicogna e l'*Opera delle Inscrizioni Veneziane*', *Miscellanea Marciana*, 15 (2009), 113–22.

38 Ugo Tucci, 'Leopold von Ranke e il mercato antiquario veneziano di manoscritti', *Quellen und Forschungen aus Italienischen Archiven und Bibliotheken*, 67 (1987), 282–310, offers an extensive description of the Venetian market.

39 E. A. Cicogna, *Diario*, BMCV, Cod. 2845, 279. While Cicogna estimated the number of books to be 150.000, Giovanni Rossi was of a different opinion: he thought they amounted to 80.000; Rossi, *Leggi e costumi*, as note 16, vol. XIV, c. 138.

40 On the library: Zorzi, *La Libreria*, as note 16, 342–43; Dorit Raines, *La famiglia Manin e la cultura libraria nel Settecento fra Friuli e Venezia* (Udine, 1997), 31–35, 52.

magnificent furniture. In the same year he bought the library of Sebastiano Zeno at the Gesuiti. In 1811 he bought 500 Aldine editions and other rare books from the nobleman Zuanne Balbi and the whole of the Mocenigo family library at S. Stae. In the same period he acquired the library formed sometime before by Lorenzo Antonio Da Ponte for his son and subsequently resold it to the Paduan scholar Daniele Francesconi. Another important library, that of Giuseppe Gradenigo, the last secretary of the Council of Ten, ended up in his hands[41].

Cesare had published his first catalogue of books for sale in January 1798, describing himself as "libraio veneto a S. Bartolammeo all'insegna dell'Americano"; in 1804 another catalogue came out, in which he called himself "librajo in Merceria dell'Orologio": a sign he had moved to a more prestigious location[42]. Another catalogue, probably of 1810, comprising 64 pages, contains only editions from the fifteenth century[43].

In 1812 he published another catalogue of 2,000 choice printed books: a manuscript note added to it says that these books came from the library of Matteo Luigi Canonici (1727–1805), a famous Jesuit collector, which had been bought by Cesare in 1810. This catalogue, of 174 pages, was itself on sale for 50 cents. The prices asked for the books in the catalogue seem rather high when compared with those for paintings. Many cost less than 5 lire, but there are some highly expensive items, such as the *Encylopédie méthodique* or the *Biblia polyglotta*, London 1657 – bibles were Canonici's main specialization as collector – which cost as much as 300 lire. Yet many other bibles belonging to Canonici do not figure in the catalogue as they had already been sold[44].

Another catalogue produced by Cesare, though lacking indications leading to him except for a manuscript note, "Cesare" in the Marciana copy, describes 5,000 books in Latin, Italian, and French. At the end of the catalogue there is a list of "Edizioni del secolo XV per ordine cronologico", 31 pages, describing 450 incunabula, starting with the works of St Cyprian, printed by Vindelin from Speyer in 1471, at the price of 150 lire. Others are much less expensive: Iacobus Philippus Foresti, *Supplementum Chronicarum*, Venice: Bernardino Benalio, 1486, was priced at 10 *lire*; the same price was asked for an edition of Dante, 1497, with Landino's commentary; but a mere 2 lire would buy a copy of the *Missale Ordinis Predicatorum* from 1497[45].

Adolfo Cesare, a cunning dealer according to Cicogna, was the first in this field; he was

---

41 For Adolfo Cesare and his acquisitions, Cicogna's *Diario* is the main source: E. A. Cicogna, *Diario*, BMCV, Cod. 2845, 4560 and passim. For the Da Ponte library in particular see Tucci, 'Leopold von Ranke', as note 38, 300–02. Ranke bought from Francesconi many manuscripts which are now at Syracuse University.

42 The first two catalogues (1798 and 1804) were identified by Dorit Raines. The first can be consulted in the Biblioteca Estense in Modena and in other libraries, the second in the Biblioteca Cameriniana at Piazzola sul Brenta, near Padua.

43 *Catalogo cronologico di edizioni del secolo 15. che si trovano vendibili appresso Adolfo Cesare librajo in Venezia*, [S.l.], [s.n.], [1810]. The catalogue of 1810 is in the Marciana Library (Misc. D 426).

44 *Catalogo di libri antichi e moderni di varie materie e in diverse lingue che trovansi vendibili in pochi esemplari nel negozio di Adolfo Cesare.* [*Raccolta Canonici*] (Venezia, stamp. Molinari, 1812). This catalogue is in the Marciana Library (227 D 238). Other prices of items included in this last catalogue: Graevius, in 33 vol., 1697, 300 *lire*; S. Gregorius Turonensis, *Opera*, 1699, 300 *lire*; *Scriptores Rerum Italicarum*, L. A. Muratori ed., 25 volumes, Milano 1723, 300 *lire*; S. Johannes Chrisostomus, 13 volumes, Monfaucon ed., Paris 1718, 200 *lire*: *Galleria* del marchese Vincenzo Giustiniani, 180 *lire*; Galland, *Bibliotheca*, Venezia 1781, 100 *lire*.

45 This catalogue is also in Biblioteca Marciana (192 C 249). Other prices: Dante, Zatta, Venezia, 1757: 44 *lire*; Apocalisse di S. Giovanni s.d., 200 *lire*. Dorit Raines kindly informs me that a small catalogue of "libri greci e latini vendibili da Adolfo Cesare" is preserved in Paris, Bibliothèque Nationale, Archives Modernes, carton 275, where 152 incunabula are listed, with their prices. In the same *carton* she found another list of 23 rare books "di ottima conservazione e pulitamente legati".

also an educated man, in whose shop scholars met frequently. Other booksellers were equally well established and esteemed, like Vincenzo Bianconi (+1817), "one of the few honest men in his profession", Giuseppe Battagia, Giuseppe Orlandelli (+1836), Antonio Canciani, the printers Nicolò Coleti (+1806) and Domenico Occhi (+after 1806)[46]. Many kept their shops in the Merceria near the Piazza of St Mark's or nearby, in accordance with a custom that dated back to the invention of printing. In a much less prestigious situation were others, those who just kept a bookseller's table in the *campi*, for example, or the pedlars: Tomaso Locatelli testified to having heard them offer in a loud voice (or singing their special song) the stories of Chiarina and Tamante[47], Allerame and Adellasia[48], Bertoldo, Bertoldino and Cacasenno[49], long enjoyed by uneducated people[50].

There were also a number of priests or former monks active in the book trade, some of them with the purpose of recovering books that had belonged to their suppressed convent, others for less noble reasons. To the first category surely

belonged Giacinto Placido Zurla (1769–1834), an illustrious scholar, a former monk at S. Michele in Murano and a future Cardinal, and perhaps also Giovanni Batttista Sanfermo, interested in buying what remained of the library of the Theatines. Unclear is the role of Don Giovanni Battista Biasiutti and Don Carlo Alessandri, who bought books coming from the suppressed Dominican friary of SS. Giovanni e Paolo, which were deposited in the suppressed Redmptorist convent known as "della Fava", where they could examine them[51].

The booksellers' community was populated by foreigners as well. The Milanese Carlo Salvi, who visited the library of S. Michele in Murano in 1806, finding it closed, and also the Armenian monastery of S. Lazzaro (the only one not depending on the *Demanio*, being subject to the Sultan of Constantinople, and therefore spared). Salvi had commercial relationships with the local booksellers Silvestro Gnoato and Adolfo Cesare. Also active was Giacomo Fuchs, partner of the company Molini, Landi & Co., probably Florentine, which had a shop in Bocca di Piazza[52].

This commercial activity required a final destination, collectors, interested in keeping the books for their use or pleasure, or even as

---

46 E. A. Cicogna, *Diario*, BMCV, Cod. 2845, 4560 (judgment on Cesare), 4451–52 on the others; see Zorzi, *La Libreria*, as note 16, 333–34, 519. An inquiry made by the Austrian government in 1815 (Marco Callegari, *L'industria del libro a Venezia durante la Restaurazione, 1815–1848* (Firenze, 2016), 104–06) declares that there were 28 bookshops in Venice: the richest were Giovanni Antonio and Nicolò Coleti, whose store was valued 150.000 *lire*, Antonio Graziosi (same value), Bettinelli, Gnoato and Adofo Cesare (all of them 100.000). There were 20 pedlars.

47 *Canzonetta di due fedelissimi amanti Chiarina e Tamante*, probably in the edition printed in Lucca by Francesco Baroni in the beginning of the nineteenth century.

48 *Nova istoria di Allerame e' Adellasia figlia di Ottone Imperatore*, or *Bellissima istoria di Allerame e' Adellasia figlia di Ottone Imperatore*, printed in various editions.

49 Three popular stories: *Le sottilissime astutie di Bertoldo*, *Le piacevoli et ridicolose simplicità di Bertoldino* and *Novella di Cacasenno, figliuolo del semplice Bertoldino*.

50 Tommaso Locatelli, *Appendice della Gazzetta di Venezia*, I (Venezia, 1837), 32.

51 Venezia, Archivio di Stato, *Direzione del Demanio*, 1806–1813, b. 328, fasc. "Vendite libri".

52 Letter dated 20 July 1806, of "Delegato di Polizia della Provincia di Venezia" addressed to "Sig. Cerosa direttore del Demanio del Dipartimento dell'Adriatico". Venezia, Archivio di Stato, *Direzione del Demanio*, 1806–1813, b. 328. The letter says also that Salvi is negotiating through Gnoato the acquisition of a portion of the library "del fu Auditore di Rota Priuli" and is also in contact with Adolfo Cesare in order to buy some manuscripts and books, belonging to a "commendator Pate", which had been transported from Udine. It is also stated that Salvi had bought two hundred books in private ownership, which were "in casa Mocenigo". Perhaps the "abbot" Celotti, close to the Mocenigo family, had been the mediator. The Priuli mentioned above was Mons. Antonio Marin 3° Priuli, born 20 June 1763, abbot of S. Gallo.

an investment. One of them, well regarded, was Gaetano Melzi, of a great Milanese family, who acquired rare books and compiled bibliographies, widely used and appreciated. He came to Venice from Milan in 1806 and tried to visit the monastery of S. Michele, together with the bookseller Salvi, hoping to be able to make good acquisitions. He also visited S. Lazzaro[53]. Another famous collector was the Florentine gentleman Angelo d'Elci, who even dared to invite the librarian Morelli to sell him books from the Library of St Mark's[54]. Antonio Rosmini, who bought the library of the Venier family, advised the bishop of Padua to buy the classical books he needed in Venice, where the prices were very favourable[55].

Probably many other citizens of the Kingdom of Italy and afterwards of the Kingdom of Lombardo-Veneto acted in the same manner. One of those was Luigi Celotti, a priest (*abate*, "abbot", as secular priests were called, from the French *abbé*, without any reference to a monastic role) who came from Cordignano, a village near Ceneda on the Venetian mainland, where the noble Venetian family Mocenigo possessed a villa and a big estate. A connoisseur, he bought some of the Mocenigo books and made important acquisitions from other noble families and from convents[56]. Another *abate*, Tommaso De Luca, a man of refined taste, expert in books, native of Belluno, formed his collection in Venice; it

was so overwhelming that even the Viceroy of Lombardo-Veneto, Archduke Rainer, expressed the wish to visit it[57]. Both Celotti and De Luca were not rich, but they had a sufficient income to be able to benefit from the state of the Venetian book market. They and others like them occupied an intermediate position between collectors and dealers: they bought, but they also sold or exchanged, often making a considerable gain. In general, their commercial interests prevailed over the connoisseurship. Other priests, as we have said, did much the same with paintings.

The British were reputed to be great buyers. Once the state of war between Britain and the French empire had come to an end with the fall of Napoleon, they started to come to Venice, some of them in order to buy books. One manuscript from the monastery of S. Michele found its way to Oxford in 1817; in 1818 the duke of Hamilton bought eight manuscripts from the same convent; in 1825 the British Museum bought another one[58]. In 1817 a gentleman called by De Luca Lord Gumbleton (the title does not appear to be correct, but there was a rich and respected family of this name), who had seen the printed catalogue of the library of the *abate*, initiated a negotiation, offering the fabulous sum of 300,000 fiorini[59]. Only one fifth of the library of De Luca was sold, for 80,000 fiorini, and sent to England, with the help of abbot Celotti, in 1824. These examples demonstrate once again the attention that British enthusiasts devoted to the Venetian market.

In the same year 1817, a famous collection ended up in England. Another *abate*, the former

---

53 The visits of Melzi to the monastery of S. Lazzaro are mentioned in the aforesaid letter. On him, see Alessia Giachery, *Jacopo Morelli e la repubblica delle lettere attraverso la sua corrispondenza (1768–1819)* (Venezia, 2012), 132.

54 Tucci, 'Leopold von Ranke', as note 38, 297.

55 Berengo, *Intellettuali e librai*, as note 23, 119. Stefano Ferrari and Giorgio Marini, *Le collezioni di stampe e di libri di Ambrogio Rosmini (1741–1818)* (Rovereto, 1997).

56 On Celotti, Anne-Marie Eze, 'Abbé Celotti and the provenance of Antonello da Messina's "The condottiere" and Antonio de Solario's "Virgin and Child with St John"', *The Burlington Magazine* (October 2009), 673–77.

57 On De Luca, Lucia Cavalet, 'Un prete bibliofilo: Don Tommaso De Luca (1752–1829)', *Miscellanea Marciana*, 17 (2002), 181–92.

58 Merolla, *La biblioteca di S. Michele*, as note 27, 36.

59 L. Cavalet, 'Un prete bibliofilo', as note 57, 186. The transaction was interrupted by Gumbleton's death. The sons were not interested. The *fiorino* was a conventional currency not used in practice, only for reckoning, and corresponded in 1815 to 2,6 Italian lire.

Jesuit Matteo Luigi Canonici, had patiently built up a very valuable library, put together mainly in Venice, and containing up to 3,550 manuscripts and 5,000 early printed editions; mention has already been made of his taste for rare bibles. When he died in 1805, the library passed on to his brother, then to his nephews, Giovanni Perissinotti and Girolamo Cardina. The collection was so important that the librarian of the Library of St Mark's, Jacopo Morelli, tried to obtain funds from the Napoleonic prefect of the region, Marco Serbelloni, in order to acquire it. He made a first valuation at 13,276 *zecchini* (about 46,000 ducats or 185,000 lire), then a second at 12,500, then a third at 11,000, hoping to entice the government by dropping the price: but the Napoleonic kingdom had other things to think about and did not reply. Morelli reported in a note about rumours concerning an offer of 50,000 *zecchini* from an Englishman, although he did not believe it: it looked exaggerated. Apparently British collectors were active already in the Napoleonic period, certainly through booksellers, and they had a reputation as lavish spenders.

Meanwhile, Cardina, who had inherited the collection of bibles and part of the other printed books, sold them to Adolfo Cesare. Perissinotti, to whom the manuscripts and the other part of the printed books had gone, waited for better times. In 1817, under the Austrian government, an Englishman – Cicogna reported in his *Diary* – came to see him, examined the manuscripts carefully, and asked to buy two of them. Perissinotti, determined not to split up the collection, said he wished to sell the whole or nothing; the Englishman then asked for the sum he wanted, and the answer was 6,000 *louis* (about 270,000 lire). After some months the University of Oxford requested a detailed catalogue, through the British consul; Anton Giovanni Bonicelli, a well-known librarian, drew it up very diligently. As soon as the consul had the catalogue in his hands, he sent it to England, having ordered his servants to lock the doors and windows of the library. In August 1817 there came the offer, 5,500 *louis*. Perissinotti immediately accepted. The librarian of St Mark's, by now Pietro Bettio, tried to persuade the government to intervene, but in vain. The books safely arrived in Oxford[60].

Perissinotti, however, still kept for himself 829 manuscripts particularly relevant to Venetian history, but in 1831 he decided to sell them. A decree of the government dated 10 February 1819, n. 3926, forbade any selling of antiquities abroad without authorization, which could be gained by consulting the directors of the Academy and of the Library; but the permission was always given. Perissinotti first offered the collection to the Library of St Mark's, asking for 5,000 lire. The government refused, and he sold the best part to the British gentleman Walter Sneyd (1752–1829), who paid 16,000 francs (about the same in lire). Sneyd and his heirs kept them at Keele Hall, near Stoke-on-Trent. In 1903 the collection was sold at auction.

The Celotti collection went on sale by Sotheby's in London on 14–18 March 1825. The title of the sale catalogue is eloquent: *A catalogue of the Hebrew, Greek, and Latin Ancient Manuscripts, containing many Greek and Latin classics, on vellum and paper; superb Hebrew bibles; fine illuminated missals, etc. Chiefly collected from the illustrious families of Nani, Gradenigo, and Mocenigo of Venice; Maffei of Verona; Salviati of Rome; and from the libraries of the celebrated monasteries of St Michele*

---

60 Cicogna, *Diario*, vol. II, Cod. 2845, 4452; Irma Merolle, *L'abate Matteo Luigi Canonici e la sua biblioteca* (Roma – Firenze, 1978), 48–55; Nereo Vianello, 'Cicognara Leopoldo', in *Dizionario Biografico degli Italiani*, 18 (Roma, 1975), 167–70; Zorzi, *La Libreria*, as note 16, 375–76, 560; Archivio della Biblioteca Marciana, year 1831. See also on this subject, and more generally, Marino Zorzi, 'The Book Trade in *Venice* under Foreign Dominations (1797–1866)', in *Habent sua fata libelli. Studies in Book History, the Classical Tradition, and Humanism in Honor of Craig Kallendorf*, eds Steven M. Oberhelman, Giancarlo Abbamonte and Patrick Baker (Leiden-Boston, 2021), 487–508.

di Murano, near Venice; of St Giustina, of Padova; and of St Giorgio Maggiore of Venice, etc., etc.[61].

Another competent book collector was the Archduke Rainer von Habsburg, who personally authorized in 1827 the acquisition by the Library of St Mark of the first book printed in Venice, Cicero's *Epistulae*, printed by Iohannes de Spira in 1469 (*GW* 6800). The seller was Celotti and the price 480 lire[62]. The Ferrarese Count Leopoldo Cicognara, president of the Accademia di Belle Arti in Venice, and a faithful follower of the Napoleonic views in artistic matters, decided in 1821 to sell his library, a collection specialized mostly in art and antiquity, and offered it to the Library of St Mark's. Having carefully examined every item, the librarian Bettio proposed a total price of 113,673 lire and submitted his conclusions to the government. In 1823 the Aulica Cancelleria, for financial reasons, had to refuse, and the Count instead sold his collection to Pope Leo XII for 18,000 *scudi* (about the same price suggested by Bettio)[63].

The former Venetian patrician families were selling too. Some sold, of course, for financial reasons, but others, even though wealthy enough, did not see any reason in keeping huge collections politically irrelevant to the present situation. Those who did not sell, donated their collection: to the Seminario Patriarcale, to the Library of St Mark, and later to the Correr Museum, or to collectors whom they trusted, such as Cicogna[64]. Some

bequeathed their collections to the city: Benedetto Valmarana (1784–1847), friend and protector of Cicogna, and Teodoro Correr (1750–1830)[65]. The *cittadini originari*, members of the former Venetian bureaucracy, acted in the same way. One exception is recorded: Ottavio Andrighetti (1777–1857), a former secretary of the Venetian Senate who assembled an impressive library which was inherited by his descendants, the Marcello family, and still exists today.

Another group of collectors, notable for both scholarship and wealth, were the doctors in medicine. The *protomedico* Francesco Aglietti (1757–1836) was so renowned that Emperor Francis I asked him to attend his wife in Vienna. Aglietti formed a collection of some ten thousand volumes, all choice and precious books[66]. His colleague, Giampietro Pellegrini (+1816), preferred paintings: he possessed ten thousand of them. His heirs were not very happy with his decision, for they would have liked to receive money, as Cicogna writes[67].

Civil servants too collected books. Although the Austrian government was rather parsimonious with high salaries, they were at least guaranteed. Thus, Lorenzo Stella, usher of the Court of Appeal, could put together a good collection

---

61 *Celotti manuscripts. A catalogue of the Hebrew, Greek, and Latin antient manuscripts, the property of the Abbé Celotti. Containing many Greek and Latin classics ... Hebrew Bibles ... illuminated missals / Which will be sold by auction by Mr Sotheby ... on Monday, March 14, 1825, and three following days ...* (London, Sotheby, 1825).

62 Zorzi, *La Libreria*, as note 16, 378.

63 Ibid., 375, 455.

64 For the following part of the text see, in addition to the indispensable *Diaries* of Cicogna, the manuscript compilations by Francesco Scipione Fapanni, Venezia, Biblioteca Marciana, Cod. It. VII, 2148 (= 9116), *Biblioteche pubbliche e private, antiche e moderne, in*

Venezia e nelle isole, e Cod. It. VII, 2291 (= 9126), *Cronache, aneddoti, biografie di Veneziani e di Veneti non patrizii, scritte da E. A. Cicogna nel "Diario"*. The catalogue of the exhibition *Una città e il suo museo. Un secolo e mezzo di collezioni civiche veneziane*, introduction by Giandomenico Romanelli, Venezia, Museo Correr, 1988, offers a series of essays about Teodoro Correr and the other donors. See also M. Zorzi, 'La gestione del patrimonio librario', as note 34, 265–90.

65 On Teodoro Correr, see Giandomenico Romanelli, 'Correr, Teodoro', in *Dizionario Biografico degli Italiani*, 29 (Roma, 1983), 509–12; Krzysztof Pomian, 'Collezionisti d'arte e di curiosità naturali', in *Storia della cultura veneta*, vol. 5/II, *Il Settecento*, eds Girolamo Arnaldi and Manlio Pastore Stocchi (Vicenza, 1986), 1–70, at 67–70.

66 Zorzi, *La Libreria*, as note 16, 345–46.

67 Cicogna, *Diario*, BMCV, Cod. 2845, 4074, 27 March 1816.

of books on Venetian ceremonies. Yet, the most extraordinary example is offered by the great scholar Emmanuele Antonio Cicogna, whose collection of manuscripts, put together in a life of passionate study, consisted of more than 4,000 items, partly donated to him, but mostly bought on his salary of about 2,000 lire. He had two unmarried sisters to provide for, and he used to divide his income into three parts, one for his sisters, one for himself, and one for the books (but probably the greatest share was devoted to the books).

Broadly speaking the book collectors in Venice can be divided into three groups in terms of taste and themes. The first group was mostly interested in rare and precious books, illuminated manuscripts, incunabula, editions by Aldus or the eighteenth-century publisher of tasteful editions Cominus, very fashionable at the time (certainly it included the three *abati*, Celotti, De Luca, and Canonici). The second group comprised those who looked for books on specific subjects, such as ancient literature, like the bibliographer and librarian Bartolomeo Gamba (1766–1841), the novelist and poet Luigi Carrer (1801–1850), the priest Antonio de Martiis (1772–1849), whose collection held 20,000 volumes; or the lawyer Carlo Roner (1844–1897), specializing in autographs.

A third group of collectors was represented by those who devoted their efforts to save the cultural heritage of the Venetian Republic. Among them one may mention Giovanni Casoni (1783–1857), engineer in the Arsenal, who assembled a collection of some 400 manuscripts; Francesco Maria Gherro (1771–1835), secretary in the office of the state lottery, who was able to collect thousands of engravings on Venetian subjects; the draper Domenico Zoppetti (+1849), who collected objects of historical interest. Their collections were bequeathed to the city. The outstanding figures in this group, however, were Giovanni Rossi (1776–1852), author of a vast unfinished work on *Le leggi e i costumi dei Veneziani*, who

collected many valuable documents to support his research and bequeathed them all to the Library of St Mark's[68]; Cicogna, the extraordinary scholar mentioned before, author of fundamental works on Venetian life and culture and the collector of a vast amount of records regarding Venetian history, all left to the city; and the "prince" of all Venetian collectors in the nineteenth century, Teodoro Correr. Of noble descent, Correr had started a conventional career in the Venetian government, but soon he had decided to become a clergyman, in order to be free to cultivate his learned interests. Not particularly rich but wealthy enough, he started to buy after the fall of the Republic, acquiring anything that had to do with Venetian history: paintings, sculptures, coins, medals, seals, documents, objects evoking the *Serenissima*, and books concerning Venetian history, among them the chronicles that patrician families used as a handbook for their political activity. He was criticized by many of his contemporaries, who thought that he had no taste, investing in things of no real value. But he wanted to preserve the memory of the Venetian past, in danger of disappearing, and ended up with a vast and outstanding collection, preserved today in the museum that bears his name.

Under the Italian government, sales and dispersions continued in Venice, although in a less dramatic atmosphere. Venice remained a great market for buying antiquities of every kind, books among them. Then followed in 1867 a second, less well-known suppression of religious houses. The Kingdom of Italy had grown out of the Kingdom of Sardinia, and the laws against the accumulation of property by the religious institutions, the so called *leggi Siccardi*, which were in force there, were automatically extended to the newly annexed territories, Venice included.

68 Dorit Raines, 'La bibliothèque manuscrite de Giovanni Rossi: un gardien du passé Vénitien et sa collection', *Miscellanea Marciana*, 5 (1990), 77–205.

The libraries that some convents had been able to rebuild under Austrian rule, sometimes due to the bequests of noblemen, though not comparable with their former libraries, were confiscated once again. This time the collections were distributed between the Library of St Mark's and other public institutions in the city[69]. Only after the "Concordato" signed by the Vatican and the Italian State in 1929 was it possible for monasteries and other religious houses to resume their activities. Today the Capuchins at the Redentore and the Franciscans at S. Francesco della Vigna have well-equipped libraries open to the public.

69 The confiscated books were distributed among the Library of St Mark, the Archivio di Stato, the Museo Civico Correr and to the Biblioteca Reale: Zorzi, *La Libreria*, as note 16, 391, 542–43.

Bibliography

Manuscript and Archival Sources

Venezia, Archivio di Stato, *Direzione del Demanio, 1806–1813*.

Venezia, Biblioteca del Civico Museo Correr, Venezia, Codd. Cicogna 2844–45, Emmanuele Antonio Cicogna, *Diario*.

Venezia, Biblioteca Nazionale Marciana, Cod. It. VII, 2148 (=9116), Francesco Scipione Fapanni, *Biblioteche pubbliche e private, antiche e moderne, in Venezia e nelle isole*.

Venezia, Biblioteca Nazionale Marciana, Cod. It. VII, 1399 (=9220), Giovanni Rossi, *Leggi e costumi dei Veneziani*, vol. XIV.

Secondary Works

Andrés, Juan, *Cartas familiares a su hermano D. Carlos Andrés*, vol. 3 (In Madrid, por Don Antonio de Sancha, 1790).

Berengo, Marino, *Intellettuali e librai nella Milano della Restaurazione* (Torino, 1980)

Bernardello, Adolfo, *Venezia nel Regno Lombardo-Veneto. Un caso atipico (1815–1866)* (Milano, 2015).

Bertoli, Bruno, *La soppressione di monasteri e conventi a Venezia dal 1797 al 1810* (Venezia, 2002).

Cadorin, Giuseppe, 'Archivi pubblici e privati', in *Venezia e le sue lagune*, vol. II, parte II (Venezia, 1847), 3–75.

Callegari, Marco, *L'industria del libro a Venezia durante la Restaurazione (1815–1848)* (Firenze, 2016).

Cavazzana Romanelli Francesca – Stefania Rossi Minutelli, 'Archivi e biblioteche', in *Storia di Venezia*, vol. VIII, eds Mario Isnenghi and Stuart Woolf, vol. II (Roma, 2002), 1081–122.

Cavalet, Lucia, 'Un prete bibliofilo: Don Tommaso De Luca (1752–1829)', *Miscellanea Marciana*, 17 (2002), 181–92.

Costantini, Massimo, *L'albero della libertà economica. Il processo di scioglimento delle corporazioni veneziane* (Venezia, 1987).

Derosas, Renzo, 'Aspetti economici della crisi del patriziato veneziano tra fine Settecento e primo Ottocento', in *Venezia nell'Ottocento*, ed. Massimo Costantini (Mantova, 1991), 11–61.

Eze, Anne-Marie, 'Abbé Celotti and the provenance of Antonello da Messina's "The condottiere" and Antonio de Solario's "Virgin and Child with St John"', *The Burlington Magazine* (October 2009), 673–77.

Ferrari, Stefano, 'Libri, storia e *Altertumwissenshaft*. Amedeo Svaier e gli eruditi danesi a Venezia sul finire del Settecento', *Analecta romana instituti danici*, 28 (2001), 135–52.

Ferrari, Stefano and Giorgio Marini, *Le collezioni di stampe e di libri di Antonio Rosmini (1741–1818)* (Rovereto, 1997).

Ferrari, Stefano, 'L'Accademia Roveretana degli Agiati e la cultura di lingua tedesca (1750–1795), in *La cultura tedesca in Italia. 1750–1850*, eds. Albero Destro and Paola Maria Filippi (Bologna, 1995), 217–76.

Fulin, Rinaldo, *E. A. Cicogna: festa letteraria nel R. Liceo Marco Polo* (Venezia, 1873).

Giacheri, Alessia, *Iacopo Morelli e la repubblica delle lettere attraverso la sua corrispondenza (1768–1819)* (Venezia, 2012).

Gottardi, Michele, *L'Austria a Venezia* (Milano, 1993).

Gar, Tommaso, 'I codici storici della collezione Foscarini conservata nella imperiale biblioteca di Vienna', *Archivio storico italiano*, 5 (1843), 281–476.

Gullino, Giuseppe, 'Economia e finanza dallo scorcio della Repubblica all'età napoleonica', in *Le metamorfosi di Venezia. Da capitale di Stato a città del mondo* (Firenze, 2001), 113–27.

Hellinga, Lotte, 'The Bibliotheca Smithiana', in *Libraries within the Library. The Origins of the British Library Printed Collections*, eds Giles Mandelbrote and Barry Taylor (London, 2009), 261–79.

La Cute, Pietro, 'Le vicende delle biblioteche monastiche veneziane dopo la soppressione napoleonica', *Rivista di Venezia*, A. VIII, no. 10 (October 1929), 597–646.

La Scuola Grande salvata, ed. Maria Agnese Chiari Moretto Wiel (Venezia, 2006).

Lamberti, Antonio, *Memorie degli ultimi cinquant'anni della Repubblica di Venezia*, eds Manlio Pastore Stocchi and Marino Zorzi (Venezia, 2019).

Locatelli, Tommaso, *Appendice della Gazzetta di Venezia* (Venezia, 1837).

Merolla, Lucia, *La biblioteca di San Michele di Murano all'epoca dell'abate G. B. Mittarelli. I codici ritrovati* (Manziana/Roma, 2010).

Merolle, Irma, *L'abate Matteo Luigi Canonici e la sua biblioteca* (Roma-Firenze, 1978).

Montecuccoli degli Erri, Francesco, 'Il console Smith. Notizie e documenti', *Ateneo Veneto*, 33 (1995), 111–81.

Moschini, Giannantonio, *Della letteratura veneziana nel secolo XVIII*, vol. II (Venezia, 1806).

Perini, Lorenza, 'Per la biografia di Francesco Pesaro (1740–1799)', *Archivio Veneto*, 145 (1995), 65–98.

Pomian, Krzysztof, 'Collezionisti d'arte e di curiosità naturali', in *Storia della cultura veneta*, vol. 5/II, *Il Settecento*, eds Girolamo Arnaldi and Manlio Pastore Stocchi (Vicenza, 1980), 1–70.

Raines, Dorit, 'La bibliothèque manuscrite de Giiovanni Rossi: un gardien du passé Vénitien et sa collection', *Miscellanea Marciana*, 5 (1990), 77–205.

Raines, Dorit, *La famiglia Manin e la cultura libraria nel Settecento fra Friuli e Venezia* (Udine, 1997).

Raines, Dorit, 'Prodromi neoclassici. Anticomania, natura e l'idea del progresso nella cultura libraria settecentesca del patriziato veneziano', in *Committenti, mecenati e collezionisti di Canova*, I, eds Giuliana Ericani and Fernando Mazzocca, Studi, Istituto di Ricerca per gli studi su Canova e il Neoclassicismo, vol. 6 (Bassano del Grappa, 2008), 47–68.

Romanelli, Giandomenico, 'Correr, Teodoro', in *Dizionario biografico degli Italiani*, 29 (Roma, 1983), 509–12.

Rosmini, Antonio, *Epistolario* (Casale, 1887), vol. I.

Rossi Minutelli, Stefania, 'Emmanuele Antonio Cicogna e l'*Opera delle Inscrizioni Veneziane*', *Miscellanea Marciana*, 15 (2009), 113–22.

Tarle, Evgenij, *Le Blocus continental et le Royaume d'Italie* (Paris, 1928).

Trombetta, Vincenzo, *L'editoria a Napoli nel decennio francese* (Milano, 2011).

Tucci, Ugo, 'Stipendi e pensioni dei pubblici impiegati nel Regno Lombardo-Veneto dal 1824 al 1866', *Archivio economico dell'unificazione italiana*, 10 (1960), fasc. 4, 1–68.

Tucci, Ugo, 'Leopold von Ranke e il mercato antiquario veneziano di manoscritti', *Quellen und Forschungen aus Italienishen Archiven und Bibliotheken*, 67 (1987), 282–310.

Una città e il suo museo. Un secolo e mezzo di collezioni civiche veneziane, introduction by Giandomenico Romanelli (Venezia, 1998).

Vianello, Nereo, 'Cicognara, Leopoldo', in *Dizionario Biografico degli Italiani*, 18 (Roma, 1975), 167–70.

Vio, Gastone, *Le scuole piccole nella Venezia dei Dogi* (Costabissara/Vicenza, 2001).

Zorzi, Alvise, *Venezia scomparsa* (Milano, 1972).

Zorzi, Marino, *La Libreria di San Marco. Libri, lettori, società nella Venezia dei Dogi* (Milano, 1987).

Zorzi, Marino, 'Le biblioteche a Venezia nel secondo Settecento', *Miscellanea Marciana*, I (1986), 253–324.

Zorzi, Marino, 'La gestione del patrimonio librario', in *Venezia e l'Austria*, eds Gino Benzoni and Gaetano Cozzi (Venezia, 1999), 265–90.

Zorzi, Marino, 'The Book Trade in Venice under Foreign Dominations (1797–1866)', in *Habent sua fata libelli. Studies in Book History, the Classical Tradition, and Humanism in Honor of Craig Kallendorf*, eds Steven N. Oberhelman, Giancarlo Abbamonte and Patrick Baker (Leiden-Boston, 2021), 487–508.

Sales Catalogues

Catalogo di libri raccolti dal fu Signor Giuseppe Smith e pulitamente legati, Venezia: MDCCLXXI.

Catalogo di libri latini, e italiani, che trovansi vendibili nel negozio di Antonio Zatta e figli libraj e stampatori di Venezia. Contenente tanto quelli di propria che di altre venete edizioni de' quali è fornito in maggior numero, ed inoltre i libri di forestiera antica e moderna impressione. Si aggiunge nel fine un elenco dei libri francesi, ed un altro copioso delle immagini e stampe in rame a bulino, carte geografiche, e musica vocale e strumentale fin'ora pubblicata, e il tutto a moneta veneta, Stampato a Venezia da Antonio Zatta e figli, 1791.

Catalogo di Libreria posta in vendita in Venezia nell'anno MDCCXCIV, [S.l., ma Venezia]: [s.n.], [1794].

Catalogo di libri con prezzi, mancante di frontespizio, interfoliato, con annotazioni autografe di Francesco Milli; ad uso di Zerletti Pietro, Venezia, [s.n.], 1798.

Catalogo della biblioteca Foscarini ai Carmini vendibile a Venezia nell'anno 1800 [Venezia, 28 novembre 1799?].

Catalogo di una Libreria che si trova vendibile in Venezia nell'anno MDCCXCIX, s.n.t.

Catalogo dei libri latini, italiani, francesi e di altre lingue straniere che trovansi vendibili da Gio. Antonio Curti q. Vito libraio in Merceria di S. Giuliano, Venezia, [s.n.], 1804.

Catalogo de' libri latini italiani e francesi che si trovano vendibili presso la ditta Antonio Zatta qu. Giacomo di Venezia, da esso stampati …, Venezia, [tip. Zatta], 1806.

Catalogo di libri latini, ed italiani, che si trovano in maggior numero nel negozio di Simon Occhi, Venezia, 1806.

Catalogo dei libri latini, italiani e francesi che si trovano vendibili da Francesco Andreola libraio e stampatore veneto in campo S. Angelo, Venezia, [s.n.], 1807.

Catalogo di libri latini, italiani e francesi che si vendono al pubblico incanto in Venezia … il giorno 15 novembre 1809, [S.n.t.].

Catalogo cronologico di edizioni del secolo 15. che si trovano vendibili appresso Adolfo Cesare libraio in Venezia, [S.l.], [s.n.], [1810].

Catalogo di libri antichi e moderni di varie materie e in diverse lingue che trovansi vendibili in pochi esemplari nel negozio di Adolfo Cesare. [*Raccolta Canonici*], Venezia, stamp. Molinari, 1812.

Celotti manuscripts. A catalogue of the Hebrew, Greek, and Latin antient manuscripts, the property of the Abbé Celotti. Containing many Greek and Latin classics … Hebrew Bibles … illuminated missals / Which will be sold by auction by Mr Sotheby … on Monday, March 14, 1825, and three following days … (London, Sotheby, 1825).

BETTINA WAGNER

"Duplum Bibliothecae regiae Monacensis". The Munich Court Library and its Book Auctions in the Nineteenth Century*

The importance of the Bayerische Staatsbibliothek in Munich as the greatest collection of mediaeval manuscripts and incunabula in Germany is largely a result of the dissolution of Bavarian monasteries in the year 1803, which led to an unprecedented increase in the holdings of the then Court Library of the Electors (from 1806 Kings) of Bavaria[1]. Within the first decade of the nineteenth century, the library expanded from about 70,000 to more than 500,000 volumes; the number of manuscripts alone grew more than tenfold, from about 2,000 to 22,000. The transfer of the Bibliotheca Palatina of Elector Carl Theodor (1777–1799) from Mannheim to Munich which began in 1782/1783 and was completed in 1804 also contributed to this expansion, but it does not concern us here[2]. The most important factor was the confiscation of manuscripts and books following the dissolution of the religious communities. The process of secularization had begun with the suppression of the Jesuit order in 1773, continued with the closure of nearly one hundred mendicant houses in 1802 and culminated in the secularization of about seventy monasteries in 1803.

---

* This paper was first published in PBSA 111 (2017), 345–77. I am grateful to the editors for granting permission to republish the text here in the context of the proceedings of the conference where the paper was originally given. The text is reprinted without alteration; references in footnotes have been brought up to date. Online resources were last checked in November 2020. I sincerely thank Richard Sharpe and Giles Mandelbrote for their comments and support in preparing the paper for publication.

1 On the history of the library and its collections, see *Handbuch der historischen Buchbestände in Deutschland*, vol. 10: *Bayern, München*, ed. Eberhard Dünninger (Hildesheim, 1996), 27–112; online version: http://fabian.sub.uni-goettingen.de/?Bayerische_Staatsbibliothek.

2 For sources and secondary literature, see Stephan Kellner and Annemarie Spethmann, *Historische Kataloge der Bayerischen Staatsbibliothek München. Münchner Hofbibliothek und andere Provenienzen*, Catalogus codicum manu scriptorum Bibliothecae Monacensis XI (Wiesbaden, 1996), 264–70 and *Die Mannheimer Hofbibliothek: Carl Theodor und seine Vorgänger als Büchersammler. Eine Ausstellung der Universitätsbibliothek Mannheim, … 17. Januar bis 30. März 2000* (Mannheim, 2000).

Bettina Wagner • Director of the Staatsbibliothek Bamberg. bettina.wagner@staatsbibliothek-bamberg.de

How the Secularization of Religious Houses Transformed the Libraries of Europe, 16th–19th Centuries, ed. by Cristina Dondi, Dorit Raines, and † Richard Sharpe, BIB, 63 (Turnhout, 2022), pp. 389–415.

BREPOLS ⚘ PUBLISHERS

DOI 10.1484/M.BIB-EB.5.128495

In 2003, two hundred years after the secularization of monasteries, the exhibition "Lebendiges Büchererbe" demonstrated the many initiatives which resulted from merging the collections of more than 150 religious houses in Munich, particularly for the development of new historical and philological disciplines such as mediaeval Latin and palaeography, German philology, history of art and legal history[3]. The exhibition catalogue also describes the difficulties with regard to logistics and administrative procedures that were encountered by the librarians responsible for stock-taking and compiling inventories of the newly acquired books from religious houses. The manuscripts and printed books that were transferred to Munich had to be stored, sorted, and catalogued, tasks that involved a considerable amount of organization to be accomplished within a reasonable time-span. Only after the completion of this work could scholars gain access to the wealth of sources that had been centralized in the Bavarian capital.

The systematic arrangement and bibliographical description of the new acquisitions were also prerequisites for a purposeful selection and subsequent de-accessioning of printed books present in multiple copies, the so-called duplicates. Given the very similar thematic focus of the various monastic libraries, it was inevitable that numerous books were taken to Munich in several copies. The members of the library committee who inspected nearly seventy monasteries in 1802–1803 were bibliographically well-versed, but even the most astute librarian could not be expected to keep track of what books had been chosen from each monastery. Within the short time available for inspection, only the most important items could be selected. Cursory lists were drawn up of those books that should be preserved, and those that were judged superfluous or even seen as dangerous were destined either for destruction as recycled paper or to be disposed of locally, thus saving the expense of transport to Munich[4]. Nonetheless, a certain amount of duplication was even intentional, because several libraries had to be provided for: in addition to the Munich Court Library, which was entitled to the first choice of books, the library of the only university in the Bavarian territory at the time – initially set up in Ingolstadt in 1472 before moving to Landshut in 1800 and finally on to Munich in 1826 – required scholarly literature, and so too did the newly-created provincial libraries and the libraries of schools.

Yet in spite of the substantial number of potential recipients, the total quantity of available editions and copies still exceeded demand. Duplicate sales were an obvious solution, since they offered a chance to free the libraries of cumbersome and unused stock and at the same time raise funds for diverse needs, some a direct result of the acquisition of monastic books, such as additional library staff, new buildings and printed catalogues, and others not related, such as widening the scope of the collections by purchasing both antiquarian and modern literature. As a result of such sales, numerous individuals and institutions benefitted from the dissolution of Bavarian monasteries, and over the course of the nineteenth century, the range of buyers extended beyond southern Germany to include nations with a growing interest in building up collections of mediaeval and early modern books, particularly France, Britain and the United States with their expanding universities and wealthy bibliophiles. Thus, the book heritage of Bavarian monasteries constitutes a core element of many

---

3 See *Lebendiges Büchererbe. Säkularisation, Mediatisierung und die Bayerische Staatsbibliothek. Eine Ausstellung der Bayerischen Staatsbibliothek München, 7.11.2003–30.1.2004,* ed. Cornelia Jahn and Dieter Kudorfer, Bayerische Staatsbibliothek, Ausstellungskataloge 74 (Munich, 2003).

4 The inventories are now preserved in the fonds *Codices bavarici Monacenses, Catalogi* (Cbm Cat.). An overview with descriptions of the individual sources relating to the earlier collections is given by Kellner and Spethmann, *Historische Kataloge,* as note 2.

libraries world-wide, and the question how and which books from Bavaria left their homeland and reached new readers and scholars is of international concern. However, research on the duplicate sales from the Munich Court Library has so far been almost exclusively published in German. This paper aims at familiarizing an English-speaking audience with the events and procedures.

The First Auction of 1815/1816

As early as 1803, the first duplicates from Bavarian monasteries had been sold individually to Munich booksellers such as Joseph von Scherer (1776–1829), who a few years later, in 1806, was appointed sub-librarian and eventually promoted to director in 1823[5]. In order to de-accession duplicates, a comprehensive and reliable catalogue of the library's printed holdings was a pre-requisite. For monastic manuscripts, which were to be preserved in Munich institutions, experts and substantial time were required[6], but the cataloguing of printed books could be carried out fairly rapidly by assistants trained on the job. In order to speed this work up, the library director Johann Christoph von Aretin (1772–1824) decided to employ daily labourers, the so-called "Diurnisten", who were paid at piece rate, i.e. by the number of books catalogued per day and at a rate of one kreutzer per book[7]. Even though this method did not ensure a high standard of description, progress at least was fast: a first alphabetical inventory of the printed books acquired from monasteries was completed as early as 1807[8]. It listed some 178,600 items and could serve as a basis for selecting and de-accessioning multiple copies. No agreement had yet been reached on the future systematic arrangement of the collection of printed books in the library[9].

5 Numerous archival sources are preserved in the BSB, particularly Scherer's papers (*Schereriana*, see Karl Dachs, *Die schriftlichen Nachlässe in der Bayerischen Staatsbibliothek München*, Catalogus codicum manu scriptorum Bibliothecae Monacensis IX,1 (Wiesbaden, 1970), 137–38, and the internal finding aids with detailed biographical information). His correspondence concerning book purchases is kept under the shelfmark *C I Scherer* in the nineteenth-century library archives, the *Alte Registratur* (until 2015 housed in the BSB and cited as A-Reg., now in the Bayerisches Hauptstaatsarchiv [BayHStA] at Munich). In 1802, Scherer had purchased the firm of the Sulzbach bookseller Johann Esaias Seidel, who in 1801 had been granted permission to conduct his entire business (printing, publishing and bookselling) in the Bavarian capital, see Pius Dirr, *Buchwesen und Schrifttum im alten München* (Munich, 1929), 126; Rudolf Schmidt, *Deutsche Buchhändler. Deutsche Buchdrucker. Beiträge zu einer Firmengeschichte des deutschen Buchgewerbes*, 6 vols (Berlin and later Eberswalde, 1902–1908); digital version on the CD-ROM *Geschichte des deutschen Buchwesens*, ed. Mark Lehmstedt, Directmedia Publishing, 2004, 5896; *Johann Esaias von Seidel (1758–1827). Zum 250. Geburtstag eines bayerischen Verlegers*, ed. Markus Lommer, Schriftenreihe des Stadtmuseums und Stadtarchivs Sulzbach-Rosenberg 23 (Sulzbach-Rosenberg, 2008). Scherer financed the purchase with a loan of 17,500 guilders, but owing to his lack

of experience in the trade and the difficult economic situation, his debts had grown to 30,000 guilders by 1806 and were only completely settled 13 years after his death. After Scherer had become librarian in 1809, his bookselling business was taken over by Maximilian Joseph Stöger, see below and note 26.

6 The largest part of this task was undertaken in the 1830s and 1840s by Johann Andreas Schmeller (1785–1852), who proposed to arrange the manuscripts by language and, within the group of Latin manuscripts, according to their monastic provenance. This decision facilitated Schmeller's work considerably, as he could draw on older library inventories which had been brought from the monasteries to Munich after the secularization and were preserved in the fonds "Cbm Cat". See Dieter Kudorfer, 'Bekanntmachung, Erschließung und Benützung der Handschriften', in *Lebendiges Büchererbe*, as note 3, 54–71.

7 Stephan Kellner, 'Vom "künstlichen Chaos" zur Ordnung "in Reih und Glied" – Der schwierige Weg zur Katalogisierung der Druckschriften', in *Lebendiges Büchererbe*, as note 3, 72–79. On Aretin, see *Lebendiges Büchererbe*, 31–33.

8 BSB, Cbm Cat. 218, see Kellner and Spethmann, *Historische Kataloge*, as note 2, 54 and 86–87.

9 After protracted disagreements between Aretin and Julius Wilhelm Hamberger who had been called in as a co-director from Göttingen in 1808, a workable solution

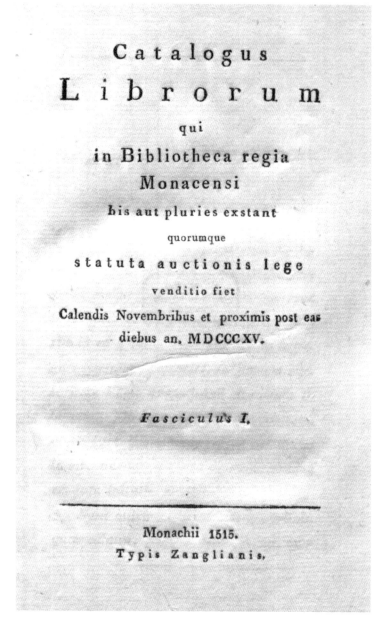

Figure 20.1. Auction catalogue of 1815, title-page (Munich, BSB, Bibl.Mont. 109)

published by the Munich printer Josef Zangl, and the auction was held 2–12 January 1816[10] (Fig. 20.1: title-page). Several interleaved copies of the catalogue with notes about sale prices and the names of buyers have been preserved in the Bayerische Staatsbibliothek[11]. They not only provide insights into what kind of private and institutional customers frequented such auctions, but also shed new light on the beginnings of the antiquarian book trade in Munich.

The auction catalogue is arranged by subject, and its range seems to be more dictated by the anticipated demand than by the duplicates available, if the number of items under each heading is anything to go by. Even though religious literature naturally dominated among the books from monastic libraries, the number of "Libri theologici" in the auction catalogues is unexpectedly small: a mere 185 titles were advertised. This may indicate that the market was already saturated by direct sales from the monasteries that had taken place immediately after the dissolution[12] and that such works met with little interest among prospective bidders at the time. On the other hand, the largest numbers of titles in the auction catalogue appear under the rubrics "Historia profana et ecclesiastica" (1167 lots), "Libri juridici" (1087 lots), and scientific works (781 lots under "Scientia mathematica et physica" and 396 lots in the subject group "Historia

In 1815, the first large-scale auction was prepared, in which about 4,000 printed books of various periods were offered. The sale catalogue was

was only found in 1824 by Martin Schrettinger. See *Lebendiges Büchererbe*, as note 3, 73.

10 *Catalogus Librorum qui in Bibliotheca regia Monacensi bis aut pluries exstant quorumque statuta auctionis lege venditio fiet Calendis Novembribus et proximis post eas diebus an. MDCCCXV* (Munich: Zangl, '1515' [recte 1815]). The 69 *Incunabula Typographiae* are listed by format and in chronological order on 231–50.

11 BSB, Bavar. 535, Cbm Cat. 292 d and Cbm Cat. 292 e. Online access via https://opacplus.bsb-muenchen.de/search?oclcno=165988813.

12 One of the earliest local booksellers involved in the dispersal was Joseph Mozler (1761–1817) in Freising, see Armin Schlechter, 'Der Briefwechsel zwischen Clemens Brentano und dem Freisinger Antiquar Joseph Matthias Mozler', *Bibliothek und Wissenschaft* (2000), 103–87.

naturalis"), all "useful" subjects for which a high demand could be expected. The surprisingly small number of 116 editions of "Autores classici" in the catalogue may be partly due to the comparatively small holdings of monasteries in this area. It is also likely that a high proportion of books in this field were retained by the Court Library, which had to catch up with editions of primary sources and scholarly publications to serve the needs of its main users, the members of the Bavarian Academy of Sciences, to which the library had been attached as an "Attribut" (adjunct) since 1759.

The total of 169 "Incunabula Typographiae" in the auction represent only a very small sample out of some 24,000 incunabula accumulated in Munich as a result of the secularization, among them large numbers of duplicates[13]. Yet without reliable methods and bibliographic tools for describing and identifying fifteenth-century printed books, not to mention assigning them to printers and dating them, cataloguing the Munich collection was a daunting task. Although some Bavarian monasteries had drawn up and even printed catalogues of incunabula in the late eighteenth century, some of which even included copy-specific information[14], the only

incunable German bibliography aiming at a wider coverage was that compiled by Georg Panzer (1729–1805), a protestant pastor of Nuremberg, before the secularization[15]. As a consequence, a substantial number of the fifteenth-century editions acquired by the Munich Court Library from dissolved monasteries were not listed there. No widely-accepted standard for describing incunabula existed before the first volume of Ludwig Hain's *Repertorium bibliographicum* was published in 1826, which was largely based on the Munich collection[16]. As a result of this unsatisfactory situation, a protracted methodological discussion took place among the librarians responsible for printed books concerning the interrelated questions of shelving system and level of descriptive cataloguing. By 1816, no agreement had been reached[17]. Meanwhile, the catalogue arranged by date of printing had only progressed up to the decade of the 1480s[18].

13   See Elmar Hertrich, 'Erschließung der Inkunabelsammlung der Bayerischen Staatsbibliothek in Vergangenheit und Gegenwart', in *Bayerische Staatsbibliothek: Inkunabelkatalog* (*BSB-Ink*), vol. 1 (Wiesbaden, 1988), XIII–XVIII, at XVI.

14   See Bettina Wagner, 'Von der Klosterbibliothek zum Gesamtkatalog der Wiegendrucke. Zur Geschichte der Inkunabelkatalogisierung in Bayern', *Gutenberg-Jahrbuch*, 81 (2006), 168–78, at 168–69. In the last decades of the eighteenth century, printed catalogues of incunabula were published for several religious houses in Bavaria, e.g. *Monumenta typographica, quae exstant in Bibliotheca collegii canonicorum in Rebdorf. Collegit, notis illustravit, et edidit eiudem collegii bibliothecarius* [i.e. Andreas Strauss] (Eichstätt, 1787); *Notitia historico-literaria de libris ab artis typographicae inventione usque ad annum MCCCCLVIIII. impressis: in bibliotheca liberi, ac imperialis monasterii ad SS. Uldaricum et Afram Augustae extantibus* (Augsburg, 1788); *Verzeichniß alter Druckdenkmale der Bibliothek*

des uralten Benediktiner-Stifts zum H. Mang in Füeßen. Mit litterarischen Anmerkungen begleitet von Joseph Maria Helmschrott (Ulm, 1790); *Druckstücke aus dem XV. Jahrhunderte, welche sich in der Bibliothek des regulirten Chorstiftes Beuerberg befinden. Beschrieben und herausgegeben* von Paul Hupfauer (Augsburg, 1794).

15   Georg W. Panzer, *Annales Typographici ab artis inventae Origine ad annum 1500 et inde usque ad annum 1536* (Nuremberg, 1793–1803).

16   On Hain, see Severin Corsten, 'Von Bernhard von Mallinckrodt zu Ludwig Hain. Ziele und Methoden der frühen Inkunabelbibliographie', *Gutenberg-Jahrbuch*, 70 (1995), 37–50; Karl Klaus Walther, 'Hains *Repertorium bibliographicum*. "Die hervorragende Leistung eines Dilettanten"?', *Aus dem Antiquariat*, 9 (1996), A369–A376; Wagner, *Geschichte der Inkunabelkatalogisierung*, as note 14, 174–77.

17   On the discussion about incunable cataloguing in 1811 and 1814, see BSB, Cbm Cat. 285, no. 1, Bernhartiana 14 e and BayHStA, BSB, A-Reg. A II Bernhart (J.B.) no. 42, and Hertrich, *Erschließung der Inkunabelsammlung*, as note 13, XVI.

18   In 1811, cataloguing of incunabula had progressed up to the year of publication 1479; ten years later, editions up to the year 1489 had been described, see Kellner and Spethmann, *Historische Kataloge*, as note 2, 82 for Cbm Cat. 221 b.

The custodian responsible for early printed books, Johann Baptist Bernhart (1759–1821), was only too well aware that multiple copies of incunabula do not constitute duplicates, since every copy has individual features with regard to typesetting, material makeup, and especially ownership and history. Bernhart's incunable catalogues and publications, particularly his study of the three copies of the Gutenberg Bible that were held by the Munich library in the early nineteenth century as a result of the secularization and the transfer of the Bibliotheca Palatina from Mannheim, demonstrate a profound familiarity with the contemporary methods of bibliographical description[19]. This was probably the reason why Bernhart, who was placed in charge of organizing the duplicate auctions, selected books for sale very restrictively.

The surviving correspondence between Bernhart and some customers, the notes about prices, *conti*, and his final report about the auction, dated 11 February 1816, all show that the range of titles offered met with great interest from bidders. Bernhart describes how the sale was conducted:

On the basis of the printed catalogue the auction was to have started on 1 November of last year [i.e. 1815]; however, it was postponed until 2 January of the current year [1816], on which day it was duly begun and continued until the 12th of the same month. The staff engaged with this consisted, in addition to myself, in the library secretary Herr Rott and the cataloguer Herr Beil, both of whom kept the manual of the auction, thus checking on each other; furthermore, two servants, Pramberger and Gubath, who issued the books and kept them in order; furthermore, the first servant to the academy, Gerzapeck, who took care of the preparations with regard to tables, seats, lights etc., and finally the bookseller Stöger, who estimated the books and called them up. The auction was held in the old session hall of the Royal Academy of Sciences; it was carried out smoothly and in an orderly way. The revenue from the duplicates sold amounted to a total of 3,838 guilders (florins) and 37 kreutzer, including the fifteenth-century printed books which – following a Supreme Order – were handed over to the bookseller Stöger for 600 guilders which were duly paid by him to the Senior Councillor for Accounts, Herr Reuss[20].

---

19 On Bernhart, see *Lebendiges Büchererbe*, as note 3, 38–40 (no. 7), 87–88 and 92–94 (no. 29); Bernhard Lübbers, 'Johann Baptist Bernhart (1759–1821) und seine Regensburger Bibliotheksreise im Winter 1811/12', in *Regensburg, Bayern und das Reich. Festschrift für Peter Schmid zum 65. Geburtstag*, ed. Tobias Appl and Georg Köglmeier (Regensburg, 2010), 597–617. For Bernhart's incunable catalogues, see Kellner and Spethmann, *Historische Kataloge*, as note 2, 77–79 and 81–84, and Wagner, *Geschichte der Inkunabelkatalogisierung*, as note 14, 170–74. Bernhart's scholarly output comprises: 'Historisch-kritische Untersuchung über das Daseyn, die Kennzeichen und das Alter der von Iohann Guttenberg und Iohann Faust in Mainz gedruckten lateinischen Bibel, dann über die Epochen der Verbreitung der Buchdruckerkunst und der Schriftgiesserey', *Beyträge zur Geschichte und Literatur, vorzüglich aus den Schätzen der Königl. Hof- und Centralbibliothek zu München*, 3,5 (1804), 91–112; 3,6, 49–112; 4,1 (1805), 49–70. – 'Gründliches Bedenken über das vom Herrn geheimen Rath Zapf angegebene hohe Alter und den Namen des Buchdruckers von des Ioannis de Turrecremata Explanatio im Psalterium Cracis impressa', ibid. 5,1 (1805), 49–66. – 'Bemerkungen über die Auflage des Theuerdanks von 1517 und über die in derselben vorkommenden Schreiberzüge', ibid. 5,1 (1805), 67–98. – 'Beyträge zur nähern Bestimmung des Druckjahres von der Kosmographie des Ptolemäus mit der Iahrzahl 1462, nebst Untersuchungen über die ersten in Metall gestochenen Landkarten', ibid. 5,5 (1805), 497–558; 5,6, 609–28. – 'Anzeige einiger von Johann Mentelin zu Straßburg gedruckten, und von ihm zum Kaufe angekündigten Bücher', *Neuer literarischer Anzeiger*,

19 (12 May 1807), 301–03. – 'Nachricht von einer merkwürdigen Ueberschwemmung von Baiern', ibid. 25 (23 June 1807), 399–400.
20 BayHStA, BSB, A-Reg. C 5, no. 30 dated 11 February 1816. In German: *Vermöge des in Druck gegebenen Katalogs hätte die Auction den 1ten November vorigen Jahres [1815] beginnen sollen; sie wurde aber auf den 2ten Januar*

The bookseller Maximilian Joseph Stöger, who acted as auctioneer, had run a printing workshop in Munich since about 1809; he mainly published small pamphlets written by members of the Academy of Sciences, including treatises by eminent Munich scholars such as the classical philologist Friedrich Wilhelm Thiersch (1784–1860), the philosopher and mineralogist Franz von Baader (1765–1841), the archaeologist Anselm von Feuerbach (1798–1851), and the numismatist and later director of the Ducal Library in Gotha, Friedrich Jacobs (1764–1847). Stöger himself also wrote essays and edited historical sources[21]. He had formed a business relationship with the Court Library when he took over Scherer's bookshop in 1809[22]. A catalogue that he published in 1810 (now apparently lost[23]) and his role in the auction of 1816 show that Stöger must be counted among the circle of early Munich antiquarian booksellers about whom only rudimentary evidence has so far come to light[24]. According to Bernhart's report, Stöger had already purchased the 169 incunable duplicates en bloc before the sale started (for an average price of 3½ guilders per item), probably in order to sell them on his own account. In addition, he successfully bid for printed books at a total outlay of 1,112 guilders during the auction, more than a third of the total realised by the sale, and itself a substantial sum, considering that the hourly wage of a cataloguer amounted to a mere 6 or 10 kreutzer in 1818[25]. In subsequent years, Stöger continued regularly to acquire duplicates from the Court Library and also offered books to the library for purchase. From about 1824 onwards, he used the title "Professor". From 1831 on, Franz Xaver Stöger, probably his son, had professional contacts with the library[26]. Another Munich antiquarian bookseller present at the sale in 1816 was Franz Josef Ehrentreich, who had exchanged books with the library as

dieß Jahres [1816] zurükgesezt: an welchem Tage sie auch angefangen und bis zum 12ten desselben Monates fortgesezt worden ist. Das hierzu gebrauchte Personale bestand, außer mir, aus dem Bibliothek-Secretaire Herrn Rott und dem Diurnisten Hrn. Beil, welche beyde das Versteigerungs Manuale miteinander hielten, und sich dadurch controllirten: auserdem zwey Diener Pramberger und Gubath, welche die Bücher hervorgaben, und in Ordnung hielten: auserdem ersten akademischen Diener Gerzapeck, welcher die Zubereitungen in Hinsicht der Tische, Sessel, Lichter u.d.g. besorgte, und endlich aus dem Buchhändler Stöger, welcher die Bücher taxirte und ausrief. Die Versteigerung wurde in dem alten Sitzungssaale der königl. Akademie der Wissenschaft gehalten; sie lief ruhig und ordentlich ab. Der Erlöß der verkauften Doubletten beträgt, mit Einschluß der Drukschriften des XV. Jahrhundert, welche dem Buchhändler Stöger nach Inhalt eines allerhöchsten Reskriptes für 600 fl. überlassen worden sind, die er auch dem Titl. Hrn. OberrechnungsRath Reuss erlegt hat, 3838 fl. 37 Kr.

21   For example, 'Versuch eines Grundrisses der Geschichte der Niederländischen Unruhen unter der Herzogin von Parma und dem Herzog von Alba' (Munich, 1804), Franz Sigl's, Franziskaners in München, Geschichte der Münchner Geißeln in schwedischer Gefangenschaft vom 7. Juni 1632 bis 3. April 1635. Aus einer gleichzeitigen Handschrift, ed. Maximilian Joseph Stöger (Munich, 1836).

22   Schmidt, Deutsche Buchhändler, as note 5, 5890 s.v. Finsterlin. See BayHStA, BSB, A-Reg. B VI Stoeger.

23   Catalogue des Livres grecs, latins … qui se trouvent chez M. J. Stoeger à Munich (1810), formerly BSB, Cat. LXVI,2, copy destroyed in World War II.

24   See Ingo Schwab, 'Der Münchner Antiquariatsbuchhandel in der ersten Hälfte des 19. Jahrhunderts', in Die Rosenthals. Der Aufstieg einer jüdischen Antiquarsfamilie zu Weltruhm (Vienna/Cologne/Weimar, 2002), 13–46. Stöger is only mentioned in passing (p. 25).

25   See BayHStA, BSB, A-Reg. C 6, no. 2. One guilder was made up of 60 kreutzer.

26   See BayHStA, BSB, A-Reg. B III Stoeger, no. 14, and B III Stoeger jun. In 1839, director Lichtenthaler wrote a reference for F. X. Stöger in which he confirmed the latter's qualification as a dealer in antiquarian books, particularly thanks to his knowledge of early woodcuts (BayHStA, BSB, A-Reg. B 167). From 1820 onwards, F. X. Stöger had produced various publications, including partial lithographical facsimiles of the prayer-book of emperor Maximilian I with marginal drawings by Albrecht Dürer (BSB, 2 L.impr.membr. 64), which were first issued in 1820 under the title Oratio Dominica Polyglotta and reprinted several times.

early as 1806; his auction purchases were however much more limited in scope, and his bill only amounted to 84 guilders[27].

Yet many of the duplicates sold were purchased not by booksellers, but by senior civil servants and academics, many of whom had close ties with the Munich Academy of Sciences. The most prominent bidder was the creator of modern Bavaria himself, the minister Graf Maximilian von Montgelas (1759–1838), who – barely one year before his sudden dismissal instigated by Crown Prince Ludwig (later King Ludwig I) on 2 February 1817 – was at the height of his political power and had accumulated a copious private library[28]. Works on historical and philological subjects were sought by bidders such as the Landshut professor Karl Sebastian Heller von Hellersberg (1772–1818), the Augsburg librarian and book historian Placidus Braun (1756–1829), the archivists Johann Ferdinand von Huschberg (1792–1852) and Georg Ferdinand Döllinger (1772–1847), and the future president of the Academy, Thiersch. Scientific books were in high demand: among the bidders were the Erlangen botanist Karl Friedrich Philipp von Martius (1794–1868), the natural scientist Franz von Paula von Schrank (1747–1835), the anatomist Samuel Thomas von Soemmering (1755–1830), and the mineralogist Karl Ehrenbert von Moll (1760–1838)[29].

In addition, members of staff from the Court Library or from the Academy bought items on behalf of some anonymous bidders. The few names on the record show that occasionally even book collectors from more remote places in Bavaria used the opportunity to acquire publications on subjects of interest, sometimes with an expressly practical purpose. Thus, the forest warden of Baron von Perfall, the appropriately named Franz Xaver Rehbock, from Greifenberg on Lake Ammersee, sent a letter to Bernhart asking him to be kind enough to sell him standard works on forestry and surveying *gegen billige Preise* [for cheap prices], as he was *kein Mann von Vermögen* [not a man of means][30]. Bernhart, however, was unable or maybe unwilling to fulfil Rehbock's request to obtain the books before the sale, and indeed in some cases the forest warden's bids proved too low. Ordinary book collectors were clearly not in a position to compete with aristocrats, civil servants, and academics, or the directors of some eminent libraries in Bavaria and beyond (e.g. Würzburg, Freiburg and Gotha) who could deploy larger budgets. On the whole, however, the 1816 sale reached mainly a local Bavarian clientèle personally known to the sellers. The rather limited range of customers may have been

---

27 See Reinhard Wittmann, *Hundert Jahre Buchkultur in München* (Munich, 1993), 29. Ehrentreich was the son of a publican in Donauwörth, a former valet and dentist, who was granted the concession to trade in bound books in 1793; his property had a value of 200 guilders, see Schwab, *Münchner Antiquariatsbuchhandel*, as note 24, 18 and 29. On Ehrentreich as the Court Library's partner in book exchanges see BayHStA, BSB, A-Reg. B III Ehrentreich. See also Michael Schaich, *Staat und Öffentlichkeit im Kurfürstentum Bayern der Spätaufklärung*, Schriftenreihe zur bayerischen Landesgeschichte 136 (Munich, 2001), 27–32.

28 In 1971, Montgelas's library was acquired by the Bayerische Staatsbibliothek; the printed books from his collection are today held separately as the fonds "Bibl. Mont.", see *Handbuch der historischen Buchbestände*, as note 1, 27–112, at 90 and 98. As a result, some duplicates disposed of by the Court Library returned to the Bayerische Staatsbibliothek. See also Kellner and Spethmann, *Historische Kataloge*, as note 2, 542–46, and Eberhard Weis, *Montgelas*, 2 vols (Munich, ²1988 and 2005).

29 Moll's library was housed together with his other collections in the dissolved monastery of Fürstenfeld near Munich; it comprised 80,000 volumes, see *Allgemeine Deutsche Biographie*, vol. 22 (1885), 113, and Kellner and Spethmann, *Historische Kataloge*, as note 2, 539–41. Some books from his library returned to the Bayerische Staatsbibliothek via donations and a posthumous sale; others are now kept in London, Moscow, Würzburg and Erlangen.

30 BayHStA, BSB, A-Reg. C 5, no. 3.

one reason why the revenue was not as large as it might have been: many books remained unsold, and less than 10 percent of the books were acquired by purchasers other than the auctioneer Stöger himself.

Plans for a Second Auction in 1820

Five years later, in the auction planned for late 1820, a noticeable change in marketing strategy and the prospective customers was to take place. Detailed records also survive concerning this second sale. Again, J. B. Bernhart was responsible for its organization and documented his work carefully[31]. In 1817, members of the library staff had inspected the last remaining books from the dissolved monasteries, which were still stored in the Munich salt depot (*die auf dem Salzstadel gelegenen letzten Bibliotheksreste aus den aufgelösten Klöstern*), and had selected items for disposal or sale[32]. In January 1818, the *Bibliothek-Administrations-Commission* (Committee for Library Administration) decided that the books from monasteries that were stored in the attics of the royal Court Library should be sold, since an inspection had found that they were exerting a heavy and dangerous pressure on the rather unsound trusses[33]. At that time, the library was still housed in the inadequate rooms of the former Jesuit college in Neuhauser Straße, which since the suppression of the order in 1773 had also accommodated the Royal Archives and the Cabinets of Coins and Engravings, as well

as the Academies of Arts and of Sciences with their substantial collections. It was to take almost another ten years before Friedrich Gärtner was commissioned to plan the new library building in Ludwigstraße, which would not open for use until 1843[34].

Under these circumstances, the compilation of a sale catalogue was an arduous task which took nearly two years to complete. When the manuscript was ready, the printer Lindner could not guarantee quick execution of the job, so the task was assigned to the firm of Lindauer that began typesetting on 1 December 1819. Printing came to a halt soon afterwards, however, when Bernhart pointed out that the books on offer had not been checked against the main catalogue of the royal Court Library, and consequently it was quite possible that several of these books were not yet present in the library and were not really duplicates[35]. These concerns proved justified, and as a result the first four sheets of the catalogue had to be revised and reset, which led to considerable delays. Printing still had not been finished by May 1820. This meant that the sale projected for the autumn had to be cancelled; in late October, members of the public were informed by the local press that the sale had been postponed indefinitely[36].

By that time, the catalogue had already been issued (Fig. 20.2), albeit with a much reduced number of books when compared to the man-

31 BayHStA, BSB, A-Reg. C 6, no. 1 und 4.

32 Archive of the Academy of Sciences, VIII. 212. Thirty-five crates with books were transferred to the Court Library.

33 BayHStA, BSB, A-Reg. C 6, no. 1: *daß die ... auf den Speichern der königlichen Hofbibliothek aufbewahrten Klosterbücher wegen dem schweren und gefährlichen Druck, den sie, nach genommenem Augenschein ..., auf den ziemlich morschen Dachstuhl machen, verkauft werden sollen.*

34 See Annemarie Kaindl, "'Nicht nur für den gegenwärtigen Bedarf, sondern für den von Jahrhunderten' – Der Bibliotheksbau in der Ludwigstraße', in *Lebendiges Büchererbe*, as note 3, 214–27.

35 BayHStA, BSB, A-Reg. C 6, no. 1: *daß die angebotenen Bücher mit dem Hauptkatalog der königl. Hofbibliothek nicht verglichen worden, und also es leicht möglich seyn kann, daß mehrere dieser Bücher in der Bibliothek noch nicht aufgestellt, und folglich keine Doubletten sind.*

36 *Münchener Politische Zeitung* 258 (31 October 1820), 1282, and 259 (1 November 1820), 1286.

Figure 20.2. Auction catalogue of 1820, title-page (Munich, BSB, Cat. 432 b)

2,980[38]. Apparently, more than a fifth of the books originally selected for deaccessioning had been added to the library's holdings after all. In addition to the folio volumes, 1,962 books in quarto were included in the catalogue, which comprised a total of more than 5,000 lots. The books in both formats are listed in alphabetical order without any classification by subject, but the contingent of theological books is clearly much larger than in the preceding sale. The 28 incunabula offered are not grouped together in a separate section, but listed among the other books.

In addition to the newspaper announcement, Bernhart notified numerous recipients of the catalogue with personal letters about the cancellation of the sale. The list of names and Bernhart's correspondence provide interesting insights into the sale's prospective customers[39]. The main difference from the auction of 1816 is the much greater variety of potential bidders. Now, the group of book collectors from within Bavaria had extended to include students and country pastors in addition to university professors, high civil servants, and members of the nobility. Furthermore, the geographical scope had widened considerably after the end of the Napoleonic Wars[40]. While in 1816, only two booksellers from Munich had been present in the auction, many more antiquarian dealers were involved now: the Munich firms of Stöger,

uscript draft:[37] while the latter contains 3,630 books in folio, the printed catalogue lists only

---

37   *Verzeichniß einer Anzahl in der Königl. Hofbibliothek zu München befindlichen Doubletten, welche daselbst vom 6. Nov. d. J. an die Meistbietenden gegen baare Bezahlung*

werden versteigert werden* (Munich, 1820). For online access to four Munich copies, see https://opacplus.bsb-muenchen.de/search?oclcno=165929622.

38   See BayHStA, BSB, A-Reg. C 6, no. 4, fol. 2v.

39   BayHStA, BSB, A-Reg. C 6, no. 3 (containing *Rechenschaft über die ausgetheilten Auktions-Katalogen vom Jahre 1820*).

40   On the development of the international book trade after 1815 see also Johann Goldfriedrich, *Geschichte des deutschen Buchhandels vom Beginn der Fremdherrschaft bis zur Reform des Börsenvereins im neuen Deutschen Reiche (1805–1889)* (Leipzig, 1913), 55.

Thienemann[41], Lindauer, and Lentner were joined by competitors from Augsburg, Freising, Fürth, Nuremberg, Würzburg, and Leipzig, who all requested catalogues. In addition, numerous private collectors in Germany were interested in purchasing Munich duplicates, among them persons of high standing such as Christian Friedrich Bernhard Augustin (1771–1856), cathedral preacher at Halberstadt, Johann Baptist Keller (1774–1845), the first bishop of the diocese of Rottenburg, Johann Gerhard Christian Thomas (1785–1838), senator and later mayor of Frankfurt. After discussing the question whether the catalogue should also be distributed abroad, the committee for library administration reached the decision that the catalogue could not very well be sent to large foreign cities such as London, Paris, or St Petersburg, because the books listed in it were not of a kind to interest great libraries[42]. Nevertheless, the list of recipients includes names that would have guaranteed an international clientèle, e.g. the firms of Treuttel & Würtz in Strasbourg, Paris and London, Payne in London, several unnamed persons from Switzerland and other "unknown strangers" (*unbekannte Fremde*).

There is reason to think that this second large sale of Munich duplicates was not merely postponed, but cancelled altogether. Bernhart's

notes end on 3 January 1821; on 19 June 1821 his sudden death from a stroke, suffered on library premises, brought his work to a halt[43]. After that time, events at the library are much less well documented, but unlike the preceding sale, no accounts survive from 1821. It may therefore be concluded that the loss of Bernhart as an organizer as well as the still unsatisfactory level of cataloguing of the monastic printed books prevented the library from going ahead with the auction.

Sales in the 1830s and 1840s

Duplicates continued to be sold to members of the library staff, however, some of whom were clearly acting as dealers on a private basis, as well as to collectors and other libraries in Germany and abroad[44]. Even an order issued by King Ludwig I

41   The information given by Schmidt, *Deutsche Buchhändler*, as note 5, 5890 concerning Thienemann's purchase of the "Buch-, Kunst-, Musik- und Landkarten-Handlung von Fr. Xav. Stöger" in 1817 seems doubtful, as the Stögers continue to be recorded as booksellers after this date. It is possible that Stöger sold only his publishing company to Thienemann, see Katharina Masel, *Kalender und Volksaufklärung in Bayern. Zur Entwicklung des Kalenderwesens 1750 bis 1830*, Forschungen zur Landes- und Regionalgeschichte 2 (St Ottilien, 1997), 328, note 629.

42   BayHStA, BSB, A-Reg. C 6, no. 1: *daß dieser Katalog nicht wohl in auswärtige grosse Städte versandt werden könnte, z.B. nach London, Paris, St Petersburg etc. weil die darin vorkommenden Bücher nicht von der Art sind, daß sie bey großen Bibliotheken Absatz finden möchten.*

43   Hertrich, *Erschließung der Inkunabelsammlung*, as note 13, XVII, gives the date erroneously as 20 July 1821, but as early as 14 July 1821 a list of the official papers found in Bernhart's desk after his death was drawn up, and according to a supplication of his widow to the library authorities (BayHStA, BSB, A-Reg. A II Bernhart (J.B.) 52, dated 11 October 1822), Bernhart had died on 19 June of the preceding year, leaving her with eight underage children.

44   One of the prominent purchasers from abroad was Earl Spencer; already in 1818, Thomas Frognall Dibdin had purchased some books for him in Munich; see *Die Bayerische Staatsbibliothek in historischen Beschreibungen* (Munich, [2]1998), 109–17. The supposed duplicates were not always checked very carefully. A former Munich copy of a Greek incunable (*Epistulae diversorum philosophorum, oratorum, rhetorum*, Venice: Aldus Manutius, 1499; GW 9367; ISTC ie00064000) is today preserved in the University Library of Heidelberg (D 4350 oct. INC), into which the following note was entered around 1830: *Die Exemplare dieses seltnen Buches sind verschieden, daher unsere drei Exemplare behalten werden müßen. Haben die Herrn Bibliothekare in München dieses gewußt, als sie hieher Duplum schrieben?* ("The copies of this rare book are different, which is the reason why our three copies have to be kept. Did the gentlemen librarians in Munich know this when they noted 'Duplum' here?");

in 1829, forbidding sales of library duplicates for the immediate future, seems to have had only a short-term effect[45]. When the move to the new library building was drawing closer, the question of duplicates became more urgent. In 1832, director Johann Philipp Lichtenthaler (1778–1857) wrote a lengthy memorandum pleading for a resumption of the sales[46], and in 1833 the library was again granted permission to sell unwanted items[47]. Lichtenthaler justified his request with the concern that the duplicates would infect the new building with *Wurmfraß und Moderdunst* (bookworms and fustiness) and would require substantial storage space, because they could not be left behind in the Jesuit college, which was already earmarked for use by the university. He stressed, however, that it would be necessary to cross-check the duplicates against the recently completed library catalogue. Lichtenthaler estimated the number of duplicates at about 30,000 volumes, including 12,000 incunabula, the component of the sale that would generate the largest income; he expected a total return of 30–36,000 guilders. The need to augment the library's budget through duplicate sales became increasingly pressing at a time when the idea of building a universal library was prevalent, a project further pursued by exchanging duplicates with booksellers for other books that were lacking in the library.

In the 1830s and 1840s, the library entertained contact with a wide-ranging network of exchange partners. Duplicates were not only passed on to German booksellers[48], but increasingly also to specialized antiquarian dealers in Italy, Great Britain, and the United States[49]. Thanks to affluent bibliophiles and expanding libraries in the Anglo-American world, a thriving new market developed at a time when demand for old books was declining in Continental Europe and prices were falling after decades of over-supply from the dissolved monasteries[50]. As a result, collecting interests came to focus more and more on older and rarer monuments of printing.

A typical example of the purchasing policy of large institutions is provided by the Bodleian Library in Oxford, where a substantial collection of incunabula was established in the course of the nineteenth century by purchases as well as through private donations[51]. About 500 incunabula in the Bodleian can be easily identified as former duplicates from the Munich Court Library, for they contain typical handwritten entries: for example the note "Duplum", duplicate numbers or

---

see *Katalog der Inkunabeln der Universitätsbibliothek Heidelberg, des Instituts für Geschichte der Medizin und des Stadtarchivs Heidelberg*, by Armin Schlechter and Ludwig Ries, Kataloge der Universitätsbibliothek Heidelberg 9 / Inkunabeln in Baden-Württemberg 3 (Wiesbaden, 2009), vol. 1, no. 644 (with two copies). The Bayerische Staatsbibliothek today owns only one copy of this edition (4 Inc.c.a. 1612 m; BSB-Ink E-86).

45 BayHStA, BSB, A-Reg. C 3, Fasz. 1, no. 7.
46 BayHStA, BSB, A-Reg. C 3, Fasz. 1, no. 8.
47 See BayHStA, BSB, A-Reg. C 3, Fasz. 2, no. 11 (references to permissions granted on 24 January 1833 and 27 September 1835).

48 See BayHStA, BSB, A-Reg. B III and C I. Among the exchange partners were the firms Seligsberg in Bayreuth (1845–46), Fincke in Berlin (1831–48), Baer (1836–69) and Sankt Goar (1844–52) in Frankfurt/Main, Weigel in Leipzig (1828–66), Thoma in Nuremberg (1840–45) and Manz in Regensburg (1840).
49 For example the firms Gnoato in Venice (1836–47), Pirotta in Milan (1836), Rodd (1834–50) and Stewart (1839) in London, and Putnam in New York (1847).
50 See Bernard M. Rosenthal, 'The history of incunabula collections in the United States. A brief account', *Aus dem Antiquariat*, 6 (2000), A350–366, and Kristian Jensen, *Revolution and the antiquarian book. Reshaping the past, 1780–1815* (Cambridge et al., 2011), 3 figure I.2 and 185–87 on the incunables acquired by the Bodleian Library.
51 See Alan Coates, 'The Bodleian Library and its Incunabula', in *A catalogue of books printed in the fifteenth century now in the Bodleian Library* by Alan Coates, Kristian Jensen, Cristina Dondi, Bettina Wagner, and Helen Dixon (Oxford, 2005) (cited as Bod-inc.), vol. 1, LVII–LXXVIII, at LXIII as well as in the index of provenances under the individual years of auction and the entry for Munich.

previous Munich shelfmarks[52] (Fig. 20.3). Those volumes were not purchased directly from the Continent, but through booksellers in London. In 1837, Thomas Rodd invoiced the Bodleian Library for 904 florins for 38 "books from Munich"[53], and even larger quantities of books were purchased via Leigh and Sotheby in the years 1840 and 1841[54]. The biggest acquisition, comprising 320 incunabula, was made in 1850 through the Berlin bookseller Adolf Asher, who enjoyed close business relations with British libraries and also ran a flourishing trade in English books in Germany[55]. In November 1849, he purchased more than 500 incunabula from the Munich Court Library for a total of 1,637 guilders, the largest portion of which (320 items) he sold on to the Bodleian Library a year later for £113 19s 6d[56]. In June 1850, he approached director Lichtenthaler in Munich with a proposal for the library to pay off unsettled bills in kind with duplicates, and he requested a complete copy of the library's catalogue of duplicates in order to select titles. This request was fulfilled gradually by 1853, even though it amounted to an enormous task – the catalogue comprised 172 *cahiers* of 500 leaves

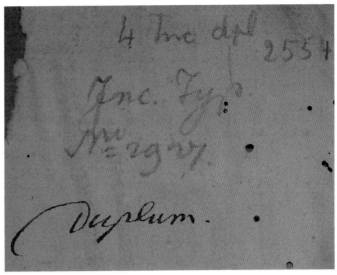

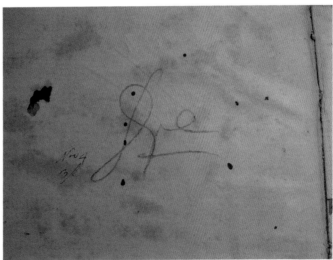

Figure 20.3. Typical nineteenth century "duplum"-entries and old shelfmarks from the Munich Court Library

each, i.e. a total of *c.* 86,000 leaves[57] – and the copyist, *scriptor* Joseph Bachlechner, complained that sending library catalogues to antiquarian booksellers was an unheard-of event in library administration[58]. Duplicate exchanges between

---

52 These numbers correspond to various handwritten inventories and indexes of duplicates, some of which have been preserved in the fonds Cbm Cat., e.g. Cbm Cat. 22 (dated 1807), Cbm Cat. 253 (for the period 1820–35), Cbm Cat. 283 (for the period 1812–16) and Cbm Cat. 292 (for the period 1841–85).

53 Bod-inc., as note 51, 2910, note 56.

54 *Catalogue of a Valuable Assemblage of Fine, Rare and Curious Books* (London: Sotheby, 27.5.1840) and *Catalogue of a Valuable Collection of Choice, and Curious Books, Consigned from Germany* (London: Sotheby, 27.8.1841).

55 On Asher see Coates, *Bodleian Library*, as note 51, LXIII note 56, and 2837 note 39 as well as David Paisey, 'Adolphus Asher (1800–1853): Berlin Bookseller, Anglophile and Friend to Panizzi', *British Library Journal*, 12 (1997), 131–53. Asher was a close friend of Antonio Panizzi (1797–1879), who was at the time in charge of the collection of printed books at the British Museum.

56 BayHStA, BSB, A-Reg. B III Asher, no. 87 und 95.

57 BayHStA, BSB, A-Reg. A 153, drawn up in the period 1843–48.

58 BayHStA, BSB, A-Reg. A 185, no. 3: *Versendung von Bibliothek-Katalogen an Antiquare* [sei] *ein in der Bibliothek-Verwaltung unerhörtes Ding.*

the Munich Court library and Asher, as well as his successor Albert Cohn, continued well into the early twentieth century.

The Butsch and Quatremère Auctions of 1858–1859

In the mid-1850s, the need to generate an income for the library within a short timespan became again more pressing, as the newly-appointed library director, the classical philologist Karl Halm (1809–1882)[59], intended to raise funds to purchase the library of the recently-deceased orientalist Étienne Quatremère (1782–1857), which would constitute a welcome expansion in an area that had been one of the library's strengths since its foundation in the sixteenth century[60]. Furthermore, Halm required financial means for the publication of the catalogue of manuscripts, which had been compiled by the late Johann Andreas Schmeller (1795–1852) in the 1830s and was still only accessible in a handwritten copy on the library's premises; its distribution in print was essential to make the Munich holdings more widely known to scholars world-wide, but the publication costs were estimated at 30,000 guilders[61]. The obvious solution seemed to

auction off duplicates, particularly copies of rare and attractive books which were likely to find considerable interest among international collectors and thus generate a high income.

While the earlier sales that had been organized in the city of Munich were mainly targeted at academics and librarians from Bavaria and Germany, the auctions arranged by director Halm were intended to attract the elite of the international antiquarian book dealers. Perhaps in order to avoid coverage in local Munich papers, the auctions were held outside the Bavarian capital: the first auction took place in May 1858 in Augsburg, where the bookseller Fidelis Butsch, who organized the sale, was resident[62]. Six months later, after the successful acquisition of the Quatremère collection by the Munich Court Library, a series of four auctions, supposedly of unwanted duplicates from the Quatremère library, began in Paris[63]. However, as hinted at in the title of the sale catalogue by

---

59   See *Allgemeine Deutsche Biographie*, vol. 49 (1904), 723–31. Halm's correspondence with Butsch is part of the collection of his personal papers at the BSB, Halmiana.

60   See Helga Rebhan, 'Johann Albrecht Widmanstetter und seine Bibliothek', in *Kulturkosmos der Renaissance. Die Gründung der Bayerischen Staatsbibliothek. Katalog der Ausstellung zum 450-jährigen Jubiläum, 7. März–1. Juni 2008 und der Schatzkammerausstellung "Musikschätze der Wittelsbacher", 9. Juni–6. Juli 2008*, Bayerische Staatsbibliothek, Ausstellungskataloge 79 (Wiesbaden, 2008), 81–83.

61   See above note 6 and *Johann Andreas Schmeller. 1785–1852. Bayerische Staatsbibliothek, Gedächtnisausstellung zum 200. Geburtsjahr* (Munich, 1985). The first volume of Schmeller's manuscript catalogue was published posthumously: *Die deutschen Handschriften der K. Hof- und Staatsbibliothek zu München nach J. A. Schmellers*

kürzerem Verzeichniss (Munich, 1866). On the printing costs of the manuscript catalogue, see Georg Leyh, 'Die Hof- und Staatsbibliothek 1826–1882', [first published 1957; reprinted] in *Beiträge zur Geschichte der Bayerischen Staatsbibliothek*, ed. Rupert Hacker (Munich, 2000), 253–62, at 259–60.

62   *Catalog einer kostbaren Sammlung von xylographischen und typographischen Seltenheiten, welche [von Holztafeldrucken, Pergamentdrucken und anderen typographischen Seltenheiten, welche nebst einer namhaften Anzahl auserlesener Bücher aus allen Fächern am] Montag den 3. Mai 1858 und folgende Tage bei Fidelis Butsch in Augsburg in dessen Haus Lit. F. Nro. 367 in der Heilig-Kreutz-Strasse öffentlich versteigert werden* (Augsburg, 1858). Online access: https://opacplus.bsb-muenchen.de/search?oclcno=162931955.

63   *Bibliothèque Quatremère. Catalogue d'une collection de livres précieux et importants provenant pour la plupart de la bibliothèque de feu M. Étienne Quatremère de l'Institut*, rédigé par M. Ch. Halm, 4 vols (Paris, 1858–1859). Online access: https://opacplus.bsb-muenchen.de/search?oclcno=162819782. The acquisition cost of the Quatremère library amounted to 340,000 Francs, and the revenue from duplicate sales was estimated at 100,000 Francs, see Leyh, 260, note 66.

the phrase *livres … provenant pour la plupart de la bibliothèque de feu M. Étienne Quatremère*, not all books offered in the Parisian sales between November 1858 and November 1859 had in fact previously been owned by the eminent orientalist himself. In order to make the sales of Quatremère duplicates more profitable, Halm – as he states explicitly in the preface to the first sale catalogue – enhanced them with precious early printed books that had entered the Munich Court Library much earlier, largely as a result of the dissolution of monasteries[64]. The director probably cherished the hope that duplicate sales abroad, in a well-established centre of the international antiquarian booktrade, would both attract a wider range of wealthy bidders and at the same time less attention from the German public and fellow-librarians who might object against such fund-raising at the expense of the national cultural heritage.

In the Augsburg sale of May 1858 and in the second of the Parisian auctions held in February 1859, numerous rare items from the Munich Court Library were offered, mostly books printed in the fifteenth and sixteenth centuries, including a copy of the Gutenberg Bible, a vellum copy of the *Catholicon*, and many rare incunabula as well as blockbooks. The kind of books on offer, the thematic arrangement of the catalogues, and the often detailed descriptions and even copy-specific notes on individual items show

that the audience targeted by these auctions was completely different from those of the 1815 and 1820 catalogues. Now, it was bibliophile collectors rather than academics of various disciplines who would be interested in buying bibliographical rarities and to whom the age of an edition or its printing technique mattered as much or even more than its contents. Such a clientèle would not be satisfied with the very limited information given for incunabula in the previous sales. While the 1815 catalogue had at least contained references to Panzer's *Annales*, the 1820 catalogue gave only very basic bibliographical records, and early printed books were treated in exactly the same manner as recent publications. Unlike the catalogue of 1815, the 1820 catalogue did not even list incunabula as a separate group. By the mid-nineteenth century, incunable bibliography had made substantial progress: Ludwig Hain's *Repertorium bibliographicum* had been published posthumuously between 1826 and 1838, making it much easier to identify duplicates among the Munich collection, which had been subsequently reshelved systematically in the groups of dated and undated incunabula, the former arranged by format and date of printing, the latter by author. The 1858 and 1859 sale catalogues exactly mirror the various subject groups of the library: they contain separate sections for books printed on vellum, books with engravings, and xylographs; in the second of the Quatremère catalogues, the dated incunabula were presented in chronological order exactly as they had been shelved[65]. Furthermore, copious notes on the condition

---

64 In his preface to the catalogue of the first Quatremère auction, as note 63, which was held at the maison A. Franck in rue Richelieu, Paris on 25 November 1858 and the following days, Karl Halm stated: "D'ailleurs pour rendre nos ventes plus intéressantes encore, nous ajouterons aux différentes catégories qu'elles embrassent, des exemplaires du fonds de doubles de notre bibliothèque, surtout un quantité d'anciens ouvrages rares, pour relever et compléter un spécialité qui dans la bibliothèque de M. Quatremère paraît être comparativement la plus faible." (p. II). A total of more than 10,000 titles were offered in the Quatremère sales, among them *c.* 400 incunabula and rare books.

---

65 In the second Quatremère auction of 3–19 February 1859, 139 "Incunables avec date", 158 "Incunables sans date", 88 "Livres rares et curieux", 11 "Livres imprimés sur vélin" and one "Xylographe" (a Biblia pauperum) were offered. This subject division mirrors exactly the main groups of valuable early printed books in the Munich library: the "Incunabula cum anno", "Incunabula sine anno", "Rariora", "Libri impressi membranacei" and "Xylographa".

of the rare books were included, sometimes even references to the existing bibliographical literature.

Unlike Bernhart, who had selected the duplicates of incunabula and other rare books which were offered in previous sales, Halm was not particularly concerned with the history of printing nor with copy-specific features of early printed books. As a professor of classical philology, the library director had no profound knowledge of scholarly bibliographical methods and apparently no previous experience of the book market, even though his father Felix Halm had been an art dealer. Karl Halm was mainly interested in overcoming the library's budgetary constraints by making a fast and easy profit from what appeared to be little-used and therefore superfluous books. He seems to have seriously underestimated the value of the duplicates offered, as he accepted a proposal from Butsch that the auctioneer should receive a commission of a third of the proceeds of the sale. Butsch is even said to have deliberately suggested low estimates in order to conceal how large his profit from the transaction might turn out to be. When the Augsburg sale of 3 May 1858 resulted in a total income of 27,798 guilders for 850 lots – the Gutenberg Bible alone fetched 2,336 guilders, and four blockbooks another 3,400 guilders – Butsch's share amounted to 9,266 guilders[66].

From the neatly annotated copy of the Augsburg auction catalogue that was used for drawing up the final accounts (Fig. 20.4), it becomes obvious that by the mid-nineteenth century, sales of antiquarian books in Bavaria had become an international event. Business was transacted mainly with the large German, French, and British firms; only very few direct private bids are recorded[67]. Apart from the well-established firm of Asher & Co., the following dealers were represented and made substantial purchases: Windprecht (Augsburg), Stargardt (Berlin), Baer (Frankfurt), Weigel (Leipzig), Zipperer (Munich), Tross and Vieweg (both Paris), Gancia (Brighton), Stark (Hull), Boone and Quaritch (both London). Butsch himself acquired a number of items, probably on commission[68].

Adolf Schmidt-Künsemüller (Munich, 1979), 146 no. 30. For the individual prices and fates of the blockbooks, see below note 72.

67 The following individual names appear, some of them repeatedly: Herberger, Metzger Reiter and Prof. Oppenrieder (all three from Augsburg), Dekan Eberhard (Kelheim), Dr Petzholdt (Dresden), Dr Förstemann (Wernigerode), Rat Herzenskron, Inspector Müller and Oberdorfer (without indication of place, probably from Munich or Augsburg).

68 A rare xylographic print that Butsch sold on to the Bibliothèque nationale et universitaire at Strasbourg has recently come to light again: the unique woodcut broadside of the "Acht Schalkheiten" produced c. 1460. The broadside (shelfmark K.6) must originally have been part of the Schedel collection, as a Latin distich in his hand is visible on the blank verso; it also bears an early nineteenth-century Munich shelfmark in Bernhart's hand. The broadside was probably sold by the Court Library at the Augsburg sale, but is not listed individually in the Catalog. Later, Butsch (re-)acquired the xylograph at the 1872 sale of the Leipzig collector Theodor Oswald Weigel (1812–1881) and in the following year sold it to the library at Strasbourg, which had been destroyed in the German-French war in 1870. See Bettina Wagner, 'De la planche illustrée au livre. Les *Huit grugeries* [autour de 1460]', in *Métamorphoses – un bâtiment, des collections.* [exposition … présentée à la Bibliothèque Nationale et Universitaire de Strasbourg du 11 avril au 20 septembre 2015], ed. Christophe Didier et Madeleine Zeller (Strasbourg, 2015), 244–47.

---

66 The results of the sale are documented in an annotated copy of the *Catalog* (Munich, BSB, 8 L.impr.c.n.mss. 142). The Gutenberg Bible formerly owned by the Augustinian Canons of Rottenbuch was purchased by the Frankfurt dealer Joseph Baer on behalf of the imperial library at St Petersburg and in Soviet times was sold via Maggs in London; the Swiss collector Martin Bodmer acquired it in 1928, and the copy is now kept in Cologny near Geneva: see Ilona Hubay, 'Die bekannten Exemplare der zweiundvierzigzeiligen Bibel und ihre Besitzer', in *Johannes Gutenbergs zweiundvierzigzeilige Bibel, Faksimile-Ausgabe nach dem Exemplar der Staatsbibliothek Preußischer Kulturbesitz Berlin. Kommentarband*, ed. Wieland Schmidt und Friedrich

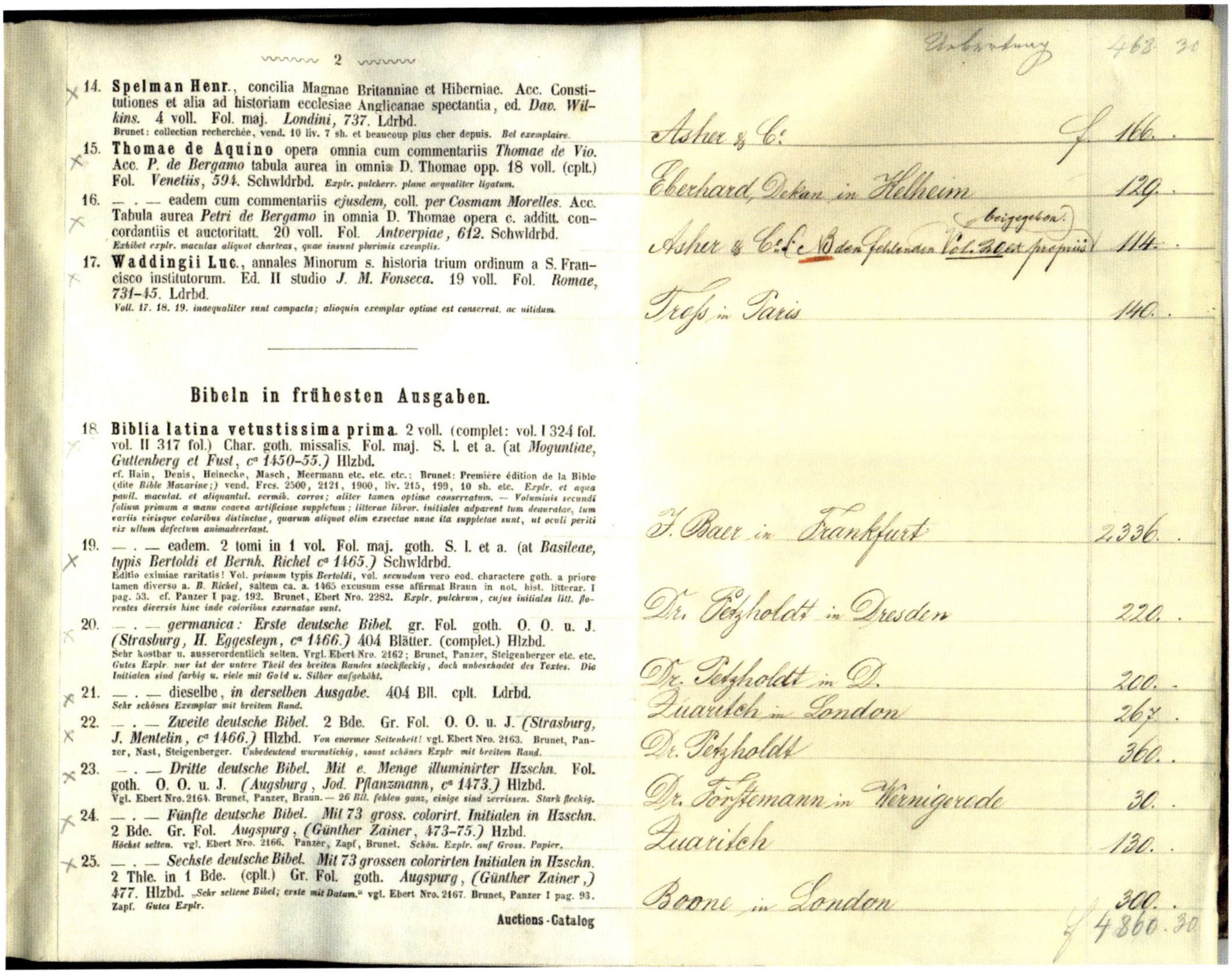
2

14. **Spelman Henr.**, concilia Magnae Britanniae et Hiberniae. Acc. Constitutiones et alia ad historiam ecclesiae Anglicanae spectantia, ed. *Dav. Wilkins.* 4 voll. Fol. maj. *Londini, 737.* Ldrbd.
Brunet: collection recherchée, vend. 10 liv. 7 sh. et beaucoup plus cher depuis. *Bel exemplaire.*

15. **Thomae de Aquino** opera omnia cum commentariis *Thomae de Vio.* Acc. *P. de Bergamo* tabula aurea in omnia D. Thomae opp. 18 voll. (cplt.) Fol. *Venetiis, 594.* Schwldrbd. *Explr. pulcherr. plane aequaliter ligatum.*

16. — . — eadem cum commentariis *ejusdem,* coll. *per Cosmam Morelles.* Acc. Tabula aurea *Petri de Bergamo* in omnia D. Thomae opera c. additt. concordantiis et auctoritatt. 20 voll. Fol. *Antverpiae, 612.* Schwldrbd.
Exhibet explr. maculas aliquot charteas, quae insunt plurimis exemplis.

17. **Waddingii Luc.**, annales Minorum s. historia trium ordinum a S. Francisco institutorum. Ed. II studio *J. M. Fonseca.* 19 voll. Fol. *Romae, 731–45.* Ldrbd.
Voll. 17. 18. 19. inaequaliter sunt compacta; alioquin exemplar optime est conservat. ac nitidum.

Bibeln in frühesten Ausgaben.

18. **Biblia latina vetustissima prima.** 2 voll. (complet: vol. I 324 fol. vol. II 317 fol.) Char. goth. missalis. Fol. maj. S. l. et a. (at *Moguntiae, Guttenberg et Fust, ca 1450–55.)* Hlzbd.
cf. Hain, Denis, Heinecke, Masch, Meermann etc. etc. etc.; Brunet: Première édition de la Bible (dite *Bible Mazarine;*) vend. Frcs. 2500, 2121, 1900, liv. 215, 199, 10 sh. etc. *Explr. et aqua paull. maculat. et aliquantul. vermib. corros; aliter tamen optime conservatum. — Voluminis secundi folium primum a manu coaeva artificiose suppletum; litterae libror. initiales adparent tum deauratae, tum variis vivisque coloribus distinctae, quarum aliquot olim exsectae nunc ita suppletae sunt, ut oculi periti vix ullum defectum animadvertant.*

19. — . — eadem. 2 tomi in 1 vol. Fol. maj. goth. S. l. et a. (at *Basileae, typis Bertoldi et Bernh. Richel ca 1465.)* Schwldrbd.
Editio eximiae raritatis! Vol. *primum* typis *Bertoldi,* vol. *secundum* vero eod. charactere goth. a priore tamen diverso a. *B. Richel,* saltem ca. a. 1465 excusum esse affirmat Braun in not. hist. litterar. I pag. 53. cf. Panzer I pag. 192. Brunet, Ebert Nro. 2282. *Explr. pulchrum, cujus initiales litt. florentes diversis hinc inde coloribus exornatae sunt.*

20. — . — *germanica: Erste deutsche Bibel.* gr. Fol. goth. O. O. u. J. *(Strasburg, H. Eggesteyn, ca 1466.)* 404 Blätter. (complet.) Hlzbd.
Sehr kostbar u. ausserordentlich selten. Vrgl. Ebert Nro. 2162; Brunet, Panzer, Steigenberger etc. etc. *Gutes Explr. nur ist der untere Theil des breiten Randes stockfleckig, doch unbeschadet des Textes. Die Initialen sind farbig u. viele mit Gold u. Silber aufgehöht.*

21. — . — dieselbe, *in derselben Ausgabe.* 404 Bll. cplt. Ldrbd.
Sehr schönes Exemplar mit breitem Rand.

22. — . — *Zweite deutsche Bibel.* 2 Bde. Gr. Fol. O. O. u. J. *(Strasburg, J. Mentelin, ca 1466.)* Hlzbd. *Von enormer Seltenheit!* vgl. Ebert Nro. 2163. Brunet, Panzer, Nast, Steigenberger. *Unbedeutend wurmstichig, sonst schönes Explr. mit breitem Rand.*

23. — . — *Dritte deutsche Bibel. Mit e. Menge illuminirter Hzschn.* Fol. goth. O. O. u. J. *(Augsburg, Jod. Pflanzmann, ca 1473.)* Hlzbd.
Vgl. Ebert Nro. 2164. Brunet, Panzer, Braun. — *26 Bll. fehlen ganz, einige sind zerrissen. Stark fleckig.*

24. — . — *Fünfte deutsche Bibel. Mit 73 gross. colorirt. Initialen in Hzschn.* 2 Bde. Gr. Fol. *Augspurg, (Günther Zainer, 473–75.)* Hzbd.
Höchst selten. vgl. Ebert Nro. 2166. Panzer, Zapf, Brunet. *Schön. Explr. auf Gross. Papier.*

25. — . — *Sechste deutsche Bibel. Mit 73 grossen colorirten Initialen in Hzschn.* 2 Thle. in 1 Bde. (cplt.) Gr. Fol. goth. *Augspurg, (Günther Zainer,) 477.* Hlzbd. *„Sehr seltene Bibel; erste mit Datum."* vgl. Ebert Nro. 2167. Brunet, Panzer I pag. 93. Zapf. *Gutes Explr.*

Auctions-Catalog

Asher & Co f. 166.
Eberhard, Dekan in Kelheim 129.
Asher & Co 114.
Tross in Paris 140.
J. Baer in Frankfurt 2336.
Dr. Petzholdt in Dresden 220.
Dr. Petzholdt in D. 200.
Quaritch in London 267.
Dr. Petzholdt 360.
Dr. Förstemann in Wernigerode 30.
Quaritch 130.
Boone in London 300.
f 4860.30

Figure 20.4. Auction catalogue of 1858, title page and p. 57 with annotations (Munich, BSB, 8 L.impr.c.n.mss. 142)

The rather unprofessional dealings of the Munich director and the outcome of the sales met with severe criticism from Halm's rather combative Würzburg colleague Anton Ruland (1809–1874)[69], who had been a member of the Bavarian Parliament since 1848 and who used this forum to voice his concerns[70]. In a parliamentary speech delivered on 10 March 1859, hardly three weeks after the second Parisian sale, Ruland

69 See *Allgemeine Deutsche Biographie*, vol. 29 (1889), 632–34, and Thomas Sauer, *Anton Ruland (1809–1874). Ein Beitrag zur Geschichte der katholischen Restauration in Bayern*, Schriftenreihe zur bayerischen Landesgeschichte 103 (Munich, 1995).

70 See Max Pauer, 'Anton Ruland und Karl Halm. Ein bibliothekarischer Streit um Dublettenverkäufe vor hundert Jahren', in *Aus der Arbeit des Bibliothekars. Festschrift Fritz Redenbacher*, ed. Bernhard Sinogowitz, Schriften der Universitäts-Bibliothek 4 (Erlangen, 1960), 121–35, and Bettina Wagner, 'Wege und Abwege bayerischer Inkunabeln', *Wolfenbütteler Notizen zur Buchgeschichte*, 18/19 (1993/1994), issue 2, 93–108.

pointed out that the printed books that had been sold were an integral part of the Bavarian cultural heritage owing to their provenances. Ruland's outrage was particularly inflamed by the deaccessioning (and often mutilation) of volumes formerly owned by the Nuremberg doctor Hartmann Schedel (1440–1514), whose collection – the largest private library of a fifteenth-century German humanist still in existence – had survived nearly intact for nearly 350 years after his death, as it had been purchased by the Bavarian Dukes as part of the library of Johann Jakob Fugger as early as 1571[71]. Many early printed items, such as blockbooks, had even been cut out of manuscripts or composite volumes to enable them to be sold separately[72]. In vain, Halm attempted to refute

this criticism by issuing a public statement, and Ruland responded at greater length with a printed pamphlet[73]. As a result of the public dispute, a committee was set up to review the duplicates which had been selected for deaccessioning. This effectively brought major sales to an end for the time being.

A Lesson Learnt? Cataloguing Duplicates and Reconstructing Dispersed Collections

In many countries, sales of duplicates from public collections have continued well into the twentieth century and beyond. Faced with budgetary constraints and conflicting priorities, some decision-makers still regard the presence of several copies of the same edition in one institution (or indeed several editions of the same work) as a waste of precious space and staff resources, as well

---

71 See 'Zur Geschichte der K. Hof- und Staatsbibliothek zu München', in *Serapeum*, 20 (1859), no. 9, 129–42, here 131. On Schedel's library and its history, see *Worlds of Learning. The Library and World Chronicle of the Nuremberg Physician Hartmann Schedel (1440–1514)*, ed. Bettina Wagner, Bayerische Staatsbibliothek, Ausstellungskataloge 89 (Munich, 2015).

72 From a volume originally containing four blockbooks, an *Apocalypse* and a *Canticum Canticorum* that were pasted together (Butsch's *Catalog*, nos 719 and 720) were purchased for 1,255 guilders by Baer; they are now in St Petersburg, Saltykow-Schtschedrin-Bibliothek, 9.2.3.13 and 9.2.3.14, see *Xylographa Bavarica. Blockbücher in bayerischen Sammlungen (Xylo-Bav)*, ed. Bettina Wagner, Beschreibungen von Rahel Bacher unter Mitarbeit von Veronika Hausler, Antonie Magen und Heike Riedel-Bierschwale (Wiesbaden, 2016), nos AP-02,04 and CC-01,04. The *Ars memorandi* which was originally part of the same volume was preserved in Munich (BSB, Xylogr. 12), as was probably the fourth item, a *Biblia pauperum*, which however cannot be identified with certainty; see *Xylographa Bavarica*, no. AS-03,03. The blockbook *Apocalypse* listed in Butsch's *Catalog* (1858), no. 718 had been removed from a manuscript (now Clm 14346) and lacked the plate no. 43; it was purchased for 1,426 guilders – probably on commission – by the Augsburg firm of Sebastian Windprecht & Co., the descendants of a blind bookseller who had died in 1837, and is now untraced; see *Xylographa Bavarica*, no. AP-05,02. On Clm 14346, see *Katalog der lateinischen Handschriften der Bayerischen Staatsbibliothek München. Die Handschriften aus St Emmeram in Regensburg. Band 3: Clm 14261–14400*,

neu beschrieben von Friedrich Helmer unter Mitarbeit von Hermann Hauke und Elisabeth Wunderle, Catalogus codicum manu scriptorum Bibliothecae Monacensis, Tomus IV, series nova pars 2,3 (Wiesbaden, 2011), 284–86, and Rahel Bacher, 'Die Provenienzen der Münchener Blockbücher', in *Vom ABC bis zur Apokalypse: Leben, Glauben und Sterben in spätmittelalterlichen Blockbüchern*, ed. Bettina Wagner (Lucerne, 2012), 130–44, here 26, 137–39. The fourth blockbook sold was an *Ars memorandi* (Butsch's *Catalog*, no. 717); it was purchased by Asher for 725 guilders and may have gone to New York, see *Xylographa Bavarica*, no. AS-03,04.

73 Karl Halm, *Erläuterungen zu den Verhandlungen der bayerischen Kammer der Abgeordneten vom 10. März 1859, die k. Hof- und Staatsbibliothek in München betreffend* (Munich, 1959). Online access: https://opacplus.bsb-muenchen.de/search?oclcno=48743959. Anton Ruland, *Die in der Schrift des Herrn Oberbibliothekars und Directors Dr Karl Halm "Erläuterungen zu den Verhandlungen der bayerischen Kammer der Abgeordneten vom 10. März 1859, die k. Hof- und Staatsbibliothek in München betreffend" gegen die Kammerverhandlungen vom selben Tage gemachten Angriffe zurückgewiesen* (Würzburg, 1859). Online access: https://opacplus.bsb-muenchen.de/search?oclcno=162752307.

as a contradiction to the strategy of aiming for the widest possible range of items within a defined area of collecting. From a short-sighted perspective, focused on immediate usefulness, the capital tied up in duplicates might appear to be better spent on increasing the number of different titles or editions in a library, thus broadening the diversity of literature available to users locally and at the same time giving other libraries and private collectors world-wide a chance to build up their own collections[74].

In the course of the twentieth century, an understanding of the intrinsic value of every individual copy of an early printed book has only gradually spread beyond the small circle of book historians of early printing who have studied features like typesetting variants, paper watermarks, bindings, provenances, painted decoration or manuscript annotations. Such research trends developed in close exchanges with rare books librarians who created copy-specific descriptions of early printed books, particularly incunabula – including, of course, duplicates. In Bavaria, various projects for systematically describing the incunabula holdings of several libraries were undertaken in the 1960s and 1970s and resulted in a series of printed catalogues[75]. The incunable

collection of the Bayerische Staatsbibliothek in Munich is covered in a multi-volume catalogue (BSB-Ink) that was published from 1988 and made accessible online in 2004[76]. However, cataloguing the Munich incunable duplicates is still an ongoing process. Even after the decimation through duplicate sales, which were only partly compensated by purchases made in recent years, the Munich collection today [2017] comprises more than 20,000 copies of 9,781 editions. Due to these large numbers, only those multiple copies of fifteenth-century editions were included in the printed catalogue which had been given a library shelfmark by 1985, but another *c.* 2,500 as yet unaccessioned duplicates from dissolved monasteries were excluded, as their poor state of conservation would have necessitated substantial conservation work before cataloguing[77]. The first step to remedy this omission was taken 2007, when all uncatalogued duplicates were recorded

74 A substantial number of Munich incunable duplicates, particularly editions from the workshop of Peter Drach in Speyer, were acquired in the nineteenth century by the Historisches Museum der Pfalz in Speyer, partly via the private collection of the eminent philologist Wilhelm Meyer (1845–1917), a student of Karl Halm's, see INKA (provenance search for "Speyer" and "München"), online at http://www.inka.uni-tuebingen.de/. As a result of the Congress of Vienna in 1815, Speyer had become part of Bavaria and was seat of the Bavarian administration of the Palatinate until 1945.

75 Ilona Hubay, *Incunabula der Universitätsbibliothek Würzburg*, Inkunabelkataloge Bayerischer Bibliotheken 1 (Wiesbaden, 1966); Id., *Incunabula Eichstätter Bibliotheken*, Inkunabelkataloge bayerischer Bibliotheken 2 (Wiesbaden, 1968); Id., *Incunabula aus der Staatlichen Bibliothek Neuburg/Donau, (Incunabula) in der Benediktinerabtei Ottobeuren*, Inkunabelkataloge bayerischer Bibliotheken 3 (Wiesbaden, 1970); Barbara Hellwig, *Inkunabelkatalog des Germanischen Nationalmuseums Nürnberg, bearb. nach*

einem Verzeichnis von Walter Matthey, Inkunabelkataloge bayerischer Bibliotheken 4 (Wiesbaden, 1970); Ilona Hubay, *Incunabula der Staats- und Stadtbibliothek Augsburg*, Inkunabelkataloge Bayerischer Bibliotheken 5 (Wiesbaden, 1966). See also Elmar Hertrich, '75 Jahre Gesamtkatalog der Wiegendrucke: zur Erschließung deutscher Inkunabelsammlungen seit der Jahrhundertwende', *Aus dem Antiquariat*, 10 (1970), A345-54.

76 Printed version: *Bayerische Staatsbibliothek: Inkunabelkatalog (BSB-Ink)*, ed. Elmar Hertrich, Günter Mayer, Bettina Wagner and Claudia Bubenik, 8 vols (Wiesbaden, 1988–2021). Online access: https://inkunabeln.digitale-sammlungen.de/sucheEin.html. See also Bettina Wagner: 'Collecting, Cataloguing, and Digitizing Incunabula at the Bayerische Staatsbibliothek Munich', *Papers of the Bibliographical Society of America*, 101 (2007), no. 4, 451–79.

77 According to the preface of the first catalogue volume (p. VII), the collection in 1985 comprised 9,573 editions in a total of 16,785 copies; an additional 2,448 duplicates were not included in this figure. Since the cutoff date of the catalogue, more than 240 further incunable editions were purchased by the library, which have been recorded in the online database and are described in *Bayerische Staatsbibliothek: Inkunabelkatalog (BSB-Ink)*, vol. 8 (Wiesbaden, 2021), 457–517.

in the online catalogue of incunabula, albeit as yet without detailed copy-specific descriptions.

Those duplicates which were sold in nineteenth-century auctions and thus dispersed raise different problems today. As a rule, it is not possible for the Bayerische Staatsbibliothek to reacquire them even if they come again onto the antiquarian market, as such purchases fall outside the remit of modern institutional acquisition profiles – partly because the nineteenth-century idea of building "universal libraries" still prevails, partly because the number of books involved would be potentially enormous, and partly because the monetary value of the books has in some cases risen beyond all expectations[78]. Such – often unpredictable – price increases raise an additional, yet fundamental question concerning the disposal of public property that constitutes an integral part of a country's heritage in return for a short-term financial profit – a gain that may in the long run, as the antiquarian book market fluctuates, turn out to be a substantial diminution of the library's assets.

As the goal of physically reconstructing the dispersed historical collections of dissolved religious houses will inevitably remain utopian, "virtual" reconstruction in printed or electronic form has emerged in recent years as an alternative approach[79]. On the basis of printed incunable catalogues of individual collections,

the database INKA was created in the 1990s as a joint enterprise by a number (currently 51) libraries in Germany and Austria[80]. The database is hosted by the University Library at Tübingen; as of late 2016, it contains records of more than 70,000 copies of incunabula, many of them with information on provenances and other copy-specific features in standardized form[81]. Since 2015, more than 300 institutions worldwide have begun to contribute to the database "Material Evidence in Incunabula" (MEI) hosted by the Consortium of European Research Libraries (CERL); so far, 60,000 copies of incunabula have been recorded[82]. The identification of marks of ownership from a wide range of different places and persons poses considerable problems for cataloguers, as familiarity with languages, scripts, names and heraldic emblems of the regions of origin is essential. Therefore, a close network of international collaboration such as the German "ProvenienzWiki" and the provenance mailing list run by HEBIS[83] or the CERL website[84] can be of enormous support. Once a high level of copy-specific cataloguing at collection level has been achieved, modern technologies make it possible to produce inventories of books from dispersed libraries[85] and even to reunite them

78 A former Munich duplicate, a copy of the "Opera" of Lactantius, printed by Sweynheym and Pannartz in Rome on 29 October 1465, was offered at an estimate of 1 million Euro in 2012, see Bernard and Stéphane Clavreuil, *Livres & manuscripts du XIIIᵉ au XXᵉ siècle* (Paris, 2012), no. 3. The copy comes from the Benedictine monastery on the Michelsberg in Bamberg suppressed in 1803 and was subsequently owned by Martin Bodmer, Hans-Peter Kraus, Adrian Flühmann, Heribert Tenschert and J. R. Ritman. The book cannot be traced in any of the auction catalogues discussed in this paper.

79 See e.g. *Rekonstruktion und Erschließung mittelalterlicher Bibliotheken. Neue Formen der Handschriftenpräsentation*, ed. Andrea Rapp and Michael Embach, Beiträge zu den Historischen Kulturwissenschaften 1 (Berlin, 2008).

80 http://www.inka.uni-tuebingen.de/.

81 See Ulrike Mehringer and Armin Schlechter, 'Der Inkunabel-Katalog deutscher Bibliotheken (INKA)', *B.I.T.online – Zeitschrift für Bibliothek, Information und Technologie*, 5 (2002), Heft 1, 41–44: URL: http://www.b-i-t-online.de/archiv/2002-01/nach1.htm.

82 https://data.cerl.org/mei/_search. See also Dondi in this volume.

83 Subscription via https://provenienz.gbv.de/Hauptseite and https://www.hebis.de/arbeitsmaterialien/mailinglisten/ with link to https://dlist.server.uni-frankfurt.de/mailman/listinfo/provenienz.

84 https://www.cerl.org/resources/provenance/main.

85 A long-term project for the reconstruction of the library of the Augsburg humanist Konrad Peutinger (1465–1547) on the basis of a printed edition of the contemporary inventories is still ongoing; so far, three volumes have been published: *Die Bibliothek Konrad Peutingers*.

in digital form on a joint website[86]. However, such reconstructions are difficult and expensive undertakings, as they involve time-consuming labour to trace books from former religious houses in institutions all over the world and to identify them in surviving historical inventories. Projects for the reconstruction of dispersed libraries often tend to miss out on books that are now owned privately or in the hands of booksellers, as such copies are extremely mobile and especially difficult to track. Yet, when successful, such enterprises provide fascinating insights into historical book collections, particularly of religious houses, and allow detailed study of monastic reading (and writing) practices and their diachronic transformations. The efforts invested in such virtual reconstruction projects are therefore well spent, for in our era of globalization, they can stimulate libraries to analyse the historical development of their collections and strengthen their individual profile. Tracing dispersed duplicates thus both helps to build up a network of institutions linked by such book transfers and makes the cultural heritage of a particular place or region more visible. Such enterprises thereby contribute to a better understanding of an institution's identity, which is shaped by the periods of growth and of losses, of expansion and migration alike, and of which the decisions of the past, may they be considered right or wrong today, constitute an integral part.

Edition der historischen Kataloge und Rekonstruktion der Bestände, vol. 1: *Die autographen Kataloge Peutingers. Der nicht-juristische Bibliotheksteil*, ed. Hans-Jörg Künast and Helmut Zäh (Tübingen, 2003); vol. 2: *Die autographen Kataloge Peutingers: Der juristische Bibliotheksteil*, ed. Hans-Jörg Künast and Helmut Zäh with Uta Goerlitz and Christoph Petersen, vol. 3: *Das Nachlassinventar, Ergänzungen zu den Drucken und Handschriften*, ed. Hans-Jörg Künast (Tübingen, 2017), *Die Bibliothek und der handschriftliche Nachlaß Konrad Peutingers*, ed. Jochen Brüning, Helmut Gier, Jan-Dirk Müller and Bernhard Schimmelpfennig. Studia Augustana 14 (Tübingen, 2005).

86 From 2008 to 2012, the Bayerische Staatsbibliothek was a partner in a project funded by the Deutsche Forschungsgemeinschaft that aimed at a comparative analysis of the written heritage from five South German nunneries: 'Schriftlichkeit aus süddeutschen Frauenklöstern', see http://www.digitale-sammlungen.de/index.html?c=kurzauswahl&adr=daten.digitale-sammlungen.de/~db/ausgaben/uni_ausgabe.html?projekt=1229072566&recherche=ja&ordnung=sig&l=de. On the project website hosted by the university of Düsseldorf, manuscripts and printed books from these nunneries are presented in a systematic arrangement based on historical sources like contemporary manuscript catalogues. The website contains hyperlinks to detailed descriptions and digital reproductions of the books. See also https://www.bayerische-landesbibliothek-online.de/sueddeutsche-frauenkloester.

Bibliography

Manuscripts and Archival Sources

Munich, Archive of the Academy of Sciences, VIII. 212.

Munich, Bayerische Staatsbibliothek (BSB), Bavar. 535.

Munich, BSB, Bernhartiana 14 e.

Munich, BSB, Bibl.Mont. 109.

Munich, BSB, Cat. 432 b.

Munich, BSB, Cbm Cat. 22.

Munich, BSB, Cbm Cat. 218.

Munich, BSB, Cbm Cat. 221 b.

Munich, BSB, Cbm Cat. 253.

Munich, BSB, Cbm Cat. 283.

Munich, BSB, Cbm Cat. 285, no. 1.

Munich, BSB, Cbm Cat. 292; Cbm Cat. 292 d; Cbm Cat. 292 e.

Munich, BSB, Clm 14346.

Munich, BSB, Xylogr. 12.

Munich, BSB, 8 L.impr.c.n.mss. 142.

Munich, Bayerisches Hauptstaatsarchiv (BayHStA), A-Reg. A II Bernhart (J.B.), no. 42 and 52.

Munich, BayHStA, BSB, A-Reg. A 153.

Munich, BayHStA, BSB, A-Reg. A 185, no. 3.

Munich, BayHStA, BSB, A-Reg. B III Asher, no. 87 and 95.

Munich, BayHStA, BSB, A-Reg. B III Ehrentreich.

Munich, BayHStA, BSB, A-Reg. B III Stoeger, no. 14; B III Stoeger jun.

Munich, BayHStA, BSB, A-Reg. B VI Stoeger.

Munich, BayHStA, BSB, A-Reg. B 167.

Munich, BayHStA, BSB, A-Reg. C I Scherer.

Munich, BayHStA, BSB, A-Reg. C 3, Fasz. 1, no. 7–8; Fasz. 2, no. 11.

Munich, BayHStA, BSB, A-Reg. C 5, no. 3 and no. 30.

Munich, BayHStA, BSB, A-Reg. C 6, no. 1–4.

St Petersburg, Saltykow-Schtschedrin-Bibliothek, 9.2.3.13 and 9.2.3.14.

Strasbourg, Bibliothèque nationale et universitaire, K.6.

Heidelberg, University Library, D 4350 oct. INC.

Primary Sources

Epistulae diversorum philosophorum, oratorum, rhetorum, Venice: Aldus Manutius, 1499. 4°. GW 9367; ISTC
   ie00064000.

Secondary Works

Allgemeine Deutsche Biographie, vol. 22 (1885), 113; vol. 29 (1889), 632–34; vol. 49 (1904), 723–31.

Rahel Bacher, 'Die Provenienzen der Münchener Blockbücher', in *Vom ABC bis zur Apokalypse: Leben, Glauben
   und Sterben in spätmittelalterlichen Blockbüchern*, ed. Bettina Wagner (Lucerne, 2012), 130–44.

Die Bayerische Staatsbibliothek in historischen Beschreibungen (Munich, ²1998).

Bayerische Staatsbibliothek: Inkunabelkatalog (*BSB-Ink*), ed. Elmar Hertrich, Günter Mayer, Bettina Wagner and
   Claudia Bubenik, 8 vols (Wiesbaden, 1988–2021). Online access: https://inkunabeln.digitale-sammlungen.
   de/sucheEin.html.

Johann Baptist Bernhart, 'Historisch-kritische Untersuchung über das Daseyn, die Kennzeichen und das Alter der
   von Iohann Guttenberg und Iohann Faust in Mainz gedruckten lateinischen Bibel, dann über die Epochen der
   Verbreitung der Buchdruckerkunst und der Schriftgiesserey', *Beyträge zur Geschichte und Literatur, vorzüglich
   aus den Schätzen der Königl. Hof- und Centralbibliothek zu München*, 3,5 (1804), 91–112; 3,6, 49–112; 4,1 (1805),
   49–70.

Johann Baptist Bernhart, 'Gründliches Bedenken über das vom Herrn geheimen Rath Zapf angegebene hohe
   Alter und den Namen des Buchdruckers von des Ioannis de Turrecremata Explanatio im Psalterium Cracis
   impressa', ibid. 5,1 (1805), 49–66.

Johann Baptist Bernhart, 'Bemerkungen über die Auflage des Theuerdanks von 1517 und über die in derselben
   vorkommenden Schreiberzüge', ibid. 5,1 (1805), 67–98.

Johann Baptist Bernhart, 'Beyträge zur nähern Bestimmung des Druckjahres von der Kosmographie des
   Ptolemäus mit der Iahrzahl 1462, nebst Untersuchungen über die ersten in Metall gestochenen Landkarten',
   ibid. 5,5 (1805), 497–558; 5,6, 609–28.

Johann Baptist Bernhart, 'Anzeige einiger von Johann Mentelin zu Straßburg gedruckten, und von ihm zum Kaufe
   angekündigten Bücher', *Neuer literarischer Anzeiger*, 19 (12 May 1807), 301–03.

Johann Baptist Bernhart, 'Nachricht von einer merkwürdigen Ueberschwemmung von Baiern', ibid. 25 (23
   June 1807), 399–400.

Die Bibliothek Konrad Peutingers. Edition der historischen Kataloge und Rekonstruktion der Bestände, vol. 1: *Die
   autographen Kataloge Peutingers. Der nicht-juristische Bibliotheksteil*, ed. Hans-Jörg Künast and Helmut
   Zäh (Tübingen, 2003); vol. 2: *Die autographen Kataloge Peutingers: Der juristische Bibliotheksteil*, ed. Hans-
   Jörg Künast and Helmut Zäh with Uta Goerlitz and Christoph Petersen, vol. 3: *Das Nachlassinventar,
   Ergänzungen zu den Drucken und Handschriften*, ed. Hans-Jörg Künast (Tübingen, 2017), *Die Bibliothek und der
   handschriftliche Nachlaß Konrad Peutingers*, ed. Jochen Brüning, Helmut Gier, Jan-Dirk Müller and Bernhard
   Schimmelpfennig. Studia Augustana 14 (Tübingen, 2005).

*Bibliothèque Quatremère. Catalogue d'une collection de livres précieux et importants provenant pour la plupart de la
   bibliothèque de feu M. Étienne Quatremère de l'Institut*, rédigé par M. Ch. Halm, 4 vols (Paris, 1858–1859).

Catalog einer kostbaren Sammlung von xylographischen und typographischen Seltenheiten, welche [*von
   Holztafeldrucken, Pergamentdrucken und anderen typographischen Seltenheiten, welche nebst einer namhaften*

Anzahl auserlesener Bücher aus allen Fächern am] Montag den 3. Mai 1858 und folgende Tage bei Fidelis Butsch in Augsburg in dessen Haus Lit. F. Nro. 367 in der Heilig-Kreutz-Strasse öffentlich versteigert werden (Augsburg, 1858).

Catalogue des Livres grecs, latins … qui se trouvent chez M. J. Stoeger à Munich (1810).

Catalogue of a Valuable Assemblage of Fine, Rare and Curious Books (London: Sotheby, 27.5.1840).

Catalogue of a Valuable Collection of Choice, and Curious Books, Consigned from Germany (London: Sotheby, 27.8.1841).

Catalogus Librorum qui in Bibliotheca regia Monacensi bis aut pluries exstant quorumque statuta auctionis lege venditio fiet Calendis Novembribus et proximis post eas diebus an. MDCCCXV (Munich, '1515' [recte 1815]).

Bernard and Stéphane Clavreuil, *Livres & manuscrits du XIIIᵉ au XXᵉ siècle* (Paris, 2012).

Alan Coates, 'The Bodleian Library and its Incunabula', in *A catalogue of books printed in the fifteenth century now in the Bodleian Library* by Alan Coates, Kristian Jensen, Cristina Dondi, Bettina Wagner, and Helen Dixon (Oxford, 2005).

Severin Corsten, 'Von Bernhard von Mallinckrodt zu Ludwig Hain. Ziele und Methoden der frühen Inkunabelbibliographie', *Gutenberg-Jahrbuch*, 70 (1995), 37–50.

Die deutschen Handschriften der K. Hof- und Staatsbibliothek zu München nach J. A. Schmellers kürzerem Verzeichniss (Munich, 1866).

Pius Dirr, *Buchwesen und Schrifttum im alten München* (Munich, 1929).

Druckstücke aus dem XV. Jahrhunderte, welche sich in der Bibliothek des regulirten Chorstiftes Beuerberg befinden, by Paul Hupfauer (Augsburg, 1794).

Johann Goldfriedrich, *Geschichte des deutschen Buchhandels vom Beginn der Fremdherrschaft bis zur Reform des Börsenvereins im neuen Deutschen Reiche (1805–1889)* (Leipzig, 1913).

Karl Halm, *Erläuterungen zu den Verhandlungen der bayerischen Kammer der Abgeordneten vom 10. März 1859, die k. Hof- und Staatsbibliothek in München betreffend* (Munich, 1959).

Handbuch der historischen Buchbestände in Deutschland, vol. 10: *Bayern, München*, ed. Eberhard Dünninger (Hildesheim, 1996).

Elmar Hertrich, '75 Jahre Gesamtkatalog der Wiegendrucke: zur Erschließung deutscher Inkunabelsammlungen seit der Jahrhundertwende', *Aus dem Antiquariat*, 10 (1970), A345–54.

Elmar Hertrich, 'Erschließung der Inkunabelsammlung der Bayerischen Staatsbibliothek in Vergangenheit und Gegenwart', in *Bayerische Staatsbibliothek: Inkunabelkatalog (BSB-Ink)*, vol. 1 (Wiesbaden, 1988), XIII–XVIII.

Historische Kataloge der Bayerischen Staatsbibliothek München. Münchner Hofbibliothek und andere Provenienzen, by Stephan Kellner and Annemarie Spethmann, Catalogus codicum manu scriptorum Bibliothecae Monacensis XI (Wiesbaden, 1996).

Ilona Hubay, 'Die bekannten Exemplare der zweiundvierzigzeiligen Bibel und ihre Besitzer', in *Johannes Gutenbergs zweiundvierzigzeilige Bibel, Faksimile-Ausgabe nach dem Exemplar der Staatsbibliothek Preußischer Kulturbesitz Berlin. Kommentarband*, ed. Wieland Schmidt and Friedrich Adolf Schmidt-Künsemüller (Munich, 1979).

Incunabula aus der Staatlichen Bibliothek Neuburg/Donau, (Incunabula) in der Benediktinerabtei Ottobeuren, by Ilona Hubay, Inkunabelkataloge bayerischer Bibliotheken 3 (Wiesbaden, 1970).

Incunabula der Staats- und Stadtbibliothek Augsburg, by Ilona Hubay, Inkunabelkataloge Bayerischer Bibliotheken 5 (Wiesbaden, 1966).

Incunabula der Universitätsbibliothek Würzburg, by Ilona Hubay, Inkunabelkataloge Bayerischer Bibliotheken 1 (Wiesbaden, 1966).

Incunabula Eichstätter Bibliotheken, by Ilona Hubay, Inkunabelkataloge bayerischer Bibliotheken 2 (Wiesbaden, 1968).

Inkunabelkatalog des Germanischen Nationalmuseums Nürnberg, bearb. nach einem Verzeichnis von Walter Matthey by Barbara Hellwig, Inkunabelkataloge bayerischer Bibliotheken 4 (Wiesbaden, 1970).

Kristian Jensen, *Revolution and the antiquarian book. Reshaping the past, 1780–1815* (Cambridge et al., 2011).

Johann Andreas Schmeller. 1785–1852. Bayerische Staatsbibliothek, Gedächtnisausstellung zum 200. Geburtsjahr (Munich, 1985).

Johann Esaias von Seidel (1758–1827). Zum 250. Geburtstag eines bayerischen Verlegers, ed. Markus Lommer, Schriftenreihe des Stadtmuseums und Stadtarchivs Sulzbach-Rosenberg 23 (Sulzbach-Rosenberg, 2008).

Annemarie Kaindl, '"Nicht nur für den gegenwärtigen Bedarf, sondern für den von Jahrhunderten" – Der Bibliotheksbau in der Ludwigstraße', in *Lebendiges Büchererbe. Säkularisation, Mediatisierung und die Bayerische Staatsbibliothek. Eine Ausstellung der Bayerischen Staatsbibliothek München, 7.11.2003–30.1.2004*, ed. Cornelia Jahn and Dieter Kudorfer, Bayerische Staatsbibliothek, Ausstellungskataloge 74 (Munich, 2003), 214–27.

Katalog der Inkunabeln der Universitätsbibliothek Heidelberg, des Instituts für Geschichte der Medizin und des Stadtarchivs Heidelberg, by Armin Schlechter and Ludwig Ries, Kataloge der Universitätsbibliothek Heidelberg 9 / Inkunabeln in Baden-Württemberg 3 (Wiesbaden, 2009).

Katalog der lateinischen Handschriften der Bayerischen Staatsbibliothek München. Die Handschriften aus St Emmeram in Regensburg. Band 3: Clm 14261–14400, neu beschrieben von Friedrich Helmer unter Mitarbeit von Hermann Hauke und Elisabeth Wunderle, Catalogus codicum manu scriptorum Bibliothecae Monacensis, Tomus IV, series nova pars 2,3 (Wiesbaden, 2011).

Stephan Kellner, 'Vom "künstlichen Chaos" zur Ordnung "in Reih und Glied" – Der schwierige Weg zur Katalogisierung der Druckschriften', in *Lebendiges Büchererbe. Säkularisation, Mediatisierung und die Bayerische Staatsbibliothek. Eine Ausstellung der Bayerischen Staatsbibliothek München, 7.11.2003–30.1.2004*, ed. Cornelia Jahn and Dieter Kudorfer, Bayerische Staatsbibliothek, Ausstellungskataloge 74 (Munich, 2003), 72–79.

Dieter Kudorfer, 'Bekanntmachung, Erschliessung und Benützung der Handschriften', in *Lebendiges Büchererbe. Säkularisation, Mediatisierung und die Bayerische Staatsbibliothek. Eine Ausstellung der Bayerischen Staatsbibliothek München, 7.11.2003–30.1.2004*, ed. Cornelia Jahn and Dieter Kudorfer, Bayerische Staatsbibliothek, Ausstellungskataloge 74 (Munich, 2003), 54–71.

Lebendiges Büchererbe. Säkularisation, Mediatisierung und die Bayerische Staatsbibliothek. Eine Ausstellung der Bayerischen Staatsbibliothek München, 7.11.2003–30.1.2004, ed. Cornelia Jahn and Dieter Kudorfer, Bayerische Staatsbibliothek, Ausstellungskataloge 74 (Munich, 2003).

Georg Leyh, 'Die Hof- und Staatsbibliothek 1826–1882', [first published 1957; reprinted] in *Beiträge zur Geschichte der Bayerischen Staatsbibliothek*, ed. Rupert Hacker (Munich, 2000), 253–62.

Bernhard Lübbers, 'Johann Baptist Bernhart (1759–1821) und seine Regensburger Bibliotheksreise im Winter 1811/12', in *Regensburg, Bayern und das Reich. Festschrift für Peter Schmid zum 65. Geburtstag*, ed. Tobias Appl and Georg Köglmeier (Regensburg, 2010), 597–617.

Die Mannheimer Hofbibliothek: Carl Theodor und seine Vorgänger als Büchersammler. Eine Ausstellung der Universitätsbibliothek Mannheim, … 17. Januar bis 30. März 2000 (Mannheim, 2000).

Katharina Masel, *Kalender und Volksaufklärung in Bayern. Zur Entwicklung des Kalenderwesens 1750 bis 1830*, Forschungen zur Landes- und Regionalgeschichte 2 (St Ottilien, 1997).

Ulrike Mehringer and Armin Schlechter, 'Der Inkunabel-Katalog deutscher Bibliotheken (INKA)', *B.I.T.online – Zeitschrift für Bibliothek, Information und Technologie*, 5 (2002), Heft 1, 41–44.

Monumenta typographica, quae exstant in Bibliotheca collegii canonicorum in Rebdorf. Collegit, notis illustravit, et edidit eiudem collegii bibliothecarius [i.e. Andreas Strauss] (Eichstätt, 1787).

Münchener Politische Zeitung 258 (31 October 1820), 1282, and 259 (1 November 1820), 1286.

Notitia historico-literaria de libris ab artis typographicae inventione usque ad annum MCCCCLVIIII. impressis: in bibliotheca liberi, ac imperialis monasterii ad SS. Uldaricum et Afram Augustae extantibus (Augsburg, 1788).

David Paisey, 'Adolphus Asher (1800–1853): Berlin Bookseller, Anglophile and Friend to Panizzi', *British Library Journal*, 12 (1997), 131–53.

Georg W. Panzer, *Annales Typographici ab artis inventae Origine ad annum 1500 et inde usque ad annum 1536* (Nuremberg, 1793–1803).

Max Pauer, 'Anton Ruland und Karl Halm. Ein bibliothekarischer Streit um Dublettenverkäufe vor hundert Jahren', in *Aus der Arbeit des Bibliothekars. Festschrift Fritz Redenbacher*, ed. Bernhard Sinogowitz, Schriften der Universitäts-Bibliothek 4 (Erlangen, 1960), 121–35.

Helga Rebhan, 'Johann Albrecht Widmanstetter und seine Bibliothek', in *Kulturkosmos der Renaissance. Die Gründung der Bayerischen Staatsbibliothek. Katalog der Ausstellung zum 450-jährigen Jubiläum, 7. März–1. Juni 2008 und der Schatzkammerausstellung "Musikschätze der Wittelsbacher", 9. Juni–6. Juli 2008*, Bayerische Staatsbibliothek, Ausstellungskataloge 79 (Wiesbaden, 2008), 81–124.

Rekonstruktion und Erschließung mittelalterlicher Bibliotheken. Neue Formen der Handschriftenpräsentation, ed. Andrea Rapp and Michael Embach, Beiträge zu den Historischen Kulturwissenschaften 1 (Berlin, 2008).

Bernard M. Rosenthal, 'The history of incunabula collections in the United States. A brief account', *Aus dem Antiquariat*, 6 (2000), A350–366.

Anton Ruland, *Die in der Schrift des Herrn Oberbibliothekars und Directors Dr Karl Halm "Erläuterungen zu den Verhandlungen der bayerischen Kammer der Abgeordneten vom 10. März 1859, die k. Hof- und Staatsbibliothek in München betreffend" gegen die Kammerverhandlungen vom selben Tage gemachten Angriffe zurückgewiesen* (Würzburg, 1859).

Thomas Sauer, *Anton Ruland (1809–1874). Ein Beitrag zur Geschichte der katholischen Restauration in Bayern*, Schriftenreihe zur bayerischen Landesgeschichte 103 (Munich, 1995).

Michael Schaich, *Staat und Öffentlichkeit im Kurfürstentum Bayern der Spätaufklärung*, Schriftenreihe zur bayerischen Landesgeschichte 136 (Munich, 2001).

Armin Schlechter, 'Der Briefwechsel zwischen Clemens Brentano und dem Freisinger Antiquar Joseph Matthias Mozler', *Bibliothek und Wissenschaft* (2000), 103–87.

Rudolf Schmidt, *Deutsche Buchhändler. Deutsche Buchdrucker. Beiträge zu einer Firmengeschichte des deutschen Buchgewerbes*, 6 vols (Berlin and later Eberswalde, 1902–1908).

Die schriftlichen Nachlässe in der Bayerischen Staatsbibliothek München, by Karl Dachs, Catalogus codicum manu scriptorum Bibliothecae Monacensis IX,1 (Wiesbaden, 1970).

Ingo Schwab, 'Der Münchner Antiquariatsbuchhandel in der ersten Hälfte des 19. Jahrhunderts', in *Die Rosenthals. Der Aufstieg einer jüdischen Antiquarsfamilie zu Weltruhm* (Vienna/Cologne/Weimar, 2002), 13–46.

Maximilian Joseph Stöger, 'Versuch eines Grundrisses der Geschichte der Niederländischen Unruhen unter der Herzogin von Parma und dem Herzog von Alba' (Munich, 1804).

Maximilian Joseph Stöger, *Franz Sigl's, Franziskaners in München, Geschichte der Münchner Geißeln in schwedischer Gefangenschaft vom 7. Juni 1632 bis 3. April 1635. Aus einer gleichzeitigen Handschrift.* (Munich, 1836).

Verzeichniß alter Druckdenkmale der Bibliothek des uralten Benediktiner-Stifts zum H. Mang in Füeßen. Mit litterarischen Anmerkungen begleitet von Joseph Maria Helmschrott (Ulm, 1790).

Verzeichniß einer Anzahl in der Königl. Hofbibliothek zu München befindlichen Doubletten, welche daselbst vom 6. Nov. d. J. an die Meistbietenden gegen baare Bezahlung werden versteigert werden (Munich, 1820).

Xylographa Bavarica. Blockbücher in bayerischen Sammlungen (Xylo-Bav), ed. Bettina Wagner, Beschreibungen von Rahel Bacher unter Mitarbeit von Veronika Hausler, Antonie Magen und Heike Riedel-Bierschwale (Wiesbaden, 2016).

Bettina Wagner, 'Wege und Abwege bayerischer Inkunabeln', *Wolfenbütteler Notizen zur Buchgeschichte,* 18/19 (1993/1994), issue 2, 93–108.

Bettina Wagner, 'Von der Klosterbibliothek zum Gesamtkatalog der Wiegendrucke. Zur Geschichte der Inkunabelkatalogisierung in Bayern', *Gutenberg-Jahrbuch,* 81 (2006), 168–78.

Bettina Wagner, 'Collecting, Cataloguing, and Digitizing Incunabula at the Bayerische Staatsbibliothek Munich', *Papers of the Bibliographical Society of America,* 101 (2007), no. 4, 451–79.

Bettina Wagner, 'De la planche illustrée au livre. Les *Huit grugeries* [autour de 1460]', in *Métamorphoses – un bâtiment, des collections.* [exposition … présentée à la Bibliothèque Nationale et Universitaire de Strasbourg du 11 avril au 20 septembre 2015], ed. Christophe Didier and Madeleine Zeller (Strasbourg, 2015), 244–47.

Karl Klaus Walther, 'Hains *Repertorium bibliographicum.* „Die hervorragende Leistung eines Dilettanten"?', *Aus dem Antiquariat,* 9 (1996), A369–A376.

Eberhard Weis, *Montgelas,* 2 vols (Munich, ²1988 and 2005).

Reinhard Wittmann, *Hundert Jahre Buchkultur in München* (Munich, 1993).

Worlds of Learning. The Library and World Chronicle of the Nuremberg Physician Hartmann Schedel (1440–1514), ed. Bettina Wagner, Bayerische Staatsbibliothek, Ausstellungskataloge 89 (Munich, 2015).

'Zur Geschichte der K. Hof- und Staatsbibliothek zu München', in *Serapeum,* 20 (1859), no. 9, 129–142.

Digital Sources

INKA, http://www.inka.uni-tuebingen.de/.

MEI, https://data.cerl.org/mei/_search.

ProvenienzWiki, https://provenienz.gbv.de/Hauptseite.

Provenienz Mailinglist, https://www.hebis.de/arbeitsmaterialien/mailinglisten/ and https://dlist.server.uni-frankfurt.de/mailman/listinfo/provenienz.

CERL, https://www.cerl.org/resources/provenance/main.

'Schriftlichkeit aus süddeutschen Frauenklöstern', http://www.digitale-sammlungen.de/index.html?c=kurzauswahl&adr=daten.digitale-sammlungen.de/~db/ausgaben/uni_ausgabe.html?projekt=1229072566&recherche=ja&ordnung=sig&l=de and https://www.bayerische-landesbibliothek-online.de/sueddeutsche-frauenkloester.

RICHARD A. LINENTHAL

Monastic Collections and the Nineteenth-Century English Book Trade: A New Interest in Early Printed Fragments

The best London bookshops in the last decades of the eighteenth century and the first decades of the nineteenth century were awash with wonderful things to buy. Continental Europe was in the throes of revolution, invading armies, and monastic secularization, and England was relatively secure and rich. Furthermore, book collecting was in fashion and a *de rigueur* pastime for men of substance from King George III downwards. The Scottish monk-turned-bookseller Alexander Horn (1762–1820) wrote to Earl Spencer in 1798: "The secularization of Swabia will make an excellent harvest for collectors of old books"[1]. Since 1789 Horn had been librarian of the Benedictine monastery of St James in Regensburg. He was an insider and he understood the situation well.

Take as a barometer of the times the ownership of Gutenberg Bibles, the first edition of the Latin Vulgate and no doubt the most iconic status symbol among book collectors over the past two centuries and more[2]. Before 1789 the only British copies were one at Hopetoun House near Edinburgh, which had probably been there from the early decades of the eighteenth century, and the single volume at Lambeth Palace Library, printed on vellum and illuminated in London. On 18 May 1789, Sotheby's auctioned "a very elegant and curious cabinet of books, lately imported from France", from which lot 723 was another Gutenberg Bible, very simply but accurately described. As far as

---

1 Kristian Jensen, *Revolution and the Antiquarian Book: Reshaping the Past, 1780–1815* (Cambridge, 2011), 59.

---

2 For some of this information I am indebted to Eric Marshall White who has unravelled the complicated history of the surviving copies of the Gutenberg Bible in his recent book, *Editio Princeps: A History of the Gutenberg Bible* (London and Turnhout, 2017). See also Eric White, 'Gutenberg Bibles on the Move in England, 1789–1834', *Transactions of the Cambridge Bibliographical Society*, vol. 15, no. 1 (2012) a special issue ed. by Ed Potten and Satoko Tokunaga; and Roland Folter, 'The Gutenberg Bible in the Antiquarian Book Trade', *Incunabula, Studies in Fifteenth-Century Printed Books presented to Lotte Hellinga*, ed. Martin Davies (London, 1999), 271–351.

Richard A. Linenthal • Antiquarian bookseller, London. richard@linenthal.com

How the Secularization of Religious Houses Transformed the Libraries of Europe, 16th–19th Centuries, ed. by Cristina Dondi, Dorit Raines, and †Richard Sharpe, BIB, 63 (Turnhout, 2022), pp. 417–428.
BREPOLS ❧ PUBLISHERS   DOI 10.1484/M.BIB-EB.5.128496

we know this has the distinction of being the first copy of the book ever sold at auction in this country, and it was acquired by the now obscure but great collector Sir George Shuckburgh-Evelyn (1751–1804). Incidentally, just one month before in the sale of the collection of Maffeo Pinelli (1735–1785), in London, 20 April 1789[3], Shuckburgh had acquired a copy of the slightly later but much rarer 36-line Bible, printed in Bamberg, probably by Albrecht Pfister, and the following year he bought the second edition of the Latin Vulgate, Strasbourg, Johann Mentelin, not after 1460, at the Crevenna Sale in Amsterdam[4]. An extraordinary achievement.

Let me return to Gutenberg Bibles: George John, second Earl Spencer of Althorp (1758–1834), who was to become the greatest English collector of our period, acquired one in 1790 from the London bookseller Thomas Payne (1737–1809), and another was bought in a Paris sale by the Bodleian Library in 1793. By the end of the Napoleonic Wars the number of Gutenberg Bibles in Britain had risen to more than nine, and by the mid-1830s there were fifteen which represented some forty changes of ownership. This was a hot market. To a much lesser extent, the same phenomenon occurred a century later among American collectors, when the concentration of wealth shifted across the Atlantic to the United States.

Consider too another iconic book, the 1457 Mainz Psalter, the earliest printed book to name its printer and place of printing, a masterpiece of book design, employing elaborate decorated initials printed in two colours, and a much rarer book than the Gutenberg Bible. In 1792 all but two of the surviving ten copies were still in the possession of continental religious institutions, and by the end of the Napoleonic Wars none was. Two had made their way to Britain by 1802, one from the Ursuline convent at Hildesheim to the Royal Library at Windsor, and another from the choir of the monastic church at Roth near Memmingen to the Spencer Library. A third copy followed in 1824, acquired by Thomas Grenville (1755–1846) also from the Continent[5]. A similar story can be told about the equally rare 1459 Mainz Psalter with copies coming to England from the Mainz Charterhouse, which at one time possessed three copies[6], and from the monastery of St Michael at Bamberg[7].

This was the golden age of English book collecting, which reached its giddy heights with the extravagant prices at the famous Roxburghe sale in 1812 and is chronicled so fully – many have said much too fully – by the bibliographer Thomas Frognall Dibdin (1776–1847). While visiting Rouen a few years later, Dibdin recalled that "I groped around in all directions; and to a hundred earnest enquiries for something curious, or rare, or ancient, was answered that I ought to have been there in the year 1814, when Paris was first taken possession of by the Allies – that my countrymen had preceded me and left nothing for future gleaners"[8].

In the course of my research I have looked at many, but by no means all of the London booksellers' catalogues and book auction catalogues of the period, I read more of Dibdin's various works than I ever have before, and was surprised by how much of real interest is actually contained among the pages of misinformation

---

3 *Bibliotheca Pinelliana. A Catalogue of the Magnificent and Celebrated Library of Maffei Pinelli, Late of Venice* (London: James Edwards, 2 Mar. 1789 and following).

4 *Catalogue des livres de M. Pierre-Antoine Bolongaro-Crevenna* (Amsterdam: Changuion and P. den Hengst, 1789).

5 Seymour de Ricci, *Catalogue Raisonné des Premières Impressions de Mayence (1445–1467)* (Mainz, 1911), nos 54 and 55.

6 British Library, George III's copy.

7 John Rylands Library, Spencer copy.

8 Thomas Frognall Dibdin, *A Bibliographical, Antiquarian and Picturesque Tour in France and Germany* 3 vols (London, 1821), I, 151.

and hyperbole, and I have struggled through some very specialist and somewhat obscure German and French antiquarian bibliographical books and pamphlets of the late eighteenth and early nineteenth centuries[9].

What I wish to focus on is how the English book trade and English collectors at the end of the eighteenth century and in the first decades of the nineteenth century were first introduced to the earliest examples of European typography, the very first productions of the printing press. I am not so concerned with the great monuments of book-collecting such as the Gutenberg Bible, the 36-line Bible, the 1462 Bible, and the Mainz Psalters, which have been studied so well by others. Instead, I want to concentrate on the more ephemeral and much rarer indulgences and Latin grammars, which were almost unknown in England before our period. For the most part they are far removed from the trophy collecting of England's golden age of book-collecting, but they are among the most important documents of early printing, and perhaps the most difficult to interpret and understand. They are also extremely rare, and mostly survive just as binding fragments, but thanks to the dispersal of German monastic libraries a trickle of these things found their way here, they stimulated serious interest, and many of them ultimately found permanent homes in our greatest institutional libraries.

As a rule, I think human beings prefer certainties to uncertainties, and book-collectors are no exception. A book that names its author, place of printing, and date is so much more comforting than something that is totally anonymous and undated. But alas, among the earliest printed books and more ephemeral publications there are far more of the latter than the former – more uncertainties than certainties. Whereas the scholar may greet this as a challenge, a collector probably finds it unsettling. This is still the case today in the antiquarian book market. There are more collectors who will pay a high price for the first edition of, say, St Augustine's *City of God*, than for an earlier manuscript of the same text, which, although undated and more difficult to pin down, might in fact be more important textually or more interesting on account of its provenance.

A clear development during our period is a marked increase in scholarship. It may seem to our modern eyes bumbling, awkward, and a real struggle, but there were attempts both on the Continent and in Britain to classify books so as to better understand them and in some cases to make them more saleable.

The story of the rediscovery of the Gutenberg Bible, for instance, in the century or more up to about the year 1800 has been told by Paul Needham[10]. There were several candidates vying for the distinction of being the *editio princeps* of the Latin Bible, and at first glance the securely dated Fust and Schoeffer Mainz edition of 1462 offered a satisfactory choice. But when European scholars such as Michael Mattaire (1668–1747), Johann Georg Schelhorn (1694–1773), Gerard Meerman (1722–1771), Guillaume-François Debure (1731–1782), and others started to look more closely, there were undated and unsigned editions which began to take precedence, namely those books that we now refer to as the 42- and 36-line Bibles. By about the year 1800 the landscape was becoming clear, and the three distinct editions were more or less recognized and placed in their correct order.

9   I have also benefitted enormously from recent scholarship such as Kristian Jensen's *Revolution and the Antiquarian Book*, as note 1; Paul Needham's account of the 'Discovery and Invention of the Gutenberg Bible, 1455–1805', in *The Medieval Book: Glosses from Friends & Colleagues of Christopher de Hamel*, ed. James. H. Marrow, Richard A. Linenthal, and William Noel ('t Goy-Houten, 2010), 208–41; and Eric White's research, as note 2 above.

10   See note 9 above.

But stumbling blocks remained along the way, perhaps in part due to the persistence of old-fashioned theories and beliefs in an age when such scholarly opinion may have been contentious, or it was in a foreign language at least from the English point of view, and it was probably slow to travel. Even as late as 1893, a scholar as eminent as E. Gordon Duff (1863–1924), the first librarian at the John Rylands Library in Manchester, concluded that we can "probably put both Bibles earlier than 1454"[11]. He knew what had been discovered up to that time, including the then recent discovery (1890) that the 36-line Bible was for the most part set from the 42-line Bible, but of course he did not have the benefit of the very important research of Gottfried Zedler and Paul Schwenke published some ten years later[12].

I am jumping ahead of myself, and out of our period, so let me return to 1796. For the first time – apparently – a copy of the Gutenberg Bible was offered in a bookseller's catalogue. It was item 1 in the catalogue for that year issued by James Edwards (1757–1816), one of the most distinguished booksellers of his day. He was a bookseller with great imagination, energy, and style. In Dibdin's words, "He travelled diligently and fearlessly abroad: was now exploring the book-gloom of dusty monasteries, and at other times marching in the rear or the front of Bonaparte's armies in Italy"[13]. When James Edwards died, he left instructions that his coffin should be made out of his library shelves[14].

Six years earlier, in 1790, Edwards had issued a catalogue with the first 98 items arranged chronologically and described as "Books of great rarity in the infancy of printing"[15]. This was the first time that a London bookseller's catalogue had a section devoted to incunabula. The first item was a copy of the 1462 Bible described as the "editio princeps", and the note only praised the quality of the copy, "I have no where found one which equals this copy in fairness of vellum, grandeur of margin, and the exquisite paintings of the initials". In fact, many of the incunabula offered in this catalogue were dull, and there are only the briefest of descriptions and occasional scholarly comments.

The new contender for the first Bible, offered by the same bookseller six years later, was bound in three volumes, and was described as "The first book produced by the inventors of printing with metal types at Mentz, by Guttenberg and Fust, in the year 1450"[16]. There followed a full-page description talking about the history of the book and commenting on its "large letter, such as was employed for church Missals and Choir books, and similar to the Donatus from wooden blocks", and it was priced £126. But alas, James Edward's Gutenberg Bible was nothing of the sort but rather a copy of the Bamberg 36-line Bible, and it was sold to the Imperial Library at Vienna and is now in the National Library. Incidentally, a few years earlier (1790), the Bodleian Library acquired a copy of Durandus' *Rationale*, printed in 1459, on the mistaken but commonly held belief that it was the first book printed with movable cast metal type[17].

It is not Edward's mistake identifying the edition of the Bible which is impressive but rather his comments about the font of type used in the book, comparing it – entirely correctly –

11 E. Gordon Duff, *Early Printed Books* (London, 1893), 26.

12 Karl Dziatzko, *Gutenbergs früheste Druckerpraxis* (Berlin, 1890); Gottfried Zedler, *Die älteste Gutenbergtype* (Mainz, 1902); Paul Schwenke, *Die Donat- und Kalender-Type* (Mainz, 1903).

13 Thomas Frognall Dibdin, *The Bibliographical Decameron*, 3 vols (London, 1817), III, 16–17.

14 Alan Noel Latimer Munby, *Connoisseurs and Medieval Miniatures 1750–1850* (Oxford, 1972), 7.

15 *Edwards' Catalogue of a select collection of ancient and modern Books* (London, 1790).

16 James Edwards, *A Catalogue of Books, in all languages, and in every branch of literature, collected from various parts of Europe now on sale* (London, 1796), item 1.

17 Bod-Inc D-178.

with that used in an edition of Donatus' Latin grammar, although with the mistaken belief that they may have been carved wooden blocks. To have any discussion of printing type in an English bookseller's catalogue was a novelty and an important one for the future history of bibliographical scholarship.

Another item in the Edwards catalogue of 1796 was the *Margarita Poetica* by Albertus de Eyb[18]. When the same copy had been offered two years earlier, it was assigned to Paris, *c.* 1472, and the note explained, "This curious edition is not noticed by any bibliographer, it has no date or register, is printed in long lines, 13 to a page, the type is semigothic", and there follows a transcription of the colophon[19]. It was priced £5/5/–. Two years later the price remained the same, but it was redated to *c.* 1471, and the note had been changed: "There is no date or printer's name to this edition, but on comparing the type, which is semigothic, it appears to be by Ulric Gering the first printer at Paris". It is not clear to me which edition this copy actually was, and I doubt that Edwards was right.

Nor am I critical of Dibdin's comments in his edition of Ames's *Typographical Antiquities*, published in 1810, where he lists with mixed results the books supposed to have been printed by Gutenberg. Among the more obvious candidates he included several unsigned and undated books that are quite rare but there seem to have been copies in the London trade at the time and they were probably familiar to Dibdin. They belonged to the eminent booksellers George Nicol (1740?–1828) and his son William, who sold their stock at auction in 1825, and these books were in the sale[20]. One is the *Speculum Sacerdotum* by

Hermannus de Saldis (otherwise Hermannus Schildesche or Schildiz), assigned to Gutenberg on the strength of research by the "late intelligent bibliographer Mr Horn of Ratisbon", and two other books said to be printed in the types of the Hermannus de Saldis, and therefore also by Gutenberg. In fact these books are now assigned to the "Printer of the 'Darmstadt' Prognostication", and dated about 1476. However, please note, that even the great bibliographer Robert Proctor (1868–1903) in the British Museum Catalogue of Incunabula noted the affinity of these types with Peter Schoeffer in Mainz[21].

We should not be surprised that mistakes occurred. What is impressive is that the hunt was on to find gold in the flood of early printed books coming from continental Europe, and the way to do this was to introduce a new level of bibliographical scholarship, however flawed that might have been.

Having begun to look at printing types, and having struggled to make sense of them, the overall picture became even more complicated when one took into account not only the big books such as the 42- and 36-line Bibles, the dated Mainz Psalters, the 1459 Durandus, the 1462 Bible, and so forth, but also the very elusive and truly rare earliest printed ephemera and Latin grammars, which survived only as binding fragments. Several key items emerged in our period which became the focus of attention both on the Continent and in England, the most significant being printed indulgences bearing the dates 1454 and 1455. Both were intended to raise money for the war against the Turks, but they were printed with different types, and significantly one had headings in the type of the 42-line Bible and the other in the slightly larger type of the 36-line Bible[22]. The

18 Edwards, *A Catalogue of Books*, as note 16, item 26.

19 James Edwards, *A Catalogue of a very select collection of Books in all languages, and every branch of literature now on sale by J Edwards* (London, 1794), item 980.

20 *Rare and Valuable Books: Property of Messrs G. and W. Nicol* (London: Evans, 18 July 1825).

21 BMC I 41.

22 Chappe, Paulinus, commissary, *Indulgentia, 1454*. For contributions to the war against the Turks. [Mainz: Printer of the 42-line Bible (Johann Gutenberg), 1454–55]. Broadside. GW 6555; ISTC ic00422400.

first copies to come to England arrived in the short space of a couple of years between 1800 and 1802, when Earl Spencer bought examples from the monastic library of St Emmeram in Regensburg through the efforts of Alexander Horn. Details of Horn's negotiations with the monks of St Emmeram and with Earl Spencer have been found by Kristian Jensen in the Spencer archive at the British Library[23]. Spencer paid prices ranging from £40 to £60 for each of three specimens, which were considerable sums.

The significance of these printed, dated indulgences was well understood. In his catalogue of the Spencer Library published in 1814 Dibdin acknowledged the work of continental scholars who first tried to make sense of these documents – Schelhorn, Meerman, the typefounder Pierre Simon Fournier (1712–1768), and Janus Gebhard (1592–1632) – and placed them among the first printed books in the Library with a note, "The celebrity of these 'printed' Letters of Indulgence, as fixing the earliest known period of the impression of metal types, with a date subjoined, is sufficiently acknowledged by the curious in typography"[24].

Twenty years later, shortly after the death of Earl Spencer, one of his indulgences, which happened to be a duplicate of the 31-line issue with heading types of the 36-line Bible, was sold through the London booksellers Payne and Foss. It was bought by the collector Sir Thomas Phillipps (1792–1872) and is now in the Morgan Library and Museum. The indulgence appeared in two Payne and Foss catalogues, for 1835 and 1836, and was described in considerable detail, citing research by George Appleyard (d. 1855),

a former Navy and Transport Office clerk, who was hired as a secretary by Earl Spencer in 1817 and assumed increasing responsibility for the library during the following years. "The large character of this letter, having the printed date of 1455, perfectly resembles the Bible printed by Pfister at Bamberg, and proves the existence of the type of that Bible in the year 1455". The note goes on to say that "The Pfister Bible … must have been finished in the interval previous to 1461, as we find that Pfister had then that same type at liberty, wherewith to print the Fables in 1461, the four Scripture histories in 1462, and the *Biblia Pauperum* and *Belial*, both without date, and possibly previous to 1461"[25].

These Pfister imprints referred to by Spencer's librarian are among the most important books that came to England as a result of monastic secularization. Not only are they extremely rare, but Pfister is celebrated as the first printer at Bamberg, the first printer to print in any vernacular language, and the first to use woodcut illustrations. Furthermore, a couple of his books contain colophons with dates (1461, 1462) and the name of the printer, and all are printed with the types of the 36-line Bible. We now know that in its earliest form this was the first European printing type – it originated with Gutenberg in Mainz, and evolved through several states before ending up with Albrecht Pfister in Bamberg. Although less well understood in the late eighteenth and early nineteenth century, the significance of books printed in this type was not lost on scholars and collectors of the time[26].

Chappe, Paulinus, commissary, *Indulgentia, 1454–1455*. For contributions to the war against the Turks. [Mainz: Printer of the 31-line indulgence and of the 36-line Bible, 1454–55]. Broadside. GW 4226; ISTC ic00422600.

23 Jensen, *Revolution and the Antiquarian Book*, as note 1, 49, 60–61.

24 Thomas Frognall Dibdin, *Bibliotheca Spenceriana*, 4 vols (London, 1814), I, xliv, no. 7.

25 Payne and Foss, *A Catalogue of Books Printed upon Vellum now on Sale* (London, 1835), no. 76; *A Selection of First Editions; and Books Printed in the Fifteenth Century; of Books Printed upon Vellum; and other Specimens Illustrating the History and Progress of Typography* (London, 1836), no. 4.

26 Donatus-Kalendar or DK type has been the subject of major new research by Paul Needham and Blaise Agüera y Arcas: 'Temporary Matrices and Elemental Punches in Gutenberg's DK Type', in *Incunabula and their Readers*, ed. Kristian Jensen (London, 2003), 1–12.

The Pfister volumes bearing colophons dated 1461, 1462 formed part of a *Sammelband* that had been found in the library of the Carmelites at Würzburg in 1792 and offered to Spencer in 1799. The dealer was the notorious Jean-Baptiste Maugérard (1735–1815), a Benedictine monk who was given official responsibility in 1802 for the spoliation of German libraries in the Rhine region annexed by the French. In a letter to Spencer dated at Erfurt, 9 August 1799, he wrote [in French] "I come back to the History of Daniel, for which your Excellency offers me 1000 francs. You will yourself, sir, judge that it seems that one should not break the binding of this volume to separate them from the others that are bound together. One of these is the Biblia pauperum also by Pfister and the other is the History of Antichrist. This has persuaded me to keep the volume as it is or sell it as a unity. So if your Excellency wishes to keep the volume as it is, you will be kind enough to pay me 1800 francs for it"[27].

Although Spencer did ultimately end up owning apparently all the contents of this *Sammelband*, it is not clear whether he bought the volume directly from Maugérard, and I suspect he did not. I imagine there was a dealer in the middle of the transaction, and it was probably James Edwards. The volume, alas, was broken up, and the contents were divided between Spencer and his contemporary, Sir Mark Masterman Sykes (1771–1823), another great English collector. Within the following ten years or so Spencer acquired the portions sold to Sykes, in exchange for some Aldine press volumes "elegantly bound in blue morocco", as we are told by Dibdin[28]. There is no doubt that Spencer got the better deal.

The *Sammelband* contained an imperfect copy of the second edition of *Ackermann von Böhmen* (*c.* 1463), one of the greatest works of early High German prose – an allegory of complaints against Death, detailing a court action in which a bereaved widower sues Death over the loss of his wife. Like most of Pfister's books it is in the vernacular and it contains woodcut illustrations. Only one leaf of this went to Spencer, indirectly via Sykes (a full-page woodcut bound with the Latin *Biblia Pauperum*). Other leaves, some with woodcuts and others with plain text, all uniformly re-margined with old paper, were distributed by James Edwards to other collectors including Sir George Shuckburgh-Evelyn, Sir Thomas Gage (1781–1820), probably William Howley (1766–1848), later archbishop of Canterbury[29], and others. The rarity and saleability of Pfister was recognized, and this is the earliest instance that I know of where a dealer distributed the leaves of a rare book as typographic specimens.

The appreciation of fragments of early printed books is essential to any study of early typography since many things of great importance survive only as fragments. With regard to the earliest Mainz printing, Paul Needham tells us that of nearly seventy distinct pieces of printing known today by physical survivals, only twelve have come down to us in the shape of one or more complete, integral books or broadsides, and more than fifty-five survive only as binder's waste[30].

On the continent we find an important vellum fragment of Donatus' Latin grammar printed in DK-type, discovered as binding

---

27 Jensen, *Revolution and the Antiquarian Book*, as note 1, 145. See also Bénédicte Savoy, 'Codicologue, incunabuliste et rabatteur. La mission de Jean-Baptiste Maugérard dans les quatre départements du Rhin (1802–1805)', *Bulletin du bibliophile* (1999), no. 2, 313–44.

28 Dibdin, *Bibliotheca Spenceriana*, as note 25, I, 103.

29 Lotte Hellinga, 'The Rylands Incunabula: an International Perspective', *Bulletin du Bibliophile* (1989), no. 1, 44.

30 Paul Needham, 'Fragments in Books', in M. McC. Gatch, '*So precious a foundation*', *The Library of Leander van Ess* ... (New York, 1996), 94–95. For details of early English fragments and collectors/scholars from the late seventeenth to early 20th centuries see Arthur Freeman, '*Everyman* and Others, Part I: Some Fragments of Early English Printing, and their Preservers', *The Library*, vol. 9, no. 3 (2008), 267–305.

waste in the Mainz city archives by Franz Josef Bodmann and given to the Bibliothèque Nationale in Paris in 1803 through the help of Johann Gotthelf Fischer von Waldheim (1771–1853), University Librarian at Mainz. Both men have tarnished reputations, but that is another story. The year before (1802), Fischer had published this fragment and several others in his *Essai sur les monuments typographiques de Jean Gutenberg, Mayençais, Inventeur de l'imprimerie*[31]. In 1799, in a guide to Bamberg, there is mention of one Father Alexander, a Capuchin friar, who collected nine vellum leaves of the 36-line Bible, and other examples used to bind volumes in the library of the Cistercian Abbey at Langheim near Bamberg[32]. In 1840 l'archéologue Léon de Laborde (1807–1869), in his book on the origins of printing in Mainz and Bamberg, spoke of the many fragments of the 36-line Bible found in the convents of Bavaria[33]. There can be no doubt that the monastic secularization of the late eighteenth and early nineteenth centuries also provided an "excellent harvest for collectors of old [fragments]", to change slightly the words of Fr Horn to Earl Spencer.

I should like to conclude by describing two nineteenth-century London auctions that included important groups of early printed fragments – the best that had ever been offered for sale to that time, and there has been nothing comparable since. This first was the sale at Sotheby's in May 1835 of the greater part of the library of Dr Georg Kloss (1787–1854), a citizen of Frankfurt, medical practitioner, historian of freemasonry, and book collector. Taking full advantage of the superabundance of books from dissolved monastic collections, Kloss collected

books printed before 1536 with the intention of supplementing Georg Wolfgang Panzer's *Annales Typographici* (1793–1803), the fullest account of fifteenth-century printed books published to that time. Kloss had offered his collection to various German libraries but without success, and the library was sent to London for sale at Sotheby's. The catalogue was prepared by Samuel Leigh Sotheby (1805–1861), a prodigious enthusiast if not a great scholar, and it is an admirable job in spite of over-excited attribution, or rather misattribution, of so many books as coming from the library of the sixteenth-century German reformer Philipp Melanchthon[34].

Lots 1287–1303 are described as "A collection of Donatuses, illustrative of the discovery of the art of printing, the most extensive ever brought before the public". All but two of the lots are single leaves or fragments of leaves, and alas they were all removed from the bindings in which they had survived – but this was common practice. Prior to this sale you have to search long and hard to find single-leaf fragments of early printed books offered for sale in auction or booksellers' catalogues, and here, among others, there are as many as seventeen Donatuses. What strikes me is that although the catalogue descriptions repeat misunderstandings common at the time, they are surprisingly good, and many even allow for the identification of the same fragments today.

The first lot (1287) contains two leaves, printed on vellum, with 33 lines to the page, said to be "printed with the same type as was used for the commonly called the 'Mazarine' Bible, said to be printed by Guttenberg, in 1450 and 1455". It goes on to say "The 'Littera Indulgentiae' of Pope Nicholas V, in 1454, now in the possession of Earl Spencer, contains two lines printed with the same type". This fragment is now in the Bodleian Library and in the library's new

31 Mainz, 1802.

32 Murr, Christoph Gottlieb von, *Merkwürdigkeiten der fürstbischöflichen Residenzstadt Bamberg* (Munich, 1799), 261.

33 Léon de Laborde, *Débuts de l'imprimerie à Mayence et à Bamberg* (Paris, 1840).

34 Frank Herrmann, *Sotheby's, Portrait of an Auction House* (London, 1980), 27.

catalogue of incunabula the description has not much changed[35]! The next lot (1288), also two vellum leaves, but with 35 lines to the page, is said to be printed from wooden blocks and "the letter with which this is printed bears the same character with the type used by Pfister for his Latin Bible, 1461 and 1462". The next lot (1289) is described as "Printed at Bamberg, by Pfister", as is the following lot.

One lot (1291) is described as perhaps printed by Laurens Janszoon Coster at Haarlem (a remnant of the old Gutenberg/Coster debate)[36], and another (1295) with the types used in the first or second edition of the Dutch *Speculum* printed at Haarlem. Both are now in the Bodleian Library and described as examples of Dutch prototypography. There are fragments in the types of Friedrich Creussner (1298), Conrad Winters de Homborch (1296), and a paper bifolium from a blockbook edition containing a colophon naming Conrad Dinckmut of Ulm. All are in the Bodleian Library with descriptions that have hardly changed.

Perhaps the most intriguing lot is the last (1303), described as "A Large collection of fragments of various manuscript and printed Donatusses, in two portfolios". This bundle, presumably contained things that neither Kloss nor Samuel Leigh Sotheby was able to pin down, and it fetched the highest price of all the Donatus lots, £8/8/–. The buyer was the London firm of Longman, Hurst, Rees, Orme, Brown & Green, and altogether they bought ten of the seventeen Donatus lots. I would like to know more about Longman, who catalogued two copies of the Gutenberg Bible for sale in 1816 and 1818, and issued the ambitious but largely unprofitable

Bibliotheca Anglo-Poetica in 1815[37], but their antiquarian department which operated until 1849 was apparently a relatively small part of their publishing business, and their catalogues are scarce and difficult to locate[38].

The British Museum bought two of the Donatus fragments in DK-type, the type of the 36-line Bible, which are now among the earliest examples of European printing in the British Library (lots 1290 and 1292)[39]. Single lots were bought by the booksellers Payne and Foss, and by the historian of early prints and keeper at the British Museum, William Young Ottley (1771–1836).

Interestingly, the Bodleian Library bought only one Donatus at the sale and this was not a fragment, but rather one of only two bound volumes, an edition of eighteen leaves printed at Augsburg by Günther Zainer[40]. In 1835 the library was apparently not yet ready to buy fragments. However, they were given a second chance. The ten Longman lots were all acquired on behalf of Samuel Butler (1774–1839), headmaster of Shrewsbury School and in the last few years of his life bishop of Lichfield. Butler must be considered a very serious collector, if only on account of his Donatuses, and it is worth noting

35 Donatus, Aelius, *Ars minor*. [Mainz: Type of the 42-line Bible, undated]. 4°. 33-line edition. Bod-Inc D-126; GW 8708; ISTC id00317400.

36 The Gutenberg/Coster debate is summarized by Janet Ing, *Johann Gutenberg and his Bible* (New York, 1988), 37–39.

37 Seymour de Ricci, *English Collectors of Books and Manuscripts (1530–1930) and their Marks of Ownership* (Cambridge, 1930), 90; *Bibliotheca anglo-poetica or, A descriptive catalogue of a rare and rich collection of early English poetry: in the possession of Longman, Hurst, Rees, Orme, and Brown. Illustrated by occasional extracts and remarks, critical and biographical* (London, 1815). For the two copies of the Gutenberg Bible see Eric White, *Editio Princeps*, as note 2, 149 and 171–72.

38 Harold Cox and John E. Chandler, *The House of Longman: With a Record of their Bicentenary Celebration* (London, 1925); *Essays in the History of Publishing in Celebration of the 250th Anniversary of the House of Longman, 1724–1974*, ed. Asa Briggs (London, 1974); and Asa Briggs, *A History of Longmans and their Books 1724–1990* (London, 2008).

39 BMC, I 16.

40 Donatus, Aelius, *Ars minor*. [Augsburg: Günther Zainer, c. 1475]. Folio. Bod-Inc D-131; GW 8817; ISTC id00327580.

that his manuscripts were acquired *en bloc* by the British Museum. Following his death in 1839, when part of the library was sold by the London booksellers Payne and Foss[41], the Kloss Donatus fragments together with a couple of additions made by Butler were acquired by the Bodleian Library as a single purchase.

The second substantial offering of Donatus fragments, and aside from the Kloss sale the only time that such an opportunity has existed, was at Sotheby's in February 1870 at the sale of the *Bibliotheca Typographica* of Friedrich Georg Hermann Culemann (1811–1886), a bookseller and printer, collector, and senator of Hannover[42]. The collection, another by-product of monastic secularization, had been bought by the London bookseller Frederick Startridge Ellis (1830–1901), who wrote the descriptions in the catalogue and consigned the books to Sotheby's. The title-page advertises in bold type "A Most Important Series of the Editions of Donatus". There are eleven lots (217–27) with a short introduction explaining "M. Brunet well observes of the various early Editions of the Donatus, that to give any satisfactory account of them it would be necessary to have the fragments of the different Editions under one's eyes. This is an opportunity for some

of our Public Libraries to secure these valuable relics of the first efforts of Typography. Perfect copies do not exist at all". The selection is not as rich as the Kloss material, containing only a single fragment printed by Gutenberg, in this case with the types of the 42-line Bible. It was acquired by the British Museum together with three other Donatuses[43]. The Bodleian Library was quiet in this sale, and it was Cambridge's turn to shine. The newly appointed University Librarian Henry Bradshaw (1831–1886) was allowed a budget of £500 and of approximately one hundred and ten lots on his shopping list he was successful in buying ninety (including a 42-line Bible leaf on vellum and three 36-line Bible leaves)[44].

In concentrating on the trade in the earliest printed books I have limited myself to a small part only of the antiquarian book trade, and even within that specialized framework I have found myself most interested in the even smaller but still very significant field of fragments of books. Think of this as a case study, and I hope I have suggested one of the ways that monastic imports of the late eighteenth and nineteenth centuries changed the bibliographical landscape in this country.

41   Payne and Foss, *Bibliotheca Butleriana, A Catalogue of the Library of the late Right Rev. Samuel Butler* (London, 1841).

42   *Catalogue of a Bibliotheca Typographica* [*the property of F. G. H. Culemann*] ... *which will be sold by auction, by Messrs. Sotheby, Wilkinson & Hodge, 7th Feb. 1870 and 3 following days* (London, 1870).

43   BMC I 18.

44   John Claud Trewinard Oates, *A Catalogue of the Fifteenth-Century Printed Books in the University Library, Cambridge* (Cambridge, 1954), 29–30, 63.

Bibliography

Primary Sources

Chappe, Paulinus, commissary, *Indulgentia, 1454*. For contributions to the war against the Turks. [Mainz: Printer of the 42-line Bible (Johann Gutenberg), 1454–55]. Broadside. GW 6555; ISTC ic00422400.

Chappe, Paulinus, commissary, *Indulgentia, 1454–1455*. For contributions to the war against the Turks. [Mainz: Printer of the 31-line indulgence and of the 36-line Bible, 1454–55]. Broadside. GW 6556; ISTC ic00422600.

Donatus, Aelius, *Ars minor*. [Mainz: Type of the 42-line Bible, undated]. 4°. 33-line edition. Bod-Inc D-126; GW 8708; ISTC id00317400.

Donatus, Aelius, *Ars minor*. [Augsburg: Günther Zainer, *c.* 1475]. Folio. Bod- Inc D-131; GW 8817; ISTC id00327580.

Secondary Works

Blaise Agüera y Arcas and Paul Needham, 'Temporary Matrices and Elemental Punches in Gutenberg's DK Type', in *Incunabula and their Readers*, ed. Kristian Jensen (London, 2003).

Bibliotheca anglo-poetica or, A descriptive catalogue of a rare and rich collection of early English poetry: in the possession of Longman, Hurst, Rees, Orme, and Brown. Illustrated by occasional extracts and remarks, critical and biographical (London, 1815).

Bibliotheca Pinelliana. A Catalogue of the Magnificent and Celebrated Library of Maffei Pinelli, Late of Venice (London: James Edwards, 2 Mar. 1789 and following).

BMC = *Catalogue of Books Printed in the XVth Century Now in the British Museum*, 13 vols (London, 1908–2007).

Bod-Inc = *A Catalogue of Books Printed in the Fifteenth Century now in the Bodleian Library*, ed. Alan Coates, Kristian Jensen, Cristina Dondi, Bettina Wagner, and Helen Dixon, with the assistance of Carolinne White and Elizabeth Mathew; blockbooks by Nigel Palmer, and an inventory of Hebrew incunabula by Silke Schaeper, 6 vols (Oxford, 2005).

Asa Briggs, *A History of Longmans and their Books 1724–1990* (London, 2008).

Catalogue des livres de M. Pierre-Antoine Bolongaro-Crevenna (Amsterdam: Changuion and P. den Hengst, 1789).

Catalogue of a Bibliotheca Typographica [*the property of F. G. H. Culemann*] ... *which will be sold by auction, by Messrs. Sotheby, Wilkinson & Hodge, 7th Feb. 1870 and 3 following days* (London, 1870).

Harold Cox and John E. Chandler, *The House of Longman: With a Record of their Bicentenary Celebration* (London, 1925).

Léon de Laborde, *Débuts de l'imprimerie à Mayence et à Bamberg* (Paris, 1840).

Seymour de Ricci, *Catalogue Raisonné des Premières Impressions de Mayence (1445–1467)* (Mainz, 1911).

Seymour de Ricci, *English Collectors of Books and Manuscripts (1530–1930) and their Marks of Ownership* (Cambridge, 1930).

Thomas Frognall Dibdin, *Bibliotheca Spenceriana*, 4 vols (London, 1814).

Thomas Frognall Dibdin, *The Bibliographical Decameron*, 3 vols (London, 1817).

Thomas Frognall Dibdin, *A Bibliographical, Antiquarian and Picturesque Tour in France and Germany*, 3 vols (London, 1821).

E. Gordon Duff, *Early Printed Books* (London, 1893).

Karl Dziatzko, *Gutenbergs früheste Druckerpraxis* (Berlin, 1890).

James Edwards, *Catalogue of a select collection of ancient and modern Books* (London, 1790).

James Edwards, *A Catalogue of a very select collection of Books in all languages, and every branch of literature now on sale by J Edwards* (London, 1794).

James Edwards, *A Catalogue of Books, in all languages, and in every branch of literature, collected from various parts of Europe now on sale* (London, 1796).

Essays in the History of Publishing in Celebration of the 250th Anniversary of the House of Longman, 1724–1974, ed. Asa Briggs (London, 1974).

Roland Folter, 'The Gutenberg Bible in the Antiquarian Book Trade', *Incunabula, Studies in Fifteenth-Century Printed Books presented to Lotte Hellinga*, ed. Martin Davies (London, 1999), 271–351.

Arthur Freeman, '*Everyman* and Others, Part I: Some Fragments of Early English Printing, and their Preservers', *The Library*, vol. 9, no. 3 (2008), 267–305.

Lotte Hellinga, 'The Rylands Incunabula: an International Perspective', *Bulletin du Bibliophile* (1989), no. 1, 34–52.

Frank Herrmann, *Sotheby's, Portrait of an Auction House* (London, 1980).

Janet Ing, *Johann Gutenberg and his Bible* (New York, 1988).

Kristian Jensen, *Revolution and the Antiquarian Book: Reshaping the Past, 1780–1815* (Cambridge, 2011).

Alan Noel Latimer Munby, *Connoisseurs and Medieval Miniatures 1750–1850* (Oxford, 1972).

Christoph Gottlieb von Murr, *Merkwürdigkeiten der fürstbischöflichen Residenzstadt Bamberg* (Munich, 1799).

Paul Needham, 'Fragments in Books', in M. McC. Gatch, '*So precious a foundation*', *The Library of Leander van Ess* … (New York, 1996), 85–110.

Paul Needham, 'Discovery and Invention of the Gutenberg Bible, 1455–1805', in *The Medieval Book: Glosses from Friends & Colleagues of Christopher de Hamel*, ed. James H. Marrow, Richard A. Linenthal, and William Noel ('t Goy-Houten, 2010), 208–41.

John Claud Trewinard Oates, *A Catalogue of the Fifteenth-Century Printed Books in the University Library, Cambridge* (Cambridge, 1954).

Payne and Foss, *A Catalogue of Books Printed upon Vellum now on Sale* (London, 1835).

Payne and Foss, *Bibliotheca Butleriana, A Catalogue of the Library of the late Right Rev. Samuel Butler* (London, 1841).

Rare and Valuable Books: Property of Messrs G. and W. Nicol (London: Evans, 18 July 1825).

Paul Schwenke, *Die Donat- und Kalender-Type* (Mainz, 1903).

Bénédicte Savoy, 'Codicologue, incunabuliste et rabatteur. La mission de Jean-Baptiste Maugérard dans les quatre départements du Rhin (1802–1805)', *Bulletin du bibliophile* (1999), no. 2, 313–44.

A Selection of First Editions; and Books Printed in the Fifteenth Century; of Books Printed upon Vellum; and other Specimens Illustrating the History and Progress of Typography (London, 1836).

Eric Marshall White, 'Gutenberg Bibles on the Move in England, 1789–1834', *Transactions of the Cambridge Bibliographical Society*, vol. 15, no. 1 (2012) a special issue ed. by Ed Potten and Satoko Tokunaga.

Eric Marshall White, *Editio Princeps: A History of the Gutenberg Bible* (London and Turnhout, 2017).

Gottfried Zedler, *Die älteste Gutenbergtype* (Mainz, 1902).

PART 5

Migration of Books, Access to New Publics

▼ TRACING THE MONASTIC BOOK FROM ITS LEAVING
THE MONASTIC LIBRARY TO ITS NEW SECULAR USES:
THE MONASTIC PRACTICE OF "REJUVENATING" THE
COLLECTIONS, THE ACCESS TO NEW PUBLICS, THE
CHANGE IN READING HABITS, AND THE NEW PUBLICS
WHO GAIN ACCESS TO THE BOOKS

BART OP DE BEECK

Jesuit Libraries in the Southern Netherlands and their Dispersal after 1773

"La sensation qu'on éprouve en parcourant les anciens inventaires de la Bibliothèque royale et les catalogues des livres des jésuites, n'a rien de bien agréable: les titres des ouvrages ont quelque chose d'effrayant"[1].

The history of the libraries of religious institutions in the Early Modern period has still to be written. Collections of books from Jesuit colleges, abbeys and cloisters have often been neglected. Attention predominantly went to the medieval manuscript collections, scriptoria and library catalogues[2]. Research has most certainly been hampered by the sheer amount of the material. Library catalogues of the Early Modern period – if they happen to survive at all – often contain thousands of titles and it is difficult to get to grips with such a mass

of books[3]. From most of these libraries a vast number of books and manuscripts can be found still in existence in deposit libraries. It is, however, rare to find reliable provenance catalogues in

---

1 Edouard Mailly, *Histoire de l'Académie impériale et royale des sciences et belles-lettres de Bruxelles*, 2 vols (Bruxelles, 1883) I, 178.

2 e.g. Albert Derolez, *Les catalogues de bibliothèques*, Typologie des sources du moyen âge occidental, 31 (Turnhout, 1979), 60.

3 See Christian Coppens, '"L'ignorance a fait de terribles ravages". Le catalogue de la bibliothèque de Saint-Hubert (1665) dans son contexte', in *La bibliothèque de l'abbaye de Saint-Hubert en Ardenne au dix-septième siècle. Première partie: Vie intellectuelle et religieuse d'une communauté bénédictine*, ed. Luc Knapen (Leuven, 1999), 384–401 at 384–85: "Contrairement aux prévisions, on a accordé apparemment peu ou presque pas d'attention aux bibliothèques monastiques postérieures au moyen âge. […] La bibliothèque particulière d'un illustre savant ou d'un dignitaire a-t-elle donné lieu à une publication, les bibliothèques monastiques s'y prêtent peu ou pas du tout. Même si leur reconstruction sur base d'exemplaires disséminés est presqu'un travail de Sisyphe, des catalogues manuscrits ou imprimés sont conservés ça et là. Ils constituent un matériel sur mesure pour l'histoire du livre et n'attendent qu'à sortir de l'oubli." Dominique Varry, 'L'histoire des bibliothèques en France. État des lieux', *Bulletin des Bibliothèques de France*, 50.2 (2005), 16–22, at 19: "Pour leur part, les bibliothèques religieuses n'ont fait ces dernières années l'objet que de timides incursions, malgré tout prometteuses."

Bart op de Beeck • Curator of the general collection of printed books and the reading rooms, the Royal Library of Belgium. bart.opdebeeck@kbr.be

How the Secularization of Religious Houses Transformed the Libraries of Europe, 16th–19th Centuries, ed. by Cristina Dondi, Dorit Raines, and † Richard Sharpe, BIB, 63 (Turnhout, 2022), pp. 431–448.

BREPOLS ❧ PUBLISHERS   DOI 10.1484/M.BIB-EB.5.128497

these libraries and we hope that librarians and scholars will continue to work to remedy this deplorable situation. The identification of this primary material takes a lot of time and has to be carried out by the researcher himself – if he is lucky enough to have been granted free access to the collections of these institutional libraries. The search for these books and manuscripts can be compared to an archaeological excavation. Meaningless numbers, letters, etc., only make sense when one has seen them in many books. Provenance research is furthermore hindered by injudicious rebinding and other interventions. In many cases we will never be able securely to recover where a book has come from.

The dismantling of the libraries at the end of the eighteenth century is the greatest stumbling block. A vast amount of books got lost, was sold, neglected or destroyed. The Austrian government, who ruled the Southern Netherlands, abolished the Jesuit order in 1773 in compliance with the breve *Dominus ac Redemptor* of Pope Clement XIV[4]. Contemplative orders were abolished in 1781 and the remaining orders during the French occupation. In the case of the Jesuit order, Georges Joseph Gérard (1734–1814), perpetual secretary of the "Académie de Bruxelles", director of the Brussels Royal Library, official and scholar, was appointed in 1775 to handle the sale of the Jesuit libraries. The Austrian authorities decided to set aside a large quantity of printed books, as well as practically all the manuscripts for the Brussels Royal Library which had been opened to the public in 1772 under the auspices of the Brussels Academy. The remains of the collection

of this "old" Royal Library are now kept in the present Royal Library of Belgium (Koninklijke Bibliotheek van België or Bibliothèque royale de Belgique), which was founded in 1837 after the independence of Belgium. Manuscripts from the Jesuit colleges are kept in the collections of the Manuscript Room and the printed books in the collection "Ville de Bruxelles" which forms part of the Section of Old and Rare Books. These remains – be it partially – reflect the collections of the former Jesuit libraries[5].

Libraries and Books in the Residences of the Jesuit Order in the Southern Netherlands

The main library in each Jesuit residence was the *Bibliotheca Major*. In the regular colleges, which provided a secondary school education, these libraries were never for the use of the pupils but for the members of the order. The size of these libraries depended upon the importance and the wealth of the college. The libraries of smaller colleges contained a few thousand books, whereas an important college such as that in Brussels contained more than ten thousand books[6].

---

4   For a general history of the Southern Netherlands: *History of the Low Countries*, ed. Johannes Cornelis Hendrik Blom and Emiel Lamberts (repr. New York; Oxford, 2009). Simply put: the Southern Netherlands were in the sixteenth century until 1715 Spanish, from 1715 until 1794 Austrian, from 1794 until 1815 French and from 1815 until 1830 Dutch. In 1830 Belgium became an independent state.

5   This article is based on my dissertation: Bart Op de Beeck, 'Jezuïetenbibliotheken in de Zuidelijke Nederlanden: de liquidatie 1773–1828', unpublished Ph.D. diss. (Catholic University of Louvain, 2008). For other realms where the Jesuit Order was abolished, see Wifried Enderle, 'Die Jesuitenbibliothek im 17. Jahrhundert. Das Beispiel der Bibliothek des Düsseldorfer Kollegs 1619–1773', *Archiv für Geschichte des Buchwesens*, 41 (1994), 147–213; Hendrik Dijkgraaf, *The Library of a Jesuit Community at Holbeck, Nottinghamshire* (1679), Libri Pertinentes, 8 (Cambridge, 2003); Dolores García Gómez, *Testigos de la memoria: los inventarios de las bibliotecas de la compañía de Jesús en la expulsión de 1767* (San Vicente del Raspeig, 2010).

6   For the library of this college see: Bart Op de Beeck, 'De bibliotheek van het Brusselse jezuïetencollege tijdens het Ancien Régime', in *Quatre siècles de présence jésuite*

Residences where the higher education for future Jesuits was organised, like the college at Louvain, the noviciates in Tournai and Mechelen and the *Domus Professa* in Antwerp, also had a main library. When such a residence also harboured a college, it would have two separate libraries. Tournai had a *Bibliotheca Major* for the college and another one for the noviciate. Mechelen had a library for the college, one for the noviciate and the Museum Bellarminum as well[7]. The principal libraries contained a wide range of books. The core of the collection of course lay in the field of theology. But for other disciplines, and especially in the field of history, these libraries often possessed a considerable number of books. Particular excellence in one field might result from a specific donation or from the activities of certain individuals.

At the head of each library stood a library prefect. His tasks and responsibilities were prescribed in the *Regulae praefecti bibliothecae* published in 1580[8]. The *catalogi personarum* of the Jesuit colleges of the Southern Netherlands often do not mention this function implying that it was not that important and that there were often more urgent problems needing attention than the management of the library. The *Regulae praefecti bibliothecae* also stipulated that forbidden books could not be kept in the library. Consequently they were often kept apart in the "hell" (*Infernum, Enfer* or *Helle*), but certainly not destroyed. The Princess of Gavre, Marie-Amour-Désirée de Rouvroy, deposited in 1760 the complete works of Voltaire in the "hell" of Namur college library: "La princesse de Gavre leur remit en 1760 les Oeuvres de Voltaire en 17. volumes. Il s'ij trouve cette Note: *Ces 17. volumes ont été envoiés aux R.P. Jesuites par la Princesse de Gavre en 1760 pour être mis a l'Enfer: s'il arrivoit que le Prince Francois de Gavre son mari le redemandat il faudroit les lui rendre*"[9]. The responsible for the sales of the Jesuit collections, Gérard, mentions also a small separate library in the college of Mons: "La chambre dite l'Enfer n'avoit sans

---

à Bruxelles = *Vier eeuwen jezuïeten te Brussel*, ed. Alain Deneef and Xavier Rousseaux (Bruxelles; Leuven, 2012), 49–89.

7 The Museum Bellarminum is discussed further down in this paper; see also Augustin De Backer, *Bibliothèque des écrivains de la Compagnie de Jésus* (Liège, 1859), 140–41. Alfred Poncelet, *Histoire de la Compagnie de Jésus dans les anciens Pays-Bas. Etablissement de la Compagnie de Jésus en Belgique et ses développements jusqu'à la fin du règne d'Albert et d'Isabelle. Deuxième partie: Les œuvres,* Académie royale de Belgique, Classe des lettres et des sciences morales et politiques, Mémoires, Collection in 8°, XXI, 2 (Bruxelles, 1928), 473–75; Louis Brouwers, *De jezuïeten te Mechelen in de 17e en 18e eeuw en hun Xaveriuskerk, de huidige parochiekerk S.S. Petrus en Paulus* (Mechelen, 1977), 83–84.

8 Brendan Connolly, *The Roots of Jesuit Librarianship: 1540–1599. A dissertation submitted to the Faculty of the Graduate Library School in candidacy for the degree of Doctor of Philosophy, University of Chicago* (Chicago, 1955), more specifically at 61–96 and in Appendix A the first rules of 1567 and the rules of 1935. Alfred Franklin, *Les anciennes Bibliothèques de Paris*, 3 vols (Paris, 1867–1873), II (1870). Franklin gives in his chapter on

the Collège Louis-le-Grand (245–65) the Latin text of 1580 and the French translation of 1620 (246–47). Paul Mech, 'Les bibliothèques de la Compagnie de Jésus', in *Histoire des bibliothèques françaises*, II: *Les bibliothèques sous l'Ancien Régime 1530–1789*, ed. Claude Jolly (Paris, 1988), 56–63, at 57; Ernst Manfred Wermter, 'Studien und Quellen zur Geschichte der Jesuitenbibliotheken in Mainz 1561–1773', in *De Bibliotheca Moguntina. Festschrift der Stadtbibliothek Mainz zum fünfzigjährigen Bestehen ihres Gebäudes 1962*, ed. Jürgen Busch, Veröffentlichung der Stadtbibliothek und der Städtischen Volksbüchereien Mainz, 28 (Mainz, 1963), 51–70, at 51 and a Latin text and German translation at 66–68 (Abhang 1); Enderle, *Die Jesuitenbibliothek*, as note 5, 154–55.

9 National Archives of Belgium, 'Secretarie van State en Oorlog 1893', report of Gérard dated 6 May 1777. Marie-Amour-Désirée de Rouvroy was married to François Joseph Rasse Léopold, prince of Gavre (1731–1797). See Claude Bruneel and Jean-Paul Hoyois, *Les grands commis du gouvernement des Pays-Bas autrichiens. Dictionnaire biographique du personnel des institutions centrales,* Archives générales du Royaume et Archives de l'Etat dans les Provinces. Studia, 84 (Bruxelles, 2001), 279–80.

doute point été frequentée depuis plusieurs années, les livres etoient garnis de poussiere, et d'une malpropreté inexprimable"[10].

In the college and noviciate of Tournai, Gérard found two separate places where these books were kept. The first was located in the college:

L'autre chambre qu'on nommoit l'enfer devoit contenir les livres deffendus, je n'ij trouvai qu'environ cent cinquante volumes tous in octavo et duodecimo mal conditionnés et de peu d'importance, il ij avoit cependant des caisses ou tablettes en assez grand nombre et je remarquai par la poussiere qui se trouvoit encore sur les planches que ces caisses avoient eté remplies et qu'il devoit ij avoir eu des livres in folio et in quarto. je n'ai cependant pas trouvé dans la grande Bibliothèque des livres in folio et in quarto qui pourroient etre envisagés comme deffendus et il est par consequent apparent qu'il ij a des livres soustraits, qui n'ont pas eté restitués.

and the second in the noviciate:

selon ce que le preposé Herier me dit il ij avoit encore eu des livres dans un cinquieme place qu'on nommoit l'enfer, par ce que les livres deffendus par la cour de Rome ij etoient deposés; mais ces livres, selon le dire du preposé, avoient eté transportés a Bruxelles par ordre du Gouvernement[11].

In the course of the present research we discovered only a few copies which had been censored and we are not even sure if these had been censored by a previous owner or in the Jesuit library. However, there must have been a number of books which had been censored, but those were not reserved by Gérard for the collection of the Royal Library. Censorship also contributed to the low profits of the book sales as explained by Gérard: "quantité de livres etoient endommagés les cidevant jesuites aiant dechiré les feuilles qui contenoient des passages contre la Cour de Rome, contre les Instituts et contre les Moeurs …"[12].

Outside the main *Bibliotheca Major* the teachers or professors often had a reference library which supported their teaching activities. In Louvain the library of the professors (*Bibliotheca Professorum*) largely consisted of forbidden books, which were of course very useful for the compilation of the pamphlets they produced in large quantities, and which were aimed at the protestants and the Jansenists[13]. Also the college *convict* at Antwerp or the seminary in Mons – both boarding schools – possessed their proper libraries. These libraries were probably for the use of the students who would read the books under supervision[14]. Every residence had as well an infirmary and a pharmacy. They also possessed a small library. The library of the infirmary contained a number of illustrated works, emblem books and collections of engravings which were on the one hand for meditation and on the other hand for distraction of the sick. In the library of the pharmacy we find herbals, pharmacopoeia and medical works.

The Sodalities or Marian Congregations, attached to the Jesuit colleges, also possessed their own libraries. In the first place they had to contribute to the spiritual edification of their members. In a number of these congregational libraries the books could also be borrowed. The

10 National Archives of Belgium, 'Secretarie van State en Oorlog 1893', report of Gérard dated 6 May 1777.

11 National Archives of Belgium, 'Comité Jésuitique 38B', report of Gérard dated 18 March 1776. Herrier was appointed guardian of this college after the dissolution.

12 National Archives of Belgium, 'Oostenrijkse Geheime Raad 847/A', report of Gérard dated 28 August 1779.

13 Brussels, Royal Library of Belgium, shelfmark MS 4714 C, dated around 1665.

14 Pierre Delsaerdt, 'The inheritors of loss. Seized libraries and bibliophily in late 18th-century Antwerp', *De Gulden Passer*, 92.1 (2014), 53–70, at 59.

surviving copies from these libraries demonstrate that they – at least in the eighteenth century – also contained travel literature and historical publications. This evolution has to be seen as an attempt to increase the attraction of these Sodalities and they are in some way the ancestors of the public lending library[15].

During the seventeenth and eighteenth century the Jesuits formed various scholarly circles which sometimes turned into real institutions. These institutions were attached to a particular Jesuit residence. Mechelen (Malines) thus housed the Museum Bellarminum, named after Saint Robertus Bellarminus (1542–1621), Jesuit theologian and cardinal. The Jesuit members of this "Museum" focused on controversial writings against protestants and dissidents, and they tried by all means to defend the interests and ideas of the order and the catholic faith. In Antwerp a small group of Jesuits devoted to hagiographical studies flourished in the "maison professe" from the beginning of the seventeenth century; known as the Bollandists after the editor of their first volumes, they published their monumental *Acta Sanctorum* from 1643 in Antwerp until the dissolution of the Order. Both of these scholarly institutions built a considerable specialized library in the Jesuit residence in which they were housed[16].

When an individual Jesuit needed certain books for his research he could borrow them in the library of his own college or even from another residence. For example, in 1754 the provincial of the order, Joannes Fraeys, gave to the teacher of the *repetentes* (juvenate) in Courtrai, Albertus van Rijn, permission to borrow a copy of the Greek-Latin *Opera* of Lucianus. This permission had to be renewed each year "donec eadem opera collegio Bruxellensi restituantur"[17]. It might also happen that books were loaned to outsiders (under Rule 12 of the *Regulae*). A lending register with dates, titles of books and names of borrowers is known for the college at Liège[18]. Gérard found a similar one at Marche: "Le catalogue ci joint sub N. 233 se trouvoit dans la Bibliotheque de Marche, j'ij remarque que les ci devant Jesuites pretoient a des demoiselles, l'histoire du Peuple de Dieu quoique ce livre soit proscrit par la Cour de Rome et l'ait été par le Parlement de Paris"[19]. The book in question is of course the history of Israël, *Histoire du peuple de Dieu*, written by the French Jesuit Isaac-Joseph Berruyer (1681–1758) and published in seven volumes in 1728 with further parts added in 1753 and 1757. Despite the fact that the first part was condemned by the papacy and put on the Index in 1732, and later condemnations by the Parliament of Paris (1756) and by the Jesuit Order itself, this work was highly successful.

---

15 On the foundation of the Marian Congregations in Belgium under the leadership of the Belgian Jesuit Jan Leunis in 1563, Lance Lazar, 'The formation of the pious soul: Trans-Alpine demand for Jesuit devotional texts, 1548–1615', in *Confessionalization in Europe, 1555–1700: Essays in Honor and Memory of Bodo Nischan*, ed. John Headley, Hans Hillerbrand, and Anthony J. Papalas (Aldershot, Hampshire; Burlington, Vt., 2004), 289–318.

16 For the libraries of the Bollandists, see Bart Op de Beeck, 'La Bibliothèque des Bollandistes à la fin de l'Ancien Régime', in *De Rosweyde aux Acta Sanctorum. La recherche hagiographique des Bollandistes à travers quatre siècles. Actes du Colloque international* (Bruxelles, 5 octobre 2007), ed. Robert Godding, Bernard Joassart, Xavier Lequeux, and François De Vriendt, Subsidia hagiographica, 88 (Bruxelles, 2009), 149–284.

See further details in François Dolbeau, 'Nouvelles recherches sur les manuscrits des anciens bollandistes', *Analecta Bollandiana*, 129 (2011), 395–457.

17 Brussels, Royal Library of Belgium, shelfmark VB 7.332 C: *Luciani opera cum interpretatione J. Bourdelotii*. Lutetiae: Jul. Bertault, 1615, in Folio; Greek and Latin text. Provenance note on the title page: "Coll[eg].ij Soc[ieta]tis Jesu Bruxellis 1639 M.B.", "Q.", "D9/7".

18 Carmélia Opsomer-Halleux, 'Nouveaux matériaux pour l'histoire des bibliothèques liégeoise', *Bulletin de la Société royale Le Vieux-Liège*, 13 (1994), 206–15, especially 213–14. Liège was not part of the Southern Netherlands, but an independent prince-bishopric.

19 National Archives of Belgium, 'Secretarie van State en Oorlog 1893'.

Last but not least each Jesuit had in his private room a small collection of books that he needed for meditation or for his religious or teaching activities. At the time of the dissolution, Franciscus Erix complained that, when he was living in Courtrai, the library prefect had mistakenly placed his personal books in the main library and that he would like to keep in exchange the books he then possessed[20]. There were of course exceptions such as Heribertus Rosweyde (1569–1629), founding father of the Bollandists, who kept more than 500 works in his private study in Antwerp[21].

Each residence almost always tried to complete their collections of theological works even when the budget of the libraries was not very large. Books were bought from publishers, from booksellers, and at book auctions. Most libraries received gifts from private persons: either (Jesuit) authors donated their own publications, benefactors donated books or funds for the library, etc. For the Southern Netherlands we have evidence of some large gifts: from the Antwerp bishop and humanist, Laevinus Torrentius (1525–1595), and the Louvain university professor, Justus Lipsius (1547–1606) to the Louvain college library; from the theologian Jacobus Pamelius

(1536–1587) and the bishop of Bruges and Ghent, Carolus van den Bosch (1597–1665), to the Bruges college, etc. The Bollandists donated copies of their publications to each college library in the Southern Netherlands, but in the eighteenth century they also played a major role as go-between in the acquisition of books, and this service was rendered to various college libraries in the Southern Netherlands. Their network consisted not only of correspondents of the Jesuit order or catholic academics, but they also had dealings with members of other religious orders or of protestant scholars[22].

Dozens of surviving books illustrate how, particularly in the Flemish province, books migrated from one college library to another. Books of the Jesuit residence of 's-Hertogenbosch, which closed down in 1629, were distributed among the other libraries of the province. Books and manuscripts were exchanged and in the case of the Bollandists or the Historiographical Institute they were bought from other colleges of the same province or from other religious institutions[23].

Although the Jesuit order tried to organize its libraries uniformly, the reality was somewhat different. All the library catalogues we studied were organized by subject. The number of subjects

20 National Archives of Belgium, 'Comité Jésuitique', 38, fol. 758–59: "ik had tot Cortryk gelaten veele van myne boeken maer eenen pater die praefect was van de bibliotheque niet wetende dat het mijne boeken waren, heeft de zelve onder andere op de bibliotheque geplaetst. Zoo dat het mij onmogelijk is voor de zelve weder te crijgen aengezien deze myne boeken hare majesteijt zullen toebehooren, zoo vrage ik dat deez wynige boeken welkers weerde minder is als die van de myne, my zouden overgelaten worden". On Franciscus Erix (1742–1815), see Willem Audenaert, *Prosopographia Iesuitica Belgica Antiqua (PIBA). A biographical Dictionary of the Jesuits in the Low Countries 1542–1773* (Leuven-Heverlee, 2000), I, 327.

21 Brussels, Royal Library of Belgium, MS 8523 D: "Libri in cubiculo P. Heribertus Roswey, Ultraiectensis Societatis Jesu". See Op de Beeck, *La Bibliothèque*, as note 16, 195–97.

22 Antwerp, State Archives, 'Archief Nederlandse Provincie 1045'. For the Jesuit archives kept in the State Archives at Antwerp, see Hendrik Callewier, *Inventaris van het archief van de Nederduitse provincie der jezuïeten (Provincia Belgica, vervolgens Provincia Flandro-Belgica) en van het archief van het professenhuis te Antwerpen (1388) 1564–1773*, Rijksarchief te Antwerpen. Inventarissen, 59 (Brussel, 2006).

23 The Historiographical institute or "Museum Historiographicum" was erected in 1771. At the head stood the Jesuit and former Bollandist, Joseph Ghesquière (1731–1802). Ghesquière was able to form in a few years a library of several hundreds of historical printed works and more than 50 manuscripts. The members were supposed to write a general history of the Netherlands, the "Analecta Belgica". Op de Beeck, as note 5, passim.

and the way they were ordered depended on the person who compiled the catalogue. We are convinced that each library possessed a catalogue. Often these catalogues were not complete: most of them were compiled in the course of the seventeenth century to be further augmented with later acquisitions. This was mostly done in an orderly way, but later on disorder flourished. What survived are an eighteenth-century catalogue of the Bollandist library and one of the library of the college of Maastricht[24]. The Bollandist catalogue, drawn up about 1740, has more than 17% of eighteenth-century books and the main bulk, about 68%, was printed in the seventeenth century.

In the course of the eighteenth century the library catalogues were replaced by new ones. The latest shelfmarks present in the surviving books are not to be found in the library catalogues at our disposition, which date from the seventeenth century. In Brussels the eighteenth-century library catalogue was probably destroyed by the Jesuits themselves. Gérard failed to recognize the historical value of these sources and sold about 40 volumes of library catalogues to be pulped after May 1782. The surviving registers with donations all date from the seventeenth century and testify to a policy which stimulated donations to the colleges. When we compare the contents of these registers with the surviving books and manuscripts we find that they are incomplete and that even gifts dating from the period in which the register was used are missing in these lists of donations.

The eighteenth-century catalogues might have given us a clear answer about the acquisitions of the libraries since the beginning of the eighteenth century. The surviving books and the editions in the auction catalogues which date from the eighteenth century represent only a small percentage of the total number of books. In the collection *Ville de Bruxelles* of the Royal Library only one percent of the books coming from Jesuit colleges is dated after 1750. We are however certain that books were inscribed in the library until the dissolution in 1773. In the Bollandist catalogue some works have been published in 1771, and in some books coming from the library of the Ghent college the provenance is accompanied by the date 1773. Our actual knowledge of the libraries leads us to the conclusion that the hey-day of these libraries is to be situated in the seventeenth century and that they grew much slower in the eighteenth century.

The Closure of the Libraries and the Acquisitions of the Royal Library

After the dissolution of the Jesuit order in 1773, Georges-Joseph Gérard was appointed by the *Comité Jésuitique* (the council for the suppression of the Jesuit order) to sell the books in the colleges. He began his inventory in 1775 and the last books were sold in 1780. It is clear that a number of books just disappeared. In Brussels, books were sold just before the dissolution to Jacob Goyers (1719–1809), a church historian, and to François-Xavier Burtin (1743–1818), a physician, and – from 1784 on – a member of the Brussels Academy. Amongst these books were eighteenth-century editions, a set of Aldrovandus and the *Hortus Eystettensis*[25]. Teachers of the

24 Bollandist Library: Bruxelles, Bibliothèque des Bollandistes, MS Boll. 20–24; Maestricht College: Maastricht, Regionaal Historisch Centrum Limburg, Archief, Klooster der Jezuïeten te Maastricht, 30. The content of this catalogue has not been examined.

25 National Archives of Belgium, 'Comité Jésuitique, 11/A', fol. 726. On Burtin see Marie-Jeanne Stallaert, 'François-Xavier Burtin. Portretten van een verzamelaar', *Het Tijdschrift van Dexia Bank*, 54 (2002.2), n. 212, 53–62; Bruneel and Hoyois, *Les grands commis du gouvernement des Pays-Bas autrichiens*, as note 9, 138–42. On Goyers see Jan Roegiers in *Dictionnaire d'histoire et de géographie ecclésiastique*, 21 (1986), 982–83; Tom Verschaffel,

Table 22.1. Sales catalogues: lots by subject.

SALE	THEOLOGY	JURISPRUDENCE	ARTS	LITERATURE	HISTORY	NO SUBJECT*	TOTAL	TOTAL %
Nivelles	896	73	67	90	360	–	1.486	1,6%
Roermond	1.587	103	176	543	722	–	3.131	3,3%
Namur	755	139	167	237	507	–	1.805	1,9%
Ypres	1.612	213	160	254	613	–	2.852	3%
Courtrai	667	228	211	319	557	–	1.982	2,1%
Ghent	4.217	644	163	849	1.866	–	7.739	8,2%
Luxembourg	2.066	615	381	730	1.088	94	4.974	5,3%
Aalst	978	63	84	149	302	–	1.576	1,7%
Mons	3.233	661	818	499	1.246	–	6.457	6,8%
Tournai	4.192	489	604	1.613	1.778	96	8.772	9,3%
Bruges	2.850	644	825	801	1.696	–	6.816	7,2%
Brussels	4.081	645	729	1.120	2.153	–	8.728	9,2%
Mechelen	2.146	516	345	571	1.299	–	4.877	5,2%
Louvain	5.651	1.305	1.535	1.522	2.297	–	12.293	13%
Antwerp	7.503	1.082	1.653	3.290	2.586	502	16.616	17,6%
Livres choisis	840	197	617	513	2.131	–	4.298	4,5%
Total	43.274	7.617	8.535	13.100	21.201	692	94.419	100%
Total %	45,8%	8%	9%	13,9%	22,5%	0,7%	100%	

*No subject could be attributed because the lots were not sufficiently described.

new Royal Colleges, which replaced the Jesuit colleges, were given some books – sometimes the relevance with their teaching activities was quite inexistant – and there is also proof that books were stolen, even after the libraries had been sealed. Most of the books Gérard inventoried and sold naturally came from the main libraries of the colleges, but he also found stocks of schoolbooks, instructions and rules of the Jesuit order as well as devotional works (mostly for the use of the sodalities).

The reports and the correspondence of Gérard make it possible to reconstruct the course of events from the compilation of the inventories till the sales of the libraries. Five small libraries were sold without a catalogue (Ath, Halle, Lier,

Marche and Oudenaarde) and 15 libraries with a printed sales catalogue (Nivelles, Roermond, Namur, Ypres, Courtrai, Ghent, Luxembourg, Aalst, Mons, Tournai, Bruges, Brussels, Mechelen, Louvain, Antwerp). Finally in September 1780 the "Livres choisis" were brought under the hammer: a selection of the best books from all the college collections[26]. The sales catalogues are based on the inventories Gérard had compiled. This is clearly demonstrated in the sloppy sales catalogue of the Antwerp residence. Although the quality of the sales catalogues leaves much to be desired, they give us nevertheless a general view of the books present at the time of the dissolution. When we compare these eighteenth-century sales catalogues with the seventeenth-century library catalogues, we have to draw the same conclusions:

Historici in de Oostenrijkse Nederlanden (1715–1794). Proeve van een repertorium, Facultés universitaires Saint-Louis. Studiecentrum 18de-eeuwse Zuidnederlandse Letterkunde. Cahiers, 15 (Brussel, 1996), 55.

26 For these sales catalogues, see Appendix: Sales catalogues of Jesuit libraries in the Southern Netherlands.

the libraries stagnated in the eighteenth century. About 94.000 lots were sold by auction. When we arrange them by subject, theology represents more than 45%, history with its auxiliary sciences 22,5%, followed by literature (13,9%), arts (9%) and jurisprudence (8%). When we arrange the books by format about 50% were octavo books and 25% quarto and folio editions each. Typically, jurisprudence has the largest number of books in folio (35%) and philology has the largest number of octavo books (76%). For the sale of the "livres choisis" we were able to classify the books by date. The main bulk was published between 1601 and 1650: 40,5%, followed by books published in the second half of the sixteenth century (21%), and books published in the second half of the seventeenth century (15,3%). About 60% of the books are in Latin with a slow decrease in the eighteenth century.

The sales catalogues were censored by both a royal censor appointed by the Austrian government and an ecclesiastical censor appointed by the bishop. Forbidden books were indicated by an asterisk and could only be bought by "des personnes connues par leur état & leurs lumieres, ou qui ont la permission de les lire", according to a warning printed in each sales catalogue. In reality books were sold to anyone who wanted to buy them:

> Il ij a dans les Bibliotheques des ci devant jesuites une grande quantité d'ouvrages fait par des protestans et proscrits par la cour de Rome, ainsi que par les edits Roiaux; plusieurs centaines d'exemplaires des oeuvres de Machiavel, un nombre considérable de livres concernant le Jansenisme et quantité d'ouvrages soit contre les moeurs ou la religion. La pluspart de ces ouvrages étant mal conditionnés, et consistant dans de mauvaises editions, ne seront achettés que par des gens du peuple, ou par des ecoliers. Il est vrai que ces livres seront annoncés comme deffendus par les censeurs (qui cependant en ont deja

> laissé échapper de ce genre dans les catalogues de Nivelles et Ruremonde). Nous observons que la defense annoncée par le catalogue ne sert à rien, puisque depuis quelques années on laisse suivre à toutes sortes de personnes les livres annoncés comme deffendus. L'auditeur Gerard nous a, à la verité, informés, qu'il avoit ordre de ne point laisser suivre les livres deffendus à des jeunes-gens et à des personnes non lettrées, ce qu'il avoit executé dans les villes d'Ath, Lierre, Halle, et Nivelles; mais qu'il en étoit résulté des contestations, qui avoient arreté la vente, et qu'il croioit qu'il ne pourroit en agir de même dans les grandes villes où l'usage etoit établi depuis longtemps de ne point faire de distinction des livres defendus avec les autres – qu'il prevoioit qu'il en résulteroit des contestations sans nombre, et que ne pouvant pas faire exhiber les permissions de lire les livres deffendus qu'après la vente de ces sortes de livres, on devroit a chaque instant remettre en vente des livres deja ajugés; ce qui seroit cause que les ventes traineroient, et que souvent on ne trouveroit point d'achetteurs pour les livres reprouvés.

> C'est là sans doute un grand inconvenient, mais ce seroit un bien plus grand mal, si cette multitude de livres pernicieux tomboit entre les mains du peuple, qui pourra facilement s'empoisonner par le venin de ces ouvrages. Les loix et les édits de ces livres, à la vérité ne s'observent plus; mais dans un cas extraordinaire comme celui-ci, il seroit à propos de les reveiller, de s'ij conformer, en prévenant le public, soit par des annonces à la tête des catalogues, soit dans le lieu même de la vente. Ce seroit satisfaire à ce que dicte la conscience, et obvier du moins en partie aux inconvéniens apprehendés par l'auditeur Gerard[27].

---

27 National Archives of Belgium, 'Secretarie van State en Oorlog 1893', Report of Gérard dated 12 February 1778.

A number of schoolbooks were sold separately and a number of books were pulped (profit: 161 guilders). Nevertheless the sales were responsible for a benefit of about 132.000 guilders.

The details and specific titles of books communicated by Gérard in his reports and the overviews of his activities are of immeasurable value. Regularly Gérard mentions the titles of publications which were reserved for the Royal Library. A number of these editions is now kept in the Collection *Ville de Bruxelles*. Since practically all inventories with editions reserved for the Royal Library are lost, the surviving copies are the only concrete proof of the selection by Gérard[28]. More than 4.400 imprints came directly from the Jesuit libraries. The assumption that only a few books from the Jesuit libraries arrived in the Royal Library is herewith refuted[29]. According to Gérard about 30 to 40.000 volumes were reserved for the Royal Library. If these volumes correspond to some 15.000 editions, this means that 2/3 of the reserved volumes is no longer present in the Royal Library. Some of these books indeed never arrived, and a large quantity later disappeared from the library. Only 5% of these books was published after 1700 and, just as with the sales catalogues, the period 1601–1650 accounts for 44%, followed by 22% of books printed in the

second half of the sixteenth century and 16% in the second half of the seventeenth century. Only 20% of the books are of a theological nature, 36% are historical books, followed by 19% of philological works and 13 and 9% for respectively the arts and jurisprudence.

We already investigated the book collections of some Jesuit residences more thoroughly. The Antwerp residence contained not only the largest collection of books but harboured at the time of the suppression also two institutions. The Antwerp Bollandist library and the library of the Historiographical Institute have survived the suppression of the order and the suppression of the contemplative orders. They were finally dispersed in 1796. The fate of these libraries hung often by a thread. On the basis of a thorough research of the shelfmarks in the actual copies, we were able to determine that certain imprints with the provenance of the "Maison Professe" in reality belonged to the Bollandist library. Only a small part of the collections of Bollandists and Historiographs was reserved for the Royal Library. Nevertheless a considerable amount of the manuscripts from these collections is kept in this institution. The larger part of these manuscripts was bought in 1828 by the Dutch government who occupied the Southern Netherlands and arrived after the independence of Belgium (1830) in the Royal Library of Belgium through the Burgundian library. The inventories which Gérard drew up were anything but complete and a part of the manuscripts kept in the "Maison Professe" had not been inventoried by him.

After an extensive provenance research we were able, for the first time, to offer a survey of the editions presently held by the Royal Library and which were originally reserved for the "old" Royal Library. New Royal Colleges replaced the abolished Jesuit colleges and the books reserved for them are also very important to obtain an insight into the composition of the collections of books and this not only for the end of the eighteenth century. These books

28 The only surviving library inventory is the one which Gérard made of the libraries of the English Jesuit colleges in Bruges. After the abolition of the Jesuit order in France in 1762 the English Jesuits received the permission from the Austrian government to settle in Bruges. The inventory is kept in the Royal Library: pamphlet volume MS 20.373. Bart Op de Beeck, 'Boeken uit de bibliotheken van de Engelse jezuïetencolleges te Brugge, bewaard in de verzameling "Ville de Bruxelles"', in *Boekgeschiedenis in Vlaanderen. Nieuwe instrumenten en benaderingen. [Handelingen van het contactforum] 28 november 2003*, ed. Pierre Delsaerdt and Koen De Vlieger-De Wilde (Brussel, 2004), 79–89.

29 Jérome Machiels, *Van religieuze naar openbare bibliotheek*, Algemeen Rijksarchief en Rijksarchief in de Provinciën. Educatieve Dienst. Dossiers, Tweede reeks, 20 (Brussel, 2000), 55.

also passed through the hands of Gérard and once again his lists are of immeasurable value for the reconstruction of the Jesuit ownership of books. The selected books were defined as "livres classiques", principally meaning dictionaries, grammars, teaching manuals, schoolbooks and editions of mainly Latin classical authors. The "Commission royale des Etudes" or Royal Educational Commission received books from the Jesuit colleges until 1792. These hundreds of books – like the books reserved for the Royal Library – had not been sold.

The book historian Goran Proot could not find a copy of the *Ratio discendi et docendi* by the Jesuit Joseph de Jouvancy or Josephus Juvencius in the sales catalogues of the Jesuit libraries of the Southern Netherlands or in the collections of a number of present-day Belgian depository libraries[30]. When we take into account the opinions of the members of the Academy, the *Comité Jésuitique* and thus also Gérard, this is not in the least surprising. The book could easily have been part of a lot of educational books in the sales catalogues. Yet, if we look at the lists of books reserved for the new colleges we can immediately trace three copies[31].

That the edition is lacking in Belgian public depository libraries is not strange at all. This applies e.g. for all the printed regulations of the Jesuit order, the manuals the Jesuits used for the teaching in the colleges and for the theological courses of the future members of the order. After

Gérard inventoried the books the imprints with these subjects were not selected for the Royal Library. Both Gérard and the librarians Charles de la Serna Santander (1752–1813) and Joseph Marchal (1780–1858) adopted a clear policy of eliminating this material from the catalogue drawn for the use of the new Central School. Consequently, a large number of works related to the Jesuit order or written by well-known Jesuit authors are presently not available in the collections of the Royal Library. Works used by the Louvain Jesuit professors for their courses are only rarely present. The *Analogia* of Martin Becanus (1563–1624) is missing and not a single work of Hermann Busenbaum (1600–1668), Jacques Platel (1608–1681) or Vitus Pichler (1670–1736) is to be found in the Royal Library. The Royal Library does not possess a large collection of devotional printed literature, jansenistica or protestant literature and pamphlets. From the successful Jesuit author Hieremias Drexelius (1581–1638) we find only two works in the collection *Ville de Bruxelles*. The editions presently preserved in the collections of the Royal Library are not part of its founding collections *Ville de Bruxelles* or Van Hulthem, but were rather bought in the course of the nineteenth and the first half of the twentieth century[32]. Printed books were selected for their content and not as witnesses of the art of printing in the seventeenth and eighteenth century or as valuable historical material for the study of the religious and social life in the Southern Netherlands. A large number of these books was probably already lost in the eighteenth century. About 37.000 volumes, coming from the suppressed Jesuit colleges and cloisters, were sold from the 2nd till the 13th of June 1806 in Brussels by de la Serna Santander, the city librarian at

---

30 Goran Proot, *Het schooltoneel van de jezuïeten in de Provincia Flandro-Belgica tijdens het ancien régime (1575–1773)*, Onuitgegeven proefschrift Universiteit Antwerpen (Antwerpen, 2008), 91.

31 National Archives of Belgium, 'Koninklijke Commissie voor de Studies 32A', List dated 28 October 1778 with books reserved for the new college at Oudenaarde: "[number] 29 item alius libellus sine authoris nomine: ra[ti]o discendi et docendi. sine loco et anno". List dated 24 June 1778 with books reserved for the new college at Bruges: "[number] 27 Josephi juvencii ratio dicendi in 8°. Parisiis 1725 bis [the second copy is dated 1711]".

32 Bart Op de Beeck, 'Karel van Hulthem (1764–1832)', in *In de ban van boeken, grote verzamelaars uit de negentiende eeuw in de Koninklijke Bibliotheek van België*, ed. Marcus De Schepper, Ann Kelders, and Jan Pauwels (Brussel, 2008), 14–16.

that time[33]. The same situation occurred in other French "Départements" of the Southern Netherlands. Here, of course, only books from the suppressed convents were sold.

Conclusions

The Jesuit colleges – even when only founded at the end of the sixteenth or the beginning of the seventeenth century – had without any doubt, in comparison to other religious libraries of the *ancien régime*, rich libraries and with their collections of printed works were at the top of the religious institutional libraries. The Jesuits have, principally in Antwerp and Louvain, perpetuated the heritage of the sixteenth-century humanists and their libraries. Books and manuscripts from the library of the cartographer Abraham Ortelius, sold at Antwerp in 1598, were during the *ancien régime* mostly kept in the libraries of the Jesuit colleges of the Southern Netherlands[34]. When Henri Omont (1857–1940) described in 1885 the small collection of Greek manuscripts in the Royal Library, some 82 of the 121 manuscripts came from the libraries of the Antwerp Jesuits[35]. Gérard had found more than 1.300 manuscripts in the colleges and more than 40% of them were kept at the Antwerp residence, especially in the libraries of the Bollandists (36,6%) and Historiographes (4%). Louvain counts for about 25%.

From their book collections we can deduce the theological, literary and historical activities the Jesuits developed. It is clear from their numerous publications – mostly in the field of theology, moral theology and polemics – that the libraries were really exploited[36]. The pragmatism they showed in their theological opinions, e.g. molinism or their accommodating role towards the Chinese rites, is also noticeable in their views concerning their book collections: forbidden books were kept apart, but not destroyed.

The sale of the Jesuit book collections yielded about 132.000 guilders. Furthermore a large quantity of books was reserved for the Royal Library and these editions and manuscripts remained part of the patrimony of the Southern Netherlands. When we compare these results with the sale of the paintings of the Jesuit order in the Southern Netherlands, we can certainly speak of a success. Here the best paintings were bought by the Viennese court and the collectors could acquire for a bargain price the remaining most interesting paintings[37]. The projects to secure the patrimony and to keep these works of art in the Southern Netherlands failed. The *Comité Jésuitique* found in Gérard the perfect ally to inventory and to sell the books in a short term and with a reasonable result.

---

33 Archives of the City of Brussels, Instruction Publique, 101.

34 Annie De Coster and Bart Op de Beeck, 'Books and bindings from the library of Abraham Ortelius', in *Bibliophilies et reliures. Mélanges offerts à Michel Wittock*, ed. Annie De Coster and Claude Sorgeloos (Bruxelles, 2006), 374–409. For the manuscripts: Steven Gysens, '"Gekocht op de openbare veiling op 7 oktober 1598": handschriften uit Ortelius' bibliotheek "teruggevonden" in Brussel', *De Gulden Passer*, 86 (2008), 29–42.

35 Henri Omont, *Catalogue des manuscrits grecs de la Bibliothèque royale de Bruxelles et des autres bibliothèques publiques de Belgique* (Gand, 1885).

36 e.g. for the Southern Netherlands: *The Jesuits of the Low Countries: identity and impact (1540–1773): proceedings of the international congress at the faculty of theology and religious studies, KU Leuven (3–5 December 2009)*, ed. Rob Faesen and Leo Kenis, Bibliotheca ephemeridum theologicarum Lovaniensium, 251 (Leuven; Paris; Walpole, MA, 2012). *Jesuit Books in the Low Countries 1540–1773: a selection from the Maurits Sabbe Library*, ed. Paul Begheyn, Bernard Deprez and Rob Faesen, Jesuitica Neerlandica, 3 (Leuven, 2009).

37 Walter Scheelen, 'Het lot van de schilderijencollecties van de Zuidnederlandse jezuïetencolleges na de opheffing van de Orde in 1773', *Jaarboek van het Koninklijk Museum voor Schone Kunsten Antwerpen* (1988), 261–341; Christophe Loir, *La sécularisation des oeuvres d'art dans le Brabant (1773–1842). La création du musée de Bruxelles*, Études sur le XVIIIe siècle, Volume hors série, 8 (Bruxelles, 1998), 13–23.

Appendix: Sales Catalogues of Jesuit Libraries in the Southern Netherlands

* Shelfmarks are of copies in the Royal Library of Belgium. VB = *Ville de Bruxelles*; VH = Van Hulthem. Accents as in the title-pages.

Nivelles 20 September 1777
Catalogue des livres de la bibliothéque du collége des ci-devant jésuites de Nivelles, Dont la vente se fera audit collége le 20 Septembre 1777 & jours suivans, à neuf heures du main & à deux heures l'après-midi. – A Bruxelles, chez J. Vanden Berghen, Libraire, & Imprimeur de S.A.R., rue de la Magdelaine, où on distribue le Catalogue; & à Nivelles au dit Collège, [1777].
8vo. [2], 38, [2] p. Sig. [p]1 A-B8 C4; last leaf bl. Copies: VB 12.150 A vol. 5; VH 22.570 A vol. I.

Roermond 20 October 1777
Catalogue des livres de la bibliotheque du college des ci-devant jesuites de Ruremonde, Dont la Vente se fera audit Collège le vingt Octobre 1777. & jours suivans à neuf heures du Matin & à deux heures & demie l'Après-Midi. – A Bruxelles, chez François T'Serstevens Imprimeur de la Ville, dans la Bergh-straet, [1777].
8vo. 87, [3] p. Sig. [p]1 A-L4; last leaf bl.(?). Copies: VB 12.150 A vol. 5; VH 22.570 A vol. I.

Namur 30 March 1778
Catalogue de livres de la bibliothéque du collége des ci-devant jésuites de Namur, dont la vente se fera audit Collége Lundi 30 Mars 1778 & jours suivans, à huit heures & demie du matin & à deux heures

l'après-midi. Après la vente de cette Bibliothéque l'on vendra au dit Collége à Namur les Livres de la Bibliothéque des ci-devant Jésuites de Marche. – A Bruxelles: chez J. Vanden Berghen, Libraire, & Imprimeur de S.A.R., rue de la Magdelaine, où on distribue le Catalogue, [1778].
8vo. [2], 69, [3] p. Sig. [p]1 A-D8 E4, last leaf bl.(?) Copies: VB 12.150 A vol. 7; VB 12.150 A vol. 5.

Ypres 7 May 1778
Catalogue de livres de la bibliothéque du collége des ci-devant jésuites d'Ipres, Dont la vente se fera audit Collége jeudi 7 mai 1778 & jours suivans, à huit heures & demie du matin & à deux heures l'après-midi. – A Bruxelles, chez J. Vanden Berghen, Libraire, & Imprimeur de S.A.R., rue de la Magdelaine, où on distribue le Catalogue, [1778].
[2], 73, [7] p. Sig. [p]1 A-E8, last 3 leaves bl.(?). Copies: VB 12.150 A vol. 7; VB 12.150 A vol. 5; VH 22.570 A vol. IV.

Courtrai 18 May 1778
Catalogue de livres de la bibliotheque du college des ci-devant jesuites de Courtray, dont la Vente se fera audit collège le 18 May 1778. & jours suivans à huit heures & demie du Matin & à deux heures l'Après-Midi. – A Bruxelles: chez François T'Serstevens Imprimeur de la Ville, [1778].
[2], 63, [1] p.; last leaf bl. Sig. [p]1 A-H4. Copies: VB 12.150 A vol. 7; VB 12.150 A vol. 5; VH 22.570 A vol. IV.

Ghent 25 May 1778

Catalogue de livres des bibliotheques du collége des ci-devant jesuites a Gand, dont la Vente se fera audit Collége le 25 May 1778 & jours suivans, à huit heures & demie le matin & à deux heures l'après-midi. – Les Catalogues se distribuent à Gand chez Beggyn & chez Gimblet Libraires, à Bruxelles chez D'Ours & dans les autres Villes des Pays Bas chez les principaux Libraires, [1778]. 8vo. 196, [2], 72 p. Sig. [p]1 A-Z4 2A4 2B2 A-I4. 2B2 bl.(?). Copies: VB 12.150 A vol. 8; VH 22.572 A; VI 87.084 A 331; VH 22.570 A vol. IV.

Luxembourg 9 June 1778

Catalogue de livres de la bibliotheque du collége des ci-devant jesuites à Luxembourg, dont la vente se fera audit collége le Mardi 9 juin 1778 & jours suivans, à neuf heures du matin & à deux heures l'après-midi. – Les catalogues se distribuent à Luxembourg chez M. Leonardy Receveur des Domaines de S.M. & preposé à la Recette des Biens des ci-devant Jésuites; [Bruxelles: A. D'Ours, 1778]. 8vo. 145, [1] p. Sig. [p]1 A-S4. Copies: VB 12.150 A vol. 5; VH 22.570 A vol. III.

Aalst 22 June 1778

Catalogue de livres de la bibliotheque du collége des ci-devant jesuites d'Alost, Dont la Vente se fera audit Collége le 22 Juin 1778 & jours suivans à huit heures & demie du matin & à une heure & demie l'après-midi. – A Bruxelles chez A. D'Ours, Imprimeur-Libraire rue de Pondermerckt, où on distribue le Catalogue, [1778]. 8vo. 56, [2] p. Sig. [p]1 A-G4; last leaf bl. Copies: VB 12.150 A vol. 5; VH 22.570 A vol. III.

Mons 06 July 1778

Catalogue de livres, des bibliothéques du college et du seminaire des ci-devant jésuites de Mons, Dont la Vente se fera audit collége le 6 Juillet 1778, & jours suivans à huit heures & demie du matin, & à deux heures l'après-midi. – A Bruxelles, chez J. B. Jorez, Imprimeur-Libraire, rue au Beurre, où on distribue le Catalogue; à Mons, chez Henri Bottin, Imprimeur-Libraire, rue de la Clef; & chez les principaux Libraires, des autres Villes des Pays-Bas, [1778]. 8vo. [2], 211, [1] p.; last p. bl. Sig. [p]1 A-Z4 2A–2C4 2D4. Copies: VB 12.150 A vol. 8; VI 87.084 A 332; VH 22.570 A vol. III.

Tournai 3 August 1778

Catalogue de livres des bibliotheques du college et du seminaire des ci-devant jesuites a Tournay, Dont la Vente se fera audit Collége & Seminaire le 3 Août 1778. & jours suivans, à huit heures & demie du Matin, & à deux heures l'Après-Midi. Après la Vente de Livres, on vendra les Belles Caisses des bibliotheques. Les Catalogues se distribuent à Tournay, chez Jouvenau Libraire, & chez les Principaux Libraires des autres Villes des Pays-Bas. – A Bruxelles, chez François T'Serstevens Imprimeur de la Ville, [1778]. 8vo. [2], 226, [6] p. Sig. [p]1 A-Z4 2A–2D4 2E8; last 3 leaves bl.(?). Copies: VB 12.150 A vol. 4; VB 12.150 A vol. 6; VI 87.084 A 330.

Bruges 7 September 1778

Catalogue de livres, des bibliothéques des ci-devant jésuites du college de Bruges. Dont la Vente se fera audit Collége le 7 Septembre 1778, & jours suivans, à huit heures & demie du matin, & à deux heures l'après-midi. Après la Vente de Livres, on vendra les Caisses de Bibliothéques. – A Bruxelles, chez J. B. Jorez, Imprimeur-Libraire, rue au Beurre, où on distribue le Catalogue; à Bruges chez Van Praet, Imprimeur-Libraire, & chez les principaux Libraires des autres villes des Pays-Bas, [1778]. 8vo. [2], 207, [1] p. Sig. [p]1 A-Z4 2A–2C4. Copies: VB 12.150 A vol. 8; VB 12.150 A vol. 6.

Brussels & Mechelen 5 October 1778

Catalogues de livres des bibliothéques des colléges des ci-devant jésuites de Bruxelles et de Malines, dont la vente se fera au Collége des ci-devant Jésuites à Bruxelles le 5 Octobre 1778 & jours suivans, à huit heures & demie du matin & à deux heures l'après-midi. – A Bruxelles: chez J. Vanden Berghen,

Libraire, & Imprimeur de S.A.R., rue de la Magdelaine, où on distribue le Catalogue, [1778]. 8vo. [2], 277, [3]; [2], 109, [3] p. Sig. [p]1 A-E8 E8 F-Q8 R4; [p]1 A-G8; R3verso and R4 bl.(?) and in fine G8 bl.(?). Copies: VB 12.150 A vol. 4; VI 87.084 A 328; VH 22.570 A vol. II.

Louvain 12 April 1779
Catalogues de livres du collège des ci-devant jésuites de Louvain, Dont la vente se fera audit Collège Lundi 12 Avril 1779 & jours suivans, (en argent de change) à huit heures & demie du matin & à deux heures l'après-midi. La vente commencera par le Nº. 1º. du Catalogue, & on vendra au moins quatre cens Numeros par jour. – Les catalogues se distribuent A Louvain, chez Michel, Imprimeur-Libraire; [A] Bruxelles, chez J. Vanden Berghen, Imprimeur de S.A.R., rue de la Magdelaine, [1779].
8vo. [2], 418 [= 420], 36 p. Sig. [p]1 A-V8 W8 X-Z8 2A–2B8 2C2 A-B8 C2. Copies: VB 12.150 A vol. 1; VH 22.570 A vol. V; VI 87.084 A 334.

Antwerp 26 May 1779
Catalogue de livres, des bibliothéques de la Maison Professe, du Collége & du Couvent des ci-devant jésuites d'Anvers. Dont la vente se fera (en argent de change) dans la sale du Theatre attenante au Pensionat Roial rue du Prince en la dit Ville le 26. Mai 1779. & jours suivans à huit heures & demie du matin, & à deux heures l'après-midi. Tome I[-II]. – A Louvain, de l'Imprimerie de J. P. G. Michel. Les Catalogues se distribuent à Anvers, chez M. Beltiens Préposé à la Recette des Biens des ci-devant Jesuites; & chez les principaux Libraires des autres Villes des Pais-Bas, [1779].
8vo. [2], 426[=442], [2]; [2], 180 p. Sig. [p]1 A-Z4 2A–2Z4 3A–3I4 3K2; [p]1 A-Y4 Z2; 3K2verso bl. The second part has its own title page. Since the catalogues were already printed in August 1778

only the title pages were printed in 1779. Copies: VB 12.150 A vol. 2; VI 87.084 A 329; VH 22.575 A 1 & 2.

Livres choisis 4 September 1780
Catalogue des livres choisis dans les différentes bibliotheques des ci-devant jesuites des Pays-Bas, Contenant un grand Nombre d'Ouvrages rares & curieux en tout genre, dont la Vente se fera à Bruxelles, dans le College des ci-devant Jesuites le 4 du mois de Septembre 1780 & jours suivans. – A Bruxelles, Chez Jos. Ermens Imprimeur-Libraire, Marché aux Charbons, [1780].
8vo. [4], x, [2], 302, [2] p. Sig. [p]4 *4 A-T8; *4 bl.(?). Copies: VB 12.150 A vol. 3; VI 87.084 A 167; VI 87.084 A 166; VI 87.554 A; VH 22.570 A vol. VI.

Index
Table alphabetique des auteurs des livres choisis dans les bibliotheques des ci-devant jesuites des Pays-Bas, Avec l'indication de leurs Ouvrages & le renvoi aux Numéros du Catalogue, & une autre des ouvrages anonymes, sur les Frontispices desquels les Auteurs ne sont pas nommés. Par Jos. Ermens. – A Bruxelles, chez Jos. Ermens, Imprimeur-Libraire, Marché aux Charbons, où se trouvent ces Tables, au prix de Sept Sols, [1780].
8vo. [2], 56 p. [p]1 [A]-G4. Copies: VB 12.150 A vol. 3; VI 87.084 A 167; VH 22.570 A vol. VI.

Supplement
Catalogue de livres de theologie, d'histoire etc. dont la vente se fera à Bruxelles au College des ci-devant Jésuites, après la vente des livres qui commence le 4 septembre 1780. – A Bruxelles: chez Jos. Ermens, imprimeur-libraire, Marché aux Charbons, [1780].
8vo. 16 p. Sig. A8. Copy: VB 12.150 A vol. 3.

Bibliography

Manuscripts and Archival Sources

Antwerp, State Archives, 'Archief Nederlandse Provincie 1045'.

Bruges, Royal Library: pamphlet volume MS 20.373.

Brussels, Archives of the City of Brussels, Instruction Publique, 101.

Brussels, Bibliothèque des Bollandistes, MS Boll. 20–24.

Brussels, National Archives of Belgium, 'Comité Jésuitique, 11/A', fol. 726.

Brussels, National Archives of Belgium, 'Comité Jésuitique 38B', report of Gérard dated 18 March 1776.

Brussels, National Archives of Belgium, 'Koninklijke Commissie voor de Studies 32A', List dated 28 October 1778 with books reserved for the new college at Oudenaarde.

Brussels, National Archives of Belgium, 'Oostenrijkse Geheime Raad 847/A', report of Gérard dated 28 August 1779.

Brussels, National Archives of Belgium, 'Secretarie van State en Oorlog 1893', report of Gérard dated 6 May 1777.

Brussels, National Archives of Belgium, 'Secretarie van State en Oorlog 1893', Report of Gérard dated 12 February 1778.

Brussels, Royal Library of Belgium, MS 4714 C.

Brussels, Royal Library of Belgium, MS 8523 D: *Libri in cubiculo P. Heribertus Roswey, Ultraiectensis Societatis Jesu*.

Brussels, Royal Library of Belgium, VB 7.332 C: *Luciani opera cum interpretatione J. Bourdelotii*. Lutetiae: Jul. Bertault, 1615, in Folio.

Maastricht, Regionaal Historisch Centrum Limburg, Archief, Klooster der Jezuïeten te Maastricht, 30.

Secondary Works

Willem Audenaert, *Prosopographia Iesuitica Belgica Antiqua (PIBA). A biographical Dictionary of the Jesuits in the Low Countries 1542–1773* (Leuven-Heverlee, 2000).

Louis Brouwers, *De jezuïeten te Mechelen in de 17e en 18e eeuw en hun Xaveriuskerk, de huidige parochiekerk S.S. Petrus en Paulus* (Mechelen, 1977).

Claude Bruneel and Jean-Paul Hoyois, *Les grands commis du gouvernement des Pays-Bas autrichiens. Dictionnaire biographique du personnel des institutions centrales*, Archives générales du Royaume et Archives de l'Etat dans les Provinces. Studia, 84 (Bruxelles, 2001).

Hendrik Callewier, *Inventaris van het archief van de Nederduitse provincie der jezuïeten (Provincia Belgica, vervolgens Provincia Flandro-Belgica) en van het archief van het professenhuis te Antwerpen (1388) 1564–1773*, Rijksarchief te Antwerpen. Inventarissen, 59 (Brussel, 2006).

Brendan Connolly, *The Roots of Jesuit Librarianship: 1540–1599. A dissertation submitted to the Faculty of the Graduate Library School in candidacy for the degree of Doctor of Philosophy, University of Chicago* (Chicago, 1955).

Christian Coppens, '"L'ignorance a fait de terribles ravages". Le catalogue de la bibliothèque de Saint-Hubert (1665) dans son contexte', in *La bibliothèque de l'abbaye de Saint-Hubert en Ardenne au dix-septième siècle. Première partie: Vie intellectuelle et religieuse d'une communauté bénédictine*, ed. Luc Knapen (Leuven, 1999), 384–401.

Augustin De Backer, *Bibliothèque des écrivains de la Compagnie de Jésus* (Liège, 1859).

Annie De Coster and Bart Op de Beeck, 'Books and bindings from the library of Abraham Ortelius', in *Bibliophilies et reliures. Mélanges offerts à Michel Wittock*, ed. Annie De Coster and Claude Sorgeloos (Bruxelles, 2006), 374–409.

Pierre Delsaerdt, 'The inheritors of loss. Seized libraries and bibliophily in late 18th-century Antwerp', *De Gulden Passer*, 92.1 (2014), 53–70.

Albert Derolez, *Les catalogues de bibliothèques*, Typologie des sources du moyen âge occidental, 31 (Turnhout, 1979).

Hendrik Dijkgraaf, *The Library of a Jesuit Community at Holbeck, Nottinghamshire (1679)*, Libri Pertinentes, 8 (Cambridge, 2003).

François Dolbeau, 'Nouvelles recherches sur les manuscrits des anciens bollandistes', *Analecta Bollandiana*, 129 (2011), 395–457.

Wifried Enderle, 'Die Jesuitenbibliothek im 17. Jahrhundert. Das Beispiel der Bibliothek des Düsseldorfer Kollegs 1619–1773', *Archiv für Geschichte des Buchwesens*, 41 (1994), 147–213.

Alfred Franklin, *Les anciennes Bibliothèques de Paris*, 3 vols (Paris, 1867–1873).

Dolores García Gómez, *Testigos de la memoria: los inventarios de las bibliotecas de la compañía de Jesús en la expulsión de 1767* (San Vicente del Raspeig, 2010).

Steven Gysens, '"Gekocht op de openbare veiling op 7 oktober 1598": handschriften uit Ortelius' bibliotheek "teruggevonden" in Brussel', *De Gulden Passer*, 86 (2008), 29–42.

History of the Low Countries, ed. Johannes Cornelis Hendrik Blom and Emiel Lamberts (repr. New York; Oxford, 2009).

Jesuit Books in the Low Countries 1540–1773: a selection from the Maurits Sabbe Library, ed. Paul Begheyn, Bernard Deprez and Rob Faesen, Jesuitica Neerlandica, 3 (Leuven, 2009).

The Jesuits of the Low Countries: identity and impact (1540–1773): proceedings of the international congress at the faculty of theology and religious studies, KU Leuven (3–5 December 2009), ed. Rob Faesen and Leo Kenis, Bibliotheca ephemeridum theologicarum Lovaniensium, 251 (Leuven; Paris; Walpole, MA, 2012).

Lance Lazar, 'The formation of the pious soul: Trans-Alpine demand for Jesuit devotional texts, 1548–1615', in *Confessionalization in Europe, 1555–1700: Essays in Honor and Memory of Bodo Nischan*, ed. John Headley, Hans Hillerbrand, and Anthony J. Papalas (Aldershot, Hampshire; Burlington, Vt., 2004), 289–318.

Christophe Loir, *La sécularisation des oeuvres d'art dans le Brabant (1773–1842). La création du musée de Bruxelles*, Études sur le XVIIIe siècle, Volume hors série, 8 (Bruxelles, 1998).

Jérome Machiels, *Van religieuze naar openbare bibliotheek*, Algemeen Rijksarchief en Rijksarchief in de Provinciën. Educatieve Dienst. Dossiers, Tweede reeks, 20 (Brussel, 2000).

Edouard Mailly, *Histoire de l'Académie impériale et royale des sciences et belles-lettres de Bruxelles*, 2 vols (Bruxelles, 1883).

Paul Mech, 'Les bibliothèques de la Compagnie de Jésus', in *Histoire des bibliothèques françaises*, II: *Les bibliothèques sous l'Ancien Régime 1530–1789*, ed. Claude Jolly (Paris, 1988), 56–63.

Henri Omont, *Catalogue des manuscrits grecs de la Bibliothèque royale de Bruxelles et des autres bibliothèques publiques de Belgique* (Gand, 1885).

Bart Op de Beeck, 'Boeken uit de bibliotheken van de Engelse jezuïetencolleges te Brugge, bewaard in de verzameling "Ville de Bruxelles"', in *Boekgeschiedenis in Vlaanderen. Nieuwe instrumenten en benaderingen. [Handelingen van het contactforum] 28 november 2003*, ed. Pierre Delsaerdt and Koen De Vlieger-De Wilde (Brussel, 2004), 79–89.

Bart Op de Beeck, 'Jezuïetenbibliotheken in de Zuidelijke Nederlanden: de liquidatie 1773–1828', unpublished Ph.D. diss. (Catholic University of Louvain, 2008).

Bart Op de Beeck, 'Karel van Hulthem (1764–1832)', in *In de ban van boeken, grote verzamelaars uit de negentiende eeuw in de Koninklijke Bibliotheek van België*, ed. Marcus De Schepper, Ann Kelders, and Jan Pauwels (Brussel, 2008), 14–16.

Bart Op de Beeck, 'La Bibliothèque des Bollandistes à la fin de l'Ancien Régime', in *De Rosweyde aux Acta Sanctorum. La recherche hagiographique des Bollandistes à travers quatre siècles*. Actes du Colloque international (Bruxelles, 5 octobre 2007), ed. Robert Godding, Bernard Joassart, Xavier Lequeux, and François De Vriendt, Subsidia hagiographica, 88 (Bruxelles, 2009), 149–284.

Bart Op de Beeck, 'De bibliotheek van het Brusselse jezuïetencollege tijdens het Ancien Régime', in *Quatre siècles de présence jésuite à Bruxelles = Vier eeuwen jezuïeten te Brussel*, ed. Alain Deneef and Xavier Rousseaux (Bruxelles; Leuven, 2012), 49–89.

Carmélia Opsomer-Halleux, 'Nouveaux matériaux pour l'histoire des bibliothèques liégeoise', *Bulletin de la Société royale Le Vieux-Liège*, 13 (1994), 206–15.

Alfred Poncelet, *Histoire de la Compagnie de Jésus dans les anciens Pays-Bas. Etablissement de la Compagnie de Jésus en Belgique et ses développements jusqu'à la fin du règne d'Albert et d'Isabelle. Deuxième partie: Les œuvres*, Académie royale de Belgique, Classe des lettres et des sciences morales et politiques, Mémoires, Collection in 8°, XXI, 2 (Bruxelles, 1928).

Goran Proot, *Het schooltoneel van de jezuïeten in de Provincia Flandro-Belgica tijdens het ancien régime (1575–1773)*, Onuitgegeven proefschrift Universiteit Antwerpen (Antwerpen, 2008).

Jan Roegiers in *Dictionnaire d'histoire et de géographie ecclésiastique*, 21 (1986), 982–83.

Walter Scheelen, 'Het lot van de schilderijencollecties van de Zuidnederlandse jezuïetencolleges na de opheffing van de Orde in 1773', *Jaarboek van het Koninklijk Museum voor Schone Kunsten Antwerpen* (1988), 261–341.

Marie-Jeanne Stallaert, 'François-Xavier Burtin. Portretten van een verzamelaar', *Het Tijdschrift van Dexia Bank*, 54 (2002.2), n. 212, 53–62.

Dominique Varry, 'L'histoire des bibliothèques en France. Etat des lieux', *Bulletin des Bibliothèques de France*, 50.2 (2005), 16–22.

Tom Verschaffel, *Historici in de Oostenrijkse Nederlanden (1715–1794). Proeve van een repertorium*, Facultés universitaires Saint-Louis. Studiecentrum 18de-eeuwse Zuidnederlandse Letterkunde. Cahiers, 15 (Brussel, 1996).

Ernst Manfred Wermter, 'Studien und Quellen zur Geschichte der Jesuitenbibliotheken in Mainz 1561–1773', in *De Bibliotheca Moguntina. Festschrift der Stadtbibliothek Mainz zum fünfzigjährigen Bestehen ihres Gebäudes 1962*, ed. Jürgen Busch, Veröffentlichung der Stadtbibliothek und der Städtischen Volksbüchereien Mainz, 28 (Mainz, 1963), 51–70.

ANTONELLA BARZAZI

Before Napoleon. Change and Continuity in Italian Religious Book Collections

From the late fifteenth century until the Napoleonic suppressions in the first years of the nineteenth century, the history of the libraries of religious orders in Italy registers neither any episode of large-scale secularisation and confiscation comparable to those in the European countries involved in the Protestant Reformation, nor the dramatic losses that, for instance, affected book collections during the French wars of religion or the Thirty Years war. An overall look rather suggests that there was a considerable continuity in the presence and cultural role of the conventual and monastic book collections in early modern Italy. A closer analysis, however, gives a more animated picture, marked by fractures and profound changes.

During these three centuries, the Italian religious' book collections suffered notably from the effects of the internal restructuring of the regular clergy. In the first half of the fifteenth century, the Observant movement spreading among the monastic and the mendicant orders gave rise to several new congregations. Various book collections were then established or refounded in the mendicant convents involved

in the Observance and in the abbeys leading the reform of the monastic orders, such as S. Giustina in Padua and S. Maria in Florence, both of which were to become members of the future Cassinese congregation[1]. A century later, another wave of new libraries originated either from the final separation of the Observant from the Conventual Franciscans, in 1517, and then following the foundation – between 1524 and 1550 – of the Capuchins and the Regular clerics' congregations: the Theatines, the Jesuits, the Somaschans and the Barnabites. During the seventeenth century and the first half of the eighteenth no similar reorganisation can be detected. However, within local contexts, often as a consequence of agreements between the Papacy and the civil authorities, a number of convents and minor congregations were suppressed, some individual communities moved under another obedience, and several conventual *studia* or

---

1 Mario Rosa, 'I depositi del sapere: biblioteche, accademie, archivi', in *La memoria del sapere. Forme di conservazione e strutture organizzative dall'antichità a oggi*, ed. Pietro Rossi (Roma-Bari, 1988), 165–66.

Antonella Barzazi • Antonella Barzazi is Professor of Early Modern History at the Department of Political Sciences, Law and International Studies of the University of Padua. antonella.barzazi@unipd.it

How the Secularization of Religious Houses Transformed the Libraries of Europe, 16th–19th Centuries, ed. by Cristina Dondi, Dorit Raines, and † Richard Sharpe, BIB, 63 (Turnhout, 2022), pp. 449–466.
BREPOLS ❧ PUBLISHERS   DOI 10.1484/M.BIB-EB.5.128498

colleges for laymen opened, or closed, or were transferred. These events resulted, in turn, in the rearrangement, the dissolution or the move of the book holdings, thus redesigning the map of the cultural centres of the various orders. From the late 1760s the library network of the Italian religious congregations was partly transformed by the State appropriations initiated by the governments, in the context of widespread projects for the reform of religious institutions which had different effects depending on the various political areas.

The material transformation of the libraries was the result of interaction between religious, political-economic and strictly cultural factors. During a period extending from the age of Italian humanism to the Counter-Reformation and down to the Enlightenment, book collections had had to adapt to the changing religious and intellectual needs of the regular communities and the transformation of the very idea of what a library was, inherited from the late Middle Ages. As I shall try to point out in my paper, this led to books being discarded and dispersed, to migration and reuse that affected the book collections in Italian religious houses with varying intensity and helped to shape the features of the overall network of library provision, which was to be finally dismantled by the Napoleonic confiscations.

In this perspective, the first half of the sixteenth century seems crucial for various reasons. At that time the effects of the fundamental change from manuscript to printed book on both medieval and fifteenth-century libraries became decisive, giving rise to collections quantitatively richer and materially more composite. From the turn of the century the codices containing the more frequently consulted texts – concordances, dictionaries, the Bible and the writings of the Church Fathers – had already been replaced by printed editions. The discarding of manuscripts for "daily" use was accelerated: they were removed from the benches in the libraries and gradually abandoned, thrown out or reused as binding material supports for printed volumes. The most valuable codices – in terms of material, decoration or language (the Greek texts, for example) – would survive, becoming instead, after some decades, a "conservation" nucleus, alongside the growing collections of printed books[2]. The emergence of a diversified printed market offered the more enterprising regular communities increasing opportunities for the exchange and replacement of their volumes. The expansion of the book holdings would soon make the existing rooms furnished with the traditional rows of benches inadequate[3].

In the meantime, the collections of the Regular clergy and the Capuchins began appearing on the scene. In the various urban contexts the new religious foundations began to compete with the older ones to receive donations and bequests from individuals, a common means of increasing the libraries of the religious houses, and to gain the patronage of the political authorities. The new orders adopted an approach that emphasised the original mendicants' view of the library as a working instrument and concentrated on the book as an item to be used in their manifold ministries: teaching, doctrinal controversy, preaching, and missions[4]. This utilitarian approach was distant

---

2 See, for example, Rudolf Blum, *La biblioteca della Badia fiorentina e i codici di Antonio Corbinelli* (Città Del Vaticano, 1951), 28–35; Giovanna Cantoni Alzati, *La biblioteca di S. Giustina di Padova: libri e cultura presso i benedettini padovani in età umanistica* (Padova, 1982), 21–22; Tommaso Kaeppeli, *Inventari di libri di San Domenico di Perugia (1430–80)* (Roma, 1962), 195–303; 305–10.

3 On the spaces and organisation of the fifteenth-century libraries see James O'Gorman, *The Architecture of the Monastic Library in Italy 1300–1600* (New York, 1972), and Armando Petrucci, 'Le biblioteche antiche', in *Letteratura italiana*, II: *Produzione e consumo* (Torino, 1983), 530–32; 547–51.

4 On the beginning of the Capuchins' collections see the articles by Stanislao da Campagnola, 'Ranuccio I Farnese (1569–1622) fondatore della biblioteca

from both monastic culture, which considered books as heritage to be preserved, and the attitude of humanist collecting.

Printing had equally caused an unprecedented expansion of the volumes circulating in religious houses, supporting new approaches to studying and reading, encouraging individual freedom in the ways books were used and stored. From

the fourteenth century onwards, the mendicant orders had faced the problem of balancing the obligation to share these material resources, with the custom of regarding the manuscripts prepared by individual friars or supplied by their families as subject to the beneficiary's personal use[5]. The orders' legislation had responded to this phenomenon by granting permits for use on condition that the books would be transferred to the convent following the possessor's death. However, the problem became much more complex at the end of the sixteenth century in the face of the extensive possibilities of purchasing and selling printed volumes, and the unceasing multiplication of the books that were filling convent rooms. The need to counter the "individualistic" development of possessing books seems to have been felt to a greater extent by the orders that did not yet have ample book holdings. It was at the close of the sixteenth century that the Capuchins introduced the double formula to be noted on individual copies: "to be used by … pertaining to the library of …". The aim of this was to protect the use of the books by friars who left their original community in order to carry out their ministries as well as the "right" of the community to have the books returned[6].

After the mid sixteenth century while the censorship directed by the Papacy in Rome was organizing itself and the first indices of forbidden

dei Cappuccini di Fontevivo (Parma)', *Collectanea Franciscana*, 38 (1968), 308–10, and 'Le biblioteche dei cappuccini nel passaggio tra Cinque e Seicento', in *Biblioteche cappuccine italiane*, Atti del Congresso Nazionale, Assisi, 14–16 ottobre 1987, ed. Anselmo Mattioli (Perugia, 1988), 71–79, both reprinted in Stanislao da Campagnola, *Oratoria sacra: Teologie, Ideologie, Biblioteche nell'Italia dei secoli XVI–XIX* (Roma, 2003); Dorit Raines, Simonetta Pelusi, 'Il Fondo antico della Biblioteca PP. Cappuccini SS. Redentore di Venezia: per una storia documentata delle biblioteche cappuccine nel Veneto', *Notiziario Bibliografico. Periodico della Giunta regionale del Veneto*, 16 (1994), 6–8; Elena Scrima, 'Del luogo de' PP. Capuccini di Mistretta. Libri dal convento di S. Maria, Vat. Lat. 11323', in *Dalla notitia librorum degli inventari agli esemplari. Saggi di indagine su libri e biblioteche dai codici Vaticani latini 11266–11326*, ed. Rosa Marisa Borraccini (Macerata, 2009), 455–59. A list of the sixteenth-century libraries of the Somaschans is in Carlo Pellegrini, 'Catalogo delle biblioteche somasche (1599–1600)', *Somascha*, 1 (1976), 24–25; see also Valentina Lozza, 'Libri e formazione presso l'Accademia di Somasca intorno all'anno 1600', in *Dalla notitia librorum degli inventari agli esemplari*, 410–27; on the libraries of the Barnabites and the Theatines: Sergio Pagano, 'Le biblioteche dei Barnabiti italiani nel 1599. In margine ai loro più antichi cataloghi', *Barnabiti studi*, 3 (1986), 13–41, and Domenico Antonio D'Alessandro, 'Oltre il fondo "San Martino". Le biblioteche dei teatini a Napoli tra Cinque e Ottocento', in *Sant'Andrea Avellino e i Teatini nella Napoli del Viceregno Spagnolo*, ed. Domenico Antonio D'Alessandro, I (Napoli, 2011), 327–34. On the book policies of the mendicants see Kennet W. Humphreys, *The book provisions of the mediaeval friars, 1215–1400* (Amsterdam, 1964), 129; Letizia Pellegrini, *I manoscritti dei predicatori. I domenicani dell'Italia mediana e i codici della loro predicazione (secc. XIII–XV)* (Roma, 1999); *Libri, biblioteche e letture dei frati mendicanti (secoli XIII–XIV)*, Atti del XXXII Convegno internazionale, Assisi, 7–9 ottobre 2004 (Spoleto, 2005).

5   Mario Villani, 'Cultura religiosa e patrimonio librario nella provincia francescana di S. Angelo prima e dopo il concilio di Trento', in *Il Concilio di Trento nella vita culturale e spirituale del Mezzogiorno tra XVI e XVII secolo*: Atti del convegno di Maratea, 19–21 giugno 1986, eds Gabriele De Rosa and Antonio Cestaro, II (Venosa, 1988), 442–52; some information on this issue is in Pellegrini, 'I manoscritti dei predicatori', as note 4, and in the essay by the same author 'Libri e biblioteche nella vita economica dei mendicanti', in *L'economia dei conventi dei frati minori e predicatori fino alla metà del Trecento*: Atti del XXXI Convegno internazionale, Assisi, 9–11 ottobre 2003 (Spoleto, 2004), 187–214.

6   Giovanni Pozzi, Luciana Pedroia, *Ad uso di … applicato alla libraria de' cappuccini di Lugano* (Roma, 1996).

books were being published, abbots and priors also faced the challenge of having to pay greater attention to books and libraries: they verified heterodox texts in the religious houses, exercising the prerogatives guaranteed by the privileges of the regular clergy. Purges and book burnings also took place in cloisters, as was the case in 1559 in the Benedictine monastery of S. Benedetto Po, one of the epicentres of religious dissent in the Italian monastic environment[7]. However, in both the old and new orders the aim of doctrinal and religious control was soon accompanied by concern for the integrity and collective use of the library holdings. This process tended to intensify in the last decades of the sixteenth century. The provincial and general superiors regulated in detail the return to the communities of the volumes left by deceased religious members, discouraging the exchange of copies, prohibiting the removal of printed material and seeking to prevent friars and monks from treating books as their personal property. Anyone suspected of the misappropriation of books or causing dispersal of the convents' collections was threatened with excommunication by the popes and the cardinal protectors of different orders[8]. In the

"younger" congregations the admonitions were accompanied by several detailed rules aimed at the establishment and correct administration of "common" libraries[9].

These great sixteenth century changes effectively helped to shape structures that were very different from the arrangement of the late medieval and Humanist library. This is confirmed by some extraordinary documentation held in the Vatican Library, which has been the subject of several, detailed studies over the last few years. It consists of several thousand inventories of the Italian regulars' libraries sent to Rome between 1599 and 1603, in response to an order of the Roman Congregation of the Index, then committed to the enforcement of the third Roman index of prohibited books, published by Pope Clement VIII in 1596[10]. There are some considerable gaps in the

7   Massimo Zaggia, *Tra Mantova e la Sicilia nel Cinquecento*, II, *La congregazione benedettina cassinese nel Cinquecento* (Firenze, 2003), 589. A general overview on the spread of the Protestant doctrines and other radical heretical messages among the orders is in Gigliola Fragnito, 'Gli Ordini religiosi tra Riforma e Controriforma', in *Clero e società nell'Italia moderna*, ed. Mario Rosa (Roma-Bari, 1992), 169–82.

8   See Roberto Rusconi, 'I frati Minori dell'Osservanza in Italia dopo il Concilio di Trento: circolazione di libri e strumenti di formazione intellettuale (sulla base delle biblioteche conventuali e personali)', in *Identités franciscaines à l'âge des réformes*, eds Frédéric Meyer and Ludovic Viallet (Clermont-Ferrand, 2005), 385–93, and the essays by Roberto Biondi, 'Libri, biblioteche e *studia* nella legislazione delle famiglie francescane (secc. XVI–XVII)', Giovanni Grosso, 'I Carmelitani e i libri: alcune note sulla legislazione', Silvia Alessandrini Calisti, 'Norme e consuetudini degli Eremiti camaldolesi di Montecorona su libri e

biblioteche', all in *Libri, biblioteche e cultura degli ordini regolari nell'Italia moderna attraverso la documentazione della Congregazione dell'Indice*: Atti del convegno internazionale, Macerata, 30 maggio-1 giugno 2006, eds Rosa Marisa Borraccini and Roberto Rusconi (Città del Vaticano, 2006), respectively 338–56, 381–94, 321–24; Monica Bocchetta, 'La legislazione dei Minori Conventuali sugli studi e sulle biblioteche, secoli XVI-XVII', in *Presenze francescane nel Camerinese (sec. XIII–XVII)*, eds Francesca Bartolacci e Roberto Lambertini (Ripatransone, 2008), 265–70; Venturino Alce, Alfonso D'Amato, *La biblioteca di S. Domenico in Bologna* (Firenze, 1961), 101–02. On the Augustinian Hermits see Rosa Marisa Borraccini and Sara Cosi, 'Tra prescrizioni e proibizioni. Libri e biblioteche dei mendicanti della Marca d'Ancona sul declinare del Cinquecento', in *Gli ordini mendicanti (sec. XIII–XVI)*, Atti del XLIII convegno di Studi Maceratesi, Abbadia di Fiastra (Tolentino), 24–25 novembre 2007 (Macerata 2009), 83.

9   Pagano, 'Le biblioteche dei Barnabiti italiani', as note 4, 18–27; Stanislao da Campagnola, 'Le biblioteche dei cappuccini', as note 4, 75.

10   A guide to the Vatican material is in *Codices 11266–11326: Inventari di biblioteche religiose italiane alla fine del Cinquecento*, eds Marie-Madeleine Lebreton and Luigi Fiorani (Città del Vaticano, 1985); on the origin, the specific context and the different phases of the initiative promoted by the Congregation of the Index see Roberto

corpus of inventories drawn up by the religious communities at that time – no list relating to the books of the Dominicans and the Jesuits has yet been identified and several local foundations of various orders are not represented[11] –, although it actually gives a very detailed map of the monks' book holdings at the turn of the sixteenth century.

This meticulous investigation, which raised widespread opposition among the orders, aimed first of all to ascertain the submission of the regular clergy to the prescriptions of the indices. Regarding this specific purpose, the Vatican lists show that the works most fervently condemned in Rome had been eliminated: this is the case, for example, with the key texts of the Reformation, which in the early sixteenth century had circulated widely in the convents, the works by Machiavelli and Erasmus of Rotterdam or a number of Italian translations of the Bible. The name of Erasmus was generally erased from the editions of ancient classics and of the Church Fathers he published. The local superiors also declared that they had isolated the surviving prohibited books in closed cabinets kept under their surveillance[12]. So the Roman censorship project seemed a substantial success, even though the book holdings of numerous regular communities continued to testify to philosophical, theological and historical-literary interests that were anything but in line with the bibliographic canons of the Counter Reformation.

However, the Vatican inventories as a whole also provide us with what had become the particular features of the Italian regulars' libraries. Almost everywhere – from the large convents of the capital cities to the smaller houses in minor

---

Rusconi, 'Frati e monaci, libri e biblioteche alla fine del '500' and Gigliola Fragnito, 'L'Indice clementino e le biblioteche degli Ordini religiosi', both in *Libri, biblioteche e cultura degli ordini regolari*, as note 7, 13–36, 37–59; Vittorio Frajese, *Nascita dell'Indice. La censura ecclesiastica dal Rinascimento alla Controriforma* (Brescia, 2006), 194–200. Since 2002 the imposing Vatican collection of book inventories, originally consulted for the study of the libraries belonging to some particular convent or individual notable friar, has been the object of a systematic research project organised by Rosa Maria Borraccini and Roberto Rusconi, intended also to record all the bibliographical data included in the Vatican inventories (the database is accessible online at https://rici.vatlib.it/; see also Granata in this volume). An appraisal of the research carried out so far and some additional bibliography regarding the Roman Congregation survey on the regulars' book holdings are in Roberto Rusconi, 'Libri e biblioteche degli ordini regolari in un'indagine di fine Cinquecento. Indirizzi di ricerca e prospettive', *Dimensioni e problemi della ricerca storica*, 1 (2012), 111–23, and in Rosa Marisa Borraccini, Giovanna Granata, Roberto Rusconi, 'A proposito dell'inchiesta della S. Congregazione dell'Indice dei libri proibiti di fine '500', *Il capitale culturale. Studies on the Value of Cultural Heritage*, 6 (2013), 13–45; more in R. Rusconi, 'The Devil's Trick. Impossible Editions in the Lists of Titles from the Regular Orders in Italy at the End of the Sixteenth Century', and in G. Granata, 'On the Track of Lost Editions in Italian Religious Libraries at the End of the Sixteenth Century: A Numerical Analysis of the RICI Database', both in *Lost Books. Reconstructing the Print World of Pre-Industrial Europe*, eds Flavia Bruni and Andrew Pettegree (Leiden-Boston, 2016), 310–23, 324–44.

11   Some order or congregation had been originally exempted from the papal command to record the books stored in the cloisters; Fragnito, 'L'Indice clementino e le biblioteche degli Ordini religiosi', as note 10, 53–55; Rusconi, 'Libri e biblioteche degli ordini regolari', as note 10, 118.

12   Gigliola Fragnito, *La Bibbia al rogo. La censura ecclesiastica e i volgarizzamenti della Scrittura (1471–1605)* (Bologna, 1997), 241–73; on the sporadic survival of the Erasmian works: Mario Rosa, 'Dottore o seduttor deggio appellarte: note erasmiane', *Rivista di Storia e Letteratura religiosa*, 26 (1990), 5–33. See also the essays by Flavia Bruni, 'Una *inquisitio* nel convento servita di Lucca: i libri nella cella di fra Lorenzo', Lorenzo Di Lenardo, 'I libri proibiti dei Francescani Conventuali del Triveneto' and Adelisa Malena, 'Libri "proibiti", "sospesi", "dubii d'esser cattivi": in margine ad alcune liste dei Canonici regolari lateranensi', all in *Libri, biblioteche e cultura degli ordini regolari*, as note 7, 473–523, 525–53, 555–81. The situation of the Venetian religious collections is examined in detail in Antonella Barzazi, 'Ordini religiosi e biblioteche a Venezia tra Cinque e Seicento', *Annali dell'Istituto storico italo-germanico in Trento*, 21 (1995), 141–228; in a wider perspective: Antonella Barzazi, *Collezioni librarie in una capitale d'antico regime. Venezia secoli XVI–XVIII* (Roma, 2017), 39–61.

centres – the fragmentation of the orders' book holdings had increased. The books were no longer kept for the most part in the old library rooms and the "common" libraries now coexisted with a great number of collections stored in the cells of individual monks. Here they were held – according to a formula that got around the prohibition of personal ownership for the regulars – *ad usum* of priors and abbots, of teachers and students of the conventual *studium*, of confessors and preachers, but also of simple friars and monks. Individual libraries were particularly numerous in the most important and populated urban convents. Some random examples pertaining to different orders will illustrate this. In Milan, in the Cistercian monastery of S. Ambrogio Maggiore, in addition to the common library there were a further 35 collections in the names of individual monks[13]. In the Florentine "Badia" the Cassinese monks presented lists for two *bibliothecae monasterii*, called – according to the medieval mendicants' terminology – *maior* and *minor*, and for 27 collections in the names of individual monks[14]. The same arrangement appeared in Naples, in the Benedictine monastery of SS. Severino and Sossio, which included two common collections, a collection of books for novices and more than 45 collections *ad usum* by the same number of monks[15]; the same characteristics could be seen

in the book holdings of the study convents of the mendicants in important university cities such as Pavia, Padua, Bologna and once again Naples[16]. An analogous fragmentation also applied to smaller houses that had fewer books or belonged to orders that paid less attention to cultural vocation and were more sensitive to prescriptions regarding poverty and community life. It is important to note that the libraries of orders founded in the sixteenth century – though under-represented in the Index survey – were mainly described in one single list for each house but we do not know if that decision meant that the library resources were actually subjected to unified management. The dispersed library remained, however, the most prevalent form of organisation amongst the regular clergy[17].

In this context the common library was at times a traditional heritage collection made up of precious codices, first editions and teaching material representative of the official doctrinal identity of the order. But it could also have been a residual nucleus of printed works and manuscripts that were no longer used, or have completely disappeared, replaced by the collections held in the cells of the friars, generally more updated and influenced by personal interests and generational variations. In any case, the library seemed to be a fluid entity, with an undefined legal-institutional profile, marked by the pronounced mobility of its

13 *Codices 11266–11326: Inventari di biblioteche religiose italiane*, as note 10, 210.

14 *Codices 11266–11326: Inventari di biblioteche religiose italiane*, as note 10, 4. The evolution of the Italian model of the "double library" – *maior* and *minor* or rather *magna* and *parva* or still *publica* and *secreta* (the former furnished with the best copies of fundamental reference texts, the latter with copies of less quality, to be loaned by the friars) – are described in Donatella Nebbiai, 'Modelli bibliotecari premendicanti' and Donatella Frioli, 'Gli inventari delle biblioteche degli Ordini mendicanti', both in *Libri, biblioteche e letture dei frati mendicanti*, as note 4, 157–61; 334–38.

15 *Codices 11266–11326: Inventari di biblioteche religiose italiane*, as note 10, 17–18. A list regarding the common library and another 49 lists of the collections "ad

usum" of the individual monks came from the Venetian monastery belonging to the same congregation, S. Giorgio Maggiore.

16 See, for instance, *Codices 11266–11326: Inventari di biblioteche religiose italiane*, as note 10, 99 (Conventual franciscans of Padua), 53 (Carmelites of Naples), 168 (Conventual franciscans of Pavia).

17 The Vatican inventories yield a total of 1382 book collections ascribed to the religious houses and 8,195 "personal" libraries. Borraccini-Cosi, 'Tra prescrizioni e proibizioni', as note 8, 84; see also – for a comparison among the Conventual Franciscans, the Observant Franciscans and the Capuchins – Rusconi, 'I frati minori dell'Osservanza', as note 8, 406–07.

components. In the Paduan convent of the Canons regular of S. Giovanni of Verdara, a member of the Lateran congregation, for example, one of the lists referred to a group of books belonging to the convent of Santo Spirito in Bergamo, allocated to Padua for the use of the students coming from Bergamo[18]. Another example is even more significant. It pertains to the Venetian convent of the Observant Franciscans of S. Francesco della Vigna, the largest library in the city, with about four thousand works. In S. Francesco della Vigna two libraries, called *maior* and *minor*, contained the convent's "historical" collections: all in all around 1,300 titles including manuscripts, incunabula, editions from the early decades of the sixteenth century. Among the 35 "personal" collections the largest and most up-to-date one – assigned *ad usum* to the former provincial, Fra Francesco from Vicenza – had 1,200 works and seems to have functioned as a reference collection for the community. But a note to the catalogue declares that it was intended for the Observant convent of S. Biagio in Vicenza – where Fra Francesco had presumably taken his vows – "pro bibliotheca constituenda"[19]. So the collection would have to leave Venice.

Thus, at the turn of the new century, the division of the library structures made the vast book holdings of the Italian convents distinctly vulnerable. The destiny of the collections *ad usum* of individual religious seemed at the mercy of personal events and choices – transfers, temporary absences, deaths – and of the recurring internal conflicts in the communities. Meanwhile the lack of any unitary direction or expansion policy exposed the existing "common" libraries to the risks of disuse and dispersal. Indeed, the first half of the seventeenth century was a particularly critical period for the regulars' collections.

Some orders focused their attention on the Roman libraries and two great institutions were established, the Bibliotheca Vallicelliana by the Oratorians and the Bibliotheca Angelica by the Augustinian Hermits[20]. However, on the periphery the collections of religious houses barely survived as they no longer exerted the active cultural function and capacity to attract readers they had had for most of the previous century. The available sources indicate demolitions and the abandoning of old library buildings, neglect and venality on the part of the religious and constant dispersals also affecting – like a kind of haemorrhage – the more celebrated manuscript collections.

During the Roman survey of 1599–1603 considerable dispersals had already been noted in the area around Piedmont following the wars of the sixteenth century and the connivance of religious members without any scruples. In the following years Pope Paul V ensured that groups of codices belonging to the ancient monastic collections from the Abbey of Bobbio and in the Greek Abbey of Grottaferrata were transferred to the Vatican Library where they would be conserved more appropriately[21]. The manuscripts of the abbeys of S. Maria in Florence and S. Giustina in Padua were also affected by losses[22]; similar episodes also occurred with greater frequency in Venice, traditionally one of the European

18 Vatican Apostolic Library, Cod. Vat. Lat. 11282, fol. 285r.
19 Vatican Apostolic Library, Cod. Vat. Lat. 11304, fol. 36v; Barzazi, 'Ordini religiosi e biblioteche a Venezia', as note 12, 198–203.
20 Rosa, 'I depositi del sapere', as note 1, 180; a portrait of the founder of the Angelica is in Alfredo Serrai, *Angelo Rocca fondatore della prima biblioteca pubblica europea* (Milano, 2004).
21 Rosa, 'I depositi del sapere', as note 1, 181. As the author underlines, censorial purposes and concern for preservation interwove in the Roman book policy during the Counter-Reformation.
22 Blum, *La biblioteca della Badia fiorentina*, as note 2, 35; Cantoni Alzati, *La biblioteca di S. Giustina di Padova*, as note 2, 25. The losses affecting some Florentine monasteries, due to the "incurie des abbés" and the "offensive des bibliophiles", are recalled in Emmanuelle Chapron, «*Ad utilità pubblica*». *Politique des bibliothèques et pratiques du livre à Florence au XVIIIe siècle* (Genève, 2009), 60–62.

cities with the richest book collections. In the Cassinese monastery of S. Giorgio Maggiore in Venice, the existing library room was demolished in 1614 and the books arranged in other spaces. In another prestigious library in Venice, that belonging to the Dominicans of SS. Giovanni e Paolo, codices were removed. In addition to these dispersals, libraries were equally affected by the severe decline of the European learned book market, which had flourished until about 1630[23]. Furthermore, the structural problems of the regulars' library holdings were accompanied in the mid seventeenth century by the effects of a negative economic situation and the difficulties in the governance of the orders, exacerbated by considerable tension between Roman centralism and the entrenchment of the religious houses in local contexts[24]. These processes transformed the religious libraries more into depositaries of treasures for collectors than living organisms. Thus, several prominent purchasers, such as Johann Jacob Fugger (1516–1575), a German banker and collector, and Jacques Gaffarel (1601–1681), a French Orientalist and member of Richelieu's circle, succeeded in buying a number of manuscripts of the Canons regular of S. Antonio in Castello, donated to the convent by Cardinal Domenico Grimani, including the Greek and oriental codices previously owned by Giovanni Pico della Mirandola[25]. In the forties this

continuous depletion of the Venetian collections led the canon of S. Giorgio in Alga Giacomo Filippo Tomasini to come up with the project of collecting existing inventories, which he was then to publish in 1650 in *Bibliothecae Venetae manuscriptae publicae et privatae*[26].

In 1652 Pope Innocent X began suppressing a series of minor convents belonging to mendicant orders and monastic congregations, presumably not endowed with any notable book collections[27]. A few years later, inspired by the Pope's action the Republic of Venice obtained from his successor, Alexander VII, the suppression of some ancient canonical orders – the Canons of Santo Spirito and S. Giorgio in Alga – and of the congregation of the "Crociferi", as well as permission to confiscate the assets in the Venetian territories of the three orders. The purpose was to use the proceeds for the defence of Candia (the isle of Crete), which was under attack by the Turks[28]. Thus, between 1656 and 1668, all traces were lost of printed and manuscript collections that had still been of considerable size and value at the time of the survey by the Congregation of the Index[29]. In 1687 – two years after the visit of the Maurist monks Jean Mabillon and Michel Germain – a fire

23 Ian Maclean, *Scholarship, Commerce, Religion. The Learned Book in the Age of Confessions, 1530–1630* (Cambridge MA-London, 2012), 211–34.

24 A number of suggestions on this crucial theme are in Carlo Fantappiè, *Il monachesimo moderno tra ragion di Chiesa e ragion di Stato: il caso toscano* (Firenze, 1993); see also Antonella Barzazi, 'Centri culturali camaldolesi e formazione dei monaci in età moderna', in *L'Ordine camaldolese in età moderna e contemporanea*, Atti del secondo Convegno di studi in occasione del Millenario di Camaldoli (1012–2012), eds Giuseppe M. Croce and Antonio U. Fossa (Cesena, 2015), 459–82.

25 Marino Zorzi, 'La circolazione del libro a Venezia nel Cinquecento: biblioteche private e pubbliche', *Ateneo Veneto*, 177 (1990), 140–42; Barzazi, 'Ordini religiosi e

biblioteche a Venezia', as note 12, 216–17.

26 The volume was published in Udine by the printer Nicolò Schiratti. In his congregation's *Annals* Tomasini dwells on the dispersion that affected the library of the eponymous Venetian convent of S. Giorgio in Alga. See Giacomo Filippo Tomasini, *Annales Canonicorum secularium S. Georgii in Alga* (Udine: Schiratti, 1642), 482, and Barzazi, *Collezioni librarie*, as note 12, 88–97.

27 Emanuele Boaga, *La soppressione innocenziana dei piccoli conventi in Italia* (Roma, 1971); Fiorenzo Landi, *Il tesoro dei regolari. L'inchiesta sui conventi d'Italia del 1650* (Bologna, 2013).

28 Boaga, *La soppressione innocenziana*, as note 27, 115–30.

29 Barzazi, 'Ordini religiosi e biblioteche a Venezia', as note 12, 179–82, 187–89. The documentation regarding the affair offers some clues about the destination of the paintings removed from the suppressed religious houses, but not about the books (Boaga, *La soppressione innocenziana*, as note 27, 128).

in the house of the canons regular of S. Antonio in Castello was to destroy the legacy of Cardinal Domenico Grimani's codices[30]. In these ways the Venetian library network was stripped of some of its traditional components.

However, in the last decades of the seventeenth century the negative trend was to be inverted: several communities of different orders in the main Italian centres began rebuilding works and undertook onerous restorations that were to transform the structure and organization of the regulars' libraries. The old spaces furnished with benches finally disappeared, replaced by wider rooms with a wall system able to hold increasingly large collections of printed books, based on the model inaugurated in Italy by Federico Borromeo's Ambrosiana, which was constructed between 1603 and 1609[31]. The revival of libraries was part of a complex reform project that affected all domains of life in the orders: from the economic management to regular discipline and studies. The example of the French Benedictines of St Maur became particularly influential: the Roman superiors of the orders encouraged friars and monks to commit to arduous studies and placed the library at the centre of a rigorous cultural project based on scholarship[32]. With its monumental nature, the library took on a defined institutional identity and established itself as an emblem of the orders that was both cultural and prestigious.

At the beginning of the eighteenth century the bibliographical canon of the Maurists actually played an important role in the initial increase of the restored Italian religious collections. It was in this phase that Venice became the epicentre of this broad phenomenon of renewal, also thanks to the revival of the local printing industry[33]. The wide wooden wall shelving then housed great editions of fundamental authors in both sacred and profane disciplines, collections of documents, biographical and chronological works of reference, generally in large-sized volumes. The earliest book holdings were then assessed following typical erudite criteria such as typographical quality, rarity of edition or particular publisher. The incunables gradually became more sought after and were the subject of specific interest and care[34]. The volumes printed in the sixteenth and seventeenth century were distinguished according to the quality of their printing and content. Some poor quality

---

30 Barzazi, 'Ordini religiosi e biblioteche a Venezia', as note 12, 227.

31 For some noteworthy Venetian cases see Antonella Barzazi, 'Un tempo assai ricche e piene di libri di merito. Le biblioteche dei regolari tra sviluppo e dispersione', in *Alli 10 Agosto 1806 soppressione del monastero di S. Giorgio*: Atti del convegno di studi nel bicentenario, ed. Giovanni Vian (Cesena, 2011), 72–73, and, by the author, *Collezioni librarie*, as note 12, 99–106. Francesco Ludovico Maschietto, *Biblioteca e bibliotecari di S. Giustina di Padova (1697-1827)* (Padova, 1981), 18–47; on the rebuilding of the Camaldolese library of Classe in Ravenna: Paolo Fabbri, 'L'"Escuriale de' Camaldolesi"', in *Cultura e vita civile a Ravenna*, ed. Donatino Domini (Bologna, 1981), 50–56, and the entry by Armando Petrucci, 'Canneti, Pietro', in *Dizionario Biografico degli Italiani*, 18 (Roma, 1975), 127–28; see also Alce D'Amato, *La biblioteca di S. Domenico*, as note 8, 48–53, and Chapron, *«Ad utilità pubblica»*, as note 22, 67–68. On the establishment and structure of the Ambrosiana: Enzo Bottasso, *Storia della biblioteca in Italia* (Milano, 1984), 60–61, and Alfredo Serrai, *Storia della bibliografia*, V, *Trattatistica biblioteconomica* (Roma, 1993), 201–33.

32 See Rosa, 'I depositi del sapere', as note 1, 194–95, and Antonella Barzazi, 'Una cultura per gli ordini religiosi: l'erudizione', *Quaderni Storici*, 119 (2005), 485–517: 498–99.

33 Barzazi, 'Un tempo assai ricche', as note 31, 73–74; M. Infelise, *L'editoria veneziana del '700* (Milano, 1989).

34 An overview on the growing interest for "rare" and ancient books and the development of bibliophilic practices in Europe is in Jean Viardot, 'Livre rares et pratiques bibliophiliques', in *Histoire de l'édition française*, ed. Henry-Jean Martin, II (Paris, 1984), 447–67; see also: Emmanuelle Chapron, 'Bibliothèques publiques et pratiques bibliophiliques au XVIIIe siècle: la collection d'incunables de la bibliothèque Magliabechiana de Florence', *Revue Française d'Histoire du Livre*, 118 (2003), 317–33.

seventeenth-century publications were removed from the shelves, such as a number of "baroque" spiritual and hagiographical works and booklets containing writings of astrology and practical medicine: these were considered obsolete and unfit for the new scholarly collections. Consequently this marked the beginning of a new cycle of selection and rejection that was to reach its peak in the early nineteenth century[35]. The oldest manuscript patrimony of the regular clergy was either partially destroyed, partially absorbed into other collections, or buried in old cabinets and armoires in the convents themselves. From the late seventeenth century on, however, parts began to be recovered, thanks to a marked antiquarian awareness. The religious members sought codices, including those for primary education and devotional use: previously abandoned and discarded, these were now regarded as important documents on the history of local culture and on the prominent men of the various orders, thus making them the object of purchase and exchange[36]. Some books prohibited by the sixteenth century Roman indices also re-surfaced, often mutilated and damaged by the censors. They were restored to the shelves and became part of collections now protected from ecclesiastical censorship by "universal" licences issued by the Roman Holy Office, allowing them to hold forbidden works[37].

Despite the variety of local situations and the choices made by individual orders, the erudite library thus represented a model of reference[38]. In the middle of the eighteenth century it was this model that inspired a revival of the regulars' libraries that gradually spread out from the capital and main cities to the smaller centres, supported by the expansion of the book trade and the emergence of scholarly culture in provincial areas[39]. Around the middle of the century a network of new libraries was extended to cover the peninsula, reflecting not so much the traditional

---

35 A purge of such material carried out in the Somaschan library of S. Maria della Salute in Venice during the eighteenth century is recalled, for instance, by Giannantonio Moschini, *Della letteratura veneziana del secolo XVIII*, II (Venezia, 1806), 40.

36 The salvage of manuscripts in some Florentine regular libraries, after the visit of Bernard de Montfaucon, is mentioned in Chapron, «*Ad utilità pubblica*», as note 22, 60–61.

37 The rules for consultation and the chances of obtaining such "permissions" are frequently discussed in the letters of the religious. See for example the correspondence of Giovanni Degli Agostini, librarian of the Venetian Franciscan convent of S. Francesco della Vigna in the 1740s, with Giammaria Mazzuchelli, in Vatican Apostolic

---

Library, Vat. Lat. 10003 (letters of Jan.-Jul. 1741 and Jan.-Apr. 1742). On the eighteenth-century regulation of the matter see Ugo Baldini, 'Il pubblico della scienza nei permessi di lettura di libri proibiti delle Congregazioni del Sant'Ufficio e dell'Indice (secolo XVI): verso una tipologia professionale e disciplinare', in *Censura ecclesiastica e cultura politica in Italia tra Cinquecento e Seicento*, ed. Cristina Stango (Firenze, 2001), 174–77.

38 Retrospective information about the eighteenth-century reconstruction of the regular clergy's Roman libraries can be found in Andreina Rita, *Biblioteche e requisizioni librarie a Roma in età napoleonica. Cronologia e fonti romane* (Città del Vaticano, 2012); on Naples see Vincenzo Trombetta, *Storia e cultura delle biblioteche napoletane. Librerie private, istituzioni francesi e borboniche, strutture postunitarie* (Napoli, 2002), 195–203; on the ways in which such new library arrangements enhanced the appeal of such collections also for orders which had hitherto had scarce interest in learning and erudition, such as the Capuchins, see Federica Dallasta and Benedetta D'Arezzo, *La biblioteca A. Turchi dei cappuccini di Parma. Vicende storiche, incunaboli, cinquecentine* (Roma 2005), 57–61, and in Federica Dallasta, 'I libri del convento di S. Maria Maddalena di Parma (Vat. Lat. 11326)', in *Dalla notitia librorum degli inventari agli esemplari*, as note 4, 307–11. However, the earlier models were not abandoned everywhere. The library holdings of the Jesuit college of S. Giovannino in Florence, for example, remained scattered – even after the middle of the eighteenth century – between the common rooms and the cells of the religious (Chapron, «*Ad utilità pubblica*», as note 22, 63–64).

39 The difficulties of adapting the minor libraries to the new canons can be seen very clearly in the Augustinian example of Fermo, studied in Borraccini-Cosi, 'Tra prescrizioni e proibizioni', as note 8, 86–90.

hierarchies between orders and congregations, but the social and cultural dynamics and the opportunities developed in the different political contexts. Remarkable, in this perspective, was the development of the Camaldolese system, structured on the major collections of S. Michele di Murano in Venice, S. Apollinare in Classe in Ravenna and S. Gregorio al Celio in Rome and on some minor libraries. Its success signaled the effectiveness of the challenge of the small cenobitic congregation of S. Michele di Murano to the old-time cultural leadership of the Cassinese monks[40]. The new library network – extended especially in northern and central Italy but also present in the Kingdom of Naples and Sicily – included some large collections of several tens of thousands of works, and a greater number of medium and minor libraries containing some-where between a thousand and ten thousand volumes[41]. On different scales and with their own specific characteristics, such collections tended to conform to an encyclopaedic structure, fully representing the scholarly disciplines and the various genres, and were generally endowed with special sections dedicated to manuscripts, both ancient and more recent, and incunabula.

The main figures in this radical restructuring of riches of the regulars' book collections were the librarians. During the eighteenth century they were given a more clearly defined role in the care of the book material, the drafting of catalogues and administration of the income allocated for acquisitions. After a preliminary organisation of the collections, they formulated plans for long-term increases that combined the acquisition of entire collections, the exchange of duplicate copies, dealing with printing houses and booksellers, and other institutional and domestic libraries. Personally engaged in historical and philological studies, they were equally involved in the rising eighteenth-century book market, thanks also to their habitual correspondence with the leading publishing centres, and with the most active figures of Italian scholarship, from Ludovico Antonio Muratori to the Venetian Apostolo Zeno[42]. Some of them – such as the Camaldolese librarians of S. Michele di Murano, in Venice, and of Classe, in Ravenna – exploited the internal financial links of their congregations to circulate books within them and to set up extended exchange networks including other religious houses and private scholars, both ecclesiastical and lay[43].

The activity and relationships of the librarians helped to establish the image of the

---

40 It should be noted that together with that of S. Michele (which had around 30,000 works at the end of the eighteenth century), the most important Venetian libraries were established in religious houses founded in the second half of the seventeenth century: S. Maria della Salute (Somaschans) and S. Maria del Rosario, head of the Dominican observant congregation dedicated to the blessed Giacomo Salomoni, originated in 1662. Barzazi, 'Un tempo assai ricche', as note 31, 75–76, and, by the author, *Collezioni librarie*, as note 12, 148–61.

41 For the seventeenth and eighteenth century overviews of the regular clergy's libraries are missing; consequently reference must be made to works of local history and the orders' and congregations' annals. As regards the monastic world, information is to be found in *Settecento monastico italiano*, Atti del I Convegno di studi storici sull'Italia Benedettina, Cesena 9–12 settembre 1986, eds Giustino Farnedi and Giovanni Spinelli (Cesena, 1990).

42 For the crucial role of the regular librarians in the Italian context, see Emmanuelle Chapron, 'Pour une histoire des bibliothécaires italiens au XVIIIe siècle', *Bibliothèque de l'École des chartes*, 166 (2008), 445–79; an overall look at the changing professional profile of the librarian between the seventeenth and eighteenth century is in Mario Rosa, 'Un "mediateur" dans la République des lettres: le bibliothécaire', in *Commercium litterarium: la communication dans la République des lettres, 1600–1750*, eds Hans Bots and Françoise Waquet (Amsterdam-Maarssen, 1994), 81–100.

43 Barzazi, *Collezioni librarie*, as note 12, 133–203; see also the author's entries 'Mittarelli, Giovanni Benedetto' and 'Mandelli, Fortunato', both in *Dizionario Biografico degli Italiani*, 75 (Roma, 2011), 97–102 and 68 (Roma, 2007), 559–62.

eighteenth-century regulars' library as the symbol of the orders' intellectual commitment, as well as a resource offered "for the common benefit" of a wider public of scholars and, more generally, the "republic of letters". This guiding idea marked the major development of the religious houses' collections and gave a unitary character to the expansions made until the mid-century.

From the 1760s on, the Italian picture tended to alter rather rapidly. Under pressure from the ideas promoted by Enlightenment culture and the reforming policies of governments, new secular models of public institutional library were created, and projects for State intervention on the regulars' collections were foreshadowed. The expulsion of the Jesuits from the Bourbon states of Parma and Naples in 1767, and their subsequent dissolution on the Pope's order in 1773, amounted to a widespread test-case for what was to happen thirty years later. Under the guidance of civil governments a massive transfer of book collections was carried out, to the advantage of the court libraries, and those in schools, universities and episcopal seminaries[44]. The dissolution of the Society of Jesus had an accelerating impact, particularly in the areas of Habsburg and Lorraine reformism, namely Lombardy and Tuscany. Here the book holdings of the Jesuits' houses and of other gradually suppressed convents, drastically re-sorted, allowed the creation of new professional and specialist book collections and a radical redesign of the existing library system on the basis of the criteria of functionality and

use for science and professions[45]. Elsewhere the effects of the first wave of suppressions were more limited and can barely be related to the discussion on the reform of teaching and cultural institutions. In this regard, the case of Venice seems particularly significant. Here the government's decision to suppress a number of religious houses affected several minor libraries on the mainland, although they did not touch the rich book holdings of the convents in the city. It was not until the eighties, following the initiative of the librarian of St Mark, Jacopo Morelli, that several groups of codices that had belonged to convents were transferred to the Library of St Mark[46]. The latter institution was thus given a key and unprecedented role in the control of the regular clergy's library network.

However, even where – as in Venice – the libraries of the religious houses had continued to grow, sheltered from State intervention, in the last decades of the eighteenth century they had lost their vitality. Faced by attack from civil governments, friars and monks remained firmly devoted to the erudite model of the first half of the century, accentuating their opposition to the culture of Enlightenment. As they were no longer kept up-to-date in line with the new intellectual trends, their collections tended to become marginalised in terms of contemporary cultural debate. In the meantime, the active presence of the religious in book exchanges had begun to decline severely. The suppressions achieved by

44 Trombetta, *Storia e cultura delle biblioteche napoletane*, as note 38, 144–57; Andrea De Pasquale, 'Introduzione' a *Parma città d'Europa. Le memorie del padre Paolo Maria Paciaudi sulla Regia Biblioteca Parmense* (Parma, 2008), 16–17, 33–34; Paolo Tinti, *La libraria dei Gesuiti di Modena* (Bologna, 2001); Luigi Balsamo, 'Le biblioteche dei Gesuiti', in *Dall'isola alla città. I Gesuiti a Bologna*, eds Gian Paolo Brizzi and Anna Maria Matteucci (Bologna, 1988), 183–92.

45 See Chapron, «*Ad utilità pubblica*», as note 22, ch. III–IV, and the essay of the same author in this volume; Renato Pasta, 'La biblioteca aulica e le letture dei principi lorenesi', in *Vivere a Pitti. Una reggia dai Medici ai Savoia*, eds Sergio Bertelli and Renato Pasta (Firenze, 2003), 351–87; Silvio Furlani, 'Maria Teresa fondatrice di biblioteche', *Accademie e biblioteche d'Italia*, 50 (1982), 459–74; Maria Teresa Monti, 'I libri di Haller e la nascita delle biblioteche pubbliche nella Lombardia asburgica', *Società e storia*, 46 (1989), 995–1030.

46 See the essay by Dorit Raines in this volume and Barzazi, *Collezioni librarie*, as note 12, 215–20.

several governments had also changed the circuits that had been used for internal exchanges within the orders – going beyond the borders of the individual Italian states – once and for all. The eighteenth century library system was in fact disrupted before the French occupation of the Italian peninsula in 1796–1797.

The confiscations carried out by the Napoleonic authorities from 1806 on were thus enacted in a variety of different situations. In those cases in which eighteenth-century reforms had either created or reinforced public library institutions, the books coming from the suppressed convents could be sent to these, guiding what the French commissioners selected for retention or chose to discard. Elsewhere, however, this sudden dismantling of the regular clergy's libraries led to extensive dispersion and a massive influx of a large quantity of books on the market. This was the case in Venice: the parallel dissolution of the rich religious' and patricians' collections was to transform the city, the main crossroad of the European book market during the entire early-modern period, into an emporium of cheap printed material[47].

---

47 See Marino Berengo, *Intellettuali e librai nella Milano della Restaurazione* (Torino, 1980), 119, and, in the present volume, the essays by Dorit Raines and Marino Zorzi.

Bibliography

Manuscripts and Archival Sources

Vatican Apostolic Library, Vat. Lat. 10003 (correspondence Giovanni Degli Agostini – Giammaria Mazzuchelli, 1741–1742).

Vatican Apostolic Library, Vat. Lat. 11282 (inventories of the Italian religious' libraries).

Vatican Apostolic Library, Vat. Lat. 11304 (inventories of the Italian religious' libraries).

Secondary Works

Venturino Alce and Alfonso D'Amato, *La biblioteca di S. Domenico in Bologna* (Firenze, 1961).

Silvia Alessandrini Calisti, 'Norme e consuetudini degli Eremiti camaldolesi di Montecorona su libri e biblioteche', in *Libri, biblioteche e cultura degli ordini regolari*, 309–35.

Ugo Baldini, 'Il pubblico della scienza nei permessi di lettura di libri proibiti delle Congregazioni del Sant'Ufficio e dell'Indice (secolo XVI): verso una tipologia professionale e disciplinare', in *Censura ecclesiastica e cultura politica in Italia tra Cinquecento e Seicento*, ed. Cristina Stango (Firenze, 2001), 171–201.

Luigi Balsamo, 'Le biblioteche dei Gesuiti', in *Dall'isola alla città. I Gesuiti a Bologna*, eds Gian Paolo Brizzi and Anna Maria Matteucci (Bologna, 1988), 183–92.

Antonella Barzazi, 'Ordini religiosi e biblioteche a Venezia tra Cinque e Seicento', *Annali dell'Istituto storico italo-germanico in Trento*, 21 (1995), 141–228.

Antonella Barzazi, 'Una cultura per gli ordini religiosi: l'erudizione', *Quaderni Storici*, 119 (2005), 485–517.

Antonella Barzazi, 'Mandelli, Fortunato', in *Dizionario Biografico degli Italiani*, 68 (Roma, 2007), 559–62.

Antonella Barzazi, 'Mittarelli, Giovanni Benedetto', in *Dizionario Biografico degli Italiani*, 75 (Roma, 2011), 97–102.

Antonella Barzazi, 'Un tempo assai ricche e piene di libri di merito. Le biblioteche dei regolari tra sviluppo e dispersione', in *Alli 10 Agosto 1806 soppressione del monastero di S. Giorgio*: Atti del convegno di studi nel bicentenario, ed. Giovanni Vian (Cesena, 2011), 71–91.

Antonella Barzazi, 'Centri culturali camaldolesi e formazione dei monaci in età moderna', in *L'Ordine camaldolese in età moderna e contemporanea*, Atti del secondo Convegno di studi in occasione del Millenario di Camaldoli (1012–2012), eds Giuseppe M. Croce and Antonio U. Fossa (Cesena, 2015), 459–82.

Antonella Barzazi, *Collezioni librarie in una capitale d'antico regime. Venezia secoli XVI–XVIII* (Roma, 2017).

Marino Berengo, *Intellettuali e librai nella Milano della Restaurazione* (Torino, 1980).

Roberto Biondi, 'Libri, biblioteche e *studia* nella legislazione delle famiglie francescane (secc. XVI–XVII)', in *Libri, biblioteche e cultura degli ordini regolari*, 338–56.

Rudolf Blum, *La biblioteca della Badia fiorentina e i codici di Antonio Corbinelli* (Città Del Vaticano, 1951).

Emanuele Boaga, *La soppressione innocenziana dei piccoli conventi in Italia* (Roma, 1971).

Monica Bocchetta, 'La legislazione dei Minori Conventuali sugli studi e sulle biblioteche, secoli XVI-XVII', in *Presenze francescane nel Camerinese (sec. XIII–XVII)*, eds Francesca Bartolacci e Roberto Lambertini (Ripatransone, 2008), 249–71.

Rosa Marisa Borraccini and Sara Cosi, 'Tra prescrizioni e proibizioni. Libri e biblioteche dei mendicanti della Marca d'Ancona sul declinare del Cinquecento', in *Gli ordini mendicanti (sec. XIII–XVI)*, Atti del XLIII convegno di Studi Maceratesi, Abbadia di Fiastra (Tolentino), 24–25 novembre 2007 (Macerata 2009), 69–153.

Rosa Marisa Borraccini, Giovanna Granata, and Roberto Rusconi, 'A proposito dell'inchiesta della S. Congregazione dell'Indice dei libri proibiti di fine '500', *Il capitale culturale. Studies on the Value of Cultural Heritage*, 6 (2013), 13–45.

Enzo Bottasso, *Storia della biblioteca in Italia* (Milano, 1984).

Flavia Bruni, 'Una *inquisitio* nel convento servita di Lucca: i libri nella cella di fra Lorenzo', in *Libri, biblioteche e cultura degli ordini regolari*, 473–523.

Giovanna Cantoni Alzati, *La biblioteca di S. Giustina di Padova: libri e cultura presso i benedettini padovani in età umanistica* (Padova, 1982).

Emmanuelle Chapron, 'Bibliothèques publiques et pratiques bibliophiliques au XVIIIe siècle: la collection d'incunables de la bibliothèque Magliabechiana de Florence', *Revue Française d'Histoire du Livre*, 118 (2003), 317–33.

Emmanuelle Chapron, 'Pour une histoire des bibliothécaires italiens au XVIIIe siècle', *Bibliothèque de l'École des chartes*, 166 (2008), 445–79.

Emmanuelle Chapron, «*Ad utilità pubblica*». *Politique des bibliothèques et pratiques du livre à Florence au XVIIIe siècle* (Genève, 2009).

Codices 11266–11326: Inventari di biblioteche religiose italiane alla fine del Cinquecento, eds Marie-Madeleine Lebreton and Luigi Fiorani (Città del Vaticano, 1985).

Domenico Antonio D'Alessandro, 'Oltre il fondo "San Martino". Le biblioteche dei teatini a Napoli tra Cinque e Ottocento', in *Sant'Andrea Avellino e i Teatini nella Napoli del Viceregno Spagnolo*, ed. Domenico Antonio D'Alessandro, I (Napoli, 2011), 327–85.

Dalla notitia librorum degli inventari agli esemplari. Saggi di indagine su libri e biblioteche dai codici Vaticani latini 11266–11326, ed. Rosa Marisa Borraccini (Macerata, 2009).

Federica Dallasta and Benedetta D'Arezzo, *La biblioteca A. Turchi dei cappuccini di Parma. Vicende storiche, incunaboli, cinquecentine* (Roma 2005).

Federica Dallasta, 'I libri del convento di S. Maria Maddalena di Parma (Vat. Lat. 11326)', in *Dalla notitia librorum degli inventari agli esemplari*, 303–26.

Andrea De Pasquale, 'Introduzione', in *Parma città d'Europa. Le memorie del padre Paolo Maria Paciaudi sulla Regia Biblioteca Parmense* (Parma, 2008), 13–45.

Lorenzo Di Lenardo, 'I libri proibiti dei Francescani Conventuali del Triveneto', in *Libri, biblioteche e cultura degli ordini regolari*, 525–53.

Paolo Fabbri, 'L'"Escuriale de' Camaldolesi"', in *Cultura e vita civile a Ravenna*, ed. Donatino Domini (Bologna, 1981), 27–94.

Carlo Fantappiè, *Il monachesimo moderno tra ragion di Chiesa e ragion di Stato: il caso toscano* (Firenze, 1993).

Gigliola Fragnito, 'Gli Ordini religiosi tra Riforma e Controriforma', in *Clero e società nell'Italia moderna*, ed. Mario Rosa (Roma-Bari, 1992), 169–82.

Gigliola Fragnito, *La Bibbia al rogo. La censura ecclesiastica e i volgarizzamenti della Scrittura (1471–1605)* (Bologna, 1997).

Gigliola Fragnito, 'L'Indice clementino e le biblioteche degli Ordini religiosi', in *Libri, biblioteche e cultura degli ordini regolari*, 37–59.

Vittorio Frajese, *Nascita dell'Indice. La censura ecclesiastica dal Rinascimento alla Controriforma* (Brescia, 2006).

Donatella Frioli, 'Gli inventari delle biblioteche degli Ordini mendicanti', in *Libri, biblioteche e letture dei frati mendicanti*, 301–73.

Silvio Furlani, 'Maria Teresa fondatrice di biblioteche', *Accademie e biblioteche d'Italia*, 50 (1982), 459–74.

Giovanna Granata, 'On the Track of Lost Editions in Italian Religious Libraries at the End of the Sixteenth Century: A Numerical Analysis of the RICI Database', in *Lost Books. Reconstructing the Print World of Pre-Industrial Europe*, eds Flavia Bruni and Andrew Pettegree (Leiden-Boston, 2016), 324–44.

Giovanni Grosso, 'I Carmelitani e i libri: alcune note sulla legislazione', in *Libri, biblioteche e cultura degli ordini regolari*, 381–94.

Kennet W. Humphreys, *The book provisions of the mediaeval friars, 1215–1400* (Amsterdam, 1964).

Mario Infelise, *L'editoria veneziana del '700* (Milano, 1989).

Tommaso Kaeppeli, *Inventari di libri di San Domenico di Perugia (1430–80)* (Roma, 1962).

Fiorenzo Landi, *Il tesoro dei regolari. L'inchiesta sui conventi d'Italia del 1650* (Bologna, 2013).

Libri, biblioteche e cultura degli ordini regolari nell'Italia moderna attraverso la documentazione della Congregazione dell'Indice: Atti del convegno internazionale, Macerata, 30 maggio-1 giugno 2006, eds Rosa Marisa Borraccini and Roberto Rusconi (Città del Vaticano, 2006).

Libri, biblioteche e letture dei frati mendicanti (secoli XIII–XIV), Atti del XXXII Convegno internazionale, Assisi, 7–9 ottobre 2004 (Spoleto, 2005).

Valentina Lozza, 'Libri e formazione presso l'Accademia di Somasca intorno all'anno 1600', in *Dalla notitia librorum degli inventari agli esemplari*, 409–34.

Ian Maclean, *Scholarship, Commerce, Religion. The Learned Book in the Age of Confessions, 1530–1630* (Cambridge MA-London, 2012), 211–34.

Adelisa Malena, 'Libri "proibiti", "sospesi", "dubii d'esser cattivi": in margine ad alcune liste dei Canonici regolari lateranensi', in *Libri, biblioteche e cultura degli ordini regolari*, 555–81.

Francesco Ludovico Maschietto, *Biblioteca e bibliotecari di S. Giustina di Padova (1697–1827)* (Padova, 1981).

Maria Teresa Monti, 'I libri di Haller e la nascita delle biblioteche pubbliche nella Lombardia asburgica', *Società e storia*, 46 (1989), 995–1030.

Giannantonio Moschini, *Della letteratura veneziana del secolo XVIII*, II (Venezia, 1806).

Donatella Nebbiai, 'Modelli bibliotecari premendicanti', in *Libri, biblioteche e letture dei frati mendicanti*, 141–69.

James O'Gorman, *The Architecture of the Monastic Library in Italy 1300–1600* (New York, 1972).

Sergio Pagano, 'Le biblioteche dei Barnabiti italiani nel 1599. In margine ai loro più antichi cataloghi', *Barnabiti studi*, 3 (1986), 13–41.

Renato Pasta, 'La biblioteca aulica e le letture dei principi lorenesi', in *Vivere a Pitti. Una reggia dai Medici ai Savoia*, eds Sergio Bertelli and Renato Pasta (Firenze, 2003), 351–87.

Carlo Pellegrini, 'Catalogo delle biblioteche somasche (1599–1600)', *Somascha*, 1 (1976), 24–25.

Carlo Pellegrini, 'Libri e biblioteche nella vita economica dei mendicanti', in *L'economia dei conventi dei frati minori e predicatori fino alla metà del Trecento*: Atti del XXXI Convegno internazionale, Assisi, 9–11 ottobre 2003 (Spoleto, 2004), 187–214.

Letizia Pellegrini, *I manoscritti dei predicatori. I domenicani dell'Italia mediana e i codici della loro predicazione (secc. XIII–XV)* (Roma, 1999).

Armando Petrucci, 'Canneti, Pietro', in *Dizionario Biografico degli Italiani*, 18 (Roma, 1975), 125–29.

Armando Petrucci, 'Le biblioteche antiche', in *Letteratura italiana*, II: *Produzione e consumo* (Torino, 1983), 527–54.

Giovanni Pozzi and Luciana Pedroia, *Ad uso di … applicato alla libraria de' cappuccini di Lugano* (Roma, 1996).

Dorit Raines and Simonetta Pelusi, 'Il Fondo antico della Biblioteca PP. Cappuccini SS. Redentore di Venezia: per una storia documentata delle biblioteche cappuccine nel Veneto', *Notiziario Bibliografico. Periodico della Giunta regionale del Veneto*, 16 (1994), 6–8.

Andreina Rita, *Biblioteche e requisizioni librarie a Roma in età napoleonica. Cronologia e fonti romane* (Città del Vaticano, 2012).

Mario Rosa, 'I depositi del sapere: biblioteche, accademie, archivi', in *La memoria del sapere. Forme di conservazione e strutture organizzative dall'antichità a oggi*, ed. Pietro Rossi (Roma-Bari, 1988), 165–209.

Mario Rosa, 'Dottore o seduttor deggio appellarte: note erasmiane', *Rivista di Storia e Letteratura religiosa*, 26 (1990), 5–33.

Mario Rosa, 'Un "mediateur" dans la République des lettres: le bibliothécaire', in *Commercium litterarium: la communication dans la République des lettres, 1600–1750*, eds Hans Bots and Françoise Waquet (Amsterdam-Maarssen, 1994), 81–100.

Roberto Rusconi, 'I frati Minori dell'Osservanza in Italia dopo il Concilio di Trento: circolazione di libri e strumenti di formazione intellettuale (sulla base delle biblioteche conventuali e personali)', in *Identités franciscaines à l'âge des réformes*, eds Frédéric Meyer and Ludovic Viallet (Clermont-Ferrand, 2005), 385–93.

Roberto Rusconi, 'Frati e monaci, libri e biblioteche alla fine del '500', in *Libri, biblioteche e cultura degli ordini regolari*, 13–36.

Roberto Rusconi, 'Libri e biblioteche degli ordini regolari in un'indagine di fine Cinquecento. Indirizzi di ricerca e prospettive', *Dimensioni e problemi della ricerca storica*, 1 (2012), 111–23.

Roberto Rusconi, 'The Devil's Trick. Impossible Editions in the Lists of Titles from the Regular Orders in Italy at the End of the Sixteenth Century', *Lost Books. Reconstructing the Print World of Pre-Industrial Europe*, eds Flavia Bruni and Andrew Pettegree (Leiden-Boston, 2016), 310–23.

Elena Scrima, 'Del luogo de' PP. Cappuccini di Mistretta. Libri dal convento di S. Maria, Vat. Lat. 11323', in *Dalla notitia librorum degli inventari agli esemplari*, 447–86.

Alfredo Serrai, *Storia della bibliografia*, V, *Trattatistica biblioteconomica* (Roma, 1993).

Alfredo Serrai, *Angelo Rocca fondatore della prima biblioteca pubblica europea* (Milano, 2004).

Settecento monastico italiano, Atti del I Convegno di studi storici sull'Italia Benedettina, Cesena 9–12 settembre 1986, eds Giustino Farnedi and Giovanni Spinelli (Cesena, 1990).

Stanislao da Campagnola, 'Ranuccio I Farnese (1569–1622) fondatore della biblioteca dei Cappuccini di Fontevivo (Parma)', *Collectanea Franciscana*, 38 (1968), 308–63; repr. in Stanislao da Campagnola, *Oratoria sacra: Teologie, Ideologie, Biblioteche nell'Italia dei secoli XVI–XIX* (Roma, 2003).

Stanislao da Campagnola, 'Le biblioteche dei cappuccini nel passaggio tra Cinque e Seicento', in *Biblioteche cappuccine italiane*, Atti del Congresso Nazionale, Assisi, 14–16 ottobre 1987, ed. Anselmo Mattioli (Perugia, 1988), 71–79; repr. in Stanislao da Campagnola, *Oratoria sacra: Teologie, Ideologie, Biblioteche nell'Italia dei secoli XVI–XIX* (Roma, 2003).

Paolo Tinti, *La libraria dei Gesuiti di Modena* (Bologna, 2001).

Giacomo Filippo Tomasini, *Annales Canonicorum secularium S. Georgii in Alga* (Udine: Schiratti, 1642).

Vincenzo Trombetta, *Storia e cultura delle biblioteche napoletane. Librerie private, istituzioni francesi e borboniche, strutture postunitarie* (Napoli, 2002).

Jean Viardot, 'Livre rares et pratiques bibliophiliques', in *Histoire de l'édition française*, ed. Henry-Jean Martin, II (Paris, 1984), 447–67.

Mario Villani, 'Cultura religiosa e patrimonio librario nella provincia francescana di S. Angelo prima e dopo il concilio di Trento', in *Il Concilio di Trento nella vita culturale e spirituale del Mezzogiorno tra XVI e XVII secolo*: Atti del convegno di Maratea, 19–21 giugno 1986, eds Gabriele De Rosa and Antonio Cestaro, II (Venosa, 1988), 442–52.

Massimo Zaggia, *Tra Mantova e la Sicilia nel Cinquecento*, II, *La congregazione benedettina cassinese nel Cinquecento* (Firenze, 2003).

Marino Zorzi, 'La circolazione del libro a Venezia nel Cinquecento: biblioteche private e pubbliche', *Ateneo Veneto*, 177 (1990), 117–89.

Digital Sources

Ricerca sull'Inchiesta della Congregazione dell'Indice (RICI), https://rici.vatlib.it/.

WILLIAM P. STONEMAN

North American Collection-Building: Gathering Monastic Books from Long Ago and Far Away

The subject of this contribution, the secularization of European religious houses and the subsequent migration of manuscripts and early printed books into North American collections, is, when compared to European countries, on a very different scale, in a very different timeframe and with a very different purpose[1]. The impact of this migration on North American libraries is a comparatively recent, a largely twentieth-century, phenomenon. So, if the title of this book and its timeframe of the sixteenth to the nineteenth centuries were to be strictly enforced, this contribution would effectively be over now because in the words of the modern American library historian, Phyllis Dain:

> Arguably, no great libraries existed in nine-teenth-century America. ... Not until well into the next century could the largest American libraries compare with the immense European repositories that they emulated – the royal, ducal, ecclesiastical, and private collections and the university and national libraries derived from them[2].

Dain's observation that American university and research libraries were built in emulation of European models may seem obvious; her primary concern is with the development of American libraries, but her observation that European

---

1 I extend my sincere thanks to Richard Sharpe and Cristina Dondi for stimulating conversation on this topic and also to John Lancaster and Roland Folter for incunable-related discussion over many years. I am much indebted to the work of Kenneth Carpenter, Paul Needham and Milton Gatch; my Houghton Library colleague Peter Accardo has generously shared his notes with me on George Ticknor and Joseph Green Cogswell. Their assistance in developing this paper has been invaluable; any errors or omissions that remain are my own.

2 Phyllis Dain, 'The Great Libraries', in *Print in Motion: The Expansion of Publishing and Reading in the United States, 1880–1940*, ed. Carl F. Kaestle and Janice Radway, Volume 4 of A History of the Book in America (Chapel Hill, 2009), 452.

William P. Stoneman • Retired Florence Fearrington Librarian of Houghton Library at Harvard University.
williampstoneman@gmail.com

How the Secularization of Religious Houses Transformed the Libraries of Europe, 16th–19th Centuries, ed. by Cristina Dondi, Dorit Raines, and †Richard Sharpe, BIB, 63 (Turnhout, 2022), pp. 467–486.
BREPOLS ❧ PUBLISHERS   DOI 10.1484/M.BIB-EB.5.128499

university and national libraries are derived from earlier collections is key to understanding what can often seem like random and sporadic individual efforts in Europe and in America. Also key to understanding this larger picture is an appreciation of how and why these earlier efforts to build libraries reflect the needs of their users and resources of their owners.

In a significant article published in 2004 Paul Needham argued that there is an important distinction to be made between old books, acquired and used because the matter in them is still relevant and continues to be useful, and old books, acquired as collectable antiquities, not primarily or essentially for their contents, but rather as indications of earlier use[3]. His study is focused on incunabula, but has larger implications for all books and manuscripts. Material in the first category can and will slip over time into the second and Needham suggested that the seventeenth century was an important period in which to observe this transition.

More recently in 2018 he has demonstrated in considerable detail how a closer examination of the books themselves and the documentation that surrounds them reflect this shift in the purpose of books and the libraries they are in[4]. Needham turned his critical attention to the Massachusetts Bay Colony and he begins by dismantling the myth that a copy of Cassianus' *De institutis coenobiorum* printed in Basel in 1485 (ISTC ic00233000) was presented by King William III to King's Chapel in Boston in 1698. Frederick Goff, following a suggestion by Margaret Bingham Stillwell, described it as a "royal gift … quite probably

the only fifteenth-century printed book to reach America in the seventeenth-century that is still extant"[5]. Needham shows that the book is not included in the list of books sent from London in 1697 at the instigation of the Rev. Thomas Bray, of the Society for Promoting Christian Knowledge. "It was a carefully chosen collection of mostly recent standard editions of the church fathers, ecclesiastical history, and protestant theology, within which a superannuated edition of Cassian would have been out of context"[6]. The letter of thanks dated 25 July 1698 is addressed to the Bishop of London, patron of the Chapel. The books in this gift were only bound and stamped "sub auspiciis Wilhelmi III" in 1823, but by then the Cassianus was counted among them.

A more likely contender as the first incunable to reach the United States was a *sammelband*, now in the Boston Public Library, of Venetian *Opuscula* by St Augustine printed in March and November 1491 (ISTC ia01219000 and ia01222000) owned by the Rev. John Norton (1606–1663) who came to America in 1635[7]. A partial copy of Duns Scotus' *Quaestiones in quattuor libros Sententiarum Petri Lombardi*, printed in Venice in 1481 (ISTC id00381000), probably owned by John Winthrop II (1606–1676) and now in the New-York Society Library is a second contender. A Latin Bible with

3 Paul Needham, 'The Late Use of Incunables and the Paths of Book Survival', *Wolfenbütteler Notizen zur Buchgeschichte*, 29 (2004), 35–59.

4 Paul Needham, 'Four Incunables brought to the Massachusetts Bay Colony', in *Lux Librorum: Essays on Books and History for Chris Coppens*, edited by Goran Proot, David McKitterick, Angela Nuovo and Paul F. Gehl (Mechelen, 2018), 141–64.

5 Frederick R. Goff, *Incunabula in American Libraries: A Third Census of Fifteenth-Century Books Recorded in North American Collections*, rev. ed. (Millwood, NY, 1973), ix; Bernard Rosenthal, 'The History of Incunabula Collections in the United States: A Brief Account', *Aus dem Antiquariat* (2000), no. 6, A350-A366; issued as part of *Börsenblatt für den Deutschen Buchhandel* (30 June 2000), A350.

6 Needham, 'Four Incunables', as note 4, 147.

7 In a marginal addendum reproduced in the revised edition Goff does acknowledge that this may have been the first incunable to reach America. Goff continued to track incunables in American collections. For his very preceptive analysis and the factors that affected this collecting, see his 'Interim Census Report on the Collecting of Incunabula by American Libraries', *Gutenberg Jahrbuch*, 51 (1976), 162–64.

the commentary of Nicolaus de Lyra printed in Lyons *c.* 1488 (ISTC ib00615000) now at Princeton University Library is a third. A signature and date of May 9, 1667 suggest that the book was owned by Thomas Shepard II (1635–1677) and was in North America by that date. A fourth candidate is another Latin Bible printed in Venice in 1476 (ISTC ib00548000) owned by an unidentified member of the Mather family and now at the American Antiquarian Society. Needham demonstrates that this volume has been transformed by Isaiah Thomas, founder of the Society:

> how in the course of its travels from one place and one owner to another, it underwent a metamorphosis. In the early seventeenth century it was "just" a book and undoubtedly a cheap one, convenient for reading and annotation. By the beginning of the nineteenth century it had metamorphosed into a prized antiquity … For Isaiah Thomas, the volume was "unquestionably one of the greatest typographical curiosities in the United States"[8].

It had moved from being a useful book in a local context into one that is important as indicative of that use and representative of larger global progress.

Most recently, however, in a forthcoming article Needham has argued convincingly that the first incunables to cross the Atlantic Ocean came quite early after the Spanish conquest when an ecclesiastical hierarchy was established and mendicant convents began to be founded as the base for missionary work in Mexico[9].

Needham has been able to identify 118 copies of 103 editions from 29 Mexican convents, colleges and seminaries. The secularization of church property began in 1867 and most of these books were gathered into the Biblioteca Nácional de México[10]. Other libraries which now hold this material are covered in the union catalogue of incunables in Mexican libraries[11]. This is a pattern of confiscation and institutionalization observed at different times and in many countries in Europe and surveyed in other chapters in the present volume. Seven of the nine libraries which now hold this material are in Mexico City, but the British Library collection includes three. Eleven of these incunables are from the conventual libraries of Santiago de Tlatelolco and San Antonio de Texcoco purchased by Adolph Sutro (1830–1898) from the Libreria Abadiano in Mexico City in 1889[12].

Adolf Sutro was born in Aachen, made his fortune in Nevada silver mines and was later mayor of San Francisco. He also purchased incunabula that were designated duplicates by the Königliche Bibliothek in Munich (now the Bayerische Staatsbibliothek), at the sale of the library of the Earl of Sunderland, beginning in 1881, and at the sale of the Carthusian monastery at Buxheim in 1883. An unknown number of Sutro's books were lost in the San Francisco earthquake fire of 1906, but 55 incunables survive, now in the San Francisco State University Library[13].

8 Needham, 'Four Incunables', as note 4, 164. Needham is quoting the description of the volume in Thomas's *The History of Printing in America with a biography of printers, and an account of newspapers, to which is prefixed a concise view of the discovery and process of the art in other parts of the world*, 2 vols (Worcester, Massachusetts, 1810), I, 54–57.

9 I am very grateful to Dr Needham for sharing his paper on the subject of incunables in Colonial America and especially its appendix.

10 See Jesús Yhmoff Cabrera, *Catálogo de incunables de la Biblioteca Nacional de México* (México, 1968; 2. ed. corr. y aum., 1987).

11 Elvia Carreño Velázquez, *Catálogo de incunables* (México, 2000).

12 Michael W. Mathes, 'Adolph Sutro's Incunabula from Mexico: A Study in Provenance', *Book Club of California Quarterly Newsletter*, 46.4 (1981), 103–05.

13 On Sutro, see Donald C. Dickinson, *Dictionary of American Book Collectors* (New York, 1986), 303–04 for additional bibliography and more recently see Russ Davidson, 'Adolph Sutro as Book Collector: A New Look', *California State Library Bulletin*, 75 (2003), 2–27.

This pattern of early use in Hispanophone territories in the New World may also be apparent in Francophone areas of North America. The libraries of provincial Quebec, in particular, may well contain similar traces of earlier use by French settlers to establish colonies and to spread cultural influence.

In Anglophone America the development or metamorphosis, to use Needham's term, of research libraries begins with the appreciation of the use of such libraries and the articulation of their value; two contemporary observers can serve to illustrate this point. The first, the Bostonian George Ticknor (1791–1871), wrote home to his father in November 1815 from Göttingen, where he was studying Greek:

> Every day I am filled with new astonishment at the variety and accuracy, the minuteness and readiness, of his learning.

Ticknor was writing about his tutor, Johannes Schulze (1786–1869), and the resources available to him; he continued:

> Every day I feel anew, under the oppressive weight of his admirable acquirements, what a mortifying distance there is between a European and an American scholar! We do not yet know what a Greek scholar is; we do not even know the process by which a man is to be made one. I am sure, if there is any faith to be given to the signs of the times, two or three generations at least must pass away before we can make the discovery and success in the experiment. Dr Schulze is hardly older than I am … It never entered into my imagination to conceive that any expense of time or talent could make a man so accomplished in this forgotten language as he is[14].

Schulze, the object of Ticknor's admiration, became an official in the Prussian educational bureaucracy and his library of over 20,000 volumes was offered for sale after his death by his son. An independent evaluation of Schulze's library, commissioned by Northwestern University from Wilhelm David Koner (1817–1887), the librarian of the Royal University in Berlin, concluded that:

> for a new university, where it is desired to establish a library in aid of the studies there to be pursued, the purchase of this collection remarkable in many directions, is to be warmly recommended. It would at least serve as an admirable nucleus around which a great library might gradually grow[15].

Schulze's library, which contained 17 incunables, was eventually sold in 1869 to the Northwestern University in Evanston, Illinois, funded by university trustee and benefactor Luther L. Greenleaf (1828–1894)[16].

George S. Hillard, the editor of Ticknor's letters, endeavored to put Ticknor's letter in context and reported that:

> Nothing more marked the change produced in him by his long residence in Europe than the different impressions made by the library of Harvard College before his departure and after his return. "When I went away," he said, "I thought it was a large library: when I came back, it seemed a closetful of books"[17].

---

14 *Life, Letters, and Journals of George Ticknor*, ed. George S. Hillard (Boston, 1876), I, 73.

15 Jeffrey Garrett, 'Whispers between Books: The Collections of Deering Library', in *Deering Library: An Illustrated History* (Evanston, 2008), 6. On Deering, see also Christina M. Nielson, *Devotional & Splendor: Medieval Art at the Art Institute of Chicago* (Chicago, 2004).

16 The story of this acquisition is told in Garrett, as note 15, 4–7.

17 *Ticknor*, as note 14, I, 72.

In 1833, 13 years after Ticknor wrote his letter home, a second observer, the Scottish traveler, Thomas Hamilton (1789–1842), could be no more complimentary on the state of American libraries; in his *Men and Manners in America* he commented that:

> There is at this moment nothing in the United States worthy of the name of a library. ... At present an American might study every book within the limits of the Union, and still be regarded in many parts of Europe ... as a man comparatively ignorant[18].

Kenneth Carpenter has summarized the very practical reasons for growing interest in public libraries in nineteenth-century America.

> In the early decades of the nineteenth century, American educators, church leaders, government officials, reformers, and scholars argued that social benefits would surely follow from improved access to books, among them the creation of an educated citizenry for a strong democracy; the moral and religious education of a large and rapidly growing population; a heightened sense of the country's past; and the enhancement of the new nation's standing in the world[19].

Thus in 1851 Edward Everett (1794–1865), a former governor of Massachusetts, a recently retired president of Harvard and whose collection of Greek manuscripts would eventually come to Harvard, wrote to the mayor of Boston urging support for what would become, three years later, the Boston Public Library.

> A Public Library, well supplied with books in the various departments of art and science, and open at all times for consultation and study to the citizens at large, is absolutely needed to make our admirable system of Public Education complete[20].

Everett had studied in Göttingen at the same time as George Ticknor, with whom he had travelled. Ticknor himself argued that:

> This appetite [for healthy general reading], once formed, ... will, in the majority of cases, demand better and better books; and can, I believe, by a little judicious help, rather than by direct control or restraint, be carried much higher than is generally thought possible[21].

The American public library movement was really impelled forward at the end of the nineteenth century by the industrialist turned philanthropist, Andrew Carnegie (1835–1919):

> Carnegie drew attention to the importance of libraries in the December 1889 issue of the *North American Review*, where he argued that libraries were the best single field for philanthropy because placing books within reach of aspiring citizens effectively fostered the genuine progress of the people[22].

---

18 Thomas Hamilton, *Men and Manners in New York* (London, 1833; rptd. New York, 1968), 368–69; quoted by Kenneth E. Carpenter, *Readers & Libraries: Toward a History of Libraries and Culture in America* (Washington, DC, 1996), 7.

19 Kenneth E. Carpenter, 'Libraries', in *The Industrial Book, 1840–1880*, ed. Scott E. Casper, Jeffrey D. Groves, Stephen W. Nissenbaum, and Michael Winship, Volume 3 of A History of the Book in America (Chapel Hill, 2007), 304. See also Wayne A. Wiegand, *Parts of Our Lives: A People's History of the American Public Library* (Oxford, 2015).

20 Carpenter, 'Libraries', as note 19, 309.

21 *Ticknor*, as note 14, II, 300–02; quoted by Carpenter, 'Libraries', as note 19, 309.

22 Carpenter, 'Libraries', as note 19, 311. Carpenter cites Carnegie's article 'The Best Fields for Philanthropy', *North American Review*, 149 (December 1949), 689–98

Even more influential than his persuasive powers in this article was Carnegie's decision to put his own considerable fortune behind this argument and to build literally thousands of libraries in the United States, and indeed around the world. Thus the major debate in nineteenth-century American library history is the shifting model of economic support for public libraries and the move from subscription or membership fees to Carnegie endowments and state support; the latter was not always a promising model for research libraries of international importance. Again Kenneth Carpenter has very astutely pointed out that:

> However much those in charge – members in membership libraries, trustees in public libraries – might wish to foster reading as a means of self-improvement, reading purely for pleasure was what a larger proportion of the population wanted[23].

With this ongoing debate as background let us turn to the slow rise of academic research libraries in the United States as the eventual homes of books and manuscripts sent into the market by the secularization of European religious houses.

In 1846 George Templeton Strong (1820–1875), then a young lawyer in New York, gives us a very candid idea of the contents of the new Yale University library, now known as Dwight Hall. In his diary he wrote that:

> [The new library] building [is] a preposterous caricature of King's College Chapel [in Cambridge]. Books badly chosen – ninety percent mere lumber; indeed except in modern Italian and French literature, in which it's rather strong, the collection is on the whole

rubbish – old Puritan divinity and the like. Herrick, the librarian, seems a good-natured sort of priggish little man[24].

Strong's own library was sold after his death in 1764 lots by Bangs & Co. in New York on 4 November 1878 (McKay 2429)[25] and contained 39 medieval manuscripts (including 15 Books of Hours) and 24 incunabula[26].

For the sake of comparison let us return to the Bostonian George Ticknor who in April 1822 wrote to a colleague:

> Cogswell is doing much good in the [Harvard College] library, reforming it utterly, and will, I am persuaded, when he is finished its systematic catalogue, and shown its gross deficiencies, persuade people to do something serious towards filling it up[27].

But Joseph Green Cogswell (1786–1871), who like both Everett and Ticknor had studied at

---

and George S. Bobinski, *Carnegie Libraries: The History and Impact on American Public Library Development* (Chicago, 1969).

23 Carpenter, 'Libraries', as note 19, 310.

24 George Templeton Strong, *The Diary of George Templeton Strong: Young Man in New York, 1835–1849*, ed. Allan Nevins and Milton Halsey Thomas (New York, 1952) 279; quoted by Carpenter, *Readers*, as note 18, 8.

25 George L. McKay, *American Book Auction Catalogues, 1713–1934: A Union List* (New York, 1937).

26 Strong's library is described in James Wynne, *Private Libraries of New York* (New York, 1860), 377–84. Two of Strong's incunabula have made their way to Harvard: Jacobus de Cessolis (ISTC ic00410000, Walsh 3847); Xenophon (ISTC ix00005000, Walsh 3088). His medieval manuscripts are now in the Library of Congress, the Walters Art Museum, John Hopkins University (2), the Free Library of Philadelphia, the University of Pennsylvania, Columbia University, the University of Rochester and the Pierpont Morgan Library & Museum. Seven of Strong's manuscripts were purchased by John Jacob Astor III (1822–1890); six are now in the New York Public Library and a seventh was lot no. 64 in the Astor sale at Sotheby's, London, 21 June 1988 and later was lot no. 22 in the Arcana Collection sale, III, at Christie's, London, 6 July 2011.

27 *Life of Joseph Green Cogswell as sketched in his letters* (Cambridge, Mass., 1874), 133.

Göttingen, himself wrote more modestly later that same year:

> The [Harvard College] library is now in fine order. It is arranged on the same plan with that at Göttingen, though, for want of books, the subdivisions are much fewer at present, and the Catalogues are made out in the same way, so that all possible future editions will require no alteration in any part of the system[28].

In 1846 Ticknor wrote to Dr Nikolaus Julius (1783–1862), in Hamburg, a physician who had spent two years in America ten years earlier:

> My collection of old Spanish books is doubled since you were here, and is now so large that I am anxious to make it complete as I can.

In 1849 Ticknor published his three-volume *History of Spanish Literature* and Dr Julius was to be one of its German translators, but Ticknor had ambitions for his library and went on to ask about opportunities for developing it further.

> What can I do for it in Germany? The only resource there, that I can think of, is the small bookcase that used to stand near the window in the venerable and admirable [Ludwig] Tieck's parlor [in Potsdam], where I have spent so many happy hours. Does he still preserve that little collection, and if he does preserve it, do you think he could be induced to part with it. ... Will you do me the favor, in some way or other that would be most agreeable to him, to approach him on this subject, and see if anything can be done in my behalf? I cannot but think that it would be worthy of him to permit a part of his library to be planted on this Western continent, where,

at some time or other, it will bear fruit, and where it will never cease to be remembered that it was once the property of the first man of his time in Germany. If it comes into my hands it will, I think, be kept together, and never leave the Western world[29].

Ticknor had other important contacts in building his library after his two grand tours, including Don Pascual de Gayangos (1809–1897), in Madrid, M. Hector Bossange (1795–1884), bookseller in Paris and Mr Obadiah Rich (1777–1850), an American diplomat in London[30]. Rich gave 5 incunables to Harvard between 1830 and 1845; the copy of Diogenes Laertius printed in Venice in 1475 (ISTC id00220000) and given by Rich in 1830 was singled out by the College Librarian as the oldest printed book in Harvard's library from its receipt for more than a decade[31].

Ticknor's outlook was beginning to be shared by others, such as the Boston book collector George Livermore (1809–1865), who argued in the *North American Review* in July 1850 that:

> "the nation was rich in the number of its libraries and that those libraries as a whole contained an impressive number of books." They were mostly the *same* books, however, and Livermore called on the nation and its libraries to increase and diversify their holdings. Libraries, he believed, "should contain all those works which are too costly, too voluminous, or of *too little value* in the common estimation, to be found elsewhere, down even to the

---

28 *Cogswell*, as note 27, 133–34.

29 *Ticknor*, as note 14, II, 250–51.
30 James Lyman Whitney, *Catalogue of the Spanish Library and of the Portuguese Books bequeathed by George Ticknor to the Boston Public Library* (Boston, 1879), x.
31 James Walsh, *A Catalogue of the Fifteenth-Century Printed Books in the Harvard University Library*, 5 vols (Binghamton, N.Y., 1991–1997), V, 4. The book (Walsh 1577) had previously belonged to the Jesuits at Mindelheim.

smallest tracts." Scholars need access to broad, detailed, and sometimes unpredictable forms of knowledge, because even an "old almanac or a forgotten pamphlet" might enable a scholar to verify or correct some important point which would otherwise have remained in dispute." …
In criticizing the state of American libraries as a whole, Livermore was writing not out of despair but out of a consciousness of new possibilities. The nationalist strain in his argument revealed a certain anxiety about the relationship of the United States to Europe. Americans "must have," he wrote, "a large national library, to which we can point men of other countries as the substantial evidence of interest in the promotion of literature and science." In this nationalistic rhetoric there was an expression of national pride, but also a recognition that the United States lagged behind Europe. Livermore understood that Americans wanted to see themselves as Europeans' equals and to be perceived as such. Libraries were a means to that end, not merely in literary culture and esoteric research. Library collections were also seen as vehicles for fostering an economically advanced, industrial civilization, with an infrastructure and institutions comparable to those of Europe[32].

Against this background I would like to focus more especially on fifteenth-century printed books as a way to observe changes in library collection development by North American libraries.

The 1723 catalogue of Harvard College library records at least 6 incunables, 3 of them commentaries on the *Sententiae* of Peter Lombard, probably not much consulted, and a copy of Hartmann Schedel's *Liber chronicarum* (ISTC is00307000), but they all perished in the fire

of 1764[33]. In response to a plea for assistance to rebuild the library one of its greatest donors, Thomas Hollis of Lincoln's Inn, responded by sending thousands of books, many specially decorated and inscribed to reflect his republican beliefs, including a copy of Cleonides *Harmonicum introductorium* (ISTC ic00742000)[34]. Allen Reddick has suggested that "Hollis's donations to Harvard represent what must be the largest gift of books to one destination during the eighteenth century; his efforts far exceed those of any other private individual"[35].

As early as 1729 Thomas Prince (1687–1758) of Boston owned a copy of Guido de Monte Rochen's *Manipulus curatorum* (ISTC ig00577000) now in the Boston Public Library. In 1746 Dr John Brett of Newport, Rhode Island presented to the town's library (now the Redwood Library and Athenaeum) a copy of the Bible in Latin printed in Venice in 1487/1488 (ISTC ib00586000). The 1760 catalogue of the library of James Logan (1674–1751) of Philadelphia records 4 incunabula, including Orosius's *Historiae adversus paganos* printed in Augsburg in 1471 (ISTC i000096000) bound with Plutarch's *Apophthegmata* printed in the same year in Venice (ISTC ip00816000), now in the Library Company of Philadelphia[36].

However well-intentioned these earliest efforts might seem to be, their effect is fairly random and sporadic. Paul Needham has suggested that distinctly different from these early examples is William Mackenzie (1758–1828) of Philadelphia whose incunabula would seem to reflect a tradition of collecting that originated with English connoisseurs of the early eighteenth century.

32 Carpenter, 'Libraries', as note 19, 312, quoting George Livermore, 'Public Libraries', *North American Review*, 71 (July 1850), 189.

33 Walsh, as note 31, 'Brief History of the Collection', V, 2–3.
34 Walsh, as note 31, 2529.
35 Allen Reddick, 'Introduction', in *"From the Great Desire of Promoting Learning": Thomas's Hollis's Gifts to Harvard College Library*, ed. William H. Bond (Cambridge, Mass., 2010), 11. On Hollis, see Bond's *Thomas Hollis of Lincoln's Inn: A Whig and his Books* (Cambridge, 1990).
36 Goff, as note 5, ix–x; Rosenthal, as note 5, A351.

Now in the Library Company of Philadelphia are Mackenzie's copy of Caxton's Golden Legend (ISTC ij00148000) and the Jenson Pliny of 1476 (ISTC ip00801000), Landino's long lost dedication copy to Ferrante, the Aragonese king of Naples[37].

Again, Needham provides a convenient summary:

By the 19th century incunabula were coming to America in three ways – as part of the possessions of emigrating families; as part of the tradition of collecting that originated with English connoisseurs in the early 18th century; and through the market that was a result of the secularization of monasteries in the 18th and 19th centuries[38].

In Needham's third category was the acquisition in 1838 by Union Theological Seminary of the library of Leander van Ess (1772–1847). The seminary had been founded two years earlier and the acquisition of what might be regarded by some as an old Catholic library by a new Protestant seminary reflects its ambition for a prominent educational role in civic, national and international arenas. The library of about 16,000 volumes cost just over $5,000 and "the purchase made Union's the largest or second largest American theological library at the outset of its existence"[39]. In his study and bibliographical analysis of the library Milton McC. Gatch has concluded that "most of the early books in the library of Leander van Ess came ultimately from monastic libraries, although it is clear in a number of cases that there were intermediate owners between the monasteries and van Ess"[40]. Major sources for the library included the Dominicans at Warburg in the diocese of Paderborn where van Ess received his early education and his own Benedictine community at Marienmünster, also in the diocese of Paderborn. The Benedictine monastery at Huysburg in the diocese of Halberstadt was the provenance of 50 books and manuscripts; the 36 incunabula and manuscripts from the Franciscan house at Halberstadt are likely to be the largest survival of that institution's medieval library.

Leander van Ess's library contained over four hundred incunabula. ... The former Marburg Professor had in 1824 sold about twice as many incunabula to Sir Thomas Phillipps. (Many of these are today in the Huntington Library in California.) Many (but not all) of the incunabula that were sold to the seminary in New York – at the moment of their purchase the largest collection of incunabula in America – had already been in his possession in 1824 and were probably retained by van Ess because he felt they would be useful in his research collection"[41].

37 Paul Needham, 'Incunabula in America', unpublished lecture delivered at the Library of Congress symposium on Incunabula in American Libraries, 1–2 April 1987. Highlights from Needham's lecture are reported in Rosenthal, as note 5, A351.

38 As summarized by William Matheson, 'Incunabula in American Libraries', *Library of Congress Information Bulletin*, 46.29 (20 July 1987), 319–25 at 321. Matheson reports on a symposium which took place on 1–2 April 1987 at the Library of Congress jointly sponsored by the Center for the Book and the Rare Book and Special Collections Division. This symposium was a response to a British Library Colloquium on 'Bibliography and the Study of XVth-Century Civilization: The Beginning of Printing and the ISTC Project' which took place on 26–28 September 1984. The papers from this colloquium, still well worth reading, were published as British Library Occasional Papers 5, edited by Lotte Hellinga and John Goldfinch, *Bibliography and the Study of XVth-Century Civilization* (London, 1987).

39 *"So Precious a Foundation": The Library of Leander van Ess at the Burke Library of Union Theological Seminary in the City of New York / "Welch kostbarer Grundstock": Die Bibliothek von Leander van Ess in der Burke Library des Union Theological Seminary in New York*, ed. Milton McC. Gatch (New York, 1996), 16.

40 Gatch, as note 39, 187.

41 Gatch, as note 39, 161.

In 1836 the Library of Congress was attempting to buy the library of the late Count Dimitri Buturlin (1763–1829) which contained 25,000 printed volumes and included 979 incunabula with special strengths in Greek and Latin classics. Peter M. Van Wingen recounts how politics interfered and prevented the acquisition. As a result, the December 1839 *Catalogue of the Library of Congress in the Capitol of the United States of America* included only two incunabula: the Mainz 1492 *Chronecken der Sassen* (ISTC ic00488000) and Wynkyn de Worde's 1495 edition of Higden's *Polycronicon* (ISTC ih00268000)[42]. But in 1867 the Library was able to purchase for $100,000 the 22,500-volume library of the politician and early American historian, Peter Force (1790–1868). Force's library was rich in primary documents of American history, but in the *Special Report of the Librarian of Congress to the Joint Committee on the Library Concerning the Historical Library of Peter Force, Esq.*, the recently appointed Librarian of Congress, Ainsworth Rand Spofford, commented especially on a group of books illustrating "the progress of the art of printing from its infancy"[43]. Included in the Force library were copies of the Mainz 1467 *Constitutiones* of Pope Clement V (ISTC ic00711000), Hartmann Schedel's *Liber chronicarum* (ISTC is00307000) and the Jenson Pliny of 1472 (ISTC ip00788000).

In 1844 the previously mentioned George Livermore gave the Library of Harvard College a copy of the 1469 edition of Jerome's letters (ISTC ih00162000). He was given an honorary degree in 1850 and in 1859 his library, which included at least 7 incunable Bibles, was placed on deposit at Harvard. The books remained and were included in the Harvard Library catalogue for thirty-five years until the death of Livermore's

widow, when the books were withdrawn by his son and sent to auction in Boston at Libbie's on 20 November 1894 (McKay 4336)[44].

Perhaps the first auction in the United Sates to include incunables was that of Alexander Augustus Smets (1795–1862) of Savannah, Georgia. His library was dispersed in two sales in New York conducted by George Leavitt on 1 March 1868 (McKay 1312) and 25 May 1868 (McKay 1349)[45].

Leavitt was also the auctioneer of two collections of incunables and manuscripts imported from Europe for sale. On 27 November 1886 *Medieval Manuscripts from the Trivulzio Collection* were auctioned in New York (McKay 3393) and on 6 February 1888 *Incunabulic Treasures from the Trivulzio Collection* (McKay 3551)[46].

Stanford University began its collection of incunabula in 1895 with the acquisition of the library of Leipzig philologist Rudolf Hildebrand (1824–1894). Hildebrand's more than 5600 books included 14 incunabula[47].

Scholarly developments on the European continent and in England, especially the work of Henry Bradshaw (1831–1886), began to have an enduring impact in America[48]. Bradshaw's *A*

---

42   Peter M. Van Wingen, 'The Incunabula Collections at the Library of Congress', *Rare Book and Manuscript Librarianship*, 4.2 (1989), 85–100 at 85–86.

43   *Special Report* (1867), 6; quoted by Van Wingen, as note 42, 87.

44   Walsh, as note 31, V, 5.

45   A third sale of autographs took place on 1 July 1868 (McKay, as note 25, 1350). Smets is included in the groundbreaking study by Scott Gwara, *Medieval and Renaissance Manuscripts in the American South, 1798–1868* (Cayce, SC, 2016).

46   My 'Medieval Nuggets from the Trivulzio Library of Milan: An Overlooked Chapter in the History of American Book Collecting' was delivered as a lecture at the Grolier Club on 2 April 2014 and is in the course of preparation for publication.

47   Susan V. Lenkey, *Stanford Incunabula 1975* (Stanford, 1975), 2–3.

48   In addition to Bradshaw's *Collected Papers* (Cambridge, 1889) and George Walter Prothero's *A Memoir of Henry Bradshaw* (Cambridge, 1888), see also Paul Needham, *The Bradshaw Method: Henry Bradshaw's Contribution to Bibliography*, Seventh Hanes Lecture (Chapel Hill, 1988) and Richard Beadle, *Henry Bradshaw and the Foundations of Codicology*, Sandars Lectures 2015 (Cambridge, 2017). Additional context is provided by John Claud

Classified Index of the Fifteenth Century Books in the De Meyer Collection Sold at Ghent, November 1869, Memorandum No. 2 (London, 1870)[49] was dedicated to Jan Willem Holtrop (1806–1870), the author of *Monuments typographiques des Pays-Bas au quinzième siècles* (La Haye, issued in parts 1857–1868) and who had died earlier that year. Bradshaw's classified index to the Culemann Library sale of February 1870 was never published, but his Memorandum No. 3, *List of Founts of Type and Woodcut Devices used by Printers in Holland in the Fifteenth Century*, Memorandum No. 3 (London, 1871)[50], was based on Holtrop's work. G. W. Prothero has observed that:

> To some readers it may appear that the making of these classified lists, to which Bradshaw devoted so much of his time, is a mere matter of arrangement, a work which any clerk would be capable of doing. But this is far from being the case. Not to mention the invention of a system of classification, which substitutes order for disorder, and elevates into the rank of a science what would otherwise be a mass of disconnected facts, the making of such lists involves making not only a wide knowledge of typographical history, and a minute acquaintance with the habits and characteristics of different printers, but the power of putting facts together and making correct deductions from them. Such lists are necessarily the materials out of which any general history of typography must be built[51].

Rush C. Hawkins (1831–1920) was the first in America to recognize the importance of Bradshaw's work. Hawkins' *Titles of the First Books from the Earliest Presses established in different Cities, Towns and Monasteries in Europe before the End of the Fifteenth Century, with Brief Notes Upon their Printers, Illustrated with Reproductions of Early Types and First Engravings of the Printing Press* (New York, 1884) does not mention Bradshaw specifically in his "Introduction." Hawkins' study has its origins in the Coster controversy and Bradshaw is named three times in the body of the work which includes 236 towns and the first known work printed in each. Hawkins modestly claims that:

> This list, which is intended for the use of those who are interested in the early history of the art of printing, has been compiled chiefly from the researches of others. In no sense is any claim laid to originality, save in its convenient chronological arrangement. Neither is there any pretense that this work is exhaustive or correct. The compiler has contented himself with an effort to bring together and record such statements as seemed to him to have some foundation in facts"[52].

But Hawkins' work also deserves to be recognized as the model it soon became. Recently Richard Beadle has argued that:

> E. Gordon Duff and Robert Proctor – quietly appropriated Bradshaw's innovatory method of classifying incunabula according to a hierarchical and chronological arrangement, descending from the country in which they were printed,

Trewinard Oates, 'A Brief History of the Collection', in his *A Catalogue of the Fifteenth-century Printed Books in the University Library Cambridge* (Cambridge, 1954), especially 28–33, and David J. McKitterick, *Cambridge University Library: A History: The Eighteenth and Nineteenth Centuries* (Cambridge 1986).

49 Reprinted in his *Collected Papers*, as note 48, 206–36.
50 Reprinted in his *Collected Papers*, as note 48, 258–80.
51 Prothero, *Memoir*, as note 48, 201. These rearrangement of sale catalogues lot to reflect the progress of printing have a long tradition. The latest known to me is Francis

Jenkinson, *A List of the Incunabula collected by George Dunn, arranged to illustrate the History of Printing* (Oxford, 1923), published by the Bibliographical Society. Dunn died in 1912 and the sales of his library took place in 1913, 1914, 1915 and 1917.
52 Hawkins, xi.

to the town, to the printer or press concerned, and so on, down to editions, variant imprints of the same edition, and to specific copies with different features. Such a classification went on to be almost universally adopted, and is sometimes referred to as "Proctor Order", after Robert Proctor's *Index of Early Printed Book in the British Museum* (1898–1903). Ultimately, however, it might with more justice be recognised as another of Bradshaw's Methods, since it appears fully fledged in his Memorandum no. 2 of April 1870[53].

Proctor identified over 238 places where printing had been practiced and about 1080 distinct presses[54]. Proctor order very quickly became a benchmark by which to evaluate a collection; and booksellers and book collectors quickly began to use it.

In 1899, through the generosity of P. A. B. Widener (1834–1915) the Free Library of Philadelphia acquired 500 incunabula collected by Walter Arthur Copinger (1847–1910), founder and first president of The Bibliographical Society of London and author of two Supplements[55] to Ludwig Hain's *Repertorium Bibliographicum*[56]. The collection had been described the year before in Copinger's privately printed *Handlist of a Collection of Incunabula Illustrating the Progress and Development of the Art of Printing prior to the Year 1500 by Specimens from over Three Hundred different Presses*.

In 1906 Henry Walters (1848–1931) acquired 1100 incunabula from the Florentine bookseller Leo S. Olschki. In the introduction to the catalogue of the collection prepared by Olschki, Walters wrote, clearly with some pride, that "more than three hundred distinct typographical workshops are represented in this collection …" and concluded:

It is a synthesis of book making in the second half of the XVth century which will aid the student or the curious to follow step by step the early development of the art of printing. We should be indeed pleased to think that, when some day, some one will undertake the final enumeration, which Mlle. Pellechet called "The Golden Book of the Printers of the XVth Century" not only would France, Germany, Italy and England be called upon to contribute editions, but that America also might be in possession of at least one missing abroad, and thus contribute its mite of information[57].

Then John Boyd Thacher (1847–1909) bequeathed his collection of incunabula to the Library of Congress. There are 840 entries in the catalogue and the compiler, Frederick W. Ashley, quotes a telling passage written by Thacher.

I bought at Libbie & Co.'s, Boston, and paid for it, June 3, 1899, a Benedicti Regula printed by Geoffrey Marnef, Paris, September 7, 1500. This book completed my 500 presses of the fifteenth century. I take it as a good augury that the first book of my incunabula and the one to round out my five hundredth press should have been found in America. It is seldom my collection finds specimens of incunabula already brough to America.

Ten years ago it did not seem possible that I should get from one to ten examples of 500 hundred presses of the fifteenth century. No other private collection has so great a number of separate presses[58].

---

53 Beadle, as note 48, 11.
54 Van Wingen, as note 42, 88.
55 Part I (London, 1895); Part II (London, 1902).
56 2 vols (Stuttgart and Paris, 1826–1838).

57 *Incunabula Typographica: A Descriptive Catalogue of Books Printed in the Fifteenth Century (1460–1500) in the Library of Henry Walters* (Baltimore, 1906), vi–vii.
58 Frederick W. Ashley, *Catalogue of the John Boyd Thacher Collection of Incunabula, Library of Congress* (Washington, DC, 1915), 12.

And a year later appeared the catalogue of the 542 incunabula in the collection of Rush C. Hawkins which had been compiled by Alfred W. Pollard and which had been deposited in the Annmary Brown Memorial in Providence, Rhode Island. Again, the title *Catalogue of Books Mostly from the Presses of the First Printers showing the Progress of Printing with Movable Metal Types through the Second Half of the Fifteenth Century* clearly states the reason behind the collection[59].

The progress of printing across Europe and the spread of culture are explicitly linked in the 1940 Morgan Library exhibition *The Fifteenth-Century Book* which was mounted as *An Exhibition Arranged for the 500th Anniversary of the Invention of Printing*. Well aware that as he spoke World War II engulfed Europe, Lawrence C. Wroth's delivered "Printing and the Rise of Modern Culture in the Fifteenth Century" at the preview of the exhibition on January 16th, 1940.

These are some of the reflections that arise when one examines his reasons for celebrating the invention of printing. Fascinating as the study of the mechanics of a craft may be, beautiful and moving as are many of the early products of this particular craft, it is not chiefly for these considerations that the world, or such parts of it as are at peace, devotes this year its time and treasure to memorializing the great printers of the early days. It is because, in the minds of many, the activities of these men gave record and amplification to the ideas and teachings and imaginings upon which is built the cultural life of today[60].

It is worth observing that this tradition of arranging incunables to reflect the spread of printing through Europe has continued and includes:

Pierce Butler, *A Check List of Fifteenth Century Books in the Newberry Library and in other libraries of Chicago* (Chicago, 1933);

Herman Ralph Mead, *Incunabula in the Huntington Library* (San Marino, 1937);

Ada Thurston and Kurt F. Bühler, *Check List of Fifteenth Century Printing in the Pierpont Morgan Library* (New York, 1939);

Olan V. Cook, *Incunabula in the Hanes Collection of the Library of the University of North Carolina* (Chapel Hill, 1940, 2nd edition, 1960);

C. U. Faye, *Fifteenth Century Books at the University of Illinois* (Urbana, 1949);

and most recently, James E. Walsh, *A Catalogue of the Fifteenth-Century Printed Books in the Harvard University Library*, 5 vols (1991–1997).

Likewise, important American collections of incunables have been arranged for sale at auction to reflect the spread of printing. The incunable collections of Estelle Doheny (1875–1958) sold at Christie's, New York, on 22 October 1987 (136 lots) and Ned J. Nakles (1931–1999) sold at Christie's, New York on 17 April 2000 (181 lots) were arranged in Proctor order. The collection of Eric Sexton (1902–1980) sold at Christie's, New York, on 8 April 1981, where 194 lots from 114 different printing places were arranged alphabetically by place of printing: Albi-Zwolle and chronologically within each town.

Dealers clearly recognized this interest and a market for potential customers. The New York booksellers H. P. Kraus published three special *Incunabula* catalogues arranged in Proctor order and with the same cover design of embossed

---

59 It is worth noting that there was an earlier sale of some of Hawkins books, including medieval manuscripts and incunables at Leavitt, New York on 21 March 1887 (McKay, as note 25, 3437) and another at Merwin-Clayton, New York, 14 February 1906 (McKay, as note 25, 6067).

60 Lawrence C. Wroth, 'Printing and the Rise of Modern Culture in the Fifteenth Century. An Address delivered at the Preview of the Exhibition, January 16th, 1940', in

---

The Fifteenth-Century Book: An Exhibition arranged for the 500th Anniversary of the Invention of Printing (New York, 1940), 33–18 at 18.

printers' marks: Catalogue 173 (May 1986) had 141 nos.; Catalogue 182 (September 1989) had 126 nos.; and Catalogue 209 (November 1998) had 138 nos.

Given these developments it is worth remembering that as early as 1915 in describing the saturated international market for incunables, Seymour de Ricci commented: "Vers 1890 ... la situation semblait sans issue, quand l'arrivée d'un élément nouveau vint sauver la mise et render aux incunables un prospérité qu'ils n'avaient jamais encore connue. Ce sauveur, ce facteur nouveau, c'était le dollar"[61].

De Ricci observes with considerable clarity the European dealers that American collectors use, their tendency to buy in large batches, and concludes with some sadness: "pour se former une grosse collection d'incunables, on n'eut plus qu'à signer des chèques." Perhaps not surprisingly he uses Pierpont Morgan as his prime example:

Comme ailleurs, les incursions de Morgan sur la terrain de la Bibliophilie coûtèrent forte cher à ses rivaux; pendant quelques années, il fut impossible d'acheter un livre de xvᵉ siècle sans le payer à ces tarifs que les Italiens ont justement appelés *prezzi americani*[62].

A slightly more nuanced appreciation, that America did not come immediately and completely to dominate the market, is apparent in an unpublished paper by Felix de Marez Oyens. Oyens examined in depth the two-part catalogue, *Incunabula typographica* (1900 and 1905) of the Munich bookseller, Jacques Rosenthal which included 2962 books. Based on the firm's marked copies he has demonstrated that only 99 were sold to America. And almost half of those (49) went to Herman Charles Hoskier (1864–1938) of

South Orange, New Jersey; he had ordered 59[63]. In comparison the Royal Library in Copenhagen ordered 86 books and the British Museum received 260 books having ordered even more[64].

In November 1924 the German industrialist Otto Vollbehr (1869–1946) sold Henry Huntington (1850–1927) 392 incunables, chiefly Spanish and Portuguese imprints, for $170,000. In March 1925 Huntington paid Vollbehr $770,000 for another 1,740 incunables. In February 1925 he bought a third batch bringing the total number of his incunable acquisitions from Vollbehr to 2,385. Vollbehr's stated aim, as he explained it to Huntington, was to

Make the collection of incunabula in the Huntington Library as important, if possible more important and more numerous than those contained in any of the World's Great Libraries. With your cooperation, it would be my ambition to make your collection of incunabula more important and more numerous even than that of the British Museum[65].

As incredible as this may seem now this must certainly have held some appeal for a man who was using his retirement to build a name for himself as a public philanthropist and a research library for his country that he hoped would rival or surpass its European counterparts. In March 1926 Vollbehr offered a further 1,333 incunables for $640,000, including a special thirty

61 Seymour de Ricci, 'Catalogues et Collections d'Incunables', in *Revue Archéologique*, 5e série, t. 1 (Janvier-Avril 1915), 283–302 at 294.
62 de Ricci, as note 61, 295.

63 Hoskier's collection deserves to be better known. His sale of 339 incunables took place a short time later at Sotheby's, London, on 29 June 1908.
64 Felix de Marez Oyens, 'History of the Incunabula Trade, including an Analysis of Jacques Rosenthal's *Incunabula Typographica*', unpublished lecture delivered at the Library of Congress symposium on Incunabula in American Libraries, 1–2 April 1987. Highlights from Oyens' lecture are reported in Matheson, as note 38, 323 and Rosenthal, as note 5, A355-A356.
65 Donald C. Dickinson, *Henry E. Huntington's Library of Libraries* (San Marino, 1995), 208.

percent discount, but Huntington declined. In June 1926 Vollbehr wrote to Leslie Edgar Bliss (1889–1977), Huntington's librarian who had taken a larger role in acquisitions in Huntington's declining health, announcing he had acquired a copy of "the dearest book in the world." This was the three volumes of the Gutenberg Bible which had belonged to the Benedictines of St Blasien since the fifteenth century and (as Needham has pointed out) actually belonged still to their successors, the monks of St Paul in Carinthia. Vollbehr continued: "But I make you no offer. In the first place you have treated me badly and secondly you flatly refused my last offer." Vollbehr then suggested that there had been a "change of feeling" toward him at the Huntington library and accused Bliss of listening to innuendos from "envious souls and meddlers"[66].

In 1930 Vollbehr was eventually successful in selling the Bible and an additional 3000 incunables to the Library of Congress; as it had in the 1887 acquisition of the Force library the purchase was approved by Congress, but this time for $1,500,000 and made by a special appropriation unanimously approved by Congress. Earlier Vollbehr had auctioned material at the Anderson Galleries in New York on 9 February 1928 (McKay 9085) and 24 April 1928 (McKay 9112); rumors about his financial dealings were growing and his business became questionable and he fled back to Germany under suspicion[67].

The last of his offerings were eventually sold in a sale at Gimbel Brothers' department store in New York in an attempt by one of his creditors to recoup his losses. The introduction to the catalogue assert that "many of these volumes are the only known copies in existence, while a great many others may be found in only a few

of the great libraries of this country, such as the Library of Congress, the Huntington Library and the J. P. Morgan Library"[68]. This seems to be hyperbole; many might be described as the only known copies in existence in America; they are accurately described as "the only copy in America according to the 1940 census." The reference is to Margaret Bingham Stillwell's *Incunabula in American Libraries: A Second Census of Fifteenth-Century Printed Books owned in the United States Mexico and Canada* (New York, 1940). Many are still the only known copy in America. No. 279 in the Gimbel's catalogue, a copy of Johannes Herolt's *Sermones de tempore et de sanctis* printed Cologne in 1492 (Stillwell H-108, ISTC ih00118000) is now at the University of California, Berkeley; no. 280 Theodoricus de Herxen, *Devota exercitia passionis* printed in Deventer also in 1492 (Stillwell H-123, ISTC it00146450) is now at Bryn Mawr College. By far the largest group (over 100) appears to have been strategically purchased by the University of Illinois on 3 July 1942 beginning with No. 4, Albertanus Causidicus Brixiensis (Stillwell A-186, ISTC ia00203000), now no. 10 in Marian Harman, *Incunabula in the University of Illinois Library at Urbana-Champaign* (Urbana, 1979). It is interesting to note that Harman had changed completely the orientation of the catalogue of her predecessor; as noticed earlier Faye's catalogue of 1949 is in Proctor order; Harman's 30 years later is now organized alphabetically by author[69].

In many ways American businessmen, like Huntington and Morgan, who have made a lot of money, can be seen as trying to purchase respectability through the manuscripts and books

---

66 Dickinson, *Huntington's Library of Libraries*, as note 65, 207–10.

67 Further private sales and public auctions of Vollbehr books occurred in 1939 and 1940. See Van Wingen, as note 42, 94.

68 *An Important Collection of Incunabula, 1476–1500, presented by Gimbel Brothers … under the Direction of the Hammer Galleries* (New York, 1941), 4.

69 The collection continues to grow; see Christopher D. Cook, *Supplement to Harman's Incunabula at the University of Illinois at Urbana-Champaign* (Urbana, 2005).

they acquire and the libraries they found. They gravitate towards big names that they hope reflect their own power. Royal and noble individuals hold considerably more appeal than monastic institutions; the hierarchy of the church holds more appeal than monastic provenance, and the higher up in that hierarchy and the more well known the better.

As a result of this environment in nineteenth- and twentieth-century North America, which I have sketched very briefly and attempted to illustrate with pertinent examples, manuscripts and early printed books that have migrated to North America from European religious houses are comparatively well catalogued in modern research libraries and their provenance can be retrieved. The challenge is that they are now widely dispersed with no necessarily obvious location and the return on time spent in specific provenance research is fairly low. Manuscripts and early printed books, released as a result of the secularization of European religious houses and now housed in North American collections, have arrived comparatively recently, acquired as examples of a perceived common western culture, and in an attempt by their new owners to be seen as effective participants in an international cultural arena. They really can seem as if they were gathered from long ago and far away.

Bibliography

Primary Sources

Albertanus Causidicus Brixiensis, *De arte loquendi et tacendi*, Leipzig: [Conrad Kachelofen, for] J.N.?, 25 May 1490. 4°. GW 550; ISTC ia00203000.

Augustinus, Aurelius, *Opuscula*, Venice: Dionysius Bertochus, 26 Mar. 1491. 4°. GW 2866; ISTC ia01219000.

Augustinus, Aurelius, *Opuscula*, Venice: Peregrinus de Pasqualibus, Bononiensis, 10 Nov. 1491. 4°. GW 2869; ISTC ia01222000.

Biblia latina, Venice: Franciscus Renner, de Heilbronn and Nicolaus de Frankfordia, 1476. Folio. GW 4223; ISTC ib00548000.

Biblia latina (cum postillis Nicolai de Lyra) etc., [Lyon]: Johannes Siber, [after 7 May 1485, about 1488]. Folio. GW 4290; ISTC ib00615000.

Biblia Latina, Venice: Georgius Arrivabenus, 27 Feb. 1487/88. 4°. GW 4263; ISTC ib00586000.

Cassianus, Johannes, *De institutis coenobiorum*, Basel: [Johann Amerbach, after 24 Sept.] 1485. Folio. GW 6160; ISTC ic00233000.

Chronecken der Sassen [Low German], Mainz: Peter Schoeffer, 6 Mar. 1492. Folio. GW 4963; ISTC ic00488000.

Clemens V, *Constitutiones*, Mainz: Peter Schoeffer, 8 Oct. 1467. Folio. GW 7078; ISTC ic00711000.

Cleonides, *Harmonicum introductorium*, etc. Venice: Simon Bevilaqua, 3 Aug. 1497. Folio. GW 7123; ISTC ic00742000.

Diogenes Laertius, *Vitae et sententiae philosophorum*, etc. Venice: Nicolaus Jenson, 14 Aug. 1475. Folio. GW 8379; ISTC id00220000.

Duns Scotus, Johannes, *Quaestiones in quattuor libros Sententiarum Petri Lombardi*. Ed: Thomas Penketh and Bartholomaeus Bellatus, Venice: Johannes Herbort, de Seligenstadt, for Johannes de Colonia, Nicolaus Jenson et Socii, 1481. 4°. GW 9075; ISTC id00381000.

Herolt, Johannes, *Sermones discipuli de tempore et de sanctis*, Cologne: [Heinrich Quentell], 1492. 4°. GW 12372; ISTC ih00118000.

Hieronymus, *Epistolae*, [Strasbourg: Johann Mentelin, not after 1469]. Folio. GW 12422; ISTC ih00162000.

Higden, Ranulphus, *Polycronicon*, Westminster: Wynkyn de Worde, 13 Apr. 1495. Folio. GW 12469; ISTC ih00268000.

Jacobus de Cessolis, *De ludo scachorum*, [Toulouse: Henricus Mayer, about 1494]. 4°. GW 6526; ISTC ic00410000.

Jacobus de Voragine, *Legenda aurea sanctorum, sive Lombardica historia* [English] *The Golden Legend*. Tr.: William Caxton, Westminster: William Caxton, [between 20 Nov. 1483 and Mar. 1484]. Folio. ISTC ij00148000.

Orosius, Paulus, *Historiae adversus paganos*, Augsburg: Johann Schüssler, [about 7 June] 1471. Folio. ISTC io00096000.

Plinius Secundus, Gaius, *Historia naturalis*, Venice: Nicolaus Jenson, 1472. Folio. ISTC ip00788000.

Plinius Secundus, Gaius, *Historia naturalis* [Italian]. Tr: Christophorus Landinus, Venice: Nicolaus Jenson, 1476. Folio. ISTC ip00801000.

Plutarchus, *Apophthegmata*, [Venice]: Vindelinus de Spira, 1471. 4°. ISTC ip00816000.

Schedel, Hartmann, *Liber chronicarum*, Nuremberg: Anton Koberger, for Sebald Schreyer and Sebastian Kammermeister, 12 July 1493. Folio. ISTC is00307000.

Theodoricus de Herxen, *Devota exercitia passionis*, [Deventer: Jacobus de Breda], 2 May 1492. 8°. ISTC it00146450.

Xenophon, *Cyropaedia*, [Milan: Simon Magniagus, before 18 Feb. 1477]. 4°. ISTC ix00005000.

Secondary Works

An Important Collection of Incunabula, 1476–1500, presented by Gimbel Brothers … under the Direction of the Hammer Galleries (New York, 1941).

Frederick W. Ashley, *Catalogue of the John Boyd Thacher Collection of Incunabula, Library of Congress* (Washington, DC, 1915).

Richard Beadle, *Henry Bradshaw and the Foundations of Codicology*, Sandars Lectures 2015 (Cambridge, 2017).

Bibliography and the Study of XVth-Century Civilization, ed. Lotte Hellinga and John Goldfinch, British Library Occasional Papers 5 (London, 1987).

George S. Bobinski, *Carnegie Libraries: The History and Impact on American Public Library Development* (Chicago, 1969).

William H. Bond, *Thomas Hollis of Lincoln's Inn: A Whig and his Books* (Cambridge, 1990).

Henry Bradshaw, *Collected Papers* (Cambridge, 1889).

Andrew Carnegie, 'The Best Fields for Philanthropy', *North American Review*, 149 (December 1949), 689–98.

Kenneth E. Carpenter, *Readers & Libraries: Toward a History of Libraries and Culture in America* (Washington, DC, 1996).

Kenneth E. Carpenter, 'Libraries', in *The Industrial Book, 1840–1880*, ed. Scott E. Casper, Jeffrey D. Groves, Stephen W. Nissenbaum, and Michael Winship, Volume 3 of A History of the Book in America (Chapel Hill, 2007), 303–18.

Elvia Carreño Velázquez, *Catálogo de incunables* (México, 2000).

Christopher D. Cook, *Supplement to Harman's Incunabula at the University of Illinois at Urbana-Champaign* (Urbana, 2005).

Walter Arthur Copinger, Supplement to Hain's *Repertorium Bibliographicum*, part I (London, 1895); part II (London, 1902).

Phyllis Dain, 'The Great Libraries', in *Print in Motion: The Expansion of Publishing and Reading in the United States, 1880–1940*, ed. Carl F. Kaestle and Janice Radway, Volume 4 of A History of the Book in America (Chapel Hill, 2009), 452–70.

Russ Davidson, 'Adolph Sutro as Book Collector: A New Look', *California State Library Bulletin*, 75 (2003), 2–27.

Felix de Marez Oyens, 'History of the Incunabula Trade, including an Analysis of Jacques Rosenthal's *Incunabula Typographica*', unpublished lecture delivered at the Library of Congress symposium on Incunabula in American Libraries, 1–2 April 1987.

Seymour de Ricci, 'Catalogues et Collections d'Incunables', in *Revue Archéologique*, 5e série, t. 1 (Janvier-Avril 1915), 283–302.

Donald C. Dickinson, *Dictionary of American Book Collectors* (New York, 1986).

Donald C. Dickinson, *Henry E. Huntington's Library of Libraries* (San Marino, 1995).

Jeffrey Garrett, 'Whispers between Books: The Collections of Deering Library', in *Deering Library: An Illustrated History* (Evanston, 2008), 3–11.

Frederick R. Goff, *Incunabula in American Libraries: A Third Census of Fifteenth-Century Books Recorded in North American Collections*, rev. ed. (Millwood, NY, 1973).

Frederick R. Goff, 'Interim Census Report on the Collecting of Incunabula by American Libraries', *Gutenberg Jahrbuch*, 51 (1976), 162–64.

Scott Gwara, *Medieval and Renaissance Manuscripts in the American South, 1798–1868* (Cayce, SC, 2016).

Ludwig Hain, *Repertorium Bibliographicum*, 2 vols (Stuttgart and Paris, 1826–1838).

Thomas Hamilton, *Men and Manners in New York* (London, 1833; rptd. New York, 1968).

Incunabula Typographica: A Descriptive Catalogue of Books Printed in the Fifteenth Century (1460–1500) in the Library of Henry Walters (Baltimore, 1906).

Francis Jenkinson, *A List of the Incunabula collected by George Dunn, arranged to illustrate the History of Printing* (Oxford, 1923).

Susan V. Lenkey, *Stanford Incunabula 1975* (Stanford, 1975).

Life, Letters, and Journals of George Ticknor, ed. George S. Hillard (Boston, 1876).

Life of Joseph Green Cogswell as sketched in his letters (Cambridge, Mass., 1874).

George Livermore, 'Public Libraries', *North American Review*, 71 (July 1850), no. 148, 185–220.

Michael W. Mathes, 'Adolph Sutro's Incunabula from Mexico: A Study in Provenance', *Book Club of California Quarterly Newsletter*, 46.4 (1981), 103–05.

William Matheson, 'Incunabula in American Libraries', *Library of Congress Information Bulletin*, 46.29 (20 July 1987), 319–25.

George L. McKay, *American Book Auction Catalogues, 1713–1934: A Union List* (New York, 1937).

David J. McKitterick, *Cambridge University Library: A History: The Eighteenth and Nineteenth Centuries* (Cambridge 1986).

Paul Needham, 'Incunabula in America', unpublished lecture delivered at the Library of Congress symposium on Incunabula in American Libraries, 1–2 April 1987. Highlights from Needham's lecture are reported in Rosenthal (A351).

Paul Needham, *The Bradshaw Method: Henry Bradshaw's Contribution to Bibliography*, Seventh Hanes Lecture (Chapel Hill, 1988).

Paul Needham, 'The Late Use of Incunables and the Paths of Book Survival', *Wolfenbütteler Notizen zur Buchgeschichte*, 29 (2004), 35–59.

Paul Needham, 'Four Incunables brought to the Massachusetts Bay Colony', in *Lux Librorum: Essays on Books and History for Chris Coppens*, edited by Goran Proot, David McKitterick, Angela Nuovo and Paul F. Gehl (Mechelen, 2018), 141–64.

Christina M. Nielson, *Devotional & Splendor: Medieval Art at the Art Institute of Chicago* (Chicago, 2004).

John Claud Trewinard Oates, 'A Brief History of the Collection', in *A Catalogue of the Fifteenth-century Printed Books in the University Library Cambridge* (Cambridge, 1954).

George Walter Prothero, *A Memoir of Henry Bradshaw* (Cambridge, 1888).

Allen Reddick, 'Introduction', in *"From the Great Desire of Promoting Learning": Thomas's Hollis's Gifts to Harvard College Library*, ed. William H. Bond (Cambridge, Mass., 2010), 1–31.

Bernard Rosenthal, 'The History of Incunabula Collections in the United States: A Brief Account', *Aus dem Antiquariat* (2000), no. 6, A350-A366; issued as part of *Börsenblatt für den Deutschen Buchhandel* (30 June 2000), A350.

"So Precious a Foundation": The Library of Leander van Ess at the Burke Library of Union Theological Seminary in the City of New York / "Welch kostbarer Grundstock": Die Bibliothek von Leander van Ess in der Burke Library des Union Theological Seminary in New York, ed. Milton McC. Gatch (New York, 1996).

William Stoneman, 'Medieval Nuggets from the Trivulzio Library of Milan: An Overlooked Chapter in the History of American Book Collecting' was delivered as a lecture at the Grolier Club on 2 April 2014 and is in the course of preparation for publication.

George Templeton Strong, *The Diary of George Templeton Strong: Young Man in New York, 1835–1849*, ed. Allan Nevins and Milton Halsey Thomas (New York, 1952).

Isaiah Thomas, *The History of Printing in America with a biography of printers, and an account of newspapers, to which is prefixed a concise view of the discovery and process of the art in other parts of the world*, 2 vols (Worcester, Massachusetts, 1810).

Peter M. Van Wingen, 'The Incunabula Collections at the Library of Congress', *Rare Book and Manuscript Librarianship*, 4.2 (1989), 85–100.

James Walsh, *A Catalogue of the Fifteenth-Century Printed Books in the Harvard University Library*, 5 vols (Binghamton, N.Y., 1991–1997).

James Lyman Whitney, *Catalogue of the Spanish Library and of the Portuguese Books bequeathed by George Ticknor to the Boston Public Library* (Boston, 1879).

Wayne A. Wiegand, *Parts of Our Lives: A People's History of the American Public Library* (Oxford, 2015).

Lawrence C. Wroth, 'Printing and the Rise of Modern Culture in the Fifteenth Century. An Address delivered at the Preview of the Exhibition, January 16th, 1940', in *The Fifteenth-Century Book: An Exhibition arranged for the 500th Anniversary of the Invention of Printing* (New York, 1940), 33–18.

James Wynne, *Private Libraries of New York* (New York, 1860).

Jesús Yhmoff Cabrera, *Catálogo de incunables de la Biblioteca Nacional de México* (México, 1968; 2. ed. corr. y aum., 1987).

PART 6

Destruction of Books, Spoils of War, and Clandestine Exportation

▼ THE DIFFERENT WAYS IN WHICH MONASTIC LIBRARIES
WERE BROKEN UP: THE CLANDESTINE REMOVAL OF BOOKS
FROM THE MONASTIC LIBRARY, THE CONFISCATION OF
THE LIBRARY FOR PRIVATE USES, OR ITS DESTRUCTION

TUOMAS HEIKKILÄ

The Fate of Medieval Religious Book Collections in the Swedish Realm during the Reformation

The great majority of medieval religious houses in Sweden and its dependent territories were dissolved during the Reformation of the sixteenth century. Along with the other goods belonging to these institutions their books became the property of the state, but there was no plan to put them to use as books. A large part of the parchment books of ecclesiastical libraries were torn apart and used as single *bifolia* to cover the account books of the newly-established bailiwicks. This has led many Nordic scholars to label the sixteenth century as an era of sheer vandalism from the point of view of books and library history.

Yet the destruction of medieval Catholic book culture was not as total as has been argued. As the cataloguing of the existing remains of medieval material has progressed, we can now ascertain that Swedish and Finnish archives and libraries still house the remains of more than 14,000 medieval manuscripts, incunabula, and other early printed books, mostly as parchment fragments, with whole books forming only a very small part of the surviving material[1].

This article aims to frame an overview of the fate of medieval libraries in Sweden – i.e. within the geographic area consisting of parts of modern-day Sweden and Finland – during the Reformation and to draw conclusions concerning the impact of the dissolution of religious houses on our knowledge of written culture in medieval Sweden. It further argues that the reasons for the confiscation of monasteries and convents and the consequent destruction of ecclesiastical book collections were more practical than dogmatic. All in all, the Reformation may not have been such a total catastrophe for early book history as has been previously believed.

---

1 The figure is very rough and based on different estimates by several scholars about the contents of the Swedish and Finnish collections of parchment fragments. See below for more details.

Tuomas Heikkilä • Professor in Church History at the University of Helsinki, Finland. tuomas.m.heikkila@helsinki.fi

How the Secularization of Religious Houses Transformed the Libraries of Europe, 16th–19th Centuries, ed. by Cristina Dondi, Dorit Raines, and † Richard Sharpe, BIB, 63 (Turnhout, 2022), pp. 489–505

BREPOLS ❧ PUBLISHERS
DOI 10.1484/M.BIB-EB.5.128500

Medieval Libraries in Sweden

According to the traditional view, the history of the book in medieval Sweden both began and ended with a catastrophe. This article deals with the end of the medieval Latin literary culture during the Reformation and the confiscation of medieval libraries, but the first known event in the history of Swedish book culture was already unfortunate. The first mention we have of books in the area that was later to become the kingdom of Sweden is from the ninth century. According to the *Vita Anskarii*, Ansgar (801–65), "Apostle of the North", took a whole library, as many as forty books, with him when he set out from Germany to convert the Swedes in 829. While crossing the Baltic, however, Ansgar and his companions were attacked by pirates and lost all their possessions, including the books[2].

In spite of this unlucky start in the process of conversion, the new Christian faith took root during the eleventh and twelfth centuries[3]. At the same time, the areas of Svealand and Götaland were organized to form a more coherent realm, which later went on to annex areas east of the Gulf of Bothnia. Consequently, by the end of the thirteenth century, the Swedish kingdom had reached its medieval extent with areas covering the central parts of modern Sweden and Finland[4].

In comparison to the more southerly parts of Europe, Sweden was initially a literary backwater, in most of which the use of writing played only a limited role. Whereas the western parts of the realm had an original written culture based on runic letters even prior to Christianization, in the eastern parts, now Finland, the use of written culture was limited to magical interpretations of letters in the few imported items[5]. For the whole area, books and book culture were real novelties that arrived only hand in hand with Christianity during the eleventh and twelfth centuries. Written culture, however, developed swiftly, something that was reflected by the ever-rising number of libraries.

By the dawn of the Reformation in the 1520s, there were libraries established throughout the country. The majority of them were ecclesiastical. There were seven dioceses in Sweden – Uppsala, Linköping, Västerås, Skara, Strängnäs, Växjö and Åbo (called in Finnish Turku) – and in each of them there was a cathedral library and at least a small private library of the local bishop[6]. It was

2 *Vita Anskarii*. Monumenta Germaniae Historica. Scriptores, II (Hannover, 1829), 710–12, Cap. 10. On St Ansgar's activities in Sweden, see, e.g., Birgit Sawyer and Peter Sawyer, 'Scandinavia enters Christian Europe', in *The Cambridge History of Scandinavia. Volume I, Prehistory to 1520*, ed. Knut Helle (Cambridge, 2003), 147–59. On the subsequent cult of St Ansgar, see esp. Sven Helander, *Ansgarskulten i Norden*, Bibliotheca theologiae practicae, kyrkovetenskapliga studier, 45 (Stockholm, 1989).

3 For a concise but multidisciplinary summary on the topic, see Bertil Nilsson, 'The Christianization of Sweden', in *The Pre-Christian Religions of the North. History and Structures*, Vol. IV, eds Jens Peter Schjødt, John Lindow, and Anders Andrén (Turnhout 2020), 1695–1728.

4 In the English language, see esp. Philip Line, *Kingship and State Formation in Sweden 1130–1290* (Leiden, 2007); *Christianization and the Rise of Christian Monarchy*, ed. Nora Berend (Cambridge, 2007). There are many studies on the formation of the Swedish realm in Swedish. See, e.g., Thomas Lindkvist, 'Kungamakt, kristnande, statsbildning', in *Kristnandet i Sverige. Gamla källor och nya perspektiv*, ed. Bertil Nilsson (Uppsala, 1996), 217–41.

5 See Jaakko Tahkokallio, 'Kristinuskon ja kirjoitetun kulttuurin tulo Suomeen', in *Kirjallinen kulttuuri keskiajan Suomessa*, ed. Tuomas Heikkilä (Helsinki, 2010), 67–80.

6 See the old, but still relatively accurate overview: Vilhelm Gödel, *Sveriges medeltidslitteratur. Proveniens. Tiden före Antikvitetskollegiet* (Stockholm, 1916), 76–85. See Tönnes Kleberg, 'Domkyrkobiblioteket', in *Uppsala domkyrka. Katedral genom sekler* ed. Öyvind Sjöholm (Uppsala, 1982), 205–14; Henrik Aminson, *Bibliotheca Templi cathedralis Strengnesensis, 1–2* (Stockholmiae, 1863–1864); Jesse Keskiaho, 'Papiston koulutus ja oppineen papiston kirjat', in *Kirjallinen kulttuuri*, as note 5, 147–81.

the bishop's duty to oversee the liturgical books used in his diocese, and the liturgical *libri ordinarii* were housed and copied in the cathedral library. Nowhere in the diocese was the liturgy more elaborate, and therefore dependent on the use of books, than in the cathedral, where most of the clerics received their instruction, and this was reflected in the cathedral's books. On the other hand, the episcopal sees and cathedrals were the major seats of learned culture in Sweden. Consequently, the libraries of the bishops and the cathedral churches contained a large number of university books with scholarly content in theology, philosophy, and both Canon and Roman law[7].

In the relatively poor literary landscape of medieval Sweden, the importance of the libraries of the few monastic houses was significant. There were altogether thirteen Cistercian monasteries in medieval Sweden: six for monks and seven for nuns. The role of the Cistercian houses, linked as they were into the international network of the order, seems to have been decisive in the earliest phase of domestic book production in Sweden[8]. The most important monastic libraries, however,

were those of the two Bridgettine monasteries of Vadstena and Nådendal, the first of which boasted by far the biggest book collection of the kingdom at the end of the Middle Ages. Indeed, the library of Vadstena with some 1500 volumes counted among the most significant monastic libraries of northern Europe[9].

By the early 1500s, there were nearly thirty Dominican and Franciscan convents and nunneries within the kingdom of Sweden, and all of them had some kind of library. In principle, it was not the aim of the mendicant orders to collect large libraries[10]. Most of their books were intended only for everyday liturgical use and for preaching rather than general, more varied libraries. Though all the Swedish book collections – with Vadstena as the only exception – were modest when compared to major European libraries, they varied significantly in size. This is aptly exemplified by the apparently very small library of the Franciscan convent of Kökar, situated in the Åland archipelago between Stockholm and Åbo, and its mother convent in Stockholm. Whereas the former only had a small, practically-oriented collection of manuscripts[11], the library of the latter

---

7   The number of such works is still reflected in the number of remaining fragments in Sweden and Finland. Of the parchment fragments housed in the Swedish National Archives, some 10% derive from law codices and 6% from theological works; in the fragment collection of the Finnish National Library, the figures are 11% and 12%. See Jan Brunius, 'Medieval manuscript fragments in the National Archives – a survey', in *Medieval Book Fragments in Sweden*, ed. Jan Brunius (Stockholm, 2005), 9–16, at 11–12; Tuomas Heikkilä, 'The Finnish medieval fragments', in *The Beginnings of Nordic Scribal Culture, ca 1050–1300*, ed. Åslaug Ommundsen (Bergen, 2006), 27–31; fragmenta.kansalliskirjasto.fi. On incunabula of the cathedral libraries, see Wolfgang Undorf, *From Gutenberg to Luther – Transnational Print Cultures in Scandinavia 1450–1525*. Diss. Humboldt-Universität zu Berlin 2011, 344–53.

8   Michael Gullick, 'Preliminary observations on Romanesque manuscript fragments of English, Norman and Swedish origin in the Riksarkivet (Stockholm)', in *Medieval Book Fragments*, as note 7, 31–82, here 58–67.

9   On the Vadstena library, see, e.g., *Dicit Scriptura. Studier i C-samlingen tillägnade Monica Hedlund*, ed. Sara Risberg, Runica et Mediaevalia, Scripta minora, 14 (Stockholm, 2006); Anna Fredriksson Adman, *Vadstena klosters bibliotek. En analys av förvärv och bestånd* (Uppsala, 1997); *Vadstena klosters bibliotek. Ny katalog och nya forskningsmöjligheter*, ed. Monica Hedlund and Alf Härdelin, Acta universitatis Upsaliensis, 29 (Stockholm, 1990); Aarno Malin, 'Studier i Vadstena klosters bibliotek', *Nordisk tidskrift för bok- och biblioteksväsen*, 13 (1926), 129–53. On books in Nådendal: Ville Walta, 'Naantalin luostari', in *Kirjallinen kulttuuri*, as note 5, 87–308; Jesse Keskiaho, 'En grupp handskrifter från slutet av 1400-talet – från Nådendals *scriptorium*?', *Historisk Tidskrift för Finland*, 93 (2008), 318–50.

10   *Monumenta Ordinis Fratrum Praedicatorum Historica* 4, ed. Benedictus Maria Reichert (Roma, 1897–1904), 80.

11   The remains of only three manuscript antiphonaries have been connected to Kökar library: Helsinki, National Library, F.m. IV.15, IV.16, IV.39.

was one of the most important in the country[12]. It is difficult to estimate the extent of the library of the Stockholm Franciscans, but it is likely to have contained upwards of a hundred books[13]. Sweden's first printing press was in fact located within the convent in the 1480s[14]. Libraries such as those of the Stockholm Franciscans or the important Dominican convents in Sigtuna, Skänninge, Visby or Stockholm, were – at least by medieval Nordic standards – both big in the number of their books and diverse in their contents[15]. They contained a combination of practical and learned works, and many of the surviving medieval scholarly books in Sweden come from the libraries of these significant mendicant convents[16].

In spite of the existence of some libraries of considerable size, the great majority of books were to be found scattered around the region in parish churches. The local churches and chapels normally housed a small collection of liturgical books, mainly breviaries, missals, and manuals. The fact that Swedish book culture and book production were still in their infancy was reflected at this level rather than in the cathedral or conventual libraries. Many of the books in use were old, modest, imported from abroad because outdated in their places of origin and now modified for use in Sweden. Nonetheless, with as many as 1600 parish churches in Sweden in the Middle Ages, the aggregate number of their books was not insignificant[17]. In fact, the number of books contained in these small collections was overwhelming in comparison to those of genuine libraries. Hence, in framing the big picture of medieval Swedish book history, one should forget the traditional division between library books and non-library books, but rather scrutinize all the different book collections, large or small.

In addition to those of ecclesiastical institutions, there were some private libraries, whether they belonged to members of the clergy or to laymen. None of them seems to have been very significant either for the number of books or for their contents. The largest private collections known were that of *Magister* Bero, with more than 130 volumes in 1475, and the library of Clemens Rytingh, the *lector* at the Dominican convent in Stockholm, containing some 80 volumes in the

---

12 *Diarium fratrum minorum Stockholmensium*, Scriptores rerum Suecicarum I, ed. Ericus Michael Fant (Stockholmiae, 1818), 67–83; Monica Hedlund, 'Medeltida kyrko- och klosterbibliotek i Sverige', in *Helgerånet*, ed. Kerstin Abukhanfusa, Jan Brunius and Solbritt Benneth (Stockholm, 1993), 25–36, here 31–33.

13 The identified remains of the library comprise some 27 manuscript codices and incunabula; see Isak Collijn, 'Franciskanernas bibliotek på Gråmunkeholmen i Stockholm med särskild hänsyn till Kanutus Johannis' verksamhet', *Nordisk tidskrift för bok- och biblioteksväsen*, 4 (1917), 101–71, here 101–02, 129–68. As in other libraries, the remains of the majority of books are to be found within the Swedish and Finnish collection of parchment fragments; see, e.g., Helsinki, National Library, F.m. Vc.22–24 = Stockholm, National Archives, Fr 7722–7723; possibly also Helsinki, National Library, F.m. I.112, III.136, III-160, IV.139?

14 Isak Collijn, *Katalog der Inkunabeln der Königlichen Bibliothek in Stockholm*, Vol. II:1 (Stockholm, 1916), 62.

15 Hedlund, 'Medeltida kyrko- och klosterbibliotek', as note 12, 29–33.

16 See, e.g., the donation of a number of learned books by Bishop Thomas of Finland to the Dominican convent of Sigtuna as early as in the 1240s: Keskiaho, *Papiston koulutus*, as note 6, 166–68.

17 Jan Brunius, 'Recycling of manuscripts in sixteenth-century Sweden', in *Nordic Latin Manuscript Fragments. The Destruction and Reconstruction of Medieval Books*, eds Åslaug Ommundsen and Tuomas Heikkilä (London and New York, 2017), 67–81, here 67–68; Brunius, 'Medieval manuscript fragments', as note 7, 13; Ari-Pekka Palola, 'Yleiskatsaus Suomen keskiaikaisten seurakuntien perustamisajankohdista', *Faravid*, 18–19 (1996), 67–104. The number of churches and chapels was higher: *c.* 2350 in the western parts and *c.* 140 in the diocese of Åbo. Thus, there were quite often a good number of ecclesiastical buildings in a parish. Still, as it was only the main church that celebrated the liturgy on a regular basis, there was probably no need for several whole sets of liturgical books for the parish.

late fifteenth century[18]. As a comparison, one may mention that the list of books belonging to King Magnus Eriksson contained only 14 works in 1346[19]. No doubt the list only included books kept in just one of the king's castles, but it gives an idea of the size of libraries of the highest aristocracy.

All in all, books and libraries were ubiquitous and quite numerous in Sweden at the end of the Middle Ages. Books were not only numerous, but during the last centuries of the Middle Ages they also began to play a significant role in most aspects of the society. Their role was especially decisive in moulding the Christian identity and tying the the country and its inhabitants together with the rest of the Roman church and the sphere of Latin culture. And this is why it is important to study what happened to medieval libraries during the Reformation. Their destinies are bound to be indicative of the changing ideals and ideas in the Reformation era.

The Reformation in Sweden

The Reformation began in Sweden in the 1520s. Ideologically, it was inspired by the teachings of Martin Luther and the other German reformers, but equally the Swedish Reformation was a political movement much orchestrated by King Gustav Vasa (1521/1523–1560)[20]. In the early 1520s, Gustav's army had succeeded in defeating the Danish forces, and Sweden had broken away from the Kalmar union of Sweden, Denmark and Norway. Once securely on the throne, Gustav began the costly modernization of his kingdom. The ideas of the German reformers seemed to open up possibilities of strengthening both the role and the economic means of the crown – the two major goals of the new king – and following some disputes with the pope about the election of bishops, the new ideology really began to strike a chord in Sweden[21].

The Diet of Västerås, held in 1527, was a significant milestone in the Reformation, for it authorized the king to appropriate the property of the church – although royal bailiffs had already tried to seize ecclesiastical treasures some years earlier[22]. Even though the resolution of the Diet would in time lead to the adoption of the reformed faith, no sudden changes took place as yet in matters of religious dogma or practice.

In its first stage, the Reformation was mainly about money and political power. Consequently, the Crown was first and foremost interested in those ecclesiastical institutions that held significant landed property and other wealth and which had traditionally exercised appreciable political and economic power within society. In practice this meant the bishoprics, cathedrals, mendicant convents, and monasteries. With the sole exception of the monasteries, all of them were located in towns, and their property was therefore easy to seize.

One of the most important aspects of the Swedish reformation was the promotion of the vernacular. The language of the liturgy and the whole of ecclesiastical life was to be thoroughly

18 See Gödel, *Medeltidslitteratur*, as note 6, 79; Isak Collijn, 'Svenska boksamlingar under medeltiden och deras ägare. 2. Clemens Rytinghs boksamling och bokdepositioner', *Samlaren*, 24 (1903), 125–40.

19 *Diplomatarium Suecanum* (Stockholm, 1829–), no. 3484.

20 E. I. Kouri, 'The early Reformation in Sweden and Finland, c. 1520–1560', in *The Scandinavian Reformation from evangelical movement to institutionalisation of reform*, ed. Ole Peter Grell (Cambridge, 1995), 42–69.

21 Simo Heininen, 'The early reformation in Sweden', in *Church and people in Britain and Scandinavia*, ed. Ingmar Brohed (Lund, 1996), 123–30. A more detailed description of the Swedish reformation: Kauko Pirinen, *Turun tuomiokapituli uskonpuhdistuksen murroksessa*, Suomen kirkkohistoriallisen seuran toimituksia, 62 (Helsinki, 1962).

22 Olof Källström, *Medeltida kyrksilver från Sverige och Finland förlorat genom Gustav Vasas konfiskationer* (Stockholm, 1939), 24–34.

changed into Swedish or – in the eastern parts of the country – Swedish and Finnish[23]. New books were consequently needed, and the language and contents of the old ones meant that the books themselves became obsolete.

It should be emphasized, however, that the Reformation was a lengthy process, lasting several generations, rather than a swift revolution. Old beliefs and practices did not lose their importance overnight but often continued to exist in parts of the Swedish lands until the early seventeenth century. Nor did the Reformation always proceed in a straightforward manner. Many aspects of reform remained for a long time unpopular among the people[24]. The Catholic counter-reformation gained ground especially during the reign of Gustav's son Johan III (1568–1592), who even allowed the Jesuits to establish a college in Stockholm in 1576. Although this college turned out to be a short-lived phenomenon, it left its mark in the book history of the Swedish Reformation.

Confiscation of Libraries

The majority of the ecclesiastical libraries were confiscated during the Reformation. It was not done systematically or quickly, but over several decades. In fact, the long duration of the process gives us an idea of how little importance old books had for the royal administration. Throughout, the confiscation of the libraries of ecclesiastical institutions was rather an incidental aspect of the seizure of other possessions than a goal in itself. In most cases, the administrative sources of the period do not even mention books and libraries. One exception occurred in 1531, when the various properties of the Franciscan convent

in Växjö were confiscated. The practicalities were organized by a local priest, Gudmund Spegel, who was given the books of the convent as compensation for his efforts[25].

The example of Gudmund Spegel elucidates an important aspect of the confiscation of medieval books. Interestingly, the manuscripts or the printed books that contained the teachings of the old faith do not seem to have been seen as a threat to the new order of religion. The sources reveal no sign of deliberate destruction of Catholic books. The attitude towards their contents seems to have been more one of indifference than anything else. There is an obvious analogy to this attitude in the treatment of medieval altar pieces, statues, and mural paintings: although the Reformation meant that the saints had to give up their previously central position in the devotion of the people, their depictions remained in the parish churches for generations to come.

When it comes to the practical implementation of the seizing of the libraries, very little is known. The royal bailiffs seem to have played the decisive part in it, but their *modus operandi* is not yet known in detail[26]. Still, the outcome of their activities is clear. Over a period of some decades the major part of the contents of ecclesiastical libraries were taken by the Crown. At the same time, the Crown took almost all of the churches' and ecclesiastical institutions' treasures of precious metal. This, in contrast to the fate of the books, is relatively well documented[27] – a fact that indicates what really mattered to the central administration.

In the first phase of the Reformation, the books of parish churches, cathedrals and

---

23 E.g. Christer Pahlmblad, *Mässa på svenska. Den reformatoriska mässan i Sverige mot den senmedeltida bakgrunden* (Lund, 1998).

24 See Martin Berntson, *Mässan och armborstet. Uppror och reformation i Sverige 1525–1544* (Skellefteå 2010).

25 *Konung Gustaf den förstes registratur 7*, ed. Johan Axel Almquist (Stockholm, 1877), 250–51.

26 The best introduction to the topic is Seppo Eskola, *Archives, Accounting, and Accountability: Cameral Bookkeeping in Mid-Sixteenth-Century Sweden and the Duchy of Johan (1556–1563)*, Diss. University of Helsinki 2020.

27 See esp. Källström, *Medeltida kyrksilver*, as note 22.

monasteries seem to have remained intact, whereas the libraries (and other possessions) of the mendicant convents were the first to be confiscated. The important Franciscan convent on Gråmunkeholmen ("Greyfriars Island") in Stockholm was cleared of its inhabitants as early as 1527, the very year when the Diet of Västerås was held. A few years later, in 1531, some of its buildings were converted into a town hospital and later into a school[28]. Many of the former friars became parish priests, and they may have taken with them some of the books from the substantial library of the convent. None the less, the majority of the books remained in the former convent, even though the buildings had been put to new use.

The Dominican convent of Stockholm had a similar fate. The Reformation seems to have ruined its financial viability extremely quickly, and the friars saw no other option but to leave the convent by the end of 1528[29]. The Crown gladly took possession of the valuables of the convent, but the sources do not tell us anything about the library. The fate of these two important Stockholm convents was typical of the downfall of all the nearly thirty mendicant convents of the kingdom. Within a few years most of them were abandoned, their former inhabitants moved to parish churches, and the libraries scattered. One of the last to survive was the Dominican convent of St Olaf in Åbo, which had played a central role in the development of written culture in Åbo diocese – the medieval Finnish part of the kingdom – during the fourteenth and fifteenth centuries. It was totally destroyed by fire in 1537, but it is questionable whether its library was still located in the convent at that stage, since a number of leaves of books produced in St Olaf have

been found among the collections of parchment fragments in Stockholm and Helsinki[30].

Soon after this, even cathedrals, cathedral chapters, and parish churches began to lose their book collections. Although the majority of books seem to have been confiscated in the course of the sixteenth and early seventeenth centuries, the process was not always swift or systematic, and there were, for example, medieval service-books in use in many parishes as late as the latter half of the sixteenth century[31]. Some of the books ended up in private use by members of the clergy, but the majority came into the hands of the king's bailiffs and the Crown. Even though the Reformation proceeded surprisingly peacefully, books were not always handed over to their new owners voluntarily. This is suggested by the fact that many books that ought to have been confiscated were found much later, hidden in cathedrals or in parish churches. Such was the case, e.g., in Åbo, where several such books turned up in the closets of the cathedral during the seventeenth and eighteenth centuries[32]. In much the same way, at least some of the most important relics were hidden at Åbo during the Reformation, where they were found in the early eighteenth and in the twentieth centuries[33].

Monasteries of the Cistercian order also experienced the hardships of the Reformation at an early date: all thirteen of them were closed within a few years following the Diet of Västerås[34].

---

28 E.g. Gödel, *Medeltidslitteratur*, as note 6, 113–15.

29 See, e.g., the entry on December 5, 1528 in *Stockholms stads tänkebok 1524–29*, ed. Ludvig Larsson (Lund, 1929–1940).

30 Jesse Keskiaho, 'Dominikaanit', in *Kirjallinen kulttuuri*, as note 5, 267–77 with further literature; K. G. Leinberg, *De Finska klostrens historia* (Helsingfors, 1890), 78–80.

31 Jan Brunius, *From Manuscripts to Wrappers. Medieval Book Fragments in the Swedish National Archives*, Skrifter utgivna av Riksarkivet, 35 (Stockholm, 2013), 98–99.

32 E.g., Stockholm, Royal Library, MS A49 and A58.

33 Tuomas Heikkilä, *Sankt Henrikslegenden* (Helsingfors – Stockholm 2009), 70–73; Juhani Rinne, *Pyhä Henrik. Piispa ja marttyyri* (Helsinki, 1932), 273–81.

34 See Edward Ortved, *Cistercieordenen og dens klostre i Norden II: Sveriges klostre* (København 1933); James France, *The Cistercians in Scandinavia* (Kalamazoo, Michigan, 1992).

The Bridgettine monasteries of Vadstena and Nådendal, however, were something of an exception, because they housed both men and women. Traditionally, they had had an important social function as a holy retreat for the women of the nobility. This did not change during the Reformation, and it was many decades before the last of the Bridgettine nuns died or left their monastery in the 1590s. In contrast, the brethren of these double monasteries left Vadstena and Nådendal at an early stage of the Reformation, most of them taking up a new career as parish priests[35]. The immense landed property was, naturally, confiscated by the Crown soon after the Diet of Västerås, but the libraries of the two monasteries had contrasting fates. Whereas the majority of the Vadstena books remained in place until the early seventeenth century[36], the library of Nådendal was broken up, in part because the departing brethren took books with them when they left to become parish clergy, in part because the Crown confiscated what was left[37].

From Books to Fragments: Recycling the Books

As a by-product of the confiscation of the possessions of the ecclesiastical institutions, a great number of books accumulated in the hands of the Crown. Initially, there appears to have been no clear plan as to what to do with them, but soon officials decided to start collecting the books together. As the two mendicant convents of Stockholm had had significant libraries and as they were located very close to the central government, it was a logical decision to collect most of the confiscated books at the old Franciscan library at Gråmunkeholmen in Stockholm[38]. Some of the buildings of the former convent soon became a huge storehouse of books of decidedly dated content.

But what was the Crown to do with so many outmoded books in Latin? Emblematic of the whole Swedish Reformation, the Crown soon found a new, innovative, and economically justified use for the books of the confiscated libraries. Manuscripts were mostly written on durable parchment. The ever-growing central bureaucracy of the modernizing realm, in its turn, produced vast amounts of accounts and other records written on paper. As it was essential that every detail of the public finances could be inspected and audited, the accounts had to be preserved in the archives and were therefore in need of covers. In this way, the thousands of parchment leaves of the books in the libraries and book collections of the various ecclesiastical institutions were a godsend to the bureaucrats of the early modern era. Between 1530 and 1630 thousands and thousands of parchment books were torn apart so that their double leaves could be reused as durable covers to wrap the accounts of central government[39]. The accounts were mainly bound in parchment wrappings in Stockholm, where the officials could use the almost infinite supply of parchment *bifolia* from the Gråmunkeholmen

35   Carl Silfverstolpe, *Klosterfolket i Vadstena. Personhistoriska anteckningar* (Stockholm, 1898–1899); Leinberg, *Klostrens historia*, as note 30.

36   Though the library remained far from intact; see, e.g., *Vadstenadiariet. Latinsk text med översättning och kommentar*, ed. Claes Gejrot (Stockholm, 1996), 460 no. 1190; Carl Silfverstolpe, 'En blick i Vadstena klosters arkiv och bibliotek', in *Ur Några Antecknares Samlingar* (Uppsala, 1891), 89–115, here 115.

37   Silfverstolpe, *Arkiv och bibliotek*, as note 36, 89–115; Walta, *Naantalin luostari*, as note 9.

38   Gödel, *Medeltidslitteratur*, as note 6, 123–24; Anna Wolodarski, 'De svenska medeltida bokägarna speglade i fragmentsamlingen', *Arkiv, samhälle och forskning*, 1–2 (2004) 168–75.

39   See, e.g., Heikkilä and Ommundsen, 'Piecing together the past', as note 17, 3–7; Brunius, 'Medieval manuscript fragments', as note 7; Jan Brunius, 'Landskapshandlingarna i Kammararkivet. Från kammarens register till databas', *Arkiv, samhälle och forskning*, 1 (2000), 7–27.

book storage. In addition, some of the books were used for wrapping locally[40].

It is worth mentioning that the sources tell us next to nothing about the recycling of the parchment leaves. The practice must have been so common and self-evident that the central administration did not see any reason to document the fates of the dismembered books. There was nothing new in the practice of reusing redundant parchment manuscripts and early printed works in the covers and bindings of other books. What made the recycling of medieval parchment books for this purpose exceptional in Sweden during the Reformation was the systematic way in which it was executed and the large scale on which it was carried out. Between 1530 and 1630, the central administration needed over a thousand covers every year[41]. The active reuse of parchment *bifolia* continued for a century. During the first decades of the seventeenth century administrative practices and preferences began to change, and the large-scale use of parchment leaves ended in the 1630s[42].

In spite of the need of the Crown for the parchment covers, not all the confiscated books were reused. Much of the material collected in Stockholm in fact remained as complete books. From 1576 onwards the old manuscripts, incunabula, and other early printed works found surprising new users, as the Catholic-minded King Johan III (reigned 1568–1592) founded the *Collegium Regium Stockholmense* in the old Franciscan convent on Gråmunkeholmen. It is another sign of the slow progress of reform that it was the Jesuits, under the leadership of the well-known Laurentius Nicolai Norvegus, who took charge of training new priests in the college[43]. The Jesuits brought their own books with them, but they also used whatever material they found useful in the storehouse of the previously confiscated libraries[44]. This was a brief episode for the old convent. The Jesuits were soon expelled from Sweden, and when they left in the 1580s they took a part of the Gråmunkeholmen collection with them[45]. Many books next found a use in the Jesuit college in Braunsberg (today Braniewo, Poland), from where some of the volumes were returned as war booty by Swedish troops in the seventeenth century. In Sweden the majority of them were given to Uppsala university library[46]. *Habent sua fata libelli!*

In the early seventeenth century, the Crown undertook a proper reorganisation of remnants of the confiscated libraries. In spite of the large-scale use of parchment leaves for covers of bailiffs' accounts, there was still a decent number of entire books left intact. The major part of the accumulation still housed at the Gråmunkeholmen was donated to

---

40 For a short period of time, 1556–1563, the accounts relating to the Duchy of Finland were bound in Åbo, and at the end of the century, some accounts were bound in Viborg as well.

41 Jan Brunius, 'Kammaren, fogdarna och de medeltida böckerna. Studier kring pergamentsomslagen i Riksarkivet', … *Och fram träder landbygdens människor…*, ed. P. Aronson, B. Björkman, and L. Johansson (Växjö, 1994), 109–22, here 119; Brunius, *From Manuscripts to Wrappers*, as note 31, 24–27.

42 Jan Brunius, 'MPO-projektet och dess resultat', *Arkiv, samhälle och forskning*, 1–2 (2004), 154–59, here 157.

43 Oskar Garstein, *Rome and the Counter-Reformation in Scandinavia until the establishment of the S. Congregatio de Propaganda Fide 1622. Volume I (1539–1583); Volume II (1583–1622)* (Bergen and Oslo, 1963–1980), here I, 89–112; II, 14.

44 Gunnar Bolin, *Johan III:s högskola på Gråmunkeholmen* 1–2 (Stockholm, 1912–1918); Isak Collijn, '"Bibliotheca Collegii Societatis Jesu in Suetia". Några bidrag till kännedom om jesuiternas boksamling på Gråmunkeholmen', *Nordisk tidskrift för bok- och biblioteksväsen*, 1 (1914), 151–67.

45 See Garstein, *Counter-Reformation*, as note 43, I, 255–57.

46 See *The catalogue of the book collection of the Jesuit College in Braniewo held in the University Library in Uppsala. Vol. 1. Introduction, Manuscripts, Incunabula*, ed. Józef Trypućko, Michał Spandowski, and Sławomir Szyller (Warszawa, 2007); Otto Walde, *Storhetstidens litterära krigsbyten. En kulturhistorisk-bibliografisk studie*, 2 vols (Uppsala, 1916–1920), volume one.

Uppsala university library by King Gustav II Adolph (reigned 1611–1632) in 1621[47]. The vicissitudes of the Vadstena library are a striking example of the long duration and the initial lack of orderliness in the seizure of the medieval ecclesiastical libraries. As already mentioned, some books were already taken by the royal bailiffs during the early decades of the Reformation, but the majority of the books remained in the monastery until 1619[48]. At that time, the remains of this most important monastic library of Scandinavia were moved, first to Stockholm, and then in 1621, along with other books from the Gråmunkeholmen they took further journeys. Whereas the Latin manuscripts and incunabula were donated to Uppsala, most of the books in Swedish were given to the Royal Library in Stockholm, and the archival material is nowadays found in the National Archives. It is symptomatic of the different fates of the different parts of the library that Vadstena books can even be found outside Sweden, at least in Denmark and Germany[49].

What has survived?

What books have survived from before the Reformation? As mentioned previously, the consensus of the broad public and many scholars alike has long been that the Reformation destroyed practically everything from medieval Sweden[50]. Recent studies on the medieval book culture of Sweden (including Finland) in general, and on the collections of medieval parchment fragments in Stockholm and Helsinki in particular, have revealed that the archives and libraries of modern Sweden and Finland still house a significant amount of medieval material – largely thanks to the activities of the Crown during the Reformation[51].

Due to the recycling of parchment as wrappers of bailiffs' accounts, a great deal survives only as single or double leaves. For decades, scholars have tried to reassemble such fragments, reuniting leaves in the hope that recognizable manuscripts, incunabula, or later printed books may emerge. Although the work is far from finished, the number of individual books so identified is considerable. More importantly, it has become apparent that the remains of medieval monastic libraries and other ecclesiastical book collections represent a large part of the books that were in use when the Reformation came to Sweden.

At the same time, the practices of sixteenth- and seventeenth-century recycling have resulted in a slightly distorted overall picture of the books in use in Sweden on the eve of the Reformation. The size, material, and content of a book were of decisive importance in choosing the books to be confiscated by the Crown in the first place, and in deciding on which leaves to reuse. As the administrative recycling of the leaves preferred large-sized parchment books with out-of-date content, books written or printed on paper, small

47 e.g., Olof Celsius, *Uppsala universitetsbiblioteks historia*, Acta Bibliothecae R. Universitatis Upsaliensis, 17 (Uppsala, 1971); Åke Davidsson, 'Gustav II Adolfs bokgåvor till akademien i Uppsala', in *Gustav II Adolf och Uppsala universitet* (Uppsala, 1982), 93–110; Gödel, *Medeltidslitteratur*, as note 6, 155.

48 In detail, see Gödel, *Medeltidslitteratur*, as note 6, 129–32, with references to a variety of original sources.

49 See Gödel, *Medeltidslitteratur*, as note 6, 101.

50 The sixteenth century has often been referred to as an era of "vandalism of the bailiffs". See, e.g., Malin, *Vadstena bibliotek*, as note 9, 150; Aarno Malin,

'Bidrag till nordisk bokhistoria under medeltiden. Ur finska källor meddelade', *Nordisk tidskrift för bok- och biblioteksväsen*, 9 (1922), 143–67, here 153; Tuomas M. S. Lehtonen, 'Reformaatio', in *Suomen kulttuurihistoria 1: Taivas ja maa. Esihistoriasta suureen Pohjan sotaan*, eds Tuomas M. S. Lehtonen and Timo Joutsivuo (Helsinki, 2002), 237–49, here 239.

51 See esp. Tuomas Heikkilä and Åslaug Ommundsen, 'Piecing together the past: the accidental manuscript collections of the North', as note 17, 1–23; *Kirjallinen kulttuuri*, as note 5; *Medieval Book Fragments*, as note 7; Brunius, *From Manuscripts to Wrappers*, as note 31.

books and those with content that was still useful found different fates. Their number is exceedingly low, and they are obviously underrepresented among the surviving material.

The biggest collections of medieval book remains are the parchment fragment collections in the Swedish National Archives in Stockholm and in the Finnish National Library in Helsinki[52]. In both institutions, the material comes from the parchment covers of bailiffs' accounts and so consists of single or double leaves. The division between the two institutions reflects the fact that bailiffs' accounts relating to Finnish territory were moved to Helsinki in 1809–1812 and in 1864[53].

As mentioned above, the work of reassembling the fragmentary leaves so as to restore the remains of recognizable manuscripts is still ongoing. It is therefore impossible to give the exact number of medieval books that the fragments represent. For instance, the Swedish scholars have recently changed their view on the number of books represented in the Stockholm collection and upgraded their estimate quite radically from 6,000 to 11,000[54]. The Helsinki collection, in

turn, holds the remains of approximately 1500 books[55]. There is some overlap between these big collections, because both contain fragments from the same manuscripts used to wrap accounts from different parts of the realm. Allowing for this, the total numbers of books from which something survives may rise as high as c. 12,200[56]. Still, it is too early to give exact or absolutely reliable numbers.

The absolute and relative number of reconstructed books sharing leaves in both Helsinki and Stockholm fragment collections varies significantly between different subjects. Whereas almost half of the theological and juridical manuscripts in Helsinki share leaves with the Stockholm collection, the phenomenon is decisively rarer in the case of liturgical books[57]. In

is hard to think that there would be a decisive difference in the survival rates of different parts of the fragment collection with very similar contents. One is tempted to think that the reassembly of manuscripts represented in the fragment collection has progressed further in the smaller, i.e. Helsinki collection that has been studied relatively intensively by several scholars, and that the Helsinki figures would be more reliable. Should this be the case and the same average number (6.6) of leaves per book would be applied to the Stockholm fragments, the number of reconstructed books would be c. 6,000, i.e. very close to the traditional estimate of the number of books represented in the Stockholm collection. It should be stressed that the above are speculative calculations, and we shall have to wait for new results based on the content as well as palaeographical and codicological criteria to get a clearer picture of the number of books. It seems to me obvious, however, that the number of reassembled entities standing for medieval books is bound to shrink significantly in the course of the work on the Swedish fragment collection.

52 Both collections are online: fragmenta.kansalliskirjasto.fi; https://sok.riksarkivet.se/mpo. According to the latest count, still bound to be added to in future, the Helsinki collection contains nearly 10,000 and the Stockholm collection close to 40,000 parchment leaves.

53 Martti Kerkkonen, *Suomen arkistolaitos Haminan rauhasta maan itsenäistymiseen* (Helsinki, 1988), 9–10.

54 Brunius, *From Manuscripts to Wrappers*, as note 31, 37; cf. Brunius, *MPO-projektet*, as note 42, 154; [Jan Brunius], 'Databas över medeltida pergamentomslag (MPO)' https://sok.riksarkivet.se/mpo; Brunius, 'The recycling of manuscripts in sixteenth-century Sweden', as note 17, 66–81, here 67. The new estimate is surprisingly high, and the big difference to the previous estimates is largely due to over 4,000 singleton fragments that are considered to represent one parchment book each. Should the new estimate be correct, an identified book of the Stockholm collection would be represented by just 3.6 leaves on average, whereas there are as many as 6.6 leaves per book on average in the Helsinki collection. Although these are but averages and do not tell much about individual cases, the big difference is striking, as it

55 Tuomas Heikkilä, 'Kirjallistumisen jäljillä', in *Kirjallinen kulttuuri*, as note 5, 11–66, here 50.

56 My calculations are based on the reconstructed remains of manuscript books in Helsinki and the identified leaves of the same books in Stockholm. In all, c. 300 of the c. 1500 reconstructed books in Helsinki overlap with the Stockholm collection.

57 Percentage of reconstructed Helsinki books sharing leaves in Stockholm: Missals 13%, Graduals 14%, Breviaries 4%, Antiphonaries 19%, Bibles 11%, Theological and

fact, these results shed light on a much-debated question of the local and centralized reuse of parchment leaves[58]. Previous scholars have shown that some of the accounts were bound with leaves brought by the bailiffs from their own bailiwicks, whereas – as we have seen – the Stockholm central administration used leaves of the Gråmunkeholmen book deposit to bind other account volumes[59]. Yet it has remained unclear how the two different practices worked in detail. The more frequent division of fragments from manuscripts with learned contents between Stockholm and Helsinki is now understood as showing that these leaves, used on accounts from different parts of the country, were taken directly from the Gråmunkeholmen storage containing, above all, books from the libraries of the mendicant convents and monasteries[60]. Conversely, if an account was bound in a litur-

gical fragment, there is a greater likelihood that the wrapping was used locally and brought to Stockholm by the bailiff.

One should take the numbers above as very rough estimates. In both Sweden and Finland, scholars have been trying to reassemble individual fragments of medieval books since the mid-eighteenth century, but the work is far from being completed. Furthermore, the reconstruction of individual books is based on content, as well as palaeographical and codicological criteria, and is not always certain or unambiguous. In this article, the figures go to show the surprisingly high number of remains of medieval books still extant – not the exact number of them. One needs to be very careful not to draw too far-reaching conclusions based on the estimates, as some of the reassembled aggregates consist of just one or two leaves, some of more than a hundred, and new pieces of scholarship may change the picture significantly.

When we add the more or less whole extant manuscript codices and incunabula to the number of books remaining as fragments, we discover that we have material from a very handsome number of books – well over 14,000, if the new Swedish estimate on the number of books represented in their fragment collection is true – that were in use in the Swedish lands on the eve of the Reformation[61]. The actual numbers of remaining manuscripts, incunabula, and other early printed works will tell us more if they can be seen in relation to an estimate of the number of books that may have existed originally. If finding out the number of books surviving in some form or other is exceedingly difficult, it is at least equally hard to give a reliable estimate of the books that may once have been present.

The number of liturgical books used in the kingdom of Sweden is easiest to calculate. It has

philosophical works 46%, Juridical works 46%, Varia 9%. The numbers are indicative and give only an approximate idea of the differences between the genres. The results obtained from the fragment descriptions of Helsinki and Stockholm collections (online: see note 51) may be unreliable due to the fact that the learned and scholarly works have probably been easier to identify and thus combine the individual leaves from both collections than the anonymous liturgical books.

58 On the discussion, see Brunius, *From Manuscripts to Wrappers*, as note 31, 27–33.

59 Johan Axel Almquist, *Den civila lokalförvaltningen i Sverige 1523–1630*. Vol. I (Stockholm, 1917), 122–23; Isak Collijn, *Redogörelse för på uppdrag av Kungl. Maj:t. i kammararkivet och Riksarkivet verkställd undersökning angående äldre arkivalieomslag* (Stockholm, 1914), 17–27; Gödel, *Medeltidslitteratur*, as note 6, 142; Toivo Haapanen, *Verzeichnis der mittelalterlichen Handschriftenfragmente in der Universitätsbibliothek zu Helsingfors*. I. Missalia (Helsinki, 1922), XXI–XXVII; Arnold Sandberg, *Linköpings stifts kyrkoarkivalier till och med år 1800* (Lund, 1948), 40–58; Ilkka Taitto, *Graduale Aboense 1397–1406*. *Näköispainos käsikirjoituskatkelmasta* (Helsinki, 2002), 224; Eskola, *Archives*, as note 26, 21–38.

60 The juridical and theological parchment leaves were, to all appearances, used especially in the 1540s and 1550s, during the early phase of the recycling of the leaves. See Wolodarski, *Bokägarna*, as note 38, 169.

61 On an overview of the surviving incunabula in modern-day Sweden and Finland, see Undorf, *Print Cultures*, as note 7, 338–69; unfortunately, the study misses much of the recent Finnish scholarship on the topic.

previously been estimated that Swedish parish churches had as few as five liturgical books on average[62]. According to another suggestion, however, the average might have risen to as high as eight to ten books per parish church[63]. As there were some 1600 parishes in the Swedish realm at the beginning of the sixteenth century, the number of liturgical books in use in parishes is likely to have been around 8000 according to the first and about 12,000 to 16,000 according to the second estimate of the average number of books. When we add an estimation of additional liturgical works used in the seven cathedrals, and about fifty monasteries and convents, we get even higher total numbers of manuscript books of liturgical contents. According to the present estimates, the Stockholm and Helsinki fragment collections alone contain material from over 12,000 different manuscripts and early printed works of liturgical content. In addition, it has been shown that the number of sixteenth- and early seventeenth-century bailiffs' accounts – and their medieval parchment wrappings – was originally roughly 50% higher than what presently survives[64]. Although we do not know for certain from what kinds of books the parchment covers of the lost accounts derived, speculative arithmetic leads one to think that most of the liturgical parchment books in use around 1527 were seized by the Crown and reused to wrap the accounts. Again, a caveat is in order: the numbers are estimates. Our extant material

is still bound to give a relatively reliable picture of the liturgical works once used. At the same time, the high number of surviving remnants of liturgical books shows that the previous idea of an average of only five liturgical books per parish is clearly too low.

The survival rate of the more learned genres, like books of law, philosophy, or theology, is even more difficult to estimate than that of the liturgy, since we have no means of estimating how many such books may have been in Swedish libraries prior to the Reformation. The fragment collections in Stockholm and Helsinki alone contain the remains of about 1300–1500 different books of this kind[65]. As even this figure is relatively high, it is possible that it corresponds to a considerable proportion of the manuscripts of those genres that were once in existence.

The surprisingly, even exceptionally, high survival rate of manuscript books, incunabula, and other early printed works suggests that the Reformation, the new religious ideas, and the confiscation of the medieval libraries did not annihilate the medieval written heritage. A major part of the parchment books was reused as wrappings, and this has allowed us more than just a glimpse of the written culture of medieval Sweden that was rendered obsolete by the Reformation.

All in all, the sources that we still have may be fairly representative, or at least a large sample of what there once was, and they may give us a reliable basis for framing a picture of the book culture of the late medieval Swedish realm. This picture will not be accurate in every detail, but its overall form is bound to be correct.

62   Jesse Keskiaho, 'Bortom fragmenten. Handskriftsproduktion och boklig kultur i det medeltida Åbo stift', *Historisk Tidskrift för Finland*, 93 (2008), 209–52, here 214; Brunius, 'Medieval manuscript fragments', as note 7, 12.

63   Brunius, 'The recycling of manuscripts in sixteenth-century Sweden', as note 17, 67; Brunius, *From Manuscripts to Wrappers*, as note 31, 36.

64   Brunius, *From Manuscripts to Wrappers*, as note 31, 36; cf. Brunius, *Landskapshandlingarna*, as note 39, 7–27 estimates that the original number may even have been twice as high as we have today.

65   See the databases mentioned in note 52.

Bibliography

Manuscripts and Archival Sources

Helsinki, National Library, F.m. I.112, III.136, III-160, IV.139.
Helsinki, National Library, F.m. IV.15, IV.16, IV.39 (Kökar library).
Helsinki, National Library, F.m. Vc.22–24 = Stockholm, National Archives, Fr 7722–23.
Stockholm, Royal Library, MS A49 and A58.

Secondary Works

Johan Axel Almquist, *Den civila lokalförvaltningen i Sverige 1523–1630*. Vol. I (Stockholm, 1917).
Henrik Aminson, *Bibliotheca Templi cathedralis Strengnesensis, 1–2* (Stockholmiae, 1863–1864).
Martin Berntson, *Mässan och armborstet. Uppror och reformation i Sverige 1525–1544* (Skellefteå, 2010).
Gunnar Bolin, *Johan III:s högskola på Gråmunkeholmen 1–2* (Stockholm, 1912–1918).
Jan Brunius, 'Kammaren, fogdarna och de medeltida böckerna. Studier kring pergamentsomlagen i Riksarkivet', … *Och fram träder landbygdens människor…*, ed. P. Aronson, B. Björkman, and L. Johansson (Växjö, 1994), 109–22.
Jan Brunius, 'Landskapshandlingarna i Kammararkivet. Från kammarens register till databas', *Arkiv, samhälle och forskning*, 1 (2000), 7–27.
Jan Brunius, 'MPO-projektet och dess resultat', *Arkiv, samhälle och forskning, 1–2* (2004), 154–59.
Jan Brunius, 'Medieval manuscript fragments in the National Archives – a survey', in *Medieval Book Fragments in Sweden*, ed. Jan Brunius (Stockholm, 2005), 9–16.
Jan Brunius, *From Manuscripts to Wrappers. Medieval Book Fragments in the Swedish National Archives*, Skrifter utgivna av Riksarkivet, 35 (Stockholm, 2013).
Jan Brunius, 'Recycling of manuscripts in sixteenth-century Sweden', in *Nordic Latin Manuscript Fragments. The Destruction and Reconstruction of Medieval Books*, eds Åslaug Ommundsen and Tuomas Heikkilä (London and New York, 2017), 67–81.
[Jan Brunius], 'Databas över medeltida pergamentsomslag (MPO)'.
The catalogue of the book collection of the Jesuit College in Braniewo held in the University Library in Uppsala. Vol. 1. Introduction, Manuscripts, Incunabula, ed. Józef Trypućko, Michał Spandowski, and Sławomir Szyller (Warszawa, 2007).
Olof Celsius, *Uppsala universitetsbiblioteks historia*, Acta Bibliothecae R. Universitatis Upsaliensis, 17 (Uppsala, 1971).
Christianization and the Rise of Christian Monarchy, ed. Nora Berend (Cambridge, 2007).

Diarium fratrum minorum Stockholmensium, Scriptores rerum Suecicarum I, ed. Ericus Michael Fant (Stockholmiae, 1818), 67–83.

Isak Collijn, 'Svenska boksamlingar under medeltiden och deras ägare. 2. Clemens Rytinghs boksamling och bokdepositioner', *Samlaren,* 24 (1903), 125–40.

Isak Collijn, '"Bibliotheca Collegii Societatis Jesu in Suetia". Några bidrag till kännedom om jesuiternas boksamling på Gråmunkeholmen', *Nordisk tidskrift för bok- och biblioteksväsen,* 1 (1914), 151–67.

Isak Collijn, *Redogörelse för på uppdrag av Kungl. Maj:t. i kammararkivet och Riksarkivet verkställd undersökning angående äldre arkivalieomslag* (Stockholm, 1914).

Isak Collijn, *Katalog der Inkunabeln der Königlichen Bibliothek in Stockholm,* Vol. II: 1 (Stockholm, 1916).

Isak Collijn, 'Franciskanernas bibliotek på Gråmunkeholmen i Stockholm med särskild hänsyn till Kanutus Johannis' verksamhet', *Nordisk tidskrift för bok- och biblioteksväsen,* 4 (1917), 101–71.

Åke Davidsson, 'Gustav II Adolfs bokgåvor till akademien i Uppsala', in *Gustav II Adolf och Uppsala universitet* (Uppsala, 1982), 93–110.

Dicit Scriptura. Studier i C-samlingen tillägnade Monica Hedlund, ed. Sara Risberg, Runica et Mediaevalia, Scripta minora, 14 (Stockholm, 2006).

Diplomatarium Suecanum (Stockholm, 1829–).

Seppo Eskola, *Archives, Accounting, and Accountability: Cameral Bookkeeping in Mid-Sixteenth-Century Sweden and the Duchy of Johan (1556–1563),* Diss. University of Helsinki 2020.

James France, *The Cistercians in Scandinavia* (Kalamazoo, Michigan, 1992).

Anna Fredriksson Adman, *Vadstena klosters bibliotek. En analys av förvärv och bestånd* (Uppsala, 1997).

Oskar Garstein, *Rome and the Counter-Reformation in Scandinavia until the establishment of the S. Congregatio de Propaganda Fide 1622. Volume I (1539–1583); Volume II (1583–1622)* (Bergen and Oslo, 1963–1980).

Vilhelm Gödel, *Sveriges medeltidslitteratur. Proveniens. Tiden före Antikvitetskollegiet* (Stockholm, 1916).

Michael Gullick, 'Preliminary observations on Romanesque manuscript fragments of English, Norman and Swedish origin in the Riksarkivet (Stockholm)', in *Medieval Book Fragments in Sweden,* ed. Jan Brunius (Stockholm, 2005), 31–82.

Toivo Haapanen, *Verzeichnis der mittelalterlichen Handschriftenfragmente in der Universitätsbibliothek zu Helsingfors.* I. Missalia (Helsinki, 1922).

Monica Hedlund, 'Medeltida kyrko- och klosterbibliotek i Sverige', in *Helgerånet,* ed. Kerstin Abukhanfusa, Jan Brunius and Solbritt Benneth (Stockholm, 1993), 25–36.

Tuomas Heikkilä, 'The Finnish medieval fragments', in *The Beginnings of Nordic Scribal Culture, ca 1050–1300,* ed. Åslaug Ommundsen (Bergen, 2006), 27–31.

Tuomas Heikkilä, *Sankt Henrikslegenden* (Helsingfors – Stockholm 2009).

Tuomas Heikkilä, 'Kirjallistumisen jäljillä', in *Kirjallinen kulttuuri keskiajan Suomessa,* ed. Tuomas Heikkilä (Helsinki, 2010), 11–66.

Simo Heininen, 'The early reformation in Sweden', in *Church and people in Britain and Scandinavia,* ed. Ingmar Brohed (Lund, 1996), 123–30.

Sven Helander, *Ansgarskulten i Norden,* Bibliotheca theologiae practicae, kyrkovetenskapliga studier, 45 (Stockholm, 1989).

Olof Källström, *Medeltida kyrksilver från Sverige och Finland förlorat genom Gustav Vasas konfiskationer* (Stockholm, 1939).

Martti Kerkkonen, *Suomen arkistolaitos Haminan rauhasta maan itsenäistymiseen* (Helsinki, 1988).

Jesse Keskiaho, 'En grupp handskrifter från slutet av 1400-talet – från Nådendals *scriptorium*?', *Historisk Tidskrift för Finland,* 93 (2008), 318–50.

Jesse Keskiaho, 'Bortom fragmenten. Handskriftsproduktion och boklig kultur i det medeltida Åbo stift', *Historisk Tidskrift för Finland*, 93 (2008), 209–52.

Jesse Keskiaho, 'Papiston koulutus ja oppineen papiston kirjat', in *Kirjallinen kulttuuri keskiajan Suomessa*, ed. Tuomas Heikkilä (Helsinki, 2010), 147–81.

Jesse Keskiaho, 'Dominikaanit', in *Kirjallinen kulttuuri keskiajan Suomessa*, ed. Tuomas Heikkilä (Helsinki, 2010), 267–77.

Tönnes Kleberg, 'Domkyrkobiblioteket', in *Uppsala domkyrka. Katedral genom sekler* ed. Öyvind Sjöholm (Uppsala, 1982), 205–14.

Konung Gustaf den förstes registratur 7, ed. Johan Axel Almquist (Stockholm, 1877).

E. I. Kouri, 'The early Reformation in Sweden and Finland, c. 1520–1560', in *The Scandinavian Reformation from evangelical movement to institutionalisation of reform*, ed. Ole Peter Grell (Cambridge, 1995), 42–69.

Tuomas M. S. Lehtonen, 'Reformaatio', in *Suomen kulttuurihistoria 1: Taivas ja maa. Esihistoriasta suureen Pohjan sotaan*, eds Tuomas M. S. Lehtonen and Timo Joutsivuo (Helsinki, 2002), 237–49.

K. G. Leinberg, *De Finska klostrens historia* (Helsingfors, 1890).

Thomas Lindkvist, 'Kungamakt, kristnande, statsbildning', in *Kristnandet i Sverige. Gamla källor och nya perspektiv*, ed. Bertil Nilsson (Uppsala, 1996), 217–41.

Philip Line, *Kingship and State Formation in Sweden 1130–1290* (Leiden, 2007).

Aarno Malin, 'Bidrag till nordisk bokhistoria under medeltiden. Ur finska källor meddelade', *Nordisk tidskrift för bok- och biblioteksväsen*, 9 (1922), 143–67.

Aarno Malin, 'Studier i Vadstena klosters bibliotek', *Nordisk tidskrift för bok- och biblioteksväsen*, 13 (1926), 129–53.

Monumenta Ordinis Fratrum Praedicatorum Historica 4, ed. Benedictus Maria Reichert (Roma, 1897–1904).

Bertil Nilsson, 'The Christianization of Sweden', in *The Pre-Christian Religions of the North. History and Structures, Vol. IV*, eds Jens Peter Schjødt, John Lindow, and Anders Andrén (Turnhout 2020), 1695–1728.

Edward Ortved, *Cistercieordenen og dens klostre i Norden II: Sveriges klostre* (København 1933).

Christer Pahlmblad, *Mässa på svenska. Den reformatoriska mässan i Sverige mot den senmedeltida bakgrunden* (Lund, 1998).

Ari-Pekka Palola, 'Yleiskatsaus Suomen keskiaikaisten seurakuntien perustamisajankohdista', *Faravid*, 18–19 (1996), 67–104.

Kauko Pirinen, *Turun tuomiokapituli uskonpuhdistuksen murroksessa*, Suomen kirkkohistoriallisen seuran toimituksia, 62 (Helsinki, 1962).

Juhani Rinne, *Pyhä Henrik. Piispa ja marttyyri* (Helsinki, 1932).

Arnold Sandberg, *Linköpings stifts kyrkoarkivalier till och med år 1800* (Lund, 1948).

Birgit Sawyer and Peter Sawyer, 'Scandinavia enters Christian Europe', in *The Cambridge History of Scandinavia. Volume I, Prehistory to 1520*, ed. Knut Helle (Cambridge, 2003), 147–59.

Carl Silfverstolpe, 'En blick i Vadstena klosters arkiv och bibliotek', in *Ur Några Antecknares Samlingar* (Uppsala, 1891), 89–115.

Carl Silfverstolpe, *Klosterfolket i Vadstena. Personhistoriska anteckningar* (Stockholm, 1898–1899).

Stockholms stads tänkebok 1524–29, ed. Ludvig Larsson (Lund, 1929–1940).

Jaakko Tahkokallio, 'Kristinuskon ja kirjoitetun kulttuurin tulo Suomeen', in *Kirjallinen kulttuuri keskiajan Suomessa*, ed. Tuomas Heikkilä (Helsinki, 2010), 67–80.

Ilkka Taitto, *Graduale Aboense 1397–1406. Näköispainos käsikirjoituskatkelmasta* (Helsinki, 2002).

Wolfgang Undorf, *From Gutenberg to Luther – Transnational Print Cultures in Scandinavia 1450–1525*. Diss. Humboldt-Universität zu Berlin 2011.

Vadstenadiariet. Latinsk text med översättning och kommentar, ed. Claes Gejrot (Stockholm, 1996).

Vadstena klosters bibliotek. Ny katalog och nya forskningsmöjligheter, ed. Monica Hedlund and Alf Härdelin, Acta universitatis Upsaliensis, 29 (Stockholm, 1990).

Vita Anskarii. Monumenta Germaniae Historica. Scriptores, II (Hannover, 1829), 683–725.

Otto Walde, *Storhetstidens litterära krigsbyten. En kulturhistorisk-bibliografisk studie,* 2 vols (Uppsala, 1916–1920).

Ville Walta, 'Naantalin luostari', in *Kirjallinen kulttuuri keskiajan Suomessa,* ed. Tuomas Heikkilä (Helsinki, 2010), 87–308.

Anna Wolodarski, 'De svenska medeltida bokägarna speglade i fragmentsamlingen', *Arkiv, samhälle och forskning,* 1–2 (2004) 168–75.

Digital Sources

Fragmenta Membranea, https://fragmenta.kansalliskirjasto.fi.

Riksarkivet, https://sok.riksarkivet.se/mpo.

MARTIN GERMANN

Zurich and the Books of the Monasteries: From the Reformation to the 19th Century

Introduction

Zurich, a free city of the Holy Roman Empire, member of the Old Confederation of Swiss states, situated just north of the Alps on the road to Rome: in the sixteenth century it was one of the points of origin of the European Reformation. From the fourteenth century onwards, power moved from the old aristocracy to the new, local guilds. The fifteenth century was characterized not just by wars, but by pronounced religious tendencies, of which one sign was the building of many churches in and around the city.

Zurich, Medieval City of Churches

After the city of Constance itself, Zurich was the second most important city in the bishopric of Constance, the largest bishopric north of the Alps. Its churches, abbeys, monasteries and convents were as follows. The Fraumünster, a convent of noble women, was founded by royal decree in 853 and its abbess was nominally the lady mayor of the city. On the other side of the River Limmat

lay the cathedral chapter of the Grossmünster, also dating from Carolingian times, and founded to tend the supposed martyrs' graves above the Limmat. Between these two lay the Wasserkirche, situated on an island in the Limmat where in Roman times Felix and Regula, two Christians from Thebes, were said to have endured a martyr's death; and then there was the City Church of St Peter on the morainal hill beside the former Roman customs post on the Lindenhof, itself the site of the local palace of the medieval German kings. Several years after the death of the last member of the aristocratic house of Zähringen in 1218, Zurich became a free city. In the twelfth century, the Augustinian monastery of St Martin was founded on the Zürichberg, the small mountain on the eastern banks of the River Limmat. It owned many forests and in the fifteenth century became a popular destination for pilgrims from the city. Many books were donated to it.

The mendicant orders settled in Zurich from 1230 onwards[1]: first the Dominicans, then *c.* 1238

---

[1] For a detailed history, see Magdalen Bless-Grabher, 'Zürich und seine Bettelordensklöster', in *Bettelorden, Bruderschaften und Beginen in Zürich, Stadtkultur und*

Martin Germann • Formerly Konservator der Sammlung Bongarsiana-Handschriften der Burgerbibliothek Bern.
ma.germa@bluewin.ch

How the Secularization of Religious Houses Transformed the Libraries of Europe, 16th–19th Centuries, ed. by Cristina Dondi, Dorit Raines, and † Richard Sharpe, BIB, 63 (Turnhout, 2022), pp. 507–517.
BREPOLS ☙ PUBLISHERS   DOI 10.1484/M.BIB-EB.5.128501

the Franciscans, who were also given a plot of land by the city walls. Then *c.* 1270 the Augustinian Hermits settled on the western bank of the river. These monasteries of the mendicant orders each had a church and a graveyard. They competed with each other in the pastoral care of the local people and over time they all developed good relations with the city population. Their ministry to the local women resulted in the creation of Beguine communities that devoted themselves to tending to the sick. The convents of Ötenbach and St Verena were both founded as houses of Dominican nuns.

The Reformation in Zurich

Over the course of time, much potential for conflict developed in the Old Swiss Confederation, both in political and in social matters. Alliances with foreign powers caused ill will, as did payments to the middlemen involved in organizing mercenaries for service abroad. There were arguments over the use of common land, while the increasing amount of land owned by the Church[2] together with the imposition of perpetual tithes and interest ("Zinsen und Zehnten") were a source of further strife. Here and there, protests were also to be heard against the Roman priests who crossed the country time and again with indulgences to sell.

While the scholarship of the humanists prepared the way for the Reformation, with reform-minded clerics propagating their ideas, it was nevertheless the city council of Zurich that steered the Reformation locally with a firm hand.

On 1 January 1519, Ulrich Zwingli (1484–1531) gave his first sermon as the newly elected parish priest at the Grossmünster collegiate church[3]. He had made a big impression on pilgrims from Zurich as an inspiring preacher at the nearby monastery of Einsiedeln, with the result that the Zurich authorities chose him to expound the Bible to them. After various disputes over liturgical reforms, an initial discussion of theological matters resulted in the maintenance of the status quo. But disquiet was building up and change was not to be halted. In March 1523 the city council forbade friars of the Order of Preachers from ministering to the nuns of their order in the convent of Ötenbach. The following October, members of all religious orders in the city were forbidden from preaching. The year 1524 brought far-reaching change to the life of the church in Zurich. In March, the Lindenhof Procession was abolished, and in April the act of Holy Communion was reformed, which meant abolishing the Mass and the other rites of the Roman Catholic Church. On 15 June 1524 it was decided to do away with images in the churches. This initiated a period of iconoclasm, when paintings and statues in the churches of Zurich and the surrounding region were destroyed[4].

The next steps were targeted directly at the monasteries, which were dissolved and whose possessions were confiscated. This in turn had consequences for their libraries.

The Zurich council's decision to dissolve the monasteries was taken on Saturday, 3 December 1524,

---

Seelenheil im Mittelalter, ed. Barbara Helbling, Magdalen Bless-Grabher, and Ines Buhofer (Zurich, 2002), 10–24.

2   Hans-Jörg Gilomen, 'Renten und Grundbesitz in der Toten Hand: realwirtschaftliche Probleme der Jenseitsökonomie', in *Himmel, Hölle, Fegefeuer, das Jenseits im Mittelalter: eine Ausstellung des Schweizerischen Landesmuseums*, catalogue by Peter Jezler et al. (Zurich, 1994), 135–48.

3   For a chronological overview of the events in question, see Gottfried W. Locher, *Zwingli und die schweizerische Reformation*, Die Kirche in ihrer Geschichte 3 (Göttingen, 1982), section J, 1.

4   *Bilderstreit, Kulturwandel in Zwinglis Reformation*, ed. Hans-Dietrich Altendorf and Peter Jezler (Zurich, 1984); Peter Jezler, 'Der Bildersturm in Zürich 1523–1530', in *Bildersturm: Wahnsinn oder Gottes Wille?* Exhibition catalogue for Bern and Strasbourg 2000, ed. Cécile Dupeux et al. (Zurich, 2000), 75–83.

and carried out that same day in the city[5]. Around midday, a delegation from the council, together with officials who served the council, went without warning first to the monastery of the Dominicans. They called the friars together and took them to the Franciscan monastery, "not as prisoners, but under good watch, for none was able to escape or to sneak away", as one chronicle tells the story[6]. Then the Augustinian Hermits were fetched in the same manner. They too were deprived of all signs of their secular power and possessions, including documents and keys. And they too were moved into the Franciscan friary. In accordance with the council's decree, they had to decide whether or not to accept the Reformation. It was also taken into consideration which of them might be suitable for a role in the reformed ministry, while others had to learn a trade. Friars who did not originally come from Zurich were sent home with a sum of money in compensation to provide for them in old age. But those who wished to remain faithful to their order were given the lifelong right to live in the Franciscan monastery or in the monastery of St Martin on the Zürichberg. The women who remained in Ötenbach, St Verena and Selnau were given a similar lifelong right of abode. The Beguines and brotherhoods were assigned to tend to the sick and the poor.

1. The Monastery Libraries at the Time of the Dissolution of the Zurich Monasteries[7]

It is noteworthy that the few extant sources on the dissolution of the monasteries say not a word about their libraries[8]. Their books were not a topic of discussion, for they were of no interest to those involved in the political decisions of the time.

There are, however, comprehensive sources regarding what happened in the city of Zurich, and these allow us to discern three different fates for the libraries of the dissolved monasteries during the years 1523 to 1525:

a) Confiscation by the state or sequestration as a collection;

b) Dispersal, that is they were rescued by institutions that remained Catholic, or were given as a form of compensation to monks and nuns who left the city;

c) Destruction, in particular of liturgical books, with the aim of preventing the celebration of the Mass.

a) Confiscation, sequestration

Confiscation by the state or sequestration as a collection did not, in fact, happen except in the case of the Grossmünster library, which was left in its place until Conrad Pellikan started his work as librarian. As for the books from the monastic libraries, there was no official confiscation or removal; they are just not mentioned anywhere in the records of the city. We must assume that they remained where they were for the moment. After the monks were expelled, their books were left unprotected and unguarded in the empty monastery in rooms that were now being used for other purposes. It is hardly

5 See the chapters 'Armut und Arbeit, Wandlung von Werten' by Ines Buhofer and 'Das Erbe der Klöster' by Barbara Helbling in *Bettelorden*, as note 1, 281–91, 326–27 and 293–305, 327.

6 The baker and schoolmaster Bernhard Wyss (1463–1531) writes this in his manuscript chronicle of the Reformation. Held by the Zentralbibliothek Zürich, shelfmark Ms. B 66 p. 16.

7 For greater detail see Martin Germann, *Die reformierte Stiftsbibliothek am Grossmünster Zürich im 16. Jahrhundert und die Anfänge der neuzeitlichen Bibliographie*, Beiträge

zum Buch- und Bibliothekswesen 34 (Wiesbaden, 1994), especially 101–08.

8 Paul Schweizer, 'Die Behandlung der zürcherischen Klostergüter in der Reformationszeit', in *Theologische Zeitschrift aus der Schweiz*, 2 (1885), 1–28, especially 2; Jacques Figi, *Die innere Reorganisation des Grossmünsterstifts in Zürich von 1519 bis 1531*, Zürcher Beiträge zur Geschichtswissenschaft 9 (Zurich, 1951), especially 73–79.

probable that whole libraries were taken away, not least because the folio volumes were bound in wooden covers, which made them heavy and difficult to transport. Books were probably just taken away by collectors or book-lovers one by one over the ensuing months. Since the removal of the books did not respect the preservation of libraries as such, their fate thus really belongs under section b).

b) Dispersal

The fact that the monastic libraries are not mentioned in the documents pertaining to the dissolution means that their books were treated like all other movable possessions of the monasteries. In other words, the officials appointed by the council had authority over them and gave both these and other objects to the friars, monks, and nuns who left the state of Zurich. This was in compensation for what they had brought with them into the monastery or convent, as provisions for the road, or in lieu of providing for their old age. We can be sure that the weight of the books will have prevented them from being taken away in large quantities from the libraries. Nevertheless, the Reformation marked the beginning of a gigantic dispersal of books.

The chronicler Laurenz Bosshard (c. 1490–1532), canon of the Augustinian monastery of Heiligenberg in Winterthur, wrote about the dissolution of his monastery in October 1525. The delegation from the city council of Zurich promised the canons the lifelong right to live where they were and also the right to use and enjoy the monastery's possessions. However, the delegation took away all objects of value from the monastery church, among them all the silk surplices and other textiles, goblets, crucifixes, and monstrances of gold, silver, and copper. All this was packed into a barrel and taken away to Zurich. Silver and gold were made into coins there. The canons were, however, allowed ownership of their books and their bedding. "They left us all

our books and many pillows, which we divided up between us", wrote Laurenz Bosshard in his Winterthur chronicle[9].

c) Destruction of books[10]

1525 was a fateful year for books in the canton of Zurich, on the one hand because of the social tensions that erupted in Germany and Switzerland in the form of the Peasants' War[11], on the other hand because of the reforming activities of the local authorities.

In the region around Zurich, groups of peasants began attacking monasteries in early 1525. The reason for this was the imposition of tithes and interest that had until now been perpetual. These protests are reputed to have seen the destruction of the library of the Premonstratensian monastery of Rüti in the Zurich Oberland. In the Dominican womens' convent of Töss, from which all valuables – a category that did not include books – had been brought to safety in Winterthur during Whitsun week, the peasants completed their acts of destruction after having drunk their fill with wine from the convent cellars. In the belief that by destroying the written records there they would also annul their church

---

9   'Man liess uns alle bücher und ettliche küsse, die teilten wir miteinander': Laurenz Bosshard, 'Chronik über die Jahre 1185–1532'; autograph manuscript in the Zentralbibliothek Zürich, Ms. J 86 fol. 75, p. 179. Edited by Kaspar Hauser, Quellen zur schweizerischen Reformationsgeschichte 3 (Basel, 1905), 316.

10   For more on this topic, see Marcel Beck, 'Anmerkungen zu Geschichte und Psychologie des Biblioklasmus', in Nordisk tidskrift för bok- och biblioteksväsen, 39 (1952), 1–17; Fernando Báez, Storia universale della distruzione dei libri; dalle tavolette sumere alla guerra in Iraq (Rome, 2007), Italian translation by Paolo Galloni and Marco Palma of the original edition Historia universal de la destrucción de libros (Barcelona, 2004).

11   Valentin Lötscher, Der deutsche Bauernkrieg in der Darstellung und im Urteil der zeitgenössischen Schweizer, Basler Beiträge zur Geschichtswissenschaft 11 (Basel, 1943), especially 108–14 and 144–45.

taxes, they cut up or tore apart the books of the abbey of St Blasius, wading about knee-deep in fragments of parchment and paper.

In October 1525, the Grossmünster in the city, hitherto untouched, was also reformed by the city council. There are eye-witness reports of this from the Grossmünster itself, thanks to the written accounts of the provost Felix Frey and the Grossmünster scribe Johannes Widmer. Frey made a note of the order of the council delegation on 2 October 1525 that the liturgical books – he counted over fifty of them – were to be removed from the altars of the Grossmünster and carried into the large sacristy. Johannes Widmer, who at the Second Zurich Disputation in 1523 had unsuccessfully defended the pictures in the church, described how the Grossmünster treasures were taken away on 2 October. He gave a four-page list of the relics, monstrances, goblets, and vestments that were removed, and he also mentioned the order to remove the liturgical books.

On the same day a commission comprising three priests, Ulrich Zwingli himself, Leo Jud, priest of the City Church of St Peter, and Heinrich Brennwald (1478–1551), provost of the Augustinian collegiate church at Embrach, was given the task of investigating the books. Five days later, on 7 October 1525, the rejected books were carried down to the Helmhaus on the banks of the River Limmat and were there offered for sale to anyone who wanted them. Heinrich Bullinger (1504–1575), Zwingli's successor at the Grossmünster, wrote in 1574 of the Reformation of the Grossmünster that the parchment was sold to merchants as packing material, to the apothecaries as packaging for their medicines (*Pulverhüslinen*, "powder sachets"), to the bookbinders as binding material, and to everyone else too (including schoolboys), all very cheaply[12]. But care was taken to make the parchment of liturgical books unusable. They were "zerrissen", "torn up", in other words divided up into individual double leafs, "so that choral singing should end", as Johannes Widmer put it. The aim was to make it impossible to say Mass and at the same time to forbid choral singing, an art for which Zurich's churches had hitherto been renowned.

Gerold Edlibach (1454–1530), a former treasurer (Seckelmeister) of the state of Zurich and an adherent of the old faith whom we know as a chronicler, also mentioned the large piles of books that were sold, torn apart, and defaced, saying that not even one of them remained whole[13]. He estimated the cost of their manufacture at more than 10,000 guilders. This event was later called the "Zürcher Büchersturm" or Zurich biblioclasm, by analogy with the word "iconoclasm" for the destruction of images in the churches. There is no doubt that the liturgical books were destroyed, but there were no book-burnings in Zurich.

There remains the question as to whether this act of destruction also included other books besides the purely liturgical. In 1574 Heinrich Bullinger mentioned that a few good books were kept, and everything else was cast out as sophistry, scholasticism, and fables: "Es ward ouch die libery ersucht und wenig (was man vermeint gut sin) behallten, das ander alles, als sophistery, scholastery, fabelbücher etc. hinab under das Hälmhus getragen ..."[14]. This statement suggests that considerable sections of the library were removed or destroyed, but my research suggests that this was not in fact the case. Bullinger's choice of words reminds us of Martin Luther. In his tract of 1524, addressed to city councillors

---

12 Manuscript in the Zentralbibliothek Zürich, shelfmark Ms. Car. C 44; the quotation is on p. 818.

13 Manuscript in the Zentralbibliothek Zürich, shelfmark Ms. L 104; edited and with a commentary by Peter Jezler, "'Da beschachend vil grosser endrungen': G. Edlibachs Aufzeichnungen über die Zürcher Reformation 1520–1526', in *Bilderstreit*, as note 4, 41–74, especially 65; Germann, *Stiftsbibliothek*, as note 7, 104.

14 See note 12.

across Germany about the state of the schools, he too wrote of the monastic libraries and of the "mad, useless, damaging books of monks"[15]. He recommended getting rid of them.

Zwingli's dislike of the scholastic writers of the thirteenth and fourteenth centuries was well known in Zurich. Thus one of the canons of the Grossmünster, Conrad Hofmann, an early opponent of Zwingli, had as early as 1521 submitted a complaint against him with the provost and chapter of the Grossmünster[16]. Hofmann accused him of often preaching negatively about medieval scholars and even about the much earlier church fathers. In the pulpit, before all people, he had supposedly described them as "unfit, foolish and useless teachers" and as "mad fantasists", calling their teachings a "cesspool".

Yet if we look for scholastic authors in the catalogue of books in the reformed Grossmünster library from 1532 to 1551, maintained by Konrad Pellikan (1478–1556), whom Zwingli had brought to Zurich as professor of Greek and Hebrew, we find them[17]: Thomas Aquinas's works are in Pellikan's inventory (#78–81), of which one title

(#80) was in Zwingli's own library. We also find Duns Scotus's Commentary on the Sentences (#83). Aegidius Romanus is also present – despite being disliked by Zwingli (#269); this is the only book to survive from the former library of the Augustinian Hermits in the city. The situation is similar in the case of the canonists, whom Zwingli is supposed to have hated. There is a book by Pope Innocent IV (#136.4) and the *Summa decretalium* by Henricus de Segusio (called "Hostiensis"; #379), and there are two works by the glossator of church law Johannes Andreae (#122.6 and 381). Nicolaus de Tudeschis (*alias* Panormitanus) was reputedly also an object of disdain, but his lectures on the Decretals are extant in five large volumes (#338–40 and 355–56). All these books had belonged to the canons of the Grossmünster. They had found their way into the library of the Grossmünster before the Reformation, and there they became the foundation of Pellikan's reformed Grossmünster library begun in 1531. They obviously thus remained untouched by the reformers in 1525. Other works in the catalogue were added to the library over time, especially books from the Franciscan convent, which did not reach the Grossmünster until after 1536. Other authors of the Roman church do not occur in the catalogue, but the lack of older sources means that we cannot know whether their books were in Zurich's monastery libraries before the Reformation or not.

So we see that in 1525 the Catholic liturgical books from churches and monasteries in the city and region of Zurich were destroyed. These liturgical books, taken by merchants and apothecaries, have been lost for ever. What was sold to the bookbinders in part still exists but only in fragments as part of the binding of books, and the books that contain such leaves have been dispersed across many libraries near and far. As late as 1538, the city accounts record payment from a printer, sadly unnamed, for "torn-up parchment songbooks". Until well into the seventeenth century, the bookbinders' workshops in Zurich

---

15 Martin Luther, 'An die Ratsherren aller Städte Deutschlands, dass sie christliche Schulen aufrichten und halten sollen, 1524'. This text saw 11 editions in its first year alone. It is here quoted according to the Constance edition of 1524, formerly held by the Grossmünster Library, today in the Zentralbibliothek Zürich, shelfmark III M 164 Nr. 3, fol. D4v–E3r; Germann, *Stiftsbibliothek*, as note 7, 106.

16 Alfred Schindler, 'Die Klagschrift des Chorherrn Hofmann gegen Zwingli', in *Reformiertes Erbe, Festschrift für Gottfried W. Locher* (Zurich, 1992), 325–59, especially 346.

17 See the edition and reconstruction of Pellikan's catalogue in my book cited in note 7. Conrad Pellikan was an Observant Franciscan friar, teaching in the university at Basel until deprived in 1524; in 1526 he was persuaded to leave the order and became active as a teacher of Greek, Hebrew, and the Old Testament in the reformed high school of Zurich. After the death of Zwingli in 1531 he took over the running of the reorganized Grossmünster library. He created a fourfold catalogue and continued it until 1551.

had stores of parchment leaves from medieval liturgical manuscripts that were used for various binding purposes, as limp covers for books, or as padding for leather bindings. On the shelves of the Zentralbibliothek Zürich one still finds hundreds of books, often Reformation pamphlets or other works printed in Zurich during the sixteenth and seventeenth centuries, that are bound with such waste parchment. Determining the exact context in which this material was used is very difficult, and it is impossible to form any idea of what happened to the discarded parchment that left Zurich.

2. The Reformed Grossmünster Library from 1532 onwards, a Collecting-point for Dispersed Libraries of Dissolved Churches and Monasteries

As is often the case elsewhere, no catalogues exist from Zurich's pre-Reformation libraries nor are there even any inventories. The city, however, had the good fortune that Conrad Pellikan took on the responsibility for the reorganization of the former Grossmünster library after Zwingli's death in 1531. His goal was to create a functioning library for the newly formed high school for training preachers. Pellikan made a catalogue for the library that was surprisingly modern. His first action was to convince the council to buy Zwingli's books from his widow. Pellikan himself carried some 150 books from Zwingli's house to the library at the Grossmünster.

It would be easier to research the history of the library holdings, had Pellikan also made at that time a note of the origins of the books in the library, had he kept all of Zwingli's books together on the shelves, or had he at least made a list of them. He did none of these things, so we have to look in greater detail at the course that matters took. It transpires that about half of Zwingli's books were arranged on three reading desks that had formed part of the "Pultbibliothek" between 1482 and 1515. This had been filled with

the *libri catenati*, chained books. The other half of Zwingli's library was grouped primarily according to format. Pellikan mixed them together with some 150 other pre-Reformation books that had remained in the library after the biblioclasm of 1525, and in doing so paid no regard to their different origins.

Over time, the Grossmünster library became a reservoir or collecting-point for other books, especially books displaced from dissolved monasteries, and Pellikan learnt from his mistakes. We can trace this development clearly in Pellikan's inventory. In the first phase, until about 1536[18], only a few books arrived from other monasteries in Zurich. From the friary of the Augustinian Hermits there is a single book, from the Fraumünster convent six volumes, from the Dominican friary some seven volumes[19]. They are arranged among other books and their provenance remains unmentioned.

Pellikan then obviously begins an active endeavour to acquire the remains of dispersed libraries. And he does not mix them any more with other books but keeps them together on the shelves, marks them separately in his inventory, and from now on keeps a note there of their provenance.

Since the members of the religious orders were brought together in the house of the Franciscans in 1524, their presence there meant that the books of its own library were relatively well protected. One of the friars in the house was Enoch Metzger OFM, who lived until 1535. Only after this date did the books from the library make their way into the growing library at the Grossmünster, where Pellikan entered them *en bloc* in his inventory. There were 46 volumes, and only one of them was a manuscript.

---

18 See the table regarding the phases of work from 1531 to 1551 in Germann, *Stiftsbibliothek*, as note 7, 42–44.

19 These are listed individually in Germann, *Stiftsbibliothek*, as note 7, especially in chapter 6.3, 'Besitzer- und Benutzer-Register', 358.

The same happy fate was shared by the library of the Augustinian monastery of St Martin on the Zürichberg. Here, too, the canons who remained faithful to their order were allowed to remain in their monastery for the rest of their lives, and when the last of them died in 1533, their books were saved for the time being. They remained secure for the next twenty years, until they appear in 1554, still during Pellikan's lifetime, in his inventory of the reformed Grossmünster library: nine medieval manuscripts and 57 incunabula from St Martin have survived to this day in the Zentralbibliothek Zürich, while others have survived elsewhere.

3. The Library of the St Gallen Monastery as Spoils of War in Zurich

Even two hundred years after the Reformation, religious wars were still being fought in Switzerland. In the Toggenburg War of 1712 (also known as the Second Villmerger War), the army of the Protestant cantons of Bern and Zurich overran the ancient Benedictine abbey of St Gallen and took its books as part of their spoils[20]. Several years later the authorities in Bern gave back the books that had gone there, but the council of Zurich retained a significant portion of the St Gallen manuscripts in its city library. This city library, also known as the Burghers' Library, was founded in 1629 in the midst of the Thirty Years' War under the motto "Arte et Marte" ("Through art and arms") in reaction to the fate of the best protestant library of the day, the Bibliotheca Palatina of Heidelberg, which was carried off to Rome in 1623. Not until 2006 did the cantons of Zurich and St Gallen agree on a resolution to the so-called *Kulturgüterstreit* or "cultural treasure dispute", and then only after years of debate in the press, many legal opinions,

and finally after mediation by the Swiss federal government. Some forty manuscripts were returned to St Gallen on permanent loan by the authorities in Zurich, and they are today available online in the Swiss virtual manuscript library (http://www.e-codices.unifr.ch), with explanatory texts in German, English, French and Italian.

4. The Library of the Rheinau Monastery OSB after its Dissolution in 1862

The most recent dissolution of a monastery in Switzerland was a clear act of confiscation. After the Napoleonic occupation of 1798 to 1804 and in the wake of various internal upheavals culminating in the Sonderbund War of 1847 against the conservative Catholic cantons of central Switzerland, the old Helvetic Confederation was turned in 1848 into a federal state, in which Zurich was firmly established as a liberal democracy.

Not long before the First Vatican Council, at a time when religious and political issues were a continuing source of strife, the Zurich government in 1862 decided to dissolve the thousand-year-old Benedictine abbey of Rheinau. It lay on an island in the Rhine between the Grand Duchy of Baden and the Canton of Zurich. The two governments divided the abbey's estates between themselves. By this period the monastery was active primarily as a Latin school. It had been forbidden in 1836 from taking on novices and was therefore already in a process of natural decline. After the last monks had been provided with adequate compensation and had left the abbey, the greater part of the monastic library, which comprised some 12,000 volumes in total, was taken to Zurich and added to the Cantonal Library, which was at the same time the library of the university, founded in 1833[21]. This cantonal and university

---

20 For greater detail on this topic by the St Gallen librarian Ernst Tremp, see his 'Stiftsbibliothek St Gallen, St Gallen versus Zürich: ein dreihundertjähriger Streit um Kulturgüter', in *Stanser Student*, 59.1 (2002), 1–21 (also published separately).

21 Jean-Pierre Bodmer and Martin Germann, *Kantonsbibliothek Zürich 1835–1915* (Zurich, 1986), 83–88; 'Gelehrte Mönche im Kloster Rheinau: Inkunabeln,

library was then merged with the city library in 1914 to form today's Zentralbibliothek Zürich. The Rheinau books in Zurich were from the very start assigned their own shelf mark as a distinct historical collection. Since that time, cataloguing in the Zentralbibliothek has continued to record former owners as a matter of course[22].

Like the regional state libraries in Germany and the *bibliothèques municipales* in France, it was the cantonal libraries in Switzerland in the nineteenth and twentieth centuries – in our case the Zentralbibliothek Zürich – that became a collecting-point and repository for the libraries that had formerly belonged to the church or to monasteries and convents.

Detailed indexing of former owners must now be pursued for the books today owned by these repositories, especially where holdings have been acquired intact. In our case, the former libraries that had been the previous owners can at least be reconstructed virtually. For this reason, in future, there must be no more sales of so-called "duplicates" of old books such as took place in the 1920s and 1930s in particular. A further dispersal of holdings would be a grave blow to research into the former provenance of these books. This must be obvious to anyone who takes an interest in scholarly matters: it was demonstrated by the outcry throughout Europe in 2006 when the government of Baden-Württemberg in Germany tried to auction off medieval manuscripts owned by the Baden National Library in Karlsruhe in order to raise money[23].

English translation by Chris Walton,
Solothurn
April 2012

Drucke und Handschriften', by Marlies Stähli, Christoph Eggenberger et al., in *Librarium*, 52.2–3 (2009), 65–133, also published separately (Zurich, 2009).

22 Leo Cunibert Mohlberg, *Mittelalterliche Handschriften*, Katalog der Handschriften der Zentralbibliothek Zürich 1 (Zurich, 1951), index; Christian Scheidegger, *Inkunabelkatalog der Zentralbibliothek Zürich*, 2 vols, Bibliotheca bibliographica Aureliana 220, 223 (Baden-Baden, 2008–2009), as of 2021 all incunabula descriptions have been transferred into the international database Material Evidence in Incunabula (MEI), for which see Dondi in this volume.

23 For the many reactions to this, see the blog by Klaus Graf at https://archiv.twoday.net/month?date=200610) and see Martin Germann, 'Die abenteuerliche Reise muss ein Ende haben ... Warum alte Handschriften intakt zu bewahren sind', in *Süddeutsche Zeitung*, 234 (11 October 2006), 16.

Bibliography

Manuscripts

Zürich, Zentralbibliothek, Ms. B 66 p. 16 (Bernhard Wyss, 'Chronik 1267–1530', see note 6).

Zürich, Zentralbibliothek, Ms. Car. C 44 p. 818 (Bullinger 'Von den Tigurineren', 1574, autograph, see note 12).

Zürich, Zentralbibliothek, Ms. Car. XII 4 (Pellikan's catalogue of the Grossmünster Library 1531–1551, autograph, see notes 7 and 17).

Zürich, Zentralbibliothek, Ms. J 86 fol. 75 (Laurenz Bosshard, 'Chronik über die Jahre 1185–1532', autograph, see note 9).

Zürich, Zentralbibliothek, Ms. L 104 (Gerold Edlibach, 'Aufzeichnungen 1520–1526', autograph, see note 13).

Secondary Works

Fernando Báez, *Storia universale della distruzione dei libri; dalle tavolette sumere alla guerra in Iraq* (Rome, 2007), Italian translation by Paolo Galloni and Marco Palma of the original edition *Historia universal de la destrucción de libros* (Barcelona, 2004).

Marcel Beck, 'Anmerkungen zu Geschichte und Psychologie des Biblioklasmus', in *Nordisk tidskrift för bok- och biblioteksväsen*, 39 (1952), 1–17.

Bilderstreit, Kulturwandel in Zwinglis Reformation, ed. Hans-Dietrich Altendorf and Peter Jezler (Zurich, 1984).

Magdalen Bless-Grabher, 'Zürich und seine Bettelordensklöster', in *Bettelorden, Bruderschaften und Beginen in Zürich, Stadtkultur und Seelenheil im Mittelalter*, ed. Barbara Helbling, Magdalen Bless-Grabher, and Ines Buhofer (Zurich, 2002), 10–24.

Jean-Pierre Bodmer and Martin Germann, *Kantonsbibliothek Zürich 1835–1915* (Zurich, 1986).

Laurenz Bosshard, 'Chronik über die Jahre 1185–1532', edited by Kaspar Hauser, Quellen zur schweizerischen Reformationsgeschichte 3 (Basel, 1905).

Ines Buhofer, 'Armut und Arbeit, Wandlung von Werten', in *Bettelorden, Bruderschaften und Beginen in Zürich, Stadtkultur und Seelenheil im Mittelalter*, ed. Barbara Helbling, Magdalen Bless-Grabher, and Ines Buhofer (Zurich, 2002), 280–91.

Jacques Figi, *Die innere Reorganisation des Grossmünsterstifts in Zürich von 1519 bis 1531*, Zürcher Beiträge zur Geschichtswissenschaft 9 (Zurich, 1951).

'Gelehrte Mönche im Kloster Rheinau: Inkunabeln, Drucke und Handschriften', von Marlies Stähli, Christoph Eggenberger et al., in *Librarium*, 52.2–3 (2009), 65–133, also published separately (Zurich, 2009).

Martin Germann, *Die reformierte Stiftsbibliothek am Grossmünster Zürich im 16. Jahrhundert und die Anfänge der neuzeitlichen Bibliographie*, Beiträge zum Buch- und Bibliothekswesen 34 (Wiesbaden, 1994).

Martin Germann, 'Die abenteuerliche Reise muss ein Ende haben … Warum alte Handschriften intakt zu bewahren sind', in *Süddeutsche Zeitung*, 234 (11 October 2006), 16.

Hans-Jörg Gilomen, 'Renten und Grundbesitz in der Toten Hand: realwirtschaftliche Probleme der Jenseitsökonomie', in *Himmel, Hölle, Fegefeuer, das Jenseits im Mittelalter: eine Ausstellung des Schweizerischen Landesmuseums*, catalogue by Peter Jezler et al. (Zurich, 1994), 135–48.

Barbara Helbling, 'Das Erbe der Klöster', in *Bettelorden, Bruderschaften und Beginen in Zürich, Stadtkultur und Seelenheil im Mittelalter*, ed. Barbara Helbling, Magdalen Bless-Grabher, and Ines Buhofer (Zurich, 2002), 292–305.

Peter Jezler, '"Da beschachend vil grosser endrungen": G. Edlibachs Aufzeichnungen über die Zürcher Reformation 1520–1526', in *Bilderstreit, Kulturwandel in Zwinglis Reformation*, ed. Hans-Dietrich Altendorf and Peter Jezler (Zurich, 1984), 41–74.

Peter Jezler, 'Der Bildersturm in Zürich 1523–1530', in *Bildersturm: Wahnsinn oder Gottes Wille?* Exhibition catalogue for Bern and Strasbourg 2000, ed. Cécile Dupeux et al. (Zurich, 2000), 75–83.

Gottfried W. Locher, *Zwingli und die schweizerische Reformation*, Die Kirche in ihrer Geschichte 3 (Göttingen, 1982).

Valentin Lötscher, *Der deutsche Bauernkrieg in der Darstellung und im Urteil der zeitgenössischen Schweizer*, Basler Beiträge zur Geschichtswissenschaft 11 (Basel, 1943).

Martin Luther, 'An die Ratsherren aller Städte Deutschlands, dass sie christliche Schulen aufrichten und halten sollen, 1524' (Constance, 1524).

Leo Cunibert Mohlberg, *Mittelalterliche Handschriften*, Katalog der Handschriften der Zentralbibliothek Zürich 1 (Zurich, 1951).

Christian Scheidegger, *Inkunabelkatalog der Zentralbibliothek Zürich*, 2 vols, Bibliotheca bibliographica Aureliana, 220, 223 (Baden-Baden, 2008–2009).

Alfred Schindler, 'Die Klagschrift des Chorherrn Hofmann gegen Zwingli', in *Reformiertes Erbe, Festschrift für Gottfried W. Locher* (Zurich, 1992), 325–59.

Paul Schweizer, 'Die Behandlung der zürcherischen Klostergüter in der Reformationszeit', in *Theologische Zeitschrift aus der Schweiz*, 2 (1885), 1–28.

Ernst Tremp, 'Stiftsbibliothek St Gallen, St Gallen versus Zürich: ein dreihundertjähriger Streit um Kulturgüter', *Stanser Student*, 59.1 (2002), 1–21.

Digital Sources

blog by Klaus Graf at https://archiv.twoday.net/month?date=200610.

PART 7

Tools for Research

Medieval Libraries of Great Britain: MLGB3

The dispersals of the libraries of religious houses came earlier to Great Britain and the scatter was wider and the losses more thorough than might be said for nearly any other country in Europe. It has meant that scholars who want to know what was where in Britain in the middle ages have had to work hard, and consequently provenance research is well developed; it has been proceeding in a scientific manner for more than a century. The foundational work of M. R. James (1862–1936) has been outlined by Richard Sharpe in the present volume. James was the first to make a systematic search in modern libraries for manuscripts bearing evidence of their medieval homes, and he also printed a number of surviving medieval catalogues of individual collections. These two streams of provenanced books and medieval booklists, where they combine, give the clearest view that is now possible of a medieval library. Since James's day, research in the area has been formalized in two discrete repertories: the Royal Historical Society handbook, *Medieval Libraries of Great Britain*, which reports provenanceable manuscripts, and the British Academy series, Corpus of British Medieval Library Catalogues. A new digital resource, MLGB3, unites these complementary research tools in a way that allows the evidence to be approached in an integrative manner[1].

The Corpus of British Medieval Library Catalogues aims to print and annotate the documentary evidence for the availability of texts and books in the institutional libraries of medieval Britain. The need for such a corpus was first discussed in the 1930s by two Oxford medievalists, R. W. Hunt (1908–1979) and R. A. B. Mynors (1903–1989); the latter happened also to be M. R. James's literary executor[2]. A project

---

1   An overview of the circulation and ownership of manuscripts in medieval England, which represents the first attempt to generalise on the basis of the totality of this evidence, is R. Sharpe, *Libraries and Books in Medieval England. The Role of Libraries in a Changing Book Economy. The Lyell Lectures for 2018–19* (Oxford, 2023).

2   The account of the project's genesis has been well told by R. H. and M. A. Rouse, *Registrum Anglie de libris doctorum et auctorum veterum*, Corpus of British Medieval Library Catalogues 2 (London, 1991), xxi–xxix, and in the memoirs of Hunt by Richard Southern and of Mynors by Michael Winterbottom in, respectively, *Proceedings of the British Academy* 67 (1981), 371–97, and 80 (1991), 371–401.

James Willoughby • Research Fellow of New College, Oxford. james.willoughby@history.ox.ac.uk

How the Secularization of Religious Houses Transformed the Libraries of Europe, 16th–19th Centuries, ed. by Cristina Dondi, Dorit Raines, and † Richard Sharpe, BIB, 63 (Turnhout, 2022), pp. 521–527.
BREPOLS ❧ PUBLISHERS   DOI 10.1484/M.BIB-EB.5.128502

committee, first discussed in 1961–1962, was formally established in 1976 and the first volume in the series was published in 1990. Under the General Editorship of the late Richard Sharpe, sixteen multi-authored volumes have now appeared in twenty physical books. At the time of writing, the seventeenth volume, on the secular cathedrals, is in press and there are three left to come, to be overseen now by Tessa Webber who has taken over as General Editor. Material in the Corpus is grouped by species: Augustinian libraries are gathered into one volume, Cistercians in another, mendicant libraries in another; the universities of Oxford and Cambridge are covered separately, as are collegiate churches and secular cathedrals. Some institutions are witnessed either by substantial and sophisticated catalogues, such as that of Dover priory of 1389 or Syon abbey of *c.* 1500, or else by such considerable miscellaneous evidence, such as for Peterborough abbey or Durham cathedral, that they are assigned their own volumes. So as to make the totality of this evidence indexable, volumes in the series are referred to by a letter-code and booklists are numbered, as are entries within a booklist. ("A1. 2" would indicate the second entry in the first booklist in the volume on Augustinian canons.) The cumulative index of identified authors and works, known as the List of Identifications, contains more than 40,000 entries for provenanced copies of about 8,700 texts, and is still growing.

The other stream of evidence for libraries is the positive evidence of surviving books, and this is the subject of the handbook *Medieval Libraries of Great Britain* (universally known by the acronym *MLGB*). It lists, by its modern shelf-mark, every manuscript that bears evidence of its institutional home in the middle ages. The first edition by the Oxford palaeographer Neil Ker (1908–1982) was published in 1941; it was revised and augmented by Ker in 1964, and a Supplement was published by Andrew Watson

in 1987, five years after Ker's death[3]. Preparing this handlist involved examining thousands of medieval manuscripts for physical or textual evidence of their original medieval provenance (work that Ker carried out originally with collaborators, who included Mynors and Hunt). The information was recorded on file-cards, retained in the Bodleian Library. The evidence harvested in this way allowed lists to be drawn up of extant medieval books arranged according to the libraries they had belonged to. Since its first publication, *MLGB* has been a crucial port of first call for any scholar wanting to know about a medieval book or library or wanting to trace the descent of a particular text.

Presentation of the gathered information within the scope of the printed page produced a masterpiece of lucid concision. Books are listed by their medieval institution, ordered alphabetically. The expression of a book with provenance takes no more than a line, showing at a glance the extent of known survivors for each library. Each book is represented by its modern shelf-mark and followed by a signal of its date and suggestion of its contents in a few words: "Augustinus, etc."; "Medica"; "Sermones". The evidence by which the provenance was established is signalled by an italic letter-code. For example, should the book contain an *ex libris* or *ex dono* inscription, an italic letter *e* supplies that clue to the reader. Ker's criteria for inclusion were positivist ones. He gave weight to such things as aspects of script or illumination known to be representative of a particular house (*s*), bindings likewise (*b*). His letter *c* stands for "contents", where these are locally specific, such as would pertain, for example, to a house chronicle or to obits added to a kalendar. Similar to this last, there may be other liturgical clues to ownership (*l*), such as

---

3 There is much on the project's genesis in the two memoirs referred to in the preceding note, as well as in Ian Doyle's memoir of Neil Ker in *Proceedings of the British Academy*, 80 (1991), 349–59.

the addition to a kalendar of saints known to have been culted at a particular place. Marginalia (*m*) can also be a good clue to provenance, marks made against texts by known hands, such as the so-called "Tremulous Hand" of Worcester cathedral priory or the annotator at Canterbury who used a particular set of signs to mark his interest in texts, mostly patristical, which he found in the cathedral library. Ker's letter *i* stands for an inscription of ownership by a known member of a religious house, although, as he recognised, that evidence may not always signal corporate ownership: mendicants, for example, were permitted the use of books and the freedom to carry them around as they moved house. To this list of Ker's I have added "d" to signal the evidence of *dicta probatoria* – usually a *secundo folio* – fixing a match between a manuscript and a medieval catalogue entry; the evidence is rarely definitive on its own but can combine decisively with other data[4]. The next element in the line reports any match that can be made with a medieval catalogue or booklist. Ker accepted that not every piece of evidence could be decisive and used a question mark at the end of a line to signal where there was some degree of doubt in the attribution of provenance. For Anglo-Saxon manuscripts, where evidence is frequently less firm but the desire to assign provenance more keen, Ker, himself an Anglo-Saxonist, must have known he was lowering the bar to entry; the pre-Conquest manuscripts assigned to Abingdon abbey, for example, are to be treated with some circumspection.

Ker's presentation is a model of lucidity, but the layout does restrict the quantity of information the user is able to draw on. To do more, to understand the contents of the book, gain details of its medieval or later ownership or

interrogate the evidence on which the judgement of provenance has been based, one has needed until now to go to the medieval book itself, or to the book's description in a modern catalogue, or to the original file-card on which Ker and his collaborators recorded their judgements. Digital presentation offers scope for more.

Work on the digital version, called MLGB3, began in 2009 and the first release, hosted by the Bodleian Library, has been freely available since 2015 at http://mlgb3.bodleian.ox.ac.uk[5]. The first stage of work involved entering all the information from the 8,000 *MLGB* cards into the database. These held more detail than could be made available in the print version, such as the medieval inscriptions which Ker usually troubled to transcribe, and details of post-medieval ownership, an aspect of particular value where a book remained available to the market into the nineteenth or twentieth century. A secondary stage of work has aimed to enrich these data, notably by adding images of the evidence for provenance, be that an inscription or some aspect of the book's physical appearance.

MLGB3 was envisaged from the outset as an online third edition of Ker's work, so it was a natural decision to retain the familiar and helpfully concise presentation. It was also clear that that format would map very well on to a digital platform: each variable in the expression of a line – library, shelf-mark, date, contents, evidence for provenance – could be treated as an ontological unit and form the basis for searching or filtering the whole dataset. Using the advanced search function, users may restrict

---

4 For discussion, see James Willoughby, 'The *secundo folio* and its uses, medieval and modern', *The Library*, 7th ser. 12 (2011), 237–58.

5 The project has been under the direction of Richard Sharpe and James Willoughby and was made possible by grants from the Andrew W. Mellon Foundation and the Neil Ker Memorial Fund. The resource was built by Xiaofeng Yang and Sushila Burgess of Bodleian Digital Library Systems and Services, while Jacob Currie, Peter Kidd, Daniela Mairhofer, and David Rundle have all contributed to the work of populating it.

their enquiry by any of these variables: author or title; medieval library (searchable as place, or as type of institution, e.g. "cathedral", "priory", or as species, e.g. "Franciscan", "Cistercian"); modern location; modern library; shelf-mark (reducible to any one of its elements, e.g. "Bodley", "Royal"); evidence type; medieval pressmark; medieval catalogue entry (using the alphanumerical system employed by the Corpus); later ownership; or else by words occurring in the general notes. Additional filters are available for separating books according to whether they are in print or manuscript and for restricting a search to those entries that have images. The resource currently returns entries for some 8,500 books.

A simple Browse function will present results for libraries in the familiar layout of the printed edition. But the new medium allows the user to open up any of these primary single-line entries and access more information about, and images of, the evidence of provenance or post-dissolution ownership, the contents of the medieval book, and how it was catalogued and shelf-marked in its medieval library setting, or to have an explanation of certain ambiguities that might exist around a particular provenance. There is educative potential in being able to see, for example, the wording of an inscription of ownership: the degree to which it is different or identical to other inscriptions from the same place will say something about the consistency of librarianship across the centuries of a religious house's existence. Being able to show an image alongside the transcription is a visible enhancement.

MLGB3 has also permitted integration with the Corpus, fulfilling the ambition of the sister projects' originators in a way that none of them could have foreseen. Searchability by author or title is possible across the whole dataset, opening to scholars the means of discovering quickly all known copies of a particular author or work, extant or attested, that can be provenanced to a particular medieval library. Data from the Corpus and its List of Identifications are available via two tabs

on the MLGB3 homepage: "Authors/Titles" and "Medieval catalogues". The first of these offers a means to return entries for identified authors or works across the whole Corpus, with the option of applying such filters as catalogue provenance, date range, and type of document. For example, the search term "Augustine" returns well over 3,000 records; searching for "bequests" of copies of works by Augustine between 1200 and 1500 returns more than forty results; narrowing the search to "Oxford" brings the number down to ten. The "Medieval catalogues" screen presents the data as they appear in the printed volumes of the Corpus, reconfigured into the shape of the original booklists and organized by species or place under the headings of the separate volumes. This presentation is reconstructed robotically from constituent entries in the List of Identifications and does not therefore include entries for anonymous or generic books, which have not been entered into that master index. So opening the evidence for Eton College, for example, from the list of Secular Colleges, displays headings for seventeen medieval booklists or records of bequest; of these, a dozen are live links which will display a sequence of entries of identified works from the whole booklist. The documents whose headings are not live are those that list only liturgical books, a category of text that has not been included in the List of Identifications. For the entirety of the evidence, as well as discussion of the documents themselves, one must refer, at least for the present, to the printed volumes.

A user working from either of these screens can click on index entries marked to show that the book survives and will be connected to the *MLGB* entry for the actual book, so linking documentary record and physical survivor. For example, British Library, MS Royal 5 B. xvi, a copy of Augustine's *Confessiones*, belonged to Rochester cathedral priory and was catalogued there in 1123 and again in 1202. Approaching from the Authors/Titles tab returns entries for those two catalogues, under the alphanumerical system used by the Corpus: B77. 15 and B79. 21. These references show as live, indicating that the book survives: clicking on them will take the user to the entry for the Royal manuscript on the *MLGB* side of the resource. Clicking instead on the link which explains that "B77" refers to the 1123 catalogue will take the user to the "Medieval catalogues" screen, where the entry for this book can be seen in the overall context of its list. Shortly before the dissolution the book was sequestered for the king and is visible in the inventory of the palace of Westminster of 1542 (indexed in the Corpus as H2. 576); it remains in the Royal Library to this day. The hope is that this interoperability of the two datasets will make the resource useful not only to historians wanting to know about the library of a particular house but also to scholars who are interested in the reception history of particular authors or texts.

Digital presentation also allows the expression of greater detail about post-medieval owner-ship. The printed edition relied on the user's being able to identify from a shelf-mark the sources for books, that "Selden" or "Douce" in a Bodleian shelf-mark, for example, refer to the collectors John Selden (1584–1654) and Francis Douce (1757–1834); but it could say no more in the span of the printed page about the varied sources for discrete collections such as these. Non-eponymous shelf-marks would require the user to know more, for example that many manuscripts in the Royal collection now in the British Library derived from the collection of John, Lord Lumley (1533–1609), which had absorbed the manuscript libraries gathered by Henry Fitzalan (1512–1580), 12th earl of Arundel, and Archbishop Thomas Cranmer (1489–1556), men at the eye of the storm that surrounded the dissolution of monasteries in England[6]. While it

is possible to acquire a reasonable expertise in these sorts of provenance histories without very much difficulty, it is clearly an advantage of the database that, in the augmented view for each entry in MLGB3, owners can be identified and, so far as they are recoverable, lines of transmission revealed from medieval into modern times.

A further area of enrichment has been in the scope of the data. The genius for concision in the expression of the printed page of *MLGB* extended also to the survey itself. Ker and his collaborators took the decision to exclude numerous books which survived the breach of the Reformation and have remained in their libraries since the middle ages – which in England means some cathedrals and some of the Oxford and Cambridge colleges. It is perhaps not well enough recognised that the printed edition is a handlist to books that have strayed, and that it passes over those that have not. To have aimed for more complete coverage would have swollen the extent of the handlist, and it might be remembered that the first edition of *MLGB* was printed in 1941 under wartime paper restrictions. However, the decision to exclude these static books has reinforced a general impression that the work is principally a repertory of monastic libraries. Cathedrals with medieval books still *in situ* were included in the second edition, but, with the exception of Salisbury, this might be considered an extension of the monastic bias since the additions chiefly comprised the large holdings of Durham and Worcester, both Benedictine cathedral priories in the middle ages. The university colleges were still excluded, perhaps because the extent of their holdings was considered to be common knowledge, or at least accessible from H. O. Coxe's catalogue of 1852 of manuscripts in Oxford college libraries and M. R. James's catalogues of the Cambridge colleges.

The online edition has grown to include all provenanceable medieval books and therefore all "medieval libraries" of which something can be said, including those university colleges that never

6 S. Jayne and F. R. Johnson, *The Lumley Library: the Catalogue of 1609* (London, 1956), 2–13; D. G. Selwyn, *The Library of Thomas Cranmer*, Oxford Bibliographical Society, 3rd ser. 1 (Oxford, 1996), xxvi–xxxiii.

lost their collections. This has changed the profile of the corpus very significantly. Where in the print edition university colleges accounted for just under four per cent of the total number of books, they now account for twenty-five per cent. It means that a small number of institutions of one class now proportionately outrank every other class, and the character of their libraries has become proportionately more visible. Of course, this profile is on the basis of comparisons drawn between institutions which survived and those which did not.

The continuing perception that *MLGB* is, first and foremost, a repertory of monastic manuscripts will shift again as the resource grows to include early printed books with medieval provenance. Ker included printed books in *MLGB* where he knew of them, but he made no dedicated search, doubtless seeing that modern holdings of editions printed before 1540 represented an ocean of material which bibliographers of print, guided by their own lights, had never catalogued with respect to recording provenance information. Emphases have changed in recent years, of course, as Cristina Dondi's account in this volume makes clear. For incunabula, there is good hope that books with British medieval provenance will be newly located by MEI. For books printed between 1501 and 1540, it is more difficult to envisage how the work could be done systematically, but copy-specifics are now routinely included in the cataloguing of print holdings by individual libraries, and this offers the hope that provenance notes can be harvested for MLGB3 at some point in the future. The expectation is that the English university colleges will grow still further in the profile, an effect first of the sort of institutional continuity which has preserved their libraries and second of the enthusiastic way college fellows embraced print and went on to leave their books to their colleges.

Refinement and augmentation of the data happens continually, on both sides of the resource. A larger ambition for the *MLGB* side is to provide at least one image of the evidence for provenance for every entry. Another is to provide augmented contents descriptions for every book, supplementing Ker's necessarily stark "Augustinus, etc." with a full listing of every significant work in a volume. Coverage of this aspect is currently partial, but completion will improve cross-searching between the *MLGB* side and the Corpus side of the resource. It holds out the real prospect of being able to identify every provenanced copy of a particular author or work, extant or lost, from the institutional libraries of medieval Britain.

Bibliography

Ian Doyle, [memoir of Neil Ker], in *Proceedings of the British Academy*, 80 (1991), 349–59.

S. Jayne and F. R. Johnson, *The Lumley Library: the Catalogue of 1609* (London, 1956).

Richard H. and Mary A. Rouse, *Registrum Anglie de libris doctorum et auctorum veterum*, Corpus of British Medieval Library Catalogues 2 (London, 1991).

D. G. Selwyn, *The Library of Thomas Cranmer*, Oxford Bibliographical Society, 3rd ser. 1 (Oxford, 1996).

Richard Sharpe, *Libraries and Books in Medieval England. The Role of Libraries in a Changing Book Economy. The Lyell Lectures for 2018–19* (Oxford, 2023).

Richard Southern, [memoir of Richard Hunt], *Proceedings of the British Academy*, 67 (1981), 371–97.

James Willoughby, 'The *secundo folio* and its uses, medieval and modern', *The Library*, 7th ser. 12 (2011), 237–58.

Michael Winterbottom, [memoir of Roger Mynors], *Proceedings of the British Academy*, 80 (1991), 371–401.

Digital sources

MLGB3, http://mlgb3.bodleian.ox.ac.uk.

CRISTINA DONDI

Material Evidence in Incunabula and Other Tools for Searching the Provenance of Early Printed Books

Material Evidence in Incunabula (MEI) is an international collaborative database which captures the evidence of ownership and use in surviving fifteenth-century printed books to assess the distribution, sale, and reception of books over five hundred years, and therefore the social and economic impact of the introduction of a new technology, hand-printing, on European society at the time of its transition from the medieval to the early modern period. The database also allows us to detect and understand the historical circumstances surrounding the formation and dispersal of libraries.

During the ten years which followed the 2012 conference this digital tool has grown substantially. In 2012 the database included 2,454 editions in 3,851 copies, from a dozen or two institutions. Today it includes 60,000 records from almost 500 libraries in 23 countries, contributed by over 200 editors. And over 24,000 records pertaining to private or institutional ownership[1].

Well aware of the need for the historian to capture the evidence of the impact of the secularizations on the migration of books and the formation of libraries, MEI introduced the option of "institutional transfer" among the "Methods of acquisition" field which distinguishes also purchases, donations, bequests, exchanges, dedication copies, consignments, requisitions/thefts, and restitutions.

An advanced search[2] returns 3,311 editions in 5,237 copies which entered collections because of

---

1 22 Nov. 2021: 15,610 editions in 59,809 copies, from 493 libraries. 24,969 former owners. See https://data.cerl.org/mei/_stats or type '*' in the free search window. Information on former owners is gathered in a satellite database to MEI, Owners of Incunabula and Other Early Printed Books (OOI) https://data.cerl.org/owners/_search.

2 data.provenance.acquisitionMethod:e. Guidelines for advanced searches in MEI can be found at http://15cbooktrade.ox.ac.uk/distribution-use/mei-searching-guidelines/.

Cristina Dondi • Professor of Early European Book Heritage, University of Oxford, Oakeshott Senior Research Fellow in the Humanities, Lincoln College; Secretary of the Consortium of European Research Libraries (CERL). cristina.dondi@lincoln.ox.ac.uk

How the Secularization of Religious Houses Transformed the Libraries of Europe, 16th–19th Centuries, ed. by Cristina Dondi, Dorit Raines, and † Richard Sharpe, BIB, 63 (Turnhout, 2022), pp. 529–547.

BREPOLS ❧ PUBLISHERS   DOI 10.1484/M.BIB-EB.5.128503

institutional transfer, basically 10% of the copies at present in the database. This is a very good start, but a fraction of the real amount of books displaced following governmental directives and still surviving today. First, more of these books are actually included in the database but without being associated with the "institutional transfer" tag, generally because of incomplete cataloguing, but also due to lack of knowledge about the history of the specific book or collection. The ongoing editing of these records will make the books already catalogued in MEI and involved in secularizations visible and searchable. Secondly, a large number of books known to have emerged from secularized institutions are still not in MEI. Practically no records from German libraries are currently in the database, something which is being addressed at present[3]. Secularized German books sold as duplicates and today in European and American libraries[4], for example in Oxford or at Harvard, are either not yet been included in MEI (only a fraction of Harvard records have been catalogued in MEI so far), or not yet tagged as "institutional transfer": all Bodleian incunabula are in MEI, but the electronic upload from Bod-inc to MEI could not also provide the tagging for the method of acquisition so this operation has to be done manually. As in most enterprises which attempt to assess widespread phenomena with the use of large quantities of evidence, two essential components are needed: some kind of technical means and the process of actual data gathering. In MEI we have a digital tool which is programmed to support us in the detection of books whose presence in institutional or private libraries is the consequence of the secularizations

of religious houses of Europe. But the task of "feeding the machine", of contributing data is so vast that only the international, collaborative, effort of librarians and scholars can achieve it.

Incunabula from British and European Monastic Houses in the Bodleian Library

Within the Bodleian collection it has been possible to single out quite clearly incunabula from religious houses, thanks to the *Bodleian Catalogue of Incunabula*, which describes in great detail both the text and the provenance history of each book[5]. The catalogue was prepared over a period of thirteen years, from 1992 to 2005. Its *Provenance Index* lists around 5,000 entries of personal or institutional ownership.

A specific investigation of incunabula from English and Scottish monastic libraries was conducted by Alan Coates and Kristian Jensen in 1997 and discussed in an essay published in a festschrift for Andrew Watson[6].

From the time of its foundation the Bodleian Library has been acquiring small numbers of incunabula, including books formerly owned by religious houses in England and Scotland, acquired in a variety of ways, but not as a direct result of the dissolution of monasteries, because the Bodleian Library was only founded in 1602, well

---

3   Data from the collection of incunabula of the University Library of Tübingen were extracted from the INKA database and entered in MEI in May 2020; however manual enhancing (various tagging including method of acquisition) is now ongoing. https://www.inka.uni-tuebingen.de/.

4   See the paper by Bettina Wagner in this volume.

5   *A Catalogue of Books Printed in the Fifteenth Century now in the Bodleian Library*, ed. A. Coates, K. Jensen, C. Dondi, B. Wagner, and H. Dixon, with the assistance of C. White and E. Mathew; blockbooks by N. Palmer, and an inventory of Hebrew incunabula by S. Schaeper, 6 vols (Oxford, 2005); available online at http://incunables.bodleian.ox.ac.uk/.

6   Alan Coates and Kristian Jensen, 'The Bodleian Library's Acquisition of Incunabula with English and Scottish Medieval Monastic Provenances', in *Books and Collectors 1200–1700: Essays Presented to Andrew Watson*, ed. James P. Carley and Colin G. C. Tite (London, 1997), 237–59.

after the dissolution took place. Richard Sharpe's essay in this volume outlines the complexities of the English and Scottish dissolution, and concludes by observing how fewer incunabula than manuscripts survived from monastic houses in the British Isles, and why. The dispersal of books was as varied as that of the houses they belonged to. Andrew Watson had noted the common pattern of circulation of these books: from religious houses to small collectors, then to private collections of increasing importance and size, until they reached the institutions they are in today[7]. One example may serve: Oxford, Bodleian Library, Auct. 1Q 4.2 contains three editions of William of Auvergne printed in Nuremberg in 1496–1497 and bound together[8]: the volume was first owned by Ralph, a Cistercian monk of St Bernard's College in 1533–1534, before he was executed by hanging in 1538. Then it was in the hands of Edward Medley, who appears to have been a middle man who acquired second-hand books (the price is often stated in the book), and at least five books owned by him entered the Bodleian by 1605.

Coates and Jensen identified 28 books with English monastic provenance: some show evidence of institutional ownership, for example the Carthusians of Sheen; more often, however, the books contain personal ownership marks of religious, for example Richard Gordon, a Benedictine monk at Westminster Abbey, or Anthony Adell Jackson, a Cistercian monk at Kirkstall Abbey in Yorkshire[9].

Five of these can be counted among the Bodleian's foundation copies, that is books which entered at the time of the foundation of the library or were there by the time the first catalogue was published in 1605: they were acquired with money left by the Bishop of Winchester Thomas Bilson, or donated by John Barcham, a fellow of Corpus Christi College. One arrived with Archbishop Laud's donation in 1635–1640. Also in the seventeenth century, four came from the collection of John Selden who, incidentally, was still interested in the text of these books and did not acquire them as a form of antiquarianism. One came with the books of Edward Bernard, Savillian Professor of Astronomy, which were purchased by the library in 1697.

In the eighteenth century two books arrived with Thomas Tanner's bequest. He was bishop of St Asaph, former fellow of All Souls, and canon of Christ Church. One came from the large bequest of Richard Gough, strong in pre-Reformation material. Finally two came from the largest bequest of incunabula ever received by the library, that of Francis Douce, former Keeper of Mss at the British Museum, in 1834, some 479 incunabula.

Only later in the nineteenth century was the acquisition of English monastic incunabula partly motivated by their provenance. Certainly provenance was the reason for the four purchases which were made in the course of the twentieth

7   Alan Coates, *English Medieval Books: the Reading Abbey Collections from Foundation to Dispersal* (Oxford, 1999), 126 and 122, note 2, personal communication to the author.

8   Guillermus Alvernus, Episcopus Parisiensis, *Opera*. Ed: Petrus Danhauser. Add: Johann Rosenbach. [Nuremberg: Georg Stuchs, after 31 Mar. 1496]. Folio. Bod-Inc G-296; GW 11862; ISTC ig00708000; MEI 00208185. Id., *De sacramentis*. Add: *Cur deus homo; De poenitentia*. [Nuremberg: Georg Stuchs, not after 1497]. Folio. Bod-Inc G-299; GW 11869; ISTC ig00716500; MEI 00208187. Id., *De universo*. [Nuremberg: Georg Stuchs, not after 1497]. Folio. Bod-Inc G-300; GW 11870; ISTC ig00717000; MEI 00208189. Oxford, Bodleian Library, Auct. 1Q 4.2(1–3). Coates-Jensen, as note 6, no. 22.

9   A further incunable from the Carthusians of Hull was acquired by the Bodleian in 2015, the donation of Julian Blackwell; it is a copy of the 1493 Nuremberg Chronicle; Bod-Inc S-108(7). I would like to thank Alan Coates for drawing my attention to this later acquisition and for suggesting that other cases may well be out there, but their monastic provenance may not have been recognized yet, or may indeed be no longer possible to prove because of loss of evidence (personal communication, June 2020).

century: three out of four printed in England, one actually in Oxford.

Overall, the 28 editions with English monastic provenance were printed in Paris (9), Lyon (4), and eight from either Basel, Cologne, or Speyer, the Low Countries and Nuremberg, seven from Venice and one from Rome. They are bibles, books of hours, a rule of St Benedict, collections of sermons, contemporary devotional works by Johannes Nider or Gerard of Zutphen, a Cicero's *De officiis*; and one edition in English, Caxton's *The lyff of the faders*[10].

However, the Bodleian Library also holds a very substantial collection of incunabula from religious houses elsewhere in Europe, but especially from Germany and Italy. These provenances have been carefully identified during the preparation of the Bodleian's catalogue of incunabula. On the occasion of the 2012 conference all monastic provenances were extracted and arranged geographically, and by religious order; the results were shared on the conference website and are listed in the appendix[11]. For the Bodleian collection a summary includes:

Austria: 55 books from 19 houses
Belgium: 92 books from 51 houses
Czech Republic: 15 books from 13 houses
Denmark: 1 book
France: 79 books from 56 houses
Germany: 778 books from 241 houses
Italy: 161 books from 115 houses
Lithuania: 3 books from 1 house
Luxembourg: 3 books from 2 houses
Netherlands: 38 books from 14 houses
Poland: 9 books from 6 houses
Slovakia: 1 book
Spain: 37 books from 9 houses
Switzerland: 8 books from 7 houses

United Kingdom: 42 books from 23 houses
Unidentified monastic locations: 31 books

A total of 558 different religious institutions and 1,352 books are represented, a very considerable proportion of the 7,500 or so incunabula in the Bodleian collection.

In 2012 we had one provenance from Lithuania, three books from the Franciscans of Vilnius. Today, MEI includes all incunabula from Lithuania, listing 138 former owners in the Owners of Incunabula and Other Early Printed Books database. Records of religious institutions include, in Vilnius, the Jesuits, the Observant and Conventual Franciscans, the Carmelites, the Holy Trinity monastery, the Orthodox seminary, the Dominicans, the Hospitallers, and the Cathedral Chapter. In Kaunas, the Cathedral Basilica Chapter, the Dominicans, and the Observant Franciscans. In Varniai, the Samogitian Cathedral Chapter and Seminary, and the Jesuits. Then the Benedictines of Haradzishcha; the Bernardines (OFMObs) of Dotnuva, Kretinga, Lviv, Trakai, and Tytuvėnai; the Dominicans of Palėvenė, Paparčiai and of Raseiniai; the Jesuits of Kražiai and of Pašiaušė; the Church of the Assumption of the Blessed Virgin Mary in Maišiagala, near Vilnius.

A total of 469 incunables from Lithuania are listed in MEI, including one today in Poland, one in Cambridge and four in Oxford (the three mentioned above and an Italian Hebrew edition[12]).

The ways in which many of the books from European secularized institutions entered the Bodleian were discussed and presented during the conference, some further cases can now be found in this volume[13]. I will only mention Maffeo

10 Bodleian Library, Arch. G d. 29; Bod-Inc- H-116; MEI 00204045.

11 In the appendix are also provided monastic provenances now in collections at Harvard University, extracted from a printed catalogue of the collection.

12 Copy-specific information of Hebrew incunabula was not provided in Bod-Inc. The research has recently been done as part of the 15cHEBRAICA project funded by the Rothschild Foundation Hanadiv Europe (2018–2021).

13 During the conference we held a show and tell session in Convocation House, where Richard Sharpe presented manuscripts and Cristina Dondi incunabula from

Pinelli (1735–1785), the last official state printer of the city of Venice, whose books were purchased by the London bookseller James Edwards and sold at auction in 1789. Some of his books came from monastic libraries in the Veneto, such as the Benedictines of S. Giorgio Maggiore, the Camaldolese of S. Michele di Murano in Venice, the Carthusians and Benedictines of Padua, as well as from the suppressed Jesuits of Hall in Tyrol, and of Parma. The Bodleian bought 79 incunables for £538, out of a total purchase at the sale of £1080. In the Bodleian catalogue of incunabula 108 Pinelli incunabula have been identified as now in Bodley, some of which entered the collection later on, having been purchased at the Pinelli sale by Michael Wodhull, Richard Heber, or Francis Douce. In 2021 the Owners of Incunabula and Other Early Printed Books satellite database to MEI traces 170 incunabula and 45 sixteenth-century books formerly owned by Pinelli, not only in Bodley, but also in Cambridge UL (15), the Parliament of Athens (6), the Folger Shakespeare Library in Washington (6), the British Library (6), Berkeley (5), Harvard (5), Gennadius in Athens (2), Eton College (2), Liverpool University (2), Yale (2), Oxford Taylor (2), then one copy each in Bergamo, Canterbury Cathedral, Princeton, Lugano, Manchester, Milan, Edinburgh, Glasgow, Venice, and a private collection. Many more remain to be added, from the British Library, from other sources listed in Index Possessorum Incunabulorum (IPI)[14],

and from wherever else these books ended up: while it is unfeasible to scavenge the thousands of libraries with incunabula in search for one historical collection, it is sensible to bring the cataloguing of all incunabula into one place, so that this, as well as many other thousand historical collections can be virtually brought back together and their dispersal investigated.

Early Bookowners in Britain (EBOB), MLGB3, and the *Corpus of British Medieval Library Catalogues*

In 1999 Margaret Lane Ford undertook extensive research on printed books imported into England and Scotland up to 1550 and still surviving today in libraries in the UK. The results were published in her contribution to the third volume of the *Cambridge History of the Book in Britain*[15]. The data were converted by CERL into a database, Early Bookowners in Britain (EBOB), and consist of some 4,474 entries pertaining to books, corresponding to 3,495 editions. The database lists 1885 personal and 92 institutional owners. Since it was the largest and most comprehensive such sample, it allowed a preliminary analysis of where books were coming from and when, as well as what books were circulating. It offered a picture of the intellectual climate as much as of the book trade[16].

A search in the database by religious order brings the following results: Franciscans (28),

suppressed religious houses. The incunabula included volumes from the Benedictines of San Giorgio Maggiore, Venice, of Tegernsee, and of Fiecht (Tyrol); the Augustinian Canons Regular of the Lateran Congregation of Padua; and the Premonstratensians of Weissenau.

14 https://data.cerl.org/ipi/_search. IPI contains some 32,000 entries of personal names, institutional names, monograms, and arms pertaining to the ownership of incunabula. They were extracted by Paul Needham from some 200 published catalogues of incunabula with provenance information, augmented with information

from his personal research, and placed in a word file of some 1,267 pages or 500,650 words. The file was converted into a searchable database by CERL. The version offered online dates to March 2010.

15 Margaret Lane Ford, 'Importation of printed books into England and Scotland', in *Cambridge History of the Book in Britain*, 6 vols (Cambridge, 1999–2011), iii 179–201.

16 https://data.cerl.org/ebob/_search. The focus of the data being on the 15th and 16th centuries means that unfortunately it cannot be used to investigate the cause of the survival of these books into the 21st century.

Dominicans (60), Benedictines (3), Cistercians (12).

These numbers refer to editions, each sometimes represented in multiple copies owned by various people or institutions. The research is from the perspective of the books, not of their owners. A search for "Benedictine" ("Benedictines" gives no results) offers three results:

A copy of Robertus Holkot printed in Paris in 1489, one of Nicolaus de Orbellis printed in Basel in 1494, and a *Regulae monasticorum* printed in Venice in 1500.

The Holkot copy was owned by the Benedictines of Peterborough, Northants., and it is today in London, Middle Temple Library, BAY L(1). It corresponds to MLGB3[17]; however in MLGB3's list another incunable from Peterborough is also listed, a Bible printed in Nuremberg in 1497 and today in London, Dulwich College, A. 3. fol. 3[18]. This incunable is not listed in EBOB.

A search in MLGB3 for "Type of book: Printed" will result in 483 records, part incunabula, part sixteenth-century. These are all books which still survive today in UK libraries, partly listed in EBOB or MEI. It is clear that these tools have to be used in a complementary way, and that, ideally, data pertaining to incunabula should be brought together.

A search for printed books should also be conducted through the *Corpus of British Medieval Library Catalogues*. The result would bring to light not (only) what survives today but the printed editions which did exist in these libraries at the time their catalogues were compiled, before their dissolution. These editions, when identified, as is generally the case thanks to work done by James Willoughby in matching the indication of their *secundo folio* with extant editions[19], should then be entered in MEI as "Historical Copies", that is copies of incunabula which we know did exist at some point in time and space, but were subsequently destroyed.

The category of Historical Copies in MEI is a fundamental facility which allows us to track and take stock of part of the immense quantity of fifteenth-century books which were destroyed at some point after their production.

Unfortunately for the British provenances, destruction is the most likely outcome, because of the historical period in which the dissolution took place, as explained by Richard Sharpe in this volume. A very different story pertains to the many books recorded in MEI as Historical Copies on the basis of catalogues and inventories dating from the eighteenth century and later; the dissolutions which followed Joseph II, Napoleon, the *desamortización* in the Iberian peninsula, the formation of the Italian state, and the October Revolution in 1917 facilitated the dispersal of books well beyond national boundaries, via the antiquarian book trade, but not their destruction. There is every hope that collaborative cataloguing in MEI will allow us to trace them and match a historical copy with a physical one. Several examples of this are discussed in the paper by Dondi-Prosdocimi-Raines in this volume.

Incunabula, and other books, from suppressed religious houses can be found today in most European and American libraries. Partly in the area they came from and were destined for after the

---

17　Holkot, Robertus, *Super sapientiam Salomonis*, [Paris: Georg Wolf], 21 Oct. 1489. 4°. EBOB 00008216; GW 12888; ISTC ih00290000; MEI 02003663. For the online version of Medieval Libraries of Great Britain (MLGB3) http://mlgb3.bodleian.ox.ac.uk/, see Sharpe and Willoughby in this volume.

18　*Biblia latina* (cum postillis Nicolai de Lyra et expositionibus Guillelmi Britonis in omnes prologos S. Hieronymi et additionibus Pauli Burgensis replicisque Matthiae Doering). Add: Nicolaus de Lyra: *Contra perfidiam Judaeorum*, Nuremberg: Anton Koberger, 1497. Folio. GW 4294; ISTC ib00619000.

19　J. M. W. Willoughby, 'The *secundo folio* and its uses, medieval and modern', *The Library*, 7th ser. 12 (2011), 237–58.

closure of the institutions to which they originally belonged, but equally just about anywhere else, according to paths which, initiated by political change, followed economic and commercial imperatives and ended up being totally unex-pected. The identification of books dispersed by the secularizations and still surviving today can only be properly pursued with a "bottom-up", collaborative enterprise: the work continues.

Appendix

Incunabula from European Religious Houses now in the Bodleian Library, an Extract from the Provenance Index of Bod-Inc[20]

AUSTRIA: 55 books from 19 houses
<u>Augustinian Canons</u>: Ranshofen am Inn A-157(5), H-132(1), J-156; Sankt Florian D-152, J-221(1); Vienna A-053, J-119; Wiener Neustadt C-428
<u>Augustinian Hermits</u>: Mariabrunn A-600, M-171, T-107; Vienna M-176(1), P-383(1)
<u>Benedictines</u>: Mehrerau D-197(2); Salzburg H-220(1), J-130(2), R-093
<u>Canons Regular</u>: Dürnstein G-278
<u>Carmelites</u>: Lienz J-087
<u>Carthusians</u>: Gaming B-015, L-138
<u>Congregation of the Daughters of the Divine Saviour</u>: Vienna A-600, M-171, T-107
<u>Dominicans</u>: Vienna A-562(2), B-441, C-046, C-047, C-292(2), H-023(1)?, J-011, J-124(1), K-005?, N-042?, N-081?, N-087?, P-298, P-335, Q-001?, R-035?, S-323, T-095(1), T-287?
<u>Franciscans</u>: Vienna A-246, B-610(2), I-036(1)
<u>Franciscans Observant</u>: Innsbruck N-117; Salzburg J-255(2)
<u>Jesuits</u>: Vienna N-024(2), P-265
<u>Parish church</u>: Villach XYL-18

<u>Pauline Hermits</u>: Wiener Neustadt C-428, H-016, P-076(2), T-160

BELGIUM: 86 books from 49 houses
<u>Augustinian Canons</u>: Bethlehem (Louvain) B-436, D-094, D-178, T-132(1); Brussels P-025; Groenendael R-106(3); Liège S. Crux B-157(2); Liège S. Leonardus C-304 P-026; Louvain N-078, P-343(1), R-057; Maaseik G-332(1); Roermond au der Maas R-142(1); Zoniënbos at Oudergem B-181, B-374(2), B-456, F-093, F-095(1), H-128, S-182
<u>Augustinian Hermits</u>: Mechelen S-264; Walincourt B-437(2)
<u>Augustinian Hermits of the Congr. of S. Gulielmus</u>: Bruges B-434
<u>Beghards</u>: Maastricht V-015; Mechelen B-181, B-456, F-093, F-095(1), N-031, S-182
<u>Benedictines</u>: Stavelot J-242
<u>Brigittines</u>: Termonde G-332(2)
<u>Brothers of the Common life</u>: Emmerich H-112
<u>Carmelites, discalced</u>: Ghent B-357
<u>Capuchins</u>: Ghent D-035; Maastricht G-143
<u>Carthusians</u>: Bruges A-154(2), A-157(1); Brussels B-294; Louvain P-499; Roermond au der Maas C-429; Sheen Anglorum C-505(2)
<u>Cathedrals</u>: Antwerp H-054; Tournai G-230(1), P-466?, T-055, T-219
<u>Celestines</u>: Heverlee S-240
<u>Cistercians</u>: Ter Doest P-244
<u>Cistercian nuns</u>: La Ramée S-371
<u>Franciscans</u>: Diest C-070; Roermond R-073; Tienen J-112(1), T-116(2)

---

20 These lists only include institutional ownership; if we counted individual ownership by members of religious orders the number would grow considerably.

Franciscans Observant: Emmerich T-292; Maastricht S. Antonius de Padua T-202; Maastricht Mons gratiae Dei T-202; Mons G-331

Franciscans Recollect: Mons G-331; Wavre H-231

Franciscans Recollect Irish: Louvain A-207, A-209(2)

Jesuits: Bruges G-132(2); Ghent A-073, B-449, C-450(2), M-155, S-257, XYL-21; Louvain B-292, B-616, L-160(2), P-183(1), R-129; Roermond S-134 (2)

Minims: Mons C-069

Premonstratensians: De Parc C-287(2), L-099; Dronghen B-472, C-375; Hélécine H-143(1); Tongerloo H-091, J-190(1), R-004(2), S-344

CZECH REPUBLIC: 15 books from 13 houses

Augustinian Canons: Olomouc J-220(2); Třeboň B-469(2)

Cathedral Chapter: Olomouc C-068

Cistercians: Zbraslav G-146, M-298, V-165

Dominicans: Ĉeské Budějovice/Budweis N-118; Cheb P-187(2)

Franciscans: Olomouc P-346(2)

Jesuits: Krupka A-545; Olomouc P-207; Prague G-086(2)?

Premonstratensians: Doksany/Doxan P-261; Prague G-060

Servites: Jaroměřice nad Rokytnou B-340

DENMARK: 1 book

Hospital: Randers S. Spiritus P-2134

FRANCE: 85 books from 58 houses

Antonines: Rheims A-305

Augustinian Canons: Lille H-80; Phalempin A-586, A-599, T-094(2)

Barnabites: Paris W-017

Benedictines: Auxerre L-082; Baume-Les-Moines T-276; Beauvais E-028; Corbie B-063; Le Mans R-112(1); Moyenmoutier B-555, J-100; Nice M-014; Verrie A-092?

Brothers of the Common Life: Cambrai B-183, B-450, M-158

Capuchines: Auxerre L-082; Chaumont L-073(1)

Carmelites: Chalon-sur-Saône C-074, C-242; Dijon B-158, R-110(1)

Carmelites, discalced: Cambrai B-183, B-450, M-158

Cathedral library: Strasbourg S-112(1)?

Celestines: Amiens J-197; Limay A-292, A-396, B-288(1); Marcoussis B-448, J-199(2), V-128; Metz D-162, V-007; Offémont L-086; Paris I-038(1), R-028, R-067(3); Sens R-105(1)

Cistercians: Clairvaux T-030; Fontenay C-200?; Vaux-de-Cernay H-154

Cluniac Priory: Paris B-179

College: Lyon S. Irenaeus T-034; Paris C. des Bernardins H-133

Collegiate Church: Strasbourg P-440, U-003

Congregation of St Vanne: Verdun S. Agericus P-366

Dominicans: Albi O-014; Angers H-083; Metz L-085; Paris E-085

Franciscans: Miricuria Z-002; Nantes G-093, G-103, G-107, G-124, N-082, P-206(1); Rennes C-060(1); Strasbourg L-003(1); Vienne A-246

Franciscans Recollect: Bordeaux J-062; St Omer A-533(2)

Hospitals: Paris S. Catharina N-071

Jesuits: Arras G-155, P-106; Chambéry C-282; Dole P-239(2); Ensisheim B-273; Lyon S-187; Paris B-239(1), C-476(2), M-310(2); Rouen D-087; Villefranche-sur-Saône C-282

Minims: Lunéville B-386; Toulouse A-498, B-257

Williamites: H-235

Unidentified order: Douai M-167(2); Lille M-167(2)

GERMANY: 778 books from 241 houses

Augustinian Canons: Au am Inn A-467(2), B-447(1), B-476, C-401, G-181(1), G-225; Augsburg B-303(1), B-323(1)?, T-102, V-139; Baumburg B-276(1), B-469(1), D-179, L-080, R-069(1); Beyharting A-470, A-549, G-319, H-243, L-111; Böddeken J-050(2); Diessen A-008, L-075, N-019, N-065, N-104(2), R-041, Z-001; Freiburg im Breisgau G-327; Gars G-236, J-046, P-321; Heidenfeld G-050; Herrenwörth C-029(1),

D-201(1)?; Herrieden A-169(2); Hildesheim G-324, S-267; Indersdorf A-548(2), L-077, S-266, T-146, T-179, T-272(2); Mainz J-291; Passau B-610(3), D-166, G-234, J-157, J-235, J-276, R-089(2); Polling B-315, B-329(1), B-465, E-005, G-221, G-252, J-217, J-245, T-137; Rebdorf A-169(3), A-182(2), B-041, I-039, J-122(2), J-124(2), J-129, J-143(1), N-027(2), N-093, P-163(2); Reichenhall C-104, I-013, J-084, L-084(2), N-064, T-135, T-272(3); Rottenbuch A-575, P-233, P-520(1), S-258, T-289; Stadtamhof A-469(1), R-002(1); Ulm A-099(1), B-084(1)

Augustinian Nuns: Ahlen B-241(1); Coesfeld D-188, G-088, G-219, T-165

Augustinian Hermits: Memmingen A-385, A-387(3), C-084(1), C-382, D-120, D-176, G-254, N-057(2); Munich A-550, B-240, B-241(2), S-059; Ramsau D-187; Regensburg J-111, M-294, P-316; Seemannshausen B-609(1), C-481, J-042, L-083(1), N-059, P-045(4), S-314; Trier M-028; Uttenweiler B-242, C-061, C-440?, F-012(1), N-046; Würzburg J-249, M-283, M-299, T-132(2), V-108?

Benedictines: Andechs A-113, A-120, B-077, C-126, D-174(1), G-253, H-228; Asbach an der Rott L-073(2), P-045(5), P-049, P-076(1); Attel A-390(2), C-091, D-182, H-018; Augsburg A-345, B-531(2)?, E-005, M-166(1), P-010, T-090(2), T-162(2), V-130; Auhausen an der Wörnitz I-031(2); Benediktbeuren A-094(1), A-332, C-087, F-012(2), G-086(3), G-198, G-212, G-227, M-143, S-265; Blaubeuren B-455, G-221; Brühl P-225; Donauwörth A-539(1); Erfurt B-527, C-079; Fiecht A-593(2); A-636, B-085, B-130?, C-152, F-099(1), H-242(1), J-010, N-068, P-062, R-006, T-031, V-078; Frauenzell T-239; Füssen H-086(2); Gengenbach B-076(1); Heidenfeld M-289; Helmstedt J-075; Hildesheim R-099, T-073(1); Hillersleben G-091, G-119, G-128(1), H-227(2), I-031(3); Huysburg G-163; Irsee B-084(2), B-416(1), T-023, T-101; Liesborn H-045?, H-094, J-188, J-214(2), T-157(2); Mainz C-359; Mallersdorf P-048(2); Maria Laach C-444(1), J-037(1), M-325(1); Metten B-324(2), C-080, E-082(1), J-247(1), P-321?; Niederaltaich A-469(1), G-183; Northeim D-163(1), D-167(1);

Ochsenhausen S-112(2); Ottobeuren A-499, H-013, P-012; Petershausen B-276(2), D-154; Plankstetten J-270, S-310; Prüfening B-331, I-006, N-057(1); Regensburg A-127, A-148(2), A-232, B-135, B-417(1), B-418, C-086, E-067, G-102, H-032(2), H-100(1), H-103, J-090, P-080, P-260, R-065, R-067(1), R-068(1), R-126(3), T-133, T-140(3); Rott am Inn A-471, C-135, G-216, J-044(1), J-052; St Veit an der Rott P-520(1); Scheyern B-130(1), D-203, H-031, M-096, M-306, N-036, P-514(2), S-051, S-360(1), T-086; Schönau B-296(1); Seeon B-060, B-071; Tegernsee A-173, A-194, A-197, A-221(2), A-284(2), A-351, B-154, B-332, B-499, B-610(1), D-179?, G-167, H-038, H-058, H-147(1), I-047, J-097, J-110, L-037, L-081(1), L-133(2), M-183, M-186, N-043, O-077(1), P-037, P-524, S-367, T-159, T-249(2), V-160; Thierhaupten A-556(1), B-088(2), B-517, H-085, J-051(1); Trier B-397, J-202(2), S-110, V-086; Vilmar an der Lahn B-397; Weihenstephan S-039(1); Werden an der Ruhr A-500(1), H-107, S-162; Wessobrunn G-320, M-046, N-001, S-009, S-239, T-064, V-134; Wiblingen B-255(1); Würzburg B-138, L-097, M-059, N-011, N-012, N-013, P-503

Brigittines: Altomünster, D-181, S-039(3); Cleves A-541(2), A-551(2), A-559(2), A-591, A-604(2)

Canons Regular: Augsburg Priory S. Crux A-321(1), A-561, B-373(1); Eberhardsklausen B-010; Frankenthal H-111(1)

Capuchins: house in Westphalia H-090; Deggendorf N-094; Dinkelsbühl G-210; Donauwörth D-184; Eichstätt M-296; Engelberg L-132; Erding B-305; Freiburg im Breisgau F-100, F-101?, J-279(1); Heidelberg V-158; Hildesheim B-277, B-284, B-314(2), B-314(3); Koblenz B-317; Nothgottes J-255(1); Ried B-463, C-367; Worms R-107(1)

Carmelites: Abensberg A-169(4), E-071, J-045, S-176; Bamberg J-269, L-135, N-033; Cologne B-473?, C-372?, F-099(2), P-510(2); Dinkelsbühl A-597, G-222(1), J-159(2), P-091, P-219(2), P-269; Geldern A-144, L-055(2); Heilbronn B-237(1), R-116(1); Moers B-176, B-188; Neustadt an der Saale J-264(1); Wessobrunn N-001; Würzburg P-171(2)

Carmelites, discalced: Augsburg B-507, H-131, N-103; Schongau T-169

Carthusians: Basel A-172, C-396, G-151; Buxheim [47 editions]; Cologne A-543, A-590(2), A-607(1), J-139, R-104(2); Erfurt D-174(2); Nuremberg B-243; Regensburg A-304, J-200(2), J-206, L-185(2), M-244, P-510(1); Schnals T-271(1); Trier H-064, J-203; Weddern A-510(1), B-249; Wesel J-067

Cathedrals: Freising B-107, M-320(1), N-096; Hamburg B-334; Regensburg B-135, M-030; Würzburg B-538?, M-256

Celestines: Oybin G-086(2)

Church: Nördlingen S. Georgius N-104(1)

Cistercians: Camenz D-157; Eberbach A-141, A-150, M-245(1); Fürstenfeld A-097(1), A-124, A-169(5), A-507(2), G-085, H-023(2)?, H-240, J-130(1), M-132, M-245(2), P-463, T-175; Himmerod S-194, T-222(1); Kaisheim D-056, G-298, H-132(3), H-241(2), J-273, L-134, S-363(2); Marienfeld H-060; Maulbronn P-045(1); Raitenhaslach A-097(1), J-055; Tyrol St Georgenberg M-013(2); Waldsassen G-078, M-314, V-120

Cistercian nuns: Bredelar M-166(2); Kirchheim P-520(2); Medingen XYL 28.1–2; Seligenthal A-097(1)?, H-023(2)

Collegiate churches: Altötting SS Maria, Philippus et Jacobus D-105; Freising S. Vitus T-169

Brothers of the Common Life: Münster C-062, J-164

Dominicans: Augsburg O-077(2); Bamberg B-344(1), J-202(1), J-328(1)?, P-171(2), P-201, T-293(2); Bolzano T-156; Dortmund G-242(1), T-170; Eichstätt D-200, I-031(2); Frankfurt am Main M-246; Landshut B-611(1); Nuremberg P-028, P-171(2); Regensburg A-467(1), V-136(1); Schwäbisch-Gmünd A-468(1), A-562(2), G-235, J-233, J-237, J-248, J-268, L-083(2), U-009; Soest S-183(1); Wimpfen A-192, A-342(2), T-291, W-006; Würzburg J-018

Episcopal library: Bamberg P-291(4); Eichstätt A-169(2), B-243, H-087, H-098, H-198; Regensburg G-209, O-067, P-264

Franciscans: Amberg B-460, B-470, L-074, P-187(1), P-318(2), T-116(1), V-133(1); Bamberg B-237(2)?, B-376, C-106(3)?, C-411, G-099, I-040, J-190(2); Berg am Laim C-106(2); Brühl G-182, J-253(2), J-258, J-266, J-279(2), J-303; Dingolfing P-224; Ellingen J-053; Freiburg im Breisgau G-218, G-238, M-210, P-361(1); Freising J-263; Halle Fundatio Baldaufica A-466; Ingolstadt A-326, A-386?; Kelheim A-326, D-190, H-087, H-098, M-136, P-045(3); Kenzingen G-218; Lübeck T-164; Nuremberg P-361(1); Pfreimd H-244; Regensburg B-383(1), B-453, J-175(1)?, T-090(1); Schleissheim F-088; Schrobenhausen F-088; Überlingen A-505

Franciscans Conventual: Altötting B-280; Halberstadt B-173; Schwäbisch-Gmünd A-506, A-584, B-187, B-314(1), G-152, J-234(1), J-261, J-268, L-068, V-010; Würzburg A-223(2), A-245, A-322, A-413, A-501(2), B-062, B-255(2), B-266, B-422(1), C-488, D-171, G-189, H-019, J-223, P-052(1), R-030, T-150(1)?, XYL-7?, XYL-22

Franciscans Observant: Augsburg T-173; Bolzano D-168(1); Dorsten J-107(2), J-166, J-192, P-203; Limburg an der Lahn B-397, H-107, T-196(1); Munich A-312, A-344, A-598, B-345C, G-297(1), H-144, H-237, P-031(2), T-152(2), T-153; Passau A-414

Franciscans Recollect: Dornburg C-287(1); Fremersberg S. Ursula S-209; Hamm A-408, J-331, M-315, P-204(1), R-142(3), T-139, T-279; Hammelburg E-011, M-013(1), XYL-29; Mainz M-216; Miltenberg A-141, A-150

Hospital: Nördlingen Holy Ghost N-104(1); Regensburg M-263?, A-577

Hospitallers of the Holy Ghost: Wimpfen J-247(2), J-262

Jesuits: Augsburg S. Crux T-102; Augsburg S. Salvator E-002, E-010, E-029, H-036(1), H-145, J-217, T-260; Bamberg C-106(3); Biburg C-432(2); Burghausen E-031; Cologne B-333; Gorheim S-209; Hall B-270; Horstmar B-261; unidentified B-081(1), B-536?, C-105?, C-234, H-093(2), L-125?; Koblenz P-391; Landsberg A-036, V-159(2); Mainz V-096; Mindelheim C-268, P-044(2), S-326, T-233; Münster C-235; Munich H-036(1), H-084, J-039(1); Regensburg C-078, D-113, G-239,

H-111(2), J-317, S-315; Trier P-149(2); Weiden A-394, R-018

Parish churches: Amberg S. Martin B-185, G-086(1)?, G-217; Aulendorf S. Martin S-112(2)

Piarists: Rastatt B-452

Poor Clares: Runcada G-257, P-196, W-007

Premonstratensians: Adelberg A-537, A-542, A-552(2), A-610(2); Ibenstadt V-113; Roggenburg P-331; Rommersdorf V-163; Roth A-537, A-542, A-552(2), A-610(2); Sayn B-269; Schäftlarn J-057; Steinfeld in der Eifel B-267; Steingaden N-077, P-516; Weissenau A-112, A-329, A-387(1), B-442, C-416, D-058, G-289, G-334, H-075, H-199, H-233, J-027, J-049, J-077, J-079, J-083(1), J-089, J-216, P-231, P-402(1), P-474, S-263, T-188; Windberg L-071(2), R-113, T-103

Societas Sacratissimi Rosarii BVM: Cologne M-248?

Theatines: Munich A-539(1)

Unidentified order: Eichstätt T-167; unidentified monastic house H-118, F-043(2); Halle an der Saale, Marienbibliothek B-325, C-162, P-369, S-346; Heidenfeld T-194; Lonk H-110; Regensburg A-390(1);

ITALY: 161 books from 115 houses

Augustinian Canons: Como C-267; Cremona A-578; Lucca V-016; Montecompatri R-120; Naples S-339; Padua A-520(1), G-055, T-042; Pavia A-415

Augustinian Canons Regular Observant: Trevi A-233(2)

Augustinian Hermits: Bologna C-443; Brescia A-596, P-368; Crema P-065; Gravedona P-345(3); Milan A-406, A-536, L-124, N-055, P-363; Rome P-345(7); Turin D-082(1)

Basiliens: Naples B-371(1)

Benedictines: Bologna D-009; Ferrara M-172, T-106; Florence I-038(3); Naples D-070, E-087; Padua A-517, P-270?, P-451(1); Parma T-147, T-223; Praglia G-333, J-167; Subiaco A-517; Venice B-275, C-470, P-334(1), P-356(2)

Camaldolese: Florence S. Maria Angelorum C-472(2); Venice A-163(2)

Camillians: P-143

Capuchins: Camerota P-063; Cesena T-258(2); Ferrara C-296; Monza L-087(2); Naples T-081; Piacenza T-049; Pistoia P-291(3); Vicenza L-154

Carmelites: Florence S. Clemens C-354(2), L-183(2); Milan B-022; Venice T-005(1)

Carmelites, discalced: Cremona S-303; Milan P-286; Venice S-307(1)

Carthusians: Asti P-021; Carignano T-005(2); Lucca A-331, G-004; Montello M-032(2), P-334(2); Padua D-028, P-115; Vedana T-096(1)

Chierici regolari poveri delle Scuole pie: Castiglione P-379

Church: Naples S. Maria Neviensis C-248

Cistercians: Rome V-095; Venice S. Tommaso dei Borgognoni M-033

Collegium: Saluzzo S. Maria O-039(2)

Dominicans: Bergamo B-025; Bibbiena J-329(2); Crema O-054; Cremona A-185; Faenza S-029; Fano E-043; Fermo L-004; Fiesole P-393; Florence S. Marco A-318, A-494, B-311, C-223, O-040(1), P-422(2), T-140(1), T-161, V-041(2), V-141; Cattaro (Kotor, Dalmatia) E-044(1); Legnago G-072, P-176; Milan A-357, C-495, S-214(1); Reggio Emilia T-288; Rome C-220, C-298; Salerno A-524; Siena N-126(2), T-226(1), V-034; Venice O-027(2)

Franciscans: Bergamo B-372(3); Bologna P-259; Cesena C-073; Cetona C-278; Crema B-371(3)?; Florence Ognissanti S-101; Lucca S. Cerbone P-337; Lucca A-180; Lucca S. Miniato M-267; Maciano B-352, G-187, XYL-23; Ocre P-022(1); Padua T-136; Sargiano A-010, A-180, S-350, S-358; Stroncone B-279; Vigevano S-146

Franciscans Observant: Ancona I-038(4) Assisi R-005(1); Fiesole V-032; Montemaggio B-352, XYL-23; Ripatransone C-496; Trento J-148; Verona S-118(1)

Franciscans Reformed: Gubbio S-188

Jesuats: Venice A-534(2)

Jesuits: Como L-171(1), S-003; Florence P-422(2); Naples B-318; Parma B-345, P-273(2); Siena R-061

Olivetans: Perugia D-076

Oratorians: Ripatransone B-013(2)

Servites: Florence SS. Annunziata S-065

Sylvestrines: Serrasanquirico D-165(1), D-170(1)
Theatines: Ravenna A-221(3); Venice A-068
Vallombrosan: Marradi J-325
Unidentified order or place: church dedicated to
S. Georgius T-127; Franciscan convent U-008(1);
Dominican convent O-056(3), P-138(3); Fanano
Congregation of V-73; Foligno Bibliotheca S.
Bartholomaei C-153, G-205; Murata monastero
B-425; Padua V-088(1); Siena monastero P-424(3);
Padri Somaschi P-291(1)

LITHUANIA: 3 books from 1 house
Franciscans: Vilnius C-410 C-413(2) P-293(2)

LUXEMBOURG: 3 books from 2 houses
Dominicans: Jamoigne G-181(2)
Jesuits: Luxembourg G-276?, M-086

NETHERLANDS: 38 books from 14 houses
Augustinian nuns: Thabor B-181?, B-456?, F-093?,
F-095(1), S-182
Carthusians: Utrecht A-529(1)
Celestines: Haarlem P-075
Cistercians: Ijsselstein A-541(1), A-590(1),
A-604(1), G-096, G-100, G-113, G-117(1), G-123,
G-131(1), M-150(1), P-485, T-118, T-185, T-190
Brothers of the Common Life: Doesburg
R-017(2); 's-Hertogenbosch C-101, M-029;
Utrecht A-301(1)
Sisters of the Common Life: Zwolle S-240
Dominicans: Zutphen B-013(1)
Franciscan Tertiary nuns: Haarlem J-065,
O-036(2); unidentified P-512; Utrecht L-047
Poor Clares: G-213
Premonstratensians: Berne (Utrecht) A-074,
C-101, C-128, M-029, S-322, V-053

POLAND: 9 books from 6 houses
Augustinian Canons: Wrocław N-027(1)
Cistercians: Pelplin B-389
Dominicans: Wrocław B-164
Franciscans: Poznan C-410, C-413(2), P-293(2)
Franciscan Observants: Swiecie H-110
Hospital: Wrocław P-227, V-135

SLOVAKIA: 1 book
Chapter: Bratislava E-046(3)

SPAIN: 37 books from 9 houses
Capuchins: Sanlúcar de Barrameda G-330
Carmelites: unidentified L-006
Carmelites, discalced: unidentified B-265
Cistercians: Palencia B-095, B-097, B-101, B-106,
B-116, B-120, B-121, U-001
Dominicans: Aranda de Duero D-159; Gerona
B-603
Franciscans: Medina del campo T-178(2);
Santander T-178(2)
Jesuits: Avila [22 editions]

SWITZERLAND: 8 books from 7 houses
Benedictines: Langnau E-070
Capuchin Nuns: Wonnenstein F-107(1)
Franciscans: Fribourg A-199, J-047
Franciscans reformed: Grandson (Canton de
Vaud) V-018
Jesuits: Konstanz S-017?; Porrentruy S-133(1)
Unidentified: Luzerne G-333A

UNITED KINGDOM: 42 books from 23 houses
Augustinian Canons: Bristol Hospital of St John
Baptist H-116(1); Leeds (Kent) P-518
Benedictines: Belmont N-054; Canterbury
St Augustine B-384; Durham, Cathedral Priory of
St Cuthbert R-047; Evesham M-272; Lamspringe
(Hannover) B-277, R-115(2)?; Reading F-007
Brigittine nuns: Syon A-116?, XYL-13, XYL-19, XYL-30
Carthusians: Hull S-108(7); London Smithfield
XYL-24; Sheen A-116?, B-316(1), F-095(2)?, H-188?
Cathedral Library: Exeter D-060(2); Gloucester
C-028; Worcester XYL-27
Cistercians: Coupar Angus Abbey G-083, J-199(1);
Kinloss J-281; Kirkstall A-133, C-389
Friars of the Holy Cross (Crutched): London
P-189(1)
Parish Church: Ludlow S. Laurence N-017(2);
Marlborough Vicar's Library G-026(2), G-215,
G-242(2), J-063, N-058; Newport S. Francis
A-450?, D-107

Roman Catholic See: Portsmouth C-040, F-026(2), M-252, M-269, M-283, S-008

UNIDENTIFIED: 31 books
Augustinians: Ch[ ] P-223
Benedictines: M-088
Canons Regular of the Holy Cross, possibly Germany S-210
Capuchins, Bar[ ] unidentified: G-166; U-006
Dominicans: O-056(3), O-060, P-138(3), P-198
Olivetans: P-046
Bethlehem in Holland? P-490; Brescia, S. Michael T-255(1); P[ ]ensis Parochia: C-406, G-174; Promontorium, S. Maria Angelorum D-197(1); Sabniense, monasterium B-419; Monasterii Vigoren[ ] A-223(1)

Incunabula from European Religious Houses now in Harvard College Library, an Extract from the Provenance Index of Walsh[21]

AUSTRIA: 73 books from 31 houses
Augustinian Canons: Dürnstein 508, S1–1584A; Klosterneuburg 646; Ranshofen 839, 1497; Vienna 202, 636, 1604, 1994, 2440
Benedictines: Altenburg 92, 892, 918; Bregenz 682, 1115; Feldkirch (Vorarlberg) 905, 1159; Lambach 998, 1130; Melk 745, 746, 747, S1–766.5; Ossiach 76; Salzburg 89, 165, 554, 803, 854, 2000, 2005, 2014, 2504, 2710, 3188, 3835; Seitenstetten 2804
Capuchins: Ried 843
Carmelites: Lienz 496, 2028; Vienna 547
Carthusians: Gaming 2207

Cathedral Library: Gurk 1355
Cistercians: Baumgartenberg 3271; Fürstenfeld 573; Heiligenkreuz 1998, 2001, 2003, 2008, 2015, 2018, 2021; Lilienfeld 1003, 1635, 1677
Dominicans: Retz 225; Vienna 59, 60, 515, 669, 2011
Franciscans: Innsbruck 593; Salzburg 2300
Jesuits: Vienna 591, 1603, 1641, 1688, 2603; Wiener-Neustadt 2537
Pauline Hermits: Wiener-Neustadt 1133, 3753
Premonstratensians: Geras 113
Trinitarians: Vienna 3729
Ursulines: Innsbruck 730
Unidentified: Hall Waldauff'sche Stiftung 948; Vienna Nikolaikloster 1464, 1534, 2337

BELGIUM: 10 books from 10 houses
Augustinian Canons: Bethlehem (Louvain) 3219; Louvain 3882
Augustinian Hermits: Mecheln 3920
Brothers of the Common Life: Korsendonck 665A
Carmelites: Mons 3601
Franciscans: Sint-Truiden (Saint-Trond) 236; Tongeren(?) 3798
Jesuits: Antwerp 3592; Louvain 3947A; Mons 3914

CZECH REPUBLIC: 9 books from 5 houses
Archiepiscopal Seminary: Olmütz 1160
Church of the deanery: Tachov A&C 1216
Capuchins: Teinitz 2505, 3411
Dominicans: Olmütz 553, 1055
Piarists: Schlackenwerth/Ostrov 1680, 1696, 1705
Premonstratensians: Hradisco/Hradisch (Olmütz) 1160

FRANCE: 33 books from 28 houses
Augustinian Hermits: Colmar 755
Benedictines: Saint-Denis (Paris) 2298, 2580
Capuchins: Aire-sur-la-Lys S1–3601.8; Beauvais 3738; Issoire 3739; Salins 3628
Carmelites: Dijon 3609; Lyon 3027
Carthusians: Abbeville 3593; Dijon 1328
Cathedral Chapter: Rheims 3589
Celestines: Lyon 3513, 3769; Marcoussis 2430; Sens 3513

---

21 James E. Walsh, *A Catalogue of the Fifteenth-Century Printed Books in the Harvard University Library*, 5 vols (Binghamton, NY, 1991–1997); and David R. Whitesell, *First Supplement to James E. Walsh's Catalogue of the Fifteenth-Century Printed Books in the Harvard University Library* (Harvard College Library, 2006); "A&C" followed by Walsh number stands for David Whitesell's *Additions and corrections to Walsh entries*.

Collegiate Church: Grignan 3760; Strasbourg 1673, 1942, 3133, 3286, 3431

Congregation de Montaigu: Paris 3627

Dominicans: Angers 69; Bordeaux 20; (Paris S1–3736i)

Franciscans: Digne 2280; Viviers 1878

Franciscan Recollects: Baume-les-Moines 3737; Bordeaux 1704

Minims: Avallon 1227

Metropolitan Chapter: Paris 3865

Jesuits: Limoges 3764; Paris(?) 900; Toulouse 2281

Seminary: Paris S. Sulpice 3865

Unidentified: Bourges 3152

GERMANY: 299 books from 143 houses

Augustinian Canons: Au am Inn 626; Baumburg 103, 597, 3319; Beiharting 804; (Dietramszell S1–658d); Eberhards-Klausen 221, 714; Gars 2124; Hamersleben 1113; Indersdorf 86, 889; Polling 85, 955, 1881; Rebdorf 744, 826, 1161; Reichenhall 187; Rottenbuch 698, 2299, 2320; Stadt am Hof 890

Augustinian Nuns: Marienburg 128

Augustinian Hermits: Ingolstadt 147; Mindelheim 93; Munich 2085; Regensburg 14, 123, 1634; Seemanshausen 82; Taxa 910

Benedictines: Anhausen an der Brenz 52; Amorbach 271, 318, 557, 961; Augsburg 541; Bamberg 140, 834, 940, 1222, 1330, 1331; Benediktbeuren 368, 2650, S-724A; Bursfeld 574; Chiemsee (nuns) 2055; Deggingen S. Martinus Whitesell 915; Erfurt 396, 845, 1209; Fuessen 72, 73, 778, 821, 3093; Gengenbach 867; Heidenheim 963; Hofen 905, 1159; Hohenberg 2137; Huysburg 176, 815, S1–2033A; Kempten 98, 588; Liesborn 243, 382, 413; Maria Laach 2053; Metten S. Clemens 247, 331; Metten S. Michael arch. 741; Michelfeld 443; Nuremberg 63; Ochsenhausen 193, 1065, 1168; Plankstetten 1706; Prüfening 3490; Regensburg S. Jacobus Scotorum 1180, 3490; Regensburg S. Emmeram 3801; Reichenbach 679; Rott am Inn 716, 1078; Scheyern 110, 198, 1076; Sulzbach S-147A; Tegernsee 763, 800, 820, 1064; Trier 709, 1156, 1198; Weingarten 905, 1159; Wessobrunn 565; Wiblingen 2050; Zwiefalten 937, 1159

Brigittines: Altomünster 1104, 3797; Marienbaum 3; Marienburg 3

Brothers of the Common Life: Hildesheim 740; Marienthal 114

Capitulum rurale: Stiefenhofen 109

Capuchins: Bacharach 55; Bamberg 172, 288, 1251; Coesfeld 242, 388; Munich S1–1246.5; Neumarkt 219, 1067; Vilshofen 64

Carmelites: Abensberg 886, 1069, 1111; Bamberg 1083, S1–216.5; Cologne 372, 1154, 1829; Dinkelsbühl 94; Heilbronn 322, 326, 1200; Mainz 2594, 2760; Straubing 3353; Würzburg 47, 2441

Carthusians: Buxheim 95, 118, 139, 182, 238, 240, 523, 556, 736, 759, 932, 966, 979, 1210, 1220, 1619, 2256, 2806, 3040, S-195A, S-207A, S-1229A, S1–258.5; Crimmitschau 282; Dülmen 398, 403, 414, 430, 1163, 1164; Prüll 933; Wedderen 398, 403, 414, 430, 1163, 1164; Wesel 1645

Church: Ehingen an der Donau, S. Michaelskapelle 207; Nördlingen, Church of St George: A&C 2159, 2376, 2510, 2551, 3068

Cistercians: Aldersbach 441; Arnsburg 3046; Friedenweiler S1–1135.3; Fürstenzell 697; Heilsbronn 1946, 1952; Himmerod 334, 2263; Langheim 284, 691, 725, S-819A; Marienfeld 1947; Raitenhaslach 533, 564; Salem 3149, 3150; Tennenbach 1206

Cistercian nuns: Kentrup 323, 327

Collegium: Ingolstadt St Ignatius the martyr 1881

Confraternities: Dinkelsbühl Corpus Christi 1218

Cruciferi Fratres: Schwarzenbroich 408

Deutscher Orden Priesterseminar: Mergentheim 252

Dominicans: Bamberg 287, 297, 572, 1193, 1217, 1593, 2319, 2334, 2693; Dortmund 343, 418; Frankenstein 1157; Frankfurt am Main 427, 463, 1225; Hasenpfühl 1231; Landshut 878; Obermedlingen 1074; Regensburg 164, 2241; Schwäbisch-Gmünd 115, 879, 898

Dominican Nuns: Pforzheim 539

Franciscans: Aachen 3629; Amberg 87, 253, 440, 443, 840, S-262A; Andernach 749; Augsburg 53, 280, 3062(?); Bamberg 258, 1162, 1244, 1718, 2140, S1–1199.2; Dingolfing 1756; Düren 49; Fulda 279,

672; Ingolstadt 78, 551, 602, 851, 880, 883, 1934, 3196, 3197, 3198, 3201, 3392; Kelheim 1092, 1093; Kenzingen 143; Mainz 206, 436; Munich S. Anna 51, 283, 550, 3953; Passau 536; Regensburg 614; Straubing 12
Franciscans Conventual: Maihingen 713, A&C 199; Würzburg Inventio crucis/Sancta crux 2026
Jesuits: Augsburg 2656; Bamberg 259, 268, 751, 1099; Dillingen 3796; Heiligenstadt 814; Ingolstadt 166, 703, 2960; Mainz 842; Mindelheim 93, 1577; Münster 977; Munich 647; Neuburg 207; Rhein Province 220
Oratory(?): Baden(?) 3065
Parish churches: Amberg 561; Kempen 1936
Premonstratensians: Roggenburg S-1114A; Roth 643; Schussenried 481, 2311, 2329; Steingaden 159, 1137; Weissenau 11, 339, 902, 1655, 1732
Seminary: Regensburg S. Wolfgangi 1096
Unidentified order: Bredenau St Mary the Virgin 574; Dinkelsbühl Bibl. S. Georgii 2152, 2252; Häussershaim (Hassmersheim?) Kloster 731; Schwarzach SS. Sebastianus et Felicitas 39

HUNGARY: 2 books from 1 house
Dominicans: Eger 992, 1789

ITALY: 116 books from 82 houses
Augustinian Canons: Bergamo 3059; Chivasso 3751; Florence S. Michele di Campora 2850; Naples S. Johannes ad Carbonariam 2347, A&C 2347; Padua, S. Giovanni in Verdara 1293, 1738; Pontremoli SS. Annunziata 1885; Treviso 3588; Venice S. Salvator 2274; Viadana S. Nicolas 2222
Augustinian Canons of the Congregation of the Lateran: Bologna S. Salvatore 2991
Augustian Hermits: Milan 2117
Augustinian Nuns: Florence S. Caterina del Monte e S. Gaggio 1305; Varese S. Maria Annunziata 3062
Benedictines: Brescia S. Euphemia 3425; Cingoli (nuns?) 3526; Lodi S. Marco 1911; Naples SS Severinus et Sossius 1802, 2292; Padua Cass. Congr. S. Justina 1802, 3350; Pavia 2134; Perugia 1819; Perugia Cass. Congr. S. Justina 1687; San Benedetto Po 1896A; Venice, SS. Georgius et Stephanus 3350

Benedictine Nuns: Pavia S. Gregorio 2076; Piacenza 3408
Capuchins: Bergamo 3097; Oristano 3983; Palermo 2136; Verona 2120
Carmelites: Asti 1897; Florence S. Paolo 2503, 2925, Heb-25; Piacenza 2891
Carthusians: Schnals 117, 1574
Church: Rome S. Balbina 1329
Cistercians: Torcello S. Tommaso dei Borgognoni S-1809
Collegium: Piacenza S. Lazaro? 2694
Cruciferi Fratres: Conegliano 2097
Dominicans: Arienzo 1325; Bolzano 2282, 3451; Casale 3143, 3229; Fermo 2363; Ferrara 1861, 2198; Fiesole 2318; Florence S. Marco 2318, 2486A; Genoa 2303; Morbegno 3115; Pavia S. Thomas 2134; Perugia 2109, 2155, 2411; Piacenza 1672
Franciscans: Aquara 1181, 2185; Assisi 3124A, 3584; Bolzano 61, 204, 277, 1106, 1131, S-147A, S-687A, S-748B, S-1094A; Brescia 2310, 2315; Brixen 762, 1097, 1100, 1232; Fivizzano 2267, 2706; Florence Ognissanti 1983; Genoa 2185; Genoa S. Annunziata 2141; Pavia S. Maria incoronata 2405; Pavia 2531; Pinerolo 2653; Serra San Quirico 2250, 2469; Stroncone 3433; Terni 3304; Venice S. Francesco della Vigna 1693
Franciscan Reformed: Bolzano 1713, 1866, 1943, 1944, 2125, 2131
Jesuits: Milan 1816; Perugia 3526; Piacenza 2874; Rome 3470; Turin 3399; Venice 3148
Parish Church: Ferrara S. Andrea 2222
Piarists: Genoa 1857
Poor Clares: Brixen 224, 257, 1584
Servites: Florence SS. Annunziata 2966; Treviso S. Maria 2272
Theatines: Rome 1309, 2615
Unidentified: Cava dei Tirreni, S. Stefano 2866; Cosenza, convent 3077; Florence S. Antonio 2865; Pesaro Bibl. S. Crucis 1332; Rome Bibl. S. Benedicti 1906; Urbino S. Johannes Baptista 1656

LITHUANIA: 1 book
Franciscans: Wilna/Vilnius 1054

LUXEMBOURG: 1 book
Jesuits: 3663

NETHERLANDS: 2 books from 2 houses
Dominicans: Groeningen 275
Unidentified: Gouda Domus collationariae
S. Pauli 3923

NEW ZEALAND: 2 books from 1 house
Diocesan Library: Dunedin 280, 1469

POLAND: 10 books from 8 houses
Augustinian Canons: Wrocław 27
Augustinian Hermits: Wrocław 2499
Cathedral Library: Wrocław 1707
Cistercians: Oliwa 3120; Posen 68
Collegiate Church: Glogau 664
Hospital: Wrocław St Matthew 188, 464
Jesuits: Brzeznica 2350, 2711

SLOVAKIA: 1 book
Franciscans: Nitra 2063

SLOVENIA: 1 book
Carthusians: Gairach Vallis S.Mauricii 234

SPAIN: 5 books from 5 houses
Carmelites: Barcelona 1463
Franciscans: Barcelona 3956; Borja 1695
Jesuits: Madrid 2231
Unidentified: Leon 1942

SWITZERLAND: 8 books from 6 houses
Augustinian Hermits: Schoenthal 289, 1381
Benedictines: Einsiedeln 1205

Carthusians: Ittingen 972
Franciscans: Cham 2025; Fribourg 3774; Lucerne
2235, 3144

UNITED KINGDOM: 3 books from 3 houses
Cathedral Libraries: Chichester 2868
Carthusians: Sheen 340
Dominicans: Elgin 756

**UNIDENTIFIED: 60 books from 19 different
orders**
Augustinians: 1950;
Augustinian Hermits: 1239, 2980;
Benedictines: 1338, 3699;
Capuchins: 1991, 2611, 2748, 2750, 3595;
Carmelites: 2722;
Carthusians: 476, 3593, 3651;
Celestines: 3811;
Churches(?): S. Maria Gratiana(?) 2037; S. Maria
in Sylvis 3050;
Collegium: Solebanum (Salesianum??) 3554;
(S. Maria Magdalena) 757;
Conventus: (Angelorum) 2752; (S. Himerii,
possibly of Cremona?) 3334; (S. Angelus) 2010;
(S. Barbara) 3906; (S. Maria ad Gradus) 1842;
Dominicans: 15, 1901, 2318, 2389, 2524, S-110B;
St Peter and Paul 1067;
Franciscans: 155, 2082, 2373, 3905;
Jesuits: Collegio de S. Eugenio 1744, S1–149.9;
Monastery: Annunciation, Fabriano? 1880, 1108,
1128, 1141, 2352, 2405; Conception 3779, 3791,
3794; SS Peter and Paul 1019; Montecenatio?
eremo 2974;
Oratory: S. Mary Magdalene 1883
Servites: 3809.

Bibliography

Primary Sources

Biblia latina (cum postillis Nicolai de Lyra et expositionibus Guillelmi Britonis in omnes prologos S. Hieronymi et additionibus Pauli Burgensis replicisque Matthiae Doering). Add: Nicolaus de Lyra: *Contra perfidiam Judaeorum*. Nuremberg: Anton Koberger, 1497. Folio. GW 4294; ISTC ib00619000; London, Dulwich College, A. 3. fol. 3.

Guillermus Alvernus, Episcopus Parisiensis, *Opera*. Ed: Petrus Danhauser. Add: Johann Rosenbach. [Nuremberg: Georg Stuchs, after 31 Mar. 1496]. Folio. Bod-Inc G-296; GW 11862; ISTC ig00708000; MEI 00208185; Oxford, Bodleian Library, Auct. 1Q 4.2(1).

Guillermus Alvernus, Episcopus Parisiensis, *De sacramentis*. Add: *Cur deus homo; De poenitentia*. [Nuremberg: Georg Stuchs, not after 1497]. Folio. Bod-Inc G-299; GW 11869; ISTC ig00716500; MEI 00208187; Oxford, Bodleian Library, Auct. 1Q 4.2(2).

Guillermus Alvernus, Episcopus Parisiensis, *De universo*. [Nuremberg: Georg Stuchs, not after 1497]. Folio. Bod-Inc G-300; GW 11870; ISTC ig00717000; MEI 00208189; Oxford, Bodleian Library, Auct. 1Q 4.2(3).

Hieronymus, *Vitae sanctorum patrum, sive Vitas patrum* [English] *The lyff of the faders* (Tr: William Caxton). Westminster: Wynkyn de Worde, [before 21 Aug.] 1495. Folio. Bod-Inc H-116; ISTC ih00213000; MEI 00204045; Oxford, Bodleian Library, Arch. G d. 29.

Holkot, Robertus, *Super sapientiam Salomonis*. [Paris: Georg Wolf], 21 Oct. 1489. 4°. EBOB 00008216; GW 12888; ISTC ih00290000; MEI 02003663; London, Middle Temple Library, BAY L(1).

Hartmann Schedel, *Liber chronicarum*. Nuremberg: Anton Koberger, for Sebald Schreyer and Sebastian Kammermeister, 12 July 1493. Folio. Bod-Inc S-108(7); ISTC is00307000; MEI 02137684; Oxford, Bodleian Library, Blackwell b.4.

Secondary Works

A Catalogue of Books Printed in the Fifteenth Century now in the Bodleian Library, ed. Alan Coates, Kristian Jensen, Cristina Dondi, Bettina Wagner, and Helen Dixon, with the assistance of Carolinne White and Elizabeth Mathew; blockbooks by Nigel Palmer, and an inventory of Hebrew incunabula by Silke Schaeper, 6 vols (Oxford, 2005).

Alan Coates, *English Medieval Books: the Reading Abbey Collections from Foundation to Dispersal* (Oxford, 1999).

Alan Coates and Kristian Jensen, 'The Bodleian Library's Acquisition of Incunabula with English and Scottish Medieval Monastic Provenances', in *Books and Collectors 1200–1700: Essays Presented to Andrew Watson*, ed. James P. Carley and Colin G. C. Tite (London, 1997), 237–59.

Margaret Lane Ford, 'Importation of printed books into England and Scotland', in *Cambridge History of the Book in Britain*, 6 vols (Cambridge, 1999–2011), iii 179–201.

James E. Walsh, *A Catalogue of the Fifteenth-Century Printed Books in the Harvard University Library*, 5 vols (Binghamton, NY, 1991–1997).

David R. Whitesell, *First Supplement to James E. Walsh's Catalogue of the Fifteenth-Century Printed Books in the Harvard University Library* (Harvard College Library, 2006).

James M. W. Willoughby, 'The *secundo folio* and its uses, medieval and modern', *The Library*, 7th ser. 12 (2011), 237–58.

Digital Sources

15cBOOKTRADE Project, http://15cbooktrade.ox.ac.uk/distribution-use/mei-searching-guidelines/.

Bod-Inc, http://15cbooktrade.ox.ac.uk/.

Early Bookowners in Britain (EBOB), https://data.cerl.org/ebob/_search.

INKA, https://www.inka.uni-tuebingen.de/.

Index Possessorum Incunabulorum (IPI), https://data.cerl.org/ipi/_search.

Material Evidence in Incunabula (MEI), https://data.cerl.org/mei/_search.

Medieval Libraries of Great Britain (MLGB3), http://mlgb3.bodleian.ox.ac.uk/.

Owners of Incunabula and other Early Printed Books (OOI), https://data.cerl.org/owners/_search.

GIOVANNA GRANATA

The RICI Database. A Tool for the History of Religious Libraries in Italy at the End of the Sixteenth Century

Religious libraries have attracted growing interest among scholars, motivated as much by their role in the conservation and transmission of the book heritage through the Middle Ages and the modern age as by their impact on the development of today's libraries following the secularization processes that have marked the political and social history of contemporary Europe.

The surviving volumes from their collections bear witness to their long institutional history and stratified bibliographical composition, as do the archival or bibliographical sources that lead back to episodes from their past, allowing us almost to enter into the details of their very existence.

The 'top-down approach' – in other words going backwards through the extant systematic descriptions of surviving volumes with their material characteristics (such as in library catalogues) – and the 'bottom-up approach' – which means starting from documentary sources such as inventories – are complementary, indeed inseparable methods which are by now very familiar in library historiography, currently applied in a variety of researches and studies[1].

Both approaches have been quick to exploit modern technologies, especially since the beginning of the new millennium, thanks to the development of large cooperative projects. These projects have created possibilities for wide-ranging surveys, working on a vast scale,

---

1 Studies on historical inventories and catalogues have a long tradition connected to antiquarianism, which has been particularly fruitful in Italy. Much more recent is the interest in recording evidence of provenance and 'marks in books', which Anglo-American bibliography has promoted since the late 1980s; a reconstruction of the debate and its reception by Italian scholars in Graziano Ruffini, ''Di mano in mano'. Per una fenomenologia delle tracce di possesso', *Bibliotheca*, 1 (2002), 142–60; with regard to technical and operational aspects see the manual *Provenienze. Metodologia di rilevamento, descrizione e indicizzazione per il materiale bibliografico. Documento elaborato dal Gruppo di lavoro sulle provenienze coordinato dalla Regione Toscana e dalla Provincia autonoma di Trento*, ed. Katia Cestelli and Anna Gonzo (Trento and Firenze, 2009).

Giovanna Granata • Full Professor at the University of Cagliari. ggranata@unica.it

How the Secularization of Religious Houses Transformed the Libraries of Europe, 16th–19th Centuries, ed. by Cristina Dondi, Dorit Raines, and † Richard Sharpe, BIB, 63 (Turnhout, 2022), pp. 549–565.

BREPOLS ❧ PUBLISHERS   DOI 10.1484/M.BIB-EB.5.128504

and making available materials and other data which would otherwise be difficult to access because it is distributed in many institutions[2].

This is the context in which the RICI group – an acronym for 'Ricerca sull'Inchiesta della Congregazione dell'Indice' (= Research into the Inquiry of the Congregation of the Index) – started working towards the creation of the database entitled 'Le biblioteche degli ordini regolari in Italia alla fine del secolo XVI' (= The libraries of the Italian regular Orders at the end of the sixteenth century)[3].

The project has been carried out by several Italian universities[4] and has also received the support of several religious Orders[5], cultural institutes, such as the Association Don Giuseppe

De Luca in Rome, and libraries, primarily the Vatican Library.

The goal is to digitize and make available for research and study the extensive documentation produced for the so-called Inquiry of the Congregation of the Index, currently held, as far as its most relevant portion is concerned, by the Vatican Library, which also hosts the database[6].

The importance of this documentation as a source for the cultural history of the post-Tridentine age has long been known. It contains the results of a vast censorship campaign that the Congregation of the Index undertook in the immediate aftermath of the publication of the *Index Librorum Prohibitorum* issued by Clement VIII in 1596, in order to check that its

2   The MEI database hosted and maintained by CERL, on which see the essay in this volume, is undoubtedly the most significant initiative relating to the impact of digital humanities on historical bibliography and provenance research. With regard to documentary sources, an example of using new technologies is the digital library of catalogues and inventories of private libraries 'Biblioteche dei filosofi. Biblioteche Filosofiche Private in Età Moderna e Contemporanea' (picus.unica.it), see Renzo Ragghianti and Alessandro Savorelli, 'Biblioteche filosofiche private: strumenti di lavoro, documenti e contesti', in *Il libro antico tra catalogo storico e catalogazione elettronica*, ed. Roberto Rusconi (Roma, 2012), 109–32.

3   The project, coordinated by Roberto Rusconi, started in 2001. After a preparatory phase of a more strictly technical nature, the first overall results were presented to scholars and librarians in a conference held in Macerata in 2006, the proceedings of which were published in *Libri, biblioteche e cultura degli Ordini regolari nell'Italia moderna attraverso la documentazione della Congregazione dell'Indice. Atti del convegno internazionale, Macerata, 30 maggio – 1 giugno 2006*, ed. Rosa Marisa Borraccini and Roberto Rusconi (Città del Vaticano, 2006).

4   Over the years, the universities of L'Aquila, Cagliari, Chieti, Firenze, Macerata, Roma Tre, the Catholic University of Milan and the Scuola Normale Superiore of Pisa have been involved.

5   Particularly the following Orders: Augustinians, Camaldoleses, Capuchins (Umbrian Province), Carmelites, Conventuals (Centro Studi Antoniani),

Friars Minor (Conference of Provincial Ministers), Minims, Olivetans, Servites, Somaschan Fathers, Vallombrosans.

6   The database is available at https://rici.vatlib.it/. The documentation is largely held among the Vatican Latin manuscripts in 61 volumes, the *Vaticani Latini* 11266–11326, the inventory of which has been published by Marie-Madeleine Lebreton and Luigi Fiorani, *Codices Vaticani Latini 11266–11326* (Città del Vaticano, 1985) ; some book lists are also bound in the *Reginense Latino* 2099. To this corpus a few other materials found in different institutions, probably as a result of the complex history of the original archival collection, have recently been added: Città del Vaticano, Archivio della Congregazione per la Dottrina della Fede, *Index*, Serie XXII e *Index*, Protocolli, P (II.a.14), see Gigliola Fragnito, 'L'Indice clementino e le biblioteche degli Ordini religiosi', in *Libri, biblioteche e cultura degli Ordini regolari*, as note 3, 37–59: 55 and *Catholic Church and Modern Science. Documents from the Archives of the Roman Congregations of the Holy Office and the Index*. Vol. 1, *Sixteenth Century Documents*, ed. Ugo Baldini and Leen Spruit (Città del Vaticano, 2009), 2715–2734; Paris, Archives Nationales, LL 1563, fols 5r–64r, see Rocco Benvenuto, 'I Minimi nella diocesi di Bisignano alla vigilia della soppressione innocenziana', *Bollettino ufficiale dell'Ordine dei Minimi*, 48 (2002), 474–538: 524–27; Roma, Archivio Generale dell'Ordine dei Frati Minori Cappuccini, AB 214, see Costanzo Cargnoni, 'Libri e biblioteche dei Cappuccini della Provincia di Siracusa alla fine del sec. XVI', *Collectanea Franciscana*, 77 (2007), 69–151.

rules were being applied by the Italian religious Orders.

The censorship operation had a significant focus on conventual and monastic libraries owing to the attention given to the circulation of books and the risks to orthodoxy which derived from it. The Catholic Church had shown an awareness of the problems early on, but the spread of the Lutheran Reform added increasing urgency to the issue[7].

During the sixteenth century, an extremely powerful, but also intricate repressive structure was set up. Its complex mechanisms reflected the internal tensions and debates that opened up within the ecclesiastical hierarchy, not only on the tenor of the prohibitions, but also on the prerogatives of the various bodies involved in the management of the censorship machine and, ultimately, on the government of the Church itself, between those who believed in giving more power to bishops and those who wished to reinforce the hierarchical authority of the highest ecclesiastical echelons[8].

The Clementine *Index*, which was the third official index published after the appearance of the Pauline index in 1559 and the Tridentine one in 1564[9], actually marked the point of arrival of a long process which it was hoped would lead to a phase of stability and allow the full implementation of censorship and repressive activities. In reality, in the aftermath of its publication, other jurisdictional conflicts arose that saw religious Orders as protagonists, and stemming from the rule that required the possession of prohibited or suspect books in monasteries to be denounced to local bishops and Inquisitors[10].

---

7   The first Papal attempt to regulate the printing press was, in 1487, with the bull *Inter multiplices* which forbade publishing books without prior authorization, but also provided for the control and possibly suppression of the impious books that had already come out and, consequently, the persecution of those who sold or read them. While the *imprimatur* principle has since then often been reaffirmed in more or less the same terms, over time more stringent solutions for repression were adopted, with the use of the *Index Librorum Prohibitorum* as a formidable tool. The reform of the Inquisition with the Bull *Licet ab initio* of 1542 by Pope Paul IV, acted as an accelerator, followed in 1571 with the creation, by Pope Pius V, of a special Congregation of the Index of Prohibited Books. The bibliography on the subject is vast and has increased still further after the opening of the Archive of the Congregation for the Doctrine of the Faith, formerly the Congregation of the Holy Office, in 1998, see *L'Inquisizione e gli storici: un cantiere aperto. Tavola rotonda nell'ambito della Conferenza annuale della ricerca, Roma, 24–25 giugno 1999* (Roma, 2000) and *L'Inquisizione romana e i suoi archivi. A vent'anni dall'apertura dell'ACDF. Atti del convegno, Roma, 15–17 maggio 2018*, ed. Alejandro Cifres (Roma, 2019).

8   See for example the complex debate on vernacular translations of the Bible reconstructed, also in terms of their 'political' dimensions, by Gigliola Fragnito, *La Bibbia al rogo. La censura ecclesiastica e i volgarizzamenti della Scrittura, 1471–1605* (Bologna, 1997) and Ead., *Proibito capire. La Chiesa e il volgare nella prima età moderna* (Bologna, 2005).

9   As is well known, the first was prepared by the Holy Office, the second was ratified by the assembly of bishops in the Council of Trent. For the text of the 16th-century *Indices* with commentary and annotations see *Index des livres interdits*, ed. Jesús Martinez de Bujanda (Sherbrooke, Québec, and Genève, 1984–1996). On the complex preparatory phases of the Roman *Indices*, see Vittorio Frajese, *Nascita dell'Indice. La censura ecclesiastica dal Rinascimento alla Controriforma* (Brescia, 2006).

10 The debate and problems raised by the application of the Clementine *Index* to the religious Orders have now largely been reconstructed by scholars. In addition to the aforementioned works by Fragnito and Frajese, see the contributions by Roberto Rusconi, who coordinates the RICI project, in particular Roberto Rusconi, 'I religiosi e i loro libri in Italia alla fine del secolo XVI', in Rosa Marisa Borraccini, Giovanna Granata and Roberto Rusconi, 'A proposito dell'inchiesta della S. Congregazione dell'Indice dei libri proibiti di fine '500', *Il capitale culturale. Studies on the Value of Cultural Heritage*, 6 (2013), 13–45, http://riviste. unimc.it/index.php/cap-cult/article/view/400 which also contains references to the previous bibliography. The documentation on the inquiry and relationships between the Congregation of the Index and regular

The heads of Italian convents and monasteries tried to evade the obligation, which appeared to be detrimental to their autonomy, by pointing out difficulties in interpreting the prohibition rules, since the continuous revisions of the *Indices* and of the various indications of authors or works either forbidden in their entirety or requiring expurgation had made them unclear.

Thus, a dispute that involved a crucial sector of ecclesiastical organization began, in consideration of the commitment with which the religious Orders performed their pastoral activities, their contribution to theological-doctrinal reflections, and the dense and widespread presence of their institutions on Italian territory.

To overcome the impasse, the Congregation of the Index resolved to procure a list of the titles of all the books which were present in religious communities, not only those which were prohibited or otherwise suspect. In this way identification of the latter would be carried out by the Congregation itself, provided that the description of the volumes was sufficiently analytical and made it possible to identify different editions. To this end, specific cataloguing rules were laid down which provided for the mandatory indication of author, title, complete with place of publication, name of publisher, date of printing and format.

This transformed what was an essentially repressive operation into a book census which the Orders, despite their repeated efforts to do so, were unable to avoid. At the end of 1599, the Congregation of the Index peremptorily confirmed

its request and, beginning in the first months of 1600, a vast survey of all the volumes present in religious institution across the peninsula began, with the lists of all the books, when they had been compiled, being sent to Rome by the procurators of each Order.

The manuscript documentation, consisting of more than 9,000 lists written on about 19,000 sheets, remained in the Archive of the Congregation of the Index until its suppression in 1917 when it was transferred to the Vatican Library[11].

The lists describe the books in about 2,200 convents and monasteries and provide a detailed picture of the different collections found in them: the communal libraries, available to the whole monastic community, the books used in the infirmary or refectory or for the choir, the prohibited or suspect volumes, to be removed from circulation, and, above all, the books used by individual friars and monks, which they needed for their different activities as preachers, confessors, readers, or as the heads or senior figures in the community and the Order[12].

Orders is kept in the Archive of the Congregation for the Doctrine of the Faith where the Archive of the Congregation of the Index was stored at the moment of its suppression in 1917. This documentation is now published in *La Congregazione dell'Indice, l'esecuzione dell'Index del 1596 e gli Ordini regolari in Italia. Documenti*, ed. Alessandro Serra, Libri e biblioteche degli Ordini religiosi in Italia alla fine del secolo XVI, 5 = Studi e testi, 525 (Città del Vaticano, 2018).

11   Except for a brief period during the Napoleonic era, the documentation was kept in the Archive of the Congregation of the Index. In 1917, when all the papers of the Congregation were given to the Archive of the Holy Office, the materials of bibliographic interest were extracted and delivered to the Vatican Library under the auspices of Achille Ratti, the future Pope Pius XI, then Prefect of the Library. On the history of the collection see Romeo De Maio, 'I modelli culturali della Controriforma. Le biblioteche dei conventi italiani alla fine del Cinquecento', in Id., *Riforma e miti nella Chiesa del Cinquecento* (Napoli, 1973), 365–81: 366–67, with additions by Marc Dykmans, 'Les bibliothèques des religieux d'Italie en l'an 1600', *Archivum Historiae Pontificiae*, 24 (1986), 385–404: 387. The numerical data given above are from *Codices Vaticani Latini*, as note 6.

12   This is the case for a large part of the documentation, but it should be noted that there are also cases in which cumulative lists were sent for the entire community, i.e. including in a single sequence the titles of volumes belonging to the common libraries together with those of books in use by individual friars or monks.

The communities belong to some thirty Orders with different traditions, internal organizations and cultural identities.

There are lists from monastic Orders, such as the Carthusians[13], some hermit Congregations[14] and, especially, the different branches of the Benedictines[15]. A large part of the documentation relates to mendicant Orders, particularly the Franciscans[16], Carmelites[17], Augustinians[18], Servites[19], the Brethren of St Ambrose ad Nemus and St Barnabas[20] and the Cruciferi[21]. Finally, there are lists from the Canons[22] and the Clerks Regular, particularly the Somaschan Fathers[23], Barnabites[24], Theatines[25], and Caracciolini[26].

Their convents or monasteries were located all over Italy, from the north down to the south. Besides the major Italian towns such as Milan, Pavia, Venice, Padua, Mantua, Bologna, Genoa, Florence, Rome, Naples, Palermo, where many religious Orders were present with ancient and important houses[27], some remote and peripheral areas were also covered.

We also need to take account of the fact that some information was omitted. The most notable gap concerns the Jesuits and Dominicans, who apparently were asked to provide information by the Congregation of the Index, but if so no list from them was kept and it is not known whether any were indeed provided[28]. For other religious Orders, some communities or entire areas are missing. For example, branches of the Franciscans Observant are omitted in at least six provinces, mostly in central and southern Italy[29].

Despite these gaps, the lists still contain an astonishing mass of data and it is not by chance that Romeo De Maio described them as "the largest national bibliography of the Counter-Reformation"[30]. This evocative expression is not

13 Vat. Lat. 11276.
14 Hermits of St Jerome (Vat. Lat. 11296, fols 2–26), Hermits of St Jerome of Fiesole (Vat. Lat. 11290), Poor Hermits of St Jerome of the Congregation of Blessed Peter of Pisa (Vat. Lat. 11292).
15 Camaldoleses (Vat. Lat. 11286, fols 162–88; 11287), Camaldoleses of Monte Corona (Vat. Lat. 11303), Vallombrosans (Vat. Lat. 11288), Cistercians (Vat. Lat. 11301), Benedictines of Montevergine (Vat. Lat. 11313), Celestines (Vat. Lat. 11305, 11312), Olivetans (Vat. Lat. 11274), Benedictines of Cassino (Vat. Lat. 11266, 11269, 11286 (fols 7–10, 290–347v, 376–435), 11320).
16 Conventuals (Vat. Lat. 11278, 11280, 11284, 11291), Observants (Vat. Lat. 11271, 11281, 11283, 11293 (fols 29–124v), 11302, 11304, 11307, 11308, 11309, 11311, 11314, 11315, 11317), Reformed Observants (Vat. Lat. 11268), Capuchins (Vat. Lat. 11316, 11319, 11322, 11324, 11325, 11326), Third Order (Vat. Lat. 11286 (fols 105–45), 11297).
17 Carmelites of the Ancient Observance (Vat. Lat. 11272), Discalced (Vat. Lat. 11299), of the Mantuan Congregation (Vat. Lat. 11279).
18 Vat. Lat. 11285, 11286 (fols 146–153v), 11295, 11310.
19 Vat. Lat. 11270, 11286 (fols 28–47), 11321.
20 Vat. Lat. 11294.
21 Vat. Lat. 11296 (fols 127–211).
22 Canons Regular of the Lateran (Vat. Lat. 11286 (fols 454–506v), 11273, 11277, 11282), of Santo Spirito of Venice and of San Giorgio in Alga (Vat. Lat. 11298, 11286 (fols 533–39), of San Salvatore (11289).
23 Vat. Lat. 11275.
24 Vat. Lat. 11286 (fols 445–53), 11300.
25 Vat. Lat. 11267.
26 Vat. Lat. 11318.

27 In the case of Milan, for example, 28 religious communities were surveyed, in Pavia 21, 26 in Venice, 21 in Padua, 22 in Mantua, 26 in Bologna; 23 in Genoa, 25 in Florence, 33 in Rome, 27 in Naples, 13 in Palermo.
28 On the Jesuits and Dominicans see the documentation provided by Dykmans, Les bibliothèques des religieux, as note 11, 398–99. There is some evidence to show that lists of Feuillants, Ministers to the Sick, Sylvestrines, Jesuates, Basilians, and those of the Congregation of Christian Doctrine, were sent to the Congregation of the Index, although they are missing now; by contrast, there is no trace whatsoever of any lists compiled for the Trinitarians and the Mercedarians, see Fragnito, 'L'Indice clementino e le biblioteche degli Ordini religiosi', as note 6, 57–58.
29 The provinces of Marca Anconitana, San Bernardino, Basilicata, and Terra di Lavoro are missing in the coverage of central and southern Italy; in the North, information relating to the houses in the provinces of Brescia and Genova has not been kept.
30 De Maio, 'I modelli culturali della Controriforma', as note 11, 373.

so much technically valuable as a description, but it brings out the breadth of information which is available in the lists. At the same time, it also highlights another aspect that distinctively characterizes the documentation: the substantial homogeneity of approach and presentation that makes the Vatican Corpus virtually a 'catalogue'.

It appears as a substantially homogeneous corpus for at least three reasons. The first is institutional: the survey carried out by order of the Congregation of the Index involves libraries of the same type, even when there are internal differences. It can be said that we are dealing with a library system (or a network of library systems), with reasonably defined structures which, although referable to different Orders and Congregations, still presents many similarities and is therefore widely comparable also from an organizational and cultural point of view.

This homogeneity is also evident on a chronological level, given the very short period of time in which the whole operation was carried out. While the lists were not always sent to the Congregation of the Index within the first six months of 1600, as requested, they arrived within a few years, and not later than 1603[31]. The description of the books therefore took place more or less at the same time in the different communities, which means that we can assign the description of the size and characteristics of the collections to a precise chronological window, although they are, mostly in the case of the libraries for the use of the whole community, the result of very different processes of accumulation owing to the different histories of the foundations and profiles of the religious Orders.

Finally, the third aspect to be underlined is the uniformity of the descriptive model imposed by the Congregation of the Index with regards to the bibliographical aspects: as previously mentioned, specific rules had been set out for the description of the volumes and friars and monks adhered to them with a fair degree of accuracy by completing the bibliographic module with the required elements, sometimes reporting cases in which the books were incomplete[32]. Overall, the lists therefore show a high level of standardization which, as the efforts made today for the needs of library cooperation teach us, are at the basis of integrated catalogues.

The RICI group has indeed dealt with the Vatican documentation as if it were the collective catalogue of a library network, converting it to a database capable of storing records and ordering them in logical sequences, and allowing queries following multiple search paths.

Only computer processing can grasp the entire mass of data and exploit to the fullest extent all the potential offered by the lists, as well as ensuring efficiency in terms of response time, and the completeness and reliability of results.

The database called 'Le biblioteche degli ordini regolari in Italia alla fine del secolo XVI' has been built with these purposes in mind. It contains the complete transcriptions of the documentation, which is to say all the bibliographic citations in each list and all the lists collected by the Congregation of the Index. Moreover, for the purpose of making the data available in

---

31 Some of the lists were actually sent even before 1600, in the intermediate phases in which the Congregation of the Index had asked only for the prohibited and suspected books. These lists are for the most part bound in Vat. Lat. 11286.

32 Author, title, and place and date of printing are generally indicated, while format is often neglected. Gaps are indicated by the formula *caeteris caret*, referring both to problems with the material conditions of volumes and objective difficulties in deciphering the information contained therein. In other cases, these difficulties give rise to fairly obvious errors and misleading descriptions or 'ghosts', see Roberto Rusconi, 'The Devil's Trick. Impossible Editions in the Lists of Titles from the Regular Orders in Italy at the End of the Sixteenth Century', in *Lost Books. Reconstructing the Print World of Pre-Industrial Europe*, ed. Flavia Bruni and Andrew Pettegree (Leiden-Boston, 2016), 310–23.

analytical form, all the information units have been indexed, at different levels[33].

At a first level, the database focuses on the codices containing the lists: for each codex, a description highlighting the material characteristics of the volume in question is given. Furthermore, a 'one-to-many' link to the different lists it contains allows users to move easily to another level of analysis of the documentation.

At this second level, each book list is described geographically and institutionally as it relates to an individual convent or monastery – and possibly to the particular owner, monk or nun, within each community – which holds the books, to the religious Order to which the convent/monastery belongs, to the religious province of the Order (if relevant) and to the town where the convent/monastery is located.

In this way, it is possible to use the database as a kind of 'register' of religious libraries as they existed in Italy in 1600 and obtain an overview of their readers, location, size and even internal organization, as appears from the functional (and topographical) distinction between the collections held in common for the use of the community and the nuclei of books used by single friars and monks in their cells[34].

At a third level, the hundreds of thousands of entries in the book lists are indexed. They are indicated as copies of editions the reliability of which has been checked against bibliographical repertories[35]. More often they are successfully verified, and other times unsuccessfully, and in the latter cases, excluding obvious errors in the transcription, we may be in the presence of lost books[36].

aspect, the legislation of the orders is generally clear; see in this regard the essays of the section 'La normativa su libri e biblioteche negli Ordini regolari in Italia', in *Libri, biblioteche e cultura degli Ordini regolari*, as note 3, 309–94 (papers by Silvia Alessandrini Calisti, Roberto Biondi and Giovanni Grosso) and the proceedings of the conference organized by the Società internazionale di studi francescani and the Centro interuniversitario di studi francescani, *Libri e biblioteche: le letture dei frati mendicanti tra Rinascimento ed età moderna. Atti del XLVI Convegno internazionale, Assisi, 18–20 ottobre 2018* (Spoleto, 2019).

35 Large and long-established online databases have been preferred for checking bibliographic data. They are listed at rici.vatlib.it/site/about#punta_sigle.

36 The bibliography on the subject of lost books is extensive. With regard to the documentation of the Congregation of the Index, see the volume edited by Bruni and Pettegree, *Lost Books*, as note 32, which contains, in addition to the aforementioned paper by Rusconi, 'Devil's Tricks', also the contributions by Rosa Marisa Borraccini, 'An Unknown Best-Seller: The *Confessionario* of Girolamo da Palermo', 291–309 and Giovanna Granata, 'On the Track of Lost Editions in Italian Religious Libraries at the End of the Sixteenth Century: A Numerical Analysis of the RICI Database', 324–44. See also Giuseppina Zappella, 'Alla ricerca del libro perduto: supplemento "virtuale" agli annali della tipografia napoletana del Cinquecento', in *Bibliologia e critica dantesca: saggi dedicati a Enzo Esposito, I: Saggi bibliologici*, ed. Vincenzo De Gregorio (Ravenna, 1997), 243–93; Giovanna Granata, 'Le biblioteche dei religiosi in Italia alla fine del Cinquecento attraverso l''Inchiesta' della Congregazione dell'Indice. A proposito di libri 'scomparsi': il caso dei Francescani Osservanti di Sicilia', in *'Ubi neque aerugo neque tinea demolitur': studi in onore di Luigi Pellegrini per i suoi settanta anni*, ed. Maria Grazia Del Fuoco (Napoli, 2006) 329–406; Ugo Rozzo, 'Una fonte integrativa di ISTC: l'inchiesta della Congregazione dell'Indice del 1597–1603', in *Libri, biblioteche e cultura degli Ordini regolari*, as note 3, 215–50.

33 Details on the database structure are given in Giovanna Granata, 'Struttura e funzionalità della banca dati "Le biblioteche degli Ordini regolari in Italia alla fine del secolo XVI"', in *Libri, biblioteche e cultura degli Ordini regolari*, as note 3, 285–305. Since that description was published, the database search engine has been updated to the latest standards.

34 Following the material organization of the documentation, the database describes analytically the lists of the different nuclei of books present in each convent or monastery. However, it is possible to consider all the collections of each religious house as one 'virtual' library or a kind of library system. The different nuclei of books are distinct at functional level, but not at institutional one. In particular, books in use by single friars or monks were, as such, the property of the convent or monastery to which they had to be returned after the death of the individual. On this

Finally, in the last phase of the indexing process, editions (verified or not in modern censuses or catalogues) are described with their bibliographic elements and in a standard way, through authority files for authors, places of publication, publishers. For verified editions a reference is given to the most up-to-date bibliographic repertoire, while for unverified ones the reference is the database itself.

The relationship between the entries listed in the inventories and editions is central to the use of the database. The data sample examined up to now contains about 310,000 entries. The proportion of editions that have been identified is approximately 70% of the total, a percentage that has remained stable for years, while the quantitative data obviously vary. The number of entries that have been identified correspond to 31,640 editions recorded in current bibliographic repertoires and with multiple occurrences in the lists. It is a significantly high number, representative to a very large extent of the production of the first century and a half of printing[37].

In chronological terms, this corpus of editions spans the whole period since the invention of printing, from the first incunabula up to edi-tions contemporary with the investigation of the Congregation of the Index. The distribution of the number of editions per year tends to increase, although the rate of increase is uneven[38]. The geographical distribution of the places of printing is equally vast. There are roughly two hundred places included in the database, ranging from Portugal to Eastern Europe. Among them, Venice stands out with about 40% of the total editions, followed with much lower, but no less significant, values for the main European and Italian printing centres[39]. The number of publishers – around 2700 in all – is similarly very high, including all the major Italian and international publishing houses, with a noticeable presence of the leading firms Sessa, Scoto, Giunta and Giolito, but there are also publishers with a more narrowly local activity.

There are approximately 9000 authors represented in the database. Their works reflect a firm adherence to the cultural framework of the Counter Reformation, but also to the persistent continuity of Medieval, Late Medieval and pre-Tridentine traditions, as well as a wide range of subject matter. In particular, in addition to Biblical and liturgical arguments, philosophy, law, classical, humanist, medical and scientific works are present, as well as the more foreseeable areas of scholastic, moral and pastoral theology, and those of devotional and ascetic literature.

If the bibliographic analysis of the editions reveals a comprehensive and varied picture, the possibility of linking copies to editions also adds depth to it. For each edition, it is possible to measure the impact on religious collections in terms of the number of copies and it is conse-

---

37   The bibliographic analysis of the editions has been discussed on several occasions in relation to the progress of the work on the RICI database. However, the number and characteristics of the editions checked in the bibliographic repertoires are now reasonably stable, while the data on the unverified editions vary more rapidly. For a more detailed presentation, see Giovanna Granata, 'Books without Borders. The Presence of the European Printing Press in the Italian Religious Libraries at the End of the Sixteenth Century', in *International Exchange in the Early Modern Book World*, ed. Matthew McLean and Sara Barker (Leiden, 2016), 214–38. It is to be noted that, in addition to printed editions, the lists describe manuscript volumes that are however a minor part of the book collections; see on this regard Roberto Rusconi, '"O scritti a mano": i libri manoscritti tra inquisizione e descrizione', in *Dalla notitia librorum degli inventari agli esemplari. Saggi di indagine su libri e biblioteche dai codici Vaticani latini 11266–11326*, ed. Rosa Marisa Borraccini (Macerata, 2009), 1–26. Numerical data given in the present paper are current as of 15 December 2021.

---

38   The increase in the number of editions is undoubtedly more sustained from 1540 onwards throughout the second half of the century.

39   Compared to Venice, data on editions printed in Lyon (9,5%), Paris (7,5%), Rome (5%), Florence (3,5%), Basel (2,7%), Cologne (2,5%), Milan (2,3%), Naples and Antwerp (1,8%), Bologna and Brescia (1,7%) are nevertheless interesting.

quently possible to evaluate the extent both of the presence of individual publishers and of the reception of certain authors and works.

What emerges from the quantitative analysis of the relationships between copies and editions are essential clues to the phenomenon of book circulation, which would be unfathomable, in its historical dimension, if we just looked at our library catalogues. Modern catalogues provide information about books which have survived to this day, data conditioned by a multiplicity of factors. Among these factors, quite apart from the problems inherent in the passage of time, there are some which are specifically related to the collections of religious institutions.

The natural rate of loss of volumes subjected to constant use significantly affects devotional and pastoral works. The same can be said for the rate of obsolescence deriving from their strictly functional value and which has meant that copies were continually discarded and replaced over the centuries. On the other hand, the efforts to conserve material as manifested in the practice of erudite collecting, especially with private collectors – to whom we owe a substantial part of the book patrimony preserved today in institutional libraries – has not focused to any significant degree on this type of literature.

Because of the convergence of these phenomena, the books which survive today present a very partial and distorted picture of what was being printed, published, and acquired at the time, a point which has been frequently made in the studies which deal with the theme of lost books. Indeed, the extreme rarity of some editions today can be the consequence of widespread circulation in the past. The RICI database can account for these editions in a more detailed way, as well as providing evidence on the circulation of editions which are now completely lost[40].

From this point of view, owing to its structure and content, the database usefully integrates the evidence of modern bibliographical censuses with historical data. This is interesting not only for studying the history of individual editions, but also, and even more so, in connection with the history of religious libraries.

The high rate of deterioration and obsolescence that religious literature has suffered over time is added in this case to the dispersive effects of the institutional transitions to which religious collections have been subject during their long history, and particularly following the several waves of suppressions, culminating in Italy with the events – dramatic for their extensive and systematic character – of the post-Unification period.

Piero Innocenti and Maria Antonietta De Cristofaro defined linear dispersal "a dismemberment of a collection by sets, in which individual nuclei remain together, albeit in reduced numbers compared to the original collection", while "stellar" dispersal disrupts the original nucleus and individual books from the collection take many different paths. The sorting out that was done, at the time the volumes from religious institutions entered the various collections to which they were assigned, led to processes of selection and rejection which made "linear dispersion" no less serious than the "stellar dispersion" to which religious libraries were inevitably subjected, at least in part[41]. Because

40 A concrete example is the case of the *Confessionario* by Girolamo da Palermo studied by Rosa Marisa Borraccini with reference to the data of the Inquiry of the Congregation of the Index, which reveals a much

richer variety of editions of this work than the editions recorded in the census of Italian editions of the sixteenth century, EDIT16, would suggest, see Borraccini, 'Un Unknown Best-Seller', as note 36.

41 The difference between linear and stellar dispersion is discussed by Piero Innocenti and Maria Antonietta De Cristofaro, 'Iter Lucanum. Ipotesi di una mappa di archivi e biblioteche, pubblici e privati, di Basilicata dopo il terremoto del 1980', *Annali della Facoltà di Lettere e Filosofia, Università degli studi della Basilicata, Potenza*, (1993–1994), 205–59: 210. This terminology is commonly accepted, see for example Marielisa Rossi, 'Raccolte,

of this further dispersal, only a proportion of their collections has been preserved.

Moreover, the material evidence from surviving copies does not always offer historical elements for dating their connection to the collections from which they came, indicating when they became part of a collection, the context in which they were placed and the overall physiognomy of the collection. Thus, it becomes quite difficult to understand the different strata of a collection as it has grown over time and analyse from a historical perspective the cultural legacy which religious libraries have left us.

Of equal importance is the fact that religious libraries themselves have over time modified and revised their bibliographic holdings in relation to the different cultural paradigms, informational requirements and material conditions which they have had to confront over the centuries.

Although these libraries are institutions formed in order to accumulate and store, the rationale based on conservation that has affected their growth over time has been governed by criteria which are not at all static or one-directional. This is of course true for all institutional libraries in contrast to private libraries which can adhere more straightforwardly to a guiding conceptual plan and for which one can speak more easily of bibliographic paradigms[42]. In the case of religious libraries, these paradigms have not merely overlapped over time, but, in a process of intricate alchemy, have given rise to complicated and multifaceted organisms.

These aspects need to be reconstructed on the basis of archival documentation, which is the reason why the lists which are brought together, transcribed and analysed in the database are of such great interest.

Especially in the case of the historical Orders or those which ramified extensively and which remained active until the monastic suppressions in the eighteenth and nineteenth centuries, these lists can be collated and then integrated with other bibliographical and documentary sources through which the different stages of a long history can be reconstructed.

Many research initiatives in this field are centred on the earliest book inventories[43]. However, the significant campaign of cataloguing their collections which was carried out by religious Orders during the eighteenth century, when their libraries increased greatly in size, transforming their collections permanently, is only now beginning to be studied[44]. The lists of the

---

provenienze, indici', in Ead., *Provenienze, cataloghi, esemplari. Studi sulle raccolte librarie antiche* (Manziana, Roma, 2001), 9–83.

42   Reference is made to Alfredo Serrai's studies, in particular to the expression used in his essay 'Le biblioteche private quale paradigma bibliografico (La biblioteca di Aldo Manuzio il giovane)', in *Le biblioteche private come paradigma bibliografico*. Atti del Convegno internazionale, Roma, Tempio di Adriano, 10–12 ottobre 2007, ed. Fiammetta Sabba (Roma, 2008), 19–28, at 19.

43   See the survey by Donatella Nebbiai-Dalla Guarda, *I documenti per la storia delle biblioteche medievali: secoli IX–XV* (Roma, 1992) and 'Bibliothèques en Italie jusqu'au XIIIe siècle. État des sources et premières recherches', in *Libri, lettori e biblioteche dell'Italia medievale: secoli IX–XV: fonti, testi, utilizzazione del libro*. Atti della Tavola rotonda italo-francese, Roma, 7–8 marzo 1997, ed. Giuseppe Lombardi and Donatella Nebbiai-Dalla Guarda (Roma and Paris, 2000) 7–129; to the framework outlined therein is to be added at least the project of the series *RICaBiM: Repertorio di Inventari e Cataloghi di Biblioteche Medievali dal secolo VI al 1520* (Firenze, 2009-) on which see Giovanni Fiesoli, 'Inventari al quadrato: il progetto R.I.Ca.Bi.M. Bilanci e questioni di metodo', *Bibliothecae.it*, 5 (2016), 17–54, https://bibliothecae.unibo.it/article/view/6104/5865, DOI <10.6092/Issn.2283–9364/6104>.

44   See, for example, the case of the Observant convent of San Francesco del Monte in Perugia, of which in addition to the inventory drawn up at the request of the Congregation of the Index there is a catalogue compiled at the end of the eighteenth century and now published in *La 'libraria' settecentesca di San Francesco del Monte a Perugia. Non oculis mentibus esca*, ed. Fiammetta Sabba (Perugia, 2015).

Congregation of the Index are the starting point of that crucial phase of transformation during which religious libraries passed from the closed and static structure that characterized the medieval library to being a paradigm of the modern library, a transformation which is discussed in the most recent sources[45]. In this sense, religious libraries constitute a critical juncture which can be read as a development or as an antecedent of trends of much longer duration.

The Vatican corpus is no less significant in a diachronic perspective for reconstructing aspects and phases of library history which have had as their protagonists Orders and Congregations which no longer survive or which have seen their importance diminish over the course of the modern period, leaving less abundant or less well-known documentation. In this case, the lists sent to the Congregation of the Index enable us to reconstruct and perceive the proper importance of events that would otherwise remain unknown or be easily forgotten[46].

The lists in other words help us to achieve the aims of the 'bottom-up' methodology mentioned above, with its focus on contemporary documentation. This is the reason the database pays attention to its documentary sources, in all their materiality and requires their codicological description.

In addition to this, the database has functional features which support retrospective investiga-

tions, i.e. those which work backwards from the study of surviving volumes to reconstruct the past.

Copy-specific cataloguing of early printed books, which is gradually bringing to light the presence of traces of use, is still at an early stage compared to traditional bibliographical cataloguing and, although considerable progress has been made, it is far from being able to offer yet a complete mapping of library collections. In this context, the identification and location of the volumes which come from religious Orders are far from simple. This is all the more true because of the negative effects of the processes of suppression and secularization, which add a further element of opacity. This means that volumes which come from religious institutions, even when they have been acquired *en bloc*, have in many Italian libraries usually been placed in the undifferentiated 'container' of rare books collections with no indication of their original contexts and provenance.

In the face of these difficulties, the database can offer a kind of compass capable of orienting searches and indicating the potential possible priorities or strategies which have a greater probability of success.

As mentioned, at the core of its structure is the relationship between editions and copies, made possible by the bibliographical reliability of the lists. Entries are managed as copies of editions, and each edition, as well as being linked to the instances in the lists, is also linked to the relevant entry in the current standard bibliographical reference that has been used to verify the bibliographical data.

It thus becomes possible to connect the census of the Congregation of the Index and censuses or catalogues that describe books present in today's libraries. This information, together with the study of the history of the suppression of religious Orders, provides clues to surviving volumes, to searches on marks in books and their provenance, which in turn are indispensable if we

---

45   An analysis of the documentation focusing on this aspect is in Giovanna Granata, 'Dalle povere origine alle grandi biblioteche: gli Osservanti', in *Libri e biblioteche: le letture dei frati Mendicanti tra Rinascimento ed età moderna*, as note 34, 183–221.

46   This is for example the case of the Canons Regular of San Giorgio in Alga on which see Giovanna Granata, 'I libri dei Canonici secolari di San Giorgio in Alga nella documentazione della Congregazione dell'Indice', in *'Claustrum et armarium'. Studi su alcune biblioteche ecclesiastiche italiane tra Medioevo ed Età moderna*, ed. Edoardo Barbieri and Federico Gallo (Milano and Roma, 2010), 185–254.

are to understand and reconstruct the different strata which make up library collections.

In short, a kind of circular movement occurs, from the description of the inventories to the surviving copies of a given edition by precisely identifying the copies described in the inventories among those which are held in present-day libraries[47]. Of course this is hard work and not always fruitful.

The database reflects these two directions of movement. For each entry, in addition to the bibliographic source used to identify the corresponding edition, a further descriptive element is given that indicates the library and the shelf mark where the surviving copy is possibly located, thus closing the circle.

Twenty years after the beginning of the transcription and indexing of the Vatican corpus, the database can no longer be described as a research project. Although the process of data entry has not been completed, the information which has been stored is now highly representative both in qualitative and quantitative terms.

During the implementation of the database, the RICI group produced an extensive bibliography of studies and other writings that enhance different aspects of the database and test the different methodological approaches to the study of religious libraries in the modern period[48].

In conclusion, at least one initiative should be mentioned: the series 'Libri e biblioteche degli Ordini religiosi in Italia alla fine del secolo XVI' published by the Vatican Library in the series 'Studi e Testi'. The volumes of the series make available in print the transcription of the lists produced for the Inquiry of the Congregation of the Index, arranged by religious Order.

This is not a source that can be completely superimposed on the database since it differs from it not only in the type of support. The volumes intentionally lack indexes, since the latter are offered by the database with which the print version of the lists is synchronized. The

47 This is an approach that has produced numerous studies, starting from the volume edited by Borraccini, *Dalla «notitia librorum» degli inventari agli esemplari*, as note 37, the first to offer a systematic reflection on the subject.

48 A bibliography updated to 2012 is published as an appendix to the essay by Borraccini, Granata, and Rusconi, 'A proposito dell'Inchiesta della S. Congregazione dell'Indice dei libri proibiti di fine '500', as note 10. In the context of the present essay it is not possible to bring it further up to date but some conferences which shared the research perspectives and methodologies of the RICI group in a broader context are worth indicating: the 2011, 2013 and 2014 St Andrews conferences, whose proceedings have been collected in *Documenting the Early Modern Book World:*

Inventories and Catalogues in Manuscript and Print, ed. Malcolm Walsby and Natasha Constantinidou (Leiden and Boston, 2013), 207–70 (papers by Flavia Bruni and Andrea Ottone); McLean and Barker, *International Exchange in the Early Modern Book World*, as note 37, 214–38 (paper by Giovanna Granata); Bruni and Pettegree, *Lost Books*, as note 32, 291–344 (papers by Roberto Rusconi, Rosa Marisa Borraccini and Giovanna Granata); the conference held in 2013 at the Biblioteca Nazionale Centrale in Rome, whose proceedings have been published in *Le fonti per la storia camaldolese nelle biblioteche italiane e nella Biblioteca Apostolica Vaticana*, ed. Livia Martinoli and Ugo Fossa (Roma, 2015), 7–39 (papers by Roberto Rusconi, Samuele Megli and Rosa Marisa Borraccini); the conference of the Cistercensian Congregation of Casamari, whose proceedings have been published in *'In monasterio reservetur'. Le fonti per la storia dell'Ordine cistercense in Italia dal Medioevo all'Età moderna nelle biblioteche e negli archivi italiani e della Città del Vaticano. Atti del Convegno di studi, Certosa di Pavia, 22–23 ottobre 2015*, ed. Riccardo Cataldi (Cesena, 2018), 291–314 (paper by Enrico Pio Ardolino); the conference on inventories and indexing systems, *Disciplinare la memoria: strumenti e pratiche nella cultura scritta (secc. XVI–XVIII). Convegno internazionale di studi, Bologna, 13–15 marzo 2013*, ed. Maria Gioia Tavoni, Paolo Tinti, and Paola Vecchi (Bologna, 2014), 177–89 (paper by Rosa Marisa Borraccini); finally the aforementioned proceedings of the Conference of the Società internazionale di studi francescani and the Centro interuniversitario di studi francescani held in Assisi in 2018, *Libri e biblioteche*, as note 34, focused on mendicant Orders and their libraries at the end of the sixteenth century.

publication of each volume in the series follows (and concludes) the work of entering information into the database[49]. On the other hand, each volume is provided with a historical introduction focused on individual religious Orders and on their regulations concerning the organisation of monastic libraries. These are not systematic studies aimed at analysing data, but rather are intended to be a general guide to the effective use of the documentation. In this sense, the two tools, online and printed, complement each other in making available as well as enhancing a source of extraordinary importance for the history of religious libraries.

49 *Libri e biblioteche degli ordini religiosi in Italia alla fine del secolo XVI* (Città del Vaticano, 2013-). The following volumes have so far been published: *Congregazione di Santa Maria di Vallombrosa dell'Ordine di san Benedetto*, ed. Samuele Megli and Francesco Salvestrini, Libri e biblioteche degli ordini religiosi in Italia alla fine del secolo XVI, 1 = Studi e testi, 475 (2013); *Congregazione camaldolese dell'Ordine di san Benedetto*, ed. Cécile Caby and Samuele Megli, Libri e biblioteche degli ordini religiosi in Italia alla fine del secolo XVI, 2 = Studi e testi, 487 (2014); *Chierici regolari minori*, ed. Lucia Marinelli and Paola Zito; *Congregazione dell'Oratorio*, ed. Elisabetta Caldelli and Gennaro Cassiani; *Ordine dei frati scalzi della b. Vergine Maria del Monte Carmelo*, ed. Giovanni Grosso, Libri e biblioteche degli ordini religiosi in Italia alla fine del secolo XVI, 3 = Studi e testi, 497 (2015); *Congregazione degli Eremiti di san Girolamo del beato Pietro da Pisa. Monaci eremiti di san Girolamo*, ed. Monica Bocchetta, Libri e biblioteche degli Ordini religiosi in Italia alla fine del secolo XVI, 4 = Studi e testi, 522 (2017); *La Congregazione dell'Indice, l'esecuzione dell'*Index *del 1596*, as note 10; *Congregazione dei Canonici regolari del SS. Salvatore*, ed. Gianna Del Bono, Libri e biblioteche degli Ordini religiosi in Italia alla fine del secolo XVI, 6 = Studi e testi, 530 (2018); *Ordine dei Minimi di san Francesco di Paola*, ed. Rocco Benvenuto OM and Roberto Rusconi, Libri e biblioteche degli ordini religiosi in Italia alla fine del secolo XVI, 7 = Studi e testi 539 (2020). The first volume of those dedicated to the Capuchins is to be published in 2022.

Bibliography

Manuscripts and Archival Sources

Città del Vaticano, Archivio della Congregazione per la Dottrina della Fede, *Index*, Serie XXII e *Index*, Protocolli, P (II.a.14).
Città del Vaticano, Biblioteca Apostolica Vaticana, *Reginense latino* 2099
Città del Vaticano, Biblioteca Apostolica Vaticana, *Vaticani Latini* 11266–11326.
Paris, Archives Nationales, LL 1563.
Roma, Archivio Generale dell'Ordine dei Frati Minori Cappuccini, AB 214.

Secondary Works

Rocco Benvenuto, 'I Minimi nella diocesi di Bisignano alla vigilia della soppressione innocenziana', *Bollettino ufficiale dell'Ordine dei Minimi*, 48 (2002), 474–538.
Rosa Marisa Borraccini, 'Un Unknown Best-Seller: The *Confessionario* of Girolamo da Palermo', in *Lost Books. Reconstructing the Print World of Pre-Industrial Europe*, 291–309.
Costanzo Cargnoni, 'Libri e biblioteche dei Cappuccini della Provincia di Siracusa alla fine del sec. XVI', *Collectanea Franciscana*, 77 (2007), 69–151.
Catholic Church and Modern Science. Documents from the Archives of the Roman Congregations of the Holy Office and the Index. Vol. 1, *Sixteenth Century Documents*, ed. Ugo Baldini and Leen Spruit (Città del Vaticano, 2009).
Chierici regolari minori, ed. Lucia Marinelli and Paola Zito; *Congregazione dell'Oratorio*, ed. Elisabetta Caldelli and Gennaro Cassiani; *Ordine dei frati scalzi della b. Vergine Maria del Monte Carmelo*, ed. Giovanni Grosso, Libri e biblioteche degli ordini religiosi in Italia alla fine del secolo XVI, 3 = Studi e testi, 497 (Città del Vaticano, 2015).
Congregazione camaldolese dell'Ordine di san Benedetto, ed. Cécile Caby and Samuele Megli, Libri e biblioteche degli ordini religiosi in Italia alla fine del secolo XVI, 2 = Studi e testi, 487 (Città del Vaticano, 2014).
Congregazione degli Eremiti di san Girolamo del beato Pietro da Pisa. Monaci eremiti di san Girolamo, ed. Monica Bocchetta, Libri e biblioteche degli Ordini religiosi in Italia alla fine del secolo XVI, 4 = Studi e testi, 522 (Città del Vaticano, 2017).
Congregazione dei Canonici regolari del SS. Salvatore, ed. Gianna Del Bono, Libri e biblioteche degli Ordini religiosi in Italia alla fine del secolo XVI, 6 = Studi e testi, 530 (Città del Vaticano, 2018).
*La Congregazione dell'Indice, l'esecuzione dell'*Index *del 1596 e gli Ordini regolari in Italia*, ed. Alessandro Serra, Libri e biblioteche degli Ordini religiosi in Italia alla fine del secolo XVI, 5 = Studi e testi, 525 (Città del Vaticano, 2018).

Congregazione di Santa Maria di Vallombrosa dell'Ordine di san Benedetto, ed. Samuele Megli and Francesco Salvestrini, Libri e biblioteche degli ordini religiosi in Italia alla fine del secolo XVI, 1 = Studi e testi, 475 (Città del Vaticano, 2013).

Romeo De Maio, 'I modelli culturali della Controriforma. Le biblioteche dei conventi italiani alla fine del Cinquecento', in Id., *Riforma e miti nella Chiesa del Cinquecento* (Napoli, 1973), 365–81.

Disciplinare la memoria: strumenti e pratiche nella cultura scritta (secc. XVI–XVIII). Convegno internazionale di studi, Bologna, 13–15 marzo 2013, ed. Maria Gioia Tavoni, Paolo Tinti, and Paola Vecchi (Bologna, 2014).

Documenting the Early Modern Book World: Inventories and Catalogues in Manuscript and Print, ed. Malcolm Walsby and Natasha Constantinidou (Leiden and Boston, 2013).

Marc Dykmans, 'Les bibliothèques des religieux d'Italie en l'an 1600', *Archivum Historiae Pontificiae*, 24 (1986), 385–404.

Giovanni Fiesoli, 'Inventari al quadrato: il progetto R.I.Ca.Bi.M. Bilanci e questioni di metodo', *Bibliothecae.it*, 5 (2016), 17–54, https://bibliothecae.unibo.it/article/view/6104/5865, DOI <10.6092/Issn.2283–9364/6104>.

Le fonti per la storia camaldolese nelle biblioteche italiane e nella Biblioteca Apostolica Vaticana, ed. Livia Martinoli and Ugo Fossa (Roma, 2015).

Gigliola Fragnito, *La Bibbia al rogo. La censura ecclesiastica e i volgarizzamenti della Scrittura, 1471–1605* (Bologna, 1997).

Gigliola Fragnito, *Proibito capire. La Chiesa e il volgare nella prima età moderna* (Bologna, 2005).

Gigliola Fragnito, 'L'Indice clementino e le biblioteche degli Ordini religiosi', in *Libri, biblioteche e cultura degli Ordini regolari nell'Italia moderna attraverso la documentazione della Congregazione dell'Indice*, 37–59.

Vittorio Frajese, *Nascita dell'Indice. La censura ecclesiastica dal Rinascimento alla Controriforma* (Brescia, 2006).

Giovanna Granata, 'Le biblioteche dei religiosi in Italia alla fine del Cinquecento attraverso l''Inchiesta' della Congregazione dell'Indice. A proposito di libri 'scomparsi': il caso dei Francescani Osservanti di Sicilia', in *'Ubi neque aerugo neque tinea demolitur': studi in onore di Luigi Pellegrini per i suoi settanta anni*, ed. Maria Grazia Del Fuoco (Napoli, 2006), 329–406.

Giovanna Granata, 'Struttura e funzionalità della banca dati "Le biblioteche degli Ordini regolari in Italia alla fine del secolo XVI"', in *Libri, biblioteche e cultura degli Ordini regolari nell'Italia moderna attraverso la documentazione della Congregazione dell'Indice*, 285–305.

Giovanna Granata, 'I libri dei Canonici secolari di San Giorgio in Alga nella documentazione della Congregazione dell'Indice', in *'Claustrum et armarium'. Studi su alcune biblioteche ecclesiastiche italiane tra Medioevo ed Età moderna*, ed. Edoardo Barbieri and Federico Gallo (Milano and Roma, 2010), 185–254.

Giovanna Granata, 'Books without Borders. The Presence of the European Printing Press in the Italian Religious Libraries at the End of the Sixteenth Century', in *International Exchange in the Early Modern Book World*, ed. Matthew McLean and Sara Barker (Leiden, 2016), 214–38.

Giovanna Granata, 'On the Track of Lost Editions in Italian Religious Libraries at the End of the Sixteenth Century: A Numerical Analysis of the RICI Database', in *Lost Books. Reconstructing the Print World of Pre-Industrial Europe*, 324–44.

Giovanna Granata, 'Dalle povere origine alle grandi biblioteche: gli Osservanti', in *Libri e biblioteche: le letture dei frati mendicanti tra Rinascimento ed età moderna*, 183–221.

'In monasterio reservetur'. Le fonti per la storia dell'Ordine cistercense in Italia dal Medioevo all'Età moderna nelle biblioteche e negli archivi italiani e della Città del Vaticano. Atti del Convegno di studi, Certosa di Pavia, 22–23 ottobre 2015, ed. Riccardo Cataldi (Cesena, 2018).

Index des livres interdits, ed. Jesús Martinez de Bujanda (Sherbrooke, Québec, and Genève, 1984–1996).

Piero Innocenti and Maria Antonietta De Cristofaro, 'Iter Lucanum. Ipotesi di una mappa di archivi e biblioteche, pubblici e privati, di Basilicata dopo il terremoto del 1980', *Annali della Facoltà di Lettere e Filosofia, Università degli studi della Basilicata, Potenza*, (1993–1994), 205–59.

L'Inquisizione e gli storici: un cantiere aperto. Tavola rotonda nell'ambito della Conferenza annuale della ricerca, Roma, 24–25 giugno 1999 (Roma, 2000).

L'Inquisizione romana e i suoi archivi. A vent'anni dall'apertura dell'ACDF. Atti del convegno, Roma, 15–17 maggio 2018, ed. Alejandro Cifres (Roma, 2019).

Marie-Madeleine Lebreton and Luigi Fiorani, *Codices Vaticani Latini 11266–11326* (Città del Vaticano, 1985).

La 'libraria' settecentesca di San Francesco del Monte a Perugia. Non oculis mentibus esca, ed. Fiammetta Sabba (Perugia, 2015).

Libri, biblioteche e cultura degli Ordini regolari nell'Italia moderna attraverso la documentazione della Congregazione dell'Indice. Atti del convegno internazionale, Macerata, 30 maggio – 1 giugno 2006, ed. Rosa Marisa Borraccini and Roberto Rusconi (Città del Vaticano, 2006).

Libri e biblioteche: le letture dei frati mendicanti tra Rinascimento ed età moderna. Atti del XLVI Convegno internazionale, Assisi, 18–20 ottobre 2018 (Spoleto, 2019).

Libri e biblioteche degli ordini religiosi in Italia alla fine del secolo XVI (Città del Vaticano, 2013-).

Lost Books. Reconstructing the Print World of Pre-Industrial Europe, ed. Flavia Bruni and Andrew Pettegree (Leiden-Boston, 2016).

Donatella Nebbiai-Dalla Guarda, *I documenti per la storia delle biblioteche medievali: secoli IX–XV* (Roma, 1992).

Donatella Nebbiai-Dalla Guarda, 'Bibliothèques en Italie jusqu'au XIIIe siècle. État des sources et premières recherches', in *Libri, lettori e biblioteche dell'Italia medievale: secoli IX–XV: fonti, testi, utilizzazione del libro*. Atti della Tavola rotonda italo-francese, Roma, 7–8 marzo 1997, ed. Giuseppe Lombardi and Donatella Nebbiai-Dalla Guarda (Roma and Paris, 2000) 7–129.

Ordine dei Minimi di san Francesco di Paola, ed. Rocco Benvenuto OM and Roberto Rusconi, Libri e biblioteche degli ordini religiosi in Italia alla fine del secolo XVI, 7 = Studi e testi 539 (Città del Vaticano, 2020).

Provenienze. Metodologia di rilevamento, descrizione e indicizzazione per il materiale bibliografico. Documento elaborato dal Gruppo di lavoro sulle provenienze coordinato dalla Regione Toscana e dalla Provincia autonoma di Trento, ed. Katia Cestelli and Anna Gonzo (Trento and Firenze, 2009).

Renzo Ragghianti and Alessandro Savorelli, 'Biblioteche filosofiche private: strumenti di lavoro, documenti e contesti', in *Il libro antico tra catalogo storico e catalogazione elettronica*, ed. Roberto Rusconi (Roma, 2012), 109–32.

Repertorio di Inventari e Cataloghi di Biblioteche Medievali dal secolo VI al 1520 (= RICaBiM) (Firenze, 2009-).

Marielisa Rossi, 'Raccolte, provenienze, indici', in Ead., *Provenienze, cataloghi, esemplari. Studi sulle raccolte librarie antiche* (Manziana, Roma, 2001), 9–83.

Ugo Rozzo, 'Una fonte integrativa di ISTC: l'inchiesta della Congregazione dell'Indice del 1597–1603', in *Libri, biblioteche e cultura degli Ordini regolari nell'Italia moderna, attraverso la documentazione della Congregazione dell'Indice*, 215–50.

Graziano Ruffini, ''Di mano in mano'. Per una fenomenologia delle tracce di possesso', *Bibliotheca*, 1 (2002), 142–60.

Roberto Rusconi, ''O scritti a mano'': i libri manoscritti tra inquisizione e descrizione', in *Dalla notitia librorum degli inventari agli esemplari. Saggi di indagine su libri e biblioteche dai codici Vaticani latini 11266–11326*, ed. Rosa Marisa Borraccini (Macerata, 2009), 1–26.

Roberto Rusconi, 'I religiosi e i loro libri in Italia alla fine del secolo XVI', in Rosa Marisa Borraccini, Giovanna Granata and Roberto Rusconi, 'A proposito dell'inchiesta della S. Congregazione dell'Indice dei libri proibiti di fine '500', *Il capitale culturale. Studies on the Value of Cultural Heritage*, 6 (2013), 13–45, http://riviste.unimc.it/index.php/cap-cult/article/view/400

Roberto Rusconi, 'The Devil's Trick. Impossible Editions in the Lists of Titles from the Regular Orders in Italy at the End of the Sixteenth Century', in *Lost Books. Reconstructing the Print World of Pre-Industrial Europe*, 310–23.

Alfredo Serrai, 'Le biblioteche private quale paradigma bibliografico (La biblioteca di Aldo Manuzio il giovane)', in *Le biblioteche private come paradigma bibliografico*. Atti del Convegno internazionale, Roma, Tempio di Adriano, 10–12 ottobre 2007, ed. Fiammetta Sabba (Roma, 2008), 19–28.

Giuseppina Zappella, 'Alla ricerca del libro perduto: supplemento "virtuale" agli annali della tipografia napoletana del Cinquecento', in *Bibliologia e critica dantesca: saggi dedicati a Enzo Esposito, I: Saggi bibliologici*, ed. Vincenzo De Gregorio (Ravenna, 1997), 243–93.

Digital Sources

Biblioteche dei filosofi. Biblioteche Filosofiche Private in Età Moderna e Contemporanea, http://picus.unica.it/.

Material Evidence in Incunabula (MEI), https://data.cerl.org/mei/_search.

Ricerca sull'Inchiesta della Congregazione dell'Indice (RICI), 'Le biblioteche degli ordini regolari in Italia alla fine del secolo XVI', https://rici.vatlib.it/.

CRISTINA DONDI, LAVINIA PROSDOCIMI, DORIT RAINES

The Incunabula Collection of the Benedictine Library of S. Giorgio Maggiore in Venice. Formation, Use, and Dispersal according to Documentary and Material Evidence (from MEI)

The library of the Benedictine abbey of S. Giorgio Maggiore in Venice was scattered after the dissolution of the house in 1806. The reconstruction of its incunabula collection offers a test case for studying the effectiveness of a provenance methodology that combines material evidence (collected in the Material Evidence in Incunabula (MEI) database) with various forms of documentary evidence. The assumption that underlies the database is that in the total or partial absence of documentation, the books themselves may offer material evidence to tell the history of the collection[1]. Ownership notes, historical bindings and decoration, and other marks, may be left on the books belonging to a single religious house,

---

1 Cristina Dondi, 'The Venetian Booktrade: a Methodological Approach to and First Results of Book-Based Historical Research', in *Early Printed Books as Material Objects: Proceeding of the Conference organized by the IFLA Rare Books and Manuscripts Section, Munich, 19–21 August 2009*, eds Bettina Wagner and Marcia Reed (Berlin-New York, 2010), 219–28; Cristina Dondi and Maria Alessandra Panzanelli Fratoni, 'Researching the Origin of Perugia's Public Library (1582/1623) before and after *Material Evidence in Incunabula*', *Quaerendo*, 46 (2016), 129–50; and more recently Cristina Dondi, 'The 15cBOOKTRADE Project and the Study of Incunabula as Historical Sources',

Cristina Dondi • Professor of Early European Book Heritage, University of Oxford, Oakeshott Senior Research Fellow in the Humanities, Lincoln College; Secretary of the Consortium of European Research Libraries (CERL). cristina.dondi@lincoln.ox.ac.uk

Lavinia Prosdocimi • Formerly Librarian, Sezioni Manoscritti e Incunaboli, Biblioteca Universitaria, Padova. lavinia.prosdocimi16@gmail.com

Dorit Raines • Associate Professor of History of Libraries and Documentation, Dipartimento di Studi Umanistici, Università Ca' Foscari, Venezia. raines@unive.it

How the Secularization of Religious Houses Transformed the Libraries of Europe, 16th–19th Centuries, ed. by Cristina Dondi, Dorit Raines, and † Richard Sharpe, BIB, 63 (Turnhout, 2022), pp. 567–656.

BREPOLS ✠ PUBLISHERS

DOI 10.1484/M.BIB-EB.5.128505

representing their purchase, donation, exchange, use, cataloguing, selling, or confiscation. The authors intend to show in the present article that an approach that collects and arranges these marks as they were applied over time and by different hands, on the printed books as well as the manuscript collection of the Benedictine library, may serve as a method for uncovering other histories of lost libraries. Moreover, coupling the provenance approach with archival research contributes significantly to the discovery of many more volumes no longer extant today (or whose whereabouts are not yet known) and sharpens the narrative of events regarding the circulation of the books after the dissolution of the library.

The Library of S. Giorgio Maggiore before the Dissolution in 1806

Before introducing the findings of this investigation, it will be necessary to set them in context by way of a summary history of the library[2]. The monastery of

S. Giorgio Maggiore was located on a small island in front of the Doges' Palace in Venice. Records reveal the presence of the Benedictine order there as early as 790. In the act by which Doge Tribuno Memmo gave the island to the order in 982, we find the oldest reference to books at the monastery. The act states that the books, together with the church of S. Giorgio Maggiore, will become part of the monastery's property; no further information is provided about these books, but we may presume that they were liturgical volumes[3]. Centuries later, on 16 January 1362, fifty-nine manuscripts were inventoried by the notaries Tomaso Bonincontro di Boaterii (abbot from 1369) and Nicola di Conto, along with the other goods of the monastery[4]. A second inventory, made in 1369, likewise makes no mention of a specific location for a library, although there was a room dedicated to the study of texts, a 'studium'[5].

The Benedictine order in Italy was losing its vigour in 1409, when there was an attempt to revive it with the foundation of the Congregation

---

in *Printing R-Evolution and Society 1450–1500. Fifty Years that Changed Europe*, ed. Cristina Dondi, Studi di Storia 13 (Venice, 2020), 21–54. DOI 10.30687/978-88-6969-332-8.

2 Fortunato Olmo, *Istoria dell'isola di San Giorgio Maggiore* (1619), Biblioteca Universitaria di Padova, cod. 285; Flaminio Corner, *Notizie storiche delle chiese e monasteri di Venezia e di Torcello* (Padova, 1758), 467; Giovanni Rossi, 'Storia del monastero di San Giorgio *Maggiore*', in Emmanuele Antonio Cicogna, *Delle iscrizioni veneziane* (Venezia, 1834), IV 241–401; Pietro La Cute, 'Le vicende delle biblioteche monastiche veneziane dopo la soppressione napoleonica', *Rivista di Venezia*, A. VIII, no. 10 (October 1929), 597–646; Giorgio Ravegnani, *Le biblioteche del monastero di San Giorgio maggiore*, con un saggio di Nicola Ivanoff sulla decorazione della biblioteca di San Giorgio Maggiore (Firenze, 1976); Sergio Baldan, 'La storia del monastero di S. Giorgio Maggiore scritta dal monaco Fortunato Olmo', *Studi Veneziani*, LXIII (2011), 352–546; Antonella Barzazi, '"Un tempo assai ricche e piene di libri di merito". Le biblioteche dei regolari tra sviluppo e dispersione', in *Alli 10 Agosto 1806 soppressione del monastero di S. Giorgio*, ed. Giovanni Vian (Cesena, 2011), 71–91.

3 *San Giorgio Maggiore*, II, *Documenti 982–1159*, ed. Luigi Lanfranchi, *Fonti per la storia di Venezia*, sez. II, Archivi ecclesiastici Diocesi Castellana (Venezia, 1968), 20–22; Jean-Claude Hocquet, *Les monastères vénitiens et l'argent* (Rome, 2020), 28–31.

4 Ravegnani, *Le biblioteche del monastero di San Giorgio maggiore*, as note 2, 11–13 (the inventory is at 73–76); Rossi, 'Storia del monastero di San Giorgio Maggiore', as note 2, 257; Carlo Urbani, 'I benedettini di San Giorgio maggiore di Venezia: momenti salienti', in *Alli 10 Agosto 1806*, as note 2, 93–113.

5 Gabriele Mazzucco, 'L'assetto di un monastero benedettino medioevale: San Giorgio Maggiore di Venezia nel 1369', in *Monastica et umanistica. Scritti in onore di Gregorio Penco OSB*, ed. Francesco Giovanni Trolese (Cesena, 2003), 199–225 (esp. 209–11); Francesco Giovanni Trolese, 'La riforma benedettina di S. Giustina nel Quattrocento', in *I Benedettini a Padova e nel territorio padovano attraverso i secoli: saggi storici sul movimento benedettino a Padova*, catalogo della mostra storico-artistica nel 15° centenario della nascita di San Benedetto, Padova, Abbazia di Santa Giustina, ottobre-dicembre 1980, eds Alberta De Nicolò Salmazo and Francesco Giovanni Trolese (Treviso, 1980), 55–74.

of Sta. Giustina of Padua. The Congregation was named after the monastery whose abbot, from 1408, a Venetian (of patrician descent), Ludovico Barbo (*c.* 1382–1443), was considered to be the Congregation's founder[6]. The monastery of S. Giorgio Maggiore joined the Congregation on 6 November 1429, and, following a papal bull in 1430, the incorporation of the monastery into the Congregation was enacted by the Venetian Senate on 9 February 1432. However, ten years later, following the insistence by Doge Francesco Foscari that the new pope, Eugenio IV (the Venetian Gabriele Condulmer) recognize the monastery as a ducal *giuspatronato*, the Republic and the Holy See reached a compromise: the doge renounced his claim while the pope issued a new bull on 4 February 1443 'Ad exeguendum debitum', adjusting the conditions of the union: the abbot of S. Giorgio Maggiore was to be nominated in a chapter to be held in Venice, unlike other monasteries of the Congregation whose abbots were nominated in the general chapter at Sta. Giustina[7].

As for the library, after the institution of the Congregation, the number of books increased considerably and rather quickly due to numerous purchases and/or gifts as well as legacies from monks and abbots. This growth, especially during the early decades of the fifteenth century, involved the need to build a library that could preserve the non-liturgical books of the monastery. This was to become 'the old library', probably built, as hypothesized by Giorgio Ravegnani, between 1362 and 1414–1415[8]. This library was soon abandoned for the 'new library', otherwise known as the Medicean library. In 1433 Cosimo de Medici (†1464), exiled from Florence, found

shelter in Venice. He decided to build a library at the monastery and appointed the architect Michelozzo Michelozzi (†1472), a friend who had followed him into exile. The building was probably completed only forty-five years later, through generous financing from Cosimo's son, Pietro (†1469)[9].

Another important legacy in favour of the library was that by Cardinal Bessarion of Trebisond, who, during his stay in Venice, decided to donate to the monastery his collection of Greek manuscripts. Yet, on 31 May 1468, a papal bull of Paul II revoked the donation and the books eventually ended up in the library of St Mark in Venice[10]. In the meantime, the library of S. Giorgio Maggiore continued to grow through donations[11] or the purchase of books directly from Venetian booksellers[12].

6 Idelfonso Tassi, *Ludovico Barbo (1381–1443)* (Roma, 1952), 27–74.

7 Venice, Archivio di Stato (ASVe), *S. Giorgio Maggiore*, Processi, b. 14, proc. 4: 'Possesso tolto dalla Congregazione Cassinense alias S. Giustina di Padova di questo monastero e capitoli della riforma del medemo'.

8 Ravegnani, *Le biblioteche del monastero di San Giorgio maggiore*, as note 2, 17.

9 Cicogna, *Delle iscrizioni veneziane*, as note 2, IV, 594, saw the original payment receipts from 1478 and observed that the floor was completed only in 1540. See also Antonio Foscari, 'Introduzione a una ricerca sulla costruzione della Libreria medicea nel Convento di San Giorgio Maggiore a Venezia', in *Studi per Pietro Zampetti*, ed. Ranieri Varese (Ancona, 1993), 226–36 (esp. 231–32); Ravegnani, *Le biblioteche del monastero di San Giorgio maggiore*, as note 2, 17–25.

10 Ravegnani, *Le biblioteche del monastero di San Giorgio maggiore*, as note 2, 26–27; Lotte Labowsky, *Bessarion's Library and the Biblioteca Marciana. Six Early Inventories* (Roma, 1979). Cf. Venice, Biblioteca Nazionale Marciana (BNM), Cod. Marc. Lat. XIV, 14 (= 4235).

11 Andrea Giacomo Gonella q. Alessio from the parish of S. Geremia left his books in 1479 to the library; Raffaele Regio, 'pubblico lettore' bequeathed his books in 1520; in 1546, it was Cardinal Domenico Grimani's nephew, the Patriarch of Aquileia Marino, who bequeathed his books, over 1,000 manuscripts and printed books mostly in Greek and Hebrew, to the monastery, under the condition that a library would be built for them in two years' time, otherwise the collection would pass to the monks of S. Domenico. It is not known whether the collection ever reached the library, since Grimani's sister, Paola Querini, declared in her will of 1572 that as her brother had owned her sums of money, she had taken the books in satisfaction. See Cicogna, *Delle iscrizioni veneziane*, as note 2, IV, 264, 327, note 201 and 596–98.

12 ASVe, *S. Giorgio Maggiore*, Processi, b. 27, proc. 13 B., fasc. VI. 'Libreria. 1430–1786': books bought from Luca Antonio Giunta in 1512 to 1518, from Tommaso Giunta in 1526, from Bartolomeo 'Columbin' in 1517–1519, from

In 1569, amidst renovation works to some parts of the monastery, which had begun in 1559, a fire devastated an area close to the library, although apparently without damage to the books[13]. In 1614, it was decided to build a new library and to demolish the Medici one. Due to financial constraints, it was only in 1641 that Abbot Alvise Squadron appointed the architect Baldassare Longhena to carry out the project: the building's construction was finished in 1653 and its furnishing in 1670[14]. The interiors had splendid curved wooden presses topped by fifty-six statues of the greatest philosophers and scholars of antiquity[15].

Many new books entered the library, mostly purchased from Venetian booksellers[16]; but older

books arrived too, as in 1653, when the Venetian secretary Alvise Querini bequeathed his entire collection[17]. Many other donors followed in the seventeenth and the eighteenth centuries: Abbot Francesco Soperchi, the librarian, Father Idelfonso, Abbot Alvise Ghidini, with a donation of various manuscripts, Abbot Veremondo Musitelli in 1735 and Friar Andrea Benedetto Ganassoni in 1786[18]. The library achieved some renown and was considered an essential stop in the 'grand tour' of young European nobles or scholars[19].

Domenico Nicolini in 1569 and 1577, and from Giovanni Battista Bragadin, 'libraio in Roma', in 1572. The monastery also asked Nicolini to print several liturgical books.

13 Ravegnani, *Le biblioteche del monastero di San Giorgio maggiore*, as note 2, 28–35; on the renovation works, see Hocquet, *Les monastères vénitiens*, as note 3, 286–92.

14 This is also the reason why the S. Giorgio Maggiore manuscripts are not mentioned by Giacomo Filippo Tomasini in his 1650 survey of Venetian libraries: Giacomo Filippo Tomasini, *Bibliothecae Venetae Manuscriptae publicae et privatae quibus diversi scriptores hactenus incogniti recensentur* (Utini, Typis Nicolai Schiratti, 1650). For the Longhena project and the dating of the library, see Martina Frank, *Baldassare Longhena* (Venezia, 2004), 207–11.

15 Rossi, 'Storia del monastero di San Giorgio Maggiore', as note 2, 272; Cicogna, *Delle iscrizioni veneziane*, as note 2, IV, 598–99; Ravegnani, *Le biblioteche del monastero di San Giorgio maggiore*, as note 2, 35–43.

16 ASVe, *S. Giorgio Maggiore*, Processi, b. 27, proc. 13B., fasc. VI. 'Libreria. 1430–1786': in 1648 the library paid 90 ducats for the seventeen volumes of the *Magna Bibliotheca Veterum Patrum et antiquorum scriptorum ecclesiasticorum* by Marguerin de la Bigne (Parisiis, sumptibus Ægidij Morelli architypographi Regij, 1644). In 1649 and 1650 other books were bought from Matteo Leni 'per la stampatura del Boezio' [?], 'per la stampatura del *Mancipatus* e carta del detto Mancipatus' [Gerardus Belga, *Mancipatus deiparae. Quo Augustissimae Coelitum Imperatricis diligens feruulus Ad Obsequium placitumque eiusdem quotidiana seruitii praxis pie instititur. Authore Gerardo Belga ... Opera R.P.F. Gabrielis*

Bucelini (Venetiis, Ex Typographia Leniana, 1649)], and for the 'stampatura degli *Annali* del padre Bucelino' [perhaps *Annales benedectini*, s.n.t., today at Bari, Biblioteca provinciale S. Teresa dei Maschi-De Gemmis?]. Other books were purchased in 1652 from Giovanni Bertano and in 1654 from Andrea Baba.

17 ASVe, *S. Giorgio Maggiore*, Processi, b. 42, proc. 36; Cicogna, *Delle iscrizioni veneziane*, as note 2, IV, 599; Ravegnani, *Le biblioteche del monastero di San Giorgio maggiore*, as note 2, 44.

18 Ravegnani, *Le biblioteche del monastero di San Giorgio maggiore*, as note 2, 44, 50–51.

19 François Maximilien Misson [1650–1722], *Avis de Librairies in Nouveau voyage d'Italie*, 4e édition (La Haye, Chez Henry van Bulderen, 1722), vol. I, 219 for his travels in 1687–1688: '[bibliothèque] bien entretenue, plus nombreuse & plus accessible [que celle de Saint Marc]'; Joseph de Blainville [1675–1752], *Travels through Holland, Germany, Switzerland, but especially Italy* (London, John Noon and Joseph Noon, 1757), vol. I, 533 for his travels in 1707: 'the most considerable and best provided one'; Anne-Claude-Philippe de Tubières, conte de Caylus [1692–1765], *Voyage d'Italie 1714–1715* (Paris, Librairie Fiscbacher, 1914), 83: 'La Bibliothèque [...] m'a paru remplie de choses fort rares'; Joachim Christoph Nemeitz [1679–1753], *Nachlese besonderer Nachrichten von Italien: Als ein Supplement von Misson, Burnet, Addison, und andern...* (Leipzig, Johann Gottlieb Gleditsch, 1726), 54 for his travels in 1721–1722: 'Diese Bibliothec ist zwar nicht von den nombreuse sten doch im gegentheil desto kostbahrer'; Johann Georg Keyssler [1693–1743], *Neueste Reise durch Deutschland, Böhmen, Ungran, die Schweiz, Italien und Lothringen* (Hannover, Nikolaus Förster und Sohns Erben, 1751), vol. II, 1143 for his travels in 1727: 'Istgedachte Bibliothek ist die schonste von der ganzen Stadt Venedig, ob sie gleich noch nicht garzahlreich ist'; Charles-Louis de

The Library Model of the Congregation of Sta. Giustina and the Medicean Library

While the preceding history is well known, as are the whereabouts of a certain number of

manuscripts traced by Giorgio Ravegnani to their present holding institutions, little has so far been discovered about the early printed collection of the library of S. Giorgio Maggiore. Martin Gerbert, who travelled to Italy between 1759 and 1762, published an extremely helpful list of a number of incunabula (and manuscripts) that he found there[20]. The Venetian scholar Emmanuele Antonio Cicogna refers to eighteen incunabula taken by the French as war booty in 1797 (and until now it was unclear whether some or all had been returned), while the records in the Bibliothèque nationale de France enumerate twenty of them[21]. We also have the titles of eighty-five incunabula reported by Giovanni Rossi in 1806 as belonging to the collection of S. Giorgio Maggiore[22] (although their current whereabouts were mostly unknown). Furthermore, important questions such as the relationship between the libraries belonging to the congregation of Sta. Giustina of Padua, the library management policy of S. Giorgio Maggiore, the exchange programme, the dispersal and destiny of the book collection, still remain to be investigated.

In consideration of the scarce information regarding the presence of incunabula and later

Secondat, baron de Montesquieu [1689–1755], *Voyages de Montesquieu publiés par le baron Albert de Montesquieu* (Bordeaux, G. Gounomillon, 1894), vol. I, 57 for his travels in 1728–1729: 'La bibliothèque est très bien: c'est une boisure en colonnes, et tout en ordre'; Johann Jacob Volkmann [1732–1803], *Historische-Kritischen Nachrichten von Italien* (Leipzig, der Caspar Fritsch, 1778), vol. III, 631 for his travels in 1758: 'Die Bibliothek ist die ansehnlichste in Venedig. Viele Bucher sommen vom Cosimus von Medicis her, welcher sich in seinem Exil nach Venedig begeben hatte. Der Saal, worinn sie steht, ist zwar nicht sehr gross, aber von guten Berhaltnissen; die Schranke sind mit kleinen jonichen Saulen geziert, die ihnen ein artiges Unsehen geben, so wie die allegorischen Figuren uber benselben, welche auf den Innhalt der darunter stehenden Bucher zielen'; Jérôme De La Lande [1732–1807], *Voyage d'un françois en Italie, fait dans les années 1765 et 1766. Tome huitième: contenant l'histoire & les anecdotes les plus singulières de l'Italie, & sa description; les moeurs, les usages, le gouvernement ... & les plans de toutes les grandes villes d'Italie* (A Venise, et se trouve à Paris, Chez Desaint, Librarire, rue du Foin, 1769), 132–33: 'La bibliothèque renferme beaucoup de livres provenus de Come de Medicis, qui s'Etoit retiré à Venise dans son exil [...] Les armoires qui sont décorés de petites colonnes Ioniques, produisent un très-bon effet, ainsi que les figures allégoriques qui couronnent toute cette menuiserie & indiquent ingénieusement les matières renfermées dans chaque armoire'; Jacob Jonas Björnstähl [1731–1779], *Lettere ne' suoi viaggj stranieri di Giacomo Giona Bjoernstaehl professore di filosofia in Upsala scritte al signor Gjorwell bibliotecario regio in Stoccolma* (Poschiavo, Giuseppe Ambrosioni, 1785), vol. III, 182 for his travels in 1770–1773: 'bella biblioteca con molti manoscritti'. On these travellers cf. Fiammetta Sabba, *Viaggi tra i libri. Le biblioteche italiane nella letteratura del Grand Tour* (Pisa-Roma, 2018), respectively 106, 158, 163, 168, 176, 166, 213, 200, 133. We can also mention Paul Hentzner in 1599, Jacob Spon in 1678, Jean Mabillon in 1685, Robert de Cotte in 1689, Bernard de Montfaucon in 1689, Johann Caspar Goethe in 1740. See Marino Zorzi, *La Libreria di San Marco: libri, lettori, società nella Venezia dei Dogi* (Milano, 1987), 513–14, n. 513.

20 Martin Gerbert [1720–1793], *Iter Alemannicum, accedit Italicum et Gallicum* (Sankt Blasien, typis San-Blasianis, 1765), 464–72 for his travels in 1759 and 1762. Cf. Sabba, *Viaggi tra i libri*, as note 19, 182.

21 Cicogna, *Delle iscrizioni veneziane*, as note 2, IV, 601. See Bibliothèque nationale de France (BnF), AM 269: 'Venise', fasc. 1: 'Note de plusieurs livres rares qui se trouvent dans quelques bibliothèques de Venise et que la Bibliothèque Nationale se commande aux soins des citoyens commissaires du Gouvernement pour la recherche des Mouvemens des arts en Italie, le 25 thermidor an 5 [12 August 1797]', where twenty incunabula are mentioned. See now Elisabetta Sciarra, 'Acquisizioni e asportazioni alla caduta della Repubblica di Venezia', in *Printing R-Evolution and Society*, as note 1, 374–412.

22 ASVe, *Direzione dipartimentale del demanio e diritti uniti*, Atti, b. 380, 2/15, fasc. II: 'S. Giorgio Maggiore. Libri a stampa del secolo XV della Biblioteca di S. Giorgio Maggiore', a list made by Giovanni Rossi in 1806.

printed books in the library of S. Giorgio Maggiore in the period from the fifteenth to the eighteenth centuries, it will be worthwhile to understand the library management policy during the formative century of the Congregation. The surviving records of the monastery of Sta. Giustina of Padua are of great help. A surviving inventory of the library was prepared in the years 1453–1483, and was first published by Luigi Alberto Ferrai in 1887[23] and, more recently, in 1982, by Giovanna Cantoni Alzati, with identifications of the present holding institutions of the manuscripts[24], along with transcriptions of the ownership notes found in those manuscripts that belonged to a number of monasteries within the Congregation. This information led to some preliminary insights into the policy implemented in libraries of the Congregation up to 1504, when the famous monastery of Montecassino joined the Congregation, and the name was changed to Cassinese Congregation[25].

The general chapter in 1434 ruled that every house of the Congregation should regularly prepare an inventory of property[26]. As mentioned, one such inventory survives from Sta. Giustina for the period 1453–1483, it lists 1,246 items[27], both manuscripts and incunabula. The number of incunabula, mostly referred to as 'littera stampita' or 'impressus in papiro'[28], amounts to 472, which

means that 37.8% (more than a third) of the overall number of items in the library consisted in printed material produced between 1459 and 1483. The numbering in the inventory appears to follow the accession order and is written by a number of different hands[29] – the number assigned to a book is also recorded on its first leaf (usually marked in the lower margin) and – in at least the first 340 recorded items – on the last leaf of the book (or after the *explicit*)[30]. Cantoni Alzati's palaeographic analysis of the ownership notes and the hands responsible for the inventory reveal the existence at that time of an older inventory recording 340 items. The preparation of the new inventory was due to the central role of Sta. Giustina within the Congregation and to the rapid growth of the collection during the 1430s–1440s, which induced the monks to rethink their library. It is obviously impossible that incunabula were among the books recorded as part of the original library (prior to 1453) and indeed Cantoni Alzati remarks that signs of the crossing out of entries and inserting of the titles of incunabula are visible in the inventory and were made by a later, late fifteenth-century, hand, suggesting that older books were being deaccessioned and new books put in their place[31].

For the first 454 items the inventory also provides a sort of shelf-mark consisting of a majuscule letter and an Arabic numeral, each

23 Padua, Biblioteca Civica, ms B.P. 229. Luigi Alberto Ferrai, 'La biblioteca di S. Giustina di Padova', in Giuseppe Mazzatinti, *Inventario dei manoscritti italiani nelle biblioteche di Francia*, (Roma, 1887), II, 549–661.

24 Giovanna Cantoni Alzati, *La biblioteca di S. Giustina di Padova. Libri e cultura presso i benedettini padovani in età umanistica* (Padova, 1982).

25 Fortunato Federici, *Della biblioteca di S. Giustina di Padova, dissertazione storica con note biografiche* (Padova, 1815), 14.

26 Cantoni Alzati, *La biblioteca di S. Giustina di Padova*, as note 24, 14.

27 The last number is 1,337, but a mistake made by one of the monks led to the registration after the number 709 of the number 800 instead of 710. Ibid., 142.

28 The same terms are used in the 1501 catalogue of the Benedictine monastery of Saint Emmeram in Regensburg. Bettina Wagner, 'Libri impressi Bibliothecae

Monasterii Sancti Emmerammi. The Incunable Collection of St Emmeram, Regensburg, and its Catalogue, 1501', in *Incunabula and Their Readers. Printing, Selling and Using Books in the Fifteenth Century*, ed. Kristian Jensen (London, 2003), 183.

29 In the preface to the catalogue the librarian describes it as an 'inventario'. Cantoni Alzati, *La biblioteca di S. Giustina di Padova*, as note 24, 38.

30 Ferrai, *La biblioteca di S. Giustina di Padova*, as note 24, 553; Cantoni Alzati, *La biblioteca di S. Giustina di Padova*, as note 24, 15–16.

31 The incunable numbers inserted among the 340 items in the catalogue are: 30, 44, 47, 122, 124, 139, 175, 205, 239, 262, 296, 321, 322. Cantoni Alzati, *La biblioteca di S. Giustina di Padova*, as note 24, 21.

registered at the right-hand side of the entry; each of the twenty-two letters of the Latin alphabet are found in conjunction with numerals which run from 1 to 20 (except for the letters R-Z which terminate with the number 19). This fits the description of the architecture of the library, built in 1461 by initiative of Abbot Bernardo Terzi[32]. The account left in 1606 by Giacomo Cavacio (1584–1612), a monk of Sta. Giustina, refers to 'plutei' (desks), which might explain the shelf-mark system adopted: the volumes were placed on ornamented desks lettered alphabetically[33]. Elisabetta Barile presumes that the desk system led to the abandonment of the consecutive numeration of the volumes customarily used in the 'old library'[34]. But it is not clear whether the marking system covered the total number of books present on these desks: as they are numbered in alphabetical order, we may presume twenty-two desks rows with twenty books on each, presumably divided by a central aisle. But Jacopo Filippo Tomasini, a monk of the Venetian convent of S. Giorgio in Alga, left an account of 1639 referring to thirty-two desks, on which were placed both manuscripts (twenty-seven desks) and printed books (five desks – nos VIII, XVI, XXIII, XXV, XXX). It might be that he saw a different arrangement to that made in 1461, as a certain number of manuscripts were added to

the collection and perhaps new desks were added to meet the demand for new shelving space[35].

The fact that Abbot Terzi, on whose initiative the library of Sta. Giustina was built in 1461, came from S. Giorgio Maggiore cannot be considered a mere coincidence. In those years, the Venetian monastery was trying to gather funds for the construction of the Medicean library following the project left by Michelozzo Michelozzi that Vasari may have seen. In his work, *Le vite dei più eccellenti pittori, scultori e architetti*, Vasari described the library of S. Giorgio as having wooden *plutei* and being richly decorated ('fu finita non solo di muraglia, ma di banchi, di legnami ed altri ornamenti')[36]. Michelozzi was also the architect who built the library of S. Marco in Florence, completed in 1454, and which followed the pre-existing model for Italian libraries of an oblong hall with an unvaulted basilica-like space, hosting three sections and desks to which the volumes were chained (as in the monastic libraries of Monteoliveto Maggiore, Perugia, Bologna, Ferrara, and Piacenza)[37].

The form of the Medicean library of S. Giorgio Maggiore and its inventory were both very similar to the library architecture and management

32 Federici, *Della biblioteca di S. Giustina di Padova*, as note 25, 12.

33 Giacomo Cavacio, *Historiarum coenobii D. Justinae Patavinae libri sex. Quibus Cassinensis Congregationis origo, & plurima ad Urbem Patavium, ac finitimos attinentia opportunè interferuntur*, second edition (Patavii, Ex Typographia Seminarii, 1696), 229–30: 'Bernardus Abbas triclinii vestibulum auxit, cellam vinariam amplissimam fodit, Bibliothecam super ipsius fornicem instituit, eamque codicibus, pluteis, aliisque ornamentis honestavit'.

34 Elisabetta Barile, 'La biblioteca quattrocentesca di Santa Giustina di Padova', in *La calligrafia di Dio. La miniatura celebra la parola*, eds Giordana Canova Mariani and Paola Ferraro Vettore (Modena, 1999), 59–64, at 62.

35 See for example in *pluteo* XIV: 'Exposizione mistica nella Iconologia del Chiostro del Monasterio di S. Giustina con molte cose pertinenti agl'Abbati & governo temporale & Spirituale per spatio de anni 1063, e delli Benefattori, & riformi sino all'anno 1614, in ch. fol.'. Jacopo Filippo Tomasini, *Bibliothecae Patavinae manuscriptae publicae et privatae …* (Utini, Typis Nicolai Schiratti, 1639), 42–47, at 44.

36 Ravegnani, *Le biblioteche del monastero di San Giorgio maggiore*, as note 2, 18.

37 James F. O'Gorman, *The Architecture of the Monastic Library in Italy, 1300–1600. Catalogue with Introductory Essay* (New York, 1972), 1–36. The Medicean library may have inspired the Malatestiana library project in Cesena; see Piero Lucchi, 'L'ordine dei libri nella biblioteca Malatestiana. Appunti lungo un percorso di ricerca', in *Il dono di Malatesta Novello. Atti del convegno, Cesena, 21–23 marzo 2003*, eds Loretta Righetti and Daniela Savoia (Cesena, 2006), 135–224, esp. 138–44.

system of Sta. Giustina[38]. As emerges from the record of expenditure by the Medici regarding the library[39], dated 1473, the entrance to the library was through a stone portal, accessing a large hall with six large glass windows protected by green canvas, and a carved ceiling. On the walls were hung paintings and thirteen bookshelves (*chanzeli*), while in the hall were placed benches with their desks (*lezii*) richly decorated in gilt and colours[40]. As for the library management system, the General Chapter of the Congregation decided in 1434 on a uniform system for all the convents, enacting that a book's ownership note should include specific mention of the mother house (i.e. the name of the Congregation): 'omnes libri congregacionis nostre aquisiti et aquirendi conventibus nostris per donacionem vel a fratribus nostris scripti expensis conventus sive quovis alio modo adepti, deputantur usui ipsorum conventuum ubi fuerunt aquisiti'[41]. The

fifteenth-century ownership notes of S. Giorgio Maggiore follow this same pattern: the numbering of volumes is progressive and includes both manuscripts and incunabula. In the preface to the catalogue of the library of Sta. Giustina that served as a model for others, the author provides precise instructions on how to compose the *ex libris*: 'Iste liber est monachorum congregacionis S. Iustinae ipsi monasterio S. Iustinae Patavii deputatus, numero 1 A_a, numero 2 B_1, numero 3 C_1'. The pattern of this ownership note can be divided into three parts: (1) The declaration that the book is the property of the congregation (called, until 1504, 'Sta. Giustina de Padua')[42]; (2) The assignment of the book ('deputatus') to one of the monasteries of the congregation (in this case to the same – 'ipsi' – monastery of

---

38   For various hypotheses on the architecture: Foscari, 'Introduzione a una ricerca', as note 9, 226–36.

39   The document is in ASVe, *San Giorgio Maggiore*, Processi, b. 27, proc. 13B, fasc. VI, 'Libreria. 1430–1786', published by Foscari, 'Introduzione a una ricerca', as note 9, 233–34. The *Veduta* of Jacopo de' Barbari (1500) documents the existence of the library building with its gothic windows on the right of the entrance. Gianmario Guidarelli, Gabriella Liva, Silvia Musetti, 'Il complesso medievale di San Giorgio Maggiore a Venezia. Architettura, scultura, strumenti digitali per l'analisi e l'interpretazione', *Ateneo Veneto*, an. CCVI, 3° ser., 18/II (2019), 59–93, esp. 71–73. Giovanni Rossi, who had read all the documentation in the archives of S. Giorgio Maggiore before its dispersal, testifies that the ceiling was also gilded except for some niches where the monks had placed paintings. Rossi, 'Storia del monastero di San Giorgio Maggiore', as note 2, 261.

40   The inscription at the entrance read: 'Societati Mediceae / apud Deum / fratres et studiosi omnes / linguis animisque / favere tenemur / quod sua impensa / locum bibliothecae / omni cultu et ornatu / Ioanne Lanfredino socio / faciundum curavit'; Cicogna, *Delle iscrizioni veneziane*, as note 2, IV, 594, n. 27.

41   Tommaso Leccisotti, *Congregationis S. Iustinae de Padua O.S.B. Ordinationes capitulorum generalium*, I (Montecassino, 1939), 40; Cantoni Alzati, *La biblioteca*

di S. Giustina di Padova, as note 24, 6.

42   An example of the ownership declaration: 'Iste liber est monachorum congregationis sancte Iustine de Padua ordinis sancti Benedicti de obseruantia deputatus monasterio sancti Georgii maioris Venetiarum signatus numero 903' (n. 81 in the present catalogue). See the ownership notes on incunabula belonging to other monasteries of the Congregation: 'Iste liber est monasterii sancti sisti placentiae Congregationis Cassinensis alias sanctae Justinae de padua' (n. 25 in the present catalogue); 'Iste liber est monasterii sancti sixti placentiae Congregationis Cassinensis alias sanctae Justinae de padua' (n. 87 in the present catalogue). The insistence of the Congregation on inserting this declaration in any ownership note led some scholars to mistakenly attribute the ownership of various books to the library of Sta. Giustina rather than to the libraries which really owned them. Ezio Franceschini, 'Sulle versioni latine medievali del Περὶ χρωμάτων', in *Autour d'Aristote. Recueil d'études de philosophie ancienne et médiévale offert à Monseigneur A. Mansion* (Louvain, 1955), 451–69; Paolo Marangon, *Alle origini dell'aristotelismo padovano (secc. XII–XIII)* (Padova, 1977), 16–19, 30–31; Beniamino Pagnini, *Le origini della scrittura gotica padovana* (Padua, 1933), 62–66, 87–88. Cf. Lavinia Prosdocimi, 'Codici di Andrea Contrario nel testamento di Michele Salvatico', in *L'Umanesimo librario tra Venezia e Napoli. Contributi su Michele Salvatico e su Andrea Contrario*, eds Gilda P. Mantovani, Lavinia Prosdocimi and Elisabetta Barile (Venezia, 1993), 27–52, at 33–35.

Sta. Giustina); (3) The registration of the books' inventory numbers and shelf-marks[43].

If we analyse the fifteenth-century ownership notes of the books of S. Giorgio Maggiore we recognize the same logic. The text normally runs as follows: 'Iste liber est monachorum congregationis sancte Iustine de padua ordinis sancti Benedicti de obseruantia deputatus in sancto georgio maiore venet[iarum] numero 484'[44], which may be considered the earliest version adopted in the volumes because it faithfully transcribes the congregational model for the ownership note. A slightly different *ex libris*, probably contemporary, highlights more the fact that the volumes are at the disposal ('ad usum') of the monks of S. Giorgio Maggiore. It reads: 'Iste liber est congregationis Sanctae Iustinae ordinis Sancti Benedicti deputatus ad usum monachorum habitantium in monasterio Sancti Georgii Maioris de Venetiis ac signatus numero 669'[45].

The Material Evidence in Incunabula database allows us to identify fifty-seven incunabula with registered numbers in the possession of the library of S. Giorgio Maggiore at the beginning of the sixteenth century, and therefore to draw some conclusions regarding the presence of the incunabula in the library and the relationship with the library of Sta. Giustina. If we add the twenty-three surviving manuscripts so far

known to the list of fifty-seven incunabula, we can approach an idea of the library system as it existed at the beginning of the sixteenth century in the monastery of S. Giorgio Maggiore[46].

No. 48 – **Damasus, papa, I**, *De laudibus Pauli Apostoli* [et alia], MS., 15th cent.
Rome, Biblioteca nazionale centrale Vittorio Emanuele II, Vittorio Emanuele, Vitt.Em.952, fol. 152v: 'Iste liber est Monasterii sancti georgii maioris de Venetiis Congregationis sancte iustine signatus numero 48'.

No. 89 – ***Breviarium benedictinum***, MS., 15th cent.
Padua, Biblioteca Universitaria, ms. 531, fol. 1r: 'Iste liber est congregationis monachorum Sancte Iustine deputatus monasterio Sancti Georgii Maioris Venetiarum signatus numero 89'.

No. 114 – **Picus de Mirandula, Johannes**, *Opera*, Venice: Bernardinus de Vitalibus 1498. Folio.
Jerusalem, National Library of Israel, [system number 004105905], fol. 1r: 'Reverendus dominus Andreas Mocenicus protonotarius pro anime sue salute diui Georgii maioris cenobio dicauit signatus numero 114'. See Catalogue, no. 136.

No. 115 – **Aegidius (Columna) Romanus**, *De regimine principum*, Venice: Simon Bevilaqua, 9 July 1498. Folio.
Padua, Biblioteca Universitaria, Sec. XV 959/1, on the verso of the last leaf of the second bound work: 'Reverendus dominus Andreas Mocenicus prothonotarius pro animae suae salute Divi Georgii Maioris coenobio dicavit, signatus 115'. See Catalogue, no. 1.

No. 115 – **Horatius Flaccus, Quintus**, *Opera*. Comm: Antonius Mancinellus; (Pseudo-) Acron;

---

43 The shelf-marks were assigned only to the first category of books, as explained in the preface to the inventory, those that had to do with either the Holy Scriptures or with humanistic subjects and that were either held in high regard or whose author was considered an authority: 'Quarum prima illos tantum codices de divinis ac humanis rebus tractantes continent, qui vel precio vel scribentium auctoritate digni habentur'; Cantoni Alzati, *La biblioteca di S. Giustina di Padova*, as note 24, 37.

44 See no. 15 in the present catalogue: Augustinus, *De Civitate Dei*, Venice: Nicolaus Jenson, 2 Oct. 1475. Folio.

45 See no. 107 in the present catalogue: Leonardus de Utino, *Sermones de sanctis*, Venice: Johannes de Colonia and Johannes Manthen, 1475. 4°.

46 The order follows the incunable number as marked in the ownership note. The number given at the end of the incunable entries is the one assigned in the catalogue annexed to the present article.

Pomponius Porphyrio; Christophorus Landinus. Ed: Antonius Mancinellus. Venice: Johannes Alvisius, 23 July 1498. Folio.
Padua, Biblioteca Universitaria, Sec. XV 145, on the first leaf: 'Reverendus dominus Andreas Mocenicus prothonotarius apostolicus pro animae suae salute Divi Georgii Maioris coenobio dicavit signatus 115' (number crossed out). See Catalogue, no. 94.

No. C 115 – **Plautus**, *Comoediae*, Venice: Simon Bevilaqua, 17 Sept. 1499. Folio.
Oxford, Bodleian Library, Inc. c. I4.1499.5, A1r: 'Reuerendus dominus Andreas Mocenicus prothonotarius apostolicus pro anime sue salute diui Georgii maioris cenobio dicauit signatus C.115'. See Catalogue, no. 140.

No. 118 – **Celsus, A. Cornelius**, *De medicina*, Venice: Johannes Rubeus Vercellensis, 8 July 1493. Folio (formerly bound second with: M.I. Iustinus, *Iustinus hystoricus*, Venice: per Bartolomeum de Zanis de Portesio, 1503 die tertio febrarii. Folio. CNCE 51842 (Padua, Biblioteca Universitaria, 76 a 23)).
Padua, Biblioteca Universitaria, Sec. XV 943, a note on a2r of the edition of Iustinus: 'Reverendus dominus Andreas Mocenicus prothonotarius pro animae suae salute Divi Georgii Maioris coenobio dicavit, signatus 118'. See Catalogue, no. 51.

No. 124 – **Blondus, Flavius**, *Historiarum ab inclinatione Romanorum imperii decades*. Add: Pius II: Abbreviatio supra Decades Blondi. Venice: Thomas de Blavis, de Alexandria, 28 June 1484. Folio.
Milan, Biblioteca Trivulziana, Triv. Inc. B 138: 'Reverendus dominus Andreas Mocenicus protonotarius pro anime sue salute diui Georgii maioris cenobio dicauit signatus numero 124'. See Catalogue, no. 36.

No. 129 – *De imitatione Christi libri*, MS., 15th cent.
Padua, Biblioteca Universitaria, ms. 950, fol. 1r: 'Iste liberculus est congregationis Sancte Iustine

ad monasterium Sancti Georgii Maioris de Veneciis deputatus. 129'.

No. 196 – ***Vocabula excerpta partim ab Orthographia magistri Gasparini Barzizzae, partim a Catholicon***, MS., second quarter of 15th cent.
Padua, Biblioteca Universitaria, ms. 1329, fol. 182v: 'Iste liber est congregationis Sancte Iustine seu unitatis deputatus ad usum fratrum habitantium in Sancto Georgio Maiori de Venetiis usque in sempiternum signatus numero 196'.

No. 202 – **Lorenzo Giustiniani, s.**, *Sermones per totum annum*, MS., 15th cent.
Padua, Biblioteca Universitaria, ms. 1195, fol. IIIr: 'Iste liber est monachorum congregationis Sancte Iustine deputatus ad usum fratrum habitantium in monasterio Sancti Georgii Maioris de Venetiis signatus numero 202'.

No. 227 – ***Regula s. Benedicti***, MS., 15th cent. (1447).
Padua, Biblioteca Universitaria, ms. 430, fol. 54v: 'Hec regula est monasterii Sancti Georgii Maioris de Veneciis. signatus numero 227'.

No. 231 – **Augustinus, Aurelius, s.**, pseudo, *Sermones ad heremitas*, MS., 15th cent.
Padua, Biblioteca Universitaria, ms. 1326, fol. 1r: 'Iste liber est monachorum congregationis Sancte Iustine de Padua deputatus ad usum fratrum habitantiu in monasterio Sancti Georgii Maioris de Venetiis signatus numero 231'.

No. 278 – **Thomas Aquinas**, *Opuscula* (71). Ed: Antonius Pizamanus, with a life of St Thomas, Venice: Hermannus Liechtenstein, 7 Sept. 1490. 4°.
Venice, Biblioteca Nazionale Marciana, Inc. V. 0603, aa1r: '[...] Sancti Georgii M. Venetiarum numero 278'. See Catalogue, no. 168.

No. 281 – ***Biblia latina***, Venice: Johannes Herbort, 30 Apr. 1484. 4°.

Lucca, Biblioteca Statale, INC 59, fol. 408r: 'Congregationis s. Justine de padua deputatus monachis in monasterio s. Georgij maioris […] habitantibus ac signatus numero 281'. See Catalogue, no. 33.

No. 315 – **Duranti, Guillelmus,** *Rationale divinorum officiorum,* [Mainz]: Johann Fust and Peter Schoeffer, 6 Oct. 1459. Folio.
Paris, Bibliothèque nationale de France, Rés. Vélins 125, last leaf: 'Iste liber est congregationis monachorum sancte Justine | deputatus monasterio sancti Georgii maioris venetiarum ac signatus numero 315 | Constitit ducatorum decem octo emptus anno 1461'. See Catalogue, no. 68.

No. 321 – **Iohannes a Turrecremata,** *Commentaria in Regulam s. Benedicti,* MS., 15th cent.
Padua, Biblioteca Universitaria, ms. 1058, fols 1r and 215v: 'Iste liber est monachorum congregationis Sancte Iustine ordinis Sancti Benedicti deputatus monasterio Sancti Georgii Maioris Venetiarum signatus numero 321'.

No. 349 – ***Constitutiones ordinis cisterciensis,*** MS., beginning of 14th cent.
Padua, Biblioteca Universitaria, ms. 726, fol. 94r: 'Iste liber est congregationis Sancte Iustine ordinis Sancti Benedicti deputatus monasterio Sancti Georgii Maioris de Venetiis signatus numero 349'.

No. 394 – **Guillelmus Durantis,** *Rationale divinorum officiorum* (extractum), MS., 15th cent.
Padua, Biblioteca Universitaria, ms. 1186, fol. 4v: 'Iste liber est monachorum congregationis Sancte Iustine de Padua deputatus monasterio Sancti Georgii Maioris de Venetiis signatus numero 394' and 'Iste libellus extractus ex libro divinorum offitiorum est monasterii Beatorum Martyrum de Tergesto, scriptus in eodem monasterio per dominum Vitum monachum professum monasterii Sancti Georgii Maioris et priorem eiusdem monasterii Beatorum Martyrum, anno Domini 1444 vel circa'. Written about 1444 in

the monastery of the SS. Martyrs of Trieste by the monk Don Vito, professed in S. Giorgio Maggiore and prior of the monastery in Trieste, the manuscript then passed to S. Giorgio.

No. 404 – ***Scriptores rei rusticae,*** Venice: Nicolaus Jenson, 1472. Folio.
Milan, Biblioteca Nazionale Braidense, AN. XIII. 44, [*]14v: 'Iste liber est monachorum congregationis s. justine de padua ordinis s. benedicti de observantia deputatus monasterio s. Georgij maioris venetiarum signatus numero 404'. See Catalogue, no. 157.

No. 412 – **Eusebius Caesariensis,** *De evangelica praeparatione,* Venice: Nicolaus Jenson, 1470. Folio.
London, British Library, IB.19612a, at the end of the text: 'Iste liber est Congregationis Monachorum Sancte Iustine deputatus monasterio Sancti Georgii maioris (..) signatus [..] 412'. See Catalogue, no. 73.

No. 413 – **Leo Magnus papa, s.,** *Sermones,* MS., 15th cent. (1470s–1480s).
Padua, Biblioteca Universitaria, ms. 1454, fol. 137v: 'Iste liber est congregationis monachorum Sanctae Iustinae deputatus monasterio Sancti Georgii Maioris de Venetiis ac signatus numero 413'.

Nos 418–20 – **Livius, Titus,** *Historiae Romanae decades.* Ed: Johannes Andreas, bishop of Aleria, [Venice]: Vindelinus de Spira, 1470. Folio.
Trade Copy, Sotheby, London, 2013, lot 209. Inscription at the front of vol. 1 and at the back of vols 2 and 3: 'Iste liber est Congregationis monachorum sancte Iustine deputatus monasterio Diui Georgii maioris Venetiarum signatus numero 418 / 419 / 420'. See Catalogue, no. 109.

No. 456 – ***Trattatelli diversi teologici,*** MS., 15th cent.
Padua, Biblioteca Universitaria, ms. 424, fol. 204v: 'Iste liber est congregationis Sancte Iustine ordinis sancti Benedicti deputatus monasterii Sancti Georgii Maioris de Venetiis signatus numero 456'.

No. 457 – **Valla, Laurentius**, *Elegantiæ linguæ latinæ*, Venice: Nicolaus Jenson, 1471. 4°.
Paris, Bibliothèque nationale de France, Rés. X. 640, below the colophon: 'Iste liber est congregationis s. Iustine | deputatus ad usum monachorum habitantium| in monasterio s. georgii maioris | de uenetijs signatus numero 457'. See Catalogue, no. 176.

No. 459 – *Trattatelli ascetici*, MS., 15th cent.
Padua, Biblioteca Universitaria, ms. 945, fol. Iv: 'Est Sancti Georgii Maioris de Venetiis signatus numero 459'.

No. 461 – *Libellus moralis sive practica confessorum*, MS., second quarter of 15th cent.
Padua, Biblioteca Universitaria, ms. 1502, fol. 10r: 'Iste liber est monachorum congregationis Sanctae Iustinae deputatus usui conventus Sancti Georgii Maioris de Venetiis signatus [...] 461' ('461' crossed out but it also appears at the top of the same leaf).

No. 464 – **Tortellius, Johannes**, *Orthographia*, Venice: Nicolaus Jenson, 1471. Folio.
Paris, Bibliothèque nationale de France, Rés. X. 629, inscription below the colophon: 'Iste liber est congregationis s. Iustine | de Padua deputatus ad usum monachorum ha | bitantium in monasterio s. georgij maioris | de uenetijs signatus numero 464'. See Catalogue, no. 171.

No. 467 – *Excerpta e s. Antonino archiepiscopo Florentino*, MS., end of 15th cent.
Padua, Biblioteca Universitaria, ms. 1126, fol. Ir: 'Iste liber est monasterii Sancti Georgii Maioris Venetiarum 467'.

No. 484 – **Augustinus, Aurelius, s.**, *De Civitate Dei*, Venice: Nicolaus Jenson, 2 Oct. 1475. Folio.
Paris, Bibliothèque nationale de France, Rés. Vélins 301, below the colophon: 'Iste liber est monachorum congregationis | sancte Iustine de padua ordinis sancti | Benedicti de obseruantia deputatus | in sancto georgio maiore venet[iarum] numero 484'. See Catalogue, no. 15.

No. 493 – **Lactantius**, *Opera*, Venice: Vindelinus de Spira, 1472. Folio.
Paris, Bibliothèque nationale de France, Rés. C. 350, inscription below the last text: 'Iste liber est congregationis monchorum s. Iustine de Padua ordinis s Benedicti de | obseruantia deputatus in monasterio s. Georgij maioris uenet. signatus numero 493'. See Catalogue, no. 105.

No. 520 – **Strabo**, *Geographia*, Venice: Vindelinus de Spira, 1472. Folio.
Paris, Bibliothèque nationale de France, Rés. G. 15, inscription below the colophon: 'Iste liber est congregationis s. Iustine de Padua ordinis s. Benedicti de obseruan | tia | deputatus in monasterio s. georgii maioris | uenetiarum signatus numero 520'. See Catalogue, no. 162.

No. 521 – **Dominicus de Sancto Geminiano**, *Super sexto Decretalium* (I). Venice: Jacobus Rubeus, 10 Sept. 1476. Folio.
Padua, Biblioteca Universitaria, Sec. XV Duplicato 169, at the bottom of the last leaf: 'Iste liber est monachorum congregationis Sancte Iustine de Padua, deputatus in Sancto Georgio Maiori Venetiarum, signatus numero 521'. See Catalogue, no. 66.

No. 522 – **Johannes de Imola**, *In Clementinas opus*. Venice: Jacobus Rubeus, 1475. Folio.
Padua, Biblioteca Universitaria, Sec. XV 695, at the bottom of the last leaf: 'Iste liber est monachorum congregationis Sancte Iustine de Padua deputatus in Sancto Georgio Maiori Venetiarum, signatus numero 522'. See Catalogue, no. 101.

No. 539 – **Bonifacius VIII, Pont. Max.**, *Liber sextus Decretalium* (with gloss of Johannes Andreae). Ed: Alexander de Nevo. Add: Johannes Andreae, *Super arboribus consanguinitatis et affinitatis*, Venice: Nicolaus Jenson, 1476. Folio.

Manchester, John Rylands University Library, 9961, erased inscription below the colophon: 'Iste liber est monachorum congregationis Sanctae Iustinae de Padua deputatus monasterio Sancti Georgii Maioris Venetiarum, signatus numero 539'. See Catalogue, no. 41.

No. 545 – **Plinius Secundus, Gaius**, *Historia naturalis*, Parma: Stephanus Corallus, 1476. Folio. Harvard University, Houghton Library, Inc. 6842 (A), on the lower margin of [P]3r: 'Iste liber e(st) monachorum congregationis s. Justine de Padua deputatus in s. Georgio Venetiarum signatus numero 545'. See Catalogue, no. 142.

No. 546 – **Marlianus, Raimundus**, *Index locorum in commentario Caesaris Belli gallici descriptorum* (Rev: Bonus Accursius), [Milan: Bonus Accursius, about 1478]. 4°.
Berlin, Staatsbibliothek, Inc. 3080.25, at the end of the printed text: 'Iste liber est monachorum Congregationis s. Justine de Padua deputatus in s. Georgio maiori Venetiarum signatus numero 546'. See Catalogue, no. 117.

No. 574 – **Humbertus de Romanis**, *Epistola de tribus votis substantialibus religionis*; Thomas de Aquino, s., *De perfectione spiritualis vitae*, *Compendium theologiae*, MS., 15th cent.
Padua, Biblioteca Universitaria, ms. 1501, fol. IIv: 'Iste liber congregationis Sancte Iustine deputatus monasterio Sancti Georgii Maioris de Venetiis signatus numero 574'.

No. 577 – **Lorenzo Giustiniani, s.**, *De institutione et regimine praelatorum*, MS., 15th cent.
Padua, Biblioteca Universitaria, ms. 1008, fol. 1r: 'Congregationis Sancte Justine verum deputatus usui Monasterii Sancti Georgii Maioris Venetiarum 894'; fol. 146r: 'Iste liber est monasterii Sancti Georgii Maioris de Veneciis congregationis Sanctae Iustinae numero 577'.
See no. 894 below.

No. 578 – **Albertus Magnus**, *Compendium theologicae veritatis*, Venice: Christophorus Arnoldus, 5 Apr. 1476. 4°.
Padua, Biblioteca Universitaria: Sec. XV Duplicato 47, fol. 1v: 'Iste liber est monasterii Sancti Georgii (then corrected to 'Sancte Gustine', *sic*) Maioris signatus numero 604' (then corrected to '578'). See Catalogue, no. 3.
See no. 604 below.

No. 600 – **Lorenzo Giustiniani, s.**, *De disciplina et perfectione monasticae conversationis*, MS., 15th cent.
Padua, Biblioteca Universitaria, ms. 1332, fol. 140v: 'Hic liber est monachorum congregationis Sancte Iustine de Padua: deputatus ad usum fratrum habitantium in monasterio Divi Georgii Maioris de Venetiis. Signatus numero 600'.

No. 602 – **Nicolaus de Ausmo**, *Supplementum Summae Pisanellae*. Add: Alexander de Nevo: Consilia contra Judaeos foenerantes; Astesanus de Ast: Canones poenitentiales. Venice: Leonardus Wild, '1489' [i.e. 1479]. 4°.
Padua, Biblioteca Universitaria, Sec. XV 305, on the verso of the last leaf: 'Iste liber est monachorum congregationis Sancte Iustine de Padua ordinis sancti Benedicti deputatus in Sancto Georgio Maiore Venetiarum. 602'. See Catalogue, no. 123.

No. 603 – **Guido de Monte Rocherii**, *Manipulus curatorum*, MS., second quarter of 15th cent.
Padua, Biblioteca Universitaria, ms. 1319, fol. Iv: 'Iste liber est monasterii Sancti Georgii Maioris signatus numero 603', repeated on fol. 1bis^r.

No. 604 – **Albertus Magnus**, *Compendium theologicae veritatis*, Venice: Christophorus Arnoldus, 5 Apr. 1476. 4°.
Padua, Biblioteca Universitaria, Sec. XV Duplicato 47, fol. 1v: 'Iste liber est monasterii Sancti Georgii (then corrected to 'Sancte Gustine', *sic*) Maioris signatus numero 604' (then corrected to '578'). See Catalogue, no. 3.
See no. 578 above.

No. 619 – **Platea, Franciscus de**, *Opus restitutionum, usurarum, excommunicationum*, [Venice]: Bartholomaeus Cremonensis, 1472. 4°.
Oxford, Bodleian Library, Auct. 1Q inf. 1.15, [aa1v]: 'Iste liber est congregationis sancte Justine de Padua ordinis sancti Benedicti deputatus monasterio sancti Georgii maioris de Venetiis sig[natus] no. 619'. See Catalogue, no. 137.

No. 622 – **Platina, Bartholomæus**, *Vitæ pontificum*, [Venice:] Johannes de Colonia et Johannes Manthen, 11 June 1479. Folio.
Paris, Bibliothèque nationale de France, Rés. H. 64, on the verso of the last leaf: 'Iste liber est congregationis sanctae Iustinae de padua ordinis sancti Benedicti | deputatus monasterio sancti Georgij maioris de venetijs sig(at)us numero 622'. See Catalogue, no. 138.

No. 624 – **Caracciolus, Robertus**, *Sermones de adventu, Sermo de S. Joseph, Sermo de Beatitudine, Sermones de divina caritate, Sermones de immortalitate animae*. Add: Dominicus Bollanus, *De conceptione B.V.M.* [Venice: Johannes de Colonia and Johannes Manthen, about 1477–78]. 4°.
Padua, Biblioteca Universitaria, Sec. XV 1006, verso of the last leaf: 'Iste liber est congregationis Sanctae Iustinae de Padua ordinis sancti Benedicti, deputatus monasterio Sancti Georgii Maioris Venetiarum, signatus numero 624'. See Catalogue, no. 47.

No. 644 – **Lorenzo Giustiniani, s.**, *Fasciculus amoris, Tractatus de corpore Christi, Oratio*, MS., 15th cent.
Padua, Biblioteca Universitaria, ms. 1349, fol. 108r: 'Iste liber est monachorum congregationis Sanctae Iustinae ordinis Santi Benedicti de observantia deputatus in Sancto Georgio Maiori de Venetiis signatus 644'.

No. 669 – **Leonardus de Utino**, *Sermones de sanctis*. Venice: Johannes de Colonia and Johannes Manthen, 1475. 4°.

Padua, Biblioteca Universitaria, Sec. XV 82, fol. 1: 'Iste liber est congregationis Sanctae Iustinae ordinis Sancti Benedicti deputatus ad usum monachorum habitantium in monasterio Sancti Georgii Maioris de Venetiis ac signatus numero 669' (crossed out). See Catalogue, no. 107.

No. 680 – **Lorenzo Giustiniani, s.**, *Trattatelli ascetici*, MS., 15th cent.
Padua, Biblioteca Universitaria, ms. 565, 2nd flyleaf: 'Iste liber est congregationis Sanctae Iustinae de Padua ordinis divi Benedicti deputatus monasterio Sancti Georgii Maioris de Venetiis signatusque numero 680'.

No. 708 – **Crastonus, Johannes**, *Lexicon Graecolatinum*, [Milan]: Bonus Accursius, [not after 28 Mar. 1478]. Folio.
Oxford, Bodleian Library, Auct. O inf. 2.3, [A1r]: 'Iste liber est monasterii sancti Georgii maioris Venetiarum congregationis sancte Justine signatus numero 708'. See Catalogue, no. 60.

No. 717 – **Augustinus, Aurelius, s.**, *Soliloquium animae ad Deum*; Ioannes Chrysostomus, s., *Adhortatio ad Theodorum lapsum*; Scholarius, Georgius, *De octo partibus orationis*, in Greek, MS., 15th cent.
Padua, Biblioteca Universitaria, ms. 591, fol. IIr: 'Iste liber est Sancti Georgii Maioris Venetiarum signatus numero 717', repeated on fol. 143r.

No. 773 – ***Biblia Latina***, Venice: Franciscus Renner, de Heilbronn, 1480. Folio and 4°.
Oxford, Bodleian Library, Auct. M 2.12, D11v: 'Iste liber est monachorum congregationis S. Justine de Padua deputatus in S. Georgii maioris Venetiarum | 773'. See Catalogue, no. 30.

No. 781 – **Cassianus, Johannes**, *De institutis coenobiorum*. Add: *Collationes patrum XXIV*, Basel: [Johann Amerbach, after 24 Sept.] 1485. Folio.
Mantua, Biblioteca Teresiana, Inc. 291, below the colophon: 'Est monachorum congregationis S. Justine de Padua deputatus monachis

in monasterio S. Georgij maioris Venetiarum habitantibus signatus no. 781 [crossed out and the new number, in the same hand] 886'. See Catalogue, no. 50.
See no. 886 below.

No. 789 – **Papias**, *Vocabularium*. Ed: Boninus Mombritius, Venice: Andreas de Bonetis, 30 June 1485. Folio.
Milan, Biblioteca dei Servi, 85, inscription on m11v: 'Est congregationis s. Iustine de Padua ordinis S. Benedicti deputatus in monasterio sancti Georgii maioris Venetiarum ac signatus numero 789'. See catalogue, no. 129.

No. 803 – *Biblia Latina*, [Venice: Octavianus Scotus, 1481]. Folio.
Vienna, Österreichische Nationalbibliothek, 17.c. 16, fol. 12r: 'Iste liber est monachorum congregationis S. Justine de Padua ordinis S. Benedicti deputatus ad usum fratrum habitantium in monasterio S. Georgii Maioris Venetiarum signatus numero 803'. See Catalogue, no. 32.

No. 813 – **Dante Alighieri**, *La Commedia*, Florence: Nicolò di Lorenzo, 30 Aug. 1481. Folio.
Paris, Bibliothèque nationale de France, Rés. Yd. 102, below the partly cut-out colophon the original (fifteenth-century?) ownership note: '[…]ti de observantia deputa | […] tiarum signatus 813'.
See Catalogue, no. 62.

No. 827 – **Bernardus Placentinus**, *Opuscula ascetica quinque* (in verse), MS., last quarter of 15th cent[47].

Padua, Biblioteca Universitaria, ms. 1342, fol. 68r: 'Iste liber est congregationis Sancte Iustine de Padua ordinis Sancti Benedicti de obseruantia deputatus in Sancto Georgio Maiori … signatus numero 827'.

No. 886 – **Cassianus, Johannes**, *De institutis coenobiorum*. Add: *Collationes patrum XXIV*, Basel: [Johann Amerbach, after 24 Sept.] 1485. Folio.
Mantua, Biblioteca Teresiana, Inc. 291, below the colophon: 'Est monachorum congregationis S. Justine de Padua deputatus monachis in monasterio S. Georgij maioris Venetiarum habitantibus signatus no. 781 [crossed out and the new number, in the same hand] 886'. See Catalogue, no. 50.

No. 893 – *Biblia Latina*, etc. Venice: [Johannes Herbort, de Seligenstadt], for Johannes de Colonia, Nicolaus Jenson and Socii, 31 July 1481. Folio.
Locarno, Biblioteca Madonna del Sasso, MdS 57 Ba 7–9, vol. 1, c1v and vol. 2, P1r (deleted): 'Iste liber est Congregationis S. Iustine Patavine deputatus ad usum fratrum instantium in S. Georgio Maiore Venetiae signatus nno. 893'. See Catalogue, no. 31.

No. 894 – **Lorenzo Giustiniani, s.**, *De institutione et regimine praelatorum*, MS., 15th cent.
Padua, Biblioteca Universitaria, ms. 1008, fol. 1r: 'Congregationis Sancte Justine verum deputatus usui Monasterii Sancti Georgii Maioris Venetiarum 894'; fol. 146r: 'Iste liber est monasterii Sancti Georgii Maioris de Veneciis congregationis Sanctae Iustinae numero 577'.

No. 903 – **Gellius, Aulus**, *Noctes Atticae*, Venice: Nicolaus Jenson, 1472. Folio.
Milan, Biblioteca Nazionale Braidense, AI. XI. 1, [s]6r: 'Iste liber est monachorum congregationis sancte Iustine de Padua ordinis sancti Benedicti de obseruantia deputatus monasterio sancti Georgii maioris Venetiarum signatus numero 903'. See Catalogue, no. 81.

---

47   At the end (fol. 68r): 'Carmen hoc composuit reverendus quondam pater dominus Bernardus Placentinus abbas monasterii huius Divi Georgii Maioris Venetiarum'. A note following the text, by another hand but probably written immediately or shortly after the writing of the text adds: 'Bernardo Terzi (*quondam*), era morto nel 1486'.

No. 928 – **Mesue**, *Opera medicinalia*, etc. [Padua: Laurentius Canotius de Lendenaria], 9 June 1471. Folio.
Paris, Bibliothèque interuniversitaire de santé (Pharmacie), Rés. 5913, [B6]: 'Iste liber est Sancti Georgii Maioris Venetiarum no. 928'. See Catalogue, no. 120.

No. 941 – **Antoninus Florentinus**, *Summa theologica* (Pars II), Venice: Johannes de Colonia and Johannes Manthen, 1477. Folio.
Padua, Biblioteca Universitaria, Sec. XV Duplicato 99 bis, at the bottom of pp. 5v: 'Iste liber est congregationis Sancte Iustine de Padua ordinis sancti Benedicti, deputatus in Sancto Georgio Maiore Venetiarum, signatus 941'. See Catalogue, nos 8 and 9.

No. 944 – **Cicero, Marcus Tullius**, *De oratore*, etc. Venice: Thomas de Blavis, de Alexandria, 16 May 1488. Folio.
Padua, Biblioteca Universitaria, Sec. XV 445/1, at the bottom of the last leaf of the second edition bound in this volume: 'Iste liber est monachorum congregationis Sancte Iustine de Padua deputatus ad usum fratrum habitantium in monasterio Sancti Georgii Maioris Venetiarum signatus numero 944' ('944' entered over a previous number). See Catalogue, no. 52.

No. 947 – **Perottus, Nicolaus**, *Cornucopiae linguae latinae*, Venice: Paganinus de Paganinis, 14 May 1489. Folio.
Uppsala, University Library, Ink. 35b: 'Iste liber est Congregationis monachorum s. Justine de Padua ordinis s. Benedicti deputatus in monasterio s. Georgij maioris Venetiarum signatus 947'. See Catalogue, no. 130.

No. 979 – **Augustinus, Aurelius, s., Pseudo**, *Sermones ad heremitas*, Venice: Vincentius Benalius, 26 Jan. 1492/1493. 8°.
Rome, Biblioteca Casanatense, VOL INC.1293. See Catalogue, no. 17.

Bernardus Claravallensis, *Modus bene vivendi in christianam religionem*, Venice: Bernardinus Benalius, 30 May 1492. 8°.
Rome, Biblioteca Casanatense, VOL INC.1294, a1r: 'Iste liber est Congregationis monachorum s. Justine de padua ordinis sancti Benedicti deputatus in sancto Georgio maiore venetiarum, signatus 979'. See Catalogue, no. 23.
Thomas à Kempis, *Imitatio Christi*, etc. Venice: Petrus de Quarengiis, Bergomensis, and Giovanni Maria di Occimiano, 23 Apr. 1493. 8°.
Rome, Biblioteca Casanatense, VOL INC.1292. See Catalogue, no. 166.

No. 1019 – **Alberti, Leo Baptista**, *De re aedificatoria*, Florence: Nicolaus Laurentii, Alamanus, 29 Dec. 1485. Folio.
Venice, Biblioteca Nazionale Marciana, Inc. 0570, [rum]7v: 'Est monachorum Congregationis S. Iustine de Padua Ordinis S. Benedicti deputatus, in Sancto Georgio Maior Venetiarum, signatus 1019'. See Catalogue, no. 2.

No. 1020 – **Isidorus Hispalensis**, *Etymologiae*, etc. Venice: Peter Löslein, 1483. Folio.
Venice, Fondazione Cini, FOAN TES 022, C8v: 'Iste liber est monachorum congregationis s. Justine de padua ordini s. Benedicti deputatus usui fratrum […]' and A1r, in a sixteenth-century hand: 'Est s. Georgii mayoris de venetianjs sig. n. 1020'. See Catalogue, no. 96.

No. 1049 – **Savonarola, Hieronymus**, *Triumphus crucis seu de veritate fidei*, [Florence: Bartolommeo di Libri, after Aug. 1497]. Folio.
Cesena, Biblioteca Comunale Malatestiana, 160.98, m8v: 'Iste liber est Congregationis monachorum Sancte Iustine de Padua ordinis Sancti Benedicti deputatus usui fratrum habitantium in Sancto Georgio Maiore Venetiarum signatus 1049'. See Catalogue, no. 156.

No. 1070 – **Thomas Aquinas**, *Commentaria in omnes epistolas Sancti Pauli*, Venice: Bonetus

Locatellus, for Octavianus Scotus, 22 Dec. 1498. Folio.

Treviso, Biblioteca Capitolare, Inc. 17, a1r and on the last leaf of text, erased: 'Est Monasterij Sancti Georgij Maioris signatus n° 1070' and 'Iste liber est Monasterij Sancti Georgij Maioris Venet. signatus n° 1070'. See Catalogue, no. 167.

No. 1094 – **Savonarola, Hieronymus**, *Triumphus crucis seu de veritate fidei*, [Florence: Bartolommeo di Libri, after Aug. 1497]. Folio.
Cesena, Biblioteca Comunale Malatestiana, 160.98, m8v: 'Iste liber est Congregationis monachorum Sancte Iustine de Padua ordinis Sancti Benedicti deputatus usui fratrum habitantium in Sancto Georgio Maiore Venetiarum signatus 1049'. See Catalogue, no. 156.

Nos 1122[?]-1125 – **Alexander de Ales**, *Summa universae theologiae* (i.e. *Super IV libros sententiarum Petri Lombardi*), Nuremberg: Anton Koberger, 1481–82. Folio, 4 vols.
Venice, Biblioteca Nazionale Marciana, Inc. 0152–0155, inscriptions in vols 2–4: 'Iste liber est sancti georgij maioris venetorum ordinis s. benedicti sub congregatione s. Iustine signatus numero 1123'; 'Iste liber est monachorum sancti georgij maioris venetorum ordinis s. benedicti sub congregatione s. Iustine signatus numero 1124'; 'Iste liber est monasterij sancti georgij maioris venetorum ordinis s. benedicti sub congregatione s. Iustine signatus numero 1125'. See Catalogue, no. 4.

No. [?] – **Clemens V, Pont. Max.**, *Constitutiones* (cum apparatu Johannis Andreae). Add: *Decretales extravagantes Johannis XXII*, Venice: Nicolaus Jenson, 1476. Folio.
Manchester, John Rylands University Library, 9962, erased inscription on i11r: 'Iste liber est monachorum congregationis Sanctae Iustinae de Padua deputatus monasterio Sancti Georgii Maioris Venetiarum, signatus numero [...]'. See Catalogue, no. 56.

To these we could add the manuscripts that present a similar inventory note but without the shelf mark (ms. 523) or with a number replaced by a later one (ms. 857). A manuscript by Lorenzo Giustiniani should also be included, with a fifteenth-century annotation that does not mention the ownership by the congregation (ms. 1378):
- *De exemplis naturalibus contra curiosos*, 15th cent. (Padua, Biblioteca Universitaria, ms. 523)
- Iohannes Cassianus, s., *Instituta patrum, Collationes*, 15th cent., first quarter (Padua, Biblioteca Universitaria, ms. 857)
- Lorenzo Giustiniani, s., *De disciplina et perfectione monasticae conversationis*, 15th cent. (Padua, Biblioteca Universitaria, ms. 1378)

The Library System at S. Giorgio Maggiore

On the basis of this catalogue some observations may be made regarding the library system at S. Giorgio Maggiore. The first concerns the question of the existence of an inventory similar to the one at Sta. Giustina. We may presume that such a document did indeed exist, from the care that was taken to add the book number to the ownership note; and we may also assume that there existed a locative system using shelf-marks, perhaps one that used the marks recorded in the inventory.

The second observation concerns the relationship between the Congregation and its constituent monasteries. It is clear from the inventory numbering that each monastery had its own books and that the monastery of Sta. Giustina was only one among several libraries; manuscripts or printed books did not move around the libraries of the Congregation unless a monk happened to move from one monastery to another[48]. This is

---

48 See, for example, the following manuscripts in various Benedictine monasteries, each having its own ownership note and number:

probably the case, for example, with no. 3 in our list: Albertus Magnus, *Compendium theologicae veritatis* (Venice: Christophorus Arnoldus, 1476), which bears the following ownership notes: (1) 'Hic liber est monasterij s[anc]te Iustine de' padua signat[us] n.o 156'; (2) 'Iste liber est monasterii Sancti Georgii (then corrected to 'Sancte Gustine', *sic*) Maioris signatus numero

- *Santa Maria di Praglia abbey* (province of *Padua*): Padua, Biblioteca Universitaria, ms. 1004, fol. 1r: 'Iste liber est congregationis Sancte Iustine et deputatus monasterio Sancte Marie de Pratalea diocesis Paduane';
- *San Pietro monastery* (*Perugia*): Perugia, Biblioteca comunale Augusta, Manoscritti, ms. H62, c. 1r: 'Iste liber est monachorum congregationis Sancte Iustine deputatus usui conventus Sancti Petri de Perusio, s[ignatus] 414';
- *Santa Maria del Santo Sepolcro monastery* (*Florence*): Florence, Biblioteca Nazionale Centrale, ms. Conv. Soppr. A.V.2595, first flyleaf: 'Iste liber est Congregationis sancte Iustine ordinis sancti Benedicti deputatus monasterio Sancte Marie sive Abbatie florentine. Signatus 68';
- *San Martino delle Scale abbey* (*Palermo*): Palermo, Biblioteca Centrale della Regione Siciliana, MSS I.F.6 e I.F.7, fol. 1r: 'Iste liber est Monasterii sancti Martini de Scalis Congregationis Montis Casinensis alias Sancte Iustine dedicates ad opus monachorum ibi degentium signatus numero 1174';
- *San Colombano abbey* (*Bobbio*): Turin, Biblioteca Reale, MS Varia 186bis, fol. 1r: 'Istud breviarium est monachorum congregationis sancte Iustine de observantia ordinis sancti Benedicti residentium in monasterio sancti Columbani de Bobio. Scriptum sub numero';
- *San Benedetto e Santa Scolastica monastery* (*Subiaco*): Subiaco, Biblioteca statale del Monumento nazionale di S. Scolastica, Manoscritti, MS 147, CXLIII, fol. 176r: 'Iste liber est Congregationis Casinensis alias sancte Justine, deputatus ad usum monachorum monasterii Sublacensis, signatus numero 863'.

The examples are taken from Manus Online (https://manus.iccu.sbn.it/index.php) and from the PhD thesis of Costanza Rapone, *Tra Italia e Inghilterra nel medioevo: storie di codici e di uomini giunti da Oltremanica tra i secoli XII e XIV*, Università degli Studi della Tuscia di Viterbo, a.a. 2014–15, 238–39, 253–60, 271–76 (https://dspace.unitus.it/handle/2067/2903).

604 (then corrected to '578'). The incunable is not registered in the inventory of Sta. Giustina at all, a sign that it belonged to S. Giorgio at the time the inventory was made.

The third observation concerns the question of whether manuscripts and incunabula were registered together in the same series, as they are in the inventory from Sta. Giustina. The surviving manuscripts of the library of S. Giorgio Maggiore, with the typical late fifteenth-century ownership note which includes a serial number, confirms that there was no separation made between the two categories of book, as may be seen with the incunabula integrated into the run of the twenty-three manuscripts.

The fourth observation concerns the matter of the inventory: was it carried out before, during or after the building of the Medicean library (in 1478)? In the case of the Sta. Giustina inventory, included in the first 454 items registered with majuscule letters and numerals from 1 to 20 are the first 315 titles, but also the numbers 316–454 as shelf-marked by the librarian who entered them in the inventory started in 1453. If we pursue with the assumption that the model of Sta. Giustina applied to all the Congregational monasteries, then perhaps the registration of the S. Giorgio's items began just before the building of the Medicean library[49]. It may be assumed, as in the case of Sta. Giustina, that the first three hundred titles were manuscripts which had been part of the 'old library' (the 1362 inventory of Sta. Giustina, for example, describes fifty-nine manuscripts and refers to further 'duodecim libros parvi voluminis veteres et parvi valoris in uno

49 Item no. 281 (no. 33 in the present catalogue), *Biblia latina*, Venice: J. Herbort, 30 Apr. 1484. 4°, challenges this assumption but may be explained by a later insertion of the book to replace a missing manuscript, as happened also in the inventory of the library of Sta. Giustina. See Cantoni Alzati, *La biblioteca di S. Giustina di Padova*, as note 24, 21 and note 31 in the present article.

armario sagrastie'[50] and we may assume that in the course of 110 years many more were added). The incunabula were obviously entered later, but when? We have two valuable testimonies. The first is on the last leaf of what appears to be the first incunable purchased for the library of S. Giorgio: the volume published by Johann Fust and Peter Schoeffer in Mainz in October 1459 has an inscription that follows the traditional ownership note: 'Constitit ducatorum decem octo emptus anno 1461'. Thus, it is possible that this volume was entered right after the manuscripts at no. 315[51]. Further evidence giving an actual year of registration is found in the colophon to a manuscript with the number 600, which gives 1475 as the year of its creation at S. Giorgio Maggiore: 'Expletum fuit hoc opus in monasterio Sancti Georgii Maioris Venetiarum anno Domini M°CCCC°LXXV° Sixto papa IIII° imperante ad laudem et gloriam magnitonantis necnon ad utilitatem eorum qui ad culmen vere perfectionis ascendere desiderant. Ora pro me frater'[52]. If no. 600 was made in 1475 and no. 602 is dated 1479[53], we have two dates with which to confirm that S. Giorgio Maggiore's missing inventory and registration of the collection had been made at the same time as the building of the Medicean library: as for the model, surely the librarians or monks at S. Giorgio had knowledge of the inventory of Sta. Giustina whose example they followed.

We also know that as far as no. 773, the incunable editions all date to the 1470s. From no. 773 onwards, except for the sole case of a 1477 edition[54], which may have been bought in the 1480s, all the others were printed in the 1480s. The only question that remains concerns the five books donated to the library of S. Giorgio in 1498 by the Benedictine abbot of San Michele in Coniolo (in the diocese of Brescia) and Apostolic Protonotary, Andrea Mocenigo: these are numbered 114, 115 twice, C 115, 118, and 124 in the standard donation note that runs: 'Reverendus dominus Andreas Mocenicus protonotarius pro anime sue salute diui Georgii maioris cenobio dicauit signatus numero ...'. The reference to Mocenigo as protonotary places the books' arrival between 1507, the year of his election, and 1513, the year of his death[55]. Two hypotheses can be put forward for the low serial numbers the books were given: either that the books were substituted for missing manuscripts or that they belong to a different system. The fact that the number 115 is repeated means that the former possibility can be discounted. We may presume instead that these books were put not on the desks, but on a bookpress (*chanzeli*) standing against the wall which had a separate system of shelf-marks.

One final observation may be made relating to the overall number of incunabula in the library of S. Giorgio Maggiore at the beginning of the sixteenth century. We know of the existence of at least 1,125 volumes in the library around the year 1500 (both manuscript and print). The library of Sta. Giustina had 1,246 titles in its possession in 1483. Yet what seems to be almost the same size

---

50 Ravegnani, *Le biblioteche del monastero di San Giorgio maggiore*, as note 2, 76, no. 59.

51 Item no. 315 (no. 68 in the present catalogue), Duranti, Guillelmus, *Rationale divinorum officiorum*, [Mainz]: Johann Fust and Peter Schoeffer, 6 Oct. 1459. Folio.

52 Padua, Biblioteca Universitaria, MS 1332, fol. 140v (no. 600 in the S. Giorgio Maggiore inventory).

53 Item no. 602 (no. 123 in the present catalogue), Nicolaus de Ausmo, *Supplementum Summae Pisanellae*. Add: Alexander de Nevo, *Consilia contra Judaeos foenerantes*; Astesanus de Ast, *Canones poenitentiales*. Venice: Leonardus Wild, '1489' [i.e. 1479]. 4°.

54 Item no. 941 (no. 9 in the present catalogue), Antoninus Florentinus, *Summa theologica* (Pars II), Venice: Johannes de Colonia and Johannes Manthen, 1477. Folio.

55 Federico Stefani, 'Tavola VI', in Pompeo Litta, *Famiglie celebri italiane* (Milano, 1868–1872), XI: 'Mocenigo di Venezia'; Marino Sanuto, *I Diarii*, ed. Rinaldo Fulin (Venezia, 1882), vol. VII, coll. nos 236, 485.

of both libraries overlooks the fact that between the recording of the last items by both libraries lies a gap of seventeen years – a crucial period in the history of the printing press and consequently in the history of libraries. As Marco Palma has shown, the production of the printing press was already growing exponentially as of 1488 (450 titles per year) but more importantly in the 1490s (from the production of 487 titles in 1490, the industry created 750 in 1500), whereas the production of printed books is estimated in bulk numbers to have already begun to supersede manuscript production from 1471 onwards[56]. We have no further information on the rate of annual growth of the library of Sta. Giustina after the closure of the inventory, but we may suppose that in 1500 it could have reached at least 2,000 titles, if not more (in eight years – 1475 to 1483 – it had acquired most of its incunabula, representing 37% of the whole collection). The numbers would probably make it the leading library in the Congregation. But we may also evaluate the library of S. Giorgio as a fairly large one and – on the basis of the incunable presence in Sta. Giustina and, taking into consideration the fact that the years between 1485 and 1500 were the major period of incunable production – assume that 45% of its entire collection of at least 1,125 items may have comprised incunabula, which would equate to around five hundred printed volumes. This is indeed a high number when compared to the three hundred incunabula existing in 1501 in the Benedictine monastery of St Emmeram in Regensburg – considered to

be a prominent centre of study[57]; but then, it is important to remember that the monastery of S. Giorgio Maggiore was located in what was the capital city of the printing press at the time and that the availability of books was immediate.

The ownership notes also supply us with evidence for the history of the library of S. Giorgio Maggiore from the period after the making of the inventory of the Medicean library; but these now seem more sporadic, as if the management system had changed; we may assume the use of a catalogue indicating a shelf-mark entered on a flyleaf. The sixteenth-century ownership notes abandon the tradition of recording the fact that the monastery was part of the Congregation of Sta. Giustina. They are rather rare and were probably made only when the ownership note of the Medicean library appears, as with no. 176 in the present incunable catalogue: Valla, Laurentius, *Elegantiæ linguæ latinæ*, Venice: Nicolaus Jenson, 1471. 4°[58]. However, another volume bears an ownership note in the same hand with no previous notes but underscoring the fact that the volume belonged to the library: 'Isti liber est sancti Georgii maioris Venetiarum deputatus Bibliotheca'[59]. Since we know that the Medicean library also contained books bought by the

---

56 Marco Palma, 'Aspetti quantitativi della produzione libraria manoscritta e a stampa nel Quattrocento', in *Incunabula. Printing, Trading, Collecting, Cataloguing*, Milan, 10–12 Sept. 2013, ed. Alessandro Ledda, *La Bibliofilía*, nn. 1–3, CXVI (2014), 165-78, esp. 174-77; *Printing R-Evolution and Society*, as note 1, graph at p. 51 'Printing takes over – comparison between manuscripts and incunabula', based on ongoing research by Marco Palma.

---

57 Wagner, '*Libri impressi Bibliothecae Monasterii Sancti Emmerammi*', as note 28, 180–82 and note 44 at 274.

58 Now Paris, Bibliothèque nationale de France, Rés. X. 640. The old inventory number is 457.

59 Item no. 131: Perottus, Nicolaus, *Rudimenta grammatices*, Venice: [Jacobus de Fivizzano, Lunensis], for Marcus de Comitibus and Gerardus Alexandrinus, 17 Jan. 1476 [i.e. 1477?]. Folio. Now Paris, Bibliothèque nationale de France, Rés. X. 571. See also a peculiar *ex libris* for the S. Giorgio Maggiore library which tries to imitate more or less those written at the end of the fifteenth century: 'Iste liber est sancti georgii maioris venetiarum deputatus biblioteca ipsius', and then another hand which adds a new one: 'Hic liber est diui Georgi maioris venetiarum'. No. 145. Priscianus, *Opera*, [Milan: Domenico da Vespolate for Bonino Mombrizio, after 24 Feb. 1476.] Folio. Now Paris, Bibliothèque nationale de France, Rés. X. 587.

monks themselves, it seems that at a certain point during the sixteenth century, with the donation of some collections to the library and with other acquisitions of books, the ownership notes were added to underline the fact that from that point in time, the volumes were the property of the library of S. Giorgio Maggiore[60].

From the mid-seventeenth century there seem to exist more ownership notes left on the incunabula, attributable probably to two factors: dispersal due to the chaos caused by the building of the Longhena library, and accession by donation throughout the century. With reference to the lack of security for the books, we are informed by Marco Valle, who lived at that time in the monastery, that the books were removed in 1614 from the Medicean library, placed in a room above the chapter house and divided 'per ordinem scientiarum', and then moved again to two other cells next to the dormitory, 'cum periculo nisi accuratius servarentur'[61]. They stayed there until 1670. Fortunato Olmo, another monk, commented in 1619 about the transfer: 'se non periranno (il che si deve molto temere) avranno da esser ritornati alla nuova libreria quando sia resa perfetta'[62]. The fear was probably justified. Already in 1610, a mason named Bortolo Tebaldini was accused of the theft of various items, among

them 'una cassa di libri' from the monastery[63]. And the price note by a Danish traveller, Niels Andersen Vandstad, on a volume of Marsilius Ficinus that he had bought in Venice in 1658, demonstrates that a certain number of incunabula had found their way on to the market through various routes[64]. In fact, Marco Valle recalls how the Longhena library possessed mostly new books purchased from printers, while the older books and manuscripts were present in only small numbers[65].

The donations and purchases of books had not yet yielded a different form of the ownership notes: until the library books were fully relocated, something that only occurred in 1670, the *ex libris* remained 'Est Sancti Georgii Maioris Venetiarum'[66]. Likewise, confusion and uncertainty also existed regarding the numbering of the volumes, as no shelf-mark is found on them, although there must have existed a topographical system so as to locate them. Only one volume testifies to the fact that a new numbering had begun at a certain point towards the end of the sixteenth century: in a copy of Savonarola's *Triumphus crucis* (Florence 1497) we find that a fifteenth-century hand had assigned it the number 1049, while a later hand noted: 'Est Sancti Georgii Maioris de Venetiis' and assigned it the number 13[67].

This practice changed completely after the opening of the Longhena library and the shelving of the books. An awareness that here was a library displaying the new style of the larger monastic libraries, boasting not only an impressive décor

60 On the acquisitions of books by monks in the fifteenth and sixteenth centuries, see Rossi, 'Storia del monastero di San Giorgio Maggiore', as note 2, 595, citing from Fortunato Olmo, *Istoria dell'Isola di S. Giorgio Maggiore di Venezia Iscritta da D. Fortunato Olmo Veneziano M[onaco] C[assinese]*, Venice, Biblioteca del Seminario Patriarcale, ms. 602 (681). Cf. Baldan, *La storia del monastero di S. Giorgio Maggiore*, as note 2, 351–546.

61 Ravegnani, *Le biblioteche del monastero di San Giorgio maggiore*, as note 2, 35, citing Marco Valle, *De monasterio et abbatia S. Georgii Maioris Venetiarum clara et brevis notitia*, Venice, Biblioteca del Museo Civico Correr, ms. Gradenigo-Dolfin 110 (104), fols 155r, 163v.

62 Ravegnani, *Le biblioteche del monastero di San Giorgio maggiore*, as note 2, 35 citing from Olmo, *Istoria dell'isola di San Giorgio Maggiore*, as note 60, 272.

63 ASVe, *San Giorgio Maggiore*, Processi, b. 136, proc. 566, Processo contro Bortolo murer. cart. 1608–1614.

64 The annotation is on Copenhagen, Royal Library, Inc. Haun. 1591, Ficinus, Marsilius, *De religione christiana*. Venice: Otinus de Luna 1500. 4°: 'N. Wandstad Venetiis emit 20 s. 1658' (no. 77 in the present catalogue).

65 Cicogna, *Delle iscrizioni veneziane*, as note 2, IV, 598–99.

66 See nos 35, 38, 47, 88, 116, 124, 146, 163 in the present catalogue.

67 See no. 156 in the present catalogue. The volume is now Cesena, Biblioteca Comunale Malatestiana, 160.98.

but also a high number of books, led to the making of the library itself (and not the convent) the focus of the new *ex libris*, which now read: 'Est Biliothece S. Georgij Maioris Venetiarum'[68]. The numbers on each volume show that the numbering changed at least three or four times during the eighteenth century. Whether an inventory did exist and whether it was updated is not certain. The library of S. Giorgio was considered in the century of the Grand Tour to be one of the most impressive in the city[69], whether it was also efficient in retrieving incunable titles for the reader who might have wished to consult them, we do not know. As Antonella Barzazi has observed, in the second half of the eighteenth century the library had become more 'a place of aristocratic sociability than a centre of research and study'[70].

Circulation and Dispersal

The library of S. Giorgio had undergone, as we have seen, three organizational phases throughout its existence: the old library, the Medicean library and the new Longhena one. While praised by contemporaries as one of the most renowned collections in Venice[71], it was still considered by the monks throughout its existence from a utilitarian viewpoint, unlike other religious libraries of the city, such as the Dominicans or the Jesuits, which valued the accumulation and preservation of the knowledge of the past. The acquisition of manuscripts and printed books was dependent on the fields of interest of the monks: they were accustomed to move among the monasteries of the congregation and to carry

books with them, which sometimes ended up in another monastic library if the monk died there. Another reason for the presence of a S. Giorgio incunable in some other Benedictine monastic library seems to have been the outcome of exchanges, very frequent among the libraries of the congregation, especially during the eighteenth century[72]. The catalogue in the appendix below lists nine incunabula that left the library of S. Giorgio for other monasteries before the fall of the Venetian Republic in 1797: two found their way to Sta. Giustina[73], five to other Benedictine monasteries: S. Benedictus in Polirone (Mantua) in the eighteenth century[74]; the Benedictines in Arezzo[75], and the Benedictines of Sta. Maria Montis in Cesena[76]. However, the destinations of the incunabula were not exclusively Benedictine monasteries: in the course of the seventeenth century, especially after the closure of the Medicean library and during the long period before the opening of the new 'Longhena' library, there had been a steady – official or unofficial – exodus of incunabula and manuscripts which no longer served the interests of the monks. Thus, we find one incunable ending up in the Observant Dominican library of Sta. Maria del Rosario on the Zattere in Venice[77], and another that in 1628 was already part of the Jesuit library in Trieste[78].

Eight other incunabula found their way into private hands, two of them as early as the second half of the sixteenth century[79], and one purchased

---

68 See nos 1, 8, 15, 26, 57, 62, 79, 101, 104, 112, 142, 150, 153, 174 in the present catalogue.
69 See note 19.
70 Barzazi, '"Un tempo assai ricche e piene di libri di merito"', as note 2, 76.
71 See note 19.

72 Antonella Barzazi, 'Dallo scambio al commercio del libro. Case religiose e mercato librario a Venezia nel Settecento', *Atti dell'Istituto Veneto di Scienze, Lettere ed Arti*, CLVI (1997–1998), 1–44.
73 One of them, no. 3, as early as the sixteenth century, and the other, no. 6, arrived at Sta. Giustina before 1793.
74 Nos 50 and 119.
75 No. 96 in the eighteenth century.
76 Nos 156 and 172 arrived at an unknown date.
77 No. 4.
78 No. 32.
79 Nos 167 and 168.

in 1658, during the period between the closure of the Medicean library and the opening of the new one, by a Danish scholar in Venice[80]. The other three went mostly to private collectors, among whom were Count Alfonso Alvarotti in Padua, around the beginning of the eighteenth century[81], the famous Venetian collector Maffeo Pinelli, around 1750[82], and two reportedly purchased by Cardinal Loménie de Brienne in 1789 during his stay in Venice[83].

The year 1789 marks a turning point in the history of monastic libraries in Venice. Following the disappearance of a number of manuscripts and incunabula from the monastic library of SS. Giovanni and Paolo, Jacopo Morelli, the keeper of the Library of St Mark, suggested to the authorities that he draw up lists of important and precious manuscripts and books for each religious house and that each abbot should be made responsible in case they disappeared[84]. The list drawn up by Morelli for the library of S. Giorgio forms an invaluable source for research as it documents the existence in 1789 of fifty-five valuable incunabula[85]. The criteria used by Morelli for inclusion in his list were the rarity and the philological and aesthetic value of the editions: his choices were mainly Greek and Latin authors[86] and a few Venetian printers highly appreciated during the eighteenth century: Nicolas Jenson, Vindelinus de Spira,

Erhard Ratdolt, Johannes de Colonia, Aldus and, naturally, Conradus Sweynheym and Arnoldus Pannartz[87]. The fact that a volume came from the old congregational library or from the new Longhena one did not constitute a reason for inclusion in itself. In fact, only eighteen out of fifty-five incunabula are to be traced to the Medicean library[88]. While most of the incunabula belonging to the Medicean library found their way to a public library, chiefly the BnF or the Marciana (except for no. 9, today a historical copy), the incunabula which were part of the more recent Longhena library probably ended up in private hands before or during the events of 1797[89]. As for the others, their whereabouts remain for the time being unknown[90].

The French presence in Venice in 1797 brought about disorder in the library of S. Giorgio and alienations from it. A crowd, probably instigated by the Jacobin party, broke into the monastery, taking away furniture, manuscripts, and books[91]. Without a catalogue for this period, possibly never made otherwise Morelli would have used it in 1789, it is impossible to assess the number of incunabula taken away. Morelli was asked by the French commissaries 'for the research of scientific and artistic objects in Italy', being the chemist Claude-Louis Berthollet and the mathematician Gaspard Monge, to hand over to them five hundred manuscripts of their choice, as specified in the fifth article of the peace treaty signed on 16 May 1797 between General Bonaparte and the Republic of

---

80 No. 77.

81 No. 141.

82 No. 30, but also to Luigi Lechi in Brescia (no. 85).

83 Nos 41 and 56.

84 Dorit Raines, 'The dissolution of the libraries of Venetian religious houses and the keeper Jacopo Morelli under Venetian, French, and Austrian governments (1768–1819)', in the present volume.

85 Nos 2, 7, 8, 9, 11, 15, 16, 21, 29, 37, 41, 42, 43, 46, 55, 58, 60, 61, 62, 64, 68, 71, 72, 73, 80, 81, 83, 89, 93, 98, 100, 105, 109, 114, 125, 131, 134, 138, 142, 144, 145, 147, 149, 151, 157, 158, 161, 162, 170, 171, 173, 175, 176, 177, 179.

86 Nos 46, 71, 72, 73, 81, 93, 105, 109, 125, 142, 144, 145, 147, 157, 162, 175, 177, 179.

87 Nicolaus Jenson: nos 7, 15, 29, 41, 43, 46, 55, 73, 81, 89, 100, 125, 147, 157, 171, 176; Vindelinus de Spira: nos 37, 61, 83, 105, 109, 162, 175; Johannes de Colonia: nos 8, 138; Erhard Ratdolt: nos 11, 71; Aldus: nos 58, 80. Conradus Sweynheym and Arnoldus Pannartz: no. 151.

88 Nos 2, 8, 9, 41, 60, 62, 68, 73, 81, 105, 109, 125, 138, 142, 157, 162, 171, 176.

89 Nos 7, 55.

90 Nos 16, 21, 42, 50bis, 58, 61, 98, 134, 149, 151, 158, 161, 170, 173, 179.

91 Rossi, 'Storia del monastero di San Giorgio Maggiore', as note 2, 273.

Venice[92]. The Venetian library keeper suggested that at least part of the material to hand over to the French should come from the collections of the religious houses. The French commissaries, according to the testimony of Monge, had been able to find 'only' 241 manuscripts of interest to them. They then decided to add to the list 'fifteenth-century editions, among which [are] at least 53 first editions' and another fifty-nine Aldine editions[93].

The scholar Emmanuele Antonio Cicogna fortunately listed in his work *Delle iscrizioni veneziane*[94] eighteen incunabula from the library of S. Giorgio that were sent to Paris[95]. Comparing these titles with the 1789 list by Morelli, it appears that the French commissaries used Morelli's list as a sort of 'guide' to choose the best editions, again based more on rarity and value, and less on provenance from the old or new library (only half of the titles mentioned by Cicogna as taken away by the French belonged to the Medicean library)[96]. Furthermore, later annotations by Morelli on the lists, either marking the entries with a cross '+' or striking an item out (see below on the decipherment of their meaning), supply us with twenty titles[97] that almost fit the list of eighteen incunabula which Cicogna mentioned had been handed over to the French commissaries, with the exception of: no. 145, Priscianus, *Opera*

[Milan: Domenico da Vespolate for Bonino Mombrizio, after 24 Feb. 1476], which is not included in the BnF list; no. 179, Publius Vergilius Maro, *Bucolica*, [Naples: Jodocus Hohenstein], 11 Sept. 1476, not mentioned either by Cicogna or by the BnF list (and yet crossed out by Morelli); and no. 162, Strabo, *Geographia*, Venice: Vindelinus de Spira, 1472, along with no. 176, Laurentius Valla, *Elegantiæ linguæ latinæ*, Venice: Nicolaus Jenson, 1471. The two incunabula (now historical copies) not mentioned by Cicogna but included in the BnF list are: no. 37, Giovanni Boccaccio, *De montibus, silvis, fontibus*, Venice: [Vindelinus de Spira], 13 Jan. 1473; and no. 83, Georgius Trapezuntius, *Rhetorica*, Venice: Vindelinus de Spira, [not before 1472]. The last one, in fact, was only sent in September 1806 to Milan as item no. 8[98].

Other material was further confiscated by the 'citoyen Brunet' who was at the time 'agent des contributions et finances' of the French revolutionary army under Napoleon[99]. These are three incunabula: Marcus Fabius Quintilianus, *Institutiones oratoriae*, [Venice], Nicolaus Jenson, 21 May 1471[100]; Aulus Gellius, *Noctes Atticae*, Venice, Nicolaus Jenson, 1472[101], bound with Priscianus, *Opera*, [Venice, Vindelinus de Spira], 1472[102]; and *Breviarium Romanum*, Venice, Nicolaus Jenson, [before 6 May] 1478[103].

The confusion regarding the routes of the remaining incunabula emerges when we confront

---

92 Raines, 'The dissolution', as note 84, note 73. On Monge and his role in the Italian confiscations: Luigi Pepe, 'Gaspard Monge e i prelievi nelle biblioteche italiane (1796–1797)', in *Ideologie e patrimonio storico-culturale nell'età rivoluzionaria e napoleonica. A proposito del trattato di Tolentino*. Atti del convegno Tolentino, 18–21 settembre 1997 (Roma, 2000), 415–42.

93 Paris, Ministère des Affaires étrangères, Archives: 'Venise', (1797), vol. 253, *Liste des manuscrits que la Commission…*, fols 447r–454r, doct. no. 234.

94 Cicogna, *Delle iscrizioni veneziane*, as note 2, IV, 601.

95 Nos 2, 15, 29, 60, 62, 64, 68, 72, 93, 100, 105, 125, 131, 138, 144, 145, 162, 176.

96 Nos 2, 60, 62, 68, 105, 125, 138, 162, 176.

97 Nos 2, 15, 29, 37, 60, 62, 64, 68, 72, 83, 93, 100, 105, 125, 131, 138, 144, 145, 162, 179.

98 See below, note 111.

99 Morelli testified that 'many books [were taken] in the name of Brunet and, as far as [he] knew, no actual written document specifying how many and what books were taken, and these did not pass to the Paris library'. Report of Morelli on 30 August 1806 in Cicogna, *Delle iscrizioni veneziane*, as note 2, IV, 601.

100 See no. 147 in the catalogue. See Raines, 'The dissolution', as note 84, for the case of the Quintilian volume printed by Jenson in 1471 as a testimony for the confusion between similar editions which occurred in 1797.

101 See no. 81 in the catalogue.

102 See no. 145 in the catalogue.

103 Not included in the present catalogue.

the lists at our disposal. In a book published in 1799 listing all the confiscations of books and artefacts by the French are reported ten incunabula on parchment and 111 on paper (with a note that twelve were printed before 1471); among them are the Durandus printed at Mainz in 1459 on parchment (listed apart) and more than fifty first editions[104]. The absence of a detailed list makes it impossible to verify these numbers.

During the period of Austrian rule (1797–1805), although the Library of St Mark saw the restitution of almost all the incunabula taken away by the French, small confiscations of incunabula occurred in 1802: six incunabula previously moved to the Library of St Mark found their way to Vienna[105]. The Austrians justified the confiscation saying that they were interested in having all the provinces under the Austrian emperor share the books and not let them lie concentrated in one place[106]. The incunabula taken away were[107]:

– Aulus Gellius, *Noctes Atticae*, Rome: In domo Petri de Maximis [Conradus Sweynheym and Arnoldus Pannartz], 11 Apr. 1469. Folio. ISTC ig00118000; MEI 02019878

– Lucius Apuleius Madaurensis, *Opera*. Ed: Johannes Andreas, bishop of Aleri, Rome: In domo Petri de Maximis [Conradus Sweynheym and Arnoldus Pannartz], 28 Feb. 1469. Folio. ISTC ia00934000; MEI 02019904

– Gaius Julius Hyginus, *Poetica astronomica*, [Ferrara]: Augustinus Carnerius, 1475. 4°. ISTC ih00559000; MEI 02019912

– Marcus Tullius Cicero, *Epistolae ad familiares*, Rome: Conradus Sweynheym and Arnoldus Pannartz, 1467. 4°. ISTC ic00503500; MEI 02019915

– Albius Tibullus, *Elegiae*. Add: Epitaphium Tibulli, [Venice: Federicus de Comitibus, Veronensis, about 1472]. 4°. ISTC it00366600; MEI 02019914

– Hieronymus, *Epistolae*. Ed: Johannes Andreas, bishop of Aleria, Rome: Conradus Sweynheym and Arnoldus Pannartz, 13 Dec. 1468. Folio. ISTC ih00161000; MEI 02000997 [?]

It is impossible to know whether some of them belonged to the library of S. Giorgio, but we do know that all of them eventually returned to the Marciana library.

The main blow, however, came with the return of the French in 1806. Upon their arrival, they decided on the closure of the remaining monasteries and the dispersal of their book collections. Morelli, at the request of the head of the *Demanio* (Property Department), asked Giovanni Rossi, one of the delegates to the monastic libraries, to draw a list of the remaining incunabula from the library of S. Giorgio, deposited in the meantime at the former convent of Sta. Maria dell'Umiltà[108]. The list made by Rossi includes eighty-five titles, some of which are bound together. It still included seven incunabula considered in 1789

104 *Catalogo de' Capi d'opera di pittura, scultura, antichità, libri, storia naturale ed altre curiosità trasportati dall'Italia in Francia* (Venezia, Presso Antonio Curti q. Giacomo, 1799), XXIX.

105 Morelli was tremendously upset to hear of the loss of the two incunabula, replaced by other editions: see nos 15 and 29 in the present catalogue. The letter of Baron d'Otenfels on 20 October 1816 specifically declared that 'il ne manque pas un seul des objects reclamés par votre établissement', but when Morelli discovered that three had been replaced, he noted on the letter that the act of restitution of the rare books demonstrated how ignorant d'Otenfels was. Giuseppe Valentinelli, *Libri membranacei a stampa della Biblioteca Marciana di Venezia* (Venice, 1870), 20–23. Cf. Zorzi, *La Libreria di San Marco*, as note 19, 353–57.

106 Valentinelli, *Libri membranacei*, as note 105, 20, decree dated 13 May 1802.

107 Victor Cérésole, *La verité sur les déprédations autrichiennes à Venise. Trois lettres à M. Armand Baschet* (Venice, 1867), 50, n. 1.

108 ASV, Demanio 1806–1813, b. 328, fasc. marked 'Monumenti, Belle Arti, Bibliotecge e stampe', letter dated June 25, 1806 (no. 563). See Raines, 'The dissolution', as note 84, note 100.

by Morelli to be precious[109], but curiously not selected by the French in 1797. Six other editions mentioned in the 1789 Morelli list were not included in the Rossi one because they had been previously sent to Milan following the decree of 4 September 1806[110]. The annotations by Morelli on his 1789 list then become clear: the crossing out of titles signifies incunabula handed over to the French in 1797; the mark + signals the fact that these volumes remained in his custody until 1806, when he was ordered to hand them over to be sent to Milan. Unlike the volumes that departed in 1797, these six editions (bound in eight volumes because no. 109 was composed of three) never reached a host institution in Milan or elsewhere. Four editions are now considered historical copies[111] while the other two[112] ended up in private hands.

Rossi reported that he had sent the incunabula to the Paduan deposit of Sta. Anna in March 1807. The French intention was to select the best editions from the books that were arriving at the Paduan deposit from all over the Veneto and then send them to Milan[113]. Nearly half of these incunabula (thirty) eventually ended up in the University Library of Padua in 1818[114]. Some not registered by Rossi were also included in the number assigned to the University Library[115]. Other incunabula sent to the Paduan deposit found their way to other libraries, mostly in Italy: nos 25 and 87, not registered by Rossi, came in 1806 to the Queriniana in Brescia;

nos 81 and 157, registered by Rossi, came to the Braidense in Milan in 1807, probably as part of the further selection carried out in Padua; no. 180, not registered by Rossi, ended up in 1806 in the possession of Cicogna and was bequeathed to the Correr Library in Venice. A number of volumes made their way to Great Britain: no. 73, included in the list of books sent to Milan in 1806, ended up in Torquay in the Clifford C. Rattey collection and went in 1986 to the British Library; no. 109, also included in the list of books sent to Milan in 1806, ended up in the 1830s–1840s in London; nos 137 and 142, registered by Rossi, ended up in, respectively, 1831 and 1841 at the Bodleian Library in Oxford; no. 126, registered by Rossi, arrived at an unknown date at the University Library in Edinburgh. No. 142 arrived in 1841 at Cambridge, Massachusetts, and no. 130, registered by Rossi, passed to Uppsala University Library. The most striking data are the number of incunabula – thirty-five – registered by Rossi in 1806 and Giuseppe Dainese in 1811 in his catalogue of the deposit in Padua, all of which are lost – or possibly not yet located – and describable now as historical copies[116]. Another ten editions registered only by Rossi have also disappeared[117].

Although the lists made in the course of the years by Morelli (1789), Cicogna (1797), Van Praet (1797), Rossi (1806), and Dainese (1811) may appear meticulous, it seems nevertheless that the French authorities, or their representatives, were either all at sea faced with the vast number of books arriving from different monasteries, and sometimes mistook one edition for another, or else were simply too hasty in carrying some away without caring to include them in the lists. Furthermore, one cannot exclude that some incunabula were confiscated privately, as in the

---

109 Nos 1, 8, 9, 11, 71, 164.
110 Nos 46, 73, 83, 109, 147, 175.
111 Nos 46, 83, 147 and 175.
112 Nos 73 and 109.
113 La Cute, 'Le vicende delle biblioteche monastiche veneziane', as note 2, 608–10; Zorzi, *La Libreria di San Marco*, as note 19, 358–59. See Raines, 'The dissolution', as note 84.
114 Nos 1, 8, 12, 14, 26, 34, 44, 47, 48, 51, 52, 53, 57, 69, 94, 101, 104, 107, 108, 110, 112, 116, 123, 124, 132, 135, 146, 150, 153, 160.
115 Nos 66, 174.

116 Nos 5, 10, 19, 20, 40, 49, 59, 65, 67, 70, 74, 76, 78, 80, 84, 85, 86, 90, 91, 97, 99, 102, 111, 113, 118, 122, 127, 128, 133, 143, 148, 154, 155, 159, 169.
117 Nos 18, 24, 27, 75, 95, 114, 115, 152, 165, 178.

case of the citizen Brunet, or by other people with access to the deposits. The present catalogue, then, brings to light several cases in which it is unclear whether the books left the library of S. Giorgio before or after 1797[118].

An Overview of the Reconstructed Collection of Incunabula

We have been able to trace 103 editions of incunabula from S. Giorgio in thirty-one libraries of Europe and the United States, while the attentive use of documentary and bibliographic evidence has allowed us to identify a further seventy-eight editions that were part of the collection at different points in the past, even if we do not know their current whereabouts; we call these 'historical copies'. Only some of these volumes are in predictable libraries, such as those in Padua, Venice, Paris, and Vienna. Many others we were able to locate only because the libraries which currently hold them catalogued their incunabula in MEI, and so the books came to us: we simply had to search the Owners of Incunabula satellite database to MEI for S. Giorgio Maggiore.

Out of 181 copies located so far, 37 (20%) ended up where they were supposed to, at the Biblioteca Universitaria of Padua; 25 other copies (13%) were taken away to Paris and are today either still in Paris (17), in Vienna (2), or have been returned to Venice, Marciana National Library (6). 123 copies (67%) were dispersed, mostly following the secularizations: 78 (42%) historical copies are dispersed and unlocated, 45 (25%) have been located in libraries across Europe and the United States.

Most of the editions are Venetian (126), with a notable presence of the early printers, such as Vindelinus de Spira, Nicolas Jenson, John of Cologne. Milan is the next best represented, with thirteen editions, confirming the ability of the printers of the city to market their products in Venice, or better, suggesting the established channels for the booktrade between the two cities, a trend which has already been noted in the sales of the Venetian bookseller Francesco de Madiis during the years 1484–1488[119]. It is also interesting to note the presence of six foreign editions, beginning with the *Rationale divinorum officiorum* printed in 1459 and purchased, probably in Venice, in 1461 (no. 68).

With reference to subject representation, theology is strong with forty-four editions, liturgy is under-represented with only two editions; law (twenty-four), literature (twenty-six), history (twenty-two), philosophy (eighteen) and grammar (eleven) are all well represented; literature is mostly non devotional, and pertaining to the classical period, with Dante and Boccaccio among the medieval authors and some humanist ones.

Overall, there is a balance between, on the one hand, antique and late antique literature, being patristic (nineteen) and classical (thirty-eight) works, making fifty-seven in total, and, on the other hand, medieval works (sixty-five), humanist (twenty-three), and contemporary (thirty-five) works, making fifty-eight. Altogether, it is an impressive collection of works representing the best early printing shops.

An index that follows the catalogue below offers a breakdown of the editions by present location, place of printing, and subject.

---

118   Nos 33, 36, 38, 50bis, 88, 117, 120, 121, 136, 139, 140, 163.

119   Cristina Dondi and Neil Harris, 'Exporting books from Milan to Venice in the 15th century: evidence from the *Zornale* of Francesco de Madiis', in *Incunabula. Printing, Trading, Collecting, Cataloguing*, as note 56, 121–48.

Bibliography

Manuscripts and Archival Sources

Florence, Biblioteca Nazionale Centrale, ms. Conv. Soppr. A.V.2595.
Padua, Biblioteca Civica, ms B.P. 229.
Padua, Biblioteca Universitaria, ms. 285: Fortunato Olmo, *Istoria dell'isola di San Giorgio Maggiore* (1619).
Padua, Biblioteca Universitaria, ms. 1004.
Padua, Biblioteca Universitaria, ms. 1332.
Palermo, Biblioteca Centrale della Regione Siciliana, mss I.F.6 e I.F.7.
Paris, Bibliothèque nationale de France, AM 269: 'Venise'.
Paris, Bibliothèque nationale de France, Rés. X. 640.
Paris, Ministère des Affaires étrangères, Archives: 'Venise', (1797), vol. 253, *Liste des manuscrits que la Commission…*, fols 447r–454r.
Perugia, Biblioteca comunale Augusta, Manoscritti, ms. H62.
Subiaco, Biblioteca statale del Monumento nazionale di S. Scolastica, Manoscritti, ms. 147, CXLIII.
Turin, Biblioteca Reale, ms. Varia 186bis.
Venice, Archivio di Stato, Demanio 1806–1813, b. 328, fasc. marked 'Monumenti, Belle Arti, Bibliotecge e stampe'.
Venice, Archivio di Stato, *Direzione dipartimentale del demanio e diritti uniti*, Atti, b. 380, 2/15, fasc. II: 'S. Giorgio Maggiore. Libri a stampa del secolo XV della Biblioteca di S. Giorgio Maggiore'.
Venice, Archivio di Stato, *S. Giorgio Maggiore*, Processi.
Venice, Biblioteca del Museo Civico Correr, ms. Gradenigo-Dolfin 110 (104), fols 155r, 163v: Marco Valle, *De monasterio et abbatia S. Georgii Maioris Venetiarum clara et brevis notitia*.
Venice, Biblioteca del Seminario Patriarcale, ms. 602 (681): F. Olmo, *Istoria dell'Isola di S. Giorgio Maggiore di Venezia Iscritta da D. Fortunato Olmo Veneziano M[onaco] C[assinese]*.
Venice, Biblioteca Nazionale Marciana, Cod. Marc. Lat. XIV, 14 (= 4235).

Secondary Works

Sergio Baldan, 'La storia del monastero di S. Giorgio Maggiore scritta dal monaco Fortunato Olmo', *Studi Veneziani*, LXIII (2011), 352–546.
Elisabetta Barile, 'La biblioteca quattrocentesca di Santa Giustina di Padova', in *La calligrafia di Dio. La miniatura celebra la parola*, eds Giordana Canova Mariani and Paola Ferraro Vettore (Modena, 1999), 57–64.

Antonella Barzazi, 'Dallo scambio al commercio del libro. Case religiose e mercato librario a Venezia nel Settecento', *Atti dell'Istituto Veneto di Scienze, Lettere ed Arti*, CLVI (1997–1998), 1–44.

Antonella Barzazi, '"Un tempo assai ricche e piene di libri di merito". Le biblioteche dei regolari tra sviluppo e dispersione', in *Alli 10 Agosto 1806 soppressione del monastero di S. Giorgio*, ed. Giovanni Vian (Cesena, 2011), 71–91.

Gerardus Belga, *Mancipatus deiparae. Quo Augustissimae Coelitum Imperatricis diligens feruulus Ad Obsequium placitumque eiusdem quotidiana seruitii praxis pie instituitur. Authore Gerardo Belga ... Opera R.P.F. Gabrielis Bucelini* (Venetiis, Ex Typographia Leniana, 1649).

Jacob Jonas Björnståhl, *Lettere ne' suoi viaggj stranieri di Giacomo Giona Bjoernstaehl professore di filosofia in Upsala scritte al signor Gjorwell bibliotecario regio in Stoccolma* (Poschiavo, Giuseppe Ambrosioni, 1785).

Giovanna Cantoni Alzati, *La biblioteca di S. Giustina di Padova. Libri e cultura presso i benedettini padovani in età umanistica* (Padova, 1982).

Catalogo de' Capi d'opera di pittura, scultura, antichità, libri, storia naturale ed altre curiosità trasportati dall'Italia in Francia (Venezia, Presso Antonio Curti q. Giacomo, 1799).

Giacomo Cavacio, *Historiarum coenobii D. Justinae Patavinae libri sex. Quibus Cassinensis Congregationis origo, & plurima ad Urbem Patavium, ac finitimos attinentia opportunè interferuntur*, second edition (Patavii, Ex Typographia Seminarii, 1696).

Victor Cérésole, *La verité sur les déprédations autrichiennes à Venise. Trois lettres à M. Armand Baschet* (Venice, 1867).

Emmanuele Antonio Cicogna, *Delle iscrizioni veneziane* (Venezia, 1834).

Flaminio Corner, *Notizie storiche delle chiese e monasteri di Venezia e di Torcello* (Padova, 1758).

Joseph de Blainville, *Travels through Holland, Germany, Switzerland, but especially Italy* (London, John Noon and Joseph Noon, 1757).

Marguerin de la Bigne, *Magna Bibliotheca Veterum Patrum et antiquorum scriptorum ecclesiasticorum* (Parisiis, sumptibus Ægidij Morelli architypographi Regij, 1644).

Jérôme De La Lande, *Voyage d'un françois en Italie, fait dans les années 1765 et 1766. Tome huitième: contenant l'histoire & les anecdotes les plus singulières de l'Italie, & sa description; les moeurs, les usages, le gouvernement ... & les plans de toutes les grandes villes d'Italie* (A Venise, et se trouve à Paris, Chez Desaint, Librarire, rue du Foin, 1769).

Charles-Louis de Secondat, baron de Montesquieu, *Voyages de Montesquieu publiés par le baron Albert de Montesquieu* (Bordeaux, G. Gounomillon, 1894).

Anne-Claude-Philippe de Tubières, conte de Caylus, *Voyage d'Italie 1714–1715* (Paris, Librairie Fiscbacher, 1914).

Cristina Dondi, 'The Venetian Booktrade: a Methodological Approach to and First Results of Book-Based Historical Research', in *Early Printed Books as Material Objects: Proceeding of the Conference organized by the IFLA Rare Books and Manuscripts Section, Munich, 19–21 August 2009*, eds Bettina Wagner and Marcia Reed (Berlin-New York, 2010), 219–28.

Cristina Dondi and Neil Harris, 'Exporting books from Milan to Venice in the 15th century: evidence from the *Zornale* of Francesco de Madiis', in *Incunabula. Printing, Trading, Collecting, Cataloguing*, Milan, 10–12 Sept. 2013, ed. Alessandro Ledda, *La Bibliofilía*, nn. 1–3, CXVI (2014), 121–48.

Cristina Dondi and Maria Alessandra Panzanelli Fratoni, 'Researching the Origin of Perugia's Public Library (1582/1623) before and after *Material Evidence in Incunabula*', *Quaerendo*, 46 (2016), 129–50.

Cristina Dondi, 'The 15cBOOKTRADE Project and the Study of Incunabula as Historical Sources', in *Printing R-Evolution and Society 1450–1500. Fifty Years that Changed Europe*, ed. Cristina Dondi, Studi di Storia 13 (Venice, 2020), 21–54. DOI 10.30687/978-88-6969-332-8.

Fortunato Federici, *Della biblioteca di S. Giustina di Padova, dissertazione storica con note biografiche* (Padova, 1815).

Luigi Alberto Ferrai, 'La biblioteca di S. Giustina di Padova', in Giuseppe Mazzatinti, *Inventario dei manoscritti italiani nelle biblioteche di Francia*, (Roma, 1887), II 549–661.

Antonio Foscari, 'Introduzione a una ricerca sulla costruzione della Libreria medicea nel Convento di San Giorgio Maggiore a Venezia', in *Studi per Pietro Zampetti*, ed. Ranieri Varese (Ancona, 1993), 226–36.

Ezio Franceschini, 'Sulle versioni latine medievali del Περὶ χρωμάτων', in *Autour d'Aristote. Recueil d'études de philosophie ancienne et médiévale offert à Monseigneur A. Mansion* (Louvain, 1955), 451–69.

Martina Frank, *Baldassare Longhena* (Venezia, 2004).

Martin Gerbert, *Iter Alemannicum, accedit Italicum et Gallicum* (Sankt Blasien, typis San-Blasianis, 1765).

Gianmario Guidarelli, Gabriella Liva, Silvia Musetti, 'Il complesso medievale di San Giorgio Maggiore a Venezia. Architettura, scultura, strumenti digitali per l'analisi e l'interpretazione', *Ateneo Veneto*, an. CCVI, 3° ser., 18/II (2019), 59–93.

Jean-Claude Hocquet, *Les monastères vénitiens et l'argent* (Rome, 2020).

Johann Georg Keyssler, *Neueste Reise durch Deutschland, Böhmen, Ungran, die Schweiz, Italien und Lothringen* (Hannover, Nikolaus Förster und Sohns Erben, 1751).

Lotte Labowsky, *Bessarion's Library and the Biblioteca Marciana. Six Early Inventories* (Rome, 1979).

Pietro La Cute, 'Le vicende delle biblioteche monastiche veneziane dopo la soppressione napoleonica', *Rivista di Venezia*, A. VIII, no. 10 (October 1929), 597–646.

Tommaso Leccisotti, *Congregationis S. Iustinae de Padua O.S.B. Ordinationes capitulorum generalium*, I (Montecassino, 1939).

Piero Lucchi, 'L'ordine dei libri nella biblioteca Malatestiana. Appunti lungo un percorso di ricerca', in *Il mondo di Malatesta Novello. Atti del convegno, Cesena, 21–23 marzo 2003*, eds Loretta Righetti and Daniela Savoia (Cesena, 2006), 135–224.

Paolo Marangon, *Alle origini dell'aristotelismo padovano (secc. XII–XIII)* (Padova, 1977).

Gabriele Mazzucco, 'L'assetto di un monastero benedettino medioevale: San Giorgio Maggiore di Venezia nel 1369', in *Monastica et umanistica. Scritti in onore di Gregorio Penco OSB*, ed. Francesco Giovanni Trolese (Cesena, 2003), 199–225.

François Maximilien Misson, *Avis de Librairies in Nouveau voyage d'Italie*, 4e édition (La Haye, Chez Henry van Bulderen, 1722).

Joachim Christoph Nemeitz, *Nachlese besonderer Nachrichten von Italien: Als ein Supplement von Misson, Burnet, Addison, und andern…* (Leipzig, Johann Gottlieb Gleditsch, 1726).

James F. O'Gorman, *The Architecture of the Monastic Library in Italy, 1300–1600. Catalogue with Introductory Essay* (New York, 1972).

Marco Palma, 'Aspetti quantitativi della produzione libraria manoscritta e a stampa nel Quattrocento', in *Incunabula. Printing, Trading, Collecting, Cataloguing, Milan, 10–12 Sept. 2013*, ed. Alessandro Ledda, *La Bibliofilía*, nn. 1–3, CXVI (2014), 165–78.

Beniamino Pagnini, *Le origini della scrittura gotica padovana* (Padova, 1933).

Luigi Pepe, 'Gaspard Monge e i prelievi nelle biblioteche italiane (1796-1797)', in *Ideologie e patrimonio storico-culturale nell'età rivoluzionaria e napoleonica. A proposito del trattato di Tolentino. Atti del convegno Tolentino, 18–21 settembre 1997* (Roma, 2000), 415–42.

Printing R-evolution 1450–1500. Fifty Years that Changed Europe, ed. Cristina Dondi, Studi di Storia 13 (Venice, 2018).

Lavinia Prosdocimi, 'Codici di Andrea Contrario nel testamento di Michele Salvatico', in *L'Umanesimo librario tra Venezia e Napoli. Contributi su Michele Salvatico e su Andrea Contrario*, eds Gilda P. Mantovani, Lavinia Prosdocimi and Elisabetta Barile (Venezia, 1993), 27–52.

Dorit Raines, 'The dissolution of the libraries of Venetian religious houses and the keeper Jacopo Morelli under Venetian, French, and Austrian governments (1768–1819)', in the present volume.

Costanza Rapone, *Tra Italia e Inghilterra nel medioevo: storie di codici e di uomini giunti da Oltremanica tra i secoli XII e XIV*, Università degli Studi della Tuscia di Viterbo, a.a. 2014–15, https://dspace.unitus.it/handle/2067/2903.

Giorgio Ravegnani, *Le biblioteche del monastero di San Giorgio* maggiore, con un saggio di Nicola Ivanoff sulla decorazione della biblioteca di San Giorgio Maggiore (Firenze, 1976).

Giovanni Rossi, 'Storia del monastero di San Giorgio Maggiore', in Emmanuele Antonio Cicogna, *Delle iscrizioni veneziane* (Venezia, 1834), IV, 241–401.

Fiammetta Sabba, *Viaggi tra i libri. Le biblioteche italiane nella letteratura del Grand Tour* (Pisa-Roma, 2018).

San Giorgio Maggiore, II, *Documenti 982–1159*, ed. Luigi Lanfranchi, Fonti per la storia di Venezia, sez. II, Archivi ecclesiastici Diocesi Castellana (Venezia, 1968).

Elisabetta Sciarra, 'Acquisizioni e asportazioni alla caduta della Repubblica di Venezia', in *Printing R-Evolution and Society 1450–1500. Fifty Years that Changed Europe*, ed. Cristina Dondi, Studi di Storia 13 (Venice, 2020), 374–412.

Federico Stefani, 'Tavola VI', in Pompeo Litta, *Famiglie celebri italiane* (Milano, 1868–1872), XI: 'Mocenigo di Venezia'.

Idelfonso Tassi, *Ludovico Barbo (1381–1443)* (Roma, 1952).

Marino Sanuto, *I Diarii*, ed. Rinaldo Fulin (Venezia, 1882).

Giacomo Filippo Tomasini, *Bibliothecae Patavinae manuscriptae publicae et privatae…* (Utini, Typis Nicolai Schiratti, 1639).

Giacomo Filippo Tomasini, *Bibliothecae Venetae Manuscriptae publicae et privatae quibus diversi scriptores hactenus incogniti recensentur* (Utini, Typis Nicolai Schiratti, 1650).

Francesco Giovanni Trolese, 'La riforma benedettina di S. Giustina nel Quattrocento', in *I Benedettini a Padova e nel territorio padovano attraverso i secoli: saggi storici sul movimento benedettino a Padova*, catalogo della mostra storico-artistica nel 15° centenario della nascita di San Benedetto, Padova, Abbazia di Santa Giustina, ottobre-dicembre 1980, eds Alberta De Nicolò Salmazo and Francesco Giovanni Trolese (Treviso, 1980), 55–74.

Carlo Urbani, 'I benedettini di San Giorgio maggiore di Venezia: momenti salienti', in *Alli 10 Agosto 1806 soppressione del monastero di S. Giorgio*, ed. Giovanni Vian (Cesena, 2011), 93–113.

Giuseppe Valentinelli, *Libri membranacei a stampa della Biblioteca Marciana di Venezia* (Venezia, 1870).

Johann Jacob Volkmann, *Historische-Kritischen Nachrichten von Italien* (Leipzig, der Caspar Fritsch, 1778).

Bettina Wagner, '*Libri impressi Bibliothecae Monasterii Sancti Emmerammi*. The Incunable Collection of St Emmeram, Regensburg, and its Catalogue, 1501', in *Incunabula and Their Readers. Printing, Selling and Using Books in the Fifteenth Century*, ed. Kristian Jensen (London, 2003), 179–205.

Marino Zorzi, *La Libreria di San Marco: libri, lettori, società nella Venezia dei Dogi* (Milano, 1987).

Digital Sources

Manus Online, https://manus.iccu.sbn.it/index.php.

Catalogue[120]

181 catalogue entries. 175 editions (175 editions in ISTC; two editions not identified: 115, 128; one lost edition: 22) in 181 copies (no. 4 corresponds to four MEI records; nos 12 and 13, 52 and 53, and 87 and 88 are copies of the same edition). In MEI there are 175 editions in 181 copies (because nos 22, 115, and 128 are not included, but no. 4 has four separate entries). No. 50bis was found just before going to press.

---

120 Research on post-incunabula in the library of S. Giorgio Maggiore has still to begin but promises to be fruitful; see, for example, the volume now in Subiaco, Biblioteca Statale del Monumento di Santa Scolastica, ANT.500 XXIII B 22: *Bartholomei Faccii De rebus gestis Alphonsi Aragonij regis libri VII*, Mantuae: Philoterpses et Clidanus Philoponi fratres excudebant, Feb. 1563; 4° (EDIT16 CNCE 18481); on the title-page is the inscription 'Est Bibliothecae S. Georgii Maioris Venetiarum'. We should like to thank Nathalie Coilly (Bibliothèque nationale de France), the late Lilian Armstrong (Wellesley College), Geri Della Rocca de Candal, Matilde Malaspina, Sabrina Minuzzi, and Maria Alessandra Panzanelli Fratoni (15cBOOKTRADE Project), and all the curators and scholars who contributed entries on S. Giorgio's incunabula to the Material Evidence in Incunabula (MEI) database. In addition, we should like to thank for their invaluable help Elisabetta Sciarra of the Marciana Library in Venice, for the identification of nos 29 and 125, and Julianne Simpson of the John Rylands Library in Manchester, for providing specialist imaging for no. 56, as well as Ennio Ferraglio of the Biblioteca Queriniana in Brescia, Pasquale Di Viesti of the Biblioteca Comunale Teresiana in Mantua, and Daryl Green of the University of Edinburgh Main Library.

Sources

Gerbert (1765)

Martin Gerbert (1720–1793), German theologian and historian who travelled through Germany, Italy and France between 1759 and 1762. In his book: *Iter Alemannicum, accedit Italicum et Gallicum* (Sankt Blasien, typis San-Blasianis, 1765), 470–72, he published a list of incunabula belonging to the library of S. Giorgio Maggiore apparently given to him by the monks. On his Grand Tour: Fiammetta Sabba, *Viaggi tra i libri. Le biblioteche italiane nella letteratura del Grand Tour* (Pisa-Roma, 2018), 181–84.

Indice Polinà (1789–1793)

Indice della libreria di S. Giustina, compiled by the librarian Pier Maria Polinà between 1789 and 1793, in 22 volumes (Biblioteca Universitaria di Padova, ms. 1984).

This is probably a fair copy of *Index alphabeticus Bibliothecae Sanctae Iustinae de Padua*, started by the librarian Giuseppe Maria Sandi in 1717 and continued by his successors, in 27 volumes, and which was in use in the monastery until its suppression (Padua, Biblioteca Civica, ms. BP 389); see Maschietto, *Biblioteca e bibliotecari di S. Giustina di Padova*, 332–39.

Morelli's survey (1789)

Venezia, Archivio Marciano, Corporazioni Soppresse 1789–1812, fasc. 1: 'Nota dei migliori codici manoscritti e dei più rari libri stampati della Libreria di San Giorgio Maggiore'. On an inserted leaf: 'D. Giacomo Morelli Custode della Libreria di S. Marco'. The volumes are not numbered. At the end: 'In ordine al Decreto dell'Eccelso Consiglio di Dieci dei 25 Settembre 1789, dal Custode della Libreria Pubblica di S. Marco, a ciò destinato dall'Eccellentissimo Bibliotecario, restano consegnati li soprascritti Libri Manoscritti e Stampati al Reverendissimo P. Abate del Monastero di S. Giorgio Maggiore, affinchè debbano essere sempre fedelmente custoditi e conservati nella Libreria del Monastero medesimo: al qual oggetto ne sarà di tempo in tempo, per ordine Pubblico riconosciuta la loro esistenza e conservazione. D. Giovanni Alberto Campolongo, Abbate del monastero di S. Giorgio Maggiore | Don Giacomo Morelli Custode della Libreria di S. Marco'; fasc. 2. 'S. Giorgio Magg.e', always in Morelli's hand; list of more than fifty numbered volumes, mostly incunables, probably made as a preparation for the official one which is in fasc. 1, and a list of missing volumes (*mancanze*).

BnF archives list (1797)

A list of twenty incunabula of interest that the Bibliothèque nationale recommends the French commissaries should look for in the library of S. Giorgio Maggiore. The list is found at the BnF archives: BnF, AM 269: Venise, fasc. 1: 'Note de plusieurs livres rares qui se trouvent dans quelques bibliothèques de Venise et que la Bibliothèque Nationale se commande aux soins des citoyens commissaires du Gouvernement pour la recherche des Mouvemens des arts en Italie, le 25 thermidor an 5 [12 August 1797]', inside a folio with the list: 'Bibliothèque du Monastère de S. Georges le Majeur'. The person who marked the provenance of some of the incunables as 'Sta. Justina' misunderstood the provenance note, which states that the books are the property of the Congregation of Sta. Giustina but that they were part of the library of S. Giorgio Maggiore.

Cicogna (1797)

Emmanuele Antonio Cicogna, *Delle iscrizioni veneziane*, 6 vols in 7 (Venezia, Giuseppe Orlandelli, 1824–1861), IV, 601: 'Dalla libreria di s. Giorgio Maggiore furono portati a Parigi nel 1797 i seguenti Codici manuscritti […] Edizioni del secolo XV […]'. Cicogna, who lists eighteen incunabula, appears to have used the following document: 'Fattura fatta per la seguente nota presentata al Demanio di Venezia nel dì 30 agosto 1806. Nota de' codici Mss e Libri a stampa che li commissarii francesi trasportarono dalle biblioteche dei Regolari di Venezia nell'anno 1797. Carmelitani […] San Giorgio'.

Regno d'Italia, decree no. 160, 28 July 1806

Decree of secularization disposed by Eugène di Beauharnais (1781–1824), viceroy of the Kingdom of Italy (Regno d'Italia, 1805–1814). Decree issued at Monza, 28 July 1806: 'Decreto riguardante le Corporazioni religiose ne' dipartimenti veneti riuniti al Regno'; see *Bollettino delle leggi del Regno d'Italia. Parte II. Dal 1° maggio al 31 agosto 1806; coll'aggiunta dei Decreti pubblicati negli Stati Veneti avanti la loro unione al Regno* (Milano, Dalla reale stamperia, 1806), 809–20 at 814 for S. Giorgio Maggiore and Sta. Giustina in Padua; the decree dissolves S. Giorgio Maggiore and orders a merger with the convent of Sta. Giustina of Padua.
https://www.lombardiabeniculturali.it/leggi/schede/30049/; https://books.google.it/books?id=YQMKyldtJooC&printsec=front-cover&hl=it&source=gbs_ge_summary_r&cad=0#v=onepage&q&f=false

Rossi (1806)

A list of eighty-five incunables owned by the monastery prepared by Giovanni Rossi in Venice between Aug. 1806 and March 1807: see Venice, Archivio di Stato, Direzione dipartimentale del demanio e diritti uniti, Atti, b. 380, 2/15, fasc. II: 'S. Giorgio Maggiore. Libri a stampa del secolo XV della Biblioteca di S. Giorgio Maggiore'.

Regno d'Italia, books gone to Milan, 4 Sept. 1806

Venezia, Archivio della Biblioteca nazionale Marciana, busta 'Regno Italico' among documents listing books sent to Milan, Ministry of Public Education: 'No. 27) Addì 4 settembre 1806 Venezia. Dal Sig. Ab. Morelli Bibliotecario della R. Biblioteca di S. Marco ho ricevuto io qui sottoscritto li seguenti otto libri già appartenenti alla Biblioteca di S. Giorgio Maggiore, a lui stati provisoriamente consegnati addì 20 luglio po. po.' It follows a list of books, and underneath it in another hand: 'G. Dossi [...?] ho ricevuto i soprascritti libri'. Cicogna identifies the person as 'signor Dossi (ch'era il Direttore del Demanio)', who invited Morelli to hand over the eight books in the Marciana's temporary keeping. Cicogna (1797).

Rossi (March 1807)

Venice, Archivio di Stato, Demanio 1806–1813, b. 328, fasc. marked 'Anno 1807 Biblioteche. Spedizioni Libri Padova n. 220', 2nd fasc., dated 7 March 1807 and signed Giovanni Rossi. This document lists the number of books from each religious house sent to Padua on 7 March 1807.

Regno d'Italia, decree no. 77, 25 April 1810

Decree of secularization enacted by emperor Napoleon. Decree issued at Compiègne, 25 April 1810: 'Decreto portante la soppressione delle compagnie, congregazioni, comunie ed associazioni ecclesiastiche'; see *Bollettino delle leggi del Regno d'Italia. Parte prima. Dal primo gennaio al 30 giugno 1810* (Milano, Dalla reale stamperia, 1810), 264–67; among the convents dissolved by the decree is that of Sta. Giustina of Padua. *Fondi antichi della Biblioteca Universitaria di Padova*, 52 and Maschietto, *Biblioteca e bibliotecari di Santa Giustina*, 306. https://www.lombardiabeniculturali.it/leggi/schede/300790/; https://babel.hathitrust.org/cgi/pt?id=mdp.35112103077212&view=1up&seq=280

Padua, Catalogo generale XV (1811) / Catalogo generale XVI (1811)

'Catalogo generale, ossia riunione di tutti gli elenchi di libri scelti dalle biblioteche delle Corporazioni Regolari concentrate nel già convento di S. Anna di Padova' [compilato da Giuseppe Dainese] (Padua, Biblioteca Universitaria, maggio 1811, ms. 2250), 144–46: *Libri del secolo XV*; 103–43: [*Libri dal sec. XVI-*].

Doctor Giuseppe Dainese, renowned as a surgeon but chiefly a bibliographer ('chirurgo riputatissimo, ma più di tutto dedito per antico costume alla bibliografia'), who had already reorganised the books in the warehouse of Sant'Anna, was formally appointed by the Home Secretary 'cooperatore per la compilazione del catalogo' on 25 January 1810.

When the warehouse of Sant'Anna had to be cleared, some selected volumes were transferred in part to the Pubblica Libreria (today's Biblioteca Universitaria), and in part to the Sala Carmeli within the former convent of S. Francesco Grande.

Padua, S. Francesco Grande, Sala Carmeli (1813)

Five incunables from S. Giorgio Maggiore are listed in a document, now Padua, Archivio della Biblioteca Universitaria di Padova, S.I, Ba.6.2, 108.

These books were dispersed between 4 October 1813 and 1831. The document reports five incunables which on Sunday 4 October 1813 were in S. Francesco Grande, evidently transferred from the warehouse of Sant'Anna to the rooms of the Sala Carmeli (which was part of the university library), probably because of their value: these are volumes numbered in the Catalogo generale 1811 as no. 1 (Appianus, here no. 12), no. 8 (Euclides, here no. 71), no. 38 (Caracciolus with Cesariano, here nos 48 and 110), no. 45 (Lucas de Burgo, here no. 111), and no. 46 (Platea, here no. 137). Appianus, Euclides and Lucas de Burgo are listed in MEI as historical copies, their whereabouts unknown at present. Of the other two, Carraciolus-Cesariano is now in Padua and the Platea is now in Oxford. The latter's colophon is transcribed, and it is also observed that another copy of the same edition was among the books which had belonged to Michelangelo Carmeli (1706–1766); in 1831 the volume was purchased by the bookseller Thomas Thorpe for the Bodleian.

BnF restitution list (1815)

A list of seventy-seven incunables of interest that the Austrian authorities asked to be restored in 1798, but that were sent back only on 5 October 1815, when Baron d'Ottenfels, the imperial chamberlain in charge of the restitution of artefacts from the Conservatoire de Paris to their legitimate owners, ordered the restitution. The list is found in the BnF archives: BnF, AM 272: fasc. bearing the title: 'État des livres imprimés tirés des Bibliothèques de Venise pour la Bibliothèque du Roi, et restitués le 5 octobre 1815', signed 'le Baron d'Ottenfels, Commissaire de S.M.I et R. Observatoire', inside a folio with the list: 'Livres du quinzième siècle reclamés par la ville de Venise' with volumes numbered from 226 to 302 (part of the 432 artefacts taken away by the French in 1797).

Padua, Catalogo pregio (1817)

'Catalogo de' libri di qualche pregio separati da quelli di scarto rimasti al Demanio dopo la scelta fatta dai Delegati del cessato Governo Italico per la Pubblica Istruzione', written by Giuseppe Dainese (Padua, Biblioteca Universitaria, ms. 2252). In this catalogue are listed 1,006 entries of printed books from S. Giorgio Maggiore, among which are six incunables. Five incunable editions have been identified here, one other could not be identified: p. 9, no. 361: 'De Spina, Opuscula.

Venetiis, 1499. fo.'. Editions of Alphonsus de Spina printed either in Venice or in 1499 do not appear to exist. It is likely that the imprint information belongs to another edition bound last in a volume which opened with de Spina; this is an occurrence we have encountered elsewhere in this catalogue, for example nos 1, 10, 27, 75, 90, 104, 115, 127, 128, 132, 160, 164, and 178. The Rossi catalogue (1806) was unfortunately of no help on this occasion.

Padua, Catalogo Gnocchi (1818)

A document (*Processo verbale*) dated 11 April 1818 and written by Abbot Giuseppe Gnocchi, the successor to Dainese as custodian of the warehouse of Sant'Anna, states that on 10 April 1818 the librarian of the Biblioteca Universitaria, Abbot Daniele Francesconi, had given to Gnocchi the keys to Sala Carmeli, where a section of the books from the warehouse of Sant'Anna had been placed in cupboards. Amongst them were books from S. Giorgio Maggiore, specifically 503 volumes in cupboard A, 664 volumes in cupboard B, and 57 volumes in cupboard C. The librarian reserved the right to continue the delivery of books placed in other cupboards in the following days. The document today is Padua, Archivio della Biblioteca Universitaria di Padova, I Serie, Ba. 7, 163.

After Francesconi's death, the Benedictine Fortunato Federici, his successor at the library, was granted the right to select books and transport them to the Biblioteca Universitaria. The transfer took place around 1840 (Ravegnani, *Le biblioteche*, 65–68; *Fondi antichi della Biblioteca Universitaria di Padova*, 40–41).

Bibliography

Arcangelo Bossi, *Matricula monachorum congregationis Casinensis ordinis Sancti Benedicti* (Cesena, 1983).

CIBN – Bibliothèque nationale de France, *Catalogue des incunables* (*CIBN*) (Paris, 1981–), Vol. 1:1. Xylographes et A – v. 1:2. B – v. 1:3. C–D–v.1:4. E-G et supplément – v. 2:1. H-L–v. 2:2. M-O – v. 2:3 P-R – v. 2:4 S-Z et Hebraica – v. 2. H-Z, additions et corrections.

Fondi antichi della Biblioteca Universitaria di Padova. Mostra di manoscritti e libri a stampa in occasione del 350° anniversario della fondazione. Padova, Biblioteca Universitaria di Padova, 9–18 Dicembre 1979 (Padova, 1979).

Rinaldo Fulin, 'Vicende della libreria in SS. Gio. e Paolo', *Atti dell'Ateneo Veneto*, ser. II, 5 (1868), 273–94.

Francesco L. Maschietto, *Biblioteca e bibliotecari di S. Giustina di Padova (1697–1827)* (Padova, 1981).

Lavinia Prosdocimi, 'Sulle tracce di antichi inventari e note manoscritte. Codici da librerie claustrali nella Biblioteca Universitaria di Padova', in *Splendore nella regola, Codici miniati da monasteri e conventi nella Biblioteca Universitaria di Padova*, ed. Federica Toniolo and Pietro Gnan (Padova, 2011), 53–70.

Giorgio Ravegnani, *Le biblioteche del monastero di San Giorgio* maggiore, con un saggio di Nicola Ivanoff sulla decorazione della biblioteca di San Giorgio Maggiore (Firenze, 1976).

Elisabetta Sciarra, 'Acquisizioni e asportazioni alla caduta della Repubblica di Venezia', in *Printing R-Evolution and Society 1450–1500. Fifty Years that Changed Europe*, ed. Cristina Dondi, Studi di Storia 13 (Venice, 2020), 374–412.

Giuseppe Valentinelli, *Libri membranacei a stampa della Biblioteca Marciana di Venezia* (Venezia, 1870).

Digital Sources

Censimento nazionale delle edizioni italiane del XVI secolo (EDIT16), http://edit16.iccu.sbn.it/.

Gesamtkatalog der Wiegendrucke (GW), https://www.gesamtkatalogderwiegendrucke.de/.

Incunabula Short Title Catalogue (ISTC), https://data.cerl.org/istc/_search.

Material Evidence in Incunabula (MEI), https://data.cerl.org/mei/_search.

1. Aegidius (Columna) Romanus, *De regimine principum*, Venice: Simon Bevilaqua, 9 July 1498. Folio. GW 7219; ISTC ia00089000; MEI 02008198. Bound first with: Tertullianus, Quintus Septimus Florentius, *Apologeticus contra gentes*, Venice: Bernardinus Benalius, [not after 1494]. Folio. ISTC it00117000; MEI 02008199 (no. 164 here).
-1498–1513 Andreas Mocenicus, apostolic protonotary.
-1513–1806 Venice, S. Giorgio Maggiore; sixteenth-century inscription on the verso of the last leaf of the second bound work: 'Reverendus dominus Andreas Mocenicus prothonotarius pro animae suae salute Divi Georgii Maioris coenobio dicavit, signatus 115', Andrea Mocenigo died in 1513; eighteenth-century inscription on the first leaf: 'Est Bibliothecae Sancti Georgii Maioris Venetiarum'.
-1806 Regno d'Italia, decree no. 160, 28 July 1806.
-1806 Venice, S. Giorgio Maggiore; Rossi (1806), A6: 'Aegidii Romani Opus de regimine Principum. Ven. sine an. per Bernardi Benalium F.°'.
-after March 1807/1811–1818(?) Padua, Sant'Anna: Rossi (March 1807); Catalogo generale XV (1811), 144, no. 7: 'Eggidii, Opus de regimine principum, folio, Venetiis, sine anno, per Bernardinum Benalium'; *Fondi antichi della Biblioteca Universitaria di Padova*, 40–41. The entry merges the bibliographical information of the edition bound first (author and title), and the typographical information of the edition bound second (year of publication and printer).
-1818(?)-*c.* 1840 Padua, Sala Carmeli, S. Francesco Grande. When the monastery of Sant'Anna had to be cleared, some selected volumes were transferred in part to the Pubblica Libreria (the Biblioteca Universitaria), in part to the Sala Carmeli of the former convent of S. Francesco Grande. A document dated 1818 records the transfer of books from S. Giorgio Maggiore into cupboards A, B, and C of Sala Carmeli. Padua, Catalogo Gnocchi (1818).
-*c.* 1840 transfer to the Biblioteca Universitaria: Ravegnani, *Le biblioteche*, 65–68; *Fondi antichi della Biblioteca Universitaria di Padova*, 40–41.

Padua, Biblioteca Universitaria: Sec. XV 959/1

2. Alberti, Leo Baptista, *De re aedificatoria*, Florence: Nicolaus Laurentii, Alamanus, 29 Dec. 1485. Folio. GW 579; ISTC ia00215000; MEI 02014753.
-1485-*c.* 1500 Venice, S. Giorgio Maggiore, inscription on [rum]7v: 'Est monachorum Congregationis S. Iustine de Padua Ordinis S. Benedicti deputatus, in Sancto Georgio Maior Venetiarum, signatus 1019'.
-1789 Venice, S. Giorgio Maggiore; Morelli's survey (1789), fasc. 1, 3: marked with + and crossed out.
-1797–1815 Paris, Bibliothèque nationale; BnF archives list (1797), fasc. 2, no. 20: 'Albertus de Re edif. 1485 fol. Sta Justina'; Cicogna (1797): 'Dalla libreria di s. Giorgio Maggiore furono portati a Parigi nel 1797 i seguenti Codici manuscritti [...] Edizioni del secolo XV [...] 1. Alberti Baptistae de re aedificatoria f. chart. Florentiae 1485'.
-1815– Venice, Biblioteca Nazionale Marciana; Cicogna (1797): 'Per la generosità di Francesco I di gloriosissima memoria presso che tutti cotesti libri son ritornati nel 1815, e riposti nella Marciana'.
Venice, Biblioteca Nazionale Marciana: Inc. 0570

3. Albertus Magnus, *Compendium theologicae veritatis*, Venice: Christophorus Arnoldus, 5 Apr. 1476. 4°. GW 604; ISTC ia00232000; MEI 02006857.
-1476-*c.* 1500 Venice, S. Giorgio Maggiore; inscription on the verso of the first leaf: 'Iste liber est monasterii Sancti Georgii [then corrected to 'Sancte Gustine', *sic*] Maioris signatus numero 604 [then corrected to 578]'.
-*c.* 1501–1810 Padua, Sta. Giustina. Another inscription in a sixteenth-century hand on the first leaf: 'Hic liber est monasterii Sancte Iustine de Padua signatus numero 156'. The Benedictine library was closed in 1806 and placed under the supervision of Abbot Daniele Francesconi, the librarian of the Biblioteca Universitaria of Padua; it was accessioned in 1810 following the general suppression. The books, however, remained in

Sta. Giustina for another ten years, although not as the monastery's property for the monastery was already suppressed; see Regno d'Italia, decree no. 77, 25 April 1810; Maschietto, *Biblioteca e bibliotecari di S. Giustina*, 295 ss.

-*c.* 1820-*c.* 1840 Padua, Sala Carmeli, S. Francesco Grande. After the suppression of the monastery and consequent events, the volumes were transferred to the Sala Carmeli of the former convent of S. Francesco Grande between 1820 and 1821; here they remained, on deposit, until about 1840 when they were accessioned by the Biblioteca Universitaria of Padua. There are no extant inventories of the books of Sta. Giustina which were accessioned after the suppression; see *Fondi antichi della Biblioteca Universitaria di Padova*, 51–53; Maschietto, *Biblioteca e bibliotecari di Santa Giustina*, 321; Prosdocimi, 'Sulle tracce di antichi inventari', 55.

-*c.* 1840 transfer to the Biblioteca Universitaria. Ravegnani, *Le biblioteche*, 65–68; *Fondi antichi della Biblioteca Universitaria di Padova*, 40–41.
Padua, Biblioteca Universitaria: Sec. XV Duplicato 47

4. Alexander de Ales, *Summa universae theologiae* (i.e. Super IV libros sententiarum Petri Lombardi), Nuremberg: Anton Koberger, 1481–82. Folio. GW 871; ISTC ia00383000; MEI 02019757; 02019758; 02019761; 02019759.

-*c.* 1482–1500 Venice, S. Giorgio Maggiore; inscriptions in vols 2–4: 'Iste liber est sancti georgij maioris venetorum ordinis s. benedicti sub congregatione s. Iustine signatus numero 1123'; 'Iste liber est monachorum sancti georgij maioris venetorum ordinis s. benedicti sub congregatione s. Iustine signatus numero 1124'; 'Iste liber est monasterij sancti georgij maioris venetorum ordinis s. benedicti sub congregatione s. Iustine signatus numero 1125'.

-*c.* 1701–1810 Venice, Observant Dominicans, S. Maria Rosarii (1669–1810): ex-libris.

-1823 Venice, Biblioteca Nazionale Marciana: following the suppressions of religious institutions

in 1823 and in 1832, the Marciana library received by royal decree around 20,000 books formerly belonging to the Observant Dominicans based at the Zattere (Venice).
Venice, Biblioteca Nazionale Marciana: Inc. 0152–0155

5. Alexander de Villa Dei, *Doctrinale* (Partes I–IV), Venice: Thomas de Blavis, de Alexandria, 28 July 1485. Folio. GW 993; ISTC ia00426500; MEI 02006706.

-1806 Regno d'Italia, decree no. 160, 28 July 1806.

-1806 Venice, S. Giorgio Maggiore; Rossi (1806), G34: 'De Guaschis Ludovici Interpretatio Operis Alexandri Grammatici Ven. 1485 p. Thomasinum Alexandrinum F.º'.

-1811 Padua, Sant'Anna; Catalogo generale XV (1811), 146, no. 55: 'De Guaschis, Interpretatio operis Alex. Grammatici, fol. Ven. 1485'; *Fondi antichi della Biblioteca Universitaria di Padova*, 40–41.
Historical copy, Venice

6. Angelus de Clavasio, *Summa angelica de casibus conscientiae*, Venice: Georgius Arrivabenus, 4 June 1492. 4º. GW 1934; ISTC ia00723000; MEI 02008341.

-1492–before 1793 Venice, S. Giorgio Maggiore; inscription on the first leaf: 'Est Sancti Georgii Maioris Venetiarum ad usum domini Antonii Veneti'.

-after 1793–1810 Padua, Sta. Giustina; Indice Polinà (1789–1793), 61, shelfmark: 'QQ.7'. Also visible on the verso of the front flyleaf is the former shelfmark, since deleted, 'D.4 di sopra'. The books, however, remained in Sta. Giustina for another ten years, although not as the monastery's property for the monastery was already suppressed, see Regno d'Italia, decree no. 77, 25 April 1810; Maschietto, *Biblioteca e bibliotecari di Santa Giustina*, 321.

-*c.* 1820-*c.* 1840 Padua, Sala Carmeli, S. Francesco Grande. After the suppression of the monastery and consequent events, the volumes were transferred to the Sala Carmeli of the former convent of S. Francesco Grande between 1820 and 1821; here they remained, on deposit, until about 1840 when they were accessioned by the Biblioteca Universitaria. There are no extant inventories of the books of Sta. Giustina which were accessioned after the suppression; see *Fondi antichi della Biblioteca Universitaria di Padova*, 51–53; Maschietto, *Biblioteca e bibliotecari di Santa Giustina*, 321; Prosdocimi, 'Sulle tracce di antichi inventari', 55.

-*c.* 1840 transfer to the Biblioteca Universitaria. Ravegnani, *Le biblioteche*, 65–68; *Fondi antichi della Biblioteca Universitaria di Padova*, 40–41.

Padua, Biblioteca Universitaria: Sec. XV 10

7. Antoninus Florentinus, *Summa theologica* (Partes I–IV), Venice: Nicolaus Jenson, 1477–1480. Folio. CIBN A-453; GW 2185; ISTC ia00872000; MEI 02011873.

-1765 Venice, S. Giorgio Maggiore: included in the list published in Gerbert (1765).

-1789 Venice, S. Giorgio Maggiore; Morelli's survey (1789), fasc. 1, 3: 'tomi 4 in fo. Esemplare stampato in carta pecora con miniature [added:] Vedi però l'annotazione ms.', marked with +. In the manuscript addition on a smaller sheet of paper inserted in the binding, it is specified that there are three volumes of the Jenson edition and Pars II only from Venice: Johannes de Colonia and Johannes Manthen, 1477. Folio (ISTC ia00868000). Therefore, only the three Jenson volumes were taken away. They do not show today any inscription from S. Giorgio Maggiore.

-*c.* 1797–1802 Vienna: the ambassador of Ragusa to the imperial court, Count Sebastiano d'Ayala (1744–1817). No evidence in the books.

-1802 Paris: purchased by the Bibliothèque nationale de France at d'Ayala's sale in 1802.

Paris, Bibliothèque nationale de France: Rés. Vélins 940-2

8. Antoninus Florentinus, *Summa theologica* (Pars II), Venice: Johannes de Colonia and Johannes Manthen, 1477. Folio. GW 2196; ISTC ia00868000; MEI 02008360.

Considered a bibliographical unit with: **Antoninus Florentinus**, *Summa theologica* (Partes I–IV). With Molitoris' *Tabula*, i.e. pt. V, Strasbourg: Johann (Reinhard) Grüninger, 1490. Folio. GW 2191; ISTC ia00877000; MEI 02137940 (bound second, no. 9 here).

-after 4 Dec. 1490–1789 Venice, S. Giorgio Maggiore; fifteenth-century inscription in the lower margin of 5v: 'Iste liber est congregationis Sancte Iustine de Padua ordinis sancti Benedicti, deputatus in Sancto Georgio Maiore Venetiarum, signatus 941'; eighteenth-century inscription in the lower margin of a2r: 'Est bibliothecae Sancti Georgii Maioris Venetiarum'.

-1789 Venice, S. Giorgio Maggiore; Morelli's survey (1789), fasc. 1, 3: see above, no. 7.

-1806 Regno d'Italia, decree no. 160, 28 July 1806.

-1806 Venice, S. Giorgio Maggiore; Rossi (1806), A5: 'S. Antonini Summa. Ven. 1477. impensis Io. De Colonia, et Io. Manthen de Eherretzem. Tomi 2 Fol. seguitur alter tomus Tabulae omnium partium Summae pariter in F.o, ut anni 1490. Duo priores Tomi continent. partem secundam, et tertiam, alique vero partes non inveniuntur'.

-March 1807–1818(?) Padua, Sant'Anna: Rossi (March 1807); Catalogo generale XV (1811), 145, no. 34: 'S. Antonini, Summa, Venetiis, 1477 […] in folio'; *Fondi antichi della Biblioteca Universitaria di Padova*, 40–41.

-1818(?)-*c.* 1840 Padua, Sala Carmeli, S. Francesco Grande. When the monastery of Sant'Anna had to be cleared, some selected volumes were transferred in part to the Pubblica Libreria (the Biblioteca Universitaria), in part to the Sala Carmeli of the former convent of S. Francesco Grande. A document dated 1818 records the transfer of books from S. Giorgio Maggiore into cupboards A, B, and C of Sala Carmeli. Padua, Catalogo Gnocchi (1818).

-*c.* 1840 transfer to the Biblioteca Universitaria. Ravegnani, *Le biblioteche*, 65–68; *Fondi antichi della Biblioteca Universitaria di Padova*, 40–41.

Padua, Biblioteca Universitaria: Sec. XV Duplicato 99 bis

9. Antoninus Florentinus, *Summa theologica* (Partes I–IV). With Molitoris' *Tabula*, i.e. pt. V, Strasbourg: Johann (Reinhard) Grüninger, 1490. Folio. GW 2191; ISTC ia00877000; MEI 02137940. Note: In five parts dated: I) 28 Sept. 1490; II) 17 Aug. 1490; III) 4 Dec. 1490; IV) 3 July 1490; V) [undated].

Considered a bibliographical unit with: **Antoninus Florentinus**, *Summa theologica* (Pars II), Venice: Johannes de Colonia and Johannes Manthen, 1477. Folio. GW 2196; ISTC ia00868000; MEI 02008360 (bound first, no. 8 here).

-After 4 Dec. 1490–1789 Venice, S. Giorgio Maggiore; fifteenth-century inscription in the lower margin of pp. 5v of the Venice edition: 'Iste liber est congregationis Sancte Iustine de Padua ordinis sancti Benedicti, deputatus in Sancto Georgio Maiore Venetiarum, signatus 941'; eighteenth-century inscription in the lower margin of a2r of the Venice edition: 'Est bibliothecae Sancti Georgii Maioris Venetiarum'.

-1789 Venice, S. Giorgio Maggiore; Morelli's survey (1789), fasc. 1, 3, see above, no. 7.

-1806 Regno d'Italia, decree no. 160, 28 July 1806.

-1806 Venice, S. Giorgio Maggiore; Rossi (1806), A5: 'S. Antonini Summa. Ven. 1477. impensis Io. De Colonia, et Io. Manthen de Eherretzem. Tomi 2 Fol. seguitur alter tomus Tabulae omnium partium Summae pariter in F.o, ut anni 1490. Duo priores Tomi continent. partem secundam, et tertiam, alique vero partes non inveniuntur'.

Historical Copy, Venice (only the Tabula)

10. Antonius de Butrio, *Super primo libro Decretalium* (7–28), Venice: Bernardinus Rizus, Novariensis, 1485. Folio. GW 5822; ISTC ib01342000; MEI 02018170.

Bound first with: **Panormitanus de Tudeschis, Nicolaus**, *Disceptationes* (*seu Disputationes*) *et allegationes*, of which three editions were published in Venice, in 1483, 1487, and 1490, of 38, 32, and 28 leaves respectively (bound second, no. 128 here); **Panormitanus de Tudeschis, Nicolaus**, *Consilia* (cum Ludovici Bolognini tabula), Venice:

Peregrinus de Pasqualibus, Bononiensis and Dominicus Bertochus, 14 Dec. 1486. Folio. GW M47773; ISTC ip00030000; MEI 02137941 (bound third, no. 127 here); **Guido de Baysio**, *Apparatus libri sexti decretalium*, Milan: Jacobus de Sancto Nazario, de Ripa, and Bernardinus de Castelliono, 23 Dec. 1490. Folio. GW 3743; ISTC ib00284000; MEI 02018176 (bound fourth, no. 90 here).

-1806 Venice, S. Giorgio Maggiore; Rossi (1806), B17: 'De Butrio Lectura de Translatione Prelatorum, Ven. 1485 per Bernard. de Novaria. It. Nicolai de Sicilia Allegationes Ven. 1486 per Peregrinum de Pasqualibus, et socium. – Lectura D.i Archidiaconi Bononiensis. Mediolani 1490 p. Bernardi de Castello, et socium. Omnia T.º 1, F.º'. This entry merges the detail of two editions bound second and third in this composite volume, the title of Panormitanus' *Disceptationes* (*seu Disputationes*) *et allegationes*, and the bibliographical information of Panormitanus' *Consilia*.

-1806 Regno d'Italia, decree no. 160, 28 July 1806.

-1811 Padua, Sant'Anna; Catalogo generale XV (1811), 145, no. 24: 'De Butrio, Lectura etc., fol. Ven. 1485, 1486, et 1490'; *Fondi antichi della Biblioteca Universitaria di Padova*, 40–41. The four copies were still bound together in 1811, as specifically stated in the Catalogue.

Historical copy, Venice

11. Appianus, *Historia Romana* (Partes I–II), Venice: Bernhard Maler (Pictor), Erhard Ratdolt and Peter Löslein, 1477. 4º. GW 2290; ISTC ia00928000; MEI 02006673.

-1789 Venice, S. Giorgio Maggiore; Morelli's survey (1789), fasc. 1, 3.

-1806 Regno d'Italia, decree no. 160, 28 July 1806.

-1806 Venice, S. Giorgio Maggiore; Rossi (1806), A1: 'Appiani Alexandrini Historie. Ven. 1477 per Bernardinum Pictorem, F.o'.

-March 1807–1813 Padua, Sant'Anna; Rossi (March 1807); Catalogo generale XV (1811), 144, no. 1, 'Appiani, Historiae, fol. Ven. 1477 per Bern. Pictorem'; *Fondi antichi della Biblioteca Universitaria di Padova*, 40–41.

-1813–1831(?) Padua, S. Francesco Grande, Sala Carmeli. One of the five incunables from S. Giorgio Maggiore listed in a document, now Padua, S. Francesco Grande, Sala Carmeli (1813). The document reports five incunables which on Sunday 4 October 1813 were in S. Francesco Grande, evidently transferred from the warehouse of Sant'Anna to the Sala Carmeli (which was part of the University library), probably because of their value. These books were dispersed between 4 October 1813 and 1831.
Historical copy, Venice

12. Appianus, *Historia Romana* (Partes I–II), Venice: Christophorus de Pensis de Mandello, 20 Nov. 1500. Folio. GW 2291; ISTC ia00929000; MEI 02008331.
Bound second with: **Lucianus Samosatensis**, *Vera historia* [Latin]. Tr: Lilius (Tifernas) Castellanus. Add: Diodorus Siculus: *Bibliothecae historicae libri VI* [Latin]. Tr: Poggius Florentinus, Venice: Philippus Pincius, 20 Nov. 1493. Folio. ISTC il00328000; MEI 02008330 (bound first, no. 112 here); **Laurentius Valla**, *Elegantie de lingua Latina*, Venetiis: per Christoforum de Pensis, 7 Aug. 1505. Folio. EDIT16 CNCE 33468 (Padua, Biblioteca Universitaria, A.41.a.28, bound third).
-1806 Regno d'Italia, decree no. 160, 28 July 1806.
-1806 Venice, S. Giorgio Maggiore; Rossi (1806), L48: 'Luciani Poetae, et Oratoris De Veris narrationibus – Diodori Siculi de antiquorum gestis fabulosis Ven. 1493 p. Philip. Pincium – Appiani Alexandrini de bellis civilibus Ven. 1500 p. Christophorum de Pensis; Laurentii Vallensis Opus Elegantiarum linguae latinae Ven. 1505 ap. eundem Omnia uno vol. F.°'.
-March 1807–1818(?) Padua, Sant'Anna: after the suppression of the monastery of S. Giorgio Maggiore in 1806, the volume was probably deposited in the former monastery of the Benedictine nuns of Sant'Anna in Padua, as with the other books that subsequently entered the Biblioteca Universitaria, even if it cannot be identified in the lists of books selected from that warehouse.

-1818(?)-*c.* 1840 Padua, S. Francesco Grande, Sala Carmeli. When the monastery of Sant'Anna had to be cleared, some selected volumes were transferred in part to the Pubblica Libreria (the Biblioteca Universitaria), in part to the Sala Carmeli of the former convent of S. Francesco Grande. A document dated 1818 records the transfer of books from S. Giorgio Maggiore into cupboards A, B, and C of Sala Carmeli. Padua, Catalogo Gnocchi (1818).
-*c.* 1840 transfer to the Universitaria of Padua: Ravegnani, *Le biblioteche*, 65–68; *Fondi antichi della Biblioteca Universitaria di Padova*, 40–41.
Padua, Biblioteca Universitaria: Sec. XV 377/2

13. Appianus, *Historia Romana* (Partes I–II), Venice: Christophorus de Pensis de Mandello, 20 Nov. 1500. Folio. GW 2291; ISTC ia00929000; MEI 02127882.
-1484–1513 Andreas Mocenicus, apostolic protonotary.
-1513–*c.* 1700 Venice, San Giorgio Maggiore; inscription: 'Reverendus dominus Andreas Mocenicus protonotarius pro anime sue salute diui Georgii maioris cenobio dicauit signatus numero 114', Andrea Mocenigo died in 1513.
-*c.* 1700–*c.* 1800 Domenicus Margaritis, lawyer: stamp, 'ex Biblioth. Maragaritis'.
-*c.* 1800– Milan, Biblioteca Braidense: oval-shaped stamp including the text 'Imperialis Regia Bibliotheca Mediolanensis' and the image of Minerva, in use from 1800 to circa 1830.
Milan, Biblioteca Nazionale Braidense, AO. XVII. 17

14. Athanasius, *De homousio contra Arrium*, etc. [Paris]: André Bocard, for Jean Petit, [after 5 Aug.] 1500. Folio. ISTC ia01173000; MEI 02007041.
Bound with two editions of the sixteenth century.
-1550–1806 Venice, S. Giorgio Maggiore; evidence from the position and typology of the three shelfmarks on the flyleaf in a sixteenth/seventeenth-century hand, very similar to Padua, Biblioteca Universitaria: Sec. XV, Dupl. 99 bis, flyleaf.

-after March 1807/1811–1818(?) Padua, Sant'Anna: Rossi (March 1807); Catalogo generale XVI (1811), 117, no. 360: 'Illustrium virorum opuscula, folio, Parisiis, 1500'; *Fondi antichi della Biblioteca Universitaria di Padova*, 40–41.

-1818(?)-*c.* 1840 Padua, S. Francesco Grande, Sala Carmeli. When the monastery of Sant'Anna had to be cleared, some selected volumes were transferred in part to the Pubblica Libreria (the Biblioteca Universitaria di Padova), in part to the Sala Carmeli of the former convent of S. Francesco Grande. A document dated 1818 records the transfer of books from S. Giorgio Maggiore into cupboards A, B, and C of Sala Carmeli. Padua, Catalogo Gnocchi (1818).

-*c.* 1840 transfer to the Biblioteca Universitaria of Padua: Ravegnani, *Le biblioteche*, 65–68; *Fondi antichi della Biblioteca Universitaria di Padova*, 40–41.

Padua, Biblioteca Universitaria: Sec. XV 864/3

15. Augustinus, Aurelius, *De Civitate Dei*, Venice: Nicolaus Jenson, 2 Oct. 1475. Folio. CIBN A-682; GW 2879; ISTC ia01235000; MEI 02008348.

-1475-*c.* 1700 Venice, S. Giorgio Maggiore; fifteenth-century inscription below the colophon, in brown ink: 'Iste liber est monachorum congregationis | sancte Iustine de padua ordinis sancti | Benedicti de obseruantia deputatus | in sancto georgio maiore venet[iarum] numero 484'; eighteenth-century inscription below the rubricae, in brown ink: 'Est Biliothece S. Georgij Maioris Venetiarum'.

-1765 Venice, S. Giorgio Maggiore: included in the list published in Gerbert (1765).

-1789 Venice, S. Giorgio Maggiore; Morelli's survey (1789), fasc. 1, 3: 'Esemplare stampato in cartapecora, con miniature', marked with + and crossed out; ex-libris of the Marciana library with the lion of St Mark and the motto 'Custos vel ultor', created in 1722 by the then librarian Girolamo Venier and used for quite a while afterwards – this ex-libris was used by Morelli

after his survey to mark the most precious books in each monastery.

-1797– Paris, Bibliothèque nationale: BnF archives list (1797), fasc. 2, no. 2: 'S. Augustinus de Civitate dei. Venetiis 1475 in fol. sur velin, en bois sur le dos, coll. 77 no. 13 S. Justin de Padua deput.' (unfortunately, the Library subsequently rebound the incunable, in red morocco tooled in gilt on the spine); Cicogna (1797), 'Dalla libreria di s. Giorgio Maggiore furono portati a Parigi nel 1797 i seguenti Codici manuscritti [...] Edizioni del secolo XV [...] 2. S. Augustini de civitate Dei f. membr. Venetiis 1475 Ienson'. The volume did not return to the Marciana library, as should have been the case according to Cicogna (1797): 'Per la generosità di Francesco I di gloriosissima memoria presso che tutti cotesti libri son ritornati nel 1815, e riposti nella Marciana'; a different copy was sent back, now Marciana Inc. V. 0465 (MEI 02014725); BnF Restitution list (1815), fasc. 2: 'S. Augustinus de civitate dei Venet Jenson 1475 fol. Remplacé par un exemplaire de M. Salvi'; see also Valentinelli, 22–23.

Paris, Bibliothèque nationale de France: Rés. Vélins 301

16. Augustinus, Aurelius, *De civitate dei* [Italian] *De la cita d'dio*, [Venice?: Antonio di Bartolommeo Miscomini, about 1476–78]; GW assigns to [Florence?: not after 1483]. Folio. GW 2892; ISTC ia01248000; MEI 02108478.

-1789 Venice, S. Giorgio Maggiore; Morelli's survey (1789), fasc. 1, 3: no marks.

Historical copy, Venice

17. Augustinus, Aurelius, Pseudo-, *Sermones ad heremitas*, Venice: Vincentius Benalius, 26 Jan. 1492/1493. 8°. GW 3005; ISTC ia01317000; MEI 02125177.

Formerly bound with other Casanatense incunables: **Bernardus Claravallensis, Pseudo-**, *Modus bene vivendi in christianam religionem*, Venice: Bernardinus Benalius, 30 May 1492. 8°. GW 4047; ISTC ib00413000; MEI 02125145; VOL

INC.1294 (no. 23 here) and **Thomas à Kempis,** *Imitatio Christi*, etc. Venice: Petrus de Quarengiis, Bergomensis, and Giovanni Maria di Occimiano, 23 Apr. 1493. 8°. ISTC ii00028000; MEI 02125175; VOL INC.1292 (no. 166 here); see seventeenth-/ eighteenth-century manuscript index on front flyleaf IIr of Bernardus Claravallensis. The three volumes were described as bound in a composite volume in the printed catalogue by G. B. Audiffredi, *Bibliothecae Casanatensis Catalogus librorum typis impressorum* (Romae, 1761), vol. 1, 345a.

-1493-*c.* 1600 Venice, S. Giorgio Maggiore; fifteenth-century inscription on a1r of VOL INC.1294: 'Iste liber est Congregationis monachorum s. Justine de padua ordinis sancti Benedicti deputatus in sancto Georgio maiore venetiarum, signatus 979'.

-*c.* 1600 Flavius Ciccolus of Bevagna: inscription on a1r of VOL INC.1294: 'Flavius Ciccolus Meuanas etc. habuit hunc librum dono etc'.

-*c.* 1761 Rome, Biblioteca Casanatense; acquired in the eighteenth century as the other two parts of the composite volume are listed in Audiffredi (1761).

Rome, Biblioteca Casanatense: VOL INC.1293

18. Augustinus, Aurelius, Pseudo-, *Sermones ad heremitas*, Venice: Simon Bevilaqua, 4 Nov. 1495. 8°. GW 3007; ISTC ia01319000; MEI 02018099. Bound second with: **Bernardus Claravallensis, Pseudo-**, *Modus bene vivendi in christianam religionem*, Venice: Bernardinus Benalius, 30 May 1494. 8°. GW 4048; ISTC ib00414000; MEI 02018102 (bound first, no. 24 here) and **Thomas à Kempis**, *Imitatio Christi*, etc. Venice: Bernardinus Benalius, 1488. 8°. ISTC ii00017000; MEI 02018101 (bound third, no. 165 here).

-1806 Regno d'Italia, decree no. 160, 28 July 1806.

-1806 Venice, S. Giorgio Maggiore; Rossi (1806), B18: 'S. Bernardi Meditationes Ven. 1494 per Bernard. De Benaliis. It. Sermones S. Augustini ad heremitas. Ven 1495 per Simonem Bevilaquam – Io: Gerson de contempt vanitatem Ven. 1488 p. Bernard. de Benaliis. 12°'.

-Not present in Catalogo generale XV (1811), it is therefore unlikely that the book ever reached Padua.

Historical copy, Venice

19. Avicenna, *Canon medicinae* [Latin] (Lib. I–V), etc. Venice: Petrus Maufer de Maliferis, Nicolaus de Contugo et Socii, 1482–83. Folio. GW 3119; ISTC ia01421000; MEI 02018162.

-1806 Venice, S. Giorgio Maggiore; Rossi (1806), A4: '[Avicenna], Ven. 1483 per magistrum Petrum Mauser et Nicolaum de Contengo, f.'.

-1806 Regno d'Italia, decree no. 160, 28 July 1806.

-1811 Padua, Sant'Anna; Catalogo generale XV (1811), 145, no. 32: 'Avicenna, Canon medicinae etc., Venetiis, 1483'; *Fondi antichi della Biblioteca Universitaria di Padova*, 40–41.

Historical copy, Venice

20. Avicenna, *Canon medicinae* [Latin] (Lib. I–V), etc. Venice: [Bonetus Locatellus], for Octavianus Scotus, 24 Mar. 1490. 4°. GW 3122; ISTC ia01424000; MEI 02006674.

-1806 Venice, S. Giorgio Maggiore; Rossi (1806), A3: 'Avicennae Canon Medicinae transl. a Magistro Gerardo Cremonesi. Ven. 1490. impensis Octaviani Scoti 4°'.

-1806, Regno d'Italia, decree no. 160, 28 July 1806.

-1811 Padua, Sant'Anna; Catalogo generale XV (1811), 144, no. 3: 'Avicennae, Canon medicinae, 4° Ven. 1490 impensi Octav. Scoti'; *Fondi antichi della Biblioteca Universitaria di Padova*, 40–41.

Historical copy, Venice

21. Barbarus, Hermolaus, *Castigationes Plinianae et Pomponii Melae*, Rome: Eucharius Silber, 24 Nov. 1492, 13 Feb. 1493. Folio. GW 3340; ISTC ib00100000; MEI 02108479.

-1789 Venice, S. Giorgio Maggiore; Morelli's survey (1789), fasc. 1, 4: no marks.

Historical copy, Venice

22. Barbatia, Andreas, *De praestantia cardinalium*. Ed: Johannes de Gradibus. Venice: 1493. Lost edition.

Barbatia (or Barbazza) was a Sicilian jurist active in Bologna (*c.* 1399–1479). Giovanni or Jean Gradi was a Milanese jurist and counsellor of the King of France during the French occupation of Milan, active in Italy and in France (*c.* 1490–1515), recorded as commentator and editor in 22 editions in Edit16 and in several French (mostly Lyonnaise) editions; clearly deserving of further investigation. The work *De praestantia cardinalium*, dedicated to Cardinal Bessarion, was printed twice in Bologna, apparently with the same colophon (another fact worth investigating further): Barbatia, Andreas, *De praestantia cardinalium*. Add: Troilus Malvitius, *Tabula*; *De oblationibus ecclesiae vel altaris*. Bologna: Ugo Rugerius, 12 Oct. 1487. Folio. 66 leaves. GW 3350; ISTC ib00106080. Printed again in Bologna: Ugo Rugerius, 12 Oct. 1487. Folio. 62 leaves. GW 3351; ISTC ib00106100. A close reprint of the Bologna edition, with the same *titulus* mentioning the dedication to Bessarion and the printing by Ugo Rugerius of Bologna, was put to press again in the sixteenth century, in Milan: Barbazza, Andrea, *Tractatus solemnis excellentissimi i.v. monarce domini Andree Barbatia de prestantia cardinalium feliciter incipit*. Mediolani: impressum per Leonardum Pachel: ad expensis Io. Jacobi & fratrum de Lignano, 1508 die viij Februarij. Folio. 38 leaves. EDIT16 CNCE 4147 (two copies in Naples and Trento). It is therefore possible that an edition of this work, edited by Jean Gradi, was published in Venice in 1493.

Rossi's entry (1806) reads: 'B7: Barbatiae Andreae Tractatus de praestantia Cardinalium a Io. de Gradibus emendatus Ven. 1493 absq. typ. F.°'. The entry no. 19 in Padua, Catalogo generale XV (1811), 144 also mentions the work: 'Barbate, De praestantia Cardinalium. fol. Ven. 1493'.

The alternative would be to consider the entry a conflation of two editions, an occurrence encountered elsewhere. However, the two fifteenth-century editions of Barbazza are not edited by Jean Gradi, nor any other edition edited by Gradi could be found printed in Venice in 1493,

although apparently he did edit one of Barbatia's works: *De Cardinalibus legatis a Latere* (included in *Tractatus universi iuris*, 22 vols (Venice 1584–86), XIII, 2, fol. 131).

Historical copy, Venice

23. Bernardus Claravallensis, Pseudo-, *Modus bene vivendi in christianam religionem*, Venice: Bernardinus Benalius, 30 May 1492. 8°. GW 4047; ISTC ib00413000; MEI 02125145.

Formerly bound with other Casanatense incunables: **Thomas à Kempis**, *Imitatio Christi*, etc. Venice: Petrus de Quarengiis, Bergomensis, and Giovanni Maria di Occimiano, 23 Apr. 1493. 8°. ISTC ii00028000; MEI 02125175; VOL INC.1292 (no. 166 here) and **Augustinus, Aurelius, Pseudo-**, *Sermones ad heremitas*, Venice: Vincentius Benalius, 26 Jan. 1492/1493. 8°. GW 3005; ISTC ia01317000; MEI 02125177; VOL INC.1293 (no. 17 here); see seventeenth-/ eighteenth-century manuscript index on front flyleaf IIr of this copy. The three volumes were described as bound in a composite volume in the printed catalogue by G. B. Audiffredi, *Bibliothecae Casanatensis Catalogus librorum typis impressorum* (Romae 1761), vol. 1, 345a.

-1493-*c.* 1600 Venice, S. Giorgio Maggiore; fifteenth-century inscription on a1r: 'Iste liber est Congregationis monachorum s. Justine de padua ordinis sancti Benedicti deputatus in sancto Georgio maiore venetiarum, signatus 979'.

-*c.* 1600 Flavius Ciccolus of Bevagna: inscription on a1r: 'Flavius Ciccolus Meuanas etc. habuit hunc librum dono etc'.

-*c.* 1761 Rome, Biblioteca Casanatense; acquired in the eighteenth century as the other two parts of the composite volume are listed in Audiffredi (1761).

Rome, Biblioteca Casanatense: VOL INC.1294

24. Bernardus Claravallensis, Pseudo-, *Modus bene vivendi in christianam religionem*, Venice: Bernardinus Benalius, 30 May 1494. 8°. GW 4048; ISTC ib00414000; MEI 02018102.

Bound first with: **Augustinus, Aurelius, Pseudo-**, *Sermones ad heremitas*, Venice: Simon Bevilaqua, 4 Nov. 1495. 8°. GW 3007; ISTC ia01319000; MEI 02018099 (bound second, no. 18 here) and **Thomas à Kempis**, *Imitatio Christi*, etc. Venice: Bernardinus Benalius, 1488. 8°. ISTC ii00017000; MEI 02018101 (bound third, no. 165 here).

-1806 Regno d'Italia, decree no. 160, 28 July 1806.

-1806 Venice, S. Giorgio Maggiore; Rossi (1806), B18: 'S. Bernardi Meditationes Ven. 1494 per Bernard. De Benaliis. It. Sermones S. Augustini ad heremitas. Ven 1495 per Simonem Bevilaquam – Io: Gerson de contempt vanitatem Ven. 1488 p. Bernard. de Benaliis. 12°'.

Not present in Catalogo generale XV (1811), it is therefore unlikely that the book ever reached Padua.

Historical copy, Venice

25. Bernardus Claravallensis, *Sermones super Cantica canticorum*, Brescia: Angelus Britannicus, 28 Jan. 1500. 4° and 8°. GW 3938; ISTC; ib00431000; MEI 02003644.

-1501 Piacenza, Benedictines, S. Sixtus; inscription in a sixteenth-century hand: 'Iste liber est monasterii sancti sisti placentiae Congregationis Cassinensis alias sanctae Justinae de padua'.

-*c.* 1600–1806 Venice, S. Giorgio Maggiore; on the front flyleaf in an eighteenth-century hand: 'Est Sancti Georgii Venetiarum. Ad usum D. Mauretii Bergomensi' (see no. 87 here).

-1806 Brescia, Biblioteca Queriniana; acquired in unknown circumstances following the Napoleonic suppressions.

Brescia, Biblioteca Queriniana: Inc.B.II.2m2

26. Beroaldus, Philippus, *Annotationes centum*, etc. Brescia: Bernardinus de Misintis, for Angelus Britannicus, [17 Dec.] 1496. Folio. GW 4114; ISTC ib00465000; MEI 02008343.

-after 1496–1806 Venice, S. Giorgio Maggiore; ownership note on the front flyleaf in an eighteenth-century hand: 'Est bibl.ae S. Georgij M.is Venet.um'.

-1806 Venice, S. Giorgio Maggiore; Rossi (1806), B9: 'Beroaldi Philippi annotationes centum, et alia eiusd. – Angeli Politiani miscelleanorum Centuria prima; Politiani Panepistemon; eiusd. Praelectio in Aristot. Librum cui titulus Lamia; Philippi rursus Beroaldi Appendix aliorum annotationum; Io. Baptistis Pii annotamenta. Omnia simul impressa Brixiae 1496 sumptibus Angeli Britannici. 4°'.

-1806 Regno d'Italia, decree no. 160, 28 July 1806.

-March 1807–1818(?) Padua, Sant'Anna; Rossi (March 1807); Catalogo generale XV (1811), 144, no. 4: 'Beroaldi, Annotationes et Politiani, Miscellanearum, folio, Brixiae, 1496, per Angelum Britanicum'; *Fondi antichi della Biblioteca Universitaria di Padova*, 40–41.

-1818(?)-*c.* 1840 Padua, S. Francesco Grande, Sala Carmeli. When the monastery of Sant'Anna had to be cleared, some selected volumes were transferred in part to the Pubblica Libreria (the Biblioteca Universitaria of Padua), in part to the Sala Carmeli of the former convent of S. Francesco Grande. A document dated 1818 records the transfer of books from S. Giorgio Maggiore into cupboards A, B, and C of Sala Carmeli. Padua, Catalogo Gnocchi (1818).

-*c.* 1840 transfer to the Biblioteca Universitaria of Padua: Ravegnani, *Le biblioteche*, 65–68; *Fondi antichi della Biblioteca Universitaria di Padova*, 40–41.

Padua, Biblioteca Universitaria: Sec. XV 643

27. Beroaldus, Philippus, *De felicitate*, Bologna: Franciscus (Plato) de Benedictis, 1 Apr. 1495. 4°. GW 4132; ISTC ib00482000; MEI 02018106. Bound fourth with: **Mancinellus, Antonius**, *Scribendi orandique modus* (edition unidentified; bound first, no. 115 here); **Ferettus, Nicolaus**, *De elegantia linguae latinae*, Forlì: Hieronymus Medesanus, 25 May 1495. 4°. GW 9783; ISTC if00099000; MEI 02018108 (bound second, no. 75 here); **Vergerius, Petrus Paulus**, *De ingenuis moribus ac liberalibus studiis*. Ed: Johannes Calphurnius. Comm: Johannes Bonardus. Add:

Basilius Magnus: *De legendis antiquorum libris* (Tr: Leonardus Brunus Aretinus). Xenophon: *Hiero de tyrannide* (Tr: Leonardus Brunus Aretinus). Plutarchus: *De liberis educandis* (Tr: Guarinus Veronensis). S. Hieronymus: *De officiis liberorum erga parentes admonitio*, Venice: Johannes Tacuinus, de Tridino, 22 Sept. 1497. 4°. ISTC iv00139000; MEI 02018105 (bound third, no. 178 here).

-1806 Regno d'Italia, decree no. 160, 28 July 1806.

-1806 Venice, S. Giorgio Maggiore; Rossi (1806), M52: 'Mancinelli Antonii Scribendi, orandique modus, Forilivii 1495 p. Hieron. Medasanum. – Pauli Vergerii de ingenuis moribus cum comment. Io. Bonardi – Basilii de legendis antiquorum libris opusculum – Traductio ex Xenophonte Leonardi Aretini de Tyranide – Guarini Veronensis in Plutarcum praefatio, 1497 Ven. p. Io. Tacuinum. – Philippi Beroaldi de felicitate opusculum Bononiae 1495 p. Platonem de Benedictiis. Omnia uno tantum volumine in 4°. In making an entry for this composite volume, it is clear that the cataloguer merged two editions, noting the opening of an edition of Antonius Mancinellus and the imprint information for another edition, by Nicolaus Ferettus, bound behind. Unfortunately, it is not possible to determine which of the several editions of Mancinellus' *Scribendi orandique modus* is the one represented here.

Not present in Catalogo generale XV (1811), it is therefore unlikely that the book ever reached Padua.

Historical copy, Venice

28. [**Biblia Latina**] – *Interpretationes Hebraicorum nominum*, Venice: Nicolaus Jenson, 1476. Folio. CIBN B-382; GW 4222; ISTC ib00547000; MEI 02011874.

-1476–1797 Venice, S. Giorgio Maggiore: evidence from fifteenth-century illumination (representation of St George on a5r) and erased ex-libris.

-1809 Vienna, Imperial Library, VII. E. 8, apparently taken away by the French in 1809 (CIBN).

-1809 Paris, Bibliothèque nationale.

Paris, Bibliothèque nationale de France: Rés. Vélins 81

29. Biblia latina, Venice: Nicolaus Jenson, 1479. Folio. GW 4238; ISTC ib00563000; MEI 02107092.

-1479-*c.* 1500 Bollani family of Venice; coat of arms on a5r.

-*c.* 1500–1789 Venice, S. Giorgio Maggiore; seventeenth-century inscription on a2a: 'Est Bibliothecae S. Georgij Maioris Venetiarum'.

-1789 Venice, S. Giorgio Maggiore; Morelli's survey (1789), fasc. 1, 4: marked with + and crossed out.

-1797–1815 Paris, Bibliothèque nationale: BnF archives list (1797), fasc. 2, no. 3: 'Biblia sacra. Venet 1479 in fol., sur velin, coll. 76, no. 17 velin'; Cicogna (1797): 'Dalla libreria di s. Giorgio Maggiore furono portati a Parigi nel 1797 i seguenti Codici manuscritti [...] Edizioni del secolo XV [...] 3. Biblia sacra f. membr. Venetiis 1479. Ienson'. The volume did not return to the Marciana library, as should have been the case according to Cicogna (1797): 'Per la generosità di Francesco I di gloriosissima memoria presso che tutti cotesti libri son ritornati nel 1815, e riposti nella Marciana'. At the time of restitution, in 1815, a different, paper, copy was returned to the Marciana, the copy now Inc. V. 0334 (MEI 02014726), which in fact has earlier French provenance. Between 20 and 23 March 1816 the French authorities returned to the Marciana 417 of the 432 books requisitioned at the time of the revolution; see Biblioteca Nazionale Marciana, Archivio, b. 1816, 'Nota delli codici manoscritti [ed edizioni del secolo XV] della Imp. Regia Biblioteca di Venezia consegnati alli commissarii francesi Berthollet e Monge [...] nel giorno 11 ottobre 1797'; in this list the edition, which does not correspond to the one now in the Marciana library, is so described 'n. 230: Biblia Sacra, In Membranis [underlined], Venetiis, Jenson, 1479'. The only copy on parchment now in Paris, Bibliothèque nationale de France, CIBN B-395 (Rés. Vélins 82) presents early French illumination and a French coat of arms and is said to have been

purchased by the library in 1813 at the sale of the banker Daniel Henri Schérer, *Catalogue des livres précieux et de la plus belle condition, de M. Schérer* (Paris 1812), 2, n. 2; it is not clear, therefore, the movement of the S. Giorgio copy, and whether the volume was returned to Venice in 1815 and left from there for Vienna, however Valentinelli gives an idea of the complex relationship among Paris, Venice, and Vienna at pp. 20–23.
Vienna, Österreichische Nationalbibliothek: Ink 8.E.10

30. *Biblia Latina*, Venice: Franciscus Renner, de Heilbronn, 1480. Folio and 4°. GW 4241; ISTC ib00566000; MEI 00206141.
-1480-*c.* 1750 Venice, S. Giorgio Maggiore; inscription on D11v: 'Iste liber est monachorum congregationis S. Justine de Padua deputatus in S. Georgii maioris Venetiarum | 773.'
-*c.* 1750–1787 Venice, Maffeo Pinelli (1735–1785), hereditary director of the official Venetian Press: the catalogue of his library was prepared by Jacopo Morelli, the librarian of St Mark, in 1787 (see *Bibliotheca Maphaei Pinelli veneti magno jam studio collecta a J. Morellio Bibliothecae Venetae D. Marci custode descripta et annotationibus illustrata* (Venetiis, Typis Caroli Palesii, 1787), vol. I, no. 132); all the books were purchased by the London bookseller James Edwards for £600 and auctioned by him in 1789.
-1789 Oxford, Bodleian Library; purchased in 1789 at the Pinelli sale (lot 5041), for £1.10.0.
Oxford, Bodleian Library: Auct. M 2.12

31. *Biblia Latina* (cum postillis Nicolai de Lyra), etc. Venice: [Johannes Herbort, de Seligenstadt], for Johannes de Colonia, Nicolaus Jenson et Socii, 31 July 1481. Folio. GW 4286; ISTC ib00611000; MEI 02009688.
This edition consisted originally of four volumes. Yet it seems that sometime before 1660, vols 1–3 made their way out of the library of S. Giorgio Maggiore, whereas vol. 4 remained in S. Giorgio until 1806, when it was listed by Rossi and then by the Catalogo generale XV (1811) along with

another volume: **Nicolaus de Lyra**, *Postilla super Epistolas et Evangelia quadragesimalia*, [Lyons]: Nicolaus Wolf, 10 Feb. 1500/1501. 4°. ISTC in00120600; MEI 02006855 (see no. 124 here).
-1481–1660 Venice, S. Giorgio Maggiore; inscription on vol. 1, c1v and on vol. 2, P1r (deleted): 'Iste liber est Congregatio(n)is S. Iustine Patavine deputatus ad usum fratrum instantium in S. Georgio Maiore Venetiae signatus nno. 893.' This information is in regard to all four volumes.
-1660 Venice, Giovanni Maria Zilotti, subdeacon of the parish church of SS. Simone e Giuda (S. Simeon Piccolo); inscription on the front flyleaf of vol. 2: 'Iste liber erit ad usum Presbyteri Ioannis Marie Zilotti Veneti suddiaconi Titulati Parochialis, et Collegiate Eccl(esi)e S(anc)tis Simonis et Jude Venetiarum 1660.' This information is in regard only to vols 1–3, today in Locarno.
-1806 Regno d'Italia, decree no. 160, 28 July 1806.
-1806 Venice, S. Giorgio Maggiore; Rossi (1806), L47: 'Eiusdem (Nicolaus de Lyra) commentaria in Epist. D. Pauli sine l. 1481 per Io. de Colonia, et socio F.°'. This information is in regard only to vol. 4.
March 1807–1818(?) Padua, Sant'Anna; Rossi (March 1807); Catalogo generale XV (1811), 145, no. 25: 'De Lyra, Postillae etc., folio, 1500, per Nicolaum Volf, et 1481. 8'; *Fondi antichi della Biblioteca Universitaria di Padova*, 40–41. This information is in regard only to vol. 4 (today missing) listed in the catalogue along with no. 124, although probably never bound together, as the present seventeenth-century binding shows.
-*c.* 1831-*c.* 1900 Locarno, Scuola Tecnica: erased stamp on the front flyleaf of vol. 2: 'Scuola Tecnica di Locarno'. This information is in regard to vols 1–3.
Locarno, Biblioteca Madonna del Sasso: MdS 57 Ba 7–9 (vols 1–3)
Historical copy, Venice (vol. 4)

32. *Biblia Latina* [Italian], [Venice: Octavianus Scotus, 1481]. Folio. GW 4314; ISTC ib00642000; MEI 02107193.

-1481–1628 Venice, S. Giorgio Maggiore; inscription on fol. 12r: 'Iste liber est monachorum congregationis S. Justine de Padua ordinis S. Benedicti deputatus ad usum fratrum habitantium in monasterio S. Georgii Maioris Venetiarum signatus numero 803'.

-c. 1628–1773 Trieste, Jesuits; inscription on fol. 2r: 'Collegij Tergestini Societatis Jesu inscriptus Catalogo 1628'.

-1773 Vienna, Hofbibliothek; following the dissolution of the order.

Wien, Österreichische Nationalbibliothek: 17.c. 16

33. Biblia latina, Venice: Johannes Herbort, de Seligenstadt, 30 Apr. 1484. 4°. GW 4255; ISTC ib00580000; MEI 02017632.

-1484-c. 1806 Venice, S. Giorgio Maggiore; inscription on fol. 408r: 'Congregationis s. Justine de padua deputatus monachis in monasterio s. Georgij maioris [...] habitantibus ac signatus numero 281'. The volume probably left the library during the period of the Napoleonic dissolution, although it may have left even before then.

Lucca, Biblioteca Statale: INC 59

34. Biblia latina, Venice: Simon Bevilaqua, 22 Nov. 1494. 4°. GW 4274; ISTC ib00597000; MEI 02018224.

-1806 Venice, S. Giorgio Maggiore; Rossi (1806), B11: 'Biblia sacra, Ven. 1494 per Simonem Bevilaquam, 4'.

-1806, Regno d'Italia, decree 28 July 1806.

-March 1807–1818(?) Padua, Sant'Anna: after the suppression of the monastery of S. Giorgio Maggiore in 1806, the volume was probably deposited in the former monastery of the Benedictine nuns of Sant'Anna in Padua, as with the other books that subsequently entered the Biblioteca Universitaria, even if it cannot be identified in the lists of books selected from that warehouse.

-1818(?)-c. 1840 Padua, S. Francesco Grande, Sala Carmeli. When the monastery of Sant'Anna had to be cleared, some selected volumes were transferred in part to the Pubblica Libreria (the Biblioteca Universitaria of Padua), in part to the Sala Carmeli of the former convent of S. Francesco Grande. A document dated 1818 records the transfer of books from S. Giorgio Maggiore into cupboards A, B, and C of Sala Carmeli. Padua, Catalogo Gnocchi (1818).

-c. 1840 transfer to the Biblioteca Universitaria of Padua: Ravegnani, *Le biblioteche*, 65–68; *Fondi antichi della Biblioteca Universitaria di Padova*, 40–41.

Padua, Biblioteca Universitaria: Sec. XV 772

35. Blanchellus, Menghus, *Super logicam Pauli Veneti expositio et quaestiones*, Venice: Antonius de Strata, de Cremona, 27 Aug. 1483. 4°. GW 4406; ISTC ib00693000; MEI 02008359.

after 1483–1806 Venice, S. Giorgio Maggiore; ownership note on frontleaf in a late seventeenth-century hand: 'Est S. Georgii Maioris Venetiarum'.

-1806 Regno d'Italia, decree no. 160, 28 July 1806.

-1806 Venice, S. Giorgio Maggiore; Rossi (1806), M54: 'Menghi Fayentini in Pauli Veneti Logicam Comment. Ven. 1484 per Ant.m de Strata 4' (date mistakenly given as 1484).

-March 1807–1818(?) Padua, Sant'Anna; Rossi (March 1807); Catalogo generale XV (1811), 145, no. 47: 'Menghi, In Pauli Veneti Logicam commentarius, 4, Venetiis, 1484'; *Fondi antichi della Biblioteca Universitaria di Padova*, 40–41.

-1818(?)-c. 1840 Padua, S. Francesco Grande, Sala Carmeli. When the monastery of Sant'Anna had to be cleared, some selected volumes were transferred in part to the Pubblica Libreria (the Biblioteca Universitaria of Padua), in part to the Sala Carmeli of the former convent of S. Francesco Grande. A document dated 1818 records the transfer of books from S. Giorgio Maggiore into cupboards A, B, and C of Sala Carmeli. Padua, Catalogo Gnocchi (1818).

-c. 1840 transfer to the Biblioteca Universitaria of Padua: Ravegnani, *Le biblioteche*, 65–68; *Fondi antichi della Biblioteca Universitaria di Padova*, 40–41.

Padua, Biblioteca Universitaria: Sec. XV
Duplicato 89

36. Blondus, Flavius, *Historiarum ab inclinatione Romanorum imperii decades,* etc. Venice: Thomas de Blavis, de Alexandria, 28 June 1484. Folio. GW 4420 + M33466; ISTC ib00699000; MEI 02008611.
-1484–1513 Andreas Mocenicus, apostolic protonotary.
-1513–before 1806 Venice, S. Giorgio Maggiore; inscription: 'Reverendus dominus Andreas Mocenicus protonotarius pro anime sue salute diui Georgii maioris cenobio dicauit signatus numero 124'. Andrea Mocenigo died in 1513.
-First half of the 20th century Baveno, Francesco Cazzamini Mussi (1888–1952): ex-libris; probably acquired on the market following the suppression of religious institutions.
-1958 Milan, Biblioteca Trivulziana; the book collection of the writer was purchased by the Library in 1958 from the Hospital of Abbiategrasso, to whom it had been bequeathed.
Milan, Biblioteca Trivulziana: Triv. Inc. B 138

37. Boccaccio, Giovanni, *De montibus, silvis, fontibus,* Venice: [Vindelinus de Spira], 13 Jan. 1473. Folio. GW 4482; ISTC ib00756000; MEI 02108480.
-1765 Venice, S. Giorgio Maggiore: included in the list published in Gerbert (1765) as assigned to Jenson.
-1789 Venice, S. Giorgio Maggiore; Morelli's survey (1789), fasc. 2, n.n. (but no. 16): crossed out.
Historical copy, Venice

38. Boethius, *De consolatione philosophiae,* Nuremberg: Anton Koberger, 8 June 1495. 4°. GW 4559; ISTC ib00799000; MEI 02017432.
-1600–1797(?)Venice, S. Giorgio Maggiore; seventeenth-century inscription on [*1r]: 'Est S. Georgii Maioris Venetiarum'.
-1886 Cambridge; purchased in 1886.
Cambridge, University Library, Inc. 5.A.7.2[898]

39. Boethius, *Opera,* Venice: Johannes and Gregorius de Gregoriis, de Forlivio, 1497/1498–1499. Folio. GW 4512; ISTC ib00768000; MEI 02008246.
-1806 Venice, S. Giorgio Maggiore; Rossi (1806), B10: 'Boetii Severini Opera omnia. Ven. 1497 per Io. et Gregorium de Forlivio. F.°'.
-1811 Padua, Sant'Anna; Catalogo generale XV (1811), 144, no. 21: 'Boetii, Opera omnia, folio, Venetiis, 1497'; *Fondi antichi della Biblioteca Universitaria di Padova,* 40–41.
-1818(?)-c. 1840 Padua, S. Francesco Grande, Sala Carmeli. When the monastery of Sant'Anna had to be cleared, some selected volumes were transferred in part to the Pubblica Libreria (the Biblioteca Universitaria of Padua), in part to the Sala Carmeli of the former convent of S. Francesco Grande. A document dated 1818 records the transfer of books from S. Giorgio Maggiore into cupboards A, B, and C of Sala Carmeli. Padua, Catalogo Gnocchi (1818).
-c. 1840 transfer to the Biblioteca Universitaria of Padua: Ravegnani, *Le biblioteche,* 65–68; *Fondi antichi della Biblioteca Universitaria di Padova,* 40–41.
Padua, Biblioteca Universitaria: Sec. XV 678

40. Bologninus, Ludovicus, *Syllogianthon,* Bologna: Ugo Rugerius, 10 Jan. 1486. Folio. GW 4637; ISTC ib00842000; MEI 02006700.
-1806 Regno d'Italia, decree no. 160, 28 July 1806.
-1806 Venice, S. Giorgio Maggiore; Rossi (1806), B16: 'Bolognini Ludovici Opera. Bononiae 1486 p. Hugonem Rugerium F.°'.
-1811 Padua, Sant'Anna; Catalogo generale XV (1811), 145, no. 41: 'Bolognini, Opera, fol. Bononiae 1486'; *Fondi antichi della Biblioteca Universitaria di Padova,* 40–41.
Historical copy, Venice

41. Bonifacius VIII, Pont. Max., *Liber sextus Decretalium* (with gloss of Johannes Andreae). Ed: Alexander de Nevo. Add: Johannes Andreae: *Super arboribus consanguinitatis et affinitatis,*

Venice: Nicolaus Jenson, 1476. Folio. GW 4856; ISTC ib00984000; MEI 02008353.

-1476–1789 Venice, S. Giorgio Maggiore; assigned by Lilian Armstrong on the basis of the decoration by the Pico Master (St George killing the dragon in the lower margin); an erased inscription and a manuscript index of contents can be found in this volume as well as in another edition from S. Giorgio now in the Rylands Library (**Clemens V, Pont. Max.**, *Constitutiones* (cum apparatu Johannis Andreae). Add: *Decretales extravagantes Johannis XXII*, Venice: Nicolaus Jenson, 1476. Folio. GW 7098; ISTC ic00728000; MEI 02008354; no. 56 here): 'Iste liber est monachorum congregationis Sanctae Iustinae de Padua deputatus monasterio Sancti Georgii Maioris Venetiarum, signatus numero 539' (with thanks to Julianne Simpson for providing specialist imaging). As was the custom, these two editions were sold together as one item.

-1789 Venice, S. Giorgio Maggiore; Morelli's survey (1789), fasc. 1, 3: 'esemplare stampato in carta pecora con miniature', marked with +.

-1789–1792 Étienne Charles Loménie de Brienne (1727–1794); French cardinal and politician who purchased extensively during his Italian tour in 1789–1790; not listed in François-Xavier Laire, *Index librorum ab inventa typographia ad annum 1500. Catalogue des livres de m *** par G. de Bure* (Sens, 1791) which was used as sale catalogue for the 1792 auction of the library.

-1797–1892 George John, 2nd Earl Spencer (1758–1834); acquired around 1797, according to Thomas Frognall Dibdin, *Bibliotheca Spenceriana. A Descriptive Catalogue of the Books Printed in the Fifteenth Century and of Many Valuable First Editions in the Library of George John Earl Spencer* (London, 1815), vol. IV, 292–93 apparently from the library of Lomenie de Brienne.

-1892 Manchester; purchased from the 5th Earl by Mrs Rylands in 1892 for the Rylands Library. ***Manchester, John Rylands University Library: 9961***

42. Bossius, Donatus, *Chronica. Series episcoporum et archiepiscoporum Mediolanensium*,

Milan: Antonius Zarotus, for the author, 1 Mar. 1492. Folio. GW 4952; ISTC ib01040000; MEI 02108481.

-1789 Venice, S. Giorgio Maggiore; Morelli's survey (1789), fasc. 1, 4: marked with +.

Historical copy, Venice

43. Brunus Aretinus, Leonardus, *De bello Italico adversus Gothos gesto*, [Venice]: Nicolaus Jenson, [before July] 1471. 4°. GW 5601; ISTC ib01235000; MEI 02019417.

-before 1789 Venice, S. Giorgio Maggiore; Morelli's survey (1789), fasc. 2: '*Mancanze: – A S. Giorgio Maggiore, libri notati nell'Indice, che non si trovano. Aretini Leonardi, De Bello Gothico, Venetiis, Jenson, 1471, fo.* [...] Varro, *De lingua latina*, fol., sine ulla nota, saec. XV. Degli Uberti, *Dittamondo*. Vicenza, 1474, fo. [...]'; published in Fulin, *Vicende della libreria in SS. Gio. e Paolo*, 293 n. 1.

Historical copy, Venice

44. Brutus, Jacobus, *Corona aurea*, Venice: Johannes Tacuinus, de Tridino, 15 Jan. 1496/1497. 4°. GW 5657; ISTC ib01262000; MEI 02008197.

-c. 1497–1806 Venice, S. Giorgio Maggiore; old shelfmarks and erased ownership inscription; seventeenth-century note of 'D. Faustinus Venetus' (Faustinus Spinelli), a *professo* in S. Giorgio Maggiore attested in 1638 (Arcangelo Bossi, *Matricula monachorum congregationis Casinensis ordinis Sancti Benedicti* (Cesena, 1983), 200).

-1817 Padua: Catalogo pregio (1817), 10, no. 415: 'Corona aurea. Venetiis, 1496. 4°'.

Padua, Biblioteca Universitaria: Sec. XV Duplicato 5 quater

45. Burlaeus, Gualtherus, *Expositio in Aristotelis Ethica Nicomachea* (with text), Venice: Octavianus Scotus, 10 May 1481. Folio. GW 5778; ISTC ib01300000; MEI 02008218.

-1817 Padua: Catalogo pregio (1817), 3, no. 68: 'Burlaei, In Aristotelem. Venetiis, 1481. fo.'.

Historical copy, Venice

46. Caesar, Gaius Julius, *Commentarii*, Venice: Nicolaus Jenson, 1471. Folio. GW 5864; ISTC ic00017000; MEI 02108482.

-1789 Venice, S. Giorgio Maggiore; Morelli's survey (1789), fasc. 1, 4: marked with +.

-1806–1814? Milan, Regno d'Italia: books gone to Milan, 4 Sept. 1806, item four.

Historical Copy, Venice

47. Caracciolus, Robertus, *Sermones de adventu, Sermo de S. Joseph, Sermo de Beatitudine, Sermones de divina caritate, Sermones de immortalitate animae.* Add: Dominicus Bollanus: *De conceptione B.V.M.*, [Venice: Johannes de Colonia and Johannes Manthen, about 1477–78]. 4°. GW 6047; ISTC ic00139000; MEI 02008350.

-1478–1806 Venice, S. Giorgio Maggiore; contemporary illumination, on the verso of the last leaf: 'Iste liber est congregationis Sanctae Iustinae de Padua ordinis sancti Benedicti, deputatus monasterio Sancti Georgii Maioris Venetiarum, signatus numero 624'; in a late seventeenth-century hand on fol. 1r: 'Est Sancti Georgii Maioris Venetiarum'.

-1806 Regno d'Italia, decree no. 160, 28 July 1806.

-1806 Venice, S. Giorgio Maggiore; Rossi (1806), L44: 'De Licio Roberti Praedicationes sine loco, an. et typ. 4°'.

-after March 1807/1811–1818(?) Padua, Sant'Anna; Rossi (March 1807); Catalogo generale XV (1811), 146, no. 50: 'De Licio, Praedicationes, 4 (saeculo XV)'; *Fondi antichi della Biblioteca Universitaria di Padova*, 40–41.

-1818(?)-*c.* 1840 Padua, S. Francesco Grande, Sala Carmeli. When the monastery of Sant'Anna had to be cleared, some selected volumes were transferred in part to the Pubblica Libreria (the Biblioteca Universitaria), in part to the Sala Carmeli of the former convent of S. Francesco Grande. A document dated 1818 records the transfer of books from S. Giorgio Maggiore into cupboards A, B, and C of Sala Carmeli. Padua, Catalogo Gnocchi (1818).

-*c.* 1840 transfer to the Biblioteca Universitaria of Padua: Ravegnani, *Le biblioteche*, 65–68; *Fondi antichi della Biblioteca Universitaria di Padova*, 40–41.

Padua, Biblioteca Universitaria: Sec. XV 1006

48. Caracciolus, Robertus, *Specchio della fede*, Venice: [Johannes Rubeus Vercellensis, for] Giovanni da Bergamo, [after 11 Apr. 1495]. Folio. GW 6115; ISTC ic00187000; MEI 02008264.

Bound first with: **Lucanus, Marcus Annaeus**, *Cesariano (Libro dell'origine e dei fatti di Giulio Cesare)*, Venice: Alovisius de Sancta Lucia, 1 Mar. 1492. Folio. ISTC il00311000; MEI 02008265 (no. 110 here).

-1806 Regno d'Italia, decree no. 160, 28 July 1806.

-1806 Venice, S. Giorgio Maggiore; Rossi (1806), C19: 'Caracciolo fra Roberto Specchio della fede Ven. 1495 sine typ. – Libro denominato il Cesariano, ovvero dei fatti di Cesare. Ven. 1492 s. typ. F.°'.

-March 1807–1818(?) Padua, Sant'Anna; Rossi (March 1807); Catalogo generale XV (1811), 145, no. 38: 'Caracciolo, Specchio della fede, folio, Venetiis, 1495; v'è unito Libro denominato Cesariano ovvero de' fatti di Cesare, Venetiis 1492'; *Fondi antichi della Biblioteca Universitaria di Padova*, 40–41.

-1813–1831(?) Padua, S. Francesco Grande, Sala Carmeli. When the monastery of Sant'Anna had to be cleared, some selected volumes were transferred in part to the Pubblica Libreria (the Biblioteca Universitaria), in part to the Sala Carmeli of the former convent of S. Francesco Grande. A document dated 1818 records the transfer of books from S. Giorgio Maggiore into cupboards A, B, and C of Sala Carmeli. Padua, Catalogo Gnocchi (1818).

-*c.* 1840 transfer to the Biblioteca Universitaria of Padua: Ravegnani, *Le biblioteche*, 65–68; *Fondi antichi della Biblioteca Universitaria di Padova*, 40–41.

Padua, Biblioteca Universitaria, Sec. XV 406/1

49. Carcano, Michael de, *Sermonarium de decem praeceptis per quadragesimam*, Venice: Johannes and Gregorius de Gregoriis, de Forlivio, [for Alexander Calcedonius, between 18 Jan. and 1 Mar.] 1492/1493. 4°. GW 6133; ISTC ic00193000; MEI 02006705.

-1806 Regno d'Italia, decree no. 160, 28 July 1806.
-1806 Venice, S. Giorgio Maggiore; Rossi (1806), M55: 'Michaelis de Mediolano Quadragesimale. Ven. 1492 p. Gregorium de Gregoriis 4°'.
-March 1807–1818(?) Padua, Sant'Anna; Rossi (March 1807); Catalogo generale XV (1811), 146, no. 53: 'De Mediolano, Quadragesimale, 4° Ven. 1492'; *Fondi antichi della Biblioteca Universitaria di Padova*, 40–41.
Historical copy, Venice

50. Cassianus, Johannes, *De institutis coenobiorum*. Add: *Collationes patrum XXIV*, Basel: [Johann Amerbach, after 24 Sept.] 1485. Folio. GW 6160; ISTC ic00233000; MEI 00202002.

-*c.* 1485–*c.* 1700 Venice, S. Giorgio Maggiore; inscription in a fifteenth-century hand below the colophon: 'Est monachorum congregationis S. Justine de Padua deputatus monachis in monasterio S. Georgij maioris Venetiarum habitantibus signatus no. 781 [crossed out and the new number added, in the same hand] 886'.
-1700–1797 Polirone (Mantua), Benedictines, S. Benedictus; stamp and eighteenth-century inscription on the title-page: 'Est monasterij S. Benedicti Mantuani'.
-1797 Mantua, Biblioteca Teresiana: probably acquired following the Napoleonic suppressions of religious institutions.
Mantova, Biblioteca Teresiana: Inc. 291

50 bis. Cassianus, Johannes, *De institutis coenobiorum*. Add: *Collationes patrum XXIV*, Venice: [Dionysius Bertochus], 1491. Folio. GW 6161; ISTC ic00234000; MEI 02145483.

-1491–1600 Venice, S. Giorgio Maggiore; a copy is listed as no. 29 in the Inchiesta della Congregazione dell'Indice (RICI): 'Nomina librorum omnium, qui in monasterio S. Georgii maioris Venetiarum secundum indicem librorum prohibitorum nuper Sanctissimi D. N. Clementis papae VIII iussu editum, aut omnino, aut donec emendentur prohibiti sunt, una cum nominibus eorum, quorum vsibus deputati fuerunt. […] Ad usum bibliothecae 1,7,13,23,26,29,31,32,34,35,40,43,49' (Biblioteca Apostolica Vaticana, Vat. lat. 11286, fol. 341r - 341v, c.1600), for which see https://rici.vatlib.it/elenchi/view?id=4251 (ELE 4251; BIB 13114). This list contains only 54 entries and, with the exception of this incunable, they relate to 16th century editions. This is not a list of the books found in the library, but only of books relating to prohibited books. This edition does not appear in the later documentary sources for the reconstruction of the collection.
Historical copy, Venice

51. Celsus, A. Cornelius, *De medicina*, Venice: Johannes Rubeus Vercellensis, 8 July 1493. Folio. GW 6458; ISTC ic00366000; MEI 02018218.
Bound second with: **M. I. Iustinus**, *Iustinus hystoricus*, Venetiis: per Bartolomeum de Zanis de Portesio, 1503 die tertio febrarii. Folio. CNCE 51842 (Padua, Biblioteca Universitaria, 76 a 23). Formerly a historical copy, the identification with XV 943, which presents no provenance evidence and a 19th-century binding, was possible thanks to the identification of the first edition in the volume, listed in Rossi's catalogue (1806) and in Padua's historical catalogues, as the edition of Iustinus that is now Padua, Biblioteca Universitaria, 76 a 23, which contains the donation inscription and also presents a 19th-century binding. The two editions must have been split after entering the Biblioteca Universitaria. Among former shelfmarks written inside the books there is '35.139', found in both. It has been replaced by 'Sec. XV 943' in the Celsus edition and by 'E2.263' then by '76 a 23' in the Iustinus edition.
1493-*c.* 1513 Andrea Mocenigo.
1513–1806 Venice, S. Giorgio Maggiore; a note on a2r of the edition of Iustinus: 'Reverendus dominus Andreas Mocenicus prothonotarius pro

animae suae salute Divi Georgii Maioris coenobio dicavit, signatus 118', Andrea Mocenigo died in 1513.

-1806 Regno d'Italia, decree no. 160, 28 July 1806.

-1806 Venice, S. Giorgio Maggiore; Rossi (1806), I41: 'Iustini Historia Ven. 1503 p. Barthol. De Zanis, et] Aurelii Cornelii Celsi Libri de medicina, Ven. 1493 p. Io. Rubeum, F.ᵒ'.

-March 1807–1818(?) Padua, Sant'Anna; Rossi (March 1807); Catalogo generale XV (1811), 145, no. 27: '[Iustini, Historia, folio, et] Celsi Liber de medicina, folio, Venetiis 1493'; *Fondi antichi della Biblioteca Universitaria di Padova*, 40–41.

-1818(?)-*c.* 1840 Padua, S. Francesco Grande, Sala Carmeli. When the monastery of Sant'Anna had to be cleared, some selected volumes were transferred in part to the Pubblica Libreria (the Biblioteca Universitaria of Padua), in part to the Sala Carmeli of the former convent of S. Francesco Grande. A document dated 1818 records the transfer of books from S. Giorgio Maggiore into cupboards A, B, and C of Sala Carmeli. Padua, Catalogo Gnocchi (1818).

-*c.* 1840 transfer to the Biblioteca Universitaria of Padua: Ravegnani, *Le biblioteche*, 65–68; *Fondi antichi della Biblioteca Universitaria di Padova*, 40–41.

Padua, Biblioteca Universitaria, Sec. XV 943

52. Cicero, Marcus Tullius, *De oratore*, etc. Venice: Thomas de Blavis, de Alexandria, 16 May 1488. Folio. GW 6751; ISTC ic00663000; MEI 02008328. Bound first with: **Cicero, Marcus Tullius**, *Orator*, etc. Venice: Bonetus Locatellus, for Octavianus Scotus, 16 July 1492. Folio. GW 6756; ISTC ic00653000; MEI 02008329 (no. 53 here).

-1492–1806 Venice, S. Giorgio Maggiore; on the first blank leaf in an eighteenth-century hand: 'Sancti Georgii Maioris'; on the last leaf of Cicero's *Orator*: 'Iste liber est monachorum congregationis Sancte Iustine de Padua deputatus ad usum fratrum habitantium in monasterio Sancti Georgii Maioris Venetiarum signatus numero 944', where '944' is written over a previous number.

-1806 Regno d'Italia, decree no. 160, 28 July 1806.

-1806 Venice, S. Giorgio Maggiore; Rossi (1806), C20: 'Ciceronis M.T. Opera nonnulla Rhetorica,

et Oratoria cum comm. Georgii Vallae. Ven. 1492 p. Bonettum Locatellum. F.ᵒ'.

-March 1807–1818(?) Padua, Sant'Anna; Rossi (March 1807); Catalogo generale XV (1811), 145, no. 35: 'Ciceronis, Opera varia cum cummentariis Georgii Vallae, folio, Venetiis, 1492' [commentator and dating refer to the second edition in the volume]; *Fondi antichi della Biblioteca Universitaria di Padova*, 40–41.

-1818(?)-*c.* 1840 Padua, S. Francesco Grande, Sala Carmeli. When the monastery of Sant'Anna had to be cleared, some selected volumes were transferred in part to the Pubblica Libreria (the Biblioteca Universitaria of Padua), in part to the Sala Carmeli of the former convent of S. Francesco Grande. A document dated 1818 records the transfer of books from S. Giorgio Maggiore into cupboards A, B, and C of Sala Carmeli. Padua, Catalogo Gnocchi (1818).

-*c.* 1840 transfer to the Biblioteca Universitaria of Padua: Ravegnani, *Le biblioteche*, 65–68; *Fondi antichi della Biblioteca Universitaria di Padova*, 40–41.

Padua, Biblioteca Universitaria: Sec. XV 445/1

53. Cicero, Marcus Tullius, *Orator* (comm. Victor Pisanus). *De fato, Topica, Timaeus* (comm. Georgius Valla), Venice: Bonetus Locatellus, for Octavianus Scotus, 16 July 1492. Folio. GW 6756; ISTC ic00653000; MEI 02008329.

Bound second with: **Cicero, Marcus Tullius**, *De oratore*, etc. Venice: Thomas de Blavis, de Alexandria, 16 May 1488. Folio (GW 6751; ISTC ic00663000; MEI 02008328; here no. 52).

-1806 Regno d'Italia, decree no. 160, 28 July 1806.

-1806 Venice, S. Giorgio Maggiore; Rossi (1806), C20: 'Ciceronis M.T. Opera nonnulla Rhetorica, et Oratoria cum comm. Georgii Vallae. Ven. 1492 p. Bonettum Locatellum. F.ᵒ'.

-March 1807–1818(?) Padua, Sant'Anna; Rossi (March 1807); Catalogo generale XV (1811), 145, no. 35: 'Ciceronis, Opera varia cum cummentariis Georgii Vallae, folio, Venetiis, 1492' [commentator and dating refer to this edition].

-1818(?)-*c.* 1840 Padua, S. Francesco Grande, Sala Carmeli. When the monastery of Sant'Anna had to be cleared, some selected volumes were transferred in part to the Pubblica Libreria (the Biblioteca Universitaria of Padua), in part to the Sala Carmeli of the former convent of S. Francesco Grande. A document dated 1818 records the transfer of books from S. Giorgio Maggiore into cupboards A, B, and C of Sala Carmeli. Padua, Catalogo Gnocchi (1818).

-c. 1840 transfer to the Biblioteca Universitaria of Padua: Ravegnani, *Le biblioteche*, 65–68; *Fondi antichi della Biblioteca Universitaria di Padova*, 40–41.
Padua, Biblioteca Universitaria, Sec. XV 445/2

54. Cicero, Pseudo-, *Rhetorica ad C. Herennium*, Milan: Antonius Zarottus [for Marco Roma], 12 Aug. 1474. 4°. CIBN C-465; GW 6714; ISTC ic00676000; MEI 02011875.

It is not clear whether the volume belonged to S. Giorgio Maggiore or to Sta. Giustina in Padua. In BnF, archives list (1797) it is referred to as Sta. Giustina's of Padua: 'Livres provenants de la Bibliothèque de Santa Justina de Padoue: no. 16. Ciceronis Rhetorica 1474 fol. carton G 2 [Milano?]'. Van Praet refers to provenance from a Venetian convent (CIBN C-465: 'Prov. Un couvent de Venise, d'après Van Praet. Rubriqué; notes mss.'). Since we know that sometimes S. Giorgio Maggiore's ownership notes were mistakenly read as indicating the property of Sta. Giustina, because the notes typically include the Congregation's name, the question of provenance is left open here.
Paris, Bibliothèque nationale de France, Rés. X. 306

55. Clemens V, Pont. Max., *Constitutiones* (cum apparatu Johannis Andreae). Add: *Decretales extravagantes Johannis XXII*, Venice: Nicolaus Jenson, 1476. Folio. GW 7098; ISTC ic00728000; MEI 02008355.

-1476–1789 Venice, S. Giorgio Maggiore; Ferrara-style illumination and ex-libris of Sta. Giustina, probably for S. Giorgio Maggiore, according to Lilian Armstrong; see related incunable of **Gregorius IX, Pont. Max.** (formerly Ugolino,

Count of Segni), *Decretales,* cum glossa, Venice: Nicolaus Jenson, [not before 8 Mar.] 1475. Folio. GW 11454; ISTC ig00449000; MEI 02008356, Chantilly, Musée Condé: XX.I.E.4 (here no. 89).
-1789 Venice, S. Giorgio Maggiore; Morelli's survey (1789), fasc. 1, 3: 'esemplare stampato in carta pecora con miniature', marked with +.
Chantilly, Musée Condé, XX. I. D.11

56. Clemens V, Pont. Max., *Constitutiones* (cum apparatu Johannis Andreae). Add: *Decretales extravagantes Johannis XXII*, Venice: Nicolaus Jenson, 1476. Folio. GW 7098; ISTC ic00728000; MEI 02008354.

-1476–1789 Venice, S. Giorgio Maggiore; assigned by Lilian Armstrong on the basis of the decoration by the Pico Master (St George killing the dragon); an erased inscription on iiir and a manuscript index of contents can be found in this volume as well as in another S. Giorgio's edition today in Manchester, John Rylands University Library: 9961 (**Bonifacius VIII, Pont. Max.**, *Liber sextus Decretalium* (with gloss of Johannes Andreae). Ed: Alexander de Nevo. Add: Johannes Andreae: *Super arboribus consanguinitatis et affinitatis*, Venice: Nicolaus Jenson, 1476. Folio. GW 4856; ISTC ib00984000; MEI 02008353 (here no. 41): 'Iste liber est monachorum congregationis Sanctae Iustinae de Padua deputatus monasterio Sancti Georgii Maioris Venetiarum, signatus numero [...]'.
-1789–1792 Étienne Charles Loménie de Brienne (1727–1794); French cardinal and politician who purchased extensively during his Italian tour in 1789–1790; François-Xavier Laire, *Index librorum ab inventa typographia ad annum 1500. Catalogue des livres de m *** par G. de Bure* (Sens, 1791), no. 14 (1476) which was used as sale catalogue for the 1792 auction of the library.
-1797–1892 George John, 2nd Earl Spencer (1758–1834); acquired around 1797, according to Thomas Frognall Dibdin, *Bibliotheca Spenceriana. A Descriptive Catalogue of the Books Printed in the Fifteenth Century and of Many Valuable First Editions in the Library of George John Earl Spencer*

(London, 1815), IV, 292–93 from the library of Lomenie de Brienne.
-1892 Mancester; purchased from the 5th Earl by Mrs Rylands in 1892 for the Rylands Library.
Manchester, John Rylands University Library: 9962

57. Cleomedes, *De contemplatione orbium excelsorum*. Add: Aelius Aristides, *Ad Rhodienses de concordia oratio*; Dio Chrysostomus, *Ad Nicomedenses oratio, De concordia oratio*; Plutarchus, *De virtute morali, Coniugalia praecepta*. Tr: Carolus Valgulius, Brescia: Bernardinus de Misintis, for Angelus Britannicus, 3 Apr. 1497. 4°. GW 7122; ISTC ic00741000; MEI 02006835.
Bound second with: **Lilius Zacharias**, *Orbis breviarium*, [Venice: Johannes and Gregorius de Gregoriis, de Forlivio, about 1500?]. 4°. EDIT16 CNCE 45605; GW M18353; ISTC il00220000; MEI 02137942 (no. 108 here).
-1581–1608 Girolamo Asteo (1562–1626), OFMConv from Pordenone; inscription on the first leaf of Lilius Zacharias.
-1626(?)-1806 Venice, S. Giorgio Maggiore; eighteenth-century inscription on the same leaf: 'Est Bibliothecae Sancti Georgii Maioris Venetiarum'.
-1806 Regno d'Italia, decree no. 160, 28 July 1806.
-1806 Venice, S. Giorgio Maggiore; Rossi (1806), L45: 'Lilii Zachariae Orbis Breviarium sine loco, an. et typ. Cleomedis de contemplatione Orbium excelsorum disputatio; Aristidis, et Dionis de Concordia Orationes; Plutarchi precepta connubialia, et de virtutibus morum. Brixiae 1487 [probably a typo] p. Bernardium Misintam 4°.
-March 1807–1818(?) Padua, Sant'Anna; Rossi (March 1807); Catalogo Generale XV (1811), 145 no. 49, the title is: 'Lilii et alii, Orbis breviarrium etc., 4°, Brixiae, 1488 [sic]'. After the suppression of the monastery of S. Giorgio Maggiore in 1806, the volume was deposited in the former monastery of the Benedictine nuns of Sant'Anna in Padua, as with the other books that subsequently entered the Biblioteca Universitaria of Padua.

-1818(?)-c. 1840 Padua, S. Francesco Grande, Sala Carmeli. When the monastery of Sant'Anna had to be cleared, some selected volumes were transferred in part to the Pubblica Libreria (the Biblioteca Universitaria of Padua), in part to the Sala Carmeli of the former convent of S. Francesco Grande. A document dated 1818 records the transfer of books from S. Giorgio Maggiore into cupboards A, B, and C of Sala Carmeli. Padua, Catalogo Gnocchi (1818).
-c. 1840 transfer to the Biblioteca Universitaria of Padua: Ravegnani, *Le biblioteche*, 65–68; *Fondi antichi della Biblioteca Universitaria di Padova*, 40–41.
Padua, Biblioteca Universitaria: Sec. XV 529/2

58. Columna, Franciscus, *Hypnerotomachia Poliphili*, etc. Venice: Aldus Manutius, Romanus, for Leonardus Crassus, Dec. 1499. Folio. GW 7223; ISTC ic00767000; MEI 02108483.
-1789 Venice, S. Giorgio Maggiore; Morelli's survey (1789), fasc. 1, 6: marked with +.
Historical copy, Venice

59. Conradus de Alemania, *Concordantiae bibliorum*, Nuremberg: Anton Koberger, 27 June 1485. Folio. GW 7420; ISTC ic00851000; MEI 02006694.
-1806 Regno d'Italia, decree no. 160, 28 July 1806.
-1806 Venice, S. Giorgio Maggiore; Rossi (1806), C21: 'Concordantiae Bibliae Nuremberg. 1485 ap. Koburger F.°'.
-March 1807–1818(?) Padua, Sant'Anna; Rossi (March 1807); Catalogo generale XV (1811), 144, no. 22: 'Concordantiae Bibliae, fol. Nuremberg. 1485'; *Fondi antichi della Biblioteca Universitaria di Padova*, 40–41.
Historical copy, Venice

60. Crastonus, Johannes, *Lexicon Graeco-latinum*, [Milan]: Bonus Accursius, [not after 28 Mar. 1478]. Folio. GW 7812; ISTC ic00958000; MEI 00214233.
-1478–1789 Venice, S. Giorgio Maggiore; inscription on [A1r]: 'Iste liber est monasterii sancti

Georgii maioris Venetiarum congregationis sancte Justine signatus numero 708'.

-1789 Venice, S. Giorgio Maggiore; Morelli's survey (1789), fasc. 1, 4: crossed out.

-1797 Paris, Bibliothèque nationale; BnF archives list (1797), fasc. 2, no. 11: 'Crestona fol. En bois'; Cicogna (1797): 'Dalla libreria di s. Giorgio Maggiore furono portati a Parigi nel 1797 i seguenti Codici manuscritti [...] Edizioni del secolo XV [...] 4. Crestoni Ioannis Lexicon graecum f. chart. sine loco et anno'. The volume did not return to the Marciana library, as should have been the case according to Cicogna (1797): 'Per la generosità di Francesco I di gloriosissima memoria presso che tutti cotesti libri son ritornati nel 1815, e riposti nella Marciana', but entered the international booktrade, probably because the Bibliothèque nationale de France already had several other copies of this work, including another Milanese edition [Milan, circa 1476–77?] CIBN C-658.

-1797–after 1815 Paris, Bibliothèque nationale, binding by Alexis-Pierre Bradel: 'Relié par BRADEL l'Aîné. Relieur de la Bibliothèque Nat.le et de celle des 4 Nations, Neveu et Succes.r de Derome le Jeune. Rue St Jacques n° 55 Hotel de la Couture'.

-1824 Oxford; purchased by the Bodleian in 1824 for £10. 10. 0.

Oxford, Bodleian Library. Auct. O inf. 2.3

61. Dante Alighieri, *La Commedia*. Comm: Jacopo della Lana. Ed: Christophorus Berardi, etc. [Venice]: Vindelinus de Spira, 1477. Folio. GW 7964; ISTC id00027000; MEI 02108484.

-1789 Venice, S. Giorgio Maggiore; Morelli's survey (1789), fasc. 1, 3: no marks '[...] col commento di Benvenuto da Imola'.

Historical copy, Venice

62. Dante Alighieri, *La Commedia*, Florence: Nicolò di Lorenzo, 30 Aug. 1481. Folio. CIBN D-13*; GW 7966; ISTC id00029000; MEI 02011876.

-before 1789 Venice, S. Giorgio Maggiore; below the partly excised colophon the origi-

nal fifteenth-century ownership note: '[...]ti de observantia deputa | [...] tiarum signatus 813'; on the lower border of the first leaf, in an eighteenth-century hand, brown ink, 'Est Bibl.ᵉ S. Georgii Mⁱˢ Venetᵐ'.

-1789 Venice, S. Giorgio Maggiore; Morelli's survey (1789), fasc. 1, 3: marked with + and crossed out; ex-libris of the Marciana library with the lion of St Mark and the motto 'Custos vel ultor', created in 1722 by the then librarian Girolamo Venier and used for quite a while afterwards – this ex-libris was used by Morelli after his survey to mark the most precious books in the monastery.

-1797– Paris, Bibliothèque nationale; BnF archives list (1797), fasc. 2, no. 8: 'Il Dante in fol. Velin Sta. Justina'; Cicogna (1797): 'Dalla libreria di s. Giorgio Maggiore furono portati a Parigi nel 1797 i seguenti Codici manuscritti [...] Edizioni del secolo XV [...] 5. Dante f. chart. Firenze 1481'. The volume did not return to the Marciana library, as should have been the case according to Cicogna (1797): 'Per la generosità di Francesco I di gloriosissima memoria presso che tutti cotesti libri son ritornati nel 1815, e riposti nella Marciana'. A letter of Alexander Cunningham (1650/1660–1730), the Scottish jurist and scholar, to Orlando di Francesco Franceschi, dated 13 Sept. 1728, is bound at the front.

Paris, Bibliothèque nationale de France: Rés. Yd. 102

63. Dinus de Mugello, *De regulis iuris*, Venice: Andreas Calabrensis, Papiensis, 10 June 1484. Folio. GW 8358; ISTC id00199000; MEI 02018188.

-1806 Venice, S. Giorgio Maggiore; Rossi (1806), D22: 'Dini Mugellani Regulae Iuris, Ven. 1484 p. Andream Papiensem, f.°'.

-1806 Regno d'Italia, decree no. 160, 28 July 1806.

-March 1807–1818(?) Padua, Sant'Anna; Rossi (March 1807); Catalogo generale XV (1811), 144 no. 14b: 2 [...] Dinus, De regulis iuris, folio, Venetiis 1484 per Andream Papiensem'; *Fondi antichi della Biblioteca Universitaria di Padova*, 40–41.

Historical copy, Venice

64. Dio Chrysostomus, *De regno*. Tr: Publius Gregorius Tiphernas. Ed: Pius III (Franciscus de Piccolomineis), [Venice: Christophorus Valdarfer, not after 9 Nov. 1471]. 8°. GW 8368; ISTC id00204000; MEI 02016845.

-1789 Venice, S. Giorgio Maggiore; Morelli's survey (1789), fasc. 1, 4: '[...] Romae 1469 4°', marked with + and crossed out.

-1797–1815 Paris, Bibliothèque nationale; BnF archives list (1797), fasc. 2, no. 5: 'Crisostomus 1470 in fol. En bois' (unfortunately, the Library rebound the incunable in the twentieth century, in blind-stamped leather); Cicogna (1797): 'Dalla libreria di s. Giorgio Maggiore furono portati a Parigi nel 1797 i seguenti Codici manuscritti [...] Edizioni del secolo XV [...] 6. Dionis Chrysostomi Oratio de Regno. 4. Chart. Romae. 1469'. The wrong imprint refers in fact to the dated dedicatory letter which opens the work, written by Francesco Piccolomini to Maximilian I and dated Rome 1 Jan. 1469. The volume was returned to the Marciana library, as stated by Cicogna (1797): 'Per la generosità di Francesco I di gloriosissima memoria presso che tutti cotesti libri son ritornati nel 1815, e riposti nella Marciana'.

-1816 Venice, Biblioteca Nazionale Marciana: in March 1816 the French returned 417 of the 432 books taken away; see Sciarra, 'Acquisizioni e asportazioni', 381.

Venice, Biblioteca Nazionale Marciana: Inc. 1017

65. Dominicus de Sancto Geminiano, *Super prima et secunda parte sexti libri Decretalium*, Milan: Johannes Antonius de Honate, for Petrus Antonius de Castelliono and Ambrosius de Caymis, 1480–81. Folio. GW 8649; ISTC id00311500; MEI 02018214.

-1806 Regno d'Italia, decree no. 160, 28 July 1806.
-1806 Venice, S. Giorgio Maggiore; Rossi (1806), G30: 'A S. Geminiano Dominici Lectura super sext. Decretal., sine loco 1480 p. Io. Anton. Honate, T.i 2 F.°'.
-March 1807–1818(?) Padua, Sant'Anna; Rossi (March 1807); Catalogo generale XV (1811), 145, no. 29: 'A S. Giminiano, Lectura super sextum

Decretalium, folio, sine loco 1480, tomi 2'; *Fondi antichi della Biblioteca Universitaria di Padova*, 40–41.
Historical copy, Venice

66. Dominicus de Sancto Geminiano, *Super sexto Decretalium* (I), Venice: Jacobus Rubeus, 10 Sept. 1476. Folio. GW 8646; ISTC id00309000; MEI 02008361.

-1476–1806 Venice, S. Giorgio Maggiore; inscription in the lower margin of the last leaf: 'Iste liber est monachorum congregationis Sancte Iustine de Padua, deputatus in Sancto Georgio Maiori Venetiarum, signatus numero 521'.
-1811 Padua, Biblioteca Universitaria: stamp. Not listed in any inventory documenting the institutional transfer.
Padua, Biblioteca Universitaria: Sec. XV Duplicato 169

67. Duns Scotus, Johannes, *Quaestiones in quattuor libros Sententiarum Petri Lombardi*. Ed: Philippus Bagnacavallus, Venice: Bonetus Locatellus, for Octavianus Scotus, 18 Dec. 1497. Folio. GW 9077; ISTC id00383000; MEI 02006698.

-1806 Regno d'Italia, decree no. 160, 28 July 1806.
-1806 Venice, S. Giorgio Maggiore; Rossi (1806), D23: 'Duns (alias Scoti) Ioannis Opus in quatuor lib. Sententiarum Ven. 1497 p. Bonetum Locatellum F.°'.
-March 1807–1818(?) Padua, Sant'Anna; Rossi (March 1807); Catalogo generale XV (1811), 145, no. 37: 'Duns Scoti, Opus in quat. lib. Sententiarum, fol. Ven. 1497'; *Fondi antichi della Biblioteca Universitaria di Padova*, 40–41.
Historical copy, Venice

68. Duranti, Guillelmus, *Rationale divinorum officiorum*, [Mainz]: Johann Fust and Peter Schoeffer, 6 Oct. 1459. Folio. CIBN D-278; GW 9101; ISTC id00403000; MEI 02011878.

-1461–1789 Venice, S. Giorgio Maggiore; inscription on the last leaf: 'Iste liber est congregationis monachorum sancte Justine | deputatus monasterio sancti Georgii maioris venetiarum ac signatus numero 315 | Constitit ducatorum decem octo emptus anno 1461'.

-1789 Venice, S. Giorgio Maggiore; Morelli's survey (1789), fasc. 1, 5: marked with + and crossed out.

-1797 Paris, Bibliothèque nationale; BnF archives list (1797), fasc. 2, no. 6: 'Durandus 1459 in fol. sur velin en bois, Sta. Just. De Padoue' (unfortunately, the Library subsequently rebound the incunable, in red Morocco with a gold-tooled spine); Cicogna (1797): 'Dalla libreria di s. Giorgio Maggiore furono portati a Parigi nel 1797 i seguenti Codici manuscritti [...] Edizioni del secolo XV [...] 7. Durandi Guillelmi Rationale diuinorum officiorum. f. membr. Maguntiae 1459'. The volume did not return to the Marciana library, as should have been the case according to Cicogna (1797): 'Per la generosità di Francesco I di gloriosissima memoria presso che tutti cotesti libri son ritornati nel 1815, e riposti nella Marciana'; a different copy was sent back, see Marciana Membr. 0008 (MEI 02019825), having an earlier German provenance. *Paris, Bibliothèque nationale de France: Rés. Vélins 125*

69. Duranti, Guillelmus, *Rationale divinorum officiorum*. Ed: Johannes Aloisius Tuscanus, Venice: Bonetus Locatellus, for Octavianus Scotus, 7 Apr. 1491. Folio. GW 9136; ISTC id00435000; MEI 02006764.

-*c.* 1491–1740 Venice, Camaldolese, S. Michele di Murano; inscription on the verso of the first leaf: 'Iste liber est monasterii Sancti Michaelis de Muranno ordinis Camaldulensis Torcellanae diocesis quem dompnus Gabriel Mediolanensis de Arigonibus acquisivit pro usu et utilitate omnium fratrum in ipso monasterio commorantium'.

-*c.* 1740–1797 Venice, S. Giorgio Maggiore, ex libris of Marco Molin: 'Est Sancti Georgii Majoris Venetiarum ad usum D. Marci Molin'.

-1806 Venice, S. Giorgio Maggiore; Rossi (1806), R65: 'Rationale Divinorum Officiorum 1491 p. Bonettum Locatellum 4°'.

-March 1807–1818(?) Padua, Sant'Anna; Rossi (March 1807); Catalogo generale XV (1811),

144, no. 6: 'Rationale divinorum officiorum, folio, Venetiis, 1491, per Bonettum Locatelum'.

-1818(?)-*c.* 1840 Padua, S. Francesco Grande, Sala Carmeli. When the monastery of Sant'Anna had to be cleared, some selected volumes were transferred in part to the Pubblica Libreria (the Biblioteca Universitaria of Padua), in part to the Sala Carmeli of the former convent of S. Francesco Grande. A document dated 1818 records the transfer of books from S. Giorgio Maggiore into cupboards A, B, and C of Sala Carmeli. Padua, Catalogo Gnocchi (1818).

-*c.* 1840 transfer to the Biblioteca Universitaria of Padua: Ravegnani, *Le biblioteche*, 65–68; *Fondi antichi della Biblioteca Universitaria di Padova*, 40–41. *Padua, Biblioteca Universitaria: Sec. XV 153*

70. Duranti, Guillelmus, *Speculum judiciale*, etc. Venice: Baptista de Tortis, 1493/1494. Folio. GW 9159; ISTC id00452000; MEI 02006685.

-1806 Regno d'Italia, decree no. 160, 28 July 1806.

-1806 Venice, S. Giorgio Maggiore; Rossi (1806), D24: 'Duranti Gulielmi Speculum cum additionibus Io. Andreae, et Baldi. Ven. p. Baptistam de Tortis 1494 F.°'.

-March 1807–1818(?) Padua, Sant'Anna; Rossi (March 1807); Catalogo generale XV (1811), 144, no. 10: 'Duranti, Speculum cum additionibus, fol. Ven. 1494 per Bapt. de Tortis'; *Fondi antichi della Biblioteca Universitaria di Padova*, 40–41. *Historical copy, Venice*

71. Euclides, *Elementa geometriae*. Tr: Adelardus Bathoniensis. Ed: Johannes Campanus, Venice: Erhard Ratdolt, 25 May 1482. Folio. GW 9428; ISTC ie00113000; MEI 02006683.

-1789 Venice, S. Giorgio Maggiore; Morelli's survey (1789), fasc. 1, 5.

-1806 Regno d'Italia, decree no. 160, 28 July 1806.

-1806 Venice, S. Giorgio Maggiore; Rossi (1806), E25: 'Euclidis Geometriae libri. Ven. 1482 p. Erhardum Ratbolt F.°'.

-March 1807–1813 Padua, Sant'Anna; Rossi (March 1807); Catalogo generale XV (1811),

144, no. 8: 'Euclidis, Geometriae libri, Ven. 1482 per Erhardum Ratdolt F.°'.
-1813–1831(?) Padua, S. Francesco Grande, Sala Carmeli. One of the five incunables from S. Giorgio Maggiore listed in a document, now Padua, S. Francesco Grande, Sala Carmeli (1813). The document reports five incunables which on Sunday 4 October 1813 were in S. Francesco Grande, evidently transferred from the warehouse of Sant'Anna to the Sala Carmeli (which was part of the University library), probably because of their value. These books were dispersed between 4 October 1813 and 1831.
Historical copy, Venice

72. Eusebius Caesariensis, *Chronicon*. Tr: Hieronymus. With the continuations of Prosper Aquitanus and Matthaeus Palmerius Florentinus. Prelim: Boninus Mombritius: *Epigrammata tria ad lectorem*, [Milan]: Philippus de Lavagnia, [about 1474–75]. 4°. CIBN E-90; GW 9432; ISTC ie00116000; MEI 02018229.
-1789 Venice, S. Giorgio Maggiore; Morelli's survey (1789), fasc. 1, 5: marked with + and crossed out; ex-libris of the Marciana library with the lion of St Mark and the motto 'Custos vel ultor', created in 1722 by the then librarian Girolamo Venier and used for quite a while afterwards – this ex-libris was used by Morelli after his survey to mark the most precious books in each monastery.
-1797 Paris, Bibliothèque nationale; BnF archives list (1797), fasc. 2, no. 14: 'Eusebii Hist. Eccl. Med. in fol. en bois' (probably a mistake misinterpreting the title on spine: 'S. Eusebius De Tempo'); Cicogna (1797): 'Dalla libreria di s. Giorgio Maggiore furono portati a Parigi nel 1797 i seguenti Codici manuscritti […] Edizioni del secolo XV […] 8. Eusebii Pamphili chronicon. 4. chart. sine loco et anno'. The volume did not return to the Marciana library, as should have been the case according to Cicogna (1797): 'Per la generosità di Francesco I di gloriosissima memoria presso che tutti cotesti libri son ritornati nel 1815, e riposti nella Marciana'; a different copy was sent back, see now Biblioteca nazionale Marciana Inc. 0553 (MEI 02017470).

Paris, Bibliothèque nationale de France: Rés. G 139

73. Eusebius Caesariensis, *De evangelica praeparatione*, Venice: Nicolaus Jenson, 1470. Folio. GW 9440; ISTC ie00118000; MEI 02006747.
-1470–1765 Venice, S. Giorgio Maggiore; inscription at the end of the text: 'Iste liber est Congregationis Monachorum Sancte Iustine deputatus monasterio Sancti Georgii maioris (..) signatus [..] 412'; illuminated by the Pico Master, as argued by Lilian Armstrong: on the lower margin of a1 St George, to whom the monastery is entitled, is painted within a garland.
-1765 Venice, S. Giorgio Maggiore: included in the list published in Gerbert (1765).
-1789 Venice, S. Giorgio Maggiore; Morelli's survey (1789), fasc. 1, 5: marked with +.
-1806–1814? Milan, Regno d'Italia: books gone to Milan, 4 Sept. 1806, item seven.
-1873 Milan, Legatoria Conti Borbone: binder's name engraved.
-1965 Torquay, Clifford C. Rattey (1886–1970): bookplate and listed in his catalogue, *Catalogue of the Library at Corbyns, Torquay, formed by Clifford C. Rattey* (Leamington, 1965), B82.
-1986 London, The British Library: presented to the library by Hope Rattey in 1986.
London, British Library: IB.19612a

74. Falcutius, Nicolaus, *Sermones medicinales septem*, Venice: Bernardinus Stagninus, de Tridino, 1490–91. Folio. GW 9705; ISTC if00046000; MEI 02018221.
-1806 Regno d'Italia, decree no. 160, 28 July 1806.
-1806 Venice, S. Giorgio Maggiore; Rossi (1806), N56: 'Nicoli Nicolai Florentini. De Conservatione Sanitatis, et alia opuscula, s.l. 1491 p. Bernard. de Tridino, F.°'.
-March 1807–1818(?) Padua, Sant'Anna; Rossi (March 1807); Catalogo generale XV (1811), 145, no. 30: 'Nicolai De conservatione sanitatis et alia opuscula, fol. sine loco 1491, tomi 2'; *Fondi antichi della Biblioteca Universitaria di Padova*, 40–41.
Historical copy, Venice

75. Ferettus, Nicolaus, *De elegantia linguae latinae*, Forlì: Hieronymus Medesanus, 25 May 1495. 4°. GW 9783; ISTC if00099000; MEI 02018108.
Bound second with: **Mancinellus, Antonius,** *Scribendi orandique modus* (edition unidentified; bound first, no. 115 here); **Vergerius, Petrus Paulus,** *De ingenuis moribus ac liberalibus studiis.* Ed: Johannes Calphurnius. Comm: Johannes Bonardus. Add: Basilius Magnus: *De legendis antiquorum libris* (Tr: Leonardus Brunus Aretinus). Xenophon: *Hiero de tyrannide* (Tr: Leonardus Brunus Aretinus). Plutarchus: *De liberis educandis* (Tr: Guarinus Veronensis). S. Hieronymus: *De officiis liberorum erga parentes admonitio,* Venice: Johannes Tacuinus, de Tridino, 22 Sept. 1497. 4°. ISTC iv00139000; MEI 02018105 (bound third, no. 178 here); and **Beroaldus, Philippus,** *De felicitate,* Bologna: Franciscus (Plato) de Benedictis, 1 Apr. 1495. 4°. GW 4132; ISTC ib00482000; MEI 02018106 (bound fourth, no. 27 here).
-1806 Regno d'Italia, decree no. 160, 28 July 1806.
-1806 Venice, S. Giorgio Maggiore; Rossi (1806), M52: 'Mancinelli Antonii Scribendi, orandique modus, Forilivii 1495 p. Hieron. Medasanum. – Pauli Vergerii de ingenuis moribus cum comment. Io. Bonardi – Basilii de legendis antiquorum libris opusculum – Traductio ex Xenophonte Leonardi Aretini de Tyranide – Guarini Veronensis in Plutarcum praefatio, 1497 Ven. p. Io. Tacuinum. – Philippi Beroaldi de felicitate opusculum Bononiae 1495 p. Platonem de Benedictiis. Omnia uno tantum volumine in 4°'. In making an entry for this composite volume, it is clear that the cataloguer merged two editions, noting the opening of an edition of Antonius Mancinellus and the imprint information of another edition, by Nicolaus Ferettus, bound behind. Unfortunately, it is not possible to determine which of the several editions of Mancinellus' *Scribendi orandique modus* is the one represented here.
-Not present in Catalogo generale XV (1811), it is therefore unlikely that the book ever reached Padua. A copy of this edition in Padua BU today has a different provenance.
Historical copy, Venice

76. Ferrariis, Johannes Petrus de, *Practica moderna iudicialis*. Ed: Franciscus Gardensis, Venice: Andreas de Bonetis, 25 Oct. 1484. Folio. GW 9817; ISTC if00113500; MEI 02018180.
-1806 Venice, S. Giorgio Maggiore. See below, Padua.
-1806 Regno d'Italia, decree no. 160, 28 July 1806.
-after March 1807/1811–1818(?) Padua, Sant'Anna; Rossi (March 1807); Catalogo generale XV (1811), 144, no. 14: 'De Ferrariis. Practica iudicialis […] folio […]'; *Fondi antichi della Biblioteca Universitaria di Padova*, 40–41.
Historical copy, Venice

77. Ficinus, Marsilius, *De religione christiana*, Venice: Otinus de Luna 1500. 4°. GW 9877; ISTC if00149000; MEI 02017463.
-1500–1658 Venice, S. Giorgio Maggiore; early sixteenth-century inscription on the title-page, the last part deleted: 'Est sancti Georgij maioris de Venetiis signatus numero […]'.
-1658 Denmark: Niels Andersen Vandstad (1625–1677), Danish theologian and parish priest in Torbenfeldt, Skamstrup, rural dean/warden of Tudse/Tusse Herred (district); he purchased the book in Venice in 1658 for 20 soldi; inscription on the title-page: 'N. Wandstad Venetiis emit 20 s. 1658'. On Vandstad: https://wiberg-net.dk/1013-Skamstrup.htm.
-1698 Copenhagen, Georgius Francus de Frankenau (1644–1704), German physician and botanist who moved to Denmark to be the personal physician to King Christian V; acquired in Copenhangen in 1698: inscription on the title-page: 'Georgius Francus de Frankenau | Hafniae | 1698'.
-1785 Copenhagen: Count Otto Thott (1703–1785), Danish Minister of State; part of a donation which included 6,059 books printed before 1530 and 4,154 manuscripts; nothing is specifically known on how he acquired them, but see Anders Toftgaard, 'A Private Library as a Material History of the Book. Otto Thott's Encyclopedic Library in Copenhagen', in *Private Libraries and Private*

Library Inventories, 1665–1830. Studying and Interpreting Sources, ed. Rindert Jagersma, Evelien Chayes, and Helwi Blom (Leiden, in press).
Copenhagen, Royal Library: Inc. Haun. 1591

78. Franchis, Philippus de, *Super titulo 'De regulis iuris in sexto libro Decretalium'*, Venice: Bernardinus Benalius, for Francesco Cartolari da Perugia and Bernardinus Benalius, [after 30 July] 1499. Folio. GW 10251; ISTC if00280650; MEI 02006695.
-1806 Regno d'Italia, decree no. 160, 28 July 1806.
-1806 Venice, S. Giorgio Maggiore; Rossi (1806), F27: 'Franchi Philippi Opus super tit. de regulis Iuris in Sexto. Ven. 1499 p. Bernard. Benalium F.º'.
-March 1807–1818(?) Padua, Sant'Anna; Rossi (March 1807); Catalogo generale XV (1811), 145, no. 31: 'Franchi, De regulis iuris etc., fol. Ven. 1499'; *Fondi antichi della Biblioteca Universitaria di Padova*, 40–41.
Historical copy, Venice

79. Gafurius, Franchinus, *Practica musicae*, Milan: Guillaume Le Signerre for Giovanni Pietro da Lomazzo, 30 Sept. 1496. Folio. CIBN G-2; GW 10434; ISTC ig00003000; MEI 02017555.
-Sixteenth/seventeenth-centuries *c.* Piacenza, Benedictines, S. Sixtus, used by Johannes Maria; inscription in the lower margin of the third leaf: 'Est Sancti Sixti de Plac.a S. signatus numero 302 | Ad usum Jo: marie plac.a'.
-seventeenth century-*c.* 1796 Venice, S. Giorgio Maggiore; inscriptions on front leaf, above the woodcut, in an eighteenth-century hand: 'A S Georgii maioris Venet.' and in the lower margin: 'Est Bibl.e S Georgii M.is Venet.m' (see also no. 62 here).
-1797 Paris, Bibliothèque nationale, removed in 1797; note in Van Praet's hand, brown ink, on the lower right-hand corner of the verso of the front flyleaf: 'Envoi de Venise'.
Paris, Bibliothèque nationale de France: Rés. V. 550

80. Gaza, Theodorus, *Grammatica introductiva* [Greek]. Add: Gaza: *De mensibus* [Greek];

Apollonius Dyscolus: *De constructione* [Greek]; Herodianus: *De numeris* [Greek], Venice: Aldus Manutius, Romanus, 25 Dec. 1495. Folio. GW 10562; ISTC ig00110000; MEI 02006702.
-1789 Venice, S. Giorgio Maggiore; Morelli's survey (1789), fasc. 1, 7: marked with +.
-1806 Regno d'Italia, decree no. 160, 28 July 1806.
-1806 Venice, S. Giorgio Maggiore; Rossi (1806), G35: 'Gazae Theodori Introductivae Grammatices libri IV Eiusd. Opusculum de mensibus; Apollonii Grammatici de Constructione lib. IV; Herodiani opus de numeris in Graece Ven. 1495 in aedibus Aldi F.º'.
-March 1807–1818(?) Padua, Sant'Anna; Rossi (March 1807); Catalogo generale XV (1811), 145, no. 44: 'Gazae, Introductio gramatices etc., fol. Ven. Aldus 1495 graec.'; *Fondi antichi della Biblioteca Universitaria di Padova*, 40–41.
Historical copy, Venice

81. Gellius, Aulus, *Noctes Atticae*, Venice: Nicolaus Jenson, 1472. Folio. GW 10594; ISTC ig00120000; MEI 02015857.
-1472–1765 Venice, S. Giorgio Maggiore; fifteenth-century inscription on [s]6r: 'Iste liber est monachorum congregationis sancte Iustine de Padua ordinis sancti Benedicti de obseruantia deputatus monasterio sancti Georgii maioris Venetiarum signatus numero 903'.
-1765 Venice, S. Giorgio Maggiore: included in the list published in Gerbert (1765).
-1789, Venice, S. Giorgio Maggiore; Morelli's survey (1789), fasc. 1, 5: no marks; ex-libris of the Marciana library with the lion of St Mark and the motto 'Custos vel ultor', created in 1722 by the then librarian Girolamo Venier and used for quite a while afterwards – this ex-libris was used by Morelli after his survey to mark the most precious books in each monastery.
-1806 Venice, S. Giorgio Maggiore; Rossi (1806), G28: 'Gellii Auli Noctes Atticae. Ven. 1472 Ienson F.º'.
-1806 Regno d'italia, decree no. 160, 28 July 1806.
The book must have been taken to Milan, instead of Padua.

-1807 Milan, Biblioteca Braidense: on [a]2r an oval-shaped stamp including the text 'Imperialis Regia Bibliotheca Mediolanensis' and the image of Minerva, in use from 1800 to circa 1830.
Milan, Biblioteca Nazionale Braidense: AI. XI. 1

82. Gellius, Aulus, *Noctes Atticae*, Brescia: Boninus de' Boninis, 3 Mar. 1485. Folio. CIBN G-66; GW 10597; ISTC ig00122000; MEI 02017597.
-*c.* 1485–1600 Padua, Benedictines, Sta. Justina: 'Est monasterij Diue Iustine de padua signatus numero 4005'.
-*c.* 1601–1796 Venice, S. Giorgio Maggiore: see below. Not mentioned in Morelli's survey (1789).
-1797 Paris, Bibliothèque nationale: removed in 1797, note in Van Praet's hand, brown ink, on the lower right-hand corner of the front pastedown: 'Envoi de Venise'; BnF, archives list (1797), fasc. 2, no. 10. 'Aulus Gellius Brixiae fol. Velin G 3 id.'.
Paris, Bibliothèque nationale de France: Rés. Z. 48

83. Georgius Trapezuntius, *Rhetorica*, Venice: Vindelinus de Spira, [not before 1472]. Folio. GW 10664; ISTC ig00157000; MEI 02108485.
-1789 Venice, S. Giorgio Maggiore; Morelli's survey (1789), fasc. 1, 7: marked with a + in the margin; crossed out.
-1806–1814? Milan, Regno d'Italia: books gone to Milan, 4 Sept. 1806, item eight.
Historical copy, Venice

84. Gerson, Johannes, *Opera*. Ed: Johannes Geiler von Kaisersberg, [Strasbourg: Johann (Reinhard) Grüninger, partly with the types of Johann Prüss and Martin Flach], 1488. Folio. GW 10714; ISTC ig00186000; MEI 02018192.
-1806 Regno d'Italia, decree no. 160, 28 July 1806.
-1806 Venice, S. Giorgio Maggiore; Rossi (1806), G29: 'Gerson Ioannis Opera omnia T.i 4 F.°, incipit editio an. 1488, explicit quartus tomus an. 1502 per Martinum Flaccum juniorem'.
-March 1807–1818(?) Padua, Sant'Anna; Rossi (March 1807); Catalogo generale XV (1811),

144, no. 18; 'Gerson, Opera omnia, folio, 1488 per Martinum Flaccum juniorem, tomi 4'; *Fondi antichi della Biblioteca Universitaria di Padova*, 40–41.
Historical copy, Venice

85. Gratianus, *Decretum* (cum apparatu Bartholomaei Brixiensis), Venice: Andreas Calabrensis, Papiensis, 24 Aug. 1491. Folio. GW 11376; ISTC ig00383000; MEI 02018168.
-1806 Venice, S. Giorgio Maggiore; Rossi (1806), B15: 'A Brixia Bartholomei Apparatus decretorum Canonicorum, Ven. 1491 p. Andream de Calabria, f.°'.
-1806 Regno d'Italia, decree no. 160, 28 July 1806.
-March 1807–1818(?) Padua, Sant'Anna; Rossi (March 1807); Catalogo generale XV (1811), 144, no. 20: 'A Brixia, Apparatus decretorum canonicorum, folio, Venetiis 1491'; *Fondi antichi della Biblioteca Universitaria di Padova*, 40–41.
Historical copy, Venice

86. Gregorius I, Pont. Max, *Dialogorum libri quattuor*, Venice: Hieronymus de Paganinis, 13 Nov. 1492. 4°. GW 11401; ISTC ig00405000; MEI 02006704.
-1806 Regno d'Italia, decree no. 160, 28 July 1806.
-1806 Venice, S. Giorgio Maggiore; Rossi (1806), G32: 'S. Gregorii Papae Dialogi. Ven. 1492 p. Hier. de Paganinis 4'.
-1818(?)-*c.* 1840 Padua, Sant'Anna; Catalogo generale XV (1811), 146, no. 51: 'S. Gregorii P., Dialogi, 4° Ven. 1492'; *Fondi antichi della Biblioteca Universitaria di Padova*, 40–41.
Historical copy, Venice

87. Gregorius I, Pont. Max, *Moralia, sive Expositio in Job*, Brescia: Angelus Britannicus, 2 June 1498. 4°. GW 11436; ISTC ig00434000; MEI 02003446.
-1498-*c.* 1600 Piacenza, Benedictines, S. Sixtus; inscription on 1r: 'Iste liber est monasterii sancti sixti placentiae Congregationis Cassinensis alias sanctae Justinae de padua'.
-*c.* 1600–1806 Venice, S. Giorgio Maggiore; inscription on the front flyleaf in an eighteenth-century

hand: 'Est Sancti Georgii Venetiarum. Ad usum D. Mauretii Bergomensis'. It is possible that the book left the monastery with Mauritius Bergomensis (see no. 25 here).

-1806 Brescia, Biblioteca Queriniana, acquired in unknown circumstances following the Napoleonic suppressions.

Brescia, Biblioteca Queriniana: Inc.B.II.2m1

88. Gregorius I, Pont. Max, *Moralia, sive Expositio in Job*, Brescia: Angelus Britannicus, 2 June 1498. 4°. GW 11436; ISTC ig00434000; MEI 02003447.

-after 1498 Dubrovnik (Ragusa), Dominicans, S. Domenico; inscription on *c*. 1r: 'Iste liber est conventus S. Dominici de ragusio ex provisione fratris Simonis concessus ad usum fratri Vincentio a [...]'.

-*c*. 1600–1797 Venice, S. Giorgio Maggiore; seventeenth-century inscription on 1r: 'Est S. Georgii Maioris Venetiarum'.

-*c*. 1806–1863 Brescia, Luigi Lechi (1786–1867): stamp. Bequeathed to the Queriniana in 1863.

Brescia, Biblioteca Queriniana: Lechi.124

89. Gregorius IX, Pont. Max. (formerly Ugolino, Count of Segni), *Decretales*, cum glossa, Venice: Nicolaus Jenson, [not before 8 Mar.] 1475. Folio. GW 11454; ISTC ig00449000; MEI 02008356.

-1475–1789 Venice, S. Giorgio Maggiore; Ferrara-style illumination and ex-libris of Sta. Giustina, probably for S. Giorgio Maggiore, according to Lilian Armstrong; see related incunable **Clemens V, Pont. Max.**, *Constitutiones* (cum apparatu Johannis Andreae). Add: *Decretales extravagantes Johannis XXII*, Venice: Nicolaus Jenson, 1476. Folio. GW 7098; ISTC ic00728000; MEI 02008355, now in Chantilly, Musée Condé, XX. I. D.11 (here no. 55).

-1789 Venice, S. Giorgio Maggiore; Morelli's survey (1789), fasc. 2, no. 5: 'Decretalium Liber VI cum I.s Andrea, simile [i.e. Jenson 1476 in membranis]'. Morelli mistakenly names Giovanni d'Andrea as glossator of this edition, copying the information from the title that precedes

the present one in his list: the *Constitutiones* of Clement V.

Chantilly, Musée Condé : XX.I.E.4

90. Guido de Baysio, *Apparatus libri sexti decretalium*, Milan: Jacobus de Sancto Nazario, de Ripa, and Bernardinus de Castelliono, 23 Dec. 1490. Folio. GW 3743; ISTC ib00284000; MEI 02018176. Bound fourth with: **Antonius de Butrio**, *Super primo libro Decretalium* (7–28), Venice: Bernardinus Rizus, Novariensis, 1485. Folio. GW 5822; ISTC ib01342000; MEI 02018170 (bound first, no. 10 here); **Panormitanus de Tudeschis, Nicolaus**, *Disceptationes* (*seu Disputationes*) *et allegationes*, of which three editions were published in Venice, in 1483, 1487, and 1490 of 38, 32, and 28 leaves respectively (bound second, no. 128 here); **Panormitanus de Tudeschis, Nicolaus**, *Consilia* (cum Ludovici Bolognini tabula), Venice: Peregrinus de Pasqualibus, Bononiensis and Dominicus Bertochus, 14 Dec. 1486. Folio. GW M47773; ISTC ip00030000; MEI 02137941 (bound third, no. 127 here).

-1806 Regno d'Italia, decree no. 160, 28 July 1806.

-1806 Venice, S. Giorgio Maggiore; Rossi (1806), B17: 'De Butrio Lectura de Translatione Prelatorum, Ven. 1485 per Bernard. de Novaria. It. Nicolai de Sicilia Allegationes Ven. 1486 per Peregrinum de Pasqualibus, et socium. – Lectura D.i Archidiaconi Bononiensis. Mediolani 1490 p. Bernardi de Castellio, et socium. Omnia T.° 1, F.°'. This entry merges the detail of two editions bound second and third in this composite volume, the title of Panormitanus' *Disceptationes* (*seu Disputationes*) *et allegationes*, and the bibliographical information from Panormitanus, *Consilia* (cum Ludovici Bolognini tabula).

-1818(?)-*c*. 1840 Padua, Sant'Anna; Catalogo generale XV (1811), 145, no. 24: 'De Butrio, Lectura etc., fol. Ven. 1485, 1486, et 1490'; *Fondi antichi della Biblioteca Universitaria di Padova*, 40–41. The four copies were still bound together in 1811, as specifically stated in the Catalogue.

Historical copy, Venice

91. Guido de Baysio, *Rosarium decretorum*, [Venice]: Johannes Herbort, de Seligenstadt, for Johannes de Colonia, Nicolaus Jenson et Socii, 3 Apr. 1481. Folio. GW 3747; ISTC ib00288000; MEI 02018166.
-1806 Regno d'Italia, decree no. 160, 28 July 1806.
-1806 Venice, S. Giorgio Maggiore; Rossi (1806), B13: 'De Baysio Guidi Commentaria in Decretum Gratiani. 1481 absque loco p. Io. de Selgenstat. F.º'.
-March 1807–1818(?) Padua, Sant'Anna; Rossi (March 1807); Catalogo generale XV (1811), 144, no. 11: 'De Baysio, Commentaria in Decretum Gratiani, folio, 1481 absque loco per Ioannem de Silgenstad'; *Fondi antichi della Biblioteca Universitaria di Padova*, 40–41.
Historical copy, Venice

92. Hibernia, Thomas de, *Manipulus florum, seu Sententiae Patrum*, Piacenza: Jacobus de Tyela, 5 Sept. 1483. Folio. ISTC ih00149000; MEI 02008239.
-1806 Venice, S. Giorgio Maggiore; Rossi (1806), H36: 'De Hibernia Thomae Manipulus Florum. Placentiae 1483 p. Iacobum de Tyela F.º'.
-1817 Padua; Catalogo pregio (1817), 14, no. 581: 'De Hibernia, Manipulus historiarum. Placentiae, 1483. 4º'.
Historical copy, Venice

93. Homerus, *Opera* [Greek]. Ed: Demetrius Chalcondylas, Florence: [Printer of Vergilius (C 6061)], for Bernardus and Nerius Nerlius and Demetrius Damilas, [not before 13 Jan. 1488/1489]. Folio. GW 12895; ISTC ih00300000; MEI 02017398.
-1489–1529 Andrea Matteo Acquaviva d'Aragona (1458–1529): his coat of arms in each volume.
-1653 Leonardus Miliarius, Belluno; on the verso of the front pastedown of vol. 1: 'Leonardus Miliarius Bellunensis comes et eques Caesaris possidebat et Benedictinae Venetiarum Bibliotecae munusculum dicavit 1653'.
-1653–1789 Venice, S. Giorgio Maggiore: donated in 1653.

-1789 Venice, S. Giorgio Maggiore; Morelli's survey (1789), fasc. 1, 5: marked with + and crossed out.
-1797–1815 Paris, Bibliothèque nationale; BnF archives list (1797), fasc. 2, no. 1: 'Homerus. Florent. 1488 2 vol. in fol. sur velin o velum rel. en bois, sur le dos coll. 77 no. 819 (the Marciana volume has three annotations on the recto of the flyleaf: 184 (crossed out), 272 (crossed out) and 77); Cicogna (1797): 'Dalla libreria di s. Giorgio Maggiore furono portati a Parigi nel 1797 i seguenti Codici manuscritti […] Edizioni del secolo XV […] 9. Homeri opera graecae f. Membr. Florentiae 1488 T. II.'
-1815 Venice, Biblioteca Nazionale Marciana; returned in 1815 (the Bibliothèque nationale de France has other copies); Cicogna (1797): "Per la generosità di Francesco I di gloriosissima memoria presso che tutti cotesti libri son ritornati nel 1815, e riposti nella Marciana'.
Venice, Biblioteca Nazionale Marciana: Membr. 0011–0012

94. Horatius Flaccus, Quintus, *Opera*, Venice: Johannes Alvisius, 23 July 1498. Folio. GW 13469; ISTC ih00460000; MEI 02006707.
-1498–1513 Andreas Mocenicus, apostolic protonotary.
-1513–1806 Venice, S. Giorgio Maggore; inscription on the first leaf: 'Reverendus dominus Andreas Mocenicus prothonotarius apostolicus pro animae suae salute Divi Georgii Maioris coenobio dicavit signatus 115' (number crossed out), Andrea Mocenigo died in 1513.
-1806 Regno d'Italia, decree no. 160, 28 July 1806.
-1806, Venice, S. Giorgio Maggiore; Rossi (1806), H37: 'Horatii carmina cum comment. Ven. 1498 p. Io. Aloys. De Varisio F.º'.
-March 1807–1818(?) Padua, Sant'Anna; Rossi (March 1807); Catalogo generale XV (1811), 144, no. 5: 'Horatii, Carmina cum commentariis, folio, Venetiis, 1498, per Ioannem Aloysium de Varisio'; *Fondi antichi della Biblioteca Universitaria di Padova*, 40–41.

-1818(?)-*c.* 1840 Padua, S. Francesco Grande, Sala Carmeli. When the monastery of Sant'Anna had to be cleared, some selected volumes were transferred in part to the Pubblica Libreria (the Biblioteca Universitaria of Padua), in part to the Sala Carmeli of the former convent of S. Francesco Grande. A document dated 1818 records the transfer of books from S. Giorgio Maggiore into cupboards A, B, and C of Sala Carmeli. Padua, Catalogo Gnocchi (1818).

-*c.* 1840 transfer to the Biblioteca Universitaria of Padua: Ravegnani, *Le biblioteche*, 65–68; *Fondi antichi della Biblioteca Universitaria di Padova*, 40–41.
Padua, Biblioteca Universitaria: Sec. XV 145

95. Isidorus Hispalensis, *Chronicon* [Italian] *La cronica*, Cividale: [Gerardus de Lisa, de Flandria], 24 Nov. 1480. 4°. ISTC ii00179000; MEI 02018104.
-1806 Regno d'Italia, decree no. 160, 28 July 1806.
-1806 Venice, S. Giorgio Maggiore; Rossi (1806), I40: 'S. Isidoro Cronaca con additioni cavate dal Texto, et Istorie della Biblia, e del Libro di Paolo Orosio Cividal di Friuli 1480. sine typ. 4°'.
-Not present in Catalogo generale XV (1811), it is therefore unlikely that the book ever reached Padua.
Historical copy, Venice

96. Isidorus Hispalensis, *Etymologiae*, etc. Venice: Peter Löslein, 1483. Folio. ISTC ii00184000; MEI 02020126.
-1483–1740 Venice, S. Giorgio Maggiore; deleted early inscription on C8v: 'Iste liber est monachorum congregationis s. Justine de padua ordini s. Benedicti deputatus usui fratrum habitantium monasterio sancti Georgii Maioris de Venetiis. Signatus […]'. Similar to other inscriptions found in books from S. Giorgio; sixteenth-century inscription on A1r: 'Est s. Georgii mayoris de venetianjs sig. n. 1020'.
-*c.* 1740–*c.* 1770 Arezzo, Benedictines, SS. Flora et Lucilla; Gabriele Maria Scarmalli (fl. 1740–1770):

inscription on [*]1r: 'Est Abbatiae Arretinae ad usum D. Gabrielis Mariae Scarmallii Monachi Casinensis'.
-*c.* 1920–1960 Florence, Tammaro De Marinis (1878–1969): paper ex-libris 'Tammaro De Marinis'.
-*c.* 1960 Venice, Fondazione Giorgio Cini, probably gifted by the antiquarian bookseller.
Venice, Fondazione Cini: FOAN TES 022

97. Jacobus de Voragine, *Legenda aurea sanctorum, sive Lombardica historia*, Venice: Antonius de Strata, de Cremona and Marcus Catanellus, 1 July 1480. Folio. ISTC ij00095000; MEI 02006697.
-1806 Regno d'Italia, decree no. 160, 28 July 1806.
-1806 Venice, S. Giorgio Maggiore; Rossi (1806), V71: 'De voragine Iacobi Legendae Sanctorum. Ven. 1480 per Antoni de Strata, et Socios F.°'.
-March 1807–1818(?) Padua, Sant'Anna; Rossi (March 1807); Catalogo generale XV (1811), 145, no. 36: 'De Voragine, Legendae sanctorum, fol. Ven. 1480'; *Fondi antichi della Biblioteca Universitaria di Padova*, 40–41.
Historical copy, Venice

98. Jacobus Philippus de Bergamo, *De claris mulieribus*. Ed: Albertus de Placentia and Augustinus de Casali Maiori, Ferrara: Laurentius de Rubeis, de Valentia, 29 Apr. 1497. Folio. ISTC ij00204000; MEI 02108486.
-1789 Venice, S. Giorgio Maggiore; Morelli's survey (1789), fasc. 1, 4: marked with +.
Historical copy, Venice

99. Johannes XXI, Pont. Max. (formerly Petrus Hispanus), *Summulae logicales*. Comm: Johannes de Magistris, Venice: [Bonetus Locatellus], for Octavianus Scotus, 9 Sept. 1490. 4°. ISTC ij00236840; MEI 02006689.
-1806 Regno d'Italia, decree no. 160, 28 July 1806.
-1806 Venice, S. Giorgio Maggiore; Rossi (1806), M50: 'de Magistris Io. Summularum Petri Hispani glossulae, et quaestionis super totam Philosophiam. Ven. 1490, impensis Octaviani Scoti (ut opinor) per Bonettum Locatellum T. 2. 4°, vol. I'.

-March 1807–1818(?) Padua, Sant'Anna; Rossi (March 1807); Catalogo generale XV (1811), 144, no. 15: 'De Magistris, Summula P. Hispani etc., 4, Ven. 1490'; *Fondi antichi della Biblioteca Universitaria di Padova*, 40–41.
Historical copy, Venice

100. Johannes Carthusiensis, *Nosce te,* etc. Venice: Nicolaus Jenson, 1480. 4°. ISTC ij00274000; MEI 02018230.
-1789 Venice, S. Giorgio Maggiore; Morelli's survey (1789), fasc. 1, 4: crossed out.
-1797–1815 Paris, Bibliothèque nationale; Cicogna (1797): 'Dalla libreria di s. Giorgio Maggiore furono portati a Parigi nel 1797 i seguenti Codici manoscritti [...] Edizioni del secolo XV [...]. 12. Nosce Te ipsum. 4. chart. Venetiis 1480'. The volume did not return to the Marciana library, as should have been the case according to Cicogna (1797): 'Per la generosità di Francesco I di gloriosissima memoria presso che tutti cotesti libri son ritornati nel 1815, e riposti nella Marciana'. Possibly the copy now in Paris, Bibliothèque nationale de France, Rés. D. 8237; no evidence from CIBN J-175. Not listed in BnF archives list (1797); listed in BnF, restitution list (1815): 'no. 265. Nosce te ipsum. Ven. 1480'.
Historical copy, Venice

101. Johannes de Imola, *In Clementinas opus,* Venice: Jacobus Rubeus, 1475. Folio. ISTC ij00343000; MEI 02008344.
-1475–1806 Venice, S. Giorgio Maggiore; inscription in the lower margin of the last leaf: 'Iste liber est monachorum congregationis Sancte Iustine de Padua deputatus in Sancto Georgio Maiori Venetiarum, signatus numero 522'; eighteenth-century inscription on the first leaf: 'Est bibliothecae Sancti Georgii Maioris Venetiarum'.
-1806 Regno d'Italia, decree no. 160, 28 July 1806.
-1806 Venice, S. Giorgio Maggiore; Rossi (1806), I38: 'De Imola Ioannis Commentaria in Clementinas. Ven. 1475 p. Iacobum de Rubeis F.°'.

-March 1807–1818(?) Padua, Sant'Anna; Rossi (March 1807); Catalogo generale XV (1811), 144, no. 23: 'De Imola, Commentaria in 3.m librum Decretalium et in Clementinas, folio, Venetiis, 1475 et 1489, tomi 2'; *Fondi antichi della Biblioteca Universitaria di Padova*, 40–41.
-1818(?)-*c.* 1840 Padua, S. Francesco Grande, Sala Carmeli. When the monastery of Sant'Anna had to be cleared, some selected volumes were transferred in part to the Pubblica Libreria (the Biblioteca Universitaria of Padua), in part to the Sala Carmeli of the former convent of S. Francesco Grande. A document dated 1818 records the transfer of books from S. Giorgio Maggiore into cupboards A, B, and C of Sala Carmeli. Padua, Catalogo Gnocchi (1818).
-*c.* 1840 transfer to the Biblioteca Universitaria of Padua: Ravegnani, *Le biblioteche*, 65–68; *Fondi antichi della Biblioteca Universitaria di Padova*, 40–41.
Padua, Biblioteca Universitaria: Sec. XV 695

102. Johannes de Imola, *Lectura in III librum Decretalium*, [Milan: Printer of Baldus (H 2289) (Leonardus Pachel and Uldericus Scinzenzeler?)], 1 Feb. 1489. Folio. ISTC ij00347000; MEI 02018215.
-1806 Regno d'Italia, decree no. 160, 28 July 1806.
-1806 Venice, S. Giorgio Maggiore; Rossi (1806), probably identifiable with I39: 'Eiusdem [De Imola Ioannis] Comm. in tertium librum Decretalium, Ven. 1488 sine typ F.°'.
-March 1807–1818(?) Padua, Sant'Anna; Rossi (March 1807); Catalogo generale XV (1811), 144, no. 23b; 'De Imola, Commentaria in 3.m librum Decretalium [et in Clementinas], folio, Venetiis, [1475 et] 1489 [tomi 2]'; *Fondi antichi della Biblioteca Universitaria di Padova*, 40–41.
Historical copy, Venice

103. Justinus, Marcus Junianus, *Epitomae in Trogi Pompeii historias*, Milan: Christophorus Valdarfer, 1 June 1476. 4°. ISTC ij00617000; MEI 02139823.

-before 1797 Venice, S. Giorgio Maggiore (?); see BnF archives list (1797).

-1797–1815 Paris, Bibliothèque nationale; BnF archives list (1797), fasc. 2, no. 19: 'Justinus 1476 in fol. En carton P[rinceps]. S. Just.'; the volume is not registered in Morelli's survey (1789), nor by Cicogna (1797) who gives a list of eighteen books taken away by the French in 1797, nor does the volume appear to be mentioned in the BnF restitution list (1815). CIBN J-339 mentions two copies with North-Italian Benedictine provenance, SS. Faustinus et Jovita at Brescia and S. Benedictus at Polirone.

Historical copy, Venice

104. Juvenalis, Decimus Junius, *Satyrae*, Venice: Johannes Tacuinus, de Tridino, 24 July 1498. Folio. ISTC ij00666000; MEI 02008266.

Bound first with: **Persius Flaccus, Aulus**, *Satyrae*. Comm: Johannes Britannicus and Bartholomaeus Fontius, Venice: Petrus de Quarengiis, Bergomensis, 13 Apr. 1495. Folio. ISTC ip00357000; MEI 02008268 (bound second, no. 132 here) and **Statius, Publius Papinius**, *Opera*, Venice: Petrus de Quarengiis, Bergomensis, 1498/1499. Folio. ISTC is00694000; MEI 02008269 (bound third, no. 160 here).

-1700–1797 Venice, S. Giorgio Maggiore; eighteenth-century inscription on Aii: 'Est bibliothecae Sancti Georgi Maioris Venetiarum'.

-1806 Regno d'Italia, decree no. 160, 28 July 1806.

-1806 Venice, S. Giorgio Maggiore; Rossi (1806), I42: 'Iuvenalis Decii Iunii Satyrae cum Comment. Ant. Mancinelli. Ven. 1495 p. Petrum Io. de Querengis, et Statii Poetae Sylvae Thebais, et Achilleis cum plur. Commentariis. Ibid. 1498 ap. eund. F.°'; the entry merges the bibliographical information (author, title, commentator) of the edition bound first with the typographical information (place, year, and printer) of the edition bound second; it is followed by the correct bibliographical and typographical information of the edition bound third. The bibliographical information of the edition bound second, Persius,

not specified, can be inferred by the typographical information provided and by the physical presence of the three editions in one volume today in the library of the University of Padua.

-March 1807–1818(?) Padua, Sant'Anna; Rossi (March 1807); Catalogo generale XV (1811), 145, no. 39: 'Iuvenalis, Satyrae cum cummentariis, folio, Venetiis, 1495; v'è unito Statii, Sylvae etc., folio, Venetiis, 1498'; *Fondi antichi della Biblioteca Universitaria di Padova*, 40–41.

-1818(?)-*c*. 1840 Padua, Sala Carmeli, S. Francesco Grande. When the monastery of Sant'Anna had to be cleared, some selected volumes were transferred in part to the Pubblica Libreria (the Biblioteca Universitaria of Padua), in part to the Sala Carmeli of the former convent of S. Francesco Grande. A document dated 1818 records the transfer of books from S. Giorgio Maggiore into cupboards A, B, and C of Sala Carmeli. Padua, Catalogo Gnocchi (1818).

-*c*. 1840 transfer to the Biblioteca Universitaria of Padua: Ravegnani, *Le biblioteche*, 65–68; *Fondi antichi della Biblioteca Universitaria di Padova*, 40–41.

Padua, Biblioteca Universitaria: Sec. XV 420/1

105. Lactantius, *Opera*, Venice: Vindelinus de Spira, 1472. Folio. CIBN L-5*; ISTC il00005000; MEI 02017486.

-1472–1765 Venice, S. Giorgio Maggiore; inscription below the last text in a fifteenth-century humanist hand: 'Iste liber est congregationis monachorum s. Iustine de Padua ordinis s Benedicti de obseruantia deputatus in monasterio s. Georgij maioris uenet. signatus numero 493'; on the lower margin of the first leaf, in brown ink, a seventeenth-century inscription: 'Est Bibliothece S. Georgii Maioris Venetiarum'.

-1765 Venice, S. Giorgio Maggiore: included in the list published in Gerbert (1765).

-1789 Venice, S. Giorgio Maggiore; Morelli's survey (1789), fasc. 1, 5: crossed out.

-1797 Paris, Bibliothèque nationale; BnF archives list (1797), fasc. 2, no. 10: 'Lactantius 1472 in fol.

en bois Sta. Justina' (unfortunately, the Library subsequently rebound the incunable, in red Morocco, and it is therefore impossible to verify whether the former covers were indeed made of wood); Cicogna (1797): 'Dalla libreria di s. Giorgio Maggiore furono portati a Parigi nel 1797 i seguenti Codici manuscritti [...] Edizioni del secolo XV [...] 10. Lactantii Firmiani opera f. Chart. Venetiis 1472'. The volume did not return to the Marciana library, as should have been the case according to Cicogna (1797): 'Per la generosità' di Francesco I di gloriosissima memoria presso che tutti cotesti libri son ritornati nel 1815, e riposti nella Marciana'.

Paris, Bibliothèque nationale de France: Rés. C. 350

106. Laetus, Pomponius, *Grammaticae compendium*, Venice: Baptista de Tortis, 31 Mar. 1484. 4°. CIBN P-560; ISTC il00023000; MEI 02139833.
-before 1797 Venice, S. Giorgio Maggiore (?); see BnF archives list (1797).
-1797–1815 Paris, Bibliothèque nationale; BnF archives list (1797), fasc. 2, no. 18: 'Pomponius Julius fol. velum G. C. Sta. Justina'. The volume is not registered in Morelli's survey (1789), nor by Cicogna (1797) who gives a list of eighteen books taken away by the French in 1797; nor does the volume appear to be mentioned in the BnF restitution list (1815).

Historical copy, Venice

107. Leonardus de Utino, *Sermones de sanctis*, Venice: Johannes de Colonia and Johannes Manthen, 1475. 4°. ISTC il00157000; MEI 02006856.
-1475–1806 Venice, S. Giorgio Maggiore; inscription on fol. 1r: 'Iste liber est congregationis Sanctae Iustinae ordinis Sancti Benedicti deputatus ad usum monachorum habitantium in monasterio Sancti Georgii Maioris de Venetiis ac signatus numero 669' (struck through).
-1806 Regno d'Italia, decree no. 160, 28 July 1806.

-1806 Venice, S. Giorgio Maggiore; Rossi (1806), U70: 'De Utino fratris Leonardi Sermones. Ven. 1475 p. Io. de Colonia 4°'.
-March 1807–1818(?) Padua, Sant'Anna; Rossi (March 1807); Catalogo generale XV (1811), 146, no. 52: 'De Utino, Sermones, 4, Venetiis, 1475'; *Fondi antichi della Biblioteca Universitaria di Padova*, 40–41.
-1818(?)-c. 1840 Padua, Sala Carmeli, S. Francesco Grande. When the monastery of Sant'Anna had to be cleared, some selected volumes were transferred in part to the Pubblica Libreria (the Biblioteca Universitaria of Padua), in part to the Sala Carmeli of the former convent of S. Francesco Grande. A document dated 1818 records the transfer of books from S. Giorgio Maggiore into cupboards A, B, and C of Sala Carmeli. Padua, Catalogo Gnocchi (1818).
-c. 1840 transfer to the Biblioteca Universitaria of Padua: Ravegnani, *Le biblioteche*, 65–68; *Fondi antichi della Biblioteca Universitaria di Padova*, 40–41.

Padua, Biblioteca Universitaria: Sec. XV 82

108. Lilius Zacharias, *Orbis breviarium*, [Venice: Johannes and Gregorius de Gregoriis, de Forlivio, about 1500?]. 4°. EDIT16 CNCE 45605; ISTC il00220000; MEI 02137942.
Bound first with: **Cleomedes**, *De contemplatione orbium excelsorum*. Add: Aelius Aristides: *Ad Rhodienses de concordia oratio*; Dio Chrysostomus: *Ad Nicomedenses oratio*; *De concordia oratio*; Plutarchus: *De virtute morali*; *Coniugalia praecepta*. Tr: Carolus Valgulius, Brescia: Bernardinus de Misintis, for Angelus Britannicus, 3 Apr. 1497. 4°. GW 7122; ISTC ic00741000; MEI 02006835 (no. 57 here).
-1581–1608 Girolamo Asteo (1562-1626), OFMConv from Pordenone; inscription on the first leaf of this volume: 'Fratris Hieronymi Astei'.
-1626(?)–1797 Venice, S. Giorgio Maggiore; eighteenth-century inscription on the same leaf: 'Est Bibliothecae Sancti Georgii Maioris Venetiarum'.

-1806 Regno d'Italia, decree no. 160, 28 July 1806.

-1806 Venice, S. Giorgio Maggiore; Rossi (1806), L45: 'Lilii Zachariae Orbis Breviarium sine loco, an. et typ. Cleomedis de contemplatione Orbium excelsorum disputatio; Aristidis, et Dionis de Concordia Orationes; Plutarchi precepta connubialia, et de virtutibus morum. Brixiae 1487 [probably a typo] p. Bernardium Misintam 4°'.

-March 1807–1818(?) Padua, Sant'Anna: Rossi (March 1807); Catalogo Generale XV (1811), no. 49, the title is: 'Lilii et alii, Orbis breviarrium etc., 4°, Brixiae, 1488 [sic]'. After the suppression of the monastery of S. Giorgio Maggiore in 1806, the volume was deposited in the former monastery of the Benedictine nuns of Sant'Anna in Padua, as with the other books that subsequently entered the Biblioteca Universitaria of Padua.

-1818(?)-c. 1840 Padua, Sala Carmeli, S. Francesco Grande. When the monastery of Sant'Anna had to be cleared, some selected volumes were transferred in part to the Pubblica Libreria (the Biblioteca Universitaria of Padua), in part to the Sala Carmeli of the former convent of S. Francesco Grande. A document dated 1818 records the transfer of books from S. Giorgio Maggiore into cupboards A, B, and C of Sala Carmeli. Padua, Catalogo Gnocchi (1818).

-c. 1840 transfer to the Biblioteca Universitaria of Padua: Ravegnani, *Le biblioteche*, 65–68; *Fondi antichi della Biblioteca Universitaria di Padova*, 40–41.

Padua, Biblioteca Universitaria: Sec. XV 529/1

109. Livius, Titus, *Historiae Romanae decades*. Ed: Johannes Andreas, bishop of Aleria, [Venice]: Vindelinus de Spira, 1470. Folio. ISTC il00238000; MEI 00200404.

-1470–1789 Venice, S. Giorgio Maggiore; on the first leaf of text of each volume two wreaths containing St George (or his shield and the dragon) and the she-wolf with Romulus and Remus; inscription at the front of vol. 1 and at the back of vols 2 and 3: 'Iste liber est Congregationis monachorum sancte Iustine deputatus monasterio

Diui Georgii maioris Venetiarum signatus numero 418 / 419 / 420'.

-1789 Venice, S. Giorgio Maggiore; Morelli's survey (1789), fasc. 1, 5: marked with +.

-1806–1814(?) Milan, Regno d'Italia: books gone to Milan, 4 Sept. 1806, item one to three.

-1814?-c. 1841 John Wyndham Bruce (1802–1869), London lawyer; at the centre of the front pastedown of vol. 2, armorial bookplate with his motto in Welsh: 'Duw ar fy rhan'.

-c. 1841–1862 Burton Hall (Lincoln); William John Monson, 6th Baron (1796–1862): on the front pastedown of vol. 2, above Bruce's bookplate, the armorial bookplate of Lord Monson with the motto: 'Prest pour mon pais' and 'Burton Library'.

-2013 on sale at Sotheby, London, *Music and Continental Books and Manuscripts*, London 5–6 June 2013, lot 209 (£30,000-£40,000).

Trade Copy, Sotheby, London, 2013: lot 209

110. Lucanus, Marcus Annaeus, *Cesariano (Libro dell'origine e dei fatti di Giulio Cesare)*, Venice: Alovisius de Sancta Lucia, 1 Mar. 1492. Folio. ISTC il00311000; MEI 02008265.

Bound second with: **Caracciolus, Robertus**, *Specchio della fede*, Venice: [s.n.], [after 11 Apr. 1495]. GW 6115; ISTC ic00187000; MEI 02008264 (no. 48 here).

-1806 Regno d'Italia, decree no. 160, 28 July 1806.

-1806 Venice, S. Giorgio Maggiore; Rossi (1806), C19: 'Caracciolo fra Roberto Specchio della fede Ven. 1495 sine typ. – Libro denominato il Cesariano, ovvero dei fatti di Cesare. Ven. 1492 s. typ. F.°'.

-March 1807–1813 Padua, Sant'Anna; Rossi (March 1807); Catalogo generale XV (1811), 145, no. 38: 'Caracciolo, Specchio della fede, folio, Venetiis, 1495; v'è unito Libro denominato Cesariano ovvero de' fatti di Cesare, Venetiis 1492'; *Fondi antichi della Biblioteca Universitaria di Padova*, 40–41.

-1813–1831(?) Padua, Sala Carmeli, S. Francesco Grande. One of the five incunables from S. Giorgio Maggiore listed in a document, now Padua,

S. Francesco Grande, Sala Carmeli (1813). The document reports five incunables which on Sunday 4 October 1813 were in S. Francesco Grande, evidently transferred from the warehouse of Sant'Anna to the Sala Carmeli (which was part of the University library), probably because of their value. The book arrived to the Biblioteca Universitaria di Padova somewhere between 4 October 1813 and 1831.

Padua, Biblioteca Universitaria: Sec. XV 406/2

111. Lucas de Burgo S. Sepulchri, *Somma di arithmetica, geometria, proporzioni e proporzionalità*, etc. Venice: Paganinus de Paganinis, 10–20 Nov. 14[9]4. Folio. ISTC il00315000; MEI 02006703.

-1806 Regno d'Italia, decree no. 160, 28 July 1806.
-1806 Venice, S. Giorgio Maggiore; Rossi (1806), B12: 'De Burgo Lucae Aritmetica, et Geometria. Ven. 1494 per Paganino de Paganini F.°'.
-March 1807–1813(?) Padua, Sant'Anna; Rossi (March 1807); Catalogo generale XV (1811), 145, no. 45: 'De Burgo, Aritmetica et geometria, fol. Ven. 1494'; *Fondi antichi della Biblioteca Universitaria di Padova*, 40–41.
-1813–1831(?) Padua, Sala Carmeli, S. Francesco Grande. One of the five incunables from S. Giorgio Maggiore listed in a document, now Padua, S. Francesco Grande, Sala Carmeli (1813). The document reports five incunables which on Sunday 4 October 1813 were in S. Francesco Grande, evidently transferred from the warehouse of Sant'Anna to the Sala Carmeli (which was part of the University library), probably because of their value. These books were dispersed between 4 October 1813 and 1831.

Historical copy, Venice

112. Lucianus Samosatensis, *Vera historia* [Latin]. Tr: Lilius (Tifernas) Castellanus. Add: Diodorus Siculus: *Bibliothecae historicae libri VI* [Latin]. Tr: Poggius Florentinus, Venice: Philippus Pincius, 20 Nov. 1493. Folio. ISTC il00328000; MEI 02008330.

Bound first with: **Appianus**, *Historia Romana* (Partes I–II), Venice: Christophorus de Pensis de Mandello, 20 Nov. 1500. Folio. GW 2291; ISTC ia00929000; MEI 02008331 (bound second, no. 12 here); and **Laurentius Valla**, *Elegantie de lingua Latina*, Venetiis: per Christoforum de Pensis, 7 Aug. 1505. Folio. CNCE 33468 (Padua, Biblioteca Universitaria, A.41.a.28, bound third).

-1700–1797 Venice, S. Giorgio Maggiore; eighteenth-century inscription on A2: 'Est Bibliothecae Sancti Georgii Maioris Veneti'.
-1806 Regno d'Italia, decree no. 160, 28 July 1806.
-1806 Venice, S. Giorgio Maggiore; Rossi (1806), L48: 'Luciani Poetae, et Oratoris De Veris narrationibus – Diodori Siculi de antiquorum gestis fabulosis Ven. 1493 p. Philip. Pincium – Appiani Alexandrini de bellis civilibus Ven. 1500 p. Christophorum de Pensis; Laurentii Vallensis Opus Elegantiarum linguae latinae Ven. 1505 ap. eundem Omnia uno vol. F.°'.
-March 1807(?)-1818(?) Padua, Sant'Anna: after the suppression of the monastery of S. Giorgio Maggiore in 1806, the volume was probably deposited in the former monastery of the Benedictine nuns of Sant'Anna in Padua, as with the other books that subsequently entered the Biblioteca Universitaria, even if it cannot be identified in the lists of books selected from that warehouse.
-1818(?)-*c*. 1840 Padua, Sala Carmeli, S. Francesco Grande. When the monastery of Sant'Anna had to be cleared, some selected volumes were transferred in part to the Pubblica Libreria (the Biblioteca Universitaria of Padua), in part to the Sala Carmeli of the former convent of S. Francesco Grande. A document dated 1818 records the transfer of books from S. Giorgio Maggiore into cupboards A, B, and C of Sala Carmeli. Padua, Catalogo Gnocchi (1818).
-*c*. 1840 transfer to the Biblioteca Universitaria of Padua: Ravegnani, *Le biblioteche*, 65–68; *Fondi antichi della Biblioteca Universitaria di Padova*, 40–41.

Padua, Biblioteca Universitaria: Sec. XV 377/1

113. Lucianus Samosatensis, *Vera historia* [Latin], Venice: Simon Bevilaqua, for Benedetto Bordon, 25 Aug. 1494. 4°. ISTC il00329000; MEI 02018220.
-1806 Venice, S. Giorgio Maggiore; Rossi (1806), L49: 'Luciani philosophi Opera quaedam. Ven. 1494 p. Simonem Bevilaquam, 4°'.
-1806 Regno d'Italia, decree no. 160, 28 July 1806.
-March 1807–1818(?) Padua, Sant'Anna; Rossi (March 1807); Catalogo generale XV (1811), 144, no. 9: 'Luciani, Opera, folio, Venetiis 1494 per Simonem Bevilaquam'; *Fondi antichi della Biblioteca Universitaria di Padova*, 40–41.
Historical copy, Venice

114. Mahomet II, *Epistolae magni Turci*. Add: Diogenes Cynicus: *Epistolae* (Tr: Franciscus Griffolinus Aretinus). Brutus: *Epistolae*; Hippocrates: *Epistolae* (Tr: Rinucius Aretinus), [Venice: Otinus de Luna, Papiensis, about 1500]. 4°. ISTC im00066000; MEI 02139835.
-1806 Venice, S. Giorgio Maggiore; Rossi (1806), T69: 'Turci Magni Epistolae interprete Laudivio sine loco, an. et typ. Seguitur traductio manuscripta Francisci Aretini Epistolarum nunnullarum Phaleridis [*sic*]. 4° pic.' Not mentioned in Morelli's survey (1789) nor in the Catalogo Generale XV (1811).
Editions *sine notis* appeared in Toulouse, Zaragoza, Cologne, Leipzig, and Würzburg (ISTC im00060000, im00059500, im00061000, im00063000, im00065000), of which no copies survive in Italy. The work was also printed, *sine notis*, in Rome twice (im00057500, im00062000) but with no survival in Northern Italy. Therefore, the most likely edition is probably the one by Otinus de Luna. The Correr copy of the Otinus de Luna edition is bound with an edition of Phalaris, *Epistolae* [Latin], [Venice]: Maximus de Butricis, [*c.* 1491]. ISTC ip00562000; MEI 02123913. It was owned by the Reformed Franciscans of Venice and subsequently by Giovanni Rossi himself. There must have been an established tradition which brought these two works together; and while we appear to have here a combination of printed and manuscript text, or multiple editions, joined together, towards the end of the fifteenth century we find an edition which included the two works: Mahomet II, *Epistolae magni Turci*. Prelim: Laudivius Zacchia: *Epistola ad Francinum Beltrandum*. Add: Phalaris: *Epistolae* [Latin] Tr: Franciscus Griffolinus (Aretinus). Deventer: Richardus Pafraet, [between 11 June 1491 and 25 Jan. 1492]. ISTC im00063600. However, this edition cannot be the one listed by Rossi, first because there is a colophon, and second, because the translator in the Deventer edition is actually given as 'Leonardum de Aretinum', while Rossi indicates that the book correctly states the name of the translator as Franciscus Aretinus.
Historical copy, Venice

115. Mancinellus, Antonius, *Scribendi orandique modus*.
Until we have further provenance evidence from the surviving copies of this work, it is not possible to identify the edition in question, as several editions of this work were printed in the fifteenth century, six in Venice alone. Not in MEI. Bound first with: **Ferettus, Nicolaus,** *De elegantia linguae latinae*, Forlì: Hieronymus Medesanus, 25 May 1495. 4°. GW 9783; ISTC if00099000; MEI 02018108 (bound second, no. 72 here); **Vergerius, Petrus Paulus,** *De ingenuis moribus ac liberalibus studiis*. Ed: Johannes Calphurnius. Comm: Johannes Bonardus. Add: Basilius Magnus: *De legendis antiquorum libris* (Tr: Leonardus Brunus Aretinus). Xenophon: *Hiero de tyrannide* (Tr: Leonardus Brunus Aretinus). Plutarchus: *De liberis educandis* (Tr: Guarinus Veronensis). S. Hieronymus: *De officiis liberorum erga parentes admonitio*, Venice: Johannes Tacuinus, de Tridino, 22 Sept. 1497. 4°. ISTC iv00139000; MEI 02018105 (bound third, no. 178 here); and **Beroaldus, Philippus,** *De felicitate*, Bologna: Franciscus (Plato) de Benedictis, 1 Apr. 1495. 4°. GW 4132; ISTC ib00482000; MEI 02018106 (bound fourth, no. 24 here).
-1806 Regno d'Italia, decree no. 160, 28 July 1806.

-1806 Venice, S. Giorgio Maggiore; Rossi (1806), M52: 'Mancinelli Antonii Scribendi, orandique modus, Forilivii 1495 p. Hieron. Medasanum. – Pauli Vergerii de ingenuis moribus cum comment. Io. Bonardi – Basilii de legendis antiquorum libris opusculum – Traductio ex Xenophonte Leonardi Aretini de Tyranide – Guarini Veronensis in Plutarcum praefatio, 1497 Ven. p. Io. Tacuinum. – Philippi Beroaldi de felicitate opusculum Bononiae 1495 p. Platonem de Benedictiis. Omnia uno tantum volumine in 4°. In making an entry for this composite volume, it is clear that the cataloguer merged two editions, noting the opening of an edition of Antonius Mancinellus and the imprint information for another edition, by Nicolaus Ferettus, bound behind. Unfortunately, it is not possible to determine which of the several editions of Mancinellus' *Scribendi orandique modus* is the one represented here.

-Not present in Catalogo generale XV (1811), it is therefore unlikely that the book ever reached Padua.
Historical Copy, Venice

116. Marchesinus, Johannes, *Mammotrectus super Bibliam*, Venice: Franciscus Renner, de Heilbronn, and Petrus de Bartua, 1478. 4°. ISTC im00238000; MEI 02008346.
-1478 Bologna, Benedictines, S. Proculus; inscription partly erased on a1: 'Est Sancti Proculi de Bononia'.
-1600–1797 Venice, S. Giorgio Maggiore; mid-seventeenth-century inscription on A2: 'Est Sancti Georgii Maioris Venetiarum'.
-1806 Regno d'Italia, decree no. 160, 28 July 1806.
-1806 Venice, S. Giorgio Maggiore; Rossi (1806), M51: 'Mamotrectus, seu Vocabularium Bibliae Venetiis 1478 p. Franc. de Hailbrun'.
-March 1807–1818(?) Padua, Sant'Anna; Rossi (March 1807); Catalogo generale XV (1811), 146, no. 54: 'Mamotrectus, seu vocabularium Bibliae, 4, Venetiis, 1478'; *Fondi antichi della Biblioteca Universitaria di Padova*, 40–41.
-1818(?)-*c.* 1840 Padua, Sala Carmeli, S. Francesco Grande. When the monastery of Sant'Anna

had to be cleared, some selected volumes were transferred in part to the Pubblica Libreria (the Biblioteca Universitaria of Padua), in part to the Sala Carmeli of the former convent of S. Francesco Grande. A document dated 1818 records the transfer of books from S. Giorgio Maggiore into cupboards A, B, and C of Sala Carmeli. Padua, Catalogo Gnocchi (1818).
-*c.* 1840 transfer to the Biblioteca Universitaria of Padua: Ravegnani, *Le biblioteche*, 65–68; *Fondi antichi della Biblioteca Universitaria di Padova*, 40–41.
Padua, Biblioteca Universitaria: Sec. XV 821

117. Marlianus, Raimundus, *Index locorum in commentario Caesaris Belli gallici descriptorum* (Rev: Bonus Accursius), [Milan: Bonus Accursius, about 1478]. 4°. ISTC im00276000; MEI 02127999.
-1478–1806? Venice, S. Giorgio Maggiore: inscription at the end of the printed text: 'Iste liber est monachorum Congregationis s. Justine de Padua deputatus in s. Georgio maiori Venetiarum signatus numero 546'.
The fact that this edition does not appear in any of the documents attesting to the state of the library at the time of the secularizations may suggest that the volume left the library of San Giorgio Maggiore before the end of the eighteenth century.
Berlin, Staatsbibliothek: Inc. 3080.25

118. Martinus Polonus, *Margarita decreti seu Tabula Martiniana*. [Bologna: Johannes de Nördlingen and Henricus de Harlem, not after 28 Feb. 1482]. Folio. GW M201404; ISTC ISTC im00321000; MEI 02139836.
-1806 Regno d'Italia, decree no. 160, 28 July 1806.
-1806 Venice, S. Giorgio Maggiore; Rossi (1806), M53: 'Martini Ordinis Praedicatorum Margarita Decreti, sine l. an. et typ. F.°'; Catalogo XV (1811), 145, no. 42: 'Martini, Margarita Decreti, fol. sine loco, ann. et typ. (sec. XV)'.
There are other editions, one from Nuremberg (im00326000) and two from Speyer

(im00319000; im00320000) *sine notis*, but with few or no copies surviving today in Italy, while there are several copies of the Bologna edition, including three in Padua, Biblioteca Universitaria.
Historical Copy, Venice

119. Mediavilla, Richardus de, *Commentum super quarto libro Sententiarum Petri Lombardi.* (Ed: Franciscus Gregorius), [Venice]: Bonetus Locatellus, for the heirs of Octavianus Scotus, 17 Dec. 1499. 4°. ISTC im00426000; MEI 02014160.
-*c.* 1500-*c.* 1500 Venice, S. Giorgio Maggiore; in the early sixteenth-century inscription below the colophon, 'Iste liber est S. Georgij de Venetiis signatus no.', the word 'Benedicti' has been written over 'Georgii' and 'Padulijs' over 'Venetiis', in what looks like a fairly contemporary hand.
-1550–1797 Polirone (Mantua), Benedictines, S. Benedictus; stamp of the order on the title-page.
-1797 Mantova, Biblioteca Comunale Teresiana: stamp; probably acquired following the Napoleonic suppressions of religious institutions.
Mantova, Biblioteca Teresiana: Inc. 345

120. Mesue, *Opera medicinalia*, etc. [Padua: Laurentius Canotius de Lendenaria], 9 June 1471. Folio. ISTC im00509000; MEI 02015563; *Catalogues régionaux des incunables des bibliothèques publiques de France: Bibliothèque de l'Académie de médecine [et neuf bibliothèques parisiennes de médecine et de science, etc.]* ed. Yvonne Fernillot and Pierre Aquilon, Histoire et civilisation du livre, 34; Catalogues régionaux des incunables des bibliothèques publiques de France, 15 (Geneva, 2014), 170, no. 184.
-1471–1806? Venice, S. Giorgio Maggiore: sixteenth-century inscription on [B6]: 'Iste liber est Sancti Georgii Maioris Venetiarum no. 928'.
-1893 Paris, Bibliothèque nationale de France: acquisition no. 137700; inside front pastedown, two cuttings from *Livres rares et curieux … à la librairie ancienne de A. Claudin* (Paris, Oct. 1893) no. 24072 (on sale for fr. 150) and s.d. no. 38256

describing this copy; de-accession stamps of the library on fol. 1r, exchange.
Paris, Bibliothèque interuniversitaire de santé (Pharmacie): Rés. 5913

121. Missale Romanum. (Ed: Petrus Arrivabenus?), Venice: Georgius Arrivabenus, 29 May 1499. Folio. CIBN M-469; ISTC im00716000; MEI 02008352.
-1499 Venice, S. Giorgio Maggiore: sixteenth-century illumination by Benedetto Bordon, according to Lilian Armstrong.
-1813 Paris, Royal Library: acquired in 1813 according to *Catalogue des livres imprimés sur vélin de la Bibliothèque du Roi*, [ed. Joseph Basile Bernard Van Praet], 6 vols (Paris, 1822–1828), I, 92.
Paris, Bibliothèque nationale de France: Vél. 135

122. Monte, Petrus de, *Repertorium utriusque iuris*, Padua: Johannes Herbort, de Seligenstadt, 16 Nov. 1480. Folio. ISTC im00844000; MEI 02006688.
-1806 Regno d'Italia, decree no. 160, 28 July 1806.
-1806 Venice, S. Giorgio Maggiore; Rossi (1806), B14: 'Brixiensis Petri Repertorium utriusque Iuris. Patavii 1480 per Io. Herbort de Silgenstadt T.i 2 F.°'.
-March 1807–1818(?) Padua, Sant'Anna; Rossi (March 1807); Catalogo generale XV (1811), 144, no. 13: 'Brixiensis, Repertorium utriusque iuris, fol. Patavi 1480 per Io. Herbort de Silgenstadt, t. 2'.
-1818(?)-*c.* 1840 Padua, Sala Carmeli, S. Francesco Grande. When the monastery of Sant'Anna had to be cleared, some selected volumes were transferred in part to the Pubblica Libreria (the Biblioteca Universitaria of Padua), in part to the Sala Carmeli of the former convent of S. Francesco Grande. A document dated 1818 records the transfer of books from S. Giorgio Maggiore into cupboards A, B, and C of Sala Carmeli. Padua, Catalogo Gnocchi (1818).
-*c.* 1840 transfer to the Biblioteca Universitaria of Padua: Ravegnani, *Le biblioteche*, 65–68; *Fondi antichi della Biblioteca Universitaria di Padova*, 40–41.
Historical copy, Venice

123. Nicolaus de Ausmo, *Supplementum Summae Pisanellae*, etc. Venice: Leonardus Wild, '1489' [i.e. 1479]. 4°. ISTC in00071000; MEI 02008332.

-1479–1806 Venice, S. Giorgio Maggiore; inscription on the verso of the last leaf: 'Iste liber est monachorum congregationis Sancte Iustine de Padua ordinis sancti Benedicti deputatus in Sancto Georgio Maiore Venetiarum. 602'.

-1806 Regno d'Italia, decree no. 160, 28 July 1806.

-1806 Venice, S. Giorgio Maggiore; Rossi (1806), B2: 'De Auximo Nicolai Summae Pisanellae. Ven. 1489 cura Leonardi Wild 4°'.

-March 1807–1818(?) Padua; Sant'Anna; Rossi (March 1807); Catalogo generale XV (1811), 144, no. 2: 'De Auximo, Summae Pisanellae, 4, Venetiis, cura Leonardi Vilae, 1489'; *Fondi antichi della Biblioteca Universitaria di Padova*, 40–41.

-1818(?)-*c.* 1840 Padua, Sala Carmeli, S. Francesco Grande. When the monastery of Sant'Anna had to be cleared, some selected volumes were transferred in part to the Pubblica Libreria (the Biblioteca Universitaria of Padua), in part to the Sala Carmeli of the former convent of S. Francesco Grande. A document dated 1818 records the transfer of books from S. Giorgio Maggiore into cupboards A, B, and C of Sala Carmeli. Padua, Catalogo Gnocchi (1818).

-*c.* 1840 transfer to the Biblioteca Universitaria of Padua: Ravegnani, *'Le biblioteche*, 65–68; *Fondi antichi della Biblioteca Universitaria di Padova*, 40–41.

Padua, Biblioteca Universitaria: Sec. XV 305

124. Nicolaus de Lyra, *Postilla super Epistolas et Evangelia quadragesimalia*, [Lyon]: Nicolaus Wolf, 10 Feb. 1500/1501. 4°. ISTC in00120600; MEI 02006855.

-1806 Venice, S. Giorgio Maggiore: mid-seventeenth-century inscription on the first leaf: 'Est Sancti Georgii Maioris Venetiarum'.

-1806 Regno d'Italia, decree no. 160, 28 July 1806.

-1806 Venice, S. Giorgio Maggiore; Rossi (1806), L46: 'De Lira Nicolai Postilla, seu Expositio literalis, et moralis super Epistolas, et Evangelia

quadragesimalia cum quaestionibus Fratris Antonii Betontini 1500 p. Nicolaum Wolff 8°'.

-March 1807–1818(?) Padua, Sant'Anna; Rossi (March 1807); Catalogo generale XV (1811), 145, no. 25: 'De Lyra, Postillae etc., folio, 1500, per Nicolaum Volf, et 1481. 8'; *Fondi antichi della Biblioteca Universitaria di Padova*, 40–41. In this Padua catalogue, vol. 4 (today missing) of **Biblia Latina**, etc. Venice: [Johannes Herbort, de Seligenstadt], for Johannes de Colonia, Nicolaus Jenson et Socii, 31 July 1481. Folio (see no. 31 here) is mentioned along with the Lyon 1500 edition, although Rossi refers to both separately (L46 and L47).

-1818(?)-*c.* 1840 Padua, Sala Carmeli, S. Francesco Grande. When the monastery of Sant'Anna had to be cleared, some selected volumes were transferred in part to the Pubblica Libreria (the Biblioteca Universitaria of Padua), in part to the Sala Carmeli of the former convent of S. Francesco Grande. A document dated 1818 records the transfer of books from S. Giorgio Maggiore into cupboards A, B, and C of Sala Carmeli. Padua, Catalogo Gnocchi (1818).

-*c.* 1840 transfer to the Biblioteca Universitaria of Padua: Ravegnani, *Le biblioteche*, 65–68; *Fondi antichi della Biblioteca Universitaria di Padova*, 40–41.

Padua, Biblioteca Universitaria: Sec. XV 23

125. Nonius Marcellus, *De proprietate latini sermonis*, Venice: Nicolaus Jenson, 1476. Folio. ISTC in00265000; MEI 02008357.

-1476–1765 Venice, S. Giorgio Maggiore; contemporary inscription in brown ink on leaf z12r: 'In monasterio S. Georgij Maioris Venetiarum signatus numero 530'.

-1765 Venice, S. Giorgio Maggiore: included in the list published in Gerbert (1765).

-1789 Venice, S. Giorgio Maggiore; Morelli's survey (1789), fasc. 1, 6: marked with + and crossed out.

-1797–1815 Paris, Bibliothèque nationale: BnF archives list (1797), fasc. 2, no. 4: 'Nonius Marcellus. Venet. 1476 fol., sur velin S. Just. de Pad. Velin'; Cicogna (1797): 'Dalla libreria di s.

Giorgio Maggiore furono portati a Parigi nel 1797 i seguenti Codici manuscritti […] Edizioni del secolo XV […]. 11. Marcellius [*sic*] Nonius f. membr. Venetiis 1476. Ienson'.

-1815 Venice, Biblioteca Nazionale Marciana: returned in 1815 (Bibliothèque nationale de France has two copies of this edition); Cicogna (1797): 'Per la generosità di Francesco I di gloriosissima memoria presso che tutti cotesti libri son ritornati nel 1815, e riposti nella Marciana'.

Venice, Biblioteca Nazionale Marciana: Membr. 0021

126. Odonis, **Geraldus**, *Expositio in Aristotelis Ethicam*, Venice: Simon de Luere, for A. Torresanus, 14 July 1500. Folio. ISTC io00029000; MEI 02017598.

-1500–1806 Venice, S. Giorgio Maggiore: seventeenth-century inscription on the title-page: 'Est Bibliotecae S. Georgij Maioris Venetiarum'; see *Papers of Edinburgh Bibl. Society*, IX (1913), no. 150.

-1806 Regno d'Italia, decree no. 160, 28 July 1806.

-1806 Venice, S. Giorgio Maggiore; Rossi (1806), O57: 'Odonis Geraldi Sententia, et Expositio cum quaestionibus super libros Ethicorum Aristotelis, et ejusd. textu. Ven. 1500 p. Simonem de Luere F.°'.

Edinburgh, University Library: CRC In.F.73 (formerly Inc. 117)

127. Panormitanus de Tudeschis, Nicolaus, *Consilia* (cum Ludovici Bolognini tabula), Venice: Peregrinus de Pasqualibus, Bononiensis and Dominicus Bertochus, 14 Dec. 1486. Folio. GW M47773; ISTC ip00030000; MEI 02137941.

Bound third with: **Antonius de Butrio**, *Super primo libro Decretalium* (7–28), Venice: Bernardinus Rizus, Novariensis, 1485. Folio. GW 5822; ISTC ib01342000; MEI 02018170 (bound first, no. 10 here); **Panormitanus de Tudeschis**, Nicolaus, *Disceptationes* (*seu Disputationes*) *et allegationes*, of which three editions were published in Venice, in 1483, 1487, and 1490 of 38, 32, and 28 leaves respectively (bound second, no. 128 here); **Guido de Baysio**, *Apparatus libri sexti*

decretalium, Milan: Jacobus de Sancto Nazario, de Ripa, and Bernardinus de Castelliono, 23 Dec. 1490. Folio. GW 3743; ISTC ib00284000; MEI 02018176 (bound fourth, no. 90 here).

-1806 Regno d'Italia, decree no. 160, 28 July 1806.

-1806 Venice, S. Giorgio Maggiore; Rossi (1806), B17: 'De Butrio Lectura de Translatione Prelatorum, Ven. 1485 per Bernard. de Novaria. It. Nicolai de Sicilia Allegationes Ven. 1486 per Peregrinum de Pasqualibus, et socium. – Lectura D.i Archidiaconi Bononiensis. Mediolani 1490 p. Bernardi de Castellio, et socium. Omnia T.° 1, F.°'. This entry merges the detail of two editions bound second and third in this composite volume, the title of Panormitanus' *Disceptationes* (*seu Disputationes*) *et allegationes*, and the bibliographical information from Panormitanus, *Consilia* (cum Ludovici Bolognini tabula).

-March 1807–1818(?) Padua, Sant'Anna; Rossi (March 1807); Catalogo generale XV (1811), 145, no. 24: 'De Butrio, Lectura etc., fol. Ven. 1485, 1486, et 1490'; *Fondi antichi della Biblioteca Universitaria di Padova*, 40–41. The four copies were still bound together in 1811, as specifically stated in the Catalogue.

Historical copy, Venice

128. Panormitanus de Tudeschis, Nicolaus, *Disceptationes* (*seu Disputationes*) *et allegationes*. Three editions were printed in Venice, in 1483, 1487, and 1490, of 38, 32, and 28 leaves respectively. A copy of the 1487 edition now in Padua Biblioteca Universitaria presents a different provenance, therefore the S. Giorgio copy must have been disposed of and its precise bibliographical identification is not possible until the provenance of further copies is ascertained. This historical copy is not in MEI.

Bound second with: **Antonius de Butrio**, *Super primo libro Decretalium* (7–28), Venice: Bernardinus Rizus, Novariensis, 1485. Folio. GW 5822; ISTC ib01342000; MEI 02018170 (bound first, no. 10 here); **Panormitanus de Tudeschis**, Nicolaus, *Consilia* (cum Ludovici Bolognini tabula), Venice: Peregrinus de Pasqualibus, Bononiensis and Dominicus Bertochus, 14 Dec. 1486. Folio. GW M47773; ISTC ip00030000; MEI 02137941 (bound third, no. 127 here); **Guido de Baysio**, *Apparatus libri sexti decretalium*, Milan: Jacobus de Sancto Nazario, de Ripa, and Bernardinus de Castelliono, 23 Dec. 1490. Folio. GW 3743; ISTC ib00284000; MEI 02018176 (bound fourth, no. 90 here).

-1806 Regno d'Italia, decree no. 160, 28 July 1806.

-1806 Venice, S. Giorgio Maggiore; Rossi (1806), B17: 'De Butrio Lectura de Translatione Prelatorum, Ven. 1485 per Bernard. de Novaria. It. Nicolai de Sicilia Allegationes Ven. 1486 per Peregrinum de Pasqualibus, et socium. – Lectura D.i Archidiaconi Bononiensis. Mediolani 1490 p. Bernardi de Castellio, et socium. Omnia T.º 1, F.º'. This entry merges the detail of two editions bound second and third in this composite volume, the title of Panormitanus' *Disceptationes* (*seu Disputationes*) *et allegationes*, and the bibliographical information from Panormitanus, *Consilia* (cum Ludovici Bolognini tabula).

-March 1807–1818(?) Padua, Sant'Anna; Rossi (March 1807); Catalogo generale XV (1811), 145, no. 24: 'De Butrio, Lectura etc., fol. Ven. 1485, 1486, et 1490'; *Fondi antichi della Biblioteca Universitaria di Padova*, 40–41. The four copies were still bound together in 1811, as specifically stated in the Catalogue.

Historical Copy, Venice

129. Papias, *Vocabularium*. Ed: Boninus Mombritius, Venice: Andreas de Bonetis, 30 June 1485. Folio. ISTC ip00078000; MEI 02126740.

-1485-before 1797 Venice, S. Giorgio Maggiore; inscription on m11v: 'Est congregationis s. Iustine de Padua ordinis S. Benedicti deputatus in monasterio sancti Georgii maioris Venetiarum ac signatus numero 789'.

-1797(?)-1850 Milan, Giacinto Amati (1778–1850); stamp 'Preposto | d. Giacinto | Amati'. Bequeathed to the Servites of Milan.

-1850 Milan, Biblioteca dei Servi; stamp 'Conv. Ord. Serv. Mariae Mediolani'.
Milan, Biblioteca dei Servi: 85a

130. Perottus, Nicolaus, *Cornucopiae linguae latinae*, Venice: Paganinus de Paganinis, 14 May 1489. Folio. ISTC ip00288000; MEI 02006679; Hans Sallander, *Katalog der Inkunabeln der Kgl. Universitäts-Bibliothek zu Uppsala. 1) Neuerwerbungen seit dem Jahre 1907*, Bibliotheca Ekmaniana 59 (Uppsala, 1953), no. 1885.

-1489–1806 Venice, S. Giorgio Maggiore; contemporary inscription: 'Iste liber est Congregationis monachorum s. Justine de Padua ordinis s. Benedicti deputatus in monasterio s. Georgij maioris Venetiarum signatus 947'.

-1806 Regno d'Italia, decree no. 160, 28 July 1806.

-1806 Venice, S. Giorgio Maggiore; Rossi (1806), P59: 'Perotti Nicolai Cornucopia, sive Commentarii linguae latinae Ven. 1489 p. Paganinum de Paganini F.º'.

-1811 Padua, Sant'Anna; Catalogo generale XV, 145, no. 28: 'Perotti, Cornucopia, fol. Ven. 1489'.
Uppsala, University Library: Ink. 35b

131. Perottus, Nicolaus, *Rudimenta grammatices*, Venice: [Jacobus de Fivizzano, Lunensis], for Marcus de Comitibus and Gerardus Alexandrinus, 17 Jan. 1476 [i.e. 1477?]. Folio. CIBN P-124; ISTC ip00305000; MEI 02017605.

-before 1789 Venice, S. Giorgio Maggiore; seventeenth-century inscription on a1r, light brown ink: 'Est s. Georgij maioris Venitiarum [*sic*]'; another, possibly earlier, sixteenth-century inscription: 'Hic liber est Sancti Georgi Maioris Venetiarum', and just below, 'Isti liber est sancti Georgii Venetiarum deputatus Bibliotheca'.

-1789 Venice, S. Giorgio Maggiore; Morelli's survey (1789), fasc. 1, 6: without the +, crossed out.

-1797 Paris, Bibliothèque nationale: BnF archives list (1797), fasc. 2, no. 16: 'Perotus 1476 in fol. en carton'; Cicogna (1797): 'Dalla libreria di s. Giorgio Maggiore furono portati a Parigi nel 1797 i seguenti Codici manuscritti [...] Edizioni del secolo XV [...]13. Perotti Nicolai Rudimenta gramaticae f. Chart. Venetiis 1476'. The volume did not return to the Marciana library, as should have been the case according to Cicogna (1797): 'Per la generosità di Francesco I di gloriosissima memoria presso che tutti cotesti libri son ritornati nel 1815, e riposti nella Marciana'. The Marciana copy was replaced by another unknown edition supplied by the book dealer Salvi. BnF Restitution list (1815), fasc. 2.

Paris, Bibliothèque nationale de France: Rés. X. 571

132. Persius Flaccus, Aulus, *Satyrae*, Venice: Petrus de Quarengiis, Bergomensis, 13 Apr. 1495. Folio. ISTC ip00357000; MEI 02008268.
Bound second with **Juvenalis, Decimus Junius**, *Satyrae*, Venice: Johannes Tacuinus, de Tridino, 24 July 1498. Folio. ISTC ij00666000; MEI 02008266 (bound first, no. 104 here) and **Statius, Publius Papinius**, *Opera*, Venice: Petrus de Quarengiis, Bergomensis, 1498/1499. Folio. ISTC is00694000; MEI 02008269 (bound third, no. 160 here).
-1806 Regno d'Italia, decree no. 160, 28 July 1806.
-1806 Venice, S. Giorgio Maggiore; Rossi (1806), I42: 'Iuvenalis Decii Iunii Satyrae cum Comment. Ant. Mancinelli. Ven. 1495 p. Petrum Io. de Querengis, et Statii Poetae Sylvae Thebais, et Achilleis cum plur. Commentariis. Ibid. 1498 ap. eund. F.º'; the entry merges the bibliographical information (author, title, commentator) of the edition bound first with the typographical information (place, year, and printer) of the edition bound second; followed by the correct bibliographical and typographical information of the edition bound third. The bibliographical information of the edition bound second, Persius, not specified, can be inferred by the typographical information provided and by the physical presence of the three editions in one volume today in the library of the University of Padua.
-March 1807–1818(?) Padua, Sant'Anna; Rossi (March 1807); Catalogo generale XV (1811), 145, no. 39: 'Iuvenalis, Satyrae cum cummentariis,

folio, Venetiis, 1495; v'è unito Statii, Sylvae etc., folio, Venetiis, 1498'; *Fondi antichi della Biblioteca Universitaria di Padova*, 40–41.
Padua, Biblioteca Universitaria: Sec. XV 420/2

133. Petrus de Palude, *In quartum librum Sententiarum Petri Lombardi*, Venice: Bonetus Locatellus, for Octavianus Scotus, 20 Sept. 1493. Folio. ISTC ip00502000; MEI 02006699.
-1806 Regno d'Italia, decree no. 160, 28 July 1806.
-1806 Venice, S. Giorgio Maggiore; Rossi (1806), P58: 'De Palude Petri Commentaria in quartum Sententiarum. Ven. 1493 p. Bonettum Locatellum F.º'.
-March 1807–1818(?) Padua, Sant'Anna; Rossi (March 1807); Catalogo generale XV (1811), 145, no. 40: 'De Palude, Commentarii in quart. librum Sententiarum, fol. Ven. 1493'; *Fondi antichi della Biblioteca Universitaria di Padova*, 40–41.
Historical copy, Venice

134. Philelphus, Franciscus, *Mediolanensia convivia duo*, etc. [Milan: Simon Magniagus, 1483–84]. 4º. GW M32948; ISTC ip00605000; MEI 02108487.
-1789 Venice, S. Giorgio Maggiore; Morelli's survey (1789), fasc. 1, 6: 'Absque ulla nota, saec. XV in 4º', no marks.
Historical copy, Venice

135. Philelphus, Johannes Marius, *Novum epistolarium*, Venice: Johannes Tacuinus, de Tridino, '20 Oct. 1492'. 4º. ISTC ip00622000; MEI 02018225.
Formerly bound second with: [**Guarinus Veronensis**], *Regulae Guarini nuperrime impressae & emendatae cum expositione versuum hetero-clitorum & differentialium & cum suis dipthongis expositis tam graecis quam latinis additamentis foeliciter incipiunt*, Venetiis: per Ioannem de Ceretto de Tridino alias Tacuinum, 1507 die XXV mensis Augusti. 4º. CNCE 34394 (Padua, Biblioteca Universitaria 44.a.134.1).
-1806 Regno d'Italia, decree no. 160, 28 July 1806.

-1806 Venice, S. Giorgio Maggiore; Rossi (1806), G33: 'Guarini Veronensis Grammatices, Ven. 1507 ap. Io. Tacuinum, et Epistolae Marii Philelphi, Ven. 1492 ap. eumd., 4°'.

-1817 Padua: Catalogo pregio (1817), 12, no. 488; note that while only the edition originally bound first is listed, the imprint information comes from the Philelphus edition, bound second: 'Guarini Regulae gramaticales, Venetiis 1492. 4°', however, the entry in Rossi spells out that Guarinus and Philelphus were bound together.

-1820 Padua, Biblioteca Universitaria; Ravegnani, *Le biblioteche*, 65–68; *Fondi antichi della Biblioteca Universitaria di Padova*, 40–41. The volume today contains only Philelphus. The front cover is detached, clearly since the time Guarinus was removed. On the spine the title still reads 'Guarini Reg[...]'. The binding, on parchment over pasteboards, also presents traces of a decorative motif in green, which has been found in other bindings from S. Giorgio. The Guarinus edition is today bound with another sixteenth-century edition. ***Padua, Biblioteca Universitaria: Sec. XV 488***

136. Picus de Mirandula, Johannes, *Opera*, Venice: Bernardinus de Vitalibus, 1498. Folio. ISTC ip00634000; MEI 02017608; *Treasures of the Valmadonna Trust Library: A Catalogue of the 15th-Century Books and Five Centuries of Deluxe Hebrew Printing*, ed. David Sclar (London, 2011), P-634.

-1498–1513 Andreas Mocenicus, apostolic protonotary: see below.

-1513–1806? Venice, S. Giorgio Maggiore: inscription on fol. 1r: 'Reverendus dominus Andreas Mocenicus protonotarius pro anime sue salute diui Georgii maioris cenobio dicauit signatus numero 114', Andrea Mocenigo died in 1513.

-1806?-1946 Gotha, Ducal Library: disposed as a duplicate, on fol. 1r: black oval stamp, 'DUPLUM | BIB | GOTH'.

-1946–2016 London, Valmadonna Collection (Jack Lunzer, d. 2016).

-2017 Jerusalem National Library; acquired in 2017. ***Jerusalem, National Library of Israel: 2018 C 7175***

137. Platea, Franciscus de, *Opus restitutionum, usurarum, excommunicationum*, [Venice]: Bartholomaeus Cremonensis, 1472. 4°. ISTC ip00752000; MEI 02006676.

-1472–1806 Venice, S. Giorgio Maggiore; inscription on [aa1v] in a fifteenth-century hand: 'Iste liber est congregationis sancte Justine de Padua ordinis sancti Benedicti deputatus monasterio sancti Georgii maioris de Venetiis sig[natus] no. 619'.

-1806 Regno d'Italia, decree no. 160, 28 July 1806.

-1806 Venice, S. Giorgio Maggiore; Rossi (1806), P61: 'De Platea Francisci Opus Restitutionum inscriptum, absque loco, et typ. 1472 4°'.

-March 1807–1813 Padua, Sant'Anna; Rossi (March 1807); Catalogo generale XV, 145, no. 46: 'De Platea, Opus restitutionum inscriptum, 4, 1472, absque loco et typographo, bello' (the printer's name is not provided probably because it is not very noticeable in the colophon).

-1813–1831(?) Padua, Sala Carmeli, S. Francesco Grande. One of the five incunables from S. Giorgio Maggiore listed in a document, now Padua, Padua, S. Francesco Grande, Sala Carmeli (1813). The document reports five incunables which on Sunday 4 October 1813 were in S. Francesco Grande, evidently transferred from the warehouse of Sant'Anna to the Sala Carmeli (which was part of the University library), probably because of their value. These books were dispersed between 4 October 1813 and 1831.

-1831 Oxford, Bodleian Library: purchased in 1831 from the bookseller Thomas Thorpe for £0. 10. 0. ***Oxford, Bodleian Library: Auct. 1Q inf. 1.15***

138. Platina, Bartholomæus, *Vitæ pontificum*, [Venice:] Johannes de Colonia et Johannes Manthen, 11 June 1479. Folio. CIBN P-443*; ISTC ip00768000; MEI 02017609.

-1479–1789 Venice, S. Giorgio Maggiore: contemporary inscription on the verso of the last leaf: 'Iste liber est congregationis sanctae Iustinae de padua ordinis sancti Benedicti | deputatus monasterio sancti Georgij maioris de venetijs sig(at)us numero 622'.

-1789 Venice, S. Giorgio Maggiore; Morelli's survey (1789), fasc. 1, 6: marked with + and crossed out; ex-libris of the Marciana library with the lion of St Mark and the motto 'Custos vel ultor', created in 1722 by the then librarian Girolamo Venier and used for quite a while afterwards – this ex-libris was used by Morelli after his survey to mark the most precious books in each monastery.

-1797 Paris, Bibliothèque nationale, BnF archives list (1797), fasc. 2, no. 17: 'Platina 1479 in fol. Carton Sta. Justina'; Cicogna (1797): 'Dalla libreria di s. Giorgio Maggiore furono portati a Parigi nel 1797 i seguenti Codici manuscritti […] Edizioni del secolo XV […]14. Platinae Vitae Pontificum f. Chart. Venetiis 1479'. A note in Van Praet's hand in the lower right-hand corner of the front pastedown, brown ink: 'Envoi de Venise'. The volume did not return to the Marciana library, as should have been the case according to Cicogna (1797): 'Per la generosità di Francesco I di gloriosissima memoria presso che tutti cotesti libri son ritornati nel 1815, e riposti nella Marciana'.

Paris, Bibliothèque nationale de France: Rés. H. 64

139. Plato, *Opera*, Venice: B. de Choris and Simon de Luere, for A. Torresanus, 13 Aug. 1491. Folio. ISTC ip00772000; MEI 02017610.

-*c.* 1491–1806(?) Venice, S. Giorgio Maggiore: the Rattey catalogue refers to, but does not transcribe, the customary fifteenth-century inscription which mentions both Sta. Giustina and S. Giorgio Maggiore.

-1830 Rome, Robert Finch (1783–1830).

-1830 Oxford, Taylor Institution; bequest.

-1965 Torquay, Clifford C. Rattey (1886–1970); *Catalogue of the Library at Corbyns, Torquay, formed by Clifford C. Rattey* (Leamington Spa, 1965), no. B112.

Historical Copy, Rattey

140. Plautus, *Comoediae*, Venice: Simon Bevilaqua, 17 Sept. 1499. Folio. ISTC ip00784000; MEI 00209908.

-1499–1513 Andreas Mocenicus, apostolic protonotary: see below.

-1513–1806 Venice, S. Giorgio Maggiore; inscription on A1r: 'Reuerendus dominus Andreas Mocenicus prothonotarius apostolicus pro anime sue salute diui Georgii maioris cenobio dicauit signatus C.115'; Andreas Mocenigo died in 1513.

-1956 Oxford, Bodleian Library; purchased in 1956 from the bookbinders C. & C. McLeish.

Oxford, Bodleian Library: Inc. c. I4.1499.5

141. Plinius Secundus, Gaius (Pliny, the Elder), *Historia naturalis*, Venice: Johannes de Spira, [before 18 Sept.] 1469. Folio. ISTC ip00786000; MEI 02008207.

-*c.* 1469–1700 Venice, S. Giorgio Maggiore; illuminated by the Pico Master: see Lilian Armstrong, Piero Scapecchi, Federica Toniolo, *Gli incunaboli della biblioteca del Seminario Vescovile di Padova. Catalogo e studi*, ed. Pierantonio Gios and Federica Toniolo, introduction by Giordana Mariani Canova (Padua, 2008), 92, no. 346 and 163, no. 346.

-*c.* 1700–1720 Padua, Count Alfonso Alvarotti (1687–1720): evidence from the binding.

-1720 Padua, Seminario Vescovile: the Alvarotti library was purchased in 1720.

Padua, Biblioteca del Seminario Vescovile: Forc. K.1.13

142. Plinius Secundus, Gaius, *Historia naturalis*, Parma: Stephanus Corallus, 1476. Folio ISTC ip00790000; MEI 02017611.

-1476–1789 Venice, S. Giorgio Maggiore; contemporary inscription in the lower margin of [P]3r: 'Iste liber e(st) monachorum congregationis s. Justine de Padua deputatus in s. Georgio Venetiarum signatus numero 545'; seventeenth-century inscription on [a]2r: 'Est Bibl.ae S. Georgij M.is Venet.rum'.

-1789 Venice, S. Giorgio Maggiore; Morelli's survey (1789), fasc. 1, 6: no marks.

-1806 Venice, S. Giorgio Maggiore; Rossi (1806), P62: 'Plinii Secundi Historia naturalis. Parmae impensis Stephani Coralli F.°'.

Not present in Catalogo generale XV (1811), it is therefore unlikely that the book ever reached Padua.

-1841 Cambridge Mass.; manuscript note in the upper margin of [o]2r: 'King's Chapel, Boston, to the library of Harvard University, Cambridge. 1841'. Gift of the Minister, Wardens, and Vestry of King's Chapel, Boston.

Harvard University, Houghton Library: Inc. 6842 (A)

143. Plinius Secundus, Gaius, *Historia naturalis* [Italian], Venice: Bartholomaeus de Zanis, 12 Sept. 1489. Folio. ISTC ip00803000; MEI 02018222.

-1806 Regno d'Italia, decree no. 160, 28 July 1806.
-1806 Venice, S. Giorgio Maggiore; Rossi (1806), P63: 'Plinio La Storia naturale tradotta da Cristoforo Landino, Ven. 1489 p. Bortolamio de Zani, F.º'.
-March 1807–1818(?) Padua, Sant'Anna; Rossi (March 1807); Catalogo generale XV (1811), 145, no. 26: 'Plinio, Storia naturale tradotta dal Landino, folio, Venetiis 1489'; *Fondi antichi della Biblioteca Universitaria di Padova*, 40–41.

Historical copy, Venice

144. Plotinus, *Opera*. Tr. & comm: Marsilius Ficinus, Florence: Antonio di Bartolommeo Miscomini, 7 May 1492. Folio. ISTC ip00815000; MEI 02018231.

-1789 Venice, S. Giorgio Maggiore; Morelli's survey (1789), fasc. 1, 6: crossed out.
-1797 Paris, Bibliothèque nationale; BnF archives list (1797), fasc. 2, no. 7: 'Plotinus 1492 in fol.'; Cicogna (1797): 'Dalla libreria di s. Giorgio Maggiore furono portati a Parigi nel 1797 i seguenti Codici manuscritti [...] Edizioni del secolo XV [...] 15. Plotini opera f. chart. Florentiae 1492'. The volume did not return to the Marciana library, as should have been the case according to Cicogna (1797): 'Per la generosità di Francesco I di gloriosissima memoria presso che tutti cotesti libri son ritornati nel 1815, e riposti nella Marciana'.

Possibly the copy now in Paris, Rés. Z. 291 (CIBN P-480), which had belonged to the Benedictine humanist Paschasius Berselius († 1535) and to the Benedictines of Rome, San Lorenzo al Verano.

Historical copy, Venice

145. Priscianus, *Opera*, [Milan: Dominicus de Vespolate for Boninus Mombritius, after 24 Feb. 1476.] Folio. CIBN P-595*; ISTC ip00963000; MEI 02017613.

-1789 Venice, S. Giorgio Maggiore; inscription on the front flyleaf in an early sixteenth-century hand, light brown ink, different from other inscriptions found in the library's books of the period: 'Hic liber est diui Georgi maioris venetiarum'; just below, 'Iste liber est sancti georgii maioris venetiarum deputatus biblioteca ipsius'.
-1789 Venice, S. Giorgio Maggiore; Morelli's survey (1789), fasc. 1, 6: marked with + and crossed out; ex-libris of the Marciana library with the lion of St Mark and the motto 'Custos vel ultor', created in 1722 by the then librarian Girolamo Venier and used for quite a while afterwards – this ex-libris was used by Morelli after his survey to mark the most precious books in each monastery.
-1797 Paris, Bibliothèque nationale; Cicogna (1797): 'Dalla libreria di s. Giorgio Maggiore furono portati a Parigi nel 1797 i seguenti Codici manuscritti [...] Edizioni del secolo XV [...]16. Priscianus fol. chart. sine loco 1470' (1476, mistakenly read by Cicogna as 1470). The volume did not return to the Marciana library, as should have been the case according to Cicogna (1797): 'Per la generosità di Francesco I di gloriosissima memoria presso che tutti cotesti libri son ritornati nel 1815, e riposti nella Marciana'. Not listed in BnF archives list (1797).

Paris, Bibliothèque nationale de France: Rés. X. 587

146. Psalterium. Ed: Bruno, Episcopus Herbipolensis (Würzburg), [Nuremberg]: Anton Koberger, 1497. 4º. ISTC ip01057000; MEI 02006771.

-*c.* 1497-*c.* 1600 Johannes Chosmae; inscription on a2: 'Ioannis Chosmae et amicorum suorum'.
-*c.* 1600–1806 Venice, S. Giorgio Maggiore; late seventeenth-century inscription on a1: 'Est Sancti Georgii Maioris Venetiarum'.
-1806 Regno d'Italia, decree no. 160, 28 July 1806.
-1806 Venice, S. Giorgio Maggiore; Rossi (1806), B8: 'Brunonis Episcopi Herbipolensis Psalterium absq. loco 1497 per Ant. Koburger 4°'.
-March 1807–1818(?) Padua, Sant'Anna; Rossi (March 1807); Catalogo generale XV (1811), 145, no. 48: 'Beati Brunonis, Psalterium, 4, 1497, absque loco'; *Fondi antichi della Biblioteca Universitaria di Padova*, 40–41.
Padua, Biblioteca Universitaria: Sec. XV 527

147. Quintilianus, Marcus Fabius, *Institutiones oratoriae,* [Venice]: Nicolaus Jenson, 21 May 1471. Folio. ISTC iq00026000; MEI 02108488.
-1765 Venice, S. Giorgio Maggiore: included in the list published in Gerbert (1765).
-1789 Venice, S. Giorgio Maggiore; Morelli's survey (1789), fasc. 1, 6: no marks.
-1806–1814(?) Milan, Regno d'Italia: books gone to Milan, 4 Sept. 1806, item five.
Historical copy, Venice

148. Rainerius de Pisis, *Pantheologia, sive Summa universae theologiae,* Venice: Hermannus Liechtenstein, 12 Sept. 1486. Folio. ISTC ir00010000; MEI 02006693.
-1806 Regno d'Italia, decree no. 160, 28 July 1806.
-1806 Venice, S. Giorgio Maggiore; Rossi (1806), P60: 'De Pisis Raynerii Summa Theologica Partes duae. Ven. 1486 impensis Hermanni Liechtenstein T.i 2 F.°'.
-March 1807–1818(?) Padua, Sant'Anna; Rossi (March 1807); Catalogo generale XV (1811), 144, no. 16: 'De Pisis, Summa theologica, fol. Ven. 1486, t. 2'; *Fondi antichi della Biblioteca Universitaria di Padova*, 40–41.
Historical copy, Venice

149. Regulae monasticorum: *Regulae SS. Benedicti, Basilii, Augustini, Francisci,* Venice: Johannes Emericus, de Spira, for Lucantonio Giunta, 13 Apr. 1500. 4°. ISTC ir00135000; MEI 02108489.
-1789 Venice, S. Giorgio Maggiore; Morelli's survey (1789), fasc. 1, 4: 'esemplare stampato in cartapecora con miniature', marked with +.
Historical copy, Venice

150. Regiomontanus, Johannes, *Epitoma in Almagestum Ptolemaei,* Venice: Johannes Hamman for Kaspar Grossch and Stephan Roemer, 31 Aug. 1496. Folio. ISTC ir00111000; MEI 02008349.
-1700–1797 Venice, S. Giorgio Maggiore; eighteenth-century inscription on the first leaf: 'Est bibliothecae Sancti Georgii Maioris Venetiarum'.
-1817 Padua: Catalogo pregio (1817), 6, no. 217: 'De Monteregio, In Almagestum Ptolemaei. Venetiis, 1496. fo.'.
Padua, Biblioteca Universitaria: Sec. XV 954

151. Rodericus Zamorensis, *Speculum vitae humanae,* Rome: Conradus Sweynheym and Arnoldus Pannartz, 1468. 4°. ISTC ir00214000; MEI 02108490.
-1789 Venice, S. Giorgio Maggiore; Morelli's survey (1789), fasc. 1, 7: '[…] in 4° magno', marked with +.
Historical copy, Venice

152. Rolewinck, Werner, *Fasciculus temporum,* [Venice]: Erhard Ratdolt, 21 Dec. 1481. Folio. ISTC ir00264000; MEI 02018103.
-1806 Regno d'Italia, decree no. 160, 28 July 1806.
-1806 Venice, S. Giorgio Maggiore; Rossi (1806), F26: 'Fasciculus temporum omnes antiquorum Chronicas complectens. 1481 p. Erhardum Rodolt [*sic*] de Augusta 4°'.
-Not present in Catalogo generale XV (1811), it is therefore unlikely that the book ever reached Padua.
Historical copy, Venice

153. Rolewinck, Werner, *Fasciculus temporum*, Venice: Erhard Ratdolt, 8 Sept. 1485. Folio. ISTC ir00271000; MEI 02007068.

Bound with three other sixteenth-century editions: (1) Sedulius Scotus, *In omnes Epistolas Pauli collectaneum*, Basileae: per Henricum Petrum, mense Martio 1528; (2) Galenus, Claudius, *Liber de plenitudine…*, [Paris]: prostant in vico Iacobaeo, apud Christianum VVechel sub scuto Basileiensi, 1528; (3) Leone, Ambrogio, *Nouum opus quaestionum seu problematum ut pulcherrimorum ita utilissimorum tum aliis plerisque in rebus cognoscendis tum maxime in philosophia & medicina scientia*, Venetiis: per Bernardinum & Matthiam de vitali fratres, 1523 Augusti XXVIII (EDIT16 CNCE 38060).

-1700–1797 Venice, S. Giorgio Maggiore; eighteenth-century inscription on the first leaf of the first edition of the composite volume: 'Est Bibliothecae Sancti Georgii Maioris Venetiarum'.

-after March 1807/1811–1818(?) Padua, Sant'Anna; Rossi (March 1807); Catalogo generale XVI (1811), 114, no. 288: 'Fasciculus temporum, folio, Venetiis, 1485'; *Fondi antichi della Biblioteca Universitaria di Padova*, 40–41.

-1818(?)-*c.* 1840 Padua, Sala Carmeli, S. Francesco Grande. When the monastery of Sant'Anna had to be cleared, some selected volumes were transferred in part to the Pubblica Libreria (the Biblioteca Universitaria of Padua), in part to the Sala Carmeli of the former convent of S. Francesco Grande. A document dated 1818 records the transfer of books from S. Giorgio Maggiore into cupboards A, B, and C of Sala Carmeli. Padua, Catalogo Gnocchi (1818).

-*c.* 1840 transfer to the Biblioteca Universitaria of Padua: Ravegnani, *Le biblioteche*, 65–68; *Fondi antichi della Biblioteca Universitaria di Padova*, 40–41.

Padua, Biblioteca Universitaria: 48 b 71/4

154. Sabellicus, Marcus Antonius, *Enneades ab orbe condito*, Venice: Bernardinus Venetus, de Vitalibus and Matthaeus Venetus, 31 Mar. 1498. Folio. ISTC is00007000; MEI 02006687.

-1806 Regno d'Italia, decree no. 160, 28 July 1806.

-1806 Venice, S. Giorgio Maggiore; Rossi (1806), S66: 'Sabellici Marci Antonii Enneades ab orbe condito ad inclinationem Romani Imperii. Partes duae. Vol. I F.º Prior pars ap. Bernard., et Matheum Venetos, Ven 1498; Secunda Ven 1504 ap. Bernard. Vercellensem'.

-March 1807–1818(?) Padua, Sant'Anna; Rossi (March 1807); Catalogo generale XV (1811), 144, no. 12: 'Sabellici, Enneades etc., fol. 1498 per Bernard. et Math. Venetus'; *Fondi antichi della Biblioteca Universitaria di Padova*, 40–41.

-1818(?)-*c.* 1840 Padua, Sala Carmeli, S. Francesco Grande. When the monastery of Sant'Anna had to be cleared, some selected volumes were transferred in part to the Pubblica Libreria (the Biblioteca Universitaria of Padua), in part to the Sala Carmeli of the former convent of S. Francesco Grande. A document dated 1818 records the transfer of books from S. Giorgio Maggiore into cupboards A, B, and C of Sala Carmeli. Padua, Catalogo Gnocchi (1818).

-*c.* 1840 transfer to the Biblioteca Universitaria of Padua: Ravegnani, *Le biblioteche*, 65–68; *Fondi antichi della Biblioteca Universitaria di Padova*, 40–41.

Historical copy, Venice

155. Sancto Georgio, Johannes Antonius de, *Commentaria super Decreto*, Pavia: Leonardus Gerla, 12 Mar. 1497. Folio. ISTC is00130000; MEI 02006696.

-1806 Regno d'Italia, decree no. 160, 28 July 1806.

-1806 Venice, S. Giorgio Maggiore; Rossi (1806), G31: 'De S. Georgio Antonii Commentaria super Decretorum volumina. Papiae 1497 p. Leonardum Gerla F.º'.

-March 1807–1818(?) Padua, Sant'Anna; Rossi (March 1807); Catalogo generale XV (1811), 145, no. 33: 'De S. Georgio, Commentaria super Decretorum volumina, fol. Papiae 1497'; *Fondi antichi della Biblioteca Universitaria di Padova*, 40–41.

Historical copy, Venice

156. Savonarola, Hieronymus, *Triumphus crucis seu de veritate fidei* [Florence: Bartolommeo di Libri, after Aug. 1497]. Folio. ISTC is00274000; MEI 02139534.
-1497-*c.* 1797 Venice, S. Giorgio Maggiore; fifteenth-century inscription on m8v: 'Iste liber est Congregationis monachorum Sancte Iustine de Padua ordinis Sancti Benedicti deputatus usui fratrum habitantium in Sancto Georgio Maiore Venetiarum signatus 1049'; later inscription on [*1r]: 'Est Sancti Georgii Maioris de Venetiis signatus numero 13'.
-1797 Cesena, Benedictines, Sta. Maria Montis (1026–1797); historical shelfmarks on the front pastedown: 'F 919'; 'M 150' (deleted) and label with shelfmark 'G II 387' belonging to Sta. Maria Montis. It is unclear when the book left S. Giorgio Maggiore, however it must have happened well before the Napoleonic secularizations, as this edition does not appear in any of the inventories prepared in Venice or Padua. Sta. Maria Montis became part of the Congregation of Sta. Giustina (later the Cassinese Congregation) as early as 1464; its book collection entered the Biblioteca Comunale before 1816 following the closure of the monastery's library between 1796 and 1816. Bruno Monfardini, 'Gli ordini religiosi maschili (secc. XV–XX)', in *Storia della chiesa di Cesena*, Vol. I.1, ed. Marino Mengozzi (Cesena, 1998), 379–481 at 386; Paola Errani and Marco Palma, *Incunaboli a Cesena* (Rome, 2020), 24–26.
-from 1816 Cesena, Biblioteca Comunale Malatestiana (founded in 1452); the binding, in limp parchment, presents a spine covered with marbled paper and an orange label with author and title in the hand of the Malatestiana librarian John Cooke (1764–1846), active in that role from 1816 to 1825.
Cesena, Biblioteca Comunale Malatestiana: 160.98

157. *Scriptores rei rusticae*, Venice: Nicolaus Jenson, 1472. Folio. ISTC is00346000; MEI 02126715 (former historical copy, identified when added to MEI in Sept. 2018).

1472–1789 Venice, S. Giorgio Maggiore; on [*]14v the contemporary inscription: 'Iste liber est monachorum congregationis s. justine de padua ordinis s. benedicti de observantia deputatus monasterio s. Georgij maioris venetiarum signatus numero 404'.
-1789 Venice, S. Giorgio Maggiore; Morelli's survey (1789), fasc. 1, 3: marked with +.
-1806 Regno d'Italia, decree no. 160, 28 July 1806.
-1806 Venice, S. Giorgio Maggiore; Rossi (1806), R64: 'Rei rusticae Auctores. Venetiis 1472 Ienson F.°'. Not present in Catalogo generale XV (1811), it is therefore unlikely that the book ever reached Padua; at this stage, no evidence is available as to how and when the book reached the Braidense.
Milan, Biblioteca Nazionale Braidense: AN. XIII. 44

158. Simoneta, Johannes, *Commentarii rerum gestarum Francisci Sfortiae*, Milan: Antonius Zarotus, '23 Jan.' [between 6 July 1481 and 3 Feb. 1482]. Folio. ISTC is00532000; MEI 02108491.
-1789 Venice, S. Giorgio Maggiore; Morelli's survey (1789), fasc. 1, 7: no marks.
Historical copy, Venice

159. Spiera, Ambrosius de, *Quadragesimale de floribus sapientiae*, Venice: Antonius de Stanchis de Valentia, Jacobus Britannicus et socii, 24 Mar. 1481. Folio. ISTC is00679000; MEI 02006701.
-1806 Regno d'Italia, decree no. 160, 28 July 1806.
-1806 Venice, S. Giorgio Maggiore; Rossi (1806), S67: 'Spiera Ambrosii Quadragesimale. Ven. 1481 cura Antonii de Valentia, et Zacchi Britanici F.°'.
-March 1807–1818(?) Padua, Sant'Anna; Rossi (March 1807); Catalogo generale XV (1811), 145, no. 43: 'Spiera, Quadragesimale, fol. Ven. 1481'; *Fondi antichi della Biblioteca Universitaria di Padova*, 40–41.
Historical copy, Venice

160. Statius, Publius Papinius, *Opera*, Venice: Petrus de Quarengiis, Bergomensis, 1498/1499. Folio. ISTC is00694000; MEI 02008269.

Bound third with **Juvenalis, Decimus Junius**, *Satyrae*, Venice: Johannes Tacuinus, de Tridino, 24 July 1498. Folio. ISTC ij00666000; MEI 02008266 (bound first, no. 104 here) and **Persius Flaccus, Aulus**, *Satyrae*, Venice: Petrus de Quarengiis, Bergomensis, 13 Apr. 1495. Folio. ISTC ip00357000; MEI 02008268 (bound second, no. 132 here).

-1700–1797 Venice, S. Giorgio Maggiore; eighteenth-century inscription on A2r of the first work bound in this volume: 'Est bibliothecae Sancti Georgi Maioris Venetiarum'.

-1806 Regno d'Italia, decree no. 160, 28 July 1806.

-1806 Venice, S. Giorgio Maggiore; Rossi (1806), I42: 'Iuvenalis Decii Iunii Satyrae cum Comment. Ant. Mancinelli. Ven. 1495 p. Petrum Io. de Querengis, et Statii Poetae Sylvae Thebais, et Achilleis cum plur. Commentariis. Ibid. 1498 ap. eund. F.°'; the entry merges the bibliographical information (author, title, commentator) of the edition bound first with the typographical information (place, year, and printer) of the edition bound second; it is followed by the correct bibliographical and typographical information of the edition bound third. The bibliographical information of the edition bound second, Persius, not specified, can be inferred by the typographical information provided and by the physical presence of the three editions in one volume today in the library of the University of Padua.

-March 1807–1818(?) Padua, Sant'Anna; Rossi (March 1807); Catalogo generale XV (1811), 145, no. 39: 'Iuvenalis, Satyrae cum cummentariis, folio, Venetiis, 1495; v'è unito Statii, Sylvae etc., folio, Venetiis, 1498'; *Fondi antichi della Biblioteca Universitaria di Padova*, 40–41.

-1818(?)-*c.* 1840 Padua, Sala Carmeli, S. Francesco Grande. When the monastery of Sant'Anna had to be cleared, some selected volumes were transferred in part to the Pubblica Libreria (the Biblioteca Universitaria of Padua), in part to the Sala Carmeli of the former convent of S. Francesco Grande. A document dated 1818 records the transfer of books from S. Giorgio Maggiore into cupboards A, B, and C of Sala Carmeli. Padua, Catalogo Gnocchi (1818).

-*c.* 1840 transfer to the Biblioteca Universitaria of Padua: Ravegnani, *Le biblioteche*, 65–68; *Fondi antichi della Biblioteca Universitaria di Padova*, 40–41.

Padua, Biblioteca Universitaria: Sec. XV 420/3

161. *Statuta Venetiae* [Latin and Italian], [Venice]: Dionysius Bertochus, 31 Oct. 1492. Folio. ISTC is00725000; MEI 02108492.

-1789 Venice, S. Giorgio Maggiore; Morelli's survey (1789), fasc. 1, 8: no marks.

Historical copy, Venice

162. Strabo, *Geographia*, Venice: Vindelinus de Spira, 1472. Folio. CIBN S-471; ISTC is00794000; MEI 02017614.

-1472–1789 Venice, S. Giorgio Maggiore; contemporary inscription below the colophon: 'Iste liber est congregationis s. Iustine de Padua ordinis s. Benedicti de obseruan | tia | deputatus in monasterio s. georgii maioris | uenetiarum signatus numero 520'; in the lower margin of the first page inscription in a seventeenth-century hand, brown ink: 'Est Bibl.e S. Georgij M.is Venet.m'.

-1789–1797 Venice, S. Giorgio Maggiore; Morelli's survey (1789), fasc. 1, 7: marked with + and crossed out.

-1797– Paris, Bibliothèque nationale; Cicogna (1797): 'Dalla libreria di s. Giorgio Maggiore furono portati a Parigi nel 1797 i seguenti Codici manuscritti […] Edizioni del secolo XV […] 17. Strabonis geographia f. chart. Venetiis 1472'; BnF archives list (1797), fasc. 2, no. 9: 'Strabo 1472 fol. en bois Sta Justina'. According to CIBN S-471 the volume was rebound by Bradel L'Aîné (fl. 1770–1795). The volume did not return to the Marciana library.

Paris, Bibliothèque nationale de France: Rés. G. 15

163. Suso, Henricus, *Horologium aeternae sapientiae*, etc. Venice: Petrus de Quarengiis, Bergomensis, 24 Jan. 1492/1493. 4°. ISTC is00875000; MEI 02002784.

-1600–1797 Venice, S. Giorgio Maggiore; seventeenth-century inscription on 1r: 'Est s. Georgii Maioris de Venetiis'. It is not known when the incunable entered the library in Brescia.

Brescia, Biblioteca Queriniana (IT): Inc.C.VI.7m2

164. Tertullianus, Quintus Septimus Florentius, *Apologeticus contra gentes*, Venice: Bernardinus Benalius, [not after 1494]. Folio. ISTC it00117000; MEI 02008199.

Bound second with: **Aegidius (Columna) Romanus**: *De regimine principum*, Venice: Simon Bevilaqua, 9 July 1498. Folio. GW 7219; ISTC ia00089000; MEI 02008198 (no. 1 here).

-1494–1513 Andreas Mocenicus, apostolic protonotary: see below.

-1513–1797 Venice, S. Giorgio Maggiore; on the verso of the last leaf: 'Reverendus dominus Andreas Mocenicus prothonotarius pro animae suae salute Divi Georgii Maioris coenobio dicavit, signatus 115', Andrea Mocenigo died in 1513. Eighteenth-century inscription on the first leaf of the edition bound first: 'Est Bibliothecae Sancti Georgii Maioris Venetiarum'.

-after March 1807/1811–1818(?) Padua, Sant'Anna; Catalogo generale XV (1811), 144, no. 7: 'Eggidii, Opus de regimine principum, folio, Venetiis, sine anno, per Bernardinum Benalium'; the entry merges the bibliographical information of the edition bound first (author and title), and the typographical information of the edition bound second (year of publication and printer); *Fondi antichi della Biblioteca Universitaria di Padova*, 40–41.

-1818(?)-*c.* 1840 Padua, Sala Carmeli, S. Francesco Grande. When the monastery of Sant'Anna had to be cleared, some selected volumes were transferred in part to the Pubblica Libreria (the Biblioteca Universitaria of Padua), in part to the

Sala Carmeli of the former convent of S. Francesco Grande. A document dated 1818 records the transfer of books from S. Giorgio Maggiore into cupboards A, B, and C of Sala Carmeli. Padua, Catalogo Gnocchi (1818).

-*c.* 1840 transfer to the Biblioteca Universitaria of Padua: Ravegnani, *Le biblioteche*, 65–68; *Fondi antichi della Biblioteca Universitaria di Padova*, 40–41.

Padua, Biblioteca Universitaria: Sec. XV 959/2

165. Thomas à Kempis, *Imitatio Christi*, etc. Venice: Bernardinus Benalius, 1488. 8°. ISTC ii00017000; MEI 02018101.

Bound third with: **Bernardus Claravallensis, Pseudo-**, *Modus bene vivendi in christianam religionem*, Venice: Bernardinus Benalius, 30 May 1494. 8°. GW 4048; ISTC ib00414000; MEI 02018102 (bound first, no. 24 here) and **Augustinus, Aurelius, Pseudo-**, *Sermones ad heremitas*, Venice: Simon Bevilaqua, 4 Nov. 1495. 8°. GW 3007; ISTC ia01319000; MEI 02018099 (bound second, no. 18 here).

-1806 Regno d'Italia, decree no. 160, 28 July 1806.

-1806 Venice, S. Giorgio Maggiore; Rossi (1806), B18: 'S. Bernardi Meditationes Ven. 1494 per Bernard. De Benaliis. It. Sermones S. Augustini ad heremitas. Ven 1495 per Simonem Bevilaquam – Io: Gerson de contempt vanitatem Ven. 1488 p. Bernard. de Benaliis. 12°'.

-Not present in Catalogo generale XV (1811), it is therefore unlikely that the book ever reached Padua.

Historical copy, Venice

166. Thomas à Kempis, *Imitatio Christi*, etc. Venice: Petrus de Quarengiis, Bergomensis, and Giovanni Maria di Occimiano, 23 Apr. 1493. 8°. ISTC ii00028000; MEI 02125175.

Formerly bound with two other Casanatense incunables: **Bernardus Claravallensis, Pseudo-**, *Modus bene vivendi in christianam religionem*, Venice: Bernardinus Benalius, 30 May 1492. 8°. GW 4047; ISTC ib00413000; MEI 02125145;

VOL INC.1294 (no. 23 here) and **Augustinus, Aurelius, Pseudo-**, *Sermones ad heremitas*, Venice: Vincentius Benalius, 26 Jan. 1492/1493. 8°. GW 3005; ISTC ia01317000; MEI 02125177; VOL INC.1293 (no. 17 here); see seventeenth-/eighteenth-century manuscript index on front flyleaf IIr of Bernardus Claravallensis. The three volumes were described as bound in a composite volume in the printed catalogue by G. B. Audiffredi, *Bibliothecae Casanatensis Catalogus librorum typis impressorum* (Romae, 1761), vol. 1, 345a.

-1493-*c.* 1600 Venice, S. Giorgio Maggiore; fifteenth-century inscription on a1r of VOL INC. 1294: 'Iste liber est Congregationis monachorum s. Justine de padua ordinis sancti Benedicti deputatus in sancto Georgio maiore venetiarum, signatus 979'.

-*c.* 1600 Flavius Ciccolus of Bevagna; inscription on a1r of VOL. INC. 1294: 'Flavius Ciccolus Meuanas etc. habuit hunc librum dono etc'.

-*c.* 1761 Rome, Biblioteca Casanatense; acquired in the eighteenth century as the other two parts of the composite volume are listed in Audiffredi (1761).
Rome, Biblioteca Casanatense: VOL INC.1292

167. Thomas Aquinas, *Commentaria in omnes epistolas Sancti Pauli*, Venice: Bonetus Locatellus, for Octavianus Scotus, 22 Dec. 1498. Folio. ISTC it00235000; MEI 00200283.

-1499-1550 Venice, S. Giorgio Maggiore; inscription on a1r and on the last leaf of text, erased: 'Est Monasterij Sancti Georgij Maioris signatus n° 1070' and 'Iste liber est Monasterij Sancti Georgij Maioris Venet. signatus n° 1070'.

-*c.* 1557-1573 Ceneda (now Vittorio Veneto, prov. Treviso) Giacomo Fortunio (fl. 1557-1573), notary: inscription.

-1601-1769 Valdobbiadene, Capuchins; inscription on the title-page: 'Loci Capuccinorum Valis Duplauinae'. The place name, Valdobbiadene, has been struck through by a later hand and the place name 'Tarvisii' added.

-1770-1810 Treviso, Capuchins: inscription, see above.

-1810- Treviso, Biblioteca Capitolare: ex-libris.
Treviso, Biblioteca Capitolare: Inc. 17

168. Thomas Aquinas, *Opuscula* (71). Ed: Antonius Pizamanus, with a life of St Thomas, Venice: Hermannus Liechtenstein, 7 Sept. 1490. 4°. ISTC it00258000; MEI 02122654.

-1490-1550 Venice, S. Giorgio Maggiore; erased inscription in a sixteenth-century hand on a1r: 'Monasterii Sancti Georgii M. Venetiarum numero 278'.

-1573-1592 Venice? Giulio Cesare Ballino (*c.* 1530-1592); purchase note on a1r, below the previous inscription: '1573 18 Martii l[ire]. 3 s[oldi].-- // ex libris Iulii Caesaris Ballini'.

-*c.* 1800 Venice, Biblioteca Nazionale Marciana; it is not known when the incunable entered the library; however, it probably happened in the period following the suppression of religious houses, as the title appears in the library catalogue prepared at the end of the eighteenth century (BNM, Ms. It. XI, 359 (= 10439)), under the heading 'Thomas Aquinas', among the additions of Jacopo Morelli, who reordered the collections which had entered the library after the suppressions.
Venice, Biblioteca nazionale Marciana: Inc. V. 0603

169. Thomas Aquinas, *Opuscula* (73). Ed: Antonius Pizamanus, with a life of St Thomas, Venice: Bonetus Locatellus, for Octavianus Scotus, 31 Dec. 1498. Folio. ISTC it00257000; MEI 02128491.

-1806 Regno d'Italia, decree no. 160, 28 July 1806.

-1806 Venice, S. Giorgio Maggiore; Rossi (1806), T68: 'D. Thomae Aquinatis Opuscula varia Ven. 1492 p. Bonetum Locatellum F.°'.

-March 1807-1818(?) Padua, Sant'Anna; Rossi (March 1807); Catalogo generale XV (1811), 144, no. 17: 'D. Thomae, Opuscola. Fol. Ven. 1492'; *Fondi antichi della Biblioteca Universitaria di Padova*, 40-41. In both cases the date is mistakenly given as 1492.
Historical copy, Venice

170. Thwrocz, Johannes de, *Chronica Hungarorum,* etc. Brünn: [Conrad Stahel and Mathias Preunlein], 20 Mar. 1488. Folio. ISTC it00360000; MEI 02108493.
-1789 Venice, S. Giorgio Maggiore; Morelli's survey (1789), fasc. 1, 7: no marks.
Historical copy, Venice

171. Tortellius, Johannes, *Orthographia,* Venice: Nicolaus Jenson, 1471. Folio. CIBN T-290; ISTC it00394000; MEI 02008347.
-1471–1789 Venice, S. Giorgio Maggiore; contemporary inscription below the colophon: 'Iste liber est congregationis s. Iustine | de Padua deputatus ad usum monachorum ha | bitantium in monasterio s. georgij maioris | de uenetijs signatus numero 464'.
-1789 Venice, S. Giorgio Maggiore; Morelli's survey (1789), fasc. 1, 7: marked with +.
The volume is not registered by Cicogna (1797), who gives a list of eighteen books taken away by the French in 1797, nor does the volume appear to be mentioned in the BnF restitution list (1815). Fols [a]2 and [a]3 belong to another copy from S. Benedictus at Polirone (Mantua) and replace the original ones. It is not clear whether they were pasted in during their permanence at S. Giorgio Maggiore or by the BnF after the copy's arrival in the library.
Paris, Bibliothèque nationale de France: Rés. X. 629

172. Turrecremata, Johannes de, *Summa de ecclesia contra impugnatores potestatis summi pontificis et LXXIII quaestiones super potestate et auctoritate Papali ex sententiis sancti Thomae Aquinatis,* Lyon: Johannes Trechsel, 20 Sept. 1496. Folio. GW M46324; ISTC it00556000; MEI 02139533.
-Sixteenth century–before 1806 Venice, S. Giorgio Maggiore; inscription on [*1r]: 'Est Sancti Georg(ii Maiori)s Venetiarum signatus numero 5'. It is unclear when the book left S. Giorgio Maggiore, however it must have happened well

before the Napoleonic secularizations, as this edition does not appear in any of the inventories prepared in Venice or Padua. It is possible that, like the edition of Savonarola (here no. 156), it entered the Malatestiana via the Benedictines of Sta. Maria Montis of Cesena.
-from 1816 Cesena, Biblioteca Comunale Malatestiana (founded in 1452); ex-libris. The cardboard binding presents a spine covered with marbled paper and an orange label with author and title in the hand of the Malatestiana librarian John Cooke (1764–1846), active in that role from 1816 to 1825.
Cesena, Biblioteca Comunale Malatestiana: 160.93

173. Uberti, Fazio degli, *Dittamondo* [Italian], Vicenza: Leonardus Achates de Basilea, [Nov.] 1474. Folio. ISTC iu00053000; MEI 02019418.
-before 1789 Venice, S. Giorgio Maggiore; Morelli's survey (1789), fasc. 2: '*Mancanze:* – A S. Giorgio Maggiore, libri notati nell'Indice, che non si trovano. Aretini Leonardi, *De Bello Gothico,* Venetiis, Jenson, 1471, fo. […] Varro, *De lingua latina,* fol., sine ulla nota, saec. XV. Degli Uberti, *Dittamondo.* Vicenza, 1474, fo. […]'; published in Fulin, *Vicende della libreria in SS. Gio. e Paolo,* 293, no. 1.
Historical copy, Venice

174. Urbanus Averroista, *Expositio commentarii Averrois super Physica Aristotelis,* Venice: Bernardinus Stagninus, de Tridino, 15 Nov. 1492. Folio. ISTC iu00065000; MEI 02008335.
-1550–1566 Venice, Francesco Amadi (c. 1500–1566); inscription on the first leaf: '1550. Don Francesco Amadi conte palatino'.
-1566?–1797 Venice, S. Giorgio Maggiore; on the first leaf eighteenth-century inscription: 'Est bibliothecae Sancti Georgii Maioris Venetiarum'.
-1811(?) Padua, Biblioteca Universitaria; stamp. Not listed in any inventory documenting the institutional transfer.
Padua, Biblioteca Universitaria: Sec. XV 464

175. Valerius Maximus, Gaius, *Facta et dicta memorabilia*, [Venice]: Vindelinus de Spira, 1471. Folio. ISTC iv00024000; MEI 02108495.
-1765 Venice, S. Giorgio Maggiore: included in the list published in Gerbert (1765).
-1789 Venice, S. Giorgio Maggiore; Morelli's survey (1789), fasc. 1, 7: no marks.
1806–1814(?) Milan, Regno d'Italia: books gone to Milan, 4 Sept. 1806, item six.
Historical copy, Venice

176. Valla, Laurentius, *Elegantiæ linguæ latinæ*, Venice: Nicolaus Jenson, 1471. 4°. CIBN V-37; ISTC iv00051000; MEI 02017615.
-1471–1765 Venice, S. Giorgio Maggiore; unidentified coat of arms; contemporary inscription below the colophon: 'Iste liber est congregationis s. Iustine | deputatus ad usum monachorum habitantium| in monasterio s. georgii maioris | de uenetijs signatus numero 457'; seventeenth-century inscription in the lower margin of the first leaf: 'Est s. Georgij maioris Venitiarum'.
-1765 Venice, S. Giorgio Maggiore: included in the list published in Gerbert (1765).
-1789–1797 Venice, S. Giorgio Maggiore; Morelli's survey (1789), fasc. 1, 7: no marks.
-1797– Paris, Bibliothèque nationale; Cicogna (1797): 'Dalla libreria di s. Giorgio Maggiore furono portati a Parigi nel 1797 i seguenti Codici manuscritti [...] Edizioni del secolo XV [...] 17. Valle Laurentii de elegantia f. chart. Venetiis 1471'; BnF archives list (1797), fasc. 2, no. 15: 'Valla 1471 in fol. Velum Sta. Justina'. The volume did not return to the Marciana library.
Paris, Bibliothèque nationale de France: Rés. X. 640

177. Varro, Marcus Terentius, *De lingua latina*. Add: *Analogia*. Ed: Pomponius Laetus. Prelim: Pomponius Laetus: *Epistola Bartholomaeo Platinae*, [Venice: Printer of Basilius, 'De vita solitaria', about 1471–72]. 4°. ISTC iv00095000; MEI 02141391.
Although all but one of the surviving editions are 'sine notis', the inclusion in Gerbert's list

with an attribution to Jenson 1472 allows us to tentatively identify the San Giorgio's copy with this edition.
-1765 Venice, S. Giorgio Maggiore: included in the list published in Gerbert (1765).
- before 1789 Venice, S. Giorgio Maggiore; Morelli's survey (1789), fasc. 2: '*Mancanze*: – A S. Giorgio Maggiore, libri notati nell'Indice, che non si trovano. Aretini Leonardi, *De Bello Gothico*, Venetiis, Jenson, 1471, fo. [...] Varro, *De lingua latina*, fol., sine ulla nota, saec. XV. Degli Uberti, *Dittamondo*. Vicenza, 1474, fo. [...]'; published in Fulin, *Vicende della libreria in SS. Gio. e Paolo*, 293, no. 1.
Historical copy, Venice

178. Vergerius, Petrus Paulus, *De ingenuis moribus ac liberalibus studiis*. Ed: Johannes Calphurnius. Comm: Johannes Bonardus. Add: Basilius Magnus: *De legendis antiquorum libris* (Tr: Leonardus Brunus Aretinus). Xenophon: *Hiero de tyrannide* (Tr: Leonardus Brunus Aretinus). Plutarchus: *De liberis educandis* (Tr: Guarinus Veronensis). S. Hieronymus: *De officiis liberorum erga parentes admonitio*, etc. Venice: Johannes Tacuinus, de Tridino, 22 Sept. 1497. 4°. ISTC iv00139000; MEI 02018105.
Bound third with: **Mancinellus, Antonius**, *Scribendi orandique modus* (edition unidentified; bound first, no. 115 here); **Ferettus, Nicolaus**, *De elegantia linguae latinae*, Forlì: Hieronymus Medesanus, 25 May 1495. 4°. GW 9783; ISTC if00099000; MEI 02018108 (bound second, no. 75 here); and **Beroaldus, Philippus**, *De felicitate*, Bologna: Franciscus (Plato) de Benedictis, 1 Apr. 1495. 4°. GW 4132; ISTC ib00482000; MEI 02018106 (bound fourth, no. 27 here).
-1806 Regno d'Italia, decree no. 160, 28 July 1806.
-1806 Venice, S. Giorgio Maggiore; Rossi (1806), M52: 'Mancinelli Antonii Scribendi, orandique modus, Forilivii 1495 p. Hieron. Medasanum. – Pauli Vergerii de ingenuis moribus cum comment. Io. Bonardi – Basilii de legendis antiquorum libris opusculum – Traductio ex Xenophonte Leonardi

Aretini de Tyranide – Guarini Veronensis in Plutarcum praefatio, 1497 Ven. p. Io. Tacuinum. – Philippi Beroaldi de felicitate opusculum Bononiae 1495 p. Platonem de Benedictiis. Omnia uno tantum volumine in 4°. In making an entry for this composite volume, it is clear that the cataloguer merged two editions, noting the opening of an edition of Antonius Mancinellus and the imprint information for another edition, by Nicolaus Ferettus, bound behind. Unfortunately, it is not possible to determine which of the several editions of Mancinellus' *Scribendi orandique modus* is the one represented here.

-Not present in Catalogo generale XV (1811), it is therefore unlikely that the book ever reached Padua.

Historical copy, Venice

179. Vergilius Maro, Publius, *Bucolica*, [Naples: Jodocus Hohenstein], 11 Sept. 1476. 4°. ISTC iv00203500; MEI 02108496.

-1789 Venice, S. Giorgio Maggiore; Morelli's survey (1789), fasc. 2, n.n., after no. 56: lined through.

Historical copy, Venice

180. Zerbus, Gabriel, *Quaestiones metaphysicae*, Bologna: Johannes de Nördlingen and Henricus de Harlem, 1 Dec. 1482. Folio. ISTC iz00027000; MEI 02019400.

-1700–1797 Venice, S. Giorgio Maggiore; inscription in a seventeenth-century hand on the front flyleaf: 'Est Monasterij S. Georgij Maioris Venetiarum'.
-1806–1868 Emmanuele Antonio Cicogna (1789–1868); indication on the front pastedown. Bequeathed to the Correr Museum in 1868.

Venice, Biblioteca del Museo Correr: Inc. F 042

Index by Present Location: 32

Vienna, ONB (2): 29, 32

Out of 181 copies located so far, 37 (20%) ended up where they were supposed to, at the Biblioteca Universitaria of Padua; 25 other copies (13%) were taken away to Paris and are today either still in Paris (17), in Vienna (2), or have been returned to Venice, Marciana (6).

123 copies (67%) were dispersed, mostly following the secularizations: 78 (42%) historical copies are dispersed and unlocated, 45 (25%) have been located in libraries across Europe and the United States.

Index by Place of Printing

Index by Subject

Literature (**26**): 21, 26, 27, 37, 58, 61, 62, 81, 82, 93, 94, 98, 104, 105, 114, 131, 134, 135, 140, 156, 160, 165, 166, 173, 178, 179

Liturgy (**2**): 121, 146

Medicine (**5**): 19, 20, 51, 74, 120

Music (**1**): 79

Natural history (**3**): 141, 142, 143

Philosophy (**18**): 1, 35, 38, 39, 44, 45, 64, 77, 99, 111, 126, 136, 139, 144, 168, 169, 174, 180

Rhetoric (**8**): 52, 53, 54, 75, 83, 115, 147, 176

Theology (**44**): 3, 4, 6, 7, 8, 9, 14, 15, 16, 17, 18, 23, 24, 25, 47, 48, 49, 50, 50bis, 67, 68, 69, 73, 84, 86, 87, 88, 92, 100, 107, 116, 118, 119, 123, 124, 132, 136, 147, 150, 158, 162, 163, 166, 171

Late 15th century (Catalogue No. 47)

Late 15th century (Catalogue No. 52)

Beginning 16th century (Catalogue No. 94)

Mid 16th century (Catalogue No. 174)

Mid-late 17th century (Catalogue No. 47)

Late 17th century (Catalogue No. 146)

Beginning 18th century (Catalogue No. 57)

Mid 18th century (Catalogue No. 153)

Index of Names

Index of Places[1]